An Introduction to Derivatives and Risk Management

Fifth Edition

An Introduction to Derivatives and Risk Management

Fifth Edition

Don M. Chance
Virginia Tech

HARCOURT COLLEGE PUBLISHERS

Fort Worth   Philadelphia   San Diego   New York   Orlando   Austin   San Antonio
Toronto   Montreal   London   Sydney   Tokyo

Publisher	Mike Roche
Executive Editor	Mike Reynolds
Project Editor	Jim Patterson
Art Director	Susan Journey
Production Manager	James McDonald

Cover credit: © 2001 Tony Stone Images

ISBN: 0-03-031147-0
Library of Congress Catalog Card Number: 00-100124

Address for Domestic Orders
Harcourt College Publishers, 6277 Sea Harbor Drive, Orlando, FL 32887-6777
800-782-4479

Address for International Orders
International Customer Service
Harcourt, Inc., 6277 Sea Harbor Drive, Orlando, FL 32887-6777
407-345-3800
(fax) 407-345-4060
(e-mail) hbintl@harcourt.com

Address for Editorial Correspondence
Harcourt College Publishers, 301 Commerce Street, Suite 3700, Fort Worth, TX 76102

Web Site Address
http://www.harcourtcollege.com

Printed in the United States of America

0 1 2 3 4 5 6 7 8 9   039   9 8 7 6 5 4 3 2

Harcourt College Publishers

The Harcourt Series in Finance

Amling and Droms
Investment Fundamentals

Berry and Young
Managing Investments: A Case Approach

Besley and Brigham
Essentials of Managerial Finance
Twelfth Edition

Besley and Brigham
Principles of Finance

Boone, Kurtz, and Hearth
Planning Your Financial Future
Second Edition

Brigham and Houston
Fundamentals of Financial Management
Ninth Edition

Brigham, Gapenski, and Klein
2000 Cases in Financial Management: Dryden Request

Brigham, Gapenski, and Ehrhardt
Financial Management: Theory and Practice
Ninth Edition

Brigham, Gapenski, and Daves
Intermediate Financial Management
Sixth Edition

Brigham and Houston
Fundamentals of Financial Management: Concise Second Edition

Chance
An Introduction to Derivatives and Risk Management
Fifth Edition

Clark, Gerlach, and Olson
Restructuring Corporate America

Conroy
Finance Interactive

Cooley
Advances in Business Financial Management: A Collection of Readings
Second Edition

Dickerson, Campsey, and Brigham
Introduction to Financial Management
Fourth Edition

Eaker, Fabozzi, and Grant
International Corporate Finance

Gardner, Mills, and Cooperman
Managing Financial Institutions: An Asset/Liability Approach
Fourth Edition

Gitman and Joehnk
Personal Financial Planning
Eighth Edition

Greenbaum and Thakor
Contemporary Financial Intermediation

Hall
Effective Use of a Financial Calculator

Harrington and Eades
Case Studies in Financial Decision Making
Third Edition

Hayes and Meerschwam
Financial Institutions: Contemporary Cases in the Financial Services Industry

Hearth and Zaima
Contemporary Investments: Security and Portfolio Analysis
Third Edition

Johnson
Issues and Readings in Managerial Finance
Fourth Edition

Kidwell, Peterson, and Blackwell
Financial Institutions, Markets, and Money
Seventh Edition

Koch and MacDonald
Bank Management
Fourth Edition

Leahigh
Pocket Guide to Finance

Maness and Zietlow
Short-Term Financial Management

Mayes and Shank
Financial Analysis with Lotus 1-2-3 for Windows

Mayes and Shank
Financial Analysis with Microsoft Excel
Second Edition

Mayo
Financial Institutions, Investments, and Management: An Introduction
Seventh Edition

Mayo
Investments: An Introduction
Sixth Edition

Osteryoung, Newman, and Davies
Small Firm Finance: An Entrepreneurial Analysis

Reilly and Brown
Investment Analysis and Portfolio Management
Fifth Edition

Reilly and Norton
Investments
Fifth Edition

Sandburg
Discovering Your Finance Career

Seitz and Ellison
Capital Budgeting and Long-Term Financing Decisions
Third Edition

Siegel and Siegel
Futures Markets

Smith and Spudeck
Interest Rates: Principles and Applications

Stickney and Brown
Financial Reporting and Statement Analysis: A Strategic Perspective
Fourth Edition

Preface

It has now been eleven years since the first edition of this book came out. Probably no area in finance has undergone as much change as that of derivatives and risk management. In fact, this book was once called *An Introduction to Options and Futures*. The previous edition was called *An Introduction to Derivatives*. Reflecting the continuing change in the industry, we are now calling it *An Introduction to Derivatives and Risk Management*. Who knows what the sixth edition will be called? (Any suggestions?) But looking on the bright side, a dynamic field makes for an exciting subject to study and one well worth exploring for its potential for career development.

This book is all about the study of financial instruments called derivatives. The types of derivatives you will learn about are options, forwards, futures, swaps, and a number of variations of these basic instruments. Derivatives are powerful and effective tools for altering the risk of an organization or portfolio of securities. In this book you will learn the characteristics of these instruments, how they are priced, how they are used in strategies, and how to manage the risk they create as well as how to use them to manage already existing risk.

Organization of the Book

The book is divided into four main parts. First there is an introductory chapter, which gives an overview of the subject. Then Part One, consisting of Chapters 2–7, covers options. Chapter 2 introduces you to the basic characteristics of options and their markets. Chapter 3 presents the fundamental principles of pricing options. These principles are often called boundary conditions, and while we do tend to think of them as fundamental, they are nonetheless quite challenging. Chapter 4 presents the simple binomial model for pricing options. Chapter 5 covers the Black-Scholes model, which is the premier tool for pricing options and for which a Nobel Prize was awarded in 1997. Chapters 6 and 7 cover option trading strategies.

Part Two covers forward and futures contracts and begins with Chapter 8, which introduces the basic characteristics of forward and futures markets. Chapter 9 presents the principles for pricing forward and futures contracts. Chapter 10 covers hedging strategies, which is the primary use of these contracts. Chapter 11 covers some advanced applications of futures.

Part Three deals with advanced topics, but do not let that put you off. Most of what is covered here is simply applications of material previously learned. Chapter 12 covers options on futures, which combine elements of both options and futures. Chapter 13 on foreign currency derivatives combines options, forwards, and futures into one chapter. In addition you will meet the currency swap, one of the most widely used financial derivatives. Chapter 14 covers interest rate derivatives, which are your first derivatives that are not based on the price of a security, but rather on an interest rate. These are among the most actively traded, and herein you will learn about the most popular derivative, the interest rate swap. Chapter 15 covers some advanced topics and strategies, which are mostly extensions of previous topics and strategies.

Chapter 16 is the capstone chapter and deals with a broad range of topics on risk management. Derivative instruments allow the efficient buying and selling of risk. In this chapter we learn more about how companies manage this risk. In addition we cover a variety of related topics and get a chance to see how some organizations have done a poor job of managing risk.

Key Features of the Book

Some of the key features of the book are:

- An emphasis on practical application of theory; all ideas and concepts are presented with clear illustrations. You never lose touch with the real world.

- Minimal use of technical mathematics. While derivatives is unavoidably a technical subject, calculus is not necessary to learn the material at this level. (Note: Some calculus is used in appendices, but this material is not essential.)

- Balanced emphasis on strategies and pricing.

- The book is liberally illustrated with over 100 figures and supported with over 100 tables.

- Over 300 end-of-chapter questions and problems allow you to test your skills (solutions are available to adopting instructors).

- Over 200 margin notes, which are short (a few sentences) summaries of key points, are found throughout.

- Key terms. At the end of each chapter is a list of important terms you should be able to define before going on. There are an average of 18 per chapter.

- Quotes to start each chapter. While introductory students may not always catch the meaning behind quotes, they all have some meaning related to the topic of the chapter. The individuals cited are quite a varied bunch, but are mostly practitioners in the field.

- Derivatives in Action. About every other chapter includes a section called Derivatives in Action, which contains side stories that are not critical to but supplement the material.

- Bold terms. Throughout the chapter important terms are in bold.

- Software: The book comes with software consisting of one Windows program and various Excel spreadsheets. Throughout the book are sections called Software Demonstrations, which contain explicit illustrations of how to use the software.

- Appendices containing lists of symbols, formulas, and references.

- Glossary containing over 500 terms defined.

- An index, of course.

- PowerPoint Presentation slides, which are available for instructors adopting the book. Some other PowerPoint presentations that I have seen with finance textbooks are mostly just outlines; these contain much more detail.

- An *Instructor's Manual*, which contains answers to the end-of-chapter questions and problems and true-false and multiple choice tests. The *IM* also comes with software that consists of the PowerPoint slides, the true-false and multiple choice tests and the end of chapter problem solutions, all in Adobe Acrobat format. These can be freely distributed to students, thereby saving them the cost of copying.

- A Web site, www.cob.vt.edu/finance/faculty/dmc/IDRM5E.htm, which will contain updated information and errata. Yes, the book will probably have some errors, but at least I'm willing to tell you about them.

I cannot emphasize too much how I think this book blends theory and practice. All points are illustrated as much as possible using practical situations. For example, the option results are covered by following a single company's options throughout the book. When strategies are covered, we learn the theory, examine the algebraic equations that describe what is happening, and observe the results either with a table or graph.

New Features of the Fifth Edition

For those familiar with previous editions, the following are new features:

- The option examples, which were formerly illustrated using Digital Equipment, have all been replaced with new examples using America Online. This was not a voluntary change; Digital Equipment was bought out by Compaq and no longer has its own identity. Nonetheless, the new change has brought a fresh new opportunity to invigorate the book by using a young, contemporary, and extremely well-known technology company. As of this writing, AOL is involved in a merger with Time Warner, but the new firm is expected to be called AOL Time Warner so I will just continue to call it AOL.

- A slight change of notation. The symbol for the exercise price, formerly E, is now X. My choice of E comes from the classic 1973 Nobel Prize winning article by Robert Merton, but today most everyone uses X or K, with the former being my preference. In addition where it is necessary to designate time points, the stock price today is now S with a zero subscript.

- A separation of the option pricing models chapter into two chapters. Formerly, I packed the binomial and Black-Scholes models into the same chapter. Now the binomial model is Chapter 4 and the Black-Scholes model is Chapter 5. This separation allows us to give a little more coverage to each. In particular, the Black-Scholes coverage spends more time validating the assumptions, describing the properties of the model, and showing how delta hedging works.

- Elimination of the old Chapter 8. This was formerly a chapter primarily consisting of review material from other finance courses, with an emphasis on pricing assets in the spot market. Over the years, I have received feedback that suggests that this chapter probably is not necessary and I, myself, have often skipped it or covered it only very lightly in teaching. The essential material from this chapter has been seamlessly integrated into other chapters.

- An increased emphasis on over-the-counter derivative markets. With an apology to the derivatives exchanges, I believe this growing emphasis is simply a recognition of reality. I also believe no competing book gives this much recognition to the OTC market. Rest assured, if you are using this book, that you are in touch with what's going on in the market today. Or at least at the time I am writing this. Things change fast.

- Integration of the euro. Many of the foreign currency examples have been reworked to incorporate the euro. While the British pound, Japanese yen, Swiss franc, and Canadian dollar are still around, there is no longer a German mark, French franc and nine other currencies. These should disappear from textbooks and they already have from this one.

- Further Reading. A new feature to this fifth edition, these are a short list of articles at the end of each chapter that point you in the right direction to learn more. With but a few exceptions (such as classic articles), the list was selected with practicality and readability in mind.

- Significant improvements in coverage of the following topics.

    Swaps

    Value at Risk

    Credit derivatives

    Accounting for derivatives

On the coverage of accounting, probably no other issue has occupied the concerns of users as well as regulators in this industry in recent years. FAS 133, which goes into effect in June 2000, establishes standards for the accounting for derivatives transactions. I believe this is the first derivatives text to tackle the accounting issue head-on. While the coverage is not sufficient to make you an expert, you will learn how the accounting entries are made for various types of derivatives hedges and how these affect the balance sheet and income statement.

Use of the Book

At Virginia Tech, we place considerable emphasis on derivatives and risk management. Undergraduate and MBA students can, more or less, concentrate in it. We use this book as an elective undergraduate two-semester sequence, though students can stop after the first semester. We cover eight chapters in the first semester and eight in the second. For a one-semester course, the instructor would need to decide how much to emphasize of either options or forwards/futures. I would attempt to emphasize options with a blend of forwards/futures and still try to cover as much as possible of interest rate derivatives and risk management. The latter topics usually get short-changed, but they are so important in today's world, that one ought to work them in somehow.

For a one-semester course, I would probably cover Chapters 1-10, a small part of 11, all of 14, part of 15 and most of 16. Considerable discretion would have to be used, however, in that not all of the material in Chapters 1-10 could be covered.

A number of schools use this book at the MBA level. It all depends on how one wants to approach the subject and the backgrounds and technical skills of the students. The book has also been used successfully in professional training programs.

As for prerequisites, I believe a single course in finance is sufficient as a prerequisite, but a second course of almost any finance topic, would be very helpful to have had or be taking contemporaneously.

Acknowledgments

Many individuals contributed greatly to this edition of the book. I would like to thank the following people who formally reviewed the book, provided unsolicited comments, or just responded when I asked if I should make this change or that: Mike Hemler, Steven C. Mann, Bruce Bagamery, Don Rich, Robert Brooks, Randy Billingsley, Tie Su, Jill Wetmore, James Gatti, George Longsen Ye, Jerry James, Joseph Vu, Bruce Rosser, Nancy White Huckins, and Nejat Seyhun. From previous editions, I would like to thank Bill Welch, Mark Rzepczynski, Don Chambers, Peggy Fletcher, Avraham Kamara, Ann Kremer, Jerome Duncan, Dennis Draper, Bob Klemkosky, Doug Hearth, Shanta Hegde, Hun Park, Joan Junkus, Raman Kumar, Jack Broughton, Craig Ruff, Mary Davis, Gopi Maliwal, Herald Stout, Andy Chen, Louis Scott, Eric Chang, John Mitchell, Majed Muhtaseb, Jot Yau, Jorge Urrutia, Ramon Rabinovitch, Bill Reichenstein, Nusret Cakici, Margaret Smoller, John McDonald, Kuldeep Shastri, Jeff Peterson, Patricia Smith, Don Fehrs, Ashok Robin, Jim Alexander, Tim Krehbiel, Kashi Tiwari, Meir Schneller, Trey Snow, Lucy Ackert, Dan Mohan, Dick Rendleman, Phoebe Mix, and Calin Valsan, Their comments and suggestions have greatly improved the text.

A special note of thanks goes to my graduate student, Hillary Fredericks, who worked extensively on this project, especially in the conversion of the option examples from Digital Equipment to America Online and in the notational change. She now has the unique perspective of having seen the book as a student in my class several years ago and as a contributor and hopefully some day will be teaching from it.

I would also like to thank the Harcourt editorial team, led by Mike Reynolds, finance executive editor, Terri House, senior developmental editor, and Jim Patterson, senior project editor. Others on the Harcourt team included Susan Journey, James McDonald, Linda Blundell, Charlie Watson, and Carolyn Crabtree.

I thank my wife Jan, and my children Kim and Ashley, who have grown up as this book has gone through its many revisions. They neither know nor care what the book is about but probably view it as a sibling, given the amount of time I have devoted to it.

I had always felt that the errors in a book should, through attrition over the years, disappear. I have learned otherwise. Although no one wants errors to remain, if you ever find a book in its fifth edition without any errors, you can be assured that the author is simply correcting old material and not keeping the book up-to-date. With a field as dynamic as derivatives, extensive changes are inevitable. Despite Herculean efforts to cleanse this work, there are surely some errors remaining. I feel fairly confident, however, that they are not errors of fact, but merely accidental oversights and perhaps typos that just did not get caught as I read and re-read the material. Unlike most authors, who I think would rather hide known errors, I maintain a list of the errors on the book's Web site (again, that's www.cob.vt.edu/finance/faculty/dmc/IDRM5E.htm). If you see something that does not make sense, check the Web address mentioned above and see if it's there. If not, then send me an e-mail.

Or just send me an e-mail anyway, students or faculty. Tell me what you like or don't like about the book. I would love to hear from you.

Don M. Chance
First Union Professor of Financial Risk Management
Department of Finance - 0221
Pamplin College of Business
Virginia Tech
Blacksburg, VA 24061
dmc@vt.edu
www.cob.vt.edu/finance/faculty/dmc
September 2000

Brief Contents

Contents

CHAPTER 9   **PRINCIPLES OF FORWARD AND FUTURES PRICING**   **357**

CHAPTER 14 INTEREST RATE DERIVATIVES 579

CHAPTER 15 ADVANCED DERIVATIVES AND STRATEGIES 631

Man does not live by stocks and bonds alone.

Chicago Mercantile Exchange advertisement

CHAPTER 1

Introduction

You're into derivatives whether you like it or not. Your adjustable rate mortgage is a derivative. You got a deal on a loan that was cheaper at any time than a fixed-rate mortgage. In return you're taking a risk.

P.J. O'ROURKE
Eat the Rich, 1998

In the course of running a business, decisions are made in the presence of risk. A decision maker can confront one of two types of risk. Some risks are related to the underlying nature of the business and deal with such matters as the uncertainty of future sales or the cost of inputs. These risks are called **business risks.** Another class of risks deals with the uncertainty of such factors as interest rates, exchange rates, stock prices, and commodity prices. These are called **financial risks.** Most businesses are accustomed to accepting business risks. Indeed the acceptance of business risks and the potential rewards that can come with it are the foundations of capitalism.

But financial risks are a different matter. The paralyzing uncertainty of volatile interest rates can cripple the ability of a firm to acquire financing at a reasonable cost, which will enable it to provide its products and services. Firms that operate in foreign markets can have excellent sales performance offset if its own currency is strong. Companies that use raw materials can find it difficult to obtain their basic inputs at a price that will permit profitability. Managers of stock portfolios deal on a day-to-day basis with wildly unpredictable and sometimes seemingly irrational financial markets.

Although our financial system is replete with risk, it also provides a means of dealing with risk, in the form of derivatives. **Derivatives** are financial instruments whose returns are derived from those of other financial instruments. That is, their performance depends on how other financial instruments perform. Derivatives serve a valuable purpose in providing a means of managing financial risk. By using derivatives, companies and individuals can transfer, for a price, any undesired risk to other parties who either have risks that offset or want to assume that risk.

Although derivatives have been around in some form for centuries, their growth has accelerated rapidly during the last 20 years. They are now widely used by corporations, financial institutions, professional investors, and individuals. Certain types of derivatives are traded actively in public markets, similar to the stock exchanges with which you are probably already somewhat familiar. The vast majority of derivatives, however, are created in private transactions. Just as a corporation may buy a tract of land for the purpose of ultimately putting up a factory, so may it also engage in a derivatives transaction. In neither case is the existence or amount of the transaction easy for outsiders to determine. Nonetheless, we have fairly accurate data on the amount of derivatives activity in public markets and reasonably accurate data, based on surveys, on the amount of derivatives activity in private markets. We shall explore the public market data in later chapters. If you need to be convinced that derivatives are worth studying, consider this: *The Bank for International Settlements of Basel, Switzerland, estimated that at the end of 1999, derivatives contracts outstanding worldwide covered underlying assets of over $88 trillion. In comparison, gross domestic product in the United States in 1999 was about $9 trillion.* As we shall see later, measuring the derivatives market this way can give a false impression of the size of the market. Nonetheless, the market value of these contracts totals about $2.8 trillion, making the derivatives market a sizable force in the global economy.

This book is an introductory treatment of derivatives. Derivatives can be based on **real assets,** which are physical assets and include agricultural commodities, metals, and sources of energy. Although a few of these will come up from time to time in this book, our focus will be on derivatives on **financial assets,** which are stocks, bonds/loans, and currencies. In this book you will learn about the characteristics of the institutions and markets where these instruments trade, the manner in which derivative prices are determined, and the strategies in which they are used. Toward the end of the book, we shall cover how derivatives are used in managing the risk of a company.

This chapter welcomes you to the world of derivatives and provides an introduction to or a review of some financial concepts that you will need to understand derivatives. Let us begin by exploring the derivatives markets more closely and defining what we mean by these types of instruments.

Derivative Markets

In the markets for assets, purchases and sales require that the underlying good or security be delivered either immediately or shortly thereafter. Payment usually is made immediately, although credit arrangements are sometimes used. Because of these characteristics, we refer to these markets as

cash markets or **spot markets.** The sale is made, the payment is remitted, and the good or security is delivered. In other situations, the good or security is to be delivered at a later date. Still other types of arrangements let the buyer or seller choose whether or not to go through with the sale. These types of arrangements are conducted in derivative markets.

In contrast to the market for assets, derivative markets are markets for contractual instruments whose performance is determined by how another instrument or asset performs. Notice that we referred to derivatives as contracts. Like all contracts, they are agreements between two parties—a buyer and a seller—in which each party does something for the other. These contracts have a price, and buyers try to buy as cheaply as possible while sellers try to sell as dearly as possible. This section briefly introduces the various types of derivative contracts: options, forward contracts, futures contracts, and swaps and related derivatives.

Options

An **option** is a contract between two parties—a buyer and a seller—that gives the buyer the right, but not the obligation, to purchase or sell something at a later date at a price agreed upon today.

The option buyer pays the seller a sum of money called the price or premium. The option seller stands ready to sell or buy according to the contract terms if and when the buyer so desires. An option to buy something is referred to as a **call;** an option to sell something is called a **put.** Although options trade in organized markets, a large amount of option trading is conducted privately between two parties who find that contracting with each other may be preferable to a public transaction on the exchange. This type of market, called an over-the-counter market, was actually the first type of options market. The creation of an organized options exchange in 1973 reduced the interest in over-the-counter option markets; however, the over-the-counter market has been revived and is now very large and widely used, mostly by corporations and financial institutions.

Most of the options that we shall focus on trade on organized options exchanges, but the principles of pricing and using options are pretty much the same, regardless of where the option trades. Most of the options of our interest are for the purchase or sale of financial assets, such as stocks or bonds. There are, however, also options on futures contracts, metals, and foreign currencies. Many other types of financial arrangements, such as lines of credit, loan guaranties, and insurance, are forms of options. Moreover, stock itself is equivalent to an option on the firm's assets.

Forward Contracts

A **forward contract** is an agreement between two parties—a buyer and a seller—to purchase or sell something at a later date at a price agreed upon today. A forward contract sounds a lot like an option, but an option carries the right, not the obligation, to go through with the transaction. If the price of the underlying good changes, the option holder may decide to forgo buying or selling at the fixed price. On the other hand, the two parties in a forward contract incur the obligation to ultimately buy and sell the good.

Although forward markets have existed in this country for a long time, they are somewhat less familiar. Unlike options markets, they have no physical facilities for trading; there is no building or formal corporate body organized as the market. They trade strictly in an over-the-counter market consisting of direct communications among major financial institutions.

Forward markets for foreign exchange have existed for many years. With the rapid growth of derivative markets, we have seen an explosion of growth in forward markets for other instruments. It is now just as easy to enter into forward contracts for a stock index or oil as it was formerly to trade foreign currencies. Forward contracts are also extremely useful in that they facilitate the understanding of futures contracts.

Futures Contracts

A **futures contract** is an agreement between two parties — a buyer and a seller — to buy or sell something at a future date. The contract trades on a futures exchange and is subject to a daily settlement procedure. Futures contracts evolved out of forward contracts and possess many of the same characteristics. In essence, they are like liquid forward contracts. Unlike forward contracts, however, futures contracts trade on organized exchanges, called **futures markets.** For example, the buyer of a futures contract, who has the obligation to buy the good at the later date, can sell the contract in the futures market, which relieves him or her of the obligation to purchase the good. Likewise, the seller of the futures contract, who is obligated to sell the good at the later date, can buy the contract back in the futures market, relieving him or her of the obligation to sell the good.

Futures contracts also differ from forward contracts in that they are subject to a daily settlement procedure. In the daily settlement, investors who incur losses pay them every day to investors who make profits. We shall learn more about this in Chapter 8.

Futures prices fluctuate from day to day, and contract buyers and sellers attempt to profit from these price changes and to lower the risk of transacting in the underlying goods.

Options on Futures

Options on futures, sometimes called *commodity options* or *futures options,* are an important synthesis of futures and options markets. An option on a futures contract gives the buyer the right to buy or sell a futures contract at a later date at a price agreed upon today. Options on futures trade on futures exchanges and are a rare case where the derivative contract and the instrument on which it is derived trade side by side in an open market. Although options on futures are quite similar to options on spot assets, there are a few important differences. We shall cover options on futures in more depth in Chapter 12.

Swaps and Other Derivatives

Although options, forwards, and futures compose the set of basic instruments in derivative markets, there are many more combinations and variations. One of the most popular is called a **swap.** A swap is a contract in which two parties agree to exchange cash flows. For example, one party is currently receiving cash from one investment but would prefer another type of investment in which the cash flows are different. The party goes to a swap dealer, a firm operating in the over-the-counter market, who takes the opposite side of the transaction. The firm and the dealer, in effect, swap cash flow streams. Depending on what later happens to prices or interest rates, one party might gain at the expense of the other. In another type of arrangement, a firm might elect to tie the payments it makes on the swap contract to the price of a commodity, called a commodity swap, while in a different deal, a firm might buy an option to enter into a swap, called a **swaption.** As we shall show later, swaps can be viewed as a combination of forward contracts, and swaptions are just special types of options.

Swaps make up slightly more than half of the $88 trillion national principal over-the-counter derivatives market. But swaps are only one of many types of contracts that combine elements of forwards, futures, and options. For example, a firm that borrows money at a floating rate is susceptible to rising interest rates. It can reduce that risk, however, by buying a cap, which is essentially an option that pays off whenever interest rates rise above a threshold. Another firm may choose to purchase an option whose performance depends not on how one asset performs but rather on the better or worse performing of two or even more than two assets, called an alternative option.

Some of these types of contracts are referred to as **hybrids** because they combine the elements of several other types of contracts. All of them are indications of the ingenuity of participants in today's financial markets, who are constantly creating new and useful products to meet the diverse needs of investors. This process of creating new financial products is sometimes referred to as **financial engineering.** These hybrid instruments represent the effects of progress in our financial system. They are examples of change and innovation that have led to improved opportunities for risk management. Swaps, caps, and many other hybrid instruments are covered in Chapters 14 and 15.

The different types of derivatives include options, forwards, futures, options on futures, swaps, and hybrids.

D e r i v a t i v e s   i n   A c t i o n

Home Buying Derivatives

Kevin and Sharon Colburn are a young couple, married for five years, and living in the community of Herndon, Virginia, about 20 miles west of Washington, D.C. Kevin, age 29, is a programmer for an Internet-based company in the sprawling Reston-Dulles area, and Sharon, age 30, commutes to Arlington, where she manages the office for an insurance company. They have no children. Kevin and Sharon are renting an apartment and facing a decision about whether to renew their lease. They have discussed trying to buy a home. Interest rates are attractive right now, but they wish rates were a little lower. Nonetheless, they choose not to continue renting and to start searching for a home.

Kevin and Sharon then find their home in Reston and make an offer of $200,000. With that offer, they are required to post a $5,000 check with the realtor in the form of a performance bond. If Kevin and Sharon renege, they lose the money. If not, it is applied toward the purchase of the home. The seller accepts their offer. Kevin and Sharon have, thus, entered into a con-tract to purchase their home at a specific closing date at a price they agree on today.

Now they apply for a mortgage. They will be able to put $25,000 down and will borrow the remaining amount. The mortgage lender says they can borrow at a fixed rate of 8.5 percent or a floating rate of 7.5 percent. If they take the floating-rate loan, their rate will be set at 2 percent over the rate on a two-year U.S. government Treasury note. The rate will be adjusted every year, will not rise more than 2 percent in a year, and has a lifetime cap of 13 percent. Kevin and Sharon wonder which type of loan will be better and whether, in spite of the cap features, they can handle the potentially higher interest payments.

They elect to go with the fixed-rate loan. The closing date on the house is two months from now. The bank guarantees the fixed rate but also tells them that if they are willing to pay $500, then they can have the fixed rate that is in effect on the closing date, if that rate is lower. If that rate is higher, they can have the original fixed rate. Cash is tight so they elect to take the

Some Important Concepts in Financial and Derivative Markets

Before undertaking any further study of derivative markets, let us review some introductory concepts pertaining to investment opportunities and investors. Many of these ideas may already be familiar and usually are applied in the context of trading in stocks and bonds. These concepts also apply with slight modifications to trading in derivatives.

Risk Preference

Suppose you were faced with two equally likely outcomes. If the first outcome occurs, you receive $5. If the second outcome occurs, you receive $2. From elementary statistics, you know that the expected outcome is $5(.5)+$2(.5) = $3.50, which is the amount you would expect to receive on average after playing the game many times. How much would you be willing to pay to take this risk? If you say $3.50, you are not recognizing the original fixed rate and not pay the $500 for the opportunity to get a lower fixed rate.

The mortgage that they take offers the feature that they can repay it at any time without penalty. Kevin and Sharon realize that this feature is quite valuable, for their parents both refinanced their homes when interest rates fell.

In this hypothetical, but extremely common, story, Kevin and Sharon confronted several derivatives. First, they were considering re-signing a lease. The lease requires that they make a series of fixed payments over a 12-month period, for which they receive the use of the apartment. This is a type of derivative known as a swap.

They then chose to enter into an agreement to buy an asset, the house, at a later date at a price they agree on in advance. To secure their commitment they offered a collateral deposit. What they did was enter into something similar to a forward or futures contract.

They were offered a mortgage with a fluctuating interest rate but with a cap on the increase in the rate plus an overall lifetime cap. These caps are forms of options. The options would, in effect, compensate them for increases in interest rates, thereby helping them to control some of the risk. The fixed-rate loan alternative allowed them to lock in the rate and, therefore, not to worry about the course of interest rates over the next two months. Alternatively, if they wanted to take advantage of the possibility of falling rates, they could pay $500 cash and have the right to pay a lower rate if a lower rate was in effect on the closing date. This is also an option.

Nonetheless, Kevin and Sharon chose to borrow at a fixed rate and passed up the option to borrow at a lower rate. The loan offered them the right to refinance their mortgage at any time without a penalty. This, too, is an option.

So this ordinary couple, in the course of an extremely common series of family financial decisions, confronted and, in some cases, engaged in derivative transactions. These transactions were made in light of a great deal of consideration of the risks they faced both before and after using these derivatives.

risk inherent in the situation. You are simply saying that a fair trade would be for you to give up $3.50 for the chance to make $3.50 on average. You would be described as **risk neutral,** meaning that you are indifferent to the risk. Most individuals, however, would not find this a fair trade. They recognize that the $3.50 you pay is given up for certain, while the $3.50 you expect to receive is earned only on average. In fact, if you play twice, lose $3.50 once and then gain it back, you will feel worse than if you had not played.

Thus, we say that most individuals have **risk aversion.** They would pay less than $3.50 to take this risk. How much less depends on how risk averse they are. People differ in their degrees of risk aversion. But let us say you would pay $3.25. Then the difference between $3.50 and $3.25 is considered the **risk premium.** This is the additional return you expect to earn to justify taking the risk.

Although most individuals are indeed risk averse, it may surprise you to find that in the world of derivative markets, we can actually pretend that most people are risk neutral. No, we are not making some heroic but unrealistic assumption. It turns out that we obtain the same results in a world of risk aversion as we do in a world of risk neutrality. Although this is a useful point in understanding derivative markets, we shall not explore it in much depth at the level of this book. Yet without realizing it, you will probably grow to accept and understand derivative models and the hidden implication of risk neutrality.

Short Selling

If you have already taken an investments course, you probably have been exposed to the idea of short selling. Nonetheless, the concept is not too straightforward and a little review will be beneficial.

A typical transaction in the stock market involves one party buying stock from another party. It is possible, however, that the party selling the stock does not actually own the stock. That party could borrow the stock from a broker. That person is said to be **selling short** or, sometimes, *shorting*. He or she is doing so in the anticipation of the price falling, at which time the short seller would then buy back the stock at a lower price, capturing a profit and repaying the shares to the broker. You may have heard the expression, "Don't sell yourself short," which simply means not to view yourself as being less talented or less correct than someone else. Similarly, a short seller views the stock as being worth less than the market price.

Establishing a short position creates a liability. The short seller is obligated to someday buy back the stock and return it to the broker. Unlike an ordinary loan in which a borrower knows exactly how much he or she must pay back the lender, the short seller does not know how much he or she will have to pay to buy back the shares. This makes it a rather risky type of borrowing. Indeed short selling is a very daring investment strategy.

Short selling, however, can be quite beneficial in that the risk of short positions can be useful in offsetting the risk of long positions. The short selling of derivatives is particularly helpful. Short selling of stocks can be quite complex and expensive relative to buying stocks, whereas short selling of derivatives is as simple as buying derivatives. Thus, it is common to find an investor holding a stock and protecting it by selling short a derivative.

We should note that anyone who has an obligation to purchase something at a later date has the equivalent of a short sale. It is not necessary to have borrowed stock from a broker. In either case an increase in the price will be harmful.

Return and Risk

Return is the numerical measure of investment performance. It represents the percentage increase in the investor's wealth that results from making the investment. In the case of stocks, the return is the percentage change in price plus the dividend yield. The concept of return also applies to options, but, as we shall see later, the definition of the return on a futures or forward contract is somewhat unclear.

One fundamental characteristic of investors is their desire to increase their wealth. This translates into obtaining the highest return possible — but higher returns are accompanied by greater risk. **Risk** is the uncertainty of future returns. As we noted earlier, investors generally dislike risk, and they demonstrate this by avoiding risky situations when riskless ones that offer equivalent expected returns exist; however, they cannot always avoid uncertainty. Fortunately, the competitive nature of financial and derivative markets enables investors to identify investments by their degrees of risk.

For example, the stock of a company that specializes in drilling wildcat oil wells will, all other things being equal, sell for less than the stock of a company that supplies health care.[1] That is because the drilling company is engaged in a more uncertain line of business. Risk, of course, runs the spectrum from zero risk to high risk. The prices of securities will reflect the differences in the companies' risk levels. The additional return one expects to earn from assuming risk is the risk premium, which we mentioned earlier.

What other factors influence a company's stock price and expected return? Consider a hypothetical company with no risk. Will people be willing to invest money in this company if they expect no return? Certainly not. They will require a minimum return, one sufficient to compensate them for giving up the opportunity to spend their money today. This return is called the **risk-free rate** and is the investment's opportunity cost.[2]

The return investors expect is composed of the risk-free rate and a risk premium. This relationship is illustrated in Figure 1.1, where $E(r_s)$ is the expected return on the spot asset, r is the risk-free rate, and $E(\phi)$ is the risk premium — the excess of expected return over the risk-free rate.

Note that we have not identified how risk is measured. You might recall risk measures such as standard deviation and beta. At this point, we need not be concerned with the specific measure of risk. The important point is the positive relationship between risk and return known as the **risk-return trade-off.** The risk-return trade-off arises because all investors seek to maximize return subject to a minimum level of risk. If a stock moves up the line into a higher risk level, some investors will find it too risky and will sell the

---

[1] In this context, "all other things being equal" means that the comparisons have not been distorted by differences in the number of shares outstanding or the amount of financial leverage.

[2] The concept of the risk-free rate and opportunity cost is nicely illustrated by the Biblical parable about the wealthy man who entrusted three servants to manage some of his money. Two of the servants earned 100 percent returns, while the third buried the money and returned only the principal sum. The man was infuriated that the third servant had not even earned the risk-free interest rate by putting the money in the bank, whereupon he reallocated the funds to one of the other servants' portfolios. The third servant, who was summarily discharged, evidently was not destined for a career as an investment manager.

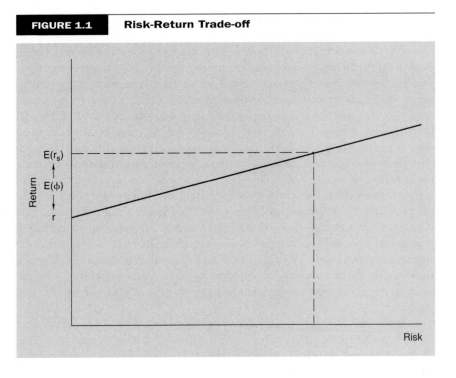

FIGURE 1.1   **Risk-Return Trade-off**

stock, which will drive down its price. New investors in the stock will expect to earn higher returns by virtue of paying a lower price for it.

The financial markets are very effective at discriminating among firms with different risk levels. Firms with low risk will find capital plentiful and inexpensive. Firms with high risk may have trouble raising capital and will pay dearly. Markets that do a good job of pricing the instruments trading therein are said to be efficient and the assets are said to be priced at their **theoretical fair values.**

Market Efficiency and Theoretical Fair Value

Market efficiency is the characteristic of a market in which the prices of the instruments trading therein reflect their true economic values to investors. In an efficient market, prices fluctuate randomly and investors cannot consistently earn returns above those that would compensate them for the level of risk they assume.

The idea that an asset has a "true economic value" is a particularly appealing concept. It suggests that somewhere out there is the *real* value of the asset. If we could determine the real value, we could perhaps make lots of money buying when the asset is priced too low and selling when it is priced too high. But finding the true economic value requires a model of how the asset is priced.

In this book we shall call the true economic value of the asset its *theoretical fair value.* There are many models that give the theoretical fair values of assets. You have probably already heard of the Capital Asset Pricing Model and perhaps the Arbitrage Pricing Theory. Derivatives also have theoretical fair values and a great deal of emphasis is placed in this book on determining the theoretical fair value of a derivative contract. Of course, these models and their respective values are correct only if the market is efficient. Fortunately, there is considerable statistical evidence supporting the notion that our markets are efficient. This is not surprising. Market efficiency is such a natural consequence of rational and knowledgeable investor behavior that we should be surprised if it did not hold.

Thus, as we weave our way through the world of derivatives, we should keep in mind that by and large these markets are efficient. Although this book presents numerous strategies for using derivatives, all of them assume that the investor has already developed expectations about the direction of the market. Derivative strategies show how to profit if those expectations prove correct and how to minimize the risk of loss if they prove wrong. These strategies are methods for managing the level of risk and thus should be considered essential tools for survival in efficient markets.

An efficient market is one in which the price of an asset equals its true economic value, which is called the **theoretical fair value.** Spot and derivative markets are normally quite efficient.

Fundamental Linkages between Spot and Derivative Markets

So far we have not established a formal connection between spot and derivative markets. Instruments such as options, forwards, and futures are available for the purchase and sale of spot market assets, such as stocks and bonds. The prices of the derivatives are related to those of the underlying spot market instruments through several important mechanisms. Chapters 3, 4, 5, and 9 examine these linkages in detail; nevertheless, a general overview of the process here will be beneficial.

Arbitrage and the Law of One Price

Arbitrage is a type of transaction in which an investor seeks to profit when the same good sells for two different prices. The individual engaging in the arbitrage, called the arbitrageur, buys the good at the lower price and immediately sells it at the higher price. Arbitrage is an attractive strategy for investors. Thousands of individuals devote their time to looking for arbitrage opportunities. If a stock sells on one exchange at one price and on another at a different price, arbitrageurs will go to work buying at the low price and selling at the high price. The low price will be driven up and the high price driven down until the two prices are equal.

In your day-to-day life, you make many purchases and sales. Sometimes you encounter the same good selling for two different prices; for example, a computer from a mail-order discount house may cost less than the same computer at a local computer store. Why is there a difference? The store may offer longer warranties, localized service, and other conveniences not available through the discounter. Likewise, a pair of running shoes purchased at a local discounter may be cheaper than the same one purchased at a sporting goods store, where you pay extra for service and product knowledge. Where real differences exist between identical goods, the prices will differ.

But sometimes the differences appear real when they actually are not. For example, suppose there are two possible outcomes that might occur. We call these states of the world. Look at the outcomes illustrated in Figure 1.2 for two securities, S1 and S2. If state 1 occurs, stock S1 will be worth $100, while if state 2 occurs, it will be worth $80. In state 1 stock S2 will be worth $50, and in state 2 it will be worth $40. It should be obvious that stock S1 is equivalent to two shares of stock S2. Or in other words, by buying two shares of stock S2, you could obtain the same outcomes as by buying one share of stock S1.

Now suppose stock S1 is selling for $85. What should be the price of S2? Suppose it is $39. Then you could buy two shares of S2, paying $78, and sell short one share of S1 by borrowing the share from your broker. The short sale of S1 means you will receive its price, $85, up front. Then when the state of the world is revealed, you can sell your two shares of S2 and

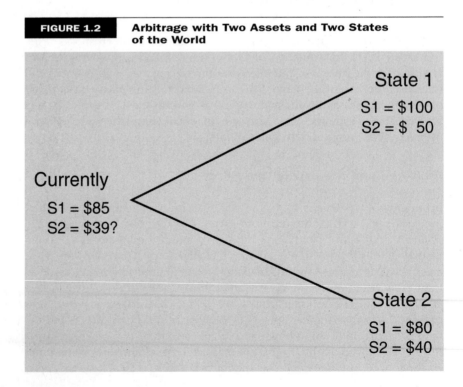

FIGURE 1.2   **Arbitrage with Two Assets and Two States of the World**

Currently
S1 = $85
S2 = $39?

State 1
S1 = $100
S2 = $ 50

State 2
S1 = $80
S2 = $40

generate exactly the amount of cash needed to buy the one share of S1 you will need to pay back your broker. Thus, there is no risk to this transaction and yet you received a net cash flow of $7 up front. This is like a loan in which you borrow $7 and do not have to pay back anything. Obviously everyone would do this, which would push up the price of S2 and push down the price of S1 until the price of S1 was exactly equal to two times the price of S2.

The rule that states that these prices must be driven into line in this manner is called the **law of one price.** The law of one price does not mean that the price of S2 must equal the price of S1. Rather it states that equivalent combinations of financial instruments must have a single price. Here the combination of two units of S2 must have the same price as one unit of S1.

The *law of one price* requires that equivalent combinations of assets, meaning those that offer the same outcomes, must sell for a single price or else there would be an opportunity for profitable arbitrage that would quickly eliminate the price differential.

Markets ruled by the law of one price have the following four characteristics:

- Investors always prefer more wealth to less.

- Given two investment opportunities, investors will always prefer one that performs at least as well as the other in all states and better in at least one state.

- If two investment opportunities offer equivalent outcomes, they must have equivalent prices.

- An investment opportunity that produces the same return in all states is risk-free and must earn the risk-free rate.

In later chapters, we shall see these rules in action.

In an efficient market, violations of the law of one price should never occur. But occasionally prices get out of line, perhaps through momentary oversight. Arbitrage is the mechanism that keeps prices in line. To make intelligent investment decisions, we need to learn how arbitrage transactions are made, which we shall do in later chapters.

The Storage Mechanism: Spreading Consumption across Time

Storage is an important linkage between spot and derivative markets. Many types of assets can be purchased and stored. Holding a stock or bond is a form of storage. Even making a loan is a form of storage. One can also buy a commodity, such as wheat or corn, and store it in a grain elevator. Storage is a form of investment in which one defers selling the item today in anticipation of selling it at a later date. Storage spreads consumption across time.

Because prices constantly fluctuate, storage entails risk. Derivatives can be used to reduce that risk by providing a means of establishing today the item's future sale price. This suggests that the risk entailed in storing the item can be removed. In that case, the overall investment should offer the risk-free rate. Therefore, it is not surprising that the prices of the storable item, the derivative contract, and the risk-free rate will all be related.

Delivery and Settlement

Another important linkage between spot and derivative markets is delivery and settlement. At expiration, a forward or futures contract calls for either immediate delivery of the item or a cash payment of the same value. Thus, an expiring forward or futures contract is equivalent to a spot transaction. The price of the expiring contract, therefore, must equal the spot price. Though options differ somewhat from forwards and futures at expiration, these instruments have an unambiguous value at expiration that is determined by the spot price.

Few derivative traders hold their positions until the contracts expire.[3] They use the market's liquidity to enter into offsetting transactions. Nonetheless, the fact that delivery or an equivalent cash payment will occur on positions open at expiration is an important consideration in pricing the spot and derivative instruments.

The foregoing properties play an important role in these markets' performance. Derivative and spot markets are inextricably linked. Nonetheless, we have not yet determined what role derivative markets play in the operations of spot markets.

The Role of Derivative Markets

Risk Management

Because derivative prices are related to the prices of the underlying spot market goods, they can be used to reduce or increase the risk of owning the spot items. For example, buying the spot item and selling a futures contract or call option reduces the investor's risk. If the good's price falls, the price of the futures or option contract will also fall. The investor can then repurchase the contract at the lower price, effecting a gain that can at least partially offset the loss on the spot item. This type of transaction is known as a hedge.

As we noted earlier, investors have different risk preferences. Some are more tolerant of risk than others. All investors, however, want to keep their investments at an acceptable risk level. Derivative markets enable those wishing to reduce their risk to transfer it to those wishing to increase it, whom we call speculators. Because these markets are so effective at reallo-

---

[3]On derivative contracts that do not call for delivery at expiration, but specify that an economically equivalent cash payment be made, positions are more likely to be held to expiration.

cating risk among investors, no one need assume an uncomfortable level of risk. Consequently, investors are willing to supply more funds to the financial markets. This benefits the economy, because it enables more firms to raise capital and keeps the cost of that capital as low as possible.

As noted, on the other side of hedging is speculation. Unless a hedger can find another hedger with opposite needs, the hedger's risk must be assumed by a speculator. Derivative markets provide an alternative and efficient means of speculating. Instead of trading the underlying stocks or bonds, an investor can trade a derivative contract. Many investors prefer to speculate with derivatives rather than with the underlying securities. The ease with which speculation can be done using derivatives in turn makes it easier and less costly for hedgers.

We would be remiss, however, if we left it at that. Speculation is controversial. Derivative markets have taken much criticism from outsiders, including accusations that their activities are tantamount to legalized gambling. We shall look at this point in a later section.

Price Discovery

Forward and futures markets are an important source of information about prices. Futures markets, in particular, are considered a primary means for determining the spot price of an asset. This should seem unusual, since a spot market for the asset must exist, but for many assets on which futures trade, the spot market is large and fragmented. Gold, oil, and commodities trade at different places and at different times. Within each asset's class, there are many varieties and quality grades. Hence, there are many potential candidates for the "spot" price of an asset. The futures market assembles that information into a type of consensus, reflecting the spot price of the particular asset on which the futures contract is based. The price of the futures contract that expires the earliest is often treated as the spot price.

Futures and forward prices also contain information about what people expect future spot prices to be. As we shall see later, spot prices contain this same information, but it may be harder to extract that information from the spot market than from the futures market. Moreover, in almost all cases, the futures market is more active and, hence, information taken from it is often considered more reliable than spot market information. While a futures or forward price should not necessarily be treated as an expected future spot price, a futures or forward price does reflect a price that a market participant could lock in today in lieu of accepting the uncertainty of the future spot price.

Hence, futures and forward markets are said to provide price discovery. Options markets do not directly provide forecasts of future spot prices. They do, however, provide valuable information about the volatility and, hence, the risk of the underlying spot asset.

Operational Advantages

Derivative markets offer several operational advantages. First, they entail lower transaction costs. This means that commissions and other trading costs are lower for traders in these markets. This makes it easy and attractive to use these markets either in lieu of spot market transactions or as a complement to spot positions.

Second, derivative markets, particularly the futures and options exchanges, have greater liquidity than the spot markets. Although spot markets generally are quite liquid for the securities of major companies, they cannot always absorb some of the large dollar transactions without substantial price changes. In some cases, one can obtain the same levels of expected return and risk by using derivative markets, which can more easily accommodate high-volume trades. This higher liquidity is at least partly due to the smaller amount of capital required for participation in derivative markets. Returns and risks can be adjusted to any level desired, but because less capital is required, these markets can absorb more trading.

Third, as noted earlier, derivative markets allow investors to sell short more easily. Securities markets impose several restrictions designed to limit or discourage short selling that are not applied to derivative transactions. Consequently, many investors sell short in these markets in lieu of selling short the underlying securities.

Market Efficiency

Spot markets for securities probably would be efficient even if there were no derivative markets. A few profitable arbitrage opportunities exist, however, even in markets that are usually efficient. The presence of these opportunities means that the prices of some assets are temporarily out of line with what they should be. Investors can earn returns that exceed what the market deems fair for the given risk level.

As noted earlier, there are important linkages among spot and derivative prices. The ease and low cost of transacting in these markets facilitate the arbitrage trading and rapid price adjustments that quickly eradicate these profit opportunities. Society benefits because the prices of the underlying goods more accurately reflect the goods' true economic values.

Derivative markets provide a means of managing risk, discovering prices, reducing costs, improving liquidity, selling short, and making the market more efficient.

Criticisms of Derivative Markets

As noted earlier, derivative markets allow the transfer of risk from those wanting to remove or decrease it to those wanting to assume or increase it. These markets require the presence of speculators willing to assume risk to accommodate the hedgers wishing to reduce it. Most speculators do not actually deal in the underlying goods and sometimes are alleged to know nothing about them. Consequently, these speculators have been characterized as little more than gamblers.

This view is a bit one-sided and ignores the many benefits of derivative markets. More important, it suggests that these markets siphon capital into wildly speculative schemes. Nothing could be further from the truth. Unlike financial markets, derivative markets neither create nor destroy wealth — they merely provide a means to transfer risk.

For example, stock markets can create wealth. Consider a firm with a new idea that offers stock to the public. Investors buy the stock, and the firm uses the capital to develop and market the idea. Customers then buy the product or service, the firm earns a profit, the stock price increases, and everyone is better off. In contrast, in derivative markets one party's gains are another's losses. These markets put no additional risk into the economy; they merely allow risk to be passed from one investor to another. More important, they allow the risk of transacting in real goods to be transferred from those not wanting it to those willing to accept it.

An important distinction between derivative markets and gambling is in the benefits provided to society. Gambling benefits only the participants and perhaps a few others who profit indirectly. The benefits of derivatives, however, extend far beyond the market participants. Derivatives help financial markets become more efficient and provide better opportunities for managing risk. These benefits spill over into society as a whole.

Misuses of Derivatives

Derivatives have occasionally been criticized for having been the source of large losses by some corporations, investment funds, state and local governments, nonprofit investors, and some individuals. Are derivatives really at fault? Is electricity to be faulted when someone with little knowledge of it mishandles it? Is fire to be blamed when someone using it becomes careless?

There is little question that derivatives are powerful instruments. They typically contain a high degree of leverage, meaning that small price changes can lead to large gains and losses. Though this would appear to be an undesirable feature of derivatives, it actually is what makes them most useful in providing the benefits discussed earlier. These are points we shall study later. At this time, however, you should recognize that to use derivatives without having the requisite knowledge is dangerous. That is all the more reason why you should be glad you have chosen to study the subject.

Having acquired that knowledge, however, does not free you of the responsibility to act sensibly. To use derivatives in inappropriate situations is dangerous. The temptation to speculate when one should be hedging is a risk that even the knowledgeable often take. Having excessive confidence in one's ability to forecast prices or interest rates and then acting on those forecasts by using derivatives can be extremely risky. You should never forget what we said about efficient markets. Regrettably in recent years many individuals have led their firms down the path of danger and destruction by forgetting these points, with the consequence that derivatives and not people are often blamed.

Fortunately derivatives are normally used by knowledgeable persons in situations where they serve an appropriate purpose. We hear far too little about the firms and investors who saved money, avoided losses, and restructured their risks successfully.

Derivatives and Your Career

It is tempting to believe that derivatives are but an interesting subject for study. You might feel that you would someday want to buy an option for your personal investment portfolio. You might think that you are unlikely to encounter derivatives in your career in business. That is simply not true.

As we noted earlier, the primary use of derivatives is in risk management. Businesses, by their very nature, face risks. Some of those risks are acceptable; indeed a business must assume some type of risk or there is no reason to be in business. But other types of risks are unacceptable and should be managed, if not eliminated. For example, a small furniture manufacturer may borrow money from a bank at a rate that will be adjusted periodically to reflect current interest rates. The furniture manufacturer is in the business of making money off the furniture market. It is not particularly suited to forecasting interest rates. Yet interest rate increases could severely hamper its ability to make a profit from its furniture business. If that firm sells its products in foreign countries, even in our nearby neighbors Canada and Mexico, it may face significant foreign exchange risk. If the raw materials it purchases and the energy it consumes are subject to uncertain future prices, as they surely are, the firm faces additional risks, all having the potential to undermine its success in its main line of business.

It was but a few years ago that a small firm would not be expected to use derivatives to manage its interest rate or foreign exchange risk, nor would it be able to do so if it wanted. The minimum sizes of transactions were too large. Times have changed now and smaller firms are more able to use derivatives.

If your career takes you into investment management, you will surely encounter derivatives. Those in public service who manage the assets of governments are finding numerous applications of derivatives. Those responsible for the commodities and energy purchased by firms will encounter situations where derivatives are or can be used. In short, derivatives are becoming commonplace and are likely to be even more so for the foreseeable future.

By taking a course and/or reading this book on derivatives, you are making the first step toward obtaining the tools necessary to understand the nature and management of risk, a subject that lies at the very heart of a business.

Summary

This chapter began by distinguishing between business and financial risk and by identifying that financial risk results from uncertainty in interest rates, exchange rates, stock prices, and commodity prices. It then introduced derivatives as a means of managing financial risk. It described the different types of derivatives and reviewed the concepts of risk preference, short selling, return and risk, and market efficiency/theoretical fair value. It introduced the principles of arbitrage and the Law of One Price, the concept of storage, and the practice of delivery/settlement. It described the role of derivative markets in terms of helping to manage risk, discovering prices, lowering transaction costs and other operational advantages, and promoting a more efficient market. It identified and responded to criticisms of derivative markets and discussed the potential misuses of derivatives.

Chapters 2 through 7 discuss options markets, and Chapters 8 through 11 cover forward and futures markets. Parts One and Two take a parallel approach. Chapters 2 and 8 discuss the characteristics of these markets; Chapters 3, 4, 5, and 9 are devoted to pricing principles; and Chapters 6, 7, 10, and 11 illustrate trading strategies.

Part Three contains five chapters that deal with advanced topics in derivatives. Chapter 12 covers options on futures. Chapter 13 focuses on foreign currency derivatives. Chapter 14 examines swaps and other interest rate derivatives. Chapter 15 covers advanced derivatives and strategies. Chapter 16 concludes the book with the subject of risk management.

Key Terms

Before continuing to Chapter 2, you should be able to give brief definitions of the following terms.

- business risk
- financial risk
- derivative
- real asset
- financial asset
- cash market/spot market
- option
- call
- put
- forward contract
- futures contract
- futures market
- option on futures
- swap
- swaption
- hybrid
- financial engineering
- risk neutrality
- risk aversion
- risk premium
- selling short
- return
- risk
- risk-free rate
- risk-return trade-off
- theoretical fair value
- market efficiency
- arbitrage
- law of one price

Further Reading

The following sources treat derivatives in a nontechnical manner.

Chance, D. M. *Essays in Derivatives*. New Hope, PA: Frank Fabozzi Associates, 1998.

Johnson, P. M. *Derivatives: A Manager's Guide to the World's Most Powerful Financial Instruments*. New York: McGraw-Hill, 1999.

Klein, R. A., and J. Lederman. *Derivatives Risk and Responsibility*. Chicago: Irwin, 1996.

McLaughlin, R. M. *Over-the-Counter Derivative Products*. New York: McGraw-Hill, 1999.

Questions and Problems

1. Distinguish between business risk and financial risk.
2. Distinguish between real assets and financial assets.
3. What is the difference between an investor who is risk neutral and one who is risk averse?
4. Explain the concept of a risk-return trade-off.
5. What are the components of the expected return?
6. What is an efficient market? Why do efficient markets benefit society?
7. Define arbitrage and the law of one price. What role do they play in our market system? What do we call the "one price" of an asset?
8. Suppose you are shopping for a new automobile. You find the same car at two dealers but at different prices. Is the law of one price being violated? Why or why not?
9. What is storage? Why is it risky? What role does it play in the economy?
10. Why is delivery important if so few futures contracts end in delivery?
11. What are the major functions of derivative markets in an economy?
12. Why is speculation controversial? How does it differ from gambling?
13. What are the three ways in which derivatives can be misused?
14. Assume you have an opportunity to visit a civilization in outer space. Its society is at roughly the same stage of development as U.S. society is now. Its economic system is virtually identical to that of the United States, but derivative trading is illegal. Compare and contrast this economy with the U.S. economy, emphasizing the differences due to the presence of derivative markets in the latter.

APPENDIX 1
Sources of Information on Derivatives

The derivative markets have become so visible in today's financial system that virtually any publication that covers the stock and bond markets contains some coverage of derivatives.

More detailed information about derivative markets is provided in numerous other publications whose web sites are listed below.

Specialized Trade Publications

These publications, targeted toward practitioners, provide the most current and practical information about the derivative markets.

Derivatives Strategy: www.derivativesstrategy.com

Derivatives Week: www.derivativesweek.com

Financial Engineering News: www.fenews.com

Futures: www.futuresmag.com

Futures and Options World: www.fow.com

Futures Industry: www.fiafii.org

Risk: www.riskpublications.com

Swaps Monitor: www.swapsmonitor.com

Specialized Derivatives Journals

The specialized derivatives journals are generally of high quality and appeal to academics as well as to practitioners.

The Journal of Computational Finance: www.riskpublications.com/jcf

The Journal of Derivatives: www.iafe.org/journal

The Journal of Futures Markets: journals.wiley.com

The Journal of Risk: www.riskpublications.com/jrisk

Review of Derivatives Research: www.wkap.nl/journalhome.htm/1380-6645

Internet Sites

With the rapidly expanding Internet, derivatives information is widely available on the World Wide Web. Given the speed with which information is updated, it is impossible to provide current information in print. Listed here are several excellent sites maintained by individuals and institutions that provide links to derivatives resources on the Internet.

Applied Derivatives Trading: www.adtrading.com

Contingency Analysis: www.contingencyanalysis.com

Finance Wat.ch: Finance.Wat.ch

FinanceWise: www.financewise.com

Gibbon's Burkes' Hot Links for Traders: www.io.com/~gibbonsb/wahoo.html

INO: www.ino.com

Numa Web Internet Resource Center for Derivatives: www.numa.com

Yahoo's List of Futures and Options Sites: dir.yahoo.com/business_and_economy/ Finance_and_Investment/Futures_and_Options

The author of this book will maintain and update this list on his home page at www.cob.vt.edu/finance/faculty/dmc/derivs/drvsites.htm

In addition, the *Financial Economics Network* provides an electronic service for delivery of abstracts of working papers and forthcoming articles in various fields of the social sciences. A series in derivatives is available at: www.ssrn.com/FEN

The two usenet groups misc.invest.options and misc.invest.futures are also useful resources.

Other Sources

The following organizations provide information, much of it free, on derivatives. In addition, the futures and options exchanges, whose addresses are given in Chapters 2 and 8, as well as brokerage firms are excellent and inexpensive sources of information.

Bank for International Settlements: www.bis.org

Commodity Futures Trading Commission: www.cftc.gov

Federal Reserve Board: www.bog.frb.fed.us/

Futures Industry Association: www.fiafii.org

Global Association of Risk Professionals: www.garp.com

International Association of Financial Engineers: www.iafe.org

International Swaps and Derivatives Association: www.isda.org

Managed Funds Association: www.mfainfo.org

National Futures Association: www.nfa.futures.org

Office of the Comptroller of the Currency: www.occ.treas.gov

The Options Industry Council: www.optionscentral.com

Securities and Exchange Commission: www.sec.gov

P A R T O N E

Options

The Structure of Options Markets

Trading is like no other profession I can think of than dragon slaying. Facing that hot breath, and those toothy jaws fearlessly, armed only with a belief in oneself, on a daily basis.

MARA KOPPEL
Women of the Pits 1998

In Chapter 1 we introduced the concept of an option, a contract between two parties—a buyer and a seller, or writer—in which the buyer purchases from the writer the right to buy or sell an asset at a fixed price. As in any contract, each party grants something to the other. The buyer pays the seller a fee called the **premium,** which is the option's price. The writer grants the buyer the right to buy or sell the asset at a fixed price.

An option to buy an asset is a **call option.** An option to sell an asset is a **put option.** The fixed price at which the option buyer can either buy or sell the asset is called the **exercise price** or **strike price,** or sometimes **striking price.** In addition, the option has a definite life. The right to buy or sell the asset at a fixed price exists up to a specified **expiration date.**

Options are often encountered in everyday life. For example, a rain check offered by a store to allow you to return and purchase a sale item that is temporarily out of stock is an option. You return to the store and buy the item, if it is really worth it. Or you can throw the rain check away. You could even give (or sell) it to someone else. A coupon clipped from the newspaper that allows you to buy an item for a special price any time up to an expiration date is also an option. Suppose you plan to purchase a deeply discounted airline ticket. You are afraid your plans might change and the airline says the ticket at that price is nonrefundable. For just $75 more, you can obtain the right to cancel the ticket at the last minute. If you pay the extra $75 for the right to cancel, you have just purchased an option. Finally, there is a good chance you are taking a college course right now, and you probably hold a valuable option: your right to drop the course up to a specific date. That right is paid for automatically with your tuition payment.

On a certain date later in the term, you will decide whether to continue with the course or drop it. This is certainly a valuable option, but one we hope you will not use, at least not in this course.

In each example, you hold the right to do something, if it turns out to be worth it to you. Although that is the essence of an option, options on securities and other assets do have a few more complicating features. But first let us take a look at how options markets developed.

The Development of Options Markets

There are plenty of examples of options in everyday life. Historians and archaeologists have even discovered primitive options. Though these arrangements may resemble modern options, the current system of options markets traces its origins to the nineteenth century, when puts and calls were offered on shares of stock. Little is known about the options world of the 1800s other than that it was fraught with corruption.

Then, in the early 1900s, a group of firms calling itself the Put and Call Brokers and Dealers Association created an options market. If someone wanted to buy an option, a member of the association would find a seller willing to write it. If the member firm could not find a writer, it would write the option itself. Thus, a member firm could be either a broker—one who matches buyer and seller—or a dealer—one who actually takes a position in the transaction.

Although this over-the-counter options market was viable, it suffered from several deficiencies. First, it did not provide the option holder the opportunity to sell the option to someone else before it expired. Options were designed to be held all the way to expiration, whereupon they were either exercised or allowed to expire. Thus, an option contract had little or no liquidity. Second, the writer's performance was guaranteed only by the broker–dealer firm. If the writer or the Put and Call Brokers and Dealers Association member firm went bankrupt, the option holder was simply out of luck.[1] Third, the cost of transacting was relatively high, due partly to the first two problems.

In 1973, a revolutionary change occurred in the options world. The Chicago Board of Trade, the world's oldest and largest exchange for the trading of commodity futures contracts, organized an exchange exclusively for trading options on stocks. The exchange was named the Chicago Board Options Exchange (CBOE). It opened its doors for call option trading on April 26, 1973, and the first puts were added in June 1977.

The CBOE created a central marketplace for options. By standardizing the terms and conditions of option contracts, it added liquidity. In other words, an investor who had previously bought or sold an option could go

---

[1]The individual or firm could, of course, pursue costly legal remedies.

back into the market prior to its expiration and sell or buy the option, thus, offsetting the original position. Most importantly, however, the CBOE added a clearinghouse that guaranteed to the buyer that the writer would fulfill his or her end of the contract. Thus, unlike in the over-the-counter market, option buyers no longer had to worry about the credit risk of the writer. This made options more attractive to the general public.

Since that time, several stock exchanges and almost all commodity futures exchanges have begun trading options. Fueled by the public's taste for options, the industry grew tremendously until the great stock market crash of 1987. Hit by the shock of the crash, many individual investors who had formerly used options have stayed away and volume has only recently recovered to its 1987 level.

Although institutional trading on the options exchanges remained fairly strong after the crash, a concurrent trend forced the exchanges to address a new competitive threat: the revival of the over-the-counter options markets. In the early 1980s, many corporations began to use currency and interest rate swaps to manage their risk. These contracts, which we briefly mentioned in Chapter 1 and shall cover in more detail in later chapters, are private transactions that are tailored to the specific needs of the two parties. They are subject to credit risk in that a party could default, leaving the opposite party holding a claim that had to be pursued in bankruptcy courts. As it turned out, however, these claims were few and far between and the market functioned exceptionally well. Soon thereafter, firms began to create other types of over-the-counter contracts, such as forwards, and, as expected, options began to be used as well. Because of the large minimum size of each transaction and the credit risk, however, the general public is unable to participate in this new, revived over-the-counter market. The growth in this institutional over-the-counter market has placed severe pressures on the options exchanges. By the early 1990s the exchanges were trying to become more innovative to win back institutional trading and to stimulate the public's interest in options. These trends, however, should not suggest that options are fading in popularity; in fact they are more popular than ever with corporations and financial institutions, but the growth is concentrated in the over-the-counter market.

Call Options

A call option is an option to buy an asset at a fixed price — the exercise price. Options are available on many types of assets, but for now we shall concentrate on options on stock.[2] Consider the following example.

---

[2]Options that trade on commodity futures exchanges are actually options on futures contracts and are covered in Chapter 12. Since a futures contract is not an asset, an option need not be an "option on an asset," although we shall continue to use that expression until Chapter 12.

On March 31, 2000, several exchanges offered options on the stock of Dell Computer. One particular call option had an exercise price of $55 and an expiration date of April 21. The Dell stock had a price of $53.9375. The buyer of this option received the right to buy the stock any time up through April 21 at $55 per share. The writer of that option therefore was obligated to sell the stock at $55 per share through April 21 whenever the buyer wanted it. For this privilege, the buyer paid the writer the premium, or price, of $2.4375.

Why would either party have entered into the call option contract? The buyer would not have done so to immediately exercise the option, because the stock could be bought in the market for $53.9375, which was less than the exercise price of $55. The buyer must have anticipated that the stock's price would rise above $55 before the option expired. Conversely, the writer expected that the stock price would not get above $55 before the option expired. The buyer and writer negotiated the premium of $2.4375, which can be viewed as the buyer's wager on the stock's price going above $55 by April 21. Alternatively, either the buyer or writer may have been using the option to protect a position in the stock — a strategy we mentioned in Chapter 1 called hedging.

Suppose that immediately after a call is purchased, the stock price increases. Because the exercise price is constant, the call option is now more valuable. New call options with the same terms will sell for higher premiums. Therefore, older call options with the same expiration date and exercise price must also sell for higher premiums. Similarly, if the stock price falls, the call's price also will decline. Clearly the buyer of a call option has bullish expectations about the stock.

A call in which the stock price exceeds the exercise price is said to be **in-the-money.** As we shall see in Chapter 3, however, in-the-money calls should not necessarily be exercised prior to expiration. If the stock price is less than the exercise price, the call option is said to be **out-of-the-money.** Out-of-the-money calls should never be exercised. We shall explore these points more thoroughly in Chapter 3. If the stock price equals the exercise price, the option is **at-the-money.**

Put Options

A put option is an option to sell an asset, such as a stock. Consider the put option on Dell stock on March 31, 2000, with an exercise price of $55 per share and an expiration date of April 21. It allowed the put holder to sell the stock at $55 per share any time up through April 21. The stock currently was selling for $53.9375. Therefore, the put holder could have elected to exercise the option, selling the stock to the writer for $55 per share. The put holder may, however, have preferred to wait and see if the stock price fell further below the exercise price. The put buyer expected the stock price to fall, while the writer expected it to remain the same or rise.

The buyer and writer negotiated a premium of $3.25, which the buyer paid to the writer. The premium can be viewed as the buyer's wager that the stock price would not rise above $55 per share by April 21. The writer accepted the premium because it was deemed to be fair compensation for the willingness to buy the stock for $55 any time up through April 21. As in the case of calls, either the buyer or the writer might have been using the put to hedge a position in the stock.

Since the put allows the holder to sell the stock for a fixed price, a decrease in the stock price will make the put more valuable. Conversely, if the stock price increases, the put will be less valuable. It should be apparent that the buyer of a put has bearish expectations for the stock.

If the stock price is less than the exercise price, the put is said to be **in-the-money.** In Chapter 3, we shall see that it is sometimes, but not always, optimal to exercise an in-the-money put prior to expiration. If the stock price is more than the exercise price, the put is **out-of-the-money.** An out-of-the-money put should never be exercised. When the stock price equals the exercise price, the put is **at-the-money.**

The Over-the-Counter Options Market

As noted earlier, there is now a rather large over-the-counter options market dominated by institutional investors. Chicago is no longer the center of the options industry. The scope of this market is worldwide. An option bought by an American corporation in Minnesota from the New York office of a Japanese bank, who in turn buys an offsetting option from the London office of a Swiss bank, would not at all be unusual. These contracts are entered into privately by large corporations, financial institutions, and sometimes even governments in which the option buyer is either familiar with the creditworthiness of the writer or has had the credit risk reduced by some type of collateral guarantee or other credit enhancement. Nonetheless, there is nearly always some credit risk faced by the buyers of these options. There are, however, several major advantages of this type of option.

The first advantage is that the terms and conditions of the options can be tailored to the specific needs of the two parties. For example, suppose the manager of a pension fund would like to protect the profit in the fund's portfolio against a general decline in the market. As we shall discuss in great detail in Chapter 6, the purchase of a put in which the holder of the portfolio can sell it to the option writer for a specific value on a certain date can assure the manager of a minimum return. Unfortunately, this type of transaction cannot always be accomplished on the options exchange. First, the options available on the exchange are based on certain stocks or stock indices. The manager would need an option on the specific portfolio, which might not match the indices on which options were available.[3] Second, the options on the exchange expire at specific dates, which might not match the manager's investment horizon. Third, even if options were available, there might not be enough liquidity to handle the large trades necessary to protect the entire portfolio. In the over-the-counter market, the manager can specify precisely which combination of stocks the option should be written on and when it should be exercised.[4] Although unusually large transactions could take some time to arrange, it is likely that most pension fund managers could get the desired transactions accomplished. Fourth, in the over-the-counter markets, options can be created on a wider range of instruments than just stocks. Options exist on bonds, interest rates, commodities, currencies, and many other types of assets as well as some instruments that are not even assets, such as insurance damage and weather.

A second advantage is that the over-the-counter market is a private market in which neither the general public nor other investors, including competitors, need know that the transactions were completed. This does not mean that the transactions are illegal or suspicious. On the options exchange, a large order to buy puts could send a signal to the market that someone might have some bad news. This could send the market reeling as it worries about what impending information might soon come out.

Another advantage is that over-the-counter trading is essentially unregulated. Its rules are those of commonsense business honesty and courtesy. Institutions that do not conform would find themselves unable to find counterparties with which to trade. This largely unregulated environment means that government approval is not needed to offer new types of options. The contracts are simply created by parties that see mutual gain in doing business with each other. There are no costly constraints or bureaucratic red tape to cut through.

Clearly there are some disadvantages to over-the-counter trading, the primary one of which is that credit risk exists and excludes many customers who are unable to establish their creditworthiness in this market. The credit risk problem is an important and highly visible contemporary issue in the swaps market and we shall discuss it more in later chapters. In addition to the credit risk problem, the sizes of the transactions in the over-the-counter market are larger than many investors can handle. It is not clear, however, that over-the-counter trading is any more or less costly than trading on the exchange.

---

[3]It would be wasteful to purchase an option on each security, even if they were available, because that would protect the portfolio against risk that is already eliminated by its diversification.

[4]Because the specific combination of stocks is called a *basket,* these types of options are called *basket options.*

The over-the-counter market is quite large, but because of the private nature of the transactions, gauging its size is difficult. The Bank for International Settlements (BIS) conducts semiannual surveys that attempt to provide some data. These surveys, however, take a long time to complete and are published with a considerable lag. The BIS's latest survey estimated that at year-end 1999, the notional principal, which is the amount of the underlying instrument, of options on interest rates, currencies, equities, and commodities was $13 trillion with a market value of about $490 billion.

Most of the options created on the over-the-counter market are not the traditional case of an option on an individual common stock. They tend to be options on bonds, interest rates, commodities, swaps, and foreign currencies and include many variations that combine options with other instruments. As noted earlier, a significant number are created on equities, meaning stock portfolios or indices. Many are on foreign stock indices. The principles behind pricing and using options, however, are pretty much the same, whether the option is created on the CBOE or in the over-the-counter market. There are obvious variations to accommodate the different types of options. We shall cover many of these in later chapters. Most of the material on options, which comprises Chapters 2 through 7, however, will use examples that come from the organized markets. Now let us take a look at how the organized options markets operate.

Organized Options Trading

An exchange is a legal corporate entity organized for the trading of securities, options, or futures. It provides a physical facility and stipulates rules and regulations governing the transactions in the instruments trading thereon. In the options markets, organized exchanges evolved in response to the lack of standardization and liquidity of over-the-counter options. Over-the-counter options were written for specific buyers by particular sellers. The terms and conditions of the contracts, such as the exercise price and expiration date, were tailored for the parties involved. Organized exchanges filled the need for standardized option contracts wherein the exchange would specify the contracts' terms and conditions. Consequently, a secondary market for the contracts was made possible. This made options more accessible and attractive to the general public.

By providing a physical trading floor, specifying rules and regulations, and standardizing contracts, options became as marketable as stocks. If an option holder wanted to sell the option before the expiration date or an option writer wished to get out of the obligation to buy or sell the stock, a closing transaction could be arranged at the options exchange. We shall examine these procedures in more detail in a later section.

The Chicago Board Options Exchange, the first organized options exchange, established the procedures that made options marketable. In addition, it paved the way for the American, Philadelphia, and Pacific Exchanges to begin option trading. The next several sections examine the CBOE's contract specifications.

Listing Requirements

The options exchange specifies the assets on which option trading is allowed. For stock options, the exchange's listing requirements prescribe the eligible stocks on which options can be traded. At one time, these requirements limited options listings to stocks of large firms, but these requirements have been relaxed, and more small firms' options are available for trading. The exchange also specifies minimum requirements that a stock must meet to maintain the listing of options on it. These requirements are similar to but slightly less stringent than those for the initial listing. In all cases, however, the exchange has the authority to make exceptions to the listing and delisting requirements.

All options of a particular type—call or put—on a given stock are referred to as an option **class.** For example, the Dell calls are one option class and the Dell puts are another. An option **series** is all the options of a given class with the same exercise price and expiration. For example, the Dell April 55 calls are a particular series, as are the Dell May 60 puts.

In recent years many options have become listed on more than one exchange. In any case, however, it should be remembered that it is the options exchanges that determine whether options of a particular stock will be listed. The company itself has no influence.

Contract Size

A standard exchange-traded option contract consists of 100 individual options. Thus, if an investor purchases one contract, it actually represents options to buy 100 shares of stock. An exception to the standard contract size occurs when either a stock splits or the company declares a stock dividend. In that case, the number of shares represented by a standard contract is adjusted to reflect the change in the company's capitalization. For example, if a company declares a 15 percent stock dividend, the number of shares represented by an outstanding contract changes from 100 to 115. In addition, the exercise price is adjusted to $1/1.15 = .8696$, rounded to the nearest eighth—.875—of its former value. If a stock split or stock dividend results in the new number of shares being an even multiple of 100, holders of outstanding contracts are credited with additional contracts. For example, if the stock splits two for one, buyers and writers are credited with two contracts for every one formerly held. In addition, the exercise price is reduced to half of its previous value.

Contract sizes for options on indexes and certain other instruments are specified as a multiple. For example, an option on the S&P 100 has a multiple of 100; an investor who buys one contract actually buys 100 options.

Exercise Prices

On options exchanges the exercise prices are standardized. The exchange prescribes the exercise prices at which options can be written. Investors must be willing to trade options with the specified exercise prices. Of course, over-the-counter transactions can have any exercise price the two participants agree on.

The exchange's objective in establishing the exercise prices is to provide options that will attract trading volume. Most option trading is concentrated in options in which the stock price is close to the exercise price. Accordingly, exchange officials tend to list options in which the exercise prices surround but are close to the current stock price. They must use their judgment as to whether an exercise price is too far above or below the stock price to generate sufficient trading volume. If the stock price moves up or down, new exercise prices close to the stock price are added.

In establishing exercise prices of stock options, the exchange generally follows the rule that the exercise prices are in $2.50 intervals if the stock price is less than $25, in $5 intervals if the stock price is between $25 and $200, and in $10 intervals if the stock price is above $200. For index options, the exercise price intervals vary due to the wide range of the various indices.

In 1993 the CBOE launched the FLEX (for flexible) option, a new type of option that represented a dramatic departure from the standardization of organized options markets. FLEX options can have any exercise price. In addition there are other variations that we shall mention when we discuss expirations. FLEX options are available with a minimum face value of $10 million for index options and 250 contracts for option on individual stocks.

When a stock pays a dividend, the stock price falls by the amount of the dividend on the ex-dividend day, which is the day after the last day on which the purchaser of the stock is entitled to receive the upcoming dividend. Because call option holders do not receive dividends and benefit from increases in the stock price and put option holders benefit from stock price decreases, the ex-dividend decrease in the stock price would arbitrarily hurt call holders and help put holders. In the old over-the-counter options market, options were said to be dividend-protected. If the company declared a $1 dividend, the exercise price was reduced by $1. Since over-the-counter options were not meant to be traded, the frequent dividend adjustments caused no problems. For exchange-listed options, however, such dividend adjustments would have generated many nonstandard exercise prices. Thus, the exchanges elected not to adjust the exercise price when a cash dividend was paid. This is also true in the current over-the-counter market.

Expiration Dates

Expiration dates of over-the-counter options are tailored to the buyers' and writers' needs. On the options exchanges, each stock is classified into a particular expiration cycle. The expiration cycles are (1) January, April, July, and October; (2) February, May, August, and November; and (3) March, June, September, and December. These were called the *January, February,* and *March cycles.* The available expirations are the current month, the next month, and the next two months within the January, February, or March cycle to which the stock is assigned. For example, in early June, IBM, which is assigned to the January cycle, will have options expiring in June and July plus the next two months in the January cycle: October and the following January. When the June options expire, the September options will be added; when the July options expire, the August options will be added; and when the August options expire, the April options will be added. Index options typically have expirations of the current and next two months.

The maturities of options on individual stocks go out about nine months with a few exceptions. LEAPS (Long-Term Equity Anticipation Shares) are options on certain stocks and indices that have expirations of up to three years. LEAPS have proven to be very popular with about 8.5 million contracts traded on the CBOE in 1998.[5] Although LEAPS are available on index options, most of the trading volume is in LEAPS on individual stocks.

As noted above, FLEX options are available on stocks and indices and permit the investor to specify any exercise price. FLEX options can also have any desired expiration up to five years for index options and three years for options on individual stocks. FLEX options are a response on the part of the options exchanges to the growing over-the-counter market in which options have tailored exercise prices and expirations.

The expiration day of an exchange-traded option is the Saturday following the third Friday of the month. The last day on which the option trades is the third Friday of the month.

Position and Exercise Limits

The Securities and Exchange Commission forces the options exchanges to impose **position limits** that define the maximum number of options an in-

---

[5]CBOE, *Market Statistics*, 1998.

vestor can hold on one side of the market. For example, because they are both bullish strategies, a long call and a short put on the same stock are transactions on the same side of the market. Likewise, a short call and a long put are both bearish strategies and thus are considered to be on the same side of the market. The options exchange publishes the position limit for each stock, which varies from 13,500 to 75,000, depending on the stock's trading volume and number of outstanding shares. Index options do not generally have position limits because they are widely used in large institutional portfolios. Certain traders called market makers have certain exemptions from these position limits.

Exercise limits are similar to position limits. An **exercise limit** is the maximum number of options that can be exercised on any five consecutive business days by any individual or group of individuals acting together. The figure for the exercise limit is the same as that for the position limit.

The purpose of position and exercise limits is to prevent a single individual or group from having a significant effect on the market. It is not clear, however, that such restrictions are necessary. They do, however, prevent many large investors from using exchange-traded options, and they reduce liquidity. They have probably hurt the options exchanges by forcing institutional investors to take their business to the over-the-counter markets.

Exchanges on Which Options Trade

Options trading currently exists on several U.S. and many foreign exchanges. The CBOE is the only U.S. exchange devoted solely to options trading; the other exchanges trade stocks as well as options. Table 2.1 lists the exchanges and their World Wide Web addresses.

Options trading is not confined to these exchanges. Chapter 12 covers options on futures, which trade on virtually every commodity futures exchange in the country. We shall defer discussing those contracts and exchanges until Chapters 8 and 12.

Figure 2.1 shows the volume of option trading on the U.S. exchanges on which options trade. Growth in option trading had been quite phenomenal until 1987. The market crash of 1987 resulted in a reduction in volume of about 35 percent in 1988 from 1987 as many individual investors shied away from the markets. The crash had an even greater impact on index option volume, which is today only about two-thirds of its pre-crash level. Some of this loss of volume, however, is not a result of the crash, but of the growing use of over-the-counter options and related contracts by institutional investors.

The CBOE's market share, as shown in Figure 2.2, is about 60 percent, and its share of the index option market is over 90 percent.

TABLE 2.1	Exchanges on Which Options on Spot Assets Trade, January 2000

United States

Chicago Board Options Exchange
   Chicago, Illinois
   www.cboe.com
American Stock Exchange
   (a division of NASDAQ)
   New York, New York
   www.amex.com
Pacific Stock Exchange
   San Francisco, California
   www.pacificex.com
Philadelphia Stock Exchange
   Philadelphia, Pennsylvania
   www.phlx.com
International Securities Exchange
   New York, New York
   www.iseoptions.com

Canada

Montreal Exchange
   Montreal, Quebec
   www.me.org

South America

Bolsa de Mercadorias & Futuros
   Sao Paulo, Brazil
   www.bmf.com.br
Santiago Stock Exchange
   Santiago, Chile
   www.sse.cl

Europe

Wiener Börse AG
   Vienna, Austria
   www.wbag.at
Brussels Exchange
   Brussels, Belgium
   www.bxs.be
Copenhagen Stock Exchange
   (FUTOP)
   Copenhagen, Denmark
   www.xcse.dk
Helsinki Securities and Derivatives
   Exchange
   Helsinki, Finland
   www.hex.fi
Paris Bourse
   Paris, France
   www.bourse-de-paris.fr
EUREX
   Frankfurt, Germany
   www.eurexchange.com
Budapest Commodity Exchange
   Budapest, Hungary
   www.bce-bat.com
Tel Aviv Stock Exchange
   Tel Aviv, Israel
   www.tase.co.il
Italian Stock Exchange
   Milan, Italy
   www.borsaitalia.it
Amsterdam Exchanges
   Amsterdam, Netherlands
   www.aex.nl
Bolsa de Derivados do Porto
   Porto, Portugal
   www.bdp.pt
Meff Renta Variable
   Madrid, Spain
   www.meffrv.es
OM Stockholm Exchange
   Stockholm, Sweden
   www.omgroup.com
London International Financial
   Futures and Options Exchange
   (LIFFE)
   London, United Kingdom
   www.liffe.com
OM London Exchange
   London, United Kingdom
   www.omgroup.com

Africa

South African Futures Exchange
   Republic of South Africa
   www.safex.co.za

Australia

Australian Stock Exchange
   Sydney, Australia
   www.asx.com.au

Asia

The Stock Exchange of Hong Kong
   Hong Kong, China
   www.sehk.com.hk
Hong Kong Futures Exchange
   Hong Kong, China
   www.hkfe.com
Tokyo Stock Exchange
   Tokyo, Japan
   www.tse.or.jp

Note: Exchanges on which options on futures trade are covered in Chapter 8.

FIGURE 2.1 **Listed Option Volume**

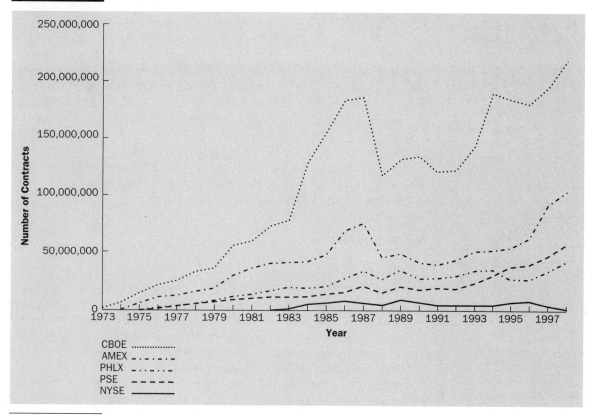

SOURCE: CBOE, *Market Statistics,* 1998

FIGURE 2.2 **Share of Option Volume**

SOURCE: CBOE, *Market Statistics,* 1998.

Option Traders

In the over-the-counter market, certain institutions, which may be banks or brokerage firms, stand ready to make markets in options. Exchange-listed options, of course, are created on an exchange, which is a legal corporate entity whose members are individuals or firms. Each membership is referred to as a **seat.** Although the organizational structures of the various exchanges differ somewhat, membership generally entitles one to physically go onto the trading floor and trade options. The following sections discuss the types of traders who operate both on and off the exchange floor. This system of traders is based on the market maker system used by the CBOE and the Pacific Stock Exchange.

The Market Maker

An individual who has purchased a seat on the CBOE can apply to be either a market maker or a floor broker. The **market maker** is responsible for meeting the public's demand for options. When someone from the public wishes to buy (sell) an option and no other member of the public is willing to sell (buy) it, the market maker completes the trade. This type of system ensures that if a private investor wishes to buy a particular option, there will be a seller willing to make an offer, and if one buys an option and later wants to sell it, there will be a buyer available. The market maker offers the public the convenience of immediate execution of trades.

The market maker is essentially an entrepreneur. To survive, the market maker must profit by buying at one price and selling at a higher price. One way this is done is by quoting a bid price and an ask price. The **bid price** is the maximum price the market maker will pay for the option. The **ask price** is the minimum price the market maker will accept for the option. The ask price is set higher than the bid price. The difference between the ask and bid price is called the **bid-ask spread.**

The bid-ask spread is a significant transaction cost for those who must trade with a market maker. To the market maker, however, it represents the reward for the willingness to buy when the public is selling and sell when the public is buying. Bid-ask spreads are discussed further in the section on transaction costs.

Market makers use a variety of techniques to trade options intelligently and profitably. Many look at fundamentals, such as interest rates, economic conditions, and company performance. Others rely on technical analysis, which purports to find signals of the direction of future stock prices in the behavior of past stock prices. Still others rely simply on intuition and experience. In addition, market makers tend to employ different trading styles. Some are **scalpers,** who try to buy at the bid and sell at the ask before the price moves downward or after the price moves just slightly upward.

Scalpers seldom hold positions for more than a few minutes. In contrast, **position traders** have somewhat longer holding periods. Many option traders, including some scalpers and position traders, are also **spreaders,** who buy one option and sell another in the hope of earning small profits at low risk. Option spreading strategies are covered in more detail in Chapter 7.

The Floor Broker

The **floor broker** is another type of trader on the exchange. The floor broker executes trades for members of the public. If someone wishes to buy or sell an option, that individual must first establish an account with a brokerage firm. That firm must either employ a floor broker or have an arrangement whereby it contracts with either an independent floor broker or a floor broker of a competing firm.

The floor broker executes orders for nonmembers and earns either a flat salary or a commission on each order executed. The floor broker generally need not be concerned about whether the price is expected to go up or down; however, a good broker will work diligently to obtain the best price for the customer.

The CBOE also has a number of Designated Primary Market Makers, or DPMs, who are allowed to be both market makers and brokers. This system is somewhat controversial because the ability to be both a market maker, who executes trades for his or her own account, and a broker, who executes trades for others, can lead to abuse. With this practice, known as dual trading, a market maker could take advantageous positions for his or her own account prior to taking a customer order to the floor. This would allow the market maker to potentially profit because of knowledge of the customer order. On the other hand, dual trading also increases liquidity. The CBOE uses the DPM system for many new listings to increase liquidity. There has been some recent discussion at the CBOE, however, of moving completely off the market maker system to a DPM system.

The Order Book Official

A third type of trader at the CBOE is the **order book official (OBO)** or **board broker,** an employee of the exchange. To see how an OBO works, suppose you place a *limit order*—an order specifying a maximum price to be paid on a purchase or a minimum acceptable price on a sale—to buy a call option at a maximum price of $3. The floor broker handling your order determines that the best quote offered by a market maker is 2 3/4 bid and 3 1/4 ask. This means that the lowest price at which a market maker will sell the call is 3 1/4. If your floor broker has other orders to execute, the OBO takes your limit order and enters it into the computer along with all the other public limit orders. The market makers are informed of the best public limit orders. If conditions change such that at least one market maker is willing to quote an ask price of $3 or lower, the OBO will execute your limit order.

Public limit orders are always executed before market maker orders; however, the market makers, being aware of the best public limit orders, know the maximum and minimum prices at which they can trade. For example, if your limit order to buy at 3 is the highest bid and the market maker is quoting an ask price of 3 1/4, the market maker chooses between accepting your bid and selling the call at 3 or holding out for an offer of 3 1/8 or higher. If no one bids 3 1/8 within a reasonable time period, the market maker might choose to take your bid of 3.

The options exchanges also have brought the benefits of modern technology to their order-processing operations, using a variety of electronic means of accelerating the rate at which orders are filled. For example, most CBOE traders now use handheld terminals instead of decks of handwritten cards and pieces of paper to submit and keep track of their trades.

Other Option Trading Systems

The CBOE and the Pacific Stock Exchange use the system of competing market makers. The American and Philadelphia Stock Exchanges use a slightly different system. Here an individual called a **specialist** is responsible for making bids and offers on options. The specialist maintains and attempts to fill public limit orders but does not disclose them to others. In addition to the specialist are individuals called **registered option traders (ROTs),** who buy and sell options for themselves or act as brokers for others. Unlike the CBOE market makers, ROTs are not obligated to make a market in the options; market making is the specialist's task.

The U.S. exchanges and many exchanges elsewhere use pit trading, the form of trading we have described here. Electronic trading systems do away with the pit and allow trading from electronic terminals, which can be placed anywhere, including offices and even homes. There are a number of different electronic trading systems, but, for the most part, they permit bids and offers to be entered into a computer that collects the information and makes it available to participants, who can then execute transactions with the stroke of a key. In the United States there are no fully automated options exchanges. The International Securities Exchange, which opened in May 2000, trades options electronically on many actively traded stocks. In addition, many foreign exchanges are fully automated, including EUREX, one of the world's largest exchanges, which was created by a merger of the German and Swiss derivatives exchanges.

Off-Floor Option Traders

The financial world consists of a vast number of institutions of all sizes, many of which participate in option trading. Some of these institutions are brokerage firms that execute orders for the public. Most brokerage firms employ individuals responsible for recommending profitable option trades to their brokers. Many, however, have specialized option-trading departments that search for mispriced options, trade in them, and in so doing contribute to their firms' profitability. Many large institutional investors, such as pension funds, trusts, and mutual funds, also trade options. In most cases, these types of investors write options on the stocks held in their portfolios. A growing contingent of foreign institutions also trade options. In addition to the large institutional investors, there are, of course, numerous individuals — some wealthy and some not — who trade options. Among those who trade options themselves are many wealthy people who turn over their financial affairs to specialized managers and thus participate in the options market without being personally involved. The dollar amounts required for trading exchange-listed options are so small that virtually anyone can afford to participate.

Cost and Profitability of Exchange Membership

An individual who decides to purchase a seat on an exchange that has option trading can take one of several routes. The most obvious is to purchase a seat from an existing member. Figure 2.3 shows the history of the price of a seat on the CBOE.

At around $400,000, the cost of obtaining membership would seem prohibitive to most individuals. There are, however, other ways to gain membership. Some seat owners lease their seats to others; rental rates run about .50 to .75 percent of the seat's price per month. Also, some members allow "trainees" to trade with their seats and charge them a percentage of the trading profits.

The CBOE has 931 members and there are 340 members of the Chicago Board of Trade who have option trading privileges at the CBOE. The AMEX has 661 full members, who primarily trade its stocks, and 203 options members. The Philadelphia Stock Exchange has 505 members with option-trading privileges, and the Pacific Stock Exchange has 551 members.

These prices are not the full cost of trading. They provide only access to the floor. Capital must be available to cover losses and a member must arrange for a firm to guarantee his or her creditworthiness. The minimum amount of capital is about $50,000. Members must also undergo training and pass an examination verifying that they know the rules and procedures, and they must agree to conform to all exchange and SEC regulations. There are additional start-up costs and monthly expenses.

It is difficult to determine how profitable option memberships are. An SEC study in 1978 showed that the average market maker earned a respectable but not unusually large amount of money. That study is outdated, however, because the options markets have changed much since that time, particularly after the crash of 1987. Anecdotal evidence suggests

FIGURE 2.3	CBOE Quarterly Seat Prices

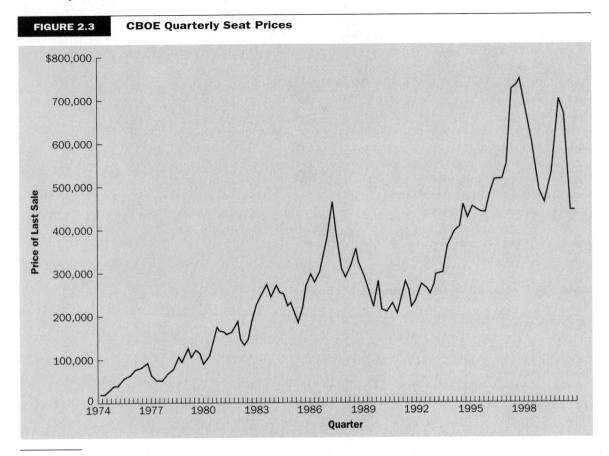

SOURCE: Chicago Board Options Exchange

that options market making is a relatively high-risk profession character-ized by extreme pressure. The temptation to take undue risks in the hope of making large profits is quite great. Many new market makers end up out of the business rather quickly. Those who are successful generally have pur-sued conservative strategies. Due to the stress, the typical market maker is a young person in his or her 20s or early 30s.

The Mechanics of Trading

Placing an Opening Order

An individual who wants to trade options must first open an account with a brokerage firm. The individual then instructs the broker to buy or sell a particular option. The broker sends the order to the firm's floor broker on the exchange on which the option trades. All orders must be executed during the normal trading hours, which vary by product from 8:30 A.M. to either 3:02 P.M. or 3:15 P.M. central time. Trading is performed within the trading pit designated for the particular option. The trading pit is a multilevel, octagonally shaped area within which the market makers and floor brokers stand.

An investor can place several types of orders. A **market order** instructs the floor broker to obtain the best price. A **limit order,** as indicated earlier, specifies a maximum price to pay if buying or a minimum price to accept if selling. Limit orders can be either good-till-canceled or day orders. A **good-till-canceled order** remains in effect until canceled. A **day order** stays in effect for the remainder of the day. Finally, an investor holding a particular option might place a **stop order** at a price lower than the current price. If the market price falls to the specified price, the broker is instructed to sell the option at the best available price. There are a number of other types of orders designed to handle different contingencies.

In addition to specifying the option the investor wishes to buy or sell, the order must indicate the number of contracts desired. The order might be a request to purchase 10 contracts at the best possible price. The market maker's quote, however, need apply to only one contract. Therefore, if multiple contracts are needed, the market maker may offer a less favorable price. In that case, the order might be only partially filled. To avoid a partial fill, the investor can place an all or none or an all or none, same price order. An **all or none order** allows the broker to fill part of the order at one price and part at another. An **all or none, same price order** requires the broker to either fill the whole order at the same price or not fill the order at all. In 1998, the CBOE reported that the average number of contracts per trade was 12.9.[6]

The Role of the Clearinghouse

After the trade is consummated, the clearinghouse enters the process. The **clearinghouse,** formally known as the **Options Clearing Corporation (OCC),** is an independent corporation that guarantees the writer's performance. The OCC is the intermediary in each transaction. A buyer exercising an option looks not to the writer but to the clearinghouse. A writer exercising an option makes payment for or delivery of the stock to the clearinghouse.

Each OCC member, known as a **clearing firm,** has an account with the OCC. Each market maker must clear all trades through a member firm, as must every brokerage firm, although in some cases a brokerage firm is also a clearing firm.

---

[6]CBOE, *Market Statistics,* 1998.

Figure 2.4 illustrates the flow of money and information as an option transaction is consummated and cleared. We shall illustrate how the clearinghouse operates by assuming that you bought the Dell April 55 call we described earlier. You contacted your broker, who, through either his or her firm's floor broker or an independent floor broker, found a seller. You bought 10 contracts at a price of $2.4375 per option, which totals $2,437.50. The seller, whose identity you do not know, has an account with another brokerage firm.

Your brokerage firm clears its trades through XYZ Trading Company, a clearing firm that is a member of the OCC. The seller's broker clears through ABC Options, another member of the OCC. You pay your broker the $2,437.50, and your broker pays XYZ Trading Company. XYZ pools the transactions of all its customers and, through a predetermined formula, deposits a sum of money with the OCC.

Let us also assume that the seller does not already own the stock, so he or she will have to deposit some additional money, called **margin,** with ABC. The amount of margin required is discussed in Appendix 2A; for now, however, just assume that the amount is 20 percent of the value of the stock, which comes to ($53.9375)(100)(10)(.2) = $10,787.50. The seller gives the $10,787.50 to the broker, who deposits it with ABC Options, which

---

FIGURE 2.4   **A Transaction on an Options Exchange**

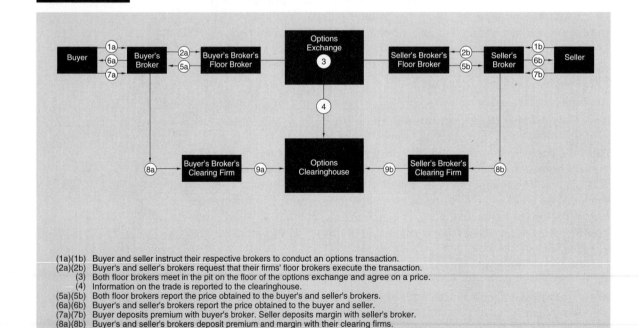

(1a)(1b)   Buyer and seller instruct their respective brokers to conduct an options transaction.
(2a)(2b)   Buyer's and seller's brokers request that their firms' floor brokers execute the transaction.
    (3)   Both floor brokers meet in the pit on the floor of the options exchange and agree on a price.
    (4)   Information on the trade is reported to the clearinghouse.
(5a)(5b)   Both floor brokers report the price obtained to the buyer's and seller's brokers.
(6a)(6b)   Buyer's and seller's brokers report the price obtained to the buyer and seller.
(7a)(7b)   Buyer deposits premium with buyer's broker. Seller deposits margin with seller's broker.
(8a)(8b)   Buyer's and seller's brokers deposit premium and margin with their clearing firms.
(9a)(9b)   Buyer's and seller's brokers' clearing firms deposit premium and margin with clearinghouse.

Note: Either buyer or seller (or both) could be a floor trader, eliminating the broker and floor broker.

also keeps the $2,437.50 premium. ABC, in turn, is required to deposit with the OCC an amount of money determined according to a formula that takes its outstanding contracts into account.

The OCC guarantees the performance of ABC, the seller's clearing firm. Thus, you, the buyer, need not worry about whether the shares will be there if you decide to exercise your option. If the shares are not delivered by the seller, the OCC will look to ABC who will look to the seller's brokerage firm, which will look to the seller's personal broker, who will look to the seller for payment or delivery of the shares.

The total number of option contracts outstanding at any given time is called the **open interest.** The open interest figure indicates the number of closing transactions that might be made before the option expires. In late March 2000, open interest in stock and index options on all exchanges was over 200 million contracts. About 99 percent of this is in options on individual stocks. Each contract covers 100 shares. Assuming an average stock, priced at about $50, the underlying asset value is about $1 trillion.[7]

The OCC thus fulfills the important responsibility of guaranteeing option writers' performances. A call buyer need not examine the writer's credit; in fact, in the case of individuals and firms off the floor, the buyers do not even know the writers' identities.

Because the member clearing firms assume some risk, the OCC imposes minimum capital requirements on them. The OCC has a claim on their securities and margin deposits in the event of their default. As a further safeguard, the OCC maintains a special fund supported by its members. If that fund is depleted, the OCC can assess its other members to ensure its survival as well as that of the options market in general.

Of course, in the over-the-counter market there is no clearinghouse, and the buyer is exposed to credit risk on the part of the writer.

Placing an Offsetting Order

Suppose an investor holds a call option. The stock price recently has been increasing, and the call's price is now much higher than the original purchase price. The liquidity of the options market makes it possible for the investor to take the profit by selling the option in the market. This is called an **offsetting order** or simply an **offset.** The order is executed in the same manner as an opening order. Continuing with our example in which you bought 10 contracts of the Dell April 55 calls, suppose the price of the calls is now $3.125. You instruct your broker to sell the calls. Your broker orders his firm's floor broker to sell the calls. The floor broker finds a buyer who agrees to the price of $3.125. The buyer pays $3,125 to her broker, who passes the funds through to the company's clearing firm, which passes the funds through to the OCC. The OCC then credits the $3,125 to the account of your broker's clearing firm, XYZ Trading Company, which credits

---

[7] *The Wall Street Journal,* April 3, 2000.

your broker's firm, which in turn credits your account. You now have $3,125 and no outstanding position in this option. The individual who bought these options from you may have been offsetting a previously established short position in the calls or may be establishing a new, long position in them.

In 1998, the CBOE reported that about 56 percent of all opening stock option transactions were closed in this manner.[8] In some cases, however, option traders may wish to exercise the option.

In the over-the-counter markets, there is no facility for selling back an option previously bought or buying back an option previously sold. These contracts are created with the objective of being held to expiration. As circumstances change, however, many holders or writers of over-the-counter options find that they need to reverse their positions. This can be done by simply entering the market and attempting to construct an offsetting position. In other words, if you had previously bought an April 6500 call on London's Financial Times 100 index and now would like to reverse the transaction before expiration, you simply call a dealer and offer to sell the same option. In the over-the-counter market, however, there is not likely to be someone trying to do the exact offsetting trade at the same time. A dealer takes the opposite position, but there are many dealers willing to do the trade. The most important difference between offsetting in the over-the-counter market and offsetting in the exchange-listed market is that in the latter the contracts cancel any obligations of the writer. In the former both contracts remain on the books so they are both subject to default risk.[9]

Exercising an Option

An American option can be exercised on any day up through the expiration date. European options, which have nothing to do with Europe, can be exercised only on the expiration date. Suppose you elect to **exercise** the Dell April 55 calls, which, like all options on stocks in the United States, are American options. You notify your brokerage firm, which in turn notifies the clearing firm through which the trade originally was cleared. The clearing firm then places an exercise order with the OCC, which randomly selects a clearing firm through which someone has written the same option. The clearing firm, using a procedure established and made known to its customers in advance, selects someone who has written that option.[10] The chosen writer is said to be **assigned.**

---

[8]CBOE, *Market Statistics*, 1998.

[9]In some cases, a reversing trade with the same dealer with whom one did the original contract can be structured as an offset, thereby terminating both contracts.

[10]Procedures such as first-in, first-out or random selection are commonly used.

If the option is a call option on an individual stock, the writer must deliver the stock. You then pay the exercise price, which is passed on to the writer. If the option had been a put option on an individual stock, you would have to deliver the stock. The writer pays the exercise price, which is passed on to you. For either type of option, however, the writer who originally wrote the contract might not be the one who is assigned the exercise.

Because an index represents a portfolio of stocks, exercise of the option ordinarily would require the delivery of the stocks weighted in the same proportions as they are in the index. This would be quite difficult and inconvenient. Instead, an alternative exercise procedure called **cash settlement** is used. With this method, if an index call option is exercised, the writer pays the buyer the contract multiple times the difference between the index level and the exercise price. For example, assume you buy one index call option that has a multiple of 100. The index is at 1500, and the exercise price is 1495. If you exercise the option, the assigned writer pays you $100(1500 - 1495) = \$500$ in cash. No stock changes hands. A put option is exercised by the writer paying the buyer the multiple times the difference between the exercise price and the index level.

An order to exercise an index option during the day is executed after the close of trading. The index value *at the end of the day*, rather than the index value when the exercise was ordered, is used to determine the amount of the settlement. Thus, an investor is well advised to wait until the end of the day to order an exercise of an index option. In addition, certain index options settle based on the index value at the opening of the next day.

On expiration day, if you find that the stock price is less than the exercise price or, for a put, that the stock price is greater than the exercise price, you allow the option to expire by doing nothing. When the expiration day passes, the option contract is removed from the records of the clearing firm and the OCC.

In 1998, about 11 percent of the calls and 14 percent of the puts on the CBOE were exercised and about 30 percent of the calls and 37 percent of the puts expired.[11] In some cases, options that should have been exercised at expiration were not, due to customer ignorance or oversight. Some brokerage firms have a policy of exercising options automatically when doing so is to the customer's advantage. Such a policy usually is stated in the agreement that the customer signs when opening the account. The OCC automatically exercises options that are at least slightly in-the-money at expiration.

Option Price Quotations

Option prices are available daily in *The Wall Street Journal* and in many daily newspapers in larger cities. Figure 2.5 illustrates how *The Wall Street Journal*

---

[11]CBOE, *Market Statistics*, 1998. These figures are for options on stocks only.

FIGURE 2.5 Stock Option Quotations in *The Wall Street Journal,* Trading Day of August 28, 2000

NOTICE TO READERS

The Wall Street Journal now publishes options quotations in decimals rather than fractions, following similar changes for the Journal's stock pages.

Monday, August 28, 2000

Composite volume and close for activity traded equity and LEAPS, or long-term options, with results for the corresponding put or call contract. Volume figures are unofficial. Open interest is total outstanding for all exchanges and reflects previous trading day. Close when possible is shown for the underlying stock or primary market. **CB**-Chicago Board Options Exchange. **AM**-American Stock Exchange. **PB** Philadelphia Stock Exchange. **PC**-Pacific Stock Exchange. **XC**-Composite. **p**-Put.

Journal Link: Complete equity option listings and data are available in the online Journal at **WSJ.com**.

reports options on individual stocks. *The Wall Street Journal* shows only the most active short-term options on stocks and the most active LEAPS on stocks.

Consider the options on Dell Computer stock (abbreviated DellCptr) in the fourth column. On the first line in the first of the seven columns is the name of the stock. In that same column below the first line is the closing New York Stock Exchange price of the stock. If more than two options are shown, the closing stock price is repeated to fill the space. For some inactive options, such as those on Amgen, there is only one line and the closing stock price is not shown. The second column contains the exercise price and the third column contains the expiration. The next column is the number of call contracts that traded that day and the following column is the closing call price. The next two columns are the put volume and closing put price. Although prices are in 16ths, they are shown in decimal form. Thus, the Dell call options expiring in November with an exercise price of 30 closed at 10 3/4 or \$10.75 (shown as 10^{75}). On that day, 6 contracts traded. The November 30 puts closed at 3/8 or \$0.375 (shown as 0^{38}) and 225 contracts traded. Ellipses (. . .) are used to fill in spaces left by option series that did not trade that day.

At the very top of the page is a list of the most active option contracts for that day. Each line also shows the volume, the exchange where it was traded, the closing price, the net change from the previous day, the stock closing price, and the open interest, which is the number of contracts currently outstanding. If the option is a put, it is indicated with a lowercase "p." Not shown here but appearing at the end of the listings is a summary of the volume and open interest by exchange.

A glance over the option pages usually reveals some options in which the stock name is followed by an *o*. With those options, the terms and conditions of the contract have been modified to reflect stock splits or stock dividends.

Figure 2.6 shows a *Wall Street Journal* listing for index options. These are grouped by exchange (e.g., CHICAGO stands for Chicago Board Options Exchange). For each index, the ticker symbol appears beside the name. Each row contains one option series, as indicated by the expiration month, the exercise price, and the letter "c" or "p" indicating call or put. The next column contains the volume in contracts and the next column contains the closing price. The next column contains the price change over the previous day, and the final column contains the open interest. The large box in the center contains information on the values of the underlying indices.

The price quotations provided in *The Wall Street Journal* are useful measures of the approximate prices at which options are bought and sold. By the time they reach the public, however, those prices are already old. In addition, they are not necessarily synchronized with one another and with the stock price. The closing price of each option and of the stock reflect only the price of the last transaction. The last transaction of the day may have

FIGURE 2.6 Index Option Quotations in *The Wall Street Journal,* Trading Day of August 28, 2000

Monday, August 28, 2000
Volume, last, net change and open interest are for all contracts. Volume figures are unofficial. Open interest reflects previous trading day p-Put c-Call

CHICAGO

STRIKE	VOL.	LAST	NET CHG.	OPEN INT.
CB TECHNOLOGY(TXX)				
Sep 980 p	20	206	− 294	42
Call Vol....0		Open Int....133		
Put Vol....20		Open Int....319		
DJ INDUS AVG(DJX)				
Dec 88 p	20	013	− 013	16,859
Dec 90 p	10	019	+ 006	11,981
Dec 96 c	32	1863	+ 063	4,313
Dec 96 p	10	038	...	7,827
Sep 100 c	14	1313	+ 163	2,281
Sep 100 p	10	006	− 006	8,414
Oct 100 c	1	13	...	47
Oct 100 p	480	019	− 006	1,806
Dec 100 c	11	15	+ 1	2,381
Dec 100 p	1	056	− 025	14,301
Mar 100 p	20	150	− 063	1,144
Sep 104 c	14	950	+ 175	670
Oct 104 c	4	044	− 025	3,141
Dec 104 c	3	1150	+ 050	3,941
Dec 104 p	550	106	− 044	3,297
Sep 106 p	190	013	− 013	9,274
Sep 108 c	45	538	+ 113	4,554
Sep 108 p	116	025	− 013	4,879
Oct 108 c	63	094	− 025	1,757
Dec 108 c	1	813	+ 025	2,296
Dec 108 p	22	175	− 050	2,908
Mar 108 c	4	11	+ 050	532
Mar 108 p	2	313	− 075	584
Sep 110 c	46	350	+ 038	8,717
Sep 110 p	250	050	− 025	8,999
Oct 110 c	20	488	+ 038	123
Oct 110 p	48	138	− 025	645
Dec 110 c	32	7	+ 063	2,822
Dec 110 p	50	231	− 031	6,304
Sep 111 c	1	275	+ 050	120
Sep 111 p	32	088	− 019	1,410
Sep 112 c	29	206	+ 050	2,145
Sep 112 p	185	1	− 038	1,917
Oct 112 c	3	363	+ 050	1,662
Oct 112 p	110	206	− 025	2,654
Dec 112 p	60	3	− 050	1,545
Mar 112 c	10	825	+ 063	1,730
Mar 112 p	2	425	− 075	132
Sep 113 c	14	169	+ 069	41
Sep 113 p	58	131	− 056	45
Sep 114 c	77	113	+ 031	100
Sep 114 p	181	175	− 088	124
Oct 114 c	1	338	− 075	10
Sep 115 c	5	063	...	3,057
Sep 115 p	30	263	− 088	37
Dec 115 p	50	425	− 075	2,115
Sep 116 p	550	031	...	3,997
Sep 116 p	22	288	− 175	1,027
Oct 116 c	11	181	+ 031	2,329
Oct 116 p	4	413	− 2	31
Dec 116 p	2	438	− 138	1,527
Sep 120 c	50	013	...	16,497
Oct 120 p	1	750	− 050	32
Nov 120 p	5	688	...	...
Dec 120 c	1	194	+ 031	2,651
Dec 120 p	32	663	− 163	518
Dec 124 c	5	088	+ 006	7,223
Call Vol....979		Open Int....172,526		
Put Vol....3,834		Open Int....232,399		
DJ TRANP AVG(DTX)				
Sep 240 c	2	4188	− 788	2
Call Vol....2		Open Int....675		
Put Vol....0		Open Int....368		

RANGES FOR UNDERLYING INDEXES

Monday, August 28, 2000

	High	Low	Close	Net Chg	From 12/31	% Chg
DJ Indus (DJX)	113.19	111.89	112.53	+ 0.60	− 2.44	− 2.1
DJ Trans (DTX)	282.24	278.67	278.67	− 0.35	− 19.05	− 6.4
DJ Util (DUX)	361.86	356.12	361.12	+ 5.17	+ 77.76	+ 27.4
S&P 100 (OEX)	834.93	823.55	829.19	+ 5.64	+ 36.36	+ 4.6
S&P 500 -A.M.(SPX)	1523.88	1506.46	1514.09	+ 7.64	+ 44.84	+ 3.1
CB-Tech (TXX)	1145.56	1128.00	1135.44	+ 2.32	+ 50.82	+ 4.7
CB-Mexico (MEX)	102.74	102.13	102.73	+ 0.39	− 9.26	− 8.3
CB-Lps Mex (VEX)	10.27	10.21	10.27	+ 0.04	− 0.93	− 8.3
MS Multinl (NFT)	936.83	923.99	929.55	+ 5.55	+ 65.75	+ 7.6
GSTI Comp (GTC)	511.20	502.97	507.59	+ 4.62	+ 50.97	+ 11.2
Nasdaq 100 (NDX)	3987.71	3928.80	3954.24	+ 22.99	+ 246.41	+ 6.6
NYSE (NYA)	678.74	672.53	675.26	+ 2.73	+ 24.96	+ 3.8
Russell 2000 (RUT)	528.83	525.11	526.48	+ 1.37	+ 21.73	+ 4.3
Lps S&P 100 (OEX)	166.99	164.71	165.84	+ 1.13	+ 7.27	+ 4.6
Lps S&P 500 (SPX)	152.39	150.65	151.41	+ 0.76	+ 4.48	+ 3.0
Volatility (VIX)	19.34	18.06	18.23	− 0.87	− 8.48	− 31.7
S&P Midcap (MID)	535.33	531.17	532.54	+ 1.25	+ 87.87	+ 19.8
Major Mkt (XMI)	1099.86	1085.80	1090.49	+ 4.46	− 75.49	− 6.5
Eurotop 100 (EUR)	384.82	383.42	384.63	+ 2.26	+ 17.30	+ 4.7
HK Fltg (HKO)	331.76	331.76	331.76	− 4.30	− 0.24	− 0.1
IW Internet (IIX)	551.03	542.27	545.24	+ 0.38	− 28.13	− 4.9
AM-Mexico (MXY)	113.65	112.31	113.55	+ 1.24	− 15.76	− 12.2
Institut'l -A.M.(XII)	920.15	908.69	913.42	+ 4.73	+ 14.25	+ 1.6
Japan (JPN)			179.80	+ 2.91	− 16.75	− 8.5
MS Cyclical (CYC)	487.34	485.18	485.23	− 1.16	− 100.55	− 17.2
MS Consumr (CMR)	523.27	518.40	519.48	+ 0.69	− 15.29	− 2.9
MS Hi Tech (MSH)	1109.72	1094.26	1103.92	+ 5.30	+ 183.14	+ 19.9
MS Internet (MOX)	77.02	75.31	75.85	+ 0.22	− 24.15	− 24.2
Pharma (DRG)	399.57	394.85	394.85	− 4.08	+ 44.27	+ 12.6
Biotech (BTK)	756.80	736.49	737.92	− 12.76	+ 346.48	+ 88.5
Gold/Silver (XAU)	51.81	51.00	51.01	− 0.79	− 16.96	− 25.0
Utility (UTY)	329.30	323.49	328.47	+ 4.76	+ 54.65	+ 20.0
Value Line (VLE)	1151.68	1145.55	1146.70	+ 1.15	+ 120.90	+ 11.8
Bank (BKX)	884.44	868.95	874.67	+ 5.73	+ 104.72	+ 13.6
Semicond (SOX)	1157.40	1130.08	1134.44	− 9.27	+ 429.88	+ 61.0
Street.com (DOT)	810.81	790.73	793.04	− 10.57	− 361.41	− 31.3
Oil Service (OSX)	138.61	133.29	137.19	+ 2.75	+ 51.23	+ 59.6
PSE Tech (PSE)	1152.38	1138.65	1146.93	+ 5.65	+ 174.86	+ 18.0

STRIKE	VOL.	LAST	NET CHG.	OPEN INT.
Sep 4020 p	3	135	− 63	321
Oct 4025 p	40	235	− 25	6
Sep 4050 c	95	93	− 525	102
Oct 4050 c	1	213	...	...
Sep 4075 p	5	17513	− 8488	16
Sep 4100 c	3	65	+ 4	446
Sep 4100 p	2	38025	− 2475	57
Sep 4150 c	2	56	+ 350	252
Sep 4200 c	22	40	+ 4	1,054
Sep 4200 p	1	245	− 180	360
Sep 4225 c	30	39	+ 1550	32
Sep 4300 c	16	17	− 350	125
Sep 4300 p	1	352	− 28	39
Sep 4350 c	25	1563	+ 113	80
Sep 4400 c	10	9	− 163	260
Oct 4400 c	6	90	...	...
Sep 4425 c	1	875	− 025	20
Sep 4450 c	4	775	− 425	79
Sep 4500 c	11	475	− 125	349
Oct 4700 c	5	26	− 2	95

STRIKE	VOL.	LAST	NET CHG.	OPEN INT.
Oct 750 p	36	238	− 088	2,591
Nov 750 p	15	425	− 250	145
Sep 755 p	80	038	− 025	1,843
Oct 755 p	4	3	...	...
Sep 760 p	583	056	− 019	3,237
Oct 760 p	44	325	− 175	979
Nov 760 p	10	538	− 438	259
Dec 760 p	2	813	− 163	124
Sep 765 p	676	056	− 044	2,263
Sep 770 p	1,004	081	− 044	3,054
Oct 770 p	107	4	− 2	494
Nov 770 p	355	750	...	...
Sep 775 p	573	1	− 031	2,306
Sep 780 c	20	5313	+ 1113	552
Sep 780 p	867	1	− 088	3,783
Oct 780 p	316	588	− 050	659
Dec 780 p	31	588	...	...
Oct 780 p	8	863	− 450	276
Sep 785 p	126	125	− 106	781
Sep 790 c	1,922	4538	+ 588	3,058
Sep 790 p	2,563	188	− 1	5,724

STRIKE	VOL.	LAST	NET CHG.	OPEN INT.
Dec 840 c	6	3550	+ 5	580
Dec 840 p	11	2950	− 750	74
Sep 845 p	179	650	+ 125	989
Sep 850 c	892	413	+ 038	2,252
Sep 850 p	51	2475	− 325	55
Oct 850 c	26	1475	+ 050	843
Sep 855 c	158	363	+ 088	601
Sep 855 p	70	2625	...	...
Sep 860 c	736	225	+ 050	4,318
Sep 860 p	53	31	− 1025	13
Oct 860 c	12	1250	+ 238	772
Nov 860 c	26	1963	+ 563	317
Dec 860 c	25	2425	+ 225	341
Sep 865 c	392	138	+ 006	1,074
Oct 870 c	50	850	+ 1	486
Oct 875 c	563	063	...	3,489
Oct 875 c	100	663	+ 013	40
Oct 880 c	343	038	− 006	4,285
Oct 880 c	217	613	+ 088	1,213
Nov 880 c	1	11	+ 1	409
Sep 890 c	1,650	025	+ 013	3,492
Oct 890 c	650	375	+ 050	406
Oct 900 c	95	013	...	1,915
Oct 900 c	253	213	...	3,469
Oct 900 c	20	1025	+ 075	1,723
Sep 920 c	15	006	...	3,035
Oct 920 c	372	088	− 013	550
Sep 920 c	10	575	+ 025	20
Call Vol....16,324		Open Int....74,462		
Put Vol....24,218		Open Int....94,500		
S & P 500 INDEX-AM(SPX)				
Dec 800 c	70	013	− 013	6,455
Dec 900 c	27	025	− 025	3,964
Dec 1050 c	50	050	− 025	7,299
Dec 1100 c	100	063	− 013	13,022
Sep 1150 p	1	006	...	8,256
Sep 1200 c	6	31750	+ 3450	1,906
Sep 1200 c	10	025	+ 013	17,785
Sep 1200 c	60	050	− 006	1,614
Nov 1200 c	25	081	− 106	1,000
Dec 1200 p	30	188	− 025	17,212
Sep 1250 c	5	27513	+ 4750	2,434
Sep 1250 p	47	013	− 006	14,040
Nov 1250 p	25	150	...	...
Dec 1250 p	32	3	− 050	23,200
Sep 1275 p	50	375	− 175	4,131
Sep 1300 c	321	218	+ 750	3,953
Sep 1300 p	312	013	− 013	23,562
Oct 1300 c	1,003	138	− 063	13,912
Dec 1300 p	2,128	538	− 063	14,926
Sep 1325 c	13	201	+ 1725	883
Sep 1325 c	8	050	+ 006	16,978
Oct 1325 p	280	2	− 1	652
Sep 1325 p	105	4	− 1	270
Sep 1350 c	471	17650	+ 1825	3,716
Sep 1350 p	700	050	...	30,495
Oct 1350 p	153	250	− 150	10,476
Nov 1350 p	3,740	6	− 175	1,943
Dec 1350 c	15	20550	+ 2275	4,969
Dec 1350 p	1,351	850	− 188	19,352
Sep 1375 p	921	152	+ 2113	2,277
Sep 1375 c	32	069	− 019	14,561
Oct 1375 p	40	375	− 075	4,012
Sep 1375 p	15	1163	− 138	7,601
Sep 1400 c	122	127	+ 14	37,870
Sep 1400 p	1,062	1	− 1	19,636
Oct 1400 c	2,097	6	− 1	7,001
Nov 1400 c	10	144	+ 3	...
Nov 1400 c	93	1050	− 225	621
Nov 1400 c	9	16075	+ 975	18,268
Dec 1400 p	3,151	14	− 25	23,477
Sep 1420 c	1	131	− 094	293
Sep 1425 c	829	104	+ 17	5,554
Sep 1425 p	2,188	188	− 063	9,637
Oct 1425 p	3,401	9	− 175	5,692
Nov 1425 c	2,983	1325	...	310
Dec 1425 c	675	13950	+ 1050	4,806
Sep 1425 p	50	18	− 5	9,551
Sep 1440 c	167	250	− 175	3,508
Sep 1450 c	9	78	+ 10	14,371

SOURCE: *The Wall Street Journal,* August 29, 2000

taken place at any time during that day. Therefore, when the last option transaction was made, the stock price may well have been something else.

Another problem with prices reported in a newspaper is that they reflect only the price of the last trade and do not indicate whether that price was a market maker's bid or ask price. For example, suppose the market maker is quoting a bid of 1 3/4 and an ask of 2. If the last trade of the day is a public order to buy, the order is filled at 2; if it is a public order to sell, the order is filled at 1 3/4. Thus, the closing price shown in the newspaper could be either 1 3/4 or 2.

Most serious option traders and certainly all institutional option traders require immediate access to bid and ask prices. This information is available free with some delay on many websites, and real-time prices can be accessed for a fee.

Types of Options

Stock Options

Options on individual stocks are often called **equity options.** As of February 2000, the CBOE had 1,379, the AMEX 1,294, the Philadelphia Stock Exchange 916, and the Pacific Stock Exchange 896. About 1,600 stocks' options are listed on more than one exchange. The total number of stocks on which options are listed is 2,736. Not all of these are active every day. For example, on April 3, 2000, options on only 328 distinct stocks traded.

Index Options

A stock index is a measure of the overall value of a group of stocks. An **index option** is an option on an index of stocks. The first index option, the CBOE 100 — since renamed the S&P 100 — was launched on March 11, 1983. The S&P 100, commonly known by its ticker symbol, OEX, had an opening-day volume of 4,575 contracts. Soon afterward other exchanges added index options, and the success of these contracts has been phenomenal. On all exchanges combined, index option volume is approximately 18 percent of the total volume of all options; however, at the CBOE, index option volume is about a third of its total volume.[12]

Table 2.2 lists the current index options. The most active index option is the CBOE's S&P 100 followed by the CBOE's S&P 500.

Index options have been popular for two reasons. First, the cash settlement feature enables investors to trade options without having to take or make delivery of stock. Cash settlement has, however, been both a blessing

---

[12]Ibid.

TABLE 2.2	Index Options Trading on U.S. Exchanges As of March 31, 2000

Chicago Board Options Exchange	American Stock Exchange
Automotive	Airline
CBOE Internet	AMEX Internet
Computer Software	Biotechnology
Dow Jones Equity REIT	Computer Technology
Dow 10	EUROTOP 100
Dow Jones Industrial Average	Hong Kong Option
Dow Jones Internet Commerce	Institutional
Dow Jones Transportation	Japan
Dow Jones Utility	Major Market
Gaming	Morgan Stanley Consumer
Gold	Morgan Stanley Cyclical
Goldman Sachs Technology Composite	Morgan Stanley High Technology
Goldman Sachs Technology Hardware	Natural Gas
Goldman Sachs Technology Internet	Networking
Goldman Sachs Technology Multimedia Networking	Oil
Goldman Sachs Technology Semiconductor	Pharmaceutical
Goldman Sachs Technology Services	S&P MidCap 400
Goldman Sachs Technology Software	Securities Broker/Dealer
Indice de Precios y Cotizaciones	
Latin 15	**Philadelphia Stock Exchange**
Mexico	
Morgan Stanley Multinational Company	Forest/Paper Products Sector
NASDAQ-100	Gold and Silver
Nikkei 300	National Over-the-Counter Sector
NYSE Composite	PHLX/KBX Bank Sector
Oil	Semiconductor Sector
Russell 2000	Utility Sector
S&P 100	Value Line Composite
S&P 500	
S&P Banks	
S&P Chemical	
S&P Health Care	
S&P Insurance	
S&P Retail	
S&P SmallCap	
S&P Transportation	
S&P Technology	

These offerings of index options change frequently as exchanges experiment with different indices and terms of the contracts. For the latest information, contact the exchanges directly. Some of these options are available with long expirations and with flexible (nonstandard) terms. Some of these options are European style and some are American style.

and a curse. Many institutional investors hold large portfolios of stocks that purport to replicate the index. They then write call options or sell futures against these portfolios. At other times, these investors sell short the stocks and buy call options or futures. When the options approach the expiration date, the institutional investors, not wanting to hold the stocks after the options expire, attempt to unwind their stock positions. Holders of stock sell the stock, and short sellers buy it back. As a result, many large stock transactions are made near expiration and are accompanied by increased volatility. The cash settlement feature of index options and futures has been blamed for this volatility, although it is not clear that it is truly the cause.

The second reason for the popularity of index options is the fact that they are options on the market as a whole. Because there are so many stocks on which options trade, few investors have the time to screen that many opportunities. Many prefer to analyze the market as a whole and use index options (and futures) to act on their forecasts.

Other Types of Options

The options exchanges have experimented with a number of different types of options, including options on bonds, though these have attracted little interest. Options on bonds and related options called *interest rate options* are, however, extremely popular in the over-the-counter markets. We shall explore these in Chapter 14. In addition, options on foreign currencies are quite popular, primarily in the over-the-counter markets. We shall cover foreign currency options in Chapter 13, when we look at foreign currency derivatives.

Many financial institutions now offer deposits on which they pay interest based on a minimum value plus the performance of the stock market above a specific level. This is like a call option plus a bond. Other innovative options include some that pay off based on how the price of a commodity, like oil, performs. It is possible to trade an option that pays off based on which stock index, say the S&P 500 or London's Financial Times 100, performs better. There are also options that expire if the stock price falls to a certain level; options that are based on the average, maximum, or minimum stock price during the life of the option; and an option that allows you to decide, after buying it but before it expires, whether to make it a put or a call. These options, often called **exotics,** are but a sampling of the tremendous number of innovations that have developed in the over-the-counter markets in recent years. We shall take a look at some of these kinds of instruments in Chapter 15.

A number of other common instruments are practically identical to options. For example, many corporations issue warrants, which are long-term options to buy the companies' stock. Warrants often are issued in conjunction with a public offering of debt or equity. Many corporations issue convertible bonds, which allow the holder to convert the bond into a certain number of shares of stock. The right to convert is itself a call option. Callable bonds, which give the issuing firm the right to repay the bonds early, contain an option-like component. Stock itself is equivalent to a call option on the firm's assets written by the bondholders with an exercise price equal to the amount due on the debt. Executive stock options, which are call options written by a corporation and given to their executives, are used extensively as compensation and to give executives an incentive to engage in activities that maximize shareholder wealth.

Transaction Costs in Option Trading

Option trading entails certain transaction costs. The costs depend on whether the trader is a member of the exchange, a nonmember institutional investor, or a member of the public who is trading through a broker. This section discusses the different types of transaction costs.

Floor Trading and Clearing Fees

Floor trading and clearing fees are the minimum charges assessed by the exchange, the clearing corporation, and the clearing firms for handling a transaction. For trades that go through a broker, these fees are included in the broker's commission, discussed in the next section. For market makers, the fees are collected by the market maker's clearing firm.

The clearing firm enters into a contractual arrangement with a market maker to clear trades for a fee usually stated on a per contract basis.

At the CBOE, the fee per transaction is about $0.24 per contract. The clearinghouse charges another $0.09. The clearing firm charges about $0.20. In addition, the CBOE charges annual dues and fees of about $2,700.

For over-the-counter options, these types of costs are not incurred, but comparable, if not higher, costs are associated with processing these customized transactions.

Commissions

One of the main advantages of owning a seat on an exchange is that it lets one avoid paying commissions on each trade. The market maker pays indirectly via the opportunity cost associated with the funds tied up in the seat price, the labor involved in trading, and forgoing the earnings that would be realized in another line of work. The savings in commissions, however, are quite substantial.

Discount brokers offer the lowest commission rates, but frequent or large trades sometimes are necessary to take advantage of their prices. A discount brokerage firm does not provide the advice and research available from full-service brokers charging higher commission rates. One should not, however, automatically assume that a full-service broker is more costly.

Options commissions are fairly simple, based on a fixed minimum and a per contract charge. Internet rates of $20 plus $1.75 per contract appear to be the most attractive rates. Some brokers may charge based on the total dollar size of the transaction, and some offer discounts to more active customers.

When exercising a stock option, the investor must pay the commission for buying or selling the stock. (Stock commissions are discussed in a later section.) If an investor exercises a cash settlement option, the transaction entails only a bookkeeping entry. Some brokerage firms do not charge to exercise a cash settlement option. When any type of option expires unexercised, there normally is no commission.

For over-the-counter options, commissions are not generally incurred, because the option buyer or seller usually trades directly with the opposite party.

Bid-Ask Spread

The market maker's spread is a significant transaction cost. Suppose the market maker is quoting a bid price of 3 and an ask price of 3 1/4 on a call. An investor who buys the call immediately incurs a "cost" of the bid-ask spread, or 1/4 point; that is, if the investor immediately sold the call, it would fetch only $3, the bid price, and the investor would immediately incur a 1/4 point, or $25, loss. This does not, however, mean that the investor cannot make a profit. The call price may well increase before the option is sold, but if the spread is constant, the bid price must increase by at least the amount of the bid-ask spread before a profit can be made.

The bid-ask spread is the cost of immediacy — the assurance that market makers are willing and able to buy and sell the options on demand. The cost is not explicitly observed, and the investor will not see it on the monthly statement from the broker. It is, however, a real cost and can be quite substantial amounting to several percent of the option's price.

It may appear that market makers can avoid the bid-ask spread transaction cost. This is true in some cases. If, however, the market maker must buy or sell an option, there may be no public orders of the opposite position. In that case, the market maker would have to trade with another market maker and thus would incur the cost of the bid-ask spread.

In the over-the-counter market, the buyer or seller trades directly with the opposite party. In many cases, one of the parties is a financial institution that makes markets in whatever options its clients want. Thus, the client will probably face a bid-ask spread that could be quite significant, but of course, the client is free to shop around.

Other Transaction Costs

Option traders incur several other types of transaction costs. Some of these costs, such as margins and taxes, are discussed in Appendixes 2A and 2B, respectively. Most option traders also trade stocks. Thus, the transaction costs of stock trades are a factor in option trading costs.

Stock trading commissions vary widely among brokerage firms; however, 1 percent to 2 percent of the stock's value for a single purchase or sale transaction is a reasonable estimate. Market makers normally obtain more favorable rates from their clearing firms. Also, large institutional investors usually can negotiate volume discounts from their brokers. Internet rates of $10 or less are sometimes seen. Stocks, however, also have bid-ask spreads and ultimately 1–2 percent is probably a good estimate of stock trading costs for public investors.

All the transaction costs discussed here are for single transactions. If the option or stock is subsequently purchased or sold in the market, the transaction cost is incurred again.

The Regulation of Options Markets

The exchange-traded options industry is regulated at several levels. Although federal and state regulations predominate, the industry also regulates itself according to rules and standards established by the exchanges and the Options Clearing Corporation.

The Securities and Exchange Commission (SEC) is the primary regulator of the options market. The SEC is a federal regulatory agency created in 1934 to oversee the securities industry, which includes stocks, bonds, options, and mutual funds. The SEC's general purpose is to ensure full disclosure of all pertinent information on publicly offered investments. It has the authority to establish certain rules and procedures and to investigate possible violations of federal securities laws. If the SEC observes a violation it may seek injunctive relief, recommend that the Justice Department press charges, or impose some sanctions itself. For more information on the SEC, see its excellent website at http://www.sec.gov.

The exchanges establish rules and procedures that apply to all members as well as to individuals and firms participating in options transactions. Rule violations are punishable by fines and/or suspensions. The Options Clearing Corporation also regulates its members to help ensure that all activities in the options markets are proper and do not pose a risk to the market's viability.

The regulatory authority of an individual state extends to any securities or options trading occurring within that state. States with significant option trading, such as Illinois and New York, actively enforce their own laws on the propriety of transactions conducted therein. Many important issues in the options industry as a whole are sometimes settled in state courts in Illinois and New York.

Other levels of regulation are imposed by the Federal Reserve System, which regulates the extension of margin credit; the Securities Investor Protection Corporation, which provides insurance against the failure of brokerage firms; and the National Association of Securities Dealers (NASD), of which most firms involved in options trading are members. In addition, several regional and national organizations, such as the Association for Investment Management and Research, indirectly regulate the industry by prescribing ethical standards for their members.

Many new exchange-traded option products were introduced in the 1980s, including options on stock indices, options on foreign currencies, and options on futures. These products created some confusion as to whether the SEC or the Commodity Futures Trading Commission (CFTC) had regulatory purview. The options on futures instrument caused the greatest confusion, because it is like an option and a futures. In an important step in resolving the matter, the then chairmen of these agencies — John Shad of the SEC and Phillip McBride Johnson of the CFTC — reached an agreement. In what has come to be known as the **Johnson-Shad agreement,** or **CFTC-SEC accord,** it was decided that the SEC would regulate options on stocks, stock indices, and foreign currencies while the CFTC would govern options on all futures contracts. Also, a CFTC-regulated contract cannot permit delivery of instruments regulated by the SEC. Although the Johnson-Shad agreement was a milestone in regulatory cooperation, continued disputes between the SEC and the CFTC characterized the regulatory environment of the early 1990s. We shall learn more about these issues when we cover futures.

The primary purpose of the exchange-traded regulatory system is to protect the public. Over the years, many controversial issues have been raised and discussed. In an industry as large as the options industry, some abuses are certain to occur. In recent years, the options industry has been subjected to criticisms that it has manipulated the stock market and abused the public's trust by charging exorbitant prices for options. There is no evidence, however, that any of these charges are true. There have even been a few defaults by writers, but, thanks to the clearinghouse, in no case has any buyer lost money because of a writer's failure to perform. The options industry works hard to maintain the public's trust by operating in an environment of self-regulation. By policing itself and punishing wrong-doers, some of the cost of having federal regulation is offset for taxpayers.

As noted earlier in the chapter, the over-the-counter market is an unregulated market, bound loosely by customs and accepted procedures. The firms that participate, however, are often regulated by the NASD, the Federal Reserve, or the Comptroller of the Currency. Of course, commercial laws always apply. The SEC and the CFTC, however, have no direct regulatory authority over the over-the-counter options market.

Summary

This chapter provided the foundation for an understanding of the types of options, individuals, and institutions involved in the options markets. It examined contract specifications, mechanics of trading, transaction costs, and regulations. This information is a prerequisite to the study of option trading strategies and the pricing of options.

Chapters 3, 4, and 5 focus on the principles and models that determine option prices. Chapters 6 and 7 concentrate on applying this knowledge to the implementation of option trading strategies.

Key Terms

Before continuing to Chapter 3, you should be able to give brief definitions of the following terms.

- premium
- call option
- put option
- exercise price/strike price/striking price
- expiration date
- in-/out-of-/at-the-money
- class
- series
- position limit
- exercise limit
- seat
- market maker
- bid price
- ask price
- bid-ask spread
- scalpers
- position traders
- spreaders
- floor broker
- order book official (OBO)/board broker
- specialist
- registered option trader (ROT)
- market order
- limit order
- good-till-canceled order
- day order
- stop order
- all or none order
- all or none, same price order
- clearinghouse
- Options Clearing Corporation (OCC)
- clearing firm
- margin
- open interest
- offsetting order/offset
- exercise
- assigned
- cash settlement
- equity option
- index option
- exotics
- Johnson-Shad agreement/CFTC-SEC accord

Further Reading

The following provide good sources of information on options:

McMillan, L. G. *McMillan on Options.* New York: Wiley, 1996.

The Options Institute. *Options: Essential Concepts and Trading Strategies,* 2d ed. New York: McGraw-Hill, 1994.

Thomsett, M. C. *Getting Started in Options.* 3d ed. New York: Wiley, 1997.

Questions and Problems

1. Determine whether each of the following arrangements is an option. If so, decide whether it is a call or a put and identify the premium.

   a. You purchase homeowner's insurance for your house.

   b. You are a high school senior evaluating possible college choices. One school promises that if you enroll, it will guarantee your tuition rate for the next four years.

   c. You enter into a noncancelable, long-term apartment lease.

2. Explain the difference between an American option and a European option. What do they have in common?

3. Explain each of the terms in the following description of an option: AT&T January 65 call.

4. What adjustments to the contract terms of CBOE options would be made in the following situations?

   a. An option has an exercise price of 60. The company declares a 10 percent stock dividend.

   b. An option has an exercise price of 25. The company declares a two-for-one stock split.

   c. An option has an exercise price of 85. The company declares a four-for-three stock split.

   d. An option has an exercise price of 50. The company declares a cash dividend of $.75.

5. Consider the January, February, and March stock option exercise cycles discussed in the chapter. For each of the following dates, indicate which expirations in each cycle would be listed for trading in stock options.

   a. February 1

   b. July 1

   c. December 1

6. Why are short puts and long calls grouped together when considering position limits?

7. Compare and contrast the roles of market maker and floor broker. Why do you think an individual cannot generally be both?

8. Explain how the CBOE's order book official (OBO) handles public limit orders.

9. Contrast the market maker system of the CBOE and Pacific Stock Exchange with the specialist system of the AMEX and Philadelphia Stock Exchange. What advantages and disadvantages do you see in each system?

10. Suppose you are an individual investor with an options account at a brokerage firm. You purchase 20 call contracts at a price of $2.25 each. Explain how your premium ends up at the clearinghouse.

11. Compare and contrast the exercise procedure for stock options with that for index options. What major advantage does exercising an index option have over exercising a stock option?

12. Discuss the limitations of prices obtained from newspapers such as *The Wall Street Journal.*

13. Discuss the three possible ways in which an open option position can be terminated. Is your answer different if the option is created in the over-the-counter market?

14. Name and briefly describe at least two other instruments that are very similar to options.

15. Identify and briefly discuss the various types of option transaction costs. How do these costs differ for market makers, floor brokers, and firms trading in the over-the-counter market?

16. Explain the major difference between the regulation of exchange-traded options and over-the-counter options.

APPENDIX 2A
Margin Requirements

Margin is the amount of money an individual puts down when entering into an investment. The remainder is borrowed from the brokerage firm. The objective of a margin trade is to earn a higher return by virtue of investing less of one's own funds. This advantage is, however, accompanied by increased risk. If the stock price does not move sufficiently in the desired direction, the profit from the investment may not be enough to pay off the loan.

Regulation T of the Federal Reserve Act authorizes the Federal Reserve to regulate the extension of credit in the United States. This authority extends to the regulation of margin credit on transactions in stocks and options.

The **initial margin** is the minimum amount of funds the investor supplies on the day of the transaction. The **maintenance margin** is the minimum amount of funds required each day thereafter. On any day on which a trade is executed, the initial margin requirement must be met.

The rules presented here apply to public investors. Specialists and market makers have more lenient margin requirements. Clearing firm margins deposited with the OCC are calculated differently based on a netting out of certain identical long and short positions and an additional amount based on the probabilities of customer defaults.

Margin Requirements on Stock Transactions

The minimum initial margin for stock purchases and short sales is 50 percent. The minimum maintenance margin is 25 percent. Many brokerage firms add an additional 5 percent or more to these requirements.

Margin Requirements on Option Purchases

All option purchases must be fully margined; that is, the investor must pay the option premium in full. This rule exists because options already contain a substantial leverage component. The additional use of margin would add leverage and thus greatly increase the risk of the investor's position.

Margin Requirements on the Uncovered Sale of Options

An **uncovered call** is a transaction in which an investor writes a call on stock not already owned. If the option is exercised, the writer must buy the stock in the market at the current price, which has no upper limit. Thus, the risk is quite high. Many brokerage firms do not allow their customers to write uncovered calls. Those that do usually restrict such trades to wealthy investors who can afford large losses; yet even these must meet the minimum margin requirements.

For an uncovered call, the investor must deposit the premium plus 20 percent of the stock's value. If the call is out-of-the-money, the requirement is reduced by the amount by which the call is out-of-the-money. The margin must be at least 10 percent of the value of the stock. Consider an investor who writes one call contract at an exercise price of $30 on a stock priced at $33 for a premium of $4.50. The required margin is .2($3,300) + $450 = $1,110. If the stock is priced at $28 and the call is at $0.50, the margin is .2($2,800) + $50 − $200 = $410. These amounts are greater than 10 percent of the value of the stock. The amount by which the call is out-of-the-money reduces the required margin.

The same rules apply for puts. If a put is written at an exercise price of $30 when the stock price is $33 and the put price is $2.375, the required margin is .2($3,300) + $237.50 − $300 = $597.50. If the stock price is $29 and the put price is $3.25, the margin is .2($2,900) + $325 = $905. These amounts are greater than 10 percent of the value of the stock.

Index options are somewhat less volatile than options on individual stocks and, appropriately, have lower margin requirements. The required margin is 15 percent, instead of 20 percent, of the stock's value.

Margin Requirements on Covered Calls

A **covered call** is a transaction in which an investor writes an option against a stock already owned. If the option's exercise price is at least equal to the stock price, the investor need not deposit any additional margin beyond that required on the stock. Also, the premium on the option can be used to reduce the margin required on the stock. If, however, the exercise price is less than the stock price, the maximum amount the investor can borrow on the stock is based on the call's exercise price rather than on the stock price. For example, if the stock price is $40 and the exercise price is $35, the investor can borrow only .5($3,500) = $1,750, not .5($4,000) = $2,000, on the purchase of the stock.

Although it is possible to hold a portfolio of stocks that is identical to the index, current margin requirements do not recognize covered index call writing. Therefore, all short positions in index options must be margined according to the rules that apply to uncovered writing.

There are exceptions to many of these rules, particularly when spreads, straddles, and more complex option transactions are used. In these cases, the margin requirements often are complicated. Investors should consult a broker or some of the trade-oriented publications for additional information on margin requirements for the more complex transactions.

Questions and Problems

1. Suppose a stock is currently priced at $50. The margin requirement is 20 percent on uncovered calls and 50 percent on stocks. Calculate the required margin, in dollars, for each of the following trades:

    a. Write 10 call contracts with an exercise price of 45 and a premium of 7.

    b. Write 10 call contracts with an exercise price of 55 and a premium of 3.

    c. Write 10 put contracts with an exercise price of 45 and a premium of 3.

    d. Write 10 put contracts with an exercise price of 55 and a premium of 7.

    e. Buy 1,000 shares of stock and write 10 call contracts with an exercise price of 45 and a premium of 7.

    f. Buy 20 put contracts with an exercise price of 50 and a premium of 5.

APPENDIX 2B
Taxation of Option Transactions

Determining the applicable taxation of many investment transactions is a complex process that requires the advice of highly trained specialists. The rules covered in this appendix outline most of the basic option transactions. There are many exceptions and loopholes, and the laws change frequently. In all cases, one should secure competent professional advice.

The ordinary income of most individuals is taxed at either 15, 28, 31, 36, or 39.6 percent. Long-term capital gains, defined as profits from positions held more than 18 months, are taxed at a maximum of 20 percent. Although there are some exceptions noted herein, most options profits are short-term.

In these examples, we ignore brokerage commissions; however, they are tax deductible. The commission on the purchase of the asset is added to the purchase price; the commission on its sale is subtracted from the sale price.

The deductibility of any losses is determined by offsetting them against other investment gains. If the losses exceed the gains, any excess up to $3,000 per year is deductible against the investor's ordinary income.

These rules apply to individual investors. Corporations and other institutions trading options, especially over-the-counter options, may be subject to different tax rules and interpretations.

For the following examples, we shall assume the investor is in the 28 percent tax bracket.

Taxation of Long Call Transactions

If an investor purchases a call and sells it back at a later date at a higher price, there is a capital gain, which is either long- or short-term, usually short-term. Thus, it is taxed at the ordinary income rate. If the investor sells the call at a loss or allows it to expire, the loss is deductible as previously described.

Consider an investor who purchases a call at $3.50 on a stock priced at $36 with an exercise price of $35. Less than 18 months later but before expiration, the investor sells the call at $4.75. The profit of $1.25 is taxed at 28 percent for a tax of $1.25(.28) = $0.35. If the call were sold at a loss, the loss would be deductible as described earlier.

If the investor exercised the call, the call price plus the exercise price would be treated as the stock's purchase price and subsequently used to determine the taxable gain on the stock. For example, if the above call were exercised when the stock price was $38, the purchase price of the stock would be considered as the $35 exercise price plus the $3.50 call price for a total of $38.50. If the investor later sold the stock for $40, the taxable gain would be $1.50 and the tax $1.50(.28) = $0.42. A tax liability or deduction arises only when the stock is subsequently sold.

Taxation of Short Call Transactions

If an investor sells a call and later repurchases it or allows it to expire, any profit is a short-term capital gain and taxed at the ordinary income rate. If the call is exercised, the exercise price plus the call price is treated as the price at which the stock is sold. Then the difference between the price at which the stock is sold and the price at which it is purchased is the taxable gain.

For example, if the above investor writes the call at a price of $5.25 and subsequently buys it at $3.50 before expiration, the profit of $1.75 will be taxed at 28 percent for a tax of $1.75(.28) = $0.49. A loss would be deductible as previously described. If the call were exercised, the writer would deliver the stock. Suppose the stock price were $38 and the writer did not already own the stock. Then the writer would purchase the stock for $38 and sell it to the buyer for $35. The sum of the exercise price plus the premium, $35 + $5.25 = $40.25, would be treated as the stock's sale price. The taxable gain to the writer would be $2.25 and the tax $2.25(.28) = $0.63. Had the writer purchased the stock at an earlier date at $30, the taxable gain would be $10.25 and the tax $10.25(.28) = $2.87.

Taxation of Long Put Transactions

If an investor purchases a put and sells it or allows it to expire less than 18 months later, the profit is a short-term capital gain and is taxed at the ordinary income rate. If the put is exercised, the exercise price minus the premium is treated as the stock's sale price. Then the profit from the stock is taxed at the ordinary income rate.

Consider an investor in the 28 percent tax bracket who purchases a put at $3 on a stock priced at $52 with an exercise price of $50. Later the investor sells the put for $4.25. The gain of $1.25 is taxed at 28 percent for a tax of $1.25(.28) = $0.35. If the put is sold at a loss, the loss is deductible as previously described.

Suppose the investor exercises the put when the stock price is $46. The law would treat this as the sale of stock at $50 less the premium of $3 for a net gain of $47. If the investor purchases the stock at $46 and exercises the put, the taxable gain is $1 and the tax is $1(.28) = $0.28. If the investor had previously purchased the stock at $40, the taxable gain would be $7 and the tax $7(.28) = $1.96. Had the investor purchased the stock at a price higher than $47, the loss would be deductible as described earlier.

Another possibility is that the investor uses the exercise of the put to sell short the stock. Recall from Chapter 1 that a short sale occurs when an investor borrows stock from the broker and sells it. If the stock price falls, the investor can buy back the stock at a lower price, repay the broker the shares, and capture a profit. A short sale is made in order to profit in a falling market. In our example, the stock is sold short at $47. When the investor later repurchases the stock, any gain on the stock is taxable or any loss is deductible.

Taxation of Short Put Transactions

If an investor writes a put and subsequently buys it back before expiration, any gain is considered a short-term capital gain and is taxed at the ordinary income rate and any loss is deductible. If the put is exercised, the put's exercise price minus the premium is considered to be the stock's purchase price. The taxable gain or loss on the stock is determined by the difference between the purchase and sale prices of the stock.

Consider the put with an exercise price of $50 written at $3 when the stock price is $52. Suppose the stock price goes to $46 and the put is exercised. The put writer is considered to have purchased the stock for $50 −$3, or $47. If the investor later sells the stock for $55, the taxable gain is $8 and the tax is $8(.28) = $2.24.

Taxation of Non-Equity Options

Index options, debt options, and foreign currency options have a special tax status. At the end of the calendar year, all realized *and unrealized* gains are taxable. All losses are deductible as previously described. The profits are taxed at a blended rate in which 60 percent are taxed at the long-term capital gains rate and 40 percent are taxed at the short-term capital gains rate, which is the ordinary income rate. For an investor in the 28 percent bracket, this is an effective rate of $.6(.20) + .4(.28) = .232$.

For example, assume that during the year an investor in the 28 percent bracket had $1,250 of net profits (profits minus losses) on index options. At the end of the year, the investor holds 1,000 index options worth $2.25 that previously had been purchased for $1.75. The unrealized profit is thus $500. The total taxable profits are $1,250 + $500 = $1,750. The tax is $1,750(.6)(.20) + $1,750(.4)(.28) = 406.

Wash and Constructive Sales

Option traders should be aware of an important tax condition called the **wash sale rule.** A wash sale is a transaction in which an investor sells a security at a loss and replaces it with essentially the same security shortly thereafter. Tax laws disallow the deduction of the loss on the sale of the original security. The purpose of the wash sale rule is to prevent investors from taking losses at the end of a calendar year and then immediately replacing the securities. The time period within which the purchase of the security cannot occur is the 61-day period from 30 days before the sale of the stock through 30 days after.

Although, as with many tax laws, there is some murkiness, the wash sale rule usually treats a call option as being the same security as the stock. Thereafter, if the investor sells the stock at a loss and buys a call within the applicable 61-day period, the loss on the stock is not deductible.

In addition, the sale of a call option on a stock owned can, under some circumstances, be treated as the investor effectively having sold the stock, thereby terminating the stock holding period. This is called a constructive sale. Again, the law is somewhat unclear as this is a new IRS regulation.

Questions and Problems

1. Suppose a stock is priced at $30 and an eight-month call on the stock with an exercise price of $25 is priced at $6. Compute the taxable gain and tax due for each of the following cases assuming your tax bracket is 28 percent. Assume 100 shares and 100 calls.

   a. You buy the call. Four months later, the stock is at $28 and the call is at $4.50. You then sell the call.

   b. You buy the call. Three months later, the stock is at $31 and the call is at $6.50. You then sell the call.

   c. You buy the call. At expiration, the stock is at $32. You exercise the call and sell the stock a month later for $35.

    d. You buy the stock and write the call. You hold the position until expiration, whereupon the stock is at $28.

    e. You write the call. Two months later, the stock is at $28 and the call is at $3.50. You buy back the call.

2. Consider an index option. The index is at 425.48, and a two-month call with an exercise price of 425 is priced at $15. You are in the 31 percent tax bracket. Compute the after-tax profit for the following cases. Assume 100 calls.

    a. You buy the call. One month later, the index is at 428 and the call is at $12. You sell the call.

    b. You buy the call and hold it until expiration, whereupon the index is at 441.35. You exercise the call.

    c. You hold the call until expiration, when the index is at 417.15.

    d. How will your answers in parts a and b be affected if the option positions are not closed out by the end of the year?

3. Which of the following would be a wash sale? Explain.

    a. You buy a stock at $30. Three weeks later, you sell the stock at $26. Two weeks later, you buy a call on the stock.

    b. You buy a stock at $40. One month later, you buy a call on the stock. One week later, you sell the stock for $38.

    c. You buy a stock for $40. Three months later, you sell the stock for $42 and buy a call on the stock.

CHAPTER 3

Principles of Option Pricing

Order and simplification are the first steps toward mastery of a subject—the actual enemy is the unknown.

THOMAS MANN
The Magic Mountain, 1924

This chapter identifies and shows why certain factors affect an option's price. It examines option boundary conditions—rules that characterize rational option prices. Then it explores the relationship between options that differ by exercise price alone and those that differ only by time to expiration. Finally, the chapter discusses how put and call prices are related as well as several other important principles. An overriding point throughout this chapter, and indeed throughout this entire book, is that arbitrage opportunities are quickly eliminated by investors.

Suppose an individual offers you the following proposition. You can play a game called Game I in which you draw a ball from a hat known to contain three red balls and three blue balls. If you draw a red ball, you receive nothing; if you draw a blue ball, you receive $10. Will you play? Because the individual did not mention an entry fee, of course you will play. You incur no cash outlay up front and have the opportunity to earn $10. Of course, this opportunity is too good to be true and only an irrational person would make such an offer without charging an entry fee.

Now suppose a fair fee to play this game is $4. Now consider a new game called Game II. The person offers to pay you $20 if you draw a blue ball and nothing if you draw a red ball. Will the entry fee be higher or lower? If you draw a red ball, you receive the same payoff as in Game I; if you draw a blue ball, you receive a higher payoff than in Game I. You should be willing to pay more to play Game II because these payoffs dominate those of Game I.

From these simple games and opportunities, it is easy to see some of the basic principles of how rational people behave when faced with risky

Chapter Objectives

■ To explain and illustrate the role of arbitrage in pricing options by applying it to demonstrate the fundamental principles that determine an option's price, such as the minimum value, maximum value, value at expiration, and the lower bound

■ To identify and explain the rationale for factors that affect an option's price, including the exercise price, the time to expiration, the risk-free rate, and the volatility

■ To explain the difference between American and European options and why early exercise may or may not occur

■ To understand the very important relationship of put-call parity

71

situations. The collective behavior of rational investors operates in an identical manner to determine the fundamental principles of option pricing. As you read the various examples in this chapter in which arbitrage is used to establish fundamental rules about option pricing, keep in mind the similarity of the investment situation to the games just described. In so doing, the rational result should become clear to you.

In this chapter, we do not derive the exact price of an option; rather, we confine the discussion to identifying upper and lower limits and factors that influence an option's price. Chapters 4 and 5 explain how the exact option price is determined.

Basic Notation and Terminology

The following symbols are used throughout the book:

$$S_0 = \text{stock price today (time 0 = today)}$$
$$X = \text{exercise price}$$
$$T = \text{time to expiration as defined below}$$
$$r = \text{risk-free rate as defined below}$$
$$S_T = \text{stock price at option's expiration, i.e., after the passage of a period of time of length T}$$
$$C(S_0,T,X) = \text{price of a call option in which the stock price is } S_0, \text{ the time to expiration is T, and the exercise price is X}$$
$$P(S_0,T,X) = \text{price of a put option in which the stock price is } S_0, \text{ the time to expiration is T, and the exercise price is X}$$

In some situations, we may need to distinguish an American call from a European call. If so, the call price will be denoted as either $C_a(S_0,T,X)$ or $C_e(S_0,T,X)$ for the American and European calls, respectively. If there is no a or e subscript, the call can be either an American or a European call. In the case where two options differ only by exercise price, the notations $C(S_0,T,X_1)$ and $C(S_0,T,X_2)$ will identify the prices of the calls with X_1 less than X_2. A good way to remember this is to keep in mind that the subscript of the lower exercise price is smaller than that of the higher exercise price. In the case where two options differ only by time to expiration, the times to expiration will be T_1 and T_2, where $T_1 < T_2$. The options' prices will be $C(S_0,T_1,X)$ and $C(S_0,T_2,X)$. Identical adjustments will be made for put option prices.

For most of the examples we shall assume that the stock pays no dividends. If, during the life of the option, the stock pays dividends of D_1, D_2, . . . , etc., then we can make a simple adjustment and obtain similar results. To do so, we simply subtract the present value of the dividends, $\sum_{j=1}^{N} D_j(1 + r)^{-t_j}$ where there are N dividends and t_j is the time to each ex-dividend day, from the stock price. We assume the dividends are known ahead of time.

The time to expiration is expressed as a decimal fraction of a year. For example, if the current date is April 9 and the option's expiration date is July 18, we simply count the number of days between these two dates. That would be 21 days remaining in April, 31 in May, 30 in June, and 18 in July for a total of 100 days. The time to expiration therefore would be $100/365 = 0.274$.

The risk-free rate, r, is the rate earned on a riskless investment. An example of such an investment is a U.S. Treasury bill, or T-bill. A Treasury bill is a security issued by the U.S. government for purchase by investors. Bills with original maturities of 91 and 182 days are auctioned by the Federal Reserve each week; bills with maturities of 365 days are auctioned every four weeks. All bills mature on a Thursday.[1] Because most exchange-traded options expire on Fridays, there is always a Treasury bill maturing the day before expiration. For other options with maturities of six months or less, there is a Treasury bill maturing within one week of the option's expiration. The rate of return on a Treasury bill of comparable maturity would be a proxy for the risk-free rate.

Treasury bills pay interest not through coupons but by selling at a discount. The bill is purchased at less than face value. The difference between the purchase price and the face value is called the discount. If the investor holds the bill to maturity, it is redeemed at face value. Therefore, the discount is the profit earned by the bill holder.

Bid and ask discounts for several T-bills for the business day of May 14 of a particular year are as follows:

Maturity	Bid	Ask
5/20	4.45	4.37
6/17	4.41	4.37
7/15	4.47	4.43

The bid and ask figures are the discounts quoted by dealers trading in Treasury bills. The bid is the discount if one is selling to the dealer, and the ask is the discount if one is buying from the dealer. Bid and ask quotes are reported daily in *The Wall Street Journal*.

Most exchange-listed options expire on the third Friday of the month. In the preceding example, the third Friday of May was May 21. To find an estimate of the T-bill rate, we use the average of the bid and ask discounts, which is $(4.45 + 4.37)/2 = 4.41$. Then we find the discount from par value as $4.41(7/360) = 0.08575$, using the fact that the option has 7 days until maturity. Thus, the price is

$$100 - 0.08575 = 99.91425.$$

Note that the price is determined by assuming a 360-day year. This is a long-standing tradition in the financial community, originating from the

---

[1] If Thursday is a holiday, such as Thanksgiving, the Treasury bill matures on Wednesday of that week.

TABLE 3.1	America Online Option Data, May 14					
	Calls			Puts		
Exercise Price	May	June	July	May	June	July
120	8 3/4	15 3/8	20 7/8	2 3/4	9 1/4	13 5/8
125	5 3/4	13 1/2	18 5/8	4 5/8	11 1/2	16 5/8
130	3 5/8	11 3/8	16 3/8	7 3/8	14 1/4	19 5/8
Current stock price:	125 15/16					
Expirations:	May 21, June 18, July 16					

days before calculators, when bank loans often were for 60, 90, or 180 days. A banker could more easily calculate the discount using the fraction 60/360, 90/360, or 180/360. This tradition survives today.

The yield on our T-bill is based on the assumption of buying it at 99.91425 and holding it for 7 days, at which time it will be worth 100.[2] This is a return of $(100 - 99.91425)/99.91425 = 0.000858$. If we repeated this transaction every seven days for a full year, the return would be

$$(1.000858)^{365/7} - 1 = .0457,$$

where 1.000858 is simply 100/99.91425, or one plus the seven-day return. Note that when we annualize the return, we use the full 365-day year. Thus, we would use 4.57 percent as our proxy for the risk-free rate for options expiring on May 21.

To illustrate the principles of option pricing with real-life options, Table 3.1 presents some prices of America Online options on May 14 of a particular year. The May option expires on May 21, the June expires on June 18, and the July expires on July 16. Following the same procedure described for the May T-bill and using the Treasury bill data from the previous example gives us risk-free rates of 4.56 and 4.63 for the June and July expirations, respectively. The times to expiration are 0.0192 (7 days) for the May options, 0.0959 (35 days) for the June options, and 0.1726 (63 days) for the July options.

Principles of Call Option Pricing

In this section we formulate rules that enable us to better understand how call options are priced. It is important to keep in mind that our objective is to determine the price of a call option *prior to* its expiration day.

---

[2]Actually the number of days is counted from the settlement day, which is the second business day after the purchase day. We shall disregard this point in the calculations in this book.

The Minimum Value of a Call

A call option is an instrument with limited liability. If the call holder sees that it is advantageous to exercise it, the call will be exercised. If exercising it will decrease the call holder's wealth, the holder will not exercise it. The option cannot have negative value, because the holder cannot be forced to exercise it. Therefore,

Because a call option need not be exercised, its minimum value is zero.

$$C(S_0, T, X) \geq 0.$$

For an American call, the statement that a call option has a minimum value of zero is dominated by a much stronger statement:

$$C_a(S_0, T, X) \geq \text{Max}(0, S_0 - X).$$

The expression $\text{Max}(0, S_0 - X)$ means "Take the maximum value of the two arguments, zero or $S_0 - X$."

The intrinsic value of an American call is the greater of zero or the difference between the stock price and the exercise price.

The minimum value of an option is called its **intrinsic value,** sometimes referred to as **parity value, parity,** or **exercise value.** Intrinsic value, which is positive for in-the-money calls and zero for out-of-the-money calls, is the value the call holder receives from exercising the option and the value the call writer gives up when the option is exercised. Note that we are not concerned about the appropriateness of immediately exercising the option; we note only that one could do so if a profit opportunity were available.

To prove the intrinsic value rule, consider the America Online June 120 call. The stock price is $125.9375, and the exercise price is $120. Evaluating the expression gives $\text{Max}(0, 125.9375 - 120) = 5.9375$. Now consider what would happen if the call were priced at less than $5.9375—say, $3. An option trader could buy the call for $3, exercise it—which would entail purchasing the stock for $120—and then sell the stock for $125.9375. This arbitrage transaction would net an immediate riskless profit of $2.9375 on each share.[3] All investors would do this, which would drive up the option's price. When the price of the option reached $5.9375, the transaction would no longer be profitable. Thus, $5.9375 is the minimum price of the call.

What if the exercise price exceeds the stock price, as do the options with an exercise price of $130? Then $\text{Max}(0, 125.9375 - 130) = 0$, and the minimum value will be zero.

Now look at all of the America Online calls. Those with an exercise price of $120 have a minimum value of $\text{Max}(0, 125.9375 - 120) = 5.9375$. All three calls with an exercise price of $120 indeed have prices of no less

---

[3]Actually, it would not be necessary to sell the stock. In the absence of transaction costs, it is immaterial whether one holds the stock—an asset valued at $125.9375—or converts it to another asset—cash—worth $125.9375.

than \$5.9375. The calls with an exercise price of \$125 have minimum values of Max(0, 125.9375 − 125) = 0.9375 and are priced at no less than 0.9375. The calls with an exercise price of 130 have minimum values of Max(0, 125.9375 − 130) = 0. All those options obviously have nonnegative values. Thus, all the America Online call options conform to the intrinsic value rule. In fact, extensive empirical testing has revealed that options in general conform quite closely to the rule.

The intrinsic value concept applies only to an American call, because a European call can be exercised only on the expiration day. If the price of a European call were less than Max(0, S_0 − X), the inability to exercise it would prevent traders from engaging in the aforementioned arbitrage that would drive up the call's price.

The price of an American call normally exceeds its intrinsic value. The difference between the price and the intrinsic value is called the **time value** or **speculative value** of the call, which is defined as $C_a(S_0,T,X)$ − Max(0, S_0 − X). The time value reflects what traders are willing to pay for the uncertainty of the underlying stock. Table 3.2 presents the intrinsic values and time values of the America Online calls. Note that the time values increase with the time to expiration.

Figure 3.1 illustrates what we have established so far. The call price lies in the shaded area. Note how the American call price lies in a smaller area. This does not mean that the American call price is less than the European call price but only that its range of possible values is narrower.

The time value of an American call is the difference between the call price and the intrinsic value.

The Maximum Value of a Call

A call option also has a maximum value:

$$C(S_0,T,X) \le S_0.$$

The maximum value of a call is the price of the stock.

The call is a conduit through which an investor can obtain the stock. The most one can expect to gain from the call is the stock's value less the exercise price. Even if the exercise price were zero, no one would pay more for the call than for the stock. However, one call that is worth the stock price is

TABLE 3.2	Intrinsic Values and Time Values of America Online Calls			
			Time Value	
Exercise Price	Intrinsic Value	May	June	July
120	5.9375	2.8125	9.4375	14.9375
125	0.9375	4.8125	12.5625	17.6875
130	0.0000	3.6250	11.3750	16.3750

| FIGURE 3.1 | Minimum Values of European and American Calls |

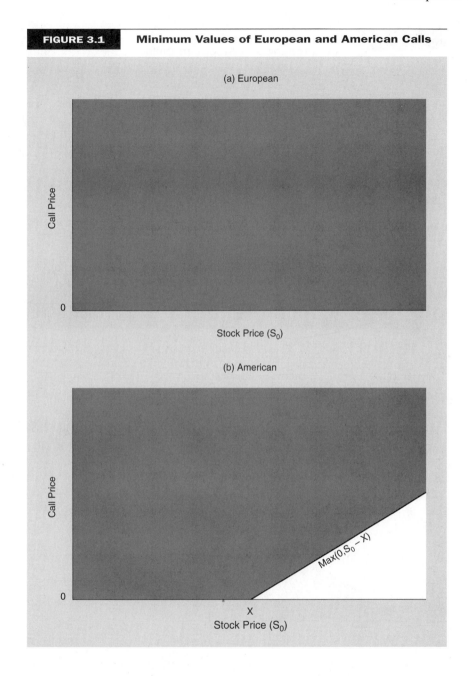

(a) European

Call Price

0

Stock Price (S_0)

(b) American

Call Price

Max(0,S_0 – X)

0

X

Stock Price (S_0)

one with an infinite maturity. It is obvious that all the America Online calls are worth no more than the value of the stock.

Figure 3.2 adds the maximum value rule to Figure 3.1. Notice that the maximum value rule has significantly reduced the range of possible option values.

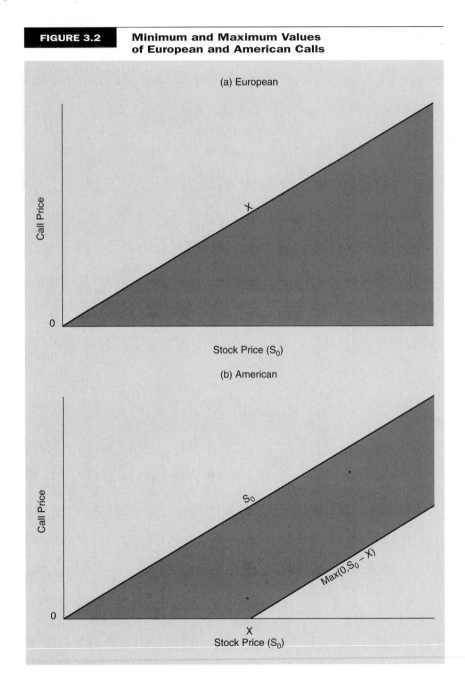

FIGURE 3.2   **Minimum and Maximum Values of European and American Calls**

The Value of a Call at Expiration

The price of a call at expiration is given as

$$C(S_T, 0, X) = Max(0, S_T - X).$$

At expiration, a call option is worth the intrinsic value.

Because no time remains in the option's life, the call price contains no time value. The prospect of future stock price increases is irrelevant to the price of the expiring option, which will be simply its intrinsic value.[4]

At expiration, an American option and a European option are identical instruments. Therefore, this rule holds for both types of options.

Figure 3.3 illustrates the value of the call at expiration. This is one situation in which the value of the call is unambiguous. But do not confuse this with our ultimate objective, which is to find the value of the call *prior to* expiration.

The Effect of Time to Expiration

Consider two American calls that differ only in their times to expiration. One has a time to expiration of T_1 and a price of $C_a(S_0, T_1, X)$; the other has a time to expiration of T_2 and a price of $C_a(S_0, T_2, X)$. Remember that T_2 is greater than T_1. Which of these two options will have the greater value?

Suppose today is the expiration day of the shorter-lived option. The stock price is S_{T_1}. The value of the expiring option is $Max(0, S_{T_1} - X)$. The second option has a time to expiration of $T_2 - T_1$. Its minimum value is $Max(0, S_{T_1} - X)$. Thus, when the shorter-lived option expires, its value is the minimum value of the longer-lived option. Therefore,

$$C_a(S_0, T_2 X) \geq C_a(S_0, T_1, X).$$

A longer-lived American call must always be worth at least as much as a shorter-lived American call with the same terms.

Normally the longer-lived call is worth more, but if it carries no time value when the shorter-lived option expires, the two options will have the same price. This can occur if the stock price is either very high or very low. Looking at the prices of the America Online calls, we can see that this is the case. The longer the time to expiration, the greater the call's value.

The time value of a call option varies with the time to expiration and the proximity of the stock price to the exercise price. Investors pay for the time value of the call based on the uncertainty of the future stock price. If the stock price is very high, the call is said to be **deep-in-the-money** and the time value will be low. If the stock price is very low, the call is said to be **deep-out-of-the-money** and the time value likewise will be low. The time value will be low because at these extremes, the uncertainty about the call expiring in- or out-of-the-money is lower. The uncertainty is greater when

---

[4]Because of the transaction cost of exercising the option, it could be worth slightly less than the intrinsic value.

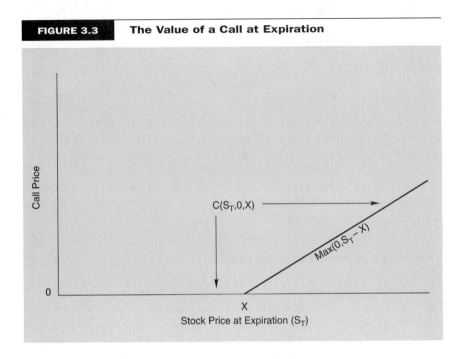

FIGURE 3.3   **The Value of a Call at Expiration**

the stock price is near the exercise price, and it is at this point that the time value is higher.

A simple analogy is useful for understanding why time value is highest when the stock price is close to the exercise price. Suppose you were watching an important basketball game between the Charlotte Hornets and the Atlanta Hawks. Let us assume that you enjoy a good game but have no sentimental attachment to either team. It is now halftime. Suppose Charlotte is ahead 65–38. How interesting is the game now? How probable is it that Charlotte will win? Are you likely to keep watching if there is something more interesting to do with your time? But suppose, instead, that the score is tied at 55–55. Isn't the game much more interesting now? Aren't you more likely to watch the second half?

An option with the stock price near the exercise price is like a close game. A deep-in- or out-of-the-money option is like a game with one team well ahead. A close game and an option nearly at-the-money are situations to which people are more willing to allocate scarce resources — for example, time to watch the game or money to buy the option.

These properties of the time value and our previous results enable us to get a general idea of what the call price looks like relative to the stock price. Figure 3.4 illustrates this point for American calls. The curved line is the price of the call, which lies above the intrinsic value, $\text{Max}(0, S_0 - X)$. As expiration approaches, the call price loses its time value, a process called

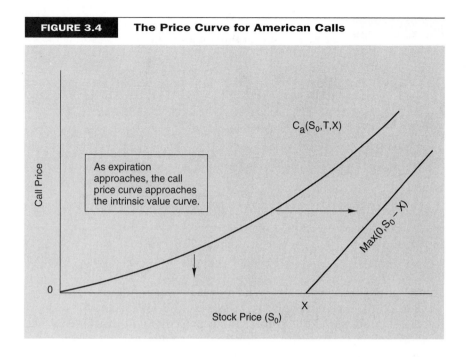

FIGURE 3.4   **The Price Curve for American Calls**

$C_a(S_0,T,X)$

As expiration approaches, the call price curve approaches the intrinsic value curve.

$Max(0,S_0-X)$

Call Price

0

X

Stock Price (S_0)

time value decay, and the curve moves gradually toward the intrinsic value. At expiration, the call price curve collapses onto the intrinsic value and the curve looks exactly like Figure 3.3.

The time value effect is evident in the America Online calls. Note that in Table 3.2, for a given exercise price the time values increase with the time to expiration. For a given time to expiration, the time values are highest for the calls with an exercise price of 125, the exercise price closest to the stock price.

The relationship between time to expiration and option price also holds for European calls. Nevertheless, we cannot yet formally accept this as fact, because we have not yet established a minimum value for a European call. That will come a bit later.

The Effect of Exercise Price

THE EFFECT ON OPTION VALUE   Consider two European calls that are identical in all respects except that the exercise price of one is X_1 and that of the other is X_2. Recall that X_2 is greater than X_1. We want to know which price is greater — $C_e(S_0,T,X_1)$ or $C_e(S_0,T,X_2)$.

Now consider two portfolios, A and B. Portfolio A consists of a long position in the call with the exercise price of X_1 and a short position in the call with the exercise price of X_2. This type of portfolio is called a money

TABLE 3.3	The Effect of Exercise Price on Call Value: Payoffs at Expiration of Portfolios A and B

Portfolio	Current Value	*Payoffs from Portfolio Given Stock Price at Expiration*		
		$S_T < X_1$	$X_1 \leq S_T < X_2$	$X_1 < X_2 \leq S_T$
A	$+C_e(S_0,T,X_1)$ $-C_e(S_0,T,X_2)$	0 0	$S_T - X_1$ 0	$S_T - X_1$ $-S_T + X_2$
		0	$S_T - X_1 \geq 0$	$X_2 - X_1 > 0$
B	$(X_2 - X_1)(1 + r)^{-T}$	$X_2 - X_1 > 0$	$X_2 - X_1 > 0$	$X_2 - X_1 > 0$

spread and is discussed further in Chapter 7. Because we pay $C_e(S_0,T,X_1)$ and receive $C_e(S_0,T,X_2)$, this portfolio will have an initial value of $C_e(S_0,T,X_1) - C_e(S_0,T,X_2)$. We do not yet know whether the initial value is positive or negative; that will depend on which option price is higher.

Portfolio B consists simply of risk-free bonds with a face value of $X_2 - X_1$. These bonds should be considered as pure discount instruments, like Treasury bills, and as maturing at the options' expiration. Thus, the value of this portfolio is the present value of the bonds' face value, or simply $(X_2 - X_1)(1 + r)^{-T}$.[5]

For the time being, we shall concentrate on portfolio A. First, we need to determine the portfolio's value at expiration. The value of any portfolio will be its cash flow or payoff when the options expire, contingent on the stock price at expiration, S_T. The stock price at expiration has three possible ranges: (1) $S_T < X_1$; (2) $X_1 \leq S_T < X_2$; or (3) $X_1 < X_2 \leq S_T$. Table 3.3 illustrates the values of portfolios A and B at expiration.

When S_T is greater than X_1, the call option with exercise price X_1 will be worth $S_T - X_1$. If S_T exceeds X_2, the call option with exercise price X_2 will be worth $S_T - X_2$. However, we are short the option with exercise price X_2. Because the buyer receives a payoff of $S_T - X_2$ when this option expires in-the-money, the writer has a payoff of $-S_T + X_2$. Adding the payoffs from the two options shows that portfolio A will always produce a payoff of no less than zero and, in some cases, more than zero. Therefore,

$$C_e(S_0,T,X_1) \geq C_e(S_0,T,X_2).$$

Why is this so? The best way to understand this rule is to look at the contradiction. Suppose $C_e(S_0,T,X_1) < C_e(S_0,T,X_2)$. Because we pay

The price of a European call must be at least as high as the price of an otherwise identical European call with a higher exercise price.

---

[5]Note that the time to expiration can be denoted as T. Technically it is the difference between time T and today, time 0, so we just use $T - 0 = T$.

$C_e(S_0,T,X_1)$ for the option bought and receive $C_e(S_0,T,X_2)$ for the option sold, we will have a net cash inflow at the beginning of the transaction. The payoffs at expiration were shown to be nonnegative. Anyone would jump at the opportunity to construct a portfolio with a positive cash inflow up front and no possibility of a cash outflow at expiration. There would be no way to lose money. Everyone would try to execute this transaction, which would drive up the price of the call with exercise price X_1 and drive down the price of the call with exercise price X_2. When the call with the lower exercise price is worth at least as much as the call with the higher exercise price, the portfolio will no longer offer a positive cash flow up front.

We have proven this result only for European calls. With American calls the long call need not be exercised, so we need only consider what would happen if the short call were exercised early.

Suppose the stock price prior to expiration is S_t and exceeds X_2. For whatever reason, the short call is exercised. This produces a negative cash flow, $-(S_t - X_2)$. The trader then exercises the long call, which produces a positive cash flow of $S_t - X_1$. The sum of these two cash flows is $X_2 - X_1$, which is positive because $X_2 > X_1$. Thus, early exercise will not generate a negative cash flow. Portfolio A therefore will never produce a negative cash flow at expiration even if the options are American calls. Thus, our result holds for American calls as well as for European calls.

The price of an American call must be at least as high as the price of another otherwise identical American call with a higher exercise price.

Note that this result shows that the price of the call with the lower exercise price cannot be less than that of the call with the higher exercise price. However, the two call prices conceivably could be equal. That could occur if the stock price were very low, in which case both calls would be deep-out-of-the-money. Neither would be expected to expire in-the-money, and both would have an intrinsic value of zero. Therefore, both prices could be approximately zero. However, with a very high stock price, the call with the lower exercise price would carry a greater intrinsic value, and thus its price would be higher than that of the call with the higher exercise price.

The prices of the America Online calls adhere to the predicted relationships. The lower the exercise price, the higher the call option price.

LIMITS ON THE DIFFERENCE IN PREMIUMS   Now compare the results of portfolio A with those of portfolio B. Note that in Table 3.3, portfolio B's return is never less than portfolio A's. Therefore, investors would not pay less for portfolio B than for portfolio A. The price of portfolio A is $C_e(S_0,T,X_1) - C_e(S_0,T,X_2)$, the price of the option purchased minus the price of the option sold. The price of portfolio B is $(X_2 - X_1)(1 + r)^{-T}$, the present value of the bond's face value. Thus,

The difference in the prices of two European calls that differ only by exercise price cannot exceed the present value of the difference in their exercise prices.

$$(X_2 - X_1)(1 + r)^{-T} \geq C_e(S_0,T,X_1) - C_e(S_0,T,X_2).$$

A related and useful statement is

$$X_2 - X_1 \geq C_e(S_0,T,X_1) - C_e(S_0,T,X_2).$$

This follows because the difference in the exercise prices is greater than the present value of the difference in the exercise prices. For two options differing only in exercise price, the difference in the premiums cannot exceed the difference in the exercise prices.

The intuition behind this result is simple: The advantage of buying an option with a lower exercise price over one with a higher exercise price will not be more than the difference in the exercise prices. For example, if you own the America Online June 125 call and are considering replacing it with the June 120 call, the most you can gain by the switch is $5. Therefore, you would not pay more than an additional $5 for the 120 over the 125. This result will be useful in Chapter 7, where we discuss spread strategies.

For American calls, the call with the lower exercise price is worth at least as much as the call with the higher exercise price. However, the statement that the difference in premiums cannot exceed the present value of the difference in exercise prices does not hold for the American call. If both calls are exercised at time t before expiration and the payoff of $X_2 - X_1$ is invested in risk-free bonds, portfolio A's return will be $(X_2 - X_1)(1 + r)^{(T - t)}$, which will exceed portfolio B's return of $X_2 - X_1$. Thus, portfolio B will not always outperform or match portfolio A.

If, however, the bonds purchased for portfolio B have a face value of $(X_2 - X_1)(1 + r)^T$, and thus a present value of $X_2 - X_1$, portfolio B will always outperform portfolio A. In that case, the current value of portfolio A cannot exceed that of portfolio B. Accordingly, we can state that for American calls

The difference in the prices of two American calls that differ only by exercise price cannot exceed the difference in their exercise prices.

$$X_2 - X_1 \geq C_a(S_0,T,X_1) - C_a(S_0,T,X_2).$$

Table 3.4 presents the appropriate calculations for examining these properties on the America Online calls. Consider the May 120 and 125 calls. The difference in their premiums is 3.

The present value of the difference in exercise prices is $5(1.0457)^{-.0192} = 4.9957$. The remaining combinations are calculated similarly using the appropriate risk-free rates and times to expiration for those options. Because these are American calls, the difference in their prices must be no greater than the difference in their exercise prices. As Table 3.4 shows, all the calls conform to this condition. In addition, all the differences in the call prices are less than the present value of the difference between the exercise prices. Remember that this result need not hold for American calls because they can be exercised early.

The Lower Bound of a European Call

We know that for an American call,

$$C_a(S_0,T,X) \geq \text{Max}(0, S_0 - X).$$

TABLE 3.4	The Relationship between Exercise Price and Call Price for America Online Calls			
		Difference between Call Prices (Present Value of Difference between Exercise Prices in Parentheses)		
Exercise Prices	Exercise Price Difference	May	June	July
120, 125	5	3.0000 (4.9957)	1.8750 (4.9787)	2.2500 (4.9611)
120, 130	10	5.1250 (9.9914)	4.0000 (9.9573)	4.5000 (9.9222)
125, 130	5	2.1250 (4.9957)	2.1250 (4.9787)	2.2500 (4.9611)

Note: Risk-free rates are 4.57% (May), 4.56% (June), and 4.63% (July); times to expiration are 0.0192 (May), 0.0959 (June), and 0.1726 (July).

Because of the requirement that immediate exercise be possible, we were unable to make such a statement for a European call. We can, however, develop a lower bound for a European call that will be higher than the intrinsic value of an American call.

Again consider two portfolios, A and B. Portfolio A consists of a single share of stock currently priced at S_0, while portfolio B contains a European call priced at $C_e(S_0,T,X)$ and risk-free bonds with a face value of X and, therefore, a present value of $X(1 + r)^{-T}$. The current value of this portfolio thus is $C_e(S_0,T,X) + X(1 + r)^{-T}$. The payoffs from these two portfolios are shown in Table 3.5.

As the table shows, the return on portfolio B is always at least as large as that of portfolio A and sometimes larger. Investors will recognize this fact and price portfolio B at a value at least as great as portfolio A's; that is,

$$C_e(S_0,T,X) + X(1 + r)^{-T} \geq S_0$$

Rearranging this expression gives

$$C_e(S_0,T,X) \geq S_0 - X(1 + r)^{-T}.$$

If $S_0 - X(1 + r)^{-T}$ is negative, we invoke the rule that the minimum value of a call is zero. Combining these results gives us a lower bound of

$$C_e(S_0,T,X) \geq Max[0, S_0 - X(1 + r)^{-T}].$$

The price of a European call must at least equal the greater of zero or the stock price minus the present value of the exercise price.

TABLE 3.5	**The Lower Bound of a European Call: Payoffs at Expiration of Portfolios A and B**		

		Payoffs from Portfolio Given Stock Price at Expiration	
Portfolio	Current Value	$S_T \leq X$	$S_T \leq X$
A	S_0	S_T	S_T
B	$C_e(S_0,T,X) + X(1 + r)^{-T}$	X	$(S_T - X) + X = S_T$

If the call price is less than the stock price minus the present value of the exercise price, we can construct an arbitrage portfolio. We buy the call and risk-free bonds and sell short the stock. This portfolio has a positive initial cash flow, because the call price plus the bond price is less than the stock price. At expiration, the payoff is $X - S_T$ if $X > S_T$ and zero otherwise. The portfolio has a positive cash flow today and either a zero or positive cash flow at expiration. Again there is no way to lose money.

Figure 3.5 shows this result for European calls. The curved line is the call price, which must lie above the lower bound. As expiration approaches, the time to expiration decreases such that the lower bound moves to the right with the call price following it. At expiration, the lower bound and price curves converge with the $\text{Max}(0, S_0 - X)$ curve.

FIGURE 3.5	**The Price Curve for European Calls**

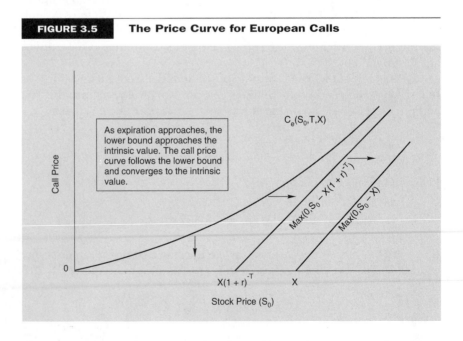

As expiration approaches, the lower bound approaches the intrinsic value. The call price curve follows the lower bound and converges to the intrinsic value.

When we showed that the intrinsic value of an American call is $\text{Max}(0, S_0 - X)$, we noted that the inability to exercise early prevents this result from holding for a European call. Now we can see that this limitation is of no consequence. Because the present value of the exercise price is less than the exercise price itself, the lower bound of a European call is greater than the intrinsic value of an American call.

For European calls, a longer-lived call will always be worth at least as much as a shorter-lived call with the same terms.

In the earlier description of how time to expiration affects the price of an American call, we could not draw the same relationship for a European call. Now we can. Consider two European calls that differ by their times to expiration, T_1 and T_2. Their prices are $C_e(S_0,T_1,X)$ and $C_e(S_0,T_2,X)$, respectively. At time T_1, the shorter-lived option expires and is worth $\text{Max}(0, S_{T_1} - X$. The minimum value of the longer-lived option is $\text{Max}(0, S_{T_1} - X(1 + r)^{-(T_2-T_1)})$. Thus, the value of the shorter-lived option is less than the lower bound of the longer-lived option. Therefore, the longer-lived call must be priced at least as high as the shorter-lived call.

Finally we should note that if the stock pays dividends such that the stock price minus the present value of the dividends is $S_0' = S_0 - \sum_{j=1}^{N} D_j (1 + r)^{-t_j}$ then the lower bound is restated as

$$C_e(S_0,T,X) \geq \text{Max}[0, S_0' - X(1 + r)^{-T}].$$

American Call versus European Call

Many of the results presented so far apply only to European calls. For example, we restricted the derivation of the lower bound to European calls. That is because an early exercise of an American call can negate the cash flows expected from the portfolio at expiration.

An American call will be at least as valuable as a European call with the same terms.

In many cases, however, American calls behave exactly like European calls. In fact, an American call can be viewed as a European call with the added feature that it can be exercised early. Since exercising an option is never mandatory,

$$C_a(S_0,T,X) \geq C_e(S_0,T,X).$$

We already proved that the minimum value of an American call is $\text{Max}(0, S_0 - X)$ while the lower bound of a European call is $\text{Max}[0, S_0 - X(1 + r)^{-T}]$. Because $S_0 - X(1 + r)^{-T}$ is greater than $S_0 - X$; as shown in Figure 3.5, the lower bound value of the American call must also be $\text{Max}[0, S_0 - X(1 + r)^{-T}]$.

Let us now examine the America Online options to determine whether their prices exceed the lower boundary. Table 3.6 presents the lower bound of each America Online call. To see how the computations are performed, take the May 120 call. The time to expiration is 0.0192, and the risk-free rate is .0457. Thus,

$$\text{Max}[\,0, S_0 - X(1 + r)^{-T}] = \text{Max}[0, 125.9375 - 120(1.0457)^{-.0192}] = 6.0404.$$

TABLE 3.6	Lower Bounds of America Online Calls

	Expiration		
Exercise Price	May	June	July
120	6.0404	6.4496	6.8713
125	1.0447	1.4709	1.9102
130	0.0000	0.0000	0.0000

Note: Risk-free rates are 4.57% (May), 4.56% (June), and 4.63% (July); times to expiration are 0.0192 (May), 0.0959 (June), and 0.1726 (July).

An American call on a non-dividend-paying stock will never be exercised early, and we can treat such a call as if it were European.

From Table 3.1, the price of the call is $8.75. Thus, this option does meet the boundary condition. Using Tables 3.1 and 3.6 reveals that the remaining calls also conform to the lower boundary. In general, studies show that call prices conform closely to the lower bound rule.

With the lower bound of an American call established, we can now examine whether an American call should ever be exercised early. If the stock price is S_0, exercising the call produces a cash flow of $S_0 - X$.[6] The call's price, however, must be at least $S_0 - X(1 + r)^{-T}$. Since the cash flow from exercising, $S_0 - X$, can never exceed the call's lower bound, $S_0 - X(1 + r)^{-T}$, it will always be better to sell the call in the market. When the transaction cost of exercising is compared to the transaction cost of selling the call, the argument that a call should not be exercised early is strengthened. Thus, if the stock pays no dividends, Figure 3.5 is also the call price curve for American calls.

Although many people find it difficult to believe that an American option on a non-dividend-paying stock would never be exercised early, it is really quite easy to see by analogy. Have you ever subscribed to a magazine and, shortly afterward, received a renewal notice mentioning the attractive rate they could offer you? You have barely begun receiving the magazine, perhaps have not yet decided if you like it, and already you are granted an option to renew. Do you immediately renew? Hardly any rational person would do so. Not only would you be giving the magazine company the interest on your money, you would also be giving up the right to decide later if you want to renew. It is almost always the case that you would still have the right to renew much later at the same rate. Likewise, exercising a call option early not only gives the writer the interest on your money, but also throws away the right to decide later if you want to own the stock.

---

[6]We are assuming that the option is in-the-money, because no one would consider exercising it if it were out-of-the-money.

If that argument is not convincing, simply consider this. The urge to exercise a deep-in-the-money call simply because you think the stock has gone as far up as you think it will should be suppressed. If your views on the stock are correct, you will not be any more pleased to own a stock that is not increasing than you would to be holding the call option. The story changes, however, if the stock pays dividends.

The Early Exercise of American Calls on Dividend-Paying Stocks

When a company declares a dividend, it specifies that the dividend is payable to all stockholders as of a certain date, called the holder-of-record date. Two business days before that date is the ex-dividend date. To be the stockholder of record by the holder-of-record date, one must buy the stock by the ex-dividend date. The stock price tends to fall by the amount of the dividend on the ex-dividend date.

When a stock goes ex-dividend, the call price drops along with it. The amount by which the call price falls cannot be determined at this point in our understanding of option pricing. Since the call is a means of obtaining the stock, however, its price could never change by more than the stock price change. Thus, the call price will fall by no more than the dividend. An investor could avoid this loss in value by exercising the option immediately before the stock goes ex-dividend. This is the only time the call should be exercised early.

Another way to see that early exercise could occur is to recall that we stated that the lower bound of a European call on a dividend-paying stock is $\text{Max}[0, S_0' - X(1 + r)^{-T}]$ where S_0' is the stock price minus the present value of the dividends. To keep things simple, assume only one dividend of the amount D, and the stock will go ex-dividend in the next instant. Then S_0' is approximately equal to $S_0 - D$ (since the present value of D is almost D). Since we would consider exercising only in-the-money calls, assume that S_0 exceeds X. Then it is easy to see that $S_0 - X$ could exceed S_0' minus the present value of X. By exercising the option, the call holder obtains the value $S_0 - X$. Suppose you were holding a European call whose value was only slightly above the lower bound. Then you might wish it were an American call because an American call could be exercised to capture the value $S_0 - X$. If you were holding a European call and wished it were an American call for at least that instant, then it should be obvious that the right to exercise early would have value. So an American call could be worth more than a European call. Note that this does not mean that exercise will definitely occur at the ex-dividend instant. It means only that exercise *could* occur. The value of the right to exercise early is what distinguishes an American call from a European call. That right is worth something only when there are dividends on the stock.

It may be optimal to exercise an American call early if the stock is about to go ex-dividend.

There is one other situation in which you can determine that the right to exercise early has no value. If the present value of all the dividends over the life of the option is less than $X(1 - (1 + r)^{-T})$, then the option would never be exercised early because the dividends are not large enough to offset the loss of interest from paying out the exercise price early.

In Chapters 4 and 5 we shall learn about option pricing models that will give us the exact price of the option. We will then be able to see the early exercise value more explicitly.

The price of a call is directly related to interest rates.

The Effect of Interest Rates

Interest rates affect a call option's price. Although the effect of interest rates is somewhat complex, an easy way to see it is to think of a call as a way to purchase stock by paying an amount of money less than the face value of the stock. By paying the call premium, you save the difference between the call price and the exercise price, the price you are willing to pay for the stock. The higher the interest rate, the more interest you can earn on the money you saved by buying the call. Thus, when interest rates are higher, calls are more attractive than buying stock.[7]

The price of a call is directly related to the volatility of the underlying stock.

The Effect of Stock Volatility

One of the basic principles of investor behavior is that individuals prefer less risk to more. For holders of stocks, higher risk means lower value. But higher risk in a stock translates into greater value for a call option on it. This is because greater volatility increases the gains on the call if the stock price increases, because the stock price can then exceed the exercise price by a larger amount. On the other hand, greater volatility means that if the stock price goes down, it can be much lower than the exercise price. To a call holder, however, this does not matter because the potential loss is limited; it is said to be truncated at the exercise price. For example, consider the America Online July 125 call. Suppose the stock price is equally likely to be at 110, 120, 130, or 140 at expiration. The call, then, is equally likely to be worth 0, 0, 5, and 15 at expiration. Now suppose the stock's volatility increases so that it has an equal chance of being at 100, 120, 130, or 150. From a stockholder's point of view, the stock is far riskier, which is less

---

[7]The exact relationship between interest rates and call prices is slightly more involved than this, however. The purchase of a call is actually more than just an option to defer purchase of the stock. Holding the call instead of the stock limits your loss to much less than if you had bought the stock. A call is said to have insurance value. Interest rates affect the insurance value of the call in a negative manner, but the overall effect on the call price is still positive. See D. M. Chance, "Translating the Greek: The Real Meaning of Call Option Derivatives," *Financial Analysts Journal* 50 (July–August 1994): 43–49.

desirable. From the option holder's perspective, the equally possible option prices at expiration are 0, 0, 5, and 25, which is more desirable. In fact, the option holder will not care how low the stock can go. If the possibility of lower stock prices is accompanied by the possibility of higher stock prices, the option holder will benefit, and the option will be priced higher when the volatility is higher.

Another way to understand the effect of volatility on the call price is to consider the extreme case of zero volatility. If the stock price is less than the exercise price, the absence of volatility guarantees that the option will expire out-of-the-money. No one would pay anything for this option. If the stock price exceeds the exercise price and has zero volatility, it will expire in-the-money and will be worth $S_0 - X$ at expiration, where S_0 is the current stock price. In this case, the call will then be worth the present value of $S_0 - X$ and thus will simply be a risk-free asset. High stock volatility is what makes call options attractive, and investors are willing to pay higher premiums on options with greater volatility.

Principles of Put Option Pricing

Many of the rules applicable to call options apply in a straightforward manner to put options. However, there are some significant differences.

The Minimum Value of a Put

A put is an option to sell a stock. A put holder is not obligated to exercise it and will not do so if exercising will decrease wealth. Thus, a put can never have a negative value:

Because a put option need not be exercised, its minimum value is zero.

$$P(S_0, T, X) \geq 0.$$

An American put can be exercised early. Therefore,

$$P_a(S_0, T, X) \geq Max(0, X - S_0).$$

Suppose that the America Online June 130 put sells for less than $X - S_0$. Let the put sell for $3. Then it would be worthwhile to buy the stock for $125.9375, buy the put for $3, and exercise the put. This would net an immediate risk-free profit of $1.0625. The combined actions of all investors conducting this arbitrage would force the put price up to at least $4.0625, the difference between the exercise price and the stock price.

Figure 3.6 illustrates these points for puts. The European put price lies somewhere in the shaded area of graph a. The American put price lies somewhere in the shaded area of graph b.

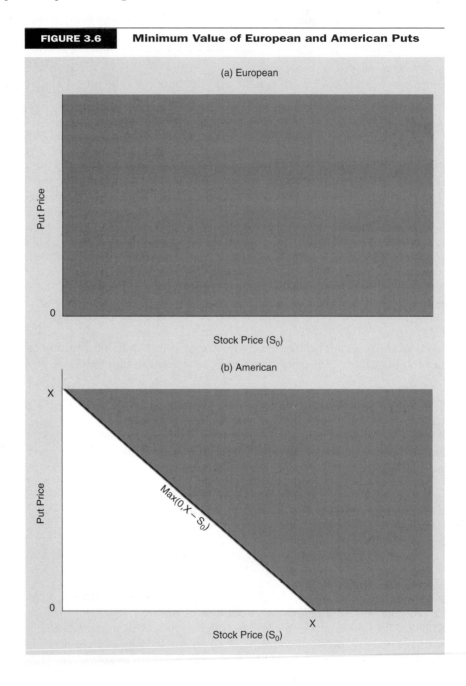

FIGURE 3.6   Minimum Value of European and American Puts

TABLE 3.7	Intrinsic Values and Time Values of America Online Puts			
			Time Value	
Exercise Price	Intrinsic Value	May	June	July
120	0.0000	2.7500	9.2500	13.6250
125	0.0000	4.6250	11.5000	16.6250
130	4.0625	3.3125	10.1875	15.5625

The value, $Max(0, X - S_0)$, is called the put's **intrinsic value.** An in-the-money put has a positive intrinsic value, while an out-of-the-money put has an intrinsic value of zero. The difference between the put price and the intrinsic value is the **time value** or **speculative value.** The time value is defined as $P_a(S_0,T,X) - Max(0, X - S_0)$. As with calls, the time value reflects what an investor is willing to pay for the uncertainty of the final outcome.

The intrinsic value of an American put is the greater of zero or the difference between the exercise price and the stock price.

Table 3.7 presents the intrinsic values and time values of the America Online puts. Note how te values increase with the time to expiration.

The intrinsic value specification, $Max(0, X - S_0)$, does not hold for European puts. That is because the option must be exercisable for an investor to execute the arbitrage transaction previously described. European puts indeed can sell for less than the intrinsic value. Later this will help us understand the early exercise of American puts.

The time value of an American put is the difference between the put price and the intrinsic value.

The Maximum Value of a Put

At expiration, the payoff from a European put is $Max(0, X - S_T)$. The best outcome that a put holder can expect is for the company to go bankrupt. In that case, the stock will be worthless and the put holder will be able to sell the shares to the put writer for X dollars.

Thus, the present value of the exercise price is the European put's maximum possible value. Since an American put can be exercised at any time, its maximum value is the exercise price.

The maximum value of a European put is the present value of the exercise price. The maximum value of an American put is the exercise price.

$$P_e(S_0,T,X) \leq X(1 + r)^{-T},$$
$$P_a(S_0,T,X) \leq X.$$

Figure 3.7 adds the maximum value rule to Figure 3.6. Although the range of possible values is reduced somewhat, there is still a broad range of possible values.

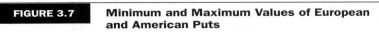

FIGURE 3.7   **Minimum and Maximum Values of European and American Puts**

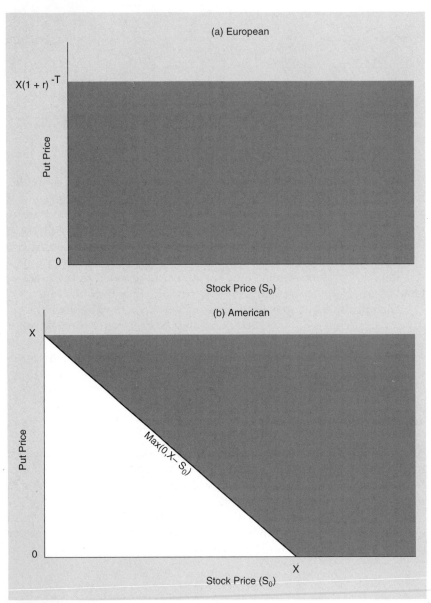

The Value of a Put at Expiration

On the put's expiration date, no time value will remain. Expiring American puts therefore are the same as European puts. The value of either type of put must be the intrinsic value. Thus,

At expiration, a put option is worth the intrinsic value.

$$P(S_T,0,X) = Max(0,X - S_T).$$

If $X > S_T$ and the put price is less than $X - S_T$, investors can buy the put and the stock and exercise the put for an immediate risk-free profit. If the put expires out-of-the-money ($X < S_T$), it will be worthless. Figure 3.8 illustrates the value of the put at expiration.

The Effect of Time to Expiration

Consider two American puts, one with a time to expiration of T_1 and the other with a time to expiration of T_2, where $T_2 > T_1$. Now assume today is the expiration date of the shorter-lived put. The stock price is S_{T_1}. The expiring put is worth $Max(0, X - S_{T_1})$. The other put, which has a remaining

---

FIGURE 3.8   **The Value of a Put at Expiration**

A longer-lived American put must always be worth at least as much as a shorter-lived American put with the same terms.

time to expiration of $T_2 - T_1$, is worth at least $Max(0, X - S_{T_1})$. Consequently, it must be true that at time 0, we must have,

$$P_a(S_0,T_2,X) \geq P_a(S_0,T_1,X).$$

Note that the two puts could be worth the same; however, this would occur only if both puts were very deep-in- or out-of-the-money. Even then, the longer-lived put would likely be worth a little more than the shorter-lived put. The longer-lived put can do everything the shorter-lived put can do and has an additional period of time in which to increase in value.

The principles that underlie the time value of a put are the same as those that underlie the time value of a call. The time value is largest when the stock price is near the exercise price and smallest when the stock price is either very high or very low relative to the exercise price. With these points in mind, we can now see that the American put price would look like Figure 3.9. As expiration approaches, the put price curve approaches the intrinsic value, which is due to the time value decay. At expiration the put price equals the intrinsic value, as in Figure 3.8.

The relationship between time to expiration and put price is more complex for European puts. Think of buying a put as deferring the sale of

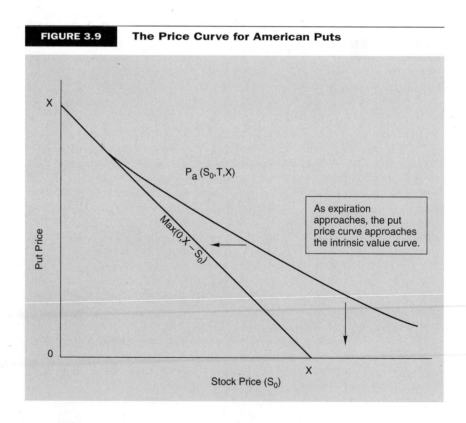

FIGURE 3.9   **The Price Curve for American Puts**

$P_a(S_0,T,X)$

$Max(0, X - S_0)$

As expiration approaches, the put price curve approaches the intrinsic value curve.

Put Price

Stock Price (S_0)

stock at the exercise price, X. The further into the future the expiration date, the longer the put holder must wait to sell the stock and receive X dollars. This can make the longer-lived European put less valuable than the shorter-lived one. This does not hold for an American put, because the holder can always exercise it and receive X dollars today. For a European put, the longer time to expiration is both an advantage—the greater time value—and a disadvantage—the longer wait to receive the exercise price. The time value effect tends to dominate, however, and in most cases longer-lived puts will be more valuable than shorter-lived puts.

Because the America Online puts are American options, the longer-term puts should be expected to show higher prices. A check of their premiums, shown in Table 3.1, confirms this point.

The Effect of Exercise Price

THE EFFECT ON OPTION VALUE   Consider two European puts identical in all respects except exercise price. One put has an exercise price of X_1 and a premium of $P_e(S_0,T,X_1)$; the other has an exercise price of X_2 and a premium of $P_e(S_0,T,X_2)$. As before $X_2 > X_1$. Which put will be more valuable?

Consider two portfolios. Portfolio A consists of a long position in the put priced at $P_e(S_0,T,X_2)$ and a short position in the put priced at $P_e(S_0,T,X_1)$. Portfolio B consists of a long position in risk-free bonds with a face value of $X_2 - X_1$ and a present value of $(X_2 - X_1)(1 + r)^{-T}$. Table 3.8 presents these portfolios' payoffs at expiration.

For portfolio A, all outcomes are nonnegative. Because this portfolio cannot produce a cash outflow for the holder, the price of the put purchased must be no less than the price of the put sold; that is,

$$P_e(S_0,T,X_2) \geq P_e(S_0,T,X_1).$$

The price of a European put must be at least as high as the price of an otherwise identical European put with a lower exercise price.

TABLE 3.8	**The Effect of Exercise Price on Put Value: Payoffs at Expiration of Portfolios A and B**

Portfolio	Current Value	Payoffs from Portfolio Given Stock Price at Expiration		
		$S_T < X_1$	$X_1 \leq S_T < X_2$	$X_1 < X_2 \leq S_T$
A	$-P_e(S_0,T,X_1)$ $+P_e(S_0,T,X_2)$	$-X_1 + S_T$ $X_2 - S_T$	0 $X_2 - S_T$	0 0
B	$(X_2 - X_1)(1 + r)^{-T}$	$X_2 - X_1 > 0$ $X_2 - X_1 > 0$	$X_2 - S_T > 0$ $X_2 - X_1 > 0$	0 $X_2 - X_1 > 0$

To understand why this is so, consider what would happen if it were not. Suppose the price of the put sold were greater than the price of the put purchased. Then an investor would receive more for the put sold than would be paid for the put purchased. That would produce a net positive cash flow up front, and, from Table 3.8, there would be no possibility of having to pay out any cash at expiration. This transaction would be like a loan that need not be paid back. Obviously, this portfolio would be very attractive and would draw the attention of other investors, who would buy the put with the higher exercise price and sell the put with the lower exercise price. This would tend to drive up the price of the former and drive down the price of the latter. The transaction would cease to be attractive when the put with the higher exercise price became at least as valuable as the put with the lower exercise price.

The intuition behind why a put with a higher exercise price is worth more than one with a lower exercise price is quite simple. A put is an option to sell stock at a fixed price. The higher the price at which the put holder can sell the stock, the more attractive the put.

The price of an American put must be at least as high as the price of an otherwise identical American put with a lower exercise price.

Suppose these were American puts. In that case, the put with the lower exercise price could be exercised early. For example, let the stock price at time t prior to expiration be S_t, where $S_t < X_1$. Let the option with exercise price X_1 be exercised. Then the investor simply exercises the option with exercise price X_2. The cash flow from these two transactions is $-(X_1 - S_t) + (X_2 - S_t) = X_2 - X_1$, which is positive. Early exercise will not generate a negative cash flow. Thus, our result holds for American puts as well as for European puts.

LIMITS ON THE DIFFERENCE IN PREMIUMS   Now let us compare the outcomes of portfolios A and B. We see that portfolio B's outcomes are never less than portfolio A's. Therefore, no one would pay more for portfolio A than for portfolio B; that is,

$$(X_2 - X_1)(1 + r)^{-T} \geq P_e(S_0,T,X_2) - P_e(S_0,T,X_1).$$

This result does not, however, hold for American puts. If the puts were American and both were exercised, the investor would receive $X_2 - X_1$ dollars. This amount would be invested in risk-free bonds and would earn interest over the options' remaining lives. At expiration, the investor would have more than $X_2 - X_1$, the payoff from portfolio B.

The difference in the prices of two European puts that differ only by exercise price cannot exceed the present value of the difference in their exercise prices.

Since the difference in exercise prices is greater than the present value of the difference in exercise prices, we can state that for European puts,

$$X_2 - X_1 \geq P_e(S_0,T,X_2) - P_e(S_0,T,X_1).$$

This means that the difference in premiums cannot exceed the difference in exercise prices. This result holds for American as well as European puts. To see this, let portfolio B's bonds have a face value of $(X_2 - X_1)(1 + r)^T$

and a present value of $X_2 - X_1$. If early exercise occurred at time t, the most the holder of portfolio A would have at expiration is $(X_2 - X_1)(1 + r)^{T-t}$. The holder of portfolio B would have a larger amount, $(X_2 - X_1)(1 + r)^T$. So again portfolio A would never pay more at expiration than would portfolio B. Therefore, the current value of portfolio A, $P_a(S_0,T,X_2) - P_a(S_0,T,X_1)$, could not exceed the current value of portfolio B, $X_2 - X_1$. Thus,

The difference in the prices of two American puts that differ only by exercise price cannot exceed the difference in their exercise prices.

$$X_2 - X_1 \geq P_a(S_0,T,X_2) - P_a(S_0,T,X_1).$$

Table 3.9 shows the differences between the put premiums and exercise prices for the America Online puts. Since these are American puts, we would expect only that the difference in their put premiums will not exceed the difference in their exercise prices—which indeed is the case. In addition, the differences in premiums do not exceed the present values of the differences in exercise prices.

The Lower Bound of a European Put

We showed that the minimum value of an American put is $\text{Max}(0, X - S_0)$. This statement does not hold for a European put, because it cannot be exercised early. However, it is possible to derive a positive lower bound for a European put.

Again consider two portfolios, A and B. Portfolio A consists of a single share of stock. Portfolio B consists of a short position in a European put priced at $P_e(S_0,T,X)$ and a long position in risk-free bonds with a face value of X and a present value of $X(1 + r)^{-T}$. The payoffs at expiration from these portfolios are shown in Table 3.10.

TABLE 3.9		The Relationship between Exercise Price and Put Price for America Online Puts		

| Exercise Prices | Exercise Price Difference | Difference between Put Prices (Present Value of Difference between Exercise Prices in Parentheses) | | |
		May	June	July
120, 125	5	1.8750 (4.9957)	2.2500 (4.9787)	3.0000 (4.9611)
120, 130	10	4.6250 (9.9914)	5.0000 (9.9573)	6.0000 (9.9222)
125, 130	5	2.7500 (4.9957)	2.7500 (4.9787)	3.0000 (4.9611)

Note: Risk-free rates are 4.57% (May), 4.56% (June), and 4.63% (July); times to expiration are 0.0192 (May), 0.0959 (June), and 0.1726 (July).

TABLE 3.10	Lower Bound of a European Put: Payoffs at Expiration of Portfolios A and B		

		Payoffs from Portfolio Given Stock Price at Expiration	
Portfolio	Current Value	$S_T < X$	$S_T \geq X$
A	S_0	S_T	S_T
B	$X(1 + r)^{-T} - P_e(S_0,T,X)$	$X - (X - S_T) = S_T$	X

Portfolio A's outcome is always at least as favorable as portfolio B's. Therefore, no one would be willing to pay more for portfolio B than for portfolio A. Portfolio A's current value must be no less than portfolio B's; that is,

$$S_0 \geq X(1 + r)^{-T} - P_e(S_0,T,X).$$

Rearranging this statement gives

$$P_e(S_0,T,X) \geq X(1 + r)^{-T} - S_0.$$

If the present value of the exercise price is less than the stock price, this lower bound will be negative. Since we know that a put cannot be worth less than zero, we can say that

$$P_e(S_0,T,X) \geq Max[0, X(1 + r)^{-T} - S_0].$$

The price of a European put must at least equal the greater of zero or the present value of the exercise price minus the stock price.

Figure 3.10 illustrates these results. The curved line is the European put price, which must lie above the lower bound. As expiration approaches, the time to expiration gets smaller so the lower bound moves to the right, with the put price curve following it. However, as time goes by, the put price gradually declines. At expiration, the put price and the lower bound converge to $Max(0, X - S_0)$, as in Figure 3.8.

Now let us compare the minimum price of the American put, its intrinsic value of $Max(0, X - S_0)$, with the lower bound of the European put, $Max[0, X(1 + r)^{-T} - S_0]$. Since $X - S_0$ is greater than $X(1 + r)^{-T} - S_0$, the American put's intrinsic value is higher than the European put's lower bound. Therefore, the European put's lower bound is irrelevant to the American put price because it is a lower minimum as seen in Figure 3.10. $Max[0, X(1 + r)^{-T} - S_0]$ is, however, relevant to the European put's price.

Finally, we can use the lower bound of a European put to examine the effect of time to expiration on the option. Earlier we stated that the direction of this effect is uncertain. Consider two puts with times to expiration of

| FIGURE 3.10 | The Price Curve for European Puts |

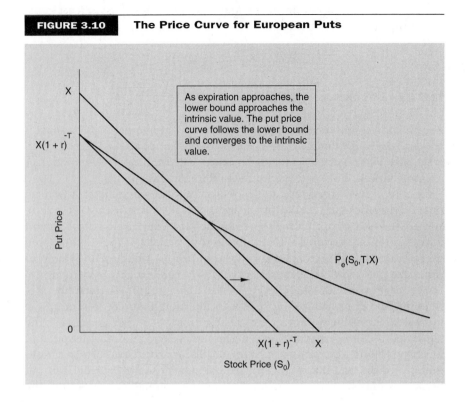

As expiration approaches, the lower bound approaches the intrinsic value. The put price curve follows the lower bound and converges to the intrinsic value.

T_1 and T_2, where $T_2 > T_1$. Suppose we are at time T_1, the stock price is S_{T_1}, and the shorter-lived put is expiring and worth $\text{Max}(0, X - S_{T_1})$. The longer-lived put has a remaining life of $T_2 - T_1$ and a lower bound of $\text{Max}[0, X(1 + r)^{-(T_2 - T_1)} - S_{T_1}]$. Although the lower bound of the longer-lived put is less than the shorter-lived put's intrinsic value, the value of the additional time on the former during which the stock price can move can more than make up the difference. Therefore, we cannot unambiguously tell whether a longer- or shorter-lived European put will be worth more.

If the stock pays dividends such that $S_0' = S_0 - \sum_{j=1}^{N} D_j (1 + r)^{-t_j}$, that is, the stock price minus the present value of the dividends, the rule becomes

$$P_e(S_0,T,X) \geq \text{Max}\,[0, X(1 + r)^{-T} - S_0'].$$

American Put versus European Put

Everything that can be done with a European put can be done with an American put. In addition, an American put can be exercised at any time

An American put will be at least as valuable as a European put with the same terms.

prior to expiration. Therefore, the American put price must at least equal the European put price; that is,

$$P_a(S_0,T,X) \geq P_e(S_0,T,X).$$

The Early Exercise of American Puts

Recall that it might be advisable to exercise an American call if the stock is about to go ex-dividend. If the stock does not pay dividends, then the call will not be exercised early and an American call will have the same value as a European call. The same cannot be said for American puts.

Let us suppose there are no dividends. Suppose you hold an American put and the stock goes bankrupt, meaning that the stock price goes to zero. You are holding an option to sell it for X dollars. There is no reason to wait until expiration to exercise it and obtain your X dollars. You might as well exercise it now. Thus, bankruptcy is one obvious situation in which an American put would be exercised early. However, *bankruptcy is not required to justify early exercise.* Look back at Figure 3.10. Note that the curved line representing the European put price crosses the straight line representing the intrinsic value of the American put. That means that at that stock price, the holder of the European put would prefer to have had an American put and would be willing to pay more to have one. This particular stock price, however, is not the one that would trigger early exercise of the American put because if the put were American, it would be optimal to hold it until the stock price dropped a little more.

If the stock pays dividends, it might still be worthwhile to exercise it early, but because dividends drive the stock price down, they make American puts less likely to be exercised early. In fact, if the dividends are sufficiently large, it can sometimes be shown that the put would never be exercised early, thus making it effectively a European put.

At this point in our material the exact situation at which an American put would be exercised early cannot be specified. We shall cover this topic again in more detail, however, in Chapter 4.

If the stock price falls to a critical level, an American put might be exercised early. The likelihood of early exercise is reduced if the stock pays dividends.

Put-Call Parity

The prices of European puts and calls on the same stock with identical exercise prices and expiration dates have a special relationship. The put price, call price, stock price, exercise price, time to expiration, and risk-free rate are all related by a formula called **put-call parity.** Let us see how this formula is derived.

Imagine a portfolio, called portfolio A, consisting of one share of stock and a European put. This portfolio will require an investment of $S_0 + P_e(S_0,T,X)$. Now consider a second portfolio, called portfolio B, consisting of a European call with the same exercise price and risk-free pure discount bonds with a face value of X. That portfolio will require an investment of

Put-call parity is the relationship among the call price, the put price, the stock price, the exercise price, the risk-free rate, and the time to expiration.

		Payoffs from Portfolio Given Stock Price at Expiration	
Payoff From	Current Value	$S_T \leq X$	$S_T > X$
A Stock	S_0	S_T	S_T
Put	$P_e(S_0,T,X)$	$\underline{X - S_T}$	$\underline{0}$
		X	S_T
B Call	$C_e(S_0,T,X)$	0	$S_T - X$
Bonds	$X(1 + r)^{-T}$	$\underline{X}$	$\underline{X}$
		X	S_T

TABLE 3.11   Put-Call Parity

$C_e(S_0,T,X) + X(1 + r)^{-T}$. Now let us look at what happens at the expiration. Table 3.11 presents the outcomes.

The stock is worth S_T regardless of whether S_T is more or less than X. Likewise the risk-free bonds are worth X regardless of the outcome. If S_T exceeds X, the call expires in-the-money and is worth $S_T - X$ and the put expires worthless. If S_T is less than or equal to X, the put expires in-the-money worth $X - S_T$ and the call expires worthless. The total values of portfolios A and B are equal. Recalling our Law of One Price from Chapter 1, the current values of the two portfolios must be equal. Thus, we require that

$$S_0 + P_e(S_0,T,X) = C_e(S_0,T,X) + X(1 + r)^{-T}.$$

This statement is referred to as put-call parity and it is probably one of the most important results in understanding options. It says that a share of stock plus a put is equivalent to a call plus risk-free bonds. It shows the relationship between the call and put prices, the stock price, the time to expiration, the risk-free rate, and the exercise price.

Suppose the combination of the put and the stock is worth less than the combination of the call and the bonds. Then you could buy the put and the stock and sell short the call and the bonds. Selling short the call just means to write the call and selling short the bonds simply means to borrow the present value of X and promise to pay back X at the options' expiration. The cash inflow of the value of the call and the bonds would exceed the cash outflow for the put and the stock. At expiration, there would be no cash inflow or outflow because you would have stock worth S_T and owe the principal on the bonds of X, but you would also have a put worth $X - S_T$ and a call worth zero or a call worth $-(S_T - X)$ and a put worth zero. All of this adds up to zero (check it). In other words, you would get some money up front but not have to pay any out at expiration. Since everyone would start doing this transaction, the prices would be forced back in line with the put-call parity equation.

By observing the signs in front of each term, we can easily determine which combinations replicate others. If the sign is positive, we should buy the option, stock, or bond. If it is negative, we should sell. For example, suppose we isolate the call price,

$$C_e(S_0,T,X) = P_e(S_0,T,X) + S_0 - X(1 + r)^{-T}.$$

Then owning a call is equivalent to owning a put, owning the stock, and selling short the bonds (borrowing). If we isolate the put price,

$$P_e(S_0,T,X) = C_e(S_0,T,X) - S_0 + X(1 + r)^{-T}.$$

This means that owning a put is equivalent to owning a call, selling short the stock, and buying the bonds. Likewise, we could isolate the stock or the bonds.

To convince yourself that these combinations on the right-hand side of the equation are equivalent to the combinations on the left-hand side, it would be helpful to set up a table like Table 3.11. Analyze the outcomes at expiration and you will see that the various combinations on the right-hand side do indeed replicate the positions taken on the left-hand side.

If the stock pays dividends, once again, we simply insert S_0', which is the stock price minus the present value of the dividends, for the stock price S_0.

While put-call parity is an extremely important and useful result, it does not hold so neatly if the options are American. The put-call parity rule for American options must be stated as inequalities,

$$C_a(S_0',T,X) + X + \sum_{j=1}^{N} D_j (1 + r)^{-t_j} \geq S_0 + P_a(S_0',T,X) \geq C_a(S_0',T,X) + X(1 + r)^{-T},$$

where S_0' is, again, the stock price minus the present value of the dividends. Although we shall skip the formal proof of this statement, it is, nonetheless, easy to make the calculations to determine if the rule is violated.

Now let us take a look at whether put-call parity holds for the America Online options. Since the stock does not pay dividends, the America Online calls are effectively European calls. However, the puts are strictly American. But first let us apply the European put-call parity rule. Panel A of Table 3.12 shows the appropriate calculations. Each cell represents a combination of exercise price and expiration and contains two figures. The upper figure is the value of the stock plus the put while the lower is the value of the call plus the bonds. If put-call parity holds, these two figures should be identical. Of course, we might not expect it to hold perfectly, because transaction costs may prevent some arbitrage opportunities from being worth exploiting. In most of the cases, the figures are very close.

Now we apply the American put-call parity rule. Panel B contains three figures for each cell. Recalling that there are no dividends, the top figure is $C_a(S_0,T,X) + X$, the middle figure is $S_0 + P_a(S_0,T,X)$, and the bottom figure is $C_a(S_0,T,X) + X(1 + r)^{-T}$. These figures should line up in descending

TABLE 3.12	Put-Call Parity for America Online Calls

A   European Put-Call Parity

Top row of cell: $S_0 + P_e(S_0,T,X)$
Bottom row of cell: $C_e(S_0,T,X) + X(1 + r)^{-T}$

Exercise Price	May	June	July
120	128.6875	135.1875	139.5625
	128.6471	134.8629	139.9412
125	130.5625	137.4375	142.5625
	130.6428	137.9666	142.6523
130	133.3125	140.1875	145.5625
	133.5135	140.8203	145.3634

B   American Put-Call Parity

Top row of cell: $C_a(S_0,T,X) + X$ (note: no dividends so $S_0' = S_0$)
Middle row of cell: $S_0 + P_a(S_0,T,X)$
Bottom row of cell: $C_a(S_0,T,X) + X(1 + r)^{-T}$

Exercise Price	May	June	July
120	128.7500	135.3750	140.8750
	128.6875	135.1875	139.5625
	128.6471	134.8629	139.9412
125	130.7500	138.5000	143.6250
	130.5625	137.4375	142.5625
	130.6428	137.9666	142.6523
130	133.6250	141.3750	146.3750
	133.3125	140.1875	145.5625
	133.5135	140.8203	145.3634

Note: Risk-free rates are 4.57% (May), 4.56% (June), and 4.63% (July); times to expiration are 0.0192 (May), 0.0959 (June), and 0.1726 (July).

order—that is, the top figure should be no lower than the middle figure, which should be no lower than the bottom figure in each cell. This is the case only for the May and June 120 options, though the discrepancies might not be large enough to justify an arbitrage transaction.

Put-call parity is the linkage between the call, put, stock, and risk-free bond. Figure 3.11 illustrates these relationships. Throughout the book, we shall further develop this figure to show other important relationships between derivative contracts, the underlying asset, and the risk-free bond market.

The Effect of Interest Rates

In contrast to call option prices, which vary directly with interest rates, put option prices vary inversely with interest rates. Purchasing a put is like deferring the sale of stock. When you finally sell the stock by exercising the

The price of a put is inversely related to interest rates.

FIGURE 3.11   **The Linkage between Calls, Puts, Stock, and Risk-Free Bonds**

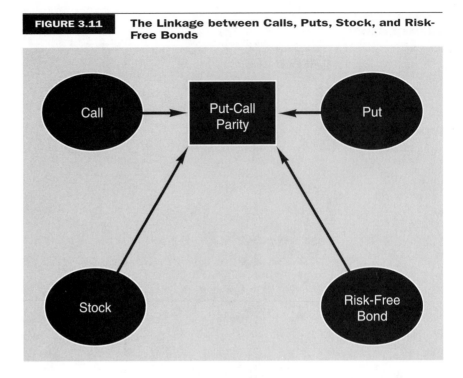

put, you receive X dollars. If interest rates increase, the X dollars will have a lower present value. Thus, a put holder forgos higher interest while waiting to exercise the option and receive the exercise price. Higher interest rates make puts less attractive to investors.

The Effect of Stock Volatility

The effect of volatility on a put's price is the same as that for a call: Higher volatility increases the possible gains for a put holder. For example, in our discussion of the effect of volatility on a call, we considered four equally likely stock prices at expiration for America Online: 110, 120, 130, and 140. The four possible put prices at expiration for a 125 put are 15, 5, 0, and 0. If the volatility increases so that the four possible stock prices at expiration are 100, 120, 130, and 150, the four possible put prices at expiration are 25, 5, 0, and 0. For the holder of a put, this increase in volatility is desirable because the put price now can rise much higher. It does not matter that the put can be even deeper out-of-the money when it expires, because its lowest possible value is still zero. The put holder's loss thus is truncated. Therefore, the put will have a higher price if the volatility is higher.

Another approach to understanding the volatility effect is to consider a European put on a stock with zero volatility. If the put is currently in-the-money, it will be worth the present value of $X - S_0$, because no further changes in the stock price will be expected. If the put is out-of-the-money, it will be worthless, because it will have no chance of expiring in-the-money. Either of these cases would be like a risk-free asset and would have no use for either hedgers or speculators.

The price of a put is directly related to the volatility of the underlying stock.

Summary

This chapter examined the basic principles of option pricing. It identified rules that impose upper and lower limits on put and call prices and examined the variables that affect an option's price. In addition, it demonstrated how put and call prices are related to each other by the put-call parity rule. Finally, the chapter examined the conditions that can induce an option trader to exercise an option prior to expiration.

We learned a number of principles that apply in some cases to European options only, in others to American options only, and in still others to both. Table 3.13 summarizes these principles.

An often confusing principle is the establishment of a minimum price. We started off by establishing a low minimum and then worked our way up until we could establish the highest possible minimum. First, we developed

TABLE 3.13	**Summary of the Principles of Option Pricing**			
	European Calls	American Calls	European Puts	American Puts
Assuming no dividends:				
Minimum value	≥ 0	≥ 0	≥ 0	≥ 0
Intrinsic value (IV)	NA	$\text{Max}(0, S_0 - X)$	NA	$\text{Max}(0, X - S_0)$
Time value	$C_e(S_0,T,X) - \text{Max}(0, S_0 - X)$	$C_a(S_0,T,X) - IV$	$P_e(S_0,T,X) - \text{Max}(0, X - S_0)$	$P_a(S_0,T,X) - IV$
Maximum value	S_0	S_0	$X(1+r)^{-T}$	X
Effect of time to	$C_e(S_0,T_2,X)$	$C_a(S_0,T_2,X)$	$P_e(S_0,T_2,X)$	$P_a(S_0,T_2,X)$
expiration	$\geq C_e(S_0,T_1,X)$	$\geq C_a(S_0,T_1,X)$	$\geqq P_e(S_0,T_1,X)$	$\geq P_a(S_0,T_1,X)$
Effect of exercise price	$C_e(S_0,T,X_1)$	$C_a(S_0,T,X_1)$	$P_e(S_0,T,X_2)$	$P_a(S_0,T,X_2)$
	$\geq C_e(S_0,T,X_2)$	$\geq C_a(S_0,T,X_2)$	$\geq P_e(S_0,T,X_1)$	$\geq P_a(S_0,T,X_1)$
Maximum difference in premiums	$(X_2 - X_1)(1+r)^{-T}$	$X_2 - X_1$	$(X_2 - X_1)(1+r)^{-T}$	$X_2 - X_1$
Lower bound	$\text{Max}[0, S_0 - X(1+r)^{-T}]$	$\text{Max}[0, S_0 - X(1+r)^{-T}]$	$\text{Max}[0, X(1+r)^{-T} - S_0]$	$\text{Max}(0, X - S_0)$
Other results:				
American versus	$C_a(S_0,T,X) \geq C_e(S_0,T,X)$			
European option	$P_a(S_0,T,X) \geq P_e(S_0,T,X)$			
prices				
Put-call parity	$P_e(S_0,T,X) = C_e(S_0,T,X) - S_0 + X(1+r)^{-T}$ (European)			
	$C_a(S_0,T,X) + X \geq S_0 + P_a(S_0,T,X) \geq C_a(S_0,T,X) + X(1+r)^{-T}$ (American)			
Effect of dividends	Replace S_0 with $S_0' = S_0 - \sum_{j=1}^{N} D_j(1+r)^{-t_j}$ and for American put-call parity add $\sum_{j=1}^{N} D_j(1+r)^{-t_j}$ to the left-hand term. The middle S_0 does not have the dividend adjustment.			

D e r i v a t i v e s   i n   A c t i o n

Some Sage Advice on Put-Call Parity

From the days of Plato and Aristotle, the lending of money at interest has sometimes been viewed as immoral. Not until the Middle Ages was it considered acceptable to profit from lending money, but even so, a maximum permissible interest rate was established. Lending at an interest rate above the maximum was called "usury" and was illegal. Even to this day, maximum interest rates are specified on certain types of transactions.

Russell Sage was a famous nineteenth-century financier. A clever man with a sharp mathematical mind, Sage was an active dealer in puts and calls. In fact, he was truly one of the first option traders in the United States and he understood the famous put-call parity relationship:

$$P_e(S_0,T,X) + S_0 = C_e(S_0,T,X) + X(1 + r)^{-T}.$$

Now turn this equation around to isolate the risk-free bonds:

$$X(1 + r)^{-T} = P_e(S_0,T,X) + S_0 - C_e(S_0,T,X).$$

The left-hand side says that the holder of a loan, in which the borrower receives the present value of X and promises to pay back X after a period of time T, is equiv-

the absolute minimum price of any call, which is zero. For American calls, the intrinsic value will provide a higher minimum if the option is in-the-money. Thus, it dominates the minimum of zero. However, it does not apply to European calls, because they cannot be exercised early. Nonetheless, there is a lower bound for European calls, which is the maximum of zero or the stock price minus the present value of the exercise price. This is at least as high as the intrinsic value of the American call. Because American calls must be worth at least as much as European calls, this lower bound applies to American calls as well. Thus, the ultimate minimum for both European and American calls on non-dividend-paying stocks is the lower bound we established for European calls.

Both American and European puts have an absolute minimum value of zero. American puts have an intrinsic value, which is the maximum of zero or the exercise price minus the stock price. This minimum does not apply to European puts, because they cannot be exercised early. European puts have a lower bound that is the maximum of zero or the present value of the exercise price minus the stock price. Because this lower bound is never greater than the intrinsic value of the American put, it does not help us raise the minimum for American puts. Thus, the lower bound is the minimum for European puts and the intrinsic value is the minimum for American puts (on non-dividend-paying stocks).

While we have identified the factors relevant to determining an option's price, we have not yet discussed how to determine the exact price. Although put-call parity appears to be a method of pricing options, it is only alent to owning a put and the stock and selling a call. Sage used put-call parity to create a synthetic loan with an interest rate that exceeded the statutory limit. This was accomplished by buying the stock and a put from his customer and then selling the customer a call. From the above formula, this is equivalent to holding a risk-free bond or loan paying off X at expiration. Sage specified the put and call prices such that the interest rate implied on the loan was greater than permitted by law.

For example, the statutory maximum in the 1860s was about 7 percent. A customer comes to Sage with stock worth $45 but needs cash and asks for a one-year loan of $50. Sage buys the stock for $45 and a put for $30 and sells the call for $25, all transactions done with the customer. The exercise price is $70. The customer receives $50 ($45 + $30 − $25 = $50). But one year later, the customer would end up buying the stock for $70 (either by exercising the call or having Sage exercise the put). The customer has borrowed $50 and, one year later, paid back $70, an interest rate of 40 percent! Of course, if the customer or the authorities had understood put-call parity, the transaction would not have occurred.

SOURCE: This material is drawn from Paul Sarnoff, *Russell Sage: The Money King* (New York: Ivan Obolensky, 1965).

a relative option pricing model. To price the put, we need to know the call's price; to price the call, we must know the put's price. Therefore, we cannot use put-call parity to price one instrument without either accepting the market price of the other as correct or having a model that first gives us the price of the other.

In short, we need an option pricing model—a formula that gives the option's price as a function of the variables that should affect it. If the option pricing model is correct, it should give option prices that conform to these boundary conditions. Most important, it should establish the theoretically correct option price. If the market price is out of line with the model price, arbitrage should force it to move toward the model price. We are now ready to look at option pricing models.

Key Terms

Before continuing to Chapter 4, you should be able to give brief definitions of the following terms.

- intrinsic value/parity value/parity/exercise value
- time value/speculative value
- deep-in-the-money/deep-out-of-the-money
- time value decay
- put-call parity

Further Reading

The classic articles where the rules presented in this chapter were developed are:

Merton, R. C. "The Relation between Put and Call Option Prices: Comment." *The Journal of Finance* 28 (1973): 183–184.

Merton, R. C. "Theory of Rational Option Pricing." *Bell Journal of Economics and Management Science* 4 (spring 1973): 41–73.

Stoll, H. R. "The Relationship between Put and Call Option Prices." *The Journal of Finance* 31 (May 1969): 319–332.

Empirical studies on whether option prices conform to these rules are:

Bhattacharya, M. "Transaction Data Tests of Efficiency of the Chicago Board Options Exchange." *Journal of Financial Economics* 12 (1983): 161–185.

Galai, D. "A Convexity Test for Traded Options." *Quarterly Review of Economics and Business* 19 (summer 1979): 83–90.

Galai, D. "Empirical Tests of Boundary Conditions for CBOE Options." *Journal of Financial Economics* 6 (1978): 187–211.

Gould, J. P., and D. Galai. "Transaction Costs and the Relationship between Put and Call Prices." *Journal of Financial Economics* 1 (1974): 105–129.

Klemkosky, R. C., and B. G. Resnick. "Put-Call Parity and Market Efficiency." *The Journal of Finance* 34 (December 1979): 1141–1155.

Klemkosky, R. C., and B. G. Resnick. "An Ex-Ante Analysis of Put-Call Parity." *Journal of Financial Economics* 8 (1980): 363–378.

Questions and Problems

1. Consider an option that expires in 68 days. The bid and ask discounts on the Treasury bill maturing in 67 days are 8.20 and 8.24, respectively. Find the approximate risk-free rate.

2. What would happen in the options market if the price of an American call were less than the value $\text{Max}(0, S_0 - X)$? Would your answer differ if the option were European?

3. In this chapter, we did not learn how to obtain the exact price of a call without knowing the price of the put and using put-call parity. In one special case, however, we can obtain an exact price for a call. Assume the option has an infinite maturity. Then use the maximum and minimum values we learned in this chapter to obtain the prices of European and American calls.

4. Why might two calls or puts alike in all respects but time to expiration have approximately the same price?

5. Why might two calls or puts alike in all respects but exercise price have approximately the same price?

6. Suppose you observe a European call option that is priced at less than the value $\text{Max}[0, S_0 - X(1 + r)^{-T}]$. What type of transaction should you execute to achieve the maximum benefit?

7. Explain why an option's time value is greatest when the stock price is near the exercise price and why it nearly disappears when the option is deep-in- or out-of-the-money.

8. Critique the following statement, made by an options investor: "My call option is very deep-in-the-money. I don't see how it can go any higher. I think I should exercise it."

9. Call prices are directly related to the stock's volatility, yet higher volatility means that the stock price can go lower. How would you resolve this apparent paradox?

10. The value $\text{Max}[0, X(1 + r)^{-T} - S_0]$ was shown to be the lowest possible value of a European put. Why is this value irrelevant for an American put?

11. Why do higher interest rates lead to higher call option prices but lower put option prices?

12. Suppose a European put price exceeds the value predicted by put-call parity. How could an investor profit?

13. Why does the justification for exercising an American call early not hold up when considering an American put?

The following option prices were observed for a stock on July 6 of a particular year. Use this information to solve problems 14 through 19. Unless otherwise indicated, ignore dividends on the stock. The stock is priced at 165 1/8. The expirations are July 17, August 21, and October 16. The risk-free rates are .0516, .0550, and .0588, respectively.

	Calls			Puts		
Strike	Jul	Aug	Oct	Jul	Aug	Oct
155	10.5	11.75	14	0.1875	1.25	2.75
160	6	8.125	11.125	0.75	2.75	4.5
165	2.6875	5.25	8.125	2.375	4.75	6.75
170	0.8125	3.25	6	5.75	7.5	9

14. Compute the intrinsic values, time values, and lower bounds of the following calls. Identify any profit opportunities that may exist.

    a. July 160

    b. October 155

    c. August 170

15. Compute the intrinsic values, time values, and lower bounds of the following puts. Identify any profit opportunities that may exist.

    a. July 165

    b. August 160

    c. October 170

16. Check the following combinations of puts and calls, and determine whether they conform to the put-call parity rule for European options. If you see any violations, suggest a strategy.

   a. July 155

   b. August 160

   c. October 170

17. Repeat Question 16 using American put-call parity, but do not suggest a strategy.

18. Examine the following pairs of calls, which differ only by exercise price. Determine whether any violate the rules regarding relationships between American options that differ only by exercise price.

   a. August 155 and 160

   b. October 160 and 165

19. Examine the following pairs of puts, which differ only by exercise price. Determine if any violate the rules regarding relationships between American options that differ only by exercise price.

   a. August 155 and 160

   b. October 160 and 170

20. (Concept Problem) Put-call parity is a powerful formula that can be used to create equivalent combinations of options, risk-free bonds, and stock. Suppose there are options available on the number of points Shaquille O'Neal will score in his next game. For example, a call option with an exercise price of 32 would pay off $Max(0, S_0 - 32)$, where S_0 is the number of points Shaq has recorded by the end of the game. Thus, if he scores 35, call holders receive $3 for each call. If he scores less than 32, call holders receive nothing. A put with an exercise price of 32 would pay off $Max(0, 32 - S_0)$. If Shaq scores more than 32, put holders receive nothing. If he scores 28, put holders receive $4 for each put. Obviously there is no way to actually buy a position in the underlying asset, a point. However, put-call parity shows that the underlying asset can be recreated from a combination of puts, calls, and risk-free bonds. Show how this would be done, and give the formula for the price of a point.

21. (Concept Question) Suppose Congress decides that investors should not profit when stock prices go down so it outlaws short selling. Congress has not figured out options, however, so there are no restrictions on option trading. Explain how to accomplish the equivalent of a short sale by using options.

Option Pricing Models:
The Binomial Model

Models are like cars: you can have the best car in the world, but it won't stop you crashing if you don't drive it properly.

MAMDOUH BARAKAT

Risk, April 1997, p. 6

This chapter examines the first of two general types of option pricing models. A **model** is a simplified representation of reality that uses certain inputs to produce an output, or result. An **option pricing model** is a mathematical formula or computational procedure that uses the factors determining the option's price as inputs. The output is the theoretical fair value of the option. If the model performs as it should, the option's market price will equal the theoretical fair value. Obtaining the theoretical fair value is a process called **option pricing.**

In Chapter 3, we examined some basic concepts in determining option prices. We saw, however, only how to price options relative to other options; for example, put-call parity demonstrates that given the price of a call, one can determine the price of a put. We also discovered relationships among the prices of options that differ by exercise prices and examined the upper and lower bounds on call and put prices. We did not, however, learn how to determine the exact option price directly from the factors that influence it.

A large body of research on option pricing exists. Much of it goes far beyond the intended level of this book. The models range from the relatively simple to the extremely complex. All of the models have much in common, and it is necessary to understand the basic models before moving on to the more complex but more realistic ones.

We begin with a simple model called the **binomial option pricing model,** which is more of a computational procedure than a formula. After taking the binomial model through several stages, we move on to Chapter 5

Chapter Objectives

- To introduce the concept of an option pricing model

- To provide a thorough treatment of the binomial option pricing model, in one- and two-period worlds, explaining how a risk-free hedge of stock and option is maintained through time

- To show how the binomial model can be used to capture the effects of early exercise of puts and calls and properly reflect those effects in the price of the option

- To illustrate how the binomial model can be extended for any number of time periods

- To present an alternative way to specify the binomial model and the **Black-Scholes option pricing model,** which is a mathematical formula. In both cases, however, we have the same objective: to obtain the theoretical fair value of the option, which is the price at which it should be trading.

The One-Period Binomial Model

First, let us consider what we mean by a one-period world. An option has a defined life, typically expressed in days. Assume the option's life is one unit of time. This time period can be as short or as long as necessary. If the time period is one day and the option has more than one day remaining, we will need a multiperiod model, which we shall examine later. For now, we will assume the option's life is a single time period.

The model is called a **binomial** model. It allows the stock price to go either up or down, possibly at different rates. A binomial probability distribution is a distribution in which there are two outcomes or states. The probability of an up or down movement is governed by the binomial probability distribution. Because of this, the model is also called a **two-state** model.

In applying the binomial model to an underlying asset, however, it is immediately obvious that the range of possible outcomes is greater than the two states the binomial distribution can accommodate; however, that makes the model no less worthwhile. Its virtues are its simplicity and its ability to present the fundamental concepts of option pricing models clearly and concisely. In so doing, it establishes a foundation that facilitates an understanding of the Black-Scholes model.

Consider a world in which there is a stock priced at S on which call options are available.[1] The call has one period remaining before it expires. The beginning of the period is today and is referred to as time 0. The end of the period is referred to as time 1. When the call expires, the stock can take on one of two values: It can go up by a factor of u or down by a factor of d. If it goes up, the stock price will be Su. If it goes down, it will be Sd.

For example, suppose the stock price is currently $50 and can go either up by 10 percent or down by 8 percent. Thus, u = 1.10 and d = 1 − .08 = 0.92. The variables u and d, therefore, are 1.0 plus the rates of return on the stock. When the call expires, the stock will be either 50(1.10) = 55 or 50(0.92) = 46.

Consider a call option on the stock with an exercise price of X and a current price of C. When the option expires, it will be worth either C_u or C_d. Because at expiration the call price is its intrinsic value,

$$C_u = Max[0, Su - X]$$
$$C_d = Max[0, Sd - X].$$

---

[1]The model can also price put options. We shall see how this is done in a later section.

Figure 4.1 illustrates the paths of both the stock and the call prices. This diagram is simple, but it will become more complex when we introduce the two-period model.

If both stock prices resulted in the option expiring in-the-money, the option would not be very speculative; however, it would still be correctly priced by the model. The writer would receive a premium compensating for the future cash outflow expected upon exercising the option. To make things more interesting, however, we shall define our variables such that the option has a chance of expiring out-of-the-money. Assume Sd is less than X; that is, if the stock price goes down, the option will expire out-of-the-money. Also assume Su is greater than X such that if the stock price goes up, the option will expire in-the-money.

As in previous chapters, let the risk-free rate be identified by the symbol r. The risk-free rate is the interest earned on a riskless investment over a time period equal to the option's remaining life. The risk-free rate falls between the rate of return if the stock goes up and the rate of return if the

FIGURE 4.1   **The One-Period Binomial Tree**

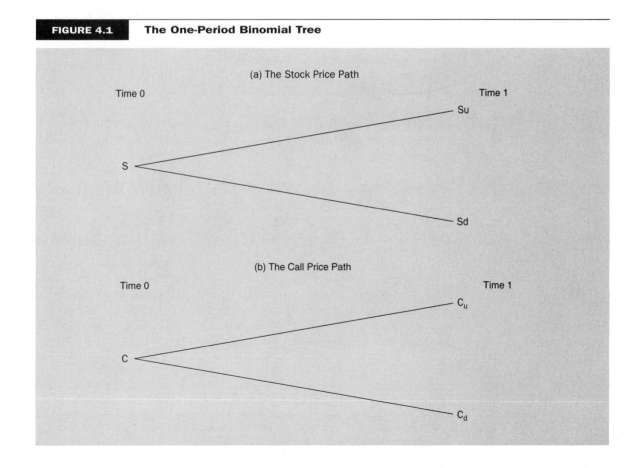

stock goes down. Thus, $d < 1 + r < u$.[2] We shall assume all investors can borrow or lend at the risk-free rate.

The objective of this model is to derive a formula for the theoretical fair value of the option, the variable C. The theoretical fair value is then compared against the actual price and reveals whether the option is over-priced, underpriced, or correctly priced. The formula for C is developed by constructing a riskless portfolio of stock and options. A riskless portfolio should earn the risk-free rate. Given the stock's values and the riskless re-turn on the portfolio, the call's value can be inferred from the other vari-ables.

This riskless portfolio is called a **hedge portfolio** and consists of h shares of stock and a single written call. The model provides the **hedge ratio,** h. The current value of the portfolio is the value of the h shares minus the value of the short call. We subtract the call's value from the value of the h shares because the shares are assets and the short call is a liability. Thus, the portfolio value is assets minus liabilities, or simply net worth. The current portfolio value is denoted as V, where $V = hS - C$.

At expiration, the portfolio value will be either V_u if the stock goes up or V_d if the stock goes down. Using the previously defined terms,

$$V_u = hSu - C_u$$
$$V_d = hSd - C_d.$$

If the same outcome is achieved regardless of what the stock price does, the position is riskless. We can choose a value of h that will make this happen. We simply set $V_u = V_d$ so that

$$hSu - C_u = hSd - C_d.$$

Solving for h,

$$h = \frac{C_u - C_d}{Su - Sd}$$

Since we know the values of S, u, and d, we can determine C_u, C_d, and h.

A riskless investment must earn a return equal to the risk-free rate. Thus, the portfolio's value one period later should equal its current value compounded for one period at the risk-free rate. If it does not, the portfo-lio will be incorrectly valued and represent a potential arbitrage opportu-nity. Later we shall see how the arbitrage would be executed.

An option is priced by combining the stock and option in a risk-free hedge portfolio such that the option price can be inferred from other known values.

---

[2]This requirement is necessary or there would be an arbitrage opportunity. If $d < u < 1 + r$, one could sell short the stock, invest the proceeds in the risk-free bond and, in the worst case, earn a return that would exceed the highest possible payout that would be owed to buy back the shorted stock. If $1 + r < d < u$, one could borrow at the rate r, invest in the stock, and al-ways earn more than the cost of the loan.

If the portfolio's current value grows at the risk-free rate, its value at the option's expiration will be $(hS - C)(1 + r)$. The two values of the portfolio at expiration, V_u and V_d, are equal, so we can select either one. Choosing V_u and setting it equal to the original value of the portfolio compounded at the risk-free rate gives

$$V(1 + r) = V_u,$$
$$(hS - C)(1 + r) = hSu - C_u.$$

Substituting the formula for h and solving this equation for C gives the option pricing formula,

$$C = \frac{pC_u + (1 - p)C_d}{1 + r},$$

The one-period binomial option pricing formula provides the option price as a weighted average of the two possible option prices at expiration, discounted at the risk-free rate.

where p is defined as $(1 + r - d)/(u - d)$. The formula gives the call option's price as a function of the variables C_u, C_d, p, and r; however, C_u and C_d are determined by the variables S, u, d, and X. Thus, the variables affecting the call option price are the current stock price, S, the exercise price, X, the risk-free rate, r, and the parameters, u and d, which define the possible future stock prices at expiration. Notice how the call price is a weighted average of the two possible call prices the next period, discounted at the risk-free rate. Notice also that we never specified the probabilities of the two stock price movements; they do not enter into the model. The option is priced relative to the stock. Therefore, given the stock price, one can obtain the option price. The stock, however, is priced independently of the option, and thus the probabilities of the stock price movements would be a factor in pricing the stock. But pricing the stock is not our concern. We already have the stock price, S.

In Chapter 1, we introduced the concept of risk neutrality and noted that we would be using it to price derivatives. The investors' feelings about risk play an important role in the pricing of securities, but in the risk-neutral option pricing framework, investors' sensitivities to risk are of no consequence. This does not mean, however, that the model assumes investors are risk neutral. The stock price is determined by how investors feel about risk. If investors are risk neutral and determine that a stock is worth $20, the model will use $20 and take no account of investors' feelings about risk. If investors are risk averse and determine that a stock is worth $20, the model will use $20 and disregard investors' feelings about risk. This does not mean that the stock will be priced equally by risk-averse and risk-neutral investors; rather, the model will accept the stock price as given and pay no attention to how risk was used to obtain the stock price. In other words, given the stock price, both an aggressive and a conservative investor will assign the same price to an option on the stock.

An Illustrative Example

Consider a stock currently priced at $100. One period later it can go up to $125, an increase of 25 percent, or down to $80, a decrease of 20 percent. Assume a call option with an exercise price of $100. The risk-free rate is 7 percent. The inputs are summarized as follows:

$$S = 100 \qquad d = 0.80$$
$$X = 100 \qquad r = .07$$
$$u = 1.25$$

First, we find the values of C_u and C_d:

$$C_u = \text{Max}\ [0,\ Su - X]$$
$$= \text{Max}\ [0,\ 100(1.25) - 100]$$
$$= 25$$
$$C_d = \text{Max}\ [0,\ Sd - X]$$
$$= \text{Max}\ [0,\ 100\ (0.80) - 100]$$
$$= 0.$$

The hedge ratio, h, is

$$h = \frac{25 - 0}{125 - 80} = 0.556$$

The hedge requires 0.556 shares of stock for each call.[3] The value of p is

$$p = \frac{1 + r - d}{u - d} = \frac{1.07 - 0.80}{1.25 - 0.80} = .6.$$

Then

$$1 - p = 1 - 0.6 = .4.$$

Plugging into the formula for C gives

$$C = \frac{25(.6) + 0(.4)}{1.07} = 14.02.$$

Thus, the theoretical fair value of the call is $14.02.

A Hedge Portfolio

Consider a hedge portfolio consisting of a short position in 1,000 calls and a long position in 556 shares of stock. The number of shares is determined

---

[3]We assume odd lots of stock can be purchased.

by the hedge ratio of 0.556 shares per written call. The current value of this portfolio is

$$556(\$100) - 1,000(\$14.02) = \$41,580.$$

Thus, you buy 556 shares at $100 per share and write 1,000 calls at $14.02. This requires a payment of $556(\$100) = \$55,600$ for the stock and takes in $1,000(\$14.02) = \$14,020$ for the calls. The net cash outlay is $\$55,600 - \$14,020 = \$41,580$. This total represents the assets (the stock) minus the liabilities (the calls) and thus is the net worth, or the amount the investor must commit to the transaction. Figure 4.2 illustrates the process.

If the stock goes up to $125, the call will be exercised for a value of $\$125 - \$100 = \$25$. The stock will be worth $556(\$125) = \$69,500$. Thus, the portfolio will be worth $556(\$125) - 1,000(\$125 - \$100) = \$44,500$. If the stock goes down to $80, the call will expire out-of-the-money. The portfolio will be worth $556(\$80) = \$44,480$. These two values of the portfolio at expiration are essentially equal, because the $20 difference is due only to the rounding off of the hedge ratio. The return on this hedge portfolio is

$$r_h = \left(\frac{\$44,500}{\$41,580}\right) - 1 \approx 0.07,$$

which is the risk-free rate. The original investment of $41,580 will have grown to $44,500—a return of about 7 percent, the risk-free rate.

FIGURE 4.2   **One-Period Binomial Example**

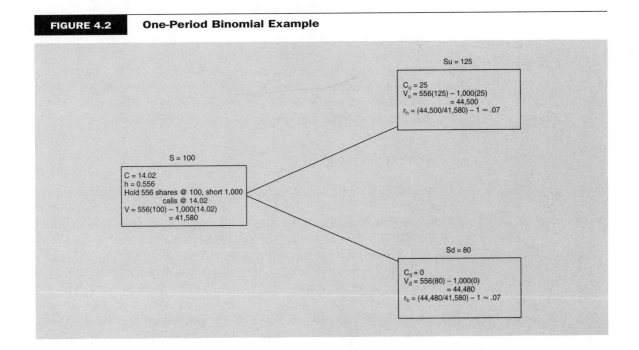

If the call price were not $14.02, an arbitrage opportunity would exist. First we will consider the case where the call is overpriced.

An Overpriced Call

If the call were overpriced, a riskless hedge could generate a riskless return in excess of the risk-free rate. Suppose the market price of the call is $15. If you buy 556 shares and write 1,000 calls, the value of the investment today is

$$556(\$100) - 1,000(\$15) = \$40,600.$$

If the stock goes up to $125, at expiration the call will be priced at $25 and the portfolio will be worth $556(\$125) - 1,000(\$25) = \$44,500$. If the stock goes down to $80, the call will be worth nothing and the portfolio will be worth $556(\$80) = \$44,480$. In either case, the portfolio will be worth the same, the difference of $20 again due to rounding. The initial investment of $40,600 will have grown to $44,500, a riskless return of

$$r_h = \left(\frac{\$44,500}{\$40,600}\right) - 1 \approx .096,$$

which is considerably higher than the risk-free rate.

A riskless portfolio that will earn more than the risk-free rate obviously is very attractive. All investors will recognize this opportunity and hurry to execute the transaction. This will increase the demand for the stock and the supply of the option. Consequently, the stock price will tend to increase and the option price to decrease until the option is correctly priced. For illustrative purposes, assume that the stock price stays at $100. Then the option price must fall from $15 to $14.02. Only at an option price of $14.02 will this risk-free portfolio offer a return equal to the risk-free rate.

Now consider what happens if the option is underpriced.

An Underpriced Call

If the option is underpriced, it is necessary to buy it. To hedge a long option position, you must sell the stock short. Suppose the call is priced at $13. Then you sell short 556 shares at $100, which generates a cash inflow of $556(\$100) = \$55,600$. Now you buy 1,000 calls at $13 each for a cost of $13,000. This produces a net cash inflow of $42,600.

If the stock goes to $125, you buy it back at $556(\$125) = \$69,500$. You exercise the calls for a gain of $1,000(\$125 - \$100) = \$25,000$. The net cash flow is $-\$69,500 + \$25,000 = -\$44,500$. If the stock goes down to $80, you buy it back, paying $556 (\$80) = \$44,480$ while the calls expire worthless. The $20 difference is again due to rounding.

In both outcomes, the returns are essentially equivalent. The overall transaction is like a loan in which you receive $42,600 up front and pay back $44,500 later. This is equivalent to an interest rate of ($44,500/ $42,600) − 1 = .0446. Because this transaction is the same as borrowing at a rate of 4.46 percent and the risk-free rate is 7 percent, it is an attractive borrowing opportunity. All investors will recognize this and execute the transaction. This will tend to drive up the call price, or possibly drive down the stock price, until equilibrium is reached. If the price of the stock stays at $100, equilibrium will be reached when the call price rises to $14.02.

This model considered only a single period. In the next section, we extend the model to a two-period world.

The Two-Period Binomial Model

In the single-period world, the stock price goes either up or down. Thus, there are only two possible future stock prices. To increase the degree of realism, we will now add another period. This will increase the number of possible outcomes at expiration. Thus, our model has three time points: today or time 0, time 1, and time 2.

Suppose that at the end of the first period the stock price has risen to Su. During the second period it could go either up or down, in which case it would end up at either Su^2 or Sud. If the stock price has gone down in the first period to Sd, during the second period it will either go down again or go back up, in which case it will end up at either Sd^2 or Sdu.

Figure 4.3 illustrates the paths of the stock price and the corresponding call prices. Viewed this way, we can see why the diagram is often called a binomial tree. The option prices at expiration are

$$C_{u^2} = Max[0, Su^2 − X]$$
$$C_{ud} = Max[0, Sud − X]$$
$$C_{d^2} = Max[0, Sd^2 − X].$$

The possible option prices at the end of the first period, C_u and C_d, initially are unknown; however, they can be found.

Suppose that in the first period the stock price increases to Su. Because there will be only one period remaining with two possible outcomes, the one-period binomial model is appropriate for finding the option price, C_u. If at the end of the first period the stock price decreases to Sd, we will again find ourselves facing a single-period world with two possible outcomes. Here we can again use the one-period binomial model to obtain the value of C_d. Using the one-period model, the option prices C_u and C_d are

$$C_u = \frac{pC_{u^2} + (1 − p)C_{ud}}{1 + r}$$

| **FIGURE 4.3** | **The Two-Period Binomial Tree** |

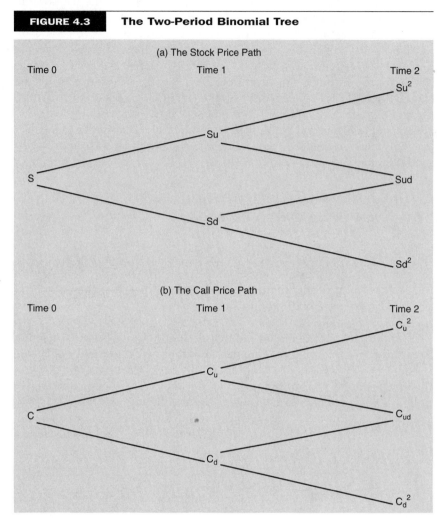

(a) The Stock Price Path

Time 0   Time 1   Time 2

S · — Su — Su^2 — Sud — Sd — Sd^2

(b) The Call Price Path

Time 0   Time 1   Time 2

C · — C_u — C_u^2 — C_{ud} — C_d — C_d^2

and

$$C_d = \frac{pC_{ud} + (1 - p)C_{d^2}}{1 + r}$$

In a single-period world, a call option's value is a weighted average of the option's two possible values at the end of the next period. The call's value if the stock goes up in the next period is weighted by the factor p; its value if the stock goes down in the next period is weighted by the factor $1 - p$. To obtain the call price at the start of the period, we discount the weighted average of the two possible future call prices at the risk-free rate for one period. The single-period binomial model is, thus, a general formula that can be used in any multiperiod world when there is but one period remaining.

Even if the call does not expire at the end of the next period, we can use the formula to find the current call price, the theoretical fair value, as a weighted average of the two possible call prices in the next period; that is,

$$C = \frac{pC_u + (1 - p)C_d}{1 + r}.$$

First, we find the values of C_u and C_d; then we substitute these into the above formula for C.

For a more direct approach, we can use

$$C = \frac{p^2C_{u^2} + 2p(1 - p)C_{ud} + (1 - p)^2C_{d^2}}{(1 + r)^2}.$$

This formula illustrates that the call's value is a weighted average of its three possible values at expiration two periods later. The denominator, $(1 + r)^2$, discounts this figure back two periods to the present.

Notice that we have not actually derived the formula by constructing a hedge portfolio. This is possible, however, and in a later section we shall see how the hedge portfolio works. First, note that the hedge is constructed by initially holding h shares of stock for each call written. At the end of the first period, the stock price is either Su or Sd. At that point, we must adjust the hedge ratio. If the stock is at Su, let the new hedge ratio be designated as h_u; if at Sd, let the new ratio be h_d. The formulas for h_u and h_d are of the same general type as that of h in the single-period model. The numerator is the call's value if the stock goes up the next period minus the call's value if the stock goes down the next period. The denominator is the price of the stock if it goes up the next period minus its price if it goes down the next period. In equation form,

$$h = \frac{C_u - C_d}{Su - Sd}, \ h_u = \frac{C_{u^2} - C_{ud}}{Su^2 - Sud}, \text{ and } h_d = \frac{C_{ud} - C_{d^2}}{Sdu - Sd^2}.$$

The two-period binomial option pricing formula provides the option price as a weighted average of the two possible option prices the next period, discounted at the risk-free rate. The two future option prices are obtained from the one-period binomial model.

An Illustrative Example

Consider the example in a two-period world from the previous section. All input values remain the same. The possible stock prices at expiration are

$$Su^2 = 100(1.25)^2$$
$$= 156.25$$
$$Sud = 100(1.25)(0.80)$$
$$= 100$$
$$Sd^2 = 100(0.80)^2$$
$$= 64.$$

The call prices at expiration are

$$
\begin{aligned}
C_{u^2} &= \text{Max}[0, Su^2 - X] \\
&= \text{Max}(0, 156.25 - 100) \\
&= 56.25 \\
C_{ud} &= \text{Max}[0, Sud - X] \\
&= \text{Max}(0, 100 - 100) \\
&= 0 \\
C_{d^2} &= \text{Max}[0, Sd^2 - X] \\
&= \text{Max}(0, 64 - 100) \\
&= 0.
\end{aligned}
$$

The value of p is the same, $(1 + r - d)/(u - d)$, regardless of the number of periods in the model.

We can find the call's value by either of the two methods discussed in the previous section. Let us first compute the values of C_u and C_d:

$$
C_u = \frac{(56.25)(.6) + (0)(.4)}{1.07} = 31.54
$$

$$
C_d = \frac{(0)(.6) + (0)(.4)}{1.07} = 0.00.
$$

Note why the value of the call is 0.00 at time 1 when the stock is at 80: The call cannot expire in-the-money at time 2. The value of the call today is a weighted average of the two possible call values one period later:

$$
C = \frac{(31.54)(.6) + (0)(.4)}{1.07} = 17.69.
$$

Note that the same call analyzed in the one-period world is worth more in the two-period world. Why? Recall from Chapter 3 that a call option with a longer maturity is never worth less than one with a shorter maturity and usually is worth more. If this principle did not hold here, something would have been wrong with the model.

A Hedge Portfolio

Now consider a hedge portfolio. Figure 4.4 illustrates this process. It would be very helpful to keep an eye on the figure as we move through the example. Let the call be trading in the market at its theoretical fair value of $17.69. The hedge will consist of 1,000 short calls. The number of shares purchased at time 0 is given by the formula for h,

$$
h = \frac{31.54 - 0.00}{125 - 80} = 0.701
$$

Thus, we buy 701 shares of stock and write 1,000 calls. The transaction can be summarized as follows:

Buy 701 shares at $100 = $70,100 (assets);
write 1,000 calls at $17.69 = −$17,690 (liabilities);
net investment = $52,410 (net worth).

STOCK GOES TO 125   The portfolio consists of 701 shares at $125 and 1,000 calls at $31.54. The value of the portfolio is $701(\$125) - 1,000(\$31.54) = \$56,085$. Our investment has grown from $52,410 to $56,085. You should be able to verify that this is a 7 percent return, the risk-free rate. To maintain a hedge through the next period, we need to revise the hedge ratio. The new hedge ratio, h_u, is

$$h_u = \frac{56.25 - 0}{156.25 - 100} = 1.$$

The new hedge ratio will be one share of stock for each call.

FIGURE 4.4   **Two-Period Binomial Example**

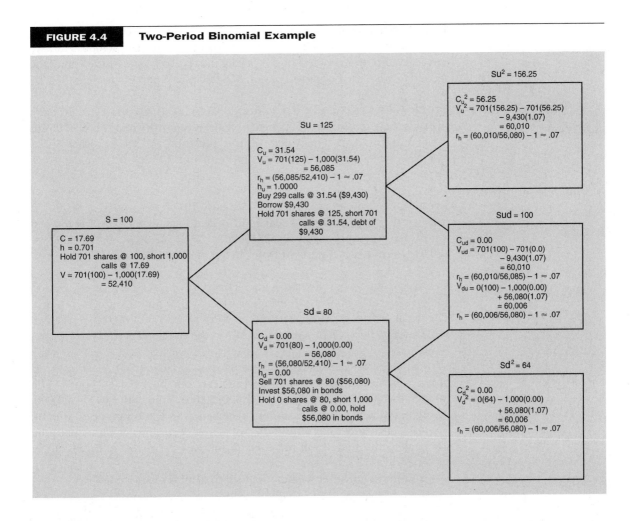

To establish the new hedge ratio, we need either 701 calls or 1,000 shares of stock. We can either buy back 299 calls, leaving us with 701, or buy 299 shares, giving us 1,000 shares. Since it is less expensive to buy the calls, let us buy back 299 calls at $31.54 each for a total cost of $9,430. To avoid putting out more of our own funds, we borrow the money at the risk-free rate.

STOCK GOES TO 80   The portfolio consists of 701 shares valued at $80 and 1,000 calls valued at $0.00. The portfolio value is $701($80) - 1,000$ ($0.00) = $56,080, which differs from the outcome at a stock price of $125 only by a round-off error. Since the return is the same regardless of the change in the stock price, the portfolio is riskless. To maintain the hedge through the next period, we adjust the hedge ratio to

$$h_d = \frac{0.00 - 0.00}{156.25 - 100.00} = .000.$$

Thus, we need zero shares of stock for the 1,000 calls. We currently hold 701 shares, so we can sell off all of the shares at $80 and receive $56,080. Then we invest this money in riskless bonds paying the risk-free rate. At the end of the second period, the bonds will pay off $56,080 plus 7 percent interest.

STOCK GOES FROM 125 TO 156.25   We sell the 701 shares at $156.25, the calls are exercised at $56.25 each, and we repay the loan of $9,430 plus 7 percent interest. The value of the portfolio is $701($156.25) - 701$ ($56.25) - $9,430(1.07) = $60,010$, a return of 7 percent from the previous period.

STOCK GOES FROM 125 TO 100   We have 701 shares valued at $100, 701 calls worth $0.00, and the repayment of the loan of $9,430 plus interest for a total portfolio value of $701($100) - 701($0.00) - $9,430 (1.07) = $60,010$, a return of 7 percent from the previous period.

STOCK GOES FROM 80 TO 100   The portfolio consists of no shares, 1,000 calls worth $0.00, and bonds worth $56,080 plus 7 percent interest. The total value of the portfolio is $0($100) - 1,000($0.00) + $56,080$ (1.07) = $60,006$, a 7 percent return from the previous period.

STOCK GOES FROM 80 TO 64   We have no shares at $64, 1,000 calls expiring worthless, and principal and interest on the risk-free bonds. The value of this portfolio is $0($64) + $1,000($0.00) + 56,080(1.07) = 60,006$. This is essentially the same amount received as in the other cases; the difference is due only to a round-off error. Thus, regardless of which path the stock takes, the hedge will produce an increase in wealth of 7 percent in each period.

Now let us consider what happens if the call is mispriced.

A Mispriced Call in the Two-Period World

If the call is mispriced at time 0, an arbitrage opportunity exists. If the call is underpriced, we should purchase it and sell short h shares of stock. If the call is overpriced, we should write it and purchase h shares of stock. Whether we earn the arbitrage return over the first period, the second period, or both periods, however, will depend on whether the call price adjusts to its theoretical fair value at the end of the first period. If it does not, we may not earn a return in excess of the risk-free rate over the first period. The call must be correctly priced at the end of the second period, however, because it expires at that time.

The two-period return will be the geometric average of the two one-period returns; that is, if 6 percent is the first-period return and 9 percent is the second-period return, the two-period return will be $\sqrt{(1.06)(1.09)} - 1 = .0749$. If one of the two returns equals the risk-free rate and the other exceeds it, the two-period return will exceed the risk-free rate. If one of the two returns is less than the risk-free rate and the other is greater, the overall return can still exceed the risk-free rate. The return earned over the full two periods will exceed the risk-free rate if the option is mispriced at time 0, the proper long or short position is taken, and the correct hedge ratio is maintained.

There are many possible outcomes of such a hedge, and it would take an entire chapter to illustrate them. We therefore shall discuss the possibilities only in general terms. In each case, we will assume the proper hedge ratio is maintained and the investor buys calls only when they are underpriced or correctly priced and sells calls only when they are overpriced or correctly priced.

Suppose the call originally was overpriced and is still overpriced at the end of the first period. Because the call has not fallen sufficiently to be correctly priced, the return over the first period actually can be less than the risk-free rate. Because the call must be correctly priced at the end of the second period, however, the return earned over the second period will more than make up for it. Overall, the return earned over the two periods will exceed the risk-free rate.

If the call originally is overpriced and becomes correctly priced at the end of the first period, the return earned over that period must exceed the risk-free rate. The return earned over the second period will equal the risk-free rate, because the call was correctly priced at the beginning of the second period and is correctly priced at the end of it. Thus, the full two-period return will exceed the risk-free rate.

If the call is overpriced at the start and becomes underpriced at the end of the first period, the return earned over that period will exceed the risk-free rate. This is because the call will have fallen in price more than is justified and now is worth considerably less than it should be. At this point, we should close out the hedge and initiate a new hedge for the second period consisting of a long position in the underpriced call and a short position in the stock. We can invest the excess proceeds in risk-free bonds. The

TABLE 4.1	Hedge Results in the Two-Period Binomial Model		
	Return from Hedge Compared to Risk-Free Rate		
	Period 1	**Period 2**	**Two-Period**
Options Overpriced at Start of Period 1			
Status of option at start of period 2			
Overpriced	indeterminate	better	better
Correctly priced	better	equal	better
Underpriced	better	better	better

second-period return will far exceed the risk-free rate. The overall two-period return obviously will be above the risk-free rate.

Table 4.1 summarizes these results. Similar conclusions apply for an underpriced call, although the interpretation differs somewhat because the hedge portfolio is short.

Extensions of the Binomial Model

Pricing Put Options

We can use the binomial model to price put options just as we can for call options. We use the same formulas, but instead of specifying the call payoffs at expiration, we use the put payoffs at expiration. To see the difference, look at Figure 4.3 on page 122. Then we simply replace every C with a P; likewise, we substitute P for C in each formula.

Let's consider the same problem we have been working on, but we shall price the two-period European put that has an exercise price of 100. The values of the put at expiration are as follows:

$$P_{u^2} = \text{Max}(0,100 - 156.25) = 0.00$$
$$P_{ud} = \text{Max}(0,100 - 100) = 0.00$$
$$P_{d^2} = \text{Max}(0,100 - 64) = 36.$$

Note how we use the put intrinsic value formula at expiration, the greater of zero or X minus the stock price. Now we step back to time 1. Using the same formulas we used for calls,

$$P_u = \frac{0(.6) + 0(.4)}{1.07} = 0.00$$
$$P_d = \frac{0(.6) + 36(.4)}{1.07} = 13.46.$$

Again, the option value is a weighted average of its two possible values the next period, where the weights are p and $1 - p$, discounted back one period at the risk-free rate. Now we find the time 0 value to be

$$P = \frac{0(.6) + 13.46(.4)}{1.07} = 5.03.$$

Pricing a put with the binomial model is the same procedure as pricing a call, except that the expiration payoffs reflect the fact that the option is the right to sell the underlying stock.

Now let us work through a hedge example. The principles are essentially the same as hedging with calls, but instead of selling calls to hedge a long position in stock, we are buying puts. Calls move directly with the stock price so to hedge, we have to sell calls. Puts, however, move inversely with the stock price, so to hedge stock we buy puts.

The formula for the hedge ratio is the same as that for calls: the option price the next period if the stock goes up minus the option price the next period if the stock goes down divided by the stock price the next period if the stock price goes up minus the stock price the next period if the stock goes down. Thus, at time 0 the hedge ratio is

$$h = \frac{0 - 13.46}{125 - 80} = -0.299.$$

The minus sign simply reflects the opposite movement of puts to stock. Here we need to buy 299 shares for a long position in 1,000 puts. This will cost

299($100)	=	$29,900 (in shares)
1,000($5.03)	=	$ 5,030 (in puts)
Total		$34,930.

STOCK GOES TO 125   We now have 299 shares worth $125 and 1,000 puts worth $0.00 for a total value of 299($125) + 1,000($0.00) = $37,375. This is approximately 7 percent more than our initial investment of $34,930. Now the new hedge ratio will be

$$h_u = \frac{0 - 0}{100 - 64} = 0.000.$$

So we need no shares for our 1,000 puts. We sell the 299 shares, collecting 299($125) = $37,375 and invest this money in risk-free bonds that will earn 7 percent.

STOCK GOES TO 80   We now have 299 shares worth $80 and 1,000 puts worth $13.46 for a total value of 299($80) + 1,000($13.46) = $37,380. This is the same as when the stock went to 125, except for a round-off difference. Again, the return is 7 percent on our initial investment of $34,930. Now the hedge ratio will be

$$h_d = \frac{0 - 36}{100 - 64} = -1.0000,$$

which means we need to buy 701 shares or sell 701 puts. Let us buy 701 shares, which will cost $56,080, by borrowing the funds at 7 percent. Now we have 1,000 shares worth $80, 1,000 puts worth $13.46, and a loan of $56,080.

STOCK GOES FROM 125 TO 156.25   We have only a bond worth $37,375(1.07) = $39,991, which is a return of 7 percent for the period.

STOCK GOES FROM 125 TO 100   Again, we have only a bond worth $37,375(1.07) = $39,991, which is a 7 percent return for the period.

STOCK GOES FROM 80 TO 100   Now we have 1,000 shares worth $100, 1,000 puts that are worthless, and we owe $56,080(1.07) = $60,006 on our loan. Thus, our total value is 1,000($100) + 1,000($0.00) − $60,006 = $39,994. This is the same total as the two outcomes above, except for a small round-off error. Again, the return for the period is 7 percent.

STOCK GOES FROM 80 TO 64   Now we have 1,000 shares worth $64, 1,000 puts worth $36, and we owe $56,080(1.07) = $60,006 on our loan. Thus, our total value is 1,000($64) + 1,000($36) − $60,006 = $39,994, the same total and 7 percent return as above.

So we see that as long as the hedge is maintained properly, we earn the risk-free return over each period. If the put were mispriced, we would take the appropriate position and hedge it with the stock. For example, if the put were selling for less than the model price, we would consider it underpriced. We would then buy it and hedge by buying the proper number of shares of stock. If the put were overpriced, we would sell it, but to hedge, we would need to sell short the stock.

American Puts and Early Exercise

The two-period binomial model is an excellent opportunity to illustrate how options can be exercised early. Let us use the same two-period put with an exercise price of 100, but make it an American put. This means that at any point in the life of the option, we can choose to exercise it early if it is best to do so. That means at any point in the binomial tree when the put is in-the-money, we need to see if it is worth more to exercise it early.

For example, go back to the values calculated for the European put at time 1. Recall that they were

$$P_u = \frac{0(.6) + 0(.4)}{1.07} = 0.00, \text{ when the stock is at 125,}$$

$$P_d = \frac{0(.6) + 36(.4)}{1.07} = 13.46, \text{ when the stock is at 80.}$$

When the stock is at 125 the put is out-of-the-money, so we do not need to worry about exercising it. When the stock is at 80, however, it is in-the-money, and we have the right to exercise it. In fact, the put is in-the-money by $20 [Max(0,100 − 80)], which is far more than its unexercised value of $13.46. So we exercise it, which means that we replace the calculated value P_d of 13.46 with 20. Thus, we now have $P_u = 0$ and $P_d = 20$. Then the value at time 0 is

$$P = \frac{0(.6) + 20(.4)}{1.07} = 7.48.$$

We would also have to consider the possibility of exercising it immediately, but since it is at-the-money, there is no reason to exercise it today. Note that its value is considerably more than its value as a European put of 5.03.

The binomial model can easily accommodate the early exercise of an American put by simply replacing the computed value with the intrinsic value if the latter is greater.

Forming a hedge portfolio with American options follows the same procedure as forming a hedge portfolio for European options, except that we use the American option values to compute the portfolio values and hedge ratios.

Dividends, European Calls, American Calls, and Early Exercise

For call options on stocks without dividends, there will, of course, never be an early exercise. Let us now consider how early exercise will affect American calls in the binomial model. To do so we must add a dividend.

There are a number of ways to incorporate dividends into the model. The simplest is to express the dividend as a yield of δ percent. Thus, when the stock price moves into the dividend period, it immediately declines by δ percent as it goes ex-dividend. We then use the ex-dividend stock prices in the binomial formulas. If the intrinsic value of the call before it goes ex-dividend exceeds the value of the call given by the binomial formula, the call should be exercised. Then the intrinsic value replaces the formula value.

Consider the same two-period problem we worked earlier in the chapter. Because we want to see a case where the call is exercised early, let us assume a fairly high dividend yield—say, 10 percent—and, let the dividend be paid and the stock go ex-dividend at time 1. At time 1, if the stock goes to 125, it then pays a 12.50 dividend and falls to 112.50. If the stock goes down to 80, it pays a dividend of 8.00 and falls to 72. The following period, its movement is based from values of either 112.50 or 72 and will be either 140.625, 90, or 57.60. This process is shown in Figure 4.5. The corresponding call prices at expiration are

$$C_{u^2} = \text{Max}(0,140.625 − 100) = 40.625$$
$$C_{ud} = C_{du} = \text{Max}(0,90.00 − 100) = 0$$
$$C_{d^2} = \text{Max}(0, 57.60 − 100) = 0.$$

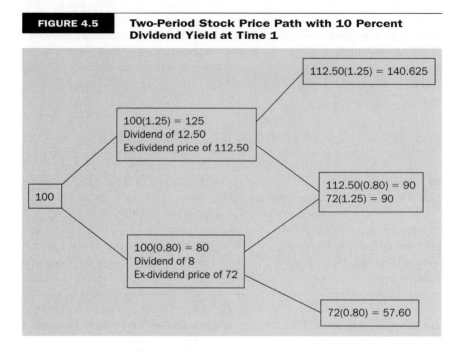

FIGURE 4.5 **Two-Period Stock Price Path with 10 Percent Dividend Yield at Time 1**

112.50(1.25) = 140.625

100(1.25) = 125
Dividend of 12.50
Ex-dividend price of 112.50

100

112.50(0.80) = 90
72(1.25) = 90

100(0.80) = 80
Dividend of 8
Ex-dividend price of 72

72(0.80) = 57.60

The European call prices after one period are

$$C_u = \frac{40.625(.6) + 0(.4)}{1.07} = 22.78$$

$$C_d = \frac{0(.6) + 0(.4)}{1.07} = 0.00.$$

Thus, the European call value at time 0 is

$$C = \frac{22.78(.6) + 0(.4)}{1.07}$$

$$= 12.77.$$

Note that this value is considerably less than its value without dividends of 17.69. Dividends will always reduce the value of a European option, because they represent a payout rather than a reinvestment of corporate cash flows for the purpose of generating growth in the stock price.

Now let the call be American. Let us move from time 0 to time 1 and let the stock move to 125. The firm is paying a dividend of 10 percent of 125 or 12.50 in just another instant. When that happens, the stock will fall to 112.50. Holding an American call, we have the right to exercise it before the stock goes ex-dividend, thereby paying 100 and receiving a stock worth 125. When the stock goes ex-dividend, its value drops to 112.50, but having acquired the stock before it goes ex-dividend, we are entitled to the dividend and have a net value of 25. Consequently, the option value at that point is 25. In other words, we simply choose to exercise the option before it goes ex-dividend and claim its intrinsic value of 25. We, consequently, replace the binomial formula value of 22.78, previously computed in the European option example, with 25. Thus, we now have $C_u = 25$. In the time 1 outcome where the stock falls to 80, we cannot justify early exercise as the call is out-of-the-money.

Stepping back to time 0, we find that the value of the American call is, therefore[4]

$$C = \frac{25(.6) + 0(.4)}{1.07} = 14.02.$$

As an alternative approach, suppose we simply have the firm pay a specific dollar dividend at time 1. Let us make it a dividend of 12. Now we run into a slight problem. As Figure 4.6 shows, at time 1 the stock goes ex-dividend to a value of either 113 or 68. If the stock is at 113 and goes down at time 2, its new price will be $113(0.80) = 90.40$. If the stock is at 68 and goes up at time 2, its new price will be $68(1.25) = 85$. Consequently, the middle state at time 2 will not be the same regardless of where the stock was at time 1. In the example illustrated here, this is not really a problem: The option value can still be computed in the normal manner. When we expand the model to include a large number of periods, however, this problem will greatly increase the computational requirements.

A binomial tree in which an up move followed by a down move puts you in the same location as a down move followed by an up move is referred to as a recombining tree. It represents the classic case of what is known as **path independence,** which means that regardless of where you are in the binomial tree, it does not matter which path you took to get there. A tree in which an up move followed by a down move does not put you in the same position as a down move followed by an up move is referred to as a non-recombining tree and is an example of **path dependence,** which means that the path taken does matter. American options with fixed dividends are a classic example of path dependence, and we shall see a few more in Chapter 15.

For a tree with n time periods, a recombining tree will have $n + 1$ final stock prices. There will be 2^n distinct paths taken to reach the final stock prices, but some of the paths will leave you in the same location; consequently, we would not have to work our way through each

---

[4]You may recall that the value of 14.02 was also the value of the one-period call. There is no connection between the one-period European option value and the two-period American option value other than that, in the latter case, we exercised the option at time 1, thereby effectively making it a one-period option.

FIGURE 4.6   **Two-Period Stock Price Path with Dividend of $12 at Time 1**

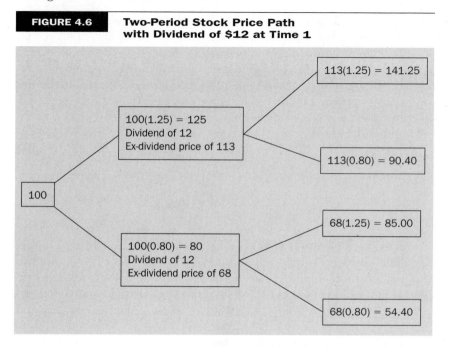

path to identify the final outcome. This greatly simplifies and reduces the computations in a tree with a large number of time periods. A non-recombining tree will have 2^n distinct paths and, therefore, 2^n final outcomes. If n is large, this number becomes astronomical quite quickly and can pose severe computational difficulties even for the fastest computers. Figure 4.7 illustrates a three-period recombining and non-recombining tree.

One special trick can greatly simplify the binomial computations for the case of an American option with dividends. Recall that in Chapter 3 in cases with dividends, we subtracted the present value of the dividends from the stock price and used this adjusted value in our formulas. We can do the same here. We are simply assuming that the dividends are fully predictable and that it is the stock price minus the present value of the dividends that follows the binomial process.

Figure 4.8 illustrates this approach. The current stock price is $100, but we adjust that value to $100 - 12/1.07 = 88.79$. Then the value 88.79 goes up or down by the factor 1.25 or 0.80. Thus, at time 0, the stock is observed to be 100, which consists of a present value of the dividend of $12/1.07 = 11.21$ and the remainder of the price, 88.79, which reflects the stock's growth potential. At time 1 if the stock goes up, the adjusted stock price is $88.79(1.25) = 110.99$. Before the stock goes ex-dividend, its actual

FIGURE 4.7 **Recombining and Non-Recombining Three-Period Binomial Trees**

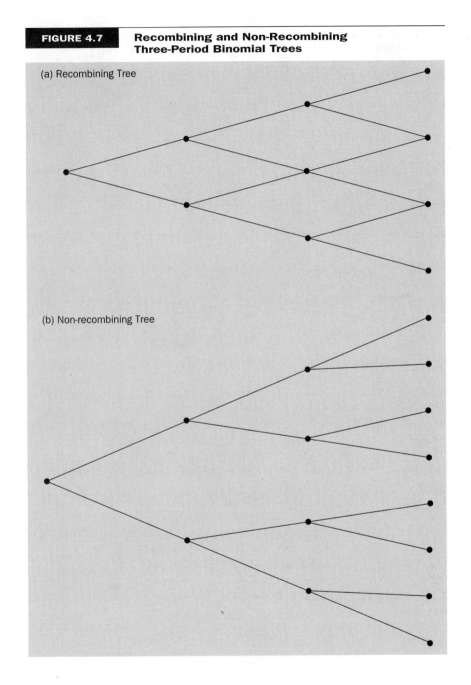

(a) Recombining Tree

(b) Non-recombining Tree

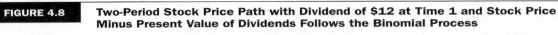

FIGURE 4.8   **Two-Period Stock Price Path with Dividend of \$12 at Time 1 and Stock Price Minus Present Value of Dividends Follows the Binomial Process**

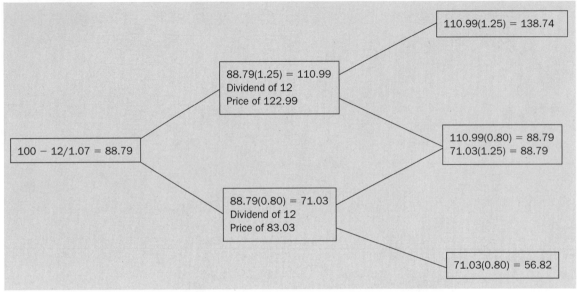

price is $110.99 + 12 = 122.99$. It then falls immediately to 110.99 as it goes ex-dividend. If at time 1, the stock went down, the adjusted price will be $88.79(0.80) = 71.03$. Before it goes ex-dividend, it will be worth 83.03. Then it goes ex-dividend and will fall to 71.03. We then see in the figure that at time 2, the middle point will be the same, with the stock at 88.79 regardless of which path was taken to get there.

Now we can easily calculate the call value.

$$C_{u^2} = \text{Max}(0,138.74 - 100) = 38.74,$$
$$C_{ud} = \text{Max}(0,88.79 - 100) = 0.00,$$
$$C_{d^2} = \text{Max}(0,56.82 - 100) = 0.00.$$

Now we step back to time 1. If the call is European, we calculate its values to be

$$C_u = \frac{38.74(.6) + 0(.4)}{1.07} = 21.72,$$
$$C_d = \frac{0(.6) + 0(.4)}{1.07} = 0.$$

If the call is American, however, at time 1 when the stock is at 122.99, we have the opportunity to exercise the call just before the stock goes ex-dividend. In that case we obtain a payoff of 22.99, resulting from acquisition of the stock for \$100, collection of the dividend of \$12, and the stock falling to a value of \$110.99. Since the payoff from exercising of 22.99 is greater than the value if not exercised, we use 22.99 for C_u. We then step back to time 1. The European option value would be

$$C = \frac{21.72(.6) + 0(.4)}{1.07} = 12.18.$$

The American option value would be

$$C = \frac{22.99(.6) + 0(.4)}{1.07} = 12.89.$$

The additional advantage of the American option in obtaining the dividend and avoiding the loss in value when the stock goes ex-dividend is worth a value of 0.71 today.

Extending the Binomial Model to n Periods

The binomial model is easily extended to any number of time periods. With n periods remaining until the option expires, the European call price is given by the formula:

$$C = \frac{\sum\limits_{j=0}^{n} \dfrac{n!}{j!(n - j)!} p^j (1 - p)^{n-j} \text{Max}[0, Su^j d^{n-j} - X]}{(1 + r)^n}$$

This seemingly difficult formula actually is not nearly as complex as it appears. It simply captures all of the possible stock price paths over the n periods until the option expires. Consider the example from the text in a three-period world where j will go from 0 to 3. First, we find the summation of the following terms.

For j = 0,

$$\frac{3!}{0!3!}(.6)^0 (.4)^3 \text{Max}[0, 100(1.25)^0 (.80)^3 - 100] = 0.$$

For j = 1,

$$\frac{3!}{1!2!}(.6)^1 (.4)^2 \text{Max}[0, 100(1.25)^1 (.80)^2 - 100] = 0.$$

For j = 2,

$$\frac{3!}{2!1!}(.6)^2 (.4)^1 \text{Max}[0, 100(1.25)^2 (.80)^1 - 100] = 10.80.$$

For j = 3,

$$\frac{3!}{3!0!}(.6)^3 (.4)^0 \text{Max}[0, 100(1.25)^3 (.80)^0 - 100] = 20.59.$$

Adding these and dividing by $(1.10)^3$ gives

$$\frac{0 + 0 + 10.80 + 20.59}{(1.07)^3} = 25.62.$$

Since we did not hold the time to expiration fixed, the value of the call is higher in the three-period world than in the two-period world. This reflects the effect of a longer time to expiration.

The n-period binomial formula works because the factorial term, $n!/j!(n - j)!$, counts the number of ways a stock price could end up at a certain level. For example, when $n = 3$, the stock price at the end of the third period could be either Sd^3, Sud^2, Su^2d, or Su^3. There is only one path the stock could have taken for it to end up at Sd^3: to go down three straight periods. There is only one path it could have taken for it to end up at Su^3: to go up three straight periods. For the stock price to end up at Sud^2, there are three possible routes: (1) up, down, down; (2) down, down, up; or (3) down, up, down. For the stock to end up at Su^2d, there are three paths: (1) up, down, up; (2) down, up, up; and (3) up, up, down. The factorial expression enumerates the routes that a stock can take to reach a certain level. The remaining terms in the formula then apply exactly as we have seen in the one- and two-period cases.

The three-period case is a good opportunity to observe one other aspect of the early exercise problem. Consider a three-period American put with an exercise price of 100. Figure 4.9 illustrates the tree. Below each stock price are two or more figures in parentheses. The first is the value of the European put expiring at time 3 with exercise price of 100, which we see is worth 7.26 today (check it for practice). The second figure in paren-

---

FIGURE 4.9   **Three-Period Binomial Stock Price Path**

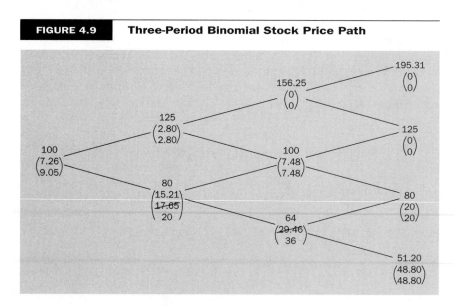

thesis is the American put value. Notice at time 2 when the stock price is 64, we show a value of 29.46 with a line drawn through it and replaced by 36. The value 29.46 is the value of the American put if not exercised at that point. It should, however, be exercised because it is $36 in the money. So we replace 29.46 with 36. Now we step back to time 2 and note what happens with the stock at 80. The European put value is 15.21, based on the next two possible values of 7.48 and 29.46. The American put value if not exercised is, however,

$$P_d = \frac{7.48(.6) + 36(.4)}{1.07} = 17.65.$$

It is $20 in the money, however, so we would exercise it and replace the value 17.65 with 20. The important point is that we can have early exercise at more than one location in the tree. Although it is optimal to exercise at time 3 if the stock is at 64, the stock would actually not get to 64 without having been at 80 at time 2 and been exercised early. Yet the only way to determine if we should exercise at 80 at time 2 is to see what would happen if we do not exercise at that time. Thus, we must evaluate the possibility of being at 64 at time 3, not having exercised at 80 at time 2. In all cases we should compare the American option value if not exercised at a given point with the intrinsic value and use the larger value for the value of the option at that point.

The Behavior of the Binomial Model for Large n and a Fixed Option Life

In the examples we have done so far, when we added a time period we simply extended the option's life. Naturally we will get a larger option value, except in those rare cases of deep-in-the-money European puts that we mentioned in Chapter 3. Suppose, however, that we keep the option's life the same and simply divide it into a larger number of increasingly smaller time periods. It turns out that when we do so, we need to make a few adjustments, but then we obtain an option value that increasingly reflects the realities of the world we live in.

For example, let us use an actual option, the June 125 America Online call. Recall that the stock price is 125.9375, the option has 35 days remaining, and the risk-free rate is 4.56 percent. The only information we have that could tell us something about the up and down factors is the volatility of the stock, a variable we briefly discussed in Chapter 3. Volatility is often measured by the statistical concept of standard deviation, which is more specifically the standard deviation of the return on the stock. This variable will become more important to us in the next chapter, but for now, let us just take a value and use it. In the case of our AOL stock, we shall use a volatility of .83, a number we shall see how to obtain in Chapter 5.

To price this option in a binomial framework with the correct volatility, we need to know what to set the risk-free rate to and what to use as the up and down parameters. The risk-free rate is simple. We adjust it in the following manner:

$$\text{risk-free rate in binomial model} = (1 + r)^{T/n}.$$

If the stock paid a dividend at a constant yield, it would be adjusted in an identical manner. There are several approaches to setting the up and down parameters. We shall initially use the following:

$$\text{binomial up parameter: } u = e^{\sigma\sqrt{T/n}}$$
$$\text{binomial down parameter: } d = 1/u,$$

where σ is the volatility. Let us do a one-period binomial model for the AOL June 125 call. Our parameters are:

$$r = (1.0456)^{0.0959/1} - 1 = .004285$$
$$u = e^{0.83\sqrt{.0959/1}} = 1.293087$$
$$d = 1/1.293087 = 0.773343.$$

Our stock prices at time 1 would be:

$$Su = 125.9375(1.293087) = 162.8481$$
$$Sd = 125.9375(0.773343) = 97.3929.$$

Thus, the option values would be

$$C_u = \text{Max}(0,162.8481 - 125) = 37.85$$
$$C_d = \text{Max}(0,97.3929 - 125) = 0.00.$$

The value of p would be $(1.004285 - 0.773343)/(1.293087 - 0.773343) = .444$ and $1 - p = .556$. The value of the call today would, therefore, be

$$C = \frac{37.85(.444) + 0.00(.556)}{1.004285} = 16.74.$$

The binomial model converges to a specific value of the option as the number of time periods increases.

The actual price of that option is 13.50, but, of course, we would not expect a one-period binomial model to accurately reflect reality. Notice in Table 4.2, however, what happens when we increase the number of time periods, each time adjusting the values of r, u, and d accordingly. We seem to be converging to the value of 13.56.

Using a binomial model to price an option is much like using a still camera to photograph something with fast action, such as a horse race. If we take a picture of the race at some point, we will not have a very good idea of what happened during the race. If we take several pictures, we begin to get a clearer view of how the race proceeded. If we take a very

TABLE 4.2	**Binomial Option Values for AOL June 125 Call When n Is Increased**

n	u	d	r	C
1	1.2931	0.7733	.004285	16.75
2	1.1993	0.8338	.002140	12.33
5	1.1218	0.8914	.000856	14.20
10	1.0847	0.9219	.000428	13.35
25	1.0528	0.9498	.000171	13.68
50	1.0370	0.9643	.000086	13.53
100	1.0260	0.9747	.000043	13.56
200	1.0183	0.9820	.000021	13.56

Note: $S = 125.9375$, $X = 100$, $r = 4.56\%$, $T = 0.0959$, $\sigma = .83$.

large number of pictures, each at very short time intervals—meaning essentially to make a movie—we obtain a near-perfect reproduction of what happened from start to finish. In the binomial model, the process of making n large is like making a movie. If we take a large enough number of pictures, meaning to make n large enough, we obtain a very accurate depiction of what happens to the stock over the option's life. Consequently, we can be confident that our estimated option value is a pretty accurate reflection of the true value of the option.

The value of the option when n approaches infinity has a very special name. It is the Black-Scholes value and is the subject of Chapter 5.

Alternative Specifications of the Binomial Model

In the preceding section we saw that the binomial model can approximate a real-life scenario if we let the number of periods be large and adjust the up and down factors and the risk-free rate to reflect the volatility of the stock and the interest accrued per period. The formulas used in that section are not, however, the only ones that can be used. Although the adjustment for the risk-free rate is the same, the up and down parameters can be adjusted as follows:

$$u = e^{(\ln(1+r)-\sigma^2/2)(T/n)+\sigma\sqrt{T/n}}$$
$$d = e^{(\ln(1+r)-\sigma^2/2)(T/n)-\sigma\sqrt{T/n}},$$

where $\ln(1 + r)$ is the continuously compounded interest rate, which we shall cover in more detail in Chapter 5.

Recall that we have been using $p = (1 + r - d)/(u - d)$. Now, however, the formula for p is

$$p = \frac{e^{\sigma^2(T/n)/2} - e^{-\sigma\sqrt{T/n}}}{e^{\sigma\sqrt{T/n}} - e^{-\sigma\sqrt{T/n}}}.$$

As it turns out, however, the above formula for p tends to be very close to .5 and will approach .5 as the number of time periods, n, increases. So for all intents and purposes, we can use .5 for p and the above formulas for u and d.

Let us make some comparisons between the two methods. Consider again the June 125 America Online call. Let us first price the option using a two-period binomial model. The risk-free rate will be

$$r = (1.0456)^{0.0959/2} - 1 = .0021.$$

Although we do not have a dividend in this problem, if there were a dividend, the rate would be adjusted in the same manner.

First, we develop the model with the formulas for u and d used earlier in the chapter. We have

$$u = e^{0.83\sqrt{0.0959/2}} = 1.1993$$
$$d = 1/1.1993 = 0.8338.$$

The value of p is $(1.0021 - 0.8338)/(1.1993 - 0.8338) = .4605$. Part a of Figure 4.10 shows the price of the option in the two-period binomial tree. The option value is shown in parentheses below the stock price. The option value today is 12.3173.

Now we develop the model with the formulas for u and d presented above in this section. We have

$$u = e^{(\ln(1.0456) - 0.83^2/2)(0.0959/2) + 0.83\sqrt{0.0959/2}} = 1.1822$$
$$d = e^{(\ln(1.0456) - 0.83^2/2)(0.0959/2) - 0.83\sqrt{0.0959/2}} = 0.8219.$$

The value of p is

$$p = \frac{e^{0.83^2(0.0959/2)/2} - e^{-0.83\sqrt{0.0959/2}}}{e^{0.83\sqrt{0.0959/2}} - e^{-0.83\sqrt{0.0959/2}}} = .500251.$$

We shall just use .5. Part b of Figure 4.10 illustrates this option's price in the two-period binomial tree. The price today is 12.6990. The difference in what we are doing here and what we previously did is that the previous formulas force the binomial model to replicate the behavior of the stock only in the limit, meaning when n is very large. These formulas force the binomial model to replicate the behavior of the stock regardless of the size of n. When we refer to replicating the behavior of the stock, we mean that the probability distribution of the stock will be of a particular form that we cover in the next chapter.

Obviously there are significant differences in the option price using the two methods. So which is best? The binomial model has two primary

FIGURE 4.10	Pricing the AOL June 125 Call in a Two-Period World

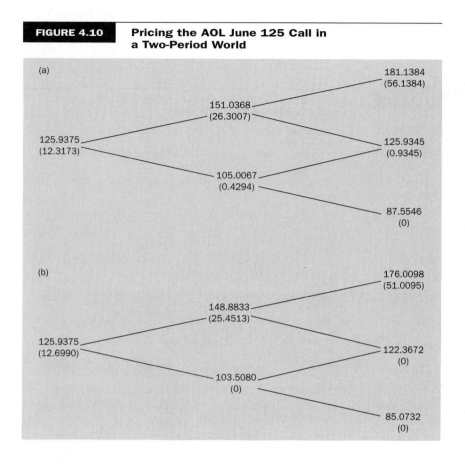

(a)

151.0368
(26.3007)

181.1384
(56.1384)

125.9375
(12.3173)

125.9345
(0.9345)

105.0067
(0.4294)

87.5546
(0)

(b)

148.8833
(25.4513)

176.0098
(51.0095)

125.9375
(12.6990)

122.3672
(0)

103.5080
(0)

85.0732
(0)

purposes: (1) to teach the underlying principles of option pricing with a minimum of mathematics, and (2) by letting the number of time periods be sufficiently large, to use in actually pricing options in real-world situations. In the case of a large number of time periods, these two methods will give nearly the same price. For example, with n = 200, we would find that the first method gives an option price of 13.56 while the second gives a price of 13.57. Note from Table 3.1 that the actual price of the option is 13.50. Provided the correct inputs are used, the binomial model, in whatever version one chooses, will do a pretty good job of pricing options. For some types of options, specifically standard European calls and puts, there is an even better method, however, called the Black-Scholes model, which is the subject of Chapter 5.

Obviously for a large number of time periods, a computer is necessary to perform the binomial option pricing calculations. This book provides Excel spreadsheets to do many of the computations. Software Demonstration 4.1 introduces you to the spreadsheet file bsbin2.xls, which computes binomial and Black-Scholes option prices. In an appendix in Chapter 5, we shall introduce the Windows program bsbwin2.1.exe, which also does binomial and Black-Scholes calculations.

SOFTWARE DEMONSTRATION 4.1   **Calculating the Binomial Price with the Excel Spreadsheet bsbin2.xls**

The Excel spreadsheet bsbin2.xls operates in Excel 97 under Windows 95 or 98. It calculates both the binomial and Black-Scholes option pricing models. The binomial model provides European and American call and put prices, as well as the delta, gamma, and theta, measures known as the option "Greeks." These concepts are covered in Chapter 5 along with the Black-Scholes model.

This spreadsheet is a read-only spreadsheet, meaning that it cannot be saved under the name bsbin2.xls, which preserves the original file. To use the spreadsheet, simply do the following:

1.   Make sure you are in Windows 95 or 98

2.   Run Excel 97

3.   Open the file bsbin2.xls

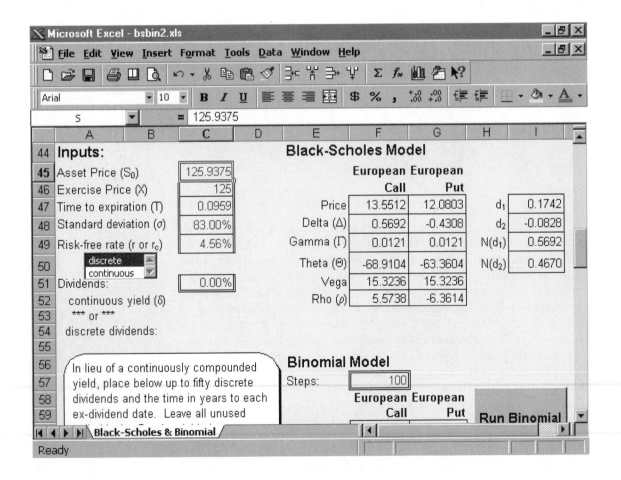

Now let us calculate an option price. Assume that you wish to find the binomial price of the option illustrated in the chapter, the America Online June 125 call. The AOL stock is at 125.9375, the exercise price is 125, the risk-free rate is 4.56 percent, the standard deviation is 0.83, and the time to expiration is 0.0959, based on 35 days to expiration. There are no dividends on the stock.

Two Excel screens are reproduced for your reference. Observe on the spreadsheet a section labeled **Inputs:** Each cell that will accept input has a double-line border and the values are in blue. Output cells have a single-line border. Enter the stock price of 125.9375 in the cell beside the words "Asset Price (S_0)" and enter the remaining inputs in the appropriate cells below. For greater accuracy, enter the time to expiration as 35/365. Leave the dividend yield and the discrete dividends blank or enter zeros. For the risk-free rate, select the choice "discrete" for now. We shall use a continuous risk-free rate in Chapter 5. The risk-free rate and volatility can be entered as either percentages or decimals. For example, you can enter either ".0456" or "4.56" for the risk-free rate.

Now note the section labeled **Binomial Model.** Enter the number of time steps. The program will handle up to 1,000. Since the binomial calculation can be time-consuming, the spreadsheet does not automatically calculate the binomial value. You must move your cursor over the button labeled **Run Binomial Option Pricing Model** and click. While the program is running, Excel's status bar will count down by showing the line "Iterating through binomial tree at times step # xxx" where "xxx" is the number of the time step the program is on. This gives you an idea of how much longer you will have to wait. Of course, the length of the wait depends on the speed of your computer. Try it with 100 time steps. Your answer for our example problem should correspond very closely to the appropriate value shown in the figure.

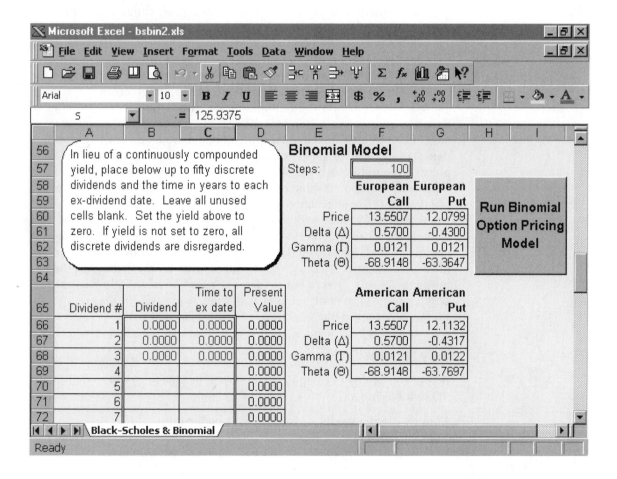

Summary

This chapter introduced the concept of an option pricing model, which is a mathematical formula or computational procedure that produces the theoretical fair value of the option. This process is called option pricing. The theoretical fair value is the price at which the option should be trading. The chapter focuses on the binomial model, which is a computational procedure for pricing the option.

We began by developing the model in a one-period world, which means that one period later the option expires. A period is defined as a specific length of time over which the underlying stock can make one of two moves—up to a specific price or down to a specific price—and there is a given interest rate. We showed that it is possible to combine a long position in the stock with a short position in a call option to produce a risk-free portfolio. Given that the return on a risk-free portfolio should be the risk-free rate, it is then possible to solve for the theoretical option price, given the other input parameters. If the option is not selling for its theoretical price, it is possible to capture an arbitrage profit at no risk.

We then extended the model to a two-period world, where we showed that the combination of long stock and short calls must be adjusted over each period to maintain the risk-free nature of the portfolio. Again, if the option is mispriced, it is possible to capture an arbitrage profit.

We examined how the binomial model will behave as the number of time periods is increased, and we showed that it seems to converge to a specific value. We also looked at how the binomial model can easily accommodate the problem of early exercise of American options. At a given time point, if the option is worth more exercised than not exercised, we simply replace the computed value of the option with the intrinsic value. We also saw that there are alternative specifications of the binomial model.

Although Chapter 4 focused only on the binomial model, we saw that as the number of time periods increased and the length of each time period decreased, we obtained a picture of a real world in which there are many possible prices over a given instant of time. This scenario, like the way in which a movie camera consolidates a collection of still photos to represent a more or less continuous view of time, leads us right into Chapter 5, where we cover the Black-Scholes model.

Key Terms

Before continuing to Chapter 5, you should be able to give brief definitions of the following terms:

- option pricing model
- binomial option pricing model
- hedge portfolio
- hedge ratio
- path independence
- path dependence

Further Reading

The binomial option pricing model was developed in the following articles:

Cox, J.C., S. A. Ross, and M. Rubinstein. "Option Pricing: A Simplified Approach." *Journal of Financial Economics* 7 (1979): 229–263.

Rendleman, R. J., Jr., and B. J. Bartter. "Two-State Option Pricing." *The Journal of Finance* 34 (1979): 1093–1110.

Further advances are presented in the following articles:

Breen, R. "The Accelerated Binomial Option Pricing Model." *Journal of Financial and Quantitative Analysis* 25 (1991): 153–164.

Brennan, M. J. "The Pricing of Contingent Claims in Discrete Time Models." *The Journal of Finance* 34 (1979): 53–68.

Stapleton, R. C., and M. J. Subrahmanyam. "The Valuation of Options When Asset Returns Are Generated by a Binomial Process." *The Journal of Finance* 39 (1984): 1525–1539.

Other good references are:

Hsia, C. C. "On Binomial Option Pricing." *The Journal of Financial Research* 6 (1983): 41–46.

McIver, J. "Tree Power." *Risk* 6 (December 1993): 58–64.

Nawalkha, S. K., and D. R. Chambers. "The Binomial Model and Risk Neutrality: Some Important Details." *The Financial Review* 30 (1995): 605–618.

Questions and Problems

1. Explain the similarities and differences between pricing an option by its boundary conditions and using an exact option pricing formula.

2. What is the principal benefit of a binomial option pricing model?

3. Describe the components of a hedge portfolio in the binomial option pricing model where the instrument being hedged is, first, a call and, second, a put.

4. If the binomial model produces an option price that is higher than the price at which the option is trading in the market, what strategy is suggested?

5. Discuss how a binomial model accommodates the possibility of early exercise of an option.

6. Explain the differences between a path independent and path dependent problem in the context of the binomial model.

7. How is the volatility of the underlying stock reflected in the binomial model?

8. Why are the up and down parameters adjusted when the number of periods is extended? Recall that in introducing the binomial model, we illustrated one- and two-period examples, but we did not adjust the parameters. What is the difference in these two examples, and why did we adjust the parameters in one case and not in the other?

9. Describe the three primary ways of incorporating dividends into the binomial model.

10. Consider a stock worth $25 that can go up or down by 15 percent per period. The risk-free rate is 10 percent. Use one binomial period.

   a. Determine the two possible stock prices for the next period.

   b. Determine the intrinsic values at expiration of a European call option with an exercise price of $25.

   c. Find the value of the option today.

   d. Construct a hedge by combining a position in stock with a position in the call. Show that the return on the hedge is the risk-free rate regardless of the outcome, assuming that the call sells for the value you obtained in part c.

   e. Determine the rate of return from a riskless hedge if the call is selling for $3.50 when the hedge is initiated.

11. Consider a two-period, two-state world. Let the current stock price be 45 and the risk-free rate be 5 percent. Each period the stock price can go either up by 10 percent or down by 10 percent. A call option expiring at the end of the second period has an exercise price of 40.

   a. Find the stock price sequence.

   b. Determine the possible prices of the call at expiration.

   c. Find the possible prices of the call at the end of the first period.

   d. What is the current price of the call?

   e. What is the initial hedge ratio?

   f. What are the two possible hedge ratios at the end of the first period?

   g. Construct an example showing that the hedge works. Make sure the example illustrates how the hedge portfolio earns the risk-free rate over both periods.

   h. What would an investor do if the call were overpriced? If it were underpriced?

12. Consider the following binomial option pricing problem involving an American call. This call has two periods to go before expiring. Its stock price is 30, and its exercise price is 25. The risk-free rate is .05. the value of u is 1.15, and the value of d is 0.90. The dividend yield is .06. Find the value of the call.

13. Find the value of an American put option using the binomial option pricing model. The parameters are S = 62, X = 70, r = .08, u = 1.10, and d = 0.95. There are no dividends. Use n = 2 periods.

14. Consider a European call with an exercise price of 50 on a stock priced at 60. The stock can go up by 15 percent or down by 20 percent each of two binomial periods. The risk-free rate is 10 percent. Determine the price today of the option. Then construct a risk-free hedge of long stock and short option. At each point in the binomial tree, show the composition and value of the hedge portfolio and demonstrate that the return is the same as the risk-free rate. On any revisions to the hedge portfolio, make the transactions (buying or selling) in stock and not options. You can borrow any additional funds required at the risk-free rate, and any excess funds should be invested at the risk-free rate.

15. Construct a table containing the up and down factors for a one-year option with a stock volatility of .55 and a risk-free rate of 7 percent for n = 1, 5, 10, 50, and 100 where n is the number of binomial periods. Let u and d be defined as

$$u = e^{\sigma\sqrt{T/n}}$$
$$d = 1/u.$$

16. Use the Excel spreadsheet bsbin2.xls and determine the value of a call option on a stock currently priced at 165.125, where the risk-free rate is 5.875 percent, the exercise price is 165, the volatility is 0.21, the option expires in 102 days, and there are no dividends on the stock. Let the number of binomial periods be 1, 5, 10, 25, and 50.

17. Use the binomial model and two time periods to determine the price of the AOL June 130 American put. Use the appropriate parameters from the information given in the chapter, which was originally given in Chapter 3, and a volatility of 0.83.

18. (Concept Problem) The binomial model can be used to price unusual features of options. Consider the following scenario. A stock priced at $75 can go up by 20 percent or down by 10 percent per period for three periods. The risk-free rate is 8 percent. A European call option expiring in three periods has an exercise price of $70. The parties to the option agree, however, that the maximum payout of this option is $40. Find the current value of the option. Then determine whether an American version of the option, also limited to a maximum payout of $40, would have any additional value over the European version. Compare your answers to the value of the option if there were no limitation on the payoff.

19. (Concept Problem) In the chapter, we obtained the binomial option pricing formula by hedging a short position in the call option with a

long position in stock. An alternative way to do this is to combine the stock and a risk-free bond to replicate the call option. Construct a one-period binomial option pricing model in which the stock and a risk-free bond are used to replicate a European call option. Assume one share of stock is used and determine the formula for the dollar amount to be invested in the risk-free bond. Then show that the option pricing formula is the same as the one developed in the text. Hint: Hold n_s shares of stock and have B dollars invested in the bond earning r percent so that the value in both outcomes matches precisely the value of the option. Then solve for n_s and B and substitute back into the formula for the value of the portfolio today to obtain the formula for C.

Option Pricing Models:
The Black-Scholes Model

[O]nce a model has been developed, we are able to improve the realism of its assumptions step by step. But unlike physics, which is a science with constant (if poorly understood) laws, the "laws" of economics and finance change constantly, even as we discover them. Sometimes they change because we have discovered them.

CHARLES SANFORD
"The Risk Management Revolution"
Proceedings of Symposia in Pure Mathematics, 1997, p. 325

Objectives

■ To present the Black-Scholes model and learn how to use it to price options

■ To understand the relationship of the model's inputs to the option price

■ To learn how to adjust the model to accommodate dividends and put options

■ To understand how volatility is estimated, both historically and as the implied volatility

■ To observe how an option position is delta hedged and how the risk can be reduced by gamma hedging

Origins of the Black-Scholes Formula

The roots of the Black-Scholes formula go back to the nineteenth century. In the 1820s, a Scottish scientist, Robert Brown, observed the motion of pollen suspended in water and noticed that the movements followed no distinct pattern, moving randomly, independent of any current in the water. This phenomenon came to be known as Brownian motion. Similar versions of Brownian motion were subsequently discovered by other scientists studying other natural phenomena. In 1900, a French doctoral student, Louis Bachelier, wrote his dissertation on the pricing of options in the Paris market and developed a model strikingly similar to the Black-Scholes model. Unfortunately, his dissertation advisor was disappointed because Bachelier's work was oriented toward such a practical issue as pricing a financial instrument. Although Bachelier received his degree, the less than enthusiastic support of his advisor damaged his career, and nothing further was heard from him.

In the early twentieth century, Albert Einstein, working on the foundations of his theories of relativity, used the principles of Brownian motion to explain movements of molecules. This work led to several research papers that earned Einstein the Nobel Prize and world renown. By that time, a fairly well developed branch of mathematics, often attributed to American mathematician Norbert Wiener, proved useful for explaining the movements of random particles. Other contributions to the mathematics were made by Japanese mathematician Kiyoshi Itô. In 1951, Itô developed an extremely important result called Itô's Lemma that 20 years later made it possible to find an option's price. Keep in mind, however, that these people were working on complex problems in physics and mathematics, not finance.

The mathematics that was used to model random movements had now evolved into its own subdiscipline, which came to be known as stochastic calculus. While ordinary calculus defined the rates of change of known functions, stochastic calculus defined the rates of change of functions in which one or more terms were random but behaved according to well-defined rules of probability.

In the late 1960s, Fischer Black finished his doctorate in mathematics at Harvard. Passing up a career as a mathematician, he went to work for Arthur Little, a management consulting firm in Boston. Black met a young MIT finance professor named Myron Scholes, and the two began an interchange of ideas on how financial markets worked. Soon Black joined the MIT finance faculty, where he made many contributions to our understanding of how assets other than options are priced. Black and Scholes then began studying options, which at that time were traded only on the over-the-counter market. They first reviewed the attempts of previous researchers to find the elusive option pricing formula.

Black and Scholes took two approaches to finding the price. One approach assumed that all assets were priced according to the Capital Asset Pricing Theory, a well-accepted model in finance. The other approach used the stochastic calculus. They obtained an equation using the first approach, but the second method left them with a differential equation they were unable to solve. This more mathematical approach was considered more important, so they continued to work on the problem, looking for a solution. Black eventually found that the differential equation could be transformed into the same one that described the movement of heat as it travels across an object. There was already a known solution, and Black and Scholes simply looked it up, applied it to their problem, and obtained the correct formula, which matched the formula they had obtained using the first method. Their paper reporting their findings was rejected by two academic journals before eventually being published in the *Journal of Political Economy,* which reconsidered an earlier decision to reject the paper.

At the same time, another young financial economist at MIT, Robert Merton, was also working on option pricing. Merton discovered many of the arbitrage rules that we covered in Chapter 3. In addition, Merton more or less simultaneously derived the formula. Merton's modesty, however, compelled him to ask a journal editor that his paper not be published

The knowledge required to develop the Black-Scholes model came from mathematics and physics.

before that of Black and Scholes. As it turned out, both papers were published, with Merton's paper appearing in the *Bell Journal of Economics and Management Science* at about the same time. Merton, however, did not initially receive as much credit as Black and Scholes, whose names became permanently associated with the model.

Fischer Black left academia in 1983 and went to work for the Wall Street firm of Goldman Sachs. Unfortunately, he died in 1995 at the age of 57. Scholes and Merton have remained in academia but have been extensively involved in real world derivatives applications.

In 1997 the Nobel Committee awarded the Nobel Prize for Economic Science to Myron Scholes and Robert Merton, while recognizing Black's contributions. You can read more about this important event at the Web site http://www.nobel.se/announcement-97/economy97.html.

The model has been one of the most significant developments in the history of the pricing of financial instruments. It has generated considerable research attempting to test the model and improve on it. A new industry of derivative products based on the Black-Scholes model has developed. Even if one does not agree with everything the model says, knowing something about it is important for surviving in the options markets.

The Black-Scholes Model as the Limit of the Binomial Model

In Chapter 4 we developed the binomial model, which served two primary purposes. It enabled us to see the basic elements underlying the principles of pricing an option without resorting to advanced mathematics. We saw that an option is priced by combining it with the underlying asset in such a manner that the risk is eliminated, and, as we move through time, the combination of stock and options must be adjusted. Since the return on a riskless portfolio is the risk-free rate, the value of that portfolio can be easily obtained by discounting its value at the option expiration by the risk-free rate. We saw that there is but a single value of the option that will result in the combined option–stock portfolio earning the risk-free rate. If the option is selling for any other price, an arbitrage profit is possible by selling an overpriced option and buying the stock or buying an underpriced option and selling short the stock. If the proper ratio of options to stock is maintained, the arbitrageur either has no risk and earns more than the risk-free rate or borrows at no risk and pays less than the risk-free rate. Another use of the binomial model is in pricing American options. The model can easily capture the value of exercising early.

In the last chapter we worked through an example in which the AOL June 125 call option was priced by using the binomial model and an increasing number of time steps. We saw that its price was 13.56 with either

FIGURE 5.1	Binomial Option Prices for Different n
	AOL June 125 call; $S_0 = 125.9375$, $r = .0456$, $T = .0959$, $\sigma = .83$

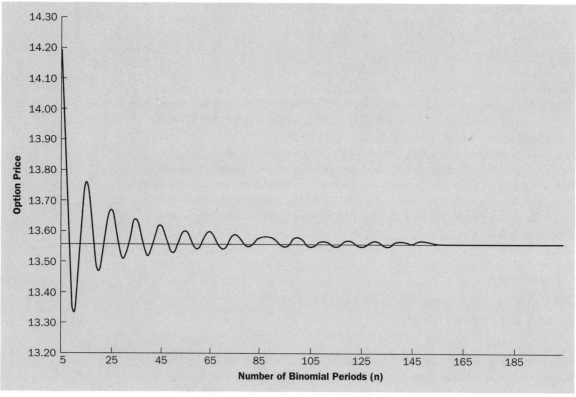

100 or 200 time steps. Figure 5.1 shows the behavior of the binomial option price in this problem as the number of time steps is increased in increments of 5, starting at n = 5 and ending at n = 200. We see that the option price bounces around and begins to stabilize at about 100 time steps. This behavior is what mathematicians call convergence. The binomial option pricing model converges to a specific value in the limit. It turns out that this value is the Black-Scholes price.

The binomial model is one of two types of models called **discrete time** models. In such models the life of the option is divided into a specific number of finite units of time. For example, if an option has a life of 100 days and we use n = 100 binomial time steps, each time step represents one day. As time elapses, the stock price jumps from one level to either of the next two levels. The real world, however, is characterized by the continuous passage of time and the fact that the stock price generally moves only in very small increments. In fact we might even characterize a stock's movements as being either up the smallest possible increment, called an uptick, or

The binomial model converges to the Black-Scholes Model as the number of time periods increases.

down the smallest possible decrement, called a downtick. Such properties are captured much better with **continuous time** models. Although in a later section we shall see how discrete and continuous time come together, let us now proceed to identify and understand the characteristics of a continuous time model. It is this continuous time framework that the Black-Scholes model uses to price options.

The Assumptions of the Model

All models are based on a specific set of assumptions. In the binomial model we assumed that the up and down factors were known and constant across time and that the risk-free rate was constant. More importantly, we made the critical assumption that the stock's movements can be characterized by the simplicity of the binomial model. We also implicitly made assumptions like no transaction costs and taxes. Let us now look at the assumptions of the Black-Scholes model.

Stock Prices Behave Randomly and Evolve According to a Lognormal Distribution

The notion that stock prices are random is central to much of the body of knowledge of pricing assets and derivatives. Are stock prices really random, however? Observe Figure 5.2. We see two panels, each purporting to be the daily closing price of America Online stock for a period of one year. One panel is the actual sequence of stock prices. The other is a set of randomly generated stock prices that have statistical properties similar to those that AOL had during that period. Can you identify which one is random?[1]

Many professional money managers claim to have the ability to predict stock prices. They observe a graph, such as Figure 5.2, and claim that such a series is at least partially predictable. They see the upward trend and believe that it can be exploited to earn large gains. Consider, however, Figure 5.3, showing the daily returns, which are simply the daily percentage price changes, on AOL stock over that same period. It is the return series that determines how an investor will perform. Can anyone predict a series like this? Not likely. Although there may be very small elements of predictability, particularly over very short time intervals, studies show that stock returns are largely unpredictable.

We also noted that stock returns are lognormally distributed. What do we mean by this? First, remember the normal, or bell-shaped, distribution. Are stock returns normally distributed? A look at the data would reveal that

---

[1]Part a of Figure 5.2 is the imposter. Part b is the actual AOL stock price. If you got it right, you probably just made a lucky guess.

| FIGURE 5.2a | **Real and Simulated Stock Prices of America Online** |

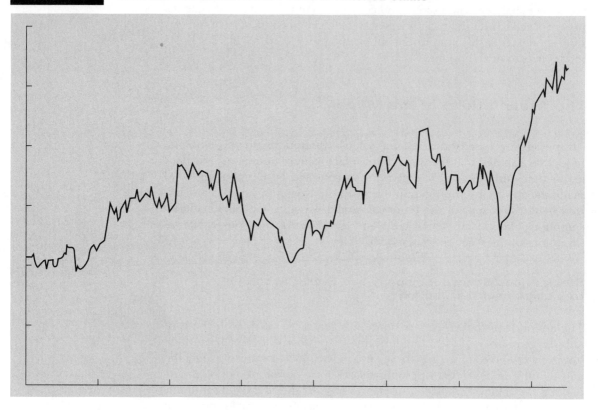

this is not the case. The return on a stock, however, can be expressed in a slightly different form known as continuous compounding. Suppose we have a $100 stock. One year later that stock is at $120. We would say that its return is 20 percent. This is what we call the simple or discrete return. It compounds only once, at the end of the year. We can obtain the future value, $120, from the present value, $100, by the simple relation $120 = $100(1.20), which has no compounding. To express this return in continuous compounding, we take the natural logarithm of one plus the return.

Recall that the logarithm of a number is the power to which a base must be raised in order to equal that number. Typical bases for logarithms are 10, the base of common logarithms, and e, which is approximately 2.718 and is the base of natural logarithms. In financial models the base is nearly always e.

The continuously compounded return, also called the log return, in our example is $\log(1.20) = 0.1812$ or 18.12 percent. The relationship between the end of year price and the beginning of year price is $120 = $100e^{.1812}$. Obviously we cannot change the prices; they were, after

FIGURE 5.2b

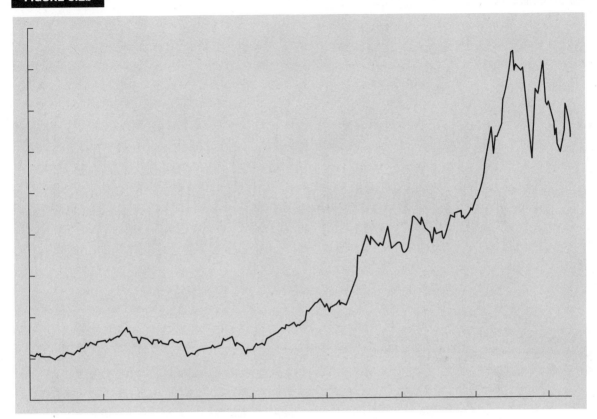

all, determined in a competitive market. But we can express the return in the form of log returns. It turns out that log returns tend to have properties that make them slightly closer to a normal distribution. Figure 5.4 shows a histogram of the log returns on AOL over the period indicated. Although we do not obtain a perfect representation of the normal distribution, we are probably not too far from it.

If the log of a variable is normally distributed, then that variable is said to be lognormally distributed. The distribution of the returns themselves has positive skewness, meaning that it has too many observations on the right side to be symmetric, as required by the normal distribution. The assumption of a lognormal distribution is quite appealing. It is fairly consistent with reality and, more importantly, does not permit stock prices to be negative. Moreover, it lends itself nicely to the high-level mathematics that were required to develop the Black-Scholes model.

| FIGURE 5.3 | Daily Returns on America Online |

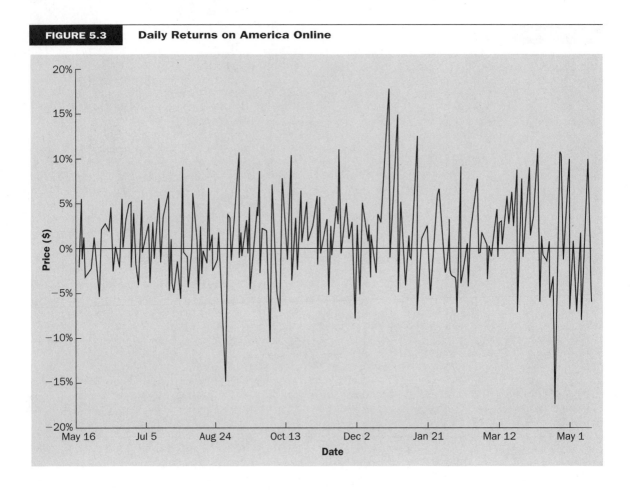

The Risk-Free Rate and Volatility of the Log Return on the Stock Are Constant throughout the Option's Life

The assumption that the risk-free rate is constant is tantamount to assuming that interest rates do not change. We know that is certainly not the case, and later in this book we shall examine risk management problems that arise in a world of changing interest rates. For now, however, it is mostly a convenience to ignore interest rate uncertainty. As it turns out, we shall see later that interest rates do not have much effect on the prices of options on stocks and some other underlying assets, so this assumption is relatively harmless at this point and keeps the model as simple as possible.

The assumption that volatility is constant is an important one. It turns out that this assumption is nearly always violated in the real world. In fact it is virtually inconceivable that any risky asset will have the same level of volatility over a period of time such as a year. Later in this chapter we learn

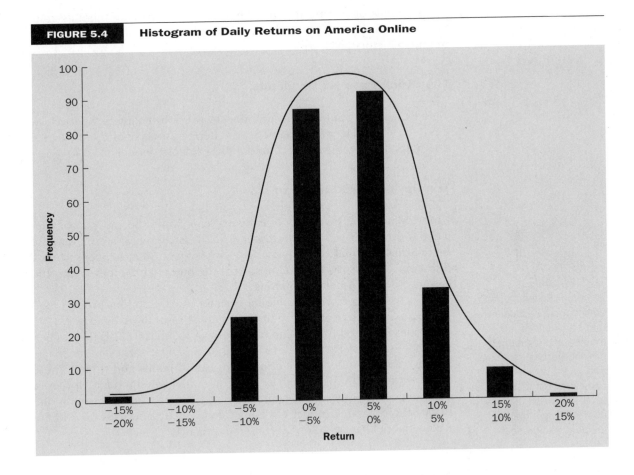

FIGURE 5.4   Histogram of Daily Returns on America Online

how volatility is estimated, but for now let us just note that estimates of the volatility of AOL over this one-year period were as low as 37 percent and as high as 150 percent.

Since we fail to meet the assumption of constant volatility, should we throw out the Black-Scholes model in favor of one that assumes that the volatility can change? We could do that, but models with changing volatility are much more complicated. Also it is not clear that such models are any better. Although changing volatility is a problem, we shall see that there are better ways to deal with it than to adopt a more complex model. Thus, we shall go ahead and assume that we meet this requirement.

There Are No Taxes or Transaction Costs

Option trading decisions are certainly affected by taxes and transaction costs, but these complexities will tend to cloud our understanding of the fundamentals of pricing options. There are ways to relax these assumptions, but this is an advanced subject and not appropriate or necessary at this introductory level.

The Stock Pays No Dividends

We have already made this assumption in previous chapters, and we saw how it can be relaxed. The same is true here, and we shall eventually see how to incorporate dividends into the Black-Scholes model.

The Options Are European

Unfortunately, the possibility of early exercise cannot be easily accommodated within the Black-Scholes framework. We shall see, however, that the **Black-Scholes model** can help us better understand what happens when a call is exercised early. For the most part, the binomial model remains the best way to price American options.

It is tempting to reject a model because its assumptions are not met. Acceptance or rejection of a model must come from three criteria: (1) Do the results obtained from the model conform to reality? (2) Is there a better model? and (3) Is the model widely used in practice? Though the Black-Scholes model results do not always conform to reality and though there are other, more complex models, it is a very widely used model. Moreover, other models nearly always come from the same basic structure as the Black-Scholes model. In fact it is fairly safe to say that perhaps no other financial model has been so widely used in practice.

The Black-Scholes option pricing model assumes that stock prices are random and lognormally distributed, that the risk-free rate and volatility are constant, that there are no taxes, transaction costs, or dividends, and that the options are European.

The Black-Scholes call option pricing formula gives the call price in terms of the stock price, exercise price, risk-free rate, time to expiration, and variance of the stock return.

A Nobel Formula

The Black-Scholes formula is:

$$C = S_0 N(d_1) - Xe^{-r_c T} N(d_2),$$

where

$$d_1 = \frac{\ln(S_o/X) + (r_c + \sigma^2/2)T}{\sigma\sqrt{T}}$$

$$d_2 = d_1 - \sigma\sqrt{T}$$

$N(d_1), N(d_2)$ = cumulative normal probabilities

σ = annualized volatility (standard deviation) of the continuously compounded (log) return on the stock

r_c = continuously compounded risk-free rate

All other variables are the same ones previously used.

FIGURE 5.5   **The Normal Probability Distribution**

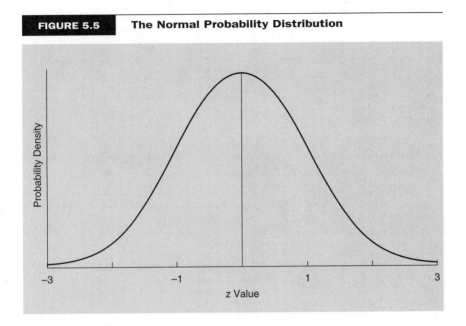

A Digression on Using the Normal Distribution

Since computation of the Black-Scholes model requires the normal probability distribution, it will probably be helpful to review this concept. Figure 5.5 illustrates the normal, or bell-shaped, curve. Recall that the curve is symmetric and everything we need to know about it is contained in the expected value, or mean, and the variance. Approximately 68 percent of the observations in a sample drawn from a normal distribution will occur within one standard deviation of the expected value. About 95 percent of the observations will lie within two standard deviations and about 99 percent within three standard deviations.

A standard normal random variable is called a **z statistic.** One can take any normally distributed random variable, convert it to a standard normal or z statistic, and use a table to determine the probability that an observed value of the random variable will be less than or equal to the value of interest.

Table 5.1 gives the cumulative probabilities of the standard normal distribution. Suppose we want to know the probability of observing a value of z less than or equal to 1.57. We go to the table and look down the first column for 1.5, then move over to the right under the column labeled 0.07; that is, the 1.5 and 0.07 add up to the z value, 1.57. The entry in the 1.5 row/0.07 column is .9418, the probability in a normal distribution of observing a value of z less than or equal to 1.57.

Suppose the value of z is less than zero—say, −1.12. We then look for the appropriate value for a positive 1.12. In the 1.1 row/0.02 column is the

TABLE 5.1		Standard Normal Probabilities								
z	0.00	0.01	0.02	0.03	0.04	0.05	0.06	0.07	0.08	0.09
0.0	.5000	.5040	.5080	.5120	.5160	.5199	.5239	.5279	.5319	.5359
0.1	.5398	.5438	.5478	.5517	.5557	.5596	.5636	.5675	.5714	.5753
0.2	.5793	.5832	.5871	.5910	.5948	.5987	.6026	.6064	.6103	.6141
0.3	.6179	.6217	.6255	.6293	.6331	.6368	.6406	.6443	.6480	.6517
0.4	.6554	.6591	.6628	.6664	.6700	.6736	.6772	.6808	.6844	.6879
0.5	.6915	.6950	.6985	.7019	.7054	.7088	.7123	.7157	.7190	.7224
0.6	.7257	.7291	.7324	.7357	.7389	.7422	.7454	.7486	.7517	.7549
0.7	.7580	.7611	.7642	.7673	.7704	.7734	.7764	.7794	.7823	.7852
0.8	.7881	.7910	.7939	.7967	.7995	.8023	.0851	.8078	.8106	.8133
0.9	.8159	.8186	.8212	.8238	.8264	.8289	.8315	.8340	.8365	.8389
1.0	.8413	.8438	.8461	.8485	.8508	.8531	.8554	.8577	.8599	.8621
1.1	.8643	.8665	.8686	.8708	.8729	.8749	.8770	.8790	.8810	.8830
1.2	.8849	.8860	.8888	.8907	.8925	.8943	.8962	.8980	.8997	.9015
1.3	.9032	.9049	.9066	.9082	.9099	.9115	.9131	.9147	.9162	.9177
1.4	.9192	.9207	.9222	.9236	.9251	.9265	.9279	.9292	.9306	.9319
1.5	.9332	.9345	.9357	.9370	.9382	.9394	.9406	.9418	.9429	.9441
1.6	.9452	.9463	.9474	.9484	.9495	.9505	.9515	.9525	.9535	.9545
1.7	.9554	.9564	.9573	.9582	.9591	.9599	.9608	.9616	.9625	.9633
1.8	.9641	.9649	.9656	.9664	.9671	.9678	.9686	.9693	.9699	.9706
1.9	.9713	.9719	.9726	.9732	.9738	.9744	.9750	.9756	.9761	.9767
2.0	.9772	.9778	.9783	.9788	.9793	.9798	.9803	.9808	.9812	.9817
2.1	.9821	.9826	.9830	.9834	.9838	.9842	.9846	.9850	.9854	.9857
2.2	.9861	.9864	.9868	.9871	.9875	.9878	.9881	.9884	.9887	.9890
2.3	.9893	.9896	.9898	.9901	.9904	.9906	.9909	.9911	.9913	.9916
2.4	.9918	.9920	.9922	.9925	.9927	.9929	.9931	.9932	.9934	.9936
2.5	.9938	.9940	.9941	.9943	.9945	.9946	.9948	.9949	.9951	.9952
2.6	.9953	.9955	.9956	.9957	.9959	.9960	.9961	.9962	.9963	.9964
2.7	.9965	.9966	.9967	.9968	.9969	.9970	.9971	.9972	.9973	.9974
2.8	.9974	.9975	.9976	.9977	.9977	.9978	.9979	.9979	.9980	.9981
2.9	.9981	.9982	.9982	.9983	.9984	.9984	.9985	.9985	.9986	.9986
3.0	.9987	.9987	.9987	.9988	.9988	.9989	.9989	.9989	.9990	.9990

value .8686. Then we subtract this number from 1. The answer is .1314. Because the table is symmetric, it is not necessary to show negative values. The probability of observing a value less than or equal to −1.12 is the same as that of observing a value greater than or equal to 1.12. The probability of observing a value greater than or equal to 1.12 is 1 minus the probability of observing a value less than or equal to 1.12. Note that we overlapped with the probability of observing a value exactly equal to 1.12. The probability of observing any single value is zero. This is so because we can observe an infinite number of possible values.

Instead of using tables, the normal probability can be accurately approximated with a polynomial equation. There are several formulas that give good approximations for the normal probability. In addition, the mathematical function = normsdist( ) in Excel is easy to use. In many applications in this book, we shall use values computed using Excel. Keep in mind, however, that Black-Scholes option values are highly sensitive to the normal probability calculation and can be off by several cents depending on which method is used.

A Numerical Example

Let us use the Black-Scholes model to price the America Online June 125 call. Recall that the inputs are a stock price of $125.9375, an exercise price of $125, and a time to expiration of .0959. We gave the risk-free rate of 4.56 percent as the Treasury bill yield that corresponds to the option's expiration. In the Black-Scholes model, however, the risk-free rate must be expressed as a continuously compounded yield. The continuously compounded equivalent of 4.56 percent is $\ln(1.0456) = 4.46$. Later in this chapter, we shall take a closer look at the basis for this transformation and at how the volatility can be determined. For now we will continue to use .83 as the standard deviation, which we used in Chapter 4.

The computation of the Black-Scholes price is a five-step process that is presented in Table 5.2. You first calculate the values of d_1 and d_2. Then you look up $N(d_1)$ and $N(d_2)$ in the normal probability table. Then you plug the values into the formula for C.

Here the theoretical fair value for the June 125 call is $13.21. The call's actual market price is $13.50. This suggests that the call is overpriced. Assuming no transaction costs, an investor should sell the call. The number of calls to sell to form a riskless hedge portfolio that will outperform the risk-free rate is discussed in a later section.

Unfortunately, the Black-Scholes model is especially sensitive to round-off error, most of which will occur in the normal probability figures. For example, consider the value of d_1 of 0.1742 and d_2 of -0.0828. To look up the d_1 and d_2 in the normal probability table, we were forced to round to two decimal places and we obtained $N(0.17) = .5675$ and $N(-0.08) = .4681$.

TABLE 5.2   **Calculating the Black-Scholes Price**

$S_o = 125.9375$ $X = 125$ $r_c = .0446$ $\sigma = 0.83$ $T = .0959$

1. Compute d_1

$$d_1 = \frac{\ln(125.9375/125) + (.0446 + (0.83)^2/2)0.0959}{0.83\sqrt{.0959}} = 0.1742$$

2. Compute d_2

$$d_2 = 0.1742 - 0.83\sqrt{0.0959} = -0.0828$$

3. Look up $N(d_1)$

$$N(0.17) = .5675$$

4. Look up $N(d_2)$

$$N(-0.08) = 1 - N(0.08) = 1 - .5319 = .4681$$

5. Plug into formula for C

$$C = 125.9375(.5675) - 125e^{-.0446(0.0959)}(.4681) = 13.21.$$

Suppose we use Excel's =normsdist() function. We simply go to a clean spreadsheet and enter the formulas, =normsdist(0.1742) and =normsdist(−0.0828). We obtain the following values:

$$N(0.1742) = .5691$$
$$N(-0.0828) = .4670,$$

and the option price would then be

$$C = 125.9375(.5691) - 125e^{-.0446(.0959)} (.4670) = 13.55,$$

which is substantially higher and quite close to the market price of $13.50. If anything, the option is now viewed as underpriced in the market. Errors of this sort are common in Black-Scholes computations. See Chance & Fredericks (1998) for further evidence on this point.

Although manual calculations are sometimes necessary, we should ultimately calculate option prices using a computer to obtain a more accurate measure for the normal probability. The accompanying Excel spreadsheet bsbin2.xls calculates the Black-Scholes price, as well as the binomial price. Software Demonstration 5.1 illustrates how to use bsbin2.xls to obtain the Black-Scholes price.

SOFTWARE DEMONSTRATION 5.1	**Calculating the Black-Scholes Price with the Excel Spreadsheet bsbin2.xls**

The Excel spreadsheet bsbin2.xls operates in Excel 97 under Windows 95 or 98. It calculates both the binomial and Black-Scholes option pricing models, the former of which is covered in Chapter 4. The Black-Scholes model provides European call and put prices, as well as the **delta, gamma, theta, vega,** and **rho,** which we know as the option "Greeks." It also provides values for d_1, d_2, $N(d_1)$, and $N(d_2)$.

This spreadsheet is a read-only spreadsheet, meaning that it cannot be saved under the name bsbin2.xls, which preserves the original file. To use the spreadsheet, simply do the following:

1. Make sure you are in Windows 95 or 98.
2. Run Excel 97.
3. Open the file bsbin2.xls.

Now let us calculate an option price. Assume that you wish to find the Black-Scholes price of the option illustrated in the chapter, the America Online June 125 call. The AOL stock is at 125.9375, the exercise price is 125, the continuously compounded risk-free rate is 4.46 percent, the standard deviation is .83, and the time to expiration is .0959, based on 35 days to expiration. There are no dividends on the stock.

Observe on the figure a section labeled **Inputs:.** Each cell that will accept input has a double-line border and the values are in blue. Output cells have a single-line border. Enter the stock price of 125.9375 in the cell beside the words "Asset Price (S_0)" and enter the remaining inputs in the appropriate cells below. For greater accuracy enter the time to expiration as 35/365. Leave the dividend yield and the discrete dividends blank or enter zeros. For the risk-free rate, select the choice "continuous". The risk-free rate and volatility can be entered as either percentages or decimals. For example, you can enter either ".0446" or "4.46" for the risk-free rate.

Observe your answers in the section labeled **Black-Scholes Model.** For those who prefer to calculate option prices outside of a spreadsheet, the Windows program bsbwin2.1.exe is provided and explained in Appendix 5B.

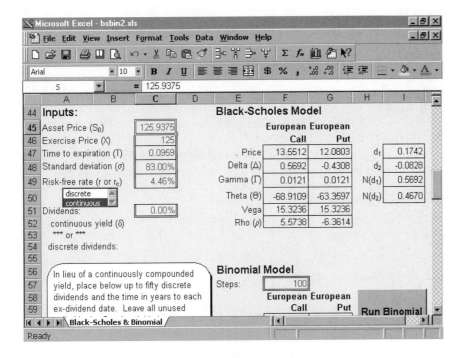

Characteristics of the Black-Scholes Formula

INTERPRETATION OF THE FORMULA   We see that the Black-Scholes formula has two main terms on the right-hand side. These terms have their own interpretation. In Chapter 4 we noted that pricing options is conducted as if investors are risk neutral. A risk neutral investor prices an asset by finding its expected future value and discounting it at the risk-free rate. For example, suppose you had the opportunity to participate in a coin toss in which you receive $10 if it lands on heads and $5 if it lands on tails. How much would you pay for it? A risk neutral investor would pay .5($10) − .5($5) = $7.50. Nearly all investors, however, are not risk neutral, but, rather, risk averse. They would recognize that half of the time, they would lose $2.50 and half of the time, they would make $2.50. A loss of $2.50 will hurt more than is offset by a profit of $2.50. Thus, a risk averse investor would pay less than $7.50, say, $6.75. The difference of $0.75 is the risk premium.

Risk averse investors determine the prices of the primary assets, stocks and bonds, in the financial markets. They do not determine the prices of derivatives. Rather, the forces of arbitrage determine the prices of derivatives. Given the price of the stock, the price of an option on the stock is determined by combining the stock and option in a risk-free portfolio. The option price is then obtained as a function of the stock price and other variables. Consequently, we can price an option as if investors were risk neutral—that is, by finding the expected future payoff of the option and discounting it at the risk-free rate.

When we did this in the binomial model we needed the probabilities p, which was $(1 + r - d)/(u - d)$, and $1 - p$. These are called **risk neutral probabilities.** We saw that they are not the actual probabilities of the up and down moves. They are what the probabilities would be if investors actually were risk neutral. In the Black-Scholes model, those probabilities are $N(d_1)$ and $N(d_2)$.

Thus, to price this option we first assume that investors are risk neutral. Then we find the expected payoff and discount it at the risk-free rate. The expected payoff is the expected value of $Max(0, S_T - X)$, or, in other words, the expected value of:

$$\begin{matrix} 0 & \text{if} & S_T \leq X \\ S_T - X & \text{if} & S_T > X. \end{matrix}$$

To ignore the outcomes where $S_T \leq X$, we must calculate the expected value of $S_T - X$, given that S_T is greater than X.

Let us multiply the first term on the right-hand side of the Black-Scholes formula by e^{r_cT},

$$S_0 N(d_1) e^{r_cT}.$$

This entire expression is the expected value of the stock price at expiration, given that the stock price exceeds the exercise price times the probability that the stock price exceeds the exercise price at expiration; however, $N(d_1)$ is not that probability. It is just a component of the entire expression. After multiplying by e^{r_cT}, the second term on the right-hand side of the Black-Scholes formula,

$$-XN(d_2),$$

is the expected value of the payment of the exercise price at expiration. Specifically, $N(d_2)$ is the probability for risk neutral investors that X will be paid at expiration. Thus, $-XN(d_2)$ is the expected payout of the exercise price at expiration. Discounting these expressions at the continuously compounded risk-free rate—that is, multiplying by e^{-r_cT}—gives

$$(S_0 N(d_1) e^{r_cT} - XN(d_2)) e^{-r_cT} = S_0 N(d_1) - Xe^{-r_cT}N(d_2),$$

which is the Black-Scholes formula.

THE BLACK-SCHOLES FORMULA AND THE LOWER BOUND OF A EUROPEAN CALL   Recall from Chapter 3 that we showed that the lower bound of a European call is

$$Max(0, S_0 - Xe^{-r_cT}).$$

For the Black-Scholes model to conform to this bound, it must always be no lower than this value. When S_0 is very high, d_1 and d_2 approach $+\infty$ which drives $N(d_1)$ and $N(d_2)$ to 1.0. Then the Black-Scholes formula becomes $S_0 - Xe^{-r_cT}$. When S_0 is very low, d_1 and d_2 approach $-\infty$, and $N(d_1)$ and $N(d_2)$ approach 0. Thus, the formula has a lower bound of $\text{Max}(0, S_0 - Xe^{-r_cT})$. The formula can never fall below this expression, because the lowest it can get is zero. When S_0 is very high, the formula is precisely the lower bound.

Next we shall examine the Black-Scholes formula when some of the variables take on extreme values.

THE FORMULA WHEN $T = 0$ It is important to remember that the purpose of the Black-Scholes formula is to price an option prior to expiration. Yet, it would not be a correct formula if it did not price an option at its expiration as well. We know that at expiration, a call option should be worth $\text{Max}(0, S_T - X)$. Would the Black-Scholes formula give this value? Yes and no.

Let us move to expiration such that $T = 0$ and the stock price is S_T. First look at d_1. Notice that we are dividing by zero. Let us write the formula as follows:

$$d_1 = \frac{\ln(S_T/X)}{\sigma\sqrt{T}} + \frac{(r + \sigma^2/2)T}{\sigma\sqrt{T}}$$
$$= \frac{\ln(S_T/X)}{\sigma\sqrt{T}} + \frac{(r + \sigma^2/2)\sqrt{T}}{\sigma}.$$

When T goes to zero, the second term on the right-hand side disappears. What happens to the first term? It would appear to be infinite, but is it $+\infty$ or $-\infty$? That depends on whether S_T is greater than X. The natural log of a number greater than one is positive and the natural log of a number that is positive but less than one is negative. (Try it on your calculator.)

Thus, if $S_T > X$,

$S_T/X > 1$, $\ln(S_T/X) > 0$, and d_1 approaches $+\infty$.

If $S_T < X$,

$S_T/X < 1$, $\ln(S_T/X) < 0$, and d_1 approaches $-\infty$.

If $S_T = X$,

$S_T/X = 1$, $\ln(S_T/X) = 0$, and d_1 approaches $-\infty$.

The third situation can be handled only by application of a special mathematical case called L'Hôpital's rule, but we shall take this result for granted. As it turns out, it will not matter whether we let d_1 approach $+\infty$ or $-\infty$.

If d_1 approaches $+\infty$, then d_2 also approaches $+\infty$. If d_1 approaches $-\infty$, then d_2 also approaches $-\infty$. If d_1 or d_2 approaches $+\infty$, then $N(d_1)$ or $N(d_2)$ approach 1.0. If d_1 or d_2 approaches $-\infty$, then $N(d_1)$ and $N(d_2)$ approach zero. Thus, when T is zero, the Black-Scholes formula behaves as follows:

If $S_T > X$,

$$S_T/X > 1, \ln(S_T/X) > 0, d_1 \text{ approaches } +\infty, d_2 \text{ approaches } +\infty,$$
$$N(d_1) \text{ approaches } 1.0, N(d_2) \text{ approaches } 1.0,$$
$$\text{and since } e^{-r_c(0)} = 1, \text{ the formula becomes } S_T - X.$$

If $S_T \leq X$,

$$S_T/X \leq 1, \ln(S_T/X) \leq 0, d_1 \text{ approaches } -\infty, d_2 \text{ approaches } -\infty,$$
$$N(d_1) \text{ approaches } 0, N(d_2) \text{ approaches } 0,$$
$$\text{and the formula becomes } 0 - 0 = 0.$$

Thus the formula becomes $\text{Max}(0, S_T - X)$. Note, however, that if you program the formula on a computer, it would blow up upon division by zero. It would have to be coded to recognize the special case of $T = 0$ so that the formula becomes $\text{Max}(0, S_T - X)$.

THE FORMULA WHEN $S_0 = 0$ Now suppose prior to expiration, the stock price goes to zero. What has happened to the underlying stock? It must be bankrupt with no chance of recovery, for if there were any chance of it recovering, a nonzero price for the option would imply an arbitrage opportunity. In other words, if there were any chance of the company recovering and the stock price were zero, everyone would want the stock. Thus, the case of $S_0 = 0$ must be reserved for the special situation of a completely dead company. A call option on it must have a value of zero.

Looking again at the above formula for d_1, we see that we must take the natural log of 0. There is no such number. We know, however, that when $S_0 < X$, the natural log of S_0/X is negative. As the stock is falling toward zero, the natural log of S_0/X approaches $-\infty$, and we can safely say that its limit is $-\infty$. Thus, we would have d_1 and d_2 approaching $-\infty$, meaning that $N(d_1)$ and $N(d_2)$ would approach 0. This would reduce the Black-Scholes formula to zero.

As in the case for $T = 0$, a computer program would require special coding to handle this case or it would simply attempt to take $\ln(0/X)$, which is undefined, without recognizing that we really want the limit of this value.

THE FORMULA WHEN $\sigma = 0$ In Chapter 3 (see p. 90), we gave an example of a case in which the volatility is zero. If the option is in-the-money, it would be like a zero coupon bond. It would pay off a positive value and that value would not change. If the option is at- or out-of-the-money, it would not pay off anything later for certain and would have a value today of zero. Thus, when σ is zero, we need the formula to reflect the payoff of a sure positive amount at expiration or zero, depending on whether S_0 is greater than, less than, or equal to zero.

Now let us write the formula for d_1 as follows:

$$d_1 = \frac{\ln(S_0/X)}{\sigma\sqrt{T}} + \frac{(r + \sigma^2/2)T}{\sigma\sqrt{T}}$$

$$= \frac{\ln\left(\dfrac{S_0}{Xe^{-r_cT}}\right)}{\sigma\sqrt{T}} + \frac{(\sigma^2/2)T}{\sigma\sqrt{T}}$$

$$= \frac{\ln\left(\dfrac{S_0}{Xe^{-r_cT}}\right)}{\sigma\sqrt{T}} + \frac{\sigma\sqrt{T}}{2}.$$

Now, when we let σ go to zero, the second term goes to 0, but what happens to the first term? It depends on whether $S_0 > Xe^{-r_cT}$. If that is true, then we are taking the log of a number greater than 1.0, so the first term goes to $+\infty$. If not, then we are taking the log of a number greater than zero and less than one, and the log will be negative. Then the term will go to $-\infty$.

Thus, if $S_0 > Xe^{-r_cT}$,

> d_1 approaches $+\infty$, $N(d_1)$ and $N(d_2)$ approach 1.0, and the call price becomes $S_0 - Xe^{-r_cT}$. This means that at expiration the call holder will pay X, which has a present value of Xe^{-r_cT}, and will receive stock that is currently worth S_0 and will have that value for sure at expiration. Thus, the call is now worth $S_0 - Xe^{-r_cT}$.

If $S_0 \leq Xe^{-r_cT}$,

> d_1 approaches $-\infty$, $N(d_1)$ and $N(d_2)$ approach 0.0, and the call price becomes zero.

Note that it is not exactly the condition of being in-the-money that determines the value of the call when the volatility is zero. In other words, it is not that $S_0 > X$, but rather that $S_0 > Xe^{-r_cT}$. Also, note again that special coding would be required to accommodate this case in a computer program.

THE FORMULA WHEN X = 0   We saw in Chapter 3 that when $X = 0$, a call is equivalent to the stock. So the Black-Scholes formula should approach S_0 when that happens. It is easy to see that this will be the case. We would be taking $\ln(+\infty)$, which is $+\infty$. Thus, d_1 and d_2 would approach $+\infty$, and $N(d_1)$ and $N(d_2)$ would approach 1.0. Then, with $X = 0$, the formula would become $S_0(1.0) - 0(1.0) = S_0$. Again, special coding would be required in a computer program.

THE FORMULA WHEN $r_c = 0$ A zero risk-free rate is no special case at all. It is not necessary to have a positive interest rate, and the Black-Scholes formula does not reduce to any special value.

The Variables in the Black-Scholes Model[2]

We have already learned that there are five variables that affect the option's price: (1) the stock price, (2) the exercise price, (3) the risk-free rate, (4) the time to expiration, and (5) the volatility or standard deviation. With the Black-Scholes model, we can see these effects more directly.

The Stock Price

A higher stock price should lead to a higher call price. Suppose the stock price is $130 instead of $125.9375. This gives values of $N(d_1)$ and $N(d_2)$ of .6171 and .5162, which gives a value of C of $15.96, which is higher than the previously obtained value, $13.55.

The value of our America Online call for a broad range of stock prices is illustrated in Figure 5.6. Note that this graph is similar to Figure 3.5, where we showed what a European call price curve should look like.

The delta is approximately the change in the option price for a small change in the stock price. It is obtained as $N(d_1)$ from the Black-Scholes model.

The relationship between the stock price and the call price is often expressed as a single value, referred to as its **delta.** The delta is obtained from the calculus procedure of differentiating the call price with respect to the stock price. The mathematical details of the procedure are a bit technical but the result is quite simple:

$$\text{Call } Delta = N(d_1).$$

Since $N(d_1)$ is a probability, the delta must range from zero to one.

Because of the assumptions behind the calculus, the delta is the change in the call price for a *very small* change in the stock price. Here our delta is .5692. This is somewhat loosely defined to mean that the option price moves 56.92 percent of the move in the stock price. Technically this is correct only for a very small move in the stock price. For example, we noted above that if the stock price were $130, a $4.0625 move, the call price would be $15.96, a move of $2.41, which is about 59 percent of the stock price move. Thus, while delta is a very important measure of the option's sensitivity to the stock price, it is precise only if the stock price makes a very small move.

---

[2]All the calculations in this section were done using the spreadsheet bsbin2.xls. In addition, we start with a base value of the AOL June 125 call of the Black-Scholes price of 13.55.

FIGURE 5.6 | **The Call Price as a Function of the Stock Price**
AOL June 125; r_c = .0446, T = .0959, σ = .83

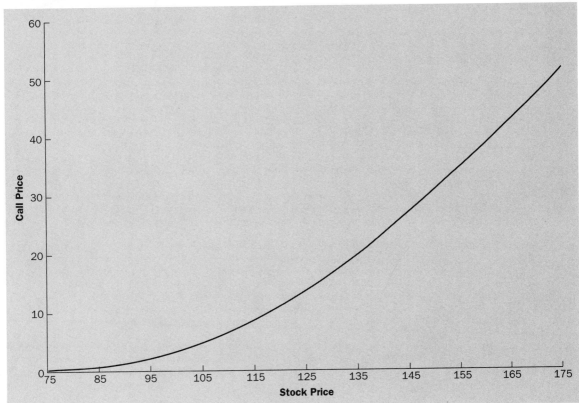

Recall that the delta ranges from zero to one. When the stock price is high relative to the exercise price, the delta is closer to one; when the stock price is low relative to the exercise price, the delta is closer to zero. The relationship between the delta and the level of the stock price for the AOL June 125 call option is illustrated in Figure 5.7.

The delta also changes as the option evolves through its life. In other words, even if the stock price did not change, the delta would change. As the life of the option decreases, for in-the-money call options the delta moves toward one; for out-of-the-money call options, the delta moves toward zero. This relationship appears in Figure 5.8, which illustrates how the deltas of two AOL calls change as the option gets closer to its expiration, assuming the stock price does not change. We look at the June 120, which is well in-the-money, and the June 130, which is well out-of-the-money. Notice how the deltas of these options change slowly until the last week of the options' lives, but then converge quickly toward 1.0 and 0.0.

FIGURE 5.7	The Delta of a Call as a Function of the Stock Price
	AOL June 125; $S_0 = 125.9375$, $r_c = .0446$, T = .0959, $\sigma = .83$

Recall from our discussion of the binomial model how we bought h shares of stock and sold one call. As long as we adjusted the number of options per share according to the formula for h, we maintained a risk-free hedge. In the Black-Scholes world, this is called a **delta hedge** and must be done continuously. A delta-hedged position is said to be **delta neutral.** For example, the stock price is $125.9375. Recall that the delta is .5691 so we construct a delta hedge by buying 569 shares and selling 1,000 calls. If the stock price falls by a small amount, say .01, we shall lose .01 (569) = 5.69 on the stock. However, the option price will fall by approximately .01 (.569) or .00569. Since we have 1,000 calls, the options collectively will fall by .00569 (1,000) = 5.69. Since we are short the options, we gain 5.69, which offsets the loss on the stock. A similar result is obtained if the price goes up. Once the price changes or time elapses, however, which it does continuously, the delta changes, a new hedge ratio must be constructed, and shares or options must be purchased or sold. If this is done properly, then a risk-

---

FIGURE 5.8   **The Delta of a Call as a Function of the Time in Days to Expiration**
AOL June 125; $S_0 = 125.9375$, $r_c = .0446$, $\sigma = .83$

In-the-money (X = 120)

Out-of-the-money (X = 130)

Delta

Days to Expiration

---

free return is earned, provided the call was correctly priced at the start. Of course, in practice it is impossible to do a perfect delta hedge because one cannot trade continuously. We shall see this more explicitly later.

An additional risk in delta hedging is that the stock price will not change by a very small amount. For example, suppose the stock went up to 130 and the call went to 15.96, as in our example. Then our 569 shares of stock would have gained $4.0625(569) = 2,312$. Our 1,000 calls would have gone up by $(15.96 - 13.55)(1,000) = 2,410$. Since we are short the calls, the overall position would have suffered a loss.

This type of risk is captured by the option's **gamma.** The gamma is the change in the delta for a very small change in the stock price. The formula for gamma is

$$\text{Call Gamma} = \frac{e^{-d_1^2/2}}{S_0\,\sigma\sqrt{2\pi T}}.$$

The gamma is the change in the delta for a change in the stock price. Its value can be obtained from the Black-Scholes model.

D e r i v a t i v e s   i n   A c t i o n

A Mathematical Snapshot of the Black-Scholes Formula

As noted in the text, the Black-Scholes formula has its origins in the work of many famous scientists and mathematicians. The detailed mathematics are somewhat difficult to follow, but the basic ideas are quite similar to the manner in which the binomial model was derived in Chapter 4.

Stock prices are assumed to be generated randomly in a manner known as *Geometric Brownian Motion*. Suppose the stock price at time 0 is S_0. At time 1, the stock price is S_1. The change in the stock price is $\Delta S_0 = S_1 - S_0$, and this change occurs over a period of time Δt. The change has two components: a drift or expected return, specified by the Greek letter μ (mu), and a variance, given by the Greek letter σ^2 (sigma squared). Both μ and σ are stated as annual rates and, consequently, the changes over a period of time are multiplied by Δt. In addition, both μ and σ are stated as percentages. Thus, the actual dollar drift is $\mu \Delta t S_0$ and the actual dollar variance is $\sigma^2 \Delta t S_0$.

The uncertainty in the change in the stock price is represented by a purely random, normally distributed variable written as ϵ (epsilon) that is multiplied by the standard deviation, which is $\sigma \sqrt{\Delta t}$. The term $\epsilon \sqrt{\Delta t}$ is called a *Brownian Motion*. Overall, the change in the stock price is written as

$$\Delta S_0 = \mu \Delta t S_0 + \sigma \sqrt{\Delta t} S_0 \epsilon,$$

which more precisely is called Geometric Brownian Motion. For example, suppose a stock priced at $100 has an expected return of 20 percent and a standard deviation of return of 45 percent. Let the length of time be

one day. Then $\Delta t = 1/365 = .00274$. Suppose the next day, the price is 101.5. This is a change of 1.5 or 1.5 percent. Then $\Delta S_0 = \$1.50$, and consists of the following:

$$\Delta S_0 = \$1.50$$
$$\text{drift} = \mu \Delta t S_0 = .20(.00274)(\$100) = \$0.0548$$
$$\text{volatility} = \sigma \sqrt{\Delta t} S_0 \epsilon = .45 \sqrt{.00274} \$100(.6135)$$
$$= \$1.4452.$$

Note that the random component, ϵ is .6135. The new price, S_1, is thus the old price, $S_0 = \$100$, plus the change in price $\Delta S_0 = \$1.50$, or $\$101.50$. The next day there will be another random component, which, through the same process as above, will lead to a new price, S_2.

Black, Scholes, and Merton assumed that the stock price evolves in this manner. In addition, they assumed that the length of time Δt is very small. Mathematicians denote small changes in time with the symbol dt. In fact, in the equation above all Δ's become d's. In general for any time t, the change in the stock price is, therefore,

$$dS_t = S_t \mu dt + S_t \sigma \sqrt{dt} \epsilon_t.$$

Then, calling upon some results from mathematical probability theory, they are able to characterize the change in the call option price as:

$$dC = \frac{\partial C}{\partial S} dS + \frac{\partial C}{\partial t} dt + \frac{1}{2} \frac{\partial^2 C}{\partial S^2} dS^2.$$

The symbol ∂ represents a partial derivative, the mathematical notion of a change in something for a very small change in something else, holding everything else

In our example with the stock at 125.9375, the gamma is calculated as $e^{-(0.1742)^2/2}/(125.9375(.83)\sqrt{2(3.14159)(.0959)}) = .0121$. This suggests that if the stock increased to 130, the delta would go from .569 to $.569 + (130 - 125.9375)(.0121) = .6182$. The actual delta if the stock goes to 130 is .6171. Of course, the gamma provides only an estimate of the change in the delta, but in this case the estimate is fairly accurate.

constant. The above formula would have the subscript "0" on the C's and S's but we drop them to reduce the notation. This complicated expression breaks down the change in the call price into three components.

The first term on the right-hand side, $\dfrac{\partial C}{\partial S}dS$, is

the change in the call price given the change in the stock price times the change in the stock price. It is the part of the call price change that comes from a small change in the stock price.

The second term on the right-hand side, $\dfrac{\partial C}{\partial t}dt$, is

the change in the call price given the change in time, times the change in time. It is the part of the call price change that comes from the time value decay, as covered in Chapter 3.

The third term on the right-hand side, $\dfrac{1}{2}\dfrac{\partial^2 C}{\partial S^2}dS^2$, is

a second-order effect representing the change in the call price from the change in the stock price times one-half the square of the change in the stock price. This is obviously a more complicated expression, but in simple terms, it represents the change in the call price resulting from large changes in the stock price.

The overall expression is known as Itô's Lemma, named after the Japanese mathematician who discovered it in the late 1940s.

Knowing how the stock price changes and how the call price changes enabled Black, Scholes, and Merton to form a risk-free hedge portfolio, consisting of h shares of stock and one short call, in a manner similar to what we did in Chapter 3. The value of such a portfolio at time 0 is

$$V_0 = hS_0 \quad C_0.$$

Notice the similarity of this formula to the one for V in the binomial model on p. 116 of Chapter 4. The change in the value of V_0 comes from a change in S_0 and a change in C_0:

$$dV_0 = hdS_0 + dC_0.$$

The two formulas we developed earlier for dS_0 and dC_0 are then substituted into the above formula. We then solve for the value of h that eliminates the uncertain term, ϵ in the formula for dS_0. With the uncertainty eliminated, the change in V_0 should represent a risk-free return. Thus, dV_0 should equal $rdtV_0$. After working through the algebra, we obtain what is known as a *partial differential equation* that looks as follows:

$$\frac{\partial C}{\partial S}rS + \frac{\partial C}{\partial t} + \frac{1}{2}\frac{\partial^2 C}{\partial S^2}S^2\sigma^2 = rC.$$

Once again we have dropped the 0 subscript to reduce the notation. The price of the option is on the right-hand side (times the risk-free rate), but the left-hand side is just a group of partial derivatives. A partial differential equation such as this, however, can, and in this case does, have a solution that provides the actual formula for C in terms of observable variables like S, σ, r, and so on. Also the solution must be a formula that, when the option expires, gives the intrinsic value.

That solution is the Black-Scholes and Merton formula given in the chapter.

The larger is the gamma, the more sensitive is the delta to a stock price change and the harder it is to maintain a delta neutral position. The gamma is always positive and is largest when the stock price is near the exercise price. When the stock price is high or low relative to the exercise price, the gamma is near zero, as shown in Figure 5.9. The gamma changes as the option approaches expiration. If the option is approximately at-the-

FIGURE 5.9　**The Gamma of a Call as a Function of the Stock Price**
AOL June 125; r_c = .0446, T = .0959, σ = .83

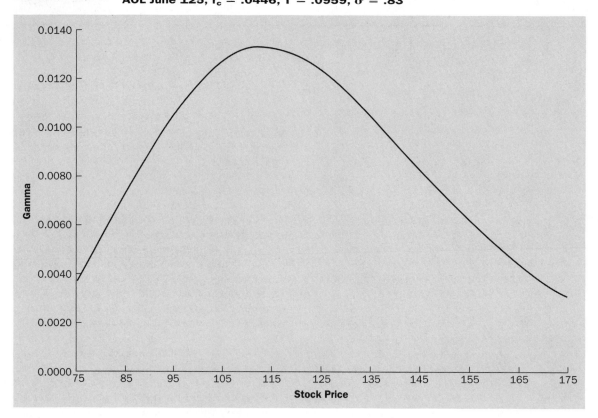

money, like our AOL June 125 call, the uncertainty of whether it will finish in- or out-of-the-money, causes the gamma to increase dramatically as expiration approaches, as seen in Figure 5.10.

Remember that the gamma represents the uncertainty of the delta. A large gamma makes it harder to delta hedge, because the delta is changing more rapidly and is more sensitive to large stock price movements. In a later section of this chapter we illustrate more explicitly the nature and solution of this problem.

The Exercise Price

Now let us change the exercise price to $130, which should decrease the call's value. Specifically, let us examine the June 130 call. We retain all of the other original values, including the stock price of $125.9375. The values

FIGURE 5.10   **The Gamma of a Call as a Function of the Time in Days to Expiration**
AOL June 125; $S_0 = 125.9375$, $r_c = .0446$, $\sigma = .83$

of d_1 and d_2 are 0.0216 and -0.2354. The normal probabilities are .5086 and .4070 and the resulting call price is $11.38, which is less than the original $13.55.

The change in the call price for a very small change in the exercise price is negative and is given by the formula $-e^{-r_cT}N(d_2)$. The exercise price of a given option does not change, however, so this concept is meaningful only in considering how much more or less a call with a different exercise price would be worth.[3] In that case, the difference in the exercise price would probably be too large to apply the formula above, which, as noted, holds only when X changes by a very small amount.

---

[3]It is possible to create an option in which the exercise price changes randomly, but we shall not cover these at this level.

The Risk-Free Rate

Chapter 3 showed how to identify the risk-free rate for the purpose of examining an option's boundary conditions. Within the Black-Scholes framework, the risk-free rate must be expressed as a continuously compounded rate.

Earlier in the chapter, we distinguished the simple or discrete return on a stock from the continuously compounded or log return on a stock. A similar distinction exists for interest rates. A simple or discrete risk-free rate assumes only annual compounding. A continuously compounded rate assumes interest compounds continuously. A simple rate can be converted to a continuously compounded rate by taking the natural logarithm of 1 plus the simple rate. For example, if the simple rate is 6 percent, $100 invested at 6 percent for one year becomes $106. The equivalent continuously compounded rate is $\ln(1.06) = .0583$. Thus, $100 invested at 5.83 percent compounded continuously grows to $106 in one year. The continuously compounded rate is always less than the simple rate. To convert a continuously compounded rate to a simple rate, use the exponential function, the inverse of the logarithmic function, that is, $e^{.0583} - 1 = .06$.

In our previous problem, the risk-free rate was 4.46 percent. We obtained this as $\ln(1.0456)$, where .0456 was the simple rate that we obtained in Chapter 3. The Black-Scholes formula requires the use of the continuously compounded rate so we specify the rate as r_c where it appears in two places in the formula. Note that in the equation for C, we compute Xe^{-r_cT}, which is the present value of the exercise price when the interest rate is continuously compounded. The same value would have been obtained had we used $X(1 + r)^{-T}$, where r is the discrete rate.

The value of our America Online call for a range of continuously compounded risk-free rates is illustrated in Figure 5.11. The call price is nearly linear in the risk-free rate and does not change much over a very broad range of risk-free rates. For example, at a risk-free rate of 4.46 percent, we obtained a call price of 13.55. If we raised the risk-free rate to 12 percent, a rather large change, the call price would increase to only 13.98. The sensitivity of the call price to the risk-free rate is called its **rho** and is given by the formula,

$$\text{Call } Rho = TXe^{-r_cT}N(d_2).$$

The rho is the change in the option price for a change in the risk-free rate. It can be obtained from the Black-Scholes model.

In our original problem, with the risk-free rate of 4.46 percent, the rho would be $(.0959)125^{-.0446(.0959)}(.4670) = 5.57$. If we let the risk-free rate go from .0446 to .12, the rho would predict a change in the call price of $(.12 - .0446)(5.57) = .42$. The actual change was $13.98 - 13.55 = 0.43$. The nearly linear relationship between the option price and the risk-free

FIGURE 5.11   The Call Price as a Function of the Risk-Free Rate
AOL June 125; $S_0 = 125.9375$, $T = .0959$, $\sigma = .83$

rate makes the rho a fairly accurate measure of the option's sensitivity to interest rate changes. One should keep in mind, however, that the Black-Scholes model assumes that interest rates do not change during the life of the option. More sophisticated models are required to accurately capture the effects of changing interest rates. We cover this topic in Chapter 14.

The rho also changes with the level of the stock price, being higher the higher the stock price, as seen in Figure 5.12.

The Volatility or Standard Deviation

As covered in Chapter 3, the volatility or standard deviation is a critical variable in valuing options. In the Black-Scholes model, the volatility is the standard deviation of the continuously compounded return on the stock. Because the volatility is the only unobservable variable, we devote an entire section later in the chapter to estimating its value.

FIGURE 5.12   **The Rho of a Call as a Function of the Stock Price**
AOL June 125; r_c = .0446, T = .0959, σ = .83

Figure 5.13 shows the option price for a range of volatilities. Because in-, at-, and out-of-the-money calls behave somewhat differently with respect to volatility, we show the graph for options with exercise prices of 120, 125, and 130. Recall that our 125 call had a price of 13.55 when its volatility was .83. If we raise that volatility to .90, the call price is about 14.62. If we lower it to .75, the call price is about 12.33. These are fairly large changes in the call price over a fairly small range of volatilities.

The sensitivity of the call price to a *very small* change in volatility is called its **vega** and is given as[4]

$$Call\ Vega = \frac{S_0 \sqrt{T} e^{-d_1^2/2}}{\sqrt{2\pi}}.$$

---

[4]It is also sometimes called its **kappa** or **lambda**.

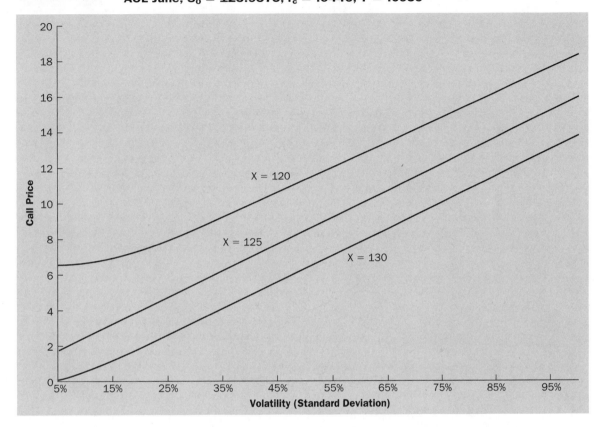

FIGURE 5.13   **The Call Price as a Function of the Volatility**
AOL June; S_0 = 125.9375, r_c = .0446, T = .0959

In our original problem the vega is $125.9375 \sqrt{.0959}e^{-(0.1742)^2/2}/$ $\sqrt{2(3.14159)} = 15.32$. This suggests that if volatility changes by a very small amount, say, .01, the call price would change by $15.32(.01) = .15$. The actual call price change if volatility went to .84, an increase of .01, would be .15. If the volatility increased .12 to .95, the vega predicts that the call price would increase by $15.32(.12) = 1.84$, when the actual call price would go to 15.39, an increase of $15.39 - 13.55 = 1.84$. This accuracy is due to the fact that, as Figure 5.13 illustrates, the volatility and the option price are nearly linear if the option is nearly at-the-money. This result will be useful in a later section. As Figure 5.13 shows, however, if the option is not at-the-money, the relationship is not quite linear and the vega will not capture all of the risk of a changing volatility.

Figure 5.14 illustrates how the vega changes with the level of the stock price for our AOL June 125 call. Notice that when the stock price is near the exercise price, the vega is largest, meaning that the option price is

The vega is the change in the option price for a change in the volatility. It can be obtained from the Black-Scholes model.

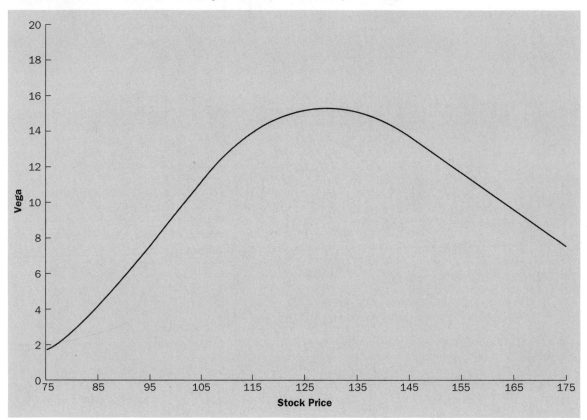

FIGURE 5.14   The Vega of a Call as a Function of the Stock Price
AOL June 125; $r_c = .0446$, T = .0959, $\sigma = .83$

more sensitive to changes in the volatility. When the stock price is large or small relative to the exercise price, the vega is smallest, and the option price is less sensitive to changes in the volatility.

Regardless of the option's "moneyness" and whether the volatility change is large or small, the option is still quite sensitive to changes in the volatility. The Black-Scholes model does not actually permit the volatility to change while the option is alive. There are more complex models that account for this phenomenon. Nonetheless, the concept of changing volatility is still considered by option traders who use the Black-Scholes model. This vega risk can be hedged by using an offsetting position in another instrument, such as another call, based on its vega risk.

The Time to Expiration

The relationship between the option price and the time to expiration is illustrated in Figure 5.15. The graph should be viewed from right to left. The

FIGURE 5.15   **The Call Price as a Function of the Time in Days to Expiration**
AOL June 125; $S_0 = 125.9375$, $r_c = .0959$, $\sigma = .83$

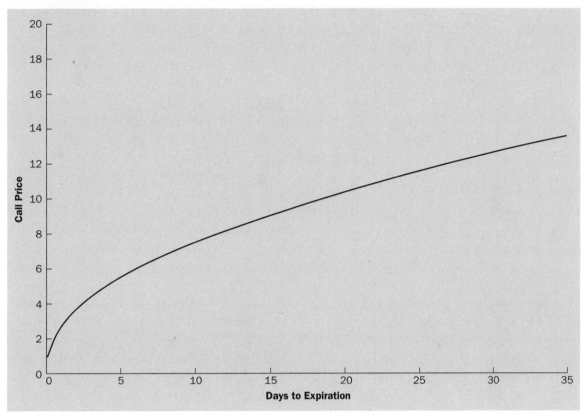

decrease in the value of the call as time elapses is the time value decay, as we discussed in Chapter 3. The rate of time value decay is measured by the option's **theta,** which is given as

$$\text{Call } Theta = -\frac{S_0 \sigma e^{-d_1^2/2}}{2\sqrt{2\pi T}} - r_c X e^{-r_c T} N\,(d_2).$$

For the June 125, d_1 is .1742, $N(d_2)$ is .4670, and theta is $-125.9375\,(.83)$ $e^{-(.1742)^2/2}/(2\sqrt{2(3.14159)(.0959)})\ -\ (.0446)\ 125e^{-.0446(.0959)}(.4670)\ =$ -68.91. Thus, in one week the time to expiration goes from .0959 to $28/365 =$ .0767, and the option price would be predicted to change by $(.0959 -$ .0767$)(-68.91) = -1.32$. The actual price changes to 12.16, so the change is $12.16 - 13.55 = -1.39$. Of course, the theta is most accurate only for a very small change in time, but the predicted price change is still very close to

The theta is the change in the option price for a change in time. It measures the time value of decay and can be obtained from the Black-Scholes model.

FIGURE 5.16   **The Theta of a Call as a Function of the Stock Price**
AOL June 125; r_c = .0446, T = .0959, σ = .83

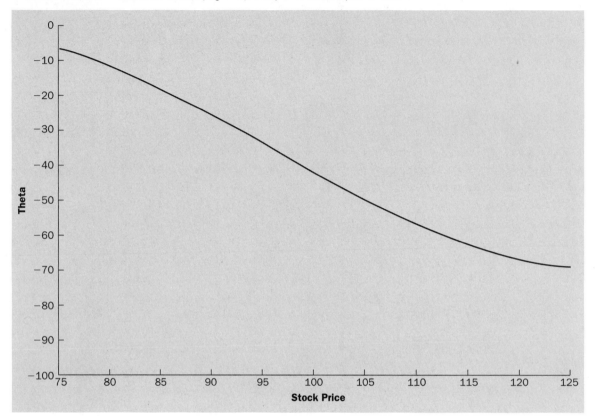

the actual price change. Since time itself is not a source of risk, however, it makes no sense to worry about it, but, of course, that does not mean that we do not need to know the rate of time value decay.

Figure 5.16 shows that the theta is inversely related to the stock price. This means that the rate of time decay is greater for in-the-money calls.

The Black-Scholes Model When the Stock Pays Dividends

The Black-Scholes model in the form we have seen so far applies to stocks that do not pay dividends, such as America Online. As we saw in Chapter 3, dividends reduce the call option's price and may induce early exercise if the options are American. Incorporating dividends into the Black-Scholes model for European options is not difficult. There are several suggested approaches, none of which has proven superior to the others. We shall discuss two here.

Known Discrete Dividends

Suppose a stock pays a dividend of D_t at some time during the option's life. This dividend is payable after a time period t, which is defined by the ex-dividend date. The dividend is assumed to be known with certainty. If we make a small adjustment to the stock price, the Black-Scholes model will remain applicable to the pricing of this option.

The adjustment is one we have done several times before. We subtract the present value of the dividend from the stock price and use the adjusted stock price in the formula. Let the stock price in the Black-Scholes formula be S_0', defined as $S_0' = S_0 - D_t e^{-r_c t}$. If there were other dividends during the life of the option, their present values would be subtracted as well.

As noted earlier, the America Online stock does not pay a dividend. For illustrative purposes, however, we will now assume that it pays a $2 dividend and has an ex-dividend date of June 4, 21 days later. All other variables are the same. The procedure for calculating the Black-Scholes price is laid out in Table 5.3. Note that now the call price is lower as we would expect.

The Black-Scholes model can price European options on stocks with known discrete dividends by subtracting the present value of the dividends from the stock price.

TABLE 5.3	Calculating the Black-Scholes Price When There Are Known Discrete Dividends

$S_0 = 125.9375$ $X = 125$ $r_c = .0446$ $\sigma = .83$ $T = .0959$
One dividend of 2, ex-dividend in 21 days (May 14 to June 4)

1. Determine the amounts of the dividend
$$D_t = 2.$$
2. Determine the times to the ex-dividend dates
$$21 \text{ days so } t = 21/365 = .0575$$
3. Subtract the present value of the dividend from the stock price to obtain S_0'
$$125.9375 - 2e^{-.0446(.0575)} = 123.9426$$
4. Compute d_1, using S_0' in place S_0
$$d_1 = \frac{\ln(123.9426/125) + (.0446 + (.83)^2/2)\,.0959}{.83\sqrt{.0959}} = 0.1121$$
5. Compute d_2
$$d_2 = 0.1121 - .83\sqrt{.0959} = -0.1449.$$
6. Look up $N(d_1)$
$$N(0.11) = .5438$$
7. Look up $N(d_2)$
$$N(-0.14) = -.5557 = .4443.$$
8. Plug into formula for C, using S_0' in place of S_0
$$C = 123.9426(.5438) - 125e^{-.0446(.0959)}(.4443) = 12.10.$$

The Excel spreadsheet bsbin2.xls, illustrated in Software Demonstration 5.1, permits you to enter up to 50 known discrete dividends. You simply enter the dividend amount and the time in years to the ex-dividend date. Be sure that you do not enter a yield or the software will ignore the discrete dividends and use the yield. For the AOL June 125 call with a $2 dividend, the spreadsheet gives the more accurate answer of $N(d_1) = .5446$, $N(d_2) = .4424$, and $C = 12.44$.

Known Continuous Dividend Yield

Another approach to the problem of adjusting the Black-Scholes formula for dividends on the stock is to assume the dividend is paid continuously at a known yield. This method assumes the dividend accrues continuously, which means that a dividend is constantly being paid. We express the annual rate as a percentage, δ. For example, let the America Online stock have an annual continuously compounded dividend yield of $\delta = .04$. Given the current stock price of $125.9375, the annual dividend is $125.9375 (.04) = 5.04$. This dividend is not paid in four quarterly installments of $1.26 each; rather, it accrues continuously in very small increments that are reinvested and accumulate over the year to $5.04.[5] Because the stock price fluctuates throughout the year, the actual dividend can change but the yield will remain constant. Thus, this model does not require the assumption that the dividend is known or is constant; it requires only that the dividend being paid at that instant be a constant percentage of the stock price.

The adjustment procedure requires substituting the value S_0' for S_0 in the Black-Scholes model, where $S_0' = S_0 e^{-\delta T}$. The expression $S_0(1 - e^{-\delta T})$ is the present value of the dividends. Subtracting this from S_0 gives S_0' as given above. The adjustment removes the present value of the dividends during the option's life from the stock price. Table 5.4 illustrates the computation of the option price. Again we see that the effect of dividends is to lower the option's price under what it would be if there were no dividends. There is, of course, no assurance that the discrete and continuous dividend adjustments will give equivalent option prices. Because the America Online stock does not pay dividends, the dividend amount and the yield are merely assumptions made for illustration purposes and are not intended to be equivalent.

The assumption of a continuous dividend is unrealistic for most options on stocks; however, the convenience of using a single yield figure in lieu of obtaining the precise dividends could justify its use for many pur-

The Black-Scholes model can price European options on stocks that pay dividends at a known continuous rate by discounting the stock price by that rate.

---

[5]The quarterly dividend of $1.26 and annual dividend of $5.04 are approximations and are not precisely equivalent to the continuously compounded yield of 4 percent, due to differences in assumptions about the times and reinvestment of the dividends.

TABLE 5.4	Calculating the Black-Scholes Price When There Are Continuous Dividends

$S_0 = 125.9375$ $X = 125$ $r_c = .0446$ $\sigma = .83$ $T = .0959$ $\delta = .04$

1. Compute the stock price minus the present value of the dividends as $S_0' = S_0 e^{-\delta T}$
$$125.9375^{-.04(.0959)} = 125.4553.$$

2. Compute d_1, using S_0' in place of S_0
$$d_1 = \frac{\ln(125.4553/125) + (.0446 + (.83)^2/2).0959}{.83\sqrt{.0959}} = 0.1593$$

3. Compute d_2
$$d_2 = 0.1593 - .83\sqrt{.0959} = -0.0977.$$

4. Look up $N(d_1)$
$$N(.16) = .5636$$

5. Look up $N(d_2)$
$$N(-.10) = 1 - N(.10) = 1 - .5398 = .4602.$$

6. Plug into formula for C, using S_0' in place of S_0
$$C = 125.4553(.5636) - 125e^{-.0446(.0959)}(.4602) = 13.43.$$

poses. For options on stocks, however, only a few dividends are paid over the life of most options; thus the discrete dividend adjustment is not especially difficult. For index options, however, the use of a yield may be preferable. The dividends on the component stocks in the index would be paid more or less continuously, and thus it would be difficult to obtain an accurate day-by-day figure for the dividends.[6]

The Excel spreadsheet bsbin2.xls, illustrated in Software Demonstration 5.1, permits you to enter a continuous dividend yield when calculating an option price. Here the AOL June 125 call with a dividend yield of 4 percent has a price of 13.28.

The Black-Scholes Model and Some Insights into American Call Options

None of the adjustments here make the Black-Scholes model capable of pricing American options. Now having seen the Black-Scholes model, however, we can use it to gain a greater understanding of why call options might be exercised early.

Consider our America Online options. Let us take an option that is well in-the-money, the June 120. Using the Black-Scholes model and the

---

[6]Dividends and ex-dividend dates are available at finance.yahoo.com. Choose "Historical quotes" in the "Chart" option. The adjustment procedure for an index option depends on how the index is constructed. Standard and Poor's produces a daily dividend series for its indices, which can be purchased or obtained by subscription from Standard and Poor's. Dividend yields are available at www.cboe.com under "Tools."

spreadsheet bsbin2.xls, we would find this option to be worth 16.03. Let us change things around a little. Suppose the stock is going to go ex-dividend in another instant. How large of a dividend would it take to justify exercising it before it goes ex-dividend? Let us assume that this is the last dividend that the stock will pay during the option's life, so after the stock has gone ex-dividend, we can safely use the Black-Scholes model to price the option.

In Table 5.5 we try dividend levels of $5–$25 in $5 increments. When the stock goes ex-dividend, it will fall by the amount of the dividend and we then can recompute the option value using the Black-Scholes model, remembering that once the stock goes ex-dividend, the Black-Scholes model will correctly price the call because there are no more dividends during the option's remaining life. The value obtained if you exercise the option just before the stock goes ex-dividend is always the intrinsic value, here $5.9375. The stock will then go ex-dividend and fall by the amount of the dividend. The third column shows the ex-dividend price of the call. You would exercise the option if the intrinsic value exceeds the ex-dividend option value. Here it would take a dividend of between $20 and $25 to justify early exercise. This would be an exceptionally large dividend, almost 20 percent of the stock price. Thus, if the AOL option were American, it is unlikely that it would be exercised. A primary reason for this is that AOL's volatility is so high that option holders would be throwing away a great deal of time value by exercising early.

Note that we never calculated the value of the option at any time before it went ex-dividend. This would require an American option pricing model. At that instant before the stock goes ex-dividend, if the dividend is not large enough to justify early exercise, the American call price would sell for the European call price. If the dividend is large enough to justify early exercise, the American call price would be $5.9375, the intrinsic value. Well before the ex-dividend instant, however, it is much more difficult to price

---

TABLE 5.5   **The Early Exercise Decision**

$S_0 = 125.9375$ $X = 120$ $r_c = .0446$ $\sigma = .83$ $T = .0959$

Dividend	Value if Exercised[1]	Value When Stock Goes Ex-Dividend[2]	Exercise?
0	5.9375	16.03	No
5	5.9375	13.03	No
10	5.9375	10.34	No
15	5.9375	7.99	No
20	5.9375	5.98	No
25	5.9375	4.32	Yes

[1]The intrinsic value before the stock goes ex-dividend.
[2]Computed using the Black-Scholes model, with an ex-dividend stock price of 125.9375 − dividend.

the option because the stock price at the ex-dividend instant is unknown. Thus, we would require an American option pricing model. In addition, if there were more than one dividend, we would need an American option pricing model to account for the remaining dividends. American option pricing models are generally beyond the scope of this book. Recall, however, that we covered the binomial model and demonstrated how it can be used to price American options. This is the preferred method used by professional option traders. Your Excel spreadsheet bsbin2.xls will calculate American call prices using the binomial model.

Estimating the Volatility

Obtaining a reliable estimate of the volatility or standard deviation is difficult. Moreover, the Black-Scholes model and option prices in general are extremely sensitive to that estimate. There are two approaches to estimating the volatility: the historical volatility and the implied volatility.

Historical Volatility

The **historical volatility** estimate is based on the assumption that the volatility that prevailed over the recent past will continue to hold in the future. First, we take a sample of returns on the stock over a recent period. We convert these returns to continuously compounded returns. Then we compute the standard deviation of the continuously compounded returns.

The returns can be daily, weekly, monthly, or any desired time interval. If we use daily returns, the result will be a daily standard deviation. To obtain the annualized standard deviation the model requires, we must multiply either the variance by the number of trading days in a year, which is about 250, or the standard deviation by $\sqrt{250}$. If we use monthly returns, the result will be a monthly variance (or standard deviation) and must be multiplied by either 12 (or $\sqrt{12}$) to obtain an annualized figure.

There is no minimum number of observations; a sample size of about 60 will be adequate in most cases. The trade-off in selecting a sample size is that the more observations one uses, the further back in time one must go. The further back one goes, the more likely the volatility will change. In the example used here, we do not use many historical observations, but this is primarily to keep the computations brief.

Assume we have a series of J continuously compounded returns, where each return is identified as r_t^c, which equals $\ln(1 + r_t)$ and to goes from 1 to J. First, we calculate the mean return as

$$\bar{r}^c = \sum_{t=1}^{J} r_t^c / J.$$

The historical volatility is estimated from a sample of recent continuously compounded returns on the stock.

TABLE 5.6	Estimating the Historical Volatility of America Online			
Date	**Price**	r_t	r_t^c	$(r_t^c - \bar{r}^c)^2$
February 17	80.1875	——	——	——
February 18	86.5000	0.0787	0.0758	0.004654
February 19	88.0000	0.0173	0.0172	0.000093
February 22	87.5625	−0.0050	−0.0050	0.000157
February 23	87.1875	−0.0043	−0.0043	0.000140
February 24	88.9375	0.0201	0.0199	0.000152
February 25	89.5625	0.0070	0.0070	0.000000
February 26	86.6875	−0.0321	−0.0326	0.001615
March 1	87.0625	0.0043	0.0043	0.000011
March 2	86.2500	−0.0093	−0.0094	0.000287
March 3	86.9375	0.0080	0.0079	0.000000
March 4	90.8750	0.0453	0.0443	0.001350
March 5	90.1250	−0.0083	−0.0083	0.000251
March 8	92.8125	0.0298	0.0294	0.000476
March 9	95.8125	0.0323	0.0318	0.000588
March 10	96.1250	0.0033	0.0033	0.000019
March 11	102.0000	0.0611	0.0593	0.002680
March 12	104.9380	0.0288	0.0284	0.000434
March 15	109.0620	0.0393	0.0385	0.000960
March 16	116.1250	0.0648	0.0628	0.003046
March 17	119.2500	0.0269	0.0266	0.000361
March 18	130.0000	0.0901	0.0863	0.006202
March 19	121.0000	−0.0692	−0.0717	0.006289
March 22	117.1250	−0.0320	−0.0325	0.001609
March 23	126.5000	0.0800	0.0770	0.004822
March 24	125.6880	−0.0064	−0.0064	0.000196
March 25	132.3750	0.0532	0.0518	0.001961
March 26	144.5000	0.0916	0.0876	0.006413
March 29	147.0000	0.0173	0.0172	0.000092
March 30	150.0000	0.0204	0.0202	0.000160
March 31	166.9380	0.1129	0.1070	0.009886
April 1	167.5000	0.0034	0.0034	0.000018
April 5	158.0000	−0.0567	−0.0584	0.004349
April 6	160.5000	0.0158	0.0157	0.000066
April 7	159.9380	−0.0035	−0.0035	0.000122

Then the variance is

$$\sigma^2 = \frac{\sum_{t=1}^{J} (r_t^c - \bar{r}^c)^2}{J - 1}$$

$$= \frac{\sum_{t=1}^{J} (r_t^c)^2 - \left(\sum_{t=1}^{J} r_t^c \right)^2 / J}{J - 1}.$$

Note that we divide the sum of the squared deviations around the mean by
J − 1. This is the appropriate divisor if the observations are a sample taken

TABLE 5.6   *(continued)*

Date	Price	r_t	r_t^c	$(r_t^c - \bar{r}^c)^2$
April 8	157.8750	−0.0128	−0.0130	0.000422
April 9	159.3120	0.0091	0.0091	0.000002
April 12	150.8750	−0.0530	−0.0544	0.003840
April 13	143.8750	−0.0464	−0.0475	0.003032
April 14	139.7500	−0.0287	−0.0291	0.001343
April 15	115.8750	−0.1780	−0.1873	0.037987
April 16	128.6880	0.1106	0.1049	0.009471
April 19	142.7500	0.1093	0.1037	0.009244
April 20	146.6880	0.0416	0.0408	0.001102
April 21	147.0000	−0.0114	−0.0114	0.000360
April 22	162.0000	0.1020	0.0972	0.008029
April 23	153.0000	−0.0556	−0.0572	0.004188
April 26	143.0000	−0.0654	−0.0676	0.005648
April 27	141.3750	−0.0114	−0.0114	0.000361
April 28	142.7500	0.0097	0.0097	0.000004
April 29	133.1250	−0.0674	−0.0698	0.005985
April 30	127.1250	−0.0451	−0.0461	0.002881
May 3	129.7500	0.0206	0.0204	0.000166
May 4	119.7500	−0.0771	−0.0802	0.007702
May 5	118.1875	−0.0130	−0.0131	0.000428
May 6	128.3125	0.0857	0.0822	0.005571
May 7	141.4375	0.1023	0.0974	0.008070
May 10	138.4375	−0.0212	−0.0214	0.000841
May 11	132.6250	−0.0420	−0.0429	0.002545
May 12	125.2500	−0.0556	−0.0572	0.004195
Totals			0.4459	0.182877

$$\bar{r}^c = \frac{0.4459}{59} = 0.0076$$

$$\sigma = \sqrt{\frac{0.182877}{58}} = 0.056152$$

Annualized $\sigma = 0.056152 \sqrt{250} = 0.8878$

from a larger population. This adjustment is necessary for the estimate of the sample variance to be an unbiased estimate of the population variance.

Table 5.6 illustrates this procedure for the America Online stock using daily closing prices. The simple return, r_t, is computed and converted to a continuously compounded return, r_t^c. Then the mean and variance of the series of continuously compounded returns are calculated. The variance is then converted to the standard deviation by taking the square root. The resulting figure is a daily volatility, so it must be multiplied by the square root of 250 to be converted to an annualized volatility, which is .8878.

The accompanying Excel spreadsheet hisv1.xls calculates the historical volatility. Software Demonstration 5.2 illustrates how to use hisv1.xls.

SOFTWARE DEMONSTRATION 5.2   **Calculating the Historical Volatility with the Excel Spreadsheet hisv1.xls**

The Excel spreadsheet hisv1.xls operates in Excel 97 under Windows 95 or 98. It calculates the historical volatility (standard deviation) for a sample of stock prices.

This spreadsheet is a read-only spreadsheet, meaning that it cannot be saved under the name hisv1.xls, which preserves the original file. To use the spreadsheet, simply do the following:

1.   Make sure you are in Windows 95 or 98.
2.   Run Excel 97.
3.   Open the file hisv1.xls.

Now let us assume that you wish to calculate a historical volatility. In the accompanying example, already entered into the cells is a set of 26 weekly prices for America Online stock. Each cell that will accept input has a double-line border and the values are in blue. Output cells have a single-line border. In the section labeled **Inputs:,** you should choose the data frequency. Directly below is a set of cells containing your data observations. Enter the prices in the column labeled "Asset Price."

To obtain the results, hit the F9 (manual recalculation) key. The output is shown in a section labeled **Results:.** The output consists of the variance, standard deviation, and the mean return. The column labeled "Periodic" provides the results in terms of the data frequency you chose. The column labeled "Annualized" provides the figures annualized by multiplying by the appropriate factor. The variance and mean are annualized by multiplying by 250 (the approximate number of trading days in a year), 52, 12, or 1, depending on your data frequency. The annualized standard deviation is then the square root of the annualized variance, which is equivalent to multiplying the periodic standard deviation by the square root of 250, 52, 12, or 1.

In this example, there are 26 prices, which leads to 25 returns. Obviously you may wish to use this spreadsheet for a different number of prices. The spreadsheet is set as a read-only file so you will need to save it under another name and then make sure the new file is not saved as a Read-Only file in the Save Options dialog box that is accessible through the Save As command. The file saved under a new name can then be edited. Enter or remove lines at the bottom by using the familiar Windows commands for adding rows and copying formulas or deleting rows. Always leave the double lines after the last row of cells, however, as the overall formulas look for those lines to determine the end of the data.

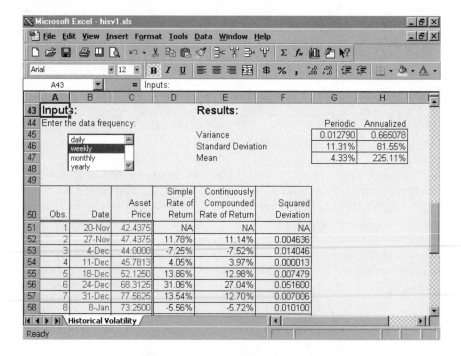

Implied Volatility

The second approach to estimating the volatility is called the **implied volatility,** which we shall denote as $\hat{\sigma}$. This procedure assumes the option's market price reflects the stock's current volatility. The Black-Scholes or any other acceptable option pricing model is used to infer a standard deviation. The implied volatility is the standard deviation that makes the Black-Scholes price equal the option's current market price.

The implied volatility is obtained by finding the standard deviation that when used in the Black-Scholes model makes the model price equal the market price of the option.

The implied volatility approach would be simple if the Black-Scholes equation could be rearranged to solve for the standard deviation. Since that cannot be done, we obtain the solution by plugging in values of σ until we find the one that makes the Black-Scholes price equal the market price. The procedure is illustrated in Figure 5.17. Because it requires a trial-and-error search, it can be quite laborious, and it is helpful to use a computer to do the calculations.[7]

Let us estimate the implied volatility for the America Online June 125 call. The input values are $S_0 = 125.9375$, $X = 125$, $r_c = .0446$, and $T = .0959$. The market price of the call is 13.50. We need to find the value of σ that will make the Black-Scholes value come to 13.50. We must also be prepared to specify a certain degree of precision in our answer; that is, how close should the model price come to the market price or how many decimal places to the right of zero do we require in our implied volatility? For illustrative purposes, we shall use two decimal places in the implied volatility and stop the trial-and-error process when we determine that the true implied volatility is within .01 of our answer.

Deriving the implied volatility will involve repetitive Black-Scholes calculations, so we will use the Excel spreadsheet bsbin2.xls. Open the file bsbin2.xls and insert the appropriate values for the asset (stock) price, exercise price, risk-free rate, and time to expiration. Let us start with a σ of .5. We see that the Black-Scholes call price is 8.48. Obviously this is too low, so let us try a σ of .6. The Black-Scholes call price is then 10.02, which is still too low. At a σ of .7, we get 11.56; a σ of .8 gives 13.09; a σ of .85 gives 13.86; and a σ of .83 gives 13.55. Thus, our answer is around .83.

Because σ is the stock's volatility, all options on a given stock with the same expiration should give the same implied volatility. For various reasons, including the possibility that the Black-Scholes model is deficient, different options on the same stock sometimes produce different implied volatilities.

Table 5.7 presents the implied volatilities obtained for the options whose exercise prices surround the stock price. The implied volatilities range from 75 percent to 86 percent. This forces us to choose a single value for the overall implied volatility.

[7]A shortcut method is presented in Appendix 5A.

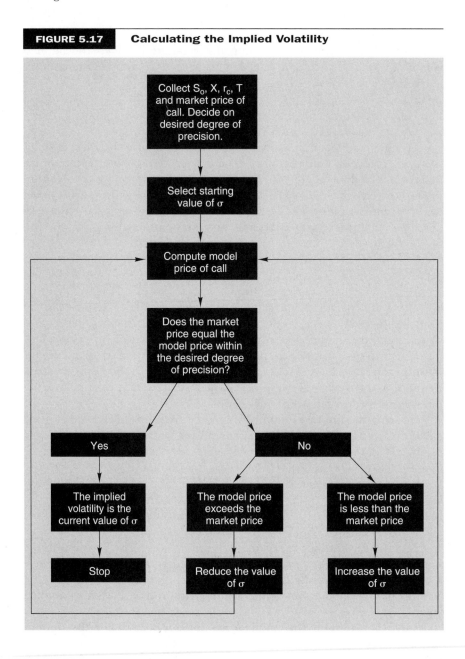

FIGURE 5.17   **Calculating the Implied Volatility**

Several methods have been suggested. Some involve taking a simple arithmetic average of the various implied volatilities. Others recommend using a weighted average. Still others simply select the implied volatility of the option whose exercise price is closest to the current stock price.

Recall from Figure 5.13 that we noticed that the call is nearly linear in the volatility if the call is at-the-money. Brenner and Subrahmanyam (1988)

| TABLE 5.7 | **Implied Volatilities of America Online Calls** | | |

		Expiration	
Exercise Price	May	June	July
120	.76	.79	.85
125	.75	.83	.86
130	.76	.83	.85

$S_0 = 125.9375$, $r_c = .0447$ (May), .0446 (June), .0453 (July),
$T = .0192$ (May), .0959 (June), .1726 (July)

exploited this fact and showed that an at-the-money call price is approximately given as

$$C \approx (0.398)S_0\,\sigma\sqrt{T},$$

where they define at-the-money as when the stock price equals the present value of the exercise price, $S_0 = Xe^{-r_cT}$. The implied volatility of an at-the-money call can then be obtained as

$$\hat{\sigma} \approx \frac{C}{(0.398)S_0\sqrt{T}},$$

where C is the market price of the call.[8] For example, our America Online June 125 has C = 13.50, $S_0 = 125.9375$, and T = .0959. Thus,

$$\hat{\sigma} \approx \frac{13.50}{(0.398)125.9375\sqrt{.0959}} = .8697.$$

Because this particular call is very close to at-the-money, the answer is fairly close to its actual implied volatility, which we obtained by trial and error.

Referring to Table 5.7, the differences in implied volatility for a given exercise price but across different expirations is called the **term structure of volatility.** By definition, the volatility in the Black-Scholes model is the volatility of the stock over the life of the option. Thus, it is reasonable to expect that the volatility might differ across expirations. Figure 5.18 illustrates the term structure of implied volatility for the AOL options expiring May, June, and July. Note that the term structure is upward sloping, meaning that the volatility is greater the further you look out on the horizon.

The differences in volatility across exercise prices for a given expiration are much more puzzling. For a given expiration, all options should

---

[8]For the curious, 0.398 is $\dfrac{1}{\sqrt{2\pi}}$, which is part of the mathematical formula that derives the normal probability.

FIGURE 5.18	The Term Structure of Implied Volatility

The Term Structure of Implied Volatility
AOL calls; r_c = .0447 (May), .0446 (June), .0453 (July),
T = .0192 (May), .0959 (June), .1726 (July), σ = .83

The pattern of implied volatility across expirations is often called the term structure of volatility, and the pattern of volatility across exercise prices is often called the volatility smile or skew.

give the same implied volatility. The implied volatilities are, after all, just the option market's opinion of the volatility of the stock. The stock's volatility should not be different across options with different exercise prices, since the options are all on the same stock. Oftentimes one observes patterns when the volatility is plotted against exercise price. A common pattern is a u-shape, referred to as the **volatility smile.** Occasionally one of the ends of the u is pointed downward instead of upward, giving the pattern the name **volatility skew.** Figure 5.19 illustrates the implied volatility for the AOL May and June options. To construct this figure, we have used options with exercise prices ranging from 100 to 180. Although the patterns shown here might be referred to as more of a smirk, it is easy to see why such names are given to patterns like these. It is much harder to understand why these patterns exist, and no satisfactory explanation has been given.

These unusual results would surely lead us to doubt the validity of the Black-Scholes model. Indeed the Black-Scholes model is not a perfect fit of

FIGURE 5.19   **The Implied Volatility Smile/Skew**
AOL calls; r_c = .0447 (May), .0446 (June),
T = .0192 (May), .0959 (June)

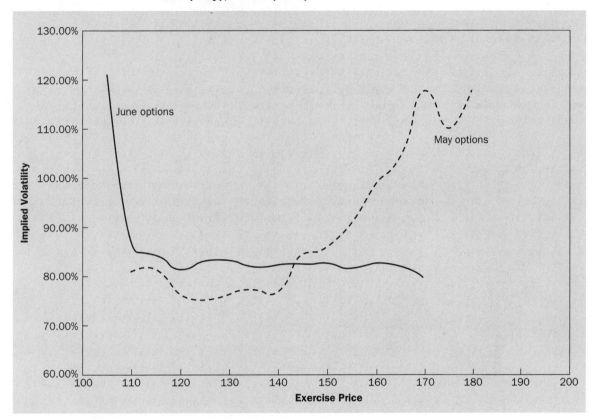

reality. Nonetheless, it is an easily understood and widely accepted model, and a great deal of research has been put into improving it. We shall not explore those improvements and variations here, but do keep in mind that the Black-Scholes model is a very basic model that does not handle all of the real world variations one might encounter.

The uncertainty of the correct value for the volatility is one reason why options attract so much speculative interest. If everyone agreed on the volatility estimate, the option would always be correctly priced and there would be far fewer reasons to buy or sell. It is the ambiguity of the volatility estimation that leads to disagreement among traders. This disagreement, in turn, leads to trading among those who believe the option is incorrectly priced.[9]

---

[9]Mark Twain in *Pudd'nhead Wilson* (1894) expressed this point succinctly by saying, "It were not best that we should think alike; it is difference of opinion that makes horse races."

Put Option Pricing Models

The Black-Scholes call option pricing model can be turned into a put option pricing model by inserting it into put-call parity.

Recall that the put-call parity formula gives the relationship between a put price and a call price. Expressing the put price as a function of the call price, we have

$$P_e(S_0,T,X) = C_e(S_0,T,X) - S_0 + X(1 + r)^{-T}.$$

In the Black-Scholes world, it is necessary to use continuous compounding and discounting. Restating put-call parity so that the present value of the exercise price is computed using continuous discounting gives

$$P_e(S_0,T,X) = C_e(S_0T,X) - S_0 + Xe^{-r_cT},$$

where, as discussed earlier, r_c is the continuously compounded rate. Then we can substitute the Black-Scholes value for the call price. Letting P stand for $P_e(S_0,T,X)$ gives the Black-Scholes European put option pricing model:

The Black-Scholes model for European puts can be obtained by applying put-call parity to the Black-Scholes model for European calls.

$$P = Xe^{-r_cT} [1 - N(d_2)] - S_0 [1 - N(d_1)],$$

where d_1 and d_2 are the same as in the call option pricing model.

In the example of the America Online June 125 call, the values of $N(d_1)$ and $N(d_2)$ using the spreadsheet bsbin2.xls were .5692 and .4670, respectively. Plugging into the formula, we get

$$P = 125e^{-(.0446)(.0959)} (1 - .4670) - 125.9375(1 - .5692)$$
$$= 12.09.$$

The actual market price of the June 125 put was 11.50. Because this price must also include a premium for the additional benefit of early exercise and the Black-Scholes model does not reflect the early exercise premium, the difference between the market and model prices is actually greater than what we see here. In other words, if the put option pricing model reflected the early exercise premium, it would produce an even higher theoretical price.

The same variables that affect the call's price affect the put's price, although in some cases in a different manner. Table 5.8 summarizes these important concepts for puts.

The Excel spreadsheet bsbin2.xls, illustrated in Software Demonstration 5.1, does the Black-Scholes calculations for puts as well as calls.

Without getting into some very advanced techniques, it is not possible to make the Black-Scholes model accommodate early exercise for American puts. If it is necessary to price an American put, we would have to use the binomial model with a large number of time periods. Thus, suppose we were attempting to price the AOL June 125 put. Using the bsbin2.xls spreadsheet with n = 100 time periods and inputs $S_0 = 125.9375$, X = 125, $r_c = 0.446$,

TABLE 5.8   **The Effects of Variables on the Black-Scholes Put Option Price**

The results for put options are obtained by using the put-call parity relationship, $P = C - S_0 + Xe^{-r_cT}$.

Stock Price

The relationship between the stock price and the put price is called the put **delta.**

$$\text{Put } Delta = N(d_1) - 1.$$

Since $N(d_1)$ is between 0 and 1, the put delta is negative. This simply means that a put option moves in an opposite direction to the stock. A delta neutral position with stock and puts will require long positions in both stock and puts. The relationship between the put delta and the stock price is called the put **gamma.**

$$\text{Put } Gamma = \frac{e^{-d_1^2/2}}{S_0\sqrt{2\pi T}}.$$

Notice that the put gamma is the same as the call gamma. Like a call, the gamma is highest when the put is at-the-money.

Exercise Price

For a difference in the exercise price, the put price will change by e^{-r_cT} $[1 - N(d_2)]$. Because both of the terms are positive, the overall expression is positive.

Risk-Free Rate

The relationship between the put price and the risk-free rate is called the put **rho.**

$$\text{Put } Rho = -TXe^{-r_cT}[1 - N(d_2)].$$

This expression is always negative, meaning that the put price moves inversely to interest rates.

Volatility

The relationship between the put price and the volatility is called the **vega.**

$$\text{Put } Vega = \frac{S_0\sqrt{T}e^{-d_1^2/2}}{\sqrt{2\pi}}.$$

This is the same expression as the vega for a call. Like a call, a put is highly sensitive to the volatility.

Time to Expiration

The relationship between the put price and the time to expiration is called the **theta.**

$$\text{Put } Theta = -\frac{S_0\sigma e^{-d_1^2/2}}{2\sqrt{2\pi T}} + r_cXe^{-r_cT}(1 - N(d_2)).$$

This expression can be positive or negative, a point we covered in Chapter 3. A European put can either increase or decrease with time. The tendency to increase occurs because there is more time for the stock to move favorably. The tendency to decrease occurs because the additional time means waiting longer to receive the exercise price at expiration.

T = .0959, and σ = .83, we would obtain an American put value of 12.11, which is only slightly higher than the European value of 12.08 obtained with the binomial model. This suggests that the premium for early exercise is not that great, a likely reflection of the fact that the volatility on AOL is so high that exercising early throws away the time value. But when would such a put be exercised? We can tell by using the binomial model. If the American put value obtained using the binomial model equals the exercise value, the put should be exercised. In fact, the put would be selling for its intrinsic value and could be exercised or sold; either value is the same. Suppose right now the stock is at $100. The intrinsic value would obviously be Max(0, 125 − 100) = 25. The American put value using the binomial model would be 27.72. So, the put is still worth more alive. Suppose the stock was at $90. Then the intrinsic value would be $35, and the American put value would be worth $35.99. The put is still worth slightly more alive. Not until somewhere between $70 and $80 is the put worth precisely its intrinsic value and at that point would be exercised early.

The critical stock price at which the put is worth exercising could be found by trial and error. As a rule, the critical stock price rises as expiration approaches, meaning that the stock does not have to get quite as low to justify exercising the put, the closer to expiration. At expiration, the critical stock price is simply the exercise price.

Managing the Risk of Options

You may have gotten the impression that investors take option positions to establish the opportunity to make money when markets move in anticipated ways. Consider, however, that on the opposite side of each option transaction is a counterparty. The options market is characterized by counterparties who are in the marketmaking or dealer business. For exchange-listed options, these are individuals at the exchanges who offer to buy or sell options. For over-the-counter options, these are institutions that offer to buy or sell options with terms tailored to their customers' needs. We shall refer to both groups of counterparties as dealers. In general, they do not take option positions to speculate or hedge; their goal is to make money from bid-ask spreads. They have no desire to speculate, so they must neutralize the risk they assume.

Earlier in the chapter we talked about delta hedging. We noted that to delta hedge an option we must buy a certain number of shares of the underlying stock. In theory a delta hedged position must be adjusted continuously to reflect the fact that the delta changes with the level of the stock price and with time. Moreover, delta hedging neutralizes only the risk of small price changes. We noted that the option's gamma reflects the possibility of larger price changes. The dealer must be able to effectively hedge away this risk.

Let us begin by considering a dealer who sells 1,000 of the AOL June 125 calls at the Black-Scholes price of 13.5512. The delta is .5692. From what we covered earlier in the chapter, we know that to hedge would require that we buy 1,000(.5692), or approximately 569 shares. The dealer cannot adjust the delta continuously, so let us say that the dealer decides to adjust the hedge at the end of each day. Let the position be held for the full 35 days remaining in the option's life. Buying 569 shares at 125.9375 and selling 1,000 calls at 13.5512 means that we must invest 569(125.9375) − 1,000(13.5512) = 58,107. So we invest $58,107.

To get some idea of the risk involved, we can simulate the daily stock prices over the remaining life of the contract. Although generating prices by simulation is covered briefly later in this book, let us for now just assume that we have simulated the daily closing prices for America Online for the next 35 days. At time 0, the time we put the delta hedge in place, AOL is at 125.9375. One day later, it closes at 120.5442. Now there are 34 days until expiration so the time remaining is T = 34/365 = .0932. We plug these values into the Black-Scholes spreadsheet, bsbin2.xls, and find that the call would then be selling for 10.4781. How have we done on our hedge?

Stock worth	569(120.5442) =	$68,590, and
options worth	−1,000(10.4781) =	−10,478, for a
total value of		$58,112.

How much should we have? If we had invested $58,107 in risk-free bonds for one day at the rate of 4.46 percent, we should have $58,107e^{.0446(1/365)} = $58,114.

How would we continue to do? Table 5.9 presents the outcomes based on a simulation of the remaining AOL prices during the option's life. Day 0 is the day we put on the hedge. We start with no shares (column 2) or calls (column 3) at all. We assume we can trade only in whole numbers of shares and calls so at the end of the day, we sell 1,000 calls (column 9) and buy 569 shares (column 11). In column 18, note that the portfolio delta is not actually zero but rather −0.1541. This comes from having 569 shares at a delta of 1.0 and 1,000 short calls at a delta of .5692 (569(1) − 1,000(.5692)) = −0.2 or, more precisely, −0.1541). Because we cannot hold fractions of shares, we have a very slight negative delta.

At the end of day 1, as explained above, our portfolio is worth $58,112(column 7) whereas the target value is $58,114(column 8). Now note the columns under the heading "End of Day Option Calculations" (columns 13–17). The new time to expiration is 34/365 = .0932. The new delta is the N(d₁) of .4999. Now we need 500 shares as indicated in column 10. Column 11 shows that we must sell off 69 shares. With the stock price of 120.5442, this generates about 69(120.5442) = $8,318, which is then invested in bonds (column 12). Let us now move forward one more day.

TABLE 5.9	Daily Adjusted Delta Hedge
	$S_0 = 125.9375$, X = 125, r_c = .0446, T = .0959, σ = .83

	Beginning of Day Holdings			End of Day Values (before adjustments)					
Day (1)	Shares (2)	Calls (3)	$ of Bonds (4)	Stock Price (5)	Call Price (6)	Portfolio Value (7)	Target Portfolio Value (8)	New Call Trades (9)
0	0	0	0	125.9375	13.5512	0	58107	−1000
1	569	−1000	0	120.5442	10.4781	58112	58114	0
2	500	−1000	8319	106.9722	4.7757	57029	58121	0
3	315	−1000	28112	123.3607	11.5535	55417	58129	0
4	534	−1000	1096	131.1649	15.9068	55231	58136	0
5	631	−1000	−11628	129.3992	14.6075	55415	58143	0
6	610	−1000	−8912	119.6825	9.0988	54995	58150	0
7	479	−1000	6767	112.0550	5.6905	54751	58157	0
8	365	−1000	19544	121.4849	9.5739	54312	58164	0
9	500	−1000	3144	120.7170	8.9847	54517	58171	0
10	487	−1000	4714	124.8160	10.8856	54613	58178	0
11	546	−1000	−2651	118.7513	7.6358	54552	58185	0
12	452	−1000	8513	119.6200	7.8155	54766	58192	0
13	463	−1000	7198	124.3584	9.9522	54824	58200	0
14	536	−1000	−1881	124.9330	10.0561	55060	58207	0
15	545	−1000	−3006	116.3448	5.7369	54665	58214	0
16	398	−1000	14099	115.3336	5.1233	54878	58221	0
17	375	−1000	16753	117.7314	5.8360	55067	58228	0
18	413	−1000	12281	130.8900	12.5225	53816	58235	0
19	640	−1000	−17433	127.6654	10.2701	54003	58242	0
20	587	−1000	−10668	124.1370	8.0310	54169	58249	0
21	521	−1000	−2475	121.2598	6.3292	54372	58257	0
22	462	−1000	4679	123.5827	7.1586	54616	58264	0
23	506	−1000	−758	121.9328	6.0472	54892	58271	0
24	468	−1000	3876	122.9043	6.1916	55203	58278	0
25	486	−1000	1664	125.1344	6.9896	55489	58285	0
26	534	−1000	−4343	126.3644	7.3050	55830	58292	0
27	562	−1000	−7883	122.2297	4.8206	55990	58299	0
28	455	−1000	5197	129.5167	8.4304	55696	58306	0
29	646	−1000	−19543	130.3376	8.5568	56098	58313	0
30	675	−1000	−23326	127.6884	6.3990	56465	58321	0
31	608	−1000	−14773	125.9571	4.8751	56934	58328	0
32	554	−1000	−7972	131.3736	7.8780	56931	58335	0
33	759	−1000	−34908	119.3439	0.9844	54690	58342	0
34	236	−1000	27512	122.4398	1.1074	55301	58349	0
35	326	−1000	16495	122.8380	0.0000	56540	58356	0

At the end of day 2, the stock takes a big jump down to 106.9722 (column 5) and the call is at 4.7757 (column 6). Our $8,318 of bonds accrued one day's interest to $8,319 (column 4). Thus, we have

Stock worth	500(106.9722) = $53,486, and
options worth	−1,000(4.7757) = −4,776, and
bonds worth	8,319, for a
total value of	$57,029 (column 7).

TABLE 5.9   *(continued)*

				End of Day Option Calculations				
Adjusted No. of Shares (10)	No. of Shares Bought or Sold (11)	$ of Bonds Purchased or Sold (12)	Time to Expiration (13)	d_1 (14)	$N(d_1)$ (15)	d_2 (16)	$N(d_2)$ (17)	Portfolio Delta (18)
569	569	0	0.0959	0.1742	0.5692	−0.0828	0.4670	−0.1541
500	−69	8318	0.0932	−0.0002	0.4999	−0.2535	0.3999	0.0897
315	−185	19790	0.0904	−0.4831	0.3145	−0.7327	0.2319	0.4935
534	219	−27016	0.0877	0.0851	0.5339	−0.1607	0.4362	0.1016
631	97	−12723	0.0849	0.3356	0.6314	0.0937	0.5373	−0.4244
610	−21	2717	0.0822	0.2797	0.6102	0.0418	0.5167	−0.1615
479	−131	15678	0.0795	−0.0537	0.4786	−0.2876	0.3868	0.4082
365	−114	12774	0.0767	−0.3457	0.3648	−0.5756	0.2824	0.2285
500	135	−16400	0.0740	0.0011	0.5005	−0.2246	0.4111	−0.4511
487	−13	1569	0.0712	−0.0323	0.4871	−0.2538	0.3998	−0.1228
546	59	−7364	0.0685	0.1159	0.5461	−0.1013	0.4596	−0.1310
452	−94	11163	0.0658	−0.1208	0.4519	−0.3336	0.3693	0.0583
463	11	−1316	0.0630	−0.0935	0.4628	−0.3018	0.3814	0.2419
536	73	−9078	0.0603	0.0898	0.5358	−0.1139	0.4546	0.2134
545	9	−1125	0.0575	0.1122	0.5446	−0.0869	0.4654	0.3518
398	−147	17103	0.0548	−0.2596	0.3976	−0.4539	0.3250	0.4147
375	−23	2653	0.0521	−0.3181	0.3752	−0.5074	0.3059	−0.2150
413	38	−4474	0.0493	−0.2209	0.4126	−0.4053	0.3426	0.4277
640	227	−29712	0.0466	0.3582	0.6399	0.1791	0.5711	0.0946
587	−53	6766	0.0438	0.2196	0.5869	0.0458	0.5183	0.1095
521	−66	8193	0.0411	0.0538	0.5215	−0.1144	0.4545	−0.4720
462	−59	7154	0.0384	−0.0951	0.4621	−0.2576	0.3983	−0.1247
506	44	−5438	0.0356	0.0157	0.5062	−0.1410	0.4439	−0.2483
468	−38	4633	0.0329	−0.0801	0.4681	−0.2306	0.4088	−0.0832
486	18	−2212	0.0301	−0.0360	0.4857	−0.1801	0.4286	0.3472
534	48	−6006	0.0274	0.0854	0.5340	−0.0520	0.4793	−0.0314
562	28	−3538	0.0247	0.1569	0.5623	0.0266	0.5106	−0.3379
455	−107	13079	0.0219	−0.1130	0.4550	−0.2359	0.4068	−0.0176
646	191	−24738	0.0192	0.3737	0.6457	0.2588	0.6021	0.3031
675	29	−3780	0.0164	0.4530	0.6747	0.3466	0.6356	0.2638
608	−67	8555	0.0137	0.2739	0.6079	0.1768	0.5702	0.0774
554	−54	6802	0.0110	0.1369	0.5544	0.0500	0.5199	−0.4277
759	205	−26932	0.0082	0.7034	0.7591	0.6282	0.7350	−0.0968
236	−523	62417	0.0055	−0.7190	0.2361	−0.7804	0.2176	−0.0813
326	90	−11020	0.0027	−0.4518	0.3257	−0.4953	0.3102	0.2958
0	−326	40045	0.0000	−∞	0.0000	−∞	0.0000	0.0000

If we had been perfectly hedged through two days, we would have $58,107e^{.0446(2/365)} = $58,121 (column 8). Thus, we are now short by over $1,000.

This process continues and on day 35, the expiration day of the option, we have a portfolio value of $56,540, while our target value is $58,356, a shortage of $1,816. Clearly this is not a perfect hedge. In fact, we have lost more than 3 percent of our investment. What is the problem?

As we discussed earlier in the chapter, delta hedging works only if done continuously and only if the stock price changes are very small. The reason for this is as follows: The delta is based on the calculus concept of a first derivative. In the context here, the first derivative is the rate of change of the option price with respect to the stock price, under the assumption that the stock price change is extremely small. Look at Figure 5.6 again and note the curvature of the graph. The delta is simply the slope of the curve at a particular value of the stock price. But with a curve as opposed to a straight line, the slope is different at every point. The slope at a given point can be accurately estimated only if we allow the stock to move by a very small amount.

Obviously the stock can move by much larger amounts, and this is much more likely the less frequently that trading can be done. When that happens, delta is not a good approximation of the risk of the option. This is a point we made earlier in the chapter. In such cases, factors known as second-order effects come into play. The second-order effect is the gamma, which we covered earlier. It turns out that using the gamma can enable us to get a better hedge.

Gamma hedging is a much more complex process, and we shall take only a brief and simple look at it. The objective of gamma hedging is to be both delta and gamma hedged, sometimes called delta neutral and gamma neutral, meaning that essentially any stock price move will be hedged. It will be impossible to be both delta and gamma hedged by holding only the stock and option. This is because the risk associated with the option's gamma must be eliminated by another instrument. The delta of a stock is 1.0, but its gamma is zero. Thus, the stock cannot hedge the option's gamma risk. What we require is an instrument that has a nonzero gamma—specifically, another option.

So let us add the June 130 call, whose Black-Scholes price is 11.3772, whose delta is .5086, and whose gamma is .0123. The gamma of our June 125 call is .0121. In what follows, we use the Greek letter delta in the form of Δ_1 and Δ_2 to represent the deltas of our June 125 call (option 1) and the June 130 call (option 2), respectively. We use the Greek letter gamma—Γ_1 and Γ_2—to represent the gammas of our June 125 call and the June 130 call. We shall hold a portfolio of h_S shares of stock, which have a delta of 1.0 and a gamma of 0.0, 1,000 short calls (the June 125), and h_C of the June 130 calls. To be delta hedged, we must meet the condition:

$$h_S(1) - 1,000\Delta_1 + h_C\Delta_2 = 0,$$

and to be gamma hedged, we must meet the condition,

$$-1,000\Gamma_1 + h_C\Gamma_2 = 0.$$

In other words, the combined gammas of the two options must equal zero. We now have two equations and two unknowns. We can solve the second one for h_C and obtain:

$$h_C = 1,000(\Gamma_1/\Gamma_2).$$

Once we have this value, we then solve the first equation for h_S:

$$h_S = 1,000(\Delta_1 - (\Gamma_1/\Gamma_2)\Delta_2).$$

Now let us set up a gamma hedge and see how it performs. First we have

$$\Delta_1 = .5692, \Delta_2 = .5086, \Gamma_1 = .0121, \text{ and } \Gamma_2 = .0123.$$

Thus, the number of the second option we need, h_C, is

$$h_C = 1,000(.0121/.0123) = 984,$$

which we change to its spreadsheet-computed value of 985. The number of shares we need is

$$h_S = 1,000(.5692 - (.0121/.0123)(.5086)) = 68.$$

Thus, we buy 68 shares, sell 1,000 of the June 125 calls, and buy 985 of the June 130 calls. This will require that we invest funds of

$$68(125.9375) - 1,000(13.5512) + 985(11.3772) = 6,219.$$

Now, at the end of the first day, the stock is at 120.5442, the 125 call is at 10.4781, and the 130 call would be worth 8.6344. The portfolio would then be worth

$$68(120.5442) - 1,000(10.4781) + 985(8.6344) = 6,224.$$

The portfolio should be worth $\$6,219e^{.0446(1/365)} = \$6,220$.

The new deltas are $\Delta_1 = .4999$ and $\Delta_2 = .4384$. The new gammas are $\Gamma_1 = .0131$ and $\Gamma_2 = .0129$. Now the new number required of the 130 call is $1,000(.0131/.0129) = 1,016$. More precise spreadsheet calculations give us an answer of 1,012 so let us use 1,012. This means we must buy $1,012 - 985 = 27$ of the 130 calls at the new price of 8.6344. This will require $27(8.6344) = \$233$.

The number of shares we will need is

$$h_S = 1,000(.4999 - (.0131/.0129).4384) = 54.70.$$

The more precise calculations of a spreadsheet give us 56. We must sell $68 - 56 = 12$ shares at 120.5442. This raises $12(120.5442) = \$1,447$, leaving $\$1,447 - \$233 = \$1,214$ of new cash that we invest in risk-free bonds.

At the end of the next day, the stock is at 106.9722, the 125 call is at 4.7757, and the 130 call is at 3.7364. Our bonds have earned a little interest but are still worth about $\$1,214$. Our portfolio is now worth

$$56(106.9722) - 1,000(4.7757) + 1,012(3.7364) + \$1,214 = \$6,210.$$

Delta hedging is difficult because trading cannot be done continuously and because there are price changes that are too large to be captured by the delta. Gamma hedging can be used to deal with these problems.

If our portfolio were hedged for two days, it should be worth $\$6,219e^{.0446(2/365)} = \$6,221$. Thus, we are $11 behind.

Because of the large number of columns required to show the full details of this transaction, we shall omit them here. The final results are that for the set of stock prices in Table 5.9, the gamma hedge ends up with a value of $6,589. The target ending value would be $6,246. The difference is $343 ahead.

Thus, gamma hedging can make the hedge better able to eliminate the risk caused by large price changes occurring over finite periods of time. Dealers have learned how to effectively delta and gamma hedge, but they also face the risk of the volatility changing. We identified this concept earlier as vega risk. We shall not cover it here at this introductory level, but do be aware that vega risk can be hedged by introducing another instrument with a nonzero vega. This would mean that we would still need another option. Then we would have three equations and three unknowns, which are the number of shares, the number of the second call, and the number of the third call. The three equations would be solved to set the delta, gamma, and vega to zero.

Summary

This chapter introduced the Black-Scholes option pricing model. We began by noting that the discovery of the Black-Scholes model was made possible by many developments in mathematics and the sciences.

We then observed that when increasing the number of time steps, the binomial model converges to a specific value, which will be the Black-Scholes value.

We identified the assumptions of the Black-Scholes model, which are that (1) stock prices behave randomly according to a lognormal distribution, (2) the risk-free rate and volatility are constant over the option's life, (3) there are no taxes or transaction costs, (4) the stock pays no dividends, and (5) the options are European.

The Black-Scholes formula was presented and illustrated, and we observed that it employs risk neutral probabilities, which are obtained from the normal probability distribution. We noted that the model conforms to the European lower bound and that it obtains the appropriate prices for extreme values, such as a zero stock price, zero time to expiration, zero volatility, and zero exercise price.

We saw that the Black-Scholes call option formula, and call options in general, are directly related to the stock price, risk-free rate, time to expiration, and volatility, and inversely related to the exercise price.

We learned that the relationship between the call price and the stock price is the delta. The relationship between the delta and the stock price is the gamma. The relationship between the call price and the risk-free rate is the rho. The relationship between the call price and the volatility is the vega. The relationship between the call price and the time to expiration is the theta.

We saw that the Black-Scholes formula can be adjusted to accommodate dividends on the underlying stock by subtracting the present value of the dividends from the stock price, under either the assumption that the dividends over the option's life are known and discrete or that the dividends are paid at a continuously compounded rate.

We found that the most critical input in the Black-Scholes model is the volatility, which must be estimated. Moreover, the model is highly sensitive to the volatility. The volatility is typically estimated using either a historical sample of stock returns or as the implied volatility, which is inferred from the current prices of options.

We adapted the Black-Scholes model to price European puts by inserting the Black-Scholes call formula into put-call parity.

We concluded by examining how a dealer would manage an option position by delta hedging. We saw the limitations of delta hedging and how gamma hedging can reduce that risk.

In Chapter 3 we used put-call parity to find relative option prices. A put, call, and stock could be priced in relation to each other. But we had to have two of the three prices already. Now we have two absolute option pricing models, the binomial and Black-Scholes, which are really the same model. Figure 5.20 shows how the Black-Scholes models for puts and calls link the call and put with the stock and risk-free bond.

FIGURE 5.20   **The Linkage between Calls, Puts, Stock, and Risk-Free Bonds**

Key Terms

Before continuing to Chapter 6, you should be able to give brief definitions of the following terms:

- discrete time
- continuous time
- lognormal distribution
- Black-Scholes option pricing model
- z statistic
- delta
- gamma
- theta
- vega

- rho
- risk neutral probability
- delta hedge/delta neutral
- historical volatility
- implied volatility
- term structure of volatility
- volatility smile/skew
- gamma hedge
- normal probability

Further Reading

The original Black-Scholes and Merton papers are:

Black, F., and M. Scholes. "The Pricing of Options and Corporate Liabilities." *Journal of Political Economy* 81 (1973): 637–659.

Merton, R. C. "Theory of Rational Call Option Pricing." *Bell Journal of Economics and Management Science* 4 (1973): 141–183.

Empirical tests of the model are in:

Black, F., and M. Scholes. "The Valuation of Option Contracts and a Test of Market Efficiency." *Journal of Finance* 27 (1972): 399–418.

Galai, D. "Tests of Market Efficiency of the Chicago Board Options Exchange." *Journal of Business* 50 (1977): 167–197.

Galai, D. "A Survey of Empirical Tests of Option Pricing Models." In *Option Pricing,* edited by M. Brenner, 45–80. Lexington, Mass.: D. C. Heath, 1983.

MacBeth, J. D., and L. J. Merville. "An Empirical Examination of the Black-Scholes Call Option Pricing Model." *Journal of Finance* 34 (1979): 1173–1186.

Other significant papers involving the Black-Scholes option pricing model are:

Cox, J. C., and S. A. Ross. "The Valuation of Options for Alternative Stochastic Processes." *Journal of Financial Economics* 3 (1976): 145–166.

Geske, R. "The Valuation of Compound Options." *Journal of Financial Economics* 7 (1979): 63–81.

Rubinstein, M. "The Valuation of Uncertain Income Streams and the Pricing of Options." *Bell Journal of Economics* 7 (1976): 407–425.

Several interesting and highly readable papers on the model by Fischer Black are:

Black, F. "Fact and Fantasy in the Use of Options." *Financial Analysts Journal* 31 (July–August 1975): 36–41, 61–72.

Black, F. "How to Use the Holes in Black-Scholes." *Journal of Applied Corporate Finance* 1 (1989): 67–73.

Black, F. "How We Came Up with the Option Formula." *Journal of Portfolio Management* 15 (winter 1989): 4–8.

Questions and Problems

1. Explain what we mean when we say that the binomial model is a discrete time model and the Black-Scholes model is a continuous time model.

2. Explain the difference between a normal and a lognormal distribution as it pertains to stock prices.

3. Which assumption in the Black-Scholes model did we drop somewhere in the chapter? What did we do in removing that assumption to make the model give the correct option price?

4. Compare the variables in the binomial model with those in the Black-Scholes model. Note any differences and explain.

5. What is the most critical variable in the Black-Scholes model? Explain.

6. Consider the right-hand side of the Black-Scholes formula as consisting of the sum of two terms. Explain what each of those terms represents.

7. Explain each of the following concepts as they relate to call options.
   a. Delta
   b. Gamma
   c. Rho
   d. Vega
   e. Theta

8. Suppose you subscribe to a service that gives you estimates of the theoretically correct volatilities of stocks. You note that the implied volatility of a particular option is substantially higher than the theoretical volatility. What action should you take?

9. Answer the following questions as they relate to implied volatilities.
   a. Can implied volatilities be expected to vary for options on the same stock with the same exercise prices but different expirations?
   b. Can implied volatilities be expected to vary for options on the same stock with the same expiration but different exercise prices?

10. What factors contribute to the difficulty of making a delta hedge be truly risk-free?

11. A stock is priced at $50 with a volatility of .35. A call option with an exercise price of $50 has an expiration in one year. The risk-free rate is 5 percent. Construct a table for stock prices of $5, 10, 15, . . ., 100. Compute the Black-Scholes price of the call and the European lower bound and verify that the former is at least as large as the latter. Use the spreadsheet bsbin2.xls or the Windows program bsbwin2.1.exe.

The following option prices were observed for calls and puts on a stock for the trading day of July 6 of a particular year. Use this information in problems 12 through 20. The stock was priced at 165 1/8. The expirations were July 17, August 21, and October 16. The continuously compounded risk-free rates associated with the three expirations were .0503, .0535, and .0571, respectively. Unless otherwise indicated, assume the options are European.

Strike	Calls			Puts		
	Jul	Aug	Oct	Jul	Aug	Oct
155	10.5	11.75	14	.1875	1.25	2.75
160	6	8.125	11.125	.75	2.75	4.5
165	2.6875	5.25	8.125	2.375	4.75	6.75
170	.8125	3.25	6	5.750	7.5	9

12. Let the standard deviation of the continuously compounded return on the stock be 0.21. Ignore dividends. Answer the following:

a. What is the theoretical fair value of the October 165 call? Calculate this answer by hand and then recalculate it using either bsbin2.xls or bsbwin2.1.exe.

b. Based on your answer in part a, recommend a riskless strategy.

c. If the stock price decreases by $1, how will the option position offset the loss on the stock?

13. Use the Black-Scholes European put option pricing formula for the October 165 put option. Repeat parts a, b, and c of question 12 with respect to the put.

14. Suppose the stock pays a $1.10 dividend with an ex-dividend date of September 10. Rework part a of problem 12 using an appropriate dividend-adjusted procedure. Calculate this answer by hand and then recalculate it using either bsbin2.xls or bsbwin2.1.exe.

15. On July 6, the dividend yield on the stock is 2.7 percent. Rework part a of problem 12 using the yield-based dividend adjustment procedure. Calculate this answer by hand and then recalculate it using either the bsbin2.xls or the bsbwin2.1.exe program.

16. Suppose on July 7 the stock will go ex-dividend with a dividend of $2. If the options were American, determine whether the July 160 call would be exercised.

17. Following is the sequence of daily prices on the stock for the preceding month of June:

Date	Price	Date	Price
6/1	159.875	6/16	162.000
6/2	157.250	6/17	161.375
6/3	160.250	6/18	160.875
6/4	161.375	6/19	161.375
6/5	160.000	6/22	163.250
6/8	161.250	6/23	164.875
6/9	159.875	6/24	166.125
6/10	157.750	6/25	167.875
6/11	157.625	6/26	166.500
6/12	156.625	6/29	165.375
6/15	159.625	6/30	162.500

Estimate the historical volatility of the stock for use in the Black-Scholes model. (Ignore dividends on the stock.)

18. Estimate the implied volatility of the August 165 call. Compare your answer with that obtained in problem 17. Use trial and error. Stop when your answer is within 0.01 of the true implied volatility. Use the Excel spreadsheet bsbin2.xls or the Windows program bsbwin2.1.exe.

19. Repeat problem 18 using the approximation for an at-the-money call. Compare your answer with the one you obtained in problem 18. Is the approximation a good one?

20. A stock is selling for $100 with a volatility of 40 percent. Consider a call option on the stock with an exercise price of 100 and an expiration of one year. The risk-free rate is 4.5 percent. Let the call be selling for its Black-Scholes value. You construct a delta-hedged position involving the sale of 10,000 calls and the purchase of an appropriate number of shares. You can buy and sell shares and calls only in whole numbers. At the end of the next day, the stock is at $99. You then adjust your position accordingly to maintain the delta hedge. The following day the stock closes at $102. In all cases use the spreadsheet bsbin2.xls or the Windows program bsbwin2.1.exe to price the call.

a. Compare the amount of money you end up with to the amount you would have had if you had invested the money in a risk-free bond. Explain why the target was or was not achieved.

b. Now add another option, one on the same stock with an exercise price of 105 and the same expiration. Reconstruct the problem by delta and gamma hedging. Explain why the target was or was not achieved.

21. (Concept Problem) Show how a delta hedge using a position in the stock and a long position in a put would be set up.

22. (Concept Problem) Suppose a stock is priced at 80 and has a volatility of .35. You buy a call option with an exercise price of 80 that expires in 3 months. The risk-free rate is 5 percent. Answer the following questions:

   a. Determine the theoretical value of the call. Use bsbin2.xls or bsbwin2.1.exe.

   b. Suppose the actual call is selling for $5. Suggest a strategy, but do not worry about hedging the risk. Simply buy or sell 100 calls.

   c. After purchasing the call, you investigate your possible profits. You expect to unwind the position one month later, at which time you expect the call to have converged to its Black-Scholes value. Of course you do not know what the stock price will be, but you can calculate the profits for stock prices over a reasonable range. You expect that the stock will not vary beyond $60 and $100. Determine your profit in increments of $10 of the stock price. Comment on your results.

Note: This problem will prepare you for Chapter 6.

APPENDIX 5A

A Shortcut to the Calculation of Implied Volatility

Solving for the implied volatility can be a tedious trial-and-error process. Manaster and Koehler (1982), however, provide a shortcut that can quickly lead to the solution. The technique employs a Newton-Raphson search procedure.

Suppose that for a given standard deviation, σ^*, the Black-Scholes formula gives the call price as $C(\sigma^*)$. The true market price, however, is $C(\sigma)$, where σ is the true volatility. Manaster and Koehler recommend an initial guess of σ_1^*, where

$$\sigma_1^* = \sqrt{\left|\ln\left(\frac{S_0}{X}\right) + r_c T\right| \left(\frac{2}{T}\right)}.$$

Then compute the value of $C(\sigma_1^*)$ and compare it to the market price, $C(\sigma)$. If this is not close enough, the next guess should be

$$\sigma_2^* = \sigma_1^* - \frac{\left[C\left(\sigma_1^*\right) - C\left(\sigma\right)\right]e^{d_1^2/2}\sqrt{2\pi}}{S_0\sqrt{T}},$$

where d_1 is computed using σ_1^*. Then compute the value $C(\sigma_2^*)$ and compare it to the market price, $C(\sigma)$. If it is not close enough, the next guess should be

$$\sigma_3^* = \sigma_2^* - \frac{\left[C\left(\sigma_2^*\right) - C\left(\sigma\right)\right]e^{d_1^2/2}\sqrt{2\pi}}{S_0\sqrt{T}},$$

with d_1 computed using σ_2^*. Repeat the process until the model price is sufficiently close to the market price. In other words, given the ith guess of the implied volatility, the $(i + 1)$th guess should be

$$\sigma_{i+1}^* = \sigma_i^* - \frac{\left[C\left(\sigma_i^*\right) - C\left(\sigma\right)\right]e^{d_1^2/2}\sqrt{2\pi}}{S_0\sqrt{T}},$$

where d_1 is computed using σ_i^*.

Let us apply this procedure to the problem in the chapter. We have $S_0 = 125.9375$, $X = 125$, $T = .0959$, $r_c = .0446$, and $C(\sigma) = 13.50$. The initial guess for the implied volatility is

$$\sigma_1^* = \sqrt{\left|\ln\left(\frac{125.9375}{125}\right) + .0446(.0959)\right|\left(\frac{2}{.0959}\right)} = .4950.$$

At a volatility of .4950, the Black-Scholes value is 8.41. The next guess should be

$$\sigma_2^* = .4950 - \frac{[8.41 - 13.50]e^{(.1533)^2/2}(2.5066)}{125.9375\sqrt{.0959}} = .8260.$$

where .1533 is the value of d_1 computed from the Black-Scholes model using .4950 as the standard deviation. The value 2.5066 is $\sqrt{2\pi}$. The Black-Scholes price using .8260 as the volatility is 13.49, which is close enough.

Thus, we have found the solution in only two steps. In the chapter we noted that the implied volatility was .83 with the slight difference being due to rounding off our answer.

APPENDIX 5B

The BSBWIN2.1 Windows Software

For those who prefer not to use a spreadsheet to calculate option prices but are comfortable with Windows, the software program bsbwin2.1.exe calculates Black-Scholes and binomial option prices along with deltas, gammas, and thetas. This Windows-based program offers many attractive features. In addition, the binomial program runs considerably faster than the Excel spreadsheet bsbin2.xls, and, thus, may be preferred if many time steps are required.

To run the program, you will need Windows 3.1, Windows 95, or Windows 98, and the file VBRUN300.DLL. This program is included in most versions of Windows. Your software diskette includes a copy of the program. If VBRUN300.DLL is already on your hard disk, it will probably be found in the \windows\system subdirectory or folder. If it is not there, copy the file from the diskette to your hard drive. To run bsbwin2.1.exe, use any of the standard Windows methods for running an executable program, such as the **Run** command in Windows 95/98. You may wish to set up a shortcut in Windows 95/98. In any case, follow the instructions for any of the numerous ways to run an executable file as demonstrated in your Windows manual.

When you run the program, you will see the following window:

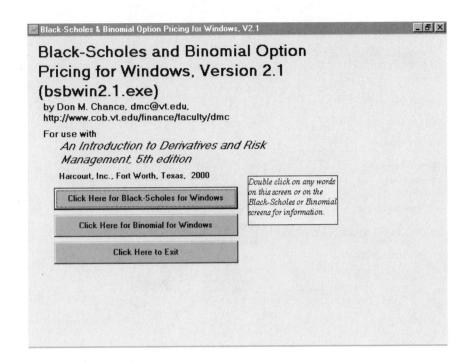

From the main screen choose either the Black-Scholes or Binomial model. You will then be taken to either a Black-Scholes or Binomial window, both of which are shown on the following pages.

At the top of each window is a bar you can click on to receive instructions for that window. Although bsbwin2.1.exe does not contain traditional Windows Help files, you can double-click on most of the key words or phrases on the main window and on the Black-Scholes and Binomial windows and see a box containing information. Try this feature out by double-clicking on any words you see on either the main window or the Black-Scholes or Binomial windows.

The program contains many error checkers, such as entering a negative asset price or dividend or forgetting to specify any time steps in the binomial model. Up to three dividends can be accommodated, but any dividend you enter that occurs after the option's life triggers a warning that deletes the dividend. Enter the risk-free rate in its continuously compounded form.

A useful feature is the Time Calculator, which enables you to enter two dates and obtain the time in years between those two dates. If you double-click on the "Time to Expiration" cell or any of the "Time to Ex-Dividend Day" cells, the Time Calculator is automatically invoked and you can insert the time into the appropriate cell as soon as you enter the dates and click on the "Time in Years" cell. When entering the year, you should

Black-Scholes for Windows

Click here for Instructions

Time Calculator (optional)

	First date	Second date
Month (1-12)		
Day (1-31)		
Year (yyyy)		
Time in Years		

Asset Price: 125.9375

Exercise Price: 125

Risk-Free Rate: .0446

Time to Expiration: .0959

Standard Deviation: .83

Dividends (click one)
- ⦿ None
- ○ Continuous Yield
- ○ Discrete

Amount   Time to Ex-Dividend Day

	Call	Put
Price	13.5768	12.1058
Delta	.5693	-.4307
Gamma	.0121	.0121
Theta	-68.9070	-63.3557
Vega	15.3244	15.3244
Rho	5.5731	-6.3633

Compute   Return

Binomial for Windows

Click here for Instructions

Time Calculator (optional)

	First date	Second date
Month (1-12)		
Day (1-31)		
Year (yyyy)		
Time in Years		

Asset Price: 125.9375

Exercise Price: 125

Risk-Free Rate: .0446

Time to Expiration: .0959

Standard Deviation: .83

# of Time Steps: 200

Dividends (Click one)
- ⦿ None
- ○ Continuous Yield
- ○ Discrete

Amount   Time to Ex-Dividend Day

	European Call	American Call	European Put	American Put
Price	13.5566	13.5566	12.0856	12.1182
Delta	.5696	.5696	-.4304	-.4320
Gamma	.0121	.0121	.0121	.0122
Theta	-68.8823	-68.8823	-63.3311	-63.7342

Compute   Return

use the format yyyy, but for any years less than 2000, the short format yy will work.

You can terminate the program the same way you close any Windows program, using the icons in the upper left- and right-hand corners or the pull down menu in the upper left-hand corner. Alternatively you can close it by clicking on the appropriate buttons in the window itself. You can minimize the window, drag it, and resize it, as with any Windows program.

CHAPTER 6

Basic Option Strategies

A bird in the hand is an apt way to describe the strategy of today's options investor. Taking the immediate income of writing a covered call, the battle-tested investor is strategically managing market risk.

LAWRENCE SEVERN
Futures and Options World, October 1995

One of the most interesting characteristics of an option is that it can be combined with stock or other options to produce a wide variety of alternative strategies. The profit possibilities are so diverse that virtually any investor can find an option strategy to suit his or her risk preference and market forecast.

In a world without options, the available strategies would be quite limited. If the market were expected to go up, one would buy stock; if it were expected to go down, one would sell short stock. As noted in Chapter 1, however, selling short stock requires an investor to meet certain requirements, such as having a minimum amount of capital to risk, selling short on an uptick or zero-plus tick, and maintaining minimum margins. Options make it simple to convert a forecast into a plan of action that will pay off if correct. Of course, any strategy will penalize if the forecast is wrong. With the judicious use of options, however, the penalties can be relatively small and known in advance.

This and the next chapter examine some of the more popular option strategies. It is not possible to cover all the strategies option traders could use. The ones we examine here should provide a basic understanding of the process of analyzing option strategies. Further study and analysis of the more advanced and complex strategies can be done using the framework presented here.

This chapter presents the basic option strategies. These strategies are the easiest to understand and involve the fewest transactions. Specifically, we

Chapter Objectives

■ To introduce the three-way procedure for examining the risk and return of an option strategy: by equation, by graph, and by numerical example

■ To examine the basic strategies of buying and selling stock, calls, and puts

■ To examine the combination strategies of covered calls, protective puts, conversions, and reversals

■ To explain how the choice of exercise price affects the possible outcomes of a strategy

■ To explain how the length of the chosen holding period affects the outcomes of a strategy

■ To illustrate the accompanying software for analyzing option strategies

219

shall cover the strategies of calls, puts, and stock, and combining calls with stock and puts with stock. We shall see how calls and stock can be combined to form puts and how puts and stock can be combined to form calls. Chapter 7 will look at spread strategies, which involve one short option and one long option, and combination strategies, which entail both puts and calls.

The approach we use here to analyze option strategies is to determine the profit a strategy will produce for a broad range of stock prices when the position is closed. This methodology is simple yet powerful enough to demonstrate its strengths. One attractive feature is that there are actually three ways to present the strategy. Because reinforcement enhances learning, we shall utilize all three presentations.

The first method is to determine an equation that gives the profit from the strategy as a function of the stock price when the position is closed. You will find that the equations are quite simple and build on skills covered in Chapters 3, 4, and 5. The second method is a graphical analysis that uses the equations to construct graphs of the profit as a function of the stock price when the position is closed. The third approach is to use a specific numerical example to illustrate how the equations and graphs apply to real-world options. We continue with the same America Online options previously examined.

Keep in mind that there are options on other types of assets, such as commodities and bonds, and there are also options on futures contracts and interest rates, which we shall encounter in later chapters. The basic principles covered in this chapter apply in a fairly straightforward manner to those cases.

As with our earlier analyses of options, we require several symbols. For convenience and because there are a few new notations, the following section presents the complete set of symbols.

Terminology and Notation

C = current call price
P = current put price
S_0 = current stock price
T = time to expiration as a fraction of a year
X = exercise price
S_T = stock price at option's expiration
Π = profit from the strategy

The following symbols indicate the number of calls, puts, or shares of stock:

N_C = number of calls
N_P = number of puts
N_S = number of shares of stock

As indicated in Chapter 2, the standard number of calls, puts, and shares is 100. For our purposes, it will not matter if we use a simple number, such as 1 or 2. When working with the numerical examples, however, we shall assume a standard contract of options or block of stock, which, of course, means 100 options or shares.

The Profit Equations

One of the powerful features of the N_C, N_P, and N_S notation is that these numbers' signs indicate whether the position is long or short. For example,

> If $N_C > (<)$ 0, the investor is buying (writing) calls.
> If $N_P > (<)$ 0, the investor is buying (writing) puts.
> If $N_S > (<)$ 0, the investor is buying (selling short) stock.

To determine the profit from a particular strategy, we need only know how many calls, puts, and shares of stock are involved, whether the position is long or short, the prices at which the options or stock were purchased or written, and the prices at which the positions were closed. With calls held to the expiration date, we already know that the call will be worth its intrinsic value at expiration. Thus, the profit can be written as

$$\Pi = N_C[\text{Max}(0, S_T - X) - C].$$

Notice how the sign of N_C allows the equation to give the profit for both the call buyer and the call writer. For example, a buyer with one call, $N_C = 1$, has a profit of

$$\Pi = \text{Max}(0, S_T - X) - C.$$

For the writer with one call, $N_C = -1$, profit is

$$\Pi = -\text{Max}(0, S_T - X) + C.$$

For a put option, the profit can be written as

$$\Pi = N_P[\text{Max}(0, X - S_T) - P].$$

For a buyer with one put, $N_P = -1$,

$$\Pi = \text{Max}(0, X - S_T) - P.$$

For a writer with one put, $N_P = -1$,

$$\Pi = -\text{Max}(0, X - S_T) + P.$$

For a transaction involving only stock, the profit equation is simply

$$\Pi = N_S(S_T - S_0).$$

For a buyer of one share of stock, $N_S = 1$, profit is

$$\Pi = S_T - S_0.$$

For a short seller of one share of stock, $N_S = -1$, profit is

$$\Pi = -S_T + S_0.$$

These profit equations make it simple to determine the profit from any transaction. Take, for example, the equations for the call buyer and the put buyer. In both cases, the profit is simply the dollar amount received from exercising the option minus the dollar amount paid for the option. This figure is then multiplied by the number of options. For the call writer and put writer, the profit is the amount received as the premium minus the amount paid out from exercising the option. This figure is then multiplied by the number of options written. Similarly, the profit for a stock buyer is simply the price at which the stock is sold minus the price paid for the stock. This figure is then multiplied by the number of shares. For the short seller, the profit is the price received from the short sale minus the price paid for repurchasing the stock. This figure is then multiplied by the number of shares sold short. To keep the analysis as simple as possible, we shall ignore the interest foregone or implicitly earned on a long or short position in options or stock.

Finally, we shall often find ourselves using the terms **bull** and **bear,** which are part of the lingo of financial markets. A bull market is one in which the price goes up. A bear market is one in which the price goes down. A bullish investor believes a bull market is coming, and a bearish investor believes a bear market is coming.

Different Holding Periods

The cases described in the previous section are strategies in which the position is held until the option expires. Because the option has no time value remaining and sells for its intrinsic value, the profit is easy to determine. It is not necessary, however, that an option trader hold the position open until the option expires. The length of the investor's holding period can be any time interval desired. In the case of a position closed out prior to the option's expiration, it is necessary to determine at what price the option would sell. How would we go about doing this?

Remember that the available information would be the exercise price and the time remaining on the option. We would want to know at what price the option would sell given a certain stock price. If the risk-free rate and an estimate of the variance of the return on the stock were available, we could use the Black-Scholes model. Here we shall assume this information is available, and we shall use the model to estimate the option's remaining time value to determine the profit from the strategy.

For illustrative purposes, we define three points in time: T_1, T_2, and T. We allow the investor to hold the position until either T_1, T_2, or all the way to expiration, T. The holding period from today until T_1 is the shortest. If an investor closes out the position at time T_1, the option will have a remaining time to expiration of $T - T_1$. The holding period from today until T_2 is of intermediate length. The investor who chooses it closes the option position with a remaining time to expiration of $T - T_2$. If the investor holds the position until expiration, the remaining time is $T - T = 0$.

Thus, the profit from a call position, if terminated at time T_1 before expiration and when the stock price is S_{T_1}, is written as

$$\Pi = N_C[C(S_{T_1}, T - T_1, X) - C],$$

where $C(S_{T_1}, T - T_1, X)$ is the value obtained from the Black-Scholes or any other appropriate call option pricing model using a stock price of S_{T_1} and a time to expiration of $T - T_1$. C is, of course, the original price of the call. The expression for puts is the same except that we use a P instead of a C and employ the Black-Scholes or any other appropriate put option pricing model to calculate $P(S_{T_1}, T - T_1, X)$. Similar expressions obviously apply when the position is closed at T_2.

Although the examples in this chapter use exchange-traded options, they are equally applicable to over-the-counter options. Although there is no specific market for liquidating over-the-counter options before expiration, the equivalent result can be obtained by simply creating a new option that offsets the old option. This procedure, of course, assumes that the writer does not default.

Assumptions

Several important assumptions underlie the analysis of option strategies.

First, we assume the stock pays no dividends. As we saw in Chapters 3, 4, and 5, dividends can complicate option decisions. Although including them here would not be especially difficult, we will intentionally omit them to keep the analysis simple. Where it is especially important, we will discuss the effect of dividends.

Second, we assume no taxes or transaction costs. These already have been covered and certainly are a consideration in option decisions, but they would add little to the analysis here. Where there are special tax and transaction cost factors, we provide an interpretation of their effects.

Recall that we have been analyzing the America Online options in previous chapters. For convenience, Table 6.1 repeats those data.

TABLE 6.1	AOL Option Data, May 14

Exercise Price	Calls			Puts		
	May	June	July	May	June	July
120	8 3/4	15 3/8	20 7/8	2 3/4	9 1/4	13 5/8
125	5 3/4	13 1/2	18 5/8	4 5/8	11 1/2	16 5/8
130	3 5/8	11 3/8	16 3/8	7 3/8	14 1/4	19 5/8

Current Stock Price: 125 15/16
Expirations: May 21, June 18, July 16
Risk-Free Rates (continuously compounded): .0447 (May); .0446 (June); .0453 (July)

Now let us move on to analyzing the strategies. The first group of strategies we shall examine are transactions involving stock.

Stock Transactions

Because combining stocks with options is sometimes an attractive strategy, it is important that we first establish the framework for stocks.

Buy Stock

The simplest transaction is the purchase of stock. The profit equation is

$$\Pi = N_S(S_T - S_0) \text{ given that } N_S > 0.$$

For illustrative purposes, let $N_S = 100$, a single round lot of stock. Figure 6.1 shows how the profit from this transaction varies with the stock price when the position is closed. The transaction is profitable if the America Online stock ultimately is sold at a price higher than $125.9375, the price paid for the stock. Dividends would lower this breakeven by the amount of the dividends, while transaction costs would raise it by the amount of those costs.

Sell Short Stock

The short sale of stock is the mirror image of the purchase of stock. The profit equation is

$$\Pi = N_S(S_T - S_0) \text{ given that } N_S < 0.$$

In this example, let $N_S = -100$, which means that 100 shares have been sold short. Figure 6.2 shows how the profit from the short sale varies with

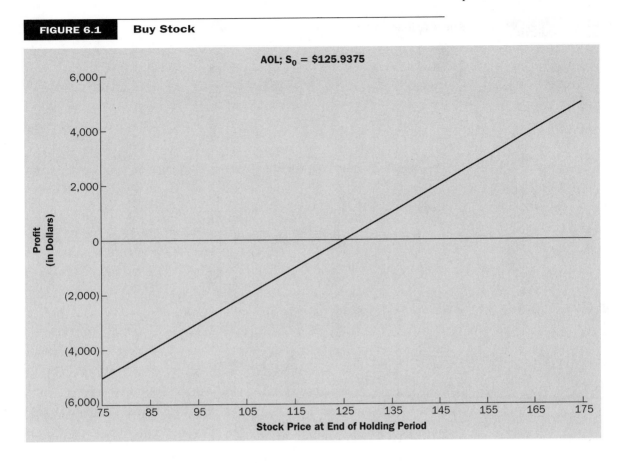

FIGURE 6.1   Buy Stock

AOL; S_0 = $125.9375

Profit (in Dollars) vs. Stock Price at End of Holding Period

the price of the America Online stock at the end of the investor's holding period. Short selling is a strategy undertaken in anticipation of a bear market. The investor borrows the stock from the broker, sells it at $125.9375, and repurchases it at—it is hoped—a lower price.[1] If the shares are repurchased at less than $125.9375, the transaction earns a profit. As Figure 6.2 shows, selling short has the potential for unlimited losses if the investor guesses wrong and the stock price rises.

Now we turn to the first of the option strategies—the call transactions.

Call Option Transactions

There are two types of call option transactions. We first examine the strategy of buying a call.

---

[1]Any dividends paid while the stock is sold short go to whoever purchased the stock from the short seller. In addition, the short seller must pay the broker the amount of the dividends.

Sell Short Stock

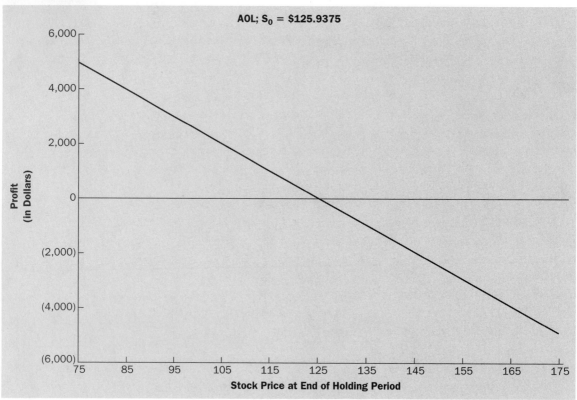

AOL; S_0 = $125.9375

Profit (in Dollars)

Stock Price at End of Holding Period

Buy a Call

The profit from a call option purchase is

$$\Pi = N_C[\text{Max}(0, S_T - X) - C] \text{ given that } N_C > 0.$$

Consider the case where the number of calls purchased is simply 1 ($N_C = 1$). Suppose the stock price at expiration is less than or equal to the exercise price so that the option expires out-of-the-money. What is the profit from the call? Since the call expires unexercised, the profit is simply $-C$. The call buyer incurs a loss equal to the premium paid for the call.

Suppose the call option ends up in-the-money. Then the call buyer will exercise the call, buying the stock for X and selling it for S_T, which will net a profit of $S_T - X - C$.[2] These results are summarized as follows:

---

[2]The stock need not be sold for this result to hold. The call buyer can retain the stock worth S_T or convert it to cash. An even better strategy would be to sell the call an instant before it expires. At that time it should have little, if any, time value left. This would avoid the high transaction cost of taking delivery of the stock.

$$\Pi = S_T - X - C \qquad \text{if } S_T > X.$$
$$\Pi = -C \qquad\qquad \text{if } S_T \le X.$$

Figure 6.3 illustrates this transaction for the America Online June 125 call, which sells for $13.50. The call has limited downside risk. The maximum possible loss for a single contract is $1,350, which is the premium times 100. At any stock price at expiration less than the exercise price of 125, the call buyer loses the maximum amount. If the stock price is above 125, the loss will be less than $1,350. Losses, however, are incurred if the stock price is below a critical stock price, which we shall call the **breakeven stock price** at expiration.

Notice in Figure 6.3 that the breakeven stock price is above the exercise price and between $135 and $145. We can find the breakeven stock price at expiration by simply setting to zero the profit for the case where stock price exceeds exercise price. We then solve for the breakeven stock price, S_T^*. Thus,

$$\Pi = S_T^* - X - C = 0.$$

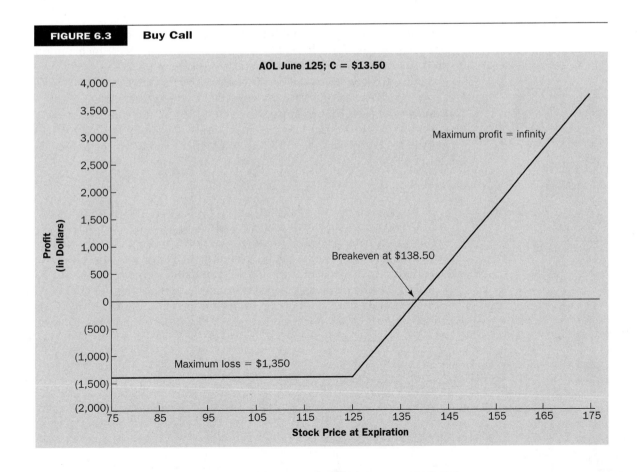

| **FIGURE 6.3** | **Buy Call** |

Solving for S_T^* gives

$$S_T^* = X + C.$$

The breakeven stock price at expiration, then, is the exercise price plus the call price. The call premium, C, is the amount already paid for the call. To break even, the call buyer must exercise the option at a price high enough to recover the option's costs. For every dollar by which the stock price at expiration exceeds the exercise price, the call buyer gains a dollar. Therefore, the stock price must exceed the exercise price by C dollars for the call buyer to recover the cost of the option. In this problem, the breakeven stock price at expiration is $125 + $13.50 = $138.50.

Notice how the call option offers the buyer a potentially unlimited profit while restricting the loss to the amount paid for the option. Although the likelihood of abnormally large profits is minimal, it is comforting to know that the potential loss is small. This makes the purchase of a call a particularly attractive strategy for those with limited budgets who wish to "play the market" while limiting their losses to a level that will not wipe them out.

Buying a call is a bullish strategy that has a limited loss (the call premium) and an unlimited potential gain.

THE CHOICE OF EXERCISE PRICE   Usually several options with the same expirations but different strike prices are available. Which option should we buy? There is no unambiguous answer.

Figure 6.4 compares the profit graphs for the America Online June calls with strike prices of 120, 125, and 130. There are advantages and disadvantages to each. First, compare the 125, which we previously examined, with the 130. If we choose a higher strike price, the gain if the stock prices rises will be less. Because the call with the higher exercise price commands a lower premium, however, the loss if the stock price falls will be smaller. The breakeven for the 130 is X + C = 130 + 11.375 = 141.375, which is higher than that for the 125.

If we choose the 120 over the 125, we have the potential for a greater profit if the stock price at expiration is higher. Also, the breakeven is X + C = 120 + 15.375 = 135.375. If the market is down, however, the loss will be greater. The potential loss is the full premium of $1,537.50. This is because the call with the lower exercise price will command a greater premium.

Buying a call with a lower exercise price has a greater maximum loss but greater upside gains.

Thus, the choice of which option to purchase is not easy and depends on how confident the call buyer is about the market outlook. If one feels strongly that the stock price will increase, the call with the lowest exercise price is preferable. Otherwise, a higher exercise price will minimize the potential loss.

THE CHOICE OF HOLDING PERIOD   The strategies previously examined assume the investor holds the option until the expiration date. Alternatively, the call buyer could sell the option prior to expiration. Let us look at what happens if a shorter holding period is chosen.

| FIGURE 6.4 | **Buy Call: Different Exercise Prices** |

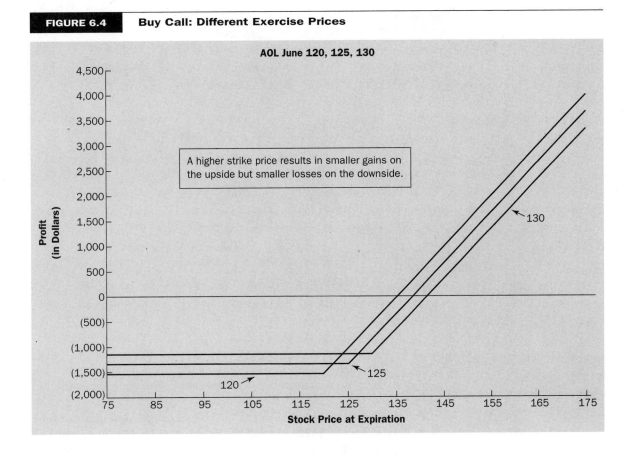

AOL June 120, 125, 130

A higher strike price results in smaller gains on the upside but smaller losses on the downside.

Recall that we plan to examine three holding periods. The shortest holding period involves the sale of the call at time T_1. The intermediate-length holding period is that in which the call is sold at time T_2. The longest holding period is that in which the option is held until expiration. If the option is sold at time T_1, the profit is the call price at the time of the sale minus the price originally paid for it. We can use the Black-Scholes model with a time to expiration of $T - T_1$ to estimate the price of the call for a broad range of possible stock prices and, thereby, determine the profit graph. Using the July 125 call, the three holding periods are (1) sell the call on June 4, T_1; (2) sell the call on June 25, T_2; and (3) hold the call until it expires on July 16, T.

For the shortest holding period, in which the position is closed on June 4, the time remaining is 42 days; that is, there are 42 days between June 4 and July 16. Thus, the call price will be based on a remaining time to expiration of $42/365 = 0.1151$. The call's time to expiration is $T - T_1 = 0.1151$. For the intermediate-length holding period, in which the position is held until June 25, the time remaining to expiration is 21 days. Thus, the time to

TABLE 6.2	Estimation of Black-Scholes Prices and Profits for AOL July 125 Call

Position Closed at: Time to Expiration:	June 4 0.1151		June 25 0.0575	
Stock Price at End of Holding Period	Black-Scholes Call Price	Profit per Contract	Black-Scholes Call Price	Profit per Contract
105	$ 5.39	$-1,323.24	$ 2.44	$-1,618.58
110	7.16	-1,146.55	3.74	-1,488.71
115	9.23	-939.10	5.43	-1,319.42
120	11.61	-701.18	7.54	-1,108.72
125	14.29	-433.80	10.06	-856.58
130	17.24	-138.48	12.98	-564.72
135	20.45	182.89	16.26	-236.18
140	23.91	528.13	19.88	125.09
145	27.57	894.98	23.77	514.71
150	31.44	1,281.14	27.91	928.27
155	35.47	1,684.36	32.24	1,361.55

Note: Calculations were done on a spreadsheet, so they may differ slightly from calculations done by hand.

expiration is $21/365 = 0.0575$ and $T - T_2 = 0.0575$. For the longest holding period, the time remaining is, of course, zero. The parameters used in the model are $X = 125$, $\sigma = 0.83$, and $r_c = 0.0453$.

The results are shown in Table 6.2. As an example, note that on June 4, at a stock price of $110, the call would have a Black-Scholes value of $7.1595. Since the investor paid $18.625 for the call, the profit per contract is $100(\$7.1595 - \$18.625) = -\$1,146.55$. If the stock price were $115, the call would be worth $9.2340 and the profit would be $100(\$9.2340 - \$18.625) = -\$939.10$. On June 25, at a stock price of $110, the call would be worth $3.7379 and the profit would be $100(\$3.7379 - \$18.625) = -\$1,488.71$. The remaining entries are computed in the same manner.

In Figure 6.5, the profit per contract is graphed as the dependent variable and the stock price at the end of the holding period is graphed as the independent variable. The graph indicates that the shortest holding period provides a higher profit for all stock prices at expiration. It would appear that the shorter the holding period, the greater the potential profit. This is because with a shorter holding period, the call can be sold to recover some of its remaining time value. The longer the call is held, the greater is the time value lost.

This seems to present a paradox: It suggests that to maximize profits, one should hold the option for the shortest time possible. Obviously option traders do not always use such short holding periods. What is missing from the explanation?

For a given stock price, the longer a call is held, the more time value it loses and the lower the profit.

FIGURE 6.5 **Buy Call: Different Holding Periods**

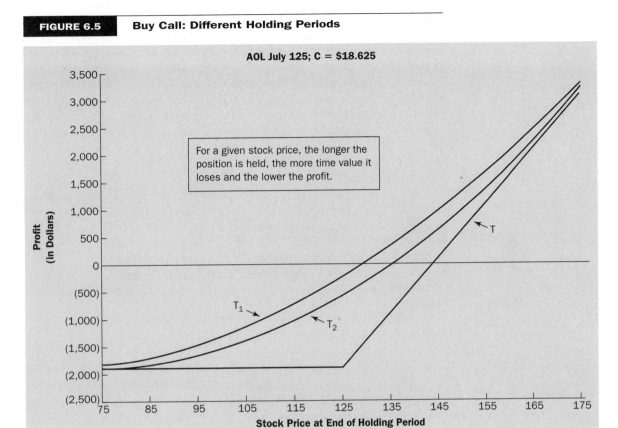

AOL July 125; C = $18.625

For a given stock price, the longer the position is held, the more time value it loses and the lower the profit.

The answer is that the shorter holding period provides superior profits *for a given stock price.* The profit graph does not indicate the likelihood that the stock price will end up high or low. In fact, with a shorter holding period, the possible range of stock prices is much lower because there is less time for the stock price to move. The longer holding period, on the other hand, gives the stock price more time to increase.

This completes our discussion of the strategy of buying a call. We now turn to the strategy of writing a call.

Write a Call

An option trader who writes a call without concurrently owning the stock is said to be writing an **uncovered** or **naked call.** The reason for this nomenclature is that the position is a high-risk strategy, one with the potential for unlimited losses. The uncovered call writer undertakes the obligation to sell stock not currently owned to the call buyer at the latter's request. The writer therefore may have to buy the stock at an unfavorable price. As a result, writing an uncovered call is a privilege restricted to those few traders with sufficient capital to risk. Because the brokerage firm must make up losses to the clearinghouse, it too is at risk. Therefore, a trader's broker must agree to handle the transaction—and that is likely to be done only for the best and wealthiest customers. Of course, traders owning seats on the exchange or low-credit-risk institutions in the over-the-counter market are less restricted and can more easily write uncovered calls, but because of the high risk even they do so infrequently. Moreover, with stocks that pay dividends, the writer faces the risk of early exercise if the calls are American, as discussed in Chapter 3.

If writing an uncovered call is such a risky strategy, why should we examine it? The reason is that writing an uncovered call can be combined with other strategies, such as buying stock or another option, to produce a strategy with very low risk. Therefore, it is necessary to establish the results for the short call before combining it with other strategies.

Because the buyer's and writer's profits are the mirror images of each other, the profit equations and graphs are already familiar. The writer's profit is

$$\Pi = N_C[\text{Max}(0, S_T - X) - C] \text{ given that } N_C < 0.$$

Assume one call, $N_C = -1$. Then the profit is

$$\Pi = C \qquad\qquad \text{if } S_T \leq X.$$
$$\Pi = -S_T + X + C \qquad \text{if } S_T > X.$$

Selling a call is a bearish strategy that has a limited gain (the premium) and an unlimited loss.

Selling a call with a lower exercise price has a greater maximum gain but greater upside losses.

Figure 6.6 illustrates the profit graph for the writer of 100 America Online June 125 calls at a price of $13.50. Note that the breakeven stock price for the writer must be the breakeven stock price for the buyer, $X + C = \$138.50$. The maximum loss for the buyer is also the maximum gain for the writer, $1,350. If the stock price ends up above the exercise price, the loss to the writer can be substantial—and, as is obvious from the graph, there is no limit to the possible loss in a bull market.

THE CHOICE OF EXERCISE PRICE   Figure 6.7 compares the strategy of writing calls at different strike prices by showing the 120, 125, and 130 calls. Figure 6.7 is the mirror image of Figure 6.4. The greatest profit potential is in the 120, which has the highest premium, $1,537.50, but is accompanied by the greatest loss potential and the lowest breakeven, $X + C = 120 + 15.375 = 135.375$. This would be the highest-risk strategy. The 130 would have the lowest risk of the three with the highest breakeven, $X + C = 130 + 11.375 = 141.375$, but also the lowest profit potential, the $1,137.50 premium.

FIGURE 6.6   Write Call

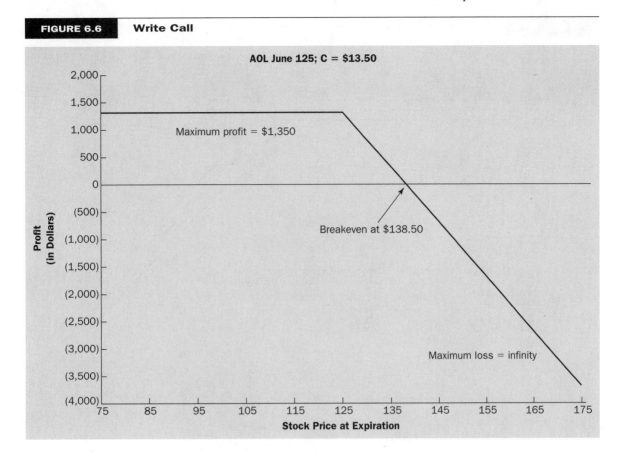

AOL June 125; C = $13.50

Maximum profit = $1,350

Breakeven at $138.50

Maximum loss = infinity

Profit (in Dollars) — Stock Price at Expiration

THE CHOICE OF HOLDING PERIOD   Figure 6.8 illustrates the profit for the three possible holding periods previously described. These are the July 130 calls in which the holding period T_1 involves the repurchase of the call on June 4; T_2 assumes the call is repurchased on June 25; and T allows the call to be held until expiration, when it either is exercised or expires out-of-the-money.

Figure 6.8 is the mirror image of Figure 6.5. A writer repurchasing the call prior to expiration will have to pay for some of the remaining time value. Therefore, for the call writer, the profit is lowest with the shortest holding period *for a given stock price*. This is because the time value repurchased is greater with the shorter holding period. With a shorter holding period, however, the stock price is less likely to move substantially; thus, the range of possible profits is far smaller. If the investor holds the position until expiration, the profit may be greater but the stock will have had more time to move—perhaps unfavorably.

For a given stock price, the longer a short call is maintained, the more time value it loses and the greater the profit.

FIGURE 6.7   **Write Call: Different Exercise Prices**

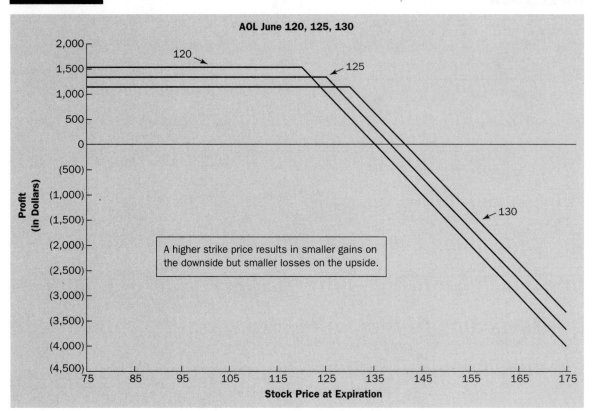

This completes our discussion of call buying and writing, which we see are mirror images of each other. We next turn to put option transactions.

Put Option Transactions

Buy a Put

Buying a put is a strategy for a bear market. The potential loss is limited to the premium paid. The gain is also limited but can still be quite substantial. The profit from the purchase of a put is given by the equation

$$\Pi = N_P[\text{Max}(0, X - S_T) - P] \text{ given that } N_P > 0.$$

As in the example for calls, assume the purchase of a single put, $N_P = 1$. If the stock price at expiration ends up less than the exercise price, the put is in-the-money and is exercised. If the stock price at expiration is greater

| FIGURE 6.8 | **Write Call: Different Holding Periods** |

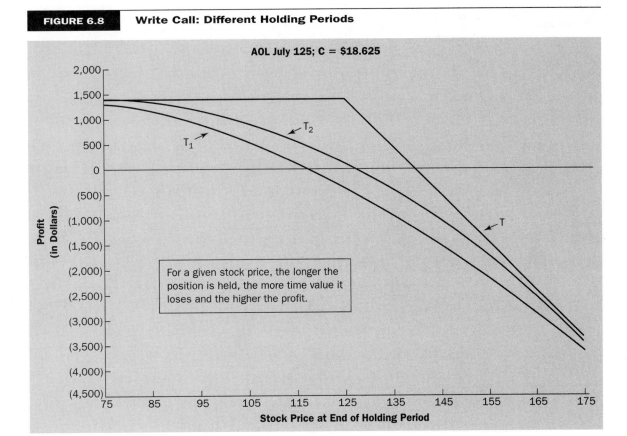

AOL July 125; C = $18.625

For a given stock price, the longer the position is held, the more time value it loses and the higher the profit.

than or equal to the exercise price, the put ends up out-of-the-money. The profits are

$$\Pi = X - S_T - P \qquad \text{if } S_T < X.$$
$$\Pi = -P \qquad\qquad \text{if } S_T \geq X.$$

Figure 6.9 illustrates the profits from the put-buying strategy for the America Online June 125 put with a premium of $11.50. The potential loss is limited to the premium paid, which in this case is $1,150. The profit is also limited, because there is a limit to how low the stock price can fall. The best outcome for a put buyer is for the company to go bankrupt. In that case, the stock would be worthless, $S_T = 0$, and the profit would be $X - P$. In this example, that would be $100(125 - 11.50) = 11,350$.

Notice that the breakeven occurs where the stock price is below the exercise price. Setting the profit equation for this case equal to zero gives

$$\Pi = X - S_T^* - P = 0.$$

FIGURE 6.9	Buy Put

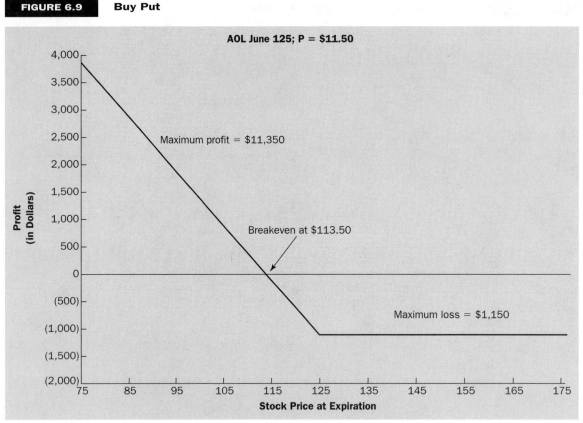

AOL June 125; P = $11.50

Maximum profit = $11,350

Breakeven at $113.50

Maximum loss = $1,150

Profit (in Dollars)

Stock Price at Expiration

Solving for the breakeven stock price, S_T^*, at expiration reveals that

$$S_T^* = X - P.$$

Buying a put is a bearish strategy that has a limited loss (the put premium) and a large, but limited, potential gain.

The put buyer must recover enough from the option's exercise to cover the premium already paid. For every dollar by which the option is in-the-money, the put buyer gains a dollar. Therefore, the stock price must fall below the exercise price by the amount of the premium. In this instance, this is $125 - 11.50 = 113.50$. For the investor to profit from this put, the stock price must fall to $113.50 or less by the expiration date.

Buying a put is an appropriate strategy when anticipating a bear market. The loss is limited to the premium paid, and the potential gain is quite high. Moreover, it is easier to execute a put transaction than a short sale. Puts need not be bought when the stock is on an uptick or zero-plus tick, and the amount paid for the put is far less than the margin on a short sale. More important, a put limits the loss while a short sale has an unlimited loss.

FIGURE 6.10   **Buy Put: Different Exercise Prices**

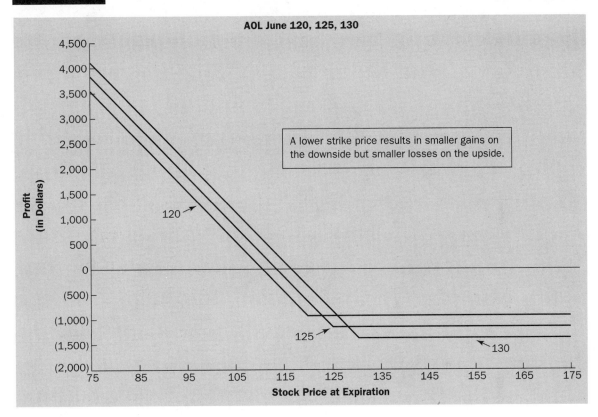

AOL June 120, 125, 130

A lower strike price results in smaller gains on the downside but smaller losses on the upside.

THE CHOICE OF EXERCISE PRICE   Figure 6.10 compares the profit graphs for puts with different strike prices using the June 120, 125, and 130 puts. The highest exercise price, the 130, has the highest premium; thus, the potential loss is greatest—in this case, $1,425. Its profit potential is highest, however, with a maximum possible profit of $100(130 − 14.25) = 11,575$ if the stock price at expiration is zero. The breakeven is $130 − 14.25 = 115.75$. The 120 has the lowest potential profit, $100(120 − 9.25) = 11,075$, and the lowest breakeven stock price, $120 − 9.25 = 110.75$. It also has the lowest loss potential, however, its premium of $925. The put chosen will be determined by the risk the option trader is willing to take. The more aggressive trader will go for the maximum profit potential and choose the highest exercise price. The more conservative trader will choose a lower exercise price to limit the potential loss.

Buying a put with a higher exercise price has a greater maximum loss but a greater downside gain.

THE CHOICE OF HOLDING PERIOD   Figure 6.11 compares the profit potential of the three holding periods for the July 125 put. The Black-Scholes

| FIGURE 6.11 | Buy Put: Different Holding Periods |

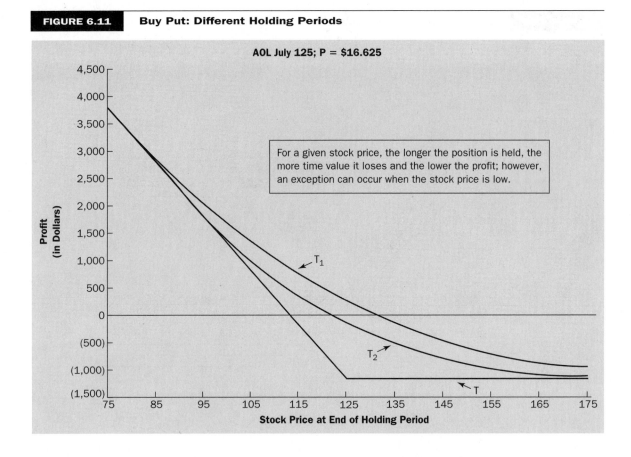

AOL July 125; P = $16.625

For a given stock price, the longer the position is held, the more time value it loses and the lower the profit; however, an exception can occur when the stock price is low.

Profit (in Dollars)

Stock Price at End of Holding Period

For a given stock price, the longer a put is held, the more time value it loses and the lower the profit. For European puts, this effect is reversed when the stock price is low.

option pricing model for European puts was used to estimate the put prices for the shorter holding periods.

By electing a shorter holding period — say, T_1 — the put buyer can sell the put back for some of the time value originally purchased. If the put buyer holds until T_2, less time value will be recovered. If held until expiration, no remaining time value will be recaptured. As with the case for calls, the shorter holding periods show greater potential profit *for a given stock price*. They allow less time, however, for the stock price to go down. Therefore, shorter holding periods are not necessarily inferior or superior to longer ones. The choice depends on the trader's forecast for the stock price, specifically how much it is expected to move, the direction, and in how much time.

An exception to the pattern of time value decay can occur at very low stock prices. Recall that it is possible that a European put can increase in value with a decrease in time.

With an understanding of the put buyer's profit potential, it should be simple to examine the case for the put writer. As you probably expect, the put writer's position is the mirror image of the put buyer's.

Write a Put

The put writer is obligated to buy the stock from the put buyer at the exercise price. The put writer profits if the stock price goes up and the put therefore is not exercised, in which case the writer keeps the premium. If the stock price falls such that the put is exercised, the put writer is forced to buy the stock at a price greater than its market value. For an American put this can, of course, occur prior to as well as at expiration.

The profit equation for the put writer is

$$\Pi = N_P[\text{Max}(0, X - S_T) - P] \text{ given that } N_P < 0.$$

Assume the simple case of a single short put, $N_P = -1$. The writer's profits are the mirror images of the buyer's:

$$\Pi = -X + S_T + P \qquad \text{if } S_T < X.$$
$$\Pi = P \qquad \text{if } S_T \geq X.$$

Selling a put is a bullish strategy that has a limited gain (the premium) and a large, but limited, potential loss.

Figure 6.12 illustrates the put writer's profits using the June 125 put written at a premium of $11.50. The writer's maximum potential profit is

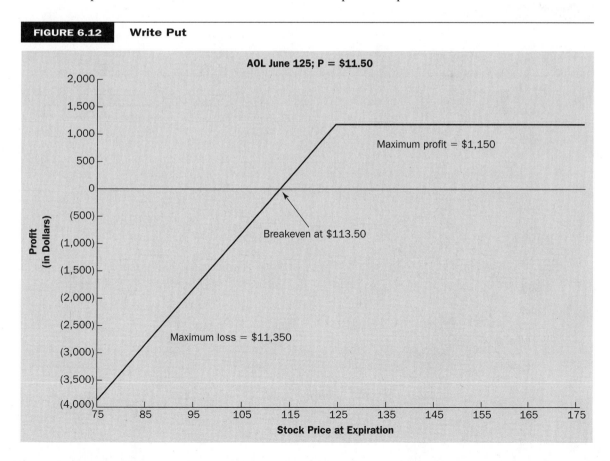

FIGURE 6.12   Write Put

AOL June 125; P = $11.50

Maximum profit = $1,150

Breakeven at $113.50

Maximum loss = $11,350

Profit (in Dollars)

Stock Price at Expiration

the buyer's maximum potential loss—the amount of the premium, $1,150. The maximum potential loss for the writer is limited, but like the buyer's maximum potential gain, it is a very large amount — here, $11,350. The breakeven stock price at expiration is the same as that for the buyer— X − P, or $113.50.

Selling a put with a higher exercise price has a greater maximum gain but a greater downside loss.

THE CHOICE OF EXERCISE PRICE   Figure 6.13 compares the put writer's profits for different strike prices using the June puts. The highest strike price, 130, offers the greatest premium income and therefore the greatest profit potential. The maximum profit is $1,425, and the breakeven is 130 − 14.25 = 115.75. The risk, however, is greatest, since any losses will be larger in a bear market. The lowest strike price offers the lowest maximum profit—the premium income of $925—but also has the lowest breakeven—120 − 9.25 = 110.75—and the lowest loss if the market is down. Once again the range of exercise prices offers the put writer several choices for assuming various degrees of risk and expected reward.

FIGURE 6.13   **Write Put: Different Exercise Prices**

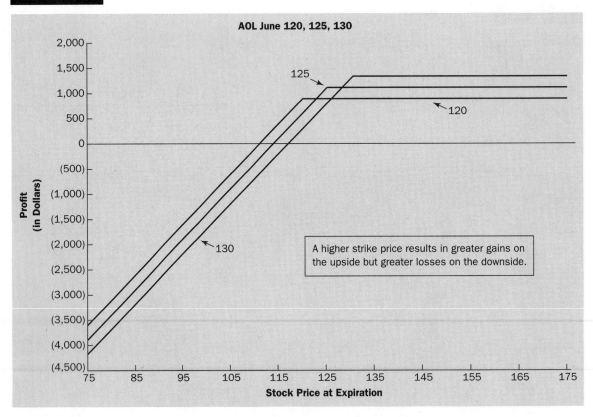

AOL June 120, 125, 130

A higher strike price results in greater gains on the upside but greater losses on the downside.

Profit (in Dollars)

Stock Price at Expiration

THE CHOICE OF HOLDING PERIOD   Figure 6.14 compares the put writer's profits for different holding periods. Like the call writer, the put writer who chooses a shorter holding period makes a smaller profit or incurs a greater loss *for a given stock price.* This is because the writer buying back the put before expiration must pay for some of the remaining time value. The advantage to the writer, however, is that with a short holding period there is a much smaller probability of a large, unfavorable stock price move. Again the choice of holding period depends on the forecast for the market price and the time frame over which the writer expects that forecast to hold.

For a given stock price, the longer a short put is maintained, the more time value it loses and the greater the profit. For European puts, this effect is reversed when the stock price is low.

With European puts, we see that at low stock prices, the pattern of time value decay reverses itself. With American puts, the writer must be aware of the possibility that they will be exercised early.

We now have covered all of the simple strategies of buying stock, selling short stock, buying calls, writing calls, buying puts, and writing puts. Figure 6.15 summarizes the profit graphs of these strategies. They can be viewed as

---

FIGURE 6.14   **Write Put: Different Holding Periods**

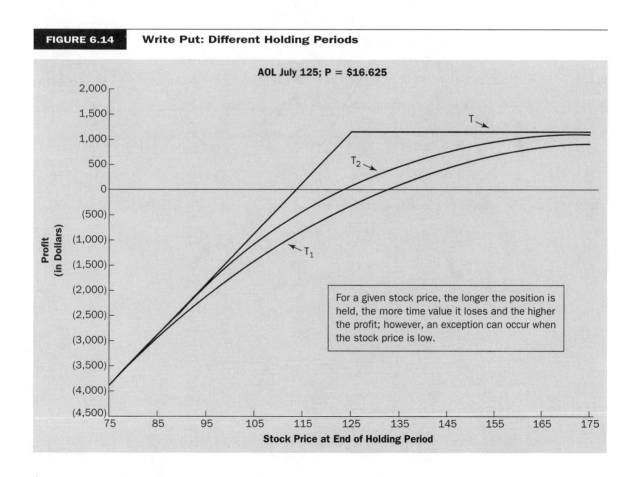

AOL July 125; P = $16.625

For a given stock price, the longer the position is held, the more time value it loses and the higher the profit; however, an exception can occur when the stock price is low.

Profit (in Dollars) vs. *Stock Price at End of Holding Period*

| FIGURE 6.15 | **Summary of Profit Graphs for Positions Held to Expiration** |

(a) Call Option Transactions

Buy Call   Write Call

(b) Put Option Transactions

Buy Put   Write Put

(c) Stock Transactions

Buy Stock   Sell Short Stock

building blocks that are combined to produce other strategies. In fact, all of the remaining strategies are but combinations of these simple ones. The remainder of this chapter examines the strategies of combining calls with stock, combining puts with stock, replicating puts with calls and stock, and replicating calls with puts and stock.

Calls and Stock: The Covered Call

Chapter 4 showed that it is possible to form a riskless hedge by buying stock and writing calls. The number of calls written must exceed the number of shares, and the appropriate hedge ratio must be maintained throughout the holding period. A simpler but nevertheless low-risk strategy involves writing one call for each share of stock owned. Although this strategy is not riskless, it does reduce the risk of holding the stock outright. It is also one of the most popular strategies among professional option traders. An investor executing this strategy is said to be writing a **covered call.**

Recall that we previously examined the uncovered call in which the investor writes a call on a stock not owned. We found the risk to be unlimited. If the option trader owns the stock, however, there is no risk of buying it in the market at a potentially high price. If the call is exercised, the investor simply delivers the stock. From another point of view, the holder of stock with no options written thereon is exposed to substantial risk of the stock price moving down. By writing a call against that stock, the investor reduces the downside risk. If the stock price falls substantially, the loss will be cushioned by the premium received for writing the call. Although in a bull market the call may be exercised and the stockholder will have to give up the stock, there are ways to minimize this possibility. We shall consider how to do this later.

Because we already examined the strategies of buying stock and writing calls, determining the profits from the covered call strategy is simple: We need only add the profit equations from these two strategies. Thus,

$$\Pi = N_S(S_T - S_0) + N_C[\text{Max}(0, S_T - X) - C]$$
$$\text{given that } N_S > 0, N_C < 0, \text{ and } N_S = -N_C.$$

The last requirement, $N_S = -N_C$, specifies that the number of calls written must equal the number of shares purchased. Consider the case of one share of stock and one short call, $N_S = 1$, $N_C = -1$.

The profit equation is

$$\Pi = S_T - S_0 - \text{Max}[0, S_T - X] + C.$$

If the option ends up out-of-the-money, the loss on the stock will be reduced by the call premium. If the option ends up in-the-money, it will be exercised and the stock will be delivered. This will reduce the gain on the stock. These results are summarized as follows:

$$\Pi = S_T - S_0 + C \qquad\qquad\qquad \text{if } S_T \le X.$$
$$\Pi = S_T - S_0 - S_T + X + C = X - S_0 + C \qquad \text{if } S_T > X.$$

Notice that in the case where the call ends up out-of-the-money, the profit increases for every dollar by which the stock price at expiration exceeds the original stock price. In the case where the call ends up in-the-money, the profit is unaffected by the stock price at expiration.

A covered call reduces downside losses on the stock at the expense of upside gains.

These results are illustrated in Figure 6.16 for the America Online June 125 call written at a premium of $13.50. The dashed line is the profit from simply holding the stock. Notice that the covered call has a smaller loss on the downside but relinquishes the upside gain and has a lower break-even. The maximum profit occurs when the stock price exceeds the exercise price; this profit is $X - S_0 + C$, which in this example is

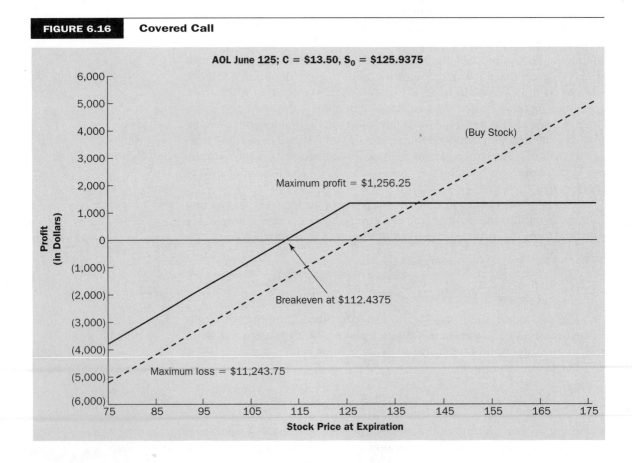

FIGURE 6.16   Covered Call

AOL June 125; C = $13.50, S_0 = $125.9375

(Buy Stock)

Maximum profit = $1,256.25

Breakeven at $112.4375

Maximum loss = $11,243.75

Profit (in Dollars) vs *Stock Price at Expiration*

$100(125 - 125.9375 + 13.50) = 1,256.25$. The maximum loss occurs if the stock price at expiration goes to zero. In that case, the profit will simply be $-S_0 + C$, which is $100(-125.9375 + 13.50) = -11,243.75$.

The breakeven stock price occurs where the profit is zero. This happens when the call ends up out-of-the-money. Setting the profit equal to zero for the case where the call is out-of-the-money,

$$\Pi = S_T^* - S_0 + C = 0,$$

and solving for S_T^* gives a breakeven of

$$S_T^* = S_0 - C.$$

Here the breakeven is $125.9375 - 13.50 = 112.4375$. At any stock price above \$112.4375, this covered call is profitable. Another way to view this is that the covered call provides a profit at any stock price at expiration down to \$112.4375. Ownership of the stock without the protection of the call provides a profit only at a stock price above \$125.9375, the current stock price.

THE CHOICE OF EXERCISE PRICE   The covered call writer has a choice of calls at different strike prices. Figure 6.17 illustrates the profit graphs for the covered call using the America Online June calls with strike prices of 120, 125, and 130. Because the highest strike price, the 130, has the lowest premium with which to cushion a stock price decrease, it offers the least amount of protection for the covered call writer. It offers the maximum profit potential, however, because the high strike price allows the writer to receive a greater amount for the stock if the call is exercised. In this example, the 130 call has a maximum profit of $100(130 - 125.9375 + 11.375) = 1,543.75$. The breakeven is $125.9375 - 11.375 = 114.5625$. The minimum profit, which occurs if the stock price at expiration is zero, is $100(-125.9375 + 11.375) = -11,456.25$.

A covered call with a lower exercise price provides greater downside protection but a lower maximum gain on the upside.

In contrast, the lowest exercise price, the 120, offers the most protection. Because it has the highest premium, the cushion on the downside is greater. If the stock moves up and the call is exercised, however, the writer will receive a lower price for the stock. The maximum profit is $100(120 - 125.9375 + 15.375) = 943.75$. The breakeven stock price is $125.9375 - 15.375 = 110.5625$. The minimum profit, which occurs at a stock price at expiration of zero, is $100(-125.9375 + 15.375) = -11,056.25$.

Writing a covered call at the lowest exercise price is the most conservative choice, because the loss on the downside is lower; however, the gain on the upside is also lower. Writing a covered call at the highest exercise price is a riskier strategy, because the upside profit potential is greater but the downside protection is less. Regardless of the exercise price chosen, writing a covered call is far less risky than owning the stock outright. The premium

FIGURE 6.17	Covered Call: Different Exercise Prices

AOL June 120, 125, 130

A lower strike price offers the most downside protection but at the expense of more of the upside gain.

For a given stock price, the longer a covered call is maintained, the more time value is lost and the greater the profit.

on the call, no matter how large or small, cushions the stockholder against a loss on the stock in a falling market.

THE CHOICE OF HOLDING PERIOD   Figure 6.18 illustrates the July 125 covered call in which the position is closed out prior to expiration. Again the Black-Scholes model was used to estimate the call's value in the manner described earlier in the chapter. The shortest holding period, T_1, which corresponds to closing out the position on June 4, gives the smallest profit *for a given stock price*. This is because the writer closes out the position by buying back the call. If there is time remaining, the writer must buy back some of the remaining time value. If a longer holding period is used, the remaining time value, which must be bought back, is less. If held to expiration, there is no time value remaining for repurchase.

Does this suggest that covered call writers should use long holding periods? Not necessarily. Again it depends on the covered call writer's forecast for the stock price and the time frame over which it applies. The investor

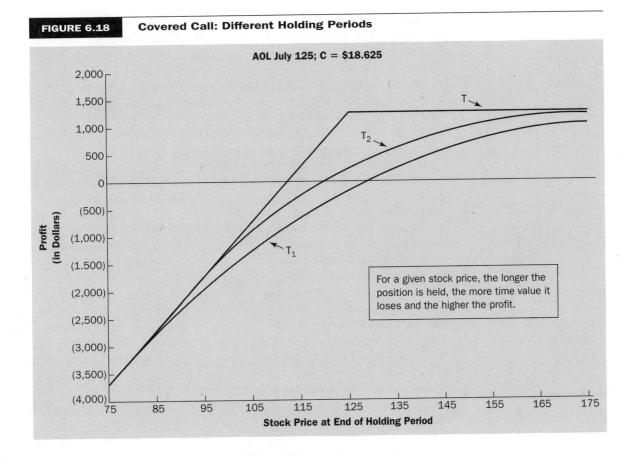

FIGURE 6.18   **Covered Call: Different Holding Periods**

might earn a larger profit by holding the position until expiration, but such a long holding period will also give the stock price more time to move down. A short holding period increases the likelihood that the stock price will not move much, and this could be more profitable for the covered call writer.

Some General Considerations with Covered Calls

As indicated earlier, covered call writing is a very popular strategy among professional option traders. This is because it is a low-risk strategy—much less risky than buying stock or options outright. There are also studies that showed that covered call writing is more profitable than simply buying options. This should make one wonder why everyone does not simply write covered calls. Obviously, if that occurred the prices of the calls would fall so low that the strategy would no longer be attractive. This superior performance of covered call writing is most likely attributable to the fact that the studies covered years in which listed options were new. Veterans of those early years widely agree that the public avidly purchased these new instruments as a cheap and exciting way to play the market. Little regard was paid to whether the calls were fairly priced. In fact, option pricing theory itself was in its infancy, and little was known about pricing options. Public demand, coupled with ignorance, most likely kept call prices artificially high and led to substantial profits for clever call writers in those years. Although there have been no similar studies recently, it seems unlikely that such superior performance could be sustained.

It is commonly believed that writing covered calls is a way to pick up extra income from a stock. Writing a call, however, imposes on the stockholder the possibility of having to sell the stock at an inconvenient or unsuitable time. If the stock price goes up, the covered call writer will be unable to participate in the resulting gains and the stock will likely be called away by exercise. If, however, the call is exercised early, the writer will be no worse off from a financial perspective. The profit will still be $X - S_0 + C$, the maximum expected profit at expiration. In fact, the writer actually will be better off, because this amount will be available before expiration.

Suppose the covered writer does not want to lose the stock by exercise. One way to minimize the likelihood of exercise is to write calls at a high exercise price so that the call is deep-out-of-the-money. This reduces the chance of the call ending up in-the-money. Suppose the stock price starts upward and it appears that the out-of-the-money call will move in-the-money and thus increase the chance of exercise. The writer can then buy the call back and write a new call at a higher exercise price, a strategy called *rolling up*. If the stock price continues to rise, the writer can buy back the new call and write another one at an even higher exercise price. In this manner, the covered call writer establishes a position in which the exercise price will always stay well ahead of the stock price. The purpose of this strategy is to avoid exercise and keep the stock in the portfolio. This may be important to someone who likes to hold on to certain stocks for various reasons. The disadvantage of this strategy is that the high exercise price means a lower premium and less downside protection. Also, transaction costs from the frequent rollovers will be higher. These factors can be weighed against the inconvenience of exercise and the investor's willingness to give up the stock.

Many institutional investors also use a covered call writing strategy. Those holding large portfolios of stocks that are expected to gain little value often believe that their portfolios' performances will improve if they write calls against the stock they own. But covered call writing — or any other strategy — cannot be the gate to unlimited wealth. In fact, it is more likely to *reduce* the portfolio's return, because it decreases its risk. It therefore should be viewed as a risk-reducing rather than return-enhancing strategy.

As one might imagine, the opposite of a long-stock/short-call position is to buy a call to protect a short-stock position. The results obtained from this strategy are the mirror image of the covered call results. We explore this strategy in an end-of-chapter problem.

Another option strategy that can be used to reduce the risk of holding stock is the protective put—the topic of the next section.

Puts and Stock: The Protective Put

As discussed in the previous section, a stockholder who wants protection against falling stock prices may elect to write a call. In a strong bull market, the stock is likely to be called away by exercise. One way to obtain protection against a bear market and still be able to participate in a bull market is to buy a **protective put;** that is, the investor simply buys stock and buys a put. The put provides a minimum selling price for the stock.

The profit equation for the protective put is found by simply adding the profit equations for the strategies of buying stock and buying a put. From this we get

$$\Pi = N_S(S_T - S_0) + N_P[\text{Max}(0, X - S_T) - P]$$
$$\text{given that } N_S > 0, N_P > 0, \text{ and } N_S = N_P.$$

As in previous examples, assume one share of stock and one put, $N_S = 1$, $N_P = 1$. If the stock price ends up above the exercise price, the put will expire out-of-the-money. If the stock price ends up less than the exercise price, the put will be exercised. The results are as follows:

$$\Pi = S_T - S_0 - P \qquad\qquad\qquad \text{if } S_T \geq X.$$
$$\Pi = S_T - S_0 + X - S_T - P = X - S_0 - P \quad \text{if } S_T < X.$$

The protective put works like an insurance policy. When you buy insurance for an asset such as a house, you pay a premium that assures you that in the event of a loss, the insurance policy will cover at least some of the loss. If the loss does not occur during the policy's life, you simply lose the premium. Similarly, the protective put is insurance for a stock. In a bear market, a loss on the stock is somewhat offset by the put's exercise. This is like filing a claim on the insurance policy. In a bull market, the insurance is not needed and the gain on the upside is reduced by the premium paid.

From the above equations, it is clear that the profit in a bull market varies directly with the stock price at expiration. The higher S_T is, the higher is the profit, Π. In a bear market, the profit is not affected by the stock price at expiration. Whatever losses are incurred on the stock are offset by gains on the put. The profit graph for a protective put is illustrated in Figure 6.19 for the America Online June 125 put purchased at a premium of $11.50. The dashed line is the profit from simply holding the stock.

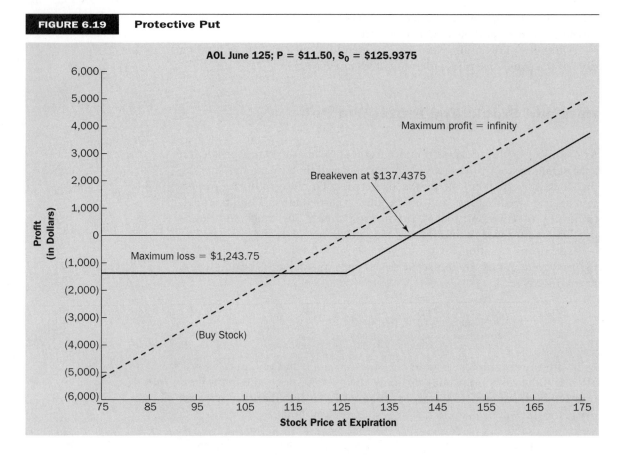

FIGURE 6.19   **Protective Put**

AOL June 125; P = $11.50, S₀ = $125.9375

A protective put sets a maximum downside loss at the expense of some of the upside gain. It is equivalent to an insurance policy on the asset.

Notice that the protective put has a smaller downside loss and smaller upside gain as well as a higher breakeven.

The maximum loss on a protective is put is found as the profit if the stock price at expiration ends up below the exercise price. Since the profit equation shows that this is $X - S_0 - P$, the America Online protective put has a minimum of $100(125 - 125.9375 - 11.50) = -1,243.75$. Clearly there is no maximum gain, because the investor profits dollar for dollar with the excess of the stock price over the exercise price. Notice how the graph of the protective put is the same shape as that of a long call. This is due to put-call parity.

The breakeven stock price at expiration occurs when the stock price at expiration exceeds the exercise price. Setting this profit to zero and solving for the breakeven stock price, S_T^*, gives

$$\Pi = S_T^* - S_0 - P = 0$$
$$S_T^* = P + S_0.$$

Thus, breakeven occurs at a stock price at expiration equal to the original stock price plus the premium. This should be apparent, since the stock price must rise above the original stock price by an amount sufficient to cover the premium paid for the put. In this example, the breakeven stock price at expiration is 11.50 + 125.9375 = 137.4375.

THE CHOICE OF EXERCISE PRICE: THE DEDUCTIBLE DECISION   The amount of coverage the protective put provides is affected by the chosen exercise price. This is equivalent to the insurance problem of deciding on the deductible. A higher deductible means that the insured bears more of the risk and thus pays a lower premium. With a lower deductible, the insurer bears more of the risk and charges a higher premium. With a protective put, a higher exercise price is equivalent to a lower deductible.

A protective put with a higher exercise price provides greater downside protection, but lower upside gains.

Figure 6.20 illustrates the comparative performances of America Online protective puts at different exercise prices. The 130 put gives the stockholder the right to sell the stock at $130 per share. The breakeven on this strategy is 125.9375 + 14.25 = 140.1875. This will be the most expensive

---

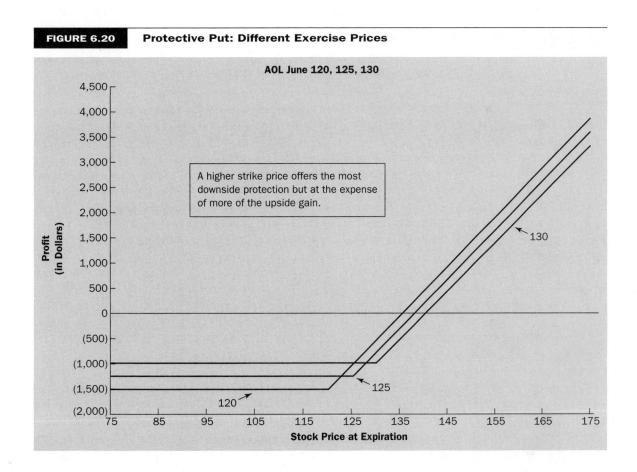

FIGURE 6.20   Protective Put: Different Exercise Prices

AOL June 120, 125, 130

A higher strike price offers the most downside protection but at the expense of more of the upside gain.

Profit (in Dollars) — vertical axis: 4,500; 4,000; 3,500; 3,000; 2,500; 2,000; 1,500; 1,000; 500; 0; (500); (1,000); (1,500); (2,000)

Stock Price at Expiration — horizontal axis: 75, 85, 95, 105, 115, 125, 135, 145, 155, 165, 175

Lines labeled 120, 125, 130

insurance but will provide the greatest coverage, with a minimum profit of $100(130 - 125.9375 - 14.25) = 1,018.75$. If the stock price rises and the put is not needed, the gain from the stock will be lower than it would be with a lower exercise price. This is because the more expensive premium was paid but the insurance was not needed.

The lowest exercise price, the 120, provides the least coverage. The breakeven is $125.9375 + 9.25 = 135.1875$. The minimum profit is $100(120 - 125.9375 - 9.25) = -1,518.75$. If the market rises, the less expensive insurance will reduce the gain by a smaller amount.

As you can see, selecting an exercise price is like choosing a deductible: The investor must balance the willingness to assume some of the risk against the ability to pay for the coverage.

THE CHOICE OF HOLDING PERIOD   Figure 6.21 illustrates the profit for different holding periods for the America Online July 125 protective put. The shorter holding period provides more coverage *for a given stock price*. This is because with a shorter holding period, the investor can sell back the

---

FIGURE 6.21   **Protective Put: Different Holding Periods**

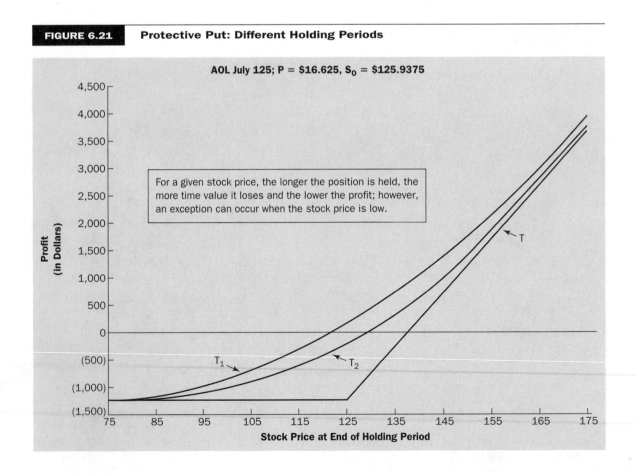

AOL July 125; P = $16.625, S_0 = $125.9375

For a given stock price, the longer the position is held, the more time value it loses and the lower the profit; however, an exception can occur when the stock price is low.

Profit (in Dollars)

Stock Price at End of Holding Period

put before expiration and recover some of the time value previously purchased. With a longer holding period, there will be less time value to recover. Again, however, we see an exception to this rule when the stock price is low. By holding all the way to expiration, there will be no time value to recover.

For a given stock price, the longer a protective put is held, the more time value is lost and the lower the profit. For European puts, this effect is reversed when the stock price is low.

The choice of holding period depends on the investor's view of the probable stock price moves and the period over which they are likely to occur. If a large stock price move is needed to provide a profit, a longer holding period will allow more time for the stock price to move. A shorter holding period is preferable if the stock price is not expected to move much. The stock price must increase by at least the amount of the premium, however, for the investor to break even. Therefore, the investor must weigh the likelihood of this occurring over the holding period.

The protective put strategy can also be turned around so that a short sale of stock is protected by a short put, or vice versa. The results would be the mirror image of those presented here. We examine this strategy as an end-of-chapter problem.

We have seen that investors holding stock can use both the covered call and the protective put to reduce risk. Which strategy is preferable? The answer depends on the investor's outlook for the market. If a bull market is believed more likely to occur, the protective put will allow the investor to participate in it. The protective put will be more expensive, however, because the investor must pay for it. The covered call writer actually receives money for writing the call. Thus, there are advantages and disadvantages to each strategy that one must carefully weigh before making a decision.

The role of put options in providing insurance is explored more thoroughly in Chapter 15. That material will show how puts, calls, Treasury bills, and futures can be used to create portfolio insurance.

The following section examines some strategies in which puts can be created from calls and calls created from puts. For obvious reasons, these are called **synthetic puts** and **calls.**

Synthetic Puts and Calls

In Chapters 3 and 5 we discussed put-call parity, the relationship between call prices and put prices:

$$P + S_0 = C + Xe^{-r_cT}.$$

The left-hand side of the equation is the value of a put and the stock; the right-hand side is the value of a call and a risk-free bond. We can rearrange put-call parity such that

$$P = C - S_0 + Xe^{-r_cT},$$

where the left-hand side is the value of a put and the right-hand side is the value of a portfolio that behaves like a put. That portfolio consists of a long call, a short sale of stock, and the purchase of a pure discount bond, or making of a loan, with a face value equal to the exercise price. Note that the signs in front of the prices in the equations indicate whether we are long or short in puts, calls, or stocks. Long positions are represented by plus ($+$) signs and short positions by minus ($-$) signs.

We actually need not buy a bond to replicate a put. The term representing the present value of the exercise price is simply a constant value that does not affect the shape of the profit graph. For example, consider a **synthetic put,** which consists of long calls and the short sale of an equal number of shares of stock. The profit is simply

$$\Pi = N_C[Max(0, S_T - X) - C] + N_S(S_T - S_0)$$
$$\text{given that } N_C > 0, N_S < 0, \text{ and } N_C = -N_S.$$

Letting the number of shares and the number of calls both be 1, the profits for the two possible ranges of stock prices at expiration are

$$\Pi = -C - S_T + S_0 \qquad\qquad \text{if } S_T \leq X.$$
$$\Pi = S_T - X - C - S_T + S_0 = S_0 - X - C \qquad \text{if } S_T > X.$$

If the stock price at expiration is equal to or below the exercise price, the profit will vary inversely with the stock price at expiration. If the stock price at expiration is above the exercise price, the profit will not be affected by the stock price at expiration. This is the same general outcome provided by a put, hence the name synthetic put.

We can see the difference between the actual put and the synthetic put from the put-call parity formula. In put-call parity, one replicates the put by buying a call, selling short a stock, and buying a pure discount bond with a face value equal to the exercise price. To replicate a put precisely, we need to buy that pure discount bond. In practice, however, most traders simply buy the call and sell short the stock.

Figure 6.22 compares the synthetic put and its actual counterpart using the America Online July 125 options. The synthetic put has a profit of

$$-C - S_T + S_0 \text{ if } S_T \leq X.$$
$$S_0 - X - C \text{ if } S_T > X.$$

The actual put has a profit of

$$X - S_T - P \text{ if } S_T \leq X.$$
$$- P \text{ if } S_T > X.$$

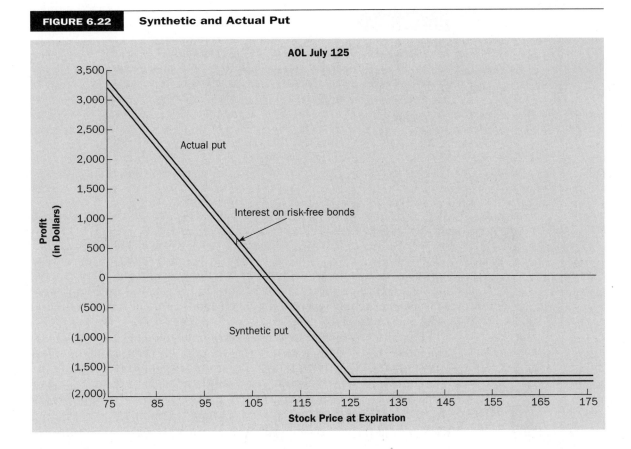

FIGURE 6.22   Synthetic and Actual Put

AOL July 125

The difference is the profit of the actual put minus the profit of the synthetic put, $X - P + C - S_0$, in either case. From put-call parity, we can substitute $C - S_0 + Xe^{-r_c T}$ for P. The difference is then

$$X(1 - e^{-r_c T}).$$

which is the interest lost by not buying the pure discount bond.

There are two reasons why someone would want to use a synthetic put. First, there once were restrictions on the listing of puts on the exchanges; puts were phased in slowly. There was also a moratorium on new option listings that started soon after the first few puts were listed in 1977. This prevented more puts from being listed until the moratorium was lifted in 1980. During the period, an investor could have created a synthetic put to use in lieu of the actual put.

Second, one can use a synthetic put to take advantage of mispricing in the relationship between puts and calls. For example, the difference

TABLE 6.3	Payoffs from Reverse Conversion

	Payoffs from Portfolio Given Stock Price at Expiration	
Position	$S_T \leq X$	$S_T > X$
Long call	0	$S_T - X$
Short stock	$-S_T$	$-S_T$
Short put	$-X + S_T$	0
	$-X$	$-X$

between the actual put price, P, and the value of the synthetic put, $C - S_0$, should be $Xe^{-r_c T}$; however, if $P - (C - S_0)$ is greater than $Xe^{-r_c T}$, either the actual put is overpriced or the synthetic put is underpriced. The investor should sell the actual put and buy the synthetic put by purchasing the call and selling short the stock. This strategy often is called a **reverse conversion** or simply **reversal.** It will generate a cash outflow at expiration of X, as shown in Table 6.3.

This property makes the reverse conversion resemble a risk-free loan. The money received when the position is opened is (1) S_0 (from the short sale of the stock), (2) P (from the sale of the put), and (3) $-C$ (from the purchase of the call). If, as we assumed, this exceeds the present value of the exercise price, we can invest the amount $S_0 + P - C$ at the risk-free rate, r_c, until the options expire. The accumulated future value of this investment will then exceed X. This means that we can repay the loan and have money left over.[3] Of course, investing this money at the risk-free rate is equivalent to buying the risk-free bonds.

We can also create **synthetic calls** by buying stock and an equal number of puts. It should be apparent that this strategy is like a call, because it is nothing more than a protective put. The graph for the protective put is, as we saw earlier, the same type of graph as that for a call.

Many investors buy the synthetic call and write the actual call when the latter is overpriced. This strategy is called a **conversion** and is used to exploit mispricing in the relationship between put and call prices.

The accompanying Excel spreadsheet stratlyz2.xls calculates and graphs the profits from any combination of positions in the asset and up to six different options on the same asset. Positions can be held to expiration or closed out prior to expiration.

Synthetic puts and calls can be constructed from options and stock.

---

[3]If the options are American and the short put is exercised early, however, we will have to pay out X dollars prior to expiration. Thus, it is possible that the interest earned on the cash inflow will be insufficient to make the required payout.

SOFTWARE DEMONSTRATION 6.1   **Analyzing Option Strategies with the Excel Spreadsheet stratlyz2.xls**

The Excel spreadsheet stratlyz2.xls operates in Excel 97 under Windows 95 or 98. It calculates and graphs the profits from option strategies with up to six options and positions in the underlying asset.

This spreadsheet is a read-only spreadsheet, meaning that it cannot be saved under the name stratlyz2.xls, which preserves the original file. To use the spreadsheet, simply do the following:

1. Make sure you are in Windows 95 or 98.
2. Run Excel 97.
3. Open the file stratlyz2.xls.

Now let us do an example. Assume you wish to find the results for a simple strategy of buying one America Online June 125 call. The call is priced at $13.50. The AOL stock is at $125.9375. First let us examine the strategy of holding the position until expiration, and then we shall close the position prior to expiration.

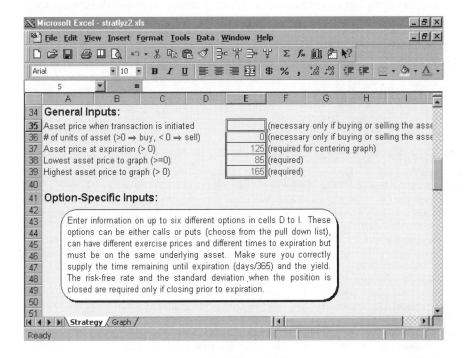

Observe the section labeled **General Inputs** in the accompanying figure. It requests five pieces of information. Each cell that will accept input has a double-line border and the values are in blue. The first input item is the asset price when the transaction is initiated, but this is required only if your strategy includes buying or selling short the asset. Insert a blank for our example. The next input is the number of units of the asset, with a positive number for buying and a negative number for selling. Insert a zero or leave it blank. The next input is the asset price at expiration. This information is required in order to center the graph. Although you obviously do not know where the asset will be at expiration, you can choose any price. Let us choose the exercise price of 125. The graph will be centered around this price, and the overall profit of the strategy for this particular price will be calculated and shown in the section below. The next two required inputs are the lowest and highest asset prices to graph. This simply defines a range over which the graph will be drawn. Let us arbitrarily choose a range of $40 on either side so the minimum is 85 and the maximum is 165.

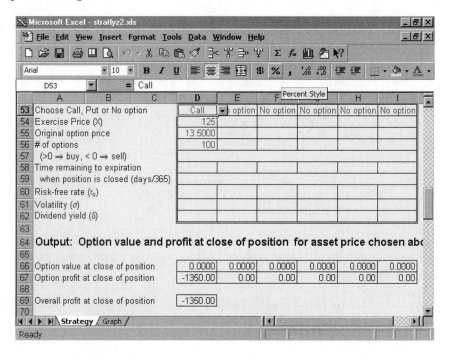

The next section is called **Option-Specific Inputs.** Here you can enter information on up to six options that differ by either time to expiration or exercise price and can be either calls or puts. Insert blanks or zeros for options not used. All options must be on the same underlying asset. In the first row use the pull down list to select either "Call," "Put," or "No option." For this strategy, select "Call." The next row should contain the exercise price, 125 in our case. The next row should contain the original option price. This is the price at which the option is either purchased or sold when the transaction is initiated — $13.50 in this example. The next line contains the number of options with a positive number for buying and a negative number for selling. Let us insert "100" for a standard long contract. The next four input cells contain information that is necessary only if the position is closed prior to expiration. If the position is held to expiration, the "Time remaining to expiration when position is closed" will be blank or zero, and the last three lines can be left blank. Leave it blank for our example. If the position is closed prior to expiration, insert the remaining time in years (i.e., days/365), and then insert the risk-free rate, volatility, and dividend yield in the next three cells below. This permits the program to use the Black-Scholes model to calculate the option's value when the position is terminated for a given asset price. We shall leave this information blank. Hit the F9 (manual recalculation) key.

The section labeled **Output: Option value and profit at close of position for asset price chosen above** shows for each option the value of the option at the close of the position, the profit on the option transaction, and the overall profit on the transaction, which includes option(s) and potential positions in the asset, for the asset price you specified above. Note that output cells have a single-line border. These answers, of course, represent only one point on the profit graph. In our example, the profit is −$1,350 because we specified an asset price at expiration of 125, which is the exercise price. The next section, **Table for Graphic Results,** shows the overall profit for the strategy for 50 possible asset prices at the end of the holding period, running from the minimum to maximum price you specified, centered around the asset price at expiration you specified. The graph is provided on a different spreadsheet, which you can access by clicking on the tab labeled **Graph** near the bottom of your screen.

As noted above, for positions closed out prior to expiration, the program automatically calculates Black-Scholes prices for the options for each possible asset price in the range specified, provided you supply it with the necessary information on the time remaining, the volatility, the interest rate, and the divided yield, if any. For example, if there are 15 days remaining until expiration (time = 15/365), the risk-free rate is 4.53 percent, the volatility is .83, and the dividend yield is zero, the call value is $8.4898, and the profit is −$501.02.

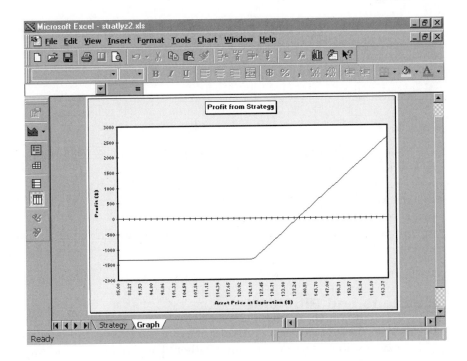

Although stratlyz2.xls will correctly graph any strategy you choose, it is possible that the graph will not look exactly as you expect it. The various possible combinations of inputs and outputs, along with the fixed parameters used to generate the graph, such as 50 asset prices, will not always produce visually appealing graphs the first time. This often happens because the graph's tick marks are not located on the exercise price. If anything looks unusual, experiment with different maximum and minimum prices until your graph looks as expected.

Summary

This chapter examined the basic option strategies. Designing the profit equations and graphs is a simple extension of material learned in previous chapters. For positions held to expiration, it is necessary only to determine the intrinsic values of puts and calls. If we elect not to hold the options until expiration, we can use the Black-Scholes model to estimate their prices. The material in this chapter, however, is basic. Option investors should always be aware of the factors that lead to early exercise, as well as tax and dividend implications. Moreover, transaction costs will lower profits, increase losses, and make breakevens higher for bullish strategies and lower for bearish strategies. The more options and stocks employed, the greater will be the transaction costs. Understanding how option transactions produce payoffs is only the first step toward using options. Unfortunately, there are no simple or even complex formulas for predicting the future. We have seen, however, that options can be used to modify risk — to increase or decrease it as needed.

The strategies examined here from the building blocks for exploring more exotic strategies. Chapter 7 looks at these advanced strategies, which combine many of the strategies discussed here to produce a much more diverse set of opportunities.

Key Terms

Before continuing to Chapter 7, you should be able to give brief definitions of the following terms.

- bear market
- bull market
- breakeven stock price
- uncovered/naked call
- covered call

- protective put
- synthetic put/call
- conversion
- reverse conversion/reversal

Questions and Problems

1. Explain the advantages and disadvantages to a call buyer of closing out a position prior to expiration rather than holding all the way until expiration.

2. Suppose one is considering buying a call at a particular exercise price. What reasons could be given for the alternative of buying a call at a higher exercise price? At a lower exercise price?

3. Explain how a protective put is like purchasing insurance on a stock.

4. Why is the choice of exercise price on a protective put like the decision on which deductible to take on an insurance policy?

5. Discuss and compare the two bullish strategies of buying a call and writing a put. Why would one strategy be preferable to the other?

6. Suppose you wish to buy stock and protect yourself against a downside movement in its price. You consider both a covered call and a protective put. What factors will affect your decision?

7. You have inherited some stock from a wealthy relative. The stock has had poor performance recently, and analysts believe it has little growth potential. You would like to write calls against the stock; however, the will stipulates that you must agree not to sell it unless you need the funds for a personal financial emergency. How can you write covered calls and minimize the likelihood of exercise?

8. We briefly mentioned the synthetic call, which consists of stock and an equal number of puts. Assume the combined value of the puts and stock exceeds the value of the actual call by less than the present value of the exercise price. Show how an arbitrage profit can be made. Note: Do not use the data from the chapter. Show your point as it was illustrated in the text for the synthetic put.

9. A short position in stock can be protected by holding a call option. Determine the profit equations for this position, and identify the breakeven stock price at expiration and maximum and minimum profits.

10. A short stock can be protected by selling a put. Determine the profit equations for this position, and identify the breakeven stock price at expiration and maximum and minimum profits.

11. Explain the advantages and disadvantages to a covered call writer of closing out the position prior to expiration.

12. Explain the considerations facing a covered call writer regarding the choice of exercise prices.

The following option prices were observed for a stock for July 6 of a particular year. Use this information in problems 13 through 18. Ignore dividends on the stock. The stock is priced at 165 1/8. The expirations are July 17, August 21, and October 16. The continuously compounded risk-free rates are .0503, .0535, and .0571, respectively. The standard deviation is .21. Assume the options are European.

	Calls			Puts		
Strike	Jul	Aug	Oct	Jul	Aug	· Oct
165	2 11/16	5 1/4	8 1/8	2 3/8	4 3/4	6 3/4
170	13/16	3 1/4	6	5 3/4	7 1/2	9

In problems 13 through 18, determine the profits for possible stock prices of 150, 155, 160, 165, 170, 175, and 180. Answer any other questions as requested. Note: Your Excel spreadsheet stratlyz2.xls will be useful here for obtaining graphs as requested, but it does not allow you to calculate the profits for several user-specified asset prices. It permits you to specify one asset price and a maximum and minimum. Use stratlyz2.xls to produce the graph for the range of prices from 150 to 180 but determine the profits for the prices of 150, 160, . . ., 180 by hand for positions held to expiration. For positions closed prior to expiration, use the spreadsheet bsbin2.xls or the Windows program bsbwin2.1.exe to determine the option price when the position is closed; then calculate the profit by hand.

13. Buy one August 165 call contract. Hold until the options expire. Determine the profits and graph the results. Then identify the breakeven stock price at expiration. What is the maximum possible loss on this transaction?

14. Repeat problem 13, but close the position on August 1. Use the spreadsheet to find the profits for the possible stock prices on August 1. Generate a graph and use it to identify the approximate breakeven stock price.

15. Buy one October 165 put contract. Hold until the options expire. Determine the profits and graph the results. Identify the breakeven stock price at expiration. What are the maximum possible gain and loss on this transaction?

16.   Buy 100 shares of stock and write one October 170 call contract. Hold the position until expiration. Determine the profits and graph the results. Identify the breakeven stock price at expiration, the maximum profit, and the maximum loss.

17.   Repeat problem 16, but close the position on September 1. Use the spreadsheet to find the profits for the possible stock prices on September 1. Generate a graph and use it to approximate the breakeven stock price.

18.   Buy 100 shares of stock and buy one August 165 put contract. Hold the position until expiration. Determine the profits and graph the results. Determine the breakeven stock price at expiration, the maximum profit, and the maximum loss.

19.   (Concept Problem) In each case examined in the chapter and in the preceding problems, we did not account for the interest on funds invested. One useful way to observe the effect of interest is to look at a conversion or a reverse conversion. Evaluate the August 165 puts and calls, and recommend a conversion or a reverse conversion. Determine the profit from the transaction if the options are held to expiration. Make sure the profit properly accounts for the interest that accrues over the holding period.

20.   (Concept Problem) Another consideration in evaluating option strategies is the effect of transaction costs. Suppose purchases and sales of an option incur a brokerage commission of 1 percent of the option's value. Purchases and sales of a share of stock incur a brokerage commission of 0.5 percent of the stock's value. If the option is exercised, there is a transaction cost on the purchase or sale of the stock. Determine the profit equations for the following strategies assuming the options are held to expiration and exercised if in-the-money rather than sold back. Assume that one option and/or share is used and that any shares left in the portfolio are sold.

a. Long call

b. Long put

c. Covered call

d. Protective put

Advanced Option Strategies

You can get as fancy as you want with your option strategies, but in this business, there's no substitute for being right. There's never been a guarantee for incremental returns.

GENE BRODY
Risk, June 1995

Chapter 6 provided a foundation for the basic option strategies. We can now move on to some of the more advanced strategies. As often noted, options can be combined in some interesting and unusual ways. In this chapter, we look at two types of advanced option strategies: spreads and combinations.

Option Spreads: Basic Concepts

A **spread** is the purchase of one option and the sale of another. There are two general types of spreads. One is the **vertical, strike,** or **money spread.** This strategy involves the purchase of an option with a particular exercise price and the sale of another option differing only by exercise price. For example, one might purchase an option on AOL expiring in June with an exercise price of 120 and sell an option on AOL also expiring in June but with an exercise price of 125; hence the terms *strike* and *money spread.* Because exercise prices were formerly arranged vertically in the option pages of newspapers, this also became known as a *vertical spread.*

Another type of spread is a **horizontal, time,** or **calendar spread.** In this spread, the investor purchases an option with an expiration of a given month and sells an otherwise identical option with a different expiration month. For example, one might purchase an AOL June 120 call and sell an AOL July 120 call. The term *horizontal spread* comes from the horizontal arrangement of expiration months in newspaper option pages, a practice since discontinued.

Sometimes spreads are identified by a special notation. The aforementioned AOL money spread is referred to as the June 120/125 spread. The month is given first; the exercise price before the slash (/) is the option purchased, and the exercise price after the slash is the option sold. If the investor buys the June 125 and sells the June 120, the result is a June 125/120 spread. The calendar spread described in the previous paragraph is identified as the June/July 120 spread. The month preceding the slash is the option purchased, while the month following the slash identifies the option sold.

Spreads can be executed using either calls or puts. A July 120/125 call spread is a net long position. This is because the 120 call costs more than the 125 call; that is, the cash outflow from buying the 120 exceeds the inflow received for selling the 125. This transaction is called **buying the spread** and is sometimes referred to as a **debit spread** for the type of accounting entry associated with it. In the July 120/125 put spread, the cash inflow received from selling the 125 put is more than the cash outflow paid in buying the 120 put. This transaction is known as **selling the spread** or a **credit spread** and results in a net short position.

For calendar spreads, the June/July 120 call spread would be net short and selling the spread, because an investor would receive more for the July call than he or she would pay for the June call. The July/June 120 call spread would be net long and buying the spread, because the July call would cost more than the June call. The terms *debit* and *credit spread* are also used here. With calendar spreads the terminology is similar for both calls and puts, because the premiums for both are greater the longer the time to expiration.

Why Investors Use Option Spreads

Spreads offer the potential for a small profit while limiting the risk. They are not, of course, the sure route to riches; we already have seen that no such strategy is. But spreads can be very useful in modifying risk while allowing profits if market forecasts prove accurate.

Risk reduction is achieved by being long in one option and short in another. If the stock price decreases, the loss on a long call will be somewhat offset by a gain on a short call. Whether the gain outweighs the loss depends on the volatility of each call. We shall illustrate this effect later. For now, consider a money spread held to expiration. Assume we buy the call with the low strike price and sell the call with the high strike price. In a bull market we will make money, because the low-exercise-price call will bring a higher payoff at expiration than will the high-exercise-price call. In a bear market, both calls will probably expire worthless and we will lose money. For that reason, the spread involving the purchase of the low-exercise-price call is referred to as a **bull spread.** Similarly, in a bear market we make money if we are long the high-exercise-price call and short the low-exercise-price call. This is called a **bear spread.** Opposite rules apply for puts: A position of long (short) the low-exercise-price put and short (long) the high-exercise-price put is a bull (bear) spread. In general, a bull spread should profit in a bull market and a bear spread should profit in a bear market.

Time spreads are not classified into bull and bear spreads. They profit by either increased or decreased volatility. We shall reserve further discussion of time spreads for a later section.

Transaction costs are an important practical consideration in spread trading. These costs can represent a significant portion of invested funds, especially for small traders. Spreads involve several option positions, and the transaction costs can quickly become prohibitive for all but floor traders and large institutional investors. As in Chapter 6, we will not build transaction costs directly into the analyses here but will discuss their special relevance where appropriate.

Notation

The notation here is the same as that used in previous chapters. We must add some distinguishing symbols, however, for the spreads' different strike prices and expirations. For a money spread, we will use subscripts to distinguish options differing by strike price. For example,

X_1, X_2, X_3 = exercise prices of calls where $X_1 < X_2 < X_3$
C_1, C_2, C_3 = prices of calls with exercise prices X_1, X_2, X_3
N_1, N_2, N_3 = quantity held of each option.

The N notation indicates the number of options where a positive N is a long position and a negative N is a short position.

In time spreads,

T_1, T_2 = times to expiration where $T_1 < T_2$
C_1, C_2 = prices of calls with times to expiration of T_1, T_2
N_1, N_2 = quantity held of each option.

The numerical illustrations will use the America Online options presented in earlier chapters. For convenience, Table 7.1 repeats the data. Unless otherwise stated, assume 100 options are employed.

TABLE 7.1   **AOL Option Data, May 14**

Exercise Price	Calls			Puts		
	May	June	July	May	June	July
120	8 3/4	15 3/8	20 7/8	2 3/4	9 1/4	13 5/8
125	5 3/4	13 1/2	18 5/8	4 5/8	11 1/2	16 5/8
130	3 5/8	11 3/8	16 3/8	7 3/8	14 1/4	19 5/8

Current Stock Price: 125 15/16
Expirations: May 21, June 18, July 16
Risk-free Rates: .0447 (May); .0446 (June); .0453 (July)

Your Excel spreadsheet stratlyz2.xls can be very useful for analyzing spreads and, indeed, all the transactions in this chapter.

Money Spreads

As indicated earlier, money spreads can be designed to profit in either a bull market or a bear market. The former is called a bull spread.

Bull Spreads

Consider two call options differing only by exercise price, X_1 and X_2, where $X_1 < X_2$. Their premiums are C_1 and C_2, and we know that $C_1 > C_2$. A bull spread consists of the purchase of the option with the lower exercise price and the sale of the option with the higher exercise price. Assuming one option of each, $N_1 = 1$ and $N_2 = -1$, the profit equations are

$$\Pi = \text{Max}(0, S_T - X_1) - C_1 - \text{Max}(0, S_T - X_2) + C_2.$$

The stock price at expiration can fall in one of three ranges: less than or equal to X_1, greater than X_1 but less than or equal to X_2, or greater than X_2. The profits for these three ranges are as follows:

$$
\begin{aligned}
\Pi &= -C_1 + C_2 && \text{if } S_T \leq X_1 < X_2. \\
\Pi &= S_T - X_1 - C_1 + C_2 && \text{if } X_1 < S_T \leq X_2. \\
\Pi &= S_T - X_1 - C_1 - S_T + X_2 + C_2 \\
&= X_2 - X_1 - C_1 + C_2 && \text{if } X_1 < X_2 < S_T.
\end{aligned}
$$

In the case where the stock price ends up equal to or below the lower exercise price, both options expire out-of-the-money. The spreader loses the premium on the long call and retains the premium on the short call. The profit is the same regardless of how far below the lower exercise price the stock price is. Because the premium on the long call is greater than the premium on the short call, however, this profit is actually a loss.

In the third case, where both options end up in-the-money, the short call is exercised on the spreader, who exercises the long call and then delivers the stock. The effect of the stock price cancels and the profit is constant for any stock price above the higher exercise price. Is this profit positive? The profit is $(X_2 - X_1) - (C_1 - C_2)$, or the difference between the exercise prices minus the difference between the premiums. Recall from Chapter 3 that the difference in premiums cannot exceed the difference in exercise prices. The spreader paid a premium of C_1, received a premium of C_2, and thus obtained the spread for a net investment of $C_1 - C_2$. The maximum payoff from the spread is $X_2 - X_1$. No one would pay more than the maximum payoff from an investment. Therefore, the profit is positive.

Only in the second case, where the long call ends up in-the-money and the short call is out-of-the-money, is there any uncertainty. The equation shows that the profit increases dollar for dollar with the stock price at expiration.

Figure 7.1 illustrates the profits from the bull spread strategy for the America Online June 125 and 130 calls with premiums of $13.50 and $11.375, respectively. The dashed line is the profit graph had we simply purchased the 125 call. The maximum loss is the net premium of $1,350 - $1,137.50, or $212.50, which occurs at any stock price at expiration at or below 125. The maximum gain is the difference in strike prices minus the difference in premiums, $100(130 - 125 - 2.125) = 287.50$, which occurs at any stock price at expiration above 130.

FIGURE 7.1 **Call Bull Spread**

A call bull spread has a limited gain, which occurs in a bull market, and a limited loss, which occurs in a bear market.

From the graph, it is apparent that the breakeven stock price at expiration is between the two exercise prices. To find this breakeven—call it S_T^*—take the profit equation for the second case, where the stock price is between both exercise prices, and set it equal to zero:

$$\Pi = S_T^* - X_1 - C_1 + C_2 = 0.$$

Then solve for S_T^*:

$$S_T^* = X_1 + C_1 - C_2.$$

The stock price must exceed the lower exercise price by the difference in the premiums. This makes sense. The spreader exercises the call with exercise price X_1. The higher the stock price, the greater the amount received from the exercise. To break even, the spreader must receive enough to recover the net premium, $C_1 - C_2$. In this problem, the breakeven stock price at expiration is $125 + 13.50 - 11.375 = 127.125$.

Note that in comparison to simply buying the 125 call, the spreader reduces the maximum loss by the premium on the short 130 call and lowers the breakeven, but gives up the chance for large gains if the stock moves up substantially.

Early exercise poses no problem with the bull spread. Suppose the stock price prior to expiration is S_t. If the short call is exercised, the stock price must be greater than X_2. This means that the stock price is also greater than X_1, and the long call can be exercised for a net payoff of $(S_t - X_1) - (S_t - X_2) = X_2 - X_1$. This is the best outcome one could obtain by holding the spread all the way to expiration.

THE CHOICE OF HOLDING PERIOD   As with any option strategy, it is possible to hold the position for a period shorter than the option's entire life. Recall that in Chapter 6 we made assumptions about closing out the option positions prior to expiration. We used short holding periods of T_1, which meant closing the position on June 4, and T_2, in which we closed the position on June 25. When a position is closed prior to expiration, we estimate the option price for a range of stock prices and use those estimates to generate the profit graph. We illustrated the general procedure in Chapter 6. Using the same methodology here, we obtain the graph in Figure 7.2, the bull spread under the assumption of three different holding periods.

Recall that T_1 is the shortest holding period, T_2 is slightly longer, and T represents holding all the way to expiration. The graph indicates that the short holding period has the lowest range of profits. If the stock price is low, the shortest holding period produces the smallest loss while the longest holding period produces the largest loss. If the stock price is high, the shortest holding period produces the smallest gain and the longest holding period the largest gain.

For a given stock price, the profit of a call bull spread increases as expiration approaches if the stock price is on the high side and decreases if the stock price is on the low side.

FIGURE 7.2   Call Bull Spread: Different Holding Periods

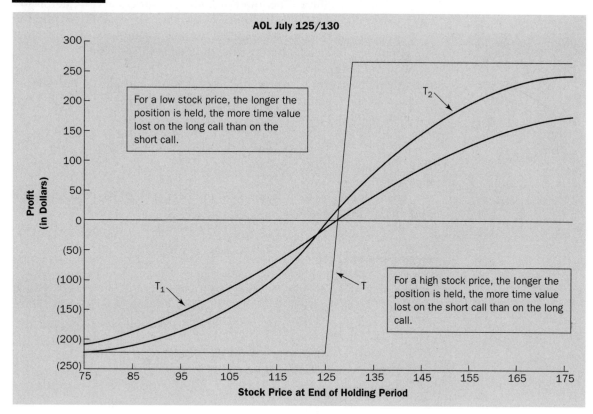

AOL July 125/130

For a low stock price, the longer the position is held, the more time value lost on the long call than on the short call.

For a high stock price, the longer the position is held, the more time value lost on the short call than on the long call.

Profit (in Dollars) vs. *Stock Price at End of Holding Period*

The logic behind these results is simple. First, recall that the low-exercise-price call will always be worth more than the high-exercise-price call; however, their relative time values will differ. An option's time value is greatest when the stock price is near the exercise price. Therefore, when stock prices are high, the high-exercise-price call will have the greater time value and when they are low, the low-exercise-price call will have the greater time value.

When we close out the spread prior to expiration, we can always expect the long call to sell for more than the short call because the long call has the lower exercise price. The excess of the long call's price over the short call's price will, however, decrease at high stock prices. This is because the time value will be greater on the short call, because the stock price is closer to the exercise price. The long call will still sell for a higher price because it has more intrinsic value, but the difference will be smaller at high stock prices. Conversely, at low stock prices the long call will have a greater time value because its exercise price is closer to the stock price.

The result of all this is that when we close the bull spread well before expiration, the profit will be lower at high stock prices and higher at low stock prices than if we did so closer to expiration. If we hold the position longer but not all the way to expiration, we will obtain the same effect, but the impact will be smaller because the time value will be less.

Which holding period should an investor choose? There is no consistently right or wrong answer. An investor who is strongly bullish should realize that the longer the position is held, the greater the profit that can be made if the forecast is correct. In addition, a long holding period allows more time for the stock price to move upward. If the forecast proves incorrect, the loss will be lower the shorter the holding period. With short holding periods, however, there is less time for a large stock price change.

The following section examines a put bear spread. We shall see that a bear spread is, in many respects, the opposite of a bull spread.

Bear Spreads

A bear spread is the mirror image of a bull spread: The trader is long the high-exercise-price put and short the low-exercise-price put. Since $N_1 = -1$ and $N_2 = 1$, the profit equation is

$$\Pi = -\mathrm{Max}(0, X_1 - S_T) + P_1 + \mathrm{Max}(0, X_2 - S_T) - P_2.$$

The outcomes are as follows

$$
\begin{aligned}
\Pi &= -X_1 + S_T + P_1 + X_2 - S_T - P_2 & \text{if } S_T \leq X_1 < X_2.\\
&= X_2 - X_1 + P_1 - P_2 \\
\Pi &= P_1 + X_2 - S_T - P_2 & \text{if } X_1 < S_T < X_2.\\
\Pi &= P_1 - P_2 & \text{if } X_1 < X_2 \leq S_T.
\end{aligned}
$$

A put bear spread has a limited gain, which occurs in a bear market, and a limited loss, which occurs in a bull market.

Figure 7.3 illustrates the put bear spread for the America Online June 125 and 130 puts with premiums of \$11.50 and \$14.25, respectively. The dashed line is a long position in the 125 put. The maximum gain is the difference in the strike prices minus the difference in the premiums, $100(130 - 125 + 11.50 - 14.25) = 225$, which occurs at any stock price at expiration below 125. The maximum loss is the net premium of $\$1,425 - \$1,150 = \$275$, which occurs at any stock price at expiration above 130.

As with the call bull spread, the breakeven stock price at expiration is between the two exercise prices. To find this breakeven, S_T^*, take the profit equation for the second case, where the stock price is between both exercise prices, and set it equal to zero:

$$\Pi = P_1 + X_2 - S_T^* - P_2 = 0.$$

FIGURE 7.3   **Put Bear Spread**

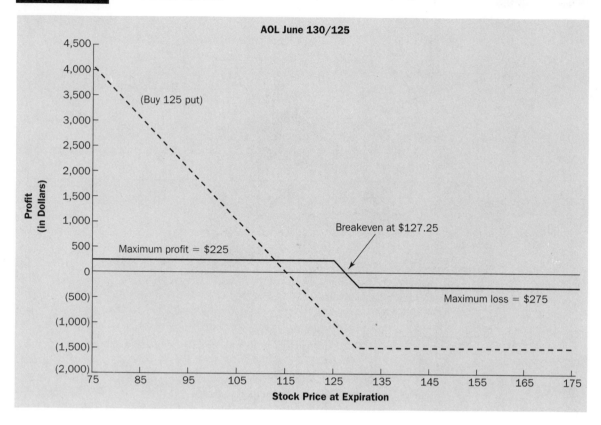

Then solve for S_T^*:

$$S_T^* = X_2 + P_1 - P_2.$$

Here the breakeven stock price is $130 + $11.50 − $14.25 = $127.25.

Relative to the long put, the bear spread has a lower maximum profit, which is limited to $225, a higher breakeven, and a lower loss on the upside by the amount of the premium from the written put.

Early exercise is not an issue for the put bear spread. This is because the put bear spread will have the long put in-the-money whenever the short put is in-the-money. If the short put is exercised, the long put can be exercised for an overall cash flow of $X_2 - X_1$, which is the maximum payoff obtainable if held to expiration.

THE CHOICE OF HOLDING PERIOD   Figure 7.4 illustrates a bear spread when different holding periods are used. The longer holding period produces higher profits in a bear market and larger losses in a bull market.

| FIGURE 7.4 | **Put Bear Spread: Different Holding Periods** |

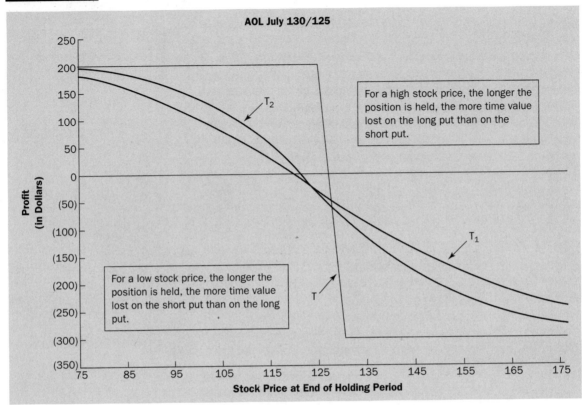

AOL July 130/125

For a high stock price, the longer the position is held, the more time value lost on the long put than on the short put.

For a low stock price, the longer the position is held, the more time value lost on the short put than on the long put.

Stock Price at End of Holding Period

For a given stock price, the profit of a put bear spread increases as expiration approaches if the stock price is on the low side and decreases if the stock price is on the high side.

Again this is because of the time value effect. The spread trader closing the position prior to expiration buys back the time value of the short put and sells the long put's remaining time value. For high stock prices, the long put has more time value than the short put and, thus, our long position loses faster than our short position. As time goes by, we lose from this effect. At low stock prices, the short put has more time value than our long put and, thus, our short position loses faster than our long position. As time goes by, we gain from this effect.

We should repeat, however, that these statements do not advocate a short or long holding period, because the length of the holding period affects the range of possible stock prices.

A Word about Call Bear Spreads and Put Bull Spreads

As we have seen, it is possible to design a call money spread that will profit in a bull market. It is also possible to construct a call spread that will profit in a bear market. There is, however, a risk of early exercise. The short call can be sufficiently in-the-money to justify early exercise, while the long call is still out-of-the-money. Even if the long call is in-the-money, the cash flow from early exercise will be negative.

For example, suppose S_t is the stock price prior to expiration. The cash flow from the exercise of the short call is $-(S_t - X_1)$, while the cash flow from the exercise of the long call is $S_t - X_2$. This gives a total cash flow of $X_1 - X_2$, which is negative. Early exercise ensures that the bear spreader will incur a cash outflow. Because the loss occurs prior to expiration, it is greater in present value terms than if it had occurred at expiration. Thus, the call bear spread entails a risk not associated with the bull spread.

Just as we can construct bear spreads with calls, we can also construct bull spreads with puts. Here we would buy the low exercise price put and sell the high exercise price put. The pattern of payoffs would be similar to those of the call bull spread, but, as with call bear spreads, early exercise would pose a risk.

Collars

Now we shall look at a popular strategy often used by professional money managers and referred to as a **collar.** A collar is very similar to a bull spread. In fact, the relationship between the two can be seen by applying what we learned about put-call parity.

Suppose you buy a stock. You wish to protect it against a loss but participate in any gains. An obvious strategy is one we covered in Chapter 6, the protective put. If you buy the put, you will have to pay out cash for the price of the put. The collar reduces the cost of the put by adding a short position in a call, where the exercise price is higher than the exercise price of the put. Although a call with any exercise price can be chosen, there is in fact one particular call that tends to be preferred: the one whose price is the same as that of the put you are buying.

Thus, let us buy the stock and buy a put with an exercise price of X_1 at a price of P_1. Now let us sell a call at an exercise price of X_2 with a premium of C_2. With $N_P = 1$ and $N_C = 1$, the profit equation is

$$\Pi = S_T - S_0 + \text{Max}(0, X_1 - S_T) - P_1 - \text{Max}(0, S_T - X_2) + C_2.$$

The profits for the three ranges are as follows:

$$
\begin{aligned}
\Pi &= S_T - S_0 + X_1 - S_T - P_1 + C_2 && \text{if } S_T \leq X_1 < X_2. \\
&= X_1 - S_0 - P_1 + C_2 \\
\Pi &= S_T - S_0 - P_1 + C_2 && \text{if } X_1 < S_T < X_2. \\
\Pi &= S_T - S_0 - P_1 - S_T + X_2 + C_2 && \text{if } X_1 < X_2 \leq S_T. \\
&= X_2 - S_0 - P_1 + C_2
\end{aligned}
$$

Since X_1 is below the current stock price, S_0, and X_2 is above it, the profit on the stock is either $X_1 - S_0$, which is negative, when S_T is at X_1 or below, or $X_2 - S_0$, which is positive, when S_T is at X_2 or above. Thus, the potential loss and gain on the stock are fixed and limited. Only in the middle range, where S_T is essentially between the two exercise prices, is there any uncertainty. As noted above, it is common to set X_2 such that $C_2 = P_1$, so these terms drop out of the above profit equations. It is not necessary, however, that we choose the call such that its price offsets the price paid for the put. In such a case, we must add $-P_1 + C_2$ to the stock profit, as indicated in the above equations.

When the call and put premiums do offset, the collar is sometimes referred to as a zero-cost collar, but this term is somewhat misleading. While there is no cash outlay for the options, the cost is in the willingness to give up all gains beyond X_2. In other words, the investor will be selling the stock at a maximum price of X_2, in exchange for which the investor receives the assurance that the stock will be sold for no worse than X_1.

Although collars are normally used with index options in conjunction with diversified portfolios, we shall stay with the example here of the single stock, America Online. Figure 7.5 illustrates the collar for the America Online July 120/136.23. The stock is bought at 125.9375. Let us say we buy the put with an exercise price of 120, which costs 13.625. Now we need to sell a call with an exercise price such that its premium is 13.625. For the July options we see that none of the calls have a price of 13.625. The 130 has a price of 16.375, so we will need a call with an exercise price greater than 130. We can use the Black-Scholes model to figure out what the exercise price should be. We use the following inputs: $S_0 = 125.9375$, $X = 136.23$, $r_c = .0453$, $\sigma = .83$, and $T = 0.1726$. We find that this call has a Black-Scholes price of 13.626, which is close enough.

Now we are faced with a problem we have not yet seen. If we use exchange-listed options, we cannot normally designate the exercise price, for this is set by the exchange. We could sell the 135 or the 140, but there is no 136.23. We have two choices. We can use an over-the-counter option, as discussed in Chapter 2, which can be customized to any exercise price. We go to an options dealer and request this specific option. Alternatively, if we trade in sufficient volume, we can use FLEX options, also mentioned in Chapter 2, which trade on the exchanges and permit us to set the exercise price. Let us assume that we do one or the other. For illustrative purposes it does not matter.

Thus, we buy the 120 put for $13.625 and sell the 136.23 call for $13.625. We do 100 of each and buy 100 shares of the AOL stock. Note that the maximum profit is capped at $100(X_2 - S_0)$, $= 100(136.23 - 125.9375) = 1{,}029.25$, and the maximum loss is $100(S_0 - X_1) = 100(125.9375 - 120) = 593.75$. The breakeven is found by setting the middle equation to zero:

$$\Pi = S_T^* - S_0 = 0,$$

A collar is a strategy in which the holder of a position in a stock buys a put with an exercise price lower than the current stock price and sells a call with an exercise price higher than the current stock price. The call premium is intended to reduce the cost of the put premium. The call exercise price is often set to make the call premium completely offset the put premium.

FIGURE 7.5 Collar

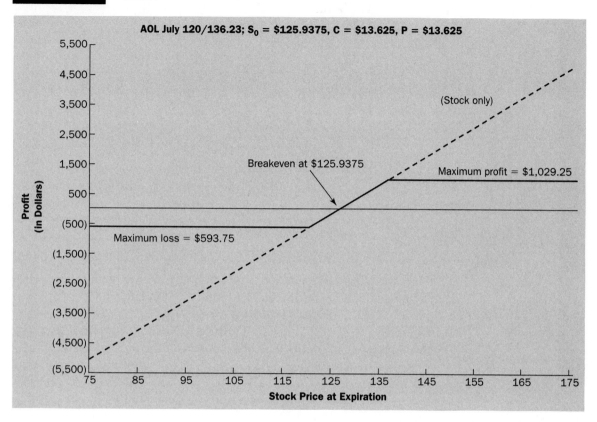

AOL July 120/136.23; S_0 = $125.9375, C = $13.625, P = $13.625

Breakeven at $125.9375

(Stock only)

Maximum profit = $1,029.25

Maximum loss = $593.75

Profit (in Dollars)

Stock Price at Expiration

which we see is obviously,

$$S_T^* = S_0,$$

and in our problem, $S_T^* = 125.9375$, the original stock price. Note in Figure 7.5 that the line for the stock profit passes right through the middle range of profit for the collar. So the investor effectively buys the stock and establishes a maximum loss of $593.75 and a maximum gain of $1,029.25.

This strategy looks a lot like a bull spread. Let us examine the difference. For the three ranges of S_T, the profit equations for the bull spread and collar are given below. For the collar, we substitute from put-call parity, $C_1 - S_0 + X_1(1 + r)^{-T}$ for P_1.

$S_T \leq X_1 < X_2$

Bull spread:	$-C_1 + C_2$
Collar:	$X_1 - S_0 - P_1 + C_2$
	$= X_1 - X_1(1 + r)^{-T} - C_1 + C_2$

$X_1 < S_T < X_2$

Bull spread:	$S_T - X_1 - C_1 + C_2$
Collar:	$S_T - S_0 - P_1 + C_2$
	$= S_T - X_1(1 + r)^{-T} - C_1 + C_2$

$X_1 < X_2 < S_T$

Bull spread:	$X_2 - X_1 - C_1 + C_2$
Collar:	$X_2 - S_0 - P_1 + C_2$
	$= X_2 - X_1(1 + r)^{-T} - C_1 + C_2.$

Thus, in all cases the collar is more profitable by the difference between X_1 and the present value of X_1.

Thus, the bull spread and the collar are similar but not identical. Note that the range of profits for the bull spread is $X_2 - X_1 - C_1 + C_2 - (C_1 + C_2)$ $= X_2 - X_1$. The range of profits for the collar is $X_2 - X_1(1 + r)^{-T} - C_1 + C_2 - (X_1 - X_1(1 + r)^{-T} - C_1 + C_2) = X_2 - X_1$. So the two strategies have the same range of profits. The initial outlay for the bull spread is $C_1 - C_2$. The initial outlay for the collar is $S_0 + P_1 - C_2$. Substituting from put-call parity for P_1, this is $X_1(1 + r)^{-T} + C_1 - C_2$. The collar is equivalent to a bull spread plus a risk-free bond paying X_1 at expiration.

THE CHOICE OF HOLDING PERIOD   In Figure 7.6 we see what the profit would look like if the position is closed early. On the downside, by closing the position at T_1, we recoup more of the time value on the long put than we pay to buy back the short call. The longer we hold the position on the downside, the less this works to our advantage. On the upside, if we close the position early, the more time value we must buy back on the short call than we receive from selling the long put. The longer we hold the position, the more this works to our disadvantage. Remember that these statements are true because the time value is greater where the stock price is close to the exercise price. On the downside, the time value is greater on the long put; on the upside, the time value is greater on the short call.

Butterfly Spreads

A **butterfly spread,** sometimes called a **sandwich spread,** is a combination of a bull spread and a bear spread. However, this transaction involves three exercise prices: X_1, X_2, and X_3, where X_2 is halfway between X_1 and X_3. Suppose we construct a call bull spread by purchasing the call with the low ex-

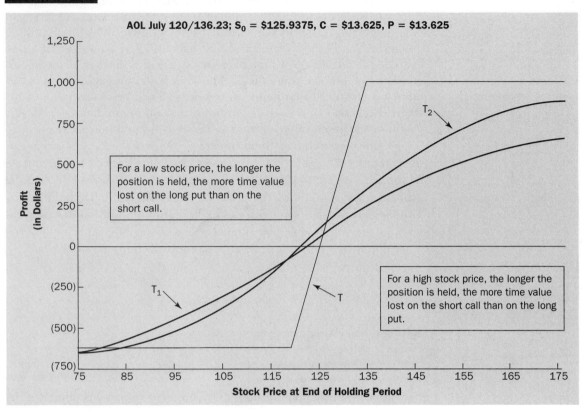

FIGURE 7.6   Collar: Different Holding Periods

AOL July 120/136.23; S_0 = $125.9375, C = $13.625, P = $13.625

For a low stock price, the longer the position is held, the more time value lost on the long put than on the short call.

For a high stock price, the longer the position is held, the more time value lost on the short call than on the long put.

ercise price, X_1, and writing the call with the middle exercise price, X_2. Then we also construct a call bear spread by purchasing the call with the high exercise price, X_3, and writing the call with the middle exercise price, X_2. Combining these positions shows that we are long one each of the low- and high-exercise-price options and short two middle-exercise-price options. Since $N_1 = 1$, $N_2 = -2$, and $N_3 = 1$, the profit equation is

$$\Pi = \text{Max}(0, S_T - X_1) - C_1 - 2\text{Max}(0, S_T - X_2) + 2C_2 + \text{Max}(0, S_T - X_3) - C_3.$$

To analyze the behavior of the profit equation, we must examine four ranges of the stock price at expiration:

$$\Pi = -C_1 + 2C_2 - C_3 \qquad\qquad\qquad \text{if } S_T \leq X_1 < X_2 < X_3.$$
$$\Pi = S_T - X_1 - C_1 + 2C_2 - C_3 \qquad\qquad \text{if } X_1 < S_T \leq X_2 < X_3.$$
$$\Pi = S_T - X_1 - C_1 - 2S_T + 2X_2 + 2C_2 - C_3$$
$$\quad = -S_T + 2X_2 - X_1 - C_1 + 2C_2 - C_3 \qquad \text{if } X_1 < X_2 < S_T \leq X_3.$$
$$\Pi = S_T - X_1 - C_1 - 2S_T + 2X_2 + 2C_2 + S_T - X_3 - C_3$$
$$\quad = -X_1 + 2X_2 - X_3 - C_1 + 2C_2 - C_3 \qquad \text{if } X_1 < X_2 < X_3 < S_T.$$

Now look at the first profit equation, $-C_1 + 2C_2 - C_3$. This can be separated into $-C_1 + C_2$ and $C_2 - C_3$. We already know that a low-exercise-price call is worth more than a high-exercise-price call. Thus, the first pair of terms is negative and the second pair is positive. Which pair will be greater in an absolute sense? The first pair will. The advantage of a low-exercise-price call over a high-exercise-price call is smaller at higher exercise prices, because there the likelihood of both calls expiring out-of-the-money is greater. If that happens, neither call will be of any value to the trader. Because $-C_1 + C_2$ is larger in an absolute sense than $C_2 - C_3$, the profit for the lowest range of stock prices at expiration is negative.

For the second range, the profit is $S_T - X_1 - C_1 + 2C_2 - C_3$. The last three terms, $-C_1 + 2C_2 - C_3$, represent the net price paid for the butterfly spread. Because the stock price at expiration has a direct effect on the profit, a graph would show the profit varying dollar for dollar and in a positive manner with the stock price at expiration. The profit in this range of stock prices can, however, be either positive or negative. This implies that there is a breakeven stock price at expiration. To find that stock price, S_T^*, set this profit equal to zero:

$$S_T^* - X_1 - C_1 + 2C_2 - C_3 = 0.$$

Solving for S_T^* gives

$$S_T^* = X_1 + C_1 - 2C_2 + C_3.$$

The breakeven equation indicates that a butterfly spread is profitable if the stock price at expiration exceeds the low exercise price by an amount large enough to cover the net price paid for the spread.

Now look at the third profit equation. Since the profit varies inversely dollar for dollar with the stock price at expiration, a graph would show the profit decreasing one for one with the stock price at expiration. The profit can be either positive or negative; hence, there is a second breakeven stock price. To find it, set the profit equal to zero:

$$S_T^* + 2X_2 - X_1 - C_1 + 2C_2 - C_3 = 0.$$

Solving for S_T^* gives

$$S_T^* = 2X_2 - X_1 - C_1 + 2C_2 - C_3.$$

Recall that in this range of stock prices, the profit declines with higher stock prices. Profit will disappear completely if the stock price is so high that it exceeds the cash flow received from the exercise of the middle-exercise-price call, $2X_2$, minus the cash flow paid for the exercise of the low-exercise-price call, X_1, minus the net premiums on the calls.

In the final range of the stock price at expiration, profit is the net premiums paid plus the difference in the exercise prices. Since X_2 is halfway between X_1 and X_3, then $X_2 - X_1$ is the same as $X_3 - X_2$. Therefore, $-X_1 + 2X_2 - X_3 = 0$. This means that the profit in this range is the same as that in the first range and is simply the difference in the premiums.

Now that we have a good idea of what a butterfly spread looks like, consider the America Online June 120, 125, and 130 calls. In this example, a plot of the results would reveal that the butterfly spread would profit at any stock price. Upon further inspection of the prices, we would see that the cost of buying the butterfly spread is less than the lowest possible value of the spread at expiration. Therefore, one or more of the options must be mispriced. To avoid any confusion about the performance of the butterfly spread, we should use theoretically correct prices, which can be obtained from the Black-Scholes model. Using the volatility of .83, we would see that at a market price of $15.375, the 120 call is significantly lower than its Black-Scholes value of about $16. Thus, let us use $16 as its price.

A butterfly spread has a limited loss, which occurs on large stock price moves, either up or down, and a limited gain, which occurs if the stock price ends up at the middle exercise price.

Figure 7.7 illustrates the butterfly spread for the June 120, 125, and 130 calls with premiums of $16.00, $13.50, and $11.375, respectively. The worst outcome is simply the net premiums or $100[-16.00 + 2(13.50) - 11.375] = -37.50$. This is obtained for any stock price less than $120 or greater than $130. The maximum profit is obtained when the stock price at expiration is at the middle exercise price. Using the second profit equation and letting $S_T = X_2$, the maximum profit is

$$\Pi = X_2 - X_1 - C_1 + 2C_2 - C_3,$$

which in this example is $100[125 - 120 - 16.00 + 2(13.50) - 11.375] = 462.50$. The lower breakeven is $X_1 + C_1 - 2C_2 + C_3$, which in this case is $120 + 16.00 - 2(13.50) + 11.375 = 120.375$. The upper breakeven is $2X_2 - X_1 - C_1 + 2C_2 - C_3$, which in this example is $2(125) - 120 - 16.00 + 2(13.50) - 11.375 = 129.625$.

The butterfly spread strategy assumes the stock price will fluctuate very little. In this example, the trader is betting that the stock price will stay within the range of $120.375 to $129.625. If this prediction of low stock price volatility proves incorrect, however, the potential loss will be limited—in this case, to $37.50. Thus, the butterfly spread is a low-risk transaction.

A trader who believes the stock price will be extremely volatile and will fall outside of the two breakeven stock prices might want to write a butterfly spread. This will involve one short position in each of the X_1 and X_3 calls and two long positions in the X_2 call. We shall leave it as an end-of-chapter problem to explore the short butterfly spread.

Early exercise can pose a problem for holders of butterfly spreads. Suppose the stock price prior to expiration is S_t, where S_t is greater than or equal to X_2 and less than or equal to X_3. Assume the short calls are

FIGURE 7.7	Call Butterfly Spread

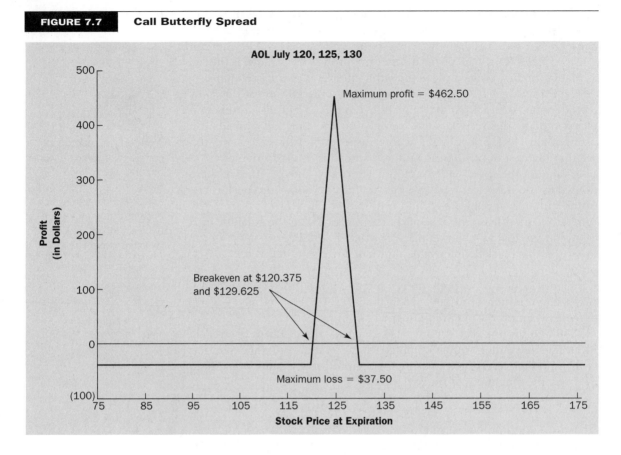

AOL July 120, 125, 130

Maximum profit = $462.50

Breakeven at $120.375
and $129.625

Maximum loss = $37.50

Profit (in Dollars)

Stock Price at Expiration

exercised shortly before the stock goes ex-dividend. The spreader then exercises the long call with exercise price X_1. The cash flow from the short calls is $-(2S_t - 2X_2)$, and the cash flow from the long call is $S_t - X_1$. This gives a total cash flow of $-S_t + X_2 + X_2 - X_1$. The minimum value of this expression is $-X_2 + X_2 + X_2 - X_1 = X_2 - X_1$, which is positive. If S_t exceeds X_3 and the two short calls are exercised, they will be offset by the exercise of both long calls, and the overall cash flow will be zero.

Thus, early exercise does not result in a cash outflow, but that does not mean that it poses no risk. If the options are exercised early, there is no possibility of achieving the maximum profit obtainable at expiration when $S_T = X_2$. If the spread were reversed and the X_1 and X_3 calls were sold while two of the X_2 calls were bought, early exercise could generate a negative cash flow.

THE CHOICE OF HOLDING PERIOD   As with any option strategy, the investor might wish to close the position prior to expiration. Consider the June 120, 125, and 130 calls. Let us continue to use the same prices used in the preceding example, $16.00, $13.50, and $11.375, respectively. Let holding period T_1 involve closing the position on June 1 and holding period T_2 close the position on June 11.[1] The graph is shown in Figure 7.8.

At high stock prices, time value will be greatest on the call with the highest exercise price. Since we are long that call, we gain the advantage of being able to sell it back early and recapture some of the time value. This advantage, however, erodes with a longer holding period because the time value decreases.

For a given stock price, the profit of a butterfly spread increases as expiration approaches if the stock price is near the middle exercise price and decreases if the stock price is on the low or high side.

FIGURE 7.8   **Call Butterfly Spread: Different Holding Periods**

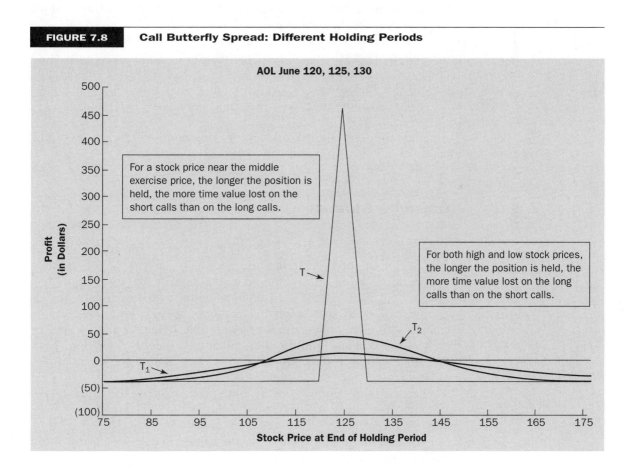

AOL June 120, 125, 130

For a stock price near the middle exercise price, the longer the position is held, the more time value lost on the short calls than on the long calls.

For both high and low stock prices, the longer the position is held, the more time value lost on the long calls than on the short calls.

---

[1]The holding period was changed in this example because the time value decay does not show up as clearly for the holding periods we have previously used.

At low stock prices, the time value will be greatest on the call with the lowest exercise price. Since we are also long that call, we can sell it back early and recapture some of its remaining time value. This advantage also decreases, however, as we hold the position longer and time value decays.

In the middle range of stock prices, the time value will be very high on the two short calls. For short holding periods, this is a disadvantage because we have to buy back these calls, which means that we must pay for the remaining time value. This disadvantage turns to an advantage, however, as the holding period lengthens and time value begins to disappear. At expiration, no time value remains; thus, profit is maximized in this range.

The breakeven stock prices are substantially further away with shorter holding periods. This is advantageous, because it will then take a much larger stock price change to produce a loss.

As always, we cannot specifically identify an optimal holding period. Because the butterfly spread is one in which the trader expects the stock price to stay within a narrow range, profit is maximized with a long holding period. The disadvantage of a long holding period, however, is that it gives the stock price more time to move outside of the profitable range.

All of the above spreads are money spreads. We now turn to an examination of calendar spreads.

Calendar Spreads

A **calendar spread,** also known as a *time* or *horizontal* spread, involves the purchase of an option with one expiration date and the sale of an otherwise identical option with a different expiration date. Because it is not possible to hold both options until expiration, analyzing a calendar spread is more complicated than analyzing a money spread. Since one option expires before the other, the longest possible holding period would be to hold the position until the shorter-maturity option's expiration. Then the other option would have some remaining time value that must be estimated.

Because both options have the same exercise prices, they will have the same intrinsic values; thus, the profitability of the calendar spread will be determined solely by the difference in their time values. The longer-term call will have more time value. This does not, however, necessarily mean that one should always buy the longer-term call and sell the shorter-term call. As with most option strategies, which option is purchased and which one is sold depends on the investor's outlook for the stock.

To best understand the calendar spread, we will again illustrate with the America Online calls. This spread consists of the purchase of the July 125 call at $18.625 and the sale of the June 125 call at $13.50. This position is net long, because you pay more for the July than you receive for the June. Consider two possible holding periods. One, T_1, will involve the spread's termination on June 1; the other, T_2, will have the spread held until June 18, the date of the June call's expiration. Using the Black-Scholes model to estimate the remaining time values produced the graph in Figure 7.9.

For a given stock price, a long calendar spread gains as expiration approaches if the stock price is near the exercise price and loses if the stock price is on the low or high side.

Like the butterfly spread, the calendar spread is one in which the stock's volatility is the major factor in its performance. The investor obtains the greatest profit if the stock has low volatility and thus trades within a narrow range. If the stock price moves substantially, the investor will likely incur a loss.

How does the calendar spread work? Recall that we are short the June call and long the July call. When closing out the position, we buy back the June call and sell the July call. If the stock price is around the exercise price, both calls will have more time value remaining than if the stock price were at the extremes. The June call will always have less time value, however, than the July call on any given date. Thus, when we close out the position, the time value repurchased on the June call will be low relative to the

---

FIGURE 7.9   Call Calendar Spread

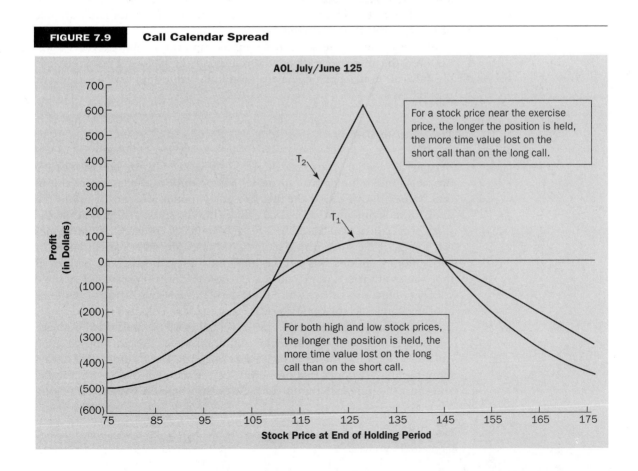

AOL July/June 125

For a stock price near the exercise price, the longer the position is held, the more time value lost on the short call than on the long call.

For both high and low stock prices, the longer the position is held, the more time value lost on the long call than on the short call.

remaining time value received from the sale of the July call. As we hold the position closer and closer to the June call's expiration, the remaining time value we must repurchase on that option will get lower and lower.

If the stock price is at the high or low extreme, the time values of both options will be low. If the stock price is high enough or low enough, there may be little, if any, time value on either option. Thus, when closing out the position there may be little time value to recover from the July option. Because the July call is more expensive, we will end up losing money on the overall transaction.

The breakeven stock prices can be obtained only by visual examination.[2] In this example, the shortest holding period has a tighter range between its two breakeven stock prices, about $115 and $145. For the longer holding period, the lower breakeven is about $110 and the higher breakeven is still around $145.

An investor who expected the stock price to move into the extremes could execute a reverse calendar spread. This would require purchasing the June call and selling the July call. If the stock price became extremely low or high, there would be little time value remaining to be repurchased on the July call. Because the spreader received more money from the sale of the July call than was paid for the purchase of the June call, a profit would be made. If the stock price ended up around the exercise price, however, the trader could incur a potentially large loss. This is because the July call would possibly have a large time value that would have to be repurchased.

Time Value Decay

Because a calendar spread is completely influenced by the behavior of the two calls' time value decay, it provides a good opportunity to examine how time values decay. Using the Black-Scholes model, we can compute the week-by-week time values for each call during the spread's life, holding the stock price constant at $125.9375. Keep in mind, of course, that time values will change if the stock price changes. Because time values are greatest for at-the-money options, we use the June and July 125 calls. The pattern of time values at various points during the options' lives is presented in Table 7.2. The table also presents the thetas, which we learned from Chapter 5 are the changes in the option prices for a very small change in time. Negative thetas imply that the option price will fall as we move forward in time.

Notice what happens as expiration approaches. Because of the June call's earlier expiration, its theta is more negative, and its time value decays more rapidly than does that of the July call. Since we are long the July call and short the June call, the spread's time value—the time value of the long

---

[2]It is possible, however, to use a computer search routine with the Black-Scholes model to find the precise breakeven.

TABLE 7.2	Time Value Decay, June and July 125 and Calendar Spread

		June 125			July 125			Spread	
Date	Time	Time Value	Theta	Time	Time Value	Theta	Time Value	Theta
May 14	0.0959	12.61	−68.91	0.1726	17.14	−51.54	4.53	17.37
May 21	0.0767	11.22	−76.92	0.1534	16.13	−54.65	4.91	22.27
May 28	0.0575	9.64	−88.63	0.1342	15.04	−58.39	5.40	30.24
June 4	0.0384	7.77	−108.18	0.1151	13.88	−63.02	6.11	45.17
June 11	0.0192	5.35	−152.11	0.0959	12.62	−68.95	7.27	83.16
June 18	0.0000	0.00	0.00	0.0767	11.22	−76.96	11.22	−76.96

$\sigma = .83$, $S = 125.9375$, r_c (June) $= .0446$, r_c (July) $= .0453$
The spread time value and theta equal the time value and theta on the long July call minus the time value and theta on the short June call. The time value of each option is obtained as the Black-Scholes value, which is the intrinsic value plus the time value, minus the intrinsic value of 0.9375.

call minus the time value of the short call—increases, as is indicated by its positive theta. Once the June call expires, however, we are left with a long position in the July call, which leaves us with a negative theta. Time value will then begin decaying.

Figure 7.10 illustrates the pattern of time value decay. As expiration approaches, the time value of the June call rapidly decreases and the overall time value of the spread increases. At expiration of the June call, the spread's time value is composed entirely of the July call's time value.

Time value decays more rapidly as expiration approaches.

Time value decay would appear to make it easy to profit with a time spread. One would simply buy the longer-term option and write the shorter-term option. As the time values decayed, the spread would gain value. In reality, however, it seldom works out like this. The pattern of time value decay illustrated here was obtained by holding the stock price constant. In the real world, the stock price probably will not remain constant. Thus, there is indeed risk to a calendar spread. This risk is mitigated somewhat by the fact that the investor is long one option and short the other. Nonetheless, the calendar spread, in which one buys the long-term option and writes the short-term option, is a good strategy if one expects the stock price to remain fairly stable.

The degree of risk of early exercise on a calendar spread depends on which call is bought and which is sold. Since both calls have the same exercise price, the extent to which they are in-the-money is the same. As discussed in Chapter 3, however, the time to expiration is a factor in encouraging early exercise. We saw that if everything else is equal, the shorter-term option is the one more likely to be exercised early. Thus, if we write the shorter-term option, it could be exercised early. We always, however, have the choice of exercising the longer-term option early. It will certainly be in-the-money if the shorter-term option is in-the-money. If S_t is the

FIGURE 7.10   **Time Value Decay**

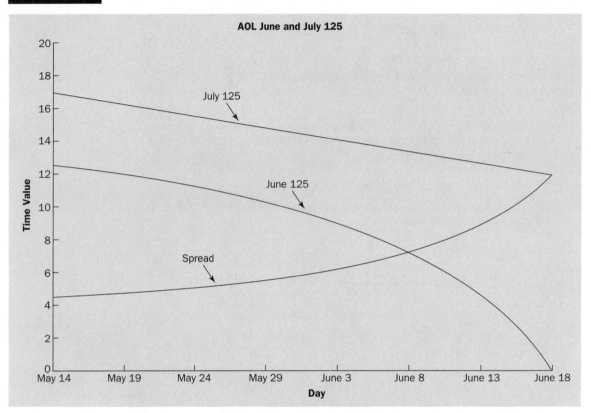

stock price prior to expiration and the shorter-term call is exercised, the cash flow will be $-(S_t - X)$ while the cash flow from exercising the longer-term option will be $S_t - X$. Thus, the total cash flow will be zero. This means that in the event of early exercise there will be no negative cash flow. It does not mean that there will be no overall loss on the transaction. The longer-term call is more expensive than the shorter-term call. This means that early exercise would ensure a loss by preventing us from waiting to capture the time value decay.

Calendar spreads can also be constructed with puts. By using the Black-Scholes model to determine the time value on the puts, similar results can be obtained. Like money spreads, put calendar spreads should not be overlooked. The puts could be mispriced, in which case a spread might offer the most profitable opportunity.

The butterfly spread and calendar spread are two of several transactions called **volatility strategies.** We shall look at the others later in this chapter. For now, however, note that all the strategies covered so far are risky. Some option traders prefer riskless strategies because if the options are mispriced, it may be possible to construct a riskless portfolio that will earn a return in excess of the risk-free rate.

Ratio Spreads

Chapter 5 examined the Black-Scholes model. It showed that when an option is mispriced, an investor can construct a riskless hedge by buying an underpriced call and selling short the stock or by buying stock and selling an overpriced call. Because of margin requirements and the uptick rule, selling short stock can be complicated. By using spreads, however, the investor can buy an underpriced call and sell an overpriced or correctly priced call, producing a ratio of one call to the other that creates a riskless position. This transaction is called a **ratio spread.**

The ratio spread can be either a money spread or a calendar spread. Consider two calls priced at C_1 and C_2. Initially we need not be concerned with which one is purchased and which one is sold, nor do we need to determine whether the two calls differ by time to expiration or by exercise price. The approach presented here can accommodate all cases.

Let the investor hold N_1 units of the call priced at C_1 and N_2 units of the call priced at C_2. The value of the portfolio is

$$V = N_1C_1 + N_2C_2.$$

Recall that the delta of a call is the change in the call price over the change in the stock price, assuming the change in the stock price is very small. Let us use the symbols Δ_1 and Δ_2 as the deltas of the two calls. Remember that the deltas are the values of $N(d_1)$ from the Black-Scholes model. If the stock price changes, the first call generates a total price change of $N_1\Delta_1$ and the second call generates a total price change of $N_2\Delta_2$. Thus, when the stock price changes, the portfolio will change in value by the sum of these two values. A hedged position is one in which the portfolio value will not change when the stock price changes. Thus, we set $N_1\Delta_1 + N_2\Delta_2$ to zero and solve for the ratio N_1/N_2.

$$\frac{N_1}{N_2} = -\frac{\Delta_2}{\Delta_1}$$

A riskless position is established if the ratio of the quantity of the first call to the quantity of the second call equals minus the inverse ratio of their deltas. The transaction would then be delta neutral.

Consider an example using the America Online June 120 and June 125 calls. Using $S_0 = 125.9375$, $r_c = .0446$, and $T = .0959$ in the Black-Scholes model gives a value of $N(d_1)$ of .630 for the June 120 and .569 for the June

A ratio spread is a risk-free transaction involving two options weighted according to their deltas.

125. Thus, the ratio of the number of June 120s to June 125s should be $-(.569/.630) = -.903$. Hence, the investor would buy 903 of the June 120s and sell 1,000 of the June 125s.

Note that the investor could have purchased 1,000 of the June 125s and sold 903 of the June 120s. The negative sign in the formula is a reminder to be long one option and short the other. An investor should, of course, always buy underpriced or correctly priced calls and sell overpriced or correctly priced calls.

If the stock price decreases by $1, the June 120 should decrease by .630 and the June 125 by .569. The investor is long 903 of the June 120s and therefore loses $.630(903) \approx 569$. Likewise, the investor is short 1,000 of the June 125s and thus gains $.569(1,000) \approx 569$. The gain on one call offsets the loss on the other.

The ratio spread, of course, does not remain riskless unless the ratio is continuously adjusted. Because this is somewhat impractical, no truly riskless hedge can be constructed. Moreover, the values of $N(d_1)$ are simply approximations of the change in the call price for a change in the stock price. They apply for only very small changes in the stock price. For larger changes in the stock price, the hedger would need to consider the gamma, which we discussed in Chapter 5. Nonetheless, spreads of this type are frequently done by option traders attempting to replicate riskless positions. Although the positions may not always be exactly riskless, they will come very close to being so as long as the ratio does not deviate too far from the optimum.

This completes our coverage of option spread strategies. The next group of strategies are called **combinations,** because they involve combined positions in puts and calls. We previously covered some combination strategies, namely conversions and reversals, which we used to illustrate put-call parity. The strategies covered in the remainder of this chapter are straddles, straps, strips, and box spreads. We will use the same approach as before; the notation should be quite familiar by now.

Straddles, Straps, and Strips

Straddles, straps, and strips, like calendar and butterfly spreads, are volatility strategies because they are based on the expectation of high or low volatility rather than the direction of the stock.

Straddles

A **straddle** is the purchase of a call and a put that have the same exercise price and expiration date. By holding both a call and a put, the trader can capitalize on stock price movements in either direction.

Consider the purchase of a straddle with the call and put having an exercise price of X and an expiration of T. Then $N_C = 1$ and $N_p = 1$, and the profit from this transaction if held to expiration is

$$\Pi = \text{Max}(0, S_T - X) - C + \text{Max}(0, X - S_T) - P.$$

Since there is only one exercise price involved, there are only two ranges of the stock price at expiration. The profits are as follows:

$$\Pi = S_T - X - C - P \text{ if } S_T \geq X.$$
$$\Pi = X - S_T - C - P \text{ if } S_T < X.$$

For the first case, in which the stock price equals or exceeds the exercise price, the call expires in-the-money.[3] It is exercised for a gain of $S_T - X$, while the put expires out-of-the-money. The profit is the gain on the call minus the premiums paid on the call and the put. For the second case, in which the stock price is less than the exercise price, the put expires in-the-money and is exercised for a gain of $X - S_T$. The profit is the gain on the put minus the premiums paid for the put and the call.

For the range of stock prices above the exercise price, the profit increases dollar for dollar with the stock price at expiration. For the range of stock prices below the exercise price, the profit decreases dollar for dollar with the stock price at expiration. When the options expire with the stock price at the exercise price, both options are at-the-money and essentially expire worthless. The profit then equals the premiums paid, which, of course, makes it a loss. These results suggest that the graph is V-shaped. Figure 7.11 illustrates the straddle for the America Online June 125 options. The dashed lines are the strategies of buying the call and the put separately.

As noted, the straddle is designed to capitalize on high stock price volatility. To create a profit, the stock price must move substantially in either direction. It is not necessary to know which way the stock will go; it is necessary only that it make a significant move. How much must it move? Look at the two breakeven points.

For the case in which the stock price exceeds the exercise price, set the profit equal to zero:

$$S_T^* - X - C - P = 0.$$

Solving for S_T^* gives a breakeven of

$$S_T^* = X + C + P.$$

-----

[3]The case in which $S_T = X$ is included in this range. Even though $S_T = X$ means that the call is at-the-money, it can still be exercised for a gain of $S_T - X = 0$.

FIGURE 7.11   **Straddle**

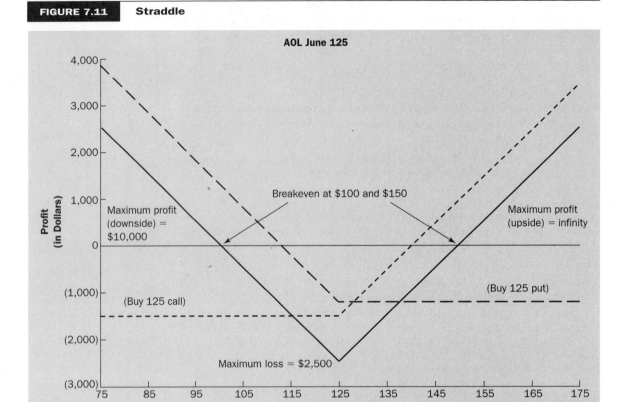

AOL June 125

Breakeven at $100 and $150

Maximum profit
(downside) =
$10,000

Maximum profit
(upside) = infinity

(Buy 125 call)

(Buy 125 put)

Maximum loss = $2,500

The upside breakeven is simply the exercise price plus the premiums paid for the options.

For the case in which the stock price is below the exercise price, set the profit equal to zero:

A straddle is a strategy designed to profit if there is a large up or down move in the stock.

$$X - S_T^* - C - P = 0.$$

Solving for S_T^* gives a breakeven of

$$S_T^* = X - C - P.$$

The downside breakeven is the exercise price minus the premiums paid on the options.

Thus, the breakeven stock prices are simply the exercise price plus or minus the premiums paid for the call and the put. This makes sense. On the upside, the call is exercised for a gain equal to the difference between the stock price and the exercise price. For the investor to profit, the stock price must exceed the exercise price by enough that the gain from exercising the call will cover the premiums paid for the call and the put. On the downside, the put is exercised for a gain equal to the difference between the exercise price and the stock price. To generate a profit, the stock price must be sufficiently below the exercise price that the gain on the put will cover the premiums on the call and the put.

In this example, the premiums are $13.50 for the call and $11.50 for the put for a total of $25. Thus, the breakeven stock prices at expiration are $125 plus or minus $25, or $100 and $150. The stock price currently is at $125.9375. To generate a profit, the stock price must increase by $24.0625 or decrease by $25.9375 in the remaining 35 days until the options expire.

The worst-case outcome for a straddle is for the stock price to end up equal to the exercise price where neither the call nor the put can be exercised for a gain.[4] The option trader will lose the premiums on the call and the put, which in this example total $100(13.50 + 11.50) = 2,500$.

The profit potential on a straddle is unlimited. The stock price can rise infinitely, and the straddle will earn profits dollar for dollar with the stock price in excess of the exercise price. On the downside, the profit is limited simply because the stock price can go no lower than zero. The downside maximum profit is found by setting the stock price at expiration equal to zero for the case in which the stock price is below the exercise price. This gives a profit of $X - C - P$, which here is $100(125 - 13.50 - 11.50) = 10,000$.

The potentially large profits on a straddle can be a temptation too hard to resist. One should be aware that the straddle normally requires a fairly large stock price move to be profitable. Even to a novice investor stock prices always seem highly volatile, but that volatility may be misleading.

For example, consider a two-month straddle on a market index. A reasonable estimate of the market's annualized standard deviation would be about 0.14. For a two-month holding period, the standard deviation would be about $\sqrt{(2/12)(0.14)^2} = .0572$. Assuming a normal distribution of returns, the stock price would be expected to fluctuate within 5.72 percent up or down about two-thirds of the time. This is a fairly small stock price change and would result in a loss in many straddle transactions. In this example, it would require about a 19 percent increase or a 21 percent decrease in the stock price to make a profit. An investor considering a straddle is advised to carefully assess the probability that the stock price will move into the profitable range.

Because both the call and the put are owned, the problem of early exercise does not exist with a straddle. The early-exercise decision is up to the straddle holder. Transaction costs also need to be considered.

When the straddle is established, there is a commission on both the call and the put. At exercise there will be a commission only on either the call or the put, whichever is in-the-money. Suppose the stock price ends up

---

[4]Either the put, the call, or both could be exercised, but the gain on either would be zero. Transaction costs associated with exercise would suggest that neither the call nor the put would be exercised when $S_T = X$.

slightly higher than the exercise price. Because of the commission on the exercise of the call, it might be inadvisable to exercise the call even though it is in-the-money. A similar argument can be made for the case against exercising the put when the stock price ends up slightly less than the exercise price. This means that, as with any option strategy, the maximum loss is slightly more than the analysis indicates because of the commission. Moreover, the stock price at which such a loss occurs is actually a range around the exercise price.

THE CHOICE OF HOLDING PERIOD   Now consider what happens upon closing the position prior to expiration. Figure 7.12 illustrates the outcomes for the America Online July 125 straddle using the same three holding periods employed in examining the other strategies;[5] that is, the shortest holding period involves closing the position on June 4, the intermediate-length holding period on June 25, and the long holding period at expiration. The profit graphs are curves that collapse onto the straight line for the case in which the position is held to expiration. The highest curve is the shortest holding period.

We should keep in mind that this graph does not imply that the shortest holding period is the best strategy. For a given stock price, the shortest holding period indeed provides the highest profit. The uncertainty of the stock price at expiration prevents the short holding period from dominating the longer holding periods. Because a straddle is designed to permit profiting from large stock price fluctuations, the short holding period leaves less time for the stock price to make a significant move.

When the straddle is closed out prior to expiration, both the call and the put will contain some remaining time value. If the stock price is extremely high or low, neither option will have much time value, but either the call or the put will have a high intrinsic value. If the stock price is close to the exercise price, both options will have a fair amount of time value. When closing out the position, the investor sells the options back and recovers this time value. As the holding period is extended closer to the expiration date, there is less time value to recover and the profit declines. The profit curve gradually decreases until at expiration it becomes the curve for the case in which the straddle is held to expiration. Thus, the higher profits from shorter holding periods come from recapturing the time value of the put and the call.

For a given stock price, a straddle, being long two options, loses value as expiration approaches.

Figure 7.12 shows that the shorter holding period leads to a lower upside and higher downside breakeven. This reduces the risk to the trader, because the range of stock prices in which a loss can be incurred is smaller. In this example, the shortest holding period has breakeven stock prices of

---

[5]Specifically, the holding period T_1 means that the remaining maturity is .1151 based on 42 days remaining, T_2 means that the remaining maturity is .0575 based on 21 days remaining, and $T = 0$ assumes holding all the way to expiration.

FIGURE 7.12   **Straddle: Different Holding Periods**

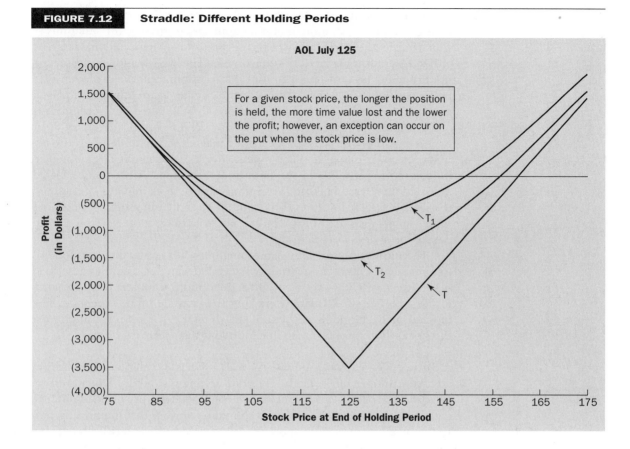

For a given stock price, the longer the position is held, the more time value lost and the lower the profit; however, an exception can occur on the put when the stock price is low.

about \$93 and \$146 and the intermediate-term holding period has breakeven stock prices of about \$90 and \$156.

APPLICATIONS OF STRADDLES   A straddle is an appropriate strategy for situations in which one suspects that the stock price will move substantially but does not know in which direction it will go. An example of this occurs when a major bank or corporation is about to fail.

Suppose a failing bank applies for a bailout from the government.[6] During the period in which the request is under consideration, a straddle will be a potentially profitable strategy. If the request is denied, the bank probably will fail and the stock will become worthless. If the bailout is granted, the bank may be able to turn itself around, in which case the stock price will rise substantially.

---

[6]Bailouts frequently take the form of loan guaranties but can also involve sale of unproductive assets, or sale of new equity or hybrid securities.

A similar scenario exists when a major corporation applies for federal loan guaranties. A straddle is also an appropriate strategy for situations in which important news is about to be released and it is expected that it will be either very favorable or very unfavorable. The weekly money supply announcements present opportunities that possibly could be exploited with index options. Corporate earnings announcements are other examples of situations in which uncertain information will be released on a specific date.

The straddle certainly is not without risk. If investors already know or expect the information, the stock price may move very little when the announcement is made. If this happens, the investor might be tempted to hold on to the straddle in the faint hope that some other, unanticipated news will be released before the options expire. In all likelihood, however, the stock price will move very little and the straddle will produce a loss. The trader might wish to cut the loss quickly by closing the position if the expected move does not materialize.

The most important thing to remember when evaluating a straddle is to note that the greater uncertainty associated with the examples described here is recognized by everyone. Thus, the options would be priced according to a higher stock volatility, making the straddle more expensive. The most attractive straddles will be those in which the investor is confident that the stock will be more volatile than everyone else believes.

A SHORT STRADDLE   An investor who expects the market to stay within a narrow trading range might consider writing a straddle. This would involve the sale of a put and a call with the same exercise price and expiration date. From the previous analysis, it should be obvious that the profit graph would be an inverted V. A short straddle would be a high-risk strategy because of the potential for large losses if the stock price moved substantially, particularly upward. Also, there would be the risk of early exercise of either the put or the call.

There are two popular variations of the straddle: the strap and the strip.

Straps

A **strap** can be more easily understood by comparing it to a straddle. Suppose an investor expects the stock price to make a large move but does not know the direction. If the stock is as likely to increase as it is to decrease, a straddle will be appropriate because it has a symmetric payoff. Large stock price increases are as profitable as equivalent stock price decreases. A straddle can be viewed as a wager in which the trader places equal bets on a bull and bear market.

Now suppose an investor is feeling slightly more bullish than bearish. He or she expects a large stock price movement, but feels it is more likely that the stock price will increase than decrease. It would make sense to increase the number of calls relative to the number of puts. The more calls used, the more bullish is the investor. A strap, then, is the special case in which two calls are purchased for each put.

In a strap, $N_C = 2$ and $N_P = 1$. The profit is

$$\Pi = 2\text{Max}(0, S_T - X) - 2C + \text{Max}(0, X - S_T) - P.$$

The profits for the two ranges of stock price at expiration are as follows:

$$\Pi = 2S_T - 2X - 2C - P \qquad \text{if } S_T \geq X$$
$$\Pi = -2C + X - S_T - P \qquad \text{if } S_T < X.$$

For the case in which the stock price equals or exceeds the exercise price, the strap's profit is greater than the straddle's by the amount $S_T - X - C$. For the case in which the stock price is less than the exercise price, the strap's profit is lower than the straddle's by the amount C, the premium on the additional call. The second call was purchased, but with this outcome it expires worthless.

Figure 7.13 illustrates the strap overlaid with the straddle for the America Online June 125 options. Notice how the maximum loss still occurs if the stock price ends up at the exercise price of 125. In this case, neither the one put.

A strap is a slightly bullish variation of a straddle, involving two calls and one put.

FIGURE 7.13   Strap

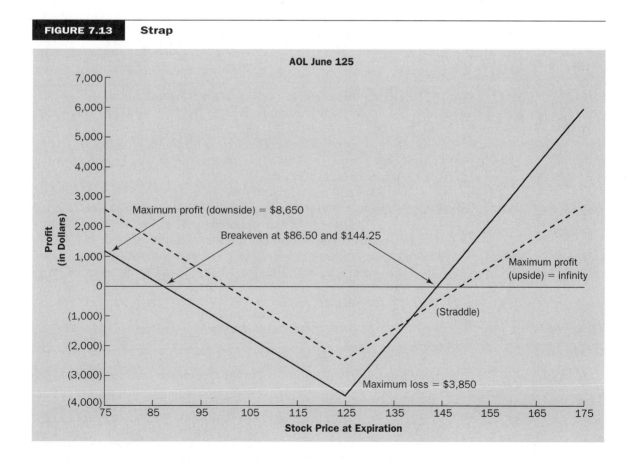

AOL June 125

Maximum profit (downside) = $8,650

Breakeven at $86.50 and $144.25

Maximum profit (upside) = infinity

(Straddle)

Maximum loss = $3,850

Profit (in Dollars)

Stock Price at Expiration

two calls nor the one put end up in-the-money. The strap is a slightly "tilted" version of the straddle. The upside profit of a strap can be greater than the straddle's if the stock price is sufficiently high. On the downside, however, the strap will always do worse than the straddle. This is because of the lost premium on the second call if the stock price ends up below the exercise price.

The two breakeven stock prices at expiration are found by setting the two profit equations to zero and solving for the stock price at expiration, S_T^*. For the case in which the stock price exceeds the exercise price,

$$2S_T^* - 2X - 2C - P = 0.$$

Solving for S_T^* gives

$$S_T^* = X + C + \frac{P}{2}.$$

For the case in which the stock price is less than the exercise price,

$$-2C + X - S_T^* - P = 0.$$

Solving for S_T^* gives

$$S_T^* = X - P - 2C.$$

The upside breakeven stock price is lower by one-half of the put premium. The downside breakeven is lower by the call premium. This means that the upside breakeven stock price is easier to reach and the downside breakeven stock price is harder. This is the price one pays with such a strategy. By increasing the "bet" on a bull market, the payoff in a bull market is higher but the payoff in a bear market is lower.

In this example, the upside breakeven is 125 + 13.50 + 11.50/2 = 144.25 as opposed to $150 for the straddle. The downside breakeven is 125 − 11.50 − 2(13.50) = 86.50 as opposed to $100 for the straddle. The maximum profit is infinity on the upside and 100(−2C + X − P) = 100[−2(13.50) + 125 − 11.50] = 8,650 on the downside. The worst outcome is the profit at a stock price at expiration equal to the exercise price. This is 100[−2(13.50) − 11.50] = −3,850. In the straddle, the worst outcome is a loss of $2,500.

Strips

A **strip** is simply a long position in two puts and one call. Compared to the straddle, the strip involves increasing one's bet that the market will go down. The investor is still uncertain which way the market will go but is feeling slightly more bearish than bullish. If the market goes down, there will be two puts to exercise. If the market goes up, the cost of the second put will cut into the profit.

In a strip, $N_C = 1$ and N_P −2. The profit equation is

$$\Pi = \text{Max}(0, S_T - X) - C + 2\text{Max}(0, X - S_T) - 2P.$$

The profit equations for the two possible ranges of stock price at expiration are as follows:

$$\Pi = S_T - X - C - 2P \qquad \text{if } S_T \geq X.$$
$$\Pi = -C + 2X - 2S_T - 2P \qquad \text{if } S_T < X.$$

When the stock price at expiration is below the exercise price, the extra put adds the amount $X - S_T - P$ to the profit. If the stock price ends up above the exercise price, the profit from the strip falls below the profit from a straddle by the amount of the second put premium.

Figure 7.14 illustrates the strip overlaid with the straddle for the America Online June 125 options. The strip "tilts" the straddle up from

A strip is a slightly bearish variation of a straddle, involving two puts and one call.

FIGURE 7.14   Strip

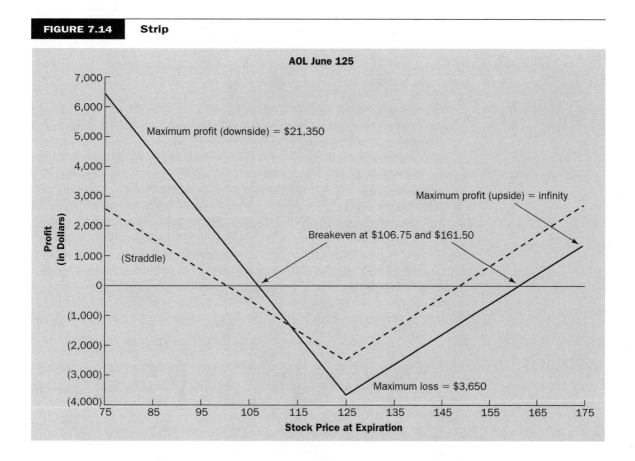

AOL June 125

Maximum profit (downside) = $21,350

Maximum profit (upside) = infinity

Breakeven at $106.75 and $161.50

(Straddle)

Maximum loss = $3,650

Profit (in Dollars)

Stock Price at Expiration

the left. The worst case is still when the stock price ends up at the exercise price, because with that outcome neither the puts nor the call are worth anything. The profit in this case is $-C - 2P$, which here equals $100[-13.50 - 2(11.50)] = -3,650$.

The upside breakeven is found by setting to zero the profit for the case in which the stock price at expiration exceeds the exercise price:

$$S_T^* - X - C - 2P = 0.$$

Solving for S_T^* gives

$$S_T^* = X + C + 2P.$$

The downside breakeven is found by setting to zero the profit for the case in which the stock price at expiration is less than the exercise price:

$$-C + 2X - 2S_T^* - 2P = 0.$$

Solving for S_T^* gives

$$S_T^* = X - P - \left(\frac{C}{2}\right).$$

The upside breakeven reflects the fact that the stock price must exceed the exercise price by the premiums on the one call and the two puts. On the downside, the breakeven is reduced by one-half of the premium on the call. In this example, the upside breakeven is $125 + 13.50 + 2(11.50) = 161.50$ and the downside breakeven is $125 - 11.50 - 13.50/2 = 106.75$. Recall that for the straddle the breakevens were $100 and $150. The downside breakeven on the strip is higher, meaning that the stock price need not fall as much to create a profit. On the upside, however, the stock price must increase more with the strip than with the straddle to generate a profit. The maximum profit is still infinity on the upside and $100(-C + 2X - 2P) = 100[-13.50 + 2(125) - 2(11.50)] = 21,350$ on the downside.

Box Spreads

A **box spread** is a combination of a bull call money spread and a bear put money spread. In contrast to the volatility strategies, the box spread is a low-risk—in fact, riskless—strategy.

Consider a group of options with two exercise prices, X_1 and X_2, and the same expiration. A bull call spread would involve the purchase of the call with exercise price X_1 at a premium of C_1 and the sale of the call with exercise price X_2 at a premium of C_2. A bear put spread would require the purchase of the put with exercise price X_2 at a premium of P_2 and the sale of the put with exercise price X_1 at a premium of P_1. Under the rules for the effect of exercise price on put and call prices, both the call and put spread would involve an initial cash outflow, because $C_1 > C_2$ and $P_2 > P_1$. Thus, the box spread would have a net cash outflow at the initiation of the strategy.

The profit at expiration is

$$\Pi = \text{Max}(0, S_T - X_1) - C_1 - \text{Max}(0, S_T - X_2) + C_2 \\ + \text{Max}(0, X_2 - S_T) - P_2 - \text{Max}(0, X_1 - S_T) + P_1$$

Because there are two exercise prices, we must examine three ranges of the stock price at expiration. The profits are

$$\begin{aligned}
\Pi &= -C_1 + C_2 + X_2 - S_T - P_2 - X_1 + S_T + P_1 \\
&= X_2 - X_1 - C_1 + C_2 - P_2 + P_1 & \text{if } S_T \le X_1 < X_2. \\
\Pi &= S_T - X_1 - C_1 + C_2 + X_2 - S_T - P_2 + P_1 \\
&= X_2 - X_1 - C_1 + C_2 - P_2 + P_1 & \text{if } X_1 < S_T \le X_2. \\
\Pi &= S_T - X_1 - C_1 + X_2 - S_T + C_2 - P_2 + P_1 \\
&= X_2 - X_1 - C_1 + C_2 - P_2 + P_1 & \text{if } X_1 < X_2 < S_T.
\end{aligned}$$

Notice that the profit is the same in each case: The box spread will be worth $X_2 - X_1$ at expiration, and the profit will be $X_2 - X_1$ minus the premiums paid, $C_1 - C_2 + P_2 - P_1$. The box spread is thus a riskless strategy. Why would anyone want to execute a box spread if one can more easily earn the risk-free rate by purchasing Treasury bills? The reason is that the box spread may prove to be incorrectly priced, as a valuation analysis can reveal.

Because the box spread is a riskless transaction that pays off the difference in the exercise prices at expiration, it should be easy to determine whether it is correctly priced. The payoff can be discounted at the risk-free rate. The present value of this amount is then compared to the cost of obtaining the box spread, which is the net premiums paid. This procedure is like analyzing a capital budgeting problem. The present value of the payoff at expiration minus the net premiums is a net present value (NPV). Since the objective of any investment decision is to maximize NPV, an investor should undertake all box spreads in which the NPV is positive. On those spreads with a negative NPV, one should execute a reverse box spread.

The net present value of a box spread is

$$\text{NPV} = (X_2 - X_1)(1 + r)^{-T} - C_1 + C_2 - P_2 + P_1,$$

where r is the risk-free rate and T is the time to expiration.[7] If NPV is positive, the present value of the payoff at expiration will exceed the net

---

[7]Alternatively, one could compute the present value of $X_2 - X_1$ as $(X_2 - X_1)e^{-r_cT}$ and obtain the same result.

D e r i v a t i v e s   i n   A c t i o n

Options Sur le Super Bowl

Société Générale (SG), a large French bank, decided to have a little fun and teach something about options using the 1992 Super Bowl between the Washington Redskins and the Buffalo Bills. SG held a large Super Bowl party and allowed participants to create puts and calls on the game. Everyone was given 200 dollars of play money with which to trade the options. The biggest winner took home a trip to Paris. Here's how it worked.

Let W = Washington's score, B = Buffalo's score. An option (call or put) can be created with any exercise price, X. Calls pay off at the end of the game according to whether the team on which the option is written won and the spread exceeded the exercise price. For example, consider a call on Washington. Its value at the end of the game is $\text{Max}(0,(W - B) - X)$. A call on Buffalo is worth $\text{Max}(0,(B - W) - X)$ when the game is over. In other words, a call on a given team pays off only if the team wins and the point spread exceeds the exercise price. Calls can be purchased or sold. In addition it is possible to trade puts and to construct straddles, spreads, and other combination strategies. Trading be-gins 20 minutes before game time and is prohibited during commercials.

During the game the option prices rise and fall with the activity of the game. Of course, they are Euro-pean and, thus, cannot be exercised until the game is over. There is not much time (60 official minutes) in their lives but a considerable amount of information is packed into that time.

Let C^W and C^B be the prices before the game is over of the calls on Washington and Buffalo. Here's how the game went. The time to expiration is the time remaining in the game. We cannot determine exactly what the options would sell for but we know any op-tion would have a minimum value of the amount by which it is in-the-money, adjusting for the present value of the exercise price. Since the option's life is so short we need not worry about the present value adjustment.

In this example, we shall assume an exercise price of 10. Thus, a call on a team pays off at the end of the game if the team wins by at least 10 points.

As the game progresses and it appears that Wash-ington is playing well, the value of its calls would have to

premiums paid. If NPV is negative, the total amount of the premiums paid will exceed the present value of the payoff at expiration. The process is illustrated in Figure 7.15.

An alternative way to view the box spread is as the difference between two put-call parities. For example, for the options with exercise price X_1, put-call parity is

$$P_1 = C_1 - S_0 + X_1 (1 + r)^{-T},$$

and for the options with exercise price X_2, put-call parity is

$$P_2 = C_2 - S_0 + X_2 (1 + r)^{-T}.$$

Quarter	Scoring	Score		Time to Expiration	Minimum Values	
		W	B		C^W	C^B
2	Washington field goal	3	0	43:02	0	0
	Washington touchdown	10	0	39:54	0	0
	Washington touchdown	17	0	37:17	7	0
3	Washington touchdown	24	0	29:44	14	0
	Buffalo field goal	24	3	26:59	11	0
	Buffalo touchdown	24	10	20:58	4	0
	Washington touchdown	31	10	16:24	11	0
4	Washington field goal	34	10	14:54	14	0
	Washington field goal	37	10	11:36	17	0
	Buffalo touchdown	37	17	5:37	10	0
	Buffalo touchdown	37	24	3:55	3	0

rise as the options traders anticipate a rout. However, with each Buffalo score the Washington calls begin to decline and the Buffalo calls begin to rise. In the end the Washington calls paid off 3 points because Washington won by 13 points.

Although SG's efforts to educate people on the use of options in some way make them appear to be gambling, they do illustrate nicely how options work and how their prices rise and fall with the uncertainty about the final outcome.

SOURCE: This material is drawn from Robert J. McCartney, "'Skins Up by 10? You Make the Call: Punt or Put?" *Washington Post,* January 26, 1992, p. H1.

FIGURE 7.15   The Box Spread

$-(C_1 - C_2 + P_2 - P_1)$ $(X_2 - X_1)$

Today   Expiration
(Find the present value of the future payoff)

$NPV = (X_2 - X_1)(1 + r)^{-T} - (C_1 - C_2 + P_2 - P_1)$

If NPV > 0, execute the box spread.
If NPV < 0, execute a reverse box spread.

Rearranging both equations to isolate the stock price gives

$$S_o = C_1 - P_1 + X_1(1 + r)^{-T}.$$
$$S_o = C_2 - P_2 + X_2(1 + r)^{-T}.$$

Since the left-hand sides are equal, the right-hand sides must also be equal; therefore,

$$C_1 - P_1 + X_1(1 + r)^{-T} = C_2 - P_2 + X_2(1 + r)^{-T}.$$

Rearranging this equation gives

$$0 = (X_2 - X_1)(1 + r)^{-T} - C_1 + C_2 - P_2 + P_1.$$

This is our put-call parity equation when the NPV is zero, which results if all puts and calls are correctly priced relative to one another.

Let us examine the America Online June box spread using the 125 and 130 options. Consider the following transaction: Buy the 125 call at $13.50, buy the 130 put at $14.25, write the 130 call at $11.375, and write the 125 put at $11.50. The premiums paid for the 125 call and 130 put minus the premiums received for the 130 call and 125 put net out to $4.875. Thus, it will cost $487.50 to buy the box spread.

The payoff at expiration is $X_2 - X_1$. The net present value is

$$NPV = 100[(130 - 125)(1.0456)^{-.0959} - 4.875] = \$10.37,$$

where .0456 is the discrete risk-free rate for June as determined in Chapter 3 and .0959 is the time to expiration from May 14 to June 18. Thus, the spread is underpriced and should be purchased. Had the NPV been negative, the box spread would have been overpriced and should be sold. In that case, an investor would buy the 130 call and 125 put and sell the 125 call and 130 put. This would generate a positive cash flow up front that exceeded the present value of the cash outflow of $X_2 - X_1$ at expiration.

A box spread is a risk-free transaction in which the value can be easily calculated as the present value of a future payoff minus the initial outlay.

If the investor is holding a long box spread, the risk of early exercise is unimportant. Suppose the short call is exercised. Because the short call is in-the-money, the long call will be even deeper in-the-money. The investor can then exercise the long call. If the short put is exercised, the investor can in turn exercise the long put, which will be even deeper in-the-money than the short put. The net effect is a cash inflow of $X_2 - X_1$, the maximum payoff at expiration. For the short box spread, however, early exercise will result in a cash outflow of $X_2 - X_1$. Thus, the early exercise problem is an important consideration for short box spreads.

Transaction costs on a box spread will be high because four options are involved. At least two of the four options, however, will expire out-of-the-money. Nonetheless, the high transaction costs will make the box spread costly to execute for all but those who own seats on the exchange.

Summary

This chapter showed how some of the basic option strategies introduced in Chapter 6 can be combined to produce more complex strategies, such as spreads and combinations. Spreads were shown to be relatively low-risk strategies. Money spreads can be designed to profit in a bull or a bear market. A collar uses both a long put and a short call, along with the underlying stock, and is similar to a bull money spread. Calendar spreads and butterfly spreads are used to profit in either the presence or absence of high volatility. Straddles, straps, and strips were also shown to be attractive in periods of high or low volatility. Straps and strips are variations of the straddle in which a trader can increase a bet on the direction of the market. Finally, the chapter introduced the box spread, a riskless transaction that lends itself to a variation of a standard capital budgeting analysis with the end result being a net present value, a concept often encountered elsewhere in finance.

The strategies covered in this and the preceding chapter are but a few of the many possible option strategies. Those interested in furthering their knowledge of option strategies can explore the many excellent books cited in the references. The framework developed here should be sufficient to get you started. At this point, you should be capable of assessing the risks and rewards of a few simple option strategies. This book is an introduction and hopefully will encourage you to explore option strategies in more depth.

At one time, options, forward, and futures markets existed almost independently of each other. Now it is sometimes difficult to tell where one market ends and the other begins. Although we shall leave the world of options for awhile, we will return to it in Chapter 11.

Key Terms

Before continuing to Chapter 8, you should be able to give brief definitions of the following terms.

- spread
- vertical/strike/money spread
- horizontal/time/calendar spread
- buying the spread/debit spread
- selling the spread/credit spread
- bull spread
- bear spread

- collar
- butterfly/sandwich spread
- volatility strategy
- ratio spread
- combination
- straddle/strap/strip
- box spread

Questions and Problems

1. Explain why option traders often use spreads instead of simple long or short options and combined positions of options and stock.

2. Suppose an option trader has a call bull spread. The stock price has risen substantially, and the trader is considering closing the position early. What factors should the trader consider with regard to closing the transaction before the options expire?

3. Suppose you are following the stock of a firm that has been experiencing severe problems. Failure is imminent unless the firm is granted government-guaranteed loans. If the firm fails, its stock will, of course, fall substantially. If the loans are granted, it is expected that the stock will rise substantially. Identify two strategies that would be appropriate for this situation. Justify your answers.

4. Explain how a short call added to a protective put forms a collar and how it changes the payoff and up-front cost.

5. Derive the profit equations for a put bull spread. Determine the maximum and minimum profits and the breakeven stock price at expiration.

6. Explain the process by which the profit of a short straddle closed out prior to expiration is influenced by the time values of the put and call.

7. Explain why selecting a strap over a straddle implies a slightly more bullish outlook.

8. The chapter showed how analyzing a box spread is like a capital budgeting problem using the net present value approach. Consider the internal rate of return method of examining capital budgeting problems and analyze the box spread in that context.

The following option prices were observed for calls and puts on a stock on July 6 of a particular year. Use this information for problems 9 through 22. The stock was priced at 165 1/8. The expirations are July 17, August 21, and October 16. The continuously compounded risk-free rates associated with the three expirations are .0503, .0535, and .0571, respectively. The standard deviation is .21.

Strike	Calls			Puts		
	Jul	**Aug**	**Oct**	**Jul**	**Aug**	**Oct**
160	6	8 1/8	11 1/8	3/4	2 3/4	4 1/2
165	2 11/16	5 1/4	8 1/8	2 3/8	4 3/4	6 3/4
170	13/16	3 1/4	6	5 3/4	7 1/2	9

For problems 9 through 13 and 16 through 19, determine the profits for the holding period indicated for possible stock prices of 150, 155, 160, 165, 170, 175, and 180 at the end of the holding period. Answer any other questions as indicated. Note: Your Excel spreadsheet stratlyz2.xls will be useful here for obtaining graphs as requested but it does not allow you to calculate the profits for several user-specified asset prices. It permits you to specify one asset price and a maximum and minimum. Use stratlyz2.xls to produce the graph for the range of prices from 150 to 180 but determine the profits for the prices of 150, 155, . . . , 180 by hand for positions held to expiration. For positions closed prior to expiration, use the spreadsheet bsbin2.xls or the Windows program bsbwin2.1.exe to determine the option price when the position is closed; then calculate the profit by hand.

9. Construct a bear money spread using the October 165 and 170 calls. Hold until the options expire. Determine the profits and graph the results. Identify the breakeven stock price at expiration and the maximum and minimum profits. Discuss any special considerations associated with this strategy.

10. Repeat problem 9, but close the position on September 20. Use the spreadsheet to find the profits for the possible stock prices on September 20. Generate a graph and use it to identify the approximate breakeven stock price.

11. Construct a collar using the October 160 put. First use the Black-Scholes model to identify a call that will make the collar have zero up-front cost. Then close the position on September 20. Use the spreadsheet to find the profits for the possible stock prices on September 20. Generate a graph and use it to identify the approximate breakeven stock price. Determine the maximum and minimum profits.

12. Suppose you are expecting the stock price to move substantially over the next three months. You are considering a butterfly spread. Construct an appropriate butterfly spread using the October 160, 165, and 170 calls. Hold the position until expiration. Determine the profits and graph the results. Identify the two breakeven stock prices and the maximum and minimum profits.

13. Construct a calendar spread using the August and October 170 calls that will profit from high volatility. Close the position on August 1. Use the spreadsheet to find the profits for the possible stock prices on August 1. Generate a graph and use it to estimate the maximum and minimum profits and the breakeven stock prices.

14. Using the Black-Scholes model, compute and graph the time value decay of the October 165 call on the following dates: July 15, July 31, August 15, August 31, September 15, September 30, and October 16. Assume the stock price remains constant. Use the spreadsheet to find the time value in all of the cases.

15. Consider a riskless spread with a long position in the August 160 call and a short position in the October 160 call. Determine the appropriate hedge ratio. Then show how a $1 stock price increase would have a neutral effect on the spread value. Discuss any limitations of this procedure.

16. Construct a long straddle using the October 165 options. Hold until the options expire. Determine the profits and graph the results. Identify the breakeven stock prices at expiration and the minimum profit.

17. Repeat problem 15, but close the positions on September 20. Use the spreadsheet to find the profits for the possible stock prices on September 20. Generate a graph and use it to identify the approximate breakeven stock prices.

18. Construct a long strap using the October 165 options. Hold the position until expiration. Determine the profits and graph the results. Identify the breakeven stock prices at expiration and the minimum profit. Compare the results with the October 165 straddle.

19. Construct a short strip using the August 170 options. Hold the position until the options expire. Determine the profits and graph the results. Identify the breakeven stock prices at expiration and the minimum profit.

20. Analyze the August 160/170 box spread. Determine whether a profit opportunity exists and, if so, how one should exploit it.

21. (Concept Problem) The chapter presented two variations of the straddle: straps and strips. Another variation of the straddle is called a *strangle*. A strangle is the purchase of a call with a higher exercise price and a put with a lower exercise price. Evaluate the strangle strategy by examining the purchase of the August 165 put and 170 call. As in the problems above, determine the profits for stock prices of 150, 155, 160, 165, 170, 175, and 180. Hold the position until expiration and graph the results. Find the breakeven stock prices at expiration. Explain why one would want to use a strangle.

22. (Concept Problem) Many option traders use a combination of a money spread and a calendar spread called a *diagonal spread*. This transaction involves the purchase of a call with a lower exercise price and longer time to expiration and the sale of a call with a higher exercise price and shorter time to expiration. Evaluate the diagonal spread that involves the purchase of the October 165 call and the sale of the August 170 call. Determine the profits for the same stock prices you previously examined under the assumption that the position is closed on August 1. Use the spreadsheet to find the profits for the possible stock prices on August 1. Generate a graph and use it to estimate the breakeven stock price at the end of the holding period.

PART TWO

Forwards and Futures

CHAPTER EIGHT

The Structure of Forward and Futures Markets

CHAPTER NINE

Principles of Forward and Futures Pricing

CHAPTER TEN

Futures Hedging Strategies

CHAPTER ELEVEN

Advanced Futures Strategies

CHAPTER 8

The Structure of Forward and Futures Markets

An exchange floor is a crucible of ideas, markets, events. Eventually ideas sprout from that for improving a market or for whole new markets. Without ideas and the interchange of ideas, you're never going to get an innovative process to work.

LEO MELAMED
Futures, October 1996

Chapter Objectives

- To define and provide examples of forward contracts and futures contracts

- To describe the institutional characteristics of forward and futures markets, especially the daily settlement procedure in futures markets and the delivery process

- To provide information on the futures contracts available for trading

- To describe the process of placing an order to trade a futures contract

- To illustrate the role of the clearinghouse in futures trading

- To show how futures prices are quoted in *The Wall Street Journal*

- To present information on the magnitude and effects of transaction costs in futures trading

- To discuss the regulatory structure of futures and forward markets

- To illustrate how taxes affect futures transactions

Part One explored the world of options markets. The next four chapters look at forward and futures markets. A **forward contract** is an agreement between two parties, a buyer and a seller, that calls for the delivery of an asset at a future point in time with a price agreed upon today. A **futures contract** is a forward contract that has standardized terms, is traded on an organized exchange, and follows a daily settlement procedure in which the losses of one party to the contract are paid to the other party.

Forward and futures contracts have many of the characteristics of option contracts. Both provide for the sale and delivery of an asset on a later date at a price agreed upon today. An option—more specifically, a call option—gives the holder the right to forgo the future purchase of the asset. This is done, as we have seen, if the asset's price is below the exercise price. A forward or futures contract does not offer the right to forgo purchase of the asset. Like an exchange-listed option, however, a futures contract can be sold in the market prior to expiration. Like an over-the-counter option, a forward contract can be offset by creating a new forward contract.

Forward contracts, sometimes called **forward commitments,** are very common in everyday life. For example, an apartment lease is a series of forward contracts. The current month's use of the apartment is a spot transaction, but the two parties also have agreed to usage of the apartment for future months at a rate agreed upon today. A magazine subscription renewed for several years locks in the rate not only for the current year (a spot transaction) but for future years (a forward transaction). Of course, some deals permit you to cancel the subscription, thus turning the forward contract into something much closer to an option. A nonrefundable airline ticket is a forward contract. As we noted in Chapter 2, however, some airline tickets permit cancellation if you are willing to pay a higher price for the ticket, which makes the agreement an option. Near and dear to the hearts of most college students (and many others) is your basic pizza delivery order, which is also a forward contract. The customer and the restaurant agree that the customer will buy the pizza at a specific price at a future point in time ("30 minutes or less"). Upon delivery, the customer must accept and pay for the pizza, even though in the interim the customer might have noticed an ad or a coupon that would make an identical pizza cost less.

Any type of contractual arrangement calling for the delivery of a good or service at a future date at a price agreed upon today is a forward contract. Neither party can legally get out of the commitment. Nonetheless, either party can enter into a new, offsetting forward contract with someone else. For example, suppose after ordering the pizza, you decide that you would prefer Chinese food. You know, however, that your neighbor next door is practically addicted to pizza so you offer to sell the pizza to your neighbor when it is delivered. You might even be able to negotiate a better price, depending on how hungry your neighbor is. In that case, you contracted to deliver the pizza to your neighbor and you agreed upon a price. You are long a forward contract with the restaurant and short a forward contract with your neighbor. In the case of the apartment lease, subleasing your apartment is a way of offsetting your forward contract with the landlord.

Of course, all of these transactions are subject to a degree of uncertainty about whether a party will perform as promised. For example, suppose the pizza delivery person shows up at your door and finds no one there because you changed your mind and went out for Chinese food. Alternatively, perhaps you accepted delivery of your pizza, but your neighbor refused to accept the pizza because he changed his mind. Likewise, a landlord may find that the tenant skipped town. This potential for default is quite similar to that of the over-the-counter options market. There the buyer faced the potential default of the writer. In a forward contract, however, each party is subject to the default of the other. The pizza restaurant faces the potential that you will default. Do you face the potential that the restaurant will default by not delivering your pizza? The risk is slight but still there. Here the pizza delivery order is an example of a forward contract between an extremely creditworthy customer, the restaurant, and one with lower credit quality, yourself.

These examples are but small-scale, familiar cases of forward contracting. If we substitute agricultural products, precious metals, securities, or currencies for pizza, apartments, magazines, and airline tickets, we have the real world of big-time forward contracting. To mitigate the risk of default, many forward markets evolved into futures markets. Futures markets permit organized trading in standardized versions of these forward contracts. To reduce the risk of default, futures contracts require a daily settling of gains and losses. As we move through the chapter, we shall look at these characteristics in more detail. But first, let us see how these markets evolved.

The Development of Forward and Futures Markets

As noted above, forward contracts are common in everyday life. Quite naturally such contracts go back to the beginnings of commerce. For example, in medieval trade fairs merchants often contracted for deferred delivery of goods at a price agreed to in advance. Over the next few hundred years, organized spot markets for commodities began to develop in major European cities. Meanwhile, a similar market for rice developed in Japan. The characteristics of these markets were not too unlike those of today's futures markets. Modern futures markets, however, generally trace back to the formation of the Chicago Board of Trade in 1848.

Chicago Futures Markets

In the 1840s, Chicago was rapidly becoming the transportation and distribution center of the Midwest. Farmers shipped their grain from the farm belt to Chicago for sale and subsequent distribution eastward along rail lines and the Great Lakes. Due to the seasonal nature of grain production, however, large quantities of grain were shipped to Chicago in the late summer and fall. The city's storage facilities were inadequate for accommodating this temporary increase in supply. Prices fell drastically at harvest time as supplies increased and then rose steadily as supplies were consumed.

In 1848, a group of businessmen took the first step toward alleviating this problem by forming the Chicago Board of Trade (CBOT). The CBOT initially was organized for the purpose of standardizing the quantities and qualities of the grains. A few years later, the first forward contract was developed. Called a to-arrive contract, it provided that a farmer could agree to deliver the grain at a future date at a price determined in advance. This meant that the farmer would not ship the grain to Chicago at harvest time but could fix the price and the date at which the grain subsequently would be sold.

These to-arrive contracts proved to be a curious instrument. Speculators soon found that rather than buy and sell the grain itself they could buy and sell the contracts. In that way, they could speculate on the price of grain to be delivered at a future date and not have to worry about taking delivery of and storing the grain. Soon thereafter, the exchange established a set of rules and regulations for governing these transactions. In the 1920s, the clearinghouse was established to provide a means of offsetting or unwinding positions and guaranteeing to each party that the other would perform. By that time, most of the essential ingredients of futures contracts were in place.

In 1874, the Chicago Produce Exchange was formed and later became the Chicago Butter and Egg Board. In 1898, it was reorganized as the Chicago Mercantile Exchange, which is now the second largest futures exchange in the United States. Over the years many new exchanges were formed. The 1990s saw an explosion in the development of futures exchanges around the world. As we shall see later, the world's largest futures exchange is no longer in the United States.

The Development of Financial Futures

For the first 120 years, futures exchanges offered trading in contracts on commodities such as agricultural goods and metals. Then, in 1971, the major Western economies began to allow their currency exchange rates to fluctuate. This opened the way for the formation in 1972 of the International Monetary Market (IMM), a subsidiary of the Chicago Mercantile Exchange that specializes in the trading of futures contracts on foreign currencies. These were the first futures contracts that could be called **financial futures.** The first interest rate futures contract appeared in 1975, when the Chicago Board of Trade originated its GNMA futures, a contract on Government National Mortgage Association pass-through certificates, whose yields reflect mortgage interest rates.

In 1976, the International Monetary Market introduced the first futures contract on a government security and a short-term financial instrument—90-day U.S. Treasury bills. This contract was actively traded for many years, but its popularity has declined somewhat, at least partly due to the remarkable success of a competing contract, the Eurodollar futures, which was launched in 1981.

In 1977, the Chicago Board of Trade started what became the most successful contract of all time—U.S. Treasury bond futures. In just a few years, this instrument became the most actively traded contract, surpassing many grain futures that had traded for more than 100 years. Recently, however, the Eurodollar contract has surpassed the bond contract as the most actively traded futures contract in the United States.

The 1980s brought the highly successful stock index futures contract. This instrument, sometimes referred to as "pin-stripe pork bellies," has helped bridge the long-standing gap between New York's stock traders and Chicago's futures traders. Interestingly, however, the first stock index futures contract appeared not in New York or Chicago but in Kansas City. The Kansas City Board of Trade completed the formal registration process ahead of its New York and Chicago counterparts and on February 16, 1982, launched the Value Line Index futures. The Index and Option Market, a division of the Chicago Mercantile Exchange, followed on April

21 with its S&P 500 futures contract. The New York Futures Exchange entered the game on May 6 with its New York Stock Exchange Index futures. Today, however, the Value Line and NYSE Index futures have little trading volume.

Interestingly, in the United States, the Dow Jones Industrial Average, the most well known measure of stock market activity, has had a futures contract on it for only a few years. Shortly after the first stock index futures contracts appeared, the Chicago Board of Trade attempted to start a contract on the Average, but was rebuffed in a lengthy legal process started by the Dow Jones Company. Dow Jones (DJ) stated that it did not want its name associated with speculative trading and believed that the CBOT and traders were profiting from its name. Standard and Poor's, on the other hand, has eagerly licensed its name to futures exchanges for contracts and has even developed new indices with an eye toward having futures contracts traded on them. Rebuffed by DJ, the CBOT then created a similar contract, called the Major Market Index, which traded successfully for a number of years but eventually died. In 1997, however, Dow Jones decided that it should enter the index futures business and licensed its famous Average to the Chicago Board of Trade for futures trading and the American Stock Exchange for options trading. Dow Jones also began licensing other averages and creating new market averages, including a number for foreign markets, with the intention of encouraging futures trading on them.

Stock index futures contracts have been extremely successful worldwide. Almost every major country has its own futures exchange with a successful stock index contract. Countries in which stock index futures are extremely popular include the United Kingdom, France, Japan, Germany, Spain, and Hong Kong.

Over the years there has been a tremendous degree of competition between the futures exchanges to introduce new contracts that would generate significant trading volume. Barely a month passes without at least one new futures contract being introduced. A few of these contracts, such as municipal bond futures, were moderately successful. Some, such as oil futures, were highly successful. Most of the contracts, like inflation futures, commercial paper futures, and corporate bond index futures, failed to attract much trading volume. Even the original GNMA futures contract died and attempts to modify and revive it failed. You should note, however, that such failures are not a sign of weakness but rather of a healthy and highly competitive business in which only those contracts that truly meet a need will survive.

The Parallel Development of Over-the-Counter Markets

The most active early forward market was the market for foreign exchange, called the **interbank market.** This market grew tremendously in response to the floating of currencies in the early 1970s, as mentioned above. It consists of hundreds of banks worldwide who make forward and spot commitments with each other, representing either themselves or their clients. The market is quite large, though the exact size is difficult to estimate, since the transactions are essentially private and unregulated. The transaction sizes are quite large as well and it would be unusual for individual investors to be able to participate in this market. We shall discuss this market in more detail in Chapter 13, when we cover foreign currency derivatives.

Forward markets for various financial instruments and commodities have also developed in recent years. The decade of the 1980s saw a tremendous jump in the level of understanding and appreciation for derivative instruments. While futures and options markets were growing, forward markets began to grow as well. The primary stimulant for forward market growth was the development of swaps. A swap is an agreement between two parties to exchange a series of payments. There are quite a few variations on this basic theme, but in general swaps are similar to forward contracts. We shall cover swaps in considerably more detail in Chapters 13–15. For now, however, let us note that the growing acceptance of swaps stimulated the development of other over-the-counter transactions, such as options as noted in Chapter 2, and a variety of other forward contracts. For example, one can enter into a forward contract, called a forward rate agreement or FRA, that is simply an arrangement for one party to pay a certain fixed amount of cash while the other party pays an amount of cash determined by the interest rate at a predetermined future date. This contract can be used to hedge or speculate on interest rates. It does not actually require delivery of a security or commodity as it is settled by simply exchanging cash. It is also possible to arrange for forward delivery of almost any security or commodity at a price agreed upon today. The forward market is a large and healthy one that competes and, yet, complements the futures market.

The Over-the-Counter Forward Market

In Chapter 2 we discussed how over-the-counter options differ from exchange-traded options. Now we shall do the same for forward and futures contracts. The forward market is large and worldwide. Its participants are banks, corporations, and governments. The two parties to a forward contract must agree to do business with each other, which means that each party accepts credit risk from the other. That is, unlike in options markets where the writer does not assume any credit risk from the buyer, in forward markets each party accepts the credit risk of the other. In spite of the credit risk, however, forward contracts offer many advantages.

The primary advantage is that the terms and conditions are tailored to the specific needs of the two parties. Suppose a firm would like to secure the future purchase price of 400,000 bushels of sorghum, a grain similar in use to corn. As we shall see later, the futures markets permit trading only in contracts on specific commodities and with certain expiration dates. There is no sorghum futures contract that would permit the company to lock in the future purchase price of the sorghum. If the firm could substitute corn, however, there is a corn futures contract on the Chicago Board of Trade, though its expiration might not match the horizon date of the firm. Moreover, it might permit the seller of the futures to deliver any of several grades of corn at any of several locations. The firm would perhaps prefer to arrange a specific contract with the terms tailored to meet its needs. Similar arguments can be made with respect to financial contracts. A portfolio manager might wish to lock in the market value of a specific portfolio on a certain date. If the futures market does not have such a contract, the manager might look to the forward market.

As noted about the over-the-counter options market, the forward market also has the advantage of being a private market in which the general public does not know that the transaction was done. This prevents other traders from interpreting the size of various trades as perhaps false signals of information.

The over-the-counter market is also an unregulated market. Although there is now much debate about whether this market should be regulated, and we shall bring this topic up again later in this chapter, the government currently views these contracts as private arrangements. This gives investors considerably more flexibility, saves money, and allows the market to quickly respond to changing needs and circumstances by developing new variations of old contracts.

Of course, all of this comes at the expense of assuming credit risk and the requirement that the transactions be of a rather large size, several million dollars or more. It is not clear which is more costly, forwards or futures, but since the markets coexist, they must be serving their clientele in an efficient manner.

How large is the market? Since the transactions are private, it is difficult to tell. A survey taken by the Bank for International Settlements of Basel, Switzerland, estimates that at year-end 1999 the size of the over-the-counter forward market is about $17 trillion of face value with an estimated market value of $430 billion.

Organized Futures Trading

Futures trading is organized around the concept of a futures exchange. The exchange is probably the most important component of a futures market and distinguishes it from forward markets.

A **futures exchange** is a corporate entity comprised of members. Although some exchanges allow corporate memberships, most members are individuals. The members elect a board of directors, which in turn selects individuals to manage the exchange. The exchange has a corporate hierarchy consisting of officers, employees, and committees. The exchange establishes rules for its members and may impose sanctions on violators.

Although futures exchanges are usually nonprofit corporations, some exchanges are considering becoming profit-making corporations and possibly even becoming publicly traded.

Contract Development

One of the exchange's important ongoing activities is identifying new and useful futures contracts. Most exchanges maintain research staffs that continuously examine the feasibility of new contracts. In the United States, when the exchange determines that a contract is likely to be successful, it writes a proposal specifying the terms and conditions and applies to the Commodity Futures Trading Commission (CFTC), the regulatory authority, for permission to initiate trading.[1]

It is becoming increasingly difficult to determine the characteristics of an asset that make it a likely candidate for a successful futures contract. At one time, it was thought that the asset had to be storable, but there are now futures contracts on nonstorable assets such as electricity. What does seem to be a common thread is the existence of an identifiable, volatile spot price and a group of potential users who face risk of loss if prices move in a certain direction. It is not necessary that the spot price be the price of an asset that one can actually buy and hold.

Thus, it is conceivable that virtually anything can have a futures contract traded on it. Whether the contract will be actively traded will depend on whether it fills the needs of hedgers and whether speculators are interested enough to take risks in it.

Contract Terms and Conditions

The contract's terms and conditions are determined by the exchange subject to CFTC approval. The specifications for each contract are the size, quotation unit, minimum price fluctuation, grade, and trading hours. In addition, the contract specifies delivery terms and daily price limits as well as delivery procedures, which are discussed in separate sections. Complete contract terms on selected financial futures contracts are provided in Appendix 8A.

Contract size means that one contract covers a specific number of units of the underlying asset. This might be a designated number of bushels of a

---

[1]The CFTC's responsibility is discussed later in the chapter.

grain or dollars of face value of a financial instrument. Contract size is an important decision. If too small, speculators will find it more costly to trade because there is a cost for trading each contract. The contracts are not divisible; thus, if they are too large, hedgers may be unable to get a matching number of contracts. For example, if the Chicago Board of Trade had established $1 million as the Treasury bond contract, a hedger with $500,000 of bonds to hedge probably would be unable to use it.[2]

The quotation unit is simply the unit in which the price is specified. For example, corn is quoted in fourths of a cent and Treasury bonds in percentage points and thirty-seconds of a point of par value. In most cases, the spot market quotation unit is used.

Closely related to the quotation unit is the minimum price fluctuation. This is usually the smallest unit of quotation. For example, Treasury bonds are quoted in a minimum unit of thirty-seconds. Thus, the minimum price change on a Treasury bond futures contract is $1/32$ of 1 percent of the contract price, or .0003125. Since the contract has a face value (contract size) of $100,000, the minimum price change is .0003125 $\times$ ($100,000) = $31.25.

The exchange also establishes the contract grade. In the case of agricultural commodities there may be numerous grades, each of which would command a quality price differential in the spot market. The contract must specify the grades that are acceptable for delivery. Financial futures contracts must indicate exactly which financial instrument or instruments are eligible for delivery. If multiple instruments are deliverable, the seller of the contract holds a potentially valuable option, which we shall discuss in Chapter 11.

The exchange also specifies the hours during which the contract trades. Most agricultural futures trade for four to five hours during the day. Most financial futures trade for about six hours. This trading occurs on the floor of the exchange, as described in a later section, but many exchanges have electronic trading systems, whereby trading occurs at terminals that can be placed in offices and even in homes. Electronic trading typically occurs during hours that the exchange is not open for floor trading, which in some cases means throughout the night. This practice is part of the exchange's attempt to keep pit trading alive in this age in which so much economic activity is conducted electronically. There are some contracts, however, that are designated solely for electronic trading and some others that trade simultaneously with floor trading. Some exchanges, such as the highly successful EUREX, a combined German-Swiss futures exchange, and MATIF of France, have exclusively electronic trading, and trading hours are usually longer than a standard business day.

---

[2]We say *probably* because if the bonds being hedged were twice as volatile as the futures contract, one contract would be the correct number. Chapter 10 explains this point.

Delivery Terms

The contract must also indicate a specific delivery date or dates, the delivery procedure, and a set of expiration months. In the case of harvestable commodities, the exchange usually establishes expiration months to correspond with harvest months. In nonharvestable commodities, such as financial futures, the exchange usually has followed the pattern of allowing expirations in March, June, September, and December. There are some exceptions, however.

The exchange also decides how far into the future the expiration dates will be set. For some contracts, the expirations extend only a year or two, while the Eurodollar contract extends about 10 years.

Once the expiration month has been set, the exchange determines a final trading day. This may be any day in the month, but the most common ones are the third Friday of the month and the business day prior to the last business day of the month. The first delivery day also must be set. Most contracts allow delivery on any day of the month following a particular day. Usually the first eligible delivery day is the first business day of the month, but for certain contracts other days may be specified. In the case of stock index futures and other cash-settled contracts, the settlement occurs on the last trading day or on the day after the last trading day.

For non-cash-settled contracts, the delivery procedure must be specified. The deliverable spot commodity must be sent to any of several eligible locations. Financial adjustments to the price received upon delivery are required when an acceptable but lower-grade commodity is delivered. We shall say more about the delivery procedure later.

Daily Price Limits and Trading Halts

During the course of a trading day prices fluctuate continuously, but many contracts have limits on the maximum daily price change. If a contract price hits the upper limit, the market is said to be **limit up.** If the price moves to the lower limit, the market is said to be **limit down.** Any such move, up or down, is called a **limit move.** Normally no transactions above or below the limit price are allowed. Some contracts have limits only during the opening minutes; others have limits that can be expanded according to prescribed rules if prices remain at the limits for extended periods.

In conjunction with price limits, some futures contracts — notably stock index futures — contain built-in trading halts sometimes called **circuit breakers.** When prices move rapidly, trading can be stopped for predetermined periods. These halts can be accompanied by similar halts in the spot market. Such cessations of trading were installed after the stock market crash of 1987 in response to concern that extremely volatile markets might need a cooling-off period. Although it is not clear that trading halts are necessarily effective, it seems likely that they will continue to be used in futures markets.

Other Exchange Responsibilities

The exchange also specifies that members meet minimum financial responsibility requirements. In some contracts it may establish position limits, which, like those in options markets, restrict the number of contracts that an individual trader can hold. The exchange establishes rules governing activities on the trading floor and maintains a department responsible for monitoring trading to determine whether anyone is attempting to manipulate the market. In some extreme cases, the exchange may elect to suspend trading if unusual events occur.[3]

Futures Exchanges

Futures trading takes place on over fifty futures exchanges around the world. Table 8.1 lists the exchanges and their Web addresses.

One advantage of such global futures trading, particularly when it is fully automated, is the potential it offers for linkages between exchanges. For example, the Chicago Mercantile Exchange and the Singapore International Monetary Exchange (SIMEX) are linked so that a trader opening a position in Eurodollars on one exchange can close the position on the other. Linkages among futures exchanges around the world are growing increasingly common, such as the proposed linkage between the two large exchanges, the Chicago Board of Trade and EUREX.

As previously noted, a trend in futures trading worldwide is the use of electronic trading systems. For a fee, computer terminals are placed in trading rooms of institutions and individuals. These terminals permit traders to submit bids and offers and to consummate trades by simply moving the computer's mouse over the bid or offer the trader wishes to accept and then clicking. Alternative systems match up bids and offers automatically. The Chicago Mercantile Exchange (CME) began the process with a system called GLOBEX, which eventually included access to trading not only in the CME's contracts but also in contracts of certain other exchanges. Several U.S. and several foreign exchanges have developed their own electronic trading systems, and some are merging their systems or working on joint ventures to combine their systems.

Figure 8.1 illustrates the volume of trading in futures contracts on U.S. futures exchanges since 1977. As can be seen, the growth of trading volume has been phenomenal. Most of the growth has come from financial futures contracts. Many futures traders who formerly traded in pork bellies and corn have switched to various financial contracts. In addition,

---

[3]The 1980 grain embargo against the Soviet Union and the 1987 stock market crash were two such cases.

TABLE 8.1	**Exchanges on Which Futures Trade, January 2000**

Argentina

Mercado a Término de
  Buenos Aires
  www.matba.com.ar

Australia

Sydney Futures Exchange
  www.sfe.com

Austria

Wiener Börse AG
  www.wbag.at

Belgium

Brussels Exchanges
  www.bxs.be

Brazil

Bolsa de Mercadorias &
  Futuros
  www.bmf.com.br

Canada

Montreal Exchange
  www.me.org
Toronto Stock Exchange
  www.tse.com
Winnipeg Commodity
  Exchange
  www.wce.mb.ca

Chile

Santiago Stock Exchange
  www.bolsantiago.cl

China

Dalian Commodity Ex-
  change
Shanghai Futures Exchange
  www.shfe.com.cn

Denmark

Copenhagen Stock Ex-
  change
  www.xcse.dk

Finland

Helsinki Securities &
  Derivatives Exchange
  www.hex.fi

France

Marché á Terme
  International de France
  www.matif.fr

Germany

EUREX
  www.eurexchange.com

Hong Kong

Hong Kong Futures
  Exchange
  www.hkfe.com

Hungary

Budapest Commodity
  Exchange
  www.bce-bat.com

Israel

Tel Aviv Stock Exchange
  www.tase.co.il

Italy

Italian Stock Exchange
  www.borsaitalia.it

Japan

Chubu Commodity
  Exchange
  www.c-com.or.jp
Kansai Commodities
  Exchange
  www.kanex.or.jp
Osaka Stock Exchange
  www.ose.or.jp
Tokyo Commodity
  Exchange
  www.tocom.or.jp
Tokyo Grain Exchange
  www.tge.or.jp
Tokyo International Finan-
  cial Futures & Options
  Exchange
  www.tiffe.or.jp
Tokyo Stock Exchange
  www.tse.or.jp

Malaysia

Commodity & Monetary
  Exchange of Malaysia
  www.commex.com.my
Kuala Lumpur Options &
  Financial Futures
  Exchange
  www.kloffe.com.my

Netherlands

Amsterdam Exchanges
  www.aex.nl

New Zealand

New Zealand Futures &
  Options Exchange

Portugal

Bolsa de Derivados do
  Porto
  www.bdp.pt

Romania

Sibiu Monetary Finan-
  cial & Commodity
  Exchange
  www.bmfms.ro

Singapore

Singapore Commodity
  Exchange
  www.sicom.com.sg
Singapore International
  Monetary Exchange
  www.simex.com.sg

South Africa

South African Futures
  Exchange
  www.safex.co.za

Spain

Meff Renta Fija
  www.meff.es
Meff Renta Variable
  www.meffrv.es

Sweden

OM Stockholm Exchange
  www.omgroup.com

Switzerland

EUREX
  www.eurexchange.com

United Kingdom

International Petroleum
  Exchange
  www.ipe.uk.com
London International
  Financial Futures
  Exchange
  www.liffe.com
London Metal Exchange
  www.lme.co.uk
OM London Exchange
  www.omgroup.com

United States

Cantor Exchange
  cx.cantor.com
Chicago Board of Trade
  www.cbot.com
Chicago Mercantile
  Exchange
  www.cme.com
Kansas City Board of Trade
  www.kcbt.com
MidAmerica Commodity
  Exchange
  www.midam.com
Minneapolis Grain
  Exchange
  www.mgex.com
New York Board of Trade
  www.nybot.com
New York Mercantile
  Exchange
  www.nymex.com
Philadelphia Stock
  Exchange
  www.phlx.com

| FIGURE 8.1 | Volume on U.S. Futures Exchanges |

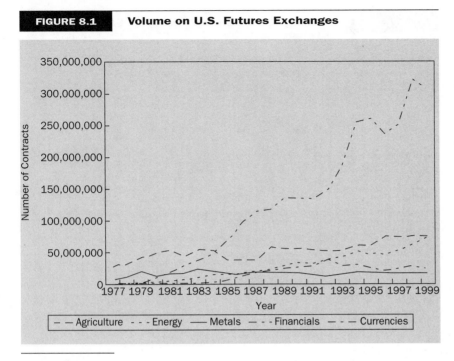

SOURCE: CFTC *Annual Report 1999*
NOTE: Figures are for the CFTC's fiscal year, which ends on September 30.

the remarkable success of stock index futures has brought many investors and institutions that formerly traded only in stocks and bonds to the arena of futures trading. It is also particularly noteworthy that energy futures are rapidly growing in popularity, a reflection of the crucial role of oil in the world's economy, and have caught up with agriculture futures as the second most popular group.

Table 8.2 presents trading volume for the 20 largest futures exchanges in the world in 1999. The Chicago Board of Trade held on to its claim as the largest U.S. futures exchange, but for the first time, it can no longer call itself the world's largest futures exchange. That title now goes to EUREX, the combined German-Swiss futures exchange. While the CBOT claims about 41 percent of volume in the U.S. market and its rival, the Chicago Mercantile Exchange, has about 36 percent of U.S. volume, it is clear that non-U.S. futures exchanges are growing in volume as well as influence. It should be noted, however, that trading volume can be a misleading measure of the size of a futures exchange as an exchange can set the size of a contract at any level it wants and small levels can stimulate trading volume number. Nonetheless, volume is pretty much the only variable by which the industry measures the size of its exchanges.

TABLE 8.2	Trading Volume on Top Twenty Global Futures Exchanges, 1999

Exchange	Number of Contracts Traded
EUREX (Germany-Switzerland)	244,686,104
Chicago Board of Trade (U.S.)	195,147,279
Chicago Mercantile Exchange (U.S.)	168,013,357
London International Financial Futures Exchange (U.K.)	97,689,714
New York Mercantile Exchange (U.S.)	92,415,006
London Metal Exchange (U.K.)	57,563,009
Bolsa de Mercadorias & Futoros (Brazil)	52,797,466
Tokyo Commodity Exchange (Japan)	48,442,161
Sydney Futures Exchange (Australia)	27,174,508
MONEP (France)	25,717,322
Singapore International Monetary Exchange (Singapore)	24,480,004
OM Stockholm (Sweden)	19,934,293
Tokyo Grain Exchange (Japan)	18,018,443
Korea Stock Exchange (Korea)	17,200,349
International Petroleum Exchange (U.K.)	17,015,778
New York Board of Trade (U.S.)	15,958,237
Tokyo International Financial Futures Exchange (Japan)	14,658,415
Tokyo Stock Exchange (Japan)	13,023,411
Osaka Securities Exchange (Japan)	10,540,224
MATIF (France)	9,411,752

Source: *Futures Industry*, February/March 2000, p. 39.

Futures Traders

The members of the exchange are individuals who physically go on the exchange floor or, on electronic systems, sit at designated terminals and trade futures contracts. There are several ways to characterize these futures traders.

General Classes of Futures Traders

All traders on the futures exchange are either commission brokers or locals.

Commission brokers simply execute transactions for other people. A commission broker can be an independent businessperson who executes trades for individuals or institutions or a representative of a major brokerage firm. In the futures industry, these brokerage firms are called **futures commission merchants (FCM).** The commission broker simply executes trades for the FCM's customers. Commission brokers make their money by charging a commission for each trade.

Locals are individuals in business for themselves who trade from their own accounts. They attempt to profit by buying contracts at a given price and selling them at a higher price. Their trading provides liquidity for the public. Locals assume the risk and reap the rewards from their skill at futures trading. It has been said that locals represent the purest form of capitalism and entrepreneurship.

Because a futures trader can be a local or an FCM, a conflict occasionally arises between traders' loyalty to themselves and their customers' interests. For example, some traders engage in **dual trading,** in which they trade for themselves and also trade as brokers for others. Dual trading has become very controversial in recent years. To illustrate the conflict that might arise, suppose a trader holds a set of orders that includes a large order for a customer. Knowing that the price may move substantially when the customer's order is placed, the trader executes a purchase for his or her own account prior to placing the customer's order. There are a number of other ways in which dual trading can be profitable to the trader at the expense of the customer. For this to occur, however, the trader must act unscrupulously. The exchanges argue that abuses of dual trading are rare. Moreover, they claim that dual trading provides liquidity to the market. Some limitations on dual trading have been enacted.

Classification by Trading Strategy

Futures traders can be further classified by the strategies they employ.

Recall that in Chapter 1 we briefly discussed hedging. A **hedger** holds a position in the spot market. This might involve owning a commodity, or it may simply mean that the individual plans or is committed to the future purchase or sale of the commodity. Taking a futures contract that is opposite to the position in the spot market reduces the risk. For example, if you hold a portfolio of stocks, you can hedge that portfolio's value by selling a stock index futures contract. If the stocks' prices fall, the portfolio will lose value, but the price of the futures contract is also likely to fall. Because you are short the futures contract, you can repurchase it at a lower price, thus making a profit. The gain from the futures position will at least partially offset the loss on the portfolio.

Hedging is an important activity in any futures or derivatives market. This section has given only a cursory overview of it. Chapter 10 is devoted exclusively to hedging.

Speculators attempt to profit from guessing the direction of the market. Speculators include locals as well as the thousands of individuals and institutions off the exchange floor. They play an important role in the market by providing the liquidity that makes hedging possible and assuming the risk that hedgers are trying to eliminate. Speculating is discussed in more detail in Chapter 11.

Spreaders use futures spreads to speculate at a low level of risk. Like an option spread, a futures spread involves a long position in one contract and a short position in another. Spreads may be intracommodity or intercommodity. An intracommodity spread is like a time spread in options. The spreader buys a contract with one expiration month and sells an otherwise identical contract with a different expiration month. An intercommodity spread, which normally is not used in options, consists of a long position in a futures contract on one commodity and a short position in a contract on another. In some cases, the two commodities even trade on different exchanges. The rationale for this type of spread rests on a perceived "normal" difference between the prices of the two futures contracts. When the prices move out of line, traders employ intercommodity spreads to take advantage of the expected price realignment.

Futures spreads work much like option time spreads in that the long position in one contract is somewhat offset by the short position in the other. There actually is no real difference between this type of spread and a hedge. For example, suppose the contract is on Treasury bills, the current month is October, and the available futures expirations are December, March, and June. A hedger holds Treasury bills and sells a December contract. A spreader holds a December contract and sells a March contract. Each holds a long position in a spot or nearby futures contract and a short position in a deferred futures contract. Each is attempting to profit from one position while expecting a loss on the other. Neither knows which position will make a profit and which will create a loss.

Arbitrageurs attempt to profit from differences in the prices of otherwise identical spot and futures positions. An analogous type of arbitrage that we already covered is the execution of conversions and reversals to take advantage of option prices that fail to conform to put-call parity. In futures markets there are some important theoretical relationships, which we shall study in Chapters 9 and 11. When prices get out of line with these theoretical predictions, arbitrageurs enter the market and execute trades that bring prices back in line. Because arbitrage is designed to be riskless, it resembles hedging and spreading. In many cases, however, it is difficult to determine whether a given strategy is arbitrage, hedging, or spreading.

Classification by Trading Style

Futures traders can also be classified by the style of trading they practice. There are three distinct trading styles: scalping, day trading, and position trading.

Scalpers attempt to profit from small changes in the contract price. Scalpers seldom hold their positions for more than a few minutes. They trade by using their skill at sensing the market's short-term direction and by buying from the public at the bid price and selling to the public at the ask price. They are constantly alert for large inflows of orders and short-term trends. Because they operate with very low transaction costs, they can profit from small moves in contract prices. The practice of making a large number of quick, small profits is referred to as scalping.

Day traders hold their positions for no longer than the duration of the trading day. Like scalpers, they attempt to profit from short-term market movements; however, they hold their positions much longer than do scalpers. Nonetheless, they are unwilling to assume the risk of adverse news that might occur overnight or on weekends.[4]

Position traders hold their transactions open for much longer periods than do scalpers and day traders. Position traders believe they can make profits by waiting for a major market movement. This may take as much as several weeks or may not come at all.

Scalpers, day traders, and position traders are not mutually exclusive. A speculator may employ any or all of these techniques in transactions.

In addition to those who trade on the floor of the exchange, there are many individuals who trade off the exchange floor and employ some of the same techniques.

Off-Floor Futures Traders

Participants in the futures markets also include thousands of individuals and institutions. Institutions include banks and financial intermediaries, investment banking firms, mutual funds, pension funds, and other corporations. In addition, some farmers and numerous individuals actively trade futures contracts, particularly today, with increasing access and low cost through the Internet. Foreign institutions are also becoming more active in U.S. futures markets.

In addition to those who directly participate in trading, U.S. federal law recognizes and regulates certain other participants. An **introducing broker (IB)** is an individual who solicits orders from public customers to trade futures contracts. IBs do not execute orders themselves, nor do their firms; rather, they subcontract with FCMs to do this. The IB and the FCM divide the commission.

A **commodity trading advisor (CTA)** is an individual or firm that analyzes futures markets and issues reports, gives advice, and makes recommendations on the purchase and sale of contracts. CTAs earn fees for their services but do not necessarily trade contracts themselves.

A **commodity pool operator (CPO)** is an individual or firm that solicits funds from the public, pools them, and uses them to trade futures contracts. The CPO profits by collecting a percentage of the assets in the fund and sometimes through sales commissions. A CPO essentially is the operator of a futures fund, a topic discussed later in this chapter. Some commodity pools are privately operated, however, and are not open for public participation.

---

[4]Day trading in this context should be distinguished from the trading of securities and derivatives on the Internet.

An **associated person (AP)** is an individual associated with any of the above individuals or institutions or any other firm engaged in the futures business. APs include directors, partners, officers, and employees but not clerical personnel.

The Cost and Profitability of Exchange Membership

Most futures exchanges have a limited number of full memberships, called **seats.** There usually is a market for seats, with the highest and lowest bids publicly reported. Seat prices tend to fluctuate with the amount of trading activity in the market and the number of new contracts introduced. Figure 8.2 illustrates the history of seat prices since 1974 for a full membership on the Chicago Board of Trade and the Chicago Mercantile Exchange. The price has been almost $1,000,000 and as low as about $70,000.

Seats can also be leased at a monthly rate of usually 1.0 to 1.5 of the seat price. Some exchanges have different levels of membership. For example, the Chicago Board of Trade has 1,402 full members and a lesser number of Associate Members; Government Instrument Market Membership Interests; Index, Debt, and Energy Membership Interests; and Commodity Options Membership Interests. Associate Members can trade in all markets except agricultural futures. Government Instrument Market Memberships allow trading in futures contracts on government securities. Index, Debt,

| FIGURE 8.2 | Quarterly Seat Prices on the Chicago Board of Trade and Chicago Mercantile Exchange |

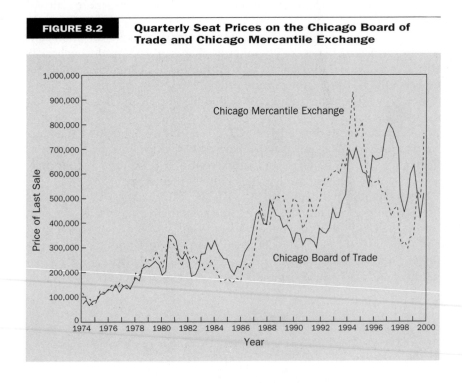

and Energy Membership Interests allow trading in futures on stock indices, bonds, and any energy-related contracts as well as options on those futures. Commodity option memberships allow trading in any options on futures contracts; these are covered in Chapter 12.

Like options markets, futures markets do not create or destroy wealth. Therefore, one trader's gains are another's losses subject to some slippage due to commissions and taxes. It has been said, however, that the vast majority of futures traders lose money. It is not surprising that a small number of individuals probably earn large profits while assuming high risks. Some are lucky and, of course, some are unlucky.

Forward Market Traders

The forward market is dominated by large institutions, such as banks and corporations. A typical forward market trader is an individual sitting at a desk with a telephone and a computer terminal. Using the computer or telephone, the trader finds out the current prices available in the market. The trader can then agree upon a price with another trader at another firm. The trader may represent his or her own firm or may execute a trade for a client. The trade may be a hedge, a spread, or an arbitrage. In fact, it is the thousands of traders off the floor whose arbitrage activities play a crucial role in making the market so efficient.

It would be remiss to suggest that the forward and futures markets are not linked. In a formal sense, forward contracts cannot be reversed by futures contracts. It is common, however, that a trader will do a forward contract and then immediately do a futures contract to hedge or offset the forward market risk. In fact, the trader might even combine these positions with an option or a swap. Why a trader might do this is a subject we shall get into later when we look at hedging, relationships between the prices in these markets, and risk management.

The Mechanics of Futures Trading

Before placing an order to trade futures contracts, an individual must open an account with a broker. Because the risk of futures trading can be quite high, the individual must make a minimum deposit — usually at least $5,000 — and sign a disclosure statement acknowledging the possible risks.

Placing an Order

One can place several types of orders. These are essentially the same as the option orders covered in Chapter 2. Stop orders and limit orders are used as well as good-till-canceled and day orders.

When an investor places an order, the broker phones the firm's trading desk on the exchange floor and relays the order to the firm's floor broker. The floor broker goes to the pit in which the contract trades. The pit is an octagonal- or polygonal-shaped ring with steps descending to the center. Hand signals and a considerable amount of verbal activity are used to place bids and make offers. This process is called **open outcry.** When the order is filled, the information is relayed back, ultimately to the broker's office, whereupon the broker telephones the customer to confirm the trade.

The process of placing and executing an order through the open-outcry system is a 140-year-old tradition. It may, however, become a thing of the past. As noted earlier, several new futures exchanges in foreign countries are fully automated so that bids and offers are submitted through a computer and trades are executed off the floor. Some systems will even match buyer and seller. As we noted in Chapter 2, the CBOE has made some progress in automating its option orders, but it too remains essentially an open-outcry market. This primarily reflects the desire of the exchange members to preserve the open-outcry system, in which they participate and indeed enjoy each day.

The Role of the Clearinghouse

At this point in the process, the clearinghouse intervenes. Each futures exchange operates its own independent clearinghouse. The clearinghouse in futures markets works like that in options markets, so its basic operations should be familiar to you from Chapter 2.

The concept of a clearinghouse as an intermediary and guarantor to every trade is not nearly as old as the futures markets themselves. The first such clearinghouse was organized in 1925 at the Chicago Board of Trade. The clearinghouse is an independent corporation, and its stockholders are its member clearing firms. Each firm maintains a margin account with the clearinghouse and must meet minimum standards of financial responsibility.

For each transaction, obviously, there is both a buyer, usually called the **long,** and a seller, typically called the **short.** In the absence of a clearinghouse, each party would be responsible to the other. If one party defaulted, the other would be left with a worthless claim. The clearinghouse assumes the role of intermediary to each transaction. It guarantees the buyer that the seller will perform and guarantees the seller that the buyer will perform. The clearinghouse's financial accounts contain separate records of contracts owned and the respective clearing firms and contracts sold and the respective clearing firms. Note that the clearinghouse keeps track only of its member firms. The clearing firms, in turn, monitor the long and short positions of individual traders and firms. All parties to futures transactions must have an account with a clearing firm or with a firm that has an account with a clearing firm.

FIGURE 8.3	A Transaction on the Futures Exchange

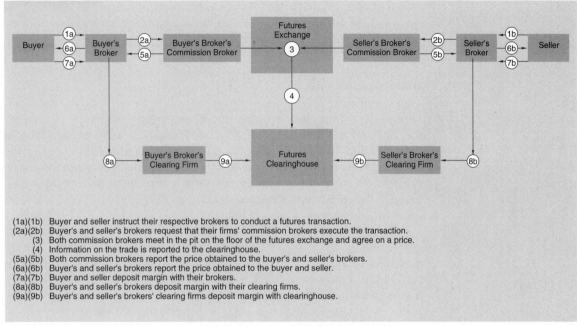

(1a)(1b)   Buyer and seller instruct their respective brokers to conduct a futures transaction.
(2a)(2b)   Buyer's and seller's brokers request that their firms' commission brokers execute the transaction.
   (3)   Both commission brokers meet in the pit on the floor of the futures exchange and agree on a price.
   (4)   Information on the trade is reported to the clearinghouse.
(5a)(5b)   Both commission brokers report the price obtained to the buyer's and seller's brokers.
(6a)(6b)   Buyer's and seller's brokers report the price obtained to the buyer and seller.
(7a)(7b)   Buyer and seller deposit margin with their brokers.
(8a)(8b)   Buyer's and seller's brokers deposit margin with their clearing firms.
(9a)(9b)   Buyer's and seller's brokers' clearing firms deposit margin with clearinghouse.

Note: Either buyer or seller (or both) could be a floor trader, eliminating the broker and the commission broker.

Figure 8.3 illustrates the flow of money and information as a futures transaction is consummated and cleared. Let us illustrate how the clearinghouse operates by assuming you sell a U.S. Treasury bond futures contract at a price of 97 27/32, which is $97,843.75. You have contacted your broker, who either is a futures commission merchant (FCM) or contracts with an FCM, whose commission broker finds a buyer in the U.S. Treasury bond futures pit of the Chicago Board of Trade. The buyer might be a local, or a commission broker, representing a customer off the floor.

Your brokerage firm clears its trades through ABC Futures, a member firm of the Chicago Board of Trade Clearing Corporation (BOTCC). The buyer's FCM clears through ACME Trading Company, a clearing firm that is also a member of the BOTCC. The required margin changes often on these contracts; we shall assume it is $2,500. You deposit this amount with ABC. ABC pools the transactions of all of its customers and deposits an amount required in its account with the BOTCC. The buyer deposits the same amount with ACME, which also deposits a sum of money, based on its customers' open positions, with the BOTCC.

The BOTCC guarantees the performance of you and the buyer. Thus, neither of you has to worry about whether the other will be able to make up the losses. The BOTCC will look to the clearing firms, ABC and ACME, for payment, and they in turn will look to you and the buyer.

Of course the forward market is an over-the-counter market. The parties to the contract deal directly with each other. There is currently no clearinghouse to guarantee to each party that the other will perform, although there are plans under way to begin a type of clearinghouse for certain over-the-counter transactions.

Daily Settlement

One way in which the clearinghouse helps ensure its survival is by using margins and the daily settlement of accounts. For each contract there is both an **initial margin,** the amount that must be deposited on the day the transaction is opened, and a **maintenance margin,** the amount that must be maintained every day thereafter. There are also initial and maintenance margins for spread and hedge transactions, which usually are lower than those for purely speculative positions.

The margin deposit is not quite like the margin on a stock trade. In stock trading, the investor deposits margin money and borrows the remainder of the stock price from the broker. In futures trading, not only is the margin requirement much smaller, but the remainder of the funds are not borrowed. The margin deposit is more like a good-faith security deposit. In fact some prefer to call them **performance bonds** rather than margins so that the distinction is clear. In any case, some large and actively trading investors are able to deposit Treasury bills for margins. Others are required to deposit cash.

At the end of each day, a committee composed of clearinghouse officials establishes a **settlement price.** This usually is an average of the prices of the last few trades of the day. Using the settlement price, each account is **marked to market.** The difference in the current settlement price and the previous day's settlement price is determined. If the difference is positive because the settlement price increased, the dollar amount is credited to the margin accounts of those holding long positions. Where does the money come from? It is charged to the accounts of those holding short positions. If the difference is negative because the settlement price decreased, the dollar amount is credited to the holders of short positions and charged to those holding long positions.

This process, sometimes called the **daily settlement,** is an important feature of futures markets and a major difference between futures and forward markets. In forward markets, the gains and losses are normally incurred at the end of the contract's life, when delivery is made. Futures markets credit and charge the price changes on a daily basis. This helps ensure the markets' integrity, because large losses are covered a little at a time rather than all at expiration, by which time the holder of the losing position may be unable to cover the loss.

To illustrate the daily settlement procedure, let us consider the transaction we previously described. We assume it was initiated on Friday, August 1. You sold one Treasury bond futures contract on the Chicago Board of

Trade at that day's opening price of 97 27/32. One such contract is for a face value of $100,000, so the price is .9784375($100,000) = $97,843.75. We shall assume that the initial margin requirement was $2,500, and the maintenance margin requirement was $2,000. You maintain the position until repurchasing the contract on August 18 at the opening price of 100 16/32, or $100,500. Table 8.3 illustrates the transactions to the account while the position was open.

Note that the account is first marked to market on the day of the trade and you made a profit of $437.50 on the first day. Each day thereafter, you must maintain $2,000 in the account so that on any given day when the

---

TABLE 8.3   **Daily Settlement Example**

Assume that on Friday, August 1, you sell one Chicago Board of Trade September Treasury bond futures contract at the opening price of 97 27/32 ($97,843.75). The initial margin requirement is $2,500, and the maintenance margin requirement is $2,000. You maintain your position every day through Friday, August 15, and then buy back the contract at the opening price on Monday, August 18. The example below illustrates the daily price changes and the flows in and out of the margin account.

Date	Settlement Price	Settlement Price ($)	Mark-to-Market	Other Entries	Account Balance	Explanation
8/1	97-13	$97,406.25	+$437.50	+$2,500	+$2,937.50	Initial margin deposit of $2,500. Price fell by 14/32 leaving profit by day-end of $437.50.
8/4	97-25	97,781.25	−375.00		2,562.50	Price rose by 12/32 giving loss of $375. Balance exceeds maintenance requirement.
8/5	96-18	96,562.50	+1,218.75		3,781.25	Price fell by 1 17/32 giving profit of $1,218.75. Balance well above maintenance requirement.
8/6	96-07	96,218.75	+343.75		4,125.00	Price fell by 11/32 giving profit of $343.75. Balance well above maintenance requirement.
8/7	97-05	97,156.25	−937.50		3,187.50	Price rose by 30/32 giving loss of $937.50. Balance still above maintenance requirement.
8/8	99-03	99,093.75	−1,937.50		1,250.00	Price rose by 1 30/32 giving loss of $1,937.50. Balance short by $750.
8/11	101-01	101,031.25	−1,937.50	+1,250.00	562.50	$1.250.00 deposited. Price rose 1 30/32 giving loss of $1,937.50. Balance short by $1,437.50.
8/12	99-25	99,781,25	+1,250.00	+1,937.50	3,750.00	$1,937.50 deposited. Price fell 1 8/32 giving profit of $1,250. Balance well above maintenance requirement.
8/13	101-01	101,031.25	−1,250.00		2,500.00	Price rose by 1 8/32 giving loss of $1,250. Balance still above maintenance requirement.
8/14	100-25	100,781.25	+250.00		2,750.00	Price fell by 8/32 giving profit of $250. Balance still above maintenance requirement.
8/15	100-25	100,781.25	0.00		2,750.00	Price did not change.
8/18	100-16	100,500.00	+281.25	−3,031.25	0.00	Bought contract back at gain of 9/32 or $281.25. Withdrew remaining balance.

balance is greater than $2,000, the excess over the initial margin can be withdrawn. We shall assume, however, that you do not withdraw the excess. If the balance falls below the $2,000 maintenance margin requirement, you receive a margin call and must deposit enough funds to bring the balance back up to the initial margin requirement. The additional funds deposited are called the **variation margin.** They are officially due within a few days but usually are required to be deposited immediately; we shall assume the money is deposited before trading begins on the day you receive the margin call. By the end of the day on Friday, August 8, the account shows a balance of $1,250. On Monday morning you receive a margin call for $1,250, which is immediately deposited. Another margin call, for $1,937.50, follows the next morning. Undaunted and still confident of ultimately turning things around, you make the deposit on August 12. When you finally buy back the contract on August 18, the account balance withdrawn is $3,031.25. In all, you have made deposits of $2,500, $1,250, and $1,937.50 for a total of $5,687.50. Thus, the overall loss on the trade is $2,656.25.

The preceding example is not at all unusual. It was selected at random. You, the seller of this contract, quickly incurred a substantial loss. For every dollar lost, however, there is a dollar gained by someone else. Traders who were bullish on Treasury bond futures from August 1 to 18 did quite well. Nonetheless, the large dollar flows from day to day serve as a stern reminder of the substantial leverage component that futures contracts offer.

It is also important to note that with futures contracts it is possible to lose more money than one has invested. For example, assume the market makes a substantial move against the investor. The account balance is depleted, and the broker asks the investor to deposit additional funds. If the investor does not have the funds, the broker will attempt to close out the position. Now assume the market moves quickly before the contracts can be closed. Ultimately the contracts are sold out, but not before the investor has incurred additional losses. Those losses must be covered in cash. In the limit, a long position can ultimately lose the full price of the contract. This would occur if the price went to zero. On a short position, however, there is no upper limit on the price. Therefore, the loss theoretically is infinite.

One method futures exchanges use to limit the losses incurred on any given day is the daily price limit, which we briefly discussed earlier. Also the clearinghouse can request that additional margin funds be deposited during a trading session rather than waiting until the end of the day.

Of course in forward markets, there is no clearinghouse, price limits, or daily settlement. There may or may not be margins required; this would depend on the creditworthiness of the party. In many cases credit is established by posting a letter of credit provided by a bank, which, in effect, stands ready to lend money to cover losses.[5]

---

[5]Some swaps and other over-the-counter contracts have begun periodically settling gains and losses but to date this is the exception and not the rule.

The total number of futures contracts outstanding at any one time is called the **open interest.** The concept is the same as it is for options markets. Each contract has both a long and a short position and counts as one contract of open interest. As an example of the potential size of open interest, the average month-ending open interest in the CFTC's 1999 fiscal year was about 8.9 million contracts, with financial and currency futures contracts accounting for about two-thirds of the total.[6]

Most futures traders do not hold their positions to expiration; rather, they simply reenter the market and execute an offsetting transaction. In other words, if one held a long position in a contract, one might elect to simply sell that contract in the market. The clearinghouse would properly note that the trader's positions were offsetting. If the position were not offset before the expiration month, delivery would become likely.

Delivery and Cash Settlement

All contracts eventually expire. As noted earlier, each contract has a delivery month. The delivery procedure varies among contracts. Some contracts can be delivered on any business day of the delivery month. Others permit delivery only after the contract has traded for the last day—a day that also varies from contract to contract. Still others are cash settled; thus, there is no delivery at all.

Most non-cash-settled financial futures contracts permit delivery any business day of the delivery month. Delivery usually is a three-day sequence beginning two business days prior to the first possible delivery day. The clearing member firms report to the clearinghouse those of their customers who hold long positions. Two business days before the intended delivery day, the holder of a short position who intends to make delivery notifies the clearinghouse of its desire to deliver. This day is called the **position day.** On the next business day, called the **notice of intention day,** the exchange selects the holder of the oldest long position to receive delivery. On the third day, the **delivery day,** delivery takes place and the long pays the short. For most financial futures, delivery is consummated by wire transfer.

Most futures contracts allow for more than one deliverable instrument. The contract usually specifies that the price paid by the long to the short be adjusted to reflect a difference in the quality of the deliverable good. We shall look at this more closely in Chapter 11.

On cash-settled contracts, such as stock index futures, the settlement price on the last trading day is fixed at the closing spot price of the underlying instrument, such as the stock index. All contracts are marked to market on that day, and the positions are deemed to be closed. One

---

[6]CFTC *Annual Report 1999.*

exception to this procedure is the S&P 500 futures contract, which closes trading on the Thursday before the third Friday of the expiration month but bases the final settlement price on the opening stock price on Friday morning. This procedure was installed to avoid some problems created when a contract settles at the closing prices, a point we shall discuss in Chapter 11.

The fact that all futures contracts can be delivered or cash settled is critical to their pricing. Most contracts, however, are not delivered. In the CFTC's fiscal year 1999, 491 million contracts were traded, but only 3.6 million — fewer than 1 percent — ended in delivery; this figure includes cash-settled contracts.[7] Thus, delivery, albeit an important feature of futures contracts, seldom takes place. Most traders close out their positions prior to expiration, a process called **offsetting.** The futures market is not the best route to acquiring a commodity, because the long contract holder is at the mercy of the short contract holder. The short can deliver on any of several delivery days and can choose to deliver any of several related but slightly different commodities. The long must accept whatever the short offers. Thus, the long usually closes out the position early. Therefore, if one needs the commodity, one often will do better to purchase it in the spot market.

Despite the flexibility sellers have in determining the delivery terms, some contracts actually are delivered through a process called **exchange for physicals (EFP),** also known as **against actuals** or **versus cash.** This is, in fact, the only type of permissible futures transaction that occurs off the floor of the exchange, or outside its electronic trading platform, if it has one. In an EFP transaction, the holders of long and short positions get together and agree on a cash transaction that would close out their futures positions. For example, farmer A holds a short position in a wheat contract and firm B holds a long position in the same contract. Firm B wants to buy farmer A's wheat, but either the wheat is not one of the grades acceptable for delivery on the contract or the farmer would find it prohibitively expensive to deliver at Chicago or Toledo as the contract requires. In either case, farmer A and firm B could arrange for A to deliver the wheat at some other acceptable location and B to pay A for the wheat at an agreed-upon price. Then A and B would be permitted to report this transaction to the CBOT as though each had offset its futures contract with a trade with the other party. Thus, the EFP market simply gives the parties additional flexibility in making delivery, choosing the terms, and conducting such business when the exchanges are closed. EFPs can also be used in cash settlement contracts. EFPs are used in several futures markets and compose almost 100 percent of deliveries made in oil futures markets.

Because forward contracts do not have standard terms and conditions like futures contracts, it is not as simple to offset them the way one can with

---

[7]Ibid.

futures. If an institution has purchased a forward contract obligating it to purchase a commodity at a future date, however, it can generally sell a new forward contract obligating it to deliver the commodity on that date. Of course, the price negotiated may lead to a profit or a loss. While this type of transaction is basically an offsetting transaction, the liquidity of the forward market may be such that it might be somewhat more difficult to find someone to do the precise transaction the institution wants. In addition, the new transaction also entails some credit risk. In the futures markets, at least in the most liquid markets such as grains, T-bonds, Eurodollars, and the S&P 500, offsetting is a fairly simple procedure, as noted above, and is subject to essentially no credit risk. In some cases, however, a forward contract can be offset by entering into the opposite transaction with the same party in which one contracted originally. By mutual agreement, the parties can treat the contracts as offsetting, thereby terminating both contracts and eliminating the credit risk.

When a forward contract is written, the intention is generally to hold it to the expiration day and take delivery. Some contracts, however, do stipulate a cash settlement. Thus, an expiring forward contract works pretty much like an expiring futures contract.

Futures Price Quotations

The best source of daily futures prices is *The Wall Street Journal*. Figure 8.4 illustrates how *The Wall Street Journal* reports futures prices. Contracts are grouped into categories: grains and oilseeds, livestock and meat, food and fiber, metals and petroleum, interest rate, currency and index.

At the top of the column are headings. Above the heading for the grains and oilseeds, we have the day's open, high, low, and settlement prices, followed by the change in the settlement price from the previous day. The next two columns give the high and low over the contract's life. The final column is the open interest.

The first line indicates the name of the commodity and the abbreviation for the exchange, followed by the contract size and the units of quotation. For example, the corn contract is traded at the Chicago Board of Trade, which is abbreviated here as CBT. One contract is for 5,000 bushels, and the prices are in cents per bushel.

Each line in the quotes indicates a particular contract. For corn we see the July, September, November, and December 2000 contracts and additional contracts expiring in 2001 and 2002. The July 2000 contract had a settlement price of 187½ cents, or $1.875, per bushel.

At the end of each contract's quotes are estimates of that day's volume (here 115,000 contracts), volume the previous day (151,352), total open interest (407,585) —which is the total as of the beginning of the trading session —and the change in open interest from the previous day (−16,167).

FIGURE 8.4   **Futures Quotations in *The Wall Street Journal*, Trading Day of June 30, 2000**

Friday, June 30, 2000

Open Interest Reflects Previous Trading Day.

GRAINS AND OILSEEDS

	Open	High	Low	Settle	Change	Lifetime High	Low	Open Interest
CORN (CBT) 5,000 bu.; cents per bu.
July	194¾	195¼	186½	187½ −	7¼	278½	186½	31,682
Sept	203½	204	195	195¾ −	8	265½	195	148,227
Nov	205	206½	204	204 −	8	268½	204	1,391
Dec	215¾	216½	205	207½ −	8½	279½	205	174,031
Mr01	227	227¼	218½	219 −	8¼	279¾	218½	28,052
May	227½	229	225¼	226¼ −	7	282½	225¼	5,798
July	233	234¾	231¼	232 −	7	287½	231¼	9,468
Sept	239½	239¾	236	236 −	7½	276½	236	903
Dec	245	247¼	245	245¼ −	5¾	275	245	7,566
Dc02	255	255	257	257 −	3	272	255	265

Est vol 115,000; vol Thu 151,352; open int 407,585, −16,167.

OATS (CBT) 5,000 bu.; cents per bu.
July	97¾	98¼	96¾	96¾ −	4½	130	96¾	1,349
Sept	108¾	108¾	103¾	103¾ −	4½	132½	103¾	6,778
Dec	113½	114½	112	112 −	4½	137	112	5,864
Mr01	123	123	120	120 −	4	142	120	801

SOYBEANS (CBT) 5,000 bu.; cents per bu.
July	491	492	477	477½ −	13½	647	440	10,907
Aug	493	494	480½	482¾ −	11	584½	441	27,136
Sept	488	488	472	473¼ −	13½	587½	450	17,492
Nov	491½	494	474	476¾ −	15	631	453	71,282
Ja01	497½	500	484	486½ −	14¾	600	481	7,321
Mar	508	509½	494	495½ −	14½	604½	492	6,121
May	516½	516½	503	503½ −	13	604	500½	5,405
July	521¾	522	512	512½ −	12½	609	505	4,322
Nov	529	529	518	518 −	11½	605	516	1,583

Est vol 65,000; vol Thu 68,459; open int 151,569, −4,336.

LIVESTOCK AND MEAT

CATTLE-FEEDER (CME) 50,000 lbs.; cents per lb.
Aug	85.90	86.95	85.90	86.45 +	.87	88.00	79.25	10,564
Sept	85.60	86.70	85.60	86.30 +	.97	88.50	83.50	2,394
Oct	86.50	87.40	86.45	87.15 +	.85	88.65	84.35	3,715
Nov	87.40	88.30	87.40	88.10 +	1.00	89.15	85.52	2,233
Ja01	88.05	88.75	88.05	88.65 +	.67	90.00	86.60	1,401
Mar	87.95	88.75	87.95	88.75 +	.85	88.75	86.30	319

Est vol 3,324; vol Thu 2,358; open int 20,810, +23.

CATTLE-LIVE (CME) 40,000 lbs.; cents per lb.
June	68.15	68.50	66.57	67.47 −	.60	70.87	65.30	1,305
Aug	66.57	67.10	66.57	66.72 +	.25	71.37	65.70	47,910
Oct	68.75	69.30	68.75	69.17 +	.45	73.30	68.00	31,883
Dec	71.00	71.50	71.00	71.05 +	.10	74.45	70.50	12,207
Fb01	72.35	72.70	72.35	72.55 +	.17	75.50	72.22	7,066
Apr	74.67	75.05	74.67	74.85 +	.17	77.30	74.45	5,295
June	72.85	73.15	72.80	72.97 +	.17	75.75	72.60	2,655

Est vol 13,913; vol Thu 7,859; open int 108,321, +784.

HOGS-LEAN (CME) 40,00 lbs.; cents per lb.
July	71.15	71.30	70.52	70.60 −	.60	74.90	51.80	8,986
Aug	69.95	70.10	68.90	69.02 −	.92	71.65	52.30	20,089
Oct	59.30	59.40	58.75	58.87 −	.60	62.35	49.00	11,122
Dec	55.90	56.05	54.70	54.95 −	1.12	59.70	49.50	7,413
Fb01	56.45	56.50	55.90	55.90 −	.50	59.85	52.40	1,982
Apr	55.45	55.50	55.05	55.05 −	.42	58.65	54.40	835
June			62.40	−	.10	65.30	60.00	147

Est vol 6,898; vol Thu 7,781; open int 50,616, −465.

PORK BELLIES (CME) 40,000 lbs.; cents per lb.
July	86.10	87.10	86.00	87.07 +	1.15	98.30	54.20	2,390
Aug	84.10	85.20	84.00	85.15 +	1.30	95.30	53.20	2,056
Fb01	73.60	73.80	72.60	72.60 −		80.00	58.50	134

Est vol 795; vol Thu 1,511; open int 4,597, +70.

INTEREST RATE

TREASURY BONDS (CBT)-$100,000; pts. 32nds of 100%
	Open	High	Low	Settle	Change	Lifetime High	Low	Open Interest
Sept	97-17	97-25	97-10	97-11 −	5	99-24	88-19	374,617
Dec	97-16	97-22	97-09	97-09 −	5	99-09	88-31	4,175
Mr01	97-19	97-19	97-06	97-08 −	5	98-06	88-06	841

Est vol 133,000; vol Thu 234,473; open int 379,646, +9,989.

TREASURY BONDS (MCE)-$50,000; pts. 32nds of 100%
| Sept | 97-19 | 97-25 | 97-07 | 97-08 − | 9 | 99-18 | 92-23 | 5,107 |

Est vol 1,300; vol Thu 2,073; open int 5,110, −48.

TREASURY NOTES (CBT)-$100,000; pts. 32nds of 100%
| Sept | 98-11 | 98-20 | 98-11 | 98-155 + | 3.5 | 99-20 | 94-22 | 598,016 |
| Dec | 98-165 | 98-165 | 98-12 | 98-13 + | 3.5 | 98-17 | 96-075 | 5,087 |

Est vol 108,000; vol Thu 141,741; open int 603,103, −8,377.

10 YR AGENCY NOTES (CBT)-$100,000; pts. 32nds of 100%
| Sept | 92-14 | 92-20 | 92-10 | 92-155 + | 5.5 | 93-045 | 88-045 | 40,387 |

Est vol 2,000; vol Thu 16,047; open int 40,388, +146.

5 YR TREAS NOTES (CBT)-$100,000; pts. 32nds of 100%
| Sept | 98-30 | 99-03 | 98-28 | 99-005 + | 3.5 | 99-24 | 96-14 | 370,998 |

Est vol 74,000; vol Thu 94,117; open int 370,998, +398.

2 YR TREAS NOTES (CBT)-$200,000; pts. 32nds of 100%
| Sept | 99-03 | 99-067 | 99-03 | 99-06 + | 1.5 | 99-07 | 98-025 | 54,070 |

Est vol 4,100; vol Thu 3,898; open int 54,070, +215.

30-DAY FEDERAL FUNDS (CBT)-$5 million; pts. of 100%
June	93.475	93.475	93.465	93.470 −	.010	94.130	93.465	8,429
July	93.46	93.46	93.46	93.46 −		94.06	93.18	20,909
Aug	93.44	93.44	93.43	93.44 +	.01	93.73	93.12	11,259
Sept	93.30	93.31	93.29	93.30 −		93.64	92.98	10,050
Oct	93.25	93.25	93.25	93.25 −		93.52	92.93	723

Est vol 4,400; vol Thu 13,197; open int 51,533, −1,788.

MUNI BOND INDEX (CBT)-$1,000; times Bond Buyer MBI
| Sept | 95-23 | 95-27 | 95-19 | 95-23 − | 1 | 96-00 | 90-03 | 20,795 |

Est vol 1,100; vol Thu 1,823; open int 21,195, +603.
Index: Close 96-07; Yield 6.02.

TREASURY BILLS (CME)-$1 mil.; pts. of 100%
	Open	High	Low	Settle	Chg	Discount Settle	Chg	Open Interest
Sept	93.86	93.86	93.85	93.85 +	.03	6.15 −	.03	537

Est vol 6; vol Thu 0; open int 537, +0.

LIBOR-1 MO. (CME)-$3,000,000; points of 100%
July	93.36	93.36	93.36	93.36	....	6.64	....	25,008
Aug	93.26	93.27	93.26	93.26	....	6.74	....	11,947
Sept	93.20	93.20	93.18	93.18	....	6.82	....	2,587
Oct				93.13	....	6.87	....	1,417
Nov				93.06	....	6.94	....	865
Dec	92.80	92.82	92.80	92.81	....	7.19	....	160

Est vol 1,167; vol Thu 3,208; open int 42,154, −456.

EURODOLLAR (CME)-$1 million; pts of 100%
	Open	High	Low	Settle	Chg	Yield Settle	Chg	Open Interest
July	93.21	93.22	93.21	93.22	....	6.78	....	48,405
Aug	93.13	93.13	93.12	93.12	....	6.88	....	12,008
Sept	93.08	93.08	93.05	93.06	....	6.94	....	622,522
Oct	92.91	92.92	92.90	92.90	....	7.10	....	2,166
Dec	92.88	92.89	92.87	92.87	....	7.13	....	511,699
Mr01	92.90	92.91	92.87	92.89	....	7.11	....	387,856
June	92.89	92.90	92.87	92.88	....	7.12	....	254,462
Sept	92.89	92.90	92.87	92.88	....	7.12	....	220,626
Dec	92.85	92.86	92.83	92.84	....	7.16	....	160,348
Mr02	92.90	92.92	92.89	92.90 +	.01	7.10 −	.01	137,787
June	92.91	92.92	92.90	92.90 +	.01	7.10 −	.01	97,871
Sept	92.90	92.93	92.89	92.91 +	.02	7.09 −	.02	105,311
Dec	92.87	92.89	92.85	92.86 +	.02	7.14 −	.02	76,128
Mr03	92.93	92.95	92.91	92.92 +	.02	7.08 −	.02	79,081
June	92.92	92.94	92.89	92.91 +	.02	7.09 −	.02	55,777
Sept	92.89	92.93	92.89	92.90 +	.03	7.10 −	.03	47,569
Dec	92.84	92.87	92.83	92.84 +	.03	7.16 −	.03	39,126
Mr04	92.91	92.91	92.86	92.88 +	.03	7.12 −	.03	36,950
June	92.86	92.88	92.83	92.86 +	.04	7.14 −	.04	36,359
Sept	92.81	92.85	92.80	92.83 +	.04	7.17 −	.04	30,206
Dec	92.73	92.77	92.72	92.75 +	.04	7.25 −	.04	27,788
Mr05	92.79	92.80	92.76	92.78 +	.04	7.22 −	.04	19,982
June	92.75	92.77	92.72	92.75 +	.04	7.25 −	.04	14,052
Sept	92.72	92.72	92.68	92.72 +	.04	7.28 −	.04	10,693
Dec	92.64	92.64	92.62	92.64 +	.04	7.36 −	.04	7,818
Mr06	92.68	92.68	92.64	92.67 +	.03	7.33 −	.03	7,706
June	92.64	92.64	92.60	92.64 +	.03	7.36 −	.03	7,286
Sept	92.62	92.62	92.57	92.61 +	.03	7.39 −	.03	6,601
Dec	92.55	92.55	92.50	92.53 +	.03	7.47 −	.03	6,484
Mr07	92.58	92.58	92.53	92.56 +	.03	7.44 −	.03	5,122
June	92.53	92.55	92.52	92.53 +	.02	7.47 −	.02	3,773
Sept	....	....	....	92.50 +	.02	7.50 −	.02	3,350
Dec	....	....	....	92.42 +	.02	7.58 −	.02	4,824
Mr08	....	....	....	92.46 +	.02	7.54 −	.02	3,970
June	....	....	....	92.43 +	.02	7.57 −	.02	4,198
Sept	....	....	....	92.40 +	.02	7.60 −	.02	3,930
Dec	....	....	....	92.32 +	.02	7.68 −	.02	2,961
Mr09	....	....	....	92.35 +	.02	7.65 −	.02	2,218
June	....	....	....	92.32 +	.02	7.68 −	.02	2,380
Sept	....	....	....	92.29 +	.02	7.71 −	.02	2,063
Dec	....	....	....	92.22 +	.02	7.78 −	.02	1,688
Mr10	....	....	....	92.25 +	.02	7.75 −	.02	1,447
June	....	....	....	92.22 +	.02	7.78 −	.02	911

Est vol 255,067; vol Thu 409,608; open int 3,113,505, +19,797.

INDEX

DJ INDUSTRIAL AVERAGE (CBOT)-$10 times average
	Open	High	Low	Settle	Change	Lifetime High	Low	Open Interest
Sept	10515	10560	10430	10550 +	30	12126	9995	11,396
Dec	10625	10697	10590	10697 +	29	12180	8100	2,126

Est vol 9,000; vol Thu 15,678; open int 13,528, −784.
Idx prl: Hi 10448.24; Lo 10336.16; Close 10447.89, +49.85.

S&P 500 INDEX (CME)-$250 times index
Sept	145570	147150	145500	146810 +	1010	159500	99000	364,855
Dec	149000	149360	147800	149070 +	1010	161860	126650	6,746
Mr01	....	....	151370 +	1010	164260	132430	1,012
June	....	....	153770 +	1060	166660	134280	629
Sept	....	....	156270 +	1060	169060	136130	143

Est vol 49,426; vol Thu 66,431; open int 373,388, −2,722.
Idx prl: Hi 1454.68; Lo 1438.71; Close 1454.60, +12.21.

MINI S&P 500 (CME)-$50 times index
| Sept | 145650 | 147100 | 145500 | 146800 + | 1000 | 156600 | 135077 | 29,836 |

Vol Thu 82,994; open int 29,855, +2,729.

S&P MIDCAP 400 (CME)- $500 times index
| Sept | 495.70 | 500.50 | 488.00 | 488.30 − | 7.30 | 514.70 | 385.25 | 13,734 |

Est vol 852; vol Thu 1,305; open int 13,734, +480.
Idx prl: Hi 493.93; Lo 481.90; Close 481.90, −9.84.

NIKKEI 225 STOCK AVERAGE (CME)-$5 times index
| Sept | 17325. | 17520. | 17325. | 17520. + | 205 | 20700. | 16000. | 14,397 |

Est vol 765; vol Thu 2,028; open int 14,408, +298.
Idx prl: Hi 17510.07; Lo 17305.81; Close 17411.05, −64.85.

NASDAQ 100 (CME)-$100 times index
| Sept | 373050 | 381000 | 371800 | 381700 + | 8600 | 483600 | 297500 | 29,491 |

Est vol 12,541; vol Thu 18,998; open int 29,505, +1,373.
Idx prl: Hi 3764.96; Lo 3666.18; Close 3763.79, +97.96.

MINI NASDAQ 100 (CME)-$20 times index
| Sept | 3726.0 | 3809.0 | 3717.5 | 3817.0 + | 86.0 | 4776.0 | 2963.0 | 19,072 |

Vol Thu 40,264; open int 19,072, +106.

GSCI (CME)-$250 times nearby index
| July | 236.85 | 238.30 | 234.40 | 235.50 − | 2.20 | 238.40 | 192.50 | 38,573 |

Est vol 556; vol Thu 209; open int 38,772, +63.
Idx prl: Hi 238.11; Lo 235.37; Close 235.71, −2.12.

RUSSELL 2000 (CME)-$500 times index
| Sept | 516.10 | 522.50 | 511.00 | 522.60 + | 6.85 | 625.90 | 423.40 | 11,545 |

Est vol 1,920; vol Thu 1,978; open int 11,545, +117.
Idx prl: Hi 517.24; Lo 509.92; Close 517.23, +4.65.

The total open interest figure normally equals the total of the open interest figures for each contract; however, the markets move so quickly that sometimes this information is not completely accurate.

The second column of quotations contains some interest rate futures. The headings vary slightly. Look at the Treasury bond futures prices. The contract is at the CBT, is for $100,000 face value, and is quoted in points and thirty-seconds of 100 percent. Thus, we can interpret the settlement price of the September 2000 contract as 97 11/32 (97.34375) or $97,343.75. The change in the settlement price is a decrease of 5/32. The next two columns give the lifetime high and low, and the final column gives the open interest. Summary figures for volume and open interest appear at the end of the list of contracts.

The quotes for the Eurodollar and Treasury bill contracts differ slightly, but that is due primarily to the manner in which their prices are quoted. We shall take a closer look at those contracts later in this book.

In the third column are the stock index futures prices. The headings are the same as those for the grains and oilseeds. Below the volume and open interest figures is information on the spot index.

As you might expect, these prices will be dated by the time you read them, but they are, nonetheless, important measures of recent market activity.

Types of Futures Contracts

Many types of futures contracts trade on U.S. futures exchanges. Some of these contracts are essentially the same underlying commodity. Many of those listed are not actively traded; some have not been traded at all for some time. Table 8.4 lists all registered contracts on U.S. futures exchanges covered in *The Wall Street Journal* on March 31, 2000, the exchanges that list them, and contract sizes. Keep in mind that new contracts are frequently introduced and old contracts are sometimes delisted. A brief discussion of some of the characteristics of each major group of contracts follows. A more detailed discussion is provided for the contracts we focus on for the remainder of the book.

Grains and Oilseeds

Grains and oilseeds compose the oldest category of futures contracts. For many years, these contracts were the most actively traded futures; however, in recent years their volume has been surpassed by the financials. The primary trading interest comes from speculative activity and hedging by farmers, food processors, grain storage firms, exporters, and an increasing number of foreign countries that import grain. These futures prices are heavily influenced by agricultural production, weather, government farm policies, and international trade, among other factors.

TABLE 8.4	Registered Futures Contracts on U.S. Futures Exchanges Covered in *The Wall Street Journal* (as of March 31, 2000)

Exchange symbols:
Cantor Exchange (CANTOR)
Chicago Board of Trade (CBOT)
Chicago Mercantile Exchange (CME)
COMEX division of New York
  Mercantile Exchange (COMEX)
FINEX division of New York Cotton
  Exchange (FINEX)
Kansas City Board of Trade (KCBT)

MidAmerica Commodity Exchange
  (MCE)
Minneapolis Grain Exchange (MGE)
New York Board of Trade (NYBOT)
New York Cotton Exchange (NYCTN)
New York Futures Exchange division
  of New York Cotton Exchange (NYFE)
New York Mercantile Exchange (NYMEX)

Contract	Exchange	Contract Size
Grains and Oilseeds		
Corn	CBOT	5,000 bu.
Corn	MCE	1,000 bu.
Oats	CBOT	5,000 bu.
Soybeans	CBOT	5,000 bu.
Soybeans	MCE	1,000 bu.
Soybean meal	CBOT	100 tons
Soybean oil	CBOT	60,000 lbs.
Rough rice	CBOT	2,000 cwt.
Wheat	CBOT	5,000 bu.
Wheat	KCBT	5,000 bu.
Wheat	MCE	1,000 bu.
Wheat	MGE	5,000 bu.
Livestock and Meat		
Feeder cattle	CME	50,000 lbs.
Hogs	CME	40,000 lbs.
Live cattle	CME	40,000 lbs.
Pork bellies	CME	40,000 lbs.
Food and Fiber		
Cocoa	NYBOT	10 metric tons
Coffee	NYBOT	37,500 lbs.
Cotton	NYBOT	50,000 lbs.
Domestic sugar	NYBOT	112,000 lbs.
Milk	CME	200,000 lbs.
Orange juice	NYBOT	15,000 lbs.
World sugar	NYBOT	112,000 lbs.
Metals and Energy		
Copper	COMEX	25,000 lbs.
Crude oil	NYMEX	1,000 bbls.
Gold	COMEX	100 troy ozs.
Heating oil—no. 2	NYMEX	42,000 gals.
Natural gas	NYMEX	10,000 million BTUs
Western Natural Gas	KCBT	10,000 million BTUs
Electricity	NYMEX	736 megawatts

Livestock and Meat

In the livestock and meat category of futures contracts are the celebrated pork bellies, so often acclaimed as the quintessential speculative instrument. In reality, however, pork bellies are no more speculative than most

TABLE 8.4   *(continued)*

Palladium	NYMEX	100 troy ozs.
Platinum	NYMEX	50 troy ozs.
Propane	NYMEX	42,000 gals.
Silver	COMEX	5,000 troy ozs.
Unleaded gasoline	NYMEX	42,000 gals.
Miscellaneous		
Lumber	CME	80,000 board ft
Foreign Currency/Eurodollar		
Australian dollar	CME	100,000 $A
British pound	CME	62,500 £
Canadian dollar	CME	100,000 CD
Euro	CME	125,000 €
Euro	NYBOT	200,000 €
Eurodollar—90-day	CME	1,000,000 $
Eurodollar—30-day	CME	3,000,000 $
Eurosterling	NYBOT	100,000 €
Euroyen	CME	100 million ¥
German mark	CME	125,000 DM
Japanese yen	CME	12,500,000 ¥
Swiss franc	CME	125,00 SF
U.S. Dollar Index	NYBOT	$1,000 × Index
Economic Indices		
Goldman Sachs Commodity Index	CME	$250 × Index
Stock Indices		
Bridge CRB Index	NYBOT	$500 × Index
Dow Jones Industrial Average	CBOT	$10 × Index
Eurotop 300 Index	CME	$200 × Index
Mini NASDAQ 100	CME	$20 × Index
Mini S&P 500	CME	$50 × Index
Mini Value Line	KCBT	$100 × Index
NASDAQ 100	CME	$100 × Index
New York Stock Exchange Index	NYBOT	$500 × Index
Nikkei 225 Index	CME	$5 × Index
Russell 1000	NYBOT	$500 × Index
Russell 2000 Index	CME	$500 × Index
S&P 400 Midcap Index	CME	$500 × Index
S&P 500 Index	CME	$500 × Index
Treasury bonds	CANTOR	$100,000
Interest Rates		
Municipal Bond Index	CBOT	$1,000 × Index
30-day Federal Funds	CBOT	$5,000,000
Treasury bills	CME	$1,000,000
Treasury bonds	CBOT	$100,000
Treasury bonds	MCE	$50,000
Treasury notes (6 1/2–10 yr.)	CBOT	$100,000
Treasury notes (5 yr.)	CBOT	$100,000
Treasury notes (2 yr.)	CBOT	$200,000

other futures contracts; neither are hogs, live cattle, or feeder cattle, the other contracts in this category. Prices of livestock and meat futures are influenced not only by the obvious — domestic and worldwide demand for meat — but by the not so obvious — prices of grains used as feed, as well as government policies, demographic trends, and international trade. Traders in this category include farmers, slaughterhouses, meat packers, and major users of beef and pork, such as fast-food restaurant chains.

Food and Fiber

Food and fiber is a diverse category that includes coffee, cocoa, cotton, orange juice, and sugar. Prices are influenced by many of the same factors cited for the previous categories. Other factors include weather in central Florida (orange juice), Africa (cocoa and coffee), and Central and South America (coffee). Because most of these commodities are imported, international economic and political conditions also are major considerations.

Metals and Energy

The metal and energy category includes metals used in jewelry and industry and in energy-related products. Each of these commodities is considered a nonrenewable natural resource. Many are produced in politically unstable foreign countries. A considerable volume of spot and futures trading in these commodities takes place in foreign cities, such as London, Paris, Amsterdam, and Zurich. Without question, international economic and political factors are critical influences in these markets. The risks, particularly political, are quite high, as are the stakes.

Miscellaneous

This is a relatively small group. It includes a lumber futures contract, and has formerly included futures on fertilizers. These contracts have not been very actively traded.

Foreign Currency

Foreign currency futures were introduced in 1972 and were the forerunners of the pure interest rate futures contracts. In recent years their popularity has decreased considerably, primarily due to the growing use of over-the-counter foreign currency derivatives. These futures contracts are covered in more detail in Chapter 13.

Treasury Bills and Eurodollars

Treasury bill and Eurodollar contracts trade on the International Monetary Market of the Chicago Mercantile Exchange. In the United States, the Eurodollar contract is the most actively traded futures contract. Although the Treasury bill contract is not very actively traded, it is, nonetheless, a useful instrument for understanding futures markets and applications. We shall explore these contracts in great detail in later chapters.

Treasury Notes and Bonds

Treasury note and bond contracts, which are traded on the Chicago Board of Trade, are virtually identical except that there are three T-note contracts that are based on 2-year, 5-year, and 10-year maturities while the T-bond contract is based on Treasury bonds with maturities of at least 15 years that are not callable for at least 15 years. Thus, the T-note contracts are inter-mediate-term interest rate futures contracts and the T-bond contract is a long-term interest rate futures contract. The T-note contracts are traded quite actively, but the T-bond contract is one of the most active of all futures contracts. Other than the difference in maturity of the underlying instruments and the margin requirements, the contract terms are essentially identical. We shall use these contracts extensively in later chapters.

Economic Indices

The first economic index futures contract, the Consumer Price Index futures, was launched with much fanfare in June 1985. Although promoted as a means of hedging the uncertainty of inflation, the contract never generated much trading volume. Exchange officials attributed this to the relatively low and stable inflation rate since the contract's initiation, although the lack of a clearly defined spot market and the unavailability of continuous information on the true spot price probably were more serious impediments.

This category includes the Goldman Sachs Commodity Index, which is based on an index of other futures, but it has not attracted much trading volume.

Stock Indices

Stock index futures have been one of the spectacular success stories of the financial markets in recent years. These cash-settled contracts are indices of combinations of stocks. Investors use them to hedge positions in stock, speculate on the direction of the stock market in general, and arbitrage the contracts against comparable combinations of stocks.

Stock index futures contracts are based on indices of common stocks. The most widely traded contract is the S&P 500 futures at the Chicago Mercantile Exchange. The futures price is quoted in the same manner as the index. The futures contract, however, has an implicit multiplier of $250. Thus, if the futures price is 1500, the actual price is 1500($250) = $375,000. At expiration, the settlement price is set at the price of the S&P

500 index and the contract is settled in cash. The expirations are March, June, September, and December. The last trading day is the Thursday before the third Friday of the expiration month.

As previously noted, futures exchanges are extremely innovative, frequently introducing new contracts, most of which do not succeed. Among the more interesting recent and forthcoming products are futures on electricity and weather. Electricity is clearly a widely used product and has an extremely volatile price, but unlike most underlying assets, it cannot be stored. As we see in later chapters, this poses a special difficulty in pricing futures contracts. The over-the-counter forward, swap, and options markets for electricity are widely used today.

Weather is another new underlying instrument that is currently popular in over-the-counter forward, swap, and options markets and is being developed for trading in the futures markets. Weather, like electricity, cannot be stored, but it is, nonetheless, a key determinant of the financial performance of numerous companies. Weather derivatives are usually is based on heating and cooling degree days, which are the number of days where the average temperature is below or above 65 degrees Fahrenheit.

One instrument conspicuously absent from the list of assets on which futures trade is individual stocks. In Chapter 2 we discussed the Johnson-Shad agreement, in which CFTC Chairman Phillip McBride Johnson and SEC Chairman John Shad decided on how options on futures would be regulated. At that time they also formally agreed to not permit futures on narrow indices and individual stocks. A narrow index is one in which there are a small number of stocks, though how many stocks constitutes a small index is not specified. In 1999 a court ruling opened the door for indices containing a small number of stocks, permitting, for example, a futures on the Dow Jones Transportation Average, which contains only 20 stocks. In the United States, however, individual stock futures continue to be prohibited, though that restriction may be relaxed someday. One problem in permitting individual stock futures is that although the SEC has firm authority with respect to insider trading on individual securities, it is not clear who would regulate insider trading on individual stock futures. In fact, it is not even clear whether the insider trading laws would apply to individual stock futures.

On worldwide futures exchanges, futures contracts exist on many of the same types of instruments. Naturally, exchanges of certain countries specialize in contracts on products locally produced. For example, Australia is a major wool-producing country and, consequently, wool futures are traded on the Sydney Futures Exchange. The Winnipeg Commodity Exchange in Canada has active trading on its key agricultural products of barley and canola, and rubber futures are traded in Singapore. For the most part, however, foreign futures exchanges have most of their volume in

TABLE 8.5	Most Active Futures Contracts in the United States, 1999

Contract (Exchange)	Volume (Number of Contracts)
Eurodollars (CME)	102,052,168
Treasury Bonds (CBOT)	97,035,915
Crude Oil (NYMEX)	36,075,778
Ten-Year Treasury Notes (CBOT)	34,400,483
S&P 500 (CME)	28,120,054
Natural Gas (NYMEX)	18,622,220
Five-Year Treasury Notes (CBOT)	17,524,751
Corn (CBOT)	15,795,337
Soybeans (CBOT)	12,756,288
Gold (NYBOT)	9,465,519

SOURCE: CFTC *Annual Report 1999*

stock indices of local countries, in local interest rates, and in the exchange rate of their currency.

Table 8.5 lists the most active futures contracts in the United States. As can be seen, financial futures contracts are among the most popular. Appendix 8A provides a detailed list of contract specifications for the actively traded financial futures contracts in the United States. Worldwide, the German-government issued bond denominated in euros is the most active contract.

Managed Funds

Recent years have witnessed the growth of the **managed funds** industry. *Managed funds* is simply a term that refers to the arrangement by which an investor hires a professional futures trader to conduct transactions on his or her behalf. The futures manager is a commodity trading advisor (CTA), which we discussed earlier. Managed funds can exist in one of four forms: futures funds, private pools, a specialized contract with one or more CTAs, or as hedge funds.[8]

Futures funds, sometimes called **commodity funds,** are essentially mutual funds that pool investors' money and trade futures. Most funds invest only about 20 percent of their money in margin positions. The remainder is kept in interest-earning assets. Futures funds offer the public a way of participating in the futures market with a very low financial commitment. Often, a fund will accept deposits of $1,000 or less. In some cases, the organizers of a fund guarantee that the investor will not lose more than the original investment.

---

[8]In addition to futures, these funds also use options and spot market instruments.

In spite of the apparent attractiveness of funds, they have been quite controversial and with just cause. Their performance has been highly volatile and their costs are quite high, often running to 20 percent of the value of the fund in a given year.

Commodity pools, mentioned earlier in the context of the pool operator or CPO, are private arrangements that operate much like futures funds. The latter, however, are open to the general public while pools normally solicit funds from specific investors. When the fund reaches a certain size, the pool is closed to other investors. Pools generally require at least a $10,000 investment. Pools have suffered some of the same problems as funds, namely inconsistent performance and heavy costs.

An increasingly popular form of managed futures is the private contractual arrangement with one or more CTAs. A typical one would involve a large institutional investor agreeing to allocate a portion of its funds to a group of CTAs. In some cases, the CTAs are supervised by a consultant or introducing broker. Since these arrangements are negotiated between the institutional investor and the introducing broker and the CTAs, the costs are usually significantly lower. Often a rather large number of CTAs, sometimes 20 to 30, is used, leading to diversified and somewhat stable performance. These arrangements are growing in popularity, particularly among pension funds.

Hedge Funds

The hedge fund industry is closely related to the managed funds industry but is much larger. A hedge fund is a privately organized pool of money that is invested in literally any financial instruments on any markets of the world. Although hedge funds actively use futures contracts, they also use options, spot instruments such as stocks and bonds, and over-the-counter instruments such as swaps, structured notes, and forward contracts. A hedge fund typically uses a high degree of leverage and takes short positions as willingly as long positions. In addition, a hedge fund frequently borrows heavily. It should be apparent that a hedge fund is a very risky form of investment. These funds normally take in only investors who have large amounts of money and a willingness to take high risks. Also, hedge funds tend to be quite secretive, often registering their legal status in offshore locations, such as the Cayman Islands. Many hedge funds even maintain a great deal of secrecy from their investors, who trust that the fund organizers will invest their money wisely and manage the risk carefully. This has not always been the case.

The term *hedge fund* is probably a misnomer. The general idea of calling this type of company a hedge fund is that the fund would take short positions, which in some sense hedge long positions. That was the original design of a hedge fund. Today, however, these funds are probably as far from the practice of hedging as one can get. That does not mean they are not legitimate investment outlets, as their success and popularity are well established in the financial system.

Indices of Futures Market Activity

In Chapter 2, we noted that indices of options market activity are relatively rare and difficult to construct. This is also true of futures market indices. There are so many diverse futures contracts with different expirations and quotations in different units that futures indices never have attracted much attention. The best-known index is the aforementioned Goldman Sachs Commodity Index, which is an average of the prices of a number of futures contracts. The prices are weighted by world production of the commodity. As a result, the index is highly influenced by oil. In general, however, few investors pay much attention to futures indices since they mostly reflect the spot market, which is well covered with indices.

Transaction Costs in Forward and Futures Trading

In Chapter 2, we discussed the different types of option trading costs that the public and professional traders incur. In this section, we shall do the same for forwards and futures. There is, however, less material available on the trading costs in these markets. One reason is that futures markets have very low trading costs—indeed, that is one of their major advantages. In addition, the costs of trading futures contracts are less documented than the costs of trading options and stocks. Also, forward markets are private and the costs are less publicized; however, forward contracting, being tailored to the specific needs of the parties, can be quite costly.

Commissions

Commissions paid by the public to brokers are assessed on the basis of a dollar charge per contract. The commission is paid at the order's initiation and includes both the opening and closing commissions; that is, a round-trip commission is charged regardless of whether the trader ultimately closes out the contract, makes or takes delivery, or makes a cash settlement. There is no typical commission rate, but, for example, a Web discount brokerage firm recently advertised a round-trip price of $7.50 for online trading.

All traders, whether on or off the exchange floor, incur a minimum charge that is paid to the clearing firm and includes the exchange fee and a fee assessed by the National Futures Association, an organization we shall discuss in a later section. These fees are usually less than $2.00 per contract.

In the forward market, transactions are usually conducted directly with dealers so there is typically no commission. There are, however, significant costs associated with processing the paperwork.

Bid-Ask Spread

A second type of trading cost is the bid-ask spread. Chapter 2 explained the concept of the spread for options. Unlike for options and stock markets, however, there is no real market maker. Many floor traders, particularly spreaders and scalpers, quote prices at which they are willing to simultaneously buy at the bid price and sell at the ask price. The bid-ask spread is the cost to the public of liquidity—the ability to buy and sell quickly without a large price concession. Because the spread is not captured and reported electronically, there is little statistical evidence on its size. The spread usually is the value of a minimum price fluctuation, called a **tick,** but occasionally equals a few more ticks for less liquid markets.

In the forward markets, bid-ask spreads are set by dealers in much the same way as they are on the exchange floor. These spreads can be quite large, depending on how eager the dealer and its competitors are to make a trade.

Delivery Costs

A futures trader who holds a position to delivery faces the potential for incurring a substantial delivery cost. In the case of most financial instruments, this cost is rather small. For commodities, however, it is necessary to arrange for the commodity's physical transportation, delivery, and storage. Although the proverbial story of the careless futures trader who woke up to find thousands of pounds of pork bellies dumped on the front lawn certainly is an exaggeration, anyone holding a long position in the delivery month must be aware of the delivery possibility. This no doubt explains part of the popularity of cash settlement contracts.

In forward markets, transactions are tailored to the needs of the parties. Consequently, the terms are usually set to keep delivery costs at a minimum. Cash settlement is frequently used.

The Regulation of Futures Markets

As noted previously, forward markets are largely unregulated. Futures markets, however, have been heavily regulated. Many regulators and legislators have taken a dim view of futures trading, likening it to gambling. In the nineteenth century, there were numerous attempts to outlaw futures trading. Most of the early regulation was at the state and local levels.

The Commodity Futures Trading Commission

The Commodity Futures Trading Commission (CFTC) was created by the United States Congress as part of the Commodity Futures Trading Act of

1974. It is a federal agency that regulates U.S. futures markets. The CFTC is responsible for licensing futures exchanges and contracts. It approves all terms and conditions of each proposed contract as well as modifications of the terms of existing contracts. To be approved by the CFTC, a contract must have an economic purpose and not be contrary to the "public interest." An "economic purpose" generally is construed to mean that it can be used for hedging.

The CFTC is responsible for ensuring that the exchanges make price information available to the public. It also establishes requirements for **reportable positions,** stipulating that futures traders report their outstanding positions if they exceed certain levels, which vary from contract to contract. The CFTC also establishes **position limits,** the maximum number of contracts a trader can have at any one time.

The commission is responsible for the authorization or licensing of individuals offering their services to the public. This includes floor brokers, FCMs, APs, CTAs, and CPOs as discussed earlier. These individuals must meet minimum capital requirements, and their backgrounds must be investigated.

The CFTC has the authority to require exchanges to establish and enforce disciplinary actions against members found to be in violation of the exchange's rules. The CFTC can also seek court injunctions and impose certain disciplinary actions itself.

The CFTC is also authorized to establish a system of addressing complaints brought by the public against brokers, traders, and other licensed futures professionals. As we shall see shortly, much of this authority has been turned over to the National Futures Association (NFA).

One of the CFTC's primary responsibilities is market surveillance. Federal law makes it a felony to attempt to manipulate the futures market. The CFTC monitors trading for indications of possible manipulation.

As part of the requirements of the 1974 law, the CFTC was formally reviewed and reauthorized in 1978 and again in 1982, when several changes were instituted into law. The CFTC's registration requirements for individuals were expanded, and authority was granted for a test program in agricultural options, which until that time had been banned. The 1982 amendment also confirmed the Johnson-Shad agreement, discussed in Chapter 2, which helped establish the lines of regulatory authority over options and options on futures.

In 1986 Congress passed the Futures Trading Act, which reauthorized the CFTC for three more years. The act extended the agency's powers to include regulation of any futures transaction, whether conducted on or off an exchange.

More information on the CFTC can be obtained at its excellent website: http://www.cftc.gov.

Over the years, the states have been restricted from regulating futures trading. That too changed in 1982, when the states were given some limited regulatory authority. Also, individuals were allowed to pursue private lawsuits against brokers and firms involved in futures trading. The most significant regulatory development of that year, however, was the establishment of the National Futures Association.

The National Futures Association

The National Futures Association (NFA) is an organization of individuals and firms that participate in the U.S. futures industry. The NFA is an industry self-regulatory agency. The 1974 law had encouraged the development of such an organization, and in 1982 the NFA was formally chartered.

All FCMs, CPOs, IBs, APs, and CTAs are required to join the NFA, and no NFA member may accept a transaction from anyone other than an NFA member. Floor traders, floor brokers, and exchanges are not required to join; they are regulated solely by the CFTC.

The NFA's objective is to prevent fraud and manipulation, protect the public interest, and encourage free markets. The NFA requires registration of its members, who must meet strict requirements and pass an examination. Like the CFTC, the NFA is authorized to monitor trading and identify rule violations as well as impose disciplinary action. Thus, it relieves the CFTC of some of this responsibility and turns the regulatory authority over to the market participants themselves.

The NFA has established a system of arbitrating disputes between individuals and registered futures markets participants. The system is designed so that individuals can obtain faster, more efficient claim settlements than would be possible with the CFTC or through the legal system.

The NFA's website is http://www.nfa.futures.org.

It would be remiss to suggest that futures market regulation is restricted to governmental agencies and self-regulatory organizations, such as the NFA. Because banks are heavy users of futures, banking regulators, such as the Federal Reserve and the Office of the Comptroller of the Currency in the United States, monitor futures activities of commercial banks. For public companies using futures, the SEC has some indirect regulatory authority by virtue of its responsibility for the laws requiring public disclosure of financial statements. The accounting profession, through its Financial Accounting Standards Board, also indirectly regulates the futures markets with its disclosure requirements. Finally, and most importantly, the industry polices itself through its futures exchanges and trade associations.

Regulation of Futures Markets Worldwide

The regulatory structure of the futures markets in most countries is similar to that of the United States. Nonetheless, it is more common in other countries for a single regulator to be responsible for futures and options markets and sometimes stock and bond markets. For example, in the United Kingdom, the Financial Services Authority is responsible for the entire investment industry, which includes the futures and options markets.

The Regulation of Futures Markets versus the Over-the-Counter Markets

The over-the-counter markets for forward contracts, swaps, and options are not regulated directly. Most of the institutions are subject to the types of regulations noted above. Currently, the CFTC feels that it should not regulate over-the-counter products, though this position can change depending on who is in charge of the CFTC and on attitudes in Congress. As such, the over-the-counter market is considerably less regulated than the futures market. This has led futures exchanges to complain of an inequity that hinders their ability to offer new and innovative products. In the 1990s, the CFTC relaxed many of its restrictions to help the futures exchanges compete with the over-the-counter market. In late 1999, the CFTC's new commissioner, William Rainer, called for further deregulation that, with regard to products that compete directly with over-the-counter products, would position the CFTC to provide oversight more than direct regulation.

Summary

This chapter provided the descriptive material necessary for understanding how the forward and futures markets operate. We learned what a futures contract is, which contracts trade in U.S. markets, the characteristics of the markets and traders, the role of the exchange, and the mechanics of trading. We also examined the nature of transaction costs and the structure of regulation. We learned what forward contracts are and how they differ from futures contracts.

The next three chapters deal with specific aspects of futures and forward trading. Chapter 9 explains the concepts of pricing futures contracts. Chapter 10 examines hedging strategies and provides illustrations of hedge transactions. Chapter 11 looks at some advanced strategies, including arbitrage, speculation, and spread transactions.

Key Terms

Before continuing to Chapter 9, you should be able to give brief definitions of the following terms.

- forward contract/forward commitment
- futures contract
- financial futures
- interbank market
- futures exchange
- limit move/limit up/limit down
- circuit breaker
- futures commission merchant (FCM)

- local
- dual trading
- hedger
- speculator
- spreader
- arbitrageur
- scalper
- day trader
- position trader
- commodity trading advisor (CTA)

- commodity pool operator (CPO)
- associated person (AP)
- seat
- open outcry
- long
- short
- initial margin
- maintenance margin
- performance bond
- settlement price
- daily settlement/marking to market
- variation margin
- open interest
- position day
- notice of intention day
- delivery day
- offsetting
- exchange for physicals (EFP)/against accruals/versus cash
- managed funds
- futures fund/commodity fund
- commodity pool
- tick
- reportable positions
- position limits

Further Reading

Two articles on the existence and role of futures markets are:

Telser, L. G. "Why There Are Organized Futures Markets." *Journal of Law and Economics* 24(1981): 1–22.

Telser, L. G., and H. N. Higinbotham. "Organized Futures Markets: Costs and Benefits." *Journal of Political Economy* 85(1977): 969–1000.

Studies of the performance and profitability of futures trading are:

Hartzmark, M. L. "Returns to Individual Traders of Futures: Aggregate Results." *Journal of Political Economy* 95 (1987): 1292–1306.

Hartzmark, M. L. "Luck versus Forecasting Ability: Determinants of Trader Performance in Futures Markets." *Journal of Business* 64 (1991): 49–74.

Hieroynmous, T. A. *The Economics of Futures Trading.* New York: Commodity Research Bureau, 1977.

Kuserk, G. J., and P. R. Locke. "Scalper Behavior in Futures Markets: An Empirical Examination." *The Journal of Futures Markets* 13 (June 1993): 409–431.

Silber, W. L. "Marketmaker Behavior in an Auction Market: An Analysis of Scalpers in Futures Markets." *The Journal of Finance* 39 (September 1984): 937–953.

Studies of trading on futures exchanges include:

Kuserk, G. J., and P. R. Locke. "Market Maker Competition on Futures Exchanges." *The Journal of Derivatives* 1 (summer 1994): 56–66.

Kuserk, G. J., and P. R. Locke. "Market Making with Price Limits." *The Journal of Futures Markets* 16 (September 1996): 677–696.

Manaster, S., and S. C. Mann. "Life in the Pits: Competitive Market Making and Inventory Control." *Review of Financial Studies* 9 (fall 1996): 953–975.

Pirrong, C. "Market Liquidity and Depth on Computerized and Open Outcry Trading Systems." *The Journal of Futures Markets* 16 (August 1996): 519–543.

Questions and Problems

1. Explain the difference between a forward contract and an option.

2. What factors distinguish a forward contract from a futures contract? What do forward and futures contracts have in common? What advantages does each have over the other?

3. Identify the most actively traded contract from each of the following groups of futures contracts: (a) financial futures, (b) nonagricultural commodity futures, and (c) agricultural commodity futures.

4. The open interest in a futures contract changes from day to day. Suppose investors holding long positions are divided into two groups: A is an individual investor and OL represents other investors. Investors holding short positions are denoted as S. Currently A holds 1,000 contracts and OL holds 4,200; thus, S is short 5,200 contracts. Determine the holdings of A, OL, and S after each of the following transactions.

    a. A sells 500 contracts, OL buys 500 contracts.

    b. A buys 700 contracts, OL sells 700 contracts.

    c. A buys 200 contracts, S sells 200 contracts.

    d. A sells 800 contracts, S buys 800 contracts.

    What determines whether volume increases or decreases open interest?

5. List and briefly explain the important contributions provided by futures exchanges.

6. How do locals differ from commission brokers? How do the latter differ from futures commission merchants?

7. Explain the basic differences between open-outcry and electronic trading systems.

8. What factors would determine whether a particular strategy is a hedge or a speculative strategy?

9. How are spread and arbitrage strategies forms of speculation? How can they be interpreted as hedges?

10. What are the differences among scalpers, day traders, and position traders?

11. What are the various ways in which an individual may obtain the right to go on to the floor of an exchange and trade futures?

12. What are daily price limits, and why are they used?

13. What are circuit breakers? What are their advantages and disadvantages?

14. Explain how the clearinghouse operates to protect the futures market.

15. Explain the differences among the three means of terminating a futures contract: an offsetting trade, cash settlement, and delivery. How is a forward contract terminated?

16. Suppose you buy a stock index futures contract at the opening price of 452.25 on July 1. The multiplier on the contract is 500, so the price is $500 (452.25) = $226,125. You hold the position open until selling it on July 16 at the opening price of 435.50. The initial margin requirement is $9,000, and the maintenance margin requirement is $6,000. Assume you deposit the initial margin and do not withdraw the excess on any given day. Construct a table showing the charges and credits to the margin account. The daily prices on the intervening days are as follows:

Day	Settlement Price
7/1	453.95
7/2	454.50
7/3	452.00
7/7	443.55
7/8	441.65
7/9	442.85
7/10	444.15
7/11	442.25
7/14	438.30
7/15	435.05
7/16	435.50

17. The crude oil futures contract on the New York Mercantile Exchange covers 1,000 barrels of crude oil. The contract is quoted in dollars and cents per barrel, e.g., $27.42, and the minimum price change is $0.01. The initial margin requirement is $3,375 and the maintenance margin requirement is $2,500. Suppose you bought a contract at $27.42, putting up the initial margin. At what price would you get a margin call?

18. Explain the difference between hedge funds and futures funds.

19. Explain in general terms the responsibility of the CFTC.

20. What role does the National Futures Association play in regulating the futures industry?

Selected Financial Futures Contract Specifications

Contract	Exchange	Trading Hours	Delivery Months	Contract Size	Minimum Price Change	Daily Price Limits	Last Trading Day	First Delivery Day	Margin
U.S. Treasury bonds	CBOT	7:20–2:00	M,J,S,D	$100,000	1/32 = $31.25	96/32 = $3,000	Business day prior to last seven business days	First business day of month	$ 2,498 (1) $ 1,850 (M)
U.S. Treasury notes (5-year)	CBOT	7:20–2:00	M,J,S,D	$100,000	1/32 = $31.25	96/32 = $3,000	Business day prior to last seven business days	First business day of month	$ 1,013 (1) $ 750 (M)
U.S. Treasury notes (6 1/2–10-year)	CBOT	7:20–2:00	M,J,S,D	$100,000	1/32 = $31.25	96/32 = $3,000	Business day prior to last seven business days	First business day of month	$ 1,620 (1) $ 1,200 (M)
Eurodollars (90-day)	CME	7:20–2:00	M,J,S,D plus next two months	$1,000,000	.005 = $12.50	None	2nd London business day before 3rd Wednesday	Cash settled on last trading day	$ 675 (1) $ 500 (M)
U.S. Treasury bills	CME	7:20–2:00	M,J,S,D	$1,000,000	.005 = $12.50	None	Business day prior to issue date	First business day of month	$ 203 (1) $ 150 (M)
S&P 500 Index	CME	8:30–3:15	M,J,S,D	$250 × Index	0.1 = $25	Varies (contract exchange)	Thursday prior to third Friday	Cash settled on Friday after last trade date	$23,438 (1) $18,750 (M)

Notes: All times are local. All trading days are Monday through Friday. Additional trading hours are available on the CBOT's electronic trading system Project A, and the CME's GLOBEX2. Margins shown are initial (1) and maintenance (M). These are for speculators. Hedge and spread margins are usually lower. This material is believed to be current as of April 2000. Contract specifications sometimes change and margins and price limits often change. Investors should consult the exchanges for the latest information. Currency contract specifications are provided in Appendix 13.

SOURCE: The exchanges

APPENDIX 8B

Taxation of Futures Transactions

Investors and traders' profits from futures contracts, as well as index options, are considered to be 60 percent capital gains and 40 percent ordinary income. Capital gains are taxed at the ordinary income rate, but subject to a maximum of 20 percent. Thus, an investor in the 31 percent tax bracket would have futures profits taxed at a blended rate of .6(.20) + .4(.31) = .244.

In addition, all futures and index options profits are subject to a mark-to-market rule in which accumulated profits are taxable in the current year even if the contract has not been closed out. For example, assume you bought a futures contract on October 15 at a price of $1,000. Your account was, of course, marked to market daily. At the end of the year, the accumulated profit in the account was $400, meaning that the futures price at the end of the year was $1,400. Then you would have to pay the tax that year on $400 even though you had not closed out the contract. In other words, realized and unrealized profits are taxed and losses are recognized.

These rules apply only to speculative transactions. Taxation of hedge transactions is more complex and will be examined in Chapter 10.

Consider the following example. Suppose an investor in the 31 percent tax bracket purchases a futures contract at $1,000 on October 15 and ultimately sells it at $1,300 on January 20 of the next year. Assume the contract price was $1,400 at the end of the year. The first year the tax liability is on $400, so the tax is $400(.6)(.20) + $400(4)(.31) = $97.60, an effective rate of 24.4 percent. In the second year, there is a taxable loss of $1,400 − $1,300 = $100. This can be used to offset taxable gains; thus, it will save the trader .244($100) = $24.40 in taxes on profitable futures trades in that year. Losses can be used to offset gains, but not more than the total amount of taxable gains. Any losses not used can be carried back to offset prior trading profits for up to three years.

Suppose the contract expired in February and the investor took delivery of the commodity. Let the price at expiration be $1,500. Then it would be assumed that the commodity was purchased at $1,500. The investor would have paid tax on the $400 profit at the end of the year in which the contract was bought; the investor would owe tax on the $100 profit that accrued between the end of the year and the expiration.

Although recent tax laws have greatly simplified the taxation of futures contracts, many complexities remain. Competent tax advice is necessary to keep up with the many changes and ensure compliance with the various rules.

Questions and Problems

1. On October 1, you purchase one March stock index futures contract at the opening price of 410.30. The contract multiplier is $500, so the price of 410.30 is really $500(410.30) = $205,150. You hold the position open until February 20, whereupon you sell the contract at the opening price of 427.30. The settlement price on December 31 was 422.40. You are in the 31 percent tax bracket. Compute your tax liability.

2. In November you buy a futures contract on a commodity at a price of $10,000. At the end of the year, the futures price is $10,500. You hold your position open until January 20, at which time the commodity price is $11,200, the contract expires, and you take delivery. You are in the 31 percent tax bracket. Compute your tax liability in both years.

Principles of Forward and Futures Pricing

A good part of the pricing is about sticking a wet finger in the air, and hoping you get it right.

ERIC BAKKER
AsiaRisk, February, 1999, p. 22

We are now ready to move directly into the pricing of forward and futures contracts. The very nature of the word *futures* suggests that futures prices concern prices in the future. The word *forward* suggests a looking ahead. In this chapter, we shall see how futures prices, forward prices, spot prices, expectations, and the cost of carry are interrelated. As with options, our objective is to link the price of the futures or forward contract to the price of the underlying instrument and to identify factors that influence the relationship between these prices.

In the early part of this chapter, we shall treat forward and futures contracts as though they were entirely separate instruments. Recall that a forward contract is an agreement between two parties to exchange an asset for a fixed price at a future date. No money changes hands, and the agreement is binding. In order to reverse the transaction, it is necessary to find someone willing to take the opposite side of a new, offsetting forward contract calling for delivery of the asset at the same time as the original contract. A forward contract is created in the over-the-counter market and is subject to default risk. A futures contract is also an agreement between two parties to exchange an asset for a fixed price at a future date. The agreement is made on a futures exchange, however, and is regulated by that exchange. The contract requires that the parties make margin deposits, and their accounts are marked to market every day. The contracts are standardized and can be bought and sold during regular trading hours. These differences between forward and futures contracts, particularly the marking to market, create some differences in their prices and values. As we shall see later, these differences may prove quite minor; for now, we shall proceed as though forward and futures contracts were entirely different instruments.

Some Properties of Forward and Futures Prices

The Concept of Price versus Value

In Chapter 1, we discussed how an efficient market means that the price of an asset equals its true economic value. The holder of an asset has money tied up in the asset. If the holder is willing to retain the asset, the asset must have a value at least equal to its price. If the asset's value were less than its price, the owner would sell it. The value is the present value of the future cash flows, with the discount rate reflecting the opportunity cost of money and a premium for the risk assumed.

Although this line of reasoning is sound in securities markets, it can get one into trouble in forward and futures markets. A forward or futures contract is not an asset. You can buy a futures contract, but do you actually pay for it? A futures contract requires a small margin deposit, but is this really the price? You can buy 100 shares of a $20 stock by placing $1,000 in a margin account and borrowing $1,000 from a broker. Does that make the stock worth $10 per share? Certainly not. The stock is worth $20 per share: You have $10 per share invested and $10 per share borrowed.

The margin requirement on a futures contract is not really a margin in the same sense as the margin on a stock. You might deposit 3 percent to 5 percent of the price of the futures contract in a margin account, but you do not borrow the remainder. The margin is only a type of security deposit. Thus, the buyer of a futures contract does not actually "pay" for it, and, of course, the seller really receives no money for it. As long as the price does not change, neither party can execute an offsetting trade that would generate a profit.

As noted previously, a forward contract may or may not require a margin deposit or some type of credit enhancement, but if it does, the principle is still the same: The forward price is not the margin.

The value of a futures contract when written is zero.

When dealing with futures contracts, we must be careful to distinguish between **price** and **value.** The futures price is an observable number. The value is less obvious. The contract's initial value, however, is zero. This is because neither party pays anything and neither party receives anything of monetary value. That does not imply, however, that neither party will pay or receive money at a later date. This point is equally applicable to forward contracts. The values of futures and forward contracts during their lives, however, are not necessarily equal either to each other or to zero.

The Value of a Forward Contract

We let $V_t(0,T)$ and $v_t(T)$ represent the values of forward and futures contracts at time t that were created at time 0 and expire at time T. Similarly, $F(0,T)$ and $f_t(T)$ are the prices at time t of forward and futures contracts created at time 0 that expire at time T. Since a forward price is fixed at a given time, conditional on the expiration date, it does not change and, therefore, does not require a time subscript. Also, since a futures price does change, it does not matter when the contract was established. Given our statement above that the value of each contract is zero when established, we can initially say that $V_0(0,T) = 0$ and $v_0(T) = 0$.

The value of a forward contract when written is zero.

THE FORWARD PRICE AT EXPIRATION   The first and most important principle is that the price of a forward contract that is created at expiration must be the spot price. Such a contract will call for delivery, an instant later, of the asset. Thus, the contract is equivalent to a spot transaction, and its price must, therefore, equal the spot price. Thus, we can say

$$F(T,T) = S_T.$$

The price of a forward contract that expires immediately is the spot price.

If this statement were not true, it would be possible to make an immediate arbitrage profit by either buying the asset and selling an expiring forward contract or selling the asset and buying an expiring forward contract.

THE VALUE OF A FORWARD CONTRACT AT EXPIRATION   At expiration, the value of a forward contract is easily found. Ignoring delivery costs, the value of a forward contract at expiration, $V_T(0,T)$, is the profit on the forward contract. The profit is the spot price minus the original forward price. Thus,

$$V_T(0,T) = S_T - F(0,T).$$

When you enter into a long forward contract with a price of $F(0,T)$, you agree to buy the asset at T, paying the price $F(0,T)$. Thus, your profit will be $S_T - F(0,T)$. This is the value of owning the forward contract. At the time the contract was written, the contract had zero value. At expiration, however, anyone owning a contract permitting him or her to buy an asset worth S_T by paying a price $F(0,T)$ has a guaranteed profit of $S_T - F(0,T)$. Thus, the contract has a value of $S_T - F(0,T)$. Of course, this value can be either positive or negative. The value to the holder of the short position is simply minus one times the value to the holder of the long position.

The value of a forward contract at expiration is the spot price minus the original forward price.

THE VALUE OF A FORWARD CONTRACT PRIOR TO EXPIRATION   To explain how a forward contract can have value during its life but prior to expiration, let us introduce $F(t,T)$ as the price of a new forward contract written at time t (prior to expiration) calling for delivery of the same underlying asset at T. Note that we have two distinct forward contracts on the same asset, one written today that we shall call the "old" contract, and a new one written at t that we shall call the "new" contract. We wish to determine what the value of the old contract will be at t, which is during its life. When we find its value, we will know what it would be worth to an investor to own it.

Before we begin, however, let us take note of why it is important to place a value on the forward contract. If a firm enters into a forward contract, it does not initially appear on the balance sheet. Although it may appear in a footnote, the contract is not an asset or liability. During the life of the forward contract, however, value may be created or destroyed as a result of changing market conditions. For example, we already saw that the forward contract has a value at expiration of $S_T - F(0,T)$, which may be positive or negative. To give a fair assessment of the assets and liabilities of the company, it would be important to determine the value of the contract before expiration. If that value is positive, the contract can be properly viewed and recorded as an asset; if it is negative, the contract should be viewed and recorded as a liability. Investors should be informed about the values of forward contracts and, indeed, all derivatives so that they can make informed decisions about the impact of derivative transactions on the overall value of the firm.

Table 9.1 illustrates how we determine the value. Today we simply enter into a long forward contract. At t we enter into a new short forward contract. At expiration we shall end up buying the asset using the old long forward contract and delivering the asset using the new short forward contract, thus guaranteeing a cash flow of $F(t,T) - F(0,T)$ at expiration. This amount is known at t so its present value can be found by discounting it at the risk-free rate over the period $T - t$. This present value should equal the value of the position at t. At t, the value of the position consists solely of the value of the old long forward contract because the value of the new short forward contract is zero. Thus, the value of the old long forward contract at t is the present value of the difference between the new forward contract price and the old forward contract price:

The value of a forward contract prior to expiration is the present value of the difference between the prices of a newly written forward contract calling for delivery of the same asset at the same expiration and the original forward contract.

$$V_t(0,T) = (F(t,T) - F(0,T))(1 + r)^{-(T-t)}.$$

You should note that this value can be negative.

A NUMERICAL EXAMPLE   Suppose you buy a forward contract today at a price of $100. The contract expires in 45 days. The risk-free rate is 10 percent. The forward contract is an agreement to buy the asset at a price of $100 in 45 days. Now, 20 days later, new forward contracts expiring at the same time — in 25 days — are being written at a price of $104. The value of your forward contract is

$$(104 - 100)(1.10)^{-25/365} = 3.974.$$

TABLE 9.1	**Valuing a Forward Contract Prior to Expiration**

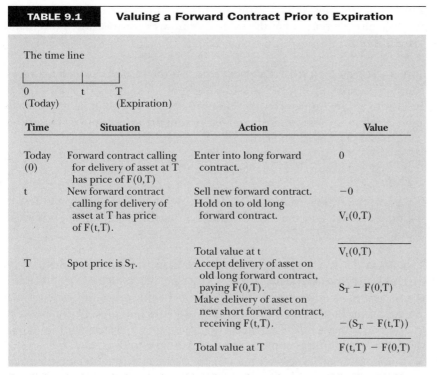

The time line

```
|_____|_____|
0               t        T
(Today)              (Expiration)
```

Time	Situation	Action	Value
Today (0)	Forward contract calling for delivery of asset at T has price of $F(0,T)$	Enter into long forward contract.	0
t	New forward contract calling for delivery of asset at T has price of $F(t,T)$.	Sell new forward contract. Hold on to old long forward contract.	-0 $V_t(0,T)$
		Total value at t	$V_t(0,T)$
T	Spot price is S_T.	Accept delivery of asset on old long forward contract, paying $F(0,T)$. Make delivery of asset on new short forward contract, receiving $F(t,T)$.	$S_T - F(0,T)$ $-(S_T - F(t,T))$
		Total value at T	$F(t,T) - F(0,T)$

Conclusion: At time t, the investor's position (long a forward contract, obligating purchase of the asset at T at a price $F(0,T)$ and short a forward contract, obligating delivery of the asset at T for a price $F(t,T)$ guarantees a value of $F(t,T) - F(0,T)$ at the expiration. Thus, the value of the investor's position at t ($V_t(0,T)$ is the present value of $F(t,T) - F(0,T)$. Since $F(t,T) - F(0,T)$ is a known amount at t, the risk-free rate can be used to find the present value. Thus,

$$V_t(0,T) = (F(t,T) - F(0,T))(1 + r)^{-(T-t)}.$$

Because the value of the new forward contract at t is zero, the value of the position at t consists solely of the value of the old forward contract. Thus, the value of the old forward contract at t is given by the above formula.

Why is your contract worth $3.974? You cannot liquidate the contract, but you can sell a new forward contract at the new price of $104. When both contracts expire in 25 days, you will buy the asset at $100 using your first contract and sell it at $104 using your second contract. Your total payoff will be $4. At 25 days before expiration, you know you will receive $4 at expiration. The present value of $4 at the risk-free rate is $3.974. To the seller, the first forward contract has a value at t of $-$3.974.

The Value of a Futures Contract

In this section, we shall look at the valuation of futures contracts. As noted previously, we shall use $f_t(T)$ for the futures price and $v_t(T)$ for the value of a futures. Let us recall that a futures contract is marked to market each day. We have already noted that the value of a futures contract when originally written is zero.

THE FUTURES PRICE AT EXPIRATION   At the instant at which a futures contract is expiring, its price must be the spot price. In other words, if you enter into a long futures contract that will expire an instant later, you have agreed to buy the asset an instant later, paying the futures price. This is the same as a spot transaction. Thus,

$$f_T(T) = S_T.$$

If this statement were not true, buying the spot and selling the futures or selling the spot and buying the futures would generate an arbitrage profit.

THE VALUE OF A FUTURES CONTRACT DURING THE TRADING DAY BUT BEFORE BEING MARKED TO MARKET   When we looked at forward contracts, the second result we obtained was the value of a forward contract at expiration. In the case of futures contracts, it is more useful to look next at how one values a futures contract before it is marked to market. In other words, what is a futures contract worth during the trading day?

Suppose we arbitrarily let the time period between settlements be one day. Suppose you purchase a futures contract at $t - 1$, when the futures price is $f_{t-1}(T)$. Let us assume that this is the opening price of the day and that it equals the settlement price the previous day. Now let us say we are at the end of the day, but the market is not yet closed. The price is $f_t(T)$. What is the value of the contract? If you sell the contract, it generates a gain of $f_t(T) - f_{t-1}(T)$. Thus, we can say that the value of the futures contract is

$$v_t(T) = f_t(T) - f_{t-1}(T) \text{ before the contract is marked to market.}$$

The value of the futures contract is simply the price change since the time the contract was opened or, if it was opened on a previous day, the last price change since marking to market. Note, of course, that the value could be negative. If we were considering the value of the futures to the holder of the short position, we would simply change the sign.

THE VALUE OF A FUTURES CONTRACT IMMEDIATELY AFTER BEING MARKED TO MARKET   When a futures contract is marked to market, the price change since the last marking to market or, if the contract was opened during the day, the price change since it was opened is distributed to the party in whose favor the price moved and charged to the party to whom the price moved against. This, of course, is the mark-to-market pro-

The price of a futures contract that expires immediately is the spot price.

The value of a futures contract during a trading day but before it is marked to market is the amount by which the price changed since the contract was opened or last marked to market, whichever comes later.

As soon as a futures contract is marked to market, its value goes back to zero.

cedure. As soon as the contract is marked to market, the value of the contract goes back to zero. Thus,

$$v_t(T) = 0 \text{ as soon as the contract is marked to market.}$$

If the futures price was still at the last settlement price and the futures trader then tried to sell the contract to capture its value, it would generate no profit, which is consistent with its zero value.

Thus, to summarize these two results, we find that the value of a long futures contract at any point in time is the profit that would be generated if the contract were sold. Because of the daily marking to market, the value of a futures contract reverts back to zero as soon as it is marked to market. The value for the holder of a short futures contract is minus one times the value for the holder of the long futures contract. For a long futures contract, value is created by positive price changes; for a short futures contract, value is created by negative price changes.

In this section we have seen how the prices and the values of futures and forward contracts are two entirely different concepts. For most assets we think that price equals value in an efficient market. For forward and futures contracts, no cash is paid out up front so the contracts have zero value when first written. The confusion over price and value could perhaps be avoided if we thought of the forward or futures price as a concept more akin to the exercise price of an option. We know that the exercise price does not equal an option's value. It simply represents the figure that the two parties agreed would be the price paid by the call buyer or received by the put buyer if the option is ultimately exercised. In a similar sense, the futures or forward price is simply the figure that the two parties agreed will be paid by the buyer to the seller at expiration in exchange for the underlying asset. This price is sometimes called the "delivery price." While we could call the forward price or the futures price the "exercise price" of the contract, the use of the terms "forward price" and "futures price" or the "delivery price" is so traditional that it would be unwise not to use them.

Forward versus Futures Prices

At expiration, forward and futures prices equal the spot price. Are they equal at any other time? Do forward and futures contracts accomplish the same result? In this section we shall see. We shall examine two cases: (1) one day prior to expiration (time t) and (2) two days or more prior to expiration.

ONE DAY PRIOR TO EXPIRATION   Table 9.2 illustrates how we examine the difference between forward and futures prices one day prior to expiration. One day prior to expiration at time t, we go long a forward contract and short a futures contract. Such a transaction has zero initial value. At expiration, we end up buying the asset with the forward contract and selling

TABLE 9.2	The Difference between Forward and Futures Prices One Day Prior to Expiration

The time line

```
——————————————— 1 day ———————————————
|                                                        |
t                                            T (expiration)
```

Time	Situation	Action	Value
t	Forward contract calling for delivery of asset at T has price of $F(t,T)$.	Enter into long forward contract.	0
	Futures contract calling for delivery of asset at T has price of $f_t(T)$.	Enter into short futures contract.	-0
		Total value at t	0
T	Spot price is S_T.	Accept delivery of asset on long forward contract, paying $F(t,T)$.	$S_T - F(t,T)_t$
		Make delivery of asset on short futures contract, receiving $f_t(T)$.	$-(S_T - f_t(T))$
		Total value at T	$f_t(T) - F(t,T)$

Conclusion: At time t, the investor's position—long a forward contract, obligating purchase of the asset at T at a price $F(t,T)$, and short a futures contract, obligating delivery of the asset at T for a price $f_t(T)$—guarantees a value of $f_t(T) - F(t,T)_t$ at the expiration. Thus, the value of the investor's position at t, which is zero, must equal the present value of $f_t(T) - F(t,T)$. The only way this can hold is that

$$f_t(T) = F(t,T).$$

So the futures price must equal the forward price when there is one day remaining.

it with the futures contract. Since we put up no money and this transaction is risk-free, the forward price would have to equal the futures price or we would make a guaranteed profit at no cost.[1] Thus,

$$f_t(T) = F(t,T) \text{ where t is one day prior to expiration.}$$

An important assumption here is that there is no default risk. We can reasonably assume this holds on the futures contract. Forward contracts are clearly subject to some default risk. With one day remaining, however, the default risk should be fairly small.

Now let us back up one day.

Provided that there is no default risk, forward and futures prices are equal one day prior to expiration.

---

[1] If the forward price were larger than the futures price, we would initially do the opposite transaction—go short the forward contract and long the futures contract. If the futures price were higher, we would initially do the transaction as indicated in Table 9.2.

TABLE 9.3	The Difference between Forward and Futures Prices Two Days Prior to Expiration

The time line

$$\text{—— 1 day ——} \quad \text{—— 1 day ——}$$

```
|_____|_____|
t−1              t              T (expiration)
```

Time	Situation	Action	Value
t−1	Forward contract calling for delivery of asset at T has price of $F(t-1, T)$.	Enter into long forward contract.	0
	Futures contract calling for delivery of asset at T has price of $f_{t-1}(T)$.	Enter into $(1 + r)^{-1/365}$ short futures contracts.	−0
		Total value at t−1	$\overline{0}$
t	The futures price is $f_t(T)$.	Buy back the $(1 + r)^{-1/365}$ futures contracts.	0
	The futures position is marked to market for a cash flow of $-(1 + r)^{-1/365} (f_t (T) - f_{t-1} (T))$	Invest the mark-to-market profit of $-(1 + r)^{-1/365} (f_t (T) - f_{t-1} (T))$ in risk-free bonds. (If this amount is negative, borrow it at the risk-free rate.)	$-(1 + r)^{-1/365}(f_t(T) - f_{t-1}(T))$
		Sell one new futures contract.	−0
		Total value at t	$\overline{-(1 + r)^{-1/365} (f_t(T) - f_{t-1}(T))}$
T	Spot price is S_T. Futures price, $f_T(T)$, converges to spot price, S_T. Bonds (or loan) matures for a value of $-(1 + r)^{-1/365} (f_t(T) - f_{t-1}(T))$ $(1 + r)^{1/365} = -(f_t(T) - f_{t-1}(T))$.	Accept delivery of asset on long forward contract, paying $F(t-1,T)$.	$S_T - F(t-1,T)$
		Make delivery of asset on short futures contract, receiving $f_t(T)$	$-(S_T - f_t(T))$
		Redeem bonds (or pay off loan).	$-(f_t(T) - f_{t-1}(T))$
		Total value at T	$\overline{f_{t-1}(T) - F(t-1,T)}$

Conclusion: The investor's position today (long a forward contract, obligating purchase of the asset at T at a price $F(t-1,T)$, and short $(1 + r)^{-1/365}$ futures contracts, obligating delivery of the asset at T for a price $f_{t-1}(T)$ guarantees a value of $f_{t-1}(T) - F(t-1,T)$ at expiration. Thus, the value of the investor's position today, which is zero, must equal the present value of $f_{t-1}(T) - F(t-1,T)$. The only way this can happen is if

$$f_{t-1}(T) = F(t-1,T).$$

So the futures price must equal the forward price when there are two days remaining.

TWO DAYS OR MORE PRIOR TO EXPIRATION   In stepping back to day t−1, we must make an important assumption: The interest rate on both days is r; that is, r does not change.[2] The futures price is $f_{t-1}(T)$ and the forward price is $F(t-1,T)$. Table 9.3 demonstrates that we should construct a portfolio consisting of a long forward contract and $(1 + r)^{-1/365}$ short

[2]Technically, the interest rate can change as long as we know what it will change to.

futures contracts. The reason we use such a seemingly strange number of futures contracts $(1 + r)^{-1/365}$) is to adjust for the marking to market that will occur once before expiration. If there were three days before expiration, we would use 2/365 in the exponent.

One day later, at t, the futures account is marked to market. If there is a profit we take the cash and reinvest it for one day at the risk-free rate, r. If there is a loss, we replace the funds in the margin account by borrowing the necessary amount for one day at the risk-free rate, r. We close out the $(1 + r)^{-1/365}$ futures contracts by buying them back and sell one new futures contract.[3]

One day later at T, both contracts expire. We accept delivery on the forward contract and make delivery on the futures contract. If we had reinvested a mark-to-market profit or borrowed to cover a mark-to-market loss at t, it would now be worth $-(f_t(T) - f_{t-1}(T)$. The overall cash flow at expiration is $f_{t-1}(T) - F(t-1,T)$, the difference in the original futures and forward prices. Since this transaction never required that we pay out or receive any funds, $f_{t-1}(T) - F(t-1,T)$ must be zero. Otherwise, we could generate an arbitrage profit by doing the transaction or doing the opposite if necessary. This argument can be repeatedly applied so as to show that forward and futures prices are equivalent at any time prior to expiration. Thus, in general,

$$f_{t-1}(T) = F(t-1,T).$$

If interest rates are known and constant and there is no default risk, forward prices will equal futures prices at any time prior to expiration.

where t is more than one day prior to expiration. It is important, however, to remember two key assumptions. We already mentioned the assumption that there is no default risk. If the contracts have many days remaining, the assumption of no default risk is less plausible. As we have noted many times, forward contracts are clearly subject to default risk that can be quite large if traders of somewhat lower quality engage in such contracts. Another key assumption is that interest rates are constant or at least known in advance. We shall cover this point one section later. But first let us take a look at an example.

A NUMERICAL EXAMPLE   Consider a September S&P 500 futures contract. On September 18, two days prior to expiration, the contract was priced at 1,332.15. There are no forward markets for the S&P 500, but assume one can buy a forward contract at 1,330. Thus, the futures price exceeds the forward price by 2.15. The interest rate is 6 percent and will not

---

[3]This procedure of closing out contracts and buying a new one can be done by buying back the $(1 + r)^{-1/365}$ contracts an instant before the close of the day and then selling one new contract or by selling $1 - (1 + r)^{-1/365}$ additional contracts at the close.

change for two days. An arbitrageur would observe that the futures price is too high and/or the forward price is too low. Suppose the arbitrageur has sufficient capital to undertake a forward contract of 10,000 units of the index. Thus, the arbitrageur will attempt to capture a risk-free profit of 10,000($2.15) = $21,500 by selling futures contracts and buying forward contracts. The number of futures contracts is $10,000 \times (1.06)^{-1/365}$ = 9,998, and the number of forward contracts is 10,000.

The next day, the futures price is 1,333.25. The arbitrageur has incurred a loss on the futures contracts of 9,998(1,333.25 − 1,332.15) = 10,998. The loss must be made up, so the arbitrageur borrows $10,998 for one day at 6 percent. The futures contracts are closed out, and a new position of 10,000 short futures is opened.

At expiration, the loan is due and the arbitrageur owes $10,998(1.06)^{1/365}$ = 11,000. Let the S&P spot index be 1,334 on the expiration day. To keep things simple we will assume the S&P forward contract is cash settled, so the arbitrageur settles the forward contract by receiving a payment equal to the spot price at expiration minus the original forward price times the number of units, or 10,000(1,334 − 1,330) = 40,000. The futures is settled in cash, so the arbitrageur makes a payment of 10,000(1,334 − 1,333.25) = 7,500. Thus, the net cash flow to the arbitrageur on the expiration day is −11,000 + 40,000 − 7,500 = 21,500. This is the original amount the arbitrageur set out to capture with this riskless hedge. The combined effects of numerous arbitrageurs buying forward contracts and selling futures contracts will drive the forward and the futures prices together.

WHY FORWARD AND FUTURES PRICES MAY NOT BE EQUAL   Under the assumptions of known or constant interest rates and no default risk, we see that forward and futures prices should be equal. Let us now consider what happens when we relax the interest rate assumption. Note that we sold $(1 + r)^{-1/365}$ futures contracts for every forward contract. If $f_t(T) >$ $f_{t-1}(T)$, we covered the loss by borrowing additional funds. The amount of interest paid on the loan was completely offset by the fact that we had only $(1 + r)^{-1/365}$ contracts for every forward contract. We borrowed $(1 + r)^{-1/365} (f_t(T) - f_{t-1}(T))$ times the number of units covered in the forward contract and the next day paid back $(1 + r)^{-1/365} (f_t(T) - f_{t-1}(T))(1 + r)^{1/365} = (f_t(T) - f_{t-1}(T))$ times the number of units covered in the forward contract. If $f_t(T) < f_{t-1}(T)$, the interest earned on the reinvested profit was offset by having only $(1 + r)^{-1/365}$ futures contracts for every unit covered in the forward contract.

When short-term interest rates are known in advance, forward prices will equal futures prices. When short-term interest rates are uncertain, arbitrageurs will not know how many futures contracts to trade to ensure a risk-free profit. Then futures and forward prices may differ. With a little intuition, we can see which would be greater.

Suppose the futures price increases over the contract's life. Then holders of long futures contracts will receive positive cash flows from marking to

Derivatives in Action

A Hill of Beans

The relationship between the futures price and the spot price is based on the idea that at expiration, a futures contract can be settled by delivering the underlying asset. The futures price converges to the spot price, and holders of long positions will be forced to accept delivery made by holders of short positions. If the market works properly, prices will behave normally and holders of the short contracts should have no difficulty buying up a sufficient quantity of the asset to deliver. We should not expect sharp price changes at expiration. Nearly all of the time this is precisely what happens. But on rare occasions, some investors attempt to buy up the deliverable supply of the asset, while simultaneously holding a large number of long futures positions. Then as the contract approaches expiration, the holders of the short positions are forced to buy the asset from this person or firm, who exacts an inflated price. This is called a "short squeeze." It can have severe impacts on holders of short positions, which often includes farmers and processors. In July 1989, just such an occurrence happened at the Chicago Board of Trade. Ferruzzi Finanziaria S.p.A. is an Italian conglomerate with annual sales of about $30 billion and international activities in the financial and commodities markets. Its efforts to control the delivery of soybeans on the July futures sent the Chicago Board of Trade and the Commodity Futures Trading Commission on a controversial course of actions.

First let us take a look at how exchanges attempt to prevent such actions. As we noted in Chapter 8, there are position limits, which represent the maximum number of contracts that can be held by one trader. However, businesses that deal in the underlying commodity often require exceptions to these limits in order to hedge a large quantity of the underlying commodity. The limit for speculators in soybean futures, called the speculative limit, is 3 million bushels. Businesses that can demonstrate a genuine hedging need routinely apply for and are granted exceptions to the limit.

In 1988 a severe drought damaged much of the corn and soybean crops. Supplies of soybeans that could be carried over to meet delivery requirements in 1989 were quite low. In the spring of 1989, the CBOT and CFTC noticed that Ferruzzi was accumulating an unusually large number of contracts in the May futures which, it contended, had been authorized by the CFTC on the basis of Ferruzzi's expressed need for large supplies of soybeans for its American subsidiary, Central Soya, a soybean processor. It argued that it was simply hedging the purchase of these soybeans. With one day remaining before the May contract expired, the CFTC revoked Ferruzzi's position limit exemption and or-

Ignoring default risk, futures prices will exceed forward prices when futures prices and interest rates move together. Forward prices will exceed futures prices when futures prices and interest rates move opposite.

market. If, during the same time, interest rates increase, the daily reinvestment of the profits will earn more interest. If futures prices decrease, the holder of a long position will incur losses. If those losses occur during a period of falling interest rates, they can be covered by borrowing at increasingly lower rates. Thus, if interest rates and futures prices move together, futures contracts will offer an advantage over forward contracts and will be priced higher.

If futures prices and interest rates move in opposite directions, profits from rising futures prices will be reinvested in a falling interest rate environment. Losses from falling futures prices will be covered by borrowing in a rising interest rate environment. This will create a preference for forward contracts and will cause forward prices to exceed futures prices. Table 9.4 summarizes these points.

dered it to immediately liquidate all contracts in excess of the speculative limit of 3 million bushels. Ferruzzi sold the May futures but immediately purchased the July futures, setting the stage for a showdown in mid-summer.

Ferruzzi was also accumulating supplies of soybeans. By early July, Ferruzzi owned 85 percent of the deliverable supply of soybeans and 53 percent of the outstanding long futures contracts. As July approached, the CBOT and CFTC began worrying that Ferruzzi was attempting a short squeeze. Ferruzzi argued that it was simply hedging its anticipated purchase of soybeans. If that were the case, however, Ferruzzi would be bidding competitively in the various spot markets that were located near its processor. Instead it placed bids well below the spot price, clearly indicating that hedging was not its intention. Simple computations showed that Ferruzzi's intent to take delivery would result in it paying far more for the soybeans than it would have to have paid had it done what hedgers typically do. Of course, such calculations assume a competitive market. If Ferruzzi had executed a short squeeze, it could have hiked the price of soybeans and exacted a stiff premium from holders of short positions.

Over a period of about six weeks the CFTC and CBOT, in a series of increasingly stronger statements, advised Ferruzzi to begin liquidating its 22 million bushel position. Ferruzzi made little effort to comply. On July 11, nine days before expiration, the CBOT invoked an emergency provision in its rules and ordered Ferruzzi to liquidate its contracts down to the 3 million speculative limit by July 18 and down to 1 million by July 20. In addition the CBOT ordered all holders of long positions to do likewise. Many traders criticized the CBOT for, in effect, intervening in the free-market process.

What happened? The soybeans held by Ferruzzi as of fall 1989 had not yet been entered into production, suggesting that it never actually needed the beans. In September 1989, its three principal traders resigned. Ferruzzi filed a complaint and a lawsuit against the CBOT, which in turn fined Ferruzzi $2 million plus $1 million in legal costs and demanded that Ferruzzi turn over its membership on the CBOT to its subsidiary, Central Soya. Ferruzzi, while not admitting guilt, paid the fines.

While the potential for extreme price movements was clearly quite real, a study showed that there were practically no price effects from the incident. Attempts to squeeze the shorts are quite rare and fraught with risk. Fortunately, the futures markets have proven to have an effective mechanism for detecting and dealing with such attempts to manipulate the market as the contracts expire.

The effect of default risk on futures and forward prices is a controversial subject that is currently being studied by many academics, practitioners, and regulators. It is difficult to determine which would be higher—the futures or forward price—in the presence of default risk. Suppose the two parties to a contract consist of a risk-free party and a party who might default. The risk-free party wants to go long and the risky party wants to go short. If the two parties traded a forward contract, they should be able to negotiate a deal that would permit the higher-risk party to compensate the lower-risk party. This could be done by having them agree to a lower forward price than would be the case if they were both risk-free. Thus, the risk-free counterparty would be committing to paying less for the asset as compensation for the possibility that the risky counterparty might not fulfill his or her end of the deal. If the risk-free party wanted to go short, the forward

| TABLE 9.4 | **Why Futures Prices Can Differ from Forward Prices with More Than One Day Remaining** |

Condition	When	Why
Futures price > Forward price	Futures prices and interest rates move together.	Long futures contracts are preferred over long forward contracts because profits will occur when interest rates are rising and losses will occur when interest rates are falling. Thus, the marking to market of futures contracts benefits the holder of a long futures contract.
Futures price < Forward price	Futures prices and interest rates move opposite.	Long forward contracts are preferred over long futures contracts because profits will occur when interest rates are falling and losses will occur when interest rates are rising. Thus, realizing all gains and losses at the end of the life of the contract benefits the holder of a long forward contract.

Note: The default risks of the two parties can raise or lower forward prices above or below futures prices.

price should be higher. So for an individual contract, it is possible to identify whether there would be a higher or lower forward price, depending on the credit risks of the two parties and the sides of the contract they desire. It is impossible to make any comments about what would happen in the market as a whole since that would depend on the composition of participants in terms of credit quality and their preferences for long or short positions. Thus, it is impossible to say whether forward prices would be higher than futures prices. For the sake of comparison, however, let us assume that the forward price on this transaction is discounted to compensate for the credit risk of the risky counterparty. Now let us compare what would happen with that same contract if it were created on a futures exchange.

In order for any party to trade futures, it must qualify by having a minimum acceptable level of credit quality. All qualifying parties, however, are not of equivalent credit risk. Our risk-free party obviously qualifies. Let us assume our risky party does also and so the parties decide to trade on the futures exchange. On the surface it might appear that both parties benefit because the clearinghouse guarantees the risky party. It does so at a cost, however, which is reflected in the required margins, trading costs, and price limits. Since it imposes the same cost on all participants, the risk-free firm pays an excessive cost to trade. Its unimpeachable credit quality is further enhanced at a cost. If the risky party is of lower risk than average, its credit is enhanced at a bargain price. In other words, each party is treated as if it were of average credit quality. Thus, the risk-free firm would find futures somewhat less attractive and it would prefer forward contracts. The risky counterparty, assuming its risk were greater than average, would prefer futures contracts. Because this party is selling, the futures price would tend to be lower. Thus, both parties would agree that a forward contract would carry a higher price.

Of course, we can make such a statement only about a specific transaction, given the characteristics of the two parties. On another trade the risk-free firm might prefer to be selling. Then its preference for forward contracts would tend to make the forward price higher. If both parties were risk-free, they would both prefer forward contracts, and the forward price should be equivalent to what it would have been had the contract been created in the futures market. If both parties were of lower than average credit risk, they would both prefer futures contracts, and we would likely see only a small difference between the price of the futures contract and the price that would exist had the contract been created on the forward market.

There may yet be other reasons for a forward-futures price differential, such as liquidity and transaction cost differences. So in the market as a whole, it is impossible to say how default risk affects the difference between futures and forward prices. We can, however, look at an empirical example.

Default risk can affect the forward-futures price differential but the direction of the effect is unclear.

A COMPARISON OF SOME ACTUAL FORWARD AND FUTURES PRICES
Are forward and futures prices equal? Let us examine some forward and futures prices of Treasury bills.

Figure 9.1 shows the forward and futures prices over a period of 10 weeks. The forward prices are computed as implied from Treasury bill spot prices. We show how this is done in a later section. With the exception of one week, the futures price is above the forward price.

Ignoring for the moment the credit risk, T-bill futures prices should not exceed forward prices. The futures price definitely moves opposite to interest rates. Holders of long futures positions will earn profits when interest rates are falling and incur losses when interest rates are rising. The observed preference for futures over forwards, as indicated in the higher price of the former, is puzzling, at least with regard to the interest rate effect. The explanation may involve the credit risk. It would be preferable if we had prices of actual forward contracts on T-bills. Such data do not exist because the contracts are created privately and the prices are not reported to the public. So in computing the implied forward rates, we are acting as though a counterparty, who could sell short a shorter-term T-bill and buy a longer-term T-bill, had entered into a long forward contract with the government. The counterparty could default when buying back the T-bill to cover the short sale, but the government is risk-free. The actual market for forward contracts involves direct rather than implied forward contracts. One party typically commits to buying the T-bill at a future time while the other party commits to selling it. Neither party is the government. Thus,

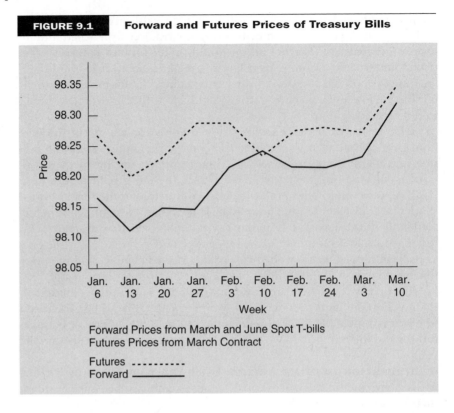

FIGURE 9.1   **Forward and Futures Prices of Treasury Bills**

Forward Prices from March and June Spot T-bills
Futures Prices from March Contract

Futures - - - - - - - - -
Forward ———————

the credit risk in a direct forward contract may differ substantially from that in an implied forward contract, where one party is implicitly the government.

Our look at the forward-futures price differential has left us with no clear explanation for what to expect. Fortunately, empirical studies have shown that the differential is actually quite small and can usually be ignored. In many of the remaining examples in this book, we shall ignore the marking to market of futures contracts and assume that the entire payoff is received at the end. We shall, however, look at some examples of forward contracts, primarily for the purpose of underscoring the fact that some types of specialized situations require contracts that do not exist on futures exchanges. For all intents and purposes, however, most of what we cover in the remainder of this chapter and the examples in other chapters will treat the contracts as economically equivalent, which means that their prices are the same.

The Term Structure Constructed with Futures

Since we feel safe in treating forward prices as futures prices, let us see how we might extract some valuable information about forward prices from futures prices.

The **term structure of interest rates** is the relationship between the interest rate on a zero coupon bond and its maturity. For example, the rate on a one-year bond might be 6 percent. The rate on a two-year bond might be 8 percent. These are called spot rates since they are rates that apply to transactions on the spot—that is, for immediate delivery. There are several explanations for why these spot rates differ, but that is not our concern. Suppose we wanted to know the rate on a forward contract to purchase a one-year zero coupon bond in one year. We would obtain this by the following argument. We could invest \$1 in a two-year zero coupon bond, which would mature to a value of $(1.08)^2 = 1.1664$. As an alternative way to invest for two years, we might invest \$1 in a one-year zero coupon bond, which would mature to a value of \$1.06, and enter into a forward contract to invest \$1.06 in a one-year bond that would mature one year later to a value of $(1.06)(1 + r)$ where r stands for the unknown forward rate. What would r be? Setting up the equation $(1.08)^2 = (1.06)(1 + r)$, we obtain r = 0.1004. Thus, 10.04 percent should be the rate established for the bond specified in the forward contract.

The term structure of interest rates is the set of spot rates on zero coupon bonds. From those spot rates one can derive the forward rates, which determine the prices of forward contracts on zero coupon bonds like Treasury bills. If forward prices can be treated as futures prices, it is also possible to go the opposite direction—that is, derive the term structure from futures prices.

The Treasury bill futures contract at the International Monetary Market (IMM) of the Chicago Mercantile Exchange calls for delivery of a 91-day Treasury bill. The contract expirations are March, June, September, and December, with maturities extending out about two years. Consider the prices on November 15 of a particular year.

The December contract is quoted at a price of 96.84, which is interpreted as a discount of $100 - 96.84 = 3.16$. This quoted value is called the **IMM Index.** Using the convention of the Treasury bill spot market, the price per \$100 of par value is

$$100 - 3.16(91/360) = 99.2012.$$

Although the actual futures price is based on a 90-day bill, we have computed it here as a 91-day T-bill price. That is because we are using the T-bill futures market to derive an implied forward price for 91-day T-bills. From Chapter 3, the yield on the purchase of a 91-day T-bill at 99.2012 is

$$(100/99.2012)^{(365/91)} - 1 = .0327.$$

This can be interpreted as the yield on a 91-day T-bill purchased by accepting delivery on the futures contract on its expiration day, December 17. We denote this rate as $r(32,123)$ because it applies to a bill that starts in 32 days and matures in 123 days. On November 15, the spot T-bill maturing

December 17 has a discount rate of 2.96. Using the same procedure as above and noting that this is a 32-day bill, we get a spot yield of 3.05 percent.[4] This is the rate $r(0,32)$.

Thus, we have found a spot rate of 3.05 percent for the next 32/365 of a year, followed by a futures (forward) rate of 3.27 percent for the next 91/365 of a year. We can now derive a spot rate for the next 32/365 + 91/365 = 123/365 of a year as

$$[(1.0305)^{32/365}(1.0327)^{(91/365)}]^{(365/123)} - 1 = r(0,123) = .0321.$$

So now we know that the annualized spot rate for 32 days is 3.05 percent and the annualized spot rate for 123 days is 3.21 percent. The latter is the rate $r(0,123)$.

There are also futures contracts expiring in later months that can be used to extend the term structure out further. The March contract has a price of 96.69, implying a discount rate of 3.31. The contract expiration is March 18, which is 91 days after the December contract expiration. Now we can extend the term structure out 123 + 91 = 214 days. The futures price for a discount of 3.31 is

$$100 - 3.31(91/360) = 99.1633,$$

which implies a yield of

$$(100/99.1633)^{(365/91)} - 1 = .0343.$$

Thus, a bill purchased by accepting delivery on the March contract would have a yield of 3.43 percent. This is the rate $r(123,214)$. So far we know that the rate $r(0,123)$ is 3.21 and the rate $r(123,214) = 3.43$. Thus, we can find the rate $r(0,214)$ as follows:

$$[(1.0321)^{(123/365)}(1.0343)^{(91/365)}]^{(365/214)} - 1 = .0330.$$

Thus, the 214-day rate is 3.30 percent. We can extend this 91 days further by using the June contract. Its price is quoted at 96.45 and it expires on June 17. With a 91-day bill delivered on June 17, we can extend the term structure out 91 days past June 17 to September 16. As a good exercise, work out this part of the problem on your own. You should find that the June T-bill implied yield would be 3.68 percent, which is $r(214,305)$. The 305-day spot rate, $r(0,305)$, is 3.41 percent.

Figure 9.2 summarizes what we have just done. We want to find the spot rates for maturities as far out as the futures market will reveal. The spot rate

---

[4]This is found as

$$100 - 2.96(32/360) = 99.7369.$$
$$(100/99.7369)^{(365/32)} - 1 = .0305.$$

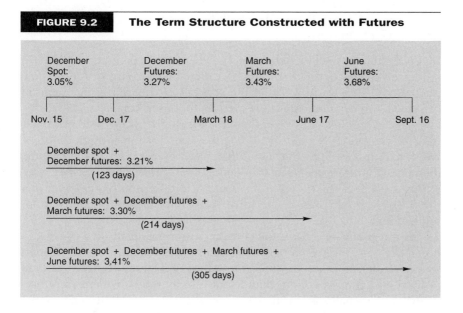

FIGURE 9.2   The Term Structure Constructed with Futures

December Spot: 3.05%

December Futures: 3.27%

March Futures: 3.43%

June Futures: 3.68%

Nov. 15   Dec. 17   March 18   June 17   Sept. 16

December spot + December futures: 3.21%
(123 days)

December spot + December futures + March futures: 3.30%
(214 days)

December spot + December futures + March futures + June futures: 3.41%
(305 days)

for the first 32 days is revealed by the spot T-bill maturing on December 17. The forward rate for the period December 17 to March 18 is revealed by the implied rate on the December futures contract, which calls for delivery of a bill maturing March 18. That rate is 3.27 percent. Linking the December spot rate of 3.05 percent to the December futures rate of 3.27 percent gives a March spot rate of 3.21 percent. In a similar manner, the March futures, calling for delivery of a bill maturing June 17, reveals the forward rate from March 18 to June 17 as 3.43 percent. Linking this rate to the previously determined March spot rate of 3.21 percent gives the June spot rate of 3.30 percent. Linking this rate with the June futures, which calls for delivery of a bill maturing September 16 with an implied yield of 3.68 percent, gives the September spot rate of 3.41 percent.

So now we have pieced together at least part of the term structure. Why did we do this? We have to defer a full answer until a later chapter but we can get a peek right now. Suppose an actual spot T-bill maturing in March were yielding more or less than the March spot rate of 3.21 percent. Then something would be out of line, and we could make an arbitrage profit. In this case, however, the actual spot March 17 T-bill was yielding 3.22 percent, practically the same rate. Markets being pretty efficient, arbitrage opportunities are indeed quite rare, but making the calculations and verifying that there is no arbitrage possibility is as important as finding that there is one.

We have now established some important results in forward and futures pricing. In the next section, we develop a forward and futures pricing model.

The term structure of spot rates can be constructed by linking the nearby spot rate with the forward rates implied by the futures market.

A Forward and Futures Pricing Model

In this section we shall learn how a forward or futures contract is priced. In other words, what is the theoretical fair price of a forward or futures contract? Recall that we introduced the concept of theoretical fair value in Chapter 1 and examined it with respect to options in Chapters 4 and 5. We saw that the binomial and Black-Scholes models give us the theoretical fair value of an option. Now we are doing the same for forwards and futures. We should, however, keep in mind that, as covered earlier in the chapter, the value of a futures contract is not equal to its price. Thus, we shall refer to this concept as the theoretical fair price, but we should remember that the theoretical fair price is the price that would imply a theoretical fair value of zero.

The theoretical fair price of a futures or forward contract is the price that would imply a theoretical fair value of zero.

In the previous section we saw that forward and futures prices can differ but that the differences are usually quite small. To make things sound a little smoother, we shall stop referring to these contracts as both forward and futures contracts and shall simply refer to them as futures contracts. We shall assume that marking to market is done only on the expiration day, thus making a futures contract be essentially a forward contract.

Before looking at the pricing of futures and forward contracts, we must establish a few principles of how spot prices are determined from risk premiums and the cost of carry.

Spot Prices, Risk Premiums, and the Cost of Carry

Let us first establish a simple framework for valuing spot assets. Let S_0 be the spot price, s be the cost of storing the asset over a period of time from 0 to T, and iS_0 be the interest forgone on S_0 dollars invested in the asset over that period of time.

First, let us assume that there is no uncertainty of the future asset price. Then we can say that S_T will be the asset price at T for sure. Then the current price of the asset would have to be

Under certainty, today's spot price equals the future spot price minus the cost of storage and the interest forgone.

$$S_0 = S_T - s - iS_0.$$

In other words, the asset price today would simply be the future price less the cost of storage and interest. No one would pay more than this amount, because storage and interest costs would wipe out any profit from holding it. No one would sell it for less than this amount, because someone would always be willing to pay more, up to the amount given in the above formula.

If we relax the assumption of a certain future asset price, then we must use the expected future asset price, $E(S_T)$. If investors are risk neutral, however, they will be willing to hold the asset without any expectation of receiving a reward for bearing risk. In that case,

$$S_0 = E(S_T) - s - iS_0.$$

In other words, the price today is the expected future price, less the storage and interest costs.

Most investors, however, are risk averse and consequently would not pay this much for the asset. They would pay a smaller amount, the difference being the risk premium. Let us denote that risk premium by $E(\phi)$. Then the current price would be

$$S_0 = E(S_T) - s - iS_0 - E(\phi).$$

In other words, in the real world of risk-averse investors, the current spot price is the expected future spot price, less any storage costs, less the interest forgone, and less the risk premium.

This statement is quite general and does not tell us anything about how the risk premium is determined. For financial assets, there are few if any storage costs, but in that case we just set $s = 0$. The above statement is a powerful reminder that asset prices must reflect expectations, costs of ownership — both explicit and implicit —, and reward for bearing risk.

Let us make one final refinement. Suppose the asset pays a cash return in the form of interest or a dividend. Let us capture this effect by reducing the interest opportunity cost by any such cash flows paid by the asset. So from now on let us remember that iS_0 is the interest forgone, less any cash flow — interest or dividends — received. We shall call this the **net interest.** Note that if the dividend or coupon interest rate is high enough, it can exceed the interest opportunity cost, making i be negative. This is not a problem and is, in fact, not all that rare. When a bond with a high coupon rate is held in an environment in which rates are low, the net interest can easily be negative.

The combination of storage costs and net interest, $s + iS_0$, is referred to as the **cost of carry.** We shall denote it with the Greek symbol θ (theta). The cost of carry is positive if the cost of storage exceeds the net interest and negative if the net interest is negative and large enough to offset the cost of storing. Sometimes, however, this concept is referred to as the **carry.** An asset that has a negative cost of carry, meaning that the net interest is a net inflow and exceeds the cost of storage, is said to have positive carry. An asset that has a positive cost of carry is said to have negative carry. For our purposes in this book, we shall refer to the concept as strictly the cost of carry.

For nonstorable goods, such as electricity, there would not necessarily be a relationship between today's spot price and the expected future spot price. Supply and demand conditions today and in the future would be independent. The risk of uncertain future supplies could not be reduced by storing some of the good currently owned. Large price fluctuations likely would occur. The cost of carry would be a meaningless concept.

At the other extreme, a commodity might be indefinitely storable. Stocks, metals, and some natural resources, such as oil, are either indefinitely or almost indefinitely storable. Their spot prices would be set in accordance with current supply and demand conditions, the cost of carry, investors' expected risk premia, and expected future supply and demand conditions.

For many agricultural commodities, limited storability is the rule. Grains have a fairly long storage life, while frozen concentrated orange juice has a more limited life. In the financial markets, Treasury bills, which mature in less than a year, have a short storage life. Treasury bonds, with their longer maturities, have a much longer storage life.

For any storable assets, the spot price is related to the expected future spot price by the cost of carry and the expected risk premium. We shall use this relationship to help understand forward and futures pricing.

The Theoretical Fair Price

Consider the following transaction: Buy the spot asset at a price of S_0, and sell a futures contract at a price of $f_0(T)$. At expiration, the spot price is S_T and the futures price is $f_T(T)$, which equals S_T. At expiration, you deliver the asset. The profit on the transaction is $f_0(T) - S_0$ minus the storage costs incurred and the opportunity cost of the funds tied up:

$$\Pi = f_0(T) - S_0 - s - iS_0 = f_0(T) - S_0 - \theta.$$

Since the expression $f_0(T) - S_0 - \theta$ involves no unknown terms, the profit is riskless, meaning the transaction should not generate a risk premium. The amount invested is S_0, the original price of the spot asset. The profit from the transaction is $f_0(T) - S_0 - \theta$, which should equal zero. Thus,

$$f_0(T) = S_0 + \theta.$$

In equilibrium, the futures price equals the spot price plus the cost of carry.

The futures price equals the spot price plus the cost of carry. The cost of carry therefore is the difference between the futures price and the spot price and is sometimes referred to as the basis.[5] We shall say much more about the basis in Chapter 10.

An alternative interpretation of this transaction is seen in Figure 9.3. The value of the position when initiated is S_0; the value at expiration is

---

[5]The basis usually is defined as the spot price minus the futures price, and we shall use this definition in Chapter 10.

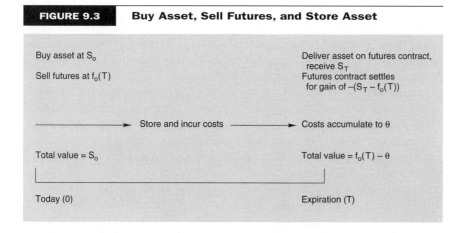

FIGURE 9.3   Buy Asset, Sell Futures, and Store Asset

Buy asset at S_0

Sell futures at $f_0(T)$

Deliver asset on futures contract,
 receive S_T
Futures contract settles
 for gain of $-(S_T - f_0(T))$

⟶ Store and incur costs ⟶ Costs accumulate to θ

Total value = S_0

Total value = $f_0(T) - \theta$

Today (0)

Expiration (T)

$f_0(T) - \theta$. Since $f_0(T) - \theta$ is known when the transaction is initiated, the transaction is risk-free. So S_0 should equal the present value of $f_0(T) - \theta$, using the risk-free rate. But the present value adjustment has already been made since θ includes the interest lost on S_0 over the holding period. Thus, $f_0(T) = S_0 + \theta$.

What makes this relationship hold? Assume the futures price is higher than the spot price plus the cost of carry:

$$f_0(T) > S_0 + \theta.$$

Arbitrageurs will then buy the spot asset and sell the futures contract. This will generate a positive profit equal to $f_0(T) - S_0 - \theta$. Many arbitrageurs will execute the same transaction, which will put downward pressure on the futures price. When $f_0(T) = S_0 + \theta$, the opportunity to earn this profit will be gone.

Now suppose the futures price is less than the spot price plus the cost of carry; that is,

$$f_0(T) < S_0 + \theta.$$

First, let us assume the asset is a financial instrument. Then arbitrageurs will sell short the asset and buy the futures. When the instrument is sold short, the short seller will not incur the storage costs. Instead of incurring the opportunity cost of funds tied up in the asset, the short seller can earn interest on the funds received from the short sale.

Thus, the cost of carry is not paid but received. The profit thus is $S_0 + \theta - f_0(T)$, which is positive. The combined actions of arbitrageurs will put downward pressure on the spot price and upward pressure on the futures price until the profit is eradicated. At that point, $f_0(T) = S_0 + \theta$.

Short selling may not actually be necessary for inducing the arbitrage activity. Consider an investor who holds the asset unhedged. That person could sell the asset and buy a futures contract. While the asset is not owned, the arbitrageur avoids the storage costs and earns interest on the funds received from its sale. At expiration, the arbitrageur takes delivery and again owns the asset unhedged. The profit from the transaction is $S_0 + \theta - f_0(T)$, which is positive. Thus, the transaction temporarily removes the asset from the investor's total assets, earns a risk-free profit, and then replaces the asset into the investor's total assets. Because many arbitrageurs will do this, it will force the spot price down and the futures price up until no further opportunities exist. This transaction is called **quasi arbitrage.**

There has been some confusion even among experts over whether futures prices reflect expectations about future spot prices. Some have said that futures prices provide expectations about future spot prices, while others have argued that futures prices reflect only the cost of carry. Still others have said that part of the time futures reveal expectations and part of the time they reveal the cost of carry. We shall more fully address the issue of whether futures prices reveal expectations in a later section; here we should note that both positions are correct. Because the futures price equals the spot price plus the cost of carry, the futures price definitely reflects the cost of carry. The spot price, however, reflects expectations. This is a fundamental tenet of spot pricing. Because the futures price will include the spot price, it too reflects expectations; however, it does so indirectly through the spot price. The overall process is illustrated in Figure 9.4.

So far we have been ignoring the fact that a small margin requirement is imposed on futures traders. Suppose in the transaction involving the purchase of the asset at S_0 and sale of the futures at $f_0(T)$, the trader was required to deposit M dollars in a margin account. Let us assume that the M dollars will earn interest at the risk-free rate. Then at expiration the trader will have delivered the asset and received an effective price of $f_0(T)$ and have incurred the cost of carry of θ. In addition, the trader will be able to release the margin deposit of M dollars plus the interest on it. Since the total value at expiration, $f_0(T) - \theta + M +$ interest on M, is known in advance, the overall transaction remains risk-free. On the front end, however, the trader put up S_0 dollars to buy the asset and M dollars for the margin account. The present value of the total value at expiration should, therefore, equal $S_0 + M$. Obviously the present value of M plus the interest on M equals M. This means that S_0 must still equal $f_0(T) - \theta$, giving us our **cost of carry model,** $f_0(T) = S_0 + \theta$. If, however, interest is not paid on the margin deposit, the futures price can be affected by the loss of interest on the margin account. How the futures price is affected is not clear, because the trader who does the reverse arbitrage, selling or selling short the asset and buying the futures, also faces the same margin requirement. Does it really matter? Probably not. Large traders typically are able to deposit interest-bearing securities. The price we observe is almost surely being determined by large traders. So it seems reasonable to assume that the margin deposit is irrelevant to the pricing of futures.

FIGURE 9.4   **How Futures Prices Are Determined**

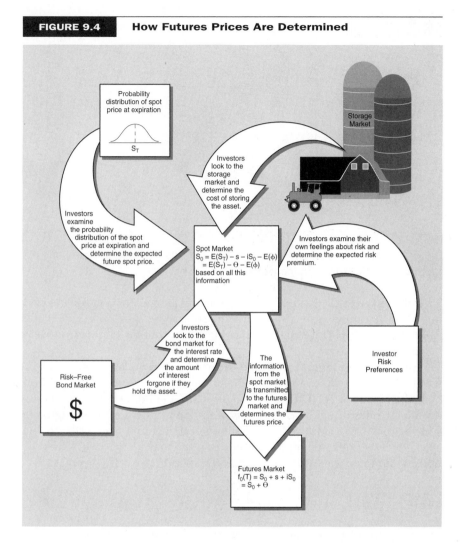

For storable assets, as well as for securities that do not pay interest or dividends, the cost of carry normally is positive. This would cause the futures price to lie above the current spot price. A market of this type is referred to as a **contango.**

Table 9.5 presents some spot and futures prices from a contango market. The example is for cotton traded on the New York Cotton Exchange. The cost of carry implied for the October contract is $41.60 - 36.75 = 4.85$. Remember that this figure includes the interest forgone on the investment of 36.75 cents for a pound of cotton and the actual physical costs of storing the cotton from late September until the contract's expiration in October.

It would be convenient if fact always conformed to theory. If that were the case, we would never observe the spot price in excess of the futures

In a contango market, the futures price exceeds the spot price.

| TABLE 9.5 | A Contango Market: Cotton, September 26 |

Expiration	Settlement Price (Cents per Pound)
Spot	36.75
October	41.60
December	42.05
March	42.77
May	43.50
July	43.80
October	45.20
December	45.85

price. In reality, spot prices sometimes exceed futures prices. A possible explanation is the convenience yield.

THE CONVENIENCE YIELD We are seeking an explanation for the case in which the futures price is less than the spot price. If $f_0(T) = S_0 + \theta$ and $f_0(T) < S_0$, then $\theta < 0$. What type of market condition might produce a negative cost of carry?

Suppose the commodity is in short supply; current consumption is unusually high relative to supplies of the good. This is producing an abnormally high spot price. The current tight market conditions discourage individuals from storing the commodity. If the situation is severe enough, the current spot price could be above the expected future spot price. If the spot price is sufficiently high, the futures price may lie below it. The relationship between the futures price and the spot price is then given as

$$f_0(T) = S_0 + \theta - \chi,$$

The convenience yield is the additional return earned by holding a commodity in short supply or a nonpecuniary gain from an asset.

where χ (chi) is simply a positive value that accounts for the difference between $f_0(T)$ and $S_0 + \theta$. If χ is sufficiently large, the futures price will lie below the spot price. This need not be the case, however, since χ can be small.

The value χ often is referred to as the **convenience yield.** It is the premium earned by those who hold inventories of a commodity that is in short supply. By holding inventories of a good in short supply, one could earn an additional return, the convenience yield. Note that we are not saying that the commodity is stored for future sale or consumption. Indeed, when the spot price is sufficiently high, the return from storage is negative. There is no incentive to store the good. In fact, there is an incentive to borrow as much of the good as possible and sell short.

For some assets a convenience yield can be viewed as a type of nonpecuniary return. For example, consider a person who owns a house, which usually offers some potential for price appreciation but the expected gain is rarely sufficient to compensate for the risk involved. In some cases, the expected gain may be no more or even less than the risk-free rate. The house, however, provides a nonpecuniary yield, which is the utility from living in the house. The buyer of the house is normally willing to pay more, thereby reducing the expected return, for the right to live in the house.

When the commodity has a convenience yield, the futures price may be less than the spot price plus the cost of carry. In that case, the futures is said to be at **less than full carry.**

A market in which the futures price lies below the current spot price is referred to as **backwardation** or sometimes an **inverted market.** An example of a backwardation market is presented in Table 9.6. Notice how the October futures price is lower than the spot price. In fact 9 out of 10 of the futures prices are lower than the spot price. If a commodities dealer bought the soybean meal on September 10 at 198.10 and sold a futures contract expiring in October at 195, it would be guaranteeing a loss of 3.10 over a period of about one month. Soybeans are harvested in the months of September to October. Meal is produced as a residual after soybean oil is extracted from the raw soybeans. At this point in time, the supply of soybeans is undoubtedly somewhat low since it is just before the harvest. Buying the soybean meal, storing it, and bringing it to the market at a time when the harvest will bring a large supply onto the market is not an economically attractive thing to do. The spot price is high, however, because at least for a few weeks, soybean meal is in short supply. Thus, someone who holds soybeans, knowing that its price is likely to fall, would be doing so to avoid the costs of not having the commodity on hand when customers want it.

It is not uncommon to see characteristics of both backwardation and contango in a market at the same time. For example, suppose the commodities dealer went long the January contract and short the March contract. The dealer would be committing to buying the soybean meal at

In a backwardation market, the spot price exceeds the futures price.

| TABLE 9.6 | A Backwardation Market: Soybean Meal, September 10 |

Expiration	Price ($ per Ton)
Spot	198.10
October	195.00
December	194.30
January	194.60
March	196.10
May	196.80
July	198.70
August	198.00
September	197.50
October	198.00
December	197.00

194.60 and selling it for 196.10. This would imply a contango market with a cost of carry from January to March of 1.50. Note as you go down the list of futures prices, you see some that are higher than the previous one and some that are lower. This occurs because the futures market reflects expectations as well as the cost of carry. It does so because any futures contract is priced off of the spot price and the cost of carry. The former will always reflect the expected future spot price, which will be influenced by what people feel about the likely success of the next harvest. In some cases the expectations effect will dominate the cost of carry effect.

Another factor that can produce backwardation in commodity markets is the inability to sell the commodity short and the reluctance on the part of holders of the commodity to sell it when its price is higher than it should be and replace it with an underpriced long futures contract. In the previous section we referred to this as quasi arbitrage. If quasi arbitrage is not executed in sufficient volume to bring the futures price to its theoretical fair price, then we could see backwardation. The spot price becomes too high and there is no one willing to sell the asset and replace it with a futures or no one able to sell short the asset.

Of course for financial assets, the cost of storage is negligible, and supply of the commodity is fairly constant. Yet we still often observe an inverted market. For interest-sensitive assets like Treasury bills and bonds, either backwardation or contango can be observed. Later in this chapter we shall look at some other reasons why financial futures prices can be below spot prices.

With these concepts in mind, we now turn to an important and highly controversial issue in futures markets: Do futures prices contain a risk premium?

Futures Prices and Risk Premia

We already discussed the concept of a risk premium in spot prices. No one would hold the spot commodity unless a risk premium were expected. Although investors do not always earn a risk premium, they must do so on average. Is there a risk premium in futures prices? Are speculators in futures contracts rewarded, on average, with a risk premium? There are two schools of thought on the subject.

THE NO RISK PREMIUM HYPOTHESIS   Consider a simple futures market in which there are only speculators. The underlying commodity is the total amount of snowfall in inches in Vail, Colorado in a given week. The contracts are cash settled at expiration. Individuals can buy or sell contracts at whatever price they agree on. Similar derivatives exist on the over-the-counter market.

For example, suppose two individuals make a contract at a price of 30. If the total snowfall is above 30 at expiration, the trader holding the short position pays the holder of the long position a sum equal to the total snow-fall minus 30. Though the ski resorts and merchants have exposures highly correlated with the level of snowfall, no one can actually "hold" the commodity, so there is no hedging or arbitrage.

Now suppose that after a period of several weeks, it is obvious that the longs are consistently beating the shorts. The shorts conclude that it is a good winter for skiing. Determined to improve their lot, those individuals who have been going short begin to go long. Of course, those who have been going long have no desire to go short. Now everyone wants to go long, and no one will go short. This drives up the futures price to a level at which someone finds it so high that it looks good to go short. Now suppose the price has been driven up so high that the opposite occurs: The shorts begin to consistently beat the longs. This causes the longs to turn around and go short. Ultimately an equilibrium must be reached in which neither the longs nor the shorts consistently beat the other side. In such a market, there is no risk premium. Neither side wins at the expense of the other.

In futures markets, this argument means that on average the futures price today equals the expected price of the futures contract at expiration; that is, $f_0(T) = E(f_T(T))$. Because the expected futures price at expiration equals the expected spot price at expiration, $E(f_T(T)) = E(S_T)$, we obtain the following result:

If the futures price does not contain a risk premium, then speculators are not rewarded for taking on risk. Futures prices will then be unbiased expectations of future spot prices.

$$f_0(T) = E(S_T).$$

This is an extremely important and powerful statement. It says that *the futures price is the market's expectation of the future spot price.* If one wishes to obtain a forecast of the future spot price, one need only observe the futures price. In the language of economists, *futures prices are unbiased expectations of future spot prices.*

As an example, on September 26 of a particular year the spot price of silver was $5.58 per troy ounce. The December futures price was $5.64 per troy ounce. If futures prices contain no risk premium, the market is forecasting that the spot price of silver in December will be $5.64. Futures traders who buy the contract at $5.64 expect to sell it at $5.64.

Figure 9.5 illustrates a situation that is reasonably consistent with this view. The May wheat futures contract is shown along with the spot price for a period of 20 weeks prior to expiration. Both prices fluctuate, and the spot price exhibits a small risk premium as suggested by the slight upward trend.[6] The futures price, however, follows no apparent trend.

We must caution, of course, that this is just an isolated case. The question of whether futures prices contain a risk premium must be answered by empirical studies. First, however, let us turn to the arguments supporting the view that futures prices do contain a risk premium.

---

[6]The upward drift, however, could also be due to the risk-free rate or possibly the storage costs.

FIGURE 9.5	No Risk Premium: May Wheat

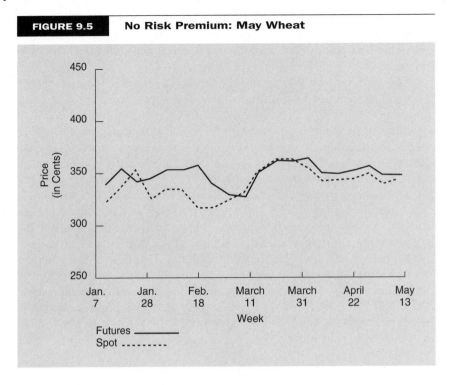

THE RISK PREMIUM HYPOTHESIS   If a risk premium were observed, we would see that

$$E(f_T(T)) > f_0(T).$$

The futures price would be expected to increase. Buyers of futures contracts at price $f_0(T)$ would expect to sell them at $E(f_T(T))$. Since futures and spot prices should converge at expiration, $E(f_T(T)) = E(S_T)$,

$$E(f_T(T)) = E(S_T) > f_0(T).$$

From this we conclude that the futures price is a low estimate of the expected future spot price.

Consider a contango market in which the cost of carry is positive. Holders of the commodity expect to earn a risk premium, $E(\phi)$, given by the following formula covered earlier in this chapter:

$$E(S_T) = S_0 + \theta + E(\phi),$$

where θ is the cost of carry and $E(\phi)$ is the risk premium. Because $f_0(T) = S_0 + \theta$, then $S_0 = f_0(T) - \theta$. Substituting for S_0 in the formula for $E(S_T)$, we get

$$E(S_T) = f_0(T) - \theta + \theta + E(\phi),$$

or simply,

$$E(S_T) = f_0(T) + E(\phi) = E(f_T(T)).$$

The expected futures price at expiration is higher than the current futures price by the amount of the risk premium. This means that buyers of futures contracts expect to earn a risk premium. They do not, however, earn a risk premium because the futures contract is risky. They earn the risk premium that existed in the spot market; it was merely transferred to the futures market.

Now consider the silver example in the previous section. The spot price is \$5.58, and the December futures price is \$5.64. The interest lost on \$5.58 for two months is about \$0.05. Let us assume that the cost of storing silver for two months is \$0.01. Let us also suppose that buyers of silver expect to earn a \$0.02 risk premium. Thus, the variables are

$$\begin{aligned} S_0 &= 5.58 \\ f_0(T) &= 5.64 \\ \theta &= .05 + .01 = .06 \\ E(\phi) &= .02. \end{aligned}$$

The expected spot price of silver in December is

$$E(S_T) = S_0 + \theta + E(\phi) = 5.58 + .06 + .02 = 5.66.$$

Because the expected spot price of silver in December equals the expected futures price in December, $E(f_T(T)) = 5.66$. This can also be found as

$$E(f_T(T)) = f_0(T) + E(\phi) = 5.64 + .02 = 5.66.$$

Futures traders who buy the contract at 5.64 expect to sell it at 5.66 and earn a risk premium of 0.02. The futures price of 5.64 is an understatement of the expected spot price in December by the amount of the risk premium.

The process is illustrated as follows:

Spot:	Buy silver $5.58	Store and incur costs + $0.06	Expected risk premium + $0.02	Expected selling price = $5.66
Futures:	Buy silver futures $5.64		Expected risk premium + $0.02	Expected selling price = $5.66

If the futures price contains a risk premium, then speculators are rewarded for taking on risk. Futures prices will then be biased expectations of future spot prices.

The idea that futures prices contain a risk premium was proposed by two famous economists, Keynes (1930) and Hicks (1939). They argued that futures and spot markets are dominated by individuals who hold long positions in the underlying commodities. These individuals desire the protection afforded by selling futures contracts. That means they need traders who are willing to take long positions in futures. To induce speculators to take long positions in futures, the futures price must be below the expected price of the contract at expiration, which is the expected future spot price. Keynes and Hicks argued, therefore, that *futures prices are biased expectations of future spot prices,* with the bias attributable to the risk premium. The risk premium in futures prices exists only because it is transferred from the spot market.

An example of such a case is shown in Figure 9.6, which illustrates a June S&P 500 futures contract. Both the spot and futures prices exhibit an upward trend.[7] Again, however, we must caution that this is only an isolated case.

FIGURE 9.6   **Risk Premium — S&P 500 Futures and Spot**

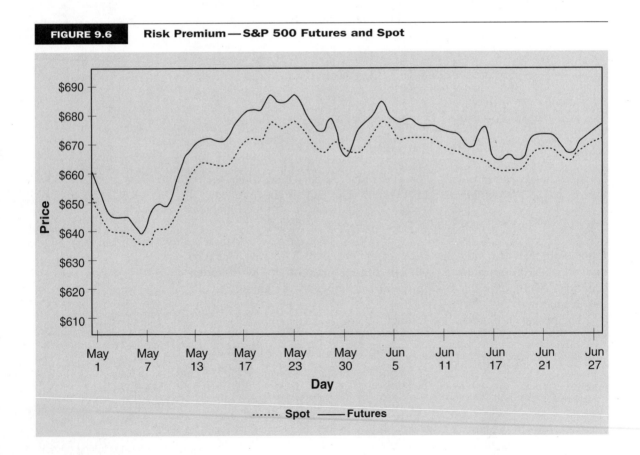

---

[7]Again the upward drift in the spot price could be due to the risk-free rate.

How can we explain the existence of a risk premium when we argued earlier that neither longs nor shorts would consistently win at the expense of the other side? The major difference in the two examples is the nature of the spot market. In the first example, in which the futures contract was on snowfall, there was no opportunity to take a "position" in the spot market. In fact, there was no spot market; futures traders were simply competing with one another in a pure gambling situation. When we allow for a spot market, we introduce individuals who hold speculative long positions in commodities. If the positions are unhedged, these individuals expect to earn a risk premium. If they are unwilling to accept the risk, they sell futures contracts. They are, in effect, purchasing insurance from the futures traders, and in so doing they transfer the risk and the risk premium to the futures markets.

This explanation is useful in seeing why futures markets should not be viewed as a form of legalized gambling. There are probably no greater risk takers in our society than farmers. They risk nearly all of their wealth on the output of their farms, which are subject to the uncertainties of weather, government interference, and foreign competition, not to mention the normal fluctuations of supply and demand. Farmers can lay off some or all of that risk by hedging in the futures markets. In so doing, they transfer the risk to parties willing to bear it. Yet no one would call farming legalized gambling. Nor would anyone criticize pension fund portfolio managers for gambling. Futures markets, and indeed all derivative markets, serve a purpose in facilitating risk transfer from parties not wanting it to parties willing to take it—for a price.

What about situations in which the hedgers buy futures? This would occur if hedgers were predominantly short the commodity. This would drive up futures prices, and futures prices would, on average, exhibit a downward trend as contracts approached expiration. Futures prices would overestimate future spot prices. Speculators who sold futures would earn a risk premium.

A market in which the futures price is below the expected future spot price is called **normal backwardation,** and one in which the futures price is above the expected future spot price is called **normal contango.** The choice of names for these markets is a bit confusing, and they must be distinguished from simply contango and backwardation.

$$
\begin{aligned}
\text{Contango:} \quad & S_0 < f_0(T) \\
\text{Backwardation:} \quad & f_0(T) < S_0 \\
\text{Normal contango:} \quad & E(S_T) < f_0(T) \\
\text{Normal backwardation:} \quad & f_0(T) < E(S_T)
\end{aligned}
$$

Because the spot price can lie below the futures price, which in turn can lie below the expected future spot price, we can have contango and normal backwardation simultaneously; indeed, this is the more typical occurrence. We can also have backwardation and normal contango simultaneously, although this is less likely.

Which view on the existence of a risk premium is correct? Since there is almost certainly a risk premium in spot prices, the existence of hedgers who hold spot positions means that the risk premium is transferred to futures traders. Thus, there would seem to be a risk premium in futures prices. If there are not enough spot positions being hedged, however, or if most hedging is being done by investors who are short in the spot market, there may be no observable risk premium in futures prices. Empirical studies have given us no clear-cut answer and suggest that the issue is still unresolved.

The Effect of Intermediate Cash Flows

Until now we have avoided any consideration of how intermediate cash flows, such as interest and dividends, affect the futures price. We did note earlier in the chapter that these cash payments would have an effect on the cost of carry, possibly making it negative. Now we shall look more closely at how they affect futures prices.

The contracts in which these factors apply are stock index and bond futures. We shall concentrate on stock index futures, although the general principles are the same in both cases.

For simplicity, assume there is only one stock in the index, which pays a sure dividend of D_T on the expiration date. Now suppose an investor buys the stock at a spot price of S_0 and sells a futures contract at a price of $f_0(T)$.

At expiration, the stock is sold at S_T, the dividend D_T is collected, and the futures contract generates a cash flow of $-(f_T(T) - f_0(T))$, which equals $-(S_T - f_0(T))$. Thus, the total cash flow at expiration is $D_T + f_0(T)$. This amount is known in advance; therefore, the current value of the portfolio must equal the present value of $D_T + f_0(T)$. The current portfolio value is simply the amount paid for the stock, S_0. Putting these results together gives

$$S_0 = (f_0(T) + D_T)(1 + r)^{-T},$$

or

$$f_0(T) = S_0(1 + r)^T - D_T.$$

Here we see that the futures price is the spot price compounded at the risk-free rate minus the dividend. A sufficiently large dividend could obviously bring the futures price down below the spot price.

To take our model one step closer to reality, let us assume the stock pays several dividends. In fact, our stock could actually be a portfolio of stocks that is identical to an index such as the S&P 500. Suppose N dividends will be paid during the life of the futures. Each dividend is denoted as D_j and is paid t_j years from today. Now suppose we buy the stock and sell the futures. During the life of the futures, we collect each dividend and reinvest it in risk-free bonds earning the rate r. Thus, dividend D_1 will grow to a value of $D_1(1 + r)^{T-t_1}$ at expiration. By the expiration day, the dividends will have grown to a value of

$$\sum_{j=1}^{N} D_j(1 + r)^{T-t_j},$$

which we shall write compactly as D_T. Thus, now we let D_T be the accumulated value at T of all dividends over the life of the futures plus the interest earned on them. In the previous example, we had only one dividend but D_T was still the same concept, the accumulated future value of the dividends. At expiration the stock is sold for S_T, and the futures is settled and generates a cash flow of $-(f_T(T) - f_0(T))$, which equals $-(S_T - f_0(T))$. Thus, the total cash flow at expiration is

$$S_T - (S_T - f_0(T)) + D_T,$$

or

$$f_0(T) + D_T.$$

This amount is also known in advance, so its present value, discounted at the risk-free rate, must equal the current value of the portfolio, which is the value of the stock, S_0. Setting these terms equal and solving for $f_0(T)$ gives

$$f_0(T) = S_0(1 + r)^T - D_T.$$

Thus, the futures price is the spot price compounded at the risk-free rate minus the compound future value of the dividends. The entire process of buying the stock, selling a futures, and collecting and reinvesting dividends to produce a risk-free transaction is illustrated in Figure 9.7 for a stock that

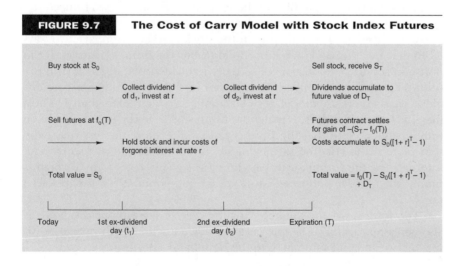

FIGURE 9.7   **The Cost of Carry Model with Stock Index Futures**

pays two dividends during the life of the futures. The total value accumulated at expiration is set equal to the total value today.

It might appear that our futures pricing model is inconsistent with the cost of carry equation we previously developed, in which $f_0(T) = S_0 + \theta$. We can show, however, that the formulas are identical and that the cost of carry will reflect the interest minus any offsetting dividends. Suppose we add and subtract S_0 on the right-hand side of the above equation:

$$f_0(T) = S_0 + S_0(1 + r)^T - S_0 - D_T.$$

Then rearranging terms gives

$$f_0(T) = S_0 + \{S_0[(1 + r)^T - 1] - D_T\}.$$

The term in braces is θ, the cost of carry. Within the braces, the first term, $S_0[(1 + r)^T - 1]$, is the interest forgone on an investment of S_0 dollars for a period of T years. The second term represents the compound future value of the dividends earned. Thus, the entire term added to S_0 is the cost of carry.

A stock index is a weighted combination of securities, most of which pay dividends. In reality, the dividend flow is more or less continuous, although not of a constant amount. As we did with options, however, we can fairly safely assume a continuous flow of dividends at a constant yield, δ. Using r_c as the continuously compounded risk-free rate and S_0 as the spot price of the index, the model is written as

$$f_0(T) = S_0 e^{(r_c - \delta)T}.$$

It is worth noting that this formula is precisely what one would obtain if all of the assumptions of the Black-Scholes model were applied to futures.

This format makes an interpretation somewhat easier. Suppose an investor is considering speculating on the stock market. There are two ways to do this: buy the stock index portfolio or buy the futures contract. If the portfolio is purchased, the investor receives dividends at a rate of δ. If the futures contract is purchased, the investor receives no dividends. The dividend yield enters the model as the factor $e^{-\delta T}$, which is less than 1. Thus, the effect of dividends is to make the futures price lower than it would be without them. Note that the futures price will exceed (be less than) the spot price if the risk-free rate is higher (lower) than the dividend yield. Alternatively, the formula can be written as $f_0(T) = (S_0 e^{-\delta T})e^{r_c T}$, which is simply the dividend-adjusted stock price compounded at the risk-free rate.

The futures pricing equation for the case of continuous dividends is also consistent with our simple cost of carry equation, $f_0(T) = S_0 + \theta$. To see this, we add and subtract S_0 to the right-hand side, giving

A stock index futures price is the stock price compounded at the risk-free rate minus the future value of the dividends. Alternatively it can be viewed as the dividend-adjusted stock price compounded at the risk-free rate.

$$f_0(T) = S_0 e^{(r_c - \delta)T} + S_0 - S_0,$$

which we can then express as

$$f_0(T) = S_0 + \{S_0[e^{(r_c - \delta)T} - 1]\}.$$

The term in braces on the right-hand side is the cost of carry, θ. The exponential function determines the compound future value of S_0 growing at the rate of $r_c - \delta$. Subtracting the 1 removes the original value of S_0, leaving the interest minus the dividends that accumulate over the life of the futures.

A **NUMERICAL EXAMPLE**   Consider the following problem. A stock index is at 50, the continuously compounded risk-free rate is 8 percent, the continuously compounded dividend yield is 6 percent, and the time to expiration is 60 days, so T is $60/365 = 0.164$. Then the futures price is

$$f_0(T) = 50e^{(.08 - .06)(.164)} = 50.16$$

If the risk-free rate were 5 percent, the futures price would be

$$f_0(T) = 50e^{(.05 - .06)(.164)} = 49.92.$$

The stock index futures pricing model is used extensively by traders and institutions to evaluate stock index futures contracts. If the futures price does not conform to the model, an opportunity to earn a riskless profit in excess of the risk-free rate is possible. Empirical research tends to support the pricing model, but we shall defer further discussion and illustration of this issue until Chapter 11. For now, let us look at how futures contracts of different expirations are related.

Prices of Futures Contracts of Different Expirations

Earlier we presented the important relationship

$$f_0(T) = S_0 + \theta,$$

which, with no dividend or interest payments or a shortage of the good, means that the futures price is above the spot price. Now consider two futures contracts on the same commodity but with different expirations. Let those two expirations be T_1 and T_2, where $T_2 > T_1$. We shall use the notation 1 and 2 to denote the respective time points. Thus,

$$f_0(1), f_0(2) = \text{futures prices}$$
$$\theta_1, \theta_2 = \text{cost of carry on each contract, respectively.}$$

The futures–spot price relationships for the two contracts are

$$f_0(1) = S_0 + \theta_1$$
$$f_0(2) = S_0 + \theta_2.$$

Solving each of these for the spot price, S_0, gives

$$S_0 = f_0(1) - \theta_1$$
$$S_0 = f_0(2) - \theta_2.$$

The spread between the prices of two futures contracts is the difference in their costs of carry and represents the cost of carry over the period starting at the expiration of the nearby contract and ending at the expiration of the deferred contract.

We then can set these equal to each other and solve for $f_0(2) - f_0(1)$:

$$f_0(2) - f_0(1) = \theta_2 - \theta_1.$$

This equation defines the spread between futures prices. The spread between the nearby and deferred contracts is the difference in their respective costs of carry. The term $\theta_2 - \theta_1$ is the cost of the carry for the time interval between T_1 and T_2.

As an example, consider the following soybean oil contract. On September 26 of a particular year, the December contract was priced at 14.64

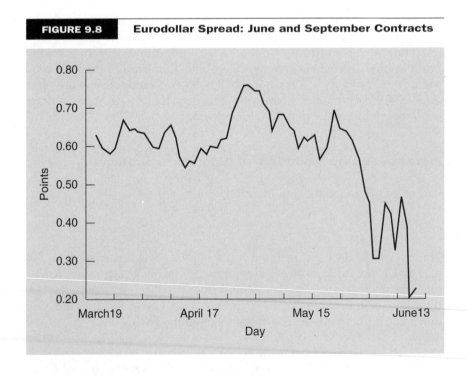

FIGURE 9.8   **Eurodollar Spread: June and September Contracts**

cents per pound and the January contract at 14.75 cents per pound. The difference of .11 cents per pound is the cost of carry of soybean oil from December to January.

It is helpful to examine the behavior of the spread through time. Figures 9.8 and 9.9 illustrate these relationships for June and September Eurodollar contracts. Figure 9.8 is the spread—the June futures price minus the September futures price—starting at about 60 trading days prior to the June expiration. Figure 9.9 presents the June and September futures prices and the spot price. Note that the September contract price is less than the June contract price. As the two contracts approach the June expiration, the spread narrows. This reflects the fact that the cost of carry of the June contract is approaching zero. The June contract is beginning to behave like the spot Eurodollar. The cost of carry of the September contract also declines, but less rapidly than that of the June contract. The spread obviously does not change in a perfectly predictable manner, which is one reason spread trading is so popular among futures traders. As we shall see in Chapter 11, there are strategies to take advantage of changes in the spread.

FIGURE 9.9   **Spot, Nearby, and Deferred Prices: June and September Eurodollar Contracts**

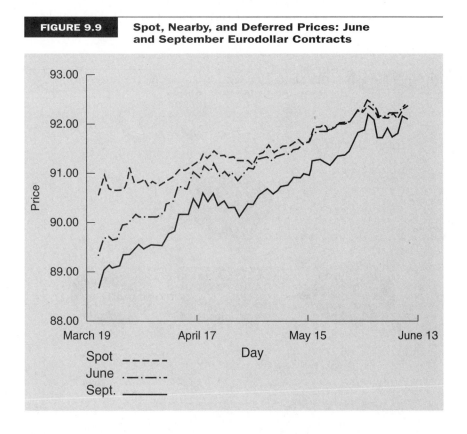

Summary

This chapter introduced several approaches to understanding the pricing of forward and futures contracts. It first established that the spot price is determined by the cost of carry and the risk premium. It then examined the relationship between futures and spot prices. It also addressed the joint issues of whether futures prices are unbiased estimators of future spot prices and whether futures prices offer risk premiums to speculators. The chapter examined the relationship between forward and futures prices. We saw that if future interest rates are uncertain, forward prices need not equal futures prices. We also saw that credit risk can affect the relationship between futures and forward prices.

So far in this book we have endeavored to understand the relationship between derivative prices and the prices of their underlying assets. We saw how put-call parity and the Black-Scholes model explain these relationships for options. The cost of carry model explains this relationship for forwards and futures. With our primary asset of interest being stock, Figure 9.10 illustrates this linkage.

As we move into Chapter 10, we should keep a few points in mind. We can reasonably accept the fact that forward and futures prices and spot prices are described by the cost of carry relationship. We do not know

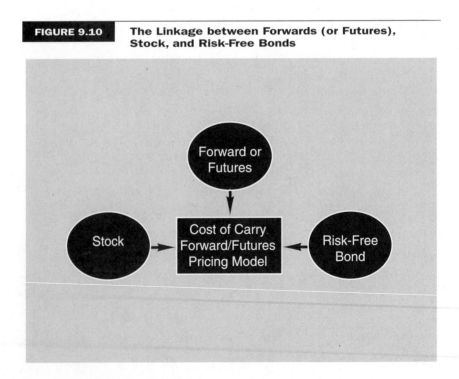

FIGURE 9.10   **The Linkage between Forwards (or Futures), Stock, and Risk-Free Bonds**

whether forward and futures prices are unbiased, but it seems logical to believe that holders of spot positions expect to earn a risk premium. When they hedge, they transfer the risk to forward and futures traders. It is, therefore, reasonable to expect forward and futures traders to demand a risk premium. Finally, although we have good reason to believe that forward prices are not precisely equal to futures prices, we see little reason to give much weight to the effect of marking to market on the performance of trading strategies. Accordingly, we shall ignore its effects in Chapter 10, which covers hedging strategies, and Chapter 11, which presents advanced strategies.

Key Terms

Before continuing to Chapter 10, you should be able to give brief definitions of the following terms.

- term structure of interest rates
- net interest
- cost of carry/cost of carry model
- quasi arbitrage
- contango

- convenience yield
- backwardation/inverted market
- normal backwardation
- normal contango
- risk premium hypothesis

Further Reading

An excellent explanation of futures pricing is in

French, K.C. "Pricing Financial Futures Contracts: An Introduction." *The Journal of Applied Corporate Finance* 1 (1989): 59–66.

The relationships between futures and forward prices were first derived in

Cox, J.C., J.E. Ingersoll, Jr., and S.A. Ross. "The Relation between Forward Prices and Futures Prices." *Journal of Financial Economics* 9 (1981): 321–346.

Jarrow, R.A., and G.S. Oldfield. "Forward Contracts and Futures Contracts." *Journal of Financial Economics* 9 (1981): 373–382.

Some empirical studies on several of the pricing relationships studied in this chapter are in

Cornell, B., and M. Reinganum. "Forward and Futures Prices: Evidence from the Foreign Exchange Markets." *The Journal of Finance* 36 (1981): 1035–1046.

French, K.R. "A Comparison of Futures and Forward Prices." *Journal of Financial Economics* 12 (1983): 311–342.

French, K.R. "Detecting Spot Price Forecasts in Futures Prices." *The Journal of Business* 59 (1986): S39—S54.

Questions and Problems

1. Assume there is a forward market for a commodity. The forward price of the commodity is $45. The contract expires in one year. The risk-free rate is 10 percent. Now, six months later, new forward contracts are being written at a price of $54. What is the original forward contract worth at this time? Explain why this is the correct value of the forward contract in six months by showing how the contract holder can capture that value even though the original contract does not have a liquid market like a futures contract.

2. Why is the value of a futures contract at the time it is purchased equal to zero? Contrast this with the value of the corresponding spot commodity.

3. Identify and provide a brief explanation of the factors that affect the spot price of a storable asset.

4. On a particular day, the S&P 500 futures settlement price was 899.30. You buy one contract at around the close of the market at the settlement price. The next day, the contract opens at 899.70 and the settlement price at the close of the day is 899.10. Determine the value of the futures contract at the opening, an instant before the close, and after the close. Remember that the S&P futures contract has a $500 multiplier.

5. A particular stock index futures expires on March 15. On March 13, the contract is selling at 353.625. Assume that there is a forward contract that also expires on March 15. The current forward price is 353. The risk-free rate is 5 percent per year, and you can assume that this rate will remain in effect for the next two days. Answer the following questions:

   a. Identify the existence of an arbitrage opportunity. What transactions should be executed on March 13?

   b. On March 14 the futures price is 353.35, and on March 15 the futures expires at 350.125. Show that the arbitrage works.

   c. Given your answer in part b, what effect will this have on market prices?

6. Identify and explain five conditions under which forward and futures prices would be equal.

7. On June 28, the price of the September Treasury bill futures is 92.95. The spot price of 91-day Treasury bills is quoted at a discount of 7.06, while the spot price of 182-day Treasury bills is 7.24. Estimate the forward rate on 91-day Treasury bills, and compare it to the rate implied by the futures market.

8. On March 15, the spot discount rate on 97-day T-bills is 8.48. This rate is based on a 360-day year. The following rates are discount rates

on that day for the 90-day T-bill futures contracts expiring on the dates indicated. Derive the futures term structure.

Contract	Rate	Expiration
June	9.22	June 20
September	9.74	September 19
December	10.06	December 19

9. Construct an arbitrage example involving an asset that can be sold short, and use it to explain the cost of carry model for pricing futures.

10. Comment on the following statement made by a futures trader: "Futures prices are determined by either expectations or the cost of carry."

11. If futures prices are less than spot prices, the explanation usually given is the convenience yield. Explain what the convenience yield is. Then identify certain assets on which convenience yields are more likely to exist and other assets on which they are not likely to be found.

12. Suppose there is an asset on which you know there is no convenience yield, yet the futures price is below the spot price. Can you think of an explanation for this?

13. What is a contango market? How do we interpret the cost of carry in a contango market? What is a backwardation market? How do we explain the cost of carry in a backwardation market?

14. On September 26, the spot price of wheat was $3.5225 per bushel and the price of a December wheat futures was $3.64 per bushel. How do you interpret the futures price if there is no risk premium in the futures market?

15. Reconsider the wheat example in problem 14. The interest forgone on money tied up in a bushel until expiration is 0.03, and the cost of storing the wheat is 0.0875 per bushel. The risk premium is 0.035 per bushel.

   a. What is the expected price of wheat on the spot market in December?

   b. Show how the futures price is related to the spot price.

   c. Show how the expected spot price at expiration, your answer in part a, is related to the futures price today.

   d. Show how the expected futures price at expiration is related to the futures price today.

   e. Explain who earns the risk premium and why.

16. On a particular day, the September S&P 500 stock index futures was priced at 960.50. The S&P 500 index was at 956.49. The contract

expires 73 days later. The risk-free rate is 5.96 percent, and the dividend yield on the index is 2.75 percent. Is the futures overpriced or underpriced?

17. How do you interpret the difference between the January frozen concentrated orange juice futures price of $1.077 per pound and the March futures price of $1.0785? The prices are as of the previous September. Explain why these values differ.

18. Suppose there is a commodity in which the expected future spot price is $60. To induce investors to buy futures contracts, a risk premium of $4 is required. To store the commodity for the life of the futures contract would cost $5.50. Find the futures price.

19. On July 10, a farmer observes that the spot price of corn is $2.735 per bushel and the September futures price is $2.76. The farmer would like a prediction of the spot price in September but believes the market is dominated by hedgers holding long positions in corn. Explain how the farmer would use this information in a forecast of the future price of corn.

20. Suppose the futures contract with the earliest expiration is priced higher than the one with the next earliest expiration. What explanation can you give for this condition?

21. The cost of carry futures pricing equation may appear slightly flawed to some people. To derive it, we equated a payoff at expiration with the initial outlay for the asset. Since these cash flows occur at different points in time, the time value of money seems to have been omitted. Explain why this interpretation is not correct.

22. (Concept Problem) Suppose there is a futures contract on a portfolio of stocks that currently are worth $100. The futures has a life of 90 days, and during that time the stocks will pay dividends of $0.75 in 30 days, $0.85 in 60 days, and $0.90 in 90 days. The simple interest rate is 12 percent.

   a. Find the price of the futures contract assuming no arbitrage opportunities are present.

   b. Find the value of θ, the cost of carry in dollars.

23. (Concept Problem) Suppose a futures margin account pays interest but at a rate that is less than the risk-free rate. Consider a trader who buys the asset and sells a futures to form a risk-free hedge. Would the trader believe the futures price should be lower or higher than if the margin account paid interest at the risk-free rate?

Futures Hedging Strategies

The law of the conservation of risk is like the law of the conservation of misery. You can only pass it around. You cannot get rid of it.

TANYA STYBLO BEDER
Risk, February 1999

Hedging is a transaction designed to reduce or, in some cases, eliminate risk. Our material on options presented numerous examples of hedges, the most obvious being the covered call and protective put. Now we shall find that it is also possible, in some cases preferable, to use forwards or futures to hedge.

Until now we have emphasized that there are many similarities and differences between forward and futures contracts. Both can be used for hedging. When choosing a forward or futures hedge over an option hedge, the hedger agrees to give up future gains and losses. No up-front cost is incurred. In contrast, an option hedge such as a protective put preserves future gains but at the expense of an up-front cost, the option premium. Forward contracting, as we previously noted, involves some credit risk and is generally available only in very large transaction sizes. We shall eventually study a number of types of forward hedges, but we defer that discussion until a later chapter, after which we have introduced swaps, a more popular type of forward hedge. In this chapter our focus is on the use of futures in hedging.

Chapter Objectives

■ To explain some of the reasons for and against hedging

■ To present the basic concepts associated with hedging, such as the basis, short and long hedging, and the risks of hedging

■ To identify the factors that are involved in deciding to undertake a hedge

■ To illustrate the different methods (price sensitivity, minimum variance) of determining the number of futures contracts to use in a hedge

■ To illustrate examples of short-term interest rate futures hedges, intermediate- and long-term interest rate futures hedges, and stock index futures hedges

Why Hedge?

Before we begin with the technical aspects of hedging, it is worthwhile to ask two questions: (1) Why do firms hedge? and (2) Should they hedge? Hedging is done to reduce risk, but is this desirable? If everyone hedged, would we not simply end up with an economy in which no one takes risks? This would surely lead to economic stagnancy. Moreover, we must wonder whether hedging can actually increase shareholder wealth.[1]

If the famous Modigliani-Miller propositions are correct, then the value of the firm is independent of any financial decisions, which include hedging. Hedging, however, may be desired by the shareholders simply to find a more acceptable combination of return and risk. It can be argued, however, that firms need not hedge since shareholders, if they wanted hedging, could do it themselves. But this ignores several important points. It assumes that shareholders can correctly assess all the firm's hedgeable risks. If a company is exposed to the risk associated with volatile raw materials prices, can the shareholders properly determine the degree of risk? Can they determine the periods over which that risk is greatest? Can they determine the correct number of futures contracts necessary to hedge their share of the total risk? Do they even qualify to open a futures brokerage account? Will their transaction costs be equal to or less than their proportional share of the transaction costs incurred if the firm did the hedging? The answer to each of these questions is "maybe not." It should be obvious that hedging is not something that shareholders can always do as effectively as firms.

Firms hedge to save taxes, reduce bankruptcy costs, and, in some cases, because managers want to reduce the risk of their own wealth, which is tied to their firms' performance. Hedging is also done in the course of offering risk management services for clients and possibly because shareholders cannot hedge as effectively as firms.

In addition, there may be other reasons why firms hedge, such as tax advantages. Low-income firms, for example those that are below the highest corporate tax rate, can particularly benefit from the interaction between hedging and the progressive corporate income tax structure. Hedging also reduces the probability of bankruptcy. This is not necessarily valuable to the shareholders except that it can reduce the expected costs that are incurred if the firm does go bankrupt. Finally, a firm may choose to hedge because its managers' livelihoods may be heavily tied to the performance of the firm. The managers may then benefit from reducing the firm's risk. This may not be in the shareholders' best interests, but it can at least explain why some firms hedge. Finally, hedging may send a signal to potential creditors that the firm is making a concerted effort to protect the value of the underlying assets. This can result in more favorable credit terms and less costly, restrictive covenants.

Many firms, such as financial institutions, are constantly trading over-the-counter financial products like swaps and forwards on behalf of their clients. They offer these services to help their clients manage their risks. These financial institutions then turn around and hedge the risk they have assumed on behalf of their clients. How do they make money? They quote rates and prices to their clients that reflect a spread sufficient to cover their

---

[1]The material in this section draws heavily from C. W. Smith and R. M. Stulz, "The Determinants of Firms' Hedging Policies," *Journal of Financial and Quantitative Analysis* 20 (1985): 391–405; D. Duffie, "Corporate Risk Management 101: Why Hedge?" *Corporate Risk Management* 3 (May 1991): 22–25; and D. R. Nance, C. W. Smith Jr., and C. W. Smithson, "On the Determinants of Corporate Hedging," *The Journal of Finance* 48 (March 1993): 267–284.

hedging costs and include a profit. In this manner, they become retailers of hedging services.

Lest we give a one-sided view of hedging, it is important to consider some reasons not to hedge. One reason is that hedging can give a misleading impression of the amount of risk reduced. There is an old saying in derivatives: "The only perfect hedge is in a Japanese garden." Hedges nearly always leave some risk and some hedges leave a surprising amount of risk that was supposed to have been eliminated. Hedging should always be viewed as risk reducing but not eliminating, thus requiring that the remaining risk be identified and monitored.

Another problem with hedging is that it eliminates the opportunity to take advantage of favorable market conditions. In other words, hedging reduces the gain potential as well as the loss potential. Carried to an extreme, hedging can nearly eliminate any reason for being in business in the first place. The creation of wealth does not come about by indiscriminate hedging. Hedging should be selective—that is, reducing certain risks while maintaining exposures where an advantage is perceived.

Finally, we should add that *there is really no such thing as a hedge.* As surprising as that sounds, consider this. When an investor moves all funds from stock to cash, he may think he is hedging, but he is really taking a position that the market will go down. When a corporation hedges away the risk associated with borrowing at a floating rate, it is taking a position that interest rates will go up. In either case, the elimination of risk is taking a position based on a view that an unfavorable event will occur in the market. This is as much of a speculative action as is investing all of one's money in the stock market or borrowing at a floating rate. In other words, reducing risk is a bet that bad things will happen in the market.

Of course, in line with the tradition in financial markets, we shall still call the act of reducing risk *hedging*.

Hedging Concepts

Before we can understand why a certain hedge is placed or how it works, we must become acquainted with a few basic hedging concepts. We have mentioned some of these points before but have not specifically applied them to hedging strategies.

Short Hedge and Long Hedge

The terms **short hedge** and **long hedge** distinguish hedges that involve short and long positions in the futures contract, respectively. A hedger who holds the commodity and is concerned about a decrease in its price might consider hedging it with a short position in futures. If the spot price and futures price move together, the hedge will reduce some of the risk.

A short hedge means to hedge by going short in the futures market. A long hedge means to hedge by going long in the futures market.

For example, if the spot price decreases, the futures price also will decrease. Since the hedger is short the futures contract, the futures transaction produces a profit that at least partially offsets the loss on the spot position. This is called a *short hedge* because the hedger is short futures.

Another type of short hedge can be used in anticipation of the future sale of an asset. An example of this occurs when a firm decides that it will need to borrow money at a later date. Borrowing money is equivalent to issuing or selling a bond or promissory note. If interest rates increase before the money is borrowed, the loan will be more expensive. A similar risk exists if a firm has issued a floating rate liability. Since the rate is periodically reset, the firm has contracted for a series of future loans at unknown rates. To hedge this risk, the firm might short an interest rate futures contract. If rates increase, the futures transaction will generate a profit that will at least partially offset the higher interest rate on the loan. Because it is taken out in anticipation of a future transaction in the spot market, this type of hedge is known as an **anticipatory hedge.**

Another type of anticipatory hedge involves an individual who plans to purchase a commodity at a later date. Fearing an increase in the commodity's price, the investor might buy a futures contract. Then, if the price of the commodity increases, the futures price also will increase and produce a profit on the futures position. That profit will at least partially offset the higher cost of purchasing the commodity. This is a *long hedge,* because the hedger is long in the futures market.

Another type of long hedge might be placed when one is short an asset. Although this hedge is less common, it would be appropriate for someone who has sold short a stock and is concerned that the market will go up. Rather than close out the short position, one might buy a futures and earn a profit on the long position in futures that will at least partially offset the loss on the short position in the stock.

In each of these cases, the hedger held a position in the spot market that was subject to risk. The futures transaction served as a temporary substitute for a spot transaction. Thus, when one holds the spot commodity and is concerned about a price decrease but does not want to sell it, one can execute a short futures trade. Selling the futures contract would substitute for selling the commodity. Table 10.1 summarizes these various hedging situations.

The Basis

The basis is the difference between the spot price and the futures price.

The **basis** is one of the most important concepts in futures markets. The basis usually is defined as the spot price minus the futures price. Some books and articles, however, define it as the futures price minus the spot price. In this book, we shall use the former definition:

$$\text{Basis} = \text{Spot price} - \text{Futures price.}$$

TABLE 10.1	Summary of Hedging Situations	
Condition Today	**Risk**	**Appropriate Hedge**
Hold asset	Asset price may fall	Short hedge
Plan to buy asset	Asset price may rise	Long hedge
Sold short asset	Asset price may rise	Long hedge
Issued floating-rate liability	Interest rates may rise	Short hedge
Plan to issue liability	Interest rates may rise	Short hedge

Note: Short hedge means long spot, short futures; long hedge means short spot, long futures.

HEDGING AND THE BASIS   The basis plays an important role in understanding the process of hedging. Here we will look at the concept of hedging and how the basis affects the performance of a hedge. Ultimately we shall need to understand the factors that influence the basis.

Let us define the following terms:

T = time to expiration
t = a time point prior to expiration
S_0 = spot price today
f_0 = futures price today
S_T = spot price at expiration
f_T = futures price at expiration
S_t = spot price at time t prior to expiration
f_t = futures price at time t prior to expiration
Π = profit from the strategy

For the time being, we shall ignore marking to market, any costs of storing the asset, and other transaction costs.

The concept of a hedge is not new. When we looked at options, we constructed several types of hedges, some of which were riskless. By taking a position in a stock and an opposite position in an option, gains (losses) on the stock are offset by losses (gains) on the option. We can do the same thing with futures: hold a long (short) position in the spot market and a short (long) position in the futures market. For a long position in the spot market, the profit from a hedge held to expiration is

$$\Pi \text{ (short hedge)} = S_T - S_0 \text{ (from the spot market)} - (f_T - f_0) \text{ (from the futures market)}.$$

For a short position in the spot market and a long position in the futures market, the sign of each term in the above equation is reversed; that is,

$$\Pi \text{ (long hedge)} = -S_T + S_0 \text{ (from the spot market)} + (f_T - f_0) \text{ (from the futures market)}.$$

D e r i v a t i v e s   i n   A c t i o n

Hedging: It's the Law

There are many good reasons for hedging and occasionally good reasons for not hedging. Rarely does a firm have to worry about whether failing to hedge is breaking the law. In Indiana, it just might be. Take the case of *Brane v. Roth* (590 NE 2nd, 587).

Farmers Cooperative is a grain elevator co-op engaged in the business of buying, storing, and selling grain. The co-op's profits had been declining steadily over the period of 1977–1979. In 1979 its accountant recommended to its board of directors that the co-op begin hedging in the futures market. The board did authorize the co-op's manager to begin hedging, but a total of only about $20,000 of grain was hedged, during a period in which its grain sales were over $7 million. The co-op experienced substantial operating losses. Shareholders determined that a hedge would have saved them significant amounts of money and sued the board of directors. The plaintiffs argued that the board breached its duty by using a manager inexperienced in hedging and by failing to supervise the manager. The plaintiffs also argued that the board members failed to learn enough about hedging to protect the shareholders' interests. The Superior Court of Miami County, Indiana, agreed and ordered the directors to pay over $400,000 to the plaintiffs. The case was appealed to the Indiana Court of Appeals, which upheld the judgment in April 1992. The Appeals court stated that the losses were caused by a failure to hedge and that the directors had made no effort to learn about hedging.

Of course, after the fact it is always easy to say that losses could have been avoided had hedging been done. Consider the counterargument, however. Suppose the co-op had made money before accounting for any hedging activities. Now suppose it had been fully hedged. Then it would have made little if any money. Could the shareholders then have sued it for hedging? It seems that where the directors erred was in failing to be properly informed about the advantages and disadvantages of hedging while authorizing, but not supervising, a modest hedging program. Had they made the effort to learn about the futures market, they might well have easily justified the small hedging program as experimental, with an eye toward gathering more information about the costs and benefits of hedging before launching into a more comprehensive hedging program.

Is failing to hedge illegal in general? Probably not, at least not yet. But it is clear that boards of directors, and probably management, are vulnerable to the charge that they failed to learn how derivative markets can help them run a business.

In some cases, we might wish to close out the position at time t, that is, before expiration. Then the profit from the hedge that is long in the spot market is

$$\Pi \text{ (short hedge)} = S_t - S_0 - (f_t - f_0).$$

At expiration, a person buying a futures contract can expect to receive immediate delivery of the good. Thus, an expiring futures contract is the same as the purchase of the spot commodity; therefore, $S_T = f_T$. Thus, the profit if the hedge is held to expiration is simply $f_0 - S_0$. That means that the hedge is equivalent to buying the asset at price S_0 and immediately guaranteeing a sale price of f_0.

As an example, suppose you buy an asset for $100 and sell a futures contract on the asset at $103. At expiration, the spot and futures prices are both \$97. You sell the asset for \$97, taking a \$3 loss, and close your futures contract at \$97, making a \$6 gain, for a net profit of \$3. Alternatively, you could deliver the asset on your futures contract, receiving \$97, and collect the \$6 that has accumulated in your futures account, making the effective sale price of the asset \$103. In either case, the transaction is equivalent to selling the asset for \$103, the original futures price.

Since the basis is defined as the spot price minus the futures price, we can write it as a variable, b, where

$$b_0 = S_0 - f_0 \text{ (initial basis)}$$
$$b_t = S_t - f_t \text{ (basis at time t)}$$
$$b_T = S_T - f_T \text{ (basis at expiration)}.$$

Thus, for a position closed out at time t,

$$\Pi \text{ (short hedge)} = S_t - f_t - (S_0 - f_0),$$
$$= b_t - b_0.$$

The profit from the hedge is simply the change in the basis. The uncertainty regarding how the basis will change is called **basis risk.** A hedge substitutes the change in the basis for the change in the spot price. The basis change is far less variable than the spot price change; hence, the hedged position is less risky than the unhedged position. Because basis risk results from the uncertainty over the change in the basis, hedging is a speculative activity but produces a risk level much lower than that of an unhedged position.

Hedging entails the assumption of basis risk, the uncertainty of the basis over the hedge period. The hedge profit is the change in the basis.

Hedging can also be viewed as a transaction that attempts to establish the expected future sale price of an asset (or purchase price, if a long hedge). For example, the equation for the profit on a short hedge can be written as $f_0 + (S_t - f_t) - S_0$. Since the hedger paid S_0 dollars to purchase the asset, then the effective sale price of the asset can be viewed as $f_0 + (S_t - f_t)$, which can be written as $f_0 + b_t$. In other words, a short hedge establishes the future sale price of the asset as the current futures price plus the basis. Since f_0 is known, the effective future sale price is uncertain only to the extent that the basis is uncertain. If the hedge is held to expiration, the effective sale price becomes $f_0 + b_T$, which is simply f_0 since the basis at expiration is zero. Thus, the sale price of the asset is established as f_0 when the transaction is initiated. The hedger would be absolutely certain that he or she would be able to effectively sell the asset for the futures price. This would be a perfect hedge. Most hedges are imperfect for a variety of reasons but often because the hedger does not typically hold the position to expiration.

If the spot price increases by more than the futures price, the basis will increase. This is said to be a strengthening basis, and it improves the performance of the short hedge. If the futures price increases by more than the spot price, the basis will decrease, reducing the performance on the hedge. In that case, the basis is said to be weakening.

TABLE 10.2	Hedging Profitability and the Basis

Type of Hedge	Benefits from	Which Occurs if
Short hedge	Strengthening basis	Spot price rises more than futures price rises
		or
		Spot price falls less than futures price falls
		or
		Spot price rises and futures price falls
Long hedge	Weakening basis	Spot price rises less than futures price rises
		or
		Spot price falls more than futures price falls
		or
		Spot price falls and futures price rises

Note: Short hedge means long spot, short futures; long hedge means short spot, long futures.

For a long hedger, however, everything is reversed. The profit equation is $-(S_t - S_0) + (f_t - f_0) = -b_t + b_0$. Now a weakening basis improves the performance and a strengthening basis reduces the performance. These relationships between hedging profitability and the basis are summarized in Table 10.2.

As noted above, if a hedge is held all the way to expiration, the basis goes to zero. In that case, the profit is simply $-b_0$ from a short hedge and $+b_0$ from a long hedge.

Finally, we should remember that hedging incurs costs, such as the transaction costs of the futures. In addition, if the asset is held, it will incur costs of storage. These will reduce the profit but their effects are generally known in advance and, thus, do not impose any additional risk.

A HEDGING EXAMPLE Let us consider an example using gold. On March 30, the price of a gold futures expiring in June was $388.60 per troy ounce. The spot price of gold was $387.15. Suppose a gold dealer held 100 troy ounces of gold worth $100(387.15) = 38,715$. To protect against a decrease in the price of gold, the dealer might sell one futures contract on 100 troy ounces. In our notation,

$$S_0 = 387.15$$
$$f_0 = 388.60$$
$$b_0 = 387.15 - 388.60 = -1.45.$$

If the hedge is held to expiration, the basis should converge to zero. It might not go precisely to zero, however, and we shall see why later. If it does, the profit should be -1 times the original basis times the number of ounces:

$$\Pi = -1(-1.45)(100) = 145.$$

Suppose that at expiration the spot price of gold is \$408.50. Then the dealer sells the gold in the spot market for a profit of $100(408.50 - 387.15) = 2,135$. The short futures contract is offset by purchasing it in the futures market for a profit of $-100(408.50 - 388.60) = -1,990$. The overall profit therefore is $-1,990 + 2,135 = 145$, as we predicted.

Now suppose we close the position prior to expiration. For example, on May 5 the spot price of gold was \$377.52 and the June futures price was \$378.63. In our notation, $S_t = 377.52$ and $f_t = 378.63$. If the gold is sold in the spot market, the profit is $100(377.52 - 387.15) = -963$. The futures contract is bought back at 378.63 for a profit of $-100(378.63 - 388.60) = 997$. The net gain is $-963 + 997 = 34$. As we said earlier, this should equal the change in the basis, $b_t - b_0$. The original basis was -1.45. The basis when the position is closed is $S_t - f_t$, or $377.52 - 378.63 = -1.11$. The profit, therefore, is

$$-1.11 - (-1.45) = .34,$$

which is the gain on the hedge per ounce of gold.

THE BEHAVIOR OF THE BASIS   Figure 10.1 shows the basis on a June Eurodollar contract for a period of 60 days prior to expiration. Notice how

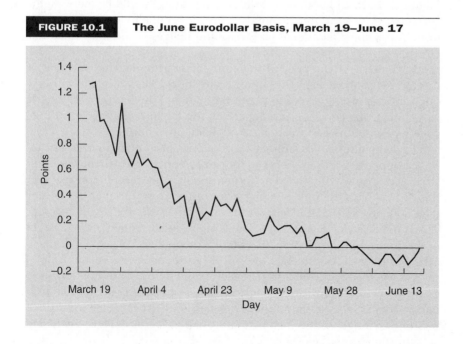

FIGURE 10.1   **The June Eurodollar Basis, March 19–June 17**

the basis starts off at about 1.3 and then gradually decreases as expiration nears. At around two weeks before expiration, the basis actually becomes negative. Because the Eurodollar contract is settled in cash, the basis on the expiration day automatically is zero.

In some cases, however, the basis does not converge exactly to zero. In the case of gold, for example, an investor who purchased gold on the spot market and immediately sold a futures contract that is about to expire would have to deliver the gold. There is a potentially significant delivery cost that could leave the futures price slightly above the spot price. For some commodities, there are several acceptable grades that can be delivered, so there are multiple spot prices. The short has control over the delivery and will choose to deliver the most economical grade. The futures price will tend to converge to the spot price of the commodity that is most likely to be delivered.

Some Risks of Hedging

Cross hedging involves an additional source of basis risk arising from the fact that the asset being hedged is not the same as the asset underlying the futures.

Sometimes the commodity being hedged and the commodity underlying the futures contract differ. A typical example, which we shall illustrate later, is the hedging of a corporate bond with a Treasury bond futures contract. This is referred to as a **cross hedge** and is a type of basis risk much greater than that encountered by hedging government bonds with Treasury bond futures. Corporate and government bond prices tend to move together, but the relationship is weaker than that of two government bonds. In addition, bonds with higher ratings would be more highly correlated with government bonds. Thus, lower-quality corporate bonds would carry some additional basis risk, and hedges would tend to be less effective.

In some cases, the price of the commodity being hedged and that of the futures contract move in opposite directions. Then a hedge will produce either a profit or a loss on both the spot and the futures positions. If one chooses the correct futures contract, this is unlikely to occur. If it occurs frequently, the hedger should find a different contract.

Hedging also entails another form of risk called **quantity risk.** For instance, suppose a farmer wishes to lock in the price at which an as yet unharvested crop will be sold. The farmer might sell a futures contract and thereby establish the future selling price of the crop. Yet what the farmer does not know and cannot hedge is the uncertainty over the size of the crop. This is the farmer's quantity risk. The farmer's total revenue is the product of the crop's price and its size. In a highly competitive market, the farmer's crop is too small to influence the price, but there are systematic factors, such as weather, that could influence everyone's crop. Thus, the crop size could be small when prices are high and large when prices are low. This situation creates its own natural hedge. When the farmer hedges, the price volatility no longer offsets the uncertainty of the crop size. Thus, the hedge actually can *increase* the overall risk.

Quantity uncertainty is common in farming but is by no means restricted to it. Many corporations and financial institutions do not know the sizes of future cash flows and thus must contend with quantity risk.

Contract Choice

The choice of futures contract actually consists of four decisions: (1) which futures commodity, (2) which expiration month, (3) whether to be long or short, and (4) the number of contracts. The number of contracts is so important that we defer it to the next main section.

WHICH FUTURES COMMODITY?   From the previous section, we can see that it is important to select a futures contract on a commodity that is highly correlated with the underlying commodity being hedged. In many cases the choice is obvious, but in some it is not.

The futures contract used for hedging should be liquid and should be on an asset that is highly correlated with the asset being hedged.

For example, suppose one wishes to hedge the rate on bank CDs, which are short-term money market instruments issued by commercial banks. There is no bank CD futures contract so the hedger must choose from among some other similar contracts. Liquidity is important, because the hedger must be able to close the contract easily. If the futures contract lacks the necessary liquidity, the hedger should select a contract that has sufficient liquidity and is highly correlated with the spot commodity being hedged. Since a Eurodollar is a short-term money market instrument, its futures contract, which is quite liquid, would seem appropriate for hedging bank CD rates. Of course, if the hedger wanted the hedging instrument to be identical to the underlying spot asset, he or she could go to the over-the-counter market and request a forward contract, but, as we have previously emphasized, that would entail some other considerations.

Another factor one should consider is whether the contract is correctly priced. A short hedger will be selling futures contracts and therefore should look for contracts that are overpriced or, in the worst case, correctly priced. A long hedger should hedge by buying underpriced contracts or, in the worst case, correctly priced contracts.

Sometimes the best hedge can be obtained by using more than one futures commodity. For example, a hedge of a corporate bond position might be more effective if both Treasury bond futures *and* municipal bond futures are used.

WHICH EXPIRATION?   Once one has selected the futures commodity, one must decide on the expiration month. As we know, only certain expiration months trade at a given time. For example, in September the Treasury bond futures contract has expirations of December of the current year, March, June, September, and December of the following year, and March, June, and September of the year after that. If the Treasury bond futures contract is the appropriate hedging vehicle, the contract used must come from this group of expirations.

The hedger should choose a contract that expires as close as possible to but after the hedge termination date.

In most cases, there will be a time horizon over which the hedge remains in effect. To obtain the maximum reduction in basis risk, a hedger should hold the futures position until as close as possible to expiration. Thus, an appropriate contract expiration would be one that corresponded as closely as possible to the expiration date. The general rule of thumb, however, is to avoid holding a futures position in the expiration month. This is because unusual price movements sometimes are observed in the expiration month, and this would pose an additional risk to hedgers. Thus, the hedger should choose an expiration month that is as close as possible to but after the month in which the hedge is terminated.[2]

Table 10.3 lists possible hedge termination dates for a Treasury bond futures hedge and the appropriate contracts for use. Consider, however, that *the longer the time to expiration, the less liquid the contract.* Therefore, the selection of a contract according to this criterion may need to be overruled by the necessity of using a liquid contract. If this happens, one should use a contract with a shorter expiration. When the contract moves into its expiration month, the futures position is closed out and a new position is opened in the next expiration month. This process, called *rolling the hedge forward,* generates some additional risk but can still be quite effective.

Of course, the time horizon problem can be handled perfectly by using a forward contract from the over-the-counter market. In fact, some hedgers have horizons of longer than 10 years, which can be hedged only by using forward contracts or swaps.

TABLE 10.3	Contract Expirations for Planned Hedge Termination Dates (Treasury Bond Futures Hedge Initiated on September 30, 2000)

Hedge Termination Date	Appropriate Contract
10/1/00–11/30/00	Dec 00
12/1/00–2/28/01	Mar 01
3/1/01–5/31/01	Jun 01
6/1/01–8/31/01	Sep 01
9/1/01–11/30/01	Dec 01
12/1/01–2/28/02	Mar 02
3/1/02–5/31/02	Jun 02
6/1/02–8/31/02	Sep 02
9/1/02–11/30/02	Dec 02

Note: The appropriate contract is based on the rule that the expiration date should be as soon as possible after the hedge termination date subject to no contract being held in its expiration month. Liquidity considerations may make some more distant contracts inappropriate.

---

[2]Not all contracts exhibit unusual price behavior in the expiration month. Thus, this rule need not always be strictly followed.

LONG OR SHORT?   After selecting the futures commodity and expiration month, the hedger must decide whether to be long or short. This decision is critical and there is absolutely no room for a mistake here. If a hedger goes long (or short) when she should have been short (or long), she has doubled the risk. The end result will be a gain or loss twice the amount of the gain or loss of the unhedged position.

    The decision of whether to go long or short requires a determination of which type of market move will result in a loss in the spot market. It then requires establishing a futures position that will be profitable while the spot position is losing. Table 10.4 summarizes three methods that will correctly identify the appropriate futures transaction. The first method requires that the hedger identify the worst case scenario and then establish a futures position that will profit if the worst case does occur. The second method

The decision of whether to go long or short futures is critical and can be made by determining whether a spot market move will help or hurt the spot position and how the futures market can be used to offset that risk.

TABLE 10.4	How to Determine Whether to Buy or Sell Futures When Hedging

Worst Case Scenario Method

1.   Assuming that the spot and futures markets move together, determine whether long and short positions in futures would be profitable if the market goes up or down.
2.   What is the worst that could happen in the spot market?
    a.   The spot market goes up.
    b.   The spot market goes down.
3.   Given your answer in 2, assume that the worst that *can* happen *will* happen.
4.   Given your answer in 3, and using your answer in 1, take a futures position that will be profitable.

Current Spot Position Method

1.   Determine whether your current position in the spot market is long or short.
    a.   If you own or plan to sell an asset, your current position is long.
    b.   If you are short an asset, your current position is short.
    c.   If you are committed to buying an asset in the future, your current position is short.
    d.   If you have issued a floating rate liability, your current position is long.
    e.   If you plan to issue a liability, your current position is long.
2.   Take a futures position that is opposite the position given by your answer in 1.

Anticipated Future Spot Transaction Method

1.   Determine what type of spot transaction you will be making when the hedge is terminated.
    a.   Sell an asset.
    b.   Buy an asset.
    c.   Issue (sell) a liability (this includes a liability with a floating rate reset).
2.   Given your answer in 1, you will need to terminate a futures position at the horizon date by doing the opposite transaction to the one in 1, e.g., if your answer in 1 is "sell," your answer here is "buy a futures."
3.   Given your answer in 2, you will need to open a futures contract today by doing the opposite, e.g., if your answer in 2 is "buy a futures," your answer here should be "sell a futures."

requires taking a futures position that is opposite to the current spot position. This is a simple method, but in some cases it is difficult to identify the current spot position. The third method identifies the spot transaction that will be conducted when the hedge is terminated. The futures transaction that will be conducted when the hedge is terminated should be the opposite of this spot transaction. The futures transaction that should be done today should be the opposite of the futures transaction that should be done at the termination of the hedge.

Margin Requirements and Marking to Market

Two other considerations in hedging are the margin requirement and the effect of marking to market. We discussed these factors earlier, but now we need to consider their implications for hedging.

Margin requirements, as we know, are very small and virtually insignificant in relation to the size of the position being hedged. Moreover, margin requirements for hedges are even smaller than speculative margins. In addition, margins can sometimes be posted with Treasury bills; thus, interest on the money can still be earned. Therefore, the initial amount of margin posted is really not a major factor in hedging.

What is important, however, is the effect of marking to market and the potential for margin calls. Remember that the profit on a futures transaction is supposed to offset the loss on the spot commodity. At least part of the time, there will be profits on the spot commodity and losses on the futures contract. On a given day when the futures contract generates a loss, the hedger must deposit additional margin money to cover that loss. Even if the spot position has generated a profit in excess of the loss on the futures contract, it may be impossible, or at least inconvenient, to withdraw the profit on the spot position to cover the loss on the futures.

This is one of the major obstacles to more widespread use of futures. Because futures profits and losses are realized immediately and spot profits and losses do not occur until the hedge is terminated, many potential hedgers tend to weigh the losses on the futures position more heavily than the gains on the spot. They also tend to think of hedges on an ex post rather than ex ante basis. If the hedge produced a profit on the spot position and a loss on the futures position, it would be apparent *after the fact* that the hedge should not have been done. But this would not be known *before the fact*.

Thus, a hedger must be aware that hedging will produce both gains and losses on futures transactions and will require periodic margin calls. The alternative to not meeting a margin call is closing the futures position. It is tempting to do this after a streak of losses and margin calls. If the futures position is closed, however, the hedge will no longer be in effect and the individual or firm will be exposed to the risk in the spot market, which is greater than the risk of the hedge.

In Chapter 9, we examined the effect of marking to market on the futures price. We concluded that the impact is fairly small. If, however, the interest earned or paid on the variation margin is not insignificant, it is possible to take it into account when establishing the optimal number of contracts. We shall cover this topic in a later section.

These are several of the most important factors one must consider before initiating a hedge. As we noted earlier, another important consideration is the correct number of futures contracts, or the hedge ratio.

Determination of the Hedge Ratio

The hedge ratio is the number of futures contracts one should use to hedge a particular exposure in the spot market.[3] The hedge ratio should be the one in which the futures profit or loss matches the spot profit or loss. There is no exact method of determining the hedge ratio before performing the hedge. There are, however, several ways to estimate it.

The hedge ratio is the number of futures contracts needed to offset the spot market risk.

The most elementary method is to take a position in the futures market equivalent in size to the position in the spot market. For example, if you hold $10 million of the commodity, you should hold futures contracts covering $10 million. If each futures contract has a price of $80,000, you should sell $10,000,000/$80,000 = 125 contracts. This approach is relatively naive, because it fails to consider that the futures and spot prices might not change in the same proportions. In some cases, however, particularly when the commodity being hedged is the same as the commodity underlying the futures contract, such a hedge ratio will be appropriate.

Nevertheless, in most other cases the futures and spot prices will change by different percentages. Suppose we write the profit from a hedge as follows:

$$\Pi = \Delta S + \Delta f N_f,$$

where the symbol Δ means *change in*. Thus, the profit is the change in the spot price (ΔS) plus the change in the futures price (Δf) multiplied by the number of futures contracts (N_f). A positive N_f means a long position and a negative N_f means a short position. For the futures profit or loss to completely offset the spot loss or profit, we set $\Pi = 0$ and find the value of N_f as

$$N_f = -\frac{\Delta S}{\Delta f}.$$

---

[3]Technically the hedge ratio is the dollar value of the futures position relative to the dollar value of the spot position. It is then used to determine the number of futures contracts necessary. In this book we shall let the hedge ratio refer to the number of futures contracts.

Because we assume futures and spot prices will move in the same direction, ΔS and Δf have the same sign; thus, N_f is negative. This example therefore is a short hedge, but the concept is equally applicable to a long hedge, where $\Pi = -\Delta S + \Delta f N_f$ and N_f would be positive.

Now we need to know the ratio $\Delta S/\Delta f$. There are several approaches to estimating this value.

Minimum Variance Hedge Ratio

The objective of a hedge — indeed, of any investment decision — is to maximize the investor's expected utility. In this book, however, we do not develop the principles of expected utility maximization. Therefore, we shall take a much simpler approach to the hedging problem and focus on risk minimization. The model used here comes from the work of Johnson (1960) and Stein (1961).

The profit from the short hedge is[4]

$$\Pi = \Delta S + \Delta f N_f.$$

The variance of the profit is

$$\sigma_\Pi^2 = \sigma_{\Delta S}^2 + \sigma_{\Delta f}^2 N_f^2 + 2\sigma_{\Delta S \Delta f} N_f,$$

where

$$\sigma_\Pi^2 = \text{variance of hedged profit}$$
$$\sigma_{\Delta S}^2 = \text{variance of change in the spot price}$$
$$\sigma_{\Delta f}^2 = \text{variance of change in the futures price}$$
$$\sigma_{\Delta S \Delta f} = \text{covariance of change in the spot price and change in the futures price.}$$

The minimum variance hedge ratio gives the optimal number of futures when the objective is to minimize risk.

The objective is to find the value of N_f that gives the minimum value of σ_Π^2. Appendix 10A presents the derivation. The formula for N_f is

$$N_f = -\frac{\sigma_{\Delta S \Delta f}}{\sigma_{\Delta f}^2}.$$

This formula gives the number of futures contracts that will produce the lowest possible variance. The negative sign means that the hedger should

---

[4]The problem as formulated here is in terms of the profit. An alternative, and in some ways preferable, formulation is in terms of the rate of return on the hedger's wealth. We shall use the profit formulation here because it is more frequently seen in the literature.

sell futures. If the problem were formulated as a long hedge, the sign would be positive.

You may recognize that the formula for N_f is very similar to that for β from a least squares regression. In fact, we can estimate N_f by running a regression with ΔS as the dependent variable and Δf as the independent variable. Of course, this can give us the correct value of N_f only for a historical set of data. We cannot know the actual value of N_f over an upcoming period. Extrapolating the future from the past is risky, but at least it is a starting point.

The effectiveness of the minimum variance hedge can be determined by examining the percentage of the risk reduced. Suppose we define hedging effectiveness as

$$e^* = \frac{\text{Risk of unhedged position} - \text{Risk of hedged position}}{\text{Risk of unhedged position.}}$$

This can be written as

$$e^* = \frac{\sigma_{\Delta S}^2 - \sigma_{\Pi}^2}{\sigma_{\Delta S}^2}.$$

Thus, e^* gives the percentage of the unhedged risk that the hedge eliminates. By substituting the formulas for σ_{Π}^2 and N_f in the formula for e^* and rearranging terms, we get

$$e^* = \frac{N_f^2 \sigma_{\Delta f}^2}{\sigma_{\Delta S}^2}.$$

This happens to be the formula for the coefficient of determination for the regression. This is the square of the correlation coefficient. It indicates the percentage of the variance in the dependent variable, ΔS, that is explained by the independent variable, Δf.

We shall see an example of the minimum variance hedge ratio in a hedging situation we examine later in this chapter.

Price Sensitivity Hedge Ratio

The price sensitivity hedge ratio comes from the work of Kolb and Chiang (1981). The objective here is to determine the value of N_f that will result in no change in the portfolio's value. Because the strategy is designed to be used with interest rate futures, we will illustrate it with reference to a bond and a bond futures contract.

In order to understand the price sensitivity formula, we must first review the concept of a bond's **duration.** The bond price, B, is the sum of the present values of each of its cash payments—coupon interest and principal. These present values can be found by discounting each cash payment at a single interest rate, which is known as the yield. Formally, we have

$$B = \sum_{t=1}^{T} \frac{CP_t}{(1 + y)^t},$$

where CP_t is the cash payment made at time t and will be either the coupon interest or principal. If the yield changes, we know that the price changes inversely. An approximation to the change in price as it relates to the change in yield is given by the formula,

$$\Delta B \approx -B \frac{DUR_B(\Delta y)}{1 + y},$$

where DUR_B represents the bond's duration and Δ represents the change in B or y. Formally, the duration is a weighted average of the time to each cash payment date and is specified in units of time. It measures the timing and size of a bond's cash flows. Bonds with high coupons and short maturities have short durations, while bonds with low coupons and long maturity have long durations. A zero coupon bond has a duration equal to its maturity, while a 30-year bond might have a duration of 8 to 14 years. From the above equation, we see that duration is a measure of a bond's price sensitivity, with longer duration bonds being more sensitive. For comparative purposes, we can say that, for example, a 10-year zero coupon bond has the same price sensitivity as a 30-year bond with a duration of 10.

Although duration has some limitations, it is a very useful concept in hedging. Knowing the duration of a bond, we can hedge it by using knowledge of the duration of an appropriate futures contract and trading enough futures to offset the duration of the bond. Now let us look at how a hedge can be designed.

Suppose changes in interest rates on all bonds are caused by a change in a single interest rate, r, which can be viewed as a default-free government bond rate. Thus, when r changes, all other bond yields change. Let S be the price of the bond held in the spot market and y_S be its yield. We will assume the bond futures contract is based on a single government bond. The futures contract has a price of f. Based upon that price, the remaining life of the deliverable bond at the expiration of the futures, and the coupon of the deliverable bond, we can infer that the deliverable bond at expiration would have a yield of y_f and a duration of DUR_f. We shall refer to these as the **implied yield** and the **implied duration** of the futures.

The profit from a hedge is the change in value of the hedger's position as a result of a change in the rate, r. If we are hedged, this change in value is zero. With details of the solution presented in Appendix 10A, the formula for N_f is

$$N_f = -\left(\frac{\Delta S}{\Delta f}\right)\left(\frac{\Delta y_f}{\Delta y_S}\right).$$

This expression can be considerably simplified. From the formula above, we can express duration as

$$DUR_S \approx -\left(\frac{\Delta S}{S}\right)\left(\frac{1 + y_S}{\Delta y_S}\right).$$

The price sensitivity hedge ratio gives the optimal number of futures to hedge against interest rate changes.

The implied duration of a futures contract can be expressed in a similar manner as

$$DUR_f \approx -\left(\frac{\Delta f}{f}\right)\left(\frac{1 + y_f}{\Delta y_f}\right).$$

Letting $\Delta y_f = \Delta y_S$ and substituting in the expression for N_f gives

$$N_f = -\left(\frac{DUR_S}{DUR_f}\right)\left(\frac{S}{f}\right)\left(\frac{1 + y_f}{1 + y_S}\right).$$

Yet another version of the price sensitivity hedge ratio is often used in practice. It is given as

$$N_f = -(\text{Yield beta})\frac{PVBP_S}{PVBP_f},$$

where $PVBP_S$ is the present value of a basis point change for the spot and is specifically defined as $\Delta S/\Delta y_S$, which we know is $-DUR_S S/(1 + y_S)$. $PVBP_f$ is the present value of a basis point change for the futures and is defined as $\Delta f/\Delta y_f$, which is $-DUR_f f/(1 + y_f)$. These variables are, in effect, the change in the price of the spot or futures for a change in the yield of Δy_S or Δy_f.

The **yield beta** is the coefficient from a regression of the spot yield on the implied yield of the futures. In the price sensitivity formula, we assumed the spot yield changes one for one with the implied yield on the futures. This makes the yield beta 1. Then, the preceding equation becomes

$$N_f = -\left(\frac{DUR_S}{DUR_f}\right)\left(\frac{S}{f}\right)\left(\frac{1 + y_f}{1 + y_S}\right),$$

which is the price sensitivity formula. If the hedger does not believe the spot and futures prices will change in a one-to-one ratio, however, the yield beta actually should be estimated. In the examples used in this chapter, we shall assume the yield beta is 1.

The price sensitivity formula takes into account the volatility of the spot and futures prices. Thus, it incorporates information from current prices rather than regressing past spot prices on past futures prices. There are merits to both approaches, and in practice one approach sometimes may be more practical than the other. We shall illustrate both methods in some hedging examples later in the chapter.

There is one final consideration in using the price sensitivity formula. Because it is derived from the calculus, the formula hedges against only very small changes in interest rates. These changes must occur over a very short period of time. Once the interest rate changes and/or a period of time elapses, the durations of the bond and the futures change and a new hedge ratio is required. This problem is much like the delta hedging we covered earlier in the Black-Scholes model. It is possible that many of our bond hedges, which are over periods of a few months at most, would not require major changes in the hedge ratio. Regardless, for our purposes here, we shall maintain the hedge ratio at the same value as obtained from the formula under the initial conditions, keeping in mind that the hedge will be less than perfect. If we desire a perfect hedge in practice, we would have to make adjustments.

We shall see examples of the price sensitivity hedge ratio in hedging situations we encounter later in this chapter.

Stock Index Futures Hedging

Because the price sensitivity hedge is not applicable to stock index futures, the minimum variance hedge usually is employed. Suppose we define ΔS as Sr_S, where r_S is the return on the stock, which is the percentage change in price. Then we define Δf as fr_f, where r_f is the percentage change in the price of the futures contract. Note that this is not the return on the futures contract. Because there is no initial outlay, there is no return on a futures contract. If we substitute Sr_S and fr_f for ΔS and Δf in the minimum variance formula for N_f, we get

$$N_f = -\frac{S\sigma_{Sf}}{f\sigma_f^2},$$

The minimum variance hedge ratio for stock index futures takes into account the stock portfolio's beta.

where σ_{Sf} is the covariance between r_S and r_f and σ_f^2 is the variance of r_f. If we run a regression of the percentage change in the spot price on the percentage change in the futures price, we obtain a regression coefficient we can call β_S. You may recognize this concept as similar to the beta from the Capital Asset Pricing Model. Is this the same beta? Not exactly, but since the futures contract is based on a market index, the beta will be very close — probably close enough for our purposes. In that case,

$$N_f = -\beta_S\left(\frac{S}{f}\right)$$

is the minimum variance hedge ratio for a stock index futures contract where β_S is the beta of the stock portfolio.

This hedge ratio is widely used in practice even though it ignores a few problems. For one, it disregards dividends on the portfolio of stocks. Also, it assumes the futures contract behaves exactly like the market portfolio or the underlying stock index. In other words, it assumes that the beta of the futures is 1. This will not be precisely the case. Thus, there is some basis risk that can impair the hedge's effectiveness. For our purposes, however, we shall stay with the above formula so we can concentrate on the essential concepts underlying the stock index futures hedge.

We shall see two examples of the stock index futures hedge later in the chapter.

Tailing the Hedge

In Chapter 9, we discussed the impact of marking to market on futures prices. We saw that the effect is likely to be small, so we can treat forward contracts as though they were futures contracts and permit the profit from the contract to be earned entirely at expiration. In reality, there are some cases where the interest earned on daily profits and losses from futures positions can be significant enough to require consideration in the design of hedging models. In that case, we should make an adjustment to the optimal hedge ratio. This is called **tailing the hedge.**

Suppose we set up a hedge consisting of a long position in the spot asset priced at S_0 and a short position in the futures priced at $f_0(T)$. We shall hold the position until the futures expires at T. During the interim at times 1 and 2, the futures will be marked to market. This implies that from today until time 1 is one day, from time 1 until time 2 is one day, and from time 2 to time T is one day. We shall assume the interest rate applied to settlement gains and losses is the risk-free rate, r, and this rate is constant until expiration.

Table 10.5 illustrates the procedure for tailing the hedge. When the hedge is set up, it is necessary to sell, not one futures, but rather $(1 + r)^{-(T-1)}$ futures. Note that this is the present value factor for the period spanned from the end of the current day until expiration. This number will be slightly less than one. At time 1, the futures will be marked to market. The amount credited to the margin account should be invested in risk-free bonds until expiration. If the amount is negative, it should be financed by borrowing (issuing risk-free bonds) until expiration. When expiration arrives, this mark-to-market cash flow will have

When marking to market is an important factor, the hedge ratio should be adjusted to reflect the effect of the interest on the marking to market. This process is called tailing the hedge.

TABLE 10.5	Tailing the Hedge

The time line

——— 1 day ———	——— 1 day ———	——— 1 day ———
0	1	2	T (Expiration)

Time	Situation	Action	Value
0	Asset is worth S_0. Futures contract on asset is selling for $f_0(T)$.	Buy asset in spot market. Sell $(1 + r)^{-(T-1)}$ futures contracts.	S_0 -0
		Total value at time 0	S_0
1	Futures price is $f_1(T)$.	Buy back the $(1 + r)^{-(T-1)}$ futures contracts.	$-(1 + r)^{-(T-1)}(f_1(T) - f_0(T))$
	Futures position is marked to market for a cash flow of $-(1 + r)^{-(T-1)}(f_1(T) - f_0(T))$.	Invest mark-to-market profit of $-(1 + r)^{-(T-1)}(f_1(T) - f_0(T))$ in risk-free bonds, which will grow to a value of $-(f_1(T) - f_0(T))$ at T. (If this amount is negative, borrow it at the risk-free rate.) Sell $(1 + r)^{-(T-2)}$ new futures contracts.	$+(1 + r)^{-(T-1)}(f_1(T) - f_0(T))$ -0
		Total value at time 1	0
2	Futures price is $f_2(T)$.	Buy back the $(1 + r)^{-(T-2)}$ futures contracts.	$-(1 + r)^{-(T-2)}(f_2(T) - f_1(T))$
	Futures position is marked to market for a cash flow of $-(1 + r)^{-(T-2)}(f_2(T) - f_1(T))$.	Invest mark-to-market profit of $-(1 + r)^{-(T-2)}(f_2(T) - f_1(T))$ in risk-free bonds, which will grow to a value of $-(f_2(T) - f_1(T))$ at T. (If this amount is negative, borrow it at the risk-free rate.) Sell one new futures contract.	$+(1 + r)^{-(T-2)}(f_2(T) - f_1(T))$ -0
		Total value at time 2	0
T	Spot asset is worth S_T. Futures price, $f_T(T)$, converges to S_T. Futures account is marked to market for a cash flow of $-(S_T - f_2(T))$.	Deliver spot asset on short futures and receive $f_T(T)$, which equals S_T. Redeem (or pay off) bonds established at times 1 and 2.	$S_T - (S_T - f_2(T))$ $-(f_1(T) - f_0(T)) - (f_2(T) - f_1(T))$
		Total value at T	$f_0(T)$

grown to a value of $-(f_1(T) - f_0(T))$. Note how the number of futures contracts we set up, $(1 + r)^{-(T-1)}$, exactly offsets the compound interest factor, $(1 + r)^{(T-1)}$, so that the futures price change at time 1 is realized at expiration. Then at time 1 the number of futures must be adjusted to reflect the interest factor, $(1 + r)^{-(T-2)}$, for the remaining time until expiration. The same procedure is followed until expiration, at which time there will be $f_0(T)$ dollars remaining. Had this adjustment to the hedge ratio not been made, then the hedge would not have been risk-free. Of course, if future interest rates were uncertain, then it would be impossible to correctly tail the hedge.

Consider the following simple example. Let S_0 be 100 and $f_0(T)$ be 105. The interest rate, r, is .10. Without tailing the hedge, the hedger would buy 1 unit of the spot at 100 and sell 1 unit of the futures at 105. With the tail, however, the hedger should sell $(1.10)^{-(2/365)}$ futures when there are three days to go and $T - 1$ is $2/365$. This amounts to 0.9995 contracts. Thus, if the investor held 10,000 units of the spot, the hedge ratio would be 0.9995(10,000) futures, or 9,995 contracts. At time 1, the hedge ratio would be changed to $(1.10)^{-(1/365)}$ or 0.9997, or 9,997 contracts. At time 2, the hedge ratio would change to 1, or 10,000 contracts.

These adjustments to the hedge ratio may seem insignificant, but that is primarily because we let the hedge begin three days before expiration. Had we extended our example to, say, 100 days before expiration, and assuming marking to market daily, the hedge ratio would have been $(1.10)^{-(99/365)}$ or 9,745 contracts. Each day this ratio would change by incrementing the exponent by $1/365$ until the day before expiration, when it would become $365/365$, or 1. In practice, many professional hedgers do not necessarily adjust the hedge ratio daily; they do so only periodically and achieve results quite close to those of a daily adjustment. To keep our hedge examples fairly basic, we shall not use this tailing procedure; nevertheless, you should keep it in mind for situations you may encounter in the real world.

Hedging Strategies

So far we have examined some basic principles underlying the practice of hedging. The next step is to illustrate how these hedges are executed. We shall look at some examples developed from a variety of economic and financial environments that illustrate several hedging principles.

The examples are divided into three groups: short-term interest rate hedges, intermediate- and long-term interest rate hedges, and stock hedges. We begin with short-term interest rate hedges.

Short-Term Interest Rate Hedges

Before getting into the details of various hedging transactions, we need to examine the characteristics of the contracts we shall use. We briefly introduced T-bill futures in Chapter 9. Suppose a T-bill futures contract is priced such that the discount is 8.25. The Chicago Mercantile Exchange quotes the price as $100 - 8.25 = 91.75$, which is called the IMM Index, which stands for the International Monetary Market, the division of the Chicago Mercantile Exchange on which the contract trades. Therefore, when you observe the futures price, it will be 91.75. That is not, however, the actual price at which you trade the contract and, thus, is not the real futures price. The actual futures price per $100 is given by the formula

$$f = 100 - (100 - \text{IMM Index})(90/360).$$

For example, if the IMM Index is 91.75,

$$f = 100 - (100 - 91.75)(90/360) = 97.9375.$$

The standard size of a single contract is $1 million face value of T-bills; thus, the futures price is $979,375.

The purpose of assuming a 90-day bill in the formula is that it implies that a one-point move in the IMM Index converts to a $25 change in the futures price. For example, if the IMM Index goes up to 91.76, the futures price will be $979,400. Thus, followers of the contract can quickly assess the dollar impact of a change in the IMM Index. If the holder of the short position elects to make delivery of a 90- or 92-day bill, the formula is adjusted on the delivery day so that 90 or 92 is used instead of 90 in calculating the final price.

The contract expiration months are March, June, September, and December, going out about two years. The last trading day is the business day prior to the date of issue of T-bills in the third week of the month. Delivery can take place on the business day after the last trading day and any day thereafter during the expiration month.

The Eurodollar contract is the most successful of the several short-term interest rate futures contracts. A **Eurodollar** is a dollar deposited in a foreign bank or foreign branch of a U.S. bank. The deposit is denominated in dollars rather than in the country's currency. Eurodollars avoid U.S. reserve requirements and many other regulations, and in recent years their use by U.S. corporations and banks has greatly increased. The primary Eurodollar interest rate, called **LIBOR** for **London Interbank Offer Rate,** is considered one of the best indicators of the cost of short-term borrowing. The Eurodollar futures contract has achieved great success, quickly surpassing in volume the Treasury bill futures contract, the first short-term interest rate futures contract. The Eurodollar contract's success is at least partly due to its cash settlement feature.

A major difference between T-bills and Eurodollars is the manner in which their rates are interpreted. The T-bill is a discount instrument, and the Eurodollar is an add-on instrument. For example, although T-bills and Eurodollars would not have equivalent rates, suppose we assume the quoted rate is 10 percent for both 90-day T-bills and Eurodollars. Then we know that the T-bill price per $100 face value would be $100 - 10(90/360) = 97.5$ and that the yield would be $(100/97.5)^{365/90} - 1 = .1081$. Thus, the investor puts down $97.50 today and receives $100 in 90 days. For a Eurodollar deposit of $97.50, the interest would be figured as $\$97.50(.10)(90/360) = \$2.44$; thus, the investor would get back $97.50 + $2.44 = 99.94 at expiration. The yield would be $(99.94/97.50)^{365/90} - 1 = .1054$. T-bills will not, however, yield more than Eurodollars in general because T-bills have no credit risk while Eurodollar borrowers could default. The Eurodollar rate would simply be quoted higher.

The Eurodollar futures contract is based on a three-month Eurodollar time deposit, which is a loan made by one bank to another. The contract is for $1 million face value and is quoted by the IMM Index method—the same procedure used for T-bills. The Eurodollar contract, however, is settled in cash. The settlement price on the last day of trading is the LIBOR rate as determined by the CME clearinghouse. Contract expirations are March, June, September, and December and extend out 10 years. The last trading day is the second London business day before the third Wednesday of the month. There is also a contract on the rate on 30-day Eurodollar deposits.

The Eurodollar contract is very actively traded and is much more liquid than the T-bill contract. It is considered an excellent contract for hedging or speculating on short-term interest rates and is also widely used for hedging by institutions who take positions as dealers in interest rate swaps and other over-the-counter interest rate derivatives, as we discuss in Chapter 14.

HEDGING THE FUTURE PURCHASE OF A TREASURY BILL   Consider the following scenario. On February 15, a corporate treasurer learns that $1 million will be available on May 17. The funds will be needed for long-term investment later in the year, but meanwhile they should be invested in liquid, interest-earning securities. The treasurer decides to purchase 91-day Treasury bills at the weekly auction on May 17.

T-bills are currently offered at a discount of 8.20. The treasurer would like to lock in this rate, but knows that the forward rate would be a more accurate reflection of the rate he would expect to receive when he buys the T-bills. That rate is 8.94. The treasurer knows that there is an active futures contract on Treasury bills that has expirations of March, June, September, and December. The treasurer knows that the risk is that interest rates will fall. Thus, using the worst case scenario method, the treasurer assumes that interest rates will fall. If that happens, Treasury bill futures prices will rise. Thus, he knows that he needs to buy futures so that he will profit in the futures market if interest rates fall.

Table 10.6 presents the hedge. The treasurer wants to lock in the yield of 9.6 percent given by the forward price of T-bills. With a $1 million

TABLE 10.6	Anticipatory Hedge of a Future Purchase of a Treasury Bill

Scenario: On February 15, a corporate treasurer learns that $1 million will become available on May 17. The treasurer plans to purchase 91-day U.S. Treasury bills at the weekly auction.

Date	Spot Market	Futures Market
February 15	The implied forward price of 91-day T-bills implies a discount of 8.94. Price per $100 face value: 100 − 8.94(91/360) = 97.74. Proceeds from $1,000,000 face value: $977,400. Implied yield: $(100/97.74)^{365/91} - 1$ = .0960	June T-bill IMM Index is at 91.32. Price per $100 face value: 100 − (100 − 91.32)(90/360) = 97.83. Price per contract: $978,300. **Buy one contract**
May 17	91-day T-bills are selling for a discount of 7.69. Price per $100 face value: 100 − 7.69(91/360) = 98.0561. Proceeds from $1,000,000 face value: $980,561. Implied yield: $(100/98.0561)^{365/91} - 1$ = .0819.	June T-bill IMM Index is at 92.54. Price per $100 face value: 100 − (100 − 92.54)(90/360) = 98.135. Price per contract: $981,350. **Sell one contract**

Analysis: When the $1,000,000 face value T-bills are purchased on May 17, the treasurer will pay $980,561, which implies a yield of 8.19 percent, which is much lower than the 9.60 percent implied forward rate in effect at the time the hedge was initiated.

The profit on the futures transaction is

$981,350 (sale price of futures)
− $978,300 (purchase price of futures)
$3,050 (profit on futures).

The profit on the futures can be considered as a reduction in the effective price of the T-bills. This makes the T-bills effectively cost $980,561 − $3,050 = $977,511.

Thus, the treasurer effectively paid $977,511 for $1,000,000 face value of T-bills. This implies a return of

$$(\$1,000,000/\$977,511)^{365/91} - 1 = .0955.$$

Thus, the effective return on the T-bills after accounting for the hedge is 9.55 percent, which is quite close to the 9.60 percent implied forward rate.

position and the futures contract covering $1 million of T-bills, the treasurer knows that he needs one contract.[5]

When the hedge is over, the treasurer is glad he did hedge. The T-bills he bought on May 17 yielded only 8.19 percent, but the futures transaction generated a profit of $3,050. This amount effectively reduces the $980,561 he paid for the T-bills, so the effective yield now becomes 9.55 percent.

This hedge worked because the spot and futures T-bill prices moved in the same direction. In this case, rates declined. Had rates risen, the T-bills would have been less expensive, thus offering a higher yield. The futures position would have produced a loss, however, and this would have offset some or all of the gain made in the spot market. In that case, the hedge would have been effective, but the treasurer would have wished that the hedge had not been done. The price one pays for hedging is that it will occasionally produce losses on the futures position that will absorb gains made in the spot market.

The above hedge is just one of many types of long hedges one can execute with interest rate futures contracts on short-term instruments. Many types of firms and some individuals determine that they will be investing funds in money market instruments at a later date. As long as the decision to invest the funds is unlikely to be reversed, a hedge is appropriate. This does not mean, however, that one should always hedge. If the hedger believes rates are abnormally low and likely to rise, the hedge will lock in the low rate while money market rates might increase. Thus, the hedger should not blindly hedge in all interest rate environments. Although in an efficient market the hedger should be unable to effectively time the interest rate cycle, it would still be inappropriate for the hedger to ignore his or her own expectations. This will be true for all of the remaining cases.

HEDGING A FUTURE COMMERCIAL PAPER ISSUE Corporations frequently borrow funds in short-term markets. These funds supply working capital used to finance inventory and accounts receivable and provide liquidity with which to meet interest payments on loans. Large, creditworthy corporations frequently borrow by issuing commercial paper, a short-term promissory note.

Suppose that on April 6 a corporate treasurer determines that on July 20, the firm will need to issue $10 million of commercial paper with a maturity of 180 days. Commercial paper rates are quoted on a 360-day basis,

---

[5]Recall that the optimal hedge ratio requires the durations and yields of the spot and futures contracts. Since we are hedging 91-day T-bills with 90-day T-bill futures, the durations are essentially the same: 0.25. The yield implied by the futures price of 97.83 is 9.31 percent and the yield on the forward T-bill is 9.60 percent. Using the price sensitivity formula gives a value of N_f of one contract. In other examples in this chapter, we shall illustrate how differences in these factors affect the hedge ratio.

and the paper is discounted.[6] Thus, commercial paper is like Treasury bills, and the calculations for determining the purchase price and effective yield are the same.

The treasurer's worst case scenario is for rates to rise. She knows that if rates rise, interest rate futures prices will fall. So to profit from an increase in interest rates, the treasurer knows to take a short position in futures. Unfortunately there is no commercial paper futures contract, so the treasurer decides to use Eurodollar futures. Recall that Eurodollar futures are quoted like Treasury bill futures and have expirations of March, June, September, and December. The treasurer decides to use the September contract.

The hedge is presented in Table 10.7. The treasurer knows that the rate she would like to lock in is not the spot rate but the forward rate, which is 10.37 percent. If the paper were issued at that rate, it would bring proceeds of $9,481,500, which would mean that its yield would be 11.40 percent. The treasurer uses the price sensitivity hedge ratio, which is necessary here because the spot and futures instruments have different durations and yields. Also the futures contract covers $1 million of Eurodollars while the treasurer's exposure is almost $10 million. Using the formula as indicated in the table results in the treasurer selling 20 contracts.

When the hedge is terminated, the treasurer ends up issuing the paper at an effective yield of 12.57 percent. The futures transaction earned $38,000, however, which can be added to the proceeds from the paper. So the effective cost of the paper is 11.65 percent, which is reasonably close to the target of 11.40 percent, especially given that the hedge instrument, Eurodollar futures, is not the same as the underlying spot instrument, commercial paper. This example illustrates the importance of properly determining the hedge ratio. Had the hedger simply noted that a $10 million spot position hedged by a $1 million futures contract should require 10 contracts, the hedge would have been far less effective.

The hedge worked because Eurodollar and commercial paper rates moved in the same direction—in this case, upward. Had rates moved downward, there would have been a loss on the futures transaction and the loan would have been less expensive without the hedge. The firm would not have known, however, that rates would decrease; thus, it bought the protection of the hedge at the risk of a decrease in interest rates.

What we have just seen is a short hedge. The example is applicable to a wide variety of similar situations. For example, the firm could take out a bank loan rather than issue commercial paper. A bank could plan to borrow funds by issuing CDs. Any type of firm that anticipated borrowing money at a future time would be able to reduce the uncertainty of the rate at which it would borrow by selling futures contracts.

---

[6]We assume the firm can get by with slightly less than $10 million in cash. Otherwise, it would need to issue more than $10 million face value of commercial paper.

TABLE 10.7	Anticipatory Hedge of a Future Commercial Paper Issue

Scenario: On April 6, a corporate treasurer learns that on July 20 the firm will have to issue $10 million face value of 180-day commercial paper.

Date	Spot Market	Futures Market
April 6	The implied forward rate on 180-day commercial paper is 10.37 percent. Proceeds per $100 face value: $100 - 10.37(180/360) = 94.815$. Proceeds from $10,000,000 face value: $9,481,500. Implied rate: $(100/94.815)^{365/180} - 1 = .1140$.	September Eurodollar futures IMM Index is at 88.23. Price per $100 face value: $100 - (100 - 88.23)(90/360) = 97.0575$. Price per contract: $970,575. Implied yield: $(100/97.0575)^{365/90} - 1 = .1288$. Appropriate number of contracts: $$N_f = -\left(\frac{180/365}{90/365}\right)\left(\frac{9,481,500}{970,575}\right)\left(\frac{1.1288}{1.1140}\right)$$ $= -19.80$. **Sell 20 contracts**
July 20	Issue 180-day commercial paper at current spot rate of 11.34. Proceeds per $100 face value: $100 - 11.34(180/360) = 94.33$. Proceeds from $10,000,000 face value: $9,433,000. Implied rate: $(100/94.33)^{365/180} - 1 = .1257$.	September Eurodollar futures IMM Index is at 87.47. Price per $100 face value: $100 - (100 - 87.47)(90/360) = 96.8675$. Price per contract: $968,675. **Buy 20 contracts**

Analysis: When the $10,000,000 face value of commercial paper is issued on July 20, the firm will receive $9,433,000, which implies a rate of 12.57 percent, which is much higher than the 11.40 percent implied forward rate in effect at the time the hedge was initiated.

The profit on the futures transaction is

$$\begin{array}{ll} 20(\$970,575) & \text{(sale price of futures)} \\ - \; 20(\$968,675) & \text{(purchase price of futures)} \\ \hline \$38,000 & \text{(profit on futures).} \end{array}$$

The profit on the futures can be considered as an increase in the proceeds received from issuing the paper. This effectively changes the proceeds to $9,433,000 + $38,000 = $9,471,000.

Thus, the firm effectively received $9,471,000 for $10,000,000 face value of commercial paper. This implies a rate of

$$(\$10,000,000/\$9,471,000)^{365/180} - 1 = .1165.$$

Thus, the effective rate paid on the commercial paper after accounting for the hedge is 11.65 percent, which is reasonably close to the 11.40 percent implied forward rate.

HEDGING A FLOATING-RATE LOAN   In addition to using interest rate futures, there are other ways to hedge the risk of changing interest rates. For example, a bank might require that the interest rate on a loan float with market interest rates. If interest rates increase, the rate the bank charges on the loan will go up and at least partially cover the additional cost to the bank of borrowing the money. Thus, the bank will pass on the interest rate risk to its loan customers.

This will place the burden of hedging on the borrower. If the loan rate is tied to a floating market rate, the borrower must get into a position to profit when interest rates increase. It can do this by selling interest rate futures contracts.

Consider the following situation. On February 3, a firm decides to take out a three-month, $10 million loan from a bank. The rate on the loan will be set on the first Friday of the month and will equal that day's 90-day LIBOR plus 100 basis points. For simplicity, we shall assume the monthly rate will be one-twelfth of the annual rate. We shall also assume a flat term structure for 90 days so that the current spot rate is also the forward rate. The firm can repay any part or all of the loan at any time.

The current LIBOR is 9.68 so the rate for the first interest payment is already fixed at 10.68 percent. The firm knows it is exposed to rising interest rates, specifically the LIBOR on March 2 and April 6, the first Fridays of March and April. So the firm is exposed to two distinct risk events and it must hedge those risks separately. To hedge the first event, the rate reset on March 2, the firm must sell a certain number of futures contracts as determined by the price sensitivity formula. The optimal number is based on a spot exposure of $10 million, the initial loan balance. The second risk event is the rate reset on April 6. The optimal number of contracts to hedge this risk is based on the price sensitivity formula using a different amount of spot exposure, specifically the loan balance on March 2. This amount will be $10,000,000(1 + .1068/12) = $10,089,000, reflecting the interest over the first period at the rate of 10.68 percent. If there were any later rate resets, the loan balance would be calculated on the assumption that the hedge works perfectly to lock in the initial loan rate or, if the term structure were not flat, the forward rates. In this case, with the term structure flat, the rate the firm is trying to lock in is 10.68 percent each period. With the firm paying one-twelfth of 10.68 percent per month, the effective annual rate is $[1 + (.1068/12)]^{12} - 1 = .1122$.

Table 10.8 presents the results of this hedge. Using the price sensitivity hedge ratio, the risk associated with each reset date requires a position of three futures contracts to hedge. Note that on the first reset date, March 2, the firm buys back three of the contracts. Since rates rose from February 3 to March 2, those contracts were profitable and the gains were used to reduce the loan balance on March 2. This helped offset the higher rate to be paid on April 6, based on the balance on March 2. The same thing happens on April 6. Rates are even higher, but the second group of three futures contracts generated a profit that is used to lower the loan balance on

TABLE 10.8 Hedging a Floating-Rate Loan with Eurodollar Futures

Scenario: On February 3 a firm decides to take out a three-month, $10 million loan from a bank. The rate for a given month will be set on the first Friday of the month and will equal that day's 90-day LIBOR plus 100 basis points. The monthly rate will be 1/12 of the annual rate. The firm can repay any or all of the loan at any time.

Date	Spot Market	Futures Market
February 3	The term structure is flat at 9.68 percent. Adding 100 basis points gives an effective rate of $[1 + (0.1068/12)]^{12} - 1 = .1122$. This is the rate the firm is trying to lock in. The rate in effect for the first month is 10.68 percent. The spot position is $10,000,000 and the duration is 1/12 (one month).	The June Eurodollar IMM Index is at 90.75. This implies a price of $(100 - (100 - 90.75)(90/360)) = 97.6875$ per $100, or $976,875 per contract. This implies a Eurodollar rate of $(100/97.6875)^{(365/90)} - 1 = .0995$. The duration is approximately 1/4 year. Appropriate number of contracts to hedge the first rate reset: $$N_f = -\left(\frac{1/12}{1/4}\right)\left(\frac{10,000,000}{976,875}\right)\left(\frac{1.0995}{1.1122}\right)$$ $$= -3.37.$$ Appropriate number of contracts to hedge the second rate reset: $$N_f = -\left(\frac{1/12}{1/4}\right)\left(\frac{10,089,000}{976,875}\right)\left(\frac{1.0995}{1.1122}\right)$$ $$= -3.40.$$ So the firm needs to sell three contracts to hedge the first rate reset and three more to hedge the second. **Sell six contracts**
March 2	Accumulated principal and interest: $10,000,000[1 + (.1068/12)] =$ $10,089,000. LIBOR is 10.09 so the rate is reset to 11.09. This is the rate that is in effect for the second month.	The June Eurodollar IMM Index is at 90.47. This implies a price of $(100 - (100 - 90.47)(90/360)) = 97.6175$ per $100, or $976,175 per contract. The profit on each futures contract is $976,875 - $976,175 = $700. **Buy back three contracts** Futures profit $= 3($700) = $2,100$. Apply futures profit to loan balance reducing it to $10,089,000 - $2,100 = $10,086,900. Three short futures contracts are left.
April 6	Accumulated principal and interest: $10,086,900[1 + (.1109/12)]$ $= $10,180,120. LIBOR is 10.79 so the rate is reset to 11.79. This is the rate that is in effect for the third month.	The June Eurodollar IMM Index is at 89.99. This implies a price of $(100 - (100 - 89.99)(90/360)) = 97.4975$ per $100, or $974,975 per contract. The profit on each futures contract is $976,875 - $974,975 = $1,900. **Buy back three contracts** Futures profit $= 3($1,900) = $5,700$. Apply futures profit to loan balance reducing it to $10,180,120 - $5,700 = $10,174,420. No futures contracts are left.
May 4	Accumulated principal and interest: $10,174,420[1 + (.1179/12)]$ $= $10,274,384. Pay back this amount.	

Analysis: The firm borrowed $10,000,000 and paid back $10,274,384 for an effective rate of

$$(10,274,384/10,000,000)^4 - 1 = .1144.$$

This rate is only slightly higher than the 11.22 percent rate the firm was attempting to lock in. Had the firm not hedged, its rate would have been

$$\{[1 + (.1068/12)][1 + (.1109/12)][1 + (.1179/12)]\}^4 - 1 = .1178.$$

April 6 so as to help offset the higher rate paid on May 4 based on the April 6 balance.

Ultimately, the loan ended up costing the firm 11.44 percent. This is reasonably close to the target of 11.22 percent and much better than the 11.78 percent it would have paid had it not hedged and simply accepted the risk of rising interest rates. Of course, had rates decreased, the hedge would have cost the firm some or all of the savings it would have otherwise generated.

Floating-rate loans are very common in our financial system. They are but one means of passing on the interest rate risk to the borrower. Some banks prefer to offer their customers fixed-rate loans, but the rates on the CDs they issue float with market interest rates. The bank can then hedge its floating-rate financing and offer its loan customers a fixed rate. Because banks are probably more knowledgeable about the benefits of hedging, this type of arrangement should be common. Unfortunately, it is not always the case. Many banks do not use interest rate futures as much as one would think given their central position in the financial system and the risk exposure they face. Fortunately, however, the use of interest rate futures by banks is on the increase.

The type of hedge described in this section is called a **strip hedge** or simply a **strip.** It can also be used as an arbitrage strategy whereby the investor effectively creates a synthetic 90-day (or longer) fixed-rate security. The return on this security can be compared against the return from actual 90-day securities. A variation of the strip hedge is called a **rolling strip hedge,** in which the hedger attempts to extend the effective maturity farther out than the availability of the futures contracts permits. In that case, the hedger simply rolls forward the expiring contracts into new contracts as they become available. When the liquidity of contracts with longer maturities raises concerns about using them, the hedger might wish to use a larger quantity of the shorter-term futures and gradually roll over into the longer-term futures as their expirations become shorter and they become more liquid. This transaction is referred to as a **stack hedge.** Of course, all the strategies involving rolling over into new contracts will entail some additional basis risk.

Finally we should note that these short-term interest rate risk problems are particularly appropriate for the use of forward rate agreements, interest rate options, and swaps, and are far more likely to be solved using those instruments, as we cover in Chapter 14.

Intermediate- and Long-Term Interest Rate Hedges

Treasury note and bond contracts, which are traded on the Chicago Board of Trade, are virtually identical except that there are three T-note contracts that are based on 2-year, 5-year, and 10-year maturities while the T-bond contract is based on Treasury bonds with maturities of at least 15 years that are not callable for at least 15 years. Thus, the T-note contracts are intermediate-term interest rate futures contracts and the T-bond contract is a long-term interest rate futures contract. The T-note contracts are traded quite actively, but the T-bond contract is one of the most active of all futures contracts. Other than the difference in maturity of the underlying instruments and the margin requirements, the contract terms are essentially identical. We shall, therefore, discuss only the T-bond contract.

The T-bond contract is based on the assumption that the underlying bond has a specific coupon rate and, as mentioned, a maturity or call date of not less than 15 years. For all contracts through December 1999, the rate is 8 percent. Starting with the March 2000 contract, the rate is 6 percent. The specific coupon requirement is not restrictive, however; the CBOT permits delivery of bonds with other coupon rates, with an appropriate adjustment made to the price received for the bonds. There can easily be 30 or more different bond issues eligible for delivery on a given contract.

T-bond futures prices are quoted in dollars and thirty-seconds of par value of $100. For example, a futures price of 93-14 is 93 14/32, or 93.4375. The face value of T-bonds underlying the contract is $100,000; therefore, a price of 93.4375 is actually $93,437.50. Expiration months are March, June, September, and December, extending out about two years. The last trading day is the business day prior to the last seven days of the expiration month. The first delivery day is the first business day of the month.

More details on the T-bond futures contract will be given when needed in Chapter 11.

HEDGING A LONG POSITION IN A GOVERNMENT BOND   Portfolio managers constantly face decisions about when to buy and sell securities. In some cases, such decisions are automatic. Securities are sold at certain times to generate cash for meeting obligations, such as pension payments. Consider the following example.

On February 25, a portfolio manager holds $1 million face value of government bonds with a coupon of 11 7/8 percent and maturing in about 25 years. The bond currently is priced at 101 per $100 par value, and the yield is 11.74 percent. The duration is 7.83 years. The bond must be sold on March 28.[7]

The portfolio manager is concerned that interest rates will increase, resulting in a lower bond price and the possibility that the proceeds from the bond's sale will be inadequate for meeting the pension obligation. The manager knows that if interest rates increase, a short futures position will yield a profit that can offset at least part of any decrease in the bond's value.

---

[7]In actual situations a portfolio manager would hold a diversified portfolio of bonds. If the intention were to hedge the entire portfolio, the hedge ratio would be based on the overall portfolio value, yield, and duration. We assume the manager needs approximately $1 million of cash on March 28 and will sell only this bond to generate the cash.

TABLE 10.9	Hedging a Long Position in a Government Bond

Scenario: On February 25, a portfolio manager holds $1 million face value of a government bond, the 11 7/8s, which mature in about 25 years. The bond is currently priced at 101, has a duration of 7.83, and has a yield of 11.74 percent. The manager will sell the bond on March 28.

Date	Spot Market	Futures Market
February 25	The current price of the bonds is 101. Value of position: $1,010,000. The short end of the term structure is flat so this is the forward price of the bonds in March.	June T-bond futures is at 70 16/32. Price per contract: $70,500. The futures price and the characteristics of the deliverable bond imply a duration of 7.20 and a yield of 14.92 percent. Appropriate number of contracts:

$$N_f = -\left(\frac{7.83}{7.20}\right)\left(\frac{1,010,000}{70,500}\right)\left(\frac{1.1492}{1.1174}\right)$$
$$= -16.02.$$

Sell 16 contracts

Date	Spot Market	Futures Market
March 28	The bonds are sold at their current price of 95 22/32. This is a price of $956.875 per bond. Value of position: $956,875.	June T-bond futures is at 66 23/32. Price per contract: $66,718.75. **Buy 16 contracts**

Analysis: When the $1 million face value bonds are sold on March 28, they are worth $956,875, a loss in value of $1,010,000 − $956,875 = $53,125.

The profit on the futures transaction is

$$
\begin{array}{ll}
16(\$70,500) & \text{(sale price of futures)} \\
-16(\$66,718.75) & \text{(purchase price of futures)} \\
\hline
\$60,500 & \text{(profit on futures).}
\end{array}
$$

Thus, the hedge eliminated the entire loss in value and resulted in an overall gain in value of $60,500 − $53,125 = $7,375.

Since this is a government bond, the Treasury bond futures contract should be used.[8]

Table 10.9 presents the results of the hedge. The manager will use the June T-bond futures contract. Using the price sensitivity hedge ratio, the manager determines that he should sell 16 contracts. When the bonds were sold on March 28 they generated a loss of over $53,000. The futures transaction produced a profit of over $60,000. Thus, the hedge eliminated all the loss and even produced a gain. Had bond prices moved up, the futures price would have increased and the futures transaction would have gener-

_____

[8]Technically, the accrued interest would be included here, but it is not subject to any uncertainty so we leave it out of the hedging examples.

ated a loss that would have reduced or perhaps eliminated all of the increase in the value of the bonds.

This short hedge represents one of the most common hedging applications, and we shall see a slight variation of it later when we examine stock index futures hedging. This hedge is applicable to many firms and institutions, such as banks, insurance companies, pension funds, and mutual funds.

ANTICIPATORY HEDGE OF A FUTURE PURCHASE OF A TREASURY NOTE   Previously we saw how one could hedge the future purchase of a Treasury bill. In this example, we do the same with a Treasury note. We also take a slightly different approach to determining the hedge ratio.

Suppose that on March 29, a portfolio manager determines that approximately $1 million will be available on July 15. The manager decides to purchase the 11 5/8 Treasury notes maturing in about nine years. The forward price of the notes is 97 28/32, or $978,750, for $1 million face value. This price implies a forward yield of 12.02 percent. If yields decline, the notes' price will increase and the manager may be unable to make the purchase. If this happens, a profit could have been made by purchasing futures contracts. Because the Treasury note futures contract is quite liquid, the manager decides to buy T-note futures. Because the hedge is to be terminated on July 15, the September contract is appropriate.

The manager has been gathering statistics on the relationship between the T-note spot and futures markets. He has run a regression of the spot price changes on the futures price changes and obtained a coefficient of 10.5. So he decides to use 11 futures contracts. The results are presented in Table 10.10.

When the bonds are ultimately purchased, they end up costing over $97,000 more, but the futures transaction generated a profit of over $82,000. Thus, the effective purchase price is actually about $15,000 higher and gives an effective yield of 11.75 percent, which is reasonably close to the target forward yield of 12.02 percent.

Had bond prices moved down, the hedger would have regretted doing the hedge. The notes would have cost less, but this would have been offset by a loss on the futures contract. Once again, this is the price of hedging — forgoing gains to limit losses.

HEDGING A CORPORATE BOND ISSUE   One interesting application of an interest rate futures hedge occurs when a firm decides to issue bonds at a future date. There is an interim period during which the firm prepares the necessary paperwork and works out an underwriting arrangement for distributing the bonds. During that period, interest rates could increase so that when the bonds ultimately are issued, they will command a higher yield. This will be more costly to the issuer.

Consider the following example. On February 24, a corporation decides to issue $5 million face value of bonds on May 24. As a standard of

TABLE 10.10	Anticipatory Hedge of a Future Purchase of a Treasury Note

Scenario: On March 29, a portfolio manager determines that approximately $1 million will be available for investment on July 15. The manager plans to purchase the 11 5/8s Treasury notes maturing in about nine years.

Date	Spot Market	Futures Market
March 29	The forward price of the notes is 97 28/32. Current forward value of notes: $978,750. This implies a yield of 12.02 percent.	September T-note futures are at 78 21/32. Price per contract: $78,656.25. A regression of the change in the note price on the change in the futures price gave a regression coefficient of 10.5. **Buy 11 contracts**
July 15	The notes are purchased at their current price of 107 19/32. This is a price of $1,075.9375 per note. Value of position: $1,075,937.50.	September T-note futures is at 86 6/32. Price per contract: $86,187.50. **Sell 11 contracts**

Analysis: When the $1 million face value notes are purchased on July 15, they cost $1,075,937.50, an increased cost of $1,075,937.50 − $978,750 = $97,187.50. The yield at this price is 10.31 percent.

The profit on the futures transaction is

$$
\begin{array}{ll}
11(\$86,187.50) & \text{(sale price of futures)} \\
-\ 11(\$78,656.25) & \text{(purchase price of futures)} \\
\hline
\$82,843.75 & \text{(profit on futures).}
\end{array}
$$

Thus, the hedge offset about 85 percent of the increased cost. The effective purchase price of the notes is $1,075,937.50 − $82,843.75 = $993,093.75, which is an effective yield of 11.75 percent.

comparison, the firm currently has a bond issue outstanding with a coupon of 9 3/8 percent, a yield of 13.76 percent, and a maturity of about 21 years. Any new bonds issued will require a similar yield. Thus, the firm expects that when the bonds are issued in May, the coupon would be set at 13.76 percent, so the bonds would go out at par.

If rates increase, the firm will have to discount the bonds or adjust the coupon upward to the new market yield. We shall assume that the coupon is fixed so that the price will decrease. In either case, the firm will incur a loss. The firm realizes that if rates increase, it can make a profit from a short transaction in futures. Thus, it decides to hedge the issue by selling futures contracts.

There is no corporate bond futures contract, so the hedger chooses the Treasury bond futures contract. Because the hedge will be closed on May 24, the June contract is chosen.

The hedge is illustrated in Table 10.11. Using the price sensitivity hedge ratio, the firm sells 67 futures contracts. When the bonds are ultimately issued, the yield is 15.25 percent. This results in a loss of over $460,000 on the bonds, but the futures transaction made over $500,000. The firm made a net gain of about $44,000. The futures profit can be

---

TABLE 10.11	Hedging a Corporate Bond Issue

Scenario: On February 24, a corporation decides to issue $5 million of bonds on May 24. The firm currently has outstanding comparable bonds with a coupon of 9 3/8, a yield of 13.76 percent, and a maturity of about 21 years. The firm anticipates that if conditions do not change, the bonds when issued in May will go out with a 13.76 percent coupon and be priced at par with a 20-year maturity and a duration of 7.22.

Date	Spot Market	Futures Market
February 24	If issued in May, it is expected that the bonds would offer a coupon of 13.76 percent and be priced at par with a duration of 7.22. Value of position: $5,000,000.	June T-bond futures are at 68 11/32. Price per contract: $68,343.75. The futures price and the characteristics of the deliverable bond imply a duration of 7.83 and a yield of 13.60 percent. Appropriate number of contracts: $$N_f = -\left(\frac{7.22}{7.83}\right)\left(\frac{5,000,000}{68,373.75}\right)\left(\frac{1.1360}{1.1376}\right)$$ $$= -67.4.$$ **Sell 67 contracts**
May 24	The yield on comparable bonds is 15.25 percent. The bonds are issued with a 13.76 percent coupon at a price of 90.74638. Price per bond: $907.46. Value of bonds: $4,537,319.	June T-bond futures is at 60 25/32. Price per contract: $60,781.25. **Buy 67 contracts**

Analysis: When the $5 million face value bonds are issued on May 24, they are worth $4,537,319, a loss in value of $5,000,000 − $4,537,319 = $462,681. The yield at this price is 15.25 percent. (Note: Alternatively, if the bonds actually were issued at par with the coupon set at the yield on May 24 of 15.25 percent, the firm would receive the full $5,000,000 but the present value of its increased interest cost would be $462,681.)

The profit on the futures transaction is

$$\begin{array}{ll} 67(\$68,343.75) & \text{(sale price of futures)} \\ -\ 67(\$60,781.25) & \text{(purchase price of futures)} \\ \hline \$506,687.50 & \text{(profit on futures).} \end{array}$$

Thus, the hedge offset more than all of the increased cost and left a net gain of $506,687.50 − $462,681 = $44,006.50. The effective issue price of the bonds is $4,537,319 + $506,687.50 = $5,044,006.50, which is an effective yield of 13.63 percent.

added to the proceeds from the bond of about $4.5 million so as to infer an effective issue price of slightly more than $5 million. This sets the effective yield on the bonds at 13.63 percent, which is quite close to the target of 13.76 percent.

Had interest rates declined, the firm would have obtained a higher price for the bonds; however, this would have been at least partially offset by a loss on the futures transaction. By executing the hedge, the firm was able to protect itself against an interest rate change while preparing the issue. In a similar vein, investment bankers might do this type of hedge. An investment banker purchases the bonds from the firm and then resells them to investors. Between the time the bonds are purchased and resold, the investment banker is exposed to the risk that bond yields will increase.[9] Therefore, a short hedge such as this would be appropriate. Many investment banking firms have been able to protect themselves against large losses by hedging with interest rate futures.

Stock Index Futures Hedges

Stock index futures have been one of the spectacular success stories of the financial markets in recent years. These cash-settled contracts are indices of combinations of stocks. Investors use them to hedge positions in stock, speculate on the direction of the stock market in general, and arbitrage the contracts against comparable combinations of stocks.

Stock index futures contracts are based on indices of common stocks. The most widely traded contract is the S&P 500 futures at the Chicago Mercantile Exchange.

The futures price is quoted in the same manner as the index. The futures contract, however, has an implicit multiplier of $250. Thus, if the futures price is 1,300, the actual price is 1,300($250) = $325,000. At expiration, the settlement price is set at the price of the S&P 500 index and the contract is settled in cash. The expirations are March, June, September, and December. The last trading day is the Thursday before the third Friday of the expiration month.

Several of the hedging examples illustrated with T-note and T-bond futures are similar to stock index futures hedges where a firm attempts to hedge a long position in a security or portfolio. The first example we shall look at is the hedge of a stock portfolio.

STOCK PORTFOLIO HEDGE   A central tenet of modern investment theory is that diversification eliminates unsystematic risk, leaving only system-

---

[9]Investment bankers do employ other means of minimizing their risk exposure. The use of a syndicate, in which a large number of investment bankers individually take a small portion of the issue, spreads out the risk. Many issues are taken on a "best efforts" basis. This allows the investment banker to return the securities to the issuing firm if market conditions make the sale of the securities impossible without substantial price concessions.

atic risk. Until the creation of stock index futures, investors had to accept the fact that systematic risk could not be eliminated. Now investors can use stock index futures to hedge the systematic risk. But should they do that? If all systematic and unsystematic risk is eliminated, the portfolio can expect to earn only the risk-free return. Why not just buy T-bills? The answer is that investors occasionally wish to change or eliminate systematic risk for brief periods. During times of unusual volatility in the market, they can use stock index futures to adjust or eliminate the systematic risk. This is much easier and less costly than adjusting the relative proportions invested in each stock. Later the portfolio manager can close out the futures position, and the portfolio systematic risk will be back at its original level.

Consider a portfolio manager who on March 31 is concerned about the market over the period ending July 27. The portfolio has accumulated an impressive profit, and the manager would like to protect the portfolio value over this time period. The manager knows that the portfolio is exposed to a loss in value resulting from a decline in the market as a whole, the systematic risk effect, as well as losses resulting from the unsystematic risk of the individual stocks. Although the portfolio contains only eight stocks, the manager is not particularly worried about the unsystematic risk. The manager knows that the systematic risk can be hedged by using S&P 500 stock index futures, specifically the September contract.

The results are shown in Table 10.12. The portfolio beta, which reflects the influence of the market as a whole on a stock or portfolio, is a weighted average of the betas of the component stocks, where each weight of a given stock is the market value of that stock divided by the total market value of the portfolio. This gives a portfolio beta of 1.06. Using the minimum variance hedge ratio results in the sale of 25 contracts. On July 27, the portfolio has declined in value by over $200,000, a loss of 2.68 percent. The futures transaction, however, generated a profit of $60,000, which reduced the effective loss to only 1.90 percent.

The objective of the hedge was to eliminate systematic risk. Clearly systematic risk was reduced but not eliminated. The stock portfolio value declined about 2.68 percent while the futures price decreased a little over 1 percent. The hedge certainly helped but was far from perfect. There are several possible explanations for this result. One is that the betas are an estimate taken from a popular investment advisory service. Beta estimates over the recent past have not necessarily been stable. It is also possible that the portfolio was not sufficiently diversified and some unsystematic risk contributed to the loss. Some of the stocks may have paid dividends during the hedge period. We did not account for these dividends in illustrating the hedge results. Dividends would have reduced the loss on the portfolio and made the hedge more effective.

Had the market moved up, the portfolio would have shown a profit, but this would have been at least partially offset by a loss on the futures transaction. In either outcome, however, the portfolio manager would have been reasonably successful in capturing at least some of the accumulated profit on the portfolio.

TABLE 10.12	**Stock Portfolio Hedge**

Scenario: On March 31, a portfolio manager is concerned about the market over the next four months. The portfolio has accumulated an impressive profit, which the manager wishes to protect over the period ending July 27. The prices, number of shares, and betas are given below:

Stock	Price (3/31)	Number of Shares	Market Value	Weight	Beta
Federal Mogul	18.875	18,000	$ 339,750	.044	1.00
Lockheed Martin	73.500	16,000	1,176,000	.152	0.80
IBM	50.875	7,000	356,125	.046	0.50
US West	43.625	10,800	471,150	.061	0.70
Bausch & Lomb	54.250	21,000	1,139,250	.147	1.10
First Union	47.750	28,800	1,375,200	.178	1.10
Walt Disney	44.500	25,000	1,112,500	.144	1.40
Delta Air Lines	52.875	33,200	1,755,450	.227	1.20
			$7,725,425		

Portfolio beta:
  .044(1.00) + .152(0.80) + .046(0.50) + .061(0.70)
    + .147(1.10) + .178(1.10) + .144(1.40) + .227(1.20) = 1.06.
S&P 500 September futures contract:
  Price on March 31: 1305
  Multiplier: $250
  Price of one contract: $250(1305) = $326,250
Optimal number of futures contracts:

$$N_f = -1.06\left(\frac{7,725,425}{326,250}\right) = -25.10.$$

Sell 25 contracts

ANTICIPATORY HEDGE OF A TAKEOVER OR ACQUISITION   The exciting world of takeovers and acquisitions offers an excellent opportunity to apply hedging concepts. The acquiring firm identifies a target firm and intends to make a bid for the latter's stock. Typically the acquiring firm plans to purchase enough stock to obtain control. Because of the large amount of stock usually involved and the speed with which takeover rumors travel, the acquiring firm frequently makes a series of smaller purchases until it has accumulated sufficient shares to obtain control. During the period in which the acquiring firm is slowly and quietly buying the stock, it is exposed to the risk that stock prices in general will increase. This means that either the shares will cost more or fewer shares can be purchased.

Consider the following situation. On July 15, a firm has identified Helix Technology Corporation as a potential acquisition.[10] Helix stock

---

[10]The choice of Helix is merely for illustrative purposes. Helix is not known to be a takeover target as of this writing.

TABLE 10.12   *(continued)*

Stock	Price (7/27)	Market Value
Federal Mogul	21.625	$ 389,250
Lockheed Martin	81.500	1,304,000
IBM	43.875	307,125
US West	47.125	508,950
Bausch & Lomb	45.875	963,375
First Union	48.125	1,386,000
Walt Disney	40.000	1,000,000
Delta Air Lines	50.000	1,660,000
		$7,518,700

Results: The values of the stocks on July 27 are shown below:
S&P 500 September futures contract:
   Price on July 27: 1,295.40
   Multiplier: $250
   Price of one contract: $250(1,295.40) = $323,850
Buy 25 contracts

Analysis: The market value of the stocks declined by $7,725,425 − $7,518,700 = $206,725, a loss of 2.68 percent.

The futures profit was

$$
\begin{array}{ll}
25(\$326,250) & \text{(sale price of futures)} \\
-\ 25(\$323,850) & \text{(purchase price of futures)} \\
\hline
\$60,000 & \text{(profit on futures).}
\end{array}
$$

Thus, the overall loss on the stocks was effectively reduced to $206,725 − $60,000 = $146,725, a loss of 1.90 percent.

currently is selling for $26.50 and has a beta of 1.80. The acquiring firm plans to buy 100,000 shares, which will cost $2.65 million. The purchase will be made on August 15. This could be viewed as one purchase in a series of purchases designed to ultimately acquire controlling interest in the target firm. The acquiring firm realizes that if stock prices as a whole increase, the shares will be more expensive. If the firm purchases stock index futures, however, any general increase in stock prices will lead to a profit in the futures market.

Because the hedge will be terminated on August 15, the acquiring firm chooses to buy September S&P 500 futures. Table 10.13 shows the results of the hedge.

On August 15, the Helix stock price is $28.75. The shares thus cost an additional $225,000.[11] The profit on the futures transaction, however, was $250,125. Thus, the effective cost of the shares is $26.25.

---

[11]It is unlikely that all of the 100,000 shares could have been purchased at the same price. Therefore, we should treat $28.75 as the average price at which the shares were acquired.

TABLE 10.13	**Anticipatory Hedge of a Takeover**

Scenario: On July 15, a firm has decided to begin buying up shares of Helix Technology Corporation with the ultimate objective of obtaining controlling interest. The acquisition will be made by purchasing lots of about 100,000 shares until sufficient control is obtained. The first purchase of 100,000 shares will take place on August 15. The stock is currently worth $26.50 and has a beta of 1.80.

Date	Spot Market	Futures Market
July 15	Current price of the stock is 26.50. Current cost of shares: 100,000($26.50) = $2,650,000. The beta is 1.80.	September S&P 500 futures is at 1,260.50. Price per contract: $315,125. Approximate number of contracts:

$$N_f = 1.80 \left(\frac{2,650,000}{315,125} \right)$$
$$= -15.14.$$

Since it should buy futures, ignore the negative sign.
Buy 15 contracts

Date	Spot Market	Futures Market
August 15	The stock is purchased at its current price of 28.75. Cost of shares: 100,000($28.75) = $2,875,000.	September S&P 500 futures is at 1,327.20. Price per contract: $331,800. **Sell 15 contracts**

Analysis: When the 100,000 shares are purchased on August 15, they cost $2,875,000, an additional $225,000.

The profit on the futures transaction is

$$
\begin{array}{ll}
15(\$331,800) & \text{(sale price of futures)} \\
- \ 15(\$315,125) & \text{(purchase price of futures)} \\
\hline
\$250,125 & \text{(profit on futures)}.
\end{array}
$$

Thus, the hedge eliminated all of the additional cost and left a small gain. The shares end up effectively costing ($2,875,000 − $250,125)/100,000 = 26.25.

The hedge was successful in reducing some of the additional cost of the shares; however, the unsystematic risk cannot be hedged. In takeover situations, the unsystematic risk is likely to be very high. For example, if word leaks out that someone is buying up the stock, the price will tend to rise substantially. This can occur even if the market as a whole is going down. Also, federal regulations require that certain takeover attempts be announced beforehand. If there were options on the target firm's stock, however, the acquiring firm could use these to hedge the unsystematic risk.

The takeover game is intense and exciting, with high risk and the potential for large profits. Stock index futures can play an important role, but the extent to which futures are used to hedge this kind of risk is not known, because much of this kind of activity is done with a minimum of publicity.

The takeover example is but one type of situation wherein a firm can use a long hedge with stock index futures. Any time someone is considering buying a stock, there is the risk that the stock price will increase before the purchase is made. Stock index futures cannot hedge the risk that factors specific to the company will drive up the stock price, but they can be used to protect against increases in the market as a whole.

Summary

This chapter looked at hedging with interest rate and stock index futures. It began by examining some basic concepts necessary for understanding and formulating hedge strategies. It explored the concepts of long and short hedging and basis risk and identified rules that help determine which contract to select, including the choice of commodity, expiration month, and whether to be long or short. The chapter also examined techniques for determining the optimal number of futures contracts for providing the volatility needed to offset the spot market risk.

The hedge examples were grouped by type of contract—short-term interest rate futures hedges, intermediate- and long-term interest rate futures hedges, and stock index futures hedges. While these examples span a broad range of applications, there are numerous similar situations in which virtually the same type of hedge would apply. The emphasis was on understanding the concept of hedging by observing it in practical situations.

Table 10.14 contains capsule descriptions of the various hedge situations that are likely to be encountered, with an identification of the nature of the risk and a prescription of what to do to hedge the risk.

Chapter 11 continues our look at futures strategies by examining arbitrage, speculative, and spread strategies. These strategies are somewhat more complex and require more frequent reference to concepts developed in previous chapters. You may wish to review Chapter 9 before reading Chapter 11.

Key Terms

Before continuing to Chapter 11, you should be able to give brief definitions of the following terms.

- short hedge/long hedge
- anticipatory hedge
- basis/basis risk
- cross hedge
- quantity risk
- hedge ratio
- duration
- implied yield
- implied duration
- yield beta
- tailing the hedge
- strip hedge
- rolling strip hedge
- stack hedge

TABLE 10.14	Hedge Situations

Scenario	The Risk	What to Do
You anticipate the purchase of a bond, note, Treasury bill, or other fixed-income security at a future date.	By the time the purchase date arrives, interest rates may have fallen, making the security sell for a higher price and lower yield.	To hedge against a decrease in interest rates, buy interest rate futures because their prices move inversely to interest rates.
You anticipate that you will issue a bond or take out a loan at a future date.	By the time the future date arrives, interest rates may have risen, making the bond or loan more costly.	To hedge against an increase in interest rates, sell interest rates futures because their prices move inversely to interest rates.
You borrow at a floating rate. Future interest payments will be adjusted directly with the given interest rate.	By the time the rate is reset, an increase in interest rates may result in higher interest payments.	To hedge against an increase in interest rates, sell interest rate futures because their prices move inversely to interest rates.
You hold a bond or fixed-income security and are either concerned about its future market value or plan to sell it at a later date.	By the time that future date arrives, interest rates may have risen, resulting in a lower market value.	To hedge against an increase in interest rates, sell interest rate futures because their prices move inversely to interest rates.
You hold a stock portfolio and are either concerned about its future market value or plan to sell it at a later date.	By the time that future date arrives, the value of the stock may have fallen.	To hedge against a decrease in stock prices in general, sell stock index futures, which move directly with the level of stock prices.
You plan to purchase a stock at a later date, possibly as part of a takeover.	By the time that future date arrives, the price of the stock may have risen, making it more expensive or requiring that you purchase fewer shares.	To hedge against an increase in stock prices in general, buy stock index futures, which move directly with the level of stock prices.

Further Reading

The theory underlying some of the hedging models in this chapter is found in

Johnson, L. L. "The Theory of Hedging and Speculation in Commodity Futures Markets." *Review of Economic Studies* 27 (1960): 139–151.

Stein, J. L. "The Simultaneous Determination of Spot and Futures Prices." *The American Economic Review* 51 (1961): 1012–1025.

Empirical research on hedging effectiveness is in

Ederington, L. H. "The Hedging Performance of the New Futures Market." *The Journal of Finance* 34 (1979): 157–170.

Figlewski, S. "Hedging Performance and Basis Risk in Stock Index Futures." *The Journal of Finance* 39 (1984): 657–669.

Figlewski, S. "Hedging with Stock Index Futures: Theory and Application in a New Market." *The Journal of Futures Markets* 5 (1985): 183–199.

The rationale for and evidence on the hedging and risk management activities of corporations can be found in

Smith, C. W., and R. M. Stulz. "The Determinants of Firms' Hedging Policies." *Journal of Financial and Quantitative Analysis* 20 (1985): 391–405.

Nance, D. R., C. W. Smith, Jr., and C. W. Smithson. "On the Determinants of Corporate Hedging." *The Journal of Finance* 48 (1993): 267–284.

Questions and Problems

1. Explain the difference between a short hedge and a long hedge.

2. What is the basis? How is the basis expected to change over the life of a futures contract?

3. Explain why a strengthening basis benefits a short hedge and hurts a long hedge.

4. Suppose you are a dealer in sugar. It is September 26, and you hold 112,000 pounds of sugar worth $0.0479 per pound. The price of a futures contract expiring in January is $0.0550 per pound. Each contract is for 112,000 pounds. Determine the original basis. Then calculate the profit from a hedge if it is held to expiration and the basis converges to zero. Show how the profit is explained by movements in the basis alone.

5. Rework problem 4, but assume the hedge is closed on December 10, when the spot price is $0.0574 and the January futures price is $0.0590.

6. What factors must one consider in deciding on the appropriate futures commodity for a hedge?

7. For each of the following hedge termination dates, identify the appropriate contract expiration. Assume the available expiration months are March, June, September, and December.

    a. August 10

    b. December 15

    c. February 20

    d. June 14

8. State and explain two reasons why firms hedge.

9. What is the minimum variance hedge ratio and the measure of hedging effectiveness? What do these two values tell us?

10. What is the price sensitivity hedge ratio? How are the price sensitivity and minimum variance hedge ratios alike? How do they differ?

11. Suppose you are an oil dealer and hold a position of 1 million barrels of crude oil. You hedge by trading futures, each of which is on 10,000 barrels. You consider the effects of marking to market to be sufficient to justify tailing the hedge. The hedge will be on for 60 days. The interest rate is 8.5 percent. You plan to hold the hedge all the way to the expiration date. Determine the number of contracts you should sell at the beginning of the hedge. Then determine the number of contracts you should be holding when the hedge has 20 days to go.

12. For each of the following situations, determine whether a long or short hedge is appropriate. Justify your answers.

a. A firm anticipates issuing stock in three months.

b. An investor plans to buy a bond in 30 days.

c. A bank holds a floating rate security issued by another bank.

d. A firm plans to borrow money in two months.

13. On October 26, a bank is considering making a $20 million, three-month, fixed-rate loan to a corporation. The loan will be taken out immediately and repaid on January 25. The bank knows it will have to finance the loan by issuing one-month CDs that will pay interest at the LIBOR. The CDs will mature on the last Friday of the month and will be repaid by issuing a new CD at the new rate.

The forward LIBOR is 10.16 percent. The bank must keep its cost of financing as low as possible and will lose money on the loan if that cost exceeds 11 percent. December Eurodollar futures currently are at 89.33. March Eurodollar futures are at 88.89. Both figures are IMM Index values. The dates on which the CDs will be rolled over are November 30 and December 28.

a. What should the firm do on October 26?

b. On November 30, the December Eurodollar futures is at 90.54. The March contract is at 89.93. The LIBOR is 9.10 percent. Describe what happens on this day.

c. On December 28, the March contract is at 90.56. The LIBOR is 8.63 percent. Describe what happens on this day.

d. On January 25, the fixed-rate loan is repaid. The March contract is at 91.28. Determine the overall outcome of the hedge. Be sure to determine whether the firm met its objective of keeping the rate below 11 percent.

14. On July 6, a firm learns that it will have approximately $10 million available for short-term investment on November 30. It believes that the best use of the funds is to make a Eurodollar deposit. The forward rate on 90-day Eurodollar deposits is 12.25 percent. The firm is concerned that Eurodollar rates will decrease over the next few months. The December Eurodollar IMM Index is 86.30.

a. Describe the transaction the firm should execute to hedge the risk of a decrease in Eurodollar rates. What is the yield on Eurodollar deposits on July 6?

b. On November 30, the December Eurodollar IMM Index is at 90.54. The three-month Eurodollar deposit rate is 9.10 percent. Determine the outcome of the hedge. Calculate the effective yield on the Eurodollar deposit.

15. On February 15, a firm learns that it will need to borrow $10 million on August 15 for 90 days. The loan will be at a fixed rate equal to the prime rate, which currently is 11 percent. The loan will be discounted and the rate stated on a 360-day basis. The company is concerned about rising interest rates and is considering hedging that risk. It is uncertain, however, whether the T-bill or Eurodollar contract is a better hedge. The prime rate is administered by the bank and is not necessarily highly correlated with market rates. Lacking any specific knowledge of how to handle this problem, the firm decides to assume the prime rate changes 1 point for every 1-point change in T-bill and Eurodollar rates. The firm elects to use T-bill futures for the hedge but, for future reference, to track the performance of a Eurodollar hedge.

   The September T-bill IMM Index is 90.25, and the September Eurodollar IMM Index is 89.06. For each of the following questions, work out the results for both a T-bill and a Eurodollar hedge.

a. Determine the transaction the firm would make on February 15 to set up the hedge. Use the price sensitivity hedge ratio. Identify the effective rate if the loan were taken out today.

b. On August 15, the prime rate is at 13 percent. The September T-bill IMM Index is at 89.84, and the Eurodollar IMM Index is at 88.14. Determine the outcome of the hedge. What is the effective cost of borrowing?

16. On January 31, a firm learns that it will have $5 million available on May 31. It will use the funds to purchase the APCO 9 1/2 percent bonds maturing in about 21 years. Interest is paid semiannually on March 1 and September 1. The bonds are rated A2 by Moody's and are selling for 78 7/8 per 100 and yielding 12.32 percent. The duration is 7.81.

   The firm is considering hedging the anticipated purchase with September T-bond futures. The futures price is 71 8/32. The firm believes the futures contract is tracking the Treasury bond with a coupon of 12 3/4 percent and maturing in about 25 years. It has determined that the implied yield on the futures contract is 11.40 percent and the duration of the contract is 8.32.

The firm believes the APCO bond yield will change 1 point for every 1-point change in the yield on the bond underlying the futures contract.

a. Determine the transaction the firm should conduct on January 31 to set up the hedge.

b. On May 31, the APCO bonds were priced at 82 3/4. The September futures price was 76 14/32. Determine the outcome of the hedge.

17. On July 1, a portfolio manager holds $1 million face value of Treasury bonds, the 11 1/4s maturing in about 29 years. The price is 107 14/32. The bond will need to be sold on August 30. The manager is concerned about rising interest rates and believes a hedge would be appropriate. The September T-bond futures price is 77 15/32.

The manager decides to compute the minimum variance hedge ratio by regressing the daily change in the portfolio value on the change in the September futures price. The regression gives a coefficient of 13 and explains 95 percent of the variation.

a. What transaction should the firm make on July 1?

b. On August 30, the bond was selling for 101 12/32 and the futures price was 77 5/32. Determine the outcome of the hedge.

18. You are the manager of a stock portfolio. On October 1, your holdings consist of the eight stocks listed in the following table, which you intend to sell on December 31. You are concerned about a market decline over the next three months. The number of shares, their prices, and the betas are shown, as well as the prices on December 31.

Stock	Number of Shares	Beta	10/1 Price	12/31 Price
R. R. Donnelley	10,000	1.00	19 5/8	27 3/8
B. F. Goodrich	6,200	1.05	31 3/8	32 7/8
Raytheon	15,800	1.15	49 3/8	53 5/8
Maytag	8,900	0.90	55 3/8	77 7/8
Kroger	11,000	0.85	42 1/8	47 7/8
Comdisco	14,500	1.45	19 3/8	28 5/8
Cessna	9,900	1.20	29 3/4	30 1/8
Foxboro	4,500	0.95	24 3/4	26

On October 1, you decide to execute a hedge using a stock index futures contract, which has a $500 multiplier. The March contract price is 376.20. On December 31, the March contract price is 424.90. Determine the outcome of the hedge.

19. On March 1, a securities analyst recommended General Cinema stock as a good purchase in the early summer. The portfolio manager plans to buy 20,000 shares of the stock on June 1 but is concerned that the market as a whole will be bullish over the next three months. General Cinema's stock currently is at 32 7/8, and the beta is 1.10.

Construct a hedge that will protect against movements in the stock market as a whole. Use the September stock index futures, which is priced at 375.30 on March 1 and which has a $500 multiplier. Evaluate the outcome of the hedge if on June 1 the futures price is 387.30 and General Cinema's stock price is 38 5/8.

20. (Concept Problem) As we discussed in the chapter, futures can be used to eliminate systematic risk in a stock portfolio, leaving it essentially a risk-free portfolio. A portfolio manager can achieve the same result, however, by selling the stocks and replacing them with T-bills. Consider the following stock portfolio.

Stock	Number of Shares	Price	Beta
Northrop Grumman	14,870	18.125	1.10
H. J. Heinz	8,755	36.125	1.05
Washington Post	1,245	264	1.05
Disney	8,750	134.5	1.25
Wang Labs	33,995	4.25	1.20
Wisconsin Energy	12,480	29	0.65
General Motors	14,750	48.75	0.95
Union Pacific	12,900	71.5	1.20
Royal Dutch Shell	7,500	78.75	0.75
Illinois Power	3,550	15.5	0.60

Suppose the portfolio manager wishes to convert this portfolio to a riskless portfolio for a period of one month. The price of a stock index futures with a $500 multiplier is 369.45. To sell each share would cost $20 per order plus $0.03 per share. Each company's shares would constitute a separate order. The futures contract would entail a cost of $27.50 per contract, round-trip. T-bill purchases cost $25 per trade for any number of T-bills. Determine the most cost-effective way to accomplish the manager's goal of converting the portfolio to a risk-free position for one month and then converting it back.

21. (Concept Problem) On January 2, a bank learns it will have about $10 million to invest in T-bills on November 28. The current T-bill discount rate is 7.11 percent. The bank believes T-bill rates will fall over the next nine months. It would like to hedge in the T-bill futures market but believes that only the nearby contract is sufficiently liquid to justify a hedge. Thus, it will use the March contract until February 28, the June contract from February 28 to May 30, the September contract from May 30 to August 29, and the December contract from August 29 to November 28. When it rolls out of one contract and into the next, it will take its futures gain (loss) and reinvest (borrow) at the market rates for the time remaining until November 28. These rates are, of course, unknown when the hedge is begun. The reinvestment (borrowing) rates turned out to be 8 percent from February

28 to November 28, 6.875 percent from May 30 to November 28, and 5.6875 percent from August 29 to November 28. Whatever amount is invested on the given date earns the rate indicated for the time remaining until November 28; however, these are annual rates, so adjust accordingly. The prices of the T-bill futures on the appropriate dates were as follows:

March contract: January 2 (93.18), February 28 (93.10)
June contract: February 28 (93.39), May 30 (93.71)
September contract: May 30 (93.77), August 29 (94.94)
December contract: August 29 (95.06), November 28 (94.71)

On November 28, the discount spot rate on 91-day T-bills was 5.41 percent. Determine the rate the bank would earn on the purchase of the spot T-bills on November 28 both with and without the hedge. Remember to account for the reinvestment of futures profits and losses as the hedge is rolled forward on the given dates.

APPENDIX 10A

Derivation of the Hedge Ratio*

Minimum Variance Hedge Ratio

The variance of the profit from the hedge is

$$\sigma_{\Pi}^2 = \sigma_{\Delta S}^2 + \sigma_{\Delta f}^2 N_f^2 + 2\sigma_{\Delta S \Delta f} N_f.$$

The value of N_f that minimizes σ_{Π}^2 is found by differentiating σ_{Π}^2 with respect to N_f.

$$\frac{\partial \sigma_{\Pi}^2}{\partial N_f} = 2\sigma_{\Delta f}^2 N_f + 2\sigma_{\Delta S \Delta f}.$$

Setting this equal to zero and solving for N_f gives

$$N_f = -\frac{\sigma_{\Delta S \Delta f}}{\sigma_{\Delta f}^2}.$$

The second derivative $(2\sigma_{\Delta f}^2 > 0)$ verifies that this is a minimum.

Price Sensitivity Hedge Ratio

The value of the position can be specified as

$$V = S + V^f N_f,$$

where V^f is the value of the futures contract. Now we wish to find the effect of a change in r on V. Since $\partial V^f / \partial r = \partial f / \partial r$,

$$\frac{\partial V}{\partial r} = \frac{\partial S}{\partial r} + \frac{\partial f}{\partial r} N_f.$$

The optimal value of N_f is the one that makes this derivative equal to zero. We do not know the derivatives $\partial S / \partial r$ and $\partial f / \partial r$, but we can use the chain rule to express the equation as

$$\frac{\partial V}{\partial r} = \frac{\partial S}{\partial y_S} \frac{\partial y_S}{\partial r} + \frac{\partial f}{\partial y_f} \frac{\partial y_f}{\partial r} N_f = 0.$$

---

*This appendix requires the use of calculus.

This procedure introduces the yield changes, ∂y_S and ∂y_f, into the problem. Usually it is assumed that $\partial y_S/\partial r = \partial y_f/\partial r$. Substituting and solving for N_f gives

$$N_f = -\frac{(\partial S/\partial y_S)}{(\partial f/\partial y_f)}.$$

This is approximated as

$$N_f = -\frac{(\Delta S/\Delta y_S)}{(\Delta f/\Delta y_f)}$$

$$= -\left(\frac{\Delta S}{\Delta f}\right)\left(\frac{\Delta y_F}{\Delta y_S}\right).$$

APPENDIX 10B

Taxation of Hedging

The tax treatment of hedging was originally established in a 1936 IRS ruling that stated that using futures contracts to reduce business risk generates ordinary income or loss. The ruling was reaffirmed in a 1955 Supreme Court case involving a firm called Corn Products Refining Company. Corn Products had purchased futures contracts to hedge the future purchase of corn it expected to need. The futures price went up and Corn Products reported the profits as capital gains, which at that time were treated more favorably for tax purposes. The IRS disagreed and the case ultimately ended up in the Supreme Court, which ruled that the purchase of the corn futures was related to the everyday operations of the firm and, thus, should be considered ordinary income for tax purposes. From that point on, the taxation of futures hedges was determined by what came to be known as the *business motive test*. Put simply, was the hedge designed to reduce the firm's business risk? If so, then any profits or losses would be treated as ordinary income.

This interpretation held for 33 years until a shocking ruling occurred on a case that had nothing to do with hedging. Arkansas Best, a holding company, sold shares of the National Bank of Commerce of Dallas at a substantial loss, which it reported as an ordinary loss. Ordinary losses are more attractive to the taxpaying entity because capital losses are limited to the total of capital gains. So capital losses can potentially be unusable as tax credits while ordinary losses are fully deductible against ordinary income. In 1988 the Supreme Court ruled that the losses were capital. It argued that the shares did not constitute a sufficient exception to the established definition of a capital asset. In other words, the shares were not part of Arkansas Best's inventory. Since Best was a holding company, it felt that the shares were a part of its inventory.

The IRS then began using the Arkansas Best case to argue that certain futures hedges could be treated as a capital transactions, thus calling into question the millions of routine hedging transactions executed by businesses. It used the case to argue that the Federal National Mortgage Association (FNMA), a firm that buys and sells mortgages, must treat over $120 million in interest rate futures and options losses as capital. Furthermore, it ruled that while long futures and options to purchase (calls) could be viewed as substitutes for inventory positions and, thus, taxable as ordinary income, short positions and put options could never be used as substitutes for inventory because they represent contracts to sell.

Such an interpretation implied that a business holding an inventory could not reduce its risk by agreeing to sell some of the inventory in advance, at least not without potentially serious tax consequences. In other words, the IRS ruling discourages conservative business practices. The implications for the futures markets and for businesses that had routinely hedged for years were far reaching. The futures markets could be effectively shut down and millions of back taxes might be owed.

The futures exchanges and many businesses lobbied Treasury Secretary Lloyd Bentsen. Finally on October 18, 1993, the IRS reversed its ruling on the FNMA case. The IRS did argue that hedgers would need to be able to prove that futures and options transactions to protect inventory were indeed hedges. In addition, the taxation of liability hedges, such as selling futures in anticipation of issuing liabilities in the future, of hedges to protect the cost of raw materials purchases, and of many over-the-counter market hedges, such as by using swaps, is still somewhat unclear.

Advanced Futures Strategies

Fund managers who aren't using futures and options are dealing with an incomplete set of resources.

PAUL DOLEY

Portfolio Managers Talk Futures and Risk Management,
Chicago Mercantile Exchange Videotape, 1995

This chapter looks at some advanced futures trading strategies. Some of these strategies are spreads and some are arbitrage strategies. Let us start out by defining these terms.

A **spread** is a strategy involving a long or short position in one futures contract and an opposite position in another. The concept of a spread certainly should not be new to you. We already covered time spreads in options, and we discussed **futures spreads** briefly in Chapter 9. A spread is a relatively low-risk strategy with several objectives. To regard a spread as a nonspeculative strategy, however, is misleading. A spread involves an element of speculation, but the risk is much lower than that in an outright long or short position.

We discussed arbitrage frequently in previous chapters. Arbitrage is the mechanism that links derivative prices to spot prices. Without arbitrage, the markets would be far less efficient. Derivative and spot prices, however, do not always conform to their theoretical relationships. When this happens, arbitrageurs step in and execute profitable transactions that quickly drive prices back to their theoretical levels. This chapter illustrates some of the arbitrage transactions important to the proper functioning and efficiency of the futures markets. It should be noted that while we sometimes ignore transaction costs in these examples, in practice any arbitrage opportunities must be evaluated by considering whether the profits cover the transaction costs.

Our approach here is to examine three groups of contracts: short-term interest rate futures contracts, intermediate- and long-term interest rate

Chapter Objectives

■ To illustrate the futures spread and arbitrage strategies using short-term interest rate futures, intermediate- and long-term interest rate futures, and stock index futures.

■ To demonstrate the accompanying software to identify the cheapest-to-deliver bond on the Treasury bond futures contract futures contracts, and stock index futures contracts. Within each group of contracts, we shall examine several popular trading strategies.

Short-Term Interest Rate Futures Strategies

In the category of short-term interest rate futures, we shall look at Treasury bill and Eurodollar futures strategies. You may first wish to review the contract specifications and hedging examples in Chapters 9 and 10.

Treasury Bill Cash-and-Carry/Implied Repo

In Chapter 9, we saw that the futures price is determined by the spot price and the cost of carry. The basic arbitrage transaction that determines this relationship often is referred to as a cash-and-carry. The investor purchases the security in the spot market and sells a futures contract. If the futures contract is held to expiration, the security's sale price is guaranteed.[1] Since the transaction is riskless, it should offer a return sufficient to cover the cost of carry. Because there is no risk, the investor will not earn a risk premium.

Another way to approach this problem is to focus on the rate at which the security's purchase can be financed. Often the financing is obtained by means of a repurchase agreement. A **repurchase agreement,** or **repo,** is an arrangement with a financial institution in which the owner of a security sells that security to the financial institution with an agreement to buy it back, usually a day later. This transaction is referred to as an overnight repo. The repo thus is a form of a secured loan. The investor obtains the use of the funds to buy the security by pledging it as collateral. The interest charged on a repo is usually quoted and calculated as if there were 360 days in a year, but here we shall use the assumption of a full 365-day year.

Repurchase agreements are frequently used in transactions involving government securities. Overnight repos are more common, but longer-term arrangements, called term repos, of up to two weeks are sometimes employed. In cash-and-carry transactions, the security is considered as being financed by using a repo. If the return from the transaction is greater than the repo rate, the arbitrage will be profitable.

From Chapter 9, the futures–spot price relationship is

$$f_0(T) = S_0 + \theta.$$

---

[1] Recall that this is true because the spot price at expiration equals the futures price at expiration. The profit on the spot transaction is $S_T - S_0$, and the profit on the futures transaction is $-(f_T(T) - f_0(T))$. The total profit is $f_0(T) - S_0$. Thus, $f_0(T)$ is the effective sale price of the underlying asset.

Since we are focusing on securities here, there is no significant storage cost; thus, the cost of carry, θ, is strictly the interest, iS_0. Now let us define the implicit interest cost as

$$\theta = f_0(T) - S_0.$$

Thus, θ is the implied cost of financing expressed in dollars. Suppose we express it as a percentage of the spot price, θ/S_0, and denote this as $\hat{r}$. Then $\hat{r}$ is the **implied repo rate.** If the cost of financing the position—the actual repo rate—is less than the implied repo rate, the arbitrage will be profitable.

The implied repo rate is the return implied by the cost-of-carry relationship between spot and futures prices and reflects the return to a cash-and-carry position.

Readers familiar with the concept of internal rate of return (IRR) will find that it is analogous to the implied repo rate. If the arbitrage brings no profit, the cost of financing is the implied repo rate. In a capital budgeting problem, a zero net present value (NPV) defines the internal rate of return. If the opportunity cost is less than the IRR, the project is attractive and produces a positive NPV. Likewise, an arbitrage is profitable if it can be financed at a rate lower than the implied repo rate.

For example, suppose there is a security that matures at time T and an otherwise identical security that matures at an earlier time, t. There is also a futures contract that expires at time t. You buy the longer-term security at a price of S_0, finance it at the rate r (an annualized rate), and sell a futures contract. At time t, the futures expires and you deliver the security. You have effectively sold the security at t for a price of $f_0(t)$. The profit from the transaction is

$$\Pi = f_0(t) - S_0(1 + r)^t.$$

The term $S_0(1 + r)^t$ reflects what you paid for the security, factored up by the cost of financing over period t. The implied repo rate, $\hat{r}$, is the cost of financing that produces no arbitrage profit; therefore, with $\Pi = 0$,

$$\hat{r} = \left(\frac{f_0(t)}{S_0}\right)^{1/t} - 1.$$

There is yet another approach to understanding the basic cash-and-carry arbitrage. Suppose we buy the security that matures at time T and simultaneously sell the futures contract that expires at time t (t < T). When the futures contract expires, we deliver the security, which has a remaining maturity of T − t. The net effect is that we have taken a security that matures at T and shortened its maturity to t. Thus, we have created a synthetic t-period instrument. If the return from the synthetic t-period instrument is greater than the return from an actual security maturing at t, prices are out of line and an arbitrage profit is possible.

An example of this strategy is to buy a six-month T-bill and sell a futures contract expiring in three months. This transaction creates a synthetic three-month T-bill, with a return that should equal the return on an actual three-month T-bill. If it does not, investors will be attracted to the strategy and their transactions will drive up the price of the six-month T-bill and drive down the futures price, or vice versa, until the synthetic T-bill and the actual T-bill have the same returns.

AN EXAMPLE   Table 11.1 illustrates the cash-and-carry transaction with Treasury bills. This is an example of a situation in which buying a longer-term T-bill, selling a futures that expires before the T-bill matures, and delivering the T-bill when the futures expires creates a synthetic shorter-term

---

TABLE 11.1	**Treasury Bill Cash-and-Carry Arbitrage**

Scenario: On September 26, the T-bill maturing on December 18, 83 days later, has a discount rate of 5.19. The T-bill maturing March 19, 174 days later, has a discount rate of 5.35. The December T-bill futures is priced at the IMM Index of 94.80. An arbitrage opportunity is available.

Date	Spot Market	Futures Market
September 26	The March 19 T-bill has a discount of 5.35. Price per $100 face value: $100 - 5.35(174/360)$ $= 97.4142$.	December T-bill IMM Index is at 94.80. Price per $100 face value: $100 - (100 - 94.80)(90/360)$ $= 98.70$.
	Buy one T-bill	**Sell one contract**
December 18	The March T-bill still has 91 days remaining but the current spot price of the T-bill is irrelevant.	Deliver the March T-bill and receive an effective price of 98.70 based on the futures price at the time the contract was initiated. This closes out the futures position.

Analysis: The T-bill was bought on September 26 at 97.4142. It was delivered on December 18 to close out the futures contract. There are 83 days between September 26 and December 18. Thus, the annualized rate of return on a security bought at 97.4142 and sold at 98.70 where the holding period is 83 days is

$$\left(\frac{98.70}{97.4142}\right)^{365/83} - 1 = .0594.$$

This rate should be compared to the return from buying an actual 83-day T-bill. Its price, based on the 5.19 discount in effect on September 26 for a T-bill maturing on December 18, is

$$100 - 5.19(83/360) = 98.8034.$$

If this bill were purchased and held until maturity on December 18, it would return its full face value of 100 for an overall return of

$$\left(\frac{100}{98.8034}\right)^{365/83} - 1 = .0544,$$

which is a full 50 basis points lower.

T-bill. The return on this synthetic T-bill is 50 basis points higher than the return on an actual T-bill with the same maturity.

There are, however, some limitations to the effectiveness of this strategy. These prices were closing prices from *The Wall Street Journal*. As we acknowledged when studying options, the prices may not necessarily be synchronized. A professional arbitrageur would, of course, have access to current synchronized prices, but even in that case the prices might change before the transaction is completed.

Another limitation to the cash-and-carry arbitrage is that the repo rate is not fixed for the full time period. As noted earlier, some term repos for up to two weeks are available, but most repo financing is overnight. In either case, the financing rate on the T-bill is unknown when the arbitrage is executed. Each time a repo matures, new financing must be arranged, and the rate may well be much higher than originally expected. A number of other limitations, such as transaction costs, come into play when determining the implied repo rate from other futures instruments.

Eurodollar Arbitrage

As described in Chapter 10, the Eurodollar market is a large market in which foreign banks and foreign branches of U.S. banks issue dollar-denominated deposits and often commit to forward and futures transactions. Although the Eurodollar market is highly efficient, there may be occasional arbitrage opportunities resulting from violations of the cost-of-carry relationship between spot and futures or forward prices.

AN EXAMPLE   Table 11.2 illustrates a situation in which a London bank, needing to issue a 180-day Eurodollar time deposit, finds that it can get a better rate by issuing a 90-day time deposit and selling a futures expiring in 90 days. By stringing the 90-day time deposit to the futures contract, the bank creates a synthetic 180-day time deposit with a better rate.

It might appear that the result was contingent on the rate on the time deposit issued on December 16—a rate that was not known back in September. In fact, the result of this transaction was known when it was executed. The 90-day time deposit was issued at a rate of $.0825(90/360) = .020625$ for the 90 days. The Eurodollar futures was sold at a rate of $.0863(90/360) = .021575$. Thus, if the bank issued a 90-day time deposit at $.020625$ and followed that with a 90-day time deposit at $.021575$, the overall rate for 180 days would be

$$(1.020625)(1.021575) - 1 = .042645.$$

Annualizing this rate gives

$$(1.042645)^{(365/180)} - 1 = .0884,$$

which is the rate obtained by the bank.

TABLE 11.2	**Eurodollar Arbitrage**

Scenario: On September 16, a London bank needs to issue $10 million of 180-day Eurodollar time deposits. The current rate on such time deposits is 8.75. The bank is considering the alternative of issuing a 90-day time deposit at its current rate of 8.25 and selling a Eurodollar futures contract. If the 180-day time deposit is issued, the bank will have to pay back

$$\$10,000,000[1 + .0875(180/360)] = \$10,437,500,$$

which is a rate of

$$\left(\frac{\$10,437,500}{\$10,000,000}\right)^{365/180} - 1 = .0907.$$

The rates available in the spot and futures markets are such that the bank can obtain a better rate by doing the following.

Date	Spot Market	Futures Market
September 16	The 90-day time deposit rate is 8.25.	December Eurodollar IMM Index is at 91.37. Price per $100 face value: 100 − (100 − 91.37)(90/360) = 97.8425.
	Issue 90-day time deposit for $10,000,000	Price per contract: $978,425. **Sell 10 contracts**
December 16	The 90-day time deposit matures and the bank owes $10,000,000 (1 + .0825(90/360)) = $10,206,250. The rate on new 90-day time deposits is 7.96.	December Eurodollar IMM Index is at 92.04. Price per $100 face value: 100 − (100 − 92.04)(90/360) = 98.01. Price per contract: $980,100.
	Issue new 90-day time deposit for $10,223,000	**Buy 10 contracts**

Analysis: On September 16, the bank received $10,000,000 from the newly issued 90-day time deposit. On December 16, it bought back its ten futures contracts at a loss of 10($980,100 − $978,425) = $16,750. It issued $10,223,000 of new time deposits, using $16,750 to cover the loss in the futures account and the remaining $10,206,250 to pay off the maturing 90-day time deposit.

On March 16 it paid off the new time deposit, owing

$$\$10,223,000[1 + .0796(90/360)] = \$10,426,438.$$

Thus, on September 16, it received $10,000,000 and on March 16, it paid out $10,426,438. It had no other cash flows in the interim. Thus, its effective borrowing cost for 180 days was

$$\left(\frac{\$10,426,438}{\$10,000,000}\right)^{365/180} - 1 = .0884,$$

which is 23 basis points less than the cost of a 180-day Eurodollar time deposit.

Intermediate- and Long-Term Interest Rate Futures Strategies

Intermediate- and long-term interest rate futures include Treasury note and Treasury bond futures. As we noted in earlier chapters, these instruments are virtually identical. Here we shall concentrate on the Treasury bond contract.

Recall that the T-bond contract is based on the assumption that the underlying bond has a specific coupon rate and a maturity or call date of not less than 15 years. The coupon assumption is 8 percent for contracts expiring through December 1999 and 6 percent for contracts expiring March 2000 or later.

Suppose you are short the March 2000 contract. As the holder of the short position, you have the choice of which day during the delivery month to make delivery and which bond from among the eligible bonds you will deliver. Let us assume you have decided to deliver the bonds with a coupon of 7 7/8 percent and maturing on February 15, 2021. Delivery will be made on Friday, March 3, 2000.

Since the contract assumes delivery of a bond with a 6 percent coupon, the delivery of the 7 7/8s requires an adjustment to the price paid by the long to the short. The adjustment is based on the CBOT's conversion factor system. The **conversion factor, CF,** is defined for each eligible bond for a given contract. The CF is the price of a bond with a face value of $1, coupon and maturity equal to that of the deliverable bond, and yield of 6 percent. The maturity is defined as the maturity of the bond on the first day of the delivery month. If the bond is callable, the call date is substituted for the maturity date. The CF for the 7 7/8s of 2021 would be the price of a bond with a face value of $1, coupon of 7 7/8 percent, maturity equal to the time remaining from March 1, 2000, the first business day of the month, to February 15, 2021, the maturity date of the bond, and yield of 6 percent. That same bond delivered on the June 2000 contract would have a different CF because it would have a different maturity—on June 2000 rather than on March 2000. A different bond delivered on the March 2000 contract would have a different conversion factor.

The conversion factor system is designed to place all bonds on an equivalent basis for delivery purposes. If the holder of the short position delivers a bond with a coupon greater than 6 percent, the CF will be greater than 1. The short will then receive more than the futures price in payment for the bond. If the coupon is less than 6 percent, the CF will be less than 1 and the short will receive less than the futures price in payment for the bond.

Tables of conversion factors are available, and there is a specific formula for determining the conversion factor, which is provided in Appendix

11A. Your software includes the Excel spreadsheet cf1.xls that calculates the conversion factor and it is explained in the appendix. In this problem, the CF for the 7 7/8s of 2021 delivered on the March 2000 contract would be 1.2207. To determine the invoice price—the amount the long pays to the short for the bond—multiply the CF by the settlement price on the position day. Then the accrued interest from the last coupon payment date until the delivery date is added:[2]

> Invoice price = (Settlement price on position day) (Conversion factor) + Accrued interest.

In this problem, assume the settlement price on Wednesday, March 1, which is called the position day, was 112-16, or $112,500. The bond has coupon payment dates of February 15 and August 15. Thus, the last coupon payment date was February 15, 2000. The number of days from February 15 to March 3 is 17, and the number of days between coupon payment dates of February 15, 2000, and August 15, 2000, is 182. Thus, the accrued interest is

$$\$100,000(.07875/2)(17/182) = \$368.$$

The invoice price therefore is

$$\$112,500(1.2207) + \$368 = \$137,697.$$

On the next day, called notice of intention day, Thursday, March 2, the holder of the long position receives an invoice of $137,697 and must pay this amount and accept the bond on the delivery day, Friday, March 3.

Table 11.3 presents CFs and invoice prices for other bonds deliverable on the March 2000 contract. Note how the CFs vary directly with the level of the coupon.

---

[2]The accrued interest is the amount of interest that has built up since the last coupon date. Most bonds pay interest semiannually on the maturity day and six months hence. Thus a bond maturing on February 15, 2015, would pay interest every year on February 15 and August 15. The accrued interest is the semiannual coupon times the number of days since the last coupon date divided by the number of days between the last coupon date and the next coupon date. It is simply a proration of the next coupon. The buyer of a bond will receive the full next coupon, but, because she is not entitled to all of it, must pay the seller the accrued interest. The actual correct bond price will accurately include the accrued interest in it, though the quoted price will not.

TABLE 11.3	**Conversion Factors and Invoice Prices for Deliverable Bonds (March 2000, T-Bond Futures Contract)**

Contract price: 112.50 ($112,500)
Delivery date: March 3, 2000

Coupon	Maturity Date	CF	Accrued Interest	Invoice Price
11 1/4	2/15/15	1.5089	$ 525	$170,276
10 5/8	8/15/15	1.4577	496	164,487
9 7/8	11/15/15	1.3875	2,957	159,051
9 1/4	2/15/16	1.3280	432	149,832
7 1/4	5/15/16	1.1274	2,171	129,004
7 1/2	11/15/16	1.1557	2,246	132,262
8 3/4	5/15/17	1.2906	2,620	147,813
8 7/8	8/15/17	1.3062	415	147,363
9 1/8	5/15/18	1.3411	2,733	153,607
9	11/15/18	1.3325	2,695	152,601
8 7/8	2/15/19	1.3208	415	149,005
8 1/8	8/15/19	1.2405	380	139,936
8 1/2	2/15/20	1.2869	397	145,173
8 3/4	5/15/20	1.3178	2,620	150,873
8 3/4	8/15/20	1.3197	409	148,875
7 7/8	2/15/21	1.2207	368	137,697
8 1/8	5/15/21	1.2518	2,433	143,261
8 1/8	8/15/21	1.2532	380	141,365
8	11/15/21	1.2398	2,396	141,874
7 1/4	8/15/22	1.1523	339	129,973
7 5/8	11/15/22	1.1992	2,283	137,193
7 1/8	2/15/23	1.1385	333	128,414
6 1/4	8/15/23	1.0310	292	116,280
7 1/2	11/15/24	1.1913	2,246	136,267
7 5/8	2/15/25	1.2080	147	136,047
6 7/8	8/15/25	1.1129	321	125,522
6	2/15/26	1.0000	280	112,780
6 3/4	8/15/26	1.0984	315	123,885
6 1/4	11/15/26	1.0330	1,872	118,085
6 5/8	2/15/27	1.0826	309	122,102
6 3/8	8/15/27	1.0499	298	118,412
6 1/8	11/15/27	1.0167	1,834	116,213
5 1/2	8/15/28	0.9323	257	105,141
5 1/4	11/15/28	0.8982	1,572	102,620
5 1/4	2/15/29	0.8977	245	101,236
6 1/8	8/15/29	1.0170	286	114,699

Determining the Cheapest-to-Deliver Bond on the Treasury Bond Futures Contract

As previously explained, the specifications on the Treasury bond contract allow delivery of many different bonds, subject to the minimum 15-year maturity or call date. At any given time prior to expiration, it is impossible to determine which bond will be delivered. It is, however, possible to identify the bond that is most likely to be delivered. That bond is referred to as the **cheapest to deliver** or **CTD.**

Suppose it is September 22, 1999, and you are interested in determining the bond that is most likely to be delivered on the upcoming March contract. The procedure involves a series of calculations that we shall illustrate for one particular bond—the 8 7/8s that mature on August 15, 2017.

If the holder of a long position in this bond also holds a short position in the T-bond futures contract, that trader can elect to maintain the position until expiration and deliver this particular bond. Even if another bond would be cheaper to deliver, the trader always has the option to deliver the bond already held. The cost of delivering the particular bond is the net profit or loss from buying the bond, selling a futures, holding the position until expiration, and then delivering the bond. Thus, the trader incurs the cost of carry on the bond held. Remember that this cost is somewhat offset by the coupons received on the bond.

For evaluating at time t the best bond to deliver at time T, the general expression for the cost of delivering a bond is

$$f(CF) + AI_T - [(B + AI_t)(1 + r)^{(T-t)} - FV \text{ of coupons at T}],$$

where AI_T is the accrued interest on the bond at T, the delivery date; AI_t is the accrued interest on the bond at t, today; and r is the risk-free rate that represents the interest lost on the funds invested in the bond. The term inside the brackets is the spot price of the bond (quoted price plus accrued interest) factored up by the cost of carry and reduced by the compound future value of any coupons received while the position is held. These coupons, of course, help offset the cost of carry, and by subtracting them we are simply reflecting the net cost of carry. The bracketed term is, thus, the forward price of the bond. The first two terms are the amount the trader would receive from delivering the bond. This is the invoice price.

The futures price is 94 1/32 or 94.03125, and the conversion factor for our bond is 1.3062. The accrued interest on September 22 is 0.92, and the accrued interest on March 3, the day we shall assume delivery, is 0.41. The price quoted for the bond is 124 21/32 or 124.65625. The repo rate is 5.8 percent. There are 163 days between September 22 and March 3. The invoice price for the futures is

$$94.03125(1.3062) + 0.41 = 123.24.$$

The coupon of 4.4375 is received on February 15 and reinvested at 5.8 percent for 17 days to grow to a value of $4.4375(1.058)^{17/365} = 4.45$. Thus, the forward price of the bond is

$$(124.65625 + 0.92)(1.058)^{(163/365)} - 4.45 = 124.33.$$

Hence, the bond would cost 1.09 more than it would return.

This conclusion by itself does not enable us to make a decision. We can only compare this figure for one bond to that for another. Let us consider a second bond, the 9 1/8s maturing on May 15, 2018. Its conversion factor is 1.3411, and its price is 127 27/32 or 127.84375. The accrued interest is 3.22 on September 22 and 2.73 on March 3. The coupon of 4.5625 received on November 15 is reinvested at 5.8 percent for 109 days and grows to a value of

$$4.5625(1.058)^{(109/365)} = 4.64.$$

Thus, the forward price of the bond is

$$(127.84375 + 3.22)(1.058)^{(163/365)} - 4.64 = 129.77.$$

The invoice price is

$$94.03125(1.3411) + 2.73 = 128.84$$

Thus, the difference between the amount received and the amount paid is $128.84 - 129.77 = -0.93$.

Therefore, it is clear that the 9 1/8 percent bond is better to deliver than the 8 7/8 percent bond. Of course, this calculation should be done for all bonds that are eligible for delivery. The bond for which the difference between the amount received and the amount paid is the maximum is the cheapest bond to deliver.

Table 11.4 presents these calculations for the March 2000 contract evaluated on September 22. Thirty-six eligible bonds are shown. The column labeled "Difference" is the difference between the invoice price and the forward price. All of these values are negative as they should be; otherwise one could earn an easy arbitrage profit. The cheapest bond to deliver is the one in which Difference is the closest to zero. In this case it is the 8 1/8 of August 15, 2021.

The Excel spreadsheet ctd2.xls will automatically do these calculations for you. Software Demonstration 11.1 illustrates how to use ctd2.xls.

The cheapest bond to deliver is important for several reasons. Any futures contract must reflect the behavior of the spot price. In the case of Treasury bond and note futures, the so-called "spot price" is not easy to determine. The cheapest bond to deliver is the bond that represents the spot instrument that the futures contract is tracking. Therefore, the cost of carry model examined in Chapter 9 would apply only to the cheapest bond to deliver. Also, the optimal hedge ratio would require knowledge of the cheapest bond to deliver.

The cheapest bond to deliver is the bond for which the difference between the revenue received from delivery of the bond and the cost incurred to buy and hold the bond is maximized.

TABLE 11.4	The Cheapest-to-Deliver Bond on the Treasury Bond Futures Contract

Current date: September 22, 1999
Delivery date: March 3, 2000
Repo rate: 5.8 percent
Futures price: 94 1/32

Coupon	Maturity	Ask Price	Forward Price	Invoice Price	Difference	Accrued Interest at t	Accrued Interest at T	Future Value of Coupon	CF
11 1/4	2/15/15	146 5/32	145.4344	142.4126	−3.0218	1.1617	0.5254	5.6398	1.5089
10 5/8	8/15/15	140 19/32	139.9772	137.5677	−2.4095	1.0971	0.4962	5.3265	1.4577
9 7/8	11/15/15	133 14/32	135.3959	133.4262	−1.9697	3.4885	2.9571	5.0213	1.3875
9 1/4	2/15/16	127 11/32	126.9331	125.3069	−1.6262	0.9552	0.4320	4.6372	1.3280
7 1/4	5/15/16	107 14/32	109.1168	108.1846	−0.9322	2.5611	2.1710	3.6866	1.1274
7 1/2	11/15/16	110 2/32	111.7722	110.9219	−0.8503	2.6495	2.2459	3.8137	1.1557
8 3/4	5/15/17	123 5/32	125.0170	123.9734	−1.0436	3.0910	2.6202	4.4493	1.2906
8 7/8	8/15/17	124 21/32	124.3253	123.2362	−1.0892	0.9164	0.4145	4.4492	1.3062
9 1/8	5/15/18	127 27/32	129.7692	128.8405	−0.9287	3.2235	2.7325	4.6400	1.3411
9	11/15/18	126 28/32	128.7940	127.9925	−0.8015	3.1793	2.6951	4.5764	1.3325
8 7/8	2/15/19	125 21/32	125.3508	124.6152	−0.7356	0.9164	0.4145	4.4492	1.3208
8 1/8	8/15/19	117 23/32	117.5075	117.0723	−0.4802	0.8390	0.3795	4.0732	1.2405
8 1/2	2/15/20	122 5/32	121.9099	121.4035	−0.5064	0.8777	0.3970	4.2612	1.2869
8 3/4	5/15/20	125 4/32	127.0360	126.5372	−0.4987	3.0910	2.6202	4.4493	1.3178
8 3/4	8/15/20	125 8/32	124.9837	124.5043	−0.4793	0.9035	0.4087	4.3865	1.3197
7 7/8	2/15/21	115 21/32	115.4913	115.1527	−0.3386	0.8132	0.3678	3.9479	1.2207
8 1/8	5/15/21	118 19/32	120.4296	120.1439	−0.2857	2.8702	2.4330	4.1315	1.2518
8 1/8	8/15/21	118 21/32	118.4689	118.2174	−0.2515	0.8390	0.3795	4.0732	1.2532
8	11/15/21	117 13/32	119.2301	118.9773	−0.2527	2.8261	2.3956	4.0679	1.2398
7 1/4	8/15/22	109 4/32	109.0406	108.6897	−0.3510	0.7486	0.3386	3.6345	1.1523
7 5/8	11/15/22	113 20/32	115.4072	115.0470	−0.3603	2.6936	2.2833	3.8772	1.1992
7 1/8	2/15/23	107 27/32	107.7761	107.3886	−0.3875	0.7357	0.3328	3.5719	1.1385
6 1/4	8/15/23	97 26/32	97.8351	97.2391	−0.5960	0.6454	0.2919	3.1332	1.0310
7 1/2	11/15/24	113 4/32	114.9128	114.2618	−0.6510	2.6495	2.2459	3.8137	1.1913
7 5/8	2/15/25	114 28/32	114.5824	113.7358	−0.8466	0.5802	0.1466	3.8166	1.2080
6 7/8	8/15/25	105 17/32	105.5035	104.9712	−0.5324	0.7099	0.3211	3.4465	1.1129
6	2/15/26	94 27/32	94.8895	94.3010	−0.5885	0.6196	0.2802	3.0079	1.0000
6 3/4	8/15/26	104 4/32	104.1109	103.5985	−0.5123	0.6970	0.3152	3.3839	1.0984
6 1/4	11/15/26	101 1/32	102.6934	99.0029	−3.6905	2.2079	1.8716	3.1781	1.0330
6 5/8	2/15/27	102 24/32	102.7502	102.1094	−0.6408	0.6841	0.3094	3.3212	1.0826
6 3/8	8/15/27	99 22/32	99.7085	99.0213	−0.6872	0.6583	0.2977	3.1959	1.0499
6 1/8	11/15/27	96 21/32	98.2252	97.4389	−0.7863	2.1637	1.8341	3.1145	1.0167
5 1/2	8/15/28	89 4/32	89.2227	87.9176	−1.3051	0.5679	0.2569	2.7572	0.9323
5 1/4	11/15/28	86 14/32	87.8738	86.0295	−1.8443	1.8546	1.5721	2.6696	0.8982
5 1/4	2/15/29	87 11/32	87.4949	84.6615	−2.8334	0.5421	0.2452	2.6319	0.8977
6 1/8	8/15/29	100 21/32	100.8008	95.9181	−4.8827	0.6325	0.2861	3.0706	1.0170

Delivery Options

The characteristics of the Treasury bond futures contract create some interesting opportunities for alert investors. Specifically, the contract contains several imbedded options. While these **delivery options** are not formally traded in the same way stock options are, they have many of the characteristics of the options we studied in earlier chapters. We shall examine some of these options here.

THE WILD CARD OPTION   The **wild card option** results from a difference in the closing times of the spot and futures markets. The Treasury bond futures contract stops trading at 3:00 P.M. eastern time. The spot market for Treasury bonds operates until 5:00 P.M. eastern time. During the delivery month, the holder of a short position knows the settlement price for that day at 3:00 P.M. Multiplying the settlement price by the conversion factor gives the invoice price the holder would receive if a given bond were delivered. This figure is locked in until the next day's trading starts.

During the two-hour period after the futures market closes, the spot market continues to trade. If the spot price declines during those two hours, the holder of a short futures position may find it attractive to buy a bond and deliver it. Because the futures market is closed and the invoice price is fixed, the futures market is unable to react to the new information that drove the spot price down. Moreover, the short has until about 9:00 P.M. to make the decision to deliver.

Let us use the following symbols:

f_3 = futures price at 3:00 P.M.
S_3 = spot price at 3:00 P.M.
CF = conversion factor of bond under consideration

You hold a short position in the futures contract that is expiring during the current month. Assume you own $1/CF$ bonds. Why this unusual amount? If you do not own any bonds, your position will be quite risky. Also, the bond under consideration should be the cheapest bond to deliver. That way your risk is quite low. Unexpected changes in the futures price will be approximately matched by changes in the value of the $1/CF$ bonds. We require the case that $CF > 1.0$.

If you make delivery that day, you will be required to deliver one bond per contract. You own only $1/CF$ bonds, so you will have to buy $1 - 1/CF$ additional bonds. If the bonds' spot price declines sufficiently between 3:00 P.M. and 5:00 P.M., you may be able to buy the additional bonds at a price low enough to make a profit. These additional bonds are called the *tail*.

Now suppose that at 5:00 P.M. the bond price is S_5. If you buy the additional $1 - 1/CF$ bonds at the price of S_5, and deliver them, your profit will be

$$\Pi = f_3(CF) - \left[\left(\frac{1}{CF}\right)S_5 + \left(1 - \frac{1}{CF}\right)S_5\right] = f_3(CF) - S_5$$

The first term, $f_3(CF)$, is the invoice price. This is simply the 3:00 P.M. settlement price on the futures contract times the conversion factor on the bond. The invoice price is the amount you receive upon delivery. The

---

SOFTWARE DEMONSTRATION 11.1   **Identifying the Cheapest-to-Deliver Bond with the Excel Spreadsheet ctd2.xls**

The Excel spreadsheet ctd2.xls operates in Excel 97 under Windows 95 or 98. It identifies the cheapest-to-deliver bond from among a set of bonds for the Chicago Board of Trade bond futures contract.

The spreadsheet is a read-only spreadsheet, meaning that it cannot be saved under the name ctd2.xls, which preserves the original file. To use the spreadsheet, simply do the following:

1.   Make sure you are in Windows 95 or 98.
2.   Run Excel 97.
3.   Open the file ctd2.xls.

Now let us work an example. Consider the problem in the text in which on September 22, 1999, you wish to identify the cheapest-to-deliver bond on the March 2000 contract. The current repo rate is 5.8 percent and the futures price is 94 1/32. You have identified 36 bonds that meet the 15-year maturity or callability requirement and are eligible for delivery.

Observe on the spreadsheet a section labeled **Inputs:**. Each cell that will accept inputs has a double-line border and the values are in blue. Enter the current date in the form mm/dd/yyyy. Insert "9/22/1999" in the appropriate box. Then enter the delivery date "3/3/2000" in its box. The repo rate can be entered as either "5.8" or ".058" in the appropriate box. The futures price

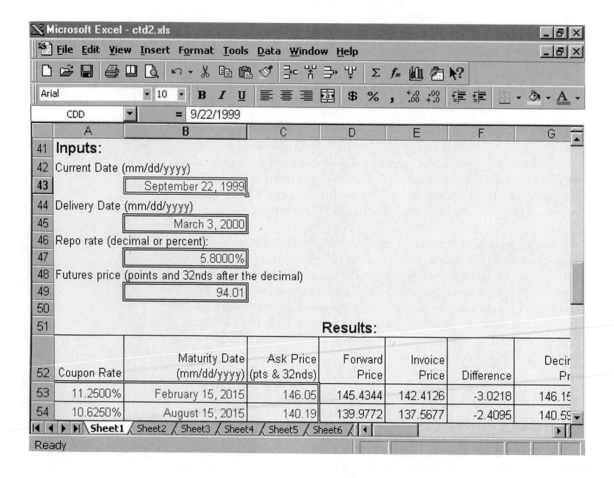

should be entered as points and thirty-seconds. Thus, 94 1/32 should be entered as "94.01". The trailing zero can be omitted for values like "103.2" for 103 20/32. List the individual bonds in the section below. Consider the first bond. Let it have a coupon rate of 11.25 percent, a maturity date of February 15, 2015, and an ask price of 146 5/32. For the coupon rate enter "11.25" or ".1125". Enter the maturity date as "2/15/2015". Enter the ask price the same way you did the futures price. Thus, 146 5/32 is entered as "146.05". Hit F9 to recalculate and the values will appear for each bond in the section labeled **Results:.** Output cells have a single-line border.

The calculations shown are the forward price, the invoice price, the difference between the invoice price and forward price, the decimal price, which is simply the ask price converted from thirty-seconds to decimals, the accrued interest on the current date, the accrued interest on the delivery date, and the value of the coupons at delivery. The last figure is the value of the coupons paid between the current date and the delivery date plus any interest paid on their reinvestment. To the right of each row are additional columns used to perform the calculations. These columns include the conversion factor and various other figures used in the calculations. The column labeled "Difference" is the value that you are looking for. The bond with the largest difference, which should be the one with the least negative value, is the cheapest bond to deliver.

The number of bonds you wish to analyze may differ. To accommodate additional bonds, copy all of the formulas from columns D through AE on new rows.

terms in brackets denote values of the bonds you are delivering. The first term, $(1/CF)S_5$, is the 5:00 P.M. value of the $1/CF$ bonds you already owned. The second term is the cost of the $1 - 1/CF$ bonds bought at the 5:00 P.M. price. As indicated above, the expression simplifies to $f_3(CF) - S_5$. Note that the 3:00 P.M. bond price does not enter into the decision to deliver because the delivery decision is made at 5:00 P.M. By that time, the $1/CF$ bonds are worth $(1/CF)S_5$ and can be sold for that amount.

If the transaction is profitable, $\Pi > 0$. This requires that

$$S_5 < f_3(CF).$$

A trader can observe the spot price at 5:00 P.M. If the price is sufficiently low, the trader should buy the remaining $1 - 1/CF$ bonds and make delivery. The wild card option thus will be profitable if the spot price at 5:00 P.M. falls below the invoice price established at 3:00 P.M.

As an example, suppose that on March 2 the March futures contract has a settlement price at 3:00 P.M. of 101.8125. The cheapest bonds to deliver were the 12 1/2s maturing in about 22 years, which have a conversion factor of 1.464. We do not have the 3:00 P.M. spot price, but let us assume it is 149.65. Suppose we are short 100 contracts, which obligates us to deliver bonds with a face value of 100($100,000) = $10,000,000. Assume each bond has a face value of $1,000. Thus, we will have to deliver 10,000 bonds. To begin this strategy, we must have a position in the spot T-bonds; otherwise, our risk will be quite high. We weight that position by the conversion factor; that is, we hold bonds with a face value of $10,000,000(1/1.464) = $6,830,601—in other words, about 6,831 bonds. To make delivery, we will need to buy 3,169 bonds. For us to make a profit, the 5:00 P.M. price must decline to

$$S_5 < 101.8125(1.464) = 149.05,$$

The wild card option is the opportunity the holder of the short futures contract has to lock in the invoice price at 3:00 P.M. and make delivery if the spot price falls below the established invoice price between 3:00 P.M. and 5:00 P.M. The option exists only during the delivery month.

or less. Thus, if the spot price declined by at least 0.60 by 5:00 P.M., it would pay to buy the remaining 3,169 bonds and make delivery.

The alternative to delivery is holding the position until the next day. In fact, that will always be the better choice if the conversion factor is less than 1.0. Note that if CF < 1.0, the hedged position will include 1/CF bonds, which exceeds 1.0. Thus, the hedger will hold more bonds than futures and there will be no tail, or additional bonds, to purchase at the lower 5:00 P.M. price. In that case, the wild card option is worthless. Moreover, if the price does not fall sufficiently by 5:00 P.M., holding the position is preferred over delivery. Of course, it is possible that the wild card option will never be worth exercising, meaning simply that it ends up, like many other options, out-of-the-money.

THE QUALITY OPTION   The holder of the short position has the right to deliver any of a number of acceptable bonds. Sometimes the holder of the short position will be holding a bond that is not the best to deliver. A profit is sometimes possible by switching to another bond. This is called the **quality option,** because the deliverable bonds are considered to be of different quality; it is also sometimes called the switching option.

The value of this option arises because of changes in the term structure of interest rates. You may be holding a hedged position in Treasury bonds and futures, anticipating that you will make delivery of the bond that you hold on the futures contract. Then if the term structure changes, another bond may become the cheapest to deliver. Although you could always deliver the bond you hold, the right to switch to a more favorably priced bond has value.

The quality option exists, not only in Treasury bond and note markets, but also in the markets for many commodity futures. For example, the Chicago Board of Trade's wheat futures contract specifies that the holder of the short position can deliver any of four different grades of wheat. Other agricultural contracts have similar options. In fact, agricultural contracts usually grant the right to deliver at one of several locations. This feature, called the location option, has essentially the same economic effect as the quality option.

In any case, however, the quality option conveys a right to the holder of the short position. Since this right has value, the futures price will tend to be lower by the value of this option. In other words, the seller of a futures receives a lower price that reflects the fact that a valuable option is attached to the contract. Likewise, the buyer pays a lower price for granting the seller this valuable right.

THE END-OF-THE-MONTH OPTION   The last day for trading a T-bond futures contract is the eighth-to-last business day of the delivery month. Delivery can take place during the remaining business days. The invoice price during those final delivery days is based on the settlement price on the last trading day. Thus, during the last seven delivery days, the holder of the

The quality option is the opportunity the holder of the short futures contract has to switch to another deliverable bond if it becomes more favorably priced. The option exists on any futures contract that permits delivery of one of several underlying assets, with the decision made by the holder of the short position.

short position has full knowledge of the price that would be received for delivery of the bonds. This gives the holder of the short position the opportunity to watch the spot market for a fall in bond prices. The trader can continue to wait for spot prices to fall until the second-to-last business day, because delivery must occur by the last business day.

The **end-of-the-month option,** thus, is similar to the wild card option. There is a period during which spot prices can change while the delivery price is fixed. It is also related to the quality option, for the holder of the short position can also switch to another bond.

THE TIMING OPTION   Since the short is often permitted to make delivery on any day during the delivery month, he or she holds another valuable option. Suppose the Treasury bond pays a coupon that exceeds the cost of financing the position, which is the repo rate. Then the short should hold the long bond–short futures position as long as possible because it pays more than it costs. If the repo rate exceeds the bond coupon, then the position costs more to hold than it yields; thus, an early delivery is advised. Ignoring all other delivery options, this **timing option** would suggest that all deliveries would occur early or late in the month. As we have already noted, however, there are many other options that are in effect and early delivery would preclude the right to take advantage of some of these other options.

Determining the values of these delivery options is very difficult. Most contracts contain more than one option and, as noted earlier, the Treasury bond futures contract contains several delivery options. Thus, it is difficult to isolate them and observe their separate effects. There have been numerous studies, which are reviewed in Chance and Hemler (1993). Most of them found that the value of delivery options is fairly small. That does not mean they should be dismissed as insignificant. To the holder of one or more of these options, the value may at times be quite large. For our purposes, however, we can safely conclude that the economic effects are minor in comparison to the more important factors that determine the futures price.

The end-of-the-month option is the opportunity the holder of the short futures contract has to deliver during the final business days of the month. The futures contract no longer trades so the invoice price is locked in, and the option can be profitable if the spot price falls during the last few trading days of the month.

The timing option is the opportunity the holder of the short futures contract has to deliver at any time during the expiration month. Early delivery is made if the cost of financing exceeds the coupon on the bond and later delivery is made if the coupon exceeds the cost of financing.

Implied Repo/Cost of Carry

Earlier in this chapter, we examined the concept of the implied repo rate in the context of the cost of carry model for Treasury bill futures. Although slightly more complex, the concept is equally applicable to Treasury bond futures.

First, we must identify the cheapest bond to deliver. If we buy that bond today (time 0), we pay the spot price plus the accrued interest. The sale of a repo finances the bond's purchase. This means that we borrow the funds by selling the bond and agreeing to buy it back at a specified later date. We simultaneously sell a futures contract expiring at T. We hold the position until expiration, deliver the bond, and effectively receive $(CF)(f_0(T))$, the

D e r i v a t i v e s   i n   A c t i o n

The Dangers of Delivery

The following talk was given by Tom Kelly, member of the Chicago Board of Trade.

All of the advantages belong to the long cash/short futures positions. I would like to point out some of the fetters that the delivery process imposes on the short futures position.

Cash securities, i.e., U.S. Treasury bills, notes, or bonds, trade for next-day settlement (I buy them today, I pay for them tomorrow). At the time of the trade, other settlement dates can be arranged. However, although I have purchased securities for settlement tomorrow, I have no idea at what time the securities will be presented for payment. A valid delivery in the government market need only be made during the time that the Fed wire is open.

While normal hours are from 9:00 A.M. to 1:30 P.M., many times the close of the wire is extended to 3:00, 4:00, and even 5:00 P.M. In addition, recognized primary dealers in government securities get an additional 15 minutes of "dealer time" during which primary dealers may deliver to one another.

As a customer of the dealers, I can expect to receive the security very close to the time of the wire closing. My back office must be very quick to turn the securities around to the firm that I intend to deliver. If I

cannot redeliver the securities in "good time," I am forced to eat a financing loss. Worse, if I have purchased a block of $1 million and $4 million pieces and have arranged to deliver a $5 million piece, and only the $4 million block arrives, I must sit on that piece until the smaller piece arrives.

Delivery on settlement does not mean a lot to securities firms. If the delivery is straightforward (no redeliveries or pieces) and the securities do not show up, I have lost nothing; indeed, I can make money by not having the securities arrive. At the very least, my clearing bank will pay me analysis on my cash position.

Contrast this to the Chicago Board of Trade (CBOT®) delivery process.

If I am short the futures contract I must inform the CBOT two business days before delivery that I intend to deliver futures contracts. On the next day, before 3:00 P.M., I must inform the CBOT as to what I am delivering, the appropriate monies, and my delivery agent. On the delivery day, my securities must be on the Fed wire by 9:00 A.M.

If I do not comply with the CBOT rules, I am subject to as much as a $7,000 per contract fine.

That potential fine is greater than all the potential option profits.

In addition, if I truly err, my CBOT firm that is carrying the short futures contracts can be closed by the

---

futures price times the conversion factor, plus accrued interest for it. In an efficient market, there should be no arbitrage profit. Therefore, the amount we receive for the bond must equal the amount we paid for it plus the cost of carry:

$$(CF)(f_0(T)) + AI_T = (S_0 + AI_0)(1 + \hat{r})^T,$$

where AI_T is the accrued interest on the bond at expiration, AI_0 is the accrued interest when the bond originally is bought, and $\hat{r}$ is the implied repo rate. The left-hand side of the formula is the amount we receive upon delivery. The right-hand side is the amount paid for the bond, $S_0 + AI_0$,

CBOT Clearing Corporation. Obviously, such draconian penalties must be avoided.

The short futures/long cash position must bank finance two business days in advance of the promised delivery date the securities that may be delivered. If the securities appear to be difficult to get in appropriate position, I must arrange to set up even earlier. Bank financing will cost a minimum of one half a percent over normal financing rates, and failure to retrieve securities that are out on repurchase agreement can and has occurred despite attempting to bank finance five business days before delivery. I can recall one time a few years ago that I asked Goldman, Sachs to please return my position that I financed with them. The securities did not show up the first day. The CBOT Office of Investigations and Audits (OIA) called up to remind me of the delivery procedures and what would happen to my firm if I did not comply. I told the OIA representative that Goldman, Sachs, a member clearing firm of the CBOT, was failing to me. "Tough." The securities did not show up.

I threatened to "buy-in" the securities. Goldman, Sachs said that they were sorry, but that they could not return the securities to me because Salomon Brothers was not delivering the securities to them. Can you imagine to whom I was to make delivery of the futures contracts? It was Plaza Clearing, Salomon Brothers' wholly owned futures clearing firm.

On the day before delivery was to be made, the OIA phoned again with the litany of possible punishments for noncompliance with the CBOT delivery rules. My clearing firm was very worried and pointed out with great explicitness that the small amount of money I had intended to make on delivery of 400 futures contracts was going to be more than offset by the $2,800,000 fine—did I have any idea how I was to pay the fine?

At 9:30 A.M. on the delivery day, no securities had appeared. An employee of Plaza Clearing phoned and asked where my securities were. I told them that he was failing to Goldman, Sachs and that they were failing to me. He also said, "Tough."

About a minute later, a block of one million bonds came in from Goldman, Sachs, who had arranged to borrow them from the New York Fed. I delivered the securities to Plaza who immediately returned them to Goldman, Sachs, who immediately delivered to me, who . . .

The entire delivery was finished by 10:00 A.M. No fines were engendered. But, I learned small profits are never offset by enormous losses.

SOURCE: Reprinted with permission from *Review of Futures Markets*, vol. 11, no. 2, published by the Chicago Board of Trade, pp. 162–164.

factored up by the cost of financing over the holding period, 0 to T. Solving for r̂,

$$\hat{r} = \left[\frac{(CF)(f_0(T)) + AI_T}{S_0 + AI_0} \right]^{(1/T)} - 1.$$

If the bond can be financed in the repo market at a rate of less than r̂, profitable arbitrage is possible.

AN EXAMPLE   On September 22 of 1999, the cheapest bond to deliver on the upcoming March contract is the 8 1/8s maturing in about 21 years. The spot price is 118 21/32, the accrued interest is 0.84, the conversion factor is 1.2532, and the futures price is 94.03125. From September 22 to March 1 is 161 days, so $T = 161/365 = 0.4411$.

If a coupon is paid during the life of this cash-and-carry arbitrage, we must make a minor adjustment: The amount AI_T must reflect the accrual of any coupons and any interest earned from reinvesting the coupons. The coupon of 4.0625 on February 15, 2000 is received and reinvested for 15 days. We must assume a reinvestment rate, so let us use 5.8 percent. There are 184 days between the bond's coupon payment dates. The forthcoming coupon accrues for 15 days, so the total for AI_T is

$$4.0625(1.058)^{(15/365)} + 4.0625(15/184) = 4.40.$$

The implied repo rate is, therefore,

$$\hat{r} = \left[\frac{94.03125(1.2532) + 4.40}{118.65625 + 0.84} \right]^{(1/0.4411)} - 1 = 0.0528.$$

If the bond can be financed in the repo market for less than 5.28 percent, the arbitrage would be profitable.

A Treasury Bond Futures Spread

Treasury bond futures traders frequently use spreads. Suppose a trader takes a long position in a futures contract. If this is the only transaction, the risk is quite high. One way to modify the risk is to sell short a Treasury bond, but short selling requires that the trader execute a transaction in the spot market. In addition, there are margin requirements on short sales. An alternative that is easy to execute is to simply sell another Treasury bond futures contract. That transaction could be executed within the same trading pit. In addition, the margin requirement on a spread is much lower than the margin requirement on either a long or a short position.

Table 11.5 presents an example of a simple spread taken in anticipation of changes in interest rates in the T-bond market. The trader goes short the September contract and long the December in the hope that a small gain will be made. If the trader's forecast is wrong, the loss is not likely to be large. This example involves a simple position of one contract long and one contract short. In practice many traders use weighted positions, taking more of either the long or short contract so as to balance their different volatilities. The proper number of each contract to provide a risk-free position is obtained by using their durations in the same manner that we did in Chapter 10 when we constructed long spot and short futures positions. In this example, the trader's expectations were not at all realized. Rates fell and bond futures prices rose. The September contract was not profitable, but the long December contract was profitable and the overall loss was negligible.

TABLE 11.5	A Treasury Bond Futures Spread

Scenario: It is July 6. Interest rates have steadily risen over the last six months. The yield on long-term government bonds is 13.54 percent. You anticipate that rates will continue upward; however, the economy remains healthy and there are no indications that the Fed will tighten the money supply, which would drive rates further upward. Thus, while you are bearish you are encouraged by other economic factors. You want to take a speculative short position in T-bond futures but are concerned that rates will fall, generating a potentially large loss. You believe that if rates have not changed by late August, they will not change at all. Thus, you short the September contract and buy the December contract.

Date	Futures Market
July 6	The September T-bond futures price is 60 22/32 or 60.6875. Price per contract: $60,687.50 **Sell one contract** The December T-bond futures price is 60 2/32 or 60.0625. Price per contract: $60,062.50 **Buy one contract**
August 31	The September T-bond futures price is 65 27/32 or 65.84375. Price per contract: $65,843.75 **Buy one contract** The December T-bond futures price is 65 5/32 or 65.15625. Price per contract: $65,156.25 **Sell one contract**

Analysis:
The profit on the September contract was

$$\$60,687.50 - \$65,843.75 = -\$5,156.25.$$

The profit on the December contract was

$$\$65,156.25 - \$60,062.50 = \$5,093.75.$$

Thus, the overall profit was

$$-\$5,156.25 + \$5,093.75 = -\$62.50.$$

Treasury Bond Spread/Implied Repo Rate

The concept of an implied repo rate also applies to Treasury bond spreads. The implied repo rate can be used to help determine if the spread is correctly priced.

Suppose there is a futures contract expiring at time t and another expiring at time T with t coming before T. Suppose today (time 0) we sell the longer-term contract and buy the shorter-term contract. At time t, the shorter-term contract expires. We take delivery of the bond, financing it at the repo rate, r, and hold it until time T, when the longer-term contract expires. Because we are short that contract, we simply deliver the bond.

Assume we can identify today the cheapest bond to be delivered on the shorter-term contract.

Consider the following notation:

$$CF(t) = \text{conversion factor for bond delivered at t}$$
$$CF(T) = \text{conversion factor for same bond delivered at T}$$
$$f_0(t) = \text{today's futures price for contract expiring at t}$$
$$f_0(T) = \text{today's futures price for contract expiring at T}$$
$$AI_t = \text{accrued interest on bond as of time t}$$
$$AI_T = \text{accrued interest on bond as of time T}$$

At time t, we take delivery of the bond and pay the invoice price,

$$(CF(t))f_0(t) + AI_t.$$

To finance the acceptance and holding of this bond, we borrow this sum at the rate r. Then, at time T, we deliver the bond and receive the invoice price,

$$(CF(T))f_0(T) + AI_T.$$

Since this transaction is riskless, the profit from it should be zero. Therefore,

$$[(CF(t))f_0(t) + AI_t](1 + \hat{r})^{T-t} = (CF(T))f_0(T) + AI_T.$$

The bracketed term on the left-hand side is the amount we paid for the bond at t. Since we borrowed this amount, we must factor it up by the interest rate compounded over the period $T - t$. The right-hand side is the amount received from delivering the bond at T. We can now solve for $\hat{r}$, the implied repo rate:

The implied repo rate on a spread is the implied cost of establishing a cash-and-carry position at the expiration of the earlier futures contract of the spread.

$$\hat{r} = \left[\frac{(CF(T))f_0(T) + AI_T}{(CF(t))f_0(t) + AI_t} \right]^{1/(T-t)} - 1.$$

The numerator is the amount received for the bond, and the denominator is the amount paid for it. Dividing these two numbers gives the rate of return over the period $T - t$. Raising this term to the power $1/(T - t)$ annualizes the rate. The implied repo thus is the return we could earn over the period $T - t$. If the bond can be financed at less than this rate, the transaction will be profitable.

AN EXAMPLE Assume that on September 22, 1999, the cheapest bond to deliver was the 8 1/8s maturing in about 21 years. Let us examine the

March–June Treasury bond futures spread. The March contract is priced at 94.03125, and the conversion factor is 1.2532. The June futures price is 93.625. The conversion factor for the 8 1/8s delivered on the June contract is 1.2518. The accrued interest on the bond on March 3, the assumed delivery date, is 0.38, and the accrued interest on June 2 is 2.41. There are no coupons between the two futures expiration dates so no adjustment to the accrued interest is required.

Since the time from March 3 to June 2 is 91 days, the implied repo rate is

$$\hat{r} = \left[\frac{93.625 \ (1.2518) + 2.41}{94.03125 \ (1.2532) + 0.38} \right]^{365/91} - 1 = .048.$$

The implied repo rate thus is 4.8 percent. Note that this is a forward rate, because it reflects the repo rate over the period from March 3 to June 2. If the bond can be financed at a rate of less than 4.8 percent from March 3 to June 2, the transaction will be profitable.

One way traders determine if the implied repo rate on the spread is attractive is to evaluate what is called a turtle trade. The implied repo rate of 4.8 percent is an implied forward rate. It can be compared to the implied rate in the T-bill futures market. If the T-bill futures rate is lower, the trader sells the T-bill futures and buys the T-bond spread. This creates a risk-free position and earns the difference between the implied repo rate on the T-bond spread and the implied rate on the T-bill futures. If the implied rate on the T-bill futures is higher, the investor reverses the T-bond spread and buys the T-bill futures.

Intermarket Spreads

We have discussed two forms of intramarket spreads. There are also a number of **intermarket spreads** or intercommodity spreads. These are transactions in which the two futures contracts are on different underlying instruments. For example, many traders execute what is called the NOB, or notes over bonds, spread. This spread involves a long (short) position in T-note futures and a short (long) position in T-bond futures. This trade would be used to capitalize on shifts in the yield curve. For example, if a trader believes that rates on the 7-to-10-year range of the yield curve will fall and rates on the 15-plus-year range will either rise or fall by less, a long position in the NOB spread might be warranted. If the investor's expectations prove correct, a profit could be made as T-note futures will rise and T-bond futures will either fall or rise by a smaller amount. Of course, if yields on the long-term end of the market fall, the trader could end up losing money because long-term bond prices will be expected to rise by a greater amount for a given yield change. So the trader might prefer to take a weighted position in which the ratio of T-note to T-bond futures is something other than one-to-one. Thus, the NOB spread is designed to capitalize on changes in the relationship between Treasury note and Treasury bond futures prices.

Another intermarket spread is the MOB, or municipals over bonds, spread. This spread involves a long (short) position in the municipal bond futures contract and a short (long) position in the T-bond futures contract. There is no specific arbitrage relationship that defines the MOB spread, simply because T-bonds and municipals are not perfect substitutes; however, a perceived historical relationship has prevailed. Traders often watch that relationship for signs of abnormal behavior that might signal profit opportunities.

Bond Market Timing with Futures

In Chapter 10, we showed how hedge ratios can be constructed using futures. The procedure essentially combines futures so that the overall investment is insensitive to interest rate changes. In effect, this changes the duration to zero. Suppose a market timer believes that interest rates will move in one direction or the other but a duration of zero may not be appropriate. If interest rates are expected to fall, the timer may wish to increase the duration; if rates are expected to rise, the timer may wish to decrease the duration but not necessarily reduce it to zero.

Suppose a portfolio of bonds has a face value of S and a duration of DUR_S. The futures contract has a duration of DUR_f and a price of f. The timer wishes to increase the spot duration to DUR_T, which we shall call the **target duration.** One way to do this is to put more money in high-duration bonds and less money in low-duration bonds, but this would incur transaction costs on the purchase and sale of at least two bonds. Futures can be used to adjust the duration easily and at lower transaction costs.

The number of futures needed to change the duration to DUR_T is

Buying or selling futures provides a simple way of increasing or decreasing a bond's duration.

$$N_f = \left(\frac{DUR_T - DUR_S}{DUR_f}\right)\left(\frac{S}{f}\right)\left(\frac{1 + y_f}{1 + y_S}\right),$$

where y_f is the yield implied by the futures price and y_S is the yield on the spot portfolio. Appendix 11B presents the derivation of this formula.

Notice how similar this formula is to the one given in Chapter 10. That formula was

$$N_f = -\left(\frac{DUR_S}{DUR_f}\right)\left(\frac{S}{f}\right)\left(\frac{1 + y_f}{1 + y_S}\right),$$

which reduces the interest sensitivity and duration to zero.[3] If the target duration were zero in our new formula, we would obtain the old formula. Thus, the new formula is a much more general restatement of the optimal hedge ratio, because it permits the duration to be adjusted to any chosen value. If the investor expected falling interest rates and wished to increase the duration, DUR_T would be larger than DUR_S. Then N_f would be positive and futures would be bought. This makes sense because adding futures to a long spot position should increase the risk. If the trader were bearish and wished to reduce the duration, DUR_T would be less than DUR_S and N_f would be negative, meaning that futures would be sold. This is so because an opposite position in futures should be required to reduce the risk.

AN EXAMPLE   Let us rework the T-bond hedging example that appeared in Table 10.9 in Chapter 10. In that problem, on February 25 the portfolio manager held $1 million face value of the 11 7/8s bond maturing in about 25 years. The bond price is 101, and the bond will be sold on March 28. In Chapter 10, we feared an increase in interest rates and lowered the duration to zero by selling 16 futures contracts. Suppose, however, that we wanted to lower the duration from its present level of 7.83 to 4. This would make the portfolio less sensitive to interest rates, but not completely unaffected by them. In that way, if the forecast proved incorrect, the positive duration would still leave room to profit.

The example is presented in Table 11.6. The bond ends up losing 2.26 percent. To determine how close the outcome was to the desired outcome, we need to know the change in the yield on the bonds. On February 25, the yield on the spot bond was 11.74 percent; on March 28, the yield that corresponded to a price of 95 22/32 was 12.50 percent. Recall that the following formula expresses the relationship between the change in the yield and the percentage change in the bond price:

$$\frac{\Delta B}{B} \approx -DUR\left(\frac{\Delta y}{1 + y}\right),$$

where B represents the bond price. With a duration reset to 4, the formula predicts that for a yield change of $.1250 - .1174 = .0076$, the percentage price change would be

$$\frac{\Delta B}{B} \approx -4\left(\frac{.0076}{1.1174}\right) = -.0272,$$

---

[3]As noted in Chapter 10, both of these formulas apply only to extremely short holding periods. Any increment of time or change in yield will require recalculation of the number of futures contracts, so the number of contracts will need adjustment throughout the holding period.

TABLE 11.6	**Bond Market Timing with Futures**

Scenario: On February 25, a portfolio manager holds $1 million face value of a government bond, the 11 7/8s, which matures in about 25 years. The bond is currently priced at 101, has a duration of 7.83, and has a yield of 11.74 percent. The manager plans to sell the bond on March 28. The manager is worried about rising interest rates and would like to reduce the bond's sensitivity to interest rates by lowering its duration to 4. This would reduce its interest sensitivity, which would help if rates increase, but would not eliminate the possibility of gains from falling rates.

Date	Spot Market	Futures Market
February 25	The current price of the bonds is 101. Value of position: $1,010,000. The short end of the term structure is flat, so this is the forward sale price of the bonds in March.	June T-bond futures is at 70 16/32. Price per contract: $70,500. The futures price and the characteristics of the deliverable bond imply a duration of 7.20 and a yield of 14.92 percent. Appropriate number of contracts: $$N_f = \left(\frac{4 - 7.83}{7.20}\right)\left(\frac{1,010,000}{70,500}\right)\left(\frac{1.1492}{1.1174}\right)$$ $$= -7.84.$$
		Sell 8 contracts
March 28	The bonds are sold a their current price of 95 22/32. This is a price of $956.875 per bond. Value of position: $956,875.	June T-bond futures is at 66 23/32. Price per contract: $66,718.75
		Buy 8 contracts

Analysis: When the $1 million face value bonds are sold on March 28, they are worth $956,875, a loss in value of $1,010,000 − $956,875 = $53,125.

The profit on the futures transaction is

$$
\begin{array}{ll}
8(\$70,500) & \text{(sale price of futures)} \\
- 8(\$66,718.75) & \text{(purchase price of futures)} \\
\hline
\$30,250 & \text{(profit on futures)}.
\end{array}
$$

Thus, the overall transaction resulted in a loss in value of $53,125 − $30,250 = $22,875, which is a 2.26 percent decline in overall value.

---

or 2.72 percent. The actual change was 2.26 percent. Without the futures position, the duration still would have been 7.83. Plugging into the formula gives a predicted percentage change in the bond price of

$$\frac{\Delta B}{B} \approx -7.83\left(\frac{.0076}{1.1174}\right) = -.0533,$$

or a loss of 5.33 percent. The actual change without the hedge would have been − $53,125/$1,010,000 = −.0526, or a 5.26 percent loss.

This completes our discussion of Treasury note and bond futures transactions. We now turn to stock index futures.

Stock Index Futures Strategies

Stock index futures contracts offer several interesting applications. We shall look at three: stock index arbitrage, speculating on unsystematic risk, and market timing.

Stock Index Arbitrage

We discussed cash-and-carry arbitrage with Treasury bill and bond futures. The concept is equally applicable to stock index futures. In fact, this type of transaction is one of the most widely used in the futures markets. It is called **stock index arbitrage.**

Recall that the model for the stock index futures price is

$$f_0(T) = S_0 e^{(r_c - \delta)T},$$

where r_c is the continuously compounded risk-free rate and δ is the continuously compounded dividend yield. Consider the following example of a futures contract that has 40 days to go until expiration. The S&P 500 index is at 1305, the risk-free rate is 5.2 percent, and the dividend yield is 3 percent. The time to expiration will be $40/365 = .1096$. Thus, the futures should be priced at

$$f_0(T) = 1305 e^{(.052 - .03)(.1096)} = 1308.15.$$

Now suppose the actual futures price is 1309.66. Thus, the futures is slightly overpriced. We would sell the futures and buy the stocks in the S&P 500 index in the same proportions as in the index. At expiration, the futures price would equal the spot price of the S&P 500 index. We then would sell the stocks. The transaction is theoretically riskless and would earn a return in excess of the risk-free rate.

Now suppose at expiration the index closes at 1300.30. The profit on the futures contract is $1309.66 - 1300.30 = 9.36$. We bought the stocks for 1305; however, over the life of the futures this investment lost interest at a rate of 5.2 percent and accumulated dividends at a rate of 3 percent. Thus, the effective cost of the stock was $1305 e^{(.052 - .03)(.1096)} = 1308.15$, which by no coincidence is the theoretical futures price. The stock is sold at 1300.30 for a profit of $1300.30 - 1308.15 = -7.85$. Thus, the overall profit is $9.36 - 7.85 = 1.51$. This is the difference between the theoretical futures price and the actual futures price. Since the actual futures price was higher than the theoretical price we were able to execute an arbitrage involving

Stock index arbitrage is the purchase or sale of a portfolio of stock that replicates a stock index and the sale or purchase of a futures contract on the index. Stock index arbitrage occurs when the futures price does not conform to the cost of carry model and, if properly executed, will earn, at no risk, the difference between the futures price and the theoretical futures price.

the purchase of stocks and sale of futures to capture the 1.51 differential. Had the actual futures price been less than the theoretical price, then we would have executed a reverse arbitrage involving the purchase of futures and short sale of stock, which would have created a synthetic loan that would have cost less than the risk-free rate.

Let us now determine the implied repo rate. Given the pricing formula, $f_0(T) = S_0 e^{(r_c - \delta)T}$, suppose the futures price is equal to its theoretical fair price. Then we solve this equation for the implied interest rate, $\hat{r}_c$, and obtain

$$\hat{r}_c = \frac{\ln(f_0(T)/S_0)}{T} + \delta.$$

In this example, we have

$$\hat{r}_c = \frac{\ln(1309.66/1305)}{.1096} + .03 = .0625.$$

If this transaction were undertaken, it would provide a risk-free return of 6.25 percent. With the risk-free rate at 5 percent, the transaction is an attractive opportunity. Also, if an arbitrageur could not borrow at 5 percent, but could borrow at any rate less than 6.25 percent, the transaction would still be worth doing.

Stock index arbitrage has proven to be particularly popular. It turns out, however, that there are a number of serious practical considerations that can limit its profitability.

SOME PRACTICAL CONSIDERATIONS   There are several problems in implementing stock index arbitrage. We referred to the arbitrageur as buying the stock index at 1305. In reality, the arbitrageur would have to purchase all 500 stocks in the appropriate proportions as the index and immediately execute all of the trades. The New York Stock Exchange has established a computerized order processing system, called the Designated Order Turnaround, or DOT, that expedites trades. Nonetheless, it is still difficult to get all the trades in before the price of any single stock changes. Thus, most arbitrageurs do not duplicate the index but use a smaller subset of the stocks. Naturally this introduces some risk into what is supposed to be a riskless transaction.

Let us assume, however, that the trades can be executed simultaneously. Let the index be 1305. Now assume an arbitrageur has $20 million to use. Then the arbitrageur will buy the appropriately weighted 500 stocks with that amount. Because of the $250 multiplier on the futures, the S&P 500 is actually priced at 1305(250) = $326,250, so the arbitrageur will need to buy $20,000,000/$326,250 = 61.30 futures contracts. Because one cannot buy fractional contracts, the transaction will not be weighted precisely.

In addition, there are transaction costs of about 0.5 percent of the market value of the stocks. Would this consume the profit in this example? If the index is 1305 and the net profit is 1.51, the profit is 0.0012 of the index and clearly would be absorbed by the transaction costs.

In addition, there are problems involved in simultaneously selling all of the stocks in the index at expiration. These transactions must be executed such that the portfolio will be liquidated at the closing values of each stock. This is very difficult to do and frequently causes unusual stock price movements at expiration.

Nonetheless, many large financial institutions execute this type of arbitrage transaction. Every day billions of dollars trade on the basis of this futures pricing model. This trading of large blocks of stock simultaneously is called **program trading.**[4] The New York Stock Exchange defines a program trade as the simultaneous or near simultaneous purchase or sale of at least 15 stocks with a total market value of at least $1 million. The NYSE requires that these program trades be reported to it and all index arbitrage trades must be reported. Figure 11.1 shows a weekly report on program trading that is published in *The Wall Street Journal* each Friday. Note that during this five-day period, there were almost 815 million shares involved in program trading, of which more than 96 million shares were associated with index arbitrage.

Program trading is the execution on a stock market of a large number of simultaneous buy or sell orders. It is normally triggered by a computer program that detects an arbitrage opportunity or suggests some other reason for quickly establishing a large portfolio of stock.

In this type of trading, the model is programmed into a computer, which continuously monitors the futures price and the individual stock prices. When the computer identifies a deviation from the model, it sends a signal to the user. Many large institutions have established procedures for immediately executing the many simultaneous transactions, usually sending the orders through the DOT system. Table 11.7 illustrates a successful index arbitrage trade using the same example as before, but with a more significantly overpriced futures.

Are stock index futures contracts correctly priced? Is it truly possible to profit from index arbitrage? This question has been studied at great length. In the early days of stock index futures trading, there was considerable evidence that stock index futures prices were too low (Figlewski, 1984). In time, prices began to conform more closely to the model, as shown by Cornell (1985). Deviations from the model remain, however, and some can be exploited by traders with sufficiently low transaction costs. MacKinlay and Ramaswamy (1988) revealed that (1) mispricing is more common the longer the remaining time to expiration and (2) when a contract becomes overpriced or underpriced, it tends to stay overpriced or underpriced rather than reversing from overpriced to underpriced or vice versa. Sofianos (1993) found that it was very difficult to profit from index

---

[4]Index arbitrage is but one form of program trading. Another is portfolio insurance, which is covered in Chapter 15. See Hill and Jones (1988) for a discussion of the different forms of program trading.

FIGURE 11.1	Weekly Program Trading As Reported in *The Wall Street Journal*

PROGRAM TRADING

NEW YORK—Program trading for the week ended Feb. 11 accounted for 15.9%, or an average 162.9 million daily shares, of New York Stock Exchange volume.

Brokerage firms executed an additional 77.4 million daily shares of program trading away from the Big Board, mostly on foreign markets. Program trading is the simultaneous purchase or sale of at least 15 different stocks with a total value of $1 million or more.

Of the program total on the NYSE, 11.9% involved stock-index arbitrage, down from 16.1% the prior week. In this strategy, traders dart between stocks and stock-index options and futures to capture fleeting price differences.

Firms executed 67% of program for their customers, while they carried out 28.2% for their own accounts, or principal trading. An additional 4.8% was designated as customer facilitation, in which firms use principal positions to facilitate customer trades.

The report includes a special profile of trading whenever the Dow Jones Industrial Average rises or falls more than 220 points from its previous close during any one-hour period. There were no such periods during the week.

Of the five most active firms, Deutsche Bank Securities, Morgan Stanley Dean Witter, BNP Securities and Lehman Brothers executed all or most of their program activity for customers. Credit Suisse First Boston executed most of its activity as principal for its own accounts.

NYSE PROGRAM TRADING
Volume (in millions of shares) for the week ended Feb. 11, 2000

Top 15 Firms	Index Arbitrage	Derivative-Related*	Other Strategies	Total
Deutsche Bank Securities	12.5	.....	87.1	99.6
Morgan Stanley Dn Wttr	7.0	.....	77.3	84.3
BNP Securities	.....	.....	77.5	77.5
CS First Boston	3.8	.....	54.5	58.3
Lehman Brothers	.....	9.5	45.3	54.8
W & D Securities	.....	.....	49.9	49.9
TLW SecuritiesLLC	6.0	0.4	41.4	47.8
CIBC World Markets	16.0	.....	29.5	45.5
Salomon Smith Barney	0.6	.....	42.6	43.2
Bear Stearns	.....	.....	39.8	39.8
Goldman, Sachs & Co.	.....	.....	34.6	34.6
Interactive Brokers	.....	.....	33.3	33.3
RBC Dominion	29.8	.....	3.2	33.0
Nomura Securities	11.7	.....	4.4	16.1
PaineWebber	.....	.....	15.5	15.5
OVERALL TOTAL	96.5	10.8	707.2	814.5

*Other derivative-related strategies besides index arbitrage
Source: New York Stock Exchange

Source: *The Wall Street Journal*, February 18, 2000, C3.

arbitrage after accounting for the problem of simultaneously executing all trades.

One consequence of program trading is that large stock price movements often occur quickly and without an apparent flow of new information. For example, when the index or futures price becomes out of line with the cost of carry model, many investors recognize this event simultaneously and react by buying and selling large quantities of stock and futures. Such actions have attracted considerable attention from the media. Critics have

TABLE 11.7   **Stock Index Arbitrage**

Scenario: On November 8, the S&P 500 index is at 1305, the dividend yield is 3 percent, and the risk-free rate is 5.2 percent. The December futures contract, which expires in 40 days, is priced at 1316.30. Its theoretical price is

$$f = 1305e^{(.052-.03)(.1096)} = 1308.15,$$

where $T = 40/365 = .1096$. Thus, the contract is overpriced. An arbitrage will be executed using $20 million. Transaction costs are 0.5 percent of the dollars invested.

Date	Spot Market	Futures Market
November 8	The S&P 500 is at 1305. The stocks have a dividend yield of 3 percent. The risk-free interest rate is 5.2 percent.	The S&P 500 futures, expiring on December 18, is at 1316.30. The appropriate number of futures is $20 million/[(1305)(250)] = 61.30.*
	Buy $20 million of stock in the same proportions as make up the S&P 500.	**Sell 61 contracts**
December 18	The S&P 500 is at 1300.36. The stocks will be worth (1300.36/1305) ($20 million) = $19.928889 million. The $20 million invested in the stocks effectively costs $20 million)$e^{(.052-.03)(.1096)}$ = $20.048282 million. Transaction costs are $20 million (0.005) = $100,000 (includes futures costs).	Futures expires at the S&P 500 price of 1300.36.
	Sell stocks	**Close out futures at expiration**

Analysis:
Profit on stocks:

$19,928,889 (received from sale of stocks)
−$20,048,282 (invested in stocks)
−$119,393.

Profit on futures:

61(250)(1,316.30) (sale price of futures)
−61(250)(1,300.36) (purchase price of futures)
$243,085.

Overall profit:

$243,085 (from futures)
−$119,393 (from stock)
−$100,000 (transaction costs)
$23,692.

*The appropriate number of futures contracts to match $20 million of stock is $20 million divided by the index price, *not the futures price*, times the multiplier. Even though the $20 million is allocated across 500 different stocks, it is equivalent to buying $20 million/1305 = 15,326 "shares" of the S&P 500. The appropriate number of futures is one for each equivalent "share" of the S&P 500. Each futures, of course, has a $250 multiplier.

charged that program trading has led to increased volatility in the spot markets. Regulators and legislators have called for restrictions on such trading in the form of circuit breakers and reduced access to the DOT system for rapidly executing orders. Others have argued for imposing higher margins on futures trading. These issues continue to generate a lot of debate.

Speculating on Unsystematic Risk

In Chapter 10, we saw that the systematic risk of a diversified portfolio can be hedged by using stock index futures. Because the portfolio is diversified, there is no unsystematic risk and therefore the portfolio is riskless. In some cases, however, an investor might wish to hedge the systematic risk and retain the unsystematic risk.

In an efficient market, investors cannot expect to earn returns by assuming unsystematic risk. Professional financial analysts, however, do not believe this is true. Thousands of analysts devote all of their time to identifying overpriced and underpriced stocks. An analyst who thinks a stock is underpriced normally recommends it for purchase. If the stock is purchased and the market goes down, the stock's overall performance can be hurt. For example, a drug firm might announce an important new drug that can help cure diabetes. If that announcement occurs during a strong bear market, the stock can be pulled down by the market effect. The extent of the stock's movement with the market is measured by its beta.

We will use the following notation:

$$S = \text{stock price}$$
$$M = \text{value of market portfolio of all risky assets}$$
$$r_S = \Delta S/S = \text{return on stock}$$
$$r_M = \Delta M/M = \text{return on market}$$
$$\beta = \text{beta of the stock}$$

The stock's return consists of its systematic return, βr_M, and its unsystematic return, which we shall call μ_S. Thus,

$$r_S = \beta r_M + \mu_S.$$

If we multiply both sides of the equation by S, we have

$$S r_S = S \beta r_M + S \mu_S,$$

which is equivalent to

$$\Delta S = S \beta (\Delta M/M) + S \mu_S.$$

This is the return on the stock expressed in dollars. The objective of the transaction is to capture a profit equal to the unsystematic return, $S \mu_S$.

The profit from a transaction consisting of the stock and N_f futures contracts is

$$\Pi = \Delta S + N_f \Delta f.$$

Recall from Chapter 10 that the formula for N_f in an ordinary stock index futures hedge is $-\beta(S/f)$. Let us substitute this for N_f:

$$\Pi = \Delta S - \beta(S/f)\Delta f.$$

Now we need to substitute $S\beta(\Delta M/M) + S\mu_S$ for ΔS and assume the futures price change will match the index price change. In that case, $\Delta M/M = \Delta f/f$. Making these substitutions gives

$$\Pi = S\mu_S.$$

Thus, if we use N_f futures contracts where N_f is the ordinary hedge ratio for stock index futures, we will eliminate systematic risk and the profit will be the unsystematic risk.

AN EXAMPLE   Table 11.8 illustrates an application of this result. In this example, you have identified what you believe to be an underpriced stock. You are worried, however, that the market as a whole will decline and drag the stock down. To hedge the market effect, you sell stock index futures.

This transaction should not be considered riskless. As the title of this section indicates, it involves speculating on unsystematic risk. Suppose your analysis is incorrect and the company announces some bad news during a bull market. Selling the futures contract would eliminate the effect of the bull market while retaining the effect of the bad news announcement. Moreover, this type of trade depends not only on the correctness of the analysis but on the beta's stability.

Stock Market Timing with Futures

Recall that in Chapter 10, we looked at an example in which a portfolio manager sold stock index futures to eliminate the systematic risk. At a later date, the futures contracts were repurchased and the portfolio was returned to its previous level of systematic risk. The number of futures contracts was given by the formula

$$N_f = -\beta(S/f).$$

In some cases, a portfolio manager may wish to change the systematic risk but not eliminate it altogether. For example, if a portfolio manager believes the market is highly volatile, the portfolio beta could be lowered but not reduced to zero. This would enable the portfolio to profit if the market

TABLE 11.8	Speculating on Unsystematic Risk

Scenario: On July 1, you are following the stock of Helene Curtis, which has a price of 17 3/8 and a beta of 1.10. Barring any change in the general level of stock prices, you expect the stock to appreciate by about 10 percent by the end of September. Your analysis of the market as a whole calls for about an 8 percent decline in stock prices in general over the same period. Since the stock has a beta of 1.10, this would bring the stock down by $1.10(.08) = .088$, or 8.8 percent, which will almost completely offset the expected 10 percent unsystematic increase in the stock price. You decide to hedge the market effect by selling stock index futures.

Date	Spot Market	Futures Market
July 1	Own 150,000 shares of Helene Curtis stock at 17.375. Value of stock: 150,000($17.375) = $2,606,250.	December stock index futures price is 444.60. Price of one contract: 444.60($500) = $222,300. Appropriate number of contracts: $$N_f = 1.10\left(\frac{\$2,606,250}{\$222,300}\right) = -12.90.$$ **Sell 13 contracts**
September 30	Stock price is 17.75. Value of stock; 150,000($17.75) = $2,662,500.	December stock index futures price is 411.30. Price of one contract: 411.30($500) = $205,650. **Buy 13 contracts**

Analysis:
Profit on stock:

$$\begin{array}{r} \$2,662,500 \\ -\$2,606,250 \\ \hline \$56,250. \end{array}$$

Profit on futures:

$$\begin{array}{r} 13(\$222,300) \\ -13(\$205,650) \\ \hline \$216,450. \end{array}$$

Overall profit:

$$\begin{array}{r} \$56,250 \\ +\$216,450 \\ \hline \$272,700. \end{array}$$

Overall rate of return:

$$\frac{\$272,700}{\$2,606,250} = .1046.$$

did move upward but would produce a smaller loss if the market moved down. At more optimistic times, the portfolio beta could be increased. In the absence of stock index futures (or options), changing the portfolio beta would require costly transactions in the individual stocks.

Assume we have a portfolio containing stock valued at S and N_f futures contracts. The return on the portfolio is given as r_{Sf}, where

$$r_{Sf} = \frac{\Delta S + N_f \Delta f}{S}.$$

The first term in the numerator, ΔS, is the change in the price of the stock. The second term, $N_f \Delta f$, is the number of contracts times the change in the price of the futures contract. The denominator, S, is the amount of money invested in the stock. The expected return on the portfolio, $E(r_{Sf})$, is

$$E(r_{Sf}) = \frac{E(\Delta S)}{S} + N_f \frac{E(\Delta f)}{S} = E(r_S) + \frac{N_f}{S} E(\Delta f),$$

where $E(r_S)$ is the expected return on the stock defined as $E(\Delta S)/S$ and $E(\Delta f)$ is the expected change in the price of the futures contract.

From modern portfolio theory, the Capital Asset Pricing Model gives the expected return on a stock as $r + [E(r_M) - r]\beta$, where the beta is the systematic risk and reflects the influence of the market as a whole on the stock. If the market is efficient, the investor's required return will equal the expected return. If the CAPM holds for stocks, it should also hold for stock index futures; however, it would be written as

$$\frac{E(\Delta f)}{f} = [E(r_M) - r]\beta_f = E(r_M) - r,$$

where β_f is the beta of the futures contract, assumed to be 1. Although in reality β_f will not be precisely equal to 1, it is sufficiently close that we shall assume it to keep the example simple. Note that this CAPM equation seems to be missing the term r from the right-hand side. The risk-free rate reflects the opportunity cost of money invested in the asset. Because the futures contract requires no initial outlay, there is no opportunity cost; thus, the r term is omitted.

The objective is to adjust the portfolio beta, β_S, and expected return, $E(r_{Sf})$, to a more preferred level. Since the CAPM holds for the portfolio, we can write the relationship between expected return and beta as

$$E(r_{Sf}) = r + [E(r_M) - r]\beta_T,$$

where β_T is the **target beta,** the desired risk level. Now we substitute for $E(r_S)$ and $E(\Delta f)$ and get

$$E(r_{Sf}) = r + [E(r_M) - r]\beta_S + N_f(f/S)[E(r_M) - r].$$

TABLE 11.9	Stock Market Timing with Futures

Scenario: On August 29, a portfolio manager is holding a portfolio of stocks worth $3,783,225. The portfolio beta is 0.95. The manager expects the stock market as a whole to appreciate substantially over the next three months and wants to increase the portfolio beta to 1.25. The manager could buy and sell shares in the portfolio, but this would incur high transaction costs and later the portfolio beta would have to be adjusted back to 0.95. The manager decides to buy stock index futures to temporarily increase the portfolio's systematic risk. The prices, number of shares, and betas are given below. The target date for evaluating the portfolio is November 29.

Stock	Price (8/29)	Number of Shares	Market Value	Weight	Beta
Beneficial Corp.	40.500	11,350	$459,675	.122	0.95
Cummins Engine	64.500	10,950	706,275	.187	1.10
Gillette	62.000	12,400	768,800	.203	0.85
Kmart	33.000	5,500	181,500	.048	1.15
Boeing	49.000	4,600	225,400	.059	1.15
W. R. Grace	42.625	6,750	287,719	.076	1.00
Eli Lilly	87.375	11,400	996,075	.263	0.85
Parker Pen	20.625	7,650	157,781	.042	0.75
			$3,783,225		

Portfolio beta:

$$.122(0.95) + .187(1.10) + .203(0.85) + .048(1.15) + .059(1.15)$$
$$+ .076(1.00) + .263(0.85) + .042(0.75) = 0.95.$$

December stock index futures contract:

Price on August 29: 759.60
Multiplier: $250
Price of one contract: $250(759.60) = $189,900.

Required number of futures contracts:

$$N_f = (1.25 - 0.95)\left(\frac{3,783,225}{189,900}\right) = 5.98.$$

Setting this equal to $r + [E(r_M - r]\beta_T$ and solving for N_f gives

$$N_f = (\beta_T - \beta_S)\left(\frac{S}{f}\right).$$

Buying or selling futures provides a simple way of increasing or decreasing a stock portfolio's beta.

This formula differs only slightly from the previous formula for N_f. In fact, that formula is but a special case of this one. For example, if the target beta is zero, the above formula reduces to $-\beta_S\left(\frac{S}{f}\right)$, where the negative sign means that you would sell N_f futures. This is the same formula we used in Chapter 10 to eliminate systematic risk.

When the manager wants to increase the beta, β_T will be greater than β_S and N_f will be positive. In that case, the manager will buy futures contracts. That makes sense, since the risk will increase. When the beta needs

TABLE 11.9	(continued)

Buy 6 contracts
Results: The values of the stocks on November 29 are shown below:

Stock	Price (11/29)	Market Value
Beneficial Corp.	45.125	$512,168
Cummins Engine	66.750	730,913
Gillette	69.875	866,450
Kmart	35.125	193,188
Boeing	49.125	225,975
W. R. Grace	40.750	275,062
Eli Lilly	103.750	1,182,750
Parker Pen	22.875	174,994
		$4,161,500

December stock index futures contract:

> Price on November 29: 809.60
> Multiplier: $250
> Price of one contract: $250(809.60) = $202,400.

Sell 6 contracts

Analysis:
The market value of the stocks increased by $4,161,500 − $3,783,225 = $378,275, a gain of about 10 percent.

The futures profit was

> 6($202,400) (sale price of futures)
> −6($189,900) (purchase price of futures)
> $75,000 (profit on futures).

Thus, the overall gain on the portfolio was effectively increased to $378,275 + $75,000 = $453,275, a return of about 12 percent.

to be reduced, β_T will be less than β_S, and the manager should sell futures to reduce the risk.

AN EXAMPLE   Table 11.9 presents an example in which a portfolio manager, whose beta is 0.95, would like to temporarily increase it to 1.25. The manager buys stock index futures, which results in an overall gain of almost 12 percent when the stocks themselves gained only 10 percent.

Arbitraging Stock Index Futures with Stock Index Options

Recall from Chapter 3 that we examined put-call parity: the relationship between put and call prices and the price of the underlying stock, the exercise price, the risk-free rate, and the time to expiration. We derived the

| TABLE 11.10 | Put-Call-Forward/Futures Parity |

		Payoffs from Portfolio Given Stock Price at Expiration	
Portfolio	Current Value	$S_T \leq X$	$S_T > X$
A. Futures	0	$S_T - f_0(T)$	$S_T - f_0(T)$
Put	$P_e(S_0,T,X)$	$\underline{X - S_T}$	$\underline{0}$
		$X - f_0(T)$	$S_T - f_0(T)$
B. Call	$C_e(S_0,T,X)$	0	$S_T - X$
Bonds	$(X - f_0(T))(1 + r)^{-T}$	$\underline{X - f_0(T)}$	$\underline{X - f_0(T)}$
		$X - f_0(T)$	$S_T - f_0(T)$

equation by constructing a risk-free portfolio. Now we shall examine **put-call-forward (futures) parity** with puts, calls, and forward or futures contracts. To keep things as simple as possible, we shall assume the risk-free rate is constant. This allows us to ignore marking to market and treat futures contracts as forward contracts. We assume the options are European.

The first step in constructing a risk-free portfolio is to recognize that if the exercise price is set to the futures price, a combination of a long call and a short put is equivalent to a (long) futures contract. In fact, a long-call/short-put combination is called a **synthetic futures contract.** A risk-free portfolio would consist of a long futures contract and a short synthetic futures contract. Selling the synthetic futures contract requires selling a call and buying a put.

Consider the portfolios illustrated in Table 11.10. We construct two portfolios, A and B. Examining the payoffs at expiration reveals that a long futures and a long put is equivalent to a long call and long risk-free bonds with a face value of the difference between the exercise price (X) and the futures price $(f_0(T))$. If $f_0(T)$ is greater than X, as it could easily be, then instead of long bonds, you will take out a loan for the present value of $f_0(T) - X$, promising to pay back $f_0(T) - X$ when the loan matures at the options' expiration. With equivalent payoffs, the value of portfolio A today must equal the value of portfolio B today. Thus,

$$P_e(S_0,T,X) = C_e(S_0,T,X) + (X - f_0(T))(1 + r)^{-T}.$$

Put-call-futures parity is the relationship between the prices of puts, calls, and futures on an asset. With minimal assumptions, futures can be replaced by forwards.

We can, of course, write this several other ways, such as

$$C_e(S_0,T,X) - P_e(S_0,T,X) = (f_0(T) - X)(1 + r)^{-T}.$$

Notice that whether the put price exceeds the call price depends on whether the exercise price exceeds the futures price. If the parity is violated, it may be possible to earn an arbitrage profit. Of course, futures can be replaced with forwards under our assumptions.

A good instrument for examining put-call-futures parity is the S&P 500 index options and futures. The options are European and trade on the CBOE, while the futures trade on the Chicago Mercantile Exchange. On May 14 the S&P 500 index was 1337.80 and the June futures was at 1339.30. The June 1340 call was at 40, and the put was at 39. The expiration date was June 18, and the risk-free rate was 4.56 percent.

Since there are 35 days between May 14 and June 18, the time to expiration is $35/365 = .0959$. The left-hand side of the first put-call-futures parity equation is

$$P_e(S_0,T,X) = 39.$$

The right-hand side is

$$C_e(S_0,T,X) + (X - f_0(T))(1 + r)^{-T}$$
$$= 40 + (1340 - 1339.30)(1.0456)^{-.0959}$$
$$= 40.70.$$

Thus, if you bought the put and futures, paying 39, and sold the call and the bond, receiving 40.70, the two portfolios will offset at expiration. So there is no risk and yet you earn a net gain of $40.70 - 39 = 1.70$. Of course transaction costs might consume the difference.

Summary

This chapter examined the application of some advanced futures trading strategies. It looked at how T-bill, Eurodollar, Treasury bond, and stock index futures can be used in arbitrage transactions. It also examined some spread strategies and the important concept of the implied repo rate. It examined speculative strategies and techniques for using stock index and bond futures in market timing.

In the final section of the chapter we discovered a parity relationship between the options on an asset and the forward or futures on the asset. This relationship, which we called put-call-futures (or forward) parity, further establishes important linkages between spot assets and their derivatives. Following the approach in previous chapters, we illustrate those linkages, using a stock as the underlying asset, in Figure 11.2, an expanded version of Figures 3.11, 5.20, and 9.10. Note that now the figure introduces put-call-forward/futures parity as linking the call, put, forward or futures, and risk-free bond while the remaining linkages, established by put-call-parity, the Black-Scholes put and call option pricing models, and the cost of carry model, are indicated. In Chapter 12, we shall study a new derivative, the option on a futures, and introduce it into the diagram.

FIGURE 11.2	The Linkage between Forwards/Futures, Stock, Bonds, and Options

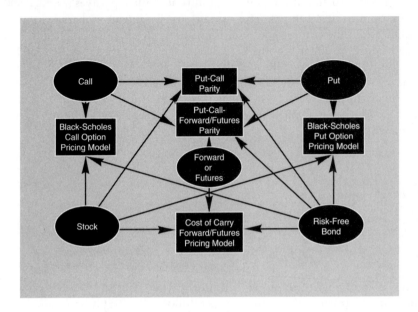

Key Terms

Before continuing to Chapter 12, you should be able to give brief definitions of the following terms.

- futures spread
- cash-and-carry
- repurchase agreement/repo
- implied repo rate
- conversion factor (CF)
- cheapest to deliver (CTD)
- delivery option
- wild card option
- quality option

- end-of-the-month option
- timing option
- intermarket spread
- target duration
- stock index arbitrage
- program trading
- put-call-forward/futures parity
- synthetic futures contract

Further Reading

A survey of the literature on delivery options is found in

Chance, D. M., and M. L. Hemler. "The Impact of Delivery Options on Futures Prices: A Survey." *The Journal of Futures Markets* 13 (1993): 127–155.

Some empirical tests of arbitrage opportunities in futures markets are found in

Elton, E. J., M. J. Gruber, and J. Rentzler. "Intra-Day Tests of Efficiency of the Treasury Bill Futures Market." *Review of Economics and Statistics* 66 (1984): 129–137.

MacKinlay, A. C., and K. Ramaswamy. "Index-Futures Arbitrage and the Behavior of Stock Index Futures Prices." *The Review of Financial Studies* 1 (1988): 137–158.

Rendleman, R. J., Jr., and C. Carabini. "The Efficiency of the Treasury Bill Futures Market." *The Journal of Finance* 44 (1979): 895–914.

Program trading and stock index arbitrage are examined in

Furbush, D. "Program Trading and Price Movement: Evidence from the October 1987 Market Crash." *Financial Management* 18 (1989): 68–83.

Stoll, H. R., and R. E. Whaley, Jr. "Program Trading and Expiration Day Effects." *Financial Analysts Journal* 43 (March–April, 1987): 16–28.

Questions and Problems

1. Explain how the repurchase agreement plays a role in the pricing of futures contracts. What is the implied repo rate?

2. On November 1, the T-bill futures contract expiring on December 19 was priced at 93 (IMM Index). The T-bill maturing at that time was priced at a discount of 7.10 and the T-bill maturing on March 20 at a discount of 7.17. Determine the implied repo rate.

3. On November 1, the March T-bill futures price was 92.85. The T-bill maturing at around the futures expiration was selling at a discount of 7.17. You are interested in using the spot T-bill and the March futures contract to construct a synthetic T-bill maturing on June 20. The March contract expires on March 21.

   a. Determine the return on this T-bill.

   b. There is no actual T-bill maturing on June 20, but based on the discounts on bills maturing around that time, such a bill probably would have a discount of 7.31. Compare your results in part a with the return on the hypothetical T-bill maturing on June 20.

4. Why is it difficult to identify the spot instrument that the Treasury bond futures contract is following? How do futures traders determine the bond that the contract is most likely following?

5. On September 26 of a particular year, the March Treasury bond futures contract settlement price was 94-22. Compare the following two bonds and determine which is the cheaper bond to deliver. Assume delivery will be made on March 1. Use 5.3 percent as the repo rate.

   a. Bond A: A 12 3/4 percent bond callable in about 19 years and maturing in about 24 years with a price of 148 9/32 and a CF of 1.4433. Coupons are paid on November 15 and May 15. The accrued interest is 4.64 on September 26 and 3.73 on March 1.

b. Bond B: A 13 7/8 percent bond callable in about 20 years and maturing in about 25 years with a price of 159 27/32 and a CF of 1.5689. Coupons are paid on November 15 and May 15. The accrued interest is 5.05 on September 26 and 4.06 on March 1.

6. It is August 20, and you are trying to determine which of two bonds is the cheaper bond to deliver on the December Treasury bond futures contract. The futures price is 89 12/32. Assume delivery will be made on December 14, and use 7.9 percent as the repo rate. Find the cheaper bond to deliver.

   a. Bond X: A 9 percent noncallable bond maturing in about 28 years with a price of 100 14/32 and a CF of 1.1106. Coupons are paid on November 15 and May 15. The accrued interest is 2.37 on August 20 and 0.72 on December 14.

   b. Bond Z: An 11 1/4 percent noncallable bond maturing in about 25 years with a price of 121 14/32 and a CF of 1.3444. Coupons are paid on February 15 and August 15. The accrued interest is 0.15 on August 20 and 3.7 on December 14.

7. Assume that on March 16, the cheapest bond to deliver on the June T-bond futures contract is the 14s callable in about 19 years and maturing in about 24 years. Coupons are paid on November 15 and May 15. The price of the bond is 161 23/32, and the CF is 1.584. The June futures price is 100 17/32. Assume a 5.5 percent reinvestment rate. Determine the implied repo rate on the contract. Interpret your result. Note that you will need to determine the accrued interest. Assume delivery on June 1.

8. During the first six months of the year, yields on long-term government debt have fallen about 100 basis points. You believe the decline in rates is over, and you are interested in speculating on a rise in rates. You are, however, unwilling to assume much risk, so you decide to do a spread. Use the following information to construct a T-bond futures spread on July 15, and determine the profit when the position is closed on November 15.

   July 15
   December futures price: 76 9/32
   March futures price: 75 9/32

   November 15
   December futures price: 79 13/32
   March futures price: 78 9/32

   ---

9. Explain how the implied repo rate on a spread transaction differs from that on a nearby futures contract.

10. On March 16, the June T-bond futures contract was priced at 100 17/32 and the September contract was at 99 17/32. Determine the implied repo rate on the spread. Assume the cheapest bond to de-

liver on both contracts is the 11 1/4 maturing in 28 years and currently priced at 140 21/32. The CF for delivery in June was 1.3593, and the CF for delivery in September was 1.3581. Delivery is on the first of the month, and the coupons are on February 15 and August 15. The accrued interest is 3.29 on June 1 and 6.16 on September 1.

11.   On July 5, a stock index futures contract was at 394.85. The index was at 392.54, the risk-free rate was 2.83 percent, the dividend yield was 2.08 percent, and the contract expired on September 20. Determine if an arbitrage opportunity was available, and explain what transactions were executed.

12.   Rework problem 11 assuming that the index was at 388.14 at expiration. Determine the profit from the arbitrage trade, and express it in terms of the profit from the spot and futures sides of the transaction. How does your answer relate to that in problem 11?

13.   On August 20 a stock index futures, which expires on September 20, was priced at 429.70. The index was at 428.51. The dividend yield was 2.7 percent. Discuss the concept of the implied repo rate on an index arbitrage trade. Determine the implied repo rate on this trade, and explain how you would evaluate it.

14.   Identify and explain some factors that make the execution of stock index futures arbitrage difficult in practice.

15.   What is program trading? Why is it so controversial?

16.   On November 1, an analyst who has been studying a firm called Computer Sciences believes the company will make a major new announcement before the end of the year. Computer Sciences currently is priced at 27 5/8 and has a beta of .95. The analyst believes the stock can advance about 10 percent if the market does not move. The analyst thinks the market might decline by as much as 5 percent, leaving the stock with a return of $.10 + (-.05)(.95)=.0525$. To capture the full 10 percent unsystematic return, the analyst recommends the sale of stock index futures. The March contract currently is priced at 393. Assume the investor owns 100,000 shares of the stock. Set up a transaction by determining the appropriate number of futures contracts. Then determine the effective return on the stock if, on December 31, the stock is sold at 28 7/8, the futures contract is at 432.30, and the multiplier is 500. Explain your results.

17.   You are the manager of a bond portfolio of $10 million face value of bonds worth $9,448,456. The portfolio has a yield of 12.25 percent and a duration of 8.33. You plan to liquidate the portfolio in six months and are concerned about an increase in interest rates that would produce a loss on the portfolio. You would like to lower its duration to 5 years. A T-bond futures contract with the appropriate expiration is priced at 72 3/32 with a face value of $100,000, an implied yield of 12 percent, and an implied duration of 8.43 years.

    a. Should you buy or sell futures? How many contracts should you use?

    b. In six months, the portfolio has fallen in value to $8,952,597. The futures price is 68 16/32. Determine the profit from the transaction.

18. You are the manager of a stock portfolio worth $10,500,000. It has a beta of 1.15. During the next three months, you expect a correction in the market that will take the market down about 5 percent; thus, your portfolio is expected to fall about 5.75 percent (5 percent times a beta of 1.15). You wish to lower the beta to 1. A stock index futures contract with the appropriate expiration is priced at 425.75 with a multiplier of $500.

    a. Should you buy or sell futures? How many contracts should you use?

    b. In three months, the portfolio has fallen in value to $9,870,000. The futures has fallen to 402.35. Determine the profit and portfolio return over the quarter. How close did you come to the desired result?

19. On March 16, the March T-bond futures settlement price was 101 21/32. Assume the 12 1/2 percent bond maturing in about 22 years is the cheapest bond to deliver. The CF is 1.4639. Assume that the price at 3:00 P.M. was 150 15/32. Determine the price at 5:00 P.M. that would be necessary to justify delivery.

20. On September 12, a stock index futures was at 423.70. The December 400 call was at 26.25, and the put was at 3.25. The index was at 420.55. The futures and options expire on December 21. The discrete risk-free rate was 2.75 percent. Determine if the futures and options are priced correctly in relation to each other. If they are not, construct a risk-free portfolio and show how it will earn a rate better than the risk-free rate.

21. (Concept Problem) Recall from the chapters on options that we learned about bull and bear spreads. Intramarket futures spreads also are considered bull and bear spreads. Describe what you think might be a bull spread with T-bonds futures. Of course, be sure to explain your reasoning.

22. (Concept Problem) Referring to problem 11, suppose transaction costs amounted to .5 percent of the value of the stock index. Explain how these costs would affect the profitability and the incidence of index arbitrage. Then calculate the range of possible futures prices within which no arbitrage would take place.

APPENDIX 11A

Determining the CBOT Treasury Bond Conversion Factor

Step 1 Determine the maturity of the bond in years, months, and days as of the first day of the expiration month. If the bond is callable, use the first call date instead of the maturity date. Let YRS be the number of years and MOS the number of months. Ignore the number of days. Let c be the coupon rate on the bond.

Step 2 Round the number of months down to 0, 3, 6, or 9. Call this MOS*.

Step 3 If MOS* = 0,

$$CF_0 = \frac{c}{2}\left[\frac{1 - (1.03)^{-2*\text{YRS}}}{.03}\right] + (1.03)^{-2*\text{YRS}}.$$

If MOS* = 3,

$$CF_3 = (CF_0 + c/2)(1.03)^{-.5} - c/4.$$

If MOS* = 6,

$$CF_6 = \frac{c}{2}\left[\frac{1 - (1.03)^{-(2*\text{YRS}+1)}}{.03}\right] + (1.03)^{-(2*\text{YRS}+1)}.$$

If MOS* = 9,

$$CF_9 = (CF_6 + c/2)(1.03)^{-.5} - c/4.$$

Example: Determine the CF for delivery of the 7 7/8s of February 15, 2021, on the March 2000 T-bond futures contract.

On March 1, 2000, the bond's remaining life is 20 years, 11 months, and 14 days. Thus, YRS = 20 and MOS = 11. Rounding down gives MOS* = 9. First, we must find CF_6:

$$CF_6 = \frac{.07875}{2}\left[\frac{1 - (1.03)^{-(2(20)+1)}}{.03}\right] + (1.03)^{-(2(20)+1)},$$
$$= 1.2195.$$

Then we find CF_9 as

$$CF_9 = (1.2195 + .07875/2)(1.03)^{-.5} - .07875/4 = 1.2207.$$

which is shown in Table 11.3 in the chapter.

The Excel spreadsheet cfl.x1s will automatically calculate the conversion factor for you. Software Demonstration 11.2 illustrates how to use cfl.xls.

SOFTWARE DEMONSTRATION 11.2   **Determining the CBOT Conversion Factor**

The Excel spreadsheet cfl.xls operates in Excel 97 under Windows 95 or 98. It calculates the conversion factor for a bond delivery on the Chicago Board of Trade's Treasury bond futures contract. These conversion factors are also valid for the various Treasury note contracts at the CBOT. Delivery is based on the assumption of a 6 percent coupon bond.

The spreadsheet is a read-only spreadsheet, meaning that it cannot be saved under the name cfl.xls, which preserves the original file. To use the spreadsheet, simply do the following:

1. Make sure you are in Windows 95 or 98.
2. Run Excel 97.
3. Open the file cfl.xls.

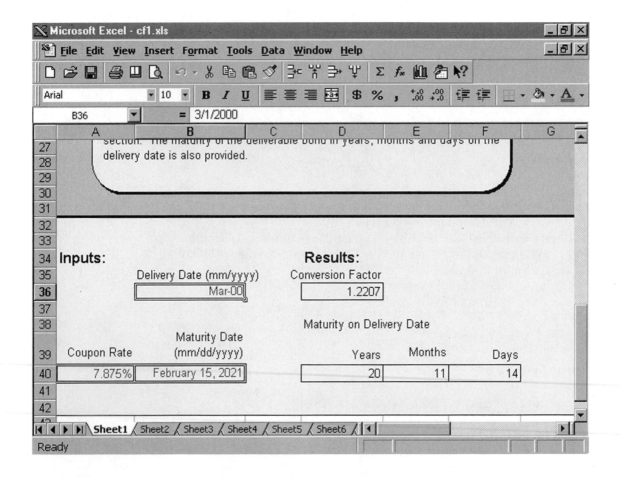

Now let us assume that you wish to calculate a conversion factor. In the example in the chapter, we wish to deliver the 7 7/8s maturing on February 15, 2021 on the March 2000 contract. Each cell that will accept input has a double-line border and the values are in blue. In the section labeled **Inputs:** you should enter the delivery date. This will always be simply a month and year. Enter it in the form mm/yyyy. Thus, you should insert "3/2000" in the cell. Several rows below, you should enter the coupon rate and maturity date. Enter the coupon rate as a percentage or decimal. For example, our bond's coupon is 7.875, so enter "7.875" or ".07875". Enter the maturity date in the format mm/dd/yyyy. Thus, in this case, you would enter "2/15/2021". The spreadsheet displays both of these dates in Excel's date format. Hit F9 (manual recalculation).

The results are automatically calculated and appear in the section labeled **Results:.** Output values have a single-line border. The conversion factor here is 1.2207. The spreadsheet also shows the maturity in years (here, 20), months (here, 11), and days (here, 14). This enables you to see if the bond has a sufficiently long maturity to be eligible for delivery on the bond or note contract.

APPENDIX 11B

Derivation of the Hedge Ratio for Adjusting Duration with Treasury Bond Futures*

The value of the position can be specified as

$$V = S + v^f N_f,$$

where v^f is the value of the futures contract. Now we wish to find the effect of a change in r or V. Since $\partial v^f / \partial r = \partial f / \partial r$, we have

$$\frac{\partial V}{\partial r} = \left(\frac{\partial S}{\partial r}\right) + \left(\frac{\partial f}{\partial r}\right) N_f.$$

The overall portfolio of bonds and futures has a yield, y_v, and a target duration, DUR_T. We can use the chain rule to rewrite the above equation as

$$\frac{\partial V/\partial y_v}{\partial r/\partial y_v} = \left(\frac{\partial S/\partial y_s}{\partial r/\partial y_s}\right) + \left(\frac{\partial f/\partial y_f}{\partial r/\partial y_f}\right) N_f.$$

From the material on duration in Chapter 10, we know that by definition $\partial S/\partial y_S = -DUR_S S/(1 + y_S)$, $\partial f/\partial y_f = -DUR_f f/(1 + y_f)$ and $\partial V/\partial y_V = -DUR_V V/(1 + y_V)$. We make the assumption that the spot and futures yields change one for one with the yield on the overall portfolio. Thus, $\partial y_S/\partial y_V = 1$ and $\partial y_f/\partial y_V = 1$. Using this result, setting DUR_V to DUR_T, the target duration, and making some algebraic rearrangements enables us to solve for the number of futures contracts;

$$N_f = -\left(\frac{DUR_S - DUR_T}{DUR_f}\right)\left(\frac{S}{f}\right)\left(\frac{1 + y_f}{1 + y_s}\right).$$

---

*This appendix requires the use of calculus.

CHAPTER 12

Options on Futures

My option gave me the right to a futures contract for that much hog [30,000 pounds] until October. Considering the average size of a hog, which I figured to be 500 pounds, this gave me a potential controlling interest in 600 animals. Right then, I vowed to eat more pork chops and bacon, and to call my friends to beg them to do the same.

JOHN ROTHCHILD
A Fool and His Money, 1997

One of the distinguishing features of U.S. financial markets is their ability to innovate. In this chapter, we shall examine one of the most successful innovations in the financial markets: **options on futures.** These instruments combine many of the most attractive features of both options and futures. As a result, they give us an opportunity to extend the principles we learned in our study of options and futures in the preceding chapters. In the latter part of the chapter we shall look at why these instruments exist in many cases alongside options on the underlying spot instrument, which are almost economically equivalent.

Options on futures are not really new instruments. They existed many years ago. As a result of several scandals, however, they were banned in 1936. They were reauthorized in 1982, when the CFTC began a pilot program allowing each exchange to offer one option on futures contract. The program was so successful that in January 1987, options on futures were authorized permanently.

Options on futures are sometimes called **commodity options,** but that term is somewhat misleading. These are not options on commodities but options on futures contracts. Though there are many options on futures contracts in which the futures is an agricultural commodity futures, the most successful have been the options on financial futures.

Options on futures are also referred to as **futures options.** In this book, however, we shall use the term *options on futures.*

Characteristics of Options on Futures

An option on a futures is a contract that grants the holder the right, but not the obligation, to buy or sell a futures contract at a fixed price — the exercise price — up to a specified expiration date. An option to buy a futures is a call, and an option to sell a futures is a put. Although an option on a futures is very similar, in fact in some cases identical, to an option on a spot, there are a number of important differences that will become apparent as we examine how they are priced.

An option on a futures contract differs from an option on the spot instrument in that upon exercise, the option holder establishes a position in the futures contract. For example, on January 31, 2000, a call option on a Treasury bond futures contract was trading at the Chicago Board of Trade with an exercise price of 90. The underlying futures is the June Treasury bond futures. The Treasury bond option on futures is an American option, meaning that it can be exercised on any day prior to and including the option expiration day.

The expiration dates of options on futures can be confusing. This is because the underlying is a futures, which itself has an expiration. Let us take a look at the two primary contracts of our interest, the Chicago Board of Trade's Treasury bond option on futures and the Chicago Mercantile Exchange's S&P 500 option on futures. The Treasury bond option on futures expires in the month prior to the month that identifies the contract. For example, a September contract expires in August. The underlying futures is the next expiring futures. The S&P 500 option on futures expires in the month in which it is identified. In other words, an October option expires in October and is exercisable into the next expiring futures, which is the December. A September option expires in September and is exercisable into the September futures.

Our T-bond option permits the purchase of the June T-bond futures at a price of 90. The option price on that day was 3 15/64, or 3.234375. The option is on one underlying futures, which, as we already learned, has a face value of $100,000. Thus, the option price per contract is $3,234.375. As with options on a spot instrument, the buyer of the option is bullish, in this case on the price of the underlying instrument, the futures.

Suppose that at expiration the futures price was at 93. Then the call holder exercises the option. This establishes for the call holder a long position in the T-bond futures contract at a price of 90. Remember that these prices are in terms of a par value of $100,000 of Treasury bonds. The futures is immediately marked to market, and the buyer thus receives a cash credit of $3,000 based on the difference between the current price, 93 — actually $93,000 — and the price at which the contract was established, 90 — actually $90,000. The investor must either deposit sufficient funds to meet the futures' initial margin requirement or liquidate the futures. Upon exercise, a short position in the futures at a price of 90, or $90,000, is established for the writer. The writer's account is immediately marked to market for a $3,000 loss and must be supplied with sufficient margin or liquidated. If at expiration the futures price is less than the exercise price, the call simply expires unexercised and the writer retains the premium paid by the buyer.

The June 90 put traded at a price of 1 18/64, or $1,281.25. If exercised, a short position in the futures at a price of 90, or $90,000, is established for the put holder. The position is marked to market, and sufficient margin funds must be deposited or the futures bought back. A long position in the futures at a price of 90, or $90,000, is established for the put writer. The position is marked to market, and sufficient margin funds must be deposited or the futures sold.

Buyers of these options are required to pay the full premium. Writers post margin for their short options in a manner similar to writers of options on spot instruments. In addition, the writers' accounts are marked to market.

Options on futures have been quite popular with investors. Figure 12.1 shows the annual volume from 1983 to 1999. Growth had been quite steady

| FIGURE 12.1 | Options on Futures Volume on U.S. Exchanges, 1983—1999 |

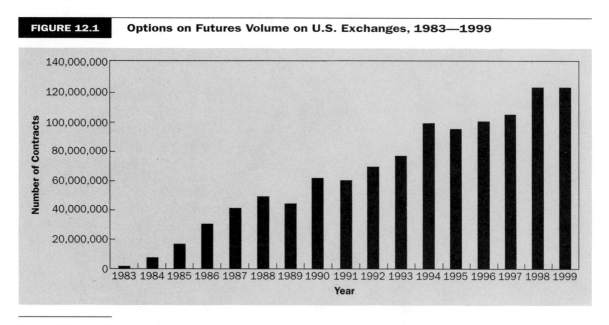

SOURCE: CFTC *Annual Report,* various years.

through 1988. Then a decline occurred in 1989. This partially reflected a decrease in public trading of these options since the market crash of 1987. Other declines occurred in 1991 and 1995, and a slight decline occurred in 1999.

Figure 12.2 illustrates the composition of the market for options on futures in terms of the type of underlying instrument. As the pie chart indicates, financials compose the largest single group, accounting for about 70 percent of volume. Agriculturals are second at 15 percent. Energy futures are third at 10 percent. Appendix 12 provides a summary of characteristics of the major contracts.

Table 12.1 presents the 1999 volume by exchange. Each of the U.S. futures exchanges has options on futures trading. The Chicago Board of Trade, which is first in futures volume, is also first in the volume of options on futures. The Chicago Mercantile Exchange is second and the New York Mercantile Exchange, with its highly successful energy futures and options, is third.

Figure 12.3 shows *The Wall Street Journal* quotations for some of the options on futures contracts. The tables are virtually the same as those for options on the spot. Beside the contract name and the exchange abbreviation is the contract size and units of quotation. Below the actual price quotations are volume and open interest figures.

Table 12.2 lists all options on futures contracts trading and regularly quoted in *The Wall Street Journal* as of January 31, 2000. Table 12.3 presents

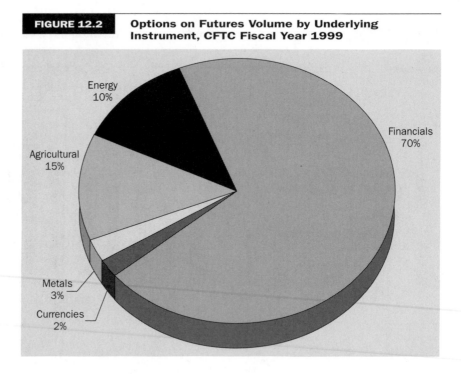

| FIGURE 12.2 | Options on Futures Volume by Underlying Instrument, CFTC Fiscal Year 1999 |

TABLE 12.1	Options on Futures Trading Volume by U.S. Exchange, CFTC Fiscal Year 1999

Exchange	Number of Contracts
Chicago Board of Trade	65,015,533
Chicago Mercantile Exchange	36,779,971
New York Mercantile Exchange	15,891,657
New York Board of Trade	5,226,733
Kansas City Board of Trade	147,848
Minneapolis Grain Exchange	57,122
MidAmerica Commodity Exchange	21,768
	123,140,632

SOURCE: CFTC *Annual Report 1999.*

the 10 most active options on futures contracts in 1999. The Treasury bond option on futures is the most active, followed by the Chicago Mercantile Exchange's Eurodollar option on futures contract. The list of most active options on futures contracts, in fact, is quite similar to that of the most active futures contracts. This is not surprising, since trading in both the options and the futures occurs side by side. As you might expect, arbitrage between the option and the underlying futures is the basis for pricing these instruments.

In addition to options on futures on U.S. exchanges, there is an active market for these instruments on some foreign futures exchanges.

Pricing Options on Futures

In this section, we shall look at some principles of pricing options on futures. These principles are closely related to the principles of pricing ordinary options that were established in Chapters 3, 4, and 5. You may wish to review those chapters before proceeding. We shall continue to employ the same notation previously used. We will make the assumptions that the options and the futures contracts expire simultaneously and the futures price equals the forward price.

The Intrinsic Value of an American Option on Futures

The minimum value of an American call on a futures is its intrinsic value. We can formally state this as

$$C_a(f_0,T,X) \geq Max(0, f_0 - X),$$

FIGURE 12.3   Options on Futures Quotations in *The Wall Street Journal*, Trading Day of June 30, 2000

AGRICULTURAL

CORN (CBT)
5,000 bu.; cents per bu.

Strike	Calls-Settle			Puts-Settle		
Price	Aug	Sep	Nov	Aug	Sep	Nov
180	....	18½	....	1¼	2¾	....
190	9⅞	12⅛	....	4⅛	6½	....
200	5	7⅝	....	9¼	12	....
210	2⅞	5	....	17	19¼	....
220	1¼	3¼	7¼	25½	27¼	22½
230	¾	2⅛	....	35	36	....

Est vol 50,000 Th 17,932 calls 10,327 puts
Op int Thur 298,704 calls 187,029 puts

SOYBEANS (CBT)
5,000 bu.; cents per bu.

Strike	Calls-Settle			Puts-Settle		
Price	Aug	Sep	Nov	Aug	Sep	Nov
425	....	....	....	¼	1½	6¼
450	35	32½	40	2¼	9½	13¾
475	17	21½	28¼	9	23½	26½
500	8½	14	19½	25½	40½	42½
525	3¼	8½	14	45⅞	60	61¼
550	1¾	4¼	10⅛	68¾	82¼	82½

Est vol 20,000 Th 11,469 calls 3,019 puts
Op int Thur 134,277 calls 50,501 puts

SOYBEAN MEAL (CBT)
100 tons; $ per ton

Strike	Calls-Settle			Puts-Settle		
Price	Aug	Sep	Oct	Aug	Sep	Oct
150	12.50	9.75	8.35	0.60	2.75	4.85
155	8.50	....	....	1.75	5.25	7.75
160	5.25	5.15	5.00	3.35	8.00	11.25
165	3.15	3.50	....	6.35	11.65	15.10
170	1.90	2.75	3.00	10.05	15.60	19.25
175	1.10	2.00	2.35	14.25	19.90	....

Est vol 3,500 Th 992 calls 589 puts
Op int Thur 25,336 calls 18,396 puts

SOYBEAN OIL (CBT)
60,000 lbs.; cents per lb.

Strike	Calls-Settle			Puts-Settle		
Price	Aug	Sep	Oct	Aug	Sep	Oct
150	....	....	....	.060	.150	.200
155	....	....	....	.160	.280	.320
160	.390	....	....	.390	.500	.500
165	.240	.560	....	.750	.800	.760
170	.150	.400	.500	1.160	1.160	1.090
175	.100	.300	.300	1.600	1.560	

Est vol 2,000 Th 3,207 calls 220 puts
Op int Thur 29,927 calls 17,398 puts

WHEAT (CBT)
5,000 bu.; cents per bu.

Strike	Calls-Settle			Puts-Settle		
Price	Aug	Sep	Dec	Aug	Sep	Dec
250	....	23	40¾	....	2	2¾
260	....	16	....	....	4¾	5¼
270	....	10¾	26¾	6½	9½	8¾
280	4	6¾	21½	13	15¼	13¼
290	2	4½	17	21	23	18½
300	1	3	13½	....	31½	24¾

Est vol 8,700 Th 2,273 calls 1,830 puts
Op int Thur 82,047 calls 43,349 puts

INDEX

DJ INDUSTRIAL AVG (CBOT)
$100 times premium

Strike	Calls-Settle			Puts-Settle		
Price	Jly	Aug	Sep	Jly	Aug	Sep
104	26.30	....	47.00	11.35	....	32.10
105	19.80	31.50	41.00	14.80	26.50	36.05
106	14.75	26.00	35.40	19.75	31.00	40.35
107	10.60	21.50	30.25	25.60	36.00	45.10
108	7.35	17.00	25.95	32.30	41.50	50.75
109	4.90	13.50	22.10	39.85	48.00	56.80

Est vol 400 Th 184 calls 146 puts
Op int Thur 3,338 calls 6,063 puts

S&P 500 STOCK INDEX (CME)
$250 times premium

Strike	Calls-Settle			Puts-Settle		
Price	Jly	Aug	Sep	Jly	Aug	Sep
1460	29.00	44.50	55.00	20.90	36.50	47.00
1465	26.10	....	52.20	23.00	....	49.10
1470	23.40	39.00	49.50	25.30	40.90	51.40
1475	20.80	36.40	46.90	27.70	43.20	53.70
1480	18.30	33.90	44.30	30.45	45.70	56.00
1485	16.10	31.50	41.90	32.90	48.20	58.60

Est vol 3,468 Th 7,106 calls 5,375 puts
Op int Thur 58,087 calls 135,424 puts

OIL

CRUDE OIL (NYM)
1,000 bbls.; $ per bbl.

Strike	Calls-Settle			Puts-Settle		
Price	Aug	Sep	Oct	Aug	Sep	Oct
3150	....	1.50	1.47	0.63	1.87	....
3200	....	1.32	1.30	0.81	....	....
3250	1.03	1.12	1.15	1.03	....	....
3300	0.81	0.96	1.01	1.31	....	....
3350	0.62	0.81	....	....	....	....
3400	0.49	0.70	0.77	....	....	....

Est vol na Th 8,611 calls 15,160 puts
Op int Thur 214,071 calls 282,691 puts

HEATING OIL No.2 (NYM)
42,000 gal.; $ per gal.

Strike	Calls-Settle			Puts-Settle		
Price	Aug	Sep	Oct	Aug	Sep	Oct
82	.0390	.0569	.0654	.0262	....	....
83	.0338	.0519	.0604	....	....	....
84	.0292	.0475	.0560	....	....	....
85	.0252	.0434	.0520	....	.0595	....
86	.0216	.0397	.0483	....	....	....
87	.0185	.0362	.0450	....	....	....

Est vol na Th 7,572 calls 2,047 puts
Op int Thur 72,589 calls 25,772 puts

GASOLINE-Unlead (NYM)
42,000 gal.; $ per gal.

Strike	Calls-Settle			Puts-Settle		
Price	Aug	Sep	Oct	Aug	Sep	Oct
102	.0346	.0304	.0183	.0467	....	....
103	.0308	.0279	....	.0528	....	....
104	.0274	.0256	.0156	....	....	....
105	.0243	.0235	....	....	....	.1878
106	.0215	.0216	.0133	....	....	.2112
107	.0190	.0198	....	.0901	....	.2010

Est vol na Th 1,083 calls 197 puts
Op int Thur 35,580 calls 24,425 puts

INTEREST RATE

T-BONDS (CBT)
$100,000; points and 64ths of 100%

Strike	Calls-Settle			Puts-Settle		
Price	Aug	Sep	Dec	Aug	Sep	Dec
95	2-34	....	....	0-12	....	....
96	1-47	2-11	2-63	0-25	0-53	1-47
97	1-04	....	....	0-47	....	....
98	0-39	1-05	1-62	1-16	1-47	2-42
99	0-19	....	....	1-61	....	....
100	0-09	0-29	1-13	....	3-06	3-57

Est vol 30,000;
Th vol 28,265 calls 30,552 puts
Op int Thur 172,739 calls 187,825 puts

T-NOTES (CBT)
$100,000; points and 64ths of 100%

Strike	Calls-Settle			Puts-Settle		
Price	Aug	Sep	Dec	Aug	Sep	Dec
96	2-35	2-44	3-06	0-04	0-14	0-47
97	1-41	1-56	....	0-10	0-26	1-02
98	0-56	1-13	1-52	0-25	0-46	1-26
99	0-24	0-45	1-20	0-57	1-14	....
100	0-09	0-24	0-59	....	1-57	....
101	0-03	0-12	0-40	....	2-44	....

Est vol 40,000 Th 12,655 calls 20,682 puts
Op int Thur 245,394 calls 190,627 puts

5 YR TREAS NOTES (CBT)
$100,000; points and 64ths of 100%

Strike	Calls-Settle			Puts-Settle		
Price	Aug	Sep	Dec	Aug	Sep	Dec
9800	....	1-15	....	0-05	0-14	0-39
9850	0-44	0-56	....	0-11	0-24	....
9900	0-24	0-38	....	0-23	0-37	....
9950	0-12	0-24	....	0-43	0-55	....
10000	0-05	0-15	....	....	1-13	....
10050	....	0-08	....	....	....	....

Est vol 4,800 Th 3,818 calls 7,970 puts
Op int Thur 49,222 calls 81,319 puts

EURODOLLAR (CME)
$ million; pts. of 100%

Strike	Calls-Settle			Puts-Settle		
Price	Jly	Aug	Sep	Jly	Aug	Sep
9275	3.15	3.20	3.25	0.02	0.07	0.15
9300	0.90	1.10	1.35	0.25	0.45	0.70
9325	0.05	0.12	0.22	1.90	1.95	2.05
9350	....	0.05	0.07	....	....	4.40
9375	....	....	0.02	....	....	6.85
9400	....	....	0.02	....	....	9.35

Est vol 54,385;
Th vol 38,846 calls 49,393 puts
Op int Thur 1,048,229 calls 949,568 puts

SOURCE: *The Wall Street Journal*, July 3, 2000.

TABLE 12.2	Listed Options on Futures Contracts on U.S. Futures Exchanges Covered in *The Wall Street Journal* (as of January 31, 2000)

Contract	Exchange	Contract Size
Interest Rates		
Treasury bonds	CBOT	$100,000
6 1/2–10-year Treasury notes	CBOT	$100,000
5-year Treasury notes	CBOT	$100,000
Municipal bond index	CBOT	$1,000 × premium
Eurodollars	CME	$1,000,000
1-year Mid-Curve Eurodollar	CME	$1,000,000
2-year Mid-Curve Eurodollar	CME	$1,000,000
Indices and Insurance		
S&P 500 Index	CME	$250 × premium
Dow Jones Industrial Average	CBOT	$100 × premium
NYSE Composite Index	NYFE	$500 × premium
NASDAQ 100 Index	CME	$100 × premium
Commodity Futures		
Corn	CBOT	5,000 bu.
Corn	MCE	1,000 bu.
Soybeans	CBOT	5,000 bu.
Soybeans	MCE	1,000 bu.
Soybean meal	CBOT	100 tons
Soybean oil	CBOT	60,000 lbs.
Wheat	CBOT	5,000 bu.
Wheat	KCBT	5,000 bu.
Oats	CBOT	5,000 bu.
Rice	CBOT	2,000 cwt.
Cotton	NYBOT	50,000 lbs.
Orange juice	NYBOT	15,000 lbs.
Coffee	NYBOT	37,500 lbs.
Sugar—world	NYBOT	112,000 lbs.
Cocoa	NYBOT	10 metric tons
Crude oil	NYMEX	1,000 bbls.
Heating oil no. 2	NYMEX	42,000 gals.
Gasoline—unleaded	NYMEX	42,000 gals.
Natural gas	NYMEX	10,000 MM Btu.
Feeder cattle	CME	50,000 lbs.
Live cattle	CME	40,000 lbs.
Lean hogs	CME	40,000 lbs.
Pork bellies	CME	40,000 lbs.
Copper	NYMEX	25,000 lbs.
Gold	NYMEX	100 troy ozs.
Silver	NYMEX	5,000 troy ozs.
Lumber	CME	80,000 bd. ft.
Foreign Currencies		
Japanese yen	CME	12,500,000 yen
German mark	CME	125,000 marks
Canadian dollar	CME	100,000 Canadian dollars
British pound	CME	62,500 pounds
Swiss franc	CME	125,000 francs

TABLE 12.3	Most Active Options on Futures Contracts in U.S., CFTC Fiscal Year 1999		

Contract	Exchange	Number of Contracts
Treasury bonds	CBOT	38,983,582
Eurodollars	CME	28,676,149
10-year Treasury notes	CBOT	10,556,981
Crude oil	NYMEX	7,668,720
Soybeans	CBOT	4,929,660
S&P 500	CME	4,652,634
Corn	CBOT	4,108,066
Natural gas	NYMEX	3,757,094
5-year Treasury notes	CBOT	2,924,388
Sugar	NYBOT	2,310,252

SOURCE: CFTC *Annual Report 1999.*

The intrinsic value of an American call option on a futures is the greater of zero or the difference between the futures price and the exercise price.

where $\text{Max}(0, f_0 - X)$ is the intrinsic value. It is easy to see that this statement must hold for options on futures in the same way as for options on the spot. If the call price is less than the intrinsic value, the call can be bought and exercised. This establishes a long position in a futures contract at the price of X. The futures is immediately sold at the price of f_0, and a risk-free profit is made.

Consider a March 1390 S&P 500 option on futures. The underlying futures price is 1401. The intrinsic value is $\text{Max}(0, 1401 - 1390) = 11$. The call is actually worth 49.20. The difference of $49.20 - 11 = 38.20$ is the time value. Like the time value on an option on the spot, the time value here decreases as expiration approaches. At expiration, the call must sell for its intrinsic value.

The intrinsic value of an American put option on futures establishes its minimum value. This is stated as

$$P_a(f_0, T, X) \geq \text{Max}(0, X - f_0),$$

The intrinsic value of an American put option on a futures is the greater of zero or the difference between the exercise price and the futures price.

where $\text{Max}(0, X - f_0)$ is the intrinsic value. Again, if this is not true, the arbitrageur can purchase the futures contract and the put, immediately exercise the put, and earn a risk-free profit.

The March 1405 S&P 500 put option on futures was priced at 44.60. The futures price was 1401. The minimum value is $\text{Max}(0, 1405 - 1401) = 4$.

The difference between the put price, 44.60, and the intrinsic value, 4, is the time value, 40.60. The time value, of course, erodes as expiration approaches. At expiration, the put is worth the intrinsic value.

The Lower Bound of a European Option on Futures

The intrinsic values apply only to American options on futures. This is because early exercise is necessary to execute the arbitrage. As you should recall from our study of options on stocks, we can establish a lower bound for a European option.

Let us first look at the call option on futures. We construct two portfolios, A and B. Portfolio A consists of a single long position in a European call. Portfolio B consists of a long position in the futures contract and a long position in risk-free bonds with a face value of $f_0 - X$. Note that if X is greater than f_0, this is actually a short position in bonds and thus constitutes a loan in which we pay back $X - f_0$ at expiration. We do not really care whether we are borrowing or lending. As long as we keep the signs correct, we will obtain the desired result in either case. Table 12.4 presents the outcomes of these portfolios.

If $f_T \leq X$, the call expires worthless. The futures contract is worth $f_T - f_0$, and the bonds are worth $f_0 - X$; thus, portfolio B is worth $f_T - X$. If $f_T > X$, the call is worth $f_T - X$, the intrinsic value, and portfolio B is still worth $f_T - X$. As you can see, portfolio A does at least as well as portfolio B in all cases; therefore, its current value should be at least as high as portfolio B's. We can state this as

$$C_e(f_0,T,X) \geq (f_0 - X)(1 + r)^{-T}.$$

Because an option cannot have negative value,

$$C_e(f_0,T,X) \geq \text{Max}[0, (f_0 - X)(1 + r)^{-T}].$$

Note that we used an important result from Chapter 9: The value of a futures contract when initially established is zero. Thus, portfolio B's value is simply the value of the risk-free bonds.

This result establishes the lower bound for a European call on the futures. Remember that a European call on the spot has a lower bound of

$$C_e(S_0,T,X) \geq S_0 - X(1 + r)^{-T}.$$

The price of a European call option on a futures must at least equal the greater of zero or the present value of the difference between the futures price and the exercise price.

TABLE 12.4   **The Lower Bound of a European Call Option on Futures: Payoffs at Expiration of Portfolios A and B**

			Payoffs from Portfolio Given Futures Price at Expiration	
Portfolio	Instrument	Current Value	$f_T \leq X$	$f_T > X$
A	Long call	$C_e(f_0,T,X)$	0	$f_T - X$
B	Long futures	0	$f_T - f_0$	$f_T - f_0$
	Bond	$(f_0 - X)(1 + r)^{-T}$	$+ f_0 - X$	$+ f_0 - X$
			$f_T - X$	$f_T - X$

As we saw in Chapter 9, in the absence of dividends on the spot instrument, the futures price is

$$f_0 = S_0(1 + r)^T.$$

Making this substitution for f_0, we see that these two lower bounds are equivalent. In fact, if the option and futures expire simultaneously, a European call on a futures is equivalent to a European call on the spot. This is because a European call can be exercised only at expiration, at which time the futures and spot prices are equivalent.

As an example of the lower bound, let us look at the March 1390 S&P 500 call option on futures on January 31 of a leap year. The option expires on March 16; thus, there are 45 days remaining and $T = 45/365 = .1233$. The futures price is 1401. The risk-free rate is 5.58 percent. The lower bound is

$$C_e(f_0,T,X) \geq \text{Max}[0, (1401 - 1390)(1.0558)^{-.1233}] = 10.93.$$

The actual call price is 49.20.

Note, however, that the lower bound established here is slightly less than the intrinsic value of 11. This should seem unusual. For ordinary equity options, the lower bound of $\text{Max}[0, S_0 - X(1 + r)^{-T}]$ exceeds the intrinsic value of $\text{Max}(0, S_0 - X)$. For options on futures, however, this is not necessarily so. As we shall see in a later section, this explains why some American call (and put) options on futures are exercised early.

Now let us look at the lower bound for a European put option on a futures. Again we shall establish two portfolios, A and B. Portfolio A consists of a long position in the put. Portfolio B consists of a short position in the futures contract and a long position in risk-free bonds with a face value of $X - f_0$. Again, if f_0 is greater than X, this is actually a short position in bonds, or taking out a loan. Table 12.5 illustrates the outcomes.

By now you should be able to explain each outcome. If $f_T < X$, the put is exercised, so portfolio A is worth $X - f_T$. If $f_T \geq X$, the put expires worthless. In both cases, the futures contract in portfolio B is worth $-(f_T - f_0)$ and the bonds are worth $X - f_0$, for a total of $X - f_T$. Portfolio A does at

TABLE 12.5	The Lower Bound of a European Put Option on Futures: Payoffs at Expiration of Portfolios A and B

Portfolio	Instrument	Current Value	Payoffs from Portfolio Given Futures Price at Expiration $f_T < X$	$f_T \geq X$
A	Long put	$P_e(f_0,T,X)$	$X - f_T$	0
B	Short futures	0	$-(f_T - f_0)$	$-(f_T - f_0)$
	Bond	$+ (X - f_0)(1 + r)^{-T}$	$+ X - f_0$	$+ X - f_0$
			$X - f_T$	$X - f_T$

least as well as portfolio B in both outcomes; therefore, the current value of A should be at least as great as the current value of B,

$$P_e(f_0, T, X) \geq (X - f_0)(1 + r)^{-T}.$$

Because the option cannot have a negative value,

$$P_e(f_0, T, X) \geq Max[0, (X - f_0)(1 + r)^{-T}].$$

The price of a European put option on a futures must at least equal the greater of zero or the present value of the difference between the exercise price and the futures price.

As we saw with calls, we can substitute S_0 for $f_0(1 + r)^{-T}$ and see that the lower bound for a put option on a futures is the same as that for a put option on the spot. As is true for calls, European put options on futures in which the put and the futures expire simultaneously are equivalent to options on the spot.

As an example, let us look at the March 1405 S&P 500 put option on futures on January 31, 2000. The futures price is 1401, the time to expiration is .1233, and the risk-free rate is 5.58 percent. The lower bound is

$$P_e(S_0, T, X) \geq Max\left[0, (1405 - 1401)(1.0558)^{-.1233}\right] = 3.97$$

The actual price of the put is 44.60. As we saw for equity puts, the European lower bound will be less than the American intrinsic value. Thus, the actual minimum price of this American put is its intrinsic value of $1405 - 1401 = 4$.

Put-Call Parity of Options on Futures

We have looked at put-call parity for options on stocks. We can also establish a put-call parity rule for options on futures.

First let us construct two portfolios, A and B. Portfolio A will consist of a long futures and a long put on the futures. This can be thought of as a protective put. Portfolio B will consist of a long call and a long bond with a face value of the exercise price minus the futures price. If X is greater than f_0, this is indeed a long position in a bond. If f_0 is greater than X, then we are simply issuing bonds with a face value of $f_0 - X$. In either case, the cash flow of the bond will be $X - f_0$ when it matures on the option expiration day. The payoffs are illustrated in Table 12.6.

As we can see, the two portfolios produce the same result. If the futures price ends up less than the exercise price, both portfolios end up worth $X - f_0$. If the futures price ends up greater than the exercise price, both portfolios end up worth $f_T - f_0$. Thus, portfolio B is also like a protective put and its current value must equal the current value of portfolio A. Since the value of the long futures in portfolio A is zero, we conclude that

$$P_e(f_0, T, X) = C_e(f_0, T, X) + (X - f_0)(1 + r)^{-T}.$$

			Payoffs from Portfolio Given Futures Price at Expiration	
Portfolio	Instrument	Current Value	$f_T \leq X$	$f_T > X$
A	Long Futures	0	$f_T - f_0$	$f_T - f_0$
	Long Put	$P_e(f_0,T,X)$	$X - f_T$	0
			$X - f_0$	$f_T - f_0$
B	Long Call	$C_e(f_0,T,X)$	0	$f_T - X$
	Bonds	$(X - f_0)(1 + r)^{-T}$	$X - f_0$	$X - f_0$
			$X - f_0$	$f_T - f_0$

TABLE 12.6　　Put-Call Parity of Options on Futures

Put-call parity of options on futures is the relationship among the call price, the put price, the futures price, the exercise price, the risk-free rate, and the time to expiration.

As with put-call parity for options on spot assets, we can write this several different ways, isolating the various terms. Note the similarity between put-call parity for options on futures and put-call parity for options on the spot:

$$P_e(S_0,T,X) = C_e(S_0,T,X) - S_0 + X(1 + r)^{-T}.$$

Because the futures price must equal $S_0(1 + r)^T$, these two versions of put-call parity are equivalent. As we stated earlier, in many ways the options themselves are equivalent.

Let us look at the March 1400 puts and calls on the S&P 500 futures on January 31. As we saw in Chapter 3, we can calculate the put price and compare it to the actual market price or calculate the call price and compare it to the actual market price. Here we shall calculate the put price. The call price is $43.40. The other input values given earlier are $f_0 = 1401$, $r = .0558$, and $T = .1233$. The put price should be

$$P_e(f_0,T,X) = 43.40 + (1400 - 1401)(1.0558)^{-.1233} = 42.41.$$

The actual put price was 42.40. This is very close, but we should expect a difference because these are American options and the formula is for European options. The formula price should be less than the market price, but in this case it is not. The effect of transaction costs, however, might explain the difference.

Early Exercise of Call and Put Options on Futures

Recall that in the absence of dividends on a stock, a call option on the stock would not be exercised early; however, a put option might be. With an option on a futures contract, either a call or a put might be exercised early. Let us look at the call.

Consider a deep-in-the-money American call. If the call is on the spot instrument, it may have some time value remaining. If it is sufficiently deep-in-the-money, it will have little time value. That does not, however, mean it should be exercised early. Disregarding transaction costs, early exercise would be equivalent to selling the call. If the call is on the futures, however, early exercise may be the better choice. The logic behind this is that a deep-in-the-money call behaves almost identically to the underlying instrument. If the call is on the spot instrument, it will move one for one with the spot price. If the call is on the futures, it will move nearly one for one with the futures price. Thus, the call on the futures will act almost exactly like a long position in a futures contract. The investor, however, has money tied up in the call but because the margin can be met by depositing interest-earning T-bills, there is no money tied up in the futures. By exercising the call and replacing it with a long position in the futures, the investor obtains the same opportunity to profit but frees up the funds tied up in the call. If the call were on the spot instrument, we could not make the same argument. The call may behave in virtually the same manner as the spot instrument, but the latter also requires the commitment of funds.

From an algebraic standpoint, the early-exercise problem is seen by noting that the minimum value of an in-the-money European call, $(f_0 - X)(1 + r)^{-T}$, is less than the value of the call if it could be exercised, $f_0 - X$. The European call cannot be exercised, but if it were an American call, it could be.

These points are illustrated in panel a of Figure 12.4. The European call option on futures approaches its lower bound of $(f_0 - X)(1 + r)^{-T}$. The American call option on futures approaches its minimum value, its intrinsic value of $f_0 - X$, which is greater than the European lower bound. There is a futures price, $f_{0(a)}{}^{\ddagger}$, at which the American call will equal its intrinsic value. Above that price, the American call will be exercised early. Recall that for calls on spot instruments, the European lower bound was higher than the intrinsic value. Thus, there was no early exercise premium—provided, of course, that the underlying asset paid no dividends.

For put options on futures, the intuitive and algebraic arguments work similarly. Deep-in-the-money American puts on futures tend to be exercised early. Panel b of Figure 12.4 illustrates the case for puts. The price of European put options on futures approaches its lower bound of $(X - f_0)(1 + r)^{-T}$, while the price of the American put option on futures approaches its intrinsic value of $X - f_0$. The American intrinsic value is greater than the European lower bound. There is a price, $f_{0(a)}{}^{\ddagger}$, at which the American put option on futures would equal its intrinsic value. Below this price, the American put would be exercised early.

Although these instruments are options on futures, it is conceivable that one would be interested in an option on a forward contract. Interestingly, these options would not be exercised early. This is because when exercised, a forward contract is established at the price of X. A forward contract is not marked to market, however, so the holder of a call does not receive an immediate cash flow of $F_0 - X$. Instead, that person receives

It may be optimal to exercise early either an American call on a futures or an American put on a futures.

FIGURE 12.4   **American and European Calls and Puts on Futures**

only a position with a value, as we learned in Chapter 9, of $(F_0 - X)$ $(1 + r)^{-T}$. This amount, however, is the lower bound of a European call on a forward contract. Early exercise cannot capture a gain over the European call value; thus, it offers no advantage. Similar arguments hold for early exercise of a European put on a forward contract.

Options on Futures Pricing Models

Fischer Black (1976) developed a variation of his own Black-Scholes model for pricing European options on futures. Using the assumption that the option and the futures expire simultaneously, the **Black model** gives the option price as follows:

$$C = e^{-r_cT} [f_0 N(d_1) - X N(d_2)],$$
where
$$d_1 = \frac{\ln(f_0/X) + (\sigma^2/2)T}{\sigma\sqrt{T}}$$
$$d_2 = d_1 - \sigma\sqrt{T}$$

Here σ is the volatility of the futures. Note that the expression for d_1 does not contain the continuously compounded risk-free rate, r_c, as it does in the Black-Scholes model. That is because the risk-free rate captures the opportunity cost of funds tied up in the stock. If the option is on a futures contract, no funds are invested in the futures and therefore there is no opportunity cost. The price of the call on the futures, however, will be the same as the price of the call on the spot. This is because when the call on the futures expires, it is exercisable into a futures position, which is immediately expiring. Thus, the call on the futures, when exercised, establishes a long position in the spot asset.

The Black call option on futures pricing model gives the call price in terms of the futures price, exercise price, risk-free rate, time to expiration, and volatility of the futures.

To prove that the Black option on futures pricing model gives the same price as the Black-Scholes model for an option on the spot, notice that in the Black model $N(d_1)$ is multiplied by $f_0 e^{-r_cT}$, while in the Black-Scholes model it is multiplied by S_0. We learned in Chapter 9 that with no dividends on the underlying asset, the futures price will equal $S_0 e^{r_cT}$. Thus, if we substitute $S_0^{r_cT}$ for f_0 in the Black model, the formula will be the same as the Black-Scholes formula.[1]

We know that in the presence of dividends, the futures price is given by the formula $f_0 = S_0 e^{(r_c - \delta)T}$. Thus, $S_0 = f_0 e^{-(r_c - \delta)T}$. If we substitute this expression for S_0 into the Black-Scholes model, we obtain the Black option on futures pricing model if the underlying spot asset—in this case, a stock

---

[1]This may not be obvious in the formula for d_1. If we substitute $S_0 e^{r_cT}$ for f_0 in the above formula for d_1, we obtain

$$d_1 = \frac{\ln(S_0 e^{r_cT}/X) + (\sigma^2/2)T}{\sigma\sqrt{T}}.$$

The expression $\ln(S_0 e^{r_cT}/X)$ is equivalent to $\ln S_0 + \ln e^{r_cT} - \ln X$. Now $\ln e^{r_cT} = r_cT$, so d_1 becomes

$$d_1 \frac{\ln(S_0/X) + (r_c + \sigma^2/2)T}{\sigma\sqrt{T}},$$

which is d_1 from the Black-Scholes formula.

—pays dividends. The dividends do not show up in the Black model, however, so we need not distinguish the Black model with and without dividends. Dividends do affect the call price, but only indirectly, as the futures price captures all the effects of the dividends.

Another useful comparison of the Black and Black-Scholes models is to consider how the Black-Scholes model might be used as a substitute for the Black model. Suppose we have available only a computer program for the Black-Scholes model, but we want to price an option on a futures contract. We can do this easily by using the version of the Black-Scholes model in Chapter 5 that had a continuous dividend yield, and inserting the risk-free rate for the dividend yield and the futures price for the spot price. The risk-free rate minus the dividend yield is the cost of carry, so it will equal zero. The Black-Scholes formula will then be pricing an option on an instrument that has a price of f_0 and a cost of carry of zero. This is precisely what the Black model prices: an option on an instrument—in this case, a futures contract—with a price of f_0 and a cost of carry of zero. Remember that the futures price reflects the cost of carry on the underlying spot asset, but the futures itself does not have a cost of carry because there are no funds tied up and no storage costs.

Let us now use the Black model to price the March 1400 call option on the S&P 500 futures. Recall that the futures price is 1401, the exercise price is 1400, the time to expiration is .1233, and the risk-free rate is $\ln(1.0558) = .0543$. We now need only the standard deviation of the continuously compounded percentage change in the futures price. For illustrative purposes, we shall use .21 as the standard deviation. Table 12.7 presents the calculations.

The actual value of the call is 43.40. Thus, the call would appear to be underpriced. As we showed in Chapter 5, an arbitrageur could create a risk-free portfolio by selling the underlying instrument and buying the call. The

TABLE 12.7	Calculating the Black Option on Futures Price

$f_0 = 1401$ $X = 1400$ $r_c = .0543$ $\sigma = .21$ $T = .1233$

1. Compute d_1.

$$d_1 = \frac{\ln(1401/1400) + ((.21)^2/2).1233}{.21\sqrt{.1233}} = 0.0466$$

2. Compute d_2.

$$d_2 = .0466 - .21\sqrt{.1233} = -0.0271$$

3. Look up $N(d_1)$.

$$N(0.05) = .5199$$

4. Look up $N(d_2)$.

$$N(-0.03) = .4880$$

5. Plug into formula for C.

$$C = e^{-(.0543)(.1233)}[1401(.5199) - 1400(.4880)] = 44.88$$

hedge ratio would be $e^{-r_cT}N(d_1)$ futures contracts for each call; however, remember that the model gives the European option price, so we expect it to be less than the actual American option price.

Your software, bsbin2.xls and bsbwin2.1.exe, introduced in Chapter 5, can be used to obtain prices of options on futures for the Black model. Simply insert the value you used for the risk-free rate for the continuously compounded dividend yield and insert the futures price for the underlying asset price.

In Chapter 5 when we studied the Black-Scholes model, we carefully examined how the model changes when any of the five underlying variables changes. Many of these effects were referred to with Greek names like delta, gamma, theta, vega, and rho. Since the Black model produces the same price as the Black-Scholes model, we will get the same effects here. The only difference is that with the Black model we express these results in terms of the futures price, rather than the spot or stock price. For any of the formulas in which S_0 appears, such as the gamma, vega, and theta, we simply replace S_0 with $f_0^{-r_cT}$. In the case of the delta, we must redefine delta as the change in the call price for a change in the futures price. For an option on a stock, we saw that the delta is $N(d_1)$. For an option on a futures, the delta is $e^{-r_cT}N(d_1)$.

We can easily develop a pricing model for European put options on futures from the Black model and put-call parity. Using the continuously compounded version, put-call parity is expressed as $C - P = (f_0 - X)e^{-r_cT}$. Rearranging this expression to isolate the put price gives

$$P = C - (f_0 - X)e^{-r_cT}.$$

Now we can substitute the Black European call option on futures pricing model for C in put-call parity and rearrange the terms to obtain the Black European put option on futures pricing model,

$$P = Xe^{-r_cT}[1 - N(d_2)] - f_0e^{-r_cT}[1 - N(d_1)].$$

Some end-of-chapter problems will allow us to use this model and examine it further.

Earlier we noted that even in the absence of dividends, American calls on futures might be exercised early. Like options on the spot, American puts on futures might be exercised early. The Black model does not price American options, and we cannot appeal to the absence of dividends, as we could for some stocks, to allow us to use the European model to price an American option. Unfortunately, American option on futures pricing models are fairly complex for this book. It is possible, however, to price American options on futures using the binomial model.

The Black call option on futures pricing model can be turned into a put option on futures pricing model by using put-call parity for options on futures.

Recall from Chapter 4 that we developed the binomial model for options on a stock. In the example we used, which you may wish to review, we had a stock that could go up by 25 percent or down by 20 percent. The risk-free rate was 7 percent. The stock was initially priced at 100. We looked at a call option that had an exercise price of 100. Let us assume that the option and the futures will expire after two periods. Figure 12.5 illustrates the binomial trees for the stock (panel a) and the futures (panel b). The futures tree is obtained by noting that at any node of the tree, the futures price would be the stock price compounded at the 7 percent interest rate for the number of periods until it expires. This is our simple futures pricing model, covered in Chapter 9, when there are no dividends. Note that at expiration the futures prices all equal the corresponding stock prices. The current futures price of 114.49 is the current stock price compounded at 7 percent for two periods.

FIGURE 12.5   **The Stock and Futures Price Paths for a Two-Period Binomial Model (S = 100, r = 7, u = 1.25, d = 0.80)**

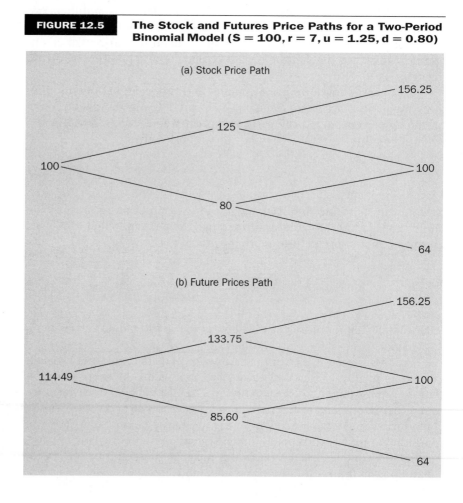

(a) Stock Price Path

(b) Future Prices Path

Recall that the price of a call on the stock, at any node, is a weighted average of the next two possible call prices, discounted at the risk-free rate. The weights are the values, $p = (1 + r - d)/(u - d)$ and $1 - p$. Here p is $(1.07 - 0.80)/(1.25 - 0.80) = .6$. The prices of the calls on the stock at expiration (with the corresponding stock prices in parentheses) are 56.25 (156.25), 0 (100), and 0 (64). Thus, the call price when the stock price is 125 is found as

$$\frac{56.25(.6) + 0(.4)}{1.07} = 31.54.$$

The other call prices are found in the same manner. For the option on the futures, the call prices at expiration are the same as those for the option on the stock. This is true because the futures expires and its price converges to the stock price. The values of p and $1 - p$ are the same so we will get the same price at any node for a European call option on a futures as for a European call option on a stock. Thus, when the stock price is at 125 and the futures price is at 133.75, the European call on the stock and the European call on the futures are both worth 31.54.

American options on futures should be priced by a model capable of capturing the impact of early exercise. One such model is the binomial model.

Suppose they are American calls. We know that the call on the stock will not be worth any more than its European counterpart because there is no dividend. Note, however, that if the futures price is 133.75, it would be possible to exercise an American call on a futures and obtain a futures contract at a price of 100.

The futures could be sold immediately for a gain of 33.75. This is more than the 31.54 it is worth unexercised. Thus, we replace the 31.54 with 33.75. When the stock is at 80 and the futures is at 85.60, the option on the futures is worth zero, exercised or not. The price of the option on the futures today would, thus, be

$$\frac{33.75(.6) + 0(.4)}{1.07} = 18.93.$$

At this point, we should still check and see if it should be exercised. Since the futures price is 114.49, it is 14.49 points in-the-money but worth less than its unexercised value of 18.93. Thus, our American call on the futures is worth 18.93, while its European counterpart, which is also the value of the American call on the spot, is worth only 17.69, as calculated in Chapter 4.

In addition to the problem of using a European option pricing model to price American options, the Black model has difficulty pricing the most actively traded options on futures, Treasury bond options on futures. That problem is related to the interest rate component. The Black model, like the Black-Scholes model, makes the assumption of a constant interest rate. This generally is considered an acceptable assumption for pricing options on commodities and sometimes even stock indices. It is far less palatable for pricing options on bonds. There is a fundamental inconsistency in assuming a constant interest rate while attempting to price an option on a futures that is on an underlying Treasury bond, whose price changes because of changing interest rates. More appropriate models are available and we explore one in Chapter 14.

Trading Strategies for Options on Futures

Virtually any strategy that can be done with options on the spot can be done with options on futures. Chapters 6 and 7 discussed many of the popular option strategies and you may wish to review them first. There is little need for much repetition here, as most of those results transfer directly to options on futures. It will be helpful, however, to briefly examine three basic option on futures strategies: buying a call, buying a put, and writing a covered call.

Buy a Call Option on Futures

Buying a call option on a futures, like buying a call option on the asset, is a bullish strategy that has a limited loss, the call premium, and an unlimited gain.

The profit from a call option on futures that is held to expiration is given by the equation

$$\Pi = \text{Max}(0, f_T - X) - C.$$

The two outcomes are

$$\Pi = -C \qquad \text{if } f_T \leq X$$
$$\Pi = f_T - X - C \qquad \text{if } f_T > X.$$

The breakeven futures price at expiration is $X + C$. The outcome of this strategy is the same as it is for an option on the spot, provided, of course, that the futures and the option expire simultaneously.

As an example, let us buy a December 110 Treasury bond call option on futures. The price of the call is \$1.234375. Because the contract is based on a \$100,000 par futures contract, the actual premium is $1,000(\$1.234375) = \$1,234.375$.[2] The graph showing the profit for various values of the futures (and spot) price at expiration is presented in Figure 12.6.

Suppose the futures price ends up at 116. Then the call is exercised, which means the futures is purchased at the exercise price of 110 and immediately sold at 116. Subtracting the cost of the call of 1.234375 gives a

---

[2]Since the exercise price is quoted in hundreds, the total exercise price is $110(1,000) = \$110,000$. Thus, the total premium is obtained by multiplying by 1,000.

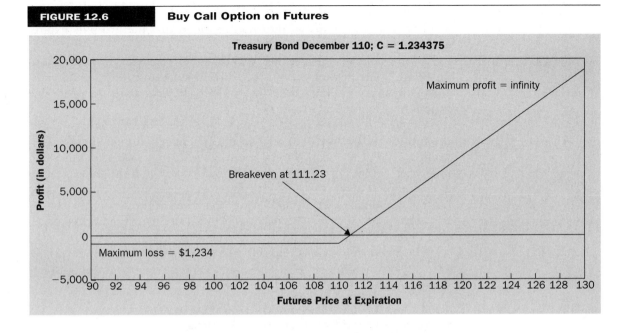

FIGURE 12.6   **Buy Call Option on Futures**

Treasury Bond December 110; C = 1.234375

Maximum profit = infinity

Breakeven at 111.23

Maximum loss = $1,234

profit of 116 − 110 − 1.234375 = 4.765625. The overall profit is 1,000(4.765625) = $4,765.625. If the futures price ends up below 110, the option expires worthless and the option holder loses the premium, $1,234.375. The breakeven futures price is 110 + 1.234375 = 111.23. The maximum gain is unlimited.

We shall not illustrate the comparison of different exercise prices and different holding periods. The issues are the same as they are for options on the spot. The lower-exercise-price call is more expensive, but it offers greater profit potential. The shorter holding period produces a higher profit for a given futures price but allows less time for the futures price to move.

Buy a Put Option on Futures

The profit for a put option on a futures contract held to expiration is given by the equation

$$\Pi = \text{Max}(0, X - f_T) - P.$$

The two possible outcomes are

$$\Pi = X - f_T - P \qquad \text{if } f_T < X$$
$$\Pi = -P \qquad\qquad\quad \text{if } f_T \geq X.$$

Buying a put option on a futures, like buying a put option on an asset, is a bearish strategy that has a limited loss, the put premium, and a large but limited potential gain.

The breakeven futures price at expiration is X − P. This is the same as that for a put option on the spot, provided that the two puts expire simultaneously.

As an example, consider the Treasury bond December 110 put option on futures. The cost of the put is $2.515625. Because the multiplier is 1,000, the total premium is $2,515.625. Figure 12.7 illustrates the profit for various futures prices at expiration.

Suppose the futures price at expiration is 102. Then the investor buys the futures at 102 and exercises the put, selling the futures at 110. The profit is 110 − 102 − 2.515625 (the cost of the put) = $5.484375 times the multiplier (1,000), or $5.484375(1,000) = $5,484.375. If the futures price at expiration is above 110, the put expires worthless and the investor loses the put premium of $2,515.625. The breakeven futures price is 110 − 2.515625 = 107.484375. The maximum profit occurs if the futures price goes to zero. The profit would then be 1,000(110 − 2.515625) = $107,484.

The investor should also consider the effect of different exercise prices and different holding periods. These issues are the same as for options on the spot.

Write a Covered Call Option on Futures

Recall from Chapter 6 that a covered call is a strategy in which the investor purchases the underlying instrument and writes a call. When the underlying instrument is a stock, the covered call protects the investor against a

| FIGURE 12.7 | Buy Put Option on Futures |

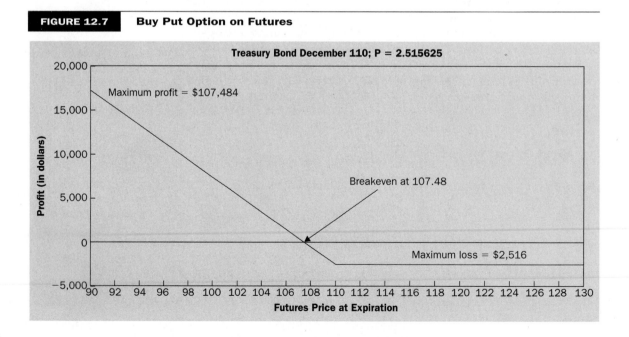

substantial decrease in the stock price. If that happens, the call will expire worthless and the investor will retain the premium. If the stock price rises above the exercise price at expiration, the call will be exercised and the investor will have effectively sold the stock for the exercise price.

The covered call option on futures is similar. A long position in a futures contract can be protected by selling a call option. If the futures price falls and the call ends up out-of-the-money, the investor retains the premium, which cushions the loss on the futures. If the futures price rises and the call is exercised, the investor effectively sells the futures contract at the exercise price.

The profit from a single long futures contract is

A covered call on a futures, like a covered call on an asset, reduces downside losses at the expense of upside gains.

$$\Pi = f_T - f_0.$$

The profit from a short call option on the futures is

$$\Pi = Max(0, f_T - X) + C.$$

Combining these into the covered call strategy gives a profit of

$$\Pi = f_T - f_0 - Max(0, f_T - X) + C.$$

The profit at expiration for the two cases is

$$\Pi = f_T - f_0 - f_T + X + C = X - f_0 + C \qquad \text{if } f_T > X$$
$$\Pi = f_T - f_0 + C \qquad \text{if } f_T \leq X.$$

The breakeven futures price at expiration is $f_0 - C$.

Figure 12.8 illustrates the possible outcomes for the covered call using the Treasury bond December 110 call. The dashed line shows the profit if only the futures position is taken. The call price is 1.234375, and the futures price is 108.71875. Suppose the futures price at expiration is 114. Then the call is exercised. The covered call writer is assigned a short futures contract at 110, which offsets the long futures position established at 108.71875. This leaves a profit of $110 - 108.71875 + 1.234375 = 2.515625$. Multiplying this by 1,000 gives the overall profit of $1,000(\$2.515625) = \$2,515.625$. If the futures price ends up at 100, the futures contract produces a loss of $108.71875 - 100 = 8.71875$. This is partially offset by the call premium of 1.234375, leaving a net loss of 7.484375. Multiplying by 1,000 gives a loss of $1,000(7.484375) = \$7,484.375$. The breakeven futures price is $108.71875 - 1.234375 = 107.484375$. The maximum loss occurs when the futures price goes to zero. The loss is $\$1,000(108.71875 - 1.234375) = \$107,484$.

Any strategy that can be executed with options on the spot can also be executed with options on futures. Some end-of-chapter problems ask you

| FIGURE 12.8 | Covered Call Option on Futures |

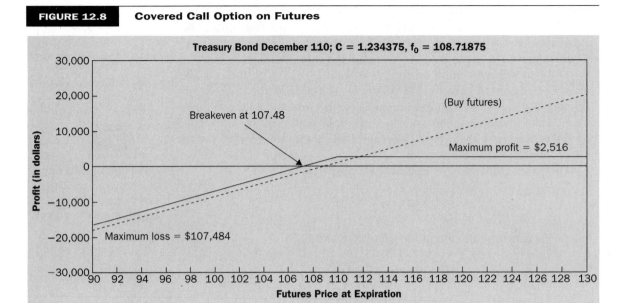

to apply options on futures to strategies that are not covered in this chapter but are covered under options on the spot.

Options on Futures versus Options on the Spot

So far, we have seen that options on futures are equivalent to options on the spot when the options are European and the futures and options expire simultaneously. In this section, we shall introduce some real-world factors that make options on futures unique.

Consider an American call option on the spot and one on the futures. Assume the spot instrument does not pay a dividend. As we already know, the call on the spot will not be exercised early. The call on the futures may be exercised early if it is sufficiently in-the-money. We know that the futures price is given by the formula

$$f_0 = S_0(1 + r)^T.$$

From the formula, it is apparent that prior to expiration the futures price is always higher than the spot price. Thus, an option on the futures is an option on a higher-priced instrument than is an option on the spot. Accordingly, its price should be higher. This is true, however, only because of the early exercise possibility. If the option could not or would not be exercised early, it would be equivalent to an option on the spot. We observed this point in our treatment of the binomial model for pricing options on futures.

A similar line of reasoning holds for puts. A put option on a futures is an option to sell a higher-priced instrument—the futures. Because of the possibility of early exercise, the put will be priced lower than the put on the spot instrument itself.

If we add dividends to the picture, things can get very complicated. Dividends lower the spread between the futures and spot prices and, if high enough, can make the futures price be less than the spot price, thus complicating the relationship further.

If the option on the futures expires before the option on the spot, it should be obvious that even European options on the spot and those on the futures are not equivalent. Even if they expire simultaneously and are European, there are other reasons why these instruments have their own unique properties.

The option on the futures can be more attractive because the underlying futures contract is more liquid, or easier to transact in, than the underlying spot instrument. As an example, options on Treasury bond futures at the Chicago Board of Trade have been far more popular than options on Treasury bonds at the Chicago Board Options Exchange. One reason is that the T-bond futures market is much more liquid than the T-bond spot market. Because exercise may require establishing a position in the underlying instrument, the underlying instrument's liquidity is important to the option trader. Even if the option is not exercised, pricing the option off of the more liquid futures market is better than pricing it off of the spot market.[3] This is particularly true in agricultural markets where the spot market is highly decentralized, which is one reason why there are no options on agricultural commodities.

While options on futures can be similar to and sometimes virtually identical to options on the spot, real world characteristics allow them to uniquely meet certain investors' needs.

Suppose an investor wishes to construct a hedge, covered call, or protective put using the S&P 500. The option on the spot would require the investor to simultaneously purchase the S&P 500 stocks in the appropriate proportions. The same strategy with the option on the futures would require only a position in the futures and the option. Obviously it would be easier to transact in the futures market than in the spot market.

Exercise of an option on the spot requires delivery of the underlying instrument. Although the possibility is somewhat remote, there is at least some likelihood that there would be a shortage of the deliverable instrument. This is more likely to occur with agricultural commodities, but it could happen with a Treasury bond or note. If using the option on the futures, one need not be concerned about obtaining the underlying commodity. Futures contracts can be created in virtually unlimited quantities. If a European option and the futures expire simultaneously, however, the option holder or writer must immediately execute an opposite transaction in the futures market to avoid having to make or take delivery on the futures contract, unless the futures is cash settled.

---

[3]The futures market still must price the futures contract off of the spot market.

Finally, we come to what may well be the key attraction of options on futures. Options on spot instruments have traded on the CBOE and several stock exchanges for many years. Individuals who held memberships in the futures exchanges could not easily trade options on the other exchanges. If they wished to trade options, they had to place orders through brokers, who would execute the trades on the CBOE and the stock exchanges. When options on futures were introduced, they gave futures traders the opportunity to trade both futures and options. For most contracts, the trading pits for the options and the underlying futures are adjacent. This greatly facilitated simultaneous trading of the option and the underlying futures. Because options on stocks do not trade side by side with the underlying stocks, futures traders have an advantage over members of the stock and option exchanges. Thus, much of the success of options on futures has come from local traders. That is not meant to imply, however, that the public has not traded these instruments. As noted earlier in this section, options on futures have many attractive features not offered by options on the spot, but neither instrument has a clear advantage over the other. Each is unique and fills the needs of a given clientele of investors and traders.

Summary

This chapter examined options on futures. These contracts are very similar to options on the spot instrument. Most of the basic rules for pricing these two types of options are similar. In particular, if the futures price equals the spot price compounded at the risk-free rate and the options expire simultaneously, a European option on the spot and a European option on the futures are equivalent. The lower bounds, put-call parity, and the Black option on futures pricing model are equivalent to their counterparts in options on the spot. The performance of trading strategies is also identical.

The chapter discussed several important differences between these two types of options. Prices of American options on the spot differ from those of American options on futures. In addition, options on futures may have more liquidity in the underlying instruments, the futures. Moreover, the options and the underlying futures trade side by side, which offers advantages to floor traders who must execute arbitrage transactions quickly.

Throughout this book we have examined linkages between spot and derivative markets. We saw that put-call parity, put-call-forward/futures parity, the cost of carry forward/futures pricing model, and the Black-Scholes model provide the linkages between these markets. We illustrated those relationships for derivatives on a stock in Figures 3.11, 5.20, 9.9, and 11.2, with each figure building on the previous one. Figure 12.9 introduces options on futures. Although the figure is now quite crowded with lines, it still provides an organized picture of the relationships between these markets. Note the important role that the risk-free bond plays in virtually all the re-

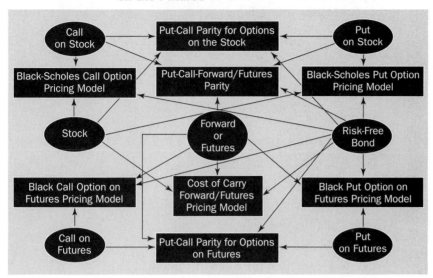

FIGURE 12.9   **The Linkage between Forwards/Futures, Stock, Bonds, Options on the Stock, and Options on the Futures**

lationships. Also remember that while the Black-Scholes call (or put) option pricing model is equivalent to the Black call (or put) option pricing model, under the usual assumptions, they are illustrated separately here. In addition, put-call forward/futures parity and put-call parity are equivalent, as a result of the cost of carry relationship between the spot and forward/futures prices. Thus, in general, these markets are all highly related by the readiness of all investors to execute the arbitrage transactions that generate risk-free profits and quickly force prices back in line.

In the next chapter, we shall examine some more widely traded but different instruments: derivatives on foreign currencies.

Key Terms

Before continuing to Chapter 13, you should be able to give brief definitions of the following terms.
• options on futures/commodity options/futures options
• Black model

Further Reading

The following provides practical information on the use of options on futures:

Labuszewski, J. *Trading Options on Futures*. New York: John Wiley, 2000.

Questions and Problems

1. Use the following data from January 31 of a particular year for a group of March 480 options on futures contract to answer parts a through g.

> Futures price: 483.10
> Expiration: March 18
> Risk-free rate: .0284 percent (simple)
> Call price: 6.95
> Put price: 5.25

   a. Determine the intrinsic value of the call.

   b. Determine the time value of the call.

   c. Determine the lower bound of the call.

   d. Determine the intrinsic value of the put.

   e. Determine the time value of the put.

   f. Determine the lower bound of the put.

   g. Determine whether put-call parity holds.

2. The put-call parity rule can be expressed as $C - P = (f_0 - X)(1 + r)^{-T}$. Consider the following data: $f_0 = 102$, $X = 100$, $r = .1$, $T = .25$, $C = 4$, and $P = 1.75$. A few calculations will show that the prices do not conform to the rule. Suggest an arbitrage strategy and show how it can be used to capture a risk-free profit. Assume no transaction costs. Be sure your answer shows the payoffs at expiration and proves these payoffs are riskless.

3. Explain why American call options on futures could be exercised early when call options on the spot are not. Assume no dividends.

4. Assume a standard deviation of .08, and use the Black model to determine if the call option in problem 1 is correctly priced. If not, suggest a riskless hedge strategy.

5. Describe two problems in using the Black option on futures pricing model for pricing options on Eurodollar futures.

6. Using the information in problem 4, calculate the price of the put described in problem 1 using the Black model for pricing puts.

7. Explain why the futures option pricing model is simply a pricing model for options on instruments with a zero cost of carry.

8. In Chapter 5, we examined the sensitivity of a call's price to different risk-free rates and volatilities. Compute the Black option on futures price using the data for the call given in problems 1 and 4 for the following risk-free rates and standard deviations. Use either the Excel spreadsheet bsbin2.xls or the Windows program bsbwin2.1.exe.

   a. Use risk-free rates of 1 through 10 percent in increments of 100 basis points. We know that the call price should increase as we increase r_c. What do you notice about the results? Try to explain. (Hint: Remember that $f_0 = S_0 e^{r_c T}$.)

  b. Use standard deviations of .05 through .50 in increments of .05. Comment on what you find.

9. An asset worth 100 can go up by 10 percent or down by 7 percent. The risk-free rate is 4 percent. There are options with an exercise price of 100. There are no dividends. Find the values of the following options. Assume two periods until expiration.

  a. A European call on the asset

  b. An American call on the asset

  c. A European call on the futures

  d. An American call on the futures

10. Find the implied volatility, to three decimal places, of the call in problem 4 if the call is worth 7.25. Use either the Excel spreadsheet bsbin2.xls or the Windows program bsbwin2.1.exe.

11. Evaluate the following statement: "Dividends are relevant to the pricing of European call options but not to the pricing of European call options on futures. Amazingly enough, this is true even though the two calls will have the same price."

Problems 12 through 15 and 17 use some options on futures prices on January 31 of a particular year. Determine the profit from the strategy for each of the following futures prices at expiration: 470, 475, 480, 485, 490, 495. Graph the results. Determine the breakeven futures price at expiration. Use a multiplier of 500.

12. The March 485 call price is 4.875. Construct a simple long call position.

13. The March 485 put price is 6.75. Construct a simple long put position.

14. The March futures price is 483.10. Using the March call data from problem 12, construct a covered call position.

15. Using the information in problems 13 and 14, construct a protective put with the March 485 put.

16. Discuss why options on futures have advantages not offered by options on the spot.

17. (Concept Problem) Redo problem 12, but close the position on March 1. The calls expire March 18. Let σ = .08 and r_c = .028. You may wish to use the Excel spreadsheet bsbin2.xls or the Windows program bsbwin2.1.exe to save time making these calculations.

18. (Concept Problem) Use the following information to calculate the call option price using the Black model: f_0 = 30, X = 25, r_c = .08, σ = .35, and T = .125. Determine the option's delta. Then recommend a risk-free hedge position, and show why the position is risk-free by evaluating its performance if the futures price decreases by $1. Use the Excel spreadsheet bsbin2.xls or the Windows program bsbwin2.1.exe.

APPENDIX 12

Selected Options on Futures Contract Specifications

This table includes only certain information for the 10 most active options on futures contracts. Other information can be obtained from the source of the table.

Contract	Size	Expirations Available	Exercise Price Increments	Minimum Price Change
Treasury Bonds (CBOT)	One $100,000 futures contract	Mar, Jun, Sep, Dec	1 point	1/64 = $15.625
Eurodollars (CME)	One $1,000,000 futures contract	Each month of current cycle	25 points	1/4 point = $6.25
10-year Treasury Notes (CBOT)	One $100,000 futures contract	Mar, Jun, Sep, Dec	1 point	1/64 = $15.625
5-year Treasury Notes (CBOT)	One $100,000 futures contract	Mar, Jun, Sep, Dec	1/2 point	1/64 = $15.625
S&P 500 (CME)	One $250 × index futures contract	Each month of current cycle	5 points	0.05 point = $12.50
Corn (CBOT)	One 5,000-bushel futures contract	Mar, May, Jul, Sep, Nov, Dec, Jan	$0.10	1/8¢/bu. = $6.25
Soybeans (CBOT)	One 5,000-bushel futures contract	Mar, May, Jul, Aug, Sep, Nov, Jan	$0.25	1/8¢/bu. = $6.25
Sugar (NYBOT)	One 112,000-lb. futures contract	Monthly	1/2¢	1/100¢ = $11.20
Crude Oil (NYMEX)	One 1,000-bbl. futures contract	Monthly	$0.50	1¢/bbl. = $10
Natural Gas (NYMEX)	One 10,000-MMBtu futures contract	Monthly	$0.05	0.01¢/MMBtu = $10

SOURCE: *The Wall Street Journal* and *Futures 2000 Source Book,* published by *Futures* magazine. This information is believed to be correct as of February 2000, but contract specifications sometimes change. Also, there are a few exceptions to the above rules for certain options. Consult the exchanges for more details.

CHAPTER 13

Foreign Currency Derivatives

People in countries with a weak currency learn fast about options.

BRIAN THOMAS, Bank of America

Asia Risk, November 1995

This chapter introduces the world of international finance and the exciting markets for currency derivatives. As in Chapter 12, it breaks away from the approach used previously, which has focused on concepts rather than on specific types of contracts. In the case of currency derivatives, a slightly different approach is necessary. Foreign currencies often are seen as exotic and confusing. While indeed some discipline is needed to organize one's thinking, in the end analyzing foreign currencies actually differs very little from analyzing ordinary stocks and bonds.

Characteristics of Foreign Currencies and Markets

The Nature of Exchange Rates

Each country has a designated currency. In the United States, of course, it is the dollar. In the United Kingdom it is the British pound (sometimes called the sterling), in Switzerland the Swiss franc, in Japan the Japanese yen, and in Canada the Canadian dollar. To settle transactions among individuals, corporations, and governments in different countries, there is a rate at which the currency of one country can be converted into the currency of another. That rate is called the **exchange rate**.

For example, suppose you wish to convert U.S. dollars into British pounds. The exchange rate is $1.40 per pound. We denote this as $1.40/£, where £ is the symbol for pounds. Each pound is convertible into $1.40. Conversely, each dollar can be converted into 1/$1.40, or .7143 pounds.

Chapter Objectives

■ To describe the structure of international financial markets

■ To illustrate how to read foreign currency spot, forward, futures, and options price quotations in *The Wall Street Journal*

■ To present the principles of pricing foreign currency forwards and futures, including the cross-rate relationship and interest rate parity

■ To present the principles of pricing foreign currency options, including the intrinsic value, lower bound, and put-call parity

■ To present the Garman-Kohlhagen foreign currency option pricing model

■ To illustrate several foreign currency forward, futures, and options trading strategies

■ To illustrate the execution and pricing of a currency swap and the valuation of a currency swap during its life

A foreign currency is simply another asset. The exchange rate is the price at which the asset can be bought.

We can express the exchange rate as the dollar cost of pounds, $1.40, or the pound cost of dollars, £.7143.

This line of thinking often causes some confusion. An easy way to understand the exchange rate is to always think in terms of a single currency—normally your domestic currency—and treat the foreign currency as if it were an asset, which it is. Just as you can buy stocks, bonds, wheat, or gold, so can you buy a foreign currency. When you convert dollars into pounds, you are simply buying an asset that happens to be pounds. When you convert back into dollars, you are selling the asset (pounds). The difference in the dollar price at which you buy the pounds and the dollar price at which you sell them generates a profit or loss that results from changes in the exchange rate.

A Brief History of Foreign Currency Markets

From the early nineteenth to the mid-twentieth century, gold was the standard to which most countries fixed their currencies. International transactions were settled in gold, and most currency rates were expressed as a fixed ratio to the price of gold. In 1944, a group of Allied nations met in Bretton Woods, New Hampshire, and established the International Monetary Fund. As part of the agreement, each nation fixed its currency in relation to the gold content of the dollar. Currency rates were allowed to fluctuate within a very narrow range, but foreign governments were obligated to execute the necessary buying and selling of their currencies and the dollar to keep the exchange rate relatively stable. For the most part, exchange rates were fixed.

The system worked well as long as there was confidence that the fixed exchange rate accurately reflected the value of a given currency. When it did not, there was significant buying and selling of that currency. For example, if investors thought, as they did in the late 1940s, that the British pound was overvalued, they would sell pounds. With the price of pounds fixed, no one wanted to hold pounds. The British government was forced to devalue the pound, which meant lowering its official exchange rate.

By the late 1960s, the United States was running a record balance-of-payments deficit. This meant the United States was paying out more dollars than it was taking in. As foreigners were accumulating large quantities of dollars that were quickly losing value in light of record U.S. inflation levels, the dollar came under pressure and finally was devalued by the U.S. government in 1971. At the same time, the dollar's convertibility to gold was suspended. The Bretton Woods system had failed.

An interim system that developed in 1972, called the Smithsonian Agreement, allowed a wider range in which currencies could fluctuate, but it all too quickly proved inadequate. In 1973, the exchange rates of several countries began to fluctuate freely. Ultimately all exchange rates of free countries fluctuated with market conditions.

Over the years the major countries of Europe have attempted to coordinate their monetary policies, with the ultimate goal being a unified Europe with a single currency. In 1979 the Federal Republic of Germany proposed a system in which the European countries attempted to keep their currencies in line with each other. Not all countries participated, however, and the weaker participating currencies came under pressure as their values were held artificially to a narrow range with respect to the stronger currencies. This system was called the European Monetary System (EMS) and currently consists of Austria, Belgium, Denmark, Finland, France, Germany, Greece, Ireland, Italy, Luxembourg, Netherlands, Portugal, Spain, Sweden, and the United Kingdom. Germany was the strongest currency, a result of a tight monetary policy that limited inflation to less than 2 percent. Other countries were forced to align their monetary policies with that of Germany. In 1990 the unification of the two Germanys placed further pressure on the system. Germany's budget deficit grew along with its inflation and interest rates. Other countries were forced to follow similar economic policies. A massive recession hit Europe at the same time that it was attempting to move toward the goal of economic integration by 1992 and a single currency. Other countries wanted to enact policies that would stimulate economic growth while Germany held the line toward tight economic policies to keep its own inflation under control. Several countries began to oppose the single currency concept. In September 1992, Great Britain and Italy, which had two of the weaker currencies, withdrew from the EMS, meaning that they would no longer support their currencies by buying them in the international markets. These currencies fell and interest rates declined. The EMS fell apart and for a few days the currency markets went into turmoil.

Since that time conditions have stabilized, and most of the major economic powers of Europe have joined forces to unite Europe with a single currency. In 1995, France, Germany, Austria, Belgium, Luxembourg, Spain, Finland, Ireland, Italy, Netherlands, and Portugal announced that they would create a new currency, called the **euro** and denoted with the symbol €, to be phased in over several years. On January 1, 1999, the euro was fixed at the following values:

6.5597	French francs
1.95583	German marks
13.7603	Austrian schillings
40.3399	Belgian francs
40.3399	Luxembourg francs
166.386	Spanish pesetas
5.94573	Finnish marks
0.787564	Irish punts
1936.27	Italian lira
2.20371	Netherlands florins
200.482	Portugese escudos

During 1999 these currencies continued to exist, but individuals and organizations began using the euro in noncash transactions. Financial market transactions (spot, forward, futures, options, and swaps) were conducted in euros as well as the preceding currencies. Individuals could open checking accounts and pay for goods and services in euros, either by check or credit card. Euro coins and paper money, however, will not be introduced until January 1, 2002. Payments can be made in the individual currencies until December 31, 2001. During the early part of 2002, these currencies will gradually be phased out. Coins can be exchanged for euros for about a year and paper notes can be exchanged for euros for about 10 more years.

The creation of the euro was probably the most significant event in international financial history. When these 11 individual country currencies cease to exist, there will be a significantly smaller number of distinct risks that a company will face. Consider a company with operations all over Europe. In the pre-euro period, it would have to deal with exchange rate risk for each currency. To send money from one country to another would require the purchase of one currency with another. Once the euro is created, the multitude of currencies will be reduced to a single currency. Of course, many major countries are not part of the euro system. In Europe, Great Britain and Switzerland are important nonparticipants as well as Norway and Sweden. Japan is obviously another major currency that continues its autonomy.

Just as we have previously discussed a Eurodollar deposit, we shall now have to use a comparable instrument. The introduction of the euro has led to the creation of a standard euro deposit, similar to the Eurodollar. There are, however, two officially quoted rates on this deposit. One is called **Euribor,** which stands for European Interbank Offered Rate, and is an average of rates quoted by various banks. It is published by the European Banking Federation, an organization of banks in the various member countries. Another rate occasionally heard is **EuroLIBOR,** which is an average of the rates for euro deposits among London banks and is published by the British Bankers Association. Although derivative transactions can be done based on either rate, Euribor is the more commonly quoted rate and the one we shall use here.

In the rest of the chapter, be careful not to confuse a European option with an option on the euro. The word "euro," like the word "dollar," is never capitalized. Thus, you may see a European option, an option on the euro, or a European option on the euro, and you should be able to easily tell the difference.

Figure 13.1 illustrates the behavior of the euro and the British pound during the euro's first year. In 1999 the dollar was quite strong, and consequently the euro, which began at about $1.18, ended the year down to about $1.01. As shown on the graph, the British pound did not fare much better against the dollar. The Japanese yen, however, strengthened against the dollar in 1999.

For our purposes in understanding the currency derivatives markets, the volatility of exchanges rates should be viewed as a source of risk for companies doing business in more than one country. What causes these currency fluctuations? One major factor is a nation's balance of payments. As a country exports more than it imports, the demand for its currency in-

FIGURE 13.1   Dollar Value of the Euro and British Pound, 1999

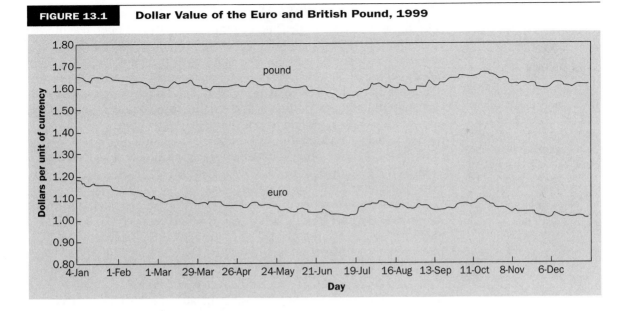

creases. At some point, however, the currency becomes so expensive that the country's goods become prohibitively costly. This leads to a decrease in exports and a lower demand for the currency. A nation running a trade deficit finds the demand for its currency weakening. This lowers its currency's value and ultimately makes its currency, and hence its goods, cheap. This reverses the cycle and turns it into a trade surplus. Unfortunately, there are so many other factors involved that the system never quite works as the theory says it should.

For example, exchange rates are clearly influenced by economic conditions in a country, such as inflation and interest rates. If inflation is high, there is little confidence in the currency, and this weakens the demand for it. High interest rates attract foreigners to the currency; however, if interest rates are high because of high inflation, the effect may be offset. Government policies and political instability are still other factors that influence currency values.

Foreign Currency Spot and Forward Markets

The market for the exchange of foreign currency is large and sophisticated. Major financial institutions and central banks in the various countries are linked through computers and telecommunication systems. Transactions are executed quickly and efficiently.

The spot market is the market for immediate delivery of the foreign currency. This is done by book entry, which is made possible by the fact that the major banks in a given country have accounts with their counterparts in

A currency forward contract is an agreement between two parties in which one party agrees to buy the currency from the other party at a later date at an exchange rate agreed upon today.

other countries. There is also a large forward market for foreign currency. Like the spot market, there is no central marketplace; it operates through telecommunication systems linking the major financial institutions. For example, if a corporation will need £1 million in 90 days, it can call a major money center bank, which will enter into a forward contract to deliver the pounds at that time. Recall that in a forward contract the price, which is the exchange rate, is agreed upon at the time the transaction is initiated. No money initially changes hands, but the bank may require a small margin deposit. Ninety days later, the corporation acquires the pounds at the forward price. As in the other forward contracts we have covered, each party assumes the credit risk of the other. This market for trading currencies by banks is called the **interbank market.**

The foreign currency interbank market is extremely large. Although the transactions are private and are not officially reported, some information is obtained by the Bank for International Settlements (BIS). The BIS conducts semiannual surveys of the derivatives positions of banks around the world. At December 1999, the BIS estimated that the notional value of foreign currency forward contracts was about $9.6 trillion, with these contracts having a market value of about $350 billion. That this market developed so rapidly and has operated so efficiently has made room for further developments in the form of foreign currency swaps and options, which we shall cover later. Today the global market for foreign currency spot, forwards, swaps, and options is one large and unified market.

Figure 13.2 illustrates a sample of foreign currency spot rates from *The Wall Street Journal* for the trading day of January 31, 2000. For many of the major countries, there are also 1-month, 3-month, and 6-month forward quotes. The rates are quoted in both U.S. dollars and foreign currency units per U.S. dollar.

Look at the Swiss franc quotes. The spot rate for Swiss francs is $0.6056, while the spot rate for dollars is 1/$0.6056, or SFR1.6512. The 1-month forward rate is $0.6073 or SFR1.6465. Because the forward rates in dollars increase the longer the horizon, the Swiss franc is said to be selling at a **forward premium** and the dollar at a **forward discount.**

Foreign Currency Futures Markets

During the transition to freely floating exchange rates in 1972, the Chicago Mercantile Exchange established the International Monetary Market for the trading of futures contracts in foreign currencies. We already are familiar with the IMM's T-bill and Eurodollar contracts. The foreign currency contracts, however, actually were the first financial futures contracts.

The foreign currency futures contracts call for delivery of a specified number of units of the foreign currency. Prices are always quoted in dollars per unit of that currency. Let us take the British pound contract as an example.

FIGURE 13.2	Foreign Currency Spot and Forward Quotations in *The Wall Street Journal*, Trading Day, July 14, 2000

CURRENCY TRADING

Friday, July 14, 2000

EXCHANGE RATES

The New York foreign exchange mid-range rates below apply to trading among banks in amounts of $1 million and more, as quoted at 4 p.m. Eastern time by Reuters and other sources. Retail transactions provide fewer units of foreign currency per dollar. Rates for the 11 Euro currency countries are derived from the latest dollar-euro rate using the exchange ratios set 1/1/99.

	U.S. $ equiv.		Currency per U.S. $	
Country	Fri	Thu	Fri	Thu
Argentina (Peso)	1.0006	1.0002	.9994	.9998
Australia (Dollar)	.5839	.5839	1.7125	1.7125
Austria (Schilling)	.06814	.06810	14.676	14.684
Bahrain (Dinar)	2.6525	2.6525	.3770	.3770
Belgium (Franc)	.0232	.0232	43.0246	43.0476
Brazil (Real)	.5548	.5520	1.8025	1.8115
Britain (Pound)	1.4993	1.5028	.6670	.6654
1-month forward	1.5001	1.5036	.6666	.6651
3-months forward	1.5019	1.5053	.6658	.6643
6-months forward	1.5050	1.5084	.6645	.6630
Canada (Dollar)	.6739	.6747	1.4840	1.4821
1-month forward	.6744	.6752	1.4829	1.4810
3-months forward	.6754	.6762	1.4807	1.4788
6-months forward	.6771	.6779	1.4769	1.4751
Chile (Peso)	.001841	.001850	543.05	540.60
China (Renminbi)	.1208	.1208	8.2796	8.2791
Colombia (Peso)	.0004658	.0004621	2146.75	2164.00
Czech. Rep. (Koruna)				
Commercial rate	.02639	.02631	37.890	38.003
Denmark (Krone)	.1257	.1256	7.9525	7.9605
Ecuador (Sucre)				
Floating rate	.00004000	.00004000	25000.00	25000.00
Finland (Markka)	.1577	.1576	6.3414	6.3448
France (Franc)	.1429	.1429	6.9961	6.9999
1-month forward	.1432	.1431	6.9829	6.9867
3-months forward	.1437	.1436	6.9582	6.9621
6-months forward	.1444	.1443	6.9242	6.9281
Germany (Mark)	.4794	.4791	2.0860	2.0871
1-month forward	.4803	.4800	2.0820	2.0832
3-months forward	.4820	.4817	2.0747	2.0759
6-months forward	.4844	.4841	2.0645	2.0657
Greece (Drachma)	.002784	.002783	359.17	359.27
Hong Kong (Dollar)	.1283	.1283	7.7961	7.7955
Hungary (Forint)	.003605	.003602	277.42	277.65
India (Rupee)	.02237	.02237	44.705	44.705
Indonesia (Rupiah)	.0001051	.0001059	9515.00	9445.00
Ireland (Punt)	1.1905	1.1899	.8400	.8404
Israel (Shekel)	.2438	.2445	4.1015	4.0900
Italy (Lira)	.0004842	.0004840	2065.13	2066.24

	U.S. $ equiv.		Currency per U.S. $	
Country	Fri	Thu	Fri	Thu
Japan (Yen)	.009261	.009240	107.98	108.22
1-month forward	.009312	.009291	107.39	107.63
3-months forward	.009415	.009394	106.22	106.46
6-months forward	.009574	.009551	104.46	104.70
Jordan (Dinar)	1.4085	1.4085	.7100	.7100
Kuwait (Dinar)	3.2563	3.2563	.3071	.3071
Lebanon (Pound)	.0006609	.0006609	1513.00	1513.00
Malaysia (Ringgit)-b	.2632	.2632	3.8000	3.8000
Malta (Lira)	2.3020	2.3026	.4344	.4343
Mexico (Peso)				
Floating rate	.1067	.1057	9.3685	9.4630
Netherland (Guilder)	.4255	.4252	2.3504	2.3516
New Zealand (Dollar)	.4610	.4598	2.1692	2.1749
Norway (Krone)	.1150	.1149	8.6978	8.7028
Pakistan (Rupee)	.01913	.01913	52.275	52.275
Peru (new Sol)	.2877	.2874	3.4758	3.4800
Philippines (Peso)	.02245	.02235	44.550	44.750
Poland (Zloty)-d	.2311	.2319	4.3270	4.3115
Portugal (Escudo)	.004677	.004674	213.82	213.94
Russia (Ruble)-a	.03590	.03591	27.855	27.848
Saudi Arabia (Riyal)	.2666	.2666	3.7508	3.7508
Singapore (Dollar)	.5736	.5737	1.7435	1.7430
Slovak Rep. (Koruna)	.02195	.02188	45.563	45.709
South Africa (Rand)	.1451	.1459	6.8900	6.8525
South Korea (Won)	.0008986	.0009005	1112.80	1110.55
Spain (Peseta)	.005635	.005632	177.46	177.55
Sweden (Krona)	.1125	.1123	8.8928	8.9083
Switzerland (Franc)	.6056	.6047	1.6512	1.6538
1-month forward	.6073	.6064	1.6465	1.6491
3-months forward	.6106	.6096	1.6376	1.6403
6-months forward	.6154	.6144	1.6249	1.6276
Taiwan (Dollar)	.03244	.03244	30.825	30.825
Thailand (Baht)	.02498	.02503	40.025	39.955
Turkey (Lira)	.00000159	.00000159	628320.00	627590.00
United Arab (Dirham)	.2723	.2723	3.6728	3.6728
Uruguay (New Peso)				
Financial	.08225	.08214	12.158	12.175
Venezuela (Bolivar)	.001460	.001460	685.00	684.75
	— — —			
SDR	1.3201	1.3226	.7575	.7561
Euro	.9376	.9371	1.0666	1.0671

Special Drawing Rights (SDR) are based on exchange rates for the U.S., German, British, French, and Japanese currencies. Source: International Monetary Fund.

a-Russian Central Bank rate. Trading band lowered on 8/17/98. b-Government rate. d-Floating rate; trading band suspended on 4/11/00. Foreign exchange rates are available from Readers' Reference Service (413) 592-3600.

A currency futures contract is an agreement between two parties in which one party agrees to buy the currency from the other party at a later date at an exchange rate agreed upon today. It trades on a futures exchange and works essentially the same as any other type of futures contract.

The pound contract calls for delivery of 62,500 pounds. The price is quoted in dollars per pound. For example, if the contract price is $1.5612, the actual price is $1.5612(62,500) = $97,575. The expiration months are March, June, September, and December. The contract expires on the second business day before the third Wednesday of the month. Contract specifications for the major IMM foreign currency contracts are provided in Appendix 13.

Figure 13.3 presents the historical volume of trading in foreign currency futures since 1981. We see that volume has declined in recent years to levels that were more characteristic of the late 1980s. Although the figure does not show the volume by contract, the most active is the Japanese yen, followed closely by the Swiss franc. The British pound, the German mark (which will be in existence only for a couple more years), the Canadian dollar, and the euro follow in trading volume.

Figure 13.4 illustrates the foreign currency futures quotations in *The Wall Street Journal*. In the quotes for the euro, the first line indicates that the contract is at the CME (Chicago Mercantile Exchange), it covers 125,000 euros, and the quote is in dollars per euro. The first four columns are the

FIGURE 13.3   **Foreign Currency Futures Volume in U.S., 1981–1999**

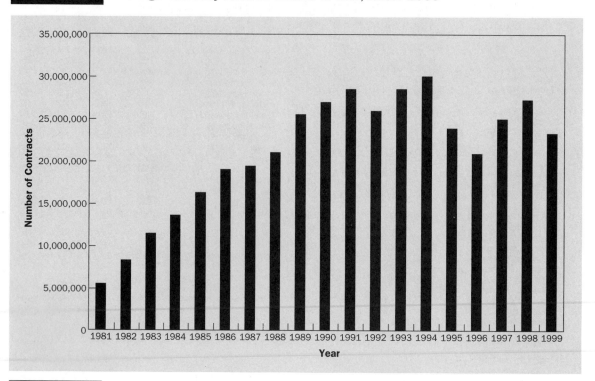

SOURCE: CFTC *Annual Reports*

FIGURE 13.4	Foreign Currency Futures Quotations in *The Wall Street Journal*, Trading Day, July 14, 2000

CURRENCY

	Open	High	Low	Settle	Change	Lifetime High	Low	Open Interest
JAPAN YEN (CME)-12.5 million yen; $ per yen (.00)								
Sept	.9352	.9405	.9327	.9372	+ .0028	1.0272	.9300	54,013
Dec	.9522	.9535	.9485	.9526	+ .0028	1.0434	.9225	3,058
Est vol 10,390; vol Thu 13,052; open int 57,141, +20.								
DEUTSCHEMARK (CME)-125,000 marks; $ per mark								
Sept	.4809	.4815	.4788	.4813	+ .0007	.5250	.4596	677
Est vol 57; vol Thu 58; open int 682, +39.								
CANADIAN DOLLAR (CME)-100,000 dlrs.; $ per Can $								
Sept	.6761	.6765	.6740	.6753	− .0009	.7017	.6623	61,123
Dec	.6762	.6770	.6755	.6770	− .0009	.7025	.6640	4,698
Mr01	....	....	....	.6787	− .0009	.7040	.6672	613
June	....	....	....	.6804	− .0009	.6990	.6695	155
Est vol 3,768; vol Thu 3,640; open int 66,603, −585.								
BRITISH POUND (CME)-62,500 pds.; $ per pound								
Sept	1.5042	1.5064	1.4986	1.4998	− .0038	1.6780	1.4700	33,055
Dec	....	....	....	1.5026	− .0038	1.6500	1.4730	286
Est vol 5,472; vol Thu 7,319; open int 33,345, +881.								
SWISS FRANC (CME)-125,000 francs; $ per franc								
Sept	.6079	.6095	.6057	.6091	+ .0014	.7063	.5783	32,844
Dec	.6104	.6137	.6104	.6140	+ .0014	.6687	.5850	104
Est vol 5,241; vol Thu 16,776; open int 32,949, −2,315.								
AUSTRALIAN DOLLAR (CME)-100,000 dlrs.; $ per A.$								
Sept	.5851	.5874	.5841	.5854	− .0003	.6699	.5672	16,475
Dec	.5865	.5870	.5855	.5864	− .0003	.6704	.5726	222
Mr01	....	....	....	.5874	− .0003	.6390	.5700	528
Est vol 375; vol Thu 2,790; open int 17,225, +578.								
MEXICAN PESO (CME)-500,000 new Mex. peso, $ per MP								
Sept	.10455	.10520	.10420	.10512	+ 00087	.10520	.08500	11,566
Dec	.10210	.10250	.10195	.10272	+ 00082	.10290	.09200	1,422
Mr01	.09950	.09980	.09950	.10020	+ 00082	.10005	.09120	591
Est vol 2,068; vol Thu 2,656; open int 13,642, −283.								
EURO FX (CME)-Euro 125,000; $ per Euro								
Sept	.9409	.9426	.9353	.9413	+ .0013	1.1136	.8991	54,769
Dec	.9423	.9465	.9410	.9460	+ .0013	1.0572	.9046	712
Est vol 11,394; vol Thu 12,534; open int 55,521, +292.								

SOURCE: *The Wall Street Journal*, July 17, 2000

open, high, low, and settlement prices. Thus, the September contract opened at $0.9409, reached a high of $0.9426, reached a low of $0.9353, and had a settlement price of $0.9413. The next column gives the change in the settlement price, which in this case was +$0.0013. The next two columns give the high and low over the contract's life, and the final column gives the open interest. The last line is a summary of the volume and open interest for all contracts.

Foreign Currency Options and Swaps Markets

Foreign currency options were introduced in 1982 at the Philadelphia Stock Exchange, and the Chicago Mercantile Exchange briefly offered them in the form of options on futures. Volume grew steadily until the early 1990s, when it stabilized and began falling. Today the Philadelphia Exchange's foreign currency options market can be considered only a moderately active market. Its quotes are available in *The Wall Street Journal*, a sample of which appears in Figure 13.5.

There is, nonetheless, an extremely large over-the-counter market for foreign currency options. These customized instruments are widely used by corporations and financial institutions to manage foreign exchange risk. As of December 1999, the Bank for International Settlements reported that over-the-counter currency options had a notional value, the amount of the underlying currency on which the option is based, of about $2.3 trillion and a market value of about $60 billion.

We have not covered swaps yet so a brief definition is necessary. A swap is a transaction in which two parties agree to exchange a series of cash payments at specific dates in the future. A currency swap is one particular type of swap that is of interest to us in this chapter. In a currency swap, the two

A currency option is an agreement between two parties in which one party pays a premium and receives the right to buy or sell a currency at a later date at an exchange rate agreed upon today.

FIGURE 13.5	**Foreign Currency Options Quotations in *The Wall Street Journal*, Trading Day, July 14, 2000**

OPTIONS
PHILADELPHIA EXCHANGE

	Calls Vol.	Last	Puts Vol.	Last
CDollr				67.53
50,000 Canadian Dollar EOM-European style				
68 Aug	20	0.27	...	0.01
Euro				93.64
62,500 Euro-cents per unit.				
92 Jul	35	1.61	...	...
94 Jul	...	...	16	0.47
94 Aug	...	0.01	15	1.18
Australian Dollar				58.50
50,000 Australian Dollars-European style.				
59½ Aug	20	0.35	...	0.01
50,000 Australian Dollars-cents per unit				
59 Jul	...	0.01	20	0.65
50,000 Australian Dollars-cents per unit.				
58½ Jul	...	...	160	0.10
British Pound				148.93
31,250 Brit. Pound EOM-European				
153 Aug	4	0.63	...	0.01

	Calls Vol.	Last	Puts Vol.	Last
31,250 Brit. Pounds-European Style.				
158 Jul	...	0.01	50	7.85
Canadian Dollar				67.47
50,000 Canadian Dollars-European Style.				
67½ Jul	...	0.01	20	0.14
Euro				93.64
62,500 Euro-European style.				
92 Jul	2	1.65	...	...
94 Jul	...	...	15	0.50
94 Aug	...	0.01	5	1.20
96 Jul	...	...	10	2.35
98 Jul	...	...	12	4.44

	Calls Vol.	Last	Puts Vol.	Last
Japanese Yen				92.32
6,250,000 J.Yen-100ths of a cent per unit.				
97 Jul	...	0.01	11	4.38
97 Sep	...	0.01	11	4.34
99 Jul	...	0.01	5	6.38
99 Sep	...	...	5	6.34
6,250,000 J.Yen-European Style.				
93 Jul	...	0.01	4	0.30
93 Aug	...	0.01	4	1.05
94 Aug	40	0.81	...	0.01
Swiss Franc				60.37
62,500 Swiss Francs-European Style.				
62½ Aug	...	0.01	16	2.15
63½ Sep	...	0.01	16	2.90
62,500 Swiss Francs-cents per unit.				
61 Jul	...	0.01	1	0.61
61 Aug	...	...	1	0.88
Call Vol 121			Open Int ...	10,139
Put Vol 459			Open Int ...	10,174

SOURCE: *The Wall Street Journal*, July 17, 2000

FIGURE 13.6	Currency Swap Notional Principal, Year-end 1987–1999

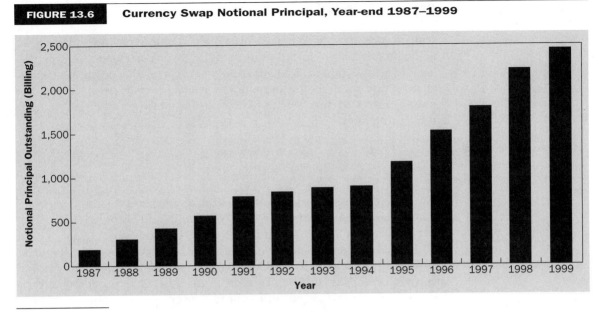

SOURCE: International Swaps and Derivatives Association, 1987–1997; Bank for International Settlements, 1998–1999.

parties agree to make a series of payments to each other in different currencies. The payments are based on interest rates in two countries. Thus, one party might make a series of interest payments to the other in U.S. dollars while the other party might make a series of payments to the first in euros. The interest payments are calculated based on a fixed amount of notional principal. The two parties also usually agree to make a final payment of the notional principal. Like forwards, futures, and options, these customized, over-the-counter instruments are widely used to manage foreign exchange risk. The Bank for International Settlements estimates that as of December 1999, the notional principal of currency swaps was about $2.4 trillion with a market value of about $250 billion. Figure 13.6 shows the history of currency swap notional principal from 1987 through 1999.

A currency swap is an agreement between two parties to exchange a series of payments at specific dates in which one series of payments is in one currency and the other is in another currency.

Pricing Foreign Currency Derivatives

Foreign currency derivatives are priced according to the same arbitrage principles we have used throughout this book. Applying these rules, however, is less straightforward than it is for ordinary derivatives. In this section, we shall look at some basic principles of pricing foreign currency derivatives.

Cross-Rate Relationships

Any three currencies are related to each other by the cross-rate relationship.

One of the most elementary principles is the **cross-rate** relationship among foreign currencies. Let us consider three currencies: the U.S. dollar, the British pound, and the euro. We express the dollar/pound exchange rate as \$/£, the euro/dollar exchange rate as €/\$, and the pound/euro exchange rate as £/€. Notice what we get when we multiply these three rates:

$$\left(\frac{\$}{£}\right)\left(\frac{€}{\$}\right)\left(\frac{£}{€}\right) = 1.$$

If this relationship does not hold, an arbitrageur can make a riskless profit. For example, consider the spot rates for pounds and euros in terms of dollars on January 31 of a particular year. The rates are \$1.6155/£ and €1.0304/\$. These rates imply that the price of euros in pounds should be £0.6007/€, since $(1.6155)(1.0304)(0.6007) = 1$. Now suppose the price of euros in pounds is £0.65/€. This means the euro is overvalued relative to the pound. An arbitrageur will want to convert euros to pounds. Here is how the transaction would be done.

Take 1 dollar and convert it to €1.0304. Then arrange for a currency dealer to convert the €1.0304 to $(1.0304)(0.65) = £0.6698$. Then convert the £0.6698 to $0.6698(1.6155) = \$1.0821$. This transaction is riskless and immediately earns a profit of 8.21 cents on a 1-dollar investment. The 8.21 percent return is the amount by which the euro is overvalued relative to the pound. In the real world, there would be a dealer bid-ask spread to cover and some modest transaction costs; however, we shall ignore these for this analysis.

The combined effects of numerous arbitrageurs would drive the exchange rate of euros for pounds down to £0.6007/€. This is the cross-rate relationship among any three currencies. Any two rates imply the third rate. The transaction that upholds this relationship is sometimes called **triangular arbitrage.** These relationships will hold for spot, forward, and futures exchange rates.

Interest Rate Parity

Interest rate parity is an important fundamental relationship between the spot and forward exchange rates and the interest rates in two countries. It is the foreign currency market's version of the cost-of-carry forward and futures pricing model that we discussed in Chapter 9. A helpful way to understand interest rate parity is to consider the position of someone who believes that a higher risk-free return can be earned by converting to a currency that pays a higher interest rate. For example, suppose a French corporate treasurer wants to earn more than the euro interest rate and be-lieves that he can convert euros to dollars and earn the higher U.S. rate. If the treasurer does so but fails to arrange a forward or futures contract to guarantee the rate at which the dollars will be converted back to euros, he runs the risk, not only of not earning the U.S. rate, but of earning less than the euro rate. If the dollar weakens while he is holding dollars, the conver-sion back to euros will be costly. This type of transaction is similar to going to a foreign country but not buying your ticket home until after you have been there a while. You are subject to whatever rates and conditions exist at the time the return ticket is purchased. Buying a round-trip ticket locks in the return price and conditions. Hence the corporate treasurer might wish to lock in the rate at which the dollars can be converted back to euros by selling a forward or futures contract on the dollar. But forward and futures prices will adjust so that the overall transaction will earn no more in euros than the euro interest rate. The cost of the return ticket will offset any in-terest rate gains while in the foreign currency. Consider the following situ-ation involving euros and U.S. dollars.

The spot exchange rate is S_0 . This quote is in euros per U.S. dollar. The U.S. risk-free interest rate is ρ, and the holding period is T. You take $S_0(1 + \rho)^{-T}$ euros and buy $(1 + \rho)^{-T}$ dollars. Simultaneously, you sell one forward contract expiring at time T. The forward exchange rate is F_0, which is also in euros per dollar. You take your $(1 + \rho)^{-T}$ dollars and invest them in U.S. T-bills that have a return of ρ.

When the forward contract expires, you will have 1 dollar. This is be-cause your $(1 + \rho)^{-T}$ dollars will have grown by the factor $(1 + \rho)^T$ so $(1 + \rho)^{-T}(1 + \rho)^T = 1$. Your forward contract obligates you to deliver the dollar, for which you receive F_0 euros. In effect, you have invested $S_0(1 + \rho)^{-T}$ and received F_0 euros. Since the transaction is riskless, your return should be the euro rate, r; that is,

$$F_0 = S_0(1 + \rho)^{-T}(1 + r)^T.$$

This relationship is called interest rate parity.[1] It is sometimes expressed as

$$F_0 = S_0(1 + r)^T/(1 + \rho)^T.$$

Interest rate parity, the relationship between futures or forward and spot exchange rates, is determined by the relationship between the risk-free interest rates in the two countries.

---

[1]There are also several common variations. The formula is sometimes approximated as $F_0 = S_0(1 + r - \rho)^T$ and sometimes as $F_0 = S_0(1 + rT)/(1 + \rho T)$ where T is days/360 or 365. The latter formula would be the case if r and ρ were in the form of LIBOR as discussed in previous chapters. Interest is added to the principal in the form of $1 + r(180/360)$. If the interest rates are continuously compounded, the formula would be $F_0 = S_0 e^{(r_c - \rho_c)T}$.

Consider the following example from a European's perspective. On January 31 of a particular year, the spot rate for dollars was €1.0304. The U.S. interest rate was 5.84 percent, while the euro interest rate was 3.59 percent. The time to expiration was $90/365 = .2466$. Thus, we have

$$F_0 = €1.0304 \, (1.0584)^{-.2466} \, (1.0359)^{.2466},$$

$$= €1.025.$$

Thus, the forward rate should be about €1.025.

Suppose, however, that the forward rate is €1.03. Then an arbitrage opportunity is available. An arbitrageur buys $(1.0584)^{-.2466} = 0.9861$ dollars for $0.9861(€1.0304) = €1.0161$ and sells one forward contract at a forward rate of €1.03. The 0.9861 dollars are invested at the U.S. risk-free rate. When the contract expires, the arbitrageur will have 1 dollar, which is delivered on the forward contract and for which €1.03 is received. Thus, the arbitrageur has invested €1.0161 and received €1.03 in 90 days. The annualized return is

$$\left(\frac{1.03}{1.0161} \right)^{365/90} - 1 = .0566,$$

which exceeds the euro risk-free rate of 3.59 percent. The combined effects of numerous arbitrageurs would push the spot rate up and/or the forward rate down until the spot and forward rates were properly aligned with the relative interest rates in the two countries.[2] Of course, some transaction costs and the dealer bid-ask spread would prevent the relationship from holding precisely.

Interest rate parity can be confusing to some people because of the difference in the way the rates can be quoted. Many times you may see interest rate parity stated as $F_0 = S_0(1 + \rho)^T (1 + r)^{-T}$. This is correct if the spot rate is quoted in units of the foreign currency. In our euro example, we could have stated the spot rate as $1/€ \, 1.0304 = 0.9705$ dollars per euro. In that case the forward rate would be stated in dollars per euro and the formula would be correctly given as $F_0 = S_0(1 + \rho)^T (1 + r)^{-T}$ with ρ being the foreign rate and r being the domestic rate. An easy way to remember is that the factor for the interest rate for a given country multiplies by the spot quote stated in that country's currency. The other interest rate factor then appears with the $-T$ in the exponent or simply in the denominator to the power T.

As we noted earlier in the chapter, when a forward rate is quoted in units of the domestic currency, here for example, the dollar quoted in

---

[2]Arbitrage could also put pressure on interest rates in the two countries. The U.S. rate could decrease, while the euro rate could increase.

euros, a higher forward than spot rate is said to be at a premium. Since the word "premium" tends to imply something higher, we have another reason to quote the currency in terms of your domestic currency. Had we quoted it the other way, a higher forward rate would imply a discount.

It has become common in discussions of international finance to interpret a forward premium (discount) as implying that the currency is expected to strengthen (weaken). Unfortunately this is a mistaken belief. The principle of arbitrage is what gives rise to a forward premium or discount. If a person could convert his or her domestic currency to a foreign currency, lock in a higher risk-free return, and convert back with the currency risk hedged, everyone would do this, which would erase any possibility of being able to earn a return better than the domestic risk-free rate. Any forward premium or discount is strictly caused by a difference in the interest rates of the two countries. If the domestic rate is lower and one forgoes the domestic risk-free return to earn the higher foreign risk-free return, the currency must sell at a forward rate proportional to the relative interest earned and given up. This has nothing to do with what people expect the spot rate to do in the future. People may have quite different beliefs about what might happen to spot rates, but we know they would agree that the forward rate must align with the spot rate by the proportional interest factors, or, in other words, by interest rate parity.

Interest rate parity is a powerful relationship and is used by all international currency traders. It is analogous to the cost of carry model for pricing other types of futures. The only difference is that the cost of carry in the two countries must be considered. For example, when funds are tied up in a foreign currency, the investor forgoes interest at the domestic rate but earns interest at the foreign rate. The difference between the domestic rate and the foreign rate is the cost of carry. The foreign interest rate thus is analogous to the dividend yield in the stock index futures pricing model.

As we saw in previous chapters, futures prices are not necessarily equal to forward prices. The differences observed in real data, however, are extremely small. Thus, as we have done previously, we shall usually assume forward exchange rates and futures exchange rates are equivalent.

The Intrinsic Value of an American Foreign Currency Option

Most of the principles of option pricing we previously covered are equally applicable to foreign currency option pricing. Thus, we shall limit our discussion to the most important principles and those that differ slightly from ordinary options. We shall use the same notation as in the option chapters. $C(S_0,T,X)$ and $P(S_0,T,X)$ are the call and put prices, with subscripts a and e used when necessary to distinguish American from European options. S_T is the spot rate at expiration. The risk-free rates and time to expiration are r, ρ, and T, as in the preceding section.

The minimum value of an American foreign currency call is

$$C_a(S_0,T,X) \geq Max(0, S_0 - X),$$

The intrinsic values of American currency options are the same as those of options on stock with the exchange rate used instead of the stock price.

which is the same as for an equity call. The term $Max(0, S_0 - X)$ is the intrinsic value. As an example, take a February 96 call on the euro quoted in U.S. dollars on January 31. The spot rate is 97.05 cents. Thus, the intrinsic value is $Max(0, 97.05 - 96) = 1.05$ cents. The call price is 1.27 cents. The difference, $1.27 - 1.05 = 0.22$ cents, is the time value.

The minimum value of an American foreign currency put is

$$P_a(S_0,T,X) \geq Max(0, X - S_0),$$

where $Max(0, X - S_0)$ is the intrinsic value. For example, on January 31, the euro February 97.5 put has an intrinsic value of $Max(0, 97.5 - 97.05) = 0.45$ cents. The put price is 0.59 cents. The difference of $0.59 - 0.45 = 0.14$ cents is the time value.

As the options move closer to expiration, their time values erode, and at expiration the options are worth only their intrinsic values. These principles are exactly like those for their equity option counterparts. Now, however, we shall establish lower bounds for European options that differ somewhat from those we did for equity options.

The Lower Bound of European Foreign Currency Options

Consider two portfolios, A and B. Portfolio A consists of a foreign currency call priced at $C_e(S_0,T,X)$ and a domestic risk-free bond with a face value of X and a present value of $X(1 + r)^{-T}$. Portfolio B is constructed by taking $S_0(1 + \rho)^{-T}$ dollars, converting it to the foreign currency, and investing it in a foreign pure discount bond with a face value equal to one unit of the foreign currency. The present value of that bond is $S_0(1 + \rho)^{-T}$ dollars. When the bond matures, it pays one unit of the foreign currency, which is converted back into S_T dollars.

Table 13.1 illustrates the payoffs from those portfolios. For portfolio A, if the spot rate at expiration does not exceed the exercise price, the call expires worthless but the bonds are worth X dollars. If the spot rate at expiration is greater than X, the call is worth $S_T - X$ and the bonds are worth X for a total of S_T. Thus, portfolio A is worth the greater of X and S_T. Portfolio B is worth S_T in either case. This is because the foreign bonds mature and are worth 1 unit of the foreign currency in either case, and that currency is converted back into S_T dollars.

The outcome of portfolio A equals or exceeds that of portfolio B in both cases. Thus, portfolio A must sell for at least as much as portfolio

| TABLE 13.1 | The Lower Bound of a European Foreign Currency Call: Payoffs at Expiration of Portfolios A and B |

Portfolio	Instrument	Current Value	Payoffs from Portfolio Given Spot Rate at Expiration	
			$S_T \leq X$	$S_T > X$
A	Long call	$C_e(S_0,T,X)$	0	$S_T - X$
	Domestic bond	$X(1 + r)^{-T}$	$\dfrac{X}{X}$	$\dfrac{X}{S_T}$
B	Foreign bond	$S_0(1 + \rho)^{-T}$	S_T	S_T

B.[3] The current value for portfolio B is $S_0(1 + \rho)^{-T}$, while the current value for portfolio A is $C_e(S_0,T,X) + X(1 + r)^{-T}$. We state this inequality as

$$C_e(S_0,T,X) + X(1 + r)^{-T} \geq S_0(1 + \rho)^{-T}.$$

This is frequently written as

$$C_e(S_0,T,X) \geq S_0(1 + \rho)^{-T} - X(1 + r)^{-T}.$$

Because an option cannot have a negative value, we can state this as

$$C_e(S_0,T,X) \geq \text{Max}[0, S_0(1 + \rho)^{-T} - X(1 + r)^{-T}].$$

The lower bound of a European currency call is the same as that of a European call on a stock except that the spot exchange rate is discounted by the foreign interest rate and appears instead of the stock price.

The call price is greater than or equal to the spot rate discounted at the foreign interest rate minus the present value of the exercise price. This is similar to the lower bound of an equity call, which is the spot price minus the present value of the exercise price. In fact, if there were a dividend on the stock, these two boundaries would be equivalent. The dividend yield would replace the foreign risk-free interest rate.

Converting dollars into a foreign currency is similar to buying a stock with a known dividend. Suppose the dividend yield is equivalent to ρ. You buy the stock, hold it, and collect the dividend; then you sell the stock at S_T. In the case of a foreign currency, you buy the currency, hold it, and collect the interest; then you sell (convert) it.

---

[3]Recall from Chapter 3 why this is true. If portfolio B sold for more than portfolio A, foreign investors would have an arbitrage opportunity. They could go short in portfolio B by selling their own currency. Then they would use the funds to construct portfolio A. This would enable them to earn a nonnegative profit and have cash left over up front.

Let us test the lower bound rule on a European option, the February 96 euro call on January 31. The spot rate was 97.05, the domestic interest rate was 5.68 percent, the euro interest rate was 3.52 percent, and the option expired 28 days later. Thus, $T = 28/365 = .0767$. The lower bound is

$$97.05(1.0352)^{-.0767} - 96(1.0568)^{-.0767} = 1.20.$$

The actual price of the call is 1.27, and it obviously exceeds the lower bound.

The lower bound for a European put is derived similarly. Portfolio A consists of a European put plus an investment of $S_0(1 + \rho)^{-T}$ dollars in a foreign pure discount bond worth one unit of the foreign currency at expiration. Portfolio B consists of a domestic pure discount bond worth X dollars at expiration. Table 13.2 illustrates the payoffs.

Portfolio A performs at least as well as portfolio B and therefore should be priced at least as high. We state this as

$$P_e(S_0,T,X) + S_0(1 + \rho)^{-T} \geq X(1 + r)^{-T}.$$

This is usually written as

$$P_e(S_0,T,X) \geq X(1 + r)^{-T} - S_0(1 + \rho)^{-T}.$$

Because an option cannot have a negative value,

$$P_e(S_0,T,X) \geq Max\,[0, X(1 + r)^{-T} - S_0(1 + \rho)^{-T}].$$

The put price must equal or exceed the present value of the exercise price minus the spot rate discounted at the foreign interest rate. This too is identical to the lower bound of a European put option on a dividend-paying stock when the dividend yield is equivalent to ρ.

The lower bound of a European currency put is the same as that of a European put on a stock except that the spot exchange rate is discounted by the foreign interest rate and appears instead of the stock price.

TABLE 13.2	**The Lower Bound of a European Foreign Currency Put: Payoffs at Expiration of Portfolios A and B**			

| | | | *Payoffs from Portfolio Given Spot Rate at Expiration* | |
Portfolio	Instrument	Current Value	$S_T \leq X$	$S_T > X$
A	Long put	$P_e(S_0,T,X)$	$(X - S_T)$	0
	Foreign bond	$S_0(1 + \rho)^{-T}$	$\dfrac{S_T}{X}$	$\dfrac{S_T}{S_T}$
B	Domestic bond	$X(1 + r)^{-T}$	X	X

As an example, consider the February 97.5 euro put on January 31 of a recent year. The lower bound is

$$97.5(1.0568)^{-.0767} - 97.05(1.0352)^{-.0767} = 0.29.$$

The actual put price is 0.59; therefore, the put conforms to the boundary condition.

As was the case with equity options, these lower bounds establish the lowest possible price for European calls and puts. For American calls and puts, the lowest possible price is the intrinsic value.

Put-Call Parity

Suppose we construct the following portfolio, called portfolio A. Take $S_0(1 + \rho)^{-T}$ dollars, convert to the foreign currency, buy a foreign bond that pays interest at the rate ρ, and buy a European put on the currency with an exercise price of X. Now consider portfolio B, consisting of a call on the currency and a position in domestic bonds with a face value of X, which pay the domestic interest rate of r. The payoffs from these portfolios are illustrated in Table 13.3. If the spot exchange rate ends up above the exercise price, both portfolios pay off the spot exchange rate. Portfolio A achieves this result because it contains a position in the $(1 + \rho)^{-T}$ units of the currency, which grow to a value of one unit of the currency worth S_T. The put ends up out-of-the-money. Portfolio B achieves this result by exercising the call to acquire the currency. The maturing domestic bond generates the cash used to pay the exercise price when exercising the call. In effect, both portfolios result in the establishment of a long position in the currency. If the spot exchange rate ends up below the exercise price, both portfolios are worth the exchange rate. Portfolio A achieves this result by selling the currency at the rate X with portfolio B results in the receipt of the face value, X, of the maturing domestic bond.

Put-call parity of European currency options is the same as for European stock options except that the spot exchange rate is discounted by the foreign interest rate and appears instead of the stock price.

| **TABLE 13.3** | **Put-Call Parity of Foreign Currency Options** |

Portfolio	Instrument	Current Value	Payoffs from Portfolio Given Spot Rate at Expiration	
			$S_T \leq X$	$S_T > X$
A	Foreign bond	$S_0(1 + \rho)^{-T}$	S_T	S_T
	Long put	$P_e(S_0,T,X)$	$\dfrac{X - S_T}{X}$	$\dfrac{0}{S_T}$
B	Long call	$C_e(S_0,T,X)$	0	$S_T - X$
	Domestic bond	$X(1 + r)^{-T}$	$\dfrac{X}{X}$	$\dfrac{X}{S_T}$

Because these two portfolios produce the same results at expiration, they should have the same initial values. Thus, we obtain the put-call parity relationship for foreign currency options:

$$S_0(1 + \rho)^{-T} + P_e(S_0,T,X) = C_e(S_0,T,X) + X(1 + r)^{-T}.$$

Stated alternatively,

$$P_e(S_0,T,X) = C_e(S_0,T,X) - S_0(1 + \rho)^{-T} + X(1 + r)^{-T},$$

or

$$C_e(S_0,T,X) = P_e(S_0,T,X) + S_0(1 + \rho)^{-T} - X(1 + r)^{-T}.$$

The only difference between this put-call parity and put-call parity for stock options is the presence of the foreign discount factor times the spot rate. Once again, however, this is equivalent to a dividend on a stock. Put-call parity for dividend-paying stocks thus would be identical to the above statement if the dividend were paid at the rate ρ.

Consider the February 96 euro put and call on January 31. The call price is 1.27. According to the formula, the put should be worth

$$1.27 - 97.05(1.0352)^{-.0767} + 96(1.0568)^{-.0767} = 0.07.$$

The actual put price is 0.07, so the put appears to be correctly priced.

American put-call parity would be analogous to American put-call parity for options on a dividend-paying stock, which we covered in Chapter 3.

Put-call parity gives the relationship between puts and calls denominated in one currency but exercisable into another. To fully understand foreign currency options, however, it is important to recognize another type of put-call parity: A call to buy currency A denominated in currency B with an exercise price of X is equivalent to a put to sell X units of currency B denominated in currency A with an exercise price of 1/X. For example, consider the February 96 euro call. This is a call to buy 1 euro at $0.96. It is equivalent to a put to sell $0.96 at $1/0.96 = €1.0417$. Let us see why this is so by considering the payoffs at expiration from these two options. If we buy the call to buy a euro at $0.96, we shall receive the following payoffs:

$$\begin{array}{ll} 0 & \text{if } S_T < \$0.96. \\ S_T - \$0.96 & \text{if } S_T \geq \$0.96 \end{array}$$

If we buy the put to sell $0.96 dollars at €1.0417, we shall receive the following payoffs:

$$
\begin{array}{ll}
0 & \text{if } 1/S_T \geq \text{€}1.0417 \\
(\$0.96)\left[\text{€}1.0417 - (1/S_T)\right] & \text{if } 1/S_T < \text{€}1.0417.
\end{array}
$$

The expression $1/S_T$ is simply the €/\$ exchange rate at expiration expressed in terms of euros. The put pays off when $1/S_T < \text{€}1.0417$. Recall that the exercise price of €1.0417 is simply the inverse of \$0.96. Thus, the put pays off when $1/S_T < \text{€}1.0417$, which is equivalent to $S_T > \$0.96$. The put payoff when this occurs is $\$0.96(\text{€}1.0417 - 1/S_T) = \text{€}1 - \$0.96/S_T$. This amount is in euros, so we convert it to dollars by multiplying by \$$S_T$, giving us $S_T - \$0.96$. Looking back at the call payoffs, we see that when the put pays off, the call also pays off, and they both pay off the same amount in dollars. It follows that when the call is out-of-the-money, the put is also out-of-the-money, and neither pays off anything. Thus, the call and the put are equivalent.

The Garman-Kohlhagen Foreign Currency Option Pricing Model

Garman and Kohlhagen (1983) derived an option pricing model for foreign currency options. Their model is a simple extension of the Black-Scholes model. The formula is

$$
C = S_0 e^{-\rho_c T} N(d_1) - X e^{-r_c T} N(d_2),
$$
where
$$
d_1 = \frac{\ln(S_0 e^{-\rho_c T}/X) + [r_c + (\sigma^2/2)]T}{\sigma\sqrt{T}}
$$
$$
d_2 = d_1 - \sigma\sqrt{T}.
$$

Table 13.4 illustrates the calculation of the Garman-Kohlhagen foreign currency option price for the euro February 96 call in dollars. Recall from Chapters 5 and 12 that the Black-Scholes and Black models require the calculation of d_1, d_2, and the normal probabilities associated with these values. Then these normal probabilities are inserted into an overall formula. The Garman-Kohlhagen model works similarly. Everywhere we would use the exchange rate S_0, we simply use S_0 discounted at the continuously compounded foreign interest rate, ρ_c. Of course, as in the Black-Scholes and Black models, we also use the continuously compounded U.S. risk-free rate. The standard deviation in this model is the standard deviation of the log of one plus the percentage change in the exchange rate, expressed in dollars per unit of the foreign currency.

Put options can also be priced by substituting the Garman-Kohlhagen formula for the call price into the put-call parity formula. Remember, of course, that the Garman-Kohlhagen model, like Black-Scholes, is a European option pricing model. American options would have higher prices

The Garman-Kohlhagen foreign currency option pricing model is equivalent to the Black-Scholes model except that the spot exchange rate is discounted by the foreign interest rate and appears instead of the stock price.

TABLE 13.4   **Calculating the Garman-Kohlhagen Foreign Currency Option Price**

$S_0 = 97.05$ $X = 96$ $r_c = .0568$ $\rho_c = .0352$
$\sigma = .045$ $T = .0767$

1. Compute d_1.

$$d_1 = \frac{\ln(97.05^{-(.0352)(.0767)}/96) + (.0568 + (.045)^2/2).0767}{.045\sqrt{.0767}} = 1.012$$

2. Compute d_2.

$$d_2 = 1.012 - .045\sqrt{.0767} = 1.000$$

3. Look up $N(d_1)$.

$$N(1.01) = .8438$$

4. Look up $N(d_2)$.

$$N(1.00) = .8413$$

5. Plug into formula C.

$$C = 97.05e^{-(.0352)(.0767)}(.8438) - 96^{-(.0568)(.0767)}(.8413) = 1.26$$

---

and would tend to be underpriced by the model. Thus, to accurately price an American foreign currency option would require an American option pricing model. As we have noted previously, most of the American models are beyond the scope of this book; however, American currency options can be priced by the binomial model, which we have covered in great detail in earlier chapters.

As you might have expected, the Garman-Kohlhagen and binomial models can be calculated using your Excel spreadsheet bsbin2.xls or your Windows program bsbwin2.1.exe.

This concludes our discussion of pricing foreign currency derivatives. In the next section, we shall briefly review several strategies using these instruments.

Trading Strategies in Foreign Currency Futures/Forwards and Options

In this section, we shall look at five applications of foreign currency instruments. The first two are long and short hedges using futures/forwards. The next two are simple speculative call and put strategies. The last is a foreign currency hedge using options.

A Long Hedge with Foreign Currency Futures

Recall that a long hedge with futures involves the purchase of a futures contract. In the case of foreign currencies, a long hedger is concerned that the value of the foreign currency will rise. An example is presented in Table 13.5.

Here an American car dealer plans to buy 20 British sports cars. Each car costs 35,000 pounds, which will have to be paid in the British currency. Based on the current forward rate of the pound, the dealer's current cost is $914,200. If, however, the pound increases in value, the cars will end up costing more. The dealer hedges by buying futures on the pound. As the table indicates, this was a good decision because the pound did appreciate; the cars ended up costing $1,009,400, which is $95,200 more, but the futures contracts generated a profit of $109,656.25, which more than covered the increased cost of the cars.

TABLE 13.5   **A Long Hedge with Foreign Currency Futures**

Scenario: On July 1, an American auto dealer enters into a contract to purchase 20 British sports cars with payment to be made in British pounds on November 1. Each car will cost 35,000 pounds. The dealer is concerned that the pound will strengthen over the next few months, causing the cars to cost more in dollars.

Date	Spot Market	Futures Market
July 1	The current exchange rate is $1.3190 per pound. The forward rate of the pound is $1.3060. Forward cost of 20 cars: $20(35,000)($1.3060) = $914,200.	December pound contract is at $1.278. Price per contract: $62,500($1.278) = $79,875.$ The appropriate number of contracts is $\dfrac{20(35,000)}{62,500} = 11.2.$
		Buy 11 contracts
November 1	The spot rate is $1.442. Buy the 700,000 pounds to purchase 20 cars. Cost in dollars: $700,000($1.442) = $1,009,400.$	December pound contract is at $1.4375. Price per contract: $62,500($1.4375) = $89,843.75.$ **Sell 11 contracts**

Analysis:
The cars ended up costing $1,009,400 − $914,200 = $95,200 more.

The profit on the futures transaction is

$$
\begin{array}{ll}
11(\$89,843.75) & \text{(sale price of futures)} \\
\underline{-11(\$79,875)} & \text{(purchase price of futures)} \\
\$109,656.25 & \text{(profit on futures).}
\end{array}
$$

The profit on the futures more than offsets the higher cost of the cars, leaving a net gain of $109,656.25 − $95,200 = $14,456.25. The dealer effectively paid $1,009,400 − $109,656.25 = $899,743.75 for the 20 cars.

As long as the pound spot and futures rates move in the same direction, the hedge will be successful in reducing some of the loss in the spot market. Had the pound weakened, there would have been a loss in the futures market that would have offset some or all of the gain in the spot market.

This transaction was executed in the futures market. Remember that futures contracts have standardized terms and provide a guarantee against default on the part of the other party. Forward contracts permit the parties to customize the terms of the contract. This transaction, however, would not be large enough to justify a forward contract. In the next example we shall execute the hedge in the forward market.

A Short Hedge with Foreign Currency Forwards

A short hedge is a commitment to sell a currency using futures or forwards and is designed to protect against a decrease in the foreign currency's value. In Table 13.6 we have a situation in which a multinational firm has 10 million pounds that it will convert at a later date. A transaction of this size can often be better executed with a customized forward contract. In addition, when the amount of exposure is large, the basis risk of a futures contract may be a risk not worth bearing. In this example the customer is long pounds and is exposed to the risk of the pound weakening. To protect against this risk, it sells a forward contract on the exact number of pounds it will convert, with the contract expiring on the day of conversion. This al-

---

TABLE 13.6	A Short Hedge with Foreign Currency Forwards

Scenario: On June 29, a multinational firm with a British subsidiary decides it will need to transfer 10 million pounds from an account in London to an account with a New York bank. Transfer will be made on September 28. The firm is concerned that over the next two months the pound will weaken.

Date	Spot Market	Forward Market
June 29	The current exchange rate is $1.362 per pound. The forward rate of the pound is $1.357. Forward value of funds: 10,000,000($1.357) = $13,570,000.	Sell pounds forward for delivery on September 28 at $1.357.
September 28	The spot rate is $1.2375.	Deliver pounds and receive 10,000,000($1.357) = $13,570,000.

Analysis:
The pounds end up worth $13,570,000 − $12,375,000 = $1,195,000 less but are delivered on the forward contract for $13,570,000, thus completely eliminating the risk. Had the transaction not been done, the firm would have converted the pounds at the spot rate of $1.2375.

lows the firm to convert the pounds to dollars by simply delivering them to the dealer on the opposite side of the forward contract. As the table indicates, the pound did depreciate, which would have caused a loss of $1,195,000. Instead the firm locked in the rate on the day it entered into the forward contract.

Buy a Foreign Currency Call

Following the notation used in Chapters 6 and 7, the profit from a single foreign currency call held to expiration is

$$\Pi = Max(0, S_T - X) - C.$$

Just as we did in Chapter 6, we will look at the outcomes in both cases, $S_T \leq X$ and $S_T > X$, and the breakeven spot rates at expiration. The results are the same as they were for equity calls:

$$\Pi = -C \qquad \text{if } S_T \leq X$$
$$\Pi = S_T - X - C \quad \text{if } S_T > X.$$

The breakeven spot rate at expiration is $X + C$.

Consider a February 96 euro call on January 31 of a particular year. Let the contract cover €100,000. The call costs 1.27 cents per euro. Figure 13.7 illustrates the profit graph with the spot rate shown in cents.

FIGURE 13.7   **Buy Foreign Currency Call**

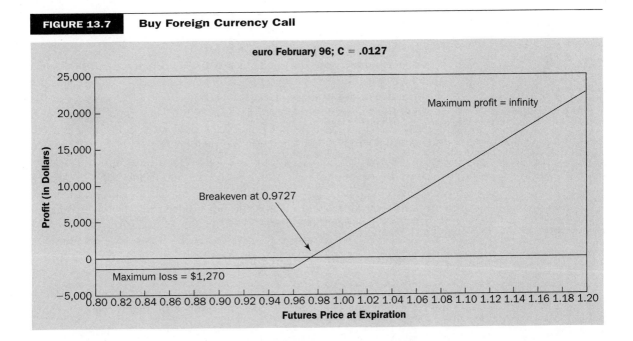

Suppose that at expiration the exchange rate is $1.10. Then the euros are worth $100{,}000(\$1.10 - \$0.96) = \$14{,}000$. The profit is $14,000 less the cost of the option, $€100{,}000(\$0.0127) = \$1{,}270$, or $12,730. If the spot rate ends up below $0.96, the call will expire worthless and the loss will be the option's cost, $1,270. To reach breakeven, the spot rate must be at least $\$0.96 + \$0.0127 = \$0.9727$. Because there is no upper limit to the spot exchange rate, the maximum profit is infinity. The maximum loss is the call premium of $1,270.

When analyzing equity options, we looked at the factors affecting the choice of exercise price and the length of the holding period. We shall not discuss those factors here; the same principles for equity options apply to foreign currency options. In addition, we shall omit a direct discussion of writing foreign currency options, as the principles are similar to those for writing equity options.

Buy a Foreign Currency Put

The profit from the purchase of a single foreign currency put held to expiration is

$$\Pi = \text{Max}(0, X - S_T) - P.$$

This is, of course, the same as the profit for an equity put. The outcomes for the two cases are

$$\Pi = -P \qquad \text{if } S_T \le X$$
$$\Pi = X - S_T - P \quad \text{if } S_T < X.$$

The breakeven spot rate at expiration is $X - P$.

As an example, consider the February 97.5 euro put on January 31 of a particular year. The cost of the put is 0.59 cents. Figure 13.8 illustrates the performance of the strategy.

Suppose the spot rate at expiration is $0.90. Then the puts are worth $100{,}000(\$0.975 - \$0.90) = \$7{,}500$. You paid 0.59 cents per put, or $100{,}000(\$0.0059) = \$590$. Thus, the net profit is $6,910. If the spot rate at expiration exceeds $0.975, the put will expire worthless and the strategy will lose the premium, $590, which is the maximum loss. The breakeven spot rate is $\$0.975 - \$0.0059 = \$0.9691$. The maximum gain occurs if the euro falls to a value of zero. Then the put holder can sell the currency at $0.975 for a profit of $100{,}000(\$0.975 - \$0.0059) = \$96{,}910$.

A Foreign Currency Option Hedge

Foreign currency forwards and futures clearly are useful tools for managing exchange rate risk. Lest we leave the impression that foreign currency

| FIGURE 13.8 | Buy Foreign Currency Put |

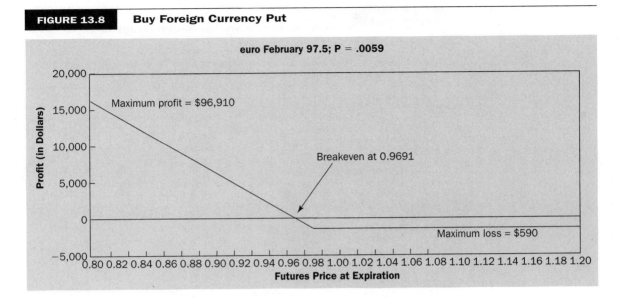

options are exclusively for speculation, we should look at an interesting hedging application using foreign currency options.

In some situations, a firm does not know for certain whether it will enter into a foreign currency transaction at a future date. For example, suppose an American firm is making a bid on a project. If it wins the bid, the foreign firm or government will pay the American firm in the foreign currency. A forward or futures contract will hedge the risk of a change in the exchange rate. Suppose, however, that the bid is awarded to another firm. This means the American firm will not receive the foreign currency. Had a forward or futures contract been used, the firm either would have a short position in the contract or, if it expired, would have to deliver the currency itself. This means the firm would be exposed to the risk of an increase in the exchange rate. An option can be used to avoid this problem.

For example, suppose an American firm is bidding for a contract to construct a sports complex in London. The bid must be submitted in British pounds. The firm plans to make a bid of £25 million. At the forward exchange rate of $1.437, the bid in dollars is equivalent to £25,000,000($1.437) = $35,925,000. Once the bid is submitted, the firm must be prepared to accept £25 million if the bid is successful. Because it is an American firm, it will convert the pounds into dollars at whatever rate prevails on the date payment is made. If the pound weakens, the firm will effectively receive fewer dollars. To simplify the example somewhat, we shall assume the payment will be made as soon as the decision is made as to which firm is awarded the construction contract.

		TABLE 13.7		Comparison of a Foreign Currency Forward Hedge and an Option Hedge

Assumption: A firm is bidding on a construction project. If the bid is successful, payment will be made in a fixed number of British pounds. The table below indicates the outcome from the forward or option contract but does not consider the profit from the construction project itself.

Outcome of Bid	No Hedge	Short Forward Hedge	Option Hedge (Buy Put)
Successful:			
Pound increases	Gain on pound	Gain on pound reduced by hedge Small profit or loss	Put expires Premium lost
Pound decreases	Loss on pound	Loss on pound reduced by hedge Small profit or loss	Loss on pound reduced by exercise of put Small profit or loss
Unsuccessful:			
Pound increases	No effect	Potentially large loss on pound	Put expires Premium lost
Pound decreases	No effect	Potentially large gain on pound	Potentially large gain on pound by exercise of put

Table 13.7 summarizes the possible outcomes and compares the general results for a forward hedge with those for an option hedge. The option would be a put, because the firm would need to protect itself against a decline in the pound's value.

If the bid is successful and the pound increases, the firm will receive the pounds, which now are valued at more dollars per pound. The forward hedge will, however, reduce this gain, because the hedge will be a short position. If the option is used, the put will expire worthless.

If the bid is successful and the pound decreases, the forward hedge will reduce the loss caused by the decline in the pound's value. The option will, however, also reduce the loss on the pound.

If the bid is unsuccessful and the pound increases, the forward hedge will result in a potentially large speculative loss. This is because the firm will not receive the pounds if the bid fails but will have a short position in a forward contract. If the option hedge is used, the put will expire worthless. The firm will have lost money—the premium on the put—but the amount lost is likely to be less than it would have been with the forward hedge.

If the bid is unsuccessful and the pound decreases, the forward hedge will result in a potentially large speculative profit, because the firm will be short forward and will not receive the pounds as a result of the failure to

Currency options provide flexibility to hedgers who are unsure of whether they will receive or make foreign cash payments.

win the bid. If the option hedge is used, the put's exercise will also result in a potentially large profit on the put.[4]

The option hedge is most beneficial when the bid is unsuccessful. Because the firm does not receive the pounds, the forward position generates a potentially large profit or loss. The option, however, can generate a large profit if the pound declines; if the pound rises, the loss will be limited to the premium. Of course, the option hedge requires payment of the option premium, while the forward hedge might require collateral. Neither type of hedge dominates the other, but each has its merits.

Let us now look at this specific hedge. The firm needs to hedge the anticipated receipt of £25 million. We shall assume it uses either forwards or over-the-counter put options. The forward price is $1.424 and the option premium is $0.025. Thus, the option will cost £25,000,000($0.025) = $625,000. The forward contract locks in £25,000,000($1.424) = $35,600,000. We can assume that the option or forward expires on the date on which the outcome of the bid is determined and that on that date the firm either receives the cash payment of £25 million or not.[5]

Figure 13.9 shows two panels that depict the value of the hedge, meaning the construction contract plus either the option or the forward, for a range of spot rates for the pound on the expiration date for the two cases of (a) the bid being successful and (b) the bid being unsuccessful.

For the case in which the bid is successful, we see that either hedge works fairly well. The option hedge is like a protective put, which benefits from a strong pound and which has limited losses from a weak pound. The forward hedge locks in $35,600,000 regardless of the value of the pound. If the firm does not hedge, note that the overall value moves one-for-one with the value of the pound.

For the case in which the bid is unsuccessful, we see that the forward hedge leaves the firm highly exposed, with the potential for a rather substantial loss. But note the option hedge: The most the firm can lose is the option premium of $625,000, yet it can gain if the pound decreases, even though it did not win the bid.

Of course, the firm could choose not to bid, but this is unlikely because bidding on contracts is the nature of the construction business. The firm could choose not to hedge, but it could win the bid and earn a much smaller profit or even a loss if the pound falls significantly. The option hedge provides an alternative that will be attractive to some firms, while the forward hedge will be better for others. The differences in their expectations and willingness to take exchange rate risk will determine whether they use options or forwards.

---

[4]Technically, we have not specified how low the pound goes, but we assume it is lower than the exercise price. There will be a profit only if the spot rate at expiration is less than the exercise price by the amount of the premium.

[5]It is unlikely that on the date the bid is awarded, the cash would actually be paid. To fine-tune the hedge, the firm would adjust the amount paid to a present value as of that date. We shall ignore this minor point here.

FIGURE 13.9 **Value of Hedge**

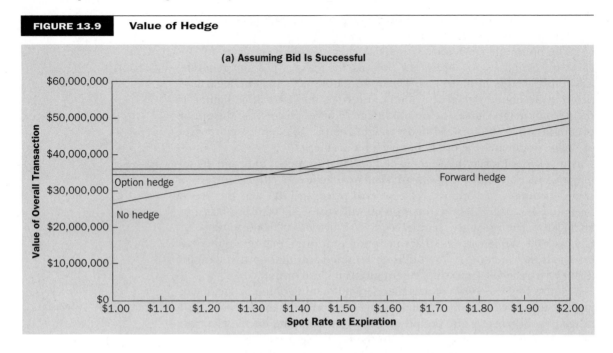

(a) Assuming Bid Is Successful

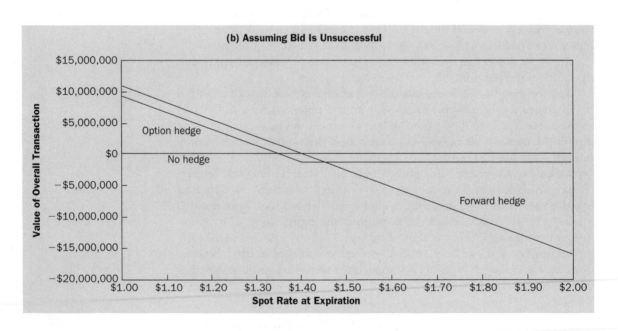

(b) Assuming Bid Is Unsuccessful

Other Instruments for Managing Foreign Exchange Risk

As we saw in previous chapters, a variety of techniques can be used to manage risk. In this chapter, we have talked about currency forwards, futures, and options; however, there are a number of other, related ways to manage foreign exchange risk. We shall briefly look at a few here.

Currency Swaps

In Chapter 14, we shall cover the most widely used interest rate derivative, the interest rate swap. In this chapter we shall cover a lesser-used but similar derivative, the **currency swap.** As described earlier, a currency swap is a transaction between two parties in which each promises to make a series of payments to the other at specific future dates, with each set of payments made in a different currency. The payments normally consist of a series of interest payments often, but not always, followed by a final principal payment. Either or both sets of payments can be at a known fixed rate or at a floating rate. In the latter case, the rate(s) is (are) determined by a specific floating interest rate, such as LIBOR or EuroLIBOR/Euribor.

Currency swaps are commonly used by firms that operate in one currency but need to borrow in another currency. A company can usually borrow less expensively in its own currency. By borrowing in its own currency, it receives funds up front and then makes interest and principal payments in its own currency. If the firm also did a currency swap, it could receive interest and principal payments in its own currency, thereby offsetting or partially offsetting its payments on its debt, and receive funds up front and make payments in the other, desired currency.

The two parties to a currency swap are usually referred to as the end user and the dealer. The former is best represented by a company such as the one described in the preceding paragraph. The dealer is usually a large bank or investment firm that makes a market in currency swaps.[6] We shall discuss the institutional features of this market more in the next few chapters. Let us look at an example of a currency swap. Reston Technology is an established Internet company in Northern Virginia's technology corridor. Reston is planning to expand its operations into Europe. To do so, it needs to borrow €10 million. It would like to issue bonds at a fixed rate and pay them back semiannually over two years. At the current exchange rate of $0.9804 per euro, Reston could borrow in U.S. dollars and convert to euros. Its expanded operations, however, will generate cash flow in euros, so it would prefer to make its interest payments in euros.

---

[6]The dealer also usually makes markets in currency spot, forward, and option transactions.

Reston's primary bank has a subsidiary, Global Swaps, Inc. (GSI), which is a large derivatives dealer, that suggests that Reston borrow in U.S. dollars and engage in a currency swap to convert its borrowing to euros. Specifically, Reston will

---

Borrow $9,804,000
Enter into a currency swap with GSI in which
  GSI pays Reston €10 million up front
  Reston pays GSI $9,804,000 up front
  GSI pays Reston interest semiannually for two years at a rate of 6.1%
  Reston pays GSI interest semiannually for two years at a rate of 4.35%
  GSI pays Reston $9,804,000 at the end of the contract
  Reston pays GSI €10 million at the end of the contract

The swap payments will be

$$.061(180/360)\$9,804,000 = \$299,022 \text{ from GSI to Reston}$$
$$.0435(180/360)€10,000,000 = €217,500 \text{ from Reston to GSI.}$$

The overall transaction, along with Reston's loan in U.S. dollars, is illustrated in Figure 13.10. Note that the swap, however, is specifically the series of payments between Reston and GSI. In this case, the bond Reston issued is simply shown as an indication of its motivation for entering into the swap, but there need not be a loan to be a swap. A company could in fact enter into a swap for purely speculative purposes.

Reston effectively borrowed €10 million at 4.35 percent. Its U.S. dollar loan at 6.5 percent is not completely offset by the payments it receives from GSI at a rate of 6.1 percent. Thus, it effectively pays an additional 0.4 percent on $9.804 million, though it does not owe the principal.

Note that the currency swap transaction itself is like Reston having borrowed €10 million at 4.35 percent and converting the proceeds to $9.804 million, which it then invests in a U.S. dollar bond at 6.1 percent. So a currency swap between two parties is equivalent to a bilateral transaction in which each party issues a bond in one currency to the other and uses the proceeds to buy the bond issued by the other party.

A currency swap can also be viewed as a series of forward contracts between the two parties. For example, on the four semiannual dates for the next two years, Reston has agreed to pay €217,500 and receive $299,022 from GSI. This is equivalent to a series of four forward contracts with Reston long the dollar and short the euro and GSI short the euro and long the dollar. Also, a fifth forward contract expires in two years with Reston agreeing to pay €10 million and receive $9,804,000.

A currency swap is equivalent to issuing a bond in one currency and using the proceeds to purchase a bond in another currency. It can also be viewed as a series of currency forward contracts.

ALTERNATIVE VARIATIONS OF CURRENCY SWAPS   In the Reston-GSI swap, both parties exchanged interest payments at a fixed rate. There are several variations that might be followed:

If Reston borrowed in dollars at a fixed rate but wanted to borrow in euros at a floating rate, it might enter into a currency swap where

> Reston pays interest at a floating rate, such as Euribor
> GSI pays interest at a fixed rate.

If Reston borrowed in dollars at a floating rate but wanted to borrow in euros at a floating rate, it might enter into a currency swap where

> Reston pays interest at a floating rate, such as Euribor
> GSI pays interest at a floating rate, such as dollar LIBOR.

FIGURE 13.10   **Example of a Currency Swap**

Scenario: Reston issues $9.804 million of bonds at 6.5 percent with interest paid semi-annually. Reston prefers to borrow in euros so it enters into a currency swap with GSI for €10 million and $9.804 million. Payments are made semiannually at 6.1 percent in dollars and 4.35 percent in euros. Principal payments are exchanged up front and at the termination date of the swap.

(a) Up Front

(b) Semiannually For Two Years

(c) At Termination Date

If Reston borrowed in dollars at a floating rate but wanted to borrow in euros at a fixed rate, it might enter into a currency swap where

> Reston pays interest at a fixed rate
> GSI pays interest at a floating rate, such as dollar LIBOR.

Although we shall cover interest rate swaps in Chapter 14, let us take a quick preview of them here by letting each currency be the same. In that case the exchange rate is one-for-one, meaning that the principal amounts need not be exchanged at the beginning nor at the end of the life of the contract. In addition it would make no sense to exchange equivalent floating or fixed rates as the payments would be the same. Thus, the typical interest rate swap is an exchange of fixed payments for floating payments, with only the interest payments and not the principal payments exchanged.

Once we see what an interest rate swap is, we can now see how a currency swap can be combined with an interest rate swap to equal another currency swap. Using euros and dollars, Figure 13.11 illustrates how each of the four currency swaps could be combined with an interest rate swap within either Europe or the United States to equal one of the other currency swaps.

Some currency swaps do not specify payment of the notional principals. A common occurrence is when a firm wants to pay interest in one currency and principal in another. In our example, if, in its loan, Reston wanted to

FIGURE 13.11　**Combining Currency Swaps with Interest Rate Swaps**

Currency Snap	+	Interest Rate Swap	=	Currency Swap
Pay € fixed Receive $ fixed	+	Pay $ fixed Receive $ floating	=	Pay € fixed Receive $ floating
Pay € fixed Receive $ floating	+	Pay € floating Receive € fixed	=	Pay € floating Receive $ floating
Pay € floating Receive $ floating	+	Pay $ floating Receive $ fixed	=	Pay € floating Receive $ fixed
Pay € floating Receive $ fixed	+	Pay € fixed Receive € floating	=	Pay € fixed Receive $ fixed

pay interest in euros but pay the principal in dollars, it would structure the swap to not involve an exchange of principals. It would, thus, receive the principal from issuing the bond in dollars, make the interest payments in dollars, receive interest on the swap in dollars, pay interest on the swap in euros, and make the final principal payment in dollars on its bonds.

PRICING OF CURRENCY SWAPS   Pricing a swap means to establish the fixed rate that would determine the fixed interest payments. The fixed rate in fact is the same one that would be paid on a fixed-for-floating interest rate swap. The process of determining the fixed rate is a simple one that we will explore more thoroughly in Chapter 14 when we cover interest rate swaps. For this chapter, we shall illustrate it lightly in the context of a currency swap using euros and dollars.

As we noted, a currency swap is equivalent to issuing a bond in one currency, converting the proceeds at the current spot rate, and using the proceeds to buy a bond in the other currency. Thus, the fixed rate on either side is simply the coupon rate on a par value bond issued in that currency. We can find that rate easily from the term structure.

Table 13.8 presents information on the term structure from dollar LIBOR and the euro term structure based on Euribor. The first thing we do is determine the discount factors based on these rates. We need a discount factor covering each period from the date of initiation of the swap to the date on which each payment is made. Using the standard Eurodollar convention, the discount factor is $1/(1 + rate(days/360))$. We see in the second panel of Table 13.8 the set of discount factors.

The formula for the fixed rate on a currency swap is

$$\text{Fixed rate on currency swap} = 2\left(\frac{1 - \text{Final discount factor}}{\text{Sum of all discount factors}}\right).$$

The "final discount factor" refers to the discount factor associated with the final swap payment. Multiplication of the term in parentheses by two results from the fact that the payments are semiannual and the discount factors used in the formula are spaced six months apart. The adjustment of multiplying by two simply annualizes the rate.

The bottom panel of Table 13.8 illustrates this calculation for the currency swap. As we shall see in Chapter 14, these two rates, 6.1 percent for dollars and 4.35 percent for euros, would be the fixed rates for interest rate swaps in each currency where that fixed rate is swapped against the floating rates, dollar LIBOR or Euribor.

So we now know that, given the term structures in Table 13.8, if a party agrees to pay dollars fixed and receive euros fixed, the dollar rate would be 6.1 percent and the euro rate would be 4.35 percent. If the swap is structured to pay dollars floating, then the terms would be to simply pay dollars at dollar LIBOR and receive euros at 4.35 percent. This is true because the

Pricing a currency swap means to determine the fixed rate that would be paid. This rate is easily determined from the term structure.

TABLE 13.8	Pricing a Currency Swap

U.S. dollar LIBOR term structure and Euribor term structure

	$ LIBOR	Euribor
6 months	5.5%	3.8%
12 months	5.5	4.2
18 months	6.2	4.4
24 months	6.4	4.5

Discount factors for U.S. dollar LIBOR and Euribor

$ LIBOR

6 months:	$1/(1 + .055(180/360)) = 0.9732$
12 months:	$1/(1 + .055(360/360)) = 0.9479$
18 months:	$1/(1 + .062(540/360)) = 0.9149$
24 months:	$1/(1 + .064(720/360)) = 0.8865$

Euribor

6 months:	$1/(1 + .038(180/360)) = 0.9814$
12 months:	$1/(1 + .042(360/360)) = 0.9597$
18 months:	$1/(1 + .044(540/360)) = 0.9381$
24 months:	$1/(1 + .045(720/360)) = 0.9174$

Swap fixed rates in each currency

$$\text{Swap rate in } \$ = 2\left(\frac{1 - 0.8865}{0.9732 + 0.9479 + 0.9149 + 0.8865}\right) = .061.$$

$$\text{Swap rate in } € = 2\left(\frac{1 - 0.9174}{0.9814 + 0.9597 + 0.9381 + 0.9174}\right) = .0435.$$

dollar fixed rate of 6.1 percent is equivalent in value to a stream of floating dollar payments at dollar LIBOR. This has to be true for 6.1 percent to be the correct rate on an interest rate swap. Likewise, if the euro rate is floating and the dollar rate is fixed, the dollar rate would be 6.1 percent. The relationships we saw in Figure 13.11 verify these points. If dollars and euros were paid floating, then both swaps would simply specify that dollar LIBOR would be paid against Euribor.

Currency swaps have one other set of terms, which is the two notional principals. Typically the end user comes to the dealer with the notional principal specified in one currency. The spot exchange rate is then used to convert that value to the notional principal in the other currency.

VALUATION OF A CURRENCY SWAP DURING ITS LIFE   When the swap is priced correctly at the start, the present value of the payments on one side of the transaction equals the present value of the payments on the other side of the transaction. During the life of the swap, the swap will gain or lose value to one party and the other as a result of changes in both interest rates and the exchange rate. To value the swap, we again resort to the term structure of interest rates as well as the new spot exchange rate.

Suppose in the Reston-GSI swap, we have now moved three months into the life of the swap. From Reston's perspective, it knows it will pay €217,500 and receive $299,022 in 3, 9, 15, and 21 months. In addition, in 21 months it will pay €10 million and receive $9,804,000. It is a simple matter to determine the value of the swap. First we must find the present value of the remaining dollar cash inflows. Then we find the present value of the remaining euro cash outflows. Recall that we observed that a currency swap is like issuing a bond in one currency and using the proceeds to buy a bond issued in another currency. What we will do is simply find the value of these implicit long and short bonds. We then convert the value of the bond issued in euros to dollars at the new spot exchange rate and subtract the present value of these dollar equivalent cash outflows from the present value of the dollar cash inflows. Table 13.9 presents the new term structure and the new spot exchange rate and shows that the swap is worth $38,560.

Valuation of a currency swap is done by finding the present value of the cash outflows in one currency and the present value of the cash outflows in the other currency. One of these present values is converted to the currency of the other using the spot exchange rate and the difference is then determined.

When the payments are floating, the valuation is a little more complex. This topic is best covered when we treat interest rate swaps in Chapter 14. We can then find the present value of the floating payments in a given currency and convert back to the other currency, if necessary.

Other Currency Derivatives

In the currency markets, there is a popular strategy referred to as an **FX swap**.[7] This type of transaction has been around longer than currency swaps, but its name makes it sound like a currency swap. This confusion is unfortunate for the transactions are quite different. An FX swap is simply a long position in a foreign currency forward contract of one expiration and a short position in a forward contract on that same currency but with a different expiration. When we studied futures, this analogous transaction was called a spread. The currency derivatives market views it as the exchange of currency at one date for that same currency at a different date; hence, the notion of "swapping" it.

In the over-the-counter currency markets, **basket options** have been particularly popular. A basket option is an option on a portfolio of currencies. For example, suppose a business has revenue coming in from several foreign countries. To protect the conversion of that revenue to dollars, the treasurer could buy puts or sell futures or forwards on each currency in the appropriate quantities. Alternatively, the treasurer could recognize that the exchange rates of all of the currencies are not perfectly correlated; thus,

---

[7]The term *FX* stands for "foreign exchange."

TABLE 13.9	Valuing a Currency Swap during Its Life

The Reston-GSI swap in Figure 13.10 is now three months into its life. The new exchange rate is $0.9790 per euro.

New U.S. dollar LIBOR term structure and Euribor term structure

	$ LIBOR	Euribor
3 months	5.7%	3.9%
9 months	6.1	4.3
15 months	6.4	4.5
21 months	6.6	4.6

New factors for U.S. dollar LIBOR and Euribor
(3 months, 9 months, 15 months and 21 months)

$ LIBOR

3 months:	$1/(1 + .057(90/360)) = 0.9860$
9 months:	$1/(1 + .061(270/360)) = 0.9563$
15 months:	$1/(1 + .064(450/360)) = 0.9259$
21 months:	$1/(1 + .066(630/360)) = 0.8965$

Euribor

3 months:	$1/(1 + .039(90/360)) = 0.9903$
9 months:	$1/(1 + .043(270/360)) = 0.9688$
15 months:	$1/(1 + .045(450/360)) = 0.9467$
21 months:	$1/(1 + .046(630/360)) = 0.9255$

Present value of the dollar payments:

$299,022(0.9860) + $299,022(0.9563) + $299,022(0.9259) + $299,022(0.8965) + $9,804,000(0.8965) = $9,915,014.

Present value of the euro payments:

€217,500(0.9903) + €217,500(0.9688) + €217,500(0.9467) + €217,500(0.9255) + €10,000,000(0.9255) = €10,088,308.

Present value of the euro payments in dollars:

€10,088,308($0.9790) = $9,876,454.

Value of the swap (receive dollars, pay euros):

$9,915,014 − $9,876,454 = $38,560.

they constitute a diversified portfolio of cash flows. A basket option is an option, denominated in dollars, on the overall value of the portfolio. Since the portfolio is less volatile than the average component, the option on the portfolio is less costly than the total cost of options on each component. Basket options are also popular in equity portfolio management.

Another popular type of currency option is called an **alternative currency option.** This is an option that pays off the better or worse of two currencies. For example, consider a Japanese yen–euro alternative currency option denominated in dollars. The option can be a "better" or "worse" "call" or "put" option. Let us assume it is a call that pays off according to the better performing currency. Now assume that when the option expires, the euro has gained more (or lost less) than the Japanese yen against the U.S. dollar. Then the option pays off as if it were a standard call option on the euro. If its payoff were based on the "worse" performing currency, it would pay off as if it were a standard call option on the Japanese yen. Such an option will cost more than a single option on either currency but less than options on both currencies. An example of when such an option might be used is when a corporate treasurer has cash flows coming from two different currencies. She is indifferent about which currency she makes payments in. She could then sell an alternative currency option and collect an option premium that rewards her for the flexibility she has to pay in either currency.

In Chapter 15 we will cover exotic options. Nearly all of the types of exotic options are on currencies as well as other assets. At this point we conclude our discussion of currency derivatives. We gave them only a brief overview, but, as we noted, most of the principles of derivative pricing already covered apply to foreign currency instruments and can easily be adapted to them. Some of the end-of-chapter problems ask you to do some of these applications.

Summary

This chapter examined foreign currency derivatives. We saw that understanding foreign currency derivatives requires an awareness of the special characteristics of foreign currency spot and forward markets. We observed how interest rate parity is the foreign currency forward/futures counterpart of the cost of carry model. We examined several basic principles for pricing foreign currency options and found that they differ only slightly from those for equity options. In particular, we saw that the Garman-Kohlhagen foreign currency option pricing model is merely a minor modification of the Black-Scholes model.

We saw that foreign currency hedge and speculative strategies are straightforward extensions of previous principles. We also observed an example of the advantage of a foreign currency option hedge. The option can be an effective hedging device when it is uncertain whether the hedger will take a position in the currency at a future date.

In this chapter we also introduced currency swaps, which can be used to convert debt issued in one currency to debt issued in another. In Chapter 14 we examine interest rate swaps. The swaps market is large and still rapidly growing, and is a natural extension of the derivative contracts we have been studying.

Key Terms

Before continuing to Chapter 14, you should be able to give brief definitions of the following terms.

- exchange rate
- euro
- EuroLIBOR/Euribor
- interbank market
- forward premium/discount
- cross-rate

- triangular arbitrage
- interest rate parity
- currency swap
- FX swap
- basket option
- alternative currency option

Further Reading

Excellent treatments of currency derivatives are in

Association for Investment Management and Research. *Managing Currency Risk.* Charlottesville, Va.: Association for Investment Management and Research, 1997.

Brown, K. C., and D. J. Smith. *Interest Rate and Currency Swaps: A Tutorial.* Charlottesville, Va.: The Research Foundation of the Institute of Chartered Financial Analysts, 1995.

Clarke, R. G., and M. P. Kritzman. *Currency Management: Concepts and Practices.* Charlottesville, Va.: The Research Foundation of the Institute of Chartered Financial Analysts, 1996.

DeRosa, D. F. *Currency Derivatives.* New York: John Wiley, 1998.

For more on international finance, see

Shapiro, A. C. *Multinational Financial Management.* 6th ed. New York: Wiley, 1999.

Solnik, B. H. *International Investments.* 4th ed. Reading, Mass.: Addison-Wesley, 1999.

Questions and Problems

1. Explain the difference between the forward and futures markets for foreign currency.

2. Discuss the differences between the use of options and forward contracts in hedging foreign exchange risk.

3. Suppose the British pound exchange rate was $1.6570 while the Swiss franc exchange rate was $0.6190. The exchange rate for Swiss francs in terms of British pounds is 2.70, that is, SF2.70/£. Explain how an arbitrageur could make a risk-free profit.

4. Suppose you are an analyst with a firm that specializes in following foreign markets and making investment strategy recommendations based on its perception of changing conditions in other countries. You observe a growing Japanese trade surplus with the United States.

You believe, however, that during the upcoming six months the trade surplus figures will narrow. Your opinion is contrary to that of most other firms. You would like to recommend a strategy that will be profitable if you are correct. Suggest one option and one futures/forward strategy, and justify your recommendations. Then discuss the risks of your strategies and ways to manage the risks so that your clients will not be wiped out if you are not as prescient as you think.

5. The following information was available:

Spot rate for Japanese yen: $0.009313
30-day forward rate for Japanese yen: $0.009356
U.S. risk-free rate: 6.15 percent
Japanese risk-free rate: 3.64 percent

Determine whether interest rate parity holds and, if not, suggest a strategy.

6. On December 9 of a particular year, a January Swiss franc call option with an exercise price of 46 had a price of 1.63. The January 46 put was at 14. The spot rate was 47.28. All prices are in cents per Swiss franc. The option expired on January 13. The U.S. risk-free rate was 7.1 percent, while the Swiss risk-free rate was 3.6 percent. Answer the following:

a. Determine the intrinsic value of the call.

b. Determine the lower bound of the call.

c. Determine the time value of the call.

d. Determine the intrinsic value of the put.

e. Determine the lower bound of the put.

f. Determine the time value of the put.

g. Determine whether put-call parity holds.

7. Use the Garman-Kohlhagen model to determine whether the Swiss franc call in problem 6 is correctly priced. Use .145 as the standard deviation of the logarithm of one plus the percentage change in the spot Swiss franc.

8. Differences would be expected in American and European call prices for foreign currency options. How is the relative level of interest rates in the two countries involved likely to affect the spread between European and American call prices?

9. On June 17 of a particular year, an American watch dealer decided to import 100,000 Swiss watches. Each watch costs SF225. The dealer would like to hedge against a change in the dollar/Swiss franc exchange rate. The forward rate was $.3881. Determine the outcome from the hedge if it was closed on August 16, when the spot rate was $.4434.

10. On January 2 of a particular year, an American firm decided to close out its account at a Canadian bank on February 28. The firm is expected to have 5 million Canadian dollars in the account at the time of the withdrawal. It would convert the funds to U.S. dollars and transfer them to a New York bank. The relevant forward exchange rate was $.7564. The March Canadian dollar futures contract was priced at $.7541. Determine the outcome of a futures hedge if on February 28 the spot rate was $.7207 and the futures rate was $.7220. All prices are in U.S. dollars per Canadian dollar.

For problems 11, 12, and 13, determine the profit for each of the following spot rates at expiration: $0.90, $0.95, $1.00, $1.05, and $1.10. Construct a profit graph. Find the breakeven spot rate at expiration. Assume each contract covers €100,000.

11. A call option on the euro expiring in six months has an exercise price of $1.00 and is priced at $0.0385. Construct a simple long position in the call.

12. A euro put with an exercise price of $1.00 is priced at $0.0435. Construct a simple long position in the put.

13. Use the information in problem 11 to construct a euro covered call. Assume the spot rate at the start is $0.9825.

14. Suppose an American firm is bidding on a contract to sell microcomputers to the German government. German officials have stipulated that the bid be made in euros and the firm receiving the bid be paid in euros. The decision will be made in January. The firm decides to use euro options to hedge its position. The current spot rate is $0.9825. The firm will bid €20 million and use an option with an exercise price of $1.00. The call is priced at $0.0241 and the put is priced at $0.0352. Which option, call or put, should the firm use? Why? Assume the day German officials will make their decision is the same day payment will be made. Also on that day, the option expires. Determine the cash flow to the firm under each of the following possible outcomes.

a. The firm wins the bid, and the spot rate is $1.05.

b. The firm wins the bid, and the spot rate is $0.95.

c. The firm loses the bid, and the spot rate is $1.05.

d. The firm loses the bid, and the spot rate is $0.95.

15. Suppose you are a U.S. firm that needs to borrow 20 million Canadian dollars ($C) for one year. You can borrow by issuing a one-year note with semiannual payments in Canada. Alternatively, you can borrow the equivalent amount in the United States and convert the proceeds to Canadian dollars by means of a currency swap. The term structures in the two countries are as follows:

	U.S.	Canada
6 months	6.50%	5.25%
12 months	6.75	5.50

Discounting is done by the LIBOR method with 30 days per month. The current spot exchange rate is $0.68 per Canadian dollar. The swap will involve fixed semiannual payments with an initial and final exchange of principal.

a. Determine the two notional principals, the swap rates, and the payment schedules for an appropriate swap, given the situation faced by the American firm.

b. Assume that three months later, the new term structures are as follows:

	U.S.	Canada
3 months	6.125%	5.00%
9 months	6.25	5.25

The new spot exchange rate is $0.675. Determine the value of the swap to the American firm.

16. (Concept Problem) Using the information in problem 11, rework the problem under the assumption that the call is closed out 30 days before expiration. Use .10 as the volatility, .06 as the U.S. interest rate, and .035 as the euro interest rate. Use the spreadsheet bsbin2.xls or the Windows program bsbwin2.1.exe to make these calculations.

17. (Concept Problem) You plan to buy 1,000 shares of Swissair stock. The current price is SF950. The current exchange rate is $0.7254/SF. You are interested in speculating on the stock but do not wish to assume any currency risk. You plan to hold the position for six months. The appropriate futures contract currently is trading at $0.7250. Construct a hedge and evaluate how your investment will do if in six months the stock is at SF926.50, the spot exchange rate is $0.7301, and the futures price is $0.7295. The Swiss franc futures contract size is SF125,000. Determine the overall profit from the transaction. Then break down the profit into the amount earned solely from the performance of the stock, the loss or gain from the currency change while holding the stock, and the loss or gain on the futures transaction.

APPENDIX 13

Foreign Currency Futures Contract Specifications*

These contracts trade on the Chicago Mercantile Exchange. Smaller versions of certain currency contracts trade on the MidAmerica Commodity Exchange and the New York Board of Trade and on some foreign exchanges. There are also contracts on the cross-rate between certain pairs of currencies.

- Delivery months: March, June, September, and December. Additional months are traded on the CME's electronic after-hours system GLOBEX2.

- Last trading day: Second business day before third Wednesday of month

- First delivery day: Third Wednesday of month

- Trading hours: 7:20 A.M. to 2:00 P.M. (local time)

- Additional currencies available are French Franc, Mexican peso, New Zealand dollar, Russian ruble, South African rand, and Brazilian real, but volume is very low.

Contract	Contract Size	Minimum Price Change	Margin (Initial/ Maintenance)[a]
euro	€125,000	$0.0001/€ = $12.50	$2,430/$1,800
Deutsche mark	DM125,000	$0.0001/DM = $12.50	$1,249/$925
Canadian dollar	C$100,000	$0.0001/$C = $10	$642/$475
Swiss franc	SF125,000	$0.0001/SF = $12.50	$1,688/$1,250
British pound	£62,500	$0.0002/£ = $12.50	$1,620/$1,200
Japanese yen	¥12,500,000	$0.000001/¥ = $12.50	$2,835/$2,100
Australian dollar	$A100,000	$0.0001/$A = $10	$1,317/$975

[a]Check with the exchange for changes to contract specifications and for spread and hedge margins, which usually are much lower than the speculative margins shown here.

---

*Source: www.cme.com. This material is believed to be correct as of March 2000. Contract specifications can change, especially margins and daily price limits. Investors should consult the exchanges for the latest information.

Interest Rate Derivatives

Derivatives are part of the vital machinery of the bank. We have put it at the heart of the business.

SAMAN MAJD, Global Head of OTC Derivatives, Deutsche Bank
Risk, May 1999.

In Chapter 13 we discussed two types of over-the-counter derivatives—the currency forward and the currency swap. Partially because of the enormous success of these instruments during the 1970s and early 1980s, the market was ripe for more financial innovation in the form of interest rate derivatives. An **interest rate derivative** is a derivative product that provides a payoff determined by how an interest rate changes. While interest rate options and forward contracts have proven to be quite popular, the most widely used interest rate derivative is the swap. In this chapter we shall take a look at these types of interest rate derivatives. We shall examine forward contracts on interest rates (called forward rate agreements), options on interest rates (commonly packaged as instruments called caps, floors, and collars), as well as interest rate swaps, options on interest rate swaps (called swaptions), and forward contracts on swaps (called forward swaps).

These instruments have grown in popularity for several reasons. Nearly all businesses face some form of interest rate risk. We have already seen several examples, such as a portfolio manager holding bonds or a corporation planning to borrow money. We showed that futures can be used to manage those risks. Since the middle 1980s, however, over-the-counter interest rate derivatives have proven to be the more popular way to manage interest rate risk. These instruments are customized to the needs of the risk manager, and an increasing number of dealer firms have gone into the business of offering these products, leading to a high degree of competition and lower bid-ask spreads.

As you know, the prices of bonds are driven by interest rates, which should make interest rate derivatives a lot like derivatives on bonds. That is true to some extent, but derivatives on bonds pay off based on movements

Chapter Objectives

- To understand the concept of an interest rate derivative as a derivative for which the underlying is an interest rate, in contrast to derivatives for which the underlying is the price of an asset

- To learn how forward contracts on interest rates, called forward rate agreements (FRAs), are used in managing interest rate risk

- To understand the structure of an interest rate swap and how it is used to hedge interest rate risk, how to price an interest rate swap, how interest rate swaps are like combinations of other financial transactions, and how to terminate an interest rate swap

- To learn how interest rate options pay off, how they are used to hedge interest rate risk, and how interest rate options are combined into caps, floors, and collars

- To understand how swaptions provide the right to buy or sell an interest rate swap and how forward swaps provide the obligation to enter into an interest rate swap

- To understand how the binomial model can represent movements in interest rates and can be used to price forward rate agreements, swaps, interest rate options, and swaptions

An interest rate derivative is a derivative product that provides a payoff determined by how an interest rate changes.

in bond prices while interest rate derivatives pay off based on movements in interest rates. Though bond prices are driven largely by interest rates, pricing interest rate derivatives is much more complex than pricing bond derivatives. In fact, pricing interest rate derivatives is one of the most complex subjects in the field of derivatives. In the latter part of this chapter we shall take an initial look at how interest rate derivative prices are driven by the term structure, which itself is a difficult process to capture in a model.

While the current chapter examines the basics of interest rate derivatives, in Chapter 15 we take it one step farther by covering advanced derivatives on stocks, stock indices, and interest rates. Then in Chapter 16 we examine the implications of the growing usage of these derivatives for managing financial risk.

The first interest rate derivative that we examine is a forward contract on an interest rate, called a forward rate agreement.

Forward Rate Agreements

A **forward rate agreement** or **FRA** is similar to any type of forward contract, but the payoff is based on an interest rate, rather than an asset price. For example, suppose a financial manager believed that interest rates were going up and wanted to lock in a specific rate to be paid on a future loan. He could do that by taking a short forward position in a fixed-income security like a Treasury bill or bond. If rates rose, the security price would fall, the forward price would also fall, and the short position would be profitable. If the hedge ratio were properly established, the position could lock in the forward rate at the time the contract was opened. Of course, as demonstrated in Chapter 10, he could also use futures.

In such a transaction, the payoff is determined directly by the price of a fixed-income security, which means that the payoff is determined indirectly by an interest rate. In an FRA the payoff is determined directly by an interest rate. Thus, our financial manager would take a long position in the FRA. The contract would specify a certain amount of notional principal on which the payment would be calculated and the terms under which the payment would be made. Typically payoffs are based on LIBOR, the Eurodollar rate, for a specific term, such as 90-day LIBOR or 180-day LIBOR. The payment is based on the difference between the resulting value of LIBOR and the contract rate, which was agreed on when the contract was taken out. This difference times the notional principal is prorated according to a specific formula over the length of the period.

The timing of the payoff in a typical FRA is much like that in a forward contract on an asset. At the expiration of the contract, LIBOR is determined and the payoff is made at that time. Surprisingly, however, this is unconventional for interest rate derivatives. As we shall see later, interest rate swaps and options provide for a payoff that occurs a specific number of days after the expiration. Though this appears to be unusual, if not inappropriate, it actually makes more sense in most cases to delay the final pay-off. This is because many of these interest rate derivatives are designed to hedge floating-rate loans, where the convention is that the interest rate is determined at the beginning of the period but the interest payment is made at the end of the period. This is because borrowers and lenders nor-mally like to know the rate during a period in which interest is accumulat-ing. Swaps and interest rate options typically follow this convention. In con-trast, most FRAs, for reasons no one seems to know, provide for the payoff to occur at the expiration. The difference in the timing of the payoff is re-ally nothing more than a present value adjustment. For illustrative pur-poses and later to show the similarity between FRAs and swaps, we shall use the more unconventional FRA payoff. That is, the rate will be determined at expiration but the payoff will occur at a later date, corresponding to the date on which the interest is paid on the spot transaction for which the FRA is used to hedge.

The exact manner in which the interest is computed is not always the same. In some cases interest is prorated as if a year has 360 days. In some cases a year is assumed to have 365 days. The number of days over which the interest is paid is sometimes the exact day count and sometimes based on the number of months with the assumption of 30 days in a month. We shall assume a 360-day year, and in most cases, we shall calculate interest over the exact number of days. Thus, six months' interest will be prorated by a factor of 181 to 184 over 360. In a few cases, we shall simply divide the interest rate by 2, effectively using 180 days as six months. This procedure may be confusing, but unfortunately, it is commonplace in the real world. In the examples here and in real-world interest rate agreements, the exact manner in which interest is calculated is stated explicitly.

Table 14.1 presents a typical situation involving an FRA. A corpora-tion wants to lock in a borrowing rate for a loan that will begin in 30 days. The loan is a 90-day loan and its rate will be set at whatever 90-day LIBOR is in 30 days plus 100 basis points, abbreviated as 100 bps.[1] Since the cor-poration is worried about rising rates, it takes a long position in the FRA and agrees on a rate of 10 percent. The terms specify that the FRA will pay off according to 90-day LIBOR 30 days from now. The payoff will be prorated over 90 days, using a 360-day year. The payment is based on the notional principal, which should correspond to the amount of the loan. In general the holder of a long FRA will have the following cash flow at expiration:

$$(\text{Notional principal})(\text{LIBOR} - \text{Agreed-upon rate})\left(\frac{\text{Days}}{360}\right),$$

---

[1]Remember that one basis point is one one-hundredth of a percent, so 100 basis points is 1 percent.

TABLE 14.1	**Hedging a Planned Loan with a Forward Rate Agreement**

Scenario: A firm plans to borrow at 90-day LIBOR plus a spread of 100 bps. The loan will be for $20 million and will be taken out in 30 days. The loan matures 90 days after that and is paid back in one lump sum. The firm would like to lock in the rate it pays on the loan so it establishes a long position in a forward rate agreement based on 90-day LIBOR. The FRA commits the firm to making an interest payment at a 10 percent rate and receiving an interest payment at LIBOR. Interest is computed on 90 days of a 360-day year.

LIBOR in 30 days	Payoff of FRA at Loan Maturity	Interest on Loan at Maturity	Total Effective Interest	Annualized Cost of Loan with FRA	Annualized Cost of Loan without FRA
6.00%	−$200,000	$350,000	$550,000	11.63%	7.29%
6.50	−175,000	375,000	550,000	11.63	7.82
7.00	−150,000	400,000	550,000	11.63	8.36
7.50	−125,000	425,000	550,000	11.63	8.90
8.00	−100,000	450,000	550,000	11.63	9.44
8.50	−75,000	475,000	550,000	11.63	9.99
9.00	−50,000	500,000	550,000	11.63	10.53
9.50	−25,000	525,000	550,000	11.63	11.08
10.00	0	550,000	550,000	11.63	11.63
10.50	25,000	575,000	550,000	11.63	12.18
11.00	50,000	600,000	550,000	11.63	12.74
11.50	75,000	625,000	550,000	11.63	13.29
12.00	100,000	650,000	550,000	11.63	13.85
12.50	125,000	675,000	550,000	11.63	14.41
13.00	150,000	700,000	550,000	11.63	14.97
13.50	175,000	725,000	550,000	11.63	15.54
14.00	200,000	750,000	550,000	11.63	16.10

where Days is the applicable number of days for the underlying interest rate. Here Days = 90 because 90-day LIBOR is used. In this example, the holder of the long FRA will have the following cash flow:

$$(\text{Notional principal})(\text{LIBOR} - .10)\left(\frac{90}{360}\right).$$

So if LIBOR in 30 days exceeds 10 percent, the corporation, being long the FRA, will receive a cash payment. If LIBOR in 30 days is less than 10 percent, the corporation will make a payment. The payment is made at the end of the life of the loan, which is 120 days from now.

Each row in Table 14.1 presents some possible outcomes, based on LIBOR in 30 days. Let us take a look at one outcome.

LIBOR at Expiration Is 12%

FRA payoff:

$$\$20,000,000(.12 - .10)(90/360) = \$100,000.$$

Interest paid on the loan:

$$\$20,000,000[.13(90/360)] = \$650,000.$$

Total effective interest paid:

$$\$650,000 - \$100,000 = \$550,000.$$

Amount borrowed: \$20,000,000
Amount paid back: \$20,550,000
Effective annual rate:

$$\left(\frac{20,550,000}{20,000,000}\right)^{365/90} - 1 = .1163.$$

Had the firm not used the FRA, it would have paid back \$650,000 in interest. Replacing \$550,000 with \$650,000 in the above calculation gives a rate of 13.85 percent.

A forward rate agreement is a contract between two parties in which one party agrees to make an interest payment at a future date at an agreed-upon rate, and the other party agrees to make an interest payment at that same date at a floating rate such as LIBOR.

Note in the table that regardless of what LIBOR is in 30 days, the cost of the loan with the FRA is always 11.63 percent. Without the FRA the cost varies directly with LIBOR. Thus, the FRA locks in a loan rate, at the expense of the interest savings that would occur if rates fell. Figure 14.1 illustrates this result graphically. The loan plus the FRA is essentially a risk-free transaction. Without the FRA, the loan is susceptible to considerable interest rate risk.

In the case where LIBOR turns out to be 12 percent, if the FRA were structured in the more conventional way, that is, with the payoff occurring at the FRA's expiration and not 90 days later, the firm would have received the FRA payoff of \$100,000 at the time it took out the loan. Thus, it would have received \$20,000,000 + \$100,000 = \$20,100,000 in 30 days and paid back \$20,000,000 + \$650,000=\$20,650,000 ninety days later. The annualized rate would, thus, have been

$$\left(\frac{\$20,650,000}{\$20,100,000}\right)^{365/90} - 1 = .1157,$$

which is just slightly different. If the contract were structured in that manner, however, the fixed rate would not have initially been set at 10 percent.

Pricing an FRA is done by determining the fixed rate, which is found as the forward rate embedded in the term structure. We shall look at FRA pricing later in the chapter.

FIGURE 14.1	**Cost of Planned Loan with and without Forward Rate Agreement**

Interest Rate Swaps

An interest rate swap is a contract between two parties in which each party agrees to exchange a series of interest payments, where at least one set of payments is determined by a variable interest rate.

An **interest rate swap** is an agreement between two parties in which each party makes a series of interest payments to the other at predetermined dates at different rates. At least one set of rates must be variable, usually called *floating*, in the sense that the rate at which the interest payment will be made is not determined until a later date. Both sets of payments could be variable but our focus in this chapter will be on the **plain vanilla swap,** in which one set of payments is fixed and the other is variable. Since each party makes a payment to the other on the same day, the convention is for only one payment, the net owed by one party to the other, to be made. Typical interest rate swap transactions are between a party called the end user and a dealer, which is normally a bank or an investment banking firm that makes a market in swaps and other interest rate derivatives. While some swaps will be conducted between dealers, few are conducted directly between end users. The dealer plays an important role in providing a counterparty with which end users can quickly and easily engage in swaps and other interest rate derivatives. As we shall see in Chapter 16, most dealers hedge the risk they assume from entering into these derivative transactions and earn a profit off of the bid-ask spreads they quote. Let us learn about interest rate swaps by examining a specific transaction.

The Structure of an Interest Rate Swap

Consider a firm called XYZ that is currently borrowing at the floating rate LIBOR but would prefer to borrow at a fixed rate. It contacts a swap dealer called ABSwaps and arranges a swap based on a $50 million notional principal. The current date is December 15. The terms of the swap call for ABSwaps to pay XYZ the 90-day LIBOR on the 15th of March, June, September, and December of the following year. The payment is determined by LIBOR at the beginning of the payment period. For example, LIBOR on March 15 determines the payment on June 15. XYZ agrees to pay ABSwaps a fixed rate of 7.5 percent on each of those payment dates. The terms of this swap also specify that the amount of interest computed for each payment period will be based on the exact number of days in the period, assuming a 360-day year. The net interest owed will be determined and only one party will make a payment to the other. In general the fixed-rate payer, floating-rate receiver has a cash flow at each interest payment date of

$$\text{(Notional principal) (LIBOR} - \text{Fixed rate)}\left(\frac{\text{Days}}{360}\right).$$

Thus, from the perspective of XYZ, the cash flow on a payment date will be

$$(\$50,000,000) (\text{LIBOR} - .075)\left(\frac{\text{Days}}{360}\right).$$

So if LIBOR exceeds 7.5 percent, XYZ will receive a payment in the above amount from ABSwaps. If LIBOR is less than 7.5 percent, XYZ will make the payment to ABSwaps.

The time pattern of XYZ's payments is illustrated in Figure 14.2. On each payment date XYZ receives a payment based on LIBOR three months prior and makes a payment based on a 7.5 percent rate. XYZ obviously does not know the cash payments it will receive; likewise, ABSwaps does not know the cash payments it will make. Table 14.2 presents an after-the-fact look at the payments on this swap. On December 15, the day the swap is negotiated, LIBOR is 7.68 percent. This determines the first swap payment,

FIGURE 14.2	Time Pattern of XYZ's Interest Rate Swap

NOTE: All payments are determined by multiplying by the notional principal of $50 million.

which will be made on March 15. There are 90 days from December 15 to March 15. Thus, ABSwaps will owe

$$\$50,000,000(.0768)\left(\frac{90}{360}\right) = \$960,000,$$

while XYZ will owe

$$\$50,000,000(.075)\left(\frac{90}{360}\right) = \$937,500.$$

The net payment will be $22,500 paid by ABSwaps to XYZ. On March 15, LIBOR turns out to be 7.50 percent, meaning that on the next payment date, each party owes the other the same amount. Thus, no payment is

TABLE 14.2	After-the-Fact Payments in Fixed-for Floating-Rate Swap

Notional principal: $50,000,000
Fixed rate: 7.5 percent
Interest based on exact number of days and 360-day year

Date	3-month LIBOR	Days	ABSwaps Owes	XYZ Owes	Net to XYZ
Dec 15	7.68				
Mar 15	7.50	90	$960,000	$937,500	$ 22,500
Jun 15	7.06	92	958,333	958,333	0
Sep 15	6.06	92	902,111	958,333	−56,222
Dec 15	—	91	765,917	947,917	−182,000

NOTE: This is but one of an infinite number of possible outcomes to the swap. It is used only to illustrate how the payments are determined and not their likely amounts.

made on June 15. The following LIBOR is 7.06, so XYZ makes a payment of $56,222. The final LIBOR is 6.06, making XYZ pay $182,000. Note in Table 14.2 that the number of days in each quarter is slightly different, resulting in the fixed payment being slightly different from quarter to quarter. Except for the different number of days in each quarter, we see that XYZ is now making fixed interest payments while receiving floating interest payments, the latter of which will offset the floating loan payments it has.

Note that no principal payments are made in an interest rate swap. Thus, the $50 million notional principal is never paid. This contrasts sharply with the currency swap where the notional principal is usually exchanged.

Why Companies Use Interest Rate Swaps

Companies use interest rate swaps primarily to convert a series of fixed interest payments to floating interest payments or floating interest payments to fixed interest payments. For example, suppose a company has taken out a loan in which it pays LIBOR plus 250 bps. If the company expects rising interest rates, the cost of its loan will go up if those expectations turn out to be true. It might, therefore, prefer a fixed-rate loan. The firm may be able to repay the loan early, refinancing it with a fixed-rate loan. Repaying a loan early and taking out a new loan is quite costly, however, and involves extensive paperwork and legal documentation. It is much simpler to enter into a swap. Suppose the firm enters into a pay-fixed, receive-floating swap, where the floating rate is LIBOR and the fixed rate is R. Now consider what its periodic payments are:

Paying LIBOR+250 bps on loan
Receiving LIBOR on swap
Paying R on swap
Net: Paying R+250 bps

Now the firm has effectively converted its floating-rate loan into a fixed-rate loan. The original floating-rate loan still exists, but the net effect is that the risk of rising interest rates has been offset. Some firms view this as a form of hedging interest rate risk, but do keep in mind that the new position of the firm is that it is exposed to falling interest rates. If rates decrease, it would have been better off without the swap, thereby keeping its position in the floating-rate loan.

Most firms use interest rate swaps in this manner, which is to manage the payment structure of their liabilities. Other firms holding interest-sensitive assets use swaps to adjust the structures of their cash inflows. Swaps, like most derivatives, are considerably easier to use than transactions in the underlying securities. They are less costly and the paperwork and legal requirements are less burdensome.

Companies use interest rate swaps to alter the structure of their asset and liability cash flows. Swaps save money by reducing paperwork and legal work.

Some firms believe that using swaps saves money by getting them better rates than they otherwise would. For example, consider a firm that wants to borrow at a fixed rate. It may find that it can get a better overall borrowing rate by borrowing at a floating rate, then entering into a receive-floating, pay-fixed swap. Notice, however, a major difference in the two transactions. If the firm merely borrows at a fixed rate, it faces no risk of a counterparty defaulting. Only the firm itself can default and that risk is assumed by the lender. If the firm borrows floating and swaps it into a fixed rate, it faces the risk that the swap counterparty might default. Counterparty credit risk is a major concern in all over-the-counter derivative transactions, and we shall discuss it more in Chapter 16.

Transactions Equivalent to Interest Rate Swaps

One consistent observation throughout our treatment of derivatives is that it is possible to construct portfolios of financial instruments with payoffs equivalent to other financial instruments and whose values will be equivalent through the principle of arbitrage. With that in mind, it is easy to see that a swap is equivalent to two other types of financial transactions.

A fixed- for floating-rate swap is equivalent to issuing either a fixed- or floating-rate note and using the proceeds to buy the other.

In our previous example, XYZ entered into a one-year swap in which it made a series of quarterly payments at a rate of 7.5 percent and received a series of quarterly payments at a rate set at LIBOR at the beginning of the quarter, with both sets of payments based on a principal value of $50 million. Suppose, instead, that XYZ had issued a $50 million one-year fixed-rate note in which it made quarterly payments at an annual rate of 7.5 percent and used the $50 million to purchase a $50 million one-year floating-rate note that would pay interest at the end of each quarter at the rate LIBOR at the beginning of the quarter. As long as the interest is computed identically, that is, based on the exact day count in the quarter and 360 days in a year, the transactions are equivalent to XYZ's swap. The $50 million received up front from issuing the fixed-rate loan is used to buy the floating-rate note. When the notes mature, XYZ receives $50 million from the floating-rate note it holds and uses it to pay off the fixed-rate note it issued. The analogy in an interest rate swap is the fact that no principal payments are made either up front or at the termination date. The net interest payments from issuing the fixed-rate note and using the proceeds to buy the floating-rate note are precisely those produced by the pay fixed–receive floating interest rate swap. Likewise, the pay floating–receive fixed side of the swap is equivalent to issuing a floating-rate note and using the proceeds to buy a fixed-rate note.

An interest rate swap is also identical to a spot transaction and a set of FRAs. Recall that in XYZ's swap, initiated on December 15, its first payment, to be made on March 15, is determined by the rate on December 15, which is 7.68 percent. As Table 14.2 showed, the first payment consists of XYZ owing $937,500 and ABSwaps owing $960,000. This is equivalent to a simple spot transaction on December 15 in which ABSwaps simply agrees to give XYZ $22,500 on March 15. Though it may seem a bit perverse for ABSwaps to do this transaction, we cannot view it in isolation. We must remember that XYZ has committed to making ABSwaps a series of fixed payments while ABSwaps is committed to giving XYZ a series of floating payments. The second swap payment is equivalent to an FRA in which XYZ agrees to pay a fixed rate and receive the LIBOR of March 15, with the payment made on June 15. There are also two other FRAs with XYZ committed to making fixed payments and receiving LIBOR. Although we shall discuss this point further later in the chapter, it should be apparent that the terms of the other three FRAs must be sufficiently favorable to ABSwaps to offset the unfavorable spot transaction represented by the first payment. With this point in mind, it is easy to see that the swap is a series of FRAs and one spot transaction at the start representing the first swap payment, which is known when the swap is taken out.

A fixed- for floating-rate swap is equivalent to a spot transaction and a set of forward rate agreements.

Swaps and many other interest rate derivatives can also be shown to be equivalent to combinations of interest rate options, as we shall explain later.

Pricing an Interest Rate Swap at the Outset

Pricing an interest rate swap means to determine the fixed rate that is appropriate for the terms of the swap. This is called the **swap rate.** We saw in the previous section that a swap can be viewed as a combination of fixed- and floating-rate bonds or as a spot transaction and a series of forward rate agreements. Since a swap involves no initial exchange of cash, it should have zero initial value. Thus, to price the swap means to determine the fixed rate that will make the swap have zero initial value.

Let us consider a simple example, which is illustrated in Table 14.3. Quantum Electronics enters into a $20 million notional principal swap in which it agrees to pay fixed and receive LIBOR. Payments will be made every six months with the floating payments based on LIBOR six months prior. For simplicity we shall assume that there are 30 days in each month and, of course, we use 360 days in a year; thus, all annual rates will simply be divided by two to obtain the semiannual rate. What is the appropriate swap rate?

Table 14.3 presents the term structure for LIBOR for six months, one year, 18 months, and two years. The quoted rates are based on LIBOR deposits of the given maturities. Recall, however, that LIBOR deposits pay interest by multiplying the rate by the number of days over 360 and adding that interest to the amount deposited. Thus, a deposit of $1 at 9 percent for six months would pay back $1(1 + .09(180/360)) = 1.045. This is a compound interest factor. To price swaps, we shall need the discount factor or present value equivalent, which is $1/1.045 = 0.9569$. As the table indicates, we obtain 0.9112, 0.8673, and 0.8264 as the discount factors for the remaining rates.

TABLE 14.3	**Pricing an Interest Rate Swap at the Outset**

Scenario: Quantum Electronics enters into a $20 million notional principal interest rate swap in which it promises to pay a fixed rate and receive payments at LIBOR. The swap specifies that payments are made every six months with the floating side determined by LIBOR at the beginning of the six-month period. All payments will assume 30 days in each month and 360 days in the year. What fixed rate will give an initial swap value of zero?

The term structure of interest rates, quoted from the LIBOR, is as follows:

Maturity	LIBOR	Discount Factor	
6 months	9.00%	$1/(1 + .09(180/360))$	$= 0.9569$
1 year	9.75	$1/(1 + .0975(360/360))$	$= 0.9112$
18 months	10.20	$1/(1 + .1020(540/360))$	$= 0.8673$
2 years	10.50	$1/(1 + .1050(720/360))$	$= 0.8264$

The first floating payment will be $20,000,000(.09/2) = $900,000$. All remaining floating payments will be determined by LIBOR at the beginning of each six-month period. Thus, the floating component of the swap has a current value of $20 million. What is the coupon that will make a fixed-rate bond have a value of $20,000,000?

Coupon (0.9569) + Coupon (0.9112) + Coupon (0.8673) +
(Coupon + 20,000,000)(0.8264) = 20,000,000.

Solving for the coupon reveals that

974,788(0.9569) + 974,788(0.9112) + 974,788(0.8673) + 20,974.788(0.8264)
= 20,000,000

So a coupon of $974,788 will set the bond's value to $20,000,000. This semiannual coupon is equivalent to an annual rate of 2($974,788/$20,000,000) = 9.75 percent.

Thus, if Quantum promises to pay a fixed rate of 9.75 percent and receive a floating rate based on LIBOR at the beginning of the six-month period, the swap will have zero initial value.

An interest rate swap has zero value at the outset. Pricing the swap means to determine the fixed rate that will give it an initial value of zero.

Using the notion that this swap is like issuing a fixed-rate bond and using the proceeds to buy a floating-rate bond means that we need to find the coupon on the fixed-rate bond that would give it an initial value of $20 million, where the coupons are discounted at the spot rates described in the previous paragraph. The floating-rate bond will automatically be worth par value of $20 million. As Table 14.3 shows, a coupon rate of 9.75 percent will make the fixed-rate bond be worth $20 million. You might observe that finding this coupon rate is similar to finding the yield on a bond. In this case, however, it is possible to solve for the coupon directly by factoring it out of the equation. In effect, pricing an interest rate swap at the outset is equivalent to finding the coupon on a par bond.

A simple alternative approach to solving for the swap rate can be stated quite easily. First, the notional principal will not affect the swap rate so it can be removed from the process, which is equivalent to setting it to $1.00. The swap rate is then found as

$$\text{Swap rate} = \frac{1 - \text{Final discount factor}}{\text{Sum of discount factors}}.$$

In our problem, we have

$$\text{Swap rate} = \frac{1 - 0.8264}{0.9569 + 0.9112 + 0.8673 + 0.8264} = .0487,$$

which is the periodic rate. If there are semiannual payments, we double this to obtain .0975, the annual quoted rate.

In the real world, the swap rate is determined by the dealer and quoted to its potential customers. The exact manner in which the rate is quoted can be somewhat confusing. Let us say that as in this example, the dealer is quoting a rate of 9.75 percent for a two-year swap. When a customer calls a dealer for a quote, if the dealer states that the rate would be 9.75 percent for a two-year swap, the quote would have to be changed almost instantaneously as interest rates change. Thus, the customer would not be able to call another dealer, then go back to the first dealer and get the same rate. In fact market interest rates could change while the dealer is on the phone making the quote.

To protect the dealer against this risk, the rate is quoted as a spread over the U.S. Treasury security with approximately the same maturity. Thus, if the two-year Treasury note was yielding 8 percent, the two-year swap would be quoted as the two-year Treasury note rate plus 175 bps. Note, however, that in making a market, a dealer would quote one rate to pay fixed and another to receive fixed. So after pricing the swap at 175 bps over the Treasury rate, the dealer might be willing to pay fixed (against receipt of LIBOR) at 174 bps and receive fixed (against paying LIBOR) at 176 bps.

An interest rate swap, as we learned with forward contracts, has zero initial value. It is neither an asset nor a liability. During its life, however, it can attain a positive or negative value. We have already seen this occur with currency swaps.

Valuing an Interest Rate Swap during Its Life

The swap rate of 9.75 percent was determined by finding the fixed rate that equates the present value of the fixed payments to the present value of the floating payments. In doing so we made the calculation easier by adding the notional principal to both sides so we could treat the two sides like bonds. The swap has an initial value of zero. The amount of money one party promises to pay has the same present value as the amount the other promises to pay.

After the swap is initiated, however, interest rates begin to change and one party can gain value at the expense of the other. For example, Quantum Electronics is paying a fixed rate and receiving a floating rate. If interest rates go up, the fixed outflows have a lower present value and the floating rates will increase. Thus, Quantum will gain from rising interest rates. Our job here is to find out how much. In effect what we need to do is assign a market value to the swap.

Suppose it is now three months into the life of the swap. We now have a new set of interest rates, as follows:

3 months	9.125%
9 months	10.000%
15 months	10.375%
21 months	10.625%

Of course there are rates for other periods, but since the swap payments remaining occur in 3, 9, 15, and 21 months, these are the only rates we need. To use these rates to find present values, we must find the discount factors as we did in pricing the swap. These are:

3 months:	$1/(1 + .09125(90/360))$	$= 0.9777$
9 months:	$1/(1 + .10(270/360))$	$= 0.9302$
15 months:	$1/(1 + .10375(450/360))$	$= 0.8852$
21 months:	$1/(1 + .10625(630/360))$	$= 0.8432$

The value of the swap will be the present value of the floating payments minus the present value of the fixed payments. Recall that in pricing the swap, we pretend as if the notional principals are paid on both sides. This allows us to treat the swap as the issuance of a fixed-rate bond with the proceeds used to buy a floating-rate bond. The whole process is illustrated in Figure 14.3.

FIGURE 14.3   **Valuation of Quantum Electronics Interest Rate Swap Three Months into Its Life**

Floating   +$20,000,000 = present value of remaining floating payments plus hypothetical notional principal

+$900,000

Fixed   −$974,788   −$974,788   −$974,788   −$974,788

−$20,000,000 (hypothetical)

0   3   6   12   18   24

(today)

Thus, including the notional principal, the present value of the fixed payments is

$$\$974{,}788(0.9777) + \$974{,}788(0.9302)$$
$$+ \$974{,}788(0.8852) + \$20{,}974{,}788(0.8432) = \$20{,}408{,}621.$$

The value of an interest rate swap changes from zero to a nonzero value as interest rates change. The swap will have positive value to one side of the contract and negative value to the other. The swap value can be determined by pricing the fixed- and floating-rate bonds that are equivalent to the swap and netting the two values.

The floating payments are a little more difficult to see, although easier to compute. The next floating payment is $\$20{,}000{,}000[.09(180/360)] = \$900{,}000$. At the next payment date, three months from now, the present value of the remaining floating payments plus the $20,000,000 principal will have a market value of $20,000,000, the par value. This is because a floating rate bond sells for par at the coupon reset date. The coupon always resets to the current interest rate. Thus, we do not need to know the remaining unknown floating payments. We know the next one. All the remaining ones plus the final principal have a value of par at the next reset date. Thus, the present value of the floating payments is

$$\$20{,}900{,}000(0.9777) = \$20{,}433{,}930.$$

So the overall swap value is

$$\$20{,}433{,}930 - \$20{,}408{,}621 = \$25{,}309.$$

To the counterparty, the value of the swap is $-\$25{,}309$.

Terminating an Interest Rate Swap

A firm that has entered into a swap may later find that it would like to get out of the swap. There are several ways to terminate a swap. One way is to do a reversal or offset, which simply involves entering into a new swap with the same terms and conditions but structured so that the cash flows on the new swap offset the cash flows on the old. For example, in the previous section, Quantum was obligated to pay a fixed rate of 9.75 percent and receive LIBOR. At three months into the swap, the transaction had a market value of $25,309. It could offset this swap by finding another party with which it could enter into a swap with identical floating payments. Suppose Quantum enters into a new swap obligating it to make floating payments at LIBOR and receive fixed payments at the going market rate. Its new swap would have zero value while its old swap would have a value of $25,309. Its LIBOR payments on the old swap would be offset by LIBOR receipts on the new swap.[2] Its fixed-rate receipts would exceed its fixed-rate payments.

---

[2]The upcoming floating payment would not match the $900,000 floating payment it has coming on the old swap, because its first payment on the new swap would be based on a new rate.

Both swaps would still be in effect so Quantum would be exposed to credit risk on both swaps.[3]

Of course, if the swap had a negative value to Quantum, it would remain on the books as a liability and the new swap would still have zero value. The LIBOR payments on both swaps would still offset, and its fixed-rate payments would exceed its fixed-rate receipts.

Another way to terminate the swap is by sale or assignment. In this case Quantum would find another party who agrees to take over its obligations and accept its receipts on the swap. Since the new party is taking over Quantum's positive-value swap, it would have to pay Quantum the swap's current market value of $25,309. If the swap had had negative value, Quantum could have paid a third party to take it. Since the original counterparty to Quantum's swap accepted Quantum as a counterparty, it would have to agree to allow Quantum to replace itself with the new counterparty.

Quantum's counterparty could also buy out of the swap by paying Quantum $25,309. This is called a **buy-back** or **close-out.** Of course, Quantum would have to agree to accept cash in lieu of continuing the swap.

Finally, had Quantum anticipated the need to terminate the swap early, it could have bought an option to terminate the swap. Quantum would have paid a premium to a dealer up front and received the right to sell the swap to the dealer. The option would most likely be offered by the original counterparty to the swap. In other words, Quantum would have arranged the swap with a counterparty to whom it would have paid a premium for the right to terminate the swap early. That right would have specified a way in which the swap is valued at the option exercise date. Later in this chapter, we look at these instruments, which are called swaptions.

Swaps can be terminated by executing an offsetting swap, by finding another party to take over the payments, by paying the market value to the counterparty, or by exercising a previously purchased option to terminate or offset the swap.

Interest Rate Options

Interest Rate Calls and Puts

Interest rate options are like forward rate agreements, but instead of being a firm commitment to receive one interest rate and pay another, they provide the right to receive one interest rate and pay another. An interest rate call pays off if interest rates end up above the agreed-upon rate. The holder pays the agreed-upon rate and receives the market rate, usually LIBOR. An interest rate put pays off if interest rates end up below the agreed-upon rate. The holder pays the market rate and receives the agreed-upon rate. This agreed-upon rate is also called the **strike rate** or **exercise rate.**

---

[3]In some cases a firm could enter into an offsetting swap with the same party with which it entered into the original swap. The two parties could then agree to cancel all remaining payments as soon as one party paid the other party the market value, here $25,309, up front.

Interest rate options usually are written by dealers and are tailored to the needs of a specific clientele. The options are typically European, meaning they can be exercised only at expiration. The expiration date is chosen, and the strike rate usually is set at the current level of the spot or forward interest rate. As noted, the options pay off on the basis of the difference between an interest rate, usually LIBOR, and an interest rate designated as the exercise or strike rate. Thus, the payoff of an interest rate call is

$$\text{(Notional principal)} \text{Max} (0, \text{LIBOR} - \text{X}) \left(\frac{\text{Days}}{360} \right),$$

where X is the exercise rate. As in interest rate swaps, when exercised, the payment by the writer is made not at the expiration but at a future date that corresponds to the maturity of the underlying spot instrument.

For example, consider a call option written on the 90-day LIBOR at an exercise rate of 10 percent, which is the current LIBOR, for a notional principal of $20 million. This option expires in 30 days. At that time, the buyer determines whether to exercise the option, which depends on whether the 90-day LIBOR is above 10 percent. If the option is exercised, the payment from the writer to the buyer is made 90 days after the exercise, or 120 days from now.

Let us consider an example using this option. A firm decides that in 30 days it will borrow $20 million at LIBOR plus 100 bps. Fearing an increase in LIBOR, it asks a dealer to write it a call option on LIBOR. The option will expire in 30 days and pay off 90 days thereafter. The bank charges a premium of $50,000. The payoff is based on 90 days and a 360-day year.

An interest rate call option gives the holder the right to receive an interest payment at a floating rate in exchange for making an interest payment at a fixed rate.

The payoff of the option is

$$(\$20,000,000) \text{ Max} (0, \text{LIBOR} - .10) \left(\frac{90}{360} \right),$$

which occurs 90 days after the expiration. If exercised, this amount helps reduce the increased cost of the loan. Table 14.4 illustrates the option payoffs for a range of possible outcomes.

Now let us examine how these results are obtained. First we must compound the premium forward for 30 days at today's LIBOR plus 100 bps:

$$\$50,000[1 + .11(30/360)] = \$50,458.$$

The effective proceeds obtained when the loan is taken out are, therefore,

$$\$20,000,000 - \$50,458 = \$19,949,542.$$

Now let us consider two outcomes, one of which leaves the call out-of-the-money and one of which leaves the call in-the-money.

LIBOR at Expiration is 6%

Interest on the loan:

$$\$20,000,000[.07(90/360)] = \$350,000.$$

Call is out-of-the-money.
Total effective interest: $350,000
Amount borrowed: $19,949,542
Amount paid back: $20,350,000
Effective annual rate:

$$\left(\frac{20,350,000}{19,949,542}\right)^{365/90} - 1 = .0839.$$

LIBOR at Expiration is 12%

Interest on the loan:

$$\$20,000,000[.13(90/360)] = \$650,000.$$

Call is in-the-money, exercised, and worth:

$$\$20,000,000(.12 - .10)(90/360) = \$100,000.$$

Total effective interest: $650,000 - $100,000 = $550,000.
Amount borrowed: $19,949,542
Amount paid back: $20,550,000
Effective annual rate:

$$\left(\frac{20,550,000}{19,949,542}\right)^{365/90} - 1 = .1278.$$

Figure 14.4 illustrates the cost of the planned fixed-rate loan with and without the interest rate call. The fixed-rate loan plus the call creates a maximum cost of 12.78 percent, which is reached if LIBOR ends up at 10 percent or above. Note that this payoff graph looks similar to a covered call or short put. In our previous option graphs, however, recall that the payoff was based on an asset price. In this case, the payoff is based on an interest rate.

Table 14.5 illustrates an interest rate put. An interest rate put might be used by a bank that lends at LIBOR plus possibly a spread. It thus is vulnerable to a decline in interest rates. Although declining interest rates generally are considered bullish, a put is appropriate because the payoff is based on LIBOR, and not on the price of a fixed-income security. In general the payoff from an interest rate put is

$$(\text{Notional principal})\text{Max}(0, \text{X} - \text{LIBOR})\left(\frac{\text{Days}}{360}\right).$$

TABLE 14.4	Hedging a Planned Loan with an Interest Rate Call

Scenario: A firm plans to borrow at 90-day LIBOR plus a spread of 100 bps. The loan will be for $20 million and will be taken out in 30 days. The loan matures 90 days after that and is paid back in one lump sum. The firm would like to establish a maximum rate it will pay on the loan so it buys an interest rate call based on 90-day LIBOR. The call gives the right to receive an interest payment based on the actual LIBOR in 30 days and has a 10 percent strike rate. The payoff is based on 90 days and a 360-day year. The call premium is $50,000. The current LIBOR is 10 percent.

LIBOR in 30 days	Payoff of Call at Loan Maturity	Interest on Loan at Maturity	Total Effective Interest	Annualized Cost of Loan with Call	Annualized Cost of Loan without Call
6.00%	$0	$350,000	$350,000	8.39%	7.29%
6.50	0	375,000	375,000	8.93	7.82
7.00	0	400,000	400,000	9.48	8.36
7.50	0	425,000	425,000	10.02	8.90
8.00	0	450,000	450,000	10.57	9.44
8.50	0	475,000	475,000	11.12	9.99
9.00	0	500,000	500,000	11.67	10.53
9.50	0	525,000	525,000	12.22	11.08
10.00	0	550,000	550,000	12.78	11.63
10.50	25,000	575,000	550,000	12.78	12.18
11.00	50,000	600,000	550,000	12.78	12.74
11.50	75,000	625,000	550,000	12.78	13.29
12.00	100,000	650,000	550,000	12.78	13.85
12.50	125,000	675,000	550,000	12.78	14.41
13.00	150,000	700,000	550,000	12.78	14.97
13.50	175,000	725,000	550,000	12.78	15.54
14.00	200,000	750,000	550,000	12.78	16.10

Like an interest rate call, exercise is determined at expiration, but the payment is made at a later date.

Here the bank plans to lend in 90 days at LIBOR plus a spread of 150 bps. The amount of the loan will be $10 million, and the loan will be for 180 days and be paid back in one lump sum. The bank finds a writer to sell it a put on LIBOR with a strike of 9 percent, the current LIBOR. The payoff is based on 180 days and a 360-day year. The put premium will be $26,500. Its payoff is

$$(\$10,000,000) \, \text{Max}(0, .09 - \text{LIBOR})\left(\frac{180}{360}\right).$$

First we must compound the premium forward for 90 days at today's LIBOR plus 150 bps:

$$\$26,500[1 + .105(90/360)] = \$27,196.$$

An interest rate put option gives the holder the right to receive an interest payment at a fixed rate in exchange for making an interest payment at a floating rate.

| **FIGURE 14.4** | **Cost of Planned Loan with and without Interest Rate Call** |

The effective proceeds paid out when the loan is taken out are

$$\$10,000,000 + \$27,196 = \$10,027,196.$$

Now let us consider two outcomes, one of which leaves the put out-of-the-money and one of which leaves the put in-the-money.

LIBOR at Expiration is 7%

Interest on the loan:

$$\$10,000,000[.085(180/360)] = \$425,000.$$

Put is in-the-money, exercised, and worth

$$\$10,000,000(.09 - .07)(180/360) = \$100,000.$$

Total effective interest received: $\$425,000 + \$100,000 = \$525,000$.
Amount paid out on loan: $\$10,027,196$
Amount received back on loan: $\$10,525,000$
Effective annual rate:

$$\left(\frac{10,525,000}{10,027,196}\right)^{365/180} - 1 = .1032.$$

| TABLE 14.5 | Hedging a Planned Loan with an Interest Rate Put |

Scenario: A bank plans to lend $10 million in 90 days at 180-day LIBOR plus a spread of 150 bps. The loan will mature 180 days after that and is paid back in one lump sum. The bank wants to lock in a minimum return on the loan so it buys an interest rate put for $26,500 with a strike rate of 9 percent. The put will pay off to the bank if LIBOR ends up below the strike rate. The payoff is based on 180 days and a 360-day year. The current LIBOR is 9 percent.

LIBOR in 90 days	Payoff of Put at Loan Maturity	Interest on Loan at Maturity	Total Effective Interest	Annualized Return on Loan with Put	Annualized Return on Loan without Put
5.00%	$200,000	$325,000	$525,000	10.32%	6.70%
5.50	175,000	350,000	525,000	10.32	7.22
6.00	150,000	375,000	525,000	10.32	7.75
6.50	125,000	400,000	525,000	10.32	8.28
7.00	100,000	425,000	525,000	10.32	8.81
7.50	75,000	450,000	525,000	10.32	9.34
8.00	50,000	475,000	525,000	10.32	9.87
8.50	25,000	500,000	525,000	10.32	10.40
9.00	0	525,000	525,000	10.32	10.93
9.50	0	550,000	550,000	10.86	11.47
10.00	0	575,000	575,000	11.39	12.00
10.50	0	600,000	600,000	11.92	12.54
11.00	0	625,000	625,000	12.46	13.08
11.50	0	650,000	650,000	13.00	13.62
12.00	0	675,000	675,000	13.54	14.16
12.50	0	700,000	700,000	14.08	14.71
13.00	0	725,000	725,000	14.62	15.25

LIBOR at Expiration is 12%

Interest on the loan:

$$\$10,000,000[.135(180/360)] = \$675,000.$$

Put is out-of-the-money.
Total effective interest: $675,000
Amount paid out on loan: $10,027,196
Amount received back on loan: $10,675,000
Effective annual rate:

$$\left(\frac{10,675,000}{10,027,196}\right)^{365/180} - 1 = .1354.$$

Figure 14.5 illustrates the return on the planned loan with and without the interest rate put. The payoff looks like what we would have formerly recognized as a call or protective put. In previous examples, these were bullish strategies that paid off if an asset price rose. Here they pay off if an interest rate increases. The floor provides a minimum return of 10.32 percent, which is reached if LIBOR is at 9 percent or below.

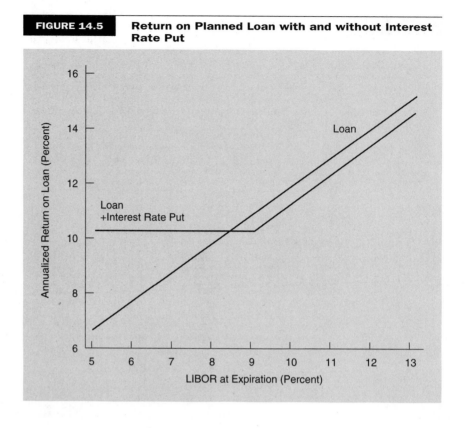

FIGURE 14.5   **Return on Planned Loan with and without Interest Rate Put**

PRICING INTEREST RATE OPTIONS   As you recall, we devoted Chapters 3, 4, and 5 to learning how to price options on stocks and stock indices and in Chapters 12 and 13 we learned how to price options on futures and currencies. The techniques were quite similar, meaning that the Black-Scholes or Black models generally apply when the options are European. The binomial model is normally required when the options are American. Unfortunately, pricing interest rate options is considerably more complex. In this part of the chapter we look at the simplest way to price interest rate options, which is the Black model that we covered in Chapter 12. Later in the chapter we develop a binomial model of the term structure and use it to price all types of interest rate derivatives.

Recall that the Black model requires the forward price of the underlying asset, the exercise price, the risk-free rate, the time to expiration, and the volatility of the forward price. Here we use the forward rate for the forward price, the strike rate for the exercise price, and the volatility of the forward rate for the volatility of the forward price. The risk-free rate and the time to expiration are the same variables as before. Because of the delay between the option expiration and the day the payoff is actually made, the computed price must be discounted using the forward rate.

For example, consider the interest rate call we examined in Table 14.4. It expires in 30 days and has a strike rate of 10 percent. Suppose the 30-day continuously compounded risk-free rate is 8 percent and the volatility (standard deviation) of the forward LIBOR is .2. Let the 30-day forward LIBOR for 90-day deposits be 11.01 percent. The time to expiration is $30/365 = .0822$. We can insert these values into the Black model and obtain an option price. The actual premium paid for the option must reflect the notional principal and the fact that the option payoff will be based on 90-day LIBOR. Thus, if C is the premium obtained from the Black model, the total cost of the option is

$$\text{(Notional principal)}\left(\frac{\text{Days}}{360}\right)\text{C,}$$

where "Days" is the number of days in the underlying LIBOR instrument. In this example, Days = 90 because the option pays off according to the 90-day LIBOR. Table 14.6 illustrates the computation of the value of our interest rate call. Note that its price of \$49,500 is very close to the price the

The Black model can be used as a simple method of pricing interest rate options. The forward rate is used for the forward price, the strike rate is used for the exercise price, and the volatility of the forward rate is the appropriate volatility. In this context, however, the model has many limitations.

TABLE 14.6   **Calculating the Black Price for an Interest Rate Call**

$f_0 = .1101$ $X = .10$ $r_c = .08$ $\sigma = .2$ $T = .0822$

1. Compute d_1:

$$d_1 = \frac{\ln(.1101/.10) + (.2^2/2).0822}{.2\sqrt{.0822}} = 1.71.$$

2. Compute d_2:

$$d_2 = 1.71 - .2\sqrt{.0822} = 1.65.$$

3. Look up $N(d_1)$:

$$N(1.71) = .9564.$$

4. Look up $N(d_2)$:

$$N(1.65) = .9505.$$

5. Plug into formula for C and discount using the forward rate over the time period between the option expiration and the payoff date:

$$C = (e^{-(.08)(.0822)}\,[.1101(.9564) - .10(.9505)])e^{-.1101(90/365)}$$
$$= .0099.$$

6. Multiply by the notional principal times days over 360:

$$(\$20,000,000)\,\frac{90}{360}\,(.0099) = \$49,500.$$

bank charged. A similar approach can be used to find the value of an interest rate put. First one should compute the call price, going up through step 5 in Table 14.6. Then using put-call parity for options on futures, $P = C - (f_0 - X)e^{-r_cT}$, one easily obtains the put price. Alternatively, one can use Black's model directly for put options where $P = e^{-r_cT}[X(1 - N(d_2)) - f_0(1 - N(d_1))]$.

While the Black model is widely used in industry to price interest rate options, it has several limitations. Interest rates are less likely than stocks to conform to the model's assumptions, such as the requirement that the volatility be constant over the life of the option. This can be a particularly severe problem for long-term options. In addition, the Black model does not guarantee that all of the fixed income assets and derivatives that a firm may deal in are priced to preclude arbitrage opportunities. More precise and arbitrage-free pricing of interest rate options is based on models that capture the evolution of the term structure as it moves through time. Although such models are complex, we shall take a look at a basic version of these models later in this chapter.

Interest Rate Caps, Floors, and Collars

Another type of transaction that can be used to protect against rising interest rates is an **interest rate cap,** which is a series of European interest rate calls that pay off at dates corresponding to interest payment dates on a loan. At each interest payment date, the holder of the cap decides whether to exercise the option based on whether the interest rate has risen above the exercise rate. A price is paid up front for the cap. The price corresponds to the sum of the prices of the series of options that make up the cap. Each option is a separate interest rate call. These individual component options are called **caplets.**

Let us look at an example. On January 2, a firm borrows $25 million over one year. It will make payments on April 2, July 2, October 2, and next January 2. On each date, starting with January 2, LIBOR in effect on that day will be the interest rate paid over the next three months. The current LIBOR is 10 percent. The firm wishes to fix its rate at 10 percent, so it buys a cap for an up-front payment of $70,000. The payoffs are based on the exact number of days and a 360-day year. At each interest payment date, the cap will be worth

$$\$25,000,000\left(\frac{\text{Days}}{360}\right)\text{Max}(0, \text{LIBOR} - .10).$$

An interest rate cap is a series of interest rate calls, designed to limit the cost of a loan with multiple interest payments.

In the formula, LIBOR is the rate that was in effect at the beginning of each quarter. Thus, as with an interest rate option, the decision to exercise is made at the beginning of the quarter but the payoff occurs at the end of the quarter. If LIBOR is greater than 10 percent, the firm will exercise the

TABLE 14.7	**After-the-Fact Payments for Interest Rate Cap**

Scenario: On January 2, a firm takes out a one-year loan with interest paid quarterly at LIBOR. The face value is $25 million. The firm buys an interest rate cap with a strike of 10 percent for a premium of $70,000. The payoffs are based on the exact number of days and a 360-day year.

Date	Days in Quarter	LIBOR (%)	Interest Due	Cap Payment	Principal Repayment	Net Cash Flow	Net Cash Flow without Cap
Jan 2	—	10.00	—	−$70,000	$ 0	$24,930,000	$25,000,000
Apr 2	91	10.68	$631,944	0	0	−631,944	−631,944
Jul 2	91	12.31	674,917	42,972	0	−631,944	−674,917
Oct 2	92	11.56	786,472	147,583	0	−638,889	−786,472
Jan 2	92	—	738,556	99,667	25,000,000	−25,638,889	−25,738,556

Effective annual rate
    Without cap: 11.7%
    With cap: 10.8%

Note: This is but one of an infinite number of possible outcomes to the cap. It is used only to illustrate how the payments are determined and not their likely amounts.

option and receive a sum as given by this equation. This helps offset the higher interest rate on the loan. Table 14.7 shows the payments associated with this interest rate cap.

For the first quarter, the firm will pay LIBOR of 10 percent in effect on January 2. Thus, on April 2 it will owe $25,000,000(.10)(91/360) = $631,944 based on 91 days from January 2 to April 2.[4] Then, on April 2, LIBOR is 10.68 percent. Because this is greater than 10 percent, the cap will pay off at the next interest payment date and the holder of the cap will receive a payment of

$$\$25,000,0000\left(\frac{91}{360}\right)(.1068 - .10) = \$42,972.$$

This will help offset the interest of $674,917, based on a rate of 10.68 percent for 91 days from April 2 to July 2. LIBOR on July 2 is 12.31 percent, so the cap will pay off on October 2. The net effect of these cash flows is seen in column 7 of Table 14.7. On January 2, the firm received $25 million from the lender but paid out $70,000 for the cap for a net cash inflow of $24,930,000. It made periodic payments as shown and, on the next January 2, repaid the principal and made the final interest payment less the cap payoff. Note that because of the cap, the interest payments differ only because of the different number of days during each interest payment period

---

[4]The first caplet expires out-of-the-money. Since the first loan interest payment is known when the cap is purchased, it need not be hedged so the first caplet is often omitted.

and not because of the rate. The interest rate is capped at LIBOR of 10 percent.

If we wish to know what annualized rate the firm actually paid, we essentially must solve for the internal rate of return, which requires a computer or financial calculator. We are solving for the cash flow that equates the present value of the four payouts to the initial receipt:

$$\$24,930,000 = \frac{\$631,944}{(1+y)^1} + \frac{\$631,944}{(1+y)^2} + \frac{\$638,889}{(1+y)^3} + \frac{\$25,638,889}{(1+y)^4}.$$

The solution is $y = .026$. Annualizing this gives a rate of $(1.026)^4 - 1 = .108$. The last column in Table 14.7 shows the cash flows if the cap had not been purchased. Solving for the internal rate of return using those numbers and annualizing the result gives a rate of .117. Thus, the cap saved the firm 90 basis points, because during the life of the loan, interest rates generally were higher than they were at the time the loan was initiated. Of course, if rates had fallen, the firm would have benefited less because the caplets would have been out-of-the-money, but the premium was paid.

Pricing caps proceeds the same as pricing interest rate calls. Each caplet is a separate interest rate call. The total value of the cap is the sum of the values of the individual caplets.

The lender in a floating-rate loan may want protection against falling rates. This type of protection can be purchased with an **interest rate floor,** which is a series of interest rate put options expiring at the interest payment dates. Each component put is called a **floorlet.**

At each interest payment date, the payoff of an interest rate floor tied to LIBOR with an exercise rate of, say, 8 percent, payoffs based on the exact number of days and a 360-day year, and a notional principal of $15 million will be

$$(\$15,000,000) \; \text{Max}(0, .08 - \text{LIBOR})\left(\frac{\text{Days}}{360}\right).$$

As previously, LIBOR is determined at the beginning of the interest payment period.

Suppose a bank makes a one-year, $15 million loan with payments made at LIBOR on March 16, June 16, September 15, and next December 16. Currently, it is December 16, and LIBOR is 7.93 percent. Thus, on March 16 the bank will receive $15,000,000[.0793(90/360)] = \$297,375$ in interest. The new rate on that day is 7.50 percent. Thus, the floor is in-the-money and will pay off

$$\$15,000,000(.08 - .075)\left(\frac{92}{360}\right) = \$19,167$$

on the next interest payment day. This will add to the interest payment of $287,500, which is lower because of the fall in interest rates. The complete results for the one-year loan are shown in Table 14.8. The floor is in-the-money and thus is exercised on each of the last three interest payment dates. This is because in this example, the year was one of interest rates lower than 8 percent.

The lender paid out $15,000,000 up front to the borrower and another $30,000 for the floor. Column 7 in Table 14.8 indicates the periodic cash flows associated with the floored loan. Following the same procedure as in the cap, we can solve for the periodic rate that equates the present value of the inflows to the outflow. This rate turns out to be about 1.97 percent. Annualizing this gives a rate of $(1.0197)^4 - 1 = .081$. The last column shows the cash flows if the floor had not been used. The annualized return associated with these cash flows is 7.4 percent. Thus, the floor boosted the bank's return by 70 basis points. Of course, in a period of rising rates, the bank will gain less from the increase in interest rates.

As with caps, the price of an interest rate floor is found by pricing each of the component floorlets and adding up their prices.

Consider a firm planning to borrow money that decides to purchase an interest rate cap. In so doing, the firm is trying to place a ceiling on the rate it will pay on its loan. If rates fall, it can gain by paying lower rates. In some cases, however, a firm will find it more advantageous to give up the right to gain from falling rates in order to lower the cost of the cap. One way to do this is to sell a floor. The combination of a long interest rate cap and short interest rate floor is called an **interest rate collar.** The premium received from selling the floor helps offset the cost of the cap. It is even possible to structure the exercise rates on the collar so that the premium received from the sale of the floor equals the premium paid for the purchase of the cap. This is called a **zero cost collar.** If interest rates fall, the options that comprise the floor will be exercised. The net effect is that the strategy will

An interest rate floor is a series of interest rate puts, designed to protect the return on a loan with multiple interest payments.

TABLE 14.8   **After-the-Fact Payments for Interest Rate Floor**

Scenario: On December 16, a bank makes a one-year loan with interest paid quarterly at LIBOR. The face value is $15 million. The firm buys an interest rate floor with a strike of 8 percent for a premium of $30,000. The payoffs are based on the exact number of days and a 360-day year.

Date	Days in Quarter	LIBOR (%)	Interest Received	Floor Payment	Principal Repayment	Net Cash Flow	Net Cash Flow without Floor
Dec 16	—	7.93	—	−$30,000	$ 0	−$15,030,000	−$15,000,000
Mar 16	90	7.50	$297,375	0	0	297,375	297,375
Jun 16	92	7.06	287,500	19,167	0	306,667	287,500
Sep 15	91	6.06	267,692	35,642	0	303,333	267,692
Dec 16	92	—	232,300	74,367	15,000,000	15,306,667	15,232,300

Effective annual rate
  Without floor: 7.4%
  With floor: 8.1%

Note: This is but one of an infinite number of possible outcomes to the floor. It is used only to illustrate how the payments are determined and not their likely amounts.

An interest rate collar is a combination of the purchase of an interest rate cap and the sale of an interest rate floor. It is used to limit the effects of interest rate increases by giving up the benefits of interest rate decreases.

establish both a floor and a ceiling on the interest cost. The existence of both limited gains and losses should remind you of a money spread with options. In fact, we covered collars with money spreads in Chapter 7.

Table 14.9 illustrates a zero cost collar in which a firm borrowing $50 million over two years buys a cap for $250,000 with an exercise price of 10 percent and sells a floor for $250,000 with an exercise price of 8.5 percent. The loan begins on March 15 and will require payments at approximately 91-day intervals at LIBOR.

By now, you should be able to verify the numbers in the table. The interest paid on June 15 is based on LIBOR on March 15 of 10.5 percent and 92 days during the period. The cap pays off on September 14 and December 14 because those are the ends of the periods in which LIBOR at the beginning of the period turned out to be greater than 10 percent. The floor pays off on September 14 and December 15 of the next year and on March 14 of the following year, the due date on the loan. Note that when the floor pays off, the firm makes, rather than receives, the payment.

Column 8 in Table 14.9 shows the cash flows associated with the collar. Following the procedure previously described to solve for the internal rate of return gives an annualized rate of 9.82 percent for the collar. Column 9 shows the cash flows had the firm done only the cap. The rate associated with this strategy would have been 9.91 percent. The last column indicates the cash flows had the firm done neither the cap nor the floor. The borrowing rate associated with that strategy would have been 10.08 percent.

TABLE 14.9　　**After-the-Fact Payments for Interest Rate Collar**

Scenario: On March 15, a firm borrows $50 million with interest paid quarterly at LIBOR. The firm buys an interest rate cap with a strike of 10 percent for $250,000. To offset the cost of the cap, the firm sells an interest rate floor with a strike of 8.5 percent for $250,000. The payoffs are based on the exact number of days and a 360-day year.

Date	Days in Quarter	LIBOR (%)	Interest Due	Cap Payment	Floor Payment	Principal Repayment	Net Cash Flow with Collar	Net Cash Flow with Cap Only	Net Cash Flow without Cap or Floor
Mar 15	——	10.50	$　　　0	−$250,000	$250,000	$　　　0	$50,000,000	$49,750,000	$50,000,000
Jun 15	92	11.56	1,341,667	0	0	0	−1,341,667	−1,341,667	−1,341,667
Sep 14	91	11.75	1,461,056	197,167	0	0	−1,263,889	−1,263,889	−1,461,056
Dec 14	91	9.06	1,485,069	221,181	0	0	−1,263,889	−1,263,889	−1,485,069
Mar 15	91	9.50	1,145,083	0	0	0	−1,145,083	−1,145,083	−1,145,083
Jun 14	91	7.62	1,200,694	0	0	0	−1,200,694	−1,200,694	−1,200,694
Sep 14	92	8.31	973,667	0	−112,444	0	−1,086,111	−973,667	−973,667
Dec 15	92	7.93	1,061,833	0	−24,278	0	−1,086,111	−1,061,833	−1,061,833
Mar 14	89	——	980,236	0	−70,458	50,000,000	−51,050,694	−50,980,236	−50,980,236

Effective annual rate
　　Without cap or floor:　　10.08%
　　With collar;　　9.82%
　　With cap:　　9.91%

Note: This is but one of an infinite number of possible outcomes to the collar. It is used only to illustrate how payments are determined and not their likely amounts.

The cap by itself would have helped lower the firm's cost of borrowing. By selling the floor and thus creating a collar, the cost of the loan was lowered from 9.91 percent to 9.82 percent.

Interest Rate Options and Swaps

Now that we have introduced caps and floors as options on interest rates, it is helpful to see how they are related to swaps. Let us consider a simple one-payment swap, which is basically an FRA. Suppose you pay the floating rate, LIBOR, and receive the swap rate. The payoff will be Swap Rate − LIBOR.

Now suppose in addition you buy a cap and sell a floor, both with a strike rate of X. The cap payoff is

$$
\begin{array}{lll}
0 & \text{if} & \text{LIBOR} \le \text{X.} \\
\text{LIBOR} - \text{X} & \text{if} & \text{LIBOR} > \text{X.}
\end{array}
$$

The floor payoff is

$$
\begin{array}{lll}
-(\text{X} - \text{LIBOR}) & \text{if} & \text{LIBOR} \le \text{X.} \\
0 & \text{if} & \text{LIBOR} > \text{X.}
\end{array}
$$

Thus, the combined payoff of the swap, cap and floor is

$$
\begin{array}{lll}
\text{Swap Rate} - \text{X} & \text{if} & \text{LIBOR} \le \text{X.} \\
\text{Swap Rate} - \text{X} & \text{if} & \text{LIBOR} > \text{X.}
\end{array}
$$

As we previously learned, the swap rate is set in the market, determined by the term structure of interest rates. We can, however, choose the strike rate X. If we choose X to be the market-determined swap rate, observe that the transaction is not only risk-free but also guarantees a payoff of zero. In that case, the transaction must have zero cash flow up front. Since the swap has no initial cash flow, that means that the long cap and short floor must have no initial cash flow. Thus, the floor premium must equal the cap premium.

The implication of this result is that a swap is equivalent to a combination of a long cap and short floor where the strikes on the cap and floor are equivalent and equal to the swap rate. A pay-fixed, receive-floating swap is equivalent to a long cap and short floor. A pay-floating, receive-fixed swap is equivalent to a short cap and long floor. This result is a type of cap-floor-swap parity.

The examples explained here, however, are for single payment swaps and caps and floors that have just one caplet and floorlet. When the swap has multiple payments, as it usually does, the cap and floor must have corresponding multiple caplets and floorlets. Each caplet and floorlet must have a strike equal to the swap rate. While the sum of the overall premiums for the cap and floor must be equal, it is not the case that the premium for an individual caplet and its corresponding floorlet will be equal.

A pay-fixed, receive-floating interest rate swap is equivalent to a long position in a cap and a short position in a floor where the exercise rate on the cap and floor is the swap rate.

We previously saw that a swap can be viewed as a combination of FRAs or as the issuance of a fixed-rate bond and purchase of a floating-rate bond or vice versa. Now we see that a swap is also equivalent to a combination of long caps and short floors or vice versa.

Interest Rate Swaptions and Forward Swaps

Earlier in this chapter we mentioned that a firm that had entered into a swap could exit the swap before it terminates if the firm had previously purchased an option on the swap. Options on swaps are called **swaptions.** A swaption is an option in which the buyer pays a premium up front and acquires the right to enter into a swap as either a fixed-rate payer, floating-rate receiver or as a floating-rate payer, fixed-rate receiver. The former is called a **payer swaption** while the latter is called a **receiver swaption.**

A swaption can be viewed as a variation of an interest rate option but there are several important differences. Like an interest rate option, a swaption specifies a strike rate stated in terms of an interest rate. A swaption is based on an underlying swap and has a fixed maturity. A swaption can also be American or European style. The parties can agree that exercise is accomplished by either a simple cash settlement or that the parties actually enter into the underlying swap.

Consider the following situation. A company called MPK Resources is considering the possibility that it will need to engage in an interest rate swap two years from now with a notional principal of $10 million. It expects that the swap would be a three-year pay fixed–receive floating swap. The firm is concerned about rising interest rates over the next two years that would force it to pay a higher fixed rate if it enters into the swap at that time. It thus decides to purchase a two-year, European-style payer swaption on a three-year, pay fixed–receive floating swap. Naturally the underlying swap should be identical to the one MPK expects to take out in two years. MPK specifies a strike rate of 11.5 percent and pays the premium in cash up front. To keep the illustration as simple as possible, assume that the underlying swap calls for annual interest payments.

Now let us consider what happens when the swaption expires in two years. Let the following discount factors for LIBOR be observed at expiration: one-year = 0.8929, two-year = 0.7901, three-year = 0.6967. Following the procedure in Table 14.3, the price of a three-year swap is found as the solution to

Coupon(0.8929) + Coupon(0.7901) + (Coupon + $10,000,000)(0.6967)
= $10,000,000.

Solving for the coupon gives Coupon = $1,274,530, which is about 12.75 percent. Thus, at expiration MPK will find that new three-year swaps will have a fixed rate of 12.75 percent. Ignoring the bid-ask spread the dealer would charge, we shall assume that a party can either pay 12.75 percent fixed and receive the floating rate or receive 12.75 percent fixed and pay the floating rate.

MPK, however, holds an expiring swaption that allows it to enter into an identical swap paying only 11.5 percent. If MPK finds that it actually does need to enter into a swap at that time, it can do so by exercising the swaption. This would allow it to enter a swap paying 11.5 percent fixed in a market where it would otherwise have to pay 12.75 percent fixed.

To better understand the payoffs of swaptions, however, let us assume that MPK finds it has no need for the swap but, having an expiring in-the-money swaption, it is worth going ahead and exercising it. Thus, MPK would exercise the swaption, thereby entering into a swap in which it pays a fixed rate of 11.5 percent and receives the floating rate. It goes into the market and enters into an otherwise identical swap in which it receives 12.75 percent fixed and pays the floating rate. The floating payments on both swaps offset, leaving MPK with a three-year annuity in which it receives a net interest payment of $12.75 - 11.5 = 1.25$ percent each year. The value of the swaption at expiration is, thus, the present value of a three-year annuity of $.0125(\$10,000,000) = \$125,000$. Using the LIBOR spot rates to discount these cash flows, we obtain

$$\$125,000(0.8929) + \$125,000(0.7901) + \$125,000(0.6967) = \$297,463.$$

Had the swaption been structured so as to provide a cash settlement instead of the actual execution of a swap, MPK would have simply received $297,463 from the counterparty.

Had the rate on new swaps been less than 11.5 percent at the swaption expiration, the swaption, like any other option, would have expired worthless. It should be apparent that when interest rates end up above the strike rate, payer swaptions are exercised, thus making payer swaptions somewhat like interest rate calls. When interest rates end up below the strike rate, receiver swaptions are exercised, making receiver swaptions like interest rate puts. An important distinction, however, is that swaptions create an annuity or the equivalent value when exercised.

Pricing swaptions is somewhat complex. The Black model, however, is often used as a reasonable approximation. The underlying variable is the forward swap rate, which we shall cover below. In the next section of this chapter we shall cover pricing swaptions with a binomial model of the term structure.

As complex as a swaption may appear to be and as different as it may seem from other instruments we have covered, it is actually quite simple to show that a swaption is equivalent to an option on a bond. Consider a payer swaption, which is an option to enter into a swap paying the fixed rate and receiving the floating rate. We can easily show that the value of this swaption when it expires is the same as the value of a put option on a bond

An interest rate swaption is an option to enter into a swap where the fixed rate is agreed upon in advance. The right to enter into a swap as a fixed-rate payer, floating-rate receiver is called a payer swaption and the right to enter into a swap as a fixed-rate receiver, floating-rate payer is called a receiver swaption. Exercise of a swaption creates an annuity equal to the difference in the fixed rate on the swaption and the fixed rate on the underlying swap at the time of exercise.

whose maturity corresponds to the maturity of the swap and whose coupon rate is the exercise rate of the swaption.

Consider, for example, the MPK swaption described earlier. It expires in two years, has an exercise rate of 11.5 percent, and a notional principal of $10 million; the underlying swap has a three-year life. Remember that the underlying swap rate at expiration was found to be 12.75 percent. The notional principal amount does not affect these results so let us just assume it is $1. Earlier in the chapter we showed a direct formula for obtaining the swap rate. As applied to this problem, we have

$$\frac{1 - 0.6967}{0.8929 + 0.7901 + 0.6967} = 0.1275.$$

The payoff value of the swaption was found as

$$\text{Max}(0,(.1275 - .115)(0.8929 + 0.7901 + 0.6967)).$$

If we substitute the above formula for the swap rate of .1275 into the swaption payoff formula, we obtain the payoff formula for the swaption as

$$\text{Max}(0, 1 - 0.6967 - .115(0.8929 + 0.7901 + 0.6967)).$$

Now suppose we consider a put option on a three-year bond with a coupon of 11.5 percent and a par value of $1. When the option expires, the bond is worth

$$.115(0.8929 + 0.7901 + 0.6967) + 1(0.6967).$$

So the payoff of the put option with an exercise price of $1 would be

$$\text{Max}(0, 1 - 0.6967 - .115(0.8929 + 0.7901 + 0.6967)),$$

which is the same as the payoff formula for the swaption.

Thus, a payer swaption is equivalent to a put option on a bond. Similarly, we could show that a receiver swaption is like a call option on a bond.

The swaptions market is quite liquid and widely used. The most obvious application is where a firm might wish to enter into a swap at a later date. It would like to obtain a favorable swap rate, but also to benefit if rates rise or fall in the interim. If the firm thinks it might need to enter into a pay-fixed swap at a later date, it might purchase a payer swaption. By paying the premium today, it has the right to enter into the swap to pay fixed. If rates increase, the payer swaption can be beneficial in allowing it to pay a lower fixed rate and not the higher market rate. If the firm thinks it might need to enter into a receive-fixed swap at a later date, it might purchase a receiver swaption. By paying the premium today, it has the right to enter into a swap to receive fixed. If rates fall, the receiver swaption can be beneficial in allowing it to receive a higher fixed rate and not the lower market rate. Similarly, firms that have entered into swaps will often purchase swaptions that allow them to offset a swap by exercising the swaption and obtaining a new swap in which the floating rates offset the floating rates on the existing swap. In that way a swaption is like an option to exit a swap.

Swaptions are also used as a substitute for an option on a bond. When firms issue bonds and consider the possibility of wanting to change them from fixed-rate to floating-rate at a later date, a swaption gives them that flexibility.

Another application of a swaption is in creating a synthetic callable bond. A callable bond is a bond in which the issuing firm has the right to call or retire it early. If a noncallable bond is issued but the firm would like to add the right to call it, it can purchase a receiver swaption. If properly structured, this swaption gives the firm the economic equivalent of an option to retire the bond early. Likewise, if the firm has issued a callable bond and no longer wants the right to call it, the firm can sell a receiver swaption, which effectively offsets the right to call the bond.

A puttable bond is a bond in which the holder of the bond has the right to sell it back to the issuer early, thereby forcing the issuer to pay off the bond before its maturity. A bond that is not puttable can be effectively made puttable by selling a payer swaption. A bond that is puttable can be made nonputtable by buying a payer swaption.

Since the use of a swaption in the context of a callable or puttable bond requires the flexibility to exercise it at any time, the swaption would have to be American-style.

As you might well imagine, if it is possible to purchase an option to enter into a swap, it is also possible to enter into a forward contract to enter into a swap. This is called a **forward swap.** One party is committed to being the fixed-rate payer on the swap and the other is committed to being the fixed-rate receiver. The fixed-rate payer is long the forward swap and the fixed-rate receiver is short the forward swap.

In our example of MPK, suppose that today the firm is looking at a five-year term structure in which the discount factors are: one-year = 0.9174, two-year = 0.8325, three-year = 0.7513, four-year = 0.6756, and five-year = 0.6070. Recall that earlier in the chapter we showed how LIBORs are converted into discount factors like these.

The two-year-ahead forward rate of the swap would be found the same way we price a swap executed at the current time except that we move ahead in time and use the implied forward discount factors. Thus, in this case we need discount factors spanning periods two to three, two to four, and two to five. Normally we would obtain these by deriving the forward rates and then converting those rates to discount factors. Given that we know the spot discount factors, however, we can go ahead and obtain the forward discount factors quite easily.

Forward discount factor for years 2 to 3: $0.7513/0.8325 = 0.9025$
Forward discount factor for years 2 to 4: $0.6756/0.8325 = 0.8115$
Forward discount factor for years 2 to 5: $0.6070/0.8325 = 0.7291$.

In other words, we simply divide the discount factor for the longer period by the discount factor for the shorter period. Thus, for example, 0.7291 is the factor we would use to convert a value at time 5 to a value at time 2.

The forward swap rate is then found as the solution to

A forward swap is a forward contract to enter into a swap in which the fixed rate is agreed upon in advance. One party is committed to paying the fixed rate and receiving the floating rate and the other is committed to receiving the fixed rate and paying the floating rate. At expiration, depending on the direction of rates on the underlying swap, one party receives an annuity paid by the other.

$$\text{Coupon } (0.9025) + \text{Coupon } (0.8115) + (\text{Coupon } + \$10,000,000)(0.7291)$$
$$= \$10,000,000.$$

The solution is \$1,108,837, which converts to a coupon of about 11.09 percent. Thus, MPK could commit to entering into a three-year swap two years from now by agreeing to pay a fixed rate of 11.09. When the forward swap expires, the difference between the fixed rate on new three-year swaps and 11.09 would determine the value at expiration. Using our previous example, MPK would be the fixed-rate payer. If, at expiration, the new rate on three-year swaps turns out to be 12.75 percent, MPK would lock in a three-year inflow of $(.1275 - .1109)(\$10,000,000) = \$166,000$. The value of the swap at expiration would, thus, be

$$\$166,000(0.8929) + \$166,000(0.7901) + \$166,000(0.6967) = \$395,030.$$

As with any type of forward contract, there may be either a positive or negative value at expiration, but for a swaption, like any option, the holder exercises only if there is positive value at expiration.

Modeling the Term Structure and Pricing Interest Rate Derivatives

We have noted several times earlier that pricing interest rate derivatives is quite difficult. Interest rates do not evolve in isolation. Interest rates of various maturities are specified by the term structure. To properly model the uncertainty in interest rates, it is necessary to model the manner in which the term structure changes through time. This means that capturing movements in bonds of many maturities is required. In addition, these movements must be arbitrage-free, meaning that it must not be possible to construct equivalent combinations of interest-paying assets that have different prices. Likewise derivatives on these interest-paying assets and interest rates must have prices consistent with no arbitrage possibilities. A good term structure model would permit arbitrage-free pricing of coupon bonds, zero coupon bonds, all kinds of derivatives on coupon and zero coupon bonds, and derivatives on interest rates. Their prices would be internally consistent. Anyone using the model to determine prices for trading in the market need not fear that a counterparty could execute arbitrage against it.

Building such a model is a difficult task, but there are many models that meet these requirements. A good model combines simplicity with realism in the manner in which it describes movements in interest rates. In this book, we shall not go too deeply into this subject for it can quickly become quite complex. We shall, however, look at one model, the Ho-Lee binomial term structure model, in a simple setting to observe how such models can be used to price interest rate derivatives.

Many interest rate derivatives are based on a short-term interest rate, like the 90-day LIBOR. In our model, we shall examine derivatives based on the shortest possible interest rate, but we leave it unnamed other than to call it the one-period rate. Thus, it might be the one-year LIBOR, but that is not important. It is simply the rate on a one-period zero coupon bond.

Figure 14.6 shows a binomial tree illustrating how the one-period rate evolves. Each node contains four pieces of information. The top piece is the one-period rate. The remaining three pieces are information about the probability that this interest rate will occur. We show how to determine that probability in the next paragraph. We observe that the rate is 10.50 percent today. This means that one could borrow or lend for one year at 10.50 percent today. One year from now, the one-period rate will be either 12 percent or 8.74 percent. This means that one year from now, one can borrow or lend for one year at either 12 percent or 8.74 percent. How these rates were obtained is illustrated in the appendix, but the important point is that the binomial tree specifies the uncertainty in future one-year borrowing and lending rates.

In Chapter 4 when we studied the binomial model for stock prices, we calculated the value of an option as a discounted probability-weighted average of future option payoffs. The probability was not actually the probability of the stock price movement but was related to the risk-free rate and the magnitudes of the up and down movements in the stock price. In our interest rate tree, we let the probability of an up move be .52 and the probability of a down move be .48. Observe on the second line at each node in Figure 14.6 a combination of u's and d's. This is the number of up and down moves the one-period rate would have to make to reach that node. For example, notice the middle interest rate at time 4 of 9.76 percent. We see the term uudd. This means that to reach 9.76 percent the one-period rate would have to go up twice and down twice though not necessarily in that order. The next row contains the number 6. This is the number of possible ways that the rate could go up twice and down twice. These are (1) up, up, down, down, (2) up, down, up, down, (3) up, down, down, up, (4) down, up, up, down, (5) down, up, down, up, and (6) down, down, up, up. Call this number Q. The final number is the probability of reaching that node. Let p be the probability of going up and $1 - p$ be the probability of going down. Then the probability of reaching that node is

A binomial tree can be used to model the evolution of interest rates and price all interest rate derivatives.

$$Q p^{(\text{\# of times the rate has gone up})} (1 - p)^{(\text{\# of times the rate has gone down})},$$

FIGURE 14.6	Binomial Model of the One-Period Interest Rate through Four Periods

Time 0	Time 1	Time 2	Time 3	Time 4
				16.45% uuuu 1 .0731
			14.95% uuu 1 .1406	
		13.47% uu 1 .2704		13.06% uuud 4 .2700
	12.00% u 1 .52		11.60% uud 3 .3894	
10.50%		10.17% ud 2 .4992		9.76% uudd 6 .3738
	8.74% d 1 .48		8.35% ddu 3 .3594	
		6.96% dd 1 .2304		6.57% dddu 4 .2300
			5.20% ddd 1 .1106	
				3.46% dddd 1 .0531

which in our example is $6.(52)^2(.48)^2 = .3738$. The same general approach is taken with all other nodes. It would be worthwhile to check a few of them to determine if you can fill in the remaining probabilities.[5]

Finally, some of our calculations require additional information, namely the spot rates on bonds of more than one year of maturity. We will introduce that information when it is necessary.

---

[5]As an aid to checking yourself, consider the probability of reaching an interest rate of 11.60 percent at time 3. This node represents two up moves and one down move and can be reached three different ways: (1) up, up, down, (2) up, down, up, and (3) down, up, up. Thus, the probability is $3(.52)^2(.48) = .3894$.

Now we proceed to show how interest rate derivatives are priced. We shall assume that the notional principal is $1 and the derivative is based on the one-period interest rate. In a real situation, the answer we obtain would have to be multiplied by the notional principal. Also, each time step would probably be less than a year so the quoted derivative price, which is stated as a rate, would need to be annualized.

Pricing Forward Rate Agreements

Let us begin by examining a one-period FRA. Recall that typical FRAs pay off on their expirations though most interest rate derivatives pay off at a later date. In our example in the earlier part of the chapter, we assumed the latter case. Here we shall look at both types of FRAs. The terminology used in practice is that when an interest rate derivative pays off at expiration, it is said to be **in arrears.** We shall refer to the other case as a **delayed settlement** FRA.

Consider a one-year in-arrears FRA. The price is the rate that would give the FRA a zero value today. For a one-year in-arrears FRA, the price is found as the rate FRA_1 in the following equation:

$$.52(.12 - FRA_1) + .48(.0874 - FRA_1) = 0.$$

Solving gives $FRA_1 = .1044$, which is interpreted as 10.44 percent per $1 of notional principal. Pricing a two-year FRA proceeds along similar lines:

$$.2704(.1347 - FRA_2) + .4992(.1017 - FRA_2) + .2304(.0696 - FRA_2) = 0.$$

Solving for FRA_2 gives .1032. The exact solution is found with the following formula:

$$FRA_t(\text{in arrears}) = \sum_{i=1}^{t+1} p_i r_i,$$

where p_i is the probability of the ith outcome and r_i is the interest rate in the ith outcome. Obviously this is simply the probability-weighted average one-period rate at the FRA expiration.

For the delayed settlement FRA, a slight adjustment is needed. For the one-period FRA, if the rate goes to .12, the FRA pays off $.12 - FRA_1$ but pays it one period later. Thus, its value would be discounted by the one-period rate, which is .12. The payoff discounted from time 2 back to time 1 would be $(.12 - FRA_1)(1.12)^{-1}$. If the one-period rate goes to 8.74, the discounted payoff would be $(.0874 - FRA_1)(1.0874)^{-1}$. Thus, the FRA rate is found as

$$.52(.12 - FRA_1(1.12)^{-1} + .48(.0874 - FRA_1)(1.0874)^{-1} = 0.$$

Solving for FRA_1 gives .1041. A two-period FRA paying off one period later than the expiration is priced as the solution to

$$.2704(.1347 - FRA_2)(1.1347)^{-1} + .4992(.1017 - FRA_2)(1.1017)^{-1}$$
$$+ .2304(.0696 - FRA_2)(1.0696)^{-1} = 0.$$

The solution is .1027. The general formula for an FRA on the one-period rate of maturity t with delayed settlement is

$$FRA_t \text{ (delayed settlement)} = \frac{\sum_{i=1}^{t+1} p_i r_i (1 + r_i)^{-1}}{\sum_{i=1}^{t+1} p_i (1 + r_i)^{-1}}.$$

The remaining rates for FRAs in arrears are .102 (three years) and .1007 (four years) and for FRAs with delayed settlement are .1012 (three years) and .0998 (four years).

Pricing Interest Rate Swaps

Consider a three-period swap with payments made annually based on the one-period rate at the beginning of the period. Let the notional principal be \$1. To determine the price of the swap we must solve for the fixed rate that would equate the present value of the fixed payments to the present value of the floating payments. Earlier we saw that this is a simple matter of finding the coupon on a bond that, when discounted at the spot rates for each period up to maturity, will equal the par value of the bond. This means that in addition to the one-period rate, we would need to know the spot rates on zero coupon bonds of maturities longer than one year. In other words, we need to know the current term structure. Let us say that this information is as follows: two-year rate = .1043 and three-year rate = .1041, and, of course, one-year rate = .105.

Now we can easily price our three-year swap. Again, this amounts to simply finding the coupon on a bond with a present value equal to par. Letting c represent the coupon rate, we have

$$c(1.105)^{-1} + c(1.1043)^{-2} + (c + 1.00)(1.1041)^{-3} = 1.00.$$

Solving for c gives .1041. For the two-year swap, the coupon would be

$$c(1.105)^{-1} + (c + 1.00)(1.1043)^{-2} = 1.00.$$

Solving for c gives .1043.[6]

Pricing Interest Rate Options

Now let us price an interest rate option expiring two years from now. Recall that although this option will expire in two years, the payoff comes three years from now. Let the option have a notional principal of $1 and, of course, be written on the one-period rate. Let the exercise rate be 9 percent and the option be a European call.

Remembering the binomial model in Chapter 4, we price the option by evaluating the discounted probability-weighted value of the option at expiration. In other words, we start at the expiration date and successively discount the probability-weighted value of the option. The values of the option at expiration are not simply the intrinsic values but must also reflect the fact that the payoffs do not occur until one period later. Thus, for example, in the upper state of time 2, where the one-period rate is .1347, the intrinsic value is $Max(0, .1347 - .09)/1.1347 = .0394$. In the middle state, the intrinsic value is $Max(0, .1017 - .09)/1.1017 = .0106$, and in the lowest state, the intrinsic value is $Max(0, .0696 - .09)/1.0696 = 0$. Obviously the discounting does not determine whether the option ends up exercised or not, but it does affect the value of the option when it is exercised. Note that in contrast to the binomial model for stocks in Chapter 4 where we discounted at a constant risk-free rate, here we discount at whatever one-period rate holds at a given time point.

The exact procedure is illustrated in Figure 14.7. After determining the intrinsic values at expiration at time 2, now step back to time 1 and look at the upper state where the one-period rate is .12. At this point the option will be worth the discounted (at 12 percent) probability-weighted average of .0394 and .0106, the next two possible option values, which is

$$\frac{.52(.0394) + .48(.0106)}{1.12} = .0228.$$

---

[6]At this point you may notice the two-year spot rate being the same as the two-year swap rate and the three-year spot rate being the same as the three-year swap rate. Actually they are not the same, but we would require greater precision to notice the difference. If the term structure is nearly flat, these rates will be very close. You may also notice that here we wrote the present value factors in the form of $(1.105)^{-1}$, $(1.1043)^{-2}$, etc. instead of their values 0.905, 0.820, etc. You should be comfortable with either format.

FIGURE 14.7	**Binomial Tree Pricing of Interest Rate Call Option, Exercise Rate of 9 Percent, European Style**

	Time 0	Time 1	Time 2
			1-period rate = .1347 Max(0, .1347 - .09)/1.1347 = .0394
		1-period rate = .12 (.52(.0394) + .48(.0106))/1.12 = .0228	
	1-period rate = .105 (.52(.0228) +.48(.0051))/1.105 = .0129		1-period rate = .1017 Max(0, .1017 - .09)/1.1017 = .0106
		1-period rate = .0874 (.52(.0106) + .48(0))/1.0874 = .0051	
			1-period rate = .0696 Max(0, .0696 - .09)/1.0696 = 0

In the lower state at time 1, where the rate is 8.74 percent, the option will be worth the discounted (at 8.74 percent) probability-weighted average of .0106 and zero, which is

$$\frac{.52(.0106) \, + \, .48(0)}{1.0874} = .0051.$$

At time 0, the option is worth the discounted (at 10.5 percent) probability-weighted average of .0228 and .0051, which is

$$\frac{.52(.0228) \, + \, .48(.0051)}{1.105} = .0129.$$

Thus, for every dollar of notional principal, the call is worth .0129. Had the option been a put, we would have followed the same procedure but the values of the option at expiration would have been zero, zero, and .0191. The resulting answer would be .0036.

To check your understanding of the process, try to determine the values of one-period puts and calls. For an exercise rate of 9 percent, the call will be worth .0126 and the put will be worth .0010. If the options were American, we would follow the same procedure we covered in Chapter 4—meaning that we insert the intrinsic values at any point where the options would be worth exercising early.

Now let us assume the options are caps. For example, consider a two-period cap with 9 percent strike consisting of caplets expiring at times 1 and 2, with payments made at times 2 and 3. We have already determined the prices of the component caplets; they are simply the prices of the one- and two-period calls, so the cap is worth .0126 + .0129 = .0255. A two-period floor would be worth .0010 + .0036 = .0046.

Pricing Swaptions

Recall that a swaption can be set up as either a payer swaption or a receiver swaption. When exercised, a payer swaption allows the holder to enter into a swap as the fixed-rate payer. When exercised, a receiver swaption allows the holder to enter into a swaption as the fixed-rate receiver. When exercised, either swaption creates an annuity of fixed payments equal to the difference between the market fixed rate and the strike rate.

The exercise of a swaption depends on whether the rate in the market on the underlying swap is above or below the strike rate. Consequently, determining if a swap is exercised is not simply a matter of looking at the one-period rate. We shall have to determine the rate on swaps for each of the possible outcomes at the swaption expiration.

Consider a two-period payer swaption with a strike rate of 10 percent. The underlying swap is a two-period swap with a notional principal of $1. In other words, this is an option to enter into a swap at time 2, where the swap will begin at time 2 and end two periods later.

Looking at the binomial tree in Figure 14.6, note the three outcomes at time 2. We shall refer to these as the upper state, where the one-period rate is 13.47 percent, the middle state, where the one-period rate is 10.17 percent, and the lower state, where the one-period rate is 6.96 percent. To price the swap, using the same approach we have used several times already, we need to know the one- and two-period spot rates in each of those three outcomes at time 2. The one-period rates are simply the rates 13.47, 10.17, and 6.96. Let us denote these rates as $r(2,3)_{uu}$, $r(2,3)_{ud}$, and $r(2,3)_{dd}$, where the subscripts identify the outcome by indicating how many times rates have gone up and down. Hence, $r(2,3)_{uu} = .1347$. Likewise, $r(2,3)_{ud} = .1017$ and $r(2,3)_{dd} = .0696$. What we need are the values of $r(2,4)_{uu}$, $r(2,4)_{ud}$, and $r(2,4)_{dd}$. This information cannot be obtained from the information we already have in hand. Since this information is nothing more than the term structure, it would be available at time 2. Let us assume that it is $r(2,4)_{uu} = .1335$, $r(2,4)_{ud} = .1011$, and $r(2,4)_{dd} = .0691$.[7]

Now we can find the swap prices for each of the outcomes at time 2. We denote these as c_{uu}, c_{ud}, and c_{dd}, and they are the solutions to the following equations:

$$c_{uu}(1.1347)^{-1} + (c_{uu} + 1.00)(1.1335)^{-2} = 1.00$$
$$c_{ud}(1.1017)^{-1} + (c_{ud} + 1.00)(1.1011)^{-2} = 1.00$$
$$c_{dd}(1.0696)^{-1} + (c_{dd} + 1.00)(1.0691)^{-2} = 1.00.$$

---

[7]Although these values were supplied to you, they were not chosen arbitrarily. They are consistent with the absence of arbitrage opportunities.

FIGURE 14.8   **Binomial Tree Pricing of Payer Swaption, Exercise Rate of 10 Percent, European-Style, Underlying Swap Has Two-Period Maturity**

Time 0	Time 1	Time 2
		$r(0,1)_{uu} = .1347$ $c_{uu} = .1336$ $\text{Max}(0, .1336 - .10)[(1.1347)^{-1} + (1.1335)^{-2}] = .0558$
	$(.52(.0558) + .48(.0019))/1.12 = .0267$	
$(.52(.0267) + .48(.0009))/1.105 = .0130$		$r(0,1)_{ud} = .1011$ $c_{uu} = .1011$ $\text{Max}(0, .1011 - .10)[(1.1017)^{-1} + (1.1011)^{-2}] = .0019$
	$(.52(.0019) + .48(0))/1.0874 = .0009$	
		$r(0,1)_{dd} = .0696$ $c_{ud} = .0691$ $\text{Max}(0, .0691 - .10)[(1.0696)^{-1} + (1.0691)^{-2}] = 0$

For any one of the c's, the solution is found as

$$c = \frac{1 - (1 + r(2,4))^{-2}}{(1 + r(2,3))^{-1} + (1 + r(2,4))^{-2}},$$

and the answers are $c_{uu} = .1336$, $c_{ud} = .1011$, and $c_{dd} = .0691$.[8]

Now after all of that work we can begin to price the swaption. Fortunately, it is an easy task, made only slightly more involved by the fact that exercise creates an annuity. For a given outcome, the value of the swaption at expiration is simply $\text{Max}(0, c - .10)[(1 + r(0,1))^{-1} + (1 + r(0,2))^{-2}]$, where the bracketed term is simply the present value factor for a two-period annuity. Once these values of the swaption at expiration are determined, the pricing proceeds as in all of our binomial examples. Each period the probability-weighted value of the next two possible swaption prices is then discounted by the appropriate one-period rate. The process is shown in Figure 14.8. Our swaption is worth .0130.

---

[8]Again, note that the swap rate would not equal the two-period rate were our calculations done with greater numerical precision.

If the swaption were a receiver swaption, then the payoff at expiration would be treated like a put, meaning that the swap rate would need to be less than the strike rate for the swaption to expire in-the-money. If the swaptions were American-style, the intrinsic value would replace the computed value in any state where the former exceeded the latter.

A forward swap would be easily priced by simply treating the swap as if it were beginning at the forward swap expiration. This means that we would require the spot rates at the forward swap expiration, which is information we have already seen how to obtain.

Now you have seen how a binomial tree is used to price interest rate derivatives. Naturally in practice, the tree must be much larger. Also, it is important that the tree be constructed so as to best mimic movements in interest rates, meaning that the volatility of interest rates should be as close as possible to the actual volatility in the market. As we have previously noted, this is an extremely complex subject that you can study in more detail in advanced courses.

Finally, we should note that although we have used the binomial process to price only interest rate derivatives, it can also be used to price any spot or derivative security whose price is determined by the interest rates modeled in the exercise. This would include zero coupon bonds, coupon bonds, and any type of derivative on zero coupon bonds or coupon bonds.

Summary

This chapter examined interest rate derivatives, which are derivatives in which the underlying asset is an interest rate. These derivatives are constructed in the over-the-counter market and are extremely popular among corporations facing interest rate risk.

We first examined the forward rate agreement, or FRA, which is a forward contract on an interest rate. The FRA requires one party to agree to make a future interest payment at a known rate and to receive a future interest payment at an unknown rate.

We also examined interest rate swaps, which are the most widely used derivative. An interest rate swap is a contract in which one party agrees to make a series of interest payments to the other, while the other makes a series of payments to the first party, with each set of payments at different rates. The standard type of interest rate swap, called the plain vanilla swap, involves one party making payments at a known rate, while the other makes payments at a rate to be determined in the future. Typical swaps have payments based on the rate at one time point, but the actual payment occurs later. This is similar to the way in which floating-rate securities pay interest.

We discovered that interest rate options are similar to options we have already covered but the payoff is based on an interest rate. Call options pay off when the interest rate ends up above the exercise rate while put options pay off when the interest rate ends up below the exercise rate. Like swaps, interest rate options make their payoffs a period of time after expiration. When borrowers need to hedge a series of possible interest rate increases, they can combine interest rate calls with different maturities into an overall transaction called a cap. When lenders need to hedge a series of possible interest rate decreases, they can combine interest rate puts with different expirations into an overall transaction called a floor. The purchase of a cap and sale of a floor, called a collar, hedges against interest rate increases by having the user give up some of the gains from falling interest rates. This can reduce or completely eliminate the amount of cash paid up front.

We also examined options on swaps, which are called swaptions. A swaption can be either a payer swaption, which gives the right to enter into a swap as the fixed-rate payer, or a receiver swaption, which gives the right to enter into the swap as a fixed-rate receiver. Exercise of a swaption creates an annuity equal to the difference in the swap rate at expiration and the exercise rate for a period equal to the life of the underlying swap. We also looked at forward swaps, which are forward contracts to enter into swaps.

Finally, we looked at how a binomial process can be used to model the term structure of interest rates, which enables one to obtain accurate, arbitrage-free prices of FRAs, swaps, options, and swaptions.

You have now seen many of the most widely used derivatives, but there are many more products and strategies. We now move on to some advanced topics in derivatives in Chapter 15.

Key Terms

Before continuing to Chapter 15, you should be able to give brief definitions of the following terms.

- interest rate derivative
- forward rate agreement (FRA)
- interest rate swap
- plain vanilla swap
- swap price/rate
- buy-back/close-out
- interest rate option
- strike rate/exercise rate
- interest rate cap
- caplet
- interest rate floor
- floorlet
- interest rate collar
- zero cost collar
- swaption
- payer swaption
- receiver swaption
- forward swap
- in arrears
- delayed settlement

Further Reading

The following describe the issues and mechanics of interest rate derivative instruments:

Abken, P. A. "Beyond Plain Vanilla: A Taxonomy of Swaps." *Federal Reserve Bank of Atlanta Economic Review* 76 (1991): 12–29.

Abken, P. A. "Interest-Rate Caps, Collars, and Floors." *Federal Reserve Bank of Atlanta Economic Review* 74 (1989): 2–25.

Arak, M., A. Estrella, L. Goodman, and A. Silver. "Interest Rate Swaps: An Alternative Explanation." *Financial Management* 17 (1988): 12–18.

Brooks, R. *Interest Rate Modeling and the Risk Premiums in Interest Rate Swaps.* Charlottesville: Association for Investment Management and Research, 1997.

Brown, K. C., and D. J. Smith. *Interest Rate and Currency Swaps: A Tutorial.* Charlottesville: Association for Investment Management and Research, 1995.

Schachter, B. "Swap Pricing and Swap Mispricing." *Derivatives Quarterly* 2 (1996): 59–64.

Smith, D. R. "A Simple Method for Pricing Interest Rate Swaptions." *Financial Analysts Journal* 47 (May–June 1991): 72–76.

Turnbull, S. M. "Swaps: A Zero Sum Game?" *Financial Management* 16 (1987): 15–21.

Wall, L. D., and J. J. Pringle. "Interest Rate Swaps: A Review of the Issues." *Federal Reserve Bank of Atlanta Economic Review* 73 (1988): 22–41.

Yaksick, R. "Swaps, Caps, and Floors: Some Parity and Price Identities." *The Journal of Financial Engineering* 1 (1992): 105–115.

Two articles that illustrate applications of these instruments are:

Brown, K., and D. J. Smith. "Forward Swaps, Swap Options, and the Management of Callable Debt." *Journal of Applied Corporate Finance* 2 (1990): 59–71.

Goodman, L. S. "The Use of Interest Rate Swaps in Managing Corporate Liabilities." *Journal of Applied Corporate Finance* 2 (1990): 35–47.

Some empirical studies include:

Brown, K. C., V. W. Harlow, and D. J. Smith. "The Empirical Analysis of Interest Rate Swap Spreads." *Journal of Fixed Income* 3 (1993): 61–78.

Duffie, D., and K. J. Singleton. "An Econometric Model of the Term Structure of Interest-Rate Swap Yields." *The Journal of Finance* 52 (1997): 1287–1321.

Sun, T.-S., S. Sundaresan, and C. Wang. "Interest Rate Swaps: An Empirical Investigation." *Journal of Financial Economics* 34 (1993): 77–99.

Wall, L. D., and J. J. Pringle. "Alternative Explanations of Interest Rate Swaps: A Theoretical and Empirical Analysis." *Financial Management* 18 (1989): 59–73.

Questions and Problems

1. Fixed- or floating-rate interest rate swaps can be viewed as equivalent to three other types of financial transactions. Identify these other transactions and explain why they perform the same as the swap.

2. Compare the use of interest rate options with forward rate agreements. Explain why a financial manager might prefer one type of contract over another.

3. If you were entering into a swap that you anticipate you might some-day wish to terminate early, what features would you want to build into the agreement to give you the flexibility to terminate the swap early?

4. How are the payment terms of an FRA in practice different from those of most interest rate derivatives?

5. Explain how a cap is similar to an interest rate call option. How is it different?

6. Explain how the two types of swaptions are like interest rate options and how they are different.

7. Explain how a forward swap is different from a swaption.

8. What is the primary advantage of pricing interest rate derivatives using a binomial term structure model?

9. What are the advantages and disadvantages of an interest rate collar over an interest rate cap?

10. Suppose a firm plans to borrow $5 million in 180 days. The loan will be taken out at whatever LIBOR is on the day the loan begins and will be repaid in one lump sum, 90 days later. The firm would like to lock in the rate it pays so it enters into a forward rate agreement with its bank. The bank agrees to lock in a rate of 12 percent. Determine the annualized cost of the loan for each of the following outcomes. Interest is based on 90 days and a 360-day year.

   a. LIBOR in 180 days is 14 percent.

   b. LIBOR in 180 days is 8 percent.

11. Determine the schedule of payments in a swap of floating- for fixed-rate interest payments. The notional principal is $20 million. The fixed-rate payer pays 11 percent. The floating-rate payer pays LIBOR, with the rate determined on the first day of the interest period. Interest payments are based on the exact number of days, which are 90, 180, 270, and 360. The LIBORs that actually result are 10.5 (90 days from now), 10.2 (180 days from now), and 9.6 (270 days from now). The current LIBOR is 11.5.

12. Jiffy Swaps, Inc. is a large swap dealer. It is in the process of pricing a $25 million fixed- for floating-rate swap. The swap will be for two years and will require semiannual payments. For simplicity assume that the payments are made exactly 180 days apart. The term structure of LIBOR is 12 percent for six months, 12.25 percent for one year, 12.75 percent for 18 months, and 13.02 percent for two years. These are annual LIBOR rates, which use a 360-day year convention and 30 days per month. First convert these rates to discount factors and then verify that a swap rate of 11.92 percent is appropriate.

13. XAC Corporation is currently engaged in a three-year swap with $10 million notional principal. Payments are made every six months. XAC pays a fixed rate of 12 percent and receives a floating rate of

LIBOR. The swap is now three-quarters of the way through the second year. The next floating payment will be at 10.25 percent. Determine the value of the swap to XAC and identify it as an asset or a liability. The appropriate discount rates are 9.75 percent (1/4 year), 9.875 percent (3/4 year), and 10 percent (1 1/4 years). Convert these rates to discount factors and use 30 days per month and 360 days per year.

14. Consider a three-year receiver swaption with a strike rate of 11.75 percent where the underlying swap is a four-year swap. The notional principal is $20,000,000. At expiration, the spot rates on zero coupon bonds of various maturities are: 10 percent (1 year), 10.5 percent (2 years), 10.9 percent (three years), and 11.2 percent (four years). Determine the payoff of the swaption. Compute your discount factors using $(1.10)^{-1}$, $(1.105)^{-2}$, etc.

15. You are the treasurer of a firm that will need to borrow $10 million at LIBOR plus 2.5 points in 45 days. The loan will have a maturity of 180 days, at which time all the interest and principal will be repaid. The interest will be determined by LIBOR on the day the loan is taken out. To hedge the uncertainty of this future rate, you purchase a call on LIBOR with a strike of 9 percent for a premium of $32,000. Determine the amount you will pay back and the annualized cost of borrowing for LIBORs of 6 percent and 12 percent. Assume the payoff is based on 180 days and a 360-day year. The current LIBOR is 9 percent.

16. A large, multinational bank has committed to lend a firm $25 million in 30 days at LIBOR plus 100 bps. The loan will have a maturity of 90 days, at which time the principal and all interest will be repaid. The bank is concerned about falling interest rates and decides to buy a put on LIBOR with a strike of 9.5 percent and a premium of $60,000, Determine the annualized loan rate for LIBORs of 6.5 percent and 12.5 percent. Assume the payoff is based on 90 days and a 360-day year. The current LIBOR is 9.5 percent.

17. As the assistant treasurer of a large corporation, your job is to look for ways your company can lock in its cost of borrowing in the financial markets. The date is June 28. Your firm is taking out a loan of $20 million, with interest to be paid on September 28, December 31, March 31, and June 29. You will pay the LIBOR in effect at the beginning of the interest payment period. The current LIBOR is 10 percent. You recommend that the firm buy an interest rate cap with a strike of 10 percent and a premium of $70,000. Determine the cash flows over the life of this loan if LIBOR turns out to be 11 percent on September 28, 11.65 percent on December 31, and 12.04 percent on March 31. The payoff is based on the exact number of days and a 360-day year. If you have a financial calculator or a spreadsheet with an IRR function, solve for the internal rate of return and annualize it to determine the effective cost of borrowing.

18. You are a funds manager for a large bank. On April 15, your bank lends a corporation $35 million, with interest payments to be made on July 16, October 15, January 16, and next April 16. The amount of interest will be determined by LIBOR at the beginning of the interest payment period. Your forecast is for declining interest rates, so you anticipate lower loan interest revenues. You decide to buy an interest rate floor with a strike set at 8 percent and a premium of $60,000. Determine the cash flows associated with the loan if LIBOR turns out to be 7.9 percent on July 16, 7.7 percent on October 15, and 8.1 percent next January 16. The payoff is based on the exact number of days and a 360-day year. If you have a financial calculator or spreadsheet with an IRR function, determine the internal rate of return and annualize it to determine your annualized return on the loan.

19. On January 15, a firm takes out a loan of $30 million, with interest payments to be made on April 16, July 15, October 14, and next January 15, when the principal will be repaid. Interest will be paid at LIBOR based on the rate at the beginning of the interest payment period, using the exact number of days and a 360-day year. The firm wants to buy a cap with a strike of 10 percent and a premium of $150,000. Its bank suggests that the firm sell a floor with a strike of 9 percent and a premium of $115,000. The current LIBOR is 10 percent. Answer the following questions.

a. What is this transaction called? Why would the firm sell the floor in addition to buying the cap? What is the firm giving up if it adds the short floor to the long cap?

b. If LIBOR turns out to be 11.35 percent on April 16, 10.2 percent on July 15, and 8.86 percent on October 14, what are the firm's cash flows associated with the loan? If you have a financial calculator or spreadsheet, determine the internal rate of return and annualize it to determine your cost of borrowing.

c. Suppose the firm did not want to pay cash up front for the collar. How could it alter the terms of the collar?

20. A bank is offering an interest rate call with an expiration of 45 days. The call pays off based on 180-day LIBOR. The volatility of forward rates is .17. The 45-day forward rate for 180-day LIBOR is .1322 and the exercise rate is .12. The risk-free rate for 45 days is .1128. Use the Black model to determine how much the bank should receive for selling this call for every $1 million of notional principal.

21. A firm is interested in purchasing an interest rate cap from a bank. It has received an offer price from the bank but would like to determine if the price is fair. The cap will consist of two caplets, one expiring in 91 days and the other in 182 days. They will both have strikes of 7 percent. The forward rate applicable to the first caplet is 8 percent and the forward rate applicable to the second caplet is 8.2 percent. The 91-day risk-free rate is 7.1 percent and the 182-day risk-free rate is 7.3 percent. The firm's best estimate of the volatility of forward rates is .166. The notional principal is $10 million, and the payoff is based on 90-day LIBOR. Use the Black model to determine a fair price for the cap.

22. The one-period spot rates in a binomial tree are as follows:

At time 0:	6 percent
At time 1:	9.47 percent or 6.28 percent
At time 2:	12.41 percent, 9.13 percent, or 5.95 percent
At time 3:	15.68 percent, 12.31 percent, 9.04 percent, and 5.86 percent
At time 4:	16.86 percent, 13.46 percent, 10.16 percent, 6.95 percent, or 3.83 percent

The probability of an up move is .55. The zero coupon rates are 6 percent (1-year), 7 percent (2-years), 7.8 percent (3-years), and 8.6 percent (4-years). Answer the following questions.

a. Draw a binomial tree with four time periods. At each node, insert the probability of reaching that node.

Each of the remaining questions asks you to price a derivative using the binomial tree developed in part a. In other words, each derivative is on the one-period rate. Make sure you check your answer to part a before moving on to parts b–g.

b. Find the price of an in-arrears FRA expiring at time 2. Also find the price of a delayed settlement FRA expiring at time 2.

c. Find the price of a three-period interest rate swap.

d. Find the price of a European interest rate put maturing in four periods where the exercise rate is 10 percent.

e. Find the price of a European interest rate cap with an exercise rate of 9 percent with caplets expiring at times 1, 2, and 3.

f. Find the price of an interest rate payer swaption expiring in two periods with an exercise rate of 9 percent where the underlying is a two-period swap. The spot rates at expiration on two-year zero coupon bonds in each of the three states are 12.33 percent, 9.08 percent, and 5.79 percent.

g. Find the price of a two-period forward swap where the underlying is a two-period swap.

23. (Concept Problem) Use the Black model to determine a fair price for an interest rate put that expires in 74 days. The forward rate is 9.79 percent, and the exercise rate is 10 percent. The appropriate risk-free rate is 8.38 percent. The volatility of forward rates is .1465. The put is based on $22 million notional principal and pays off based on 90-day LIBOR.

24. (Concept Problem) Using the binomial interest rate tree in Problem 22, find the price of an American-style interest rate put expiring at time 4 with an exercise rate of 11 percent. (Hint: You may need to review the procedure for pricing American options on stock using the binomial model in Chapter 4.)

APPENDIX 14

The Ho-Lee Model of the Term Structure

There are many models that capture movements of interest rates across the term structure. One of the easiest to use is the model of Ho and Lee (1986). Their model is based on a binomial process, which means that it captures uncertainty by permitting two outcomes to be possible. The Ho-Lee model specifies the entire term structure of zero coupon bonds and allows the term structure to shift either upward or downward. The uncertainty is reflected in shock factors that affect forward rates. In other words, the Ho-Lee model captures the uncertainty in forward rates.

We begin with some notation. Let $r(t,x,y)$ be the rate observed at time t on a bond beginning at time x and maturing at time y. Suppose we start off today with a set of spot rates, $r(0,0,1)$, $r(0,0,2)$, and $r(0,0,3)$, which are the rates today on zero coupon bonds for maturities of one to three periods. Working with the spot rates $r(0,0,1)$ and $r(0,0,2)$, we can find the forward rate $r(0,1,2)$ as $r(0,1,2) = (1 + r(0,0,2))^2(1 + r(0,0,1)) - 1$. The forward rate, $r(0,1,3)$, can be found as $r(0,1,3) = \sqrt{(1 + r(0,0,3))^3/(1 + r(0,0,1))} - 1$.

If there were no uncertainty, then the forward rates would evolve into the future spot rates. In other words, at time 1, the spot rate on one-period bonds, $r(1,1,2)$, would be the same as $r(0,1,2)$. At time 1, the spot rate on two-period bonds, $r(1,1,3)$, would be the same as $r(0,1,3)$. Ho and Lee incorporate uncertainty by permitting these spot rates to deviate from the forward rates by up and down shift factors. Bonds of different maturities have different shift factors. Thus, let us define $u(1)$ and $d(1)$ as the up and down shift factors for bonds with maturity of one year, while $u(2)$ and $d(2)$ are the shift factors for bonds with maturities of two years.

At time 1 the spot rate on a one-period bond can either shift upward,

$$r(1,1,2) = \frac{(1 + r(0,0,2))^2}{1 + r(0,0,1)} u(1) - 1,$$

or downward,

$$r(1,1,2) = \frac{(1 + r(0,0,2))^2}{1 + r(0,0,1)} d(1) - 1.$$

At time 1 the spot rate on two-period bonds can either shift upward,

$$r(1,1,3) = \sqrt{\frac{(1 + r(0,0,3))^3}{1 + r(0,0,1)}} u(2) - 1,$$

or downward,

$$r(1,1,3) = \sqrt{\frac{(1 + r(0,0,3))^3}{1 + r(0,0,1)}}\, d(2) - 1.$$

The values of $u(1)$, $d(1)$, $u(2)$, and $d(2)$ are determined by a complex theorem that prevents profitable arbitrage. We omit the details here, but the formulas for the u's and d's are easy to compute, given the required input variables. We need p, the probability of an up move, implying that $1 - p$ is the probability of a down move, and Λ, a factor reflecting the volatility. The values of the probabilities need not be the actual probabilities and, in fact, any set of probabilities can be chosen for a given value of Λ. The value of $d(i)$, where in our example $i = 1$ or 2, is given as

$$d(i) = \frac{p + (1 - p)\Lambda^i}{\Lambda^i},$$

whereas the value of $u(i)$ is

$$u(i) = d(i)\,\Lambda^i.$$

Ho and Lee show that the choice of Λ is determined by the volatility of the one-period rate according to the formula

$$\sigma = \sqrt{p(1 - p)[\ln(\Lambda)]^2}.$$

In our example, we have $r(0,0,1) = .1050$, $r(0,0,2) = .1043$, and $r(0,0,3) = .1041$. We let $p = .52$ and $1 - p = .48$. We set Λ at 1.03. This gives values of u and d of $d(1) = (.52 + .48(1.03)^1)/(1.03)^1 = .9849$, $u(1) = .9849(1.03)^1 = 1.0144$, $d(2) = (.52 + .48(1.03)^2)/(1.03)^2 = .9701$, and $u(2) = .9701(1.03)^2 = 1.0292$. The arbitrary choice of $p = .52$, $1 - p = .48$, and $\Lambda = 1.03$ implies a standard deviation of the one-period rate of $\sqrt{.52(.48)[\ln(1.03)]^2} = .0148$.

With this information we can find the spot rates at time 1. The one-period spot rate at time 1 can either be

$$r(1,1,2) = \frac{(1.1043)^2}{1.105}\, 1.0144 - 1 = .1195,$$

or

$$r(1,1,2) = \frac{(1.1043)^2}{1.105}\, .9849 - 1 = .0869.$$

The rate on two-period bonds would be

$$r(1,1,3) = \sqrt{\frac{(1.1041)^3}{1.105}\, 1.0292} - 1 = .1196,$$

or

$$r(1,1,3) = \sqrt{\frac{(1.1041)^3}{1.105}\, .9701} - 1 = .0870.$$

These results give us the possible one- and two-period spot rates at time 1. From these we can obtain the implied forward rates at time 1. Applying the up and down factors to the forward rates at time 1 will allow us to extend the tree one step farther. In order to build a tree of n time steps, it is necessary at time 0 to have the spot rates for maturities up to n + 1.

Since most derivative contracts are written on the short-term spot rate, which here is the one-period rate, we specified a tree showing the evolution of one-period rates. This was Figure 14.6. The values shown in the tree differ slightly from those computed here because the tree calculations were done on a computer and used a greater degree of precision than we used in this appendix.

Advanced Derivatives and Strategies

The best advice may be this: treat exotic derivatives like powerful medicines, large doses of which can be harmful. Use them in moderation, for a particular purpose (such as risk management) and only after having read the instructions on the bottle.

PHILIPPE JORION
Big Bets Gone Bad, 1995

In this chapter we examine some advanced derivatives and strategies. Though it may seem like we are taking a leap forward, this is not necessarily the case. While some of these derivatives are complex, others are fairly simple and some are constructed by combining derivatives we have already covered.

We shall begin the chapter with a group called equity derivatives. Although these types of derivatives have been written primarily on stocks and stock portfolios, some of them are also written on bonds, interest rates, currencies, and commodities. The second group of derivatives we cover will be strictly derivatives on fixed-income securities and interest rates. Here we shall take a look at some of the variations of the plain vanilla swap as well as structured notes and mortgage derivatives. The third group is called *exotic* options. This is a term used to classify the most advanced types of options. Some of them hardly seem exotic, but they are typically referred to that way.

Advanced Equity Derivatives and Strategies

An **equity derivative** is a derivative on a stock or stock index. While the over-the-counter market is much larger for interest rate derivatives, the over-the-counter equity derivatives market is growing rapidly. Recall that we

Chapter Objectives

■ To build on our previous coverage of the basics of derivatives by examining several new derivatives and strategies, some of which are combinations of previously studied derivatives and others of which are entirely new

■ To understand the strategy of portfolio insurance, see how it enables a portfolio to achieve a target minimum return, and illustrate how it can be implemented

■ To examine equity forwards, warrants, and equity-linked debt

■ To understand and evaluate equity swaps

■ To extend the Chapter 14 treatment of interest rate derivatives by examining some popular variations of interest rate swaps

■ To examine structured notes so as to understand how they are constructed and to gain an appreciation for their volatility

■ To understand mortgage securities, including pass-throughs, IOs, POs, and CMOs, and to gain an understanding of how their values change as interest rates change

■ To examine various exotic options, including digital and chooser options, path-dependent options, and miscellaneous exotic options, and to use the binomial model to price several of them have already studied at great length exchange-traded equity derivatives, such as options on stocks and stock indices, futures on stock indices, and options on stock index futures. While these contracts meet the needs of many investors, the specialization afforded by customized over-the-counter contracts is becoming increasingly worth the cost.

For example, many investors need derivatives that match specific portfolios. Exchange-traded derivatives are based on well-known indices, such as the S&P 500. To use a derivative on the S&P 500 to hedge a position in a portfolio that does not match the index induces some basis risk. While that risk may be acceptable for some investors, others would prefer to avoid it by using derivatives customized to their particular holdings. Such derivatives, called **baskets,** can be constructed by simply showing a derivatives dealer the composition of the portfolio. The dealer then constructs a derivative based on that specific portfolio.

Equity derivatives are especially useful in international investing. Equity derivatives on international stocks or indices allow an investor to capture the gains from investing in foreign securities without actually having to incur the additional transaction cost of acquiring those securities directly. In addition there are often costly foreign regulations to deal with and many countries impose a dividend withholding tax, which requires that some of the dividends be left in the foreign country to cover any future tax liabilities. Equity derivatives are often structured to pay off both capital gains and dividends, but since no money leaves the country, the dividend withholding tax is avoided. While investing directly in foreign securities imposes exchange rate risk, many equity derivatives are structured with a fixd exchange rate, thereby avoiding that risk.

Equity derivatives also permit fast, low-cost realignment of domestic portfolios. For example, an investor holding primarily large cap stocks and wanting to increase the allocation to small cap stocks can do so using derivatives on those two groups of stocks. This is much like our description of adjusting the risk of an equity portfolio in Chapters 10 and 11.

Naturally these features come at a cost that is incurred by the dealer and passed on to the end user. Fortunately the large size and sophisticated operations of most dealers result in efficiency and low costs, which benefit the end user.

While the emphasis in this chapter is on over-the-counter contracts and strategies, we begin with an exchange-listed derivative strategy, portfolio insurance.

Portfolio Insurance

The concept of insurance has been around for hundreds of years. Individuals and business firms routinely insure their lives and property against risk of loss. The concept extends easily to portfolios. In fact, we touched on the subject in Chapter 6 when we covered protective puts.

Suppose we own a portfolio consisting of N_S shares of stock and N_P puts. The stock price is S_0, the putprice is P, the exercise price is X, the puts are European, and we assume no dividends on the stock. The value of the portfolio is

$$V = N_S S_0 + N_P P.$$

Letting $N_S = N_P$ and calling this N, we have

$$N = \frac{V}{S_0 + P}.$$

This tells us how many shares of stock and how many puts we can buy. At expiration the portfolio's value is

$$
\begin{array}{ll}
V_T = N S_T & \text{if } S_T > X \\
V_T = N S_T + N(X - S_T) = NX & \text{if } S_T \le X,
\end{array}
$$

where S_T is the stock price when the put expires.

The worst possible outcome is that in which $S_T = 0$. Suppose we define V_{min} as the minimum value of V_T, which occurs when $S_T = 0$. Then $V_{min} = NX$ and, since N must also equal $V/(S_0 + P)$,

$$V_{min} = \frac{XV}{S_0 + P}.$$

This formula establishes the minimum value of the portfolio at expiration. Note that it occurs not only when $S_T = 0$ but also when $S_T \le X$.

Let us illustrate how this works. Suppose that on September 26 the market index is at 445.75 and the December 485 put option on the index is priced at \$38.57. The option expires on December 19, which is 84 days away, so the time to expiration is $84/365 = .2301$. The risk-free rate is 3.04 percent stated as a simple annual rate or 2.99 percent continuously compounded. The standard deviation is .155.

Suppose we hold a diversified portfolio of stocks that replicates the index. The portfolio is worth \$44,575,000, which is equivalent to 100,000 units of the index. In other words we hold a portfolio that is weighted exactly like the index and is worth 100,000 times the index level.

The minimum level of the portfolio is

$$V_{min} = \frac{XV}{S_0 + P} = \frac{(485)(44,575,000)}{445.75 + 38.57} = 44,637,585.$$

Thus, the minimum level at which we can insure the portfolio is $44,637,585. This means that if we own N shares and N puts, where

$$N = \frac{V}{S_0 + P} = \frac{44,575,000}{445.75 + 38.57} = 92,036,$$

the minimum value of the portfolio on December 19 is $44,637,585. This is a guaranteed return of .0014 for 84 days, or $(1.0014)^{(365/84)} - 1 = .0061$ per year. This figure must be below the risk-free rate or an arbitrage opportunity would be possible. After all, how could we guarantee a minimum return on a risky portfolio greater than the risk-free rate?

We buy 92,036 shares and 92,036 puts. Suppose that at expiration the index is at 510:

$$
\begin{array}{llr}
\text{Value of stock} & = 92,036(\$510) & = \$46,938,360 \\
+ \text{ Value of puts} & = 92,036(\$0) & = \underline{\hspace{1.2cm} 0} \\
\text{Total} & & = \$46,938,360.
\end{array}
$$

This exceeds the minimum value.

If at expiration the index is at 450,

Value of stock = 92,036($485) = $44,637,460 (by exercising the puts).

An appropriate combination of stock and puts establishes an insured portfolio.

While this amount appears to be slightly below the minimum, it is actually the same due to rounding off some of the previously computed values. The error is less than 1/1,000th of 1 percent.

Figure 15.1 shows the value of the insured stock-put portfolio when the put expires. The exact minimum cannot be read from the graph but is mathematically equal to $44,637,585. The graph should look familiar. It is essentially the same as that of the protective put covered in Chapter 6. In this example, however, we are looking only at the value of the investor's position at expiration and not at the profit. The dotted line shows the value of the portfolio if it were uninsured.

Like any form of insurance, **portfolio insurance** entails a cost. By *cost* we do not necessarily mean commissions, bid-ask spreads, and so on. These certainly are important, but the cost of portfolio insurance is the difference in the return of the insured portfolio and the return of the uninsured portfolio when the market goes up. In other words, it is the return that is given up in bull markets, in which the insurance was not needed. This cost varies with the uninsured value of the portfolio. When the index ended up at 510, the insured portfolio was worth $46,938,360. Had the portfolio not been insured, it would have consisted of 100,000 shares valued at $510 each for a total value of $51,000,000. The cost thus is $4,061,640, or about 9.1 percent of the portfolio's original value. The difference between 100 percent and the cost of 9.1 percent, or 90.9 percent, is called the **upside capture.** It is the percentage of the uninsured return in a bull market that is earned by

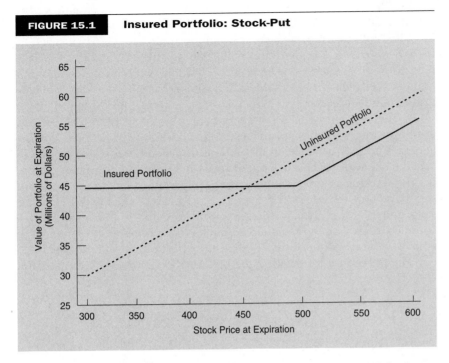

FIGURE 15.1   Insured Portfolio: Stock-Put

the insured portfolio. At low values of the portfolio, the cost of the insurance can be negative, which means that the insurance paid off more than it cost.

Because of put-call parity, an identical result is obtained with calls and Treasury bills, a strategy referred to as a **fiduciary call.** Let B be the price of a Treasury bill and B_T be its face value when it matures. Suppose we own a portfolio of N_C calls and N_B Treasury bills. At expiration, the portfolio will be worth $V_T = N_B B_T$ if $S_T < X$ and $N_C(S_T - X) + N_B B_T$ if $S_T \geq X$. Again, the worst case is S_T going to zero. Call that result V_{min}, which will be the value of the Treasury bills at maturity, i.e., $V_{min} = N_B B_T$. Thus,

$$N_B = \frac{V_{min}}{B_T}.$$

If we buy N_B Treasury bills, we can buy $N_C = (V - N_B B)/C$ calls. The number of calls can be shown to equal the number of shares and puts from the stock-put example. Thus, we also have

$$N_C = \frac{V}{S_0 + P}.$$

Continuing with our numerical example, the call is worth $2.65 and the bills have a face value of $100. Thus, we would want $44,637,585/$100

636 Chapter 15 Advanced Derivatives and Strategies

An appropriate combination of calls and Treasury bills establishes an insured portfolio.

= 446,376 Treasury bills and 92,036 calls. At expiration if the index is at 510, the calls will expire $25 in-the-money. With 92,036 calls worth $25 and 446,376 T-bills worth $100 each, the total portfolio value is $46,938,500. If the index goes to 450, there will be 92,036 worthless calls and 446,376 T-bills worth $100 each for a total of $44,637,600, which is the same minimum in the stock-put case, subject to a round-off error. The example is illustrated in Figure 15.2.

A European put (or call) with the appropriate terms and conditions would obviously be a means of insuring a portfolio. While such options generally are not available on the options exchanges, it is possible to replicate the behavior of the stock-put or call–T-bill insured portfolio by continuously adjusting a portfolio of stocks and index futures or stocks and Treasury bills. This technique is referred to as **dynamic hedging.** When using stock index futures, dynamic hedging involves selling a number of futures contracts such that the portfolio responds to stock price movements the same way the stock-put or call–T-bill insured portfolio would respond.

The procedure for deriving the hedge ratio is presented in Appendix 15A. The formula is

$$N_f = \left[\left(\frac{V_{min}}{X} \right) N(d_1) - \left(\frac{V}{S_0} \right) \right] e^{-r_c T}.$$

FIGURE 15.2   **Insured Portfolio: Call–T-bill**

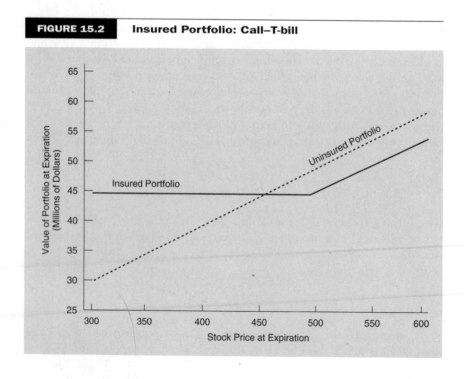

This gives the number of futures contracts. Since most futures contracts have a multiplier, this number should be divided by the multiplier. For example, if using the S&P 500 futures, the contract size is actually 250 times the quoted price. The above formula should then be divided by 250. Since futures require no outlay, the hedger can put all the funds in stock. The hedger must be sure to continuously adjust the number of futures contracts so that it always equals the value of N_f. Since the delta and T will change, this will necessitate frequent revisions.

An alternative approach to the use of futures in dynamic hedging is the use of Treasury bills. It is possible to combine stock and Treasury bills so that the portfolio behaves like the protective put or fiduciary call. The key assumption behind this result is that the Treasury bill price changes only as a result of time. It is not directly influenced by the stock price. This is a fairly reasonable assumption since the long-run correlation between stock returns and Treasury bill returns is nearly zero. Appendix 15A presents the derivation of the appropriate combination of stocks and Treasury bills. The number of Treasury bills is

$$N_B = \frac{V - N_S S_0}{B}.$$

The number of shares of stock is

$$N_S = \left(\frac{V_{min}}{X}\right)N(d_1).$$

As with the use of futures, these values will change continuously.

Both of these approaches work by equating the deltas of the dynamically hedged portfolios to the delta of the hypothetical portfolio of stock and puts. For example, for the December 485 call, the delta is .1574. This means that the put delta is $.1574 - 1 = -.8426$. A combination of one unit of stock and one put would have a delta of 1 (the stock's delta) plus $-.8426$ (the put's delta), which equals .1574, the call's delta. When using stock index futures for dynamic hedging, the combination of all $44,575,000 in stock along with N_f futures has a delta of .1574, the same delta as would have been obtained if the hedger had owned 92,036 shares and 92,036 puts. When using the combination of stock and Treasury bills, the combination of N_S shares and N_B Treasury bills also has a delta of .1574.

Table 15.1 illustrates the appropriate calculations using stock and futures in a dynamic hedge, stock and T-bills in a dynamic hedge, and the exact hedge that would result if the necessary puts were available.[1]

Dynamic hedging is the use of stock and either stock index futures or Treasury bills to achieve portfolio insurance by setting the delta of the stock-futures or stock–T-bill combination to the delta of a combination of stock and puts.

---

[1]The old and new options and futures prices were calculated using the Black-Scholes model, as covered in Chapter 5, and the cost of carry model with continuous compounding, as covered in Chapter 9.

TABLE 15.1	Dynamic Hedge Portfolio Insurance

Basic Information		*Contract Characteristics*	
Current day	September 26	Futures price	448.83
Horizon day	December 19	Futures delta	1.0069
Time to horizon	.2301	Futures multiplier	500
Stock price	445.75	Exercise price	485
Number of shares held	100,000	Put price	38.57
Market value of portfolio	$44,575,000	Call price	2.65
Risk-free rate	2.99%	Call delta	.1574
Volatility of stock	.155	Put delta	−.8426
Price of Treasury bill	99.31		
Minimum portfolio value (V_{min})	$44,637,585		

Dynamic Hedge with Futures
Number of contracts needed:

$$N_f = \left[\left(\frac{44,637,585}{485} \right)(.1574) - \left(\frac{44,575,000}{445.75} \right) \right] e^{-(.0299)(.2301)} / 500 \approx -170.$$

Dynamic Hedge with Treasury Bills
Number of shares held:

$$N_S = \left(\frac{44,637,585}{485} \right)(.1574) \approx 14,486.$$

Number of bills needed:

$$N_B = \frac{44,575,000 - 14,486(445.75)}{99.31} \approx 383,827.$$

Effects of a $1 decrease in the stock price		
New derivative prices:		
Put	$39.42	
Futures	447.82	
Stock plus put:		
Gain on stock	−$92,036	(92,036 shares × − $1)
Gain on put	78,230	(92,036 puts × ($39.42 − $38.57))
Net gain	−$13,806	(0.03% of value of portfolio)
Stock plus futures dynamic hedge:		
Gain on stock	−$100,000	(100,000 shares × −$1)
Gain on futures	85,850	(−170 contracts × (447.82 − 448.83) × 500)
Net gain	−14,150	
Stock plus Treasury bill dynamic hedge:		
Gain on stock	−$14,486	(14,486 shares × −$1)
Gain on T-bills	0	(bill price does not change due to stock price change)
Net gain	−14,486	

The lower panel shows that the differences in the three methods are very small. These differences can be explained by a combination of round-off error and the fact that a strategy equating deltas is only approximately correct if there is a non-infinitesimal change in the stock price, a point we introduced as the gamma effect in Chapter 5 and reexamine in Chapter 16. Moreover, dynamic hedging, or any delta-matching strategy, will require that the hedge ratio be adjusted continuously, which obviously cannot be done in the presence of transaction costs.

The dynamic hedging version of portfolio insurance was a widely used strategy in the mid-1980s. Its efficacy depends on the stock market having only small price changes within a short time interval. During the stock market crash of October 1987, however, stock prices experienced enormous jumps over short time intervals. While portfolios that were insured did better than those that were not, they failed to achieve their targets. The massive volume of selling done by portfolio insurers adjusting their hedge ratios was, probably wrongly, blamed for exacerbating the crash. Investors then became disillusioned with portfolio insurance. In response, however, it was not too long afterward that many new, customized equity products began to appear.

Equity Forwards

An **equity forward** contract is simply a forward contract on a stock, stock index, or portfolio. The principles are the same as those we studied previously in Chapter 9. An investor buying an equity forward simply enters into a contract with a counterparty, the seller, in which the buyer agrees to buy the stock, stock index, or portfolio from the seller at a future date at a price agreed upon today. In many cases, the equity instrument is a stock index or a portfolio of stocks. Rather than have the seller deliver stock to the buyer at expiration, the contract frequently specifies that it will be cash settled.

The price agreed upon by the two parties, called the forward price, was covered in Chapter 9. Recall that the price of a forward (or futures) contract on a stock is the current stock price, compounded at the risk-free rate minus the compound future value of the dividends. Since we have covered pricing at great length, we shall not repeat it here, but it may be useful for the reader to review the relevant parts of Chapter 9.

An equity forward is simply a forward contract on a stock, stock index, or portfolio. It is an agreement for one party to buy the stock, stock index, or portfolio from another party at a fixed price. It is usually settled in cash.

An interesting variation of a forward contract is the break forward. A **break forward** is a combination of spot and derivative positions that replicates the outcome of an ordinary call with one exception—the positions are structured such that the overall position costs nothing up front. This is like a zero-cost call, except that it would be impossible to have an instrument that costs nothing up front and returns either zero or a positive amount, like an ordinary call. The break forward achieves this result by penalizing the investor if the option ends up out-of-the-money. An ordinary call pays off $\text{Max}(0, S_T - X)$. A break forward is a call that pays off if it expires in-the-money and incurs a charge if it expires out-of-the-money. Even the in-the-money payoff, however, can be negative.

To illustrate the break forward and to keep the explanation simple, we assume no dividends on the stock. A break forward will pay off $S_T - K$ if $S_T > F$ and $F - K$ if $S_T \le F$. The value K is the sum of the compound future value of an ordinary call on the stock with exercise price F

TABLE 15.2	**Payoffs from Break Forward**		
			Payoffs from Portfolio Given Stock Price at Expiration
Instrument	**Current Value**	$S_T \leq F$	$S_T > F$
Long Call	$C(S_0, T, F)$	0	$S_T - F$
Loan	$- (K - F)e^{-r_c T}$	$-(K - F)$	$-(K - F)$
	0	$F - K$	$S_T - K$

plus the compound future value of the stock. The latter term, you know, is the forward price. Thus, K will exceed F so when $S_T \leq F$, the payoff, $F - K$, is definitely negative. It is also possible that $S_T - K$ can be negative. If the break forward were structured as a put, the exercise price would be the forward price plus the compound value of the put price.

A break forward contract is identical to an ordinary long call with an exercise price of F and a loan in which the investor receives the present value of $K - F$ and promises to pay back $K - F$. Table 15.2 illustrates this result. Recall from Chapters 2–7 that we examined some results for AOL options. We shall use the same AOL options for many of the examples in this chapter.[2] The value of the break forward at expiration is illustrated in Figure 15.3.

The example is based on a stock price of 125.9375, a time to expiration of .0959 (35 days/365), a risk-free rate of 4.46 percent continuously compounded, a volatility of 0.83, and 100 units of the break forward. The forward price of AOL is $125.9375e^{.0446(.0959)} = 126.48$. This value is the exercise price of the break forward. As noted above, the break forward is equivalent to a loan and a call with exercise price of F, so we need the price of a call expiring in 35 days with an exercise price of 126.48. Using the Black-Scholes model, that call price would be 12.88. Next we need to know the value of K. This will equal the forward price plus the compound future value of the call price. This is $126.48 + 12.88e^{.0046(.0959)} = 139.41$. Thus, the break forward will be worth $126.48 - 139.41 = -12.93$ if $S_T \leq 126.48$ and $S_T - 139.41$ if $S_T > 126.48$. In the figure all values are multiplied by $100.

Since the up-front cost is zero, the value at expiration is also the profit. While this figure looks exactly like a call, it is important to remember that a break forward incurs a payment if it expires out-of-the-money. This is the penalty for having to pay nothing for it up front.

A break forward is similar to an ordinary call in that it has a limited loss and unlimited gain; however, it requires no premium up front. Unlike an ordinary call, its value at expiration can be negative.

---

[2] In practice, many of these types of contracts are based on the S&P 500 or a specific portfolio. We use the AOL examples for convenience and because you should by now be quite familiar with these options.

FIGURE 15.3   **Break Forward**

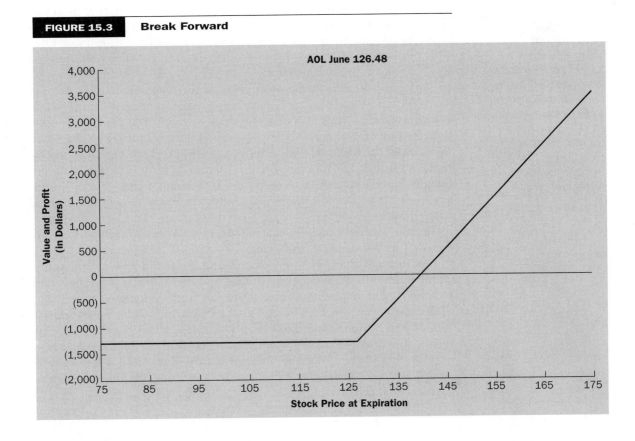

It should be apparent that a break forward is similar to a forward contract and a call option. Like a forward contract, it requires no initial outlay but can have negative value at expiration. Like a call, it has a limited loss. Due to the parity relationships that exist between puts, calls, and forwards, a break forward can also be constructed by entering into a long forward contract at the price F, borrowing the present value of K − F, and buying a put with an exercise price of F. It should also be obvious that there is no reason why break forwards cannot be constructed on interest rates, bonds, commodities, or currencies.

Equity Swaps

In Chapter 14, we examined the interest rate swap. In this chapter we shall examine the **equity swap.** Other than the manner in which the payoffs are calculated, the underlying principles are the same. In equity swaps at least one counterparty pays according to the performance of a stock or stock index. The other party pays according to any other agreeable formula. A typical equity swap would involve one side paying interest according to

An equity swap is a transaction in which at least one party agrees to make payments calculated as the return on a stock or stock index times a notional principal. The other party's payments can be calculated by any other agreeable formula.

LIBOR while the other side makes a payment based on the return on the S&P 500 times the notional principal. Such a transaction results in an investor buying the return on the S&P 500 at a cost of the Eurodollar rate. This can be a useful device for converting interest payments or bond returns to stock returns or vice versa.

Let us consider a simple equity swap of the type described above. On January 2 a portfolio manager enters into a swap with a dealer in which the manager agrees to pay LIBOR and receive the S&P 500. The S&P 500 return is based on Standard & Poor's 500 Total Return Index. This is a slight variation of the S&P 500 and includes the effect of both capital appreciation and dividends. The calculation of the return for this swap is made on the payment date and is based on the exact percentage change in the index since the last payment date. This will be (stock value on payment date − stock value on previous payment date)/stock value on previous payment date. The notional principal is $10 million. Payments will be made on April 2, July 2, October 2, and January 2 of the following year.

An unusual aspect of equity swaps is the fact that it is possible that the equity payment will be negative. In that case, payment must still be made but the direction reverses. Thus, when the stock index goes down, one counterparty receives LIBOR and also receives a payment based on the S&P 500 negative return. Table 15.3 presents a set of after-the-fact payments, based on an assumed series of LIBORs and S&P 500 index values.

The first payment is made on April 2. LIBOR on January 2 was 9 percent. There are 90 days between January 2 and April 2. The first LIBOR payment is, therefore,

$$\$10,000,000(.09)\left(\frac{90}{360}\right) = \$225,000.$$

TABLE 15.3   After-the-Fact Payments in Equity Swap with LIBOR

Notional principal: $10,000,000
Pay LIBOR, receive S&P 500 Total Return

Date	Days	LIBOR (%)	LIBOR Payment	S&P 500 Total Return Index	S&P 500 Total Return (%)	S&P 500 Payment	Net Payment
Jan 2	——	9.00	——	1324.28	——	——	——
Apr 2	90	9.15	$225,000	1350.78	2.00	$200,109	−$24,891
Jul 2	91	9.35	231,292	1430.48	5.90	590,029	358,737
Oct 2	92	8.65	238,944	1386.16	−3.10	−309,826	−548,770
Jan 2	92	——	221,056	1407.02	1.50	150,488	−70,568

Note: This is but one of an infinite number of possible outcomes to the equity swap. It is used only to illustrate how payments are determined and not their likely amounts.

The S&P 500 was at 1324.28 on January 2 and 1350.78 on April 2. The first S&P 500 payment will be the return on the S&P 500 times the notional principal:

$$\$10,000,000\left(\frac{1350.78 - 1324.28}{1324.28}\right) = \$200,109.$$

Thus, the portfolio manager owes $225,000 and is due $200,109 for a net of −$24,891. So the manager pays the swap dealer $24,891.

On the next payment date, the manager is owed more than she owes so she receives $358,737. Note, however, that from July 2 to October 2, the S&P 500 went down, so the manager not only owes the LIBOR payment of $238,944 but also *owes* an S&P 500 payment of $309,826 for a net outflow of $548,770.

In spite of the fact that the overall outcome did not turn out well for the manager, the important point is that the manager was able to obtain the S&P 500 total return on a constant investment of $10 million at a cost of LIBOR. This is similar to one of two possible alternative transactions. If the manager had held a floating rate note paying LIBOR, she could have sold that security and used the proceeds to invest in the S&P 500 Total Return portfolio. This would have produced a similar outcome. Alternatively, the swap is similar to having borrowed at LIBOR and using the proceeds to invest in the S&P 500 Total Return portfolio.

There are a couple of slight differences, however, in the actual transactions and the equity swap. In an actual transaction involving S&P 500 stock, the voting rights in the stock would have been acquired. Also, an actual investment in the S&P 500 stock would have earned a return based on a variable notional principal. For example, $10,000,000 invested in the S&P 500 on January 2 would have grown to $10,200,109 on April 2. Then $10,200,109 invested in the S&P 500 on April 2 would have grown to $10,801,945 on July 2, based on the return of 5.9 percent from April 2 to July 2. This is a dollar capital gain of $601,836, which is slightly more than the $590,029 in the swap. The discrepancy results from having the swap payoff based on a constant notional principal rather than one that changes with movements in the index. The swap could have been structured to pay off based on a notional principal that varies with the index. Many equity swaps are set up that way. This adjustment, however, overcompensates and still does not precisely replicate a true equity position. If the swap is set up with a fixed notional principal, the transaction is similar to a portfolio manager selling floating rate notes or borrowing at LIBOR and using the proceeds to invest in the S&P 500 but rebalancing the portfolio by liquidating all gains and replenishing all losses on the equity side of the transaction.

Another interesting and useful application of an equity swap is in international investing. Table 15.4 shows an example in which a U.S. portfolio manager uses an equity swap to convert S&P 500 returns into currency-hedged returns on a French stock market index, the CAC-40. In this $25

TABLE 15.4	After-the-Fact Payments in S&P 500/CAC-40 Swap

Notional principal: $25,000,000
Pay S&P 500 return, receive CAC-40 return

Date	Days	S&P 500 Total Return Index	S&P 500 Total Return (%)	S&P Payment	CAC-40 Total Return Index	CAC-40 Total Return (%)	CAC-40 Payment	Net Payment
Feb 16	——	1339.14	——	——	4459.58	——	——	——
May 17	90	1359.08	1.49	$372,254	4358.80	−2.26	−$564,964	−$937,218
Aug 17	92	1398.46	2.90	724,387	5072.48	16.37	4,093,328	3,368,941
Nov 15	90	1431.24	2.34	586,002	5028.82	−0.86	−215,181	−801,183
Feb 15	92	1458.30	1.89	472,667	5361.40	6.61	1,653,370	1,180,703

Note: This is but one of an infinite number of possible outcomes to the equity swap. It is used only to illustrate how payments are determined and not their likely amounts.

million notional principal swap, the manager agrees to pay the S&P 500 Total Return and receive the return on the CAC-40 in dollars. The swap is arranged on February 16 and payments will be made on May 17, August 17, November 15, and the next February 15. We shall again use a constant notional principal.

On May 17, the first settlement is made with the S&P 500 having risen from 1339.14 to 1359.08 and the CAC-40 having fallen from 4459.58 to 4358.80. The first S&P 500 payment is

$$\$25,000,000\left(\frac{1359.08 - 1339.14}{1339.14}\right) = \$372,254,$$

and the first CAC-40 payment is

$$\$25,000,000\left(\frac{4358.40 - 4459.58}{4459.58}\right) = -\$564,964.$$

The net payment is, therefore, an outflow of $564,964 + $372,254 = $937,218.

The swap easily accomplishes the equivalent of converting $10 million invested in the S&P 500 into $10 million invested in the CAC-40. Moreover, it does so without exchange rate risk, which is borne and probably hedged by the swap dealer, with the costs being passed on in the form of the bid-ask spread.

In these two examples we have illustrated an equity index swapped against LIBOR and one equity index swapped against another. It is also possible to swap an equity index against a fixed rate or against the return on any asset of equivalent value. Remember that a swap has a zero present value at the start. Thus, there is no reason why $10 million of stock could not be swapped against $10 million of oil, Japanese yen, corporate bonds, or any other asset. Naturally a dealer will incur some costs and will deduct those costs against the return paid to one side of the transaction.

Equity swaps are also commonly used by investment managers to convert returns from one asset class to those of another. Suppose a pension fund has its money allocated as 60 percent U.S. stocks, 30 percent foreign stocks, and 10 percent U.S. corporate bonds. It would like to change the allocation to 60-20-20. Instead of selling off foreign stock and investing in corporate bonds, it can execute a swap to pay the rate on a foreign stock index and receive the rate on an index of domestic corporate bonds. This transaction will almost surely incur a lower cost than the actual sale and purchase of the securities.

In addition to the applications shown here, equity swaps are also used by individuals who have poorly diversified portfolios and, for some reason, cannot achieve better diversification. An obvious example is an executive of a corporation. That executive has a very concentrated investment in the stock and options of the company, not to mention that the executive's income comes from the company. Equity swaps are sometimes arranged to allow the executive to sell off the risk associated with some of those shares without actually selling the shares. In addition, many portfolios are heavily concentrated in a single security that cannot be sold, such as the case of a portfolio of a family member of a founder of a company. Many charities and endowments are given large quantities of stock of a single company and for various reasons would rather not have the donor find out they had sold the stock. So the charity can instead enter into an equity swap that enables it to maintain the stock but sell off the exposure.

Equity Warrants

Warrants have been around much longer than exchange-listed options. A warrant is an option written by a firm on its own stock and usually offered with a bond issue. Anyone purchasing the bond receives one or more warrants, which give the bondholders the right to buy the stock later. The original life of a warrant is usually 3–10 years. Warrants can be priced similarly to ordinary options except that their exercise dilutes the value of the stock and this must be taken into account. Many warrants trade on stock exchanges.

From time to time, warrants are written by a financial institution, offered for sale to the public, and typically based on a stock index. Many of these warrants on foreign indices offer the interesting feature that even though the underlying index is stated in units of the foreign currency, the payoff is fixed in U.S. dollars. For example, suppose there is a call warrant on the Japanese index, the Nikkei 225 with a fixed exchange rate of ¥100 per dollar. Let the exercise price be ¥19,000. At expiration let the Nikkei be ¥19,950. Thus, the call warrant expires in-the-money by ¥950.

Because the index value is based on prices quoted in yen, the warrant ends up worth ¥950. This figure is automatically converted to dollars at ¥100 per dollar, so the warrant pays off $9.50. This type of fixed exchange rate derivative is called a **quanto.** Quantos are particularly attractive because they permit investors to earn returns in foreign markets without exchange rate risk.[3]

Equity-Linked Debt

Equity-linked debt is a combination of a call option and a bond that guarantees a return of principal and either no interest, a small amount of interest, or a guarantee of returning a given fraction of the principal. In addition, it provides an extra payment based on how a stock or stock index performed. Instruments of this sort were first offered in 1987 in the form of bank certificates of deposit and were available to the general public. These original market-indexed CDs did not prove to be very popular, and they were abandoned. In the last few years they have resurfaced with some alterations.

Suppose a bank or investment banking firm makes the following offer: Purchase a one-year zero coupon bond paying 1 percent interest and receive 50 percent of any upside gain on the S&P 500. Each unit is sold with a principal amount of $10. Currently a one-year zero coupon bond without the S&P feature would pay 5 percent compounded annually. The S&P 500 is at 1500, its standard deviation is .12, and its dividend yield is 1.5 percent. Is this a good deal?

If you invest $10, you are guaranteed to receive $10(1.01) = $10.10. Since the opportunity cost is 5 percent, the present value of this amount is $10.10/1.05 = $9.62. This means that you are implicitly paying $10.00 − $9.62 = $0.38 for 50 percent of the S&P 500 upside gain. Obviously the upside gain feature is like a call option. We can easily determine its value.

Equity-linked debt offers a guaranteed return of a fraction of the principal, the full principal, or the principal and a below-market interest rate, plus a percentage of the return on a market index.

Since the option payoff cannot be earned early, it is a European call and the Black-Scholes model applies with a slight twist. The payoff is $10(.5)\text{Max}(0, (S_T − 1500)/1500)$ where S_T is the S&P 500 at expiration. This can be written as $(5/1500)\text{Max}(0, S_T − 1500)$, making it equivalent to 5/1500th of an at-the-money call. The option value will, therefore, be 5/1500th of the Black-Scholes value. The inputs to the Black-Scholes calculation are $S = 1500$, $X = 1500$, $r = \ln(1.05) = .0488$, $T = 1$, $\sigma = .12$, and $\delta = .015$. Plugging into the model gives $C = \$96.81$. Thus, the option value to the holder of this security is $(5/1500)(\$96.81) = \$0.32$. This is slightly less than the implied cost of the option of $0.38, which is not surprising given that the firm offering the deal must cover its costs and make a profit.

---

[3]The equity swap we studied with the S&P 500 swapped against the CAC-40 is also a quanto because the CAC-40 return is applied directly to the dollar amount of notional principal, as opposed to applying it to a French franc or euro notional principal.

These equity-linked securities sometimes have other features. Some pay off based on the average price over the last 10 days before expiration. Others pay no interest or even implicitly a negative interest rate by promising to return a given percentage but less than 100 percent of the amount invested. The holder then gets a greater percentage of the gain in the S&P 500. Some of the securities make their minimum interest payments quarterly or semiannually. Others pay off based on any depreciation in the index, which makes the option feature like a put.

These securities have at times been created by stock and options exchanges but mostly trade on the over-the-counter market.

Advanced Interest Rate Derivatives

In Chapter 14 we encountered derivatives on interest rates. These consisted of forward rate agreements, swaps, options, and swaptions. When we covered swaps we discussed only the plain vanilla, fixed-for-floating swap. In this section we shall take a brief look at some variations of interest rate swaps. Later in this section we look at some other widely used interest rate instruments that are not technically derivatives but are generally considered as such.

Variations of Interest Rate Swaps

Although the plain vanilla is the most widely used type of swap, there are numerous variations. Here we shall look at four of them: basis swaps, index amortizing swaps, diff swaps, and constant maturity swaps.

BASIS SWAPS   In the plain vanilla swap, one party pays a fixed rate while the other pays a floating rate. In a **basis swap,** both parties pay a floating rate. Consequently the parties are anticipating a change in the spread between the two rates. A common basis swap would be for one party to pay LIBOR while the other party pays the Treasury bill rate. The difference between LIBOR and the T-bill rate is called the TED spread, for T-bills versus Eurodollars. If you understand the plain vanilla swap, the TED spread swap should not be difficult. From the perspective of the party paying the T-bill rate and receiving LIBOR, the transaction is equivalent to borrowing at the T-bill rate and lending at LIBOR.

A basis swap is a swap in which both parties pay a floating rate.

Since LIBOR is the borrowing rate of London banks and the T-bill rate is the borrowing rate of the U.S. government, LIBOR must always be above the T-bill rate. Consequently this swap could not have a zero value at the start. In other words, the present value of a stream of future, unknown LIBOR interest payments will always exceed the present value of a stream of future, unknown T-bill interest payments. One solution is to have the party paying the T-bill rate and receiving LIBOR make a lump-sum cash payment to the other party up front. More commonly, however, the party receiving LIBOR will receive LIBOR minus a fixed discount.

Table 15.5 illustrates an example of the determination of the basis swap spread. Here we have a one-year swap with semiannual payments. The party pays the T-bill rate and receives LIBOR. Had the party done a plain vanilla swap, paying the T-bill rate and receiving a fixed rate, it would have had a fixed rate of 6.22 percent. Had the party done another plain vanilla swap, receiving LIBOR and paying the fixed rate, it would have paid a fixed rate of 7.08 percent. Combining these two swaps produces a net of paying T-bill, receiving LIBOR, and paying .86 fixed (7.08 − 6.22).

INDEX AMORTIZING SWAPS   An **index amortizing swap** is one in which the notional principal is reduced as one moves through time. A typical application of this type of swap would be where the party holds another posi-

An index amortizing swap is one in which the notional principal is reduced through time. The amortization accelerates as interest rates decrease. This is designed to reflect the prepayments that might occur on a mortgage or other similar loan being hedged with the swap.

TABLE 15.5	Determination of the Spread on a Basis Swap

One-year swap with semiannual payments
Pay T-bill, receive LIBOR minus a spread
Payments based on (days/360)

			Current Term Structure	
Days	T-bill	Discount Factor	LIBOR	Discount Factor
180	5.05	1 − .0505(180/360) = .9478	.0701	1/(1 + .0701(180/360) = .9661
360	5.95	1 − .0595(360/360) = .9405	.0721	1/(1 + .0721(360/360) = .9327

Decompose the swap into two plain vanilla swaps:

Plain vanilla swap: pay T-bill, receive fixed
The price of that swap is found using the procedure illustrated in Chapter 14. The swap price is the solution to

$$\text{coupon} (.9748) + (\text{coupon} + 1) (.9405) = 1.00.$$

Solving gives coupon = .0311. Quoted on an annual basis gives .0311(2) = .0622.

Plain vanilla swap: pay fixed, receive LIBOR
Using the same procedure,

$$\text{coupon} (.9661) + (\text{coupon} + 1) (.9327) = 1.00.$$

Solving gives coupon = .0354. Quoted on annual basis gives .0354(2) = .0708.

Thus, the overall position can be viewed as the following:

Pay T-bill		Recieve LIBOR		Pay T-bill, Recieve LIBOR
Receive .0622	+	Pay .0708	=	Pay .0086

In practice, there would be dealer bid-ask spreads that would change the two fixed-rate quotes by a few basis points, which would increase the basis spread.

tion in which the notional principal is designed to decline through time. The most common example of this is the mortgage loan. When a homeowner takes out a mortgage, the loan balance reduces through time according to a fixed schedule. Homeowners, however, nearly always have the option to prepay and refinance their mortgages. When interest rates fall, more homeowners exercise their options. The holders of mortgages thus suffer losses by having their income streams reduced to zero and having to reinvest the prepaid principal at lower rates. In an index amortizing swap, the notional principal declines according to a schedule that specifies an acceleration of the amortization rate if interest rates fall. This results in the swap notional principal behaving much like the mortgage notional principal. There are numerous variations of this type of swap.

Securities based on mortgages have become popular instruments and are often classified as derivatives. We discuss them later in this chapter.

DIFF SWAPS   A **diff swap** is an interest rate swap based on the interest rates in two countries but where the payments are made in a single currency. For example, a U.S. firm might be concerned that German interest rates will increase relative to U.S. rates. It could hedge this position by purchasing a deutsche mark–denominated floating-rate note and selling a dollar-denominated floating-rate note. This would, however, be assuming unwanted currency risk. Alternatively, it could enter into a diff swap in which it receives the German interest rate and pays the U.S. interest rate, with all payments made in dollars. Thus, if German interest rates rise relative to U.S. interest rates, the swap will result in a net payment in dollars to the firm. Obviously the dealer in such a swap would incur the currency risk and would probably pass on to the party the cost of hedging that risk, but presumably the dealer could do it much cheaper.

It should be apparent that this swap is simply a currency-hedged basis swap. If the interest rates of one country are consistently higher than those in the other country, there would be a spread similar to that in a basis swap negotiated up front.

A diff swap is a swap in which each party makes an interest payment based on the difference between interest rates in different countries but both payments are made in the same currency. This enables the parties to speculate or hedge on relative interest rate changes of different countries without the currency risk.

CONSTANT MATURITY SWAPS   A **constant maturity swap** is similar to a plain vanilla swap or a basis swap. One party pays a floating rate such as LIBOR and the other party pays another floating rate represented by the yield on a security with a maturity longer than the reset period. In other words, if the swap settles every six months, one party pays a rate on a security with longer than six months' maturity. Typically this is the yield on a security with a maturity in the range of two to five years. In dollar-denominated swaps, that rate is often referred to as the Constant Maturity Treasury (CMT) rate. The **CMT rate** is the yield on a U.S. Treasury note with a maturity closest to the maturity of interest. Naturally there is not always a Treasury note with precisely the desired maturity. In that case, however, the parties agree that the CMT rate will be interpolated from the rates on securities with maturities slightly above and below the desired maturity.

A constant maturity swap is a swap in which one party pays a fixed rate or short-term floating rate and the other pays a floating rate tied to the yield on a treasury security of intermediate-term maturity. This security is usually called the Constant Maturity Treasury. Its maturity is typically longer than the swap settlement period.

Also, the Federal Reserve publishes its own estimate of the CMT rate, which is often used.

As an example, consider a three-year swap with semiannual payments in which one party pays the six-month LIBOR and the other pays the CMT on a five-year U.S. Treasury note. This is just a variation of a basis swap because both rates are floating. Depending on the shape of the term structure, a spread might also be paid by the party paying the lower rate. Constant maturity swaps can also have one party paying a fixed rate, with the other paying the CMT rate. It should be apparent that this is just a variation of a plain vanilla swap where the floating rate has a longer maturity than the standard LIBOR-based plain vanilla swap.

This observation gives rise to an important arbitrage relationship. If a party enters into a swap paying LIBOR and receiving the CMT and another swap paying the CMT and receiving the fixed rate, the net result is a plain vanilla swap paying LIBOR and receiving fixed. The fixed rate would reflect the fixed rate on the CMT-versus-fixed swap and the spread on the CMT-versus-LIBOR swap.

The parties to a constant maturity swap are obviously concerned about a change in the shape of the term structure. For example, if a party will be hurt if short-term rates increase more or decrease less than intermediate-term rates, it could engage in a swap to receive LIBOR and pay the CMT.

As LIBOR is widely used as an indicator of short-term interest rates, the CMT rate is also widely used as an indicator of intermediate-term interest rates. Consequently, the CMT rate is found as the underlying rate in many other types of derivatives, including caps and floors.

These examples are designed to give you a basic familiarity with the most popular variations of the plain vanilla swap. The number of variations actually seen in practice is much greater than we can show here. Moreover, many of these variations of interest rate swaps can also be used with commodity, currency, and equity swaps. If you have a good understanding of what we have covered so far, you should be ready to deal with the other types of swaps you may some day encounter.

In the next section we look at a family of instruments that is not always considered a derivative, but has been so widely associated with derivatives that it is necessary to cover it here.

Structured Notes

Corporations routinely issue debt obligations with maturities in the range of 2–10 years. These are usually called notes. Sometimes the notes carry fixed rates. Other times the notes have variable rates, such as those tied to LIBOR. In the early 1990s many corporations began issuing notes with derivative transactions attached so as to change the return pattern from the standard fixed or LIBOR-floating type. These instruments have come to be known as **structured notes.**

Most structured notes are issued by corporations of extremely high credit quality. Consequently, there is very little credit risk. The notes are typically designed with a specific user in mind. The user wants a particular exposure and normally plans to hold the notes until maturity. Thus, these tend to be fairly illiquid instruments.

A structured note is an intermediate-term debt security issued by a corporation with a good credit rating and tailored to a particular investor's needs. The coupon is altered by the use of a derivative transaction to provide an exposure not found in most other securities with similar characteristics.

Some of these notes have coupons indexed to the CMT rate. For example, the coupon could be the CMT rate plus 50 basis points. Some structured notes have leveraged coupons, meaning that, for example, the coupon might be 1.5 times the CMT rate. Let us say the CMT rate was currently 5.5 percent. Then the coupon would be 5.5(1.5) = 8.25 percent. Suppose that the CMT rate went up 100 basis points to 6.5. Then the structured note coupon would go up to 6.5(1.5) = 9.75, a 150-basis-point increase.

One interesting type of structured note is the **range floater.** This instrument pays interest only if a specified interest rate, such as LIBOR, stays within a given range. The ranges are sometimes different for each year of the note's life. As an example, consider a two-year note in which the coupon is LIBOR + 3 percent provided that:

For the first year, LIBOR is between 0 and 6 percent, and
For the second year, LIBOR is between 0 and 7 percent.

A range floater is a type of structured note in which a higher coupon is paid but only if a particular interest rate is within a specified range of rates.

In other words, if LIBOR is outside the specified range, the coupon is zero. Otherwise, the coupon is LIBOR + 3 percent, which would be considered above normal for a two-year note. You can see that this is a bet on LIBOR staying within a range. To the investor this transaction would be like a standard floating-rate note and the sale of an interest rate cap. If rates rise above a certain threshold, the investor gives up all the interest.

Probably the most widely used and most controversial type of structured note is the **inverse floater,** sometimes called the **reverse floater.** Whereas a standard floating-rate note pays interest at a rate that changes directly with interest rates in the market, an inverse floater pays interest that changes in an opposite manner to rates in the market. In other words, as interest rates go up, the coupon on an inverse floater goes down. This is usually established by setting the coupon at a formula like Y − LIBOR, where Y is a specified fixed rate. Sometimes it is simply a multiple of the fixed rate on a plain vanilla swap.

Suppose Y is 12 percent and LIBOR is currently 5.5 percent. Then the coupon will be 6.5 percent. If LIBOR moves up to 7 percent, the coupon will be 5 percent. If LIBOR moves down to 3 percent, the coupon will be 9 percent. It should be obvious that if LIBOR exceeds 12 percent, the coupon is negative, meaning that the lender rather than the borrower would pay the interest! In practice, however, most inverse floaters specify that the minimum interest rate will be zero or perhaps a very small positive rate.

An inverse floating-rate note is an intermediate-term security in which the coupon moves opposite to market interest rates.

The issuer of an inverse floater could hedge its position with a plain vanilla swap paying LIBOR and receiving a fixed rate. For the case of LIBOR < 12 percent, the issuer's payment would be 12 minus LIBOR on the structured note and + LIBOR minus the fixed rate on the swap for a total payment of 12 minus the fixed rate. The issuer would have created a synthetic fixed-rate loan at this rate. If LIBOR exceeds 12 percent, the issuer's payment would be the same as a pay floating–receive fixed swap. If the issuer does not want such a position, it might wish to buy a cap with a strike rate of 12, which would pay it LIBOR minus 12 if LIBOR exceeds 12 percent. In that case, for LIBOR of more than 12, the issuer's total payment would be $-(\text{LIBOR} - 12)$ from the cap and LIBOR minus the fixed rate on the swap for a total payment of 12 minus the fixed rate. In cases where the inverse floater payment is twice the fixed rate minus LIBOR, the net payment of the issuer after the swap will be twice the fixed rate minus the fixed rate or simply once the fixed rate. In that case, the issuer has offered an inverse floater but effectively pays only the fixed rate.

Some inverse floaters are leveraged with formulas such as three times the fixed-rate minus twice LIBOR. Many inverse floaters have caps on the maximum rate. Some are de-levered by using formulas like $Y - .75\text{LIBOR}$, where the floating coupon moves less than the movement in LIBOR.

There are many variations found in structured notes. Some have coupons determined by the difference between two interest rates, such as the TED spread, and others have coupons tied to foreign interest rates but with payments made in the domestic currency. Structured notes have also been based on complex formulas reflecting differences in rates and bond prices at different ends of the term structure.

The success of structured notes is attributed to the fact that they offer return possibilities tailored to specific investors. Unfortunately, structured notes have also been aggressively marketed in some cases to investors who were not well suited for them. Large interest rate changes coupled with high leverage resulted in large losses for investors who were not aware they had so much exposure. Primarily for this reason, original issues of structured notes have declined somewhat in the last few years.

Mortgage-Backed Securities

The fixed-rate home mortgage is the primary means by which individuals purchase houses. Most homeowners pay off their mortgages over a period of 15–30 years with fixed and equal monthly payments, consisting of interest on the remaining balance and a contribution to the principal. Nearly every mortgage also provides the homeowner the right to prepay the mortgage, which will frequently be done if interest rates decline sufficiently to cover the transaction cost of refinancing. A certain number of prepayments occur due to demographic factors, such as a family moving to another city. Mortgage lenders are primarily banks, savings and loan associations, and mortgage companies. These financial institutions that originate mortgage loans are exposed to the risk of interest rate changes. If interest rates increase, the value of a mortgage decreases. If interest rates decrease, the value of a mortgage increases but the increase is limited by the fact that lower interest rates encourage homeowners to refinance. If that happens, the mortgage holder receives the principal early and is forced to reinvest it at a lower rate. This is referred to as **prepayment risk.**

Many mortgages are combined into portfolios and claims on the portfolio are sold to investors in the form of **mortgage-backed securities.** The process of combining loans into portfolios and selling claims on the portfolio is called **securitization.** Not all securitized portfolios are mortgages. Credit card receipts and other types of loans are also securitized, but the mortgage securitization market is one of the largest and most complex. The process of securitization provides depth to the market because lenders know that they can sell the loans they hold and receive immediate cash. This increases the number of willing lenders and provides individual and institutional investors access to investment opportunities in markets that would otherwise be accessible only to financial institutions. Securitized mortgages are nearly always guaranteed against default by the purchase of credit insurance, often from a federal agency such as the Government National Mortgage Association (GNMA).

A mortgage-backed security is a security issued by a party who makes payments based on the payments it receives from a portfolio of underlying mortgages.

Securities that are issued based on mortgage portfolios are generally considered to be derivatives because they derive their values from the values of the underlying mortgages. They are, however, somewhat different from traditional derivatives. Though most mortgages have imbedded prepayment options, mortgage securities are more like mutual funds. They are investments in a security that represents holdings of another security. Nonetheless, we shall cover them here because it is important to know something about them and in practice, nearly everyone, rightly or wrongly, thinks of them as derivatives.

MORTGAGE PASS-THROUGHS AND STRIPS   Portfolios of mortgages on which claims are sold are called **mortgage pass-throughs.** An investor who purchases a mortgage pass-through receives a monthly check consisting of a proportional share of interest and principal on the portfolio of mortgages, less a servicing fee. Mortgage pass-throughs, however, are still subject to the risk of interest rate changes, which, as we noted above, result in changes to the values of the securities and affect the frequency with which homeowners refinance their mortgages. Consequently, mortgage pass-through values can change dramatically with changes in interest rates.

A mortgage pass-through is a mortgage-backed security in which the holder receives the principal and interest payments on a portfolio of mortgages, less a servicing fee.

Some mortgage pass-throughs are decomposed into **mortgage strips,** each consisting of an interest or principal stream, which are sold separately. An investor can purchase either or both strips. The **interest-only strip,** called an **IO,** provides the investor with the interest payments on the portfolio of underlying mortgages. The **principal-only strip,** called a **PO,** provides the investor with the principal payments on the portfolio of

Interest-only (IO) and principal-only (PO) strips are mortgage-backed securities entitling their holders to the interest and principal payments, respectively, of a portfolio of underlying mortgages.

underlying mortgages. If interest rates decrease and prepayments accelerate, the holder of an IO will find the value of his position decreasing, perhaps quite dramatically. Thus, it sounds as if the holder of an IO would prefer for interest rates to increase. That will be the case to a limited extent. Beyond a point, however, increases in interest rates will reduce the present value of the interest-only stream.

Understanding the mechanics of mortgage-backed securities is difficult. At this introductory level, our objective is to just grasp the fundamentals. We shall do this by looking at a simple mortgage portfolio, one consisting of a single mortgage. Let that mortgage be a $100,000 loan at 9.75 percent for 30 years. Although most mortgages have monthly payments, we shall use annual payments in this example. This enables us to show the entire amortization schedule, which is in Table 15.6.

TABLE 15.6	Amortization Schedule for a 30-Year, $100,000 Mortgage at 9.75 Percent

| | | Annual Payments | | | |
Payment No.	Balance before Payment	Payment	Interest	Principal	Balance after Payment
1	$100,000	$10,387	$9,750	$637	$99,363
2	99,363	$10,387	9,688	699	98,663
3	98,663	$10,387	9,620	768	97,896
4	97,896	$10,387	9,545	843	97,053
5	97,053	$10,387	9,463	925	96,128
6	96,128	$10,387	9,373	1,015	95,113
7	95,113	$10,387	9,274	1,114	94,000
8	94,000	$10,387	9,165	1,222	92,777
9	92,777	$10,387	9,046	1,342	91,436
10	91,436	$10,387	8,915	1,472	89,963
11	89,963	$10,387	8,771	1,616	88,348
12	88,348	$10,387	8,614	1,773	86,574
13	86,574	$10,387	8,441	1,946	84,628
14	84,628	$10,387	8,251	2,136	82,492
15	82,494	$10,387	8,043	2,344	80,147
16	80,147	$10,387	7,814	2,573	77,574
17	77,574	$10,387	7,563	2,824	74,750
18	74,750	$10,387	7,288	3,099	71,651
19	71,651	$10,387	6,986	3,401	68,250
20	68,250	$10,387	6,654	3,733	64,517
21	64,517	$10,387	6,290	4,097	60,420
22	60,420	$10,387	5,891	4,496	55,924
23	55,924	$10,387	5,453	4,935	50,989
24	50,989	$10,387	4,971	5,416	45,573
25	45,573	$10,387	4,443	5,944	39,629
26	39,629	$10,387	3,864	6,524	33,105
27	33,105	$10,387	3,228	7,160	25,946
28	25,946	$10,387	2,530	7,858	18,088
29	18,088	$10,387	1,764	8,624	9,465
30	9,465	$10,387	923	9,465	0

First let us determine the annual payment, a simple problem in the mathematics of compound interest. The payment will equal the loan amount divided by the discount factor for an annuity:

$$\text{Payment} = \frac{\$100,000}{(1 - (1.0975)^{-30})/.0975} = \$10,387.$$

Each payment consists of interest, which is .0975 times the balance owed, plus the contribution to the principal, which is $10,387 minus the interest. For example, the 10th payment of $10,387 consists of interest of $91,436(.0975) = $8,915 and the contribution to principal of $10,387 − $8,915 = $1,472, which leaves a balance of $91,436 − $1,472 = $89,964.[4]

Now let us examine the values of IOs and POs. The value of the IO strip will be the present value of the column of numbers representing the interest. The value of the PO strip will be the present value of the column of numbers representing the principal.

To determine these values we need two pieces of information. One is the rate at which to discount the cash flows. Assuming the payments are guaranteed by a federal agency, we can discount these at a rate appropriate for a Treasury security. So at the present, let us assume a rate of 7 percent. We also have to make an assumption about when the loan will be paid off. Although it is a 30-year loan, it has a good chance of being paid off early. We shall assume that it is paid off in its twelfth year, which is considered to be an average payoff date for 30-year mortgages.

At the current interest rate of 7 percent with the mortgage prepaid in the twelfth year, the value of the IO strip is found by discounting the 12 interest payments at 7 percent:

Value of IO strip at 7 percent interest and prepayment in year 12
$$= \$9,750(1.07)^{-1} + \$9,688(1.07)^{-2} \cdots + \$8,614(1.07)^{-12} = \$74,254.$$

The value of the PO strip is found by discounting the 12 principal payments, taking into account that the final principal payment will include the full payoff of $86,574:

Value of PO strip at 7 percent interest and prepayment in year 12
$$= \$637(1.07)^{-1} + \$699(1.07)^{-2} + \cdots + (\$1,773 + \$86,574)(1.07)^{-12} = \$46,690.$$

The overall pass-through would be worth the sum of these two or

$$\text{Value of pass-through} = \$74,254 + \$46,690 = \$120,944.$$

---

[4]The figures in the table reflect more precise calculations so they occasionally differ slightly from manually calculated figures.

Now assume the interest rate falls to 6 percent and we assume the homeowner prepays in two years. Then we have:

Value of IO strip at 6 percent interest and prepayment in year 2
$$= \$9,750(1.06)^{-1} + \$9,688(1.06)^{-2} = \$17,820,$$

which is a loss of 76 percent.

Value of PO strip at 6 percent interest and prepayment in year 2
$$= \$637(1.06)^{-1} + (\$699 + \$98,663)(1.06)^{-2} = \$89,034,$$

which is a gain of 91 percent. The overall pass-through is worth

$$\text{Value of pass-through} = \$17,820 + \$89,034 = \$106,854,$$

a loss of almost 12 percent.

Assume that the interest rate is at 8 percent and prepayment still occurs in year 12. Then we have:

Value of IO strip at 8 percent interest and prepayment in year 12
$$= \$9,750(1.08)^{-1} + \$9,688(1.08)^{-2} + \cdots + \$8,614(1.08)^{-12} = \$70,532,$$

a loss of 5 percent.

Value of PO strip at 8 percent interest and prepayment in year 12
$$= \$637(1.08)^{-1} + \$699(1.08)^{-2} + \cdots + (\$1,773 + \$86,574)(1.08)^{-12} = \$42,128,$$

a loss of almost 10 percent. The overall pass-through is worth

$$\text{Value of pass-through} = \$70,532 + \$42,128 = \$112,660,$$

a loss of almost 7 percent.

It would appear that IO holders lose either way, but that is not exactly how it works in practice. IO and PO strips represent portfolios of mortgages. Each mortgage will not prepay at the same time. Any increase in interest rates is likely to push the average prepayment date further out. If in our example, the interest rate change to 8 percent pushes the prepayment to year 14, we have

Value of IO strip at 8 percent interest and prepayment in year 14
$$= \$9,750(1.08)^{-1} + \$9,688(1.08)^{-2} + \cdots + \$8,251(1.08)^{-14} = \$76,445,$$

which is a gain of about 3 percent.

Value of PO strip at 8 percent interest and prepayment in year 14
$$= \$637(1.08)^{-1} + \$699(1.08)^{-2} + \cdots + (\$2,136 + \$82,492)(1.08)^{-14} = \$37,276,$$

which is a loss of about 20 percent. The overall pass-through is worth

$$\text{Value of pass-through} = \$76,445 + \$37,276 = \$113,721,$$

a loss of about 6 percent.

A mortgage pass-through decreases in value with increases in interest rates. When rates decrease, however, the gains on the pass-through are limited because of the increased prepayment rate. The pass-through is not as volatile as the IO or PO individually but it can still be fairly volatile and has limited gains because of the prepayment risk.[5]

The main point from this demonstration is that mortgage securities are complex and that POs and IOs can be extremely volatile. Not only are they affected by the discounting effect of interest rates but they are extremely sensitive to the effect that interest rate changes have on prepayments. As you might well imagine, it is difficult to predict prepayments, making it all the more difficult to get a firm grasp on the risk of these securities. This does not mean that investors should avoid them. They are priced fairly for their risk.

COLLATERALIZED MORTGAGE OBLIGATIONS (CMOs)   Another type of mortgage security is the **collateralized mortgage obligation (CMO).** CMOs, like mortgage pass-throughs, are debt securities whose payoffs are based on a portfolio of mortgages. CMOs, however, have risks and rewards that differ substantially from standard pass-throughs or IO and PO strips. In fact, some CMOs have considerably more risk and others have considerably less risk than pass-throughs or strips. This is accomplished by structuring the different types of CMO securities, called **tranches,** to have different priorities on the payments made on the underlying mortgages. In addition, some CMOs serve as equity, providing support to the liabilities and being paid after all other tranches are paid. This is called the residual tranche.

CMOs are extremely complex securities, but we can understand the basics with a few simple examples. In the mortgage pass-through described above, the combined value of the IO and PO is $120,944. Suppose we hold this mortgage and issue debt tranches with a total value of $100,000, leaving a residual or equity tranche of $20,944, which has the lowest priority of claims on the underlying mortgages. There are numerous variations of tranches in CMOs, distinguished by the different coupon rates and prepayment provisions. One type of tranche, called a planned amortization class or PAC, is characterized by a nearly fixed amortization schedule. In other words, it is designed to not be subject to prepayment risk. If, however, prepayments are dramatically above or below a specified reasonable range, some prepayments may be applied to the PAC tranche. Nonetheless, its substantially reduced prepayment risk results in a lower coupon.

With the PAC tranche protected against prepayment risk, obviously other tranches must bear more of that risk. The other tranches are arranged in priority according to which bears the greater prepayment risk. The tranches with higher coupons will receive larger percentages of any

---

[5]The limited downside gain is often referred to as the negative convexity, a concept also associated with callable bonds.

A collateralized mortgage obligation or CMO is a mortgage-backed security in which different types of CMOs, called tranches, have different risks and returns resulting from different priorities of claims on the payments generated by the underlying mortgages.

prepayments. In some cases, the tranche bearing the greatest prepayment risk must be fully paid off before the other tranches begin receiving prepayments. All tranches generally accrue interest, however, while higher-priority tranches are being paid off. In that manner the tranches accrue interest and are retired sequentially. Some tranches are called Z-bonds. They accrue interest at a given rate but no principal is paid until all other tranches are paid off.

All tranches tend to gain in value as interest rates decrease but the tranches bearing the greater prepayment risk gain less and the Z-bond gains more. It continues to accrue interest while the other tranches start receiving more prepayments. When interest rates increase, the securities bearing the greater prepayment risk do better because their prepayments are invested at higher rates. Though their values tend to fall, they fall less. The Z-bond value will then fall more.

When all tranches are paid off, there may be value left over, which is paid to the holders of the residual tranche. Any gain in value from the amount paid for the residual tranche will result from unexpected changes in interest rates and their effect on deviations in the prepayment rate from the assumptions built into the original structure.

Collateralized mortgage obligations are some of the most complicated and volatile financial instruments. Like mortgage pass-throughs, they have been aggressively marketed, sometimes to investors who had little understanding of the risks. Unfortunately, considerable misunderstanding occurred because many mortgage-backed securities were referred to as "government guaranteed." Of course, the guarantee is only that if a homeowner defaults, the payments will be made by the government agency, usually GNMA. Thus, this is only a credit guarantee; it does not guarantee against losses arising from interest rate changes and changes in the rate of prepayments. The volatility and illiquidity often seen in the market for mortgage-backed securities suggests that they be used only with caution and then only by investors who fully understand them.

Exotic Options

In recent years, the proliferation of option products has led to a new class of options called **exotic options.** Although it is difficult to identify exactly where ordinary options end and exotic options begin, it is becoming common to refer to almost any option that is not traded on an exchange or not essentially identical to one traded on an exchange as an exotic option. In some cases these options are simple; in other cases, they are quite complex. What distinguishes them from what we have previously covered, however, is the fact that they offer different types of payoffs. What makes them like what we have previously covered is that their final payoffs are determined by whether a value exceeds or is less than an exercise price.

Digital and Chooser Options

DIGITAL OPTIONS   **Digital options,** which are sometimes called **binary options,** are actually very simple options and are of two types. An **asset-or-nothing option** pays the holder the asset or its equivalent cash value if the asset price at expiration exceeds the exercise price and nothing if the asset price at expiration is less than the exercise price. A **cash-or-nothing option** pays the holder a fixed amount of cash at expiration if the asset price at expiration exceeds the exercise price and nothing if the asset price at expiration is less than the exercise price. These options can be useful for hedging positions in standard European calls. In fact, there is a simple relationship between digital options and a standard European option.

Table 15.7 illustrates the payoffs to the holder of an asset-or-nothing option who also sells a cash-or-nothing option where X is the amount of cash paid at expiration if $S_T > X$. Notice that the payoffs are $S_T - X$ if $S_T > X$ and zero otherwise. Does this look familiar? It should because it is the payoff of a standard European call. This gives us some insights into how to price digital options. Recall that the Black-Scholes price is $S_0 N(d_1) - X e^{-r_c T} N(d_2)$. The first term is the price of the asset-or-nothing option. The second term, ignoring the minus, is the price of a cash-or-nothing option that pays off X if it expires in-the-money. In other words, an asset-or-nothing option price is given as

$$O_{aon} = S_0 N(d_1),$$

and a cash-or-nothing option price is given as

$$O_{con} = X e^{-r_c T} N(d_2).$$

As an example, consider an asset-or-nothing option written on the S&P 500 Total Return Index, which is at 1440. At expiration, the option pays the full cash value of the S&P 500. The exercise price is 1440. The risk-free rate

Two types of digital options are an asset-or-nothing option, which pays the asset value if it expires in-the-money and nothing otherwise, and a cash-or-nothing option, which pays a fixed cash value if it expires in-the-money and nothing otherwise.

TABLE 15.7	Payoffs to a Position Long an Asset-or-Nothing Option and Short a Cash-or-Nothing Option	
	Payoffs from Portfolio Given Asset Price at Expiration	
Payoff from	$S_T \leq X$	$S_T > X$
Long asset-or-nothing option	0	S_T
Short cash-or-nothing option	0	$-X$
Total	0	$S_T - X$

is 4.88 percent continuously compounded, the standard deviation is .11, and the option expires in exactly one-half year. Since the option is written on the Total Return Index, which includes the dividends, we need not adjust for dividends when pricing the option. Substituting these values into d_1 for the Black-Scholes model gives $d_1 = .3526$. Using Table 5.1 on p. 162, we have $N(.35) = .6368$. Then the asset-or-nothing option is worth $1440(.6368) = 917.00$. If the option had been a cash-or-nothing option paying 1440 if it expires in-the-money, we would need d_2, which would be .2748. The $N(.27) = .6064$ and the cash-or-nothing option would be worth $1440e^{-.0488(.5)}(.6064) = 852.17$. The difference in these two values, 64.83, is the value of a standard European call.

A chooser option allows the holder to designate at a specific time prior to expiration whether the option will be a call or a put.

CHOOSER OPTIONS　A **chooser option** permits the investor to decide at a specific point during the life of the option whether it should be a call or a put. For example, suppose an investor believes the market will make a strong move but does not know which direction it will go. As we studied in Chapter 7, an investor can purchase a straddle, which is a call and a put. A cheaper alternative is to purchase a chooser option. The chooser allows the investor to decide at time t, which is prior to expiration, whether to make it a call or a put. Chooser options are also called **as-you-like-it options.**

Suppose at time t, an investor decides to make it a call. Then at expiration, the call pays off $S_T - X$ if $S_T > X$ and zero otherwise. If the investor had chosen the put, it pays off $X - S_T$ if $S_T \leq X$ and zero otherwise. Note that unless $S_T = X$, a straddle will always pay off through either the call or the put, but it is possible that a chooser will not pay off at all.

Pricing a chooser option is quite simple. At time t, the investor will make it a call if the value of the call exceeds the value of the put. At t the call price can be expressed as $C(S_t, T - t, X)$ and the put price can be expressed as $P(S_t, T - t, X)$. A little algebra using put-call parity shows that the call is worth more and would be chosen if $S_t > X(1 + r)^{-(T-t)}$. The chooser can be replicated by simply holding an ordinary call expiring at T with exercise price of X and a put expiring at t with exercise price of $X(1 + r)^{-(T-t)}$. An end-of-chapter problem asks you to verify this statement.

Let us consider a chooser option on the AOL stock. Recall that the stock price is 125.9375, the exercise price is 125, the risk-free rate is 4.56 percent discrete (4.46 percent continuous), the time to expiration is .0959 (35 days), and the volatility is .83. Let us assume the choice must be made in 20 days. First let us price an ordinary straddle. From Chapter 5, we used the Black-Scholes model and found the call to be worth 13.21 and the put to be worth 12.09. Therefore, the straddle would cost 25.30. The chooser would be worth the value of an ordinary call (13.21) and the value of a put expiring in 20 days (t = 20/365 = .0548 so T − t = .0959 − .0548 = .0411) with an exercise price of $125(1.0456)^{-.0411} = 124.77$ and a volatility of .83. Plugging into the Black-Scholes model gives a put value of 7.80. Thus, the chooser would cost 13.21 + 7.80 = 21.01. The lower cost of the chooser over the straddle comes from the fact that there is a possibility that the payoff at expiration will be zero.

A chooser option that allows the holder to designate at *any* time before expiration whether it will be a call or a put is called a complex chooser. It is much more difficult to evaluate and we do not cover it here.

Path-Dependent Options

An important distinction among options is whether the path followed by the underlying asset price matters to the price of the option. For standard European options the path taken does not matter. They can be exercised only at expiration so it does not matter how the asset reached a certain price. Standard European options are said to be path-independent. For some options, however, the path taken does matter. American options are a classic case in point. Certain paths lead to early exercise. Though we did not refer to them this way in Chapters 4 and 5, we can certainly now call them **path-dependent.**[6]

Path-dependent options are those in which the path followed by the asset during the life of the option has an effect on the option's price. Path-independent options are those in which only the asset price at expiration and not the path followed affects the options' values.

In recent years a family of new options, however, have become better known for their property of path-dependency. Some of these options are based on the average price or the maximum or minimum prices of the underlying asset during the option's life. Others have the property that they can expire worthless before expiration or can expire worthless even if they apparently are in-the-money at expiration. Today when one hears of path-dependent options, the reference is nearly always to these types of options, although these are certainly not all of the path-dependent types.

The binomial model provides a good framework within which to see how path-dependent options work. Table 15.8 presents a simple three-period binomial model where the current asset price is 50 and each period it can go up 25 percent or down 20 percent. The risk-free rate is 5 percent. We shall use an exercise price of 50. The table shows the binomial tree with the asset moving from 50 at time 0 to either 97.66, 62.50, 40, or 25.60 at time 3.

Also shown in the table is a listing of each of the eight paths the asset could take. Notice that it could go up-up-up, up-up-down, or any

---

[6]The concept of path-independence versus path-dependence is illustrated by considering the following situation encountered in traveling. Suppose you are in Baltimore and need to fly to San Francisco. There are numerous ways to get from Baltimore to San Francisco, including direct flights and many possible connecting flights. If your objective is only to get from Baltimore to San Francisco, it does not matter what route you take. This would be consistent with path independence. If your objective is to get from Baltimore to San Francisco in the least amount of time and/or at the lowest cost, then certain routings, especially direct flights, are preferred. This would be consistent with path dependence.

TABLE 15.8	**Path-Dependent Options Information**

		Time 0	Time 1	Time 2	Time 3
S_0:	50	S_0	S_1	S_2	S_3
u:	1.25				97.66
d	0.80			78.13	
r:	.05		62.50		62.50
X:	50	50.00		50.00	
p:	.556[1]		40.00		40.00
1 − p:	.444			32.00	
					25.60

Path No.	Path	Probability[2]	S_0	S_1	S_2	S_3	Average Price	S_{max}	S_{min}	European Call Payoffs	European Put Payoffs
1	uuu	.171	50.00	62.50	78.13	97.66	72.07	97.66	50.00	47.66	0.00
2	uud	.137	50.00	62.50	78.13	62.50	63.28	78.13	50.00	12.50	0.00
3	udu	.137	50.00	62.50	50.00	62.50	56.25	62.50	50.00	12.50	0.00
4	duu	.137	50.00	40.00	50.00	62.50	50.63	62.50	40.00	12.50	0.00
5	udd	.110	50.00	62.50	50.00	40.00	50.63	62.50	40.00	0.00	10.00
6	dud	.110	50.00	40.00	50.00	40.00	45.00	50.00	40.00	0.00	10.00
7	ddu	.110	50.00	40.00	32.00	40.00	40.50	50.00	32.00	0.00	10.00
8	ddd	.088	50.00	40.00	32.00	25.60	36.90	50.00	25.60	0.00	24.40

[1]Computed as $(r − d)/(u − d)$.
[2]Probability of a given path is $p^{\text{# of times price goes up}}(1 − p)^{\text{# of times price goes down}}$. For example, for path 5 (udd), the probability is $.556^1.444^2 = .110$.

of six other possible paths. Recalling from our binomial model material in Chapter 4, the probability factor, p, is $(r − d)/(u − d)$, which the table shows is .556. The probability of a given path is $p^{\text{# of times price goes up}}(1 − p)^{\text{# of times price goes down}}$. For example, the probability of going up, down, and then up is $.556^2.444^1 = .137$. Also, keep in mind that this is not the true probability but only the risk neutral probability, as discussed in Chapter 4. It is important not to combine paths, such as the fact that the stock can reach 62.50 at expiration three different ways. Each path can lead to different values of path-dependent options, so we must keep the paths separate.

The table also shows the sequence of asset prices for each path: S_0, S_1, S_2, and S_3. The eighth column shows the average price over the path, counting the original asset price. Thus, for path 1, the average is $(50.00 + 62.50 + 78.13 + 97.66)/4 = 72.07$. The next two columns show the maximum and minimum prices attained over the given path.

The last two columns show the payoffs at expiration for standard European calls. The value for a given path is $Max(0, S_3 − 50)$ for calls and $Max(0, 50 − S_3)$ for puts, which reflects those options' dependencies on only the final asset price, S_3. To find the price of those options, we simply

| TABLE 15.9 | | **Pricing an Asian Option** | | | | | |

Path No.	Path	Probability	Average Price (S_{avg})	Average Price Call Payoff[1]	Average Price Put Payoff[2]	Average Strike Call Payoff[3]	Average Strike Put Payoff[4]
1	uuu	.171	72.07	22.07	0.00	25.59	0.00
2	uud	.137	63.28	13.28	0.00	0.00	0.78
3	udu	.137	56.25	6.25	0.00	6.25	0.00
4	duu	.137	50.63	0.63	0.00	11.88	0.00
5	udd	.110	50.63	0.63	0.00	0.00	10.63
6	dud	.110	45.00	0.00	5.00	0.00	5.00
7	ddu	.110	40.50	0.00	9.50	0.00	0.50
8	ddd	.088	36.90	0.00	13.10	0.00	11.30
			Value of Option[5]	5.72	2.37	5.94	2.48

[1]$Max(0, S_{avg} - 50)$.
[2]$Max(0, 50 - S_{avg})$.
[3]$Max(0, S_3 - S_{avg})$.
[4]$Max(0, S_{avg} - S_3)$.
[5]Value of Option is found as the sum of the product of the payoffs of the option (column 5, 6, 7, or 8) by the respective probability of that payoff (column 3) discounted at the risk-free rate (i.e., divided by 1.05^3).

multiply each option payoff by the probability of that payoff occurring, sum the payoffs, and divide by $(1.05)^3$, which is simply discounting the total to the present. This is the same procedure we used in previous applications of the binomial model in Chapters 4 and 14. The European call price is 11.50 and the European put price is 4.69.[7] We now look at several types of path-dependent options.

ASIAN OPTIONS   An **Asian option** is an option where the payoff is based on the average price attained by the underlying asset during the life of the option or over a specified period of time, which does not have to correspond to the life of the option. An Asian option can take the form of either a call or a put. The average price can be used in place of either the expiration price of the asset or the exercise price. The former are called **average price options** while the latter are called **average strike options.** For the three-period case, the payoffs at expiration are as follows:

$$\text{Average price call: } Max(0, S_{avg} - X)$$
$$\text{Average price put: } Max(0, X - S_{avg})$$
$$\text{Average strike call: } Max(0, S_3 - S_{avg})$$
$$\text{Average strike put: } Max(0, S_{avg} - S_3)$$

Table 15.9 illustrates how to price an Asian option. Look at the fifth column, which shows the payoffs for the average price call. For path 1, at

An Asian option is an option in which either the final asset price or the exercise price is replaced by the average price of the asset over the option's life.

[7]As an example, the call price is found as $(.171(47.66) + .137(12.50) + \cdots + .088(0))/$ $/(1.05)^3 = 11.50$.

expiration the average price is 72.07, which makes the option be in-the-money by 22.07. The remaining payoff values are computed similarly using the first formula above. Then the values in the payoff column are multiplied by their respective probabilities (column 3). The sum of these probability-weighted outcomes is then discounted over three periods to the present. We see that both types of Asian options are considerably less valuable than their European counterparts. There are several reasons for this, but the most obvious one is that the volatility of an average of a series of numbers is less than the volatility of the series itself.

The lower prices of Asian options relative to European options make them useful for situations in which the user wants to hedge or speculate on the price series but is unwilling to spend the full price required by European options. In some cases a hedge of only an average price is satisfactory. Asian options are also used in markets where prices are unusually volatile and may be susceptible to distortion or manipulation. The averaging process results in the option payoff not being completely dependent on the price at expiration.

As we discussed in Chapter 4, the binomial model requires a large number of time steps to give an accurate approximation to the Black-Scholes price for standard European options. Unfortunately there is no formula like the Black-Scholes for Asian options.[8] The binomial model is useful for illustrative purposes, but applying it in practice with a large number of time steps is impractical for Asian options. The computer must keep track of 2^n paths, where n is the number of time periods. For our three-period model, the number of paths is $2^3 = 8$. For a realistic situation, we would require at least 50 time steps, in which case the computer must keep track of 1,125,900,000,000,000 paths! There are some Asian option approximation formulas used in practice, but the most popular method of pricing Asian options is probably by **Monte Carlo simulation.** We illustrate the Monte Carlo procedure in Appendix 15B.

LOOKBACK OPTIONS   Another widely used path-dependent option is the **lookback option.** A lookback call allows you to buy the asset at the lowest price and a lookback put allows you to sell it at the highest price attained during the life of the option. It is said that lookback options allow you to "buy low, sell high." Since you never have to miss in timing the market, a lookback option is also called a **no-regrets option.**

For the three-period binomial example, the standard lookback option has payoffs at expiration as follows:

$$\text{Lookback call: Max}(0, S_3 - S_{min})$$
$$\text{Lookback put: Max}(0, S_{max} - S_3).$$

---

[8]An exception is that if the average is a geometric average, then a formula does exist. Geometric average Asian options, however, are rarely used in practice.

In other words, the lookback call sets the exercise price at the lowest price the asset attained during the option's life. A lookback put sets the exercise price at the highest price it attained during the life of the option. In the worst case, a lookback option expires at-the-money.

Another class of lookback options, which are sometimes called **modified lookback options,** has the exercise price fixed but replaces the terminal asset price with the maximum price for a call and minimum price for a put. Thus, their payoffs are:

Lookback options base their expiration payoffs on the maximum or minimum price reached by the asset during the option's life. They allow the user to buy at the low price or sell at the high price.

$$\text{Fixed strike lookback call: Max}(0, S_{max} - X)$$
$$\text{Fixed strike lookback put: Max}(0, X - S_{min}).$$

Table 15.10 illustrates the pricing of lookback options. Consider the standard lookback call, whose payoffs are in column 6. If path 1 occurs, the asset ends up at 97.66. The minimum price along that path is 50. Thus, it expires in-the-money worth 47.66. Notice particularly path 7. From Table 15.8, we see that the asset price ended up at 40 but it went as low as 32, so the call ends up worth 8. Similarly, the basic lookback put in path 2 pays off 15.63 because the asset ended up at 62.50 but went as high as 78.13. The remaining payoffs are determined in a similar manner using the appropriate formulas shown above. The value of each option is once again found by multiplying each option payoff by the appropriate probability (column 3), summing these probability-weighted payoffs, and discounting at 5 percent over three periods.

Because lookback options allow their holders to achieve higher payoffs for some outcomes and positive payoffs for some outcomes where European options would have zero payoffs, they are worth substantially more. Is

TABLE 15.10   Pricing a Lookback Option

Path No.	Path	Probability	Maximum Price (S_{max})	Minimum Price (S_{min})	Lookback Call Payoff[1]	Lookback Put Payoff[2]	Fixed Strike Lookback Call Payoff[3]	Fixed Strike Lookback Put Payoff[4]
1	uuu	.171	97.66	50.00	47.66	0.00	47.66	0.00
2	uud	.137	78.13	50.00	12.50	15.63	28.13	0.00
3	udu	.137	62.50	50.00	12.50	0.00	12.50	0.00
4	duu	.137	62.50	40.00	22.50	0.00	12.50	10.00
5	udd	.110	62.50	40.00	0.00	22.50	12.50	10.00
6	dud	.110	50.00	40.00	0.00	10.00	0.00	10.00
7	ddu	.110	50.00	32.00	8.00	10.00	0.00	18.00
8	ddd	.088	50.00	25.60	0.00	24.40	0.00	24.40
			Value of Option[5]		13.45	7.73	14.54	6.64

[1]$\text{Max}(0, S_3 - S_{min})$.
[2]$\text{Max}(0, S_{max} - S_3)$.
[3]$\text{Max}(0, S_{max} - 50)$.
[4]$\text{Max}(0, 50 - S_{min})$.
[5]Value of Option is found as the sum of the product of the payoffs of the option (column 6, 7, 8, or 9) multiplied by the respective probability of that payoff (column 3) discounted at the risk-free rate (i.e., divided by 1.05^3).

the additional price worth it? That depends on the investor. An investor who experiences anguish over failing to buy when the price is low or sell when the price is high would probably find the extra cost worth it.

Formulas for the prices of most lookback options have been derived. Using these formulas in practice, however, is complicated by the fact that many lookback options do not provide for continuous monitoring of the asset price. Instead they consider only the closing price of the asset in determining the maximum or minimum. Because of the aforementioned large number of paths that must be followed in the binomial model, Monte Carlo methods are often used.

BARRIER OPTIONS   The final type of path-dependent option we examine is the **barrier option.** While lookback options have positive payoffs for more outcomes than do standard European options, barrier options have fewer positive payoffs than European options. This makes them less expensive than standard European options. Investors who want to save a little money and do not want to pay for outcomes they do not believe are likely to occur will be attracted to barrier options.

In one type of barrier option the holder specifies a level of the asset price that, if touched by the asset before the option expires, causes the option to terminate. In the other type of barrier option, the holder specifies a level of the asset price that must be hit by the asset to activate the option. If the asset never hits the barrier during the option's life, the option cannot be exercised even if it expires in-the-money at expiration. Options that can terminate early are called **out-options** and sometimes **knock-out options.** Options that will be unexercisable if they fail to touch the barrier are called **in-options** or sometimes **knock-in options.** Out-options, thus, can expire prematurely with no value if the barrier is hit. In-options must be activated by hitting the barrier. If they are never activated, they automatically expire worthless. If the barrier is set above the current asset price, both in- and out-options are referred to as **up-options.** If the barrier is set below the current asset price, in- and out-options are referred to as **down-options.**

Table 15.11 illustrates the pricing of barrier options. The table shows the payoffs at expiration of all eight types of barrier options. We first look at down-and-out and down-and-in options. The bold zero values are outcomes in which out-options hit the barrier and, thus, were knocked out with no value. The italicized values are outcomes in which in-options failed to hit the barrier and, thus, were never activated.

Consider the down-and-out call illustrated in column 4 where the barrier is set at 45. This means that if the asset ever hits 45, the option terminates with no value. This will occur in paths 4, 6, 7, and 8 where in each path the asset hit 40 at time 1. In path 5 the option hits the barrier but expires worthless anyway. Now move one column over to the down-and-in call. This option will never activate if the asset does not fall to 45 during the option's life. This occurs in paths 1, 2, and 3.

| TABLE 15.11 | Pricing a Barrier Option | | | | | | | |

Path No.	Path	Probability	Down-and-Out and Down-and-In Options (H = barrier)				Up-and-Out and Up-and-In Options (H = barrier)			
			Out Call Payoff (H = 45)	In Call Payoff (H = 45)	Out Put Payoff (H = 35)	In Put Payoff (H = 35)	Out Call Payoff (H = 70)	In Call Payoff (H = 70)	Out Put Payoff (H = 55)	In Put Payoff (H = 55)
1	uuu	.171	47.66	*0.00*	0.00	*0.00*	**0.00**	47.66	**0.00**	0.00
2	uud	.137	12.50	*0.00*	0.00	*0.00*	**0.00**	12.50	**0.00**	0.00
3	udu	.137	12.50	*0.00*	0.00	*0.00*	12.50	*0.00*	**0.00**	0.00
4	duu	.137	**0.00**	12.50	0.00	*0.00*	12.50	*0.00*	**0.00**	0.00
5	udd	.110	0.00	0.00	10.00	*0.00*	0.00	*0.00*	**0.00**	10.00
6	dud	.110	**0.00**	0.00	10.00	*0.00*	0.00	*0.00*	10.00	*0.00*
7	ddu	.110	**0.00**	0.00	**0.00**	10.00	0.00	*0.00*	10.00	*0.00*
8	ddd	.088	**0.00**	0.00	**0.00**	24.40	0.00	*0.00*	24.40	*0.00*
	Value of Option[1]		10.02	1.48	1.90	2.80	2.96	8.54	3.75	0.95

[1]Value of Option is found as the sum of the product of the payoffs of the option (columns 4, 5, 6, 7, 8, 9, 10, or 11) by the respective probability of that payoff (column 3) discounted at the risk-free rate (i.e., divided by 1.05^3).

Note: Bold values for out options are outcomes in which the option hit the barrier and, thus, was knocked out. Italicized values for in-options are outcomes in which the option failed to hit the barrier and, thus, was not exercisable at expiration.

The values of the options are shown in the bottom row of the table and are computed the same way as in our previous examples. Notice a very interesting result. If one combines the payoffs from the down-and-out call with those of the down-and-in call, one obtains the same payoffs of a standard European call. This should make sense. When one holds both options, if the out-option knocks out, the in-option immediately knocks in. Thus, the value of the two options combined is 10.02 + 1.48 = 11.50, which is the price we previously obtained for the standard European call. Likewise the down-and-out put and down-and-in put add up in value to the value of the standard European put, subject to a round-off error. Similar results hold for the up-options.

Some barrier options have an additional feature called a rebate. If a knock-out barrier option provides for a rebate, the holder is paid a fixed sum of cash whenever the option knocks out. If a knock-in option provides for a rebate, the holder is paid a fixed sum of cash at expiration if the option never crosses the barrier. When a barrier option has a rebate, the values of the complementary out- and in-options will add up to more than the standard European option price.

As noted above, barrier options allow investors to avoid paying a price for states they do not believe will occur. As an example of the use of a barrier option, consider a protective put. A standard European put would cost 4.69. To save a little money, an investor might purchase an up-and-out protective put with a barrier of 55 for 3.75. This option would knock out if the asset goes to 55. The holder would in effect be saying that if the asset price

Barrier options are options that either terminate early without value if the asset price hits a prespecified barrier or must be activated by the asset price hitting a prespecified barrier. The former are called out-options and the later are called in-options.

D e r i v a t i v e s   i n   A c t i o n

Financial Engineering

Financial engineering is a new and exciting field that focuses on the development of innovative financial instruments and their application to a variety of risk management problems. In the early 1980s Wall Street began hiring a few well-known academics like Fischer Black from MIT and Richard Roll from UCLA to help them develop and market financial products. As the products became more sophisticated, more and more academics were hired. Many of these academics held advanced degrees in the sciences. The term "rocket scientist," or sometimes "quant jock," was used to describe these individuals. That term, however, soon began to be used in a pejorative sense to imply that Wall Street was trying to fool the world with mathematical but useless creations. Given the efficiency of the market, deception was not possible over the long run and most of the innovations proved to be popular. In the mid-1980s, the process took on the more palatable name of "financial engineering."

Several factors have contributed to the growth of financial engineering. While risk has always been present, the volatility of interest rates and currencies has increased in recent years. In addition, the markets have

grown more efficient, making it more difficult for traditional investment and financial management strategies to squeeze out acceptable profits. Taxes and regulations have created complex problems. The fact that more small businesses are now marketing their products in foreign countries creates a need for innovative financial risk management products. World financial markets are becoming increasingly integrated, meaning that financial transactions now easily cross borders. On the academic front, innovations in financial theory have proven to be extremely applicable to real-world problems. Indeed Wall Street has benefited greatly from the research conducted in academic institutions. Last, but certainly not least, the development of the personal computer has probably done as much as anything to advance the field of financial engineering. The enormous computing power available on a desktop machine has made it possible for financial engineers to inexpensively develop and price their products.

While the evolution of derivative instruments from exchange-listed options to the exotic and complex derivatives has required a fairly high degree of quantitative ability, not all financial engineers possess the advanced technical skills of a true scientist. Indeed

rises quickly, he does not expect to need the insurance. Thus, his willingness to terminate the insurance early allows him to save money. Note, however, that this does not guarantee a better result. It simply eliminates the payoff in path 5. The knocked-out put will not pay off if the asset goes up, down, and then down because it knocked out at time 1, even though at expiration the asset price is below the exercise price. Similarly an investor interested in holding a call might consider purchasing a down-and-out call. The standard call will cost 11.50 while the down-and-out with the barrier at 45 will cost 10.02. The barrier option will not pay off in path 4 where the asset goes down, up, and up whereas the standard call would pay off if that occurred.

There are many variations of path-dependent options, including some that are American-style, i.e., with early exercise. Barrier options in particular can have many types of twists, including barriers both above and below financial engineering is a team concept, requiring the skills of many people with different backgrounds.

For example, some financial engineers have to be marketing-oriented. They find out what types of risk management problems their clients are facing. They then go back to the drawing board and design products and strategies that will help their clients deal with the risk. In some cases, these strategies are simply applications of existing products. In other cases, entirely new derivatives must be developed. In some cases the complexity of a new derivative necessitates the use of sophisticated mathematical skills to arrive at an appropriate price. In that case, it may be necessary to call on the talents of individuals who hold Ph.D.'s in physics, mathematics, engineering, or computer science. Financial engineering also requires communication skills and the ability to grasp the overall picture of a business. A global awareness and an understanding of accounting, regulatory, and taxation concerns are also important. All the members of a financial engineering team have one thing in common—a willingness to work extremely hard to earn profits or save money for their shareholders.

While financial engineers generally are found working in financial institutions, the practice of financial engineering is not one-sided. A financial institution may develop a new product, but it must sell it to customers, who are generally corporations, investment funds, and governments. For the customer to properly evaluate whether it should engage in one of these transactions, it must also possess individuals with financial engineering skills. For most customers, the financial engineering skills necessary to evaluate these products have not yet been fully developed. This is the area where growth and job opportunities are most likely. Financial engineering should someday become a major part of the knowledge base of financial and investment managers.

You can learn more about financial engineering from the various books and articles cited at the end of this chapter and in the glossary. *Risk* magazine (see Appendix 1A) gives an excellent feel for the world of financial engineering. The International Association of Financial Engineers' address is 560 Lexington Avenue, 11th Floor, New York, NY 10022; 212-317-7479; 212-371-1148 (fax); main@iafe.org. Also you can visit its website at www.iafe.org. The IAFE publishes *The Journal of Derivatives*.

the current price and requirements that the barrier be hit more than once. Another type of barrier option allows the holder to reset the exercise price if the barrier is hit. A more common and somewhat complicating factor is that often only the closing price is considered when determining whether the barrier was touched. This necessitates the use of the binomial model with a large number of time steps and special care to position the barrier on the nodes. Monte Carlo methods, as described in Appendix 15B, are also required.

Other Exotic Options

Most of the exotic options described above are reasonably simple to understand. There are many others that are quite complex and we will not attempt to tackle the pricing of these instruments. Because they are so popular, however, it is useful to examine the basic characteristics of these instruments so that you will be aware of them and perhaps recognize them when you encounter them in the future.

Compound options are options on options. For example, you can buy a call option that gives you the right to buy another call option. This is a call on a call. Likewise there are calls on puts, puts on calls, and puts on puts. The latter two give you the right to sell a call or a put. Compound options would be useful if an investor thought he might need an option later and wanted to establish a price at which the option could be bought or sold. A variation of the compound option is the **installment option,** which permits the premium to be paid in equal installments over the life of the option. At each payment date, the holder of the option decides whether it is worth paying the next installment. This is equivalent to deciding whether it is worth exercising the compound option to acquire another option.

Multi-asset options consist of a family of options whose payoffs depend on the prices of more than one asset. A simple type of multi-asset option is the **exchange option.** This option allows the holder to acquire one asset by giving up another. This kind of option is actually a special case of an ordinary European call. In a European call, the call holder has the right to give up one asset, cash, and acquire another asset, the stock. Exchange options are not commonly traded in the over-the-counter market, but they have proven to be useful in valuing many other types of options, such as the quality option in the Treasury bond futures contract that we covered in Chapter 11.

Another type of multi-asset option is the **min-max option.** This is an option that pays off according to the better or worse performing of two assets. For example, consider a call on two assets, stocks X and Y in which at expiration, we determine which asset has the higher price and then calculate the payoff based on that asset. This is an option on the maximum of two assets. In an option on the minimum of two assets, the payoff is calculated based on the asset with the lower price at expiration. These options can be puts or calls, and they are sometimes called **rainbow options.** A slight and more common variation determines the better or worse performing asset, not on the basis of how high or low its price is, but according to the rate of return on the asset during the option's life. This is also called an **alternative option.** Another variation of this is the **outperformance option,** whose payoff is determined by the difference in the prices or rates of return on two assets or indices relative to an exercise price or rate.

Shout options permit the holder at any time during the life of the option to establish a minimum payoff that will occur at expiration. For example, suppose the stock price is very high relative to the exercise price. The investor, holding such an option and fearing that the stock price will fall, can establish the minimum payoff as the amount by which it is currently in-the-money. A slight variation of this is a **cliquet option,** in which the exercise price can periodically increase as the stock price rises. Still another variation, the **lock-in option,** permits establishment of the exact payoff, as opposed to just the minimum, prior to expiration.

A **contingent premium option** permits the investor to establish an ordinary call or put option without paying a premium. The investor then pays the premium at expiration, but only if the option is in-the-money at expiration. A **pay-later option** allows the investor to pay the premium at expiration. Unlike a contingent premium option, however, the premium must still be paid regardless of whether the option ends up in-the-money. A **deferred strike option** is one in which the exercise price is not set until a specific date prior to expiration.

Forward-start options are options whose lives do not begin until a later date. The premium is paid up front and the purchaser specifies a desired degree of moneyness, such as at-the-money, 5 percent out-of-the-money, etc. Once the option begins, it is like an ordinary option. This type of option is similar to the types of executive and employee stock option plans used by firms. The firm makes a commitment that will result in its awarding options at various future dates. When the options are structured so that as one expires another begins, the combination is called a **tandem option.**

The exotic options described here are the primary ones that are used in today's markets, but there are many more. A few years ago, most of these options did not exist. The pace of creativity is quite rapid. As your career in the financial world evolves, you will likely encounter new ones quite often.

Summary

This chapter carried our treatment of derivatives one step further by examining some advanced derivatives and strategies. We learned how portfolio insurance works and saw several different ways of implementing it. We also examined various equity derivatives that trade in the over-the-counter market, including forwards, break forwards, swaps, and equity-linked debt.

Picking up where we left off with our treatment of interest rate derivatives in the previous chapter, we then looked at several variations of the plain vanilla swap, including basis swaps, index amortizing swaps, diff swaps, and constant maturity swaps. We also examined two other types of interest-sensitive instruments, structured notes and mortgage-backed securities, that are not strictly derivatives but, for better or for worse, are usually viewed as such. We saw that these instruments can have extremely volatile prices and require careful analysis.

We also looked at several types of exotic options, including digital options, chooser options, and path-dependent options. In the latter category, we examined Asian options, lookback options, and barrier options, and observed how their prices are derived in a binomial framework. All of the options classified as exotics have payoffs structured quite differently from standard European and American options.

Nearly all of these instruments are used with slight modifications in equity, currency, commodity, and interest rate markets. In particular, swaps and forwards are becoming increasingly popular in controlling the risk of price changes in raw materials. Firms with significant exposures to oil price risk are major users of derivatives. Indeed derivatives are applicable to risk management problems throughout an organization. In fact, the widespread use of derivatives has spawned the birth of a new profession, risk management.

In the first 15 chapters of this book you have gained exposure to a broad range of derivative contracts. While the coverage here is only introductory, it sets the stage for further study and eventual application of these instruments to solving risk management problems. Accordingly, we devote the final chapter to gaining an understanding of the process of risk management, the problems that risk managers must address, some techniques used by risk managers, and the consequences of good and bad risk management.

Key Terms

Before continuing to Chapter 16, you should be able to give brief definitions of the following terms.

- equity derivative
- portfolio insurance
- upside capture
- dynamic hedging
- break forward
- equity swap
- warrant
- quanto
- basis swap
- index amortizing swap
- diff swap
- CMT rate
- constant maturity swap
- structured note
- range floater
- inverse floater/reverse floater
- prepayment risk
- mortgage-backed security
- securitization
- mortgage pass-through
- interest-only strip (IO)
- principle-only strip (PO)
- collateralized mortgage obligation (CMO)
- digital/binary option
- asset-or-nothing option
- cash-or-nothing option
- chooser option
- path-dependent (independent) option
- Asian option
- lookback option
- Monte Carlo simulation
- barrier option

Further Reading

The following articles are good treatments of the topics covered here:

Portfolio insurance:

Abken, P.A. "An Introduction to Portfolio Insurance." *Federal Reserve Bank of Atlanta Economic Review* 72 (1987): 2–25.

Garcia, C.B., and F.J. Gould. "An Empirical Study of Portfolio Insurance." *Financial Analysts Journal* 43 (July–August 1987): 44–54.

O'Brien, T.J., "Portfolio Insurance Mechanics." *Journal of Portfolio Management* 14 (1988): 40–47.

Rubinstein, M. "Alternative Paths to Portfolio Insurance." *Financial Analysts Journal* 41 (July–August 1985): 42–52.

Equity Derivatives:

Beder, T.S. "Equity Derivatives for Investors." *The Journal of Financial Engineering* 1 (1992): 174–195.

Equity Derivatives: Applications in Risk Management and Investment. Risk. London: Risk Publications, Ltd. (1997).

Structured Notes:

Crabbe, L.E., and J.D. Argilagos. "Anatomy of the Structured Note Market." *Journal of Applied Corporate Finance* 7 (1994): 85–98.

L.S. Goodman. "Anatomy of the Secondary Structured Note Market." *Derivatives Quarterly* 2 (1995): 39–43.

Kawaller, I.G. "Understanding Structured Notes." *Derivatives Quarterly* 1 (1995): 29–32.

Mortgage-Backed Securities:

Becketti, S. "The Prepayment Risk of Mortgage-Backed Securities." *Federal Reserve Bank of Kansas City Economic Review* 74 (1989): 43–57.

Midanek, D.H., and J.I. Midanek. "Understanding Mortgage-Based Securities." *Derivatives Quarterly* 2 (1996): 39–46.

Stone, C.A., and A. Zissu. "The Risk of Mortgage Backed Securities and Their Derivatives." *Journal of Applied Corporate Finance* 7 (1994): 99–111.

Smith, S.D. "Analyzing Risk and Return for Mortgage-Backed Securities." *Federal Reserve Bank of Atlanta Economic Review* 76 (1991): 2–13.

Exotic Options:

Nelken, I., ed. *The Handbook of Exotic Options: Instruments, Analysis and Applications.* Chicago: Irwin (1996).

Questions and Problems

1. Explain the key differences between an equity swap and an interest rate swap.

2. Explain how a portfolio manager might justify the purchase of an inverse floating-rate note.

3. Demonstrate that the payoffs of a chooser option with an exercise price of X and a time to expiration of T, and which permits the user to designate it as a call or a put at t, can be replicated by buying a call with an exercise price X and a time to expiration of T and a put with

an exercise price equal to $X(1 + r)^{-(T - t)}$ and a time to expiration of t. This proof will require that you consider two possible outcomes at t (user designates it as a call or user designates it as a put according to the rule given in the chapter) and, for each outcome at t, there are two possible outcomes at T, which are $S_T \geq X$ or $S_T < X$. Then explain why a chooser option is less expensive than a straddle.

4. Explain why an interest-only (IO) mortgage strip has a value that is extremely volatile with respect to interest rates. What two factors determine its value?

5. Explain the difference between path-dependent options and path-independent options and give examples of each.

6. Give an example of a situation in which someone might wish to use a barrier option.

7. Construct a scenario in which a financial manager or investment manager might wish to enter into a basis swap.

8. On July 5, a market index is at 492.54. You hold a portfolio that duplicates the index and is worth 20,500 times the index. You wish to insure the portfolio at a particular value over the period until September 20. You can buy T-bills maturing on September 20 with a face value of $100 for $98.78.

   a. You plan to use puts, which are selling for $23.72 and have an exercise price of 510. Determine the appropriate number of puts and shares to hold. What is the insured value of the portfolio?

   b. Determine the value of the portfolio if the index on September 20 is at 507.35.

   c. Determine the value of the portfolio if the index on September 20 is at 515.75. Compute the upside capture and the cost of the insurance.

9. Use the information in problem 8 to set. up a dynamic hedge using stock index futures. Assume a multiplier of 500. The futures price is 496.29. The volatility is .175. The continuously compounded risk-free rate is 3.6 percent, and the call delta is .3826. Let the stock price increase by $1, and show that the change in the portfolio value is almost the same as it would have been had a put been used.

For the next three problems, use a two-period binomial model on a stock worth 100 that can go up 20 percent or down 15 percent. The risk-free rate is 6 percent each period.

10. Determine the price of an average price Asian call option. Use an exercise price of 95. Count the current price in determining the average. Comment on whether you would expect a standard European call to have a lower or higher price.

11. Determine the prices of lookback and modified lookback calls and puts. For the modified lookbacks, use an exercise price of 95.

12. Determine the prices of the following barrier options.

 a. A down-and-out call with the barrier at 90 and the exercise price at 95

 b. An up-and-out put with the barrier at 110 and the exercise price at 105

 c. Select any other barrier option but base your selection on the following instructions: Calculate the value of your selected barrier option and use it with the results you obtained in part a or b to determine the price of a standard European call or put. Then calculate the actual value of the European call or put and compare that answer with your answer obtained from the barrier options. Explain why this result is obtained.

13. A portfolio manager is interested in purchasing an instrument with a call option-like payoff but does not want to have to pay money up front. The manager learns from a banker that one can do this by entering into a break forward contract. The manager wants to learn if the banker is quoting a fair price. The stock price is 437.55. The contract expires in 270 days. The volatility is .18 and the continuously compounded risk-free rate is .0375. The exercise price will be set at the forward price of the stock.

 a. Determine the exercise price.

 b. The loan implicit in the break forward contract will have a face value of 40.19. Determine if this is a fair amount by using your answer in a and computing the value of K.

 c. Regardless of whether the break forward is found to be fairly priced, determine the value of the position if the stock price ends up at 465 and at 425.

14. An investment manager enters into an equity swap promising to pay LIBOR on the exact number of days using a 360-day year and receive the stock index return. The notional principal is $100 million. The current day is January 15. The payments will be made on each July 15 and January 15 for two years. The current LIBOR is 6.25. LIBOR turns out to be 5.97 on July 15, 5.79 on the next January 15, and 6.12 on the next July 15. The current level of the index is 412.15 and turns out to be 409.45 on July 15, 414.18 on the next January 15, 422.75 on the next July 15, and 418.61 on the next January 15. Find the payments on the swap.

15. A stock is priced at 125.37, the continuously compounded risk-free rate is 4.4 percent, and the volatility is .21. There are no dividends. Answer the following questions.

 a. Determine a fair price for a two-year asset-or-nothing option with exercise price of 120.

    b. Assuming you purchased the asset-or-nothing option at the price you determined in a, calculate your profit if the asset price at expiration is (1) 138 and (2) 114.

    c. Determine a fair price for a two-year cash-or-nothing option with exercise price of 120 that pays 120 if it expires in-the-money.

    d. Assuming you purchased the cash-or-nothing option at the price you determined in c, calculate your profit if the asset price at expiration is (1) 138 or (2) 114.

16. Consider a 10-year, fixed-rate mortgage of $500,000 that has an interest rate of 12 percent. For simplification assume that payments are made annually.

    a. Determine the amortization schedule.

    b. Using your answer in a, determine the value of both IO and PO strips with a discount rate of 10 percent under the assumption that the mortgage will not be prepaid.

    c. Now recompute the values of the IO and PO under the assumption that interest rates immediately fall to 8 percent and the mortgage is prepaid in year 6.

    d. Explain the risk characteristics of IO and PO strips.

17. An investment manager expects a stock to be quite volatile and is considering the purchase of either a straddle or a chooser option. The stock is priced at 44, the exercise price is 40, the continuously compounded risk-free rate is 5.2 percent, and the volatility is .51. The options expire in 194 days. The chooser option must be declared a call or a put exactly 90 days before expiration.

    a. Determine the prices of the straddle and the chooser.

    b. Suppose at 90 days before expiration, the stock is at 28. Find the value of the chooser option at expiration if the stock price ends up at 50 and at 30.

    c. Suppose at 90 days before expiration, the stock is at 60. Find the value of the chooser option at expiration if the stock price ends up at 50 and at 30.

    d. Compare your answers in c and d to the performance of the straddle.

18. Consider a basis swap with a maturity of 90 days in which one side will pay the rate on CDs and the other will pay LIBOR. The term structures are given as follows:

	CDs	LIBOR
30 days	4.78%	5.375%
60 days	4.84%	5.45%
90 days	4.92%	5.50%

The swap will have three payments, each 30 days apart with the first occurring 30 days from now. When discounting, convert all rates to the money market equivalent, meaning to multiply the rate by (days/360). CDs are done like T-bills and LIBOR is done as previously explained. Work out the following:

a. Determine the fixed rate on two plain vanilla swaps with the CD rate as the floating rate on one and LIBOR as the floating rate on the other. Convert your answer to an annual rate by multiplying by 12.

b. Using your answer in a, determine the spread on the basis swap of CDs against LIBOR. Be sure to make it clear which party pays the spread.

19. (Concept Problem) Suppose you are asked to assist in the design of an equity-linked security. The instrument is a five-year zero coupon bond with a guaranteed return of 1 percent, compounded annually. At the end of five years the bond will pay an additional return based on any appreciation of the Nikkei 300 stock index, a measure of the performance of 300 Japanese stocks. The risk-free rate is 5.5 percent, compounded annually, and the volatility of the index is .15. In addition the index pays a dividend of 1.7 percent continuously compounded. Presently the index is at 315.55 and the additional return is based on appreciation above the current level of the index. You expect to sell these bonds in minimum increments of $100. Overall you expect to sell $10 million of these securities. Your firm has determined that it needs a margin of $175,000 in cash today to cover costs and earn a reasonable profit. Determine the percentage of the Nikkei return that your firm should offer to cover its costs. Your firm would then set the percentage offered at less than this. If your firm sells this security, comment on the risk it creates for itself and suggest how it might deal with that risk.

20. (Concept Problem) A convertible bond is a bond that permits the holder to turn in the bond and convert it into a certain number of shares of stock. Conversion would, thus, occur only when the stock does well. As a result of the option to convert the bond to stock, the coupon rate on the bond is lower than it otherwise would be. A new type of financial instrument, the reverse convertible, pays a higher than normal coupon, but the principal payoff can be reduced if the stock falls. Let us specify that the principal payoff of the reverse convertible is FV, the face value, if $S_T > S_0$ where S_0 is the stock price when the bond is issued. If $S_T \leq S_0$, the principal payoff is $FV(S_T/S_0)$. Thus, for example, if the stock falls by 10 percent, S_T/S_0, the principal payoff, is .9FV. Show that this payoff (FV if $S_T > S_0$, and $FV(S_T/S_0)$ if $S_T \leq S_0$) is equivalent to a combination of an ordinary bond and a certain number of European puts with an exercise price of S_0. Determine how many puts you would need.

APPENDIX 15A

Derivation of the Dynamic Hedge Ratio for Portfolio Insurance*

Stock-Futures Dynamic Hedge

The stock-put portfolio of N shares and N puts initially is worth

$$V = N (S + P).$$

By this definition, N must equal $V/(S+P)$. The change in the portfolio's value for a small stock price change is given by the derivative of V with respect to S,

$$\frac{\partial V}{\partial S} = N\left(1 + \frac{\partial P}{\partial S}\right) = \left(\frac{V}{S + P}\right)\left(1 + \frac{\partial P}{\partial S}\right).$$

This is the delta of the stock-put portfolio.

We assume the put is not available, so we shall match its delta to that of an actual portfolio of N_S shares of stock and N_f futures contracts. The value of the portfolio is

$$V = N_S S + N_f V^f,$$

where V^f is the value of the futures contract. Remember that the initial value of a futures contract is zero, so $V^f = 0$. The number of shares then will be $N_S = V/S$. The delta of the stock-futures portfolio is the derivative of V with respect to S,

$$\frac{\partial V}{\partial S} = N_S + N_f\left(\frac{\partial f}{\partial S}\right).$$

Note that we must include $N_f(\partial f/\partial S)$ because $\partial V^f/\partial S = \partial f/\partial S$. Assuming no dividends, the futures price is

$$f = Se^{r_c T}.$$

---

*This appendix requires the use of calculus. To reduce the notation we remove the time 0 subscripts.

Thus,

$$\frac{\partial f}{\partial S} = e^{r_c T}.$$

We can substitute V/S and N_S and $e^{r_c T}$ for $\partial f/\partial S$, giving

$$\frac{\partial V}{\partial S} = \left(\frac{V}{S}\right) + N_f e^{r_c T}.$$

The objective is to equate the delta of the stock-futures portfolio to that of the stock-put portfolio. Thus, we should set these two derivatives equal to each other:

$$\left(\frac{V}{S + P}\right)\left(1 + \frac{\partial P}{\partial S}\right) = \left(\frac{V}{S}\right) + N_f e^{r_c T}.$$

Then we solve for N_f:

$$N_f = \left[\left(\frac{V}{S + P}\right)\left(1 + \frac{\partial P}{\partial S}\right) - \left(\frac{V}{S}\right)\right] e^{-r_c T}.$$

This formula might look somewhat simpler if we recognize that $V/(S + P)$ is simply V_{min}/X and that $1 + \partial P/\partial S = \partial C/\partial S$. Thus,

$$N_f = \left[\left(\frac{V_{min}}{X}\right)\left(\frac{\partial C}{\partial S}\right) - \left(\frac{V}{S}\right)\right] e^{-r_c T}.$$

Of course, $\partial C/\partial S = N(d_1)$ from the Black-Scholes model. Thus, if we sell N_f futures, the stock-futures portfolio has the same delta as the stock-put portfolio.

Stock–T-Bill Dynamic Hedge

In the preceding section, we derived the delta of a portfolio of N shares of stock and N puts. This value was shown to be

$$\frac{\partial V}{\partial S} = \left(\frac{V}{S + P}\right)\left(1 + \frac{\partial P}{\partial S}\right) = \left(\frac{V_{min}}{X}\right)\left(\frac{\partial C}{\partial S}\right).$$

A portfolio of stock and T-bills is worth

$$V = N_S S + N_B B.$$

Its delta is

$$\frac{\partial V}{\partial S} = N_S.$$

Note that the T-bill price does not change with a change in S. Setting this delta to the delta of the stock-put portfolio and solving for N_S gives

$$N_S = \left(\frac{V_{min}}{X}\right)\left(\frac{\partial C}{\partial S}\right).$$

and $\partial C/\partial S = N(d_1)$. Thus, if we hold N_S shares of stock and N_B T-bills according to these formulas, the delta of the stock–T-bill portfolio will equal the delta of the stock-put portfolio.

APPENDIX 15B
Monte Carlo Simulation

Simulation is a procedure in which random numbers are generated according to probabilities assumed to be associated with a source of uncertainty, such as a new product's sales or, more appropriately for our purposes, stock prices, interest rates, exchange rates, or commodity prices. Outcomes associated with these random drawings are then analyzed to determine the likely results and the associated risk. Often this technique is called **Monte Carlo simulation,** being named for the city of Monte Carlo, which is noted for its casinos.

The gambling analogy notwithstanding, Monte Carlo simulation is a legitimate and widely used technique for dealing with uncertainty in many aspects of business operations. For our purposes, it has been shown to be an accurate method of pricing options and particularly useful for path-dependent options and others for which no known formula exists.

To facilitate an understanding of the technique, we shall look at how Monte Carlo simulation has been used to price standard European options. Of course, we know that the Black-Scholes model is the correct method of pricing these options so Monte Carlo simulation is not really needed. It is useful, however, to conduct this experiment because it demonstrates the accuracy of the technique for a simple option of which the exact price is easily obtained from a known formula.

The assumptions of the Black-Scholes model imply that for a given stock price at time t, simulated changes in the stock price at a future time $t + \Delta t$ can be generated by the following formula:

$$\Delta S = Sr_c\Delta t + S\sigma\epsilon\sqrt{\Delta t},$$

where S is the current stock price, ΔS is the change in the stock price, r_c is the continuously compounded risk-free rate, σ is the volatility of the stock, and Δt is the length of the time interval over which the stock price change occurs. The variable ϵ is a random number generated from a standard normal probability distribution. Remember from Chapter 5 that the standard normal random variable has a mean of zero and a standard deviation of 1.0, and occurs with a frequency corresponding to that associated with the famous bell-shaped curve.

Generating future stock prices according to the above formula is actually quite easy. A standard normal random variable can be approximated with a slight adjustment to Excel's Rand() function. The Rand() function produces a uniform random number between 0 and 1, meaning that it generates numbers between 0 and 1 with equal probability. A good approximation for a standard normal variable is obtained by the Excel formula "= Rand() + Rand() + Rand() + Rand() + Rand() + Rand() + Rand() + Rand() + Rand() + Rand() + Rand() + Rand() − 6.0," or simply 12 uniform random numbers minus 6.0.* Alternatively, a normal random number generator is available in Excel's Data Analysis tool pack.

After generating one standard normal random variable, you then simply insert it into the right-hand side of the above formula for ΔS. This gives the price change over the life of the option, which is then added to the current price to obtain the price of the asset at expiration. You then compute the price of the option at expiration according to the standard formulas, $\text{Max}(0, S_T - X)$ for a call or $\text{Max}(0, X - S_T)$ for a put. This produces one possible option value at expiration. You then repeat this procedure many thousands of times, take the average value of the option at expiration, and discount that value at the risk-free rate. Some users compute the standard deviation of the call prices in order to obtain a feel for the possible error in estimating the price.

Let us price the AOL June 125 call that we first encountered in Chapter 3. The AOL stock price is 125.9375, the exercise price is 125, the risk-free rate is .0446, the volatility is .83, and the time to expiration is .0959. Inserting the above approximation formula for a standard normal random variable in any cell in an Excel spreadsheet produces a random number. Suppose that number is .733449. Inserting into the formula for ΔS gives $125.9375(.0446)(.0959) + 125.9375(.83)(.733449)\sqrt{.0959} = 24.28$. Thus, the simulated value of the stock at expiration is $125.9375 + 24.28 = 150.2175$. At that price, the option will be worth $\text{Max}(0, 150.2175 - 125) =$

---

*This approximation is based on the fact that the distribution of the sum of 12 uniformly distributed random numbers between 0 and 1 will have a mean of six and a standard deviation of 1. By subtracting 6.0, we adjust the mean to zero without changing the standard deviation. What we obtain is technically not normally distributed but is symmetric with mean zero and standard deviation of 1.0, which are three properties associated with the normal distribution. The procedure is widely accepted as a quick and reasonable approximation but would not pass the most demanding tests for normality.

25.22 at expiration. We then draw another random number. Suppose we get $-.18985$. Inserting into the formula for $\underline{\Delta S}$, we obtain 125.9375 $(.0446)(.0959) + 125.9375(.83)(-.18985) \sqrt{.0959} = -5.61$, which gives us a stock price at expiration of $125.9375 - 5.61 = 120.3275$, leading to an option price of $\text{Max}(0, 120.3275 - 125) = 0$. We repeat this procedure several thousand times, after which we take an average of the simulated option prices and then discount that average to the present using the present value formula $e^{-.0446(.0959)}$.

Naturally every simulation is different because each set of random numbers is different. A Monte Carlo procedure written in Excel's Visual Basic produced the following values for this call, whose actual Black-Scholes price is 13.55:

Number of Random Drawings	Call Price
1,000	12.64
10,000	13.73
50,000	13.69
100,000	13.67

It would appear that at least 100,000 random drawings are required for the simplest case of a standard European option.

Applying the Monte Carlo technique to more complicated options such as path-dependent options requires a partitioning of the option's life into time periods, as in the binomial model. For example, suppose you wanted to price an Asian call option in which the average price would be computed by collecting the daily closing price over the life of the option. Ignoring holidays and weekends, let us say that the option has a 90-day life. Then a run would consist of 90 random drawings, each used to simulate the stock price at the end of each of the 90 days. The formula for each ΔS would be based on the previous day's closing price. The value of Δt would be $1/365$. Then the average of the 90 stock prices would determine the call payoff at expiration as described in this chapter. You would then need to repeat the procedure a large number of times.

This may seem like a formidable task but that is what computers are for. More than likely computations such as these would be written in a fast and efficient language like C++. In addition, there is a considerable amount of research going on for ways to make Monte Carlo simulations run more efficiently.

For your purposes here, the important thing is to gain an understanding of the principles of option pricing with Monte Carlo simulation, which can be seen with simple European options. Each run generates a possible outcome. Provided enough runs are made, the outcomes will occur with the same relative frequency implied by the probabilities assumed by the Black-Scholes model. The option price will then become what we have so often described throughout this book—a probability-weighted average of the expiration values of the option, discounted at the risk-free rate. More complex options will naturally require modifications to the procedure.

CHAPTER 16

Financial Risk Management

Trying to control financial risk in this environment is like trying to hammer down one corner of a tent in a gale. But that's the nature of our business.

STEPHEN HODGE
Risk, March 1999

In the first 15 chapters we have studied the use of many different types of derivatives in a variety of situations. In the financial markets in recent years, derivatives are playing a major part in the decision-making process of corporations, financial institutions, and investment funds. Derivatives have been embraced not only as tools for hedging but as means of controlling risk, meaning to reduce risk when one wants to reduce risk and increase risk when one wants to increase it. The low transaction costs and ease of use of derivatives have given firms a flexibility to make adjustments to the risk of a firm or portfolio. Corporations have been particularly avid users of derivatives to manage interest rate and foreign exchange risks.

We presented charts showing volume in the exchange-listed derivatives markets in Chapters 2, 8, 12, and 13. Figures 16.1 and 16.2 illustrate the volume and market value of over-the-counter derivatives worldwide at the end of 1998 and 1999. This information is collected by the Bank for International Settlements (BIS) of Basel, Switzerland, but the BIS began its surveys to collect this information only in 1998. Thus, we do not have a long history of the OTC derivatives market. We see that the total size of this market in terms of notional principal is almost $90 trillion; however, recall that notional principal is a somewhat misleading figure, particularly with respect to swaps. Consequently, market value is a better measure. In that regard, the total market value of OTC derivatives at the end of 1999 is about $2.8 trillion. As you can see, interest rate derivatives constitute the largest group with foreign exchange derivatives being the second largest group.

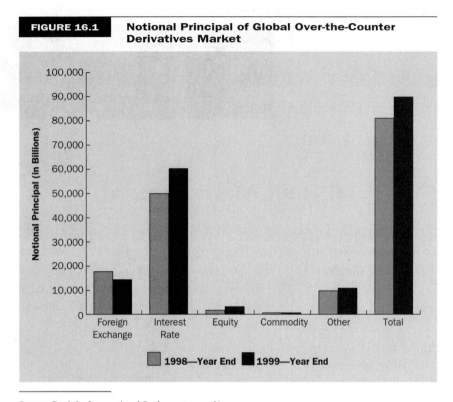

| FIGURE 16.1 | Notional Principal of Global Over-the-Counter Derivatives Market |

SOURCE: Bank for International Settlements, *www.bis.org*

Risk management is the practice of defining the risk level a firm desires, identifying the risk level it currently has, and using derivative or other financial instruments to adjust the actual risk level to the desired risk level.

As we have seen throughout this book, derivatives generally carry a high degree of leverage. When used improperly they can increase the risk dramatically, sometimes putting the survival of a firm in jeopardy. In the appendix to this chapter, we take a look at a few stories of how derivatives were used improperly, and in some cases were fatal.

The critical importance of using derivatives properly has created a whole new activity called **risk management.** Risk management is the practice of defining the risk level a firm desires, identifying the risk level a firm currently has, and using derivatives or other financial instruments to adjust the actual level of risk to the desired level of risk. Risk management has also spawned an entirely new industry of financial institutions that offer to take positions in derivatives opposite the end users, which are corporations or investment funds. These financial institutions, which we have previously identified as dealers, profit off of the spread between their buying and selling prices and generally hedge the underlying risks of their portfolios of derivatives.

FIGURE 16.2	**Market Value of Global Over-the-Counter Derivatives Market**

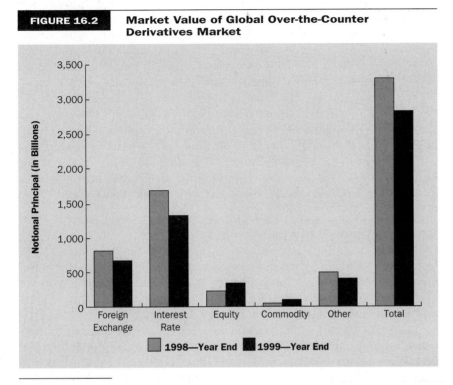

SOURCE: Bank for International Settlements, *www.bis.org*

Why Practice Risk Management?

The Impetus for Risk Management

Growth in the use of derivatives to manage risk did not occur simply because people became enamored with them. In fact, there has always been a great deal of suspicion, distrust, and outright fear of derivatives. Eventually, firms began to realize that derivatives were the best tool for coping with markets that had become increasingly volatile over the years.

The primary reason for the practice of risk management is concern over the volatility of interest rates, exchange rates, commodity prices, and stock prices. Businesses usually prefer to accept the risks internal to the industries they operate in and avoid external risks.

Some firms have begun practicing risk management because certain other firms failed to do so and incurred painful and embarrassing losses.

Several other factors have contributed to the growing use of derivatives to manage risk. The explosion in information technology made it possible to do the numerous and complex calculations necessary to price derivatives quickly and at low cost and to keep track of positions taken.[1] Another factor was the favorable regulatory environment. The CFTC adopted a pro-market position in the early 1980s, which paved the way for an increasing number of innovative futures contracts, such as Eurodollars and stock index futures. These contracts established a momentum that led to more innovation in the exchange-listed and over-the-counter markets.

We should note that the industry has gone through a significant evolution in what it calls itself. In its early stages, it was known as *commodities*. As exchange-listed options and financial futures were created, it began to call itself *futures and options*. When over-the-counter products like swaps and forwards were added, it began to be known as *derivatives*. Now the focus has shifted away from the instruments and toward the process, leaving us with the term *risk management* and sometimes **financial risk management.**

The Benefits of Risk Management

In Chapter 10, we identified several reasons why firms hedge. At this point, however, we are focusing not on the simple process of hedging, but on the more general process of managing risk. Let us restate our Chapter 10 reasons for hedging in the context of risk management.

In the Modigliani-Miller world in which there are no taxes or transaction costs and information is costless and available to everyone, financial decisions have no relevance for shareholders. Financial decisions, such as how much debt a firm issues, how large a dividend it pays, or how much risk it takes, merely determine how the pie is sliced. The size of the pie, as determined by the quality of a firm's investments in its assets, is what determines shareholder value. Modigliani-Miller argue that shareholders can do these financial transactions just as well by buying and selling stocks and bonds in their personal portfolios. Risk management is also a financial decision. Thus, risk management can, in theory, be practiced by shareholders by adjusting their personal portfolios; consequently, there is no need for firms to practice risk management.

This argument ignores the fact that most firms can practice risk management more effectively and at lower cost than shareholders. Their size and investment in information systems give firms an advantage over their shareholders. Firms can also gain from managing risk if their income fluctuates across numerous tax brackets. With a progressive tax system, they will end up with lower taxes by stabilizing their income. Risk management can also reduce the probability of bankruptcy, a costly process in which the legal system becomes a partial claimant on the firm's value. Risk management can also be done because managers, whose wealth is heavily tied to the firm's performance, are simply managing their own risk.

---

[1]In fact, one could argue that the development of the personal computer was one of the single most important events for derivatives.

Firms that are in a near-bankrupt state will find that they have little incentive to invest in seemingly attractive projects that will merely help their creditors by increasing the chance that the firm will be able to pay off its debts. This is called the underinvestment problem and is more thoroughly explored in corporate finance books. Managing risk helps avoid getting into situations like that and, as such, increases the chance that firms will always invest in attractive projects, which is good for society as a whole. Risk management also allows firms to generate the cash flow necessary to carry out their investment projects. If internal funds are insufficient, they may have to look toward external funds. Some firms would cut investment rather than raise new capital.

When a firm goes into a particular line of business, it knowingly accepts risks. Airlines, for example, accept the risks of competition in the market for transporting people from one place to another. The risk associated with volatile oil prices is an entirely different type of risk, one that they often prefer to get rid of. Hence many airlines hedge oil prices, which allows them to concentrate on their main line of business. On occasion, however, they may feel that oil prices are heading downward, suggesting that they lift their hedges. Thus, they are not just hedging but rather practicing risk management by setting the current level of risk to the desired level of risk.

Some firms use risk management as an excuse to speculate in areas where they have less expertise than they think. As we shall see in the appendix, when a consumer products company speculates on foreign interest rates, it is no longer just a consumer products company. It becomes a financial trading company and it must be prepared to suffer the consequences if its forecasts are wrong. Some firms practice risk management because they truly believe that they can time movements in the underlying source of a risk. When that source of risk is unrelated to the firm's basic line of business, the consequences of bad forecasting combined with highly leveraged derivatives can be dire.

Other firms manage risk because they believe that arbitrage opportunities are possible. For example, suppose a firm could borrow at a floating rate of LIBOR plus 110 basis points or fixed at a rate of 10.5 percent. It can enter into a swap paying a fixed rate of 9.25 percent and receiving LIBOR. Simple arithmetic shows that it would get a lower rate by issuing floating-rate debt and entering into a pay fixed–receive floating swap. The net effect is to pay LIBOR plus 110 on the floating-rate debt, receive LIBOR, and pay 9.25 on the swap, which adds up to a fixed rate of $9.25 + 1.10 = 10.35$, or 15 basis points cheaper than straight fixed-rate debt. Yet if the firm had simply issued fixed-rate debt at 10.5 percent, it would have assumed no credit risk. Now it assumes the credit risk of the swap counterparty and is compensated to the tune of a 15-basis-point reduction in the interest rate. Is this worth it? In the early days of the market, the savings were probably large enough to be worth it, but as the market has become more efficient, the savings decreased and are likely just fair compensation for

Firms manage risk to reduce taxes, to lower bankruptcy costs, because managers are concerned about their own wealth, to avoid underinvesting, to take speculative positions on occasion, to earn perceived arbitrage profits or to assume credit risks to lower borrowing costs.

the assumption of credit risk. Nonetheless, the credit risk may be worth taking in order to lower borrowing costs.

It is important to emphasize that reducing risk is not in and of itself a sufficient reason to hedge or manage risk. Firms that accept lower risks will in the long run earn lower returns. Moreover, if their shareholders truly wanted lower risks, they could easily realign their portfolios, substituting lower-risk securities for higher-risk securities. Managing risk must create value for shareholders, giving them something they cannot get themselves. To the extent that risk management reduces the costly process of bankruptcy, saves taxes, and makes it easier for firms to take on profitable investment projects, value is clearly created.

The Structure of the Risk Management Industry

The risk management industry is made up of **end users, dealers,** and other firms, including consultants and specialized software companies.

End Users

End users are generally thought of as firms that wish to engage in derivatives transactions to manage their risk. Needing to execute a derivatives transaction, end users contact derivatives dealers, whom we shall discuss in the next section. The end user could be thought of as the party who is purchasing a service while the dealer is the supplier of the service.

The end user community primarily consists of nonfinancial corporations. Other end users include investment firms, which include pension plans and mutual funds. In addition, some financial institutions that are not in the business of being derivatives dealers will still use derivatives to manage their risks. At times even a dealer, managing its own risk, will take the position of an end user opposite another dealer. Many foreign governments use derivatives. In the United States, state and local governments use derivatives, though somewhat less than corporations. With the exception of certain agencies, such as the postal service, however, the U.S. federal government does not use derivatives. Many private organizations, such as charities, endowments, and universities, use derivatives.

Obviously there are minimum firm sizes necessary to justify certain derivatives activities, but risks of as little as a few million dollars can justify over-the-counter derivatives and even smaller sizes can be managed with exchange-traded derivatives. As one might expect, larger firms use derivatives more and have more organized and sophisticated risk management operations.

In a typical corporation the treasury department has responsibility for managing the firm's cash. It operates in the financial markets on a regular basis, borrowing cash, repaying loans, and wiring funds to and from do-

An end user is a corporation, investment firm, financial institution, government, or private organization that engages in derivatives transactions with a derivatives dealer.

mestic and foreign offices. If the firm engages in derivatives transactions to manage financial risk, these transactions are typically executed and managed by the treasury department. Normally a treasury department is a cost center and not a profit center, meaning that its job is to perform a function at the lowest possible cost and not to try to earn a profit. In recent years, however, many corporate treasurers, sometimes responding to pressure placed on them by senior management, have begun using derivatives to speculate and turn a profit. Unfortunately, this is what has led some companies to speculate in markets they know little about.

Some derivatives activities are conducted outside of the treasury. For example, a firm might have a commodity purchasing manager who hedges its exposure to commodity prices. Some firms run highly decentralized derivatives activities. They may have numerous subsidiaries, each of which engages in its own hedging. We shall discuss these types of organizational issues later in the chapter.

End users have shown a preference for particular types of derivative instruments for a given type of risk. Forward contracts are preferred for foreign exchange risk with swaps being the primary instrument for managing interest rate risk and futures preferred for commodity price risk. Stock market risk is primarily managed with options, both over-the-counter and exchange-listed.

Dealers

Dealers, as previously noted, are financial institutions making markets in derivatives. These institutions include banks and numerous investment banking/brokerage firms. They quote prices indicating their willingness to take either side of derivatives transactions. These prices, as we have noted previously, are stated in terms of a bid price and an ask price, with the price they are asking higher than the price they are bidding. Dealers will not naturally have offsetting positions. Any risk that remains is usually hedged by taking on new and offsetting derivatives, which may be in the form of exchange-traded or over-the-counter contracts. Thus, the dealer is not exposed to market movements and earns a profit off of the spread between its buying and selling prices.

Most dealer firms have highly sophisticated derivatives operations. They employ individuals with training in finance, economics, mathematics, physics, computer science, and engineering. Many of their technically trained personnel design new derivatives and risk management strategies and determine how to price them. Dealers also employ sales personnel who call on potential end users, examine their risk management needs, and try to convince the end users to engage in transactions with the dealers. Dealers generally make large investments in computer hardware and software for managing their derivatives positions. Derivatives activities have been a tremendous source of profits for many dealers.

A derivatives dealer is a firm that is in the business of offering to take either side of a derivatives transaction with an end user. The dealer usually hedges its risk and earns a profit off of the difference in the prices it bids and offers.

Other Participants in the Risk Management Industry

The growth in risk management has created an industry of firms providing consulting and software services. Consulting services include general risk management consulting, legal and accounting/auditing, and personnel search. The specialized knowledge required to program computers, understand the emerging derivatives law, provide proper accounting and auditing functions, and search for specialized technical personnel has led to profitable opportunities for individuals and firms with these skills.

In previous chapters we have covered topics that have touched on the subject of how risk is managed. Our focus at that time, however, was on understanding the instruments and their uses. Now we turn more directly to the question of how risk is controlled when derivatives are used.

Although there are many types of risk, the two primary classes are market risk and credit risk. We shall cover these separately and then list and briefly discuss the other types of risk.

Managing Market Risk

Market risk is the uncertainty and potential for loss associated with movements in interest rates, foreign exchange rates, stock prices, or commodity prices.

Market risk is the uncertainty of a firm's value that is associated with movements in an underlying source of risk. For example, a firm might be concerned about movements in interest rates, foreign exchange rates, stock prices, or commodity prices.

When considering interest rate risk, there is the risk of short-, intermediate-, and long-term interest rates. Within short-term interest rate risk, there is the risk of LIBOR changing, the risk of the Treasury bill rate changing, the risk of the commercial paper rate changing, and numerous other risks associated with specific interest rates. A risk manager responsible for positions in LIBOR-based instruments and instruments tied to the commercial paper rate would have to take into account the extent to which those rates are correlated. A long position in LIBOR and a short position in commercial paper would be a partial hedge since LIBOR is correlated with the commercial paper rate. Thus, the combined effects of all sources of risk must be considered.

The effects of changes in the underlying source of risk will show up in movements in the values of spot and derivative positions. You should recall that in Chapter 5 we introduced the concept of an option's delta, which was the change in the option's price divided by the change in the underlying stock's price. We noted that a delta-hedged option would move perfectly with and be offset by an appropriately weighted position in the stock. A delta-hedged portfolio would be neutral with respect to stock price movements, but only for very small stock price changes. For large stock price changes, the delta may move too quickly. We noted that the risk of delta changing too quickly is captured by the option's gamma. We also saw that if the volatility of the underlying stock changes, the option price can change quite significantly, even without a movement in the stock price. This risk was captured by the option's vega. These risk measures, delta, gamma, and vega, are equally applicable to many instruments other than options and stocks. They are some of the tools used by risk managers to control market risk.

Let us consider a situation in which, to accommodate a customer, a derivatives dealer has taken a position in a $10 million notional principal four-year interest rate swap in which it pays a fixed rate and receives a floating rate. In addition, the dealer has sold a three-year $8 million notional principal interest rate call with an exercise rate of 12 percent. We assume that for both instruments the underlying is LIBOR. To keep things as simple as possible, we shall let the payments on the swap occur once a year. The current term structure of LIBOR and the implied forward rates are shown in Table 16.1.

Let us first price the interest rate swap. Using the procedure described in Chapter 14, we find the price per $1 of notional principal to be 11.85 percent. This is verified with the following calculation, which equates the present value of the payments on a four-year fixed-rate bond to par value, which is the present value of the payments on a four-year floating-rate bond:

$$.1185(1.10)^{-1} + .1185(1.11)^{-2} + .1185(1.116)^{-3} + (1.1185)(1.12)^{-1} = 1.00.$$

In Chapter 14 we noted that an interest rate option should be priced by using a binomial term structure model but that as an approximation we could use the Black model that we introduced in Chapter 12 to price options on futures. The inputs to the Black model for a three-year call option with an exercise rate of 12 percent are $F = .1321$ (the forward rate for a one-year Eurodollar in three years), $X = .12$, $r_c = \ln(1.116) = .1098$, $\sigma =$

TABLE 16.1   **Current Term Structure and Forward Rates**

Period	Spot Rate[1]	Forward Rate[2]
1 year	10.00%	12.01%
2 years	11.00	12.81
3 years	11.60	13.21
4 years	12.00	

[1]These are compound annual rates. For example, the quoted two-year LIBOR would be 11.61% and would compound by a factor $1 + 2(.1161)$. This is equivalent to $(1.11)^2$.
[2]Forward rate starting 1, 2, and 3 years from today. Computed as follows:

$$.1201 = (1.11)^2/(1.10) \quad - 1$$
$$.1281 = (1.116)^3 (1.11)^2 \quad - 1$$
$$.1321 = (1.12)^4/(1.116)^3 - 1.$$

.08, T = 3. Recall that the Black-Scholes software bsbin2.xls or bsbwin2.1exe can be used by inserting the forward price as the spot price and setting the dividend yield to the risk-free rate. To obtain the price of an interest rate option, however, the answer must be discounted at the current forward rate to reflect the delay between the expiration and the actual payment. The overall answer is .009215. Thus for each dollar of notional principal, the option costs .009215 or 92.15 basis points[2] Based on an $8 million notional principal, the price of the option is $8,000,000(.009215) = $73,722. Now let us look at how to delta hedge this combination of swap and option.

Delta Hedging

In order to delta hedge, we must make the portfolio be unaffected by small movements in interest rates. To do this we shall need the delta of the swap and the option. Either can be obtained by taking the mathematical first derivative of the swap or option value with respect to interest rates. In this example, however, we shall estimate the delta by repricing both instruments when the one-period spot rate and the remaining forward rates move up and down one basis point. Then we shall average the movement in the derivative's price and this will be a good approximation of the delta.[3]

If rates move up one basis point, the new one-period spot rate will be 10.01 percent and the new forward rates will be 12.02 percent, 12.82 percent, and 13.22 percent. This necessitates recalculating the spot rates, which will be 11.01 percent, 11.61 percent, and 12.01 percent.[4] Repricing the swap means to determine the present value of the new floating- and fixed-rate payments. The first floating payment is already set at 10 percent before the interest rate change. The present value of the next three floating payments can be obtained by estimating the present value of the new forward rates. The swap value will be the present value of the difference between the fixed and the floating payments: $10,000,000[(.10 − .1185) (1.1001)^{-1} + (.1202 − .1185)(1.1101)^{-2} + (.1282 − .1185)(1.1161)^{-3} + (.1322 − .1185)(1.1201)^{-4}]$. Using a spreadsheet to obtain more precise values of these calculations gives a new value of $2,130.[5] Table 16.2 shows

---

[2]This answer is obtained from the fact that the Black model gives an answer of .0105168. Discounting that answer for one year at 13.21 percent gives .009215.

[3]The price change for a one-basis-point move up is slightly different from that for a one-basis-point move down. This is why we take the average price change. This effect results from the convexity of the price curve and plays a role in gamma hedging.

[4]It appears as if the new spot rates are just one basis point above the old spot rates. This is not precisely the case, as would be indicated if we let the forward rates shift by a much larger amount or we carried our results out to more significant digits.

[5]The answer calculating manually is about $2,430. The spreadsheet calculations determine the exact forward and spot rates to a higher degree of precision.

| TABLE 16.2 | **Estimation of Swap and Option Deltas** |

	Derivative Instrument			
	4-Year Swap, Fixed Rate = .1185		**3-Year Call Option at Exercise Rate of .12**	
LIBOR change	+.0001	−.0001	+.0001	−.0001
New value	$2,130	−$2,131	$74,107	$73,338
Gain or loss*	same as new value		$74,107 − $73,722) = $385	($73,338 − $73,722) = −$384
Estimated delta	[$2,130 − (−$2,131)]/2 = $2,130.5		[$385 − (−384)]/2 = $384.5	

*The original value of the swap is zero. The original value of the option is $73,722. For a swap, the gain or loss is the new value because the old value of the swap was zero.

the results from a one-basis-point increase and decrease in the value of the swap. The delta is then the average change, which is rounded to $2,130.5.

We also need to estimate the delta of the option. Recall that it is an $8 million notional principal call with a strike rate of 12 percent. Although the Black model will give you the delta, we shall recalculate the model price and estimate the delta based on the average change from a one-basis-point move in either direction. Table 16.2 also provides this information for the option. The original price was $73,722. The new price if LIBOR moves up one basis point is $74,107, a gain of $385. If LIBOR moves down one basis point, the option is worth $73,338, a loss of $384. The average is $384.5.

Recall that we pay the fixed rate and receive the floating rate on the swap so we are long the swap. That means we have a positive delta of $2,130.5. We are short the option so we have a delta of −$384.5. This makes the overall delta $2,130.5 − $384.5 = $1,746. This means that if rates move up one basis point, we gain $1,746. If rates move down one basis point, we lose $1,746. Because we wish to be hedged, we must find an instrument that loses $1,746 if rates move up and gains $1,746 if rates move down.

Naturally we could hedge each derivative with a completely offsetting transaction in the opposite direction. In other words, we could execute a four-year swap, paying floating and receiving fixed, and buy a three-year call with a strike of 12 percent. That is not, however, how dealers normally hedge. They would rarely have a customer wanting the exact opposite transaction at that point in time and they would not be willing to take the risk of waiting until their next customer calls. The most typical hedge transaction they would execute is to trade Eurodollar futures. Recall that we

A delta-hedged position is one in which the combined spot and derivatives positions have a delta of zero. The portfolio would then have no gain or loss in value from a very small change in the underlying source of risk.

studied these instruments in Chapters 8 through 11. They are based on a $1,000,000 Eurodollar deposit and their prices move opposite to interest rates. The delta is −$25, which is based on the calculation −$1,000,000(.0001)(90/360) with .0001 representing a one-basis-point change. Note, however, that if rates move up, a long position loses and if rates move down, a long position gains. In other words, Eurodollar futures are like bonds: Their values move opposite to interest rates. Eurodollar futures are particularly attractive for dealers to hedge with, because they are extremely liquid. Also, being futures contracts and not options, they require that no cash be paid up front and their margin requirements are very low.

To offset our risk, we need a position that will gain $1,746 if rates move down and lose that amount if rates move up or, in other words, a delta of −$1,746. This would require a long position in Eurodollar futures. The number of contracts would be −$1,746/(−$25) = 69.84. Because fractional contracts are not allowed, we should probably round up to 70. This would mean our overall delta would be

$$+\$2,130.5 \text{ (from the swap)}$$
$$-\$384.5 \text{ (from the option)}$$
$$70(-\$25) \text{ (from the futures)}$$
$$= -\$4.$$

This means that the portfolio value will go down $4 if rates move up one basis point. This is basically a perfect hedge.

In practice, some minor technical problems would make this hedge less than precise. The 90-day LIBOR that the futures is based on and the one-year LIBOR that the swap and option are based on would not both be likely to move exactly one basis point. They would, however, almost always move in the same direction at the same time and certainly be highly correlated. A few minor adjustments could take care of any risk in the hedge resulting from differences in the magnitudes of their respective movements.

As we discussed in Chapter 5, a delta hedge takes care of small movements in the underlying. Larger movements, however, can bring about additional risk. This is called gamma risk. To deal with it requires a gamma hedge.

Gamma Hedging

Our estimates of the delta are based on a one-basis-point change. If rates move by a much larger amount, there will be an additional risk caused by the fact that the values of the derivatives do not move equally in both directions. For example, if rates move 50 basis points down, the swap value will change to −$107,914. A 50-basis-point increase will cause the swap value to move to $105,127. Recall that a one-basis-point move caused the swap value to change by virtually the same amount. For the option, a one-basis-point move in either direction caused a virtually equal value change. A 50-basis-point move up would cause the option value to move to $93,793, a loss of $20,071. A 50-basis-point decrease would cause the option value to move to $55,513, a gain of $18,209.[6]

As we learned in Chapter 5, the risk associated with larger price moves in which the delta does not fully capture the risk is called gamma risk. It is the risk of the delta changing. To be fully hedged a dealer would have to be delta hedged at all times. If rates move sharply, the effective delta would not equal the actual delta until the dealer could put on another transaction that would reset its delta to the appropriate value. This could be too late. This risk can be hedged, however, by combining transactions so that the delta and gamma are both zero. First, however, we must estimate the gamma. Table 16.3 illustrates the calculation of the gammas of the swap

TABLE 16.3	Estimation of Swap and Option Gammas			
Basis Point Change	Swap Value	Average Change in Swap Value*	Option Value	Average Change in Option Value
−.0002	−$4,263		$72,955	
−.0001	−2,131	$2,131.50	73,338	$383.50
.0000	0	2,130.50	73,722	384.50
+.0001	2,130	2,129	74,107	385.50
+.0002	4,258		74,493	

*Average change in swap value is computed by taking an average of the changes in the swap value around the given point. For example, at a basis point change of .0000, the change in swap value is from 0 to $2,130 and from 0 to −$2,131. This is an average change of $2,130.50. At a basis point change of −.0001, the change in swap value is from −$2,131 to −$4,263 and from −$2,131 to $0. This is an average change of $2,131.50. Similar calculations are made for the change in option value.

Swap Gamma Calculation:
The gamma is the average change in the delta divided by .0001. Thus, at a basis point change of .0000 (the current status), the delta of the swap changes from $2,130.5 to $2,131.5 and from $2,130.5 to $2,129. This is an average change of −$1.25. Dividing by .0001, the basis point move, gives a gamma of −$12,500. Although the gamma is quoted as −$12,500, it is understood that the delta moves by −$1.25 for every one-basis-point move in LIBOR.

Option Gamma Calculation:
At a basis point change of .0000 (the current status), the delta of the option changes from $384.50 to $383.50 and from $384.50 to $385.50. This is an average change of $1.00. Dividing by .0001, the basis point move, gives a gamma of $10,000. Although the gamma is quoted as $10,000, it is understood that the delta moves by $1 for every one-basis-point move in LIBOR.

---

[6]Recall that we are short the option so gains occur on rate decreases and losses occur on rate increases.

and the option. The gammas are $-\$12,500$ for the swap and $\$10,000$ for the option. This means that as LIBOR increases, the swap delta decreases in value by $\$12,500(.0001) = \$1.25$ and the option delta increases in value by $\$10,000(.0001) = \$1$. Because we are short the option, its gamma is actually $-\$10,000$. Thus, our overall gamma is $-\$22,500$.

Assuming that we have delta hedged the swap and option with the Eurodollar futures, our gamma will still be $-\$22,500$ because the gamma of the futures is zero. We are delta hedged but not gamma hedged. To become gamma hedged we will need another instrument. Let us assume that the instrument chosen is a four-year call option whose delta is $\$58$ and whose gamma is $\$10,500$, both figures under the assumption of a $\$1$ million notional principal. The problem is to determine the appropriate notional principal of this new option so that we will be delta hedged and gamma hedged. This is a simple problem answered by solving simultaneous equations.

Let us assume that we take x_1 Eurodollar futures, which have a delta of $-\$25$ and a gamma of zero, and x_2 of the four-year calls, whose delta is $\$58$ and gamma is $\$10,500$ per $\$1,000,000$ notional principal. Our swap and other option have a delta of $\$1,746$ and a gamma of $-\$22,500$. We eliminate the delta and gamma risk of the portfolio by setting the delta to zero by the equation

$$\$1,746 + x_1(-\$25) + x_2(\$58) = \$0,$$

and the gamma to zero by the equation

$$-\$22,500 + x_1(\$0) + x_2(\$10,500) = \$0.$$

These are simply two equations with two unknowns. The solution is an exercise in basic algebra, but just to make sure you understand, we shall work through the solution. Rewrite the equations as

$$x_1(-\$25) + x_2(\$58) = -\$1,746$$
$$x_2(\$10,500) = \$22,500.$$

A delta and gamma hedge is one in which the combined spot and derivatives positions have a delta of zero and a gamma of zero. The portfolio would then have no gain or loss in value from a small change in the underlying source of risk. In addition, the delta itself would be hedged, which provides protection against larger changes in the source of risk.

Solve the second equation for $x_2 = 2.14$. Insert 2.14 for x_2 in the first equation and then solve for x_1 to get $x_1 = 74.8$. This means we need to go long 74.8 Eurodollar futures. The solution $x_2 = 2.14$ means that we need to go long 2.14 times the notional principal of $\$1,000,000$ on which the new option's delta and gamma were calculated. In other words, we need $\$2,140,000$ notional principal of the four-year option. These transactions combine to set the delta and gamma of the overall position to approximately zero.[7]

---

[7]As a check, we see that the delta is $1,746 + 74.8(-25) + 2.14(58) = 0.12$ and the gamma is $-22,500 + 2.14(10,500) = -30$. The slightly negative gamma results from rounding off 2.14.

Unfortunately the use of options introduces a risk associated with possible changes in volatility. Let us take a look at how that risk arises and how we can hedge it.

Vega Hedging

In Chapter 5 we learned that the change in the option price over the change in its volatility is called its vega. A portfolio of derivatives that is both delta and gamma hedged can incur a gain or loss even when there is no change in the underlying as a result of a change in the volatility. Most options are highly sensitive to the volatility, which changes often. Consequently it is important to try to hedge vega risk.

Swaps, futures, and FRAs do not have vegas because volatility is not a determinant of their prices. In our example, we need consider only the vega of the three-year call option. Although option pricing formulas can often give the vega in its exact mathematical form, we shall estimate the vega by changing LIBOR by one basis point in each direction. Recall that under the initial term structure, the option value is $73,722. If the volatility increases from .08 to .0801, the new option value will be $73,757, a change of $35. If volatility decreases from .08 to .0799, the new option value will be $73,688, a change of −$34. This is an average change of $34.50. Since we are short this option, the vega of our portfolio of the four-year swap and this three-year option is −$34.50.

Now consider the four-year option that we introduced in the last section to use for gamma hedging. It will also have a vega that must be taken into account. Its vega is estimated to be $6.93 for every $1,000,000 notional principal. Our delta- and gamma-hedged portfolio would have $2.14 million face value of this option, making the vega $14.83. That would make our overall portfolio have a vega of $14.83 − $34.50, or −$19.67. Thus, we still have a significant risk that volatility will increase and each .0001 increase in volatility will cost us $19.67.

In order to hedge delta, gamma, and vega we will need three hedging instruments. Because of the vega risk, at least one of the instruments has to be an option. Let us use an option on a Eurodollar futures that trades at the Chicago Mercantile Exchange alongside the Eurodollar futures. The option has a delta of −$12.75, a gamma of −$500, and a vega of $2.50 per $1,000,000 notional principal. This leads to the following set of simultaneous equations:

$$\$1,746 + x_1(-\$25) + x_2(\$58) + x_3(-\$12.75) = 0$$
$$-\$22,500 + x_1(\$0) + x_2(\$10,500) + x_3(-\$500) = 0$$
$$-\$34.50 + x_1(\$0) + x_2(\$6.93) + x_3(\$2.50) = 0.$$

The first equation sets the portfolio delta to zero, the second sets the gamma to zero, and the third sets the vega to zero. The coefficients x_1, x_2, and x_3 represent quantities of $1,000,000 notional principal that should be established with Eurodollar futures, the four-year option, and the option on the Eurodollar futures. To solve these equations, we first note that the second and third equations can be written as

$$x_2(\$10,500) + x_3(-\$500) = \$22,500$$
$$x_2(\$6.93) + x_3(\$2.50) = \$34.50,$$

which is simply two equations with two unknowns. Multiplying the second equation by 200 gives us $\$1,386x_2 + \$500x_3 = \$6,900$. Then adding the two equations gives $\$11,886x_2 = \$29,400$, which gives $x_2 = 2.47$. Inserting 2.47 for x_2 in either of these equations gives $x_3 = 6.95$. Thus, we need $2.47(\$1,000,000) = \$2,470,000$ notional principal of the four-year option and $6.95(\$1,000,000) = \$6,950,000$ notional principal of the Eurodollar futures option. We then insert 2.47 and 6.95 into the first equation for x_2 and x_3, giving us $x_1(-\$25) + 2.47(\$58) + 6.95(-\$12.75) = -\$1,746$. Solving for x_1 gives a value of 72.02. This means that we would buy 72 Eurodollar futures.[8]

A vega-hedged portfolio is one in which the portfolio value will not change as a result of a change in the volatility of the underlying source of risk.

It should be apparent by now that the dealer should not hedge by setting the delta to zero and then attempting to hedge the gamma and vega risk with other instruments. As these instruments are added to eliminate gamma and vega risk, the delta hedge is destroyed. There are two possible approaches to solving the problem, one being the simultaneous equation approach that we followed here. It is guaranteed to provide the correct solutions. Another approach would be to solve the gamma and vega hedge simultaneously, which will set the gamma and vega to zero, but leave the overall delta nonzero. Then the delta hedge can be set with Eurodollar futures, which have a delta but no gamma or vega. Consequently, adding them to the position at the very end will not change the gamma or vega neutrality.

In spite of a dealer's efforts at achieving a delta-gamma-vega neutral position, it is really impossible to achieve an absolute perfect hedge. The vega hedge is accurate only for extremely small changes in volatility. Large changes would require yet another adjustment. In addition, all deltas, gammas, and vegas are valid only over the next instant in time. Even if there were no changes in LIBOR or the volatility, the position would become unhedged over time if no further adjustments were made. Eventually the portfolio would become significantly unhedged so some adjustments might be made to realign the portfolio to a delta-gamma-vega neutral position, possibly as often as once a day.

It is apt to remember a famous expression: *The only perfect hedge is in a Japanese garden.* Any dealer accepts the fact that a small amount of risk will

---

[8]Because of some rounding off, the overall position is not quite perfectly hedged. The delta is $\$1,746 + 72(-\$25) + 2.47(\$58) + 6.95(-\$12.75) = \$0.65$. The gamma is $-\$22,500 + 72(\$0) + 2.47(\$10,500) + 6.95(-\$500) = -\$40$. The vega is $-\$34.50 + 2.47(6.93) + 6.95(2.50) = -\$0.01$.

be assumed. To date, however, no major derivatives dealer who has made the effort to be hedged has suffered a significant loss and most have found market making in derivatives to be a moderately profitable activity with very low risk. This is a testament to the excellent risk management practiced by the major derivatives dealers.

On the other side of the transaction is the end user, the party who approaches the dealer about entering into a derivatives transaction. Most end users are corporations attempting to hedge their interest rate, currency, equity, or commodity price risk. Some will speculate from time to time. Most, however, already have a transaction in place that has a certain amount of risk. They contract with the dealer to lay off that risk. Rarely will the end user engage in the type of dynamic hedging illustrated above. That is because the end user is not typically a financial institution like the dealer. Financial institutions can nearly always execute transactions at lower cost and can generally afford the investment in expensive personnel, equipment, and software necessary to do dynamic hedging. Most end users enter into derivatives transactions that require little or no adjustments. You have, of course, seen many such examples throughout this book. Some end users have, however, suffered losses from being unhedged at the wrong time or from outright speculating. Yet, most end users could have obtained a better understanding about the magnitude of their risk and the potential for large losses had they applied the technique called Value at Risk or VAR.

Value at Risk (VAR)

Value at Risk or **VAR** is a dollar measure of the minimum loss that would be expected over a period of time with a given probability. For example, a VAR of $1 million for one day at a probability of .05 means that the firm would expect to lose at least $1 million in one day 5 percent of the time. Some prefer to express such a VAR as a probability of .95 that a loss will not exceed $1 million. In this manner, the VAR becomes a maximum loss with a given confidence level. How significant a million dollar loss is depends on the size of the firm and its aversion to risk. But one thing is clear from the probability statement: .05 means that it would be expected to occur once every 20 trading days, which is about once per month.

VAR is widely used by dealers, even though their hedging programs nearly always leave them with little exposure to the market. If dealers feel that it is important to use VAR, that should be a good enough reason for end users to employ it, and surveys show that an increasing number of end users are doing so.

The basic idea behind VAR is to determine the probability distribution of the underlying source of risk and to isolate the worst given percentage of outcomes. Using 5 percent as the critical percentage, VAR will determine the 5 percent of outcomes that are the worst. The performance at the 5 percent mark is the VAR.

TABLE 16.4	Probability Distribution of Change in Portfolio Value	

Change in Portfolio Value	Probability	Cumulative Probability
−$3,000,000 and lower	.05	.05
−$2 000,000 to −$2,999,999	.10	.15
−$1,000,000 to −$1,999,999	.15	.30
$0 to −$999,999	.20	.50
$0 to $999,999	.20	.70
$1,000,000 to $1,999,999	.15	.85
$2,000,000 to $2,999,999	.10	.95
$3,000,000 and higher	.05	1.00

Value at Risk or VAR is the minimum amount of money that would be lost in a portfolio with a given probability over a specific period of time.

Table 16.4 provides a simple illustration with a discrete classification of the change in the value of a hypothetical portfolio. Note that each range has a probability and a cumulative probability associated with it. Starting with the class with the worst outcome, VAR is found by examining the cumulative probability until the specified percentage is reached. In this case, VAR for 5 percent is $3,000,000 This would be interpreted as follows: There is a 5 percent probability that over the given time period, the portfolio will lose at least $3 million. Of course VAR can be expressed with respect to any chosen probability. Such statements as "There is a 15 percent probability that over the given time period, the portfolio will lose at least $2 million" and "There is a 50 percent probability that over the given time period, the portfolio will incur a loss" are both legitimate statements of the portfolio's VAR.

In a normal distribution, a 5 percent VAR occurs 1.65 standard deviations from the expected value. A 1 percent VAR occurs 2.33 standard deviations from the expected value.

Figure 16.3 illustrates the principle behind VAR when the distribution of the portfolio change in value is continuous. The familiar normal or bell-shaped curve is widely used though not necessarily appropriate in many cases. Accepting it as legitimate for our purposes, we see where the 5 percent VAR is noted, which is 1.65 standard deviations from the expected change in portfolio value, which in this example is zero. Of course, not all portfolios have an expected change of zero. In any case, the rule for determining VAR when applying normal probability theory is to move 1.65 standard deviations below the expected value. Beyond that point, 5 percent of the population of possible outcomes is found. For a VAR of 1 percent, you would move 2.33 standard deviations below the expected value.

Calculating VAR in practice is not quite this simple. The basic problem is to determine the probability distribution associated with the portfolio value. This necessitates estimating the expected values, standard deviations, and correlations among the financial instruments. The mechanics of determining the portfolio probability distribution are relatively easy once the appropriate inputs are obtained. The process is the same as the one you might already have encountered when studying investments. Let us take that process a little bit further here.

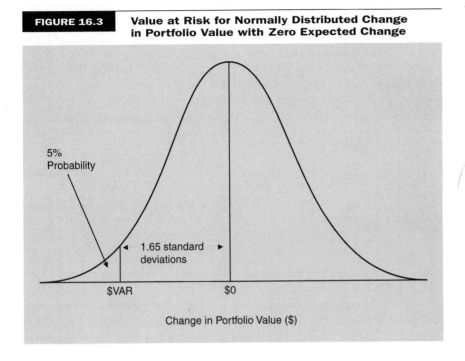

FIGURE 16.3   **Value at Risk for Normally Distributed Change in Portfolio Value with Zero Expected Change**

5%
Probability

1.65 standard
deviations

$VAR

$0

Change in Portfolio Value ($)

Assume you have two assets whose expected returns are $E(R_1)$ and $E(R_2)$ and whose standard deviations are σ_1 and σ_2, and where the correlation between their returns is ρ. The portfolio's expected return is a weighted average of the expected returns of assets 1 and 2,

$$E(R_p) = w_1 E(R_1) + w_2 E(R_2),$$

where w_1 and w_2 are the percentages of the investor's wealth that are allocated to assets 1 and 2, respectively. The portfolio standard deviation is a more complicated weighted average of the variances of assets 1 and 2 and their covariance,

$$\sigma_p = \sqrt{w_1^2 \sigma_1^2 + w_2^2 \sigma_2^2 + 2 w_1 w_2 \sigma_1 \sigma_2 \rho},$$

where the expression $\sigma_1 \sigma_2 \rho$ is recognized as the covariance between assets 1 and 2.

There are three methods of estimating VAR.

ANALYTICAL METHOD   The **analytical method,** also called the **variance-covariance method,** makes use of knowledge of the input values and any necessary pricing models along with an assumption of a normal distribution.

We illustrate the analytical method with two examples. Suppose a portfolio manager holds two distinct classes of stocks. The first class, worth $20 million, is identical to the S&P 500. It has an expected return of 12 percent and a standard deviation of 15 percent. The second class is identical to the Nikkei 300, an index of Japanese stocks, and is valued at $12 million. We shall assume the currency risk is hedged. The expected return is 10.5 percent and the standard deviation is 18 percent. The correlation between the Nikkei 300 and the S&P 500 is .55. All figures are annualized. With this information we can calculate the portfolio expected return and standard deviation as

The analytical method assumes a normal distribution and uses the expected value and variance to obtain the VAR.

$$E(R_p) = (20/32).12 + (12/32).105 = .1144$$

$$\sigma_p = \sqrt{(20/32)^2(.15)^2 + (12/32)^2(.18)^2 + 2(20/32)(12/32)(.15)(.18)(.55)}$$
$$= .1425.$$

Now let us calculate this portfolio's VAR at a 5 percent level for one week. First we must convert the annualized expected return and standard deviation to weekly equivalents. This is done by dividing the expected return by 52 (for the number of weeks in a year) and dividing the standard deviation by the square root of 52, which is 7.21. This gives us .1144/52 = .0022 and .1425/7.21 = .0198. Under the assumption of a normal distribution, the return that is 1.65 standard deviations below the expected return is

$$.0022 - 1.65(.0198) = -.0305.$$

The portfolio would be expected to lose at least 3.05 percent 5 percent of the time. VAR is always expressed in dollars, so the VAR is $32,000,000(.0305) = $976,000. In other words, the portfolio would be expected to lose at least $976,000 in one week 5 percent of the time.

Let us now calculate VAR for a portfolio containing options. In fact, let us make it an extremely risky portfolio, one consisting of a short call on a stock index. We assume that the call has one month to go before expiring, the index is at 720, the exercise price is 720, the risk-free rate is 5.8 percent, and the volatility of the index is 15 percent. We shall ignore dividends. Inserting these figures into the Black-Scholes model tells us that the call should be priced at $14.21. Assume that the index option contract has a multiplier of 500, so the total cost is 500($14.21) = $7,105. We shall assume that the investor sells 200 contracts, resulting in the receipt up front of 200($7,105) = $1,421,000. The worst outcome for an uncovered call is for the stock to increase. Let us look at the 5 percent worst outcomes, which occur on the upside. Using the same information on the index from the previous example, we must first convert to monthly data. The expected return on the index is .1144/12 = .0095 and .1425/3.46 (the square root of 12) = .0412. On the upside the 5 percent tail of the distribution is .0095

+ 1.65(.0412) = .0775. That would leave the index at 720(1.0775) = 775.80 or higher. If the option expires with the index at 775.80, it will have a value of 775.80 − 720 = 55.80. Thus, our net loss will be 55.80 − 14.21 = 41.59 per option. The total loss will be 200(500)(41.59) = $4,159,000. Thus, the VAR for this short call is $4,159,000 and we can, therefore, say that the portfolio will lose at least $4,159,000 in one month 5 percent of the time. This would be once every 20 months.

Although we calculated an expected value in these examples, it is fairly common to assume a zero expected value. This is because one day is a common period over which to calculate a VAR and the expected daily return is very small. A typical VAR calculation is much more highly influenced by the volatility than by the expected return.

The analytical method uses knowledge of the parameters of the probability distribution of the underlying sources of risk at the portfolio level. Since the expected value and variance are the only two parameters used, the method implicitly is based on the assumption of a normal distribution. If the portfolio contains options, the assumption of a normal distribution is no longer valid. Option returns are highly skewed and the expected return and variance of an option position will not accurately produce the desired result, the return that is exceeded, say, 5 percent of the time. One approach is the one used here: We identified the critical outcome of the underlying and then determined the option outcome that corresponds to it.

Another commonly used alternative employs the delta, rather than the precise option pricing model, to determine the option outcome. In fact, the analytical or variance-covariance method is also sometimes called the **delta normal method.** Although this method is only approximate, it has some advantages. The delta is a linear adjustment of the underlying price change to the option price change and linearity is a desirable and simplifying property. When the outcome of a normal distribution is adjusted in a linear manner, the result remains normally distributed. Thus, the delta normal approach linearizes the option distribution; in other words, it converts the option's distribution to a normal distribution. This can be useful, particularly when a large portfolio is concerned. For longer periods, such as the one-month period used here, the delta adjustment is sometimes supplemented with a gamma adjustment.

Another important concern in using the analytical method is that large portfolios can be very complicated to work with. In these examples, we identified only a single source of risk. For large institutions, there are literally thousands of sources of risk. The volatilities and correlations of these diverse sources of risk must be captured and consolidated into a single volatility for the portfolio. This requires massive amounts of information. Fortunately, this information is readily available. The RiskMetrics Corporation, *www.riskmetrics.com,* a spin-off of the noted Wall Street firm J. P. Morgan, has provided downloadable data sets, which are updated daily, on the Internet. This information is based on recent historical price behavior and is smoothed via a weighting of current and past volatility.

The primary advantage and disadvantage of the analytical method is its reliance on the assumption of a normal distribution. The following method gets around that assumption.

HISTORICAL METHOD   The **historical method** estimates the distribution of the portfolio's performance by collecting data on the past performance of the portfolio and using it to estimate the future probability distribution. Obviously it assumes that the past distribution is a good estimate of the future distribution.

Figure 16.4 presents an example of the information obtained from a historical sample of daily portfolio returns over approximately one year, 254 trading days in this case. The information is presented in the form of a histogram. The person doing the analysis would arbitrarily choose the intervals. In this case, the 13 worst outcomes, which is about 5.1 percent of the total possible, are shaded. This means that the critical portfolio VAR is a loss of 10 percent. If the portfolio size is $15 million, then the VAR is $15,000,000(.10) = $1,500,000. Thus, we can say that the portfolio would

The historical method uses actual data from a recent historical period to determine the VAR.

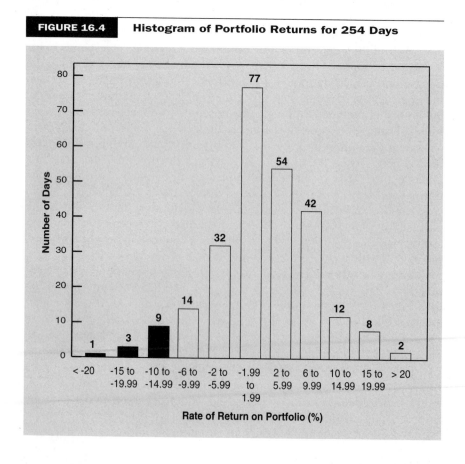

| FIGURE 16.4 | Histogram of Portfolio Returns for 254 Days |

be expected to lose at least $1.5 million in one day about 5 percent of the time, which is about once per month.

The historical method obviously produces a VAR that is consistent with the VAR of the chosen historical period. Whether this is an accurate method depends on several factors. Obviously it matters greatly whether the probability distribution of the past is repeated in the future. Also, the portfolio held in the future might differ in some way from the portfolio held in the past. For example, the S&P/Nikkei portfolio, which is currently $20 million in the S&P and $12 million in the Nikkei, could be reallocated. In fact, unless each asset performs identically, the portfolio automatically reallocates. One asset grows in value at a greater rate than the other and this changes the portfolio expected return and standard deviation. This problem, however, can be accommodated by using the historical returns but applying new weights to each asset in accordance with the current weights rather than the historical weights.

Another limitation of the historical method is that it requires the choice of a sample period. The outcome can be greatly affected by how large a sample one selects. Normally, the larger a sample, the more reliable the estimates obtained from it, but the larger the sample, the older are some of the data and the less reliable they become.

Another problem with the historical method is that the historical period may be badly representative of the future. For example, suppose the historical period included the stock market crash of October 1987, a day in which the market lost over 20 percent of its value in one day. Is this extreme outcome an accurate reflection of the VAR? Such an outcome would tremendously bias the volatility. Yet days like that are the very outcomes that risk managers should be worrying about.

The final method combines many of the best properties of the previous two methods.

MONTE CARLO SIMULATION METHOD   The **Monte Carlo simulation method** is based on the idea that portfolio returns can be fairly easily simulated. Simulation requires inputs on the expected returns, standard deviations, and correlations for each financial instrument. In an appendix to Chapter 15 we examined one procedure for simulating stock prices called the Monte Carlo method. Essentially the same procedure is used when calculating VAR except that it is necessary to ensure that the portfolio's returns properly account for the correlations among the financial instruments. This means that one cannot simply independently generate returns for, say, the S&P 500 and Treasury bonds. One set of returns can be generated but the other set of returns must reflect any correlation between the two sets of returns. This is done by making an assumption about the process in which asset returns are generated.

Monte Carlo simulation is probably the most widely used method by sophisticated firms. It is the most flexible method, because it permits the user to assume any known probability distribution and can handle relatively

Monte Carlo simulation generates random outcomes based on an assumed probability distribution to obtain the VAR.

complex portfolios; however, the more complex the portfolio, the more computational time required. Indeed Monte Carlo simulation is the most demanding method in terms of computer requirements. Nonetheless, the vast improvements in computing power in recent years have brought Monte Carlo to the forefront in risk management techniques.

A Comprehensive Calculation of VAR

Let us illustrate the three methods of calculating VAR by using a comprehensive example. Suppose we hold a very simple portfolio consisting of $25 million invested in the S&P 500. We would like to estimate VAR at 5 percent for one day using each of the three methods. First, we collect a sample of the daily returns on the S&P 500 for the past year. This gives us 253 returns. We obtain the following information, which will be useful in some of the VAR calculations:

Average daily return:	0.0457%
Daily standard deviation:	1.3327%

These numbers equate to an annual return of 0.0457 (253) = 11.56 percent and a standard deviation of $1.3327\sqrt{253}$ = 21.20 percent.

First we estimate VAR using the analytical method. Remember that we are assuming a normal distribution. Based on the above parameters, we obtain the following:

$$0.0457\% - (1.65)1.3327\% = -2.1533\%.$$

Thus, our VAR is

$$.021533(\$25,000,000) = \$538,325.$$

We might, however, believe that the parameters obtained from the historical data are not realistic. Indeed a 21 percent standard deviation is somewhat high for the S&P 500. Let us use a more realistic number of 15 percent. This equates to a daily standard deviation of $15/\sqrt{253}$ = 0.9430 percent. Let us use an expected return of 12 percent, which is a daily expected return of 12/253 = 0.0474 percent. Then

$$0.0474\% - (1.65)0.9430\% = -1.5086\%.$$

Thus, the VAR is

$$.015086(\$25,000,000) = \$377,150.$$

Which is more correct? That depends on which input seems more reasonable.

FIGURE 16.5   Historical Returns on S&P 500 for One Year

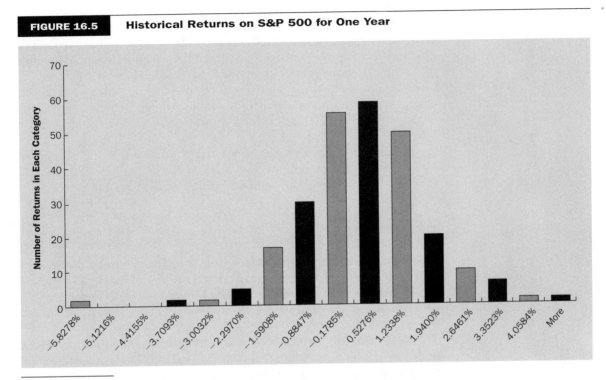

The return in a given category is more than the figure indicated and less than the figure to the right.

Remember that the analytical method is based on the assumption of a normal distribution. Is this a reasonable assumption? Figure 16.5 shows the distribution of returns for the S&P 500 that was used in this example. We see that the distribution does indeed bear some resemblance to the normal, but it probably does not completely adhere to the normal distribution.

Now let us calculate VAR based on the historical method. This method simply requires that we rank the returns from worst to best. For 253 returns, we have .05(253) = 12.65, telling us that the VAR is the twelfth or thirteenth worst outcome. Let us use the thirteenth worst outcome. If we lined up the returns from worst to best, we would find that the thirteenth worst return would be −2.0969 percent. Thus, the VAR would be

$$.020969(\$25,000,000) = \$524,225.$$

Now let us try a Monte Carlo simulation, where we have considerable flexibility. We must assume a probability distribution to generate the returns and we must choose the input values. Although one advantage of the Monte Carlo simulation is that we do not need to adhere to the normal distribution, we shall do so here for convenience and because it is the only probability distribution that you are likely to be very familiar with. In using the normal distribution we must input an expected value and volatility. Let us use the same 12 percent for the former and 15 percent for the latter that we used in the analytical method. We also have to decide on a time period, which we choose to be one day. In addition we must decide on the number of outcomes. Normally many thousands are used, but here we shall use 253, which is about one year and is the number of days over which we collected data. There is no particular reason why we should generate one year's worth of outcomes and, in practice, we would definitely want many more outcomes.

As noted earlier, the exact procedure for a Monte Carlo simulation with a normal distribution was described in the appendix to Chapter 15. Basically we generate a daily return according to the formula

$$\text{Return} = (\text{Expected Return})(1/253) + (\text{Standard Deviation}) * \epsilon\sqrt{1/253},$$

where ϵ is a random number drawn from a standard normal distribution with a mean of zero and a standard deviation of 1.0. Excel will generate such numbers with its Analysis ToolPack or a good approximation can be obtained as the sum of twelve random numbers (rand() + rand() + . . . − 6.0).

We do this 253 times, thereby obtaining 253 random returns. Once again, we simply sort them from worst to best and obtain the thirteenth worst return. Here, this is −1.3942 percent. Thus, the VAR is

$$.013942(\$25,000,000) = \$348,550.$$

Of course, different values will be obtained from one simulation to another.

We now have a number of candidates for our VAR:

$538,325, or
$377,150, or
$524,225, or
$348,550.

Which is correct? We simply do not know. The methods are so different and the inputs are so critical that this is a common result. In fact, even more variation could be obtained if we collected our data over different time periods or, for example, if we used weekly or monthly data instead of daily data. Or we could run more simulations or perhaps use a nonnormal distribution. The possibilities are almost endless. And in all honesty, the range of numbers shown here is actually quite small compared to what is frequently found in practice. Most real-world portfolios are far more complicated than this. They usually contain options, which tend to cause larger discrepancies. In short, VAR is a number that is quite sensitive to how it is calculated. That does not mean it is useless or unreliable. Knowing the potential range of VAR is itself useful. Moreover, one should always follow up the calculation with an ex post evaluation. If we settle on a VAR of, say, $400,000 in this example, we should expect that this value will be exceeded no more than 5 percent of the time. If it is exceeded far more or far less than 5 percent of the time, we know that $400,000 was not a good estimate of the VAR.

Although widely criticized, VAR has been embraced by the risk management industry. VAR, or some variation thereof, is used by nearly every major derivatives dealer and an increasing number of end users. VAR is perhaps most beneficial in communicating information to nontechnical personnel. To tell a CEO that a firm is expected to lose at least $400,000 in a day 5 percent of the time, meaning about once every month, conveys a lot of useful information that the CEO can easily grasp. The trade-off, however, is that if the number is inaccurate, the CEO will have less confidence in the number and in the person giving him or her the number. Accurate estimation with continuing ex post follow-up is critical in using VAR.

VAR is also widely used in banking regulation. The objective of banking regulators is to ensure that the banking system does not fail and that consumers and savers are protected. Most banking regulators use VAR as a measure of the risk of a bank. A common specification for VAR in this context is 10 days with a 1 percent probability.

Likewise, banks and corporations who are engaged in significant trading activities commonly use VAR as a measure to allocate capital. In other words, they set aside a certain amount of capital to protect against losses. The amount of capital set aside is often the VAR.

VAR is also used in the evaluation of the performance of investment managers and traders. The modern approach to performance evaluation is to adjust the return performance for a measure of the risk taken in achieving that performance. VAR is often used in this context as a measure of risk.

Thus, we see that VAR has a variety of practical applications. Nonetheless, VAR must be used carefully. We have barely scratched the surface of VAR, but we have encountered enough to get you started in understanding it. There is much written on VAR; in fact, it is probably one of the most written-about topics of recent years. You will not be able to turn around in the risk management world without encountering something written about it.

In addition to estimating VAR, a risk manager will often subject the portfolio to a **stress test,** which determines how badly the portfolio will do under some of the worst and most unusual circumstances. If the portfolio's return in that situation is tolerable, then the portfolio risk is assumed to be acceptable. Stress testing can be quite valuable as a supplement to VAR and other techniques of risk management. Yet, stress testing has its own criticism, including the fact that it places too much emphasis on highly unlikely events.

The important point to remember about VAR and stress testing, as well as any financial statistic, is that these are just estimates and cannot be expected to provide the full picture.

Stress testing means to estimate how a portfolio will perform if extremely rare events occur.

We have now completed our examination of market risk. We next turn to the other major type of risk: credit risk.

Managing Credit Risk

Earlier in this chapter, we mentioned a party that could borrow at a fixed rate of 10 1/2 percent or at a floating rate of LIBOR plus 1.1 percent. That party issues floating-rate debt and enters into a swap in which it pays a fixed rate of 9 1/4 percent and receives a floating rate of LIBOR, for a net fixed rate of 10.35 percent, a savings of 15 basis points over issuing fixed rate directly.

If the firm had borrowed fixed, it would have assumed no credit risk. A lender cannot default. If it borrows floating and swaps it into a synthetic fixed-rate loan, it faces the risk that the swap dealer will default, leaving it owing the floating rate of LIBOR. Perhaps the 15-basis-point saving is simply compensation for bearing the risk that the dealer will default.

Credit risk is the uncertainty and potential for loss due to a failure to pay on the part of a counterparty.

The risk of default is faced by any party that may receive obligatory payments from another party. This risk, called **credit risk** or **default risk,** is faced by any lender. We have mentioned it many times earlier in the book, especially in conjunction with over-the-counter derivatives. Because banks are used to making loans, their derivatives business is not taking on a different kind of risk than one they already have years of experience with. Since the notional principal on a derivative is not at risk, however, the credit risk of derivatives is typically much lower than the credit risk of loans. Nonbank end users typically do not make loans. When they become users of swaps, however, they become creditors.

Earlier in the book we commented on credit risk whenever we discussed over-the-counter instruments. Futures and exchange-listed options are insured against credit risk by the clearinghouse. Since there has never been a default by the clearinghouse, these contracts can be considered credit-risk free. Over-the-counter contracts are subject to credit risk that varies from party to party, from type of contract to type of contract, and from one point in time to another point in time.

In the bond market, credit risk is typically assessed by examining the credit ratings of issuers. Credit ratings are provided by several firms, most notably Standard & Poor's, Moody's, and Fitch's. Although each agency has its own labels, terms like "Triple-A" and "B-double AA" are used, with the more A's the better. Thus, you would see ratings like AAA, AA, A, BAA, BBB, BB, B, and so on down to D. Analysts for these companies base their ratings on a variety of factors, most notably the financial health of the issuer, and also the states of the economy and the issuer's industry.

There are two types of credit risk. **Current credit risk** is the risk to one party that the other party is unable to make payments that are currently due. Current credit risk is faced by only one party in a derivatives transaction, the party who holds the contract as an asset. In other words, the amount due to that party is positive so it is subject to the possibility that the other party will default. The other party currently owes more than is owed to it, so it faces no current risk of default. **Potential credit risk** is the risk that the counterparty will default in the future.

Both current and potential credit risk of over-the-counter options are faced by the buyer only. Since the buyer pays the premium to the seller and does not have to do anything else, the seller faces no credit risk. The buyer, however, may eventually choose to exercise the option, by which time the seller may be bankrupt. FRAs and swaps have two-way credit risk. Each party is obligated to do something for the other. Holding other things constant, the credit risk of an FRA or interest rate swap is determined by the credit quality of the counterparty, the terms of the contract, and the shape of the term structure. Consider, for example, a five-year plain vanilla interest rate swap. With an upward-sloping term structure, the implied forward rates are rising. These rates can be equated to the floating rates and will equal the eventual floating rates if there is no shift in interest rates during the life of the swap. When the swap is first established, the party paying the fixed rate and receiving the floating rate will initially pay more than it receives, but later the floating receipts will begin to overtake the fixed payments. At any given time current credit risk is faced by one party only, which is the party to whom the contract has positive value. Potential credit risk will reflect the combined effects of the risk of changes in interest rates and the risk of the counterparty's assets over the remaining life of the contract. Both parties face potential credit risk.

In the case of interest rate swaps, the potential credit risk is largest during the middle of the swap's life. Potential credit risk is low at the beginning of the swap's life because it is assumed that the swap would not be entered into if there were any significant problems on the near horizon. Potential credit risk is high during the middle part of the swap's life because the counterparty has had time to have its financial condition deteriorate. Potential credit risk is low during the latter part of the swap's life because there are fewer payments remaining.

Recall that interest rate swaps do not involve the exchange of principal but currency swaps often do. This also keeps the credit risk low at the end of the life of the interest rate swap but raises it somewhat for the currency swap.

The explicit prices of derivative transactions do not necessarily differ according to the credit risk of the transaction. Many derivatives dealers and end users will transact only with customers of a minimum acceptable credit quality. Thus, counterparties who barely pass the hurdle pay the same as counterparties who are essentially risk free. Assessment of a counterparty's credit risk is done much the same way as when extending credit. Financial statements and ratings are used along with simulations and other statistical techniques. VAR can even be adapted to accommodate credit risk, though it is much more difficult to do. Stress testing is commonly used to assess credit risk by assuming that extreme economic conditions occur and estimating the likelihood of default.

Current credit risk is the risk that the party owing more than the other in a derivatives transaction will default right now. Potential credit risk is the risk that either party will default at any time during the life of the contract.

The primary methods of managing derivatives credit risk are limiting exposure to a given party, collateral, marking to market, netting, credit derivatives, and, for some dealers, separately capitalized derivatives subsidiaries.

Although qualifying parties pay the same explicit rate on a derivatives transaction, there are some implicit methods of differentiating among parties with different credit risks.

The primary method used to manage credit risk is to limit the amount of exposure to a given party. The higher the credit quality of the counterparty, the greater the amount of business that can be done with it. This is similar to the principle of diversification. A party spreads out its transactions with numerous end users or dealers. An extreme case of this method is to do no business whatsoever with a counterparty whose credit quality is below a minimum level.

Collateral is commonly used in lending and is becoming increasingly used in derivatives transactions. The two parties might agree that each post collateral by depositing cash or securities with a bank or by providing a letter of credit from another bank. The parties may agree that on any settlement date, the party to whom the derivative value is negative will post collateral equal to a given percentage of the notional principal or the value of the contract. Another type of arrangement is for neither party to post collateral but if either party's credit is downgraded by one of the rating agencies, that party will post a specific amount of collateral. Some transactions are structured so that a ratings downgrade gives the other party the right to terminate the contract at that point, meaning that the value of the swap is due and payable at that time.

We discussed marking to market extensively when we studied futures markets. Marking to market is designed to reduce credit risk by forcing losing parties to pay winning parties before losses accumulate to a large amount. Some derivative contracts are structured to have marking to market on a periodic basis. For example, a swap that settles semiannually might stipulate that the contracts are marked to market every two months. When the contract is marked to market, the market value is calculated. The party to whom the value is negative owes that full amount in cash to the other party. The fixed rate is then reset to the current market fixed rate. The actual settlement, meaning the exchange of interest payments, proceeds at the regularly scheduled dates though with a new fixed rate. This procedure forces the party on the losing side to pay up before the accumulated loss is potentially much greater.

One should not always assume that the party with the weaker credit is the dealer. Many dealers are banks whose credit ratings are held down by the possibility of loan losses in their domestic and global banking business. In response to the concerns of some end users, a number of dealers have set up separate subsidiaries who do exclusively swap and derivatives transactions with end users. These subsidiaries are provided a large capital cushion and are not responsible for the debts of the parent company. Consequently, the subsidiary would have a higher credit rating than the parent company and most of these subsidiaries are rated AAA. These types of firms are called **enhanced derivatives products companies** and sometimes **special**

purpose vehicles. When these firms were first created several years ago, they were greeted with much enthusiasm. The amount of business they have generated, however, has been surprisingly little. In fact, many parent companies also maintain derivative groups within the parent company as well as the subsidiary. Most end users were content to do business with the parent company as long as its rating was reasonably high, though not necessarily AAA.

Another procedure widely used to reduce default risk is netting. Because it is used so much and it is so important, we shall devote a special section to it.

Netting

Netting is a term to describe several similar processes that are used to reduce the amount of cash paid from one party to the other by deducting any cash owed by the latter party to the former party. Netting between two parties is called **bilateral netting** while netting across several parties is called **multilateral netting.** Multilateral netting is effectively what happens when there is a clearinghouse, such as the options or futures clearinghouses we discussed in Chapters 2 and 8. At present there are no clearinghouses for over-the-counter derivatives, but the possibilities are being studied.

There are several forms of nettings. We have already seen **payment netting,** in which two parties who owe each other money on a given day agree to simply determine the net amount owed and have one party pay the other. As you should remember, this is a fairly standard procedure in interest rate swaps. If party A owes $1,250,000 to party B who owes $890,000 to party A, then party A simply makes a payment of $360,000 to party B. This eliminates the possibility of party B defaulting, at least on this payment.

In **cross product netting,** payments for one type of transaction are netted against payments for another type of transaction. Suppose, for example, that on the date on which party A owes $260,000 to party B, party B also owes A $175,000 as the interest on a loan. If the two parties had agreed to cross product netting, then A would owe B only $260,000 − $175,000 = $85,000. Of course, the two parties might seldom have transactions with payments due on the same day. Consequently, cross product netting usually comes into play in bankruptcy or in a takeover involving two parties, each owing the other various amounts arising from different transactions.

If the parties agree to **netting by novation,** the net value of their mutual obligations is replaced by a single new transaction. In our example above, if A owes B $85,000, then the transactions that have an aggregate value of $85,000 to B are replaced by a new transaction with a value of $85,000. Netting by novation is used more often in the foreign exchange markets.

Closeout netting is the stipulation that if default occurs, only the net amount is owed. This greatly reduces the credit risk by reducing the amount of cash owed by a defaulting party by the amount owed to it. Consider the following example:

Company XYZ and dealer FinSwaps are engaged in four transactions with each other. From the dealer's perspective, the market values are as follows:

Swap 1	−$1,179,580
Swap 2	+$1,055,662
Option 1	+$1,495,255
FRA 1	−$ 892,530
	+$ 478,807

XYZ defaults with no closeout netting:
Suppose XYZ demands payments on swap 1 and FRA 1 and refuses to pay on swap 2 and option 1. FinSwaps owes XYZ $2,072,110, the sum of the values of swap 1 and FRA 1. This process is commonly called *cherry picking* because the bankrupt party selects the attractive transactions and walks away from the others.
XYZ defaults but closeout netting is used:
XYZ owes FinSwaps $478,807.

Netting is the process of reducing credit risk in which amounts owed from one party to the other are netted against amounts owed from the latter to the former to arrive at an overall amount owed by one party to the other.

Today, there is hardly an issue over the use of closeout netting. It is standard in virtually every swap in most countries and bankruptcy laws of most have been revised to recognize the legitimacy of closeout netting.

In the presence of netting, the credit risk of swaps is clearly limited to the net payments, which is less than the present value of the interest payments on a loan of equivalent notional principal. Because of this and the fact that the over-the-counter derivatives market has imposed strict requirements to reduce the credit risk, its record in the matter of defaults is excellent. The default of the London borough Hammersmith and Fulham in 1988, the result of a legal ruling that permitted it to walk away from losing transactions, accounted for about half of all defaults in the over-the-counter market until that time. The record since that time has been quite good as well. In fact, the derivatives market has established a much better record on the matter of default than has the commercial loan market. Clearly the concerns expressed by some over the large size of the market as exemplified by the notional principal outstanding overstate the real risk.

Credit Derivatives

In the early 1990s an innovation in credit risk management appeared on the scene: the **credit derivative.** A credit derivative is an instrument designed to separate market risk from credit risk and to allow the separate trading of the latter. Specifically it is a derivative or derivative-like instrument whose payoff is largely determined by the credit risk of another party. Credit derivatives permit a more efficient allocation and pricing of credit risk. Parties who wish to rid themselves of credit risk can sell it to parties who are willing to buy credit risk. Ultimately, this greatly benefits those who borrow and lend and those who transact in derivatives that are subject to default, for it helps assure them that the premiums associated with the risk of default are appropriate for that level of risk. Banks, in particular, use credit derivatives both as buyers and sellers. Banks must limit the amount of exposure to a particular borrower, to a particular geographic area, or to a particular industry. They can often provide a loan, thereby servicing the borrower, but can then sell the credit risk to another party.

There are four primary types of credit derivatives, each addressing in some manner, though not perfectly, the problem of separating market risk from credit risk. The first, simplest, and most commonly used is the **total return swap.** This is a swap transaction, and in many ways is similar to an ordinary swap, in which a party agrees to pay the total return on a particular reference asset, such as a specific bond issued by a private borrower, and agrees to receive a rate such as LIBOR plus a spread. The total return includes any interest payments as well as unrealized capital gains. If the bond incurs a capital loss, the party holding the credit derivative then receives an equivalent payment from the seller of the credit derivative. The party holding a bond issued by another party is, in effect, promising to pay to another party the bond's total return and correspondingly receive an interest rate, thereby ridding itself of the risk of price changes caused by factors unrelated to interest rate movements. Presumably such price changes would occur primarily from changes in the borrower's credit risk. Note, however, that while the swap is designed to get rid of credit risk, the two parties to the swap assume the credit risk of each other. The structure of a total return swap is illustrated in Figure 16.6. Note that unrealized capital gains and losses are non-cash amounts, but the swap requires cash payment for unrealized capital gains and losses.

The total return swap keeps the bond on the books of the party who was holding it originally. The party selling the credit derivative is seeking

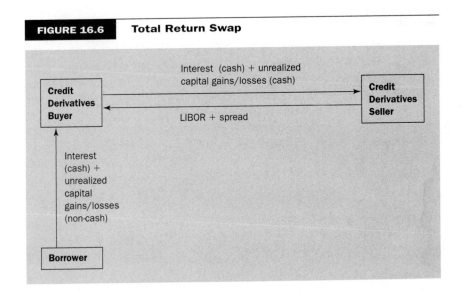

FIGURE 16.6   **Total Return Swap**

Interest (cash) + unrealized capital gains/losses (cash)

Credit Derivatives Buyer

LIBOR + spread

Credit Derivatives Seller

Interest (cash) + unrealized capital gains/losses (non-cash)

Borrower

the return on the bond without buying the bond. Note that market risk due to interest rate movements is not eliminated since those movements are reflected in the LIBOR payment. Incidentally, the LIBOR payment can, alternatively, be a fixed rate or it can be converted from LIBOR to a fixed rate with a plain vanilla swap. Note that the total return swap is much like an ordinary swap, but the interest payment corresponds to that on a specific bond and the unrealized capital gains and losses are paid.

Total return swaps are practical only for reasonably liquid bonds and not for ordinary loans. This is because the parties must be able to identify the total return over the settlement period in order to determine how much one party owes to the other. Consequently, there must be a reliable measure of the market value of the bond.

The **credit swap,** sometimes called a **credit default swap,** is perhaps misnamed. Although it is typically classified as a type of swap, it is really more like an insurance policy. A party holding a bond or loan makes a series of periodic payments to another party. In the event that the reference bond or loan defaults or has a credit downgrade, the insuring party pays the other an amount to compensate for the loss. Although this is called a swap, it is obviously just an insurance policy in which a fee is paid periodically, and the insurer compensates the insured in the event that a credit loss occurs. Credit swaps work reasonably well with both bonds and loans, but they require a careful definition of what a credit event is. A credit swap is illustrated in Figure 16.7.

Credit swaps require a very careful definition of what event triggers the payout. There are a variety of these credit events that might be specified in the contract. These include not making an interest or scheduled principal

A credit derivative is an instrument whose payoff is largely determined by the credit of another party. Credit derivatives are of the form of total return swaps, credit swaps, credit spread options, or credit-linked securities. They are used to permit the separation of market risk from credit risk and the trading of the latter.

FIGURE 16.7   **Credit Swap**

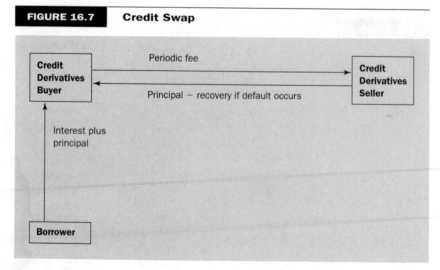

payment following a reasonable grace period, declaration of bankruptcy, a repudiation of the liability, meaning that the borrower thereby claims not to owe due to some legal technicality, a restructuring of the borrower's other debts, and an acceleration of payment of another liability. The latter could be caused by a provision in another liability that permits another creditor to require premature payment of a debt. These possibilities must be spelled out in the contract.

A **credit spread option** is just an option on the spread of a bond over a reference bond. Normally in the bond market, the spread of a bond's yield over the yield on a comparable maturity U.S. Treasury instrument is called the yield spread. It fluctuates with investors' perceptions of the credit risk in the market. Suppose the credit risk of the borrower currently dictates that it should pay 50 basis points in yield over a U.S. Treasury note of comparable maturity. The holder of the bond might buy a credit spread option with an exercise rate of 60 basis points. At expiration, or early if the option is American style, the option is in-the-money if the credit spread exceeds 60 basis points. Of course, this will occur only if the market perceives that the credit risk has increased. For this right, the holder pays a premium up front. Thus, this instrument is like an ordinary option, but the underlying is the spread of the bond over the otherwise comparable U.S. Treasury security. This type of credit derivative also requires that the underlying bond be sufficiently liquid such that a reliable assessment of its credit spread can be obtained.

The final type of credit derivative is the **credit linked security.** This type of instrument appears to be an ordinary bond or note, paying interest and principal. Underlying the note, however, is the credit quality of a third party. If that third party defaults on some other specified instrument or obligation, the credit linked security pays back less than its full principal. For example, let us say party A buys a credit linked note from party B. Party B in turn is holding a note issued by party C. If party C fails to pay party B, the latter is then able to reduce its obligation to party A. In this manner, party A assumes some credit risk of both parties A and B. Party B, often a bank, is, thus, able to lay off some unwanted credit risk. Of course, party A receives a higher interest rate on the note as compensation for acceptance of this risk.

The size of the credit derivatives market is unknown. The Bank for International Settlements does not differentiate credit derivatives from other derivatives in its surveys. Some information is available from the United States Office of the Comptroller of the Currency, which regulates federally chartered banks in the United States. Its surveys, obtainable from its website *www.occ.gov,* indicate that the notional principal of credit derivatives at these large U.S. banks grew from $55 billion at the end of 1997 to $287 billion at the end of 1999. This is relatively small compared to other derivatives, but certainly represents a rapid pace of growth that is expected to continue.

Other Types of Risks

Although market risk and credit risk comprise the two primary risks, they are by no means exhaustive. The unforeseen circumstances that can occur touch on almost all aspects of running a business.

Operational risk is the risk of a breakdown in the operations of the derivatives program or risk management system. This could include such events as power failures, computer problems such as viruses and software bugs, the failure of staff personnel to monitor and record transactions properly, the failure of staff personnel to have the necessary knowledge of potentially complex transactions, the failure to have proper documentation, and fraud perpetrated by traders or staff personnel. These risks are present in virtually any type of business operation, but because derivatives transactions are generally somewhat complex and usually involve large amounts of money, the need to avoid these problems is critical.

Perhaps the most important part of operational risk is the effectiveness of proper controls. For example, if certain persons are authorized to engage in derivatives transactions, then it is imperative that their activities be monitored by personnel who report to persons higher in the organization. Anyone authorized to trade must be restricted in what contracts and how much that person can trade. Controls must be in place to make sure that these policies are followed. As obvious as that seems, some firms have not done a good job of ensuring that well-established policies and procedures are actually followed. In fact, it is safe to say that many derivatives losses can be traced in part to operational risks. In many cases, unauthorized trades took place. An individual in a company made trades that were inappropriate or exposed the firm to excessive risks that clearly were risks the firm had not authorized its traders to take. Such an individual is often called a rogue trader, trading within the firm but outside its control parameters.

Operational risk is receiving a great deal of attention today. Unfortunately it is one of the most difficult risks to manage. First, it is difficult to identify and even define it. Second, it does not easily lend itself to analysis. Operational risk losses, fortunately, do not occur often. Yet when they do occur, they can lead to tremendous losses. The infrequency of their occurrence leads to two major problems. One is that they are not amenable to analysis by standard statistical techniques. A normal distribution or even other common statistical distributions do not fit the unusual profiles of operational risk losses. Another problem is that little data exists on operational risk losses. When companies incur such losses, they do their best to not reveal this information, for it tends to be embarrassing and suggests sloppiness in their internal systems. The infrequency of past problems and lack of data make it difficult to predict when and where such losses will occur. The risk management industry, however, is beginning to recognize this problem and some efforts to share data among firms have begun.

Operational risks are more along the lines of risks that are addressed by traditional insurance policies. When an insurance firm provides protection against a singer's voice during a concert tour, it is insuring against an infrequent event of an operational risk nature. When an insurer provides protection against employee fraud, it is insuring against operational risk. It is not surprising, therefore, that insurance companies have begun to look at marketing products for insuring against operational risk in the financial industry and, in particular, in connection with derivatives-related transactions. While there are no derivative contracts that protect against operational risk, some discussion has begun toward creating operational risk derivatives, and they will surely exist in the near future.

Model risk is the risk that in pricing a financial instrument, such as a derivative, the firm will use an inappropriate model or a model containing errors (including programming bugs and errors), or use incorrect inputs. This is a critical issue for dealers, because offering derivatives at attractive prices and then managing the risk is their business. It can also be critical for end users, because they are less likely to have the personnel and knowledge to properly price the instruments.

We have learned enough in this book to take a quick look at model risk. Suppose a customer wants to buy a three-year American put option on the S&P 500. Let the index be at 1450, the exercise price be at 1450, the risk-free rate be 6 percent, the volatility be 18 percent, the dividend yield be 1.5 percent, and, of course, the time to expiration be three years. Because this is an American option, we should use a binomial tree to properly reflect the early exercise feature. It is tempting, nonetheless, to use the Black-Scholes model, so that is what we mistakenly do. Using your spreadsheet bsbin2.xls, we obtain a value for the call of 88.05. Let us get the correct value, however, using the binomial model. Using 200 time steps, we obtain 111.82. This is an error of over 20 percent. If the customer wanted $1,000,000 of notional principal of this option, we would be losing over $200,000 just in selling the option. Further losses would undoubtedly be incurred in trying to manage the risk by delta, gamma, and vega hedging.

Here is another variation of model risk. Suppose we used the correct model, sold the option at 111.82, and then hedged away the risk with other transactions. Now suppose one year later we needed to assign a value to the option. With two years to go and the same S&P value, the put would be worth 99.56. But suppose we used a volatility of 22 percent. The put would have a value of 122.68. This is a significant difference. Yet volatility variations from, for example, 18 percent to 22 percent are common. One might be tempted not to view this as a form of model risk, but any time the inputs are unknown, model risk exists. With an input as critical as the volatility is to an option, the model risk can be tremendous.

Some major financial institutions have discovered embarrassing errors, even in simple valuation problems such as forward contracts, that have led to significant losses. The best insurance against model risk is knowledge: knowledge of the theories and models.

Liquidity risk is the risk that a firm will need to enter into a derivatives transaction and find that the market for that transaction is so thin that the price includes a significant discount or premium for that liquidity. Anyone making a market in an illiquid instrument will bear significant risk and would charge wide bid-ask spreads or even be unwilling to trade. Most plain vanilla derivatives have little such risk but exotic transactions can have significant liquidity risk. Liquidity risk is hardly confined to derivatives, however, as was evidenced in the August–September 1998 period when the famous hedge fund Long-Term Capital Management (LTCM) found itself holding positions in very illiquid bonds from around the world. LTCM had sophisticated risk management systems and some of the smartest people in the business, but it misestimated the effects of illiquidity during a global financial crisis where markets around the world were falling in unison. LTCM suffered severe losses that led to a bailout by a consortium of banks that was orchestrated by the U.S. Federal Reserve.

A great deal of research is going on to model liquidity risk or, at the minimum, to think about its effects when managing other types of risks. Some discussion has begun on the creation of liquidity risk derivatives, which would allow parties to buy and sell liquidity risk just like any other form of risk.

Accounting risk is the uncertainty over the proper accounting treatment of a derivatives transaction. Accounting for derivatives has been a significant source of controversy and risk for many years. Users of derivatives have lived with an ongoing concern that the manner in which they account for derivatives will be declared inappropriate after the fact and that they will be required to restate certain transactions with the potential to lower past earnings figures. The significance, timeliness, and critical importance of proper accounting for derivatives is a reason why we examine this subject in more detail in a later section.

Legal risk is the risk that the legal system will fail to enforce a contract. For example, suppose a dealer enters into a swap with a counterparty who, upon incurring a loss, then refuses to pay the dealer, arguing that the dealer misled it or that the counterparty had no legal authority to enter into the swap. These arguments have been successfully used in the legal system, particularly by local governments. The risk of contracts not being enforced is a serious one for dealers.[9] This risk can effectively turn a swap or an FRA into an option, because the counterparty simply walks away without paying if the market moves against it. Not too surprisingly, no counterparty has ever claimed that it was misled or had no authority to do derivatives after making money on them. We shall see this issue again

---

[9]The aforementioned Hammersmith and Fulham case illustrates the dangers of legal risk to the dealer. The case was supported on the doctrine of *ultra vires,* which means to have no legal authority.

when we look at the bankruptcy of Orange County, California in the appendix to this chapter.

Tax risk is the risk that taxes or the interpretation of tax laws will change unexpectedly. A good example of this was described in Appendix 10B where the tax status of hedging, which had been established almost a half century prior, was called into question. For a period of time, the possibility existed that certain hedging transactions would be taxed in a different manner, rendering them much less attractive. Moreover, the threat that completed transactions will have to be re-taxed always looms. Tax risk has managed to completely eliminate the use of certain transactions, such as the American Stock Exchange's PRIMES and SCORES, which were precursors to the equity-linked debt we covered in Chapter 15. As another example of tax risk, Congress has been considering for many years levying a tax on each futures transaction to pay the cost of regulating the futures markets.

In addition to market and credit risks, risk managers must consider operational risk, model risk, liquidity risk, accounting risk, legal risk, tax risk, regulatory risk, and settlement risk.

Regulatory risk is the risk that regulations or the regulatory style will change unexpectedly. For example, the Commodity Futures Trading Commission was once chaired by an individual who pursued a free-market, loose-knit style of regulation that encouraged innovation and competition. When a new administration took over the White House, a new chairman was appointed. The philosophy of the agency changed overnight to a much tighter regulatory approach. Obviously, regulatory risk means that certain existing or contemplated transactions can become illegal or regulated.

Settlement risk is commonly faced in international transactions. Let us say that a bank in country A engages in a financial transaction with a corporation in country B in which both the bank and the corporation will be required to pay each other rather than net their payments.[10] The bank and the corporation are 12 hours apart with the bank's day beginning first. On settlement day the bank wires its funds to the corporation under the assumption that when the markets open the corporation will wire its funds to the bank. When the corporation's markets open, however, the corporation announces that it is bankrupt and will suspend all payments. Thus, the bank will be out the money and will have to get in line with the corporation's other creditors. This risk is sometimes called **Herstatt risk**, named for the German bank that in 1974 failed under similar circumstances. Settlement risk can arise out of bankruptcy, insolvency, or fraud.

This enumeration of risks does not necessarily cover every possible contingency. Foreign currency transactions, for example, are subject to political risk, meaning that the government of a country may take over the financial system and declare certain transactions null and void or refuse to allow currency to leave the country. The Chicago Board of Trade was forced to suspend operations one day due to a flood in downtown Chicago.

---

[10]For example, a currency swap is usually done without netting because the payments are occurring in two different currencies.

Risk managers needing to trade CBOT products had to look for substitutes in other markets. It would be impossible to have every contingency covered, but risk managers need to be aware of as many problems as possible that could occur.

There is one final source of risk that is of considerable concern to many people, especially regulators. There is a belief that when one company defaults, it could trigger the default of one of its creditors, which could trigger further defaults. These effects could ripple through the entire financial system, leading to widespread panic and a meltdown of the whole system. This is called **systemic risk.** In modern times, the closest the world's economy has come to such a breakdown was during the stock market crash of October 1987, and on a lesser scale to a global financial crisis that occurred in September 1998. As it turned out, while there was a great deal of panic and enormous losses, the markets did not even come close to a total breakdown. Regulators worry, however, that the volume of derivatives transactions, particularly over-the-counter derivatives, is much greater now. While this might be a legitimate concern in an economy in which most financial institutions do not practice risk management, there is little cause for concern today. Nearly every major financial institution in the world practices risk management and most maintain a relatively hedged position in derivatives. There have been numerous shocks to the financial system in the 1990s but none has come remotely close to causing a systemic breakdown.

Systemic risk is the risk that failure of one or more financial institutions will trigger more failures, ultimately leading to a breakdown of the financial system.

Organizational and Accounting Issues in Risk Management

Most of this book has been focused on various market- and credit-related issues associated with the use of derivatives. At this point, we turn to a look at the organizational and accounting issues that confront any firm that engages in derivatives transactions.

Derivatives in the Organization

The quality of an organization always starts at the top. This means that senior management and the board of directors must take the initiative for being knowledgeable and aware of the derivatives activities the firm engages in. This does not mean that they must be experts in derivatives, but they should be able to define each of the instruments used by the firm and should know why the firm uses them. Most importantly, they must establish written policies and procedures governing the use of derivatives. These policies must specify a rationale for the use of derivatives, define the circumstances under which derivatives can be used, authorize the appropriate personnel to execute transactions, define trading limits, establish control procedures to ensure that all policies are followed, and address the issue of how the performance of a derivatives/risk management operation will be evaluated.

Senior management is particularly responsible for ensuring that competent personnel with sufficient technical knowledge are employed by the firm when such skills are needed. They must also authorize the expenditure of funds for the necessary hardware and software.

A dealer organization, which is in the derivatives business to earn a profit, will engage in numerous transactions and naturally should practice risk management at the centralized firmwide level. If there are relationships between movements in interest rates, stock prices, and foreign exchange rates, and there nearly always are, it would be unwise to have separate risk managers monitoring the performance of the bond department, the equities department, and the various international operations. Rather, most dealers have opted for a single risk manager, who often reports to the chief executive officer. The risk manager should have access to all of the necessary financial and statistical information and should have the authority to stop traders from trading and/or force them to unwind positions. It should not be possible for traders or derivatives sales personnel to influence the risk manager. Some dealers use a risk management committee, but in either case, the risk manager's or the committee's responsibility is usually to senior management. In any case, independent risk management is probably the most important requirement for an effective risk management system.

A corporate risk management function may be surprisingly decentralized. Some firms may have purchasing departments that hedge purchases of raw materials. Many firms will have foreign subsidiaries who hedge their subsidiary operations. Most corporations delegate domestic interest rate hedging to the treasury department. The treasury's normal responsibility is managing cash and bank loans. In recent years, many corporations have begun to centralize their risk management activities, focusing on risk management of the firm as a whole. This enables the firm to allow certain natural hedges to work. For example, a firm might be exposed long to German interest rates in one division and short in another. If each division hedges separately, unnecessary transactions are done. A centralized risk management function would determine that the risks of two divisions are at least partially offsetting.

Many corporations unfortunately do not provide for an independent risk management function. To make things worse, they sometimes operate their treasury department as a profit center. Instead of attempting to simply manage the firm's cash and bank loans efficiently, treasurers sometimes start trading in the derivatives markets with the objective of earning a profit. It is not reasonable to expect that they can do this effectively over the long run and, unfortunately, for some firms, the long run came early in the form of large derivatives losses.

Derivatives dealers have two distinct groups of derivatives specialists. One group is the sales personnel, who call on clients, analyze the clients' risks, and offer the dealer's products and services for the purpose of managing the clients' risks. The other group is made up of traders who execute derivatives transactions for the dealer. Most dealers also have research

One of the most important organizational considerations in risk management is to have an independent risk management function, meaning that the risk manager has access to necessary information, the authority to take corrective action, and immunity from the influence of traders and sales personnel.

A typical dealership operation is divided into two groups: the front office, meaning the trading function, and the back office, meaning the clerical, record-keeping function. Effective risk management requires that these two functions be separated.

departments, normally made up of technically trained personnel who conduct research, design and price new products, and provide support for sales personnel and traders. Most corporations do not have research departments but may have a few individuals on the staff with trading experience and a high degree of technical expertise.

The derivatives operations of dealers are typically segregated into what are called the **front office** and **back office.** Some firms have an additional layer in between the front office and back office, which is naturally called the middle office. The front office consists of the traders and their assistants. The back office personnel are the clerks and operations officers whose job is to process the paperwork and generate the necessary reports. It is considered critical by nearly every dealer that these two functions be separate. If they are not, as we shall see when we read in the appendix to this chapter about the failure of Barings Bank, the proverbial "fox is guarding the chicken coop." In some firms, the back office may be the only control mechanism. While this is not the optimal structure, at the very least the back office should not have to report to the front office or feel any pressure from it.

All firms should also have a legal department or have access to external legal counsel. The attorneys are responsible for ensuring that all contracts are properly documented and conform to appropriate laws.

Within most firms there is an individual called a compliance officer who is responsible for assuring that all internal and external regulations are followed.

The accounting function is an important one in all firms. We have already mentioned the complexities of derivatives accounting. Although an accounting system is not the same as a risk management system, the two must

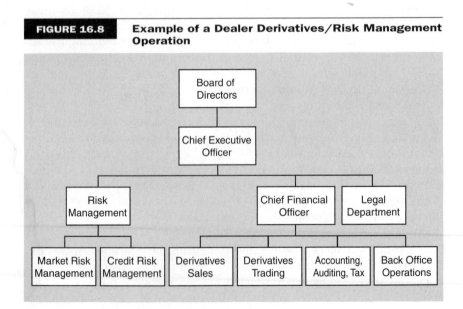

FIGURE 16.8   **Example of a Dealer Derivatives/Risk Management Operation**

not be inconsistent. An accounting system also provides for periodic auditing, but does not substitute for risk management. Auditing simply determines whether the financial records have been kept in conformance with the policies established by the accounting profession and the firm. Auditing is a periodic process. Risk management is a continuous process.

Any firm that engages in derivatives and risk management activities should provide for regular evaluation of its performance. It should define its objectives and establish a system that will provide timely and unbiased assessments of the quality of its activities. This is not a simple task since objective performance evaluation is quite difficult to do, but this issue must be addressed, nonetheless.

Although there are many effective variations, Figures 16.8 and 16.9 illustrate examples of a derivatives/risk management operation for a dealer and for a corporate end user. The dealer operation is centralized with an independent risk manager reporting to the chief executive officer. The corporate structure shown here is a little less centralized with derivatives activities undertaken by both a purchasing officer and the treasurer. This firm has established a risk management function that reports to the treasury. It is unlikely, however, that the risk manager has sufficient information to monitor the purchasing officer's hedging transactions or the authority to do much about it if policies are not followed or problems occur.

FIGURE 16.9   **Example of a Corporate Derivatives/Risk Management Operation**

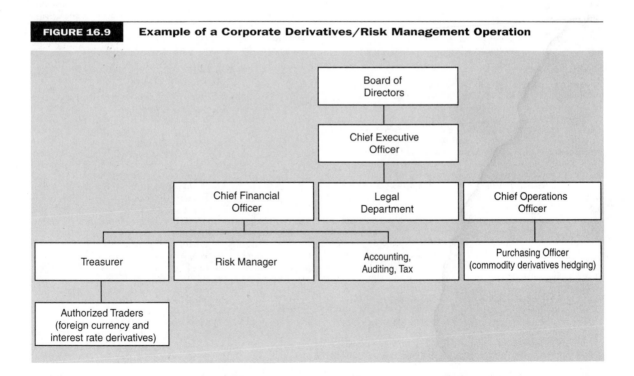

Risk Management at Coca-Cola

Coca-Cola is one of the largest and most recognized global corporations. It faces nearly every type of risk a company can have. The following section taken from its 1999 annual report tells its shareholders how the company manages its risks and how it reports its derivatives transactions. Notice that not only does the company do extensive hedging using derivatives, but it also reports its Value at Risk.

FINANCIAL RISK MANAGEMENT

Our Company uses derivative financial instruments primarily to reduce our exposure to adverse fluctuations in interest rates and foreign exchange rates and, to a lesser extent, adverse fluctuations in commodity prices and other market risks. We do not enter into derivative financial instruments for trading purposes. As a matter of policy, all our derivative positions are used to reduce risk by hedging an underlying economic exposure. Because of the high correlation between the hedging instrument and the underlying exposure, fluctuations in the value of the instruments are generally offset by reciprocal changes in the value of the underlying exposure. The derivatives we use are straightforward instruments with liquid markets.

Our Company monitors our exposure to financial market risks using several objective measurement systems, including value-at-risk models. For the value-at-risk calculations discussed below, we used a historical simulation model to estimate potential future losses our Company could incur as a result of adverse movements in foreign currency and interest rates. We have not considered the potential impact of favorable movements in foreign currency and interest rates on our calculations. We examined historical weekly returns over the previous 10 years to calculate our value at risk. Our value-at-risk calculations do not represent actual losses that our Company expects to incur.

Foreign Currency

We manage most of our foreign currency exposures on a consolidated basis, which allows us to net certain exposures and take advantage of any natural offsets. With approximately 70 percent of 1999 operating income generated outside the United States, weakness in one particular currency is often offset by strengths in others over time. We use derivative financial instruments to further reduce our net exposure to currency fluctuations.

Our Company enters into forward exchange contracts and purchases currency options (principally European currencies and Japanese yen) to hedge firm sale commitments denominated in foreign currencies. We also purchase currency options (principally European currencies and Japanese yen) to hedge certain anticipated sales. Premiums paid and realized gains and losses, including those on any terminated contracts, are included in prepaid expenses and other assets. These are recognized in income, along with unrealized gains and losses, in the same period we realize the hedged transactions. Gains and losses on derivative financial instruments that are designated and effective as hedges of net investments in international operations are included in shareowners' equity as a foreign currency translation adjustment, a component of other comprehensive income.

Our value-at-risk calculation estimates foreign currency risk on our derivatives and other financial instruments. The av-

erage value at risk represents the simple average of quarterly amounts for the past year. We have not included in our calculation the effects of currency movements on anticipated foreign currency denominated sales and other hedged transactions. We performed calculations to estimate the impact to the fair values of our derivatives and other financial instruments over a one-week period resulting from an adverse movement in foreign currency exchange rates. As a result of our calculations, we estimate with 95 percent confidence that the fair values would decline by less than $71 million using 1999 average fair values and by less than $56 million using December 31, 1999, fair values. On December 31, 1998, we estimated the fair value would decline by less than $60 million. However, we would expect that any loss in the fair value of our derivatives and other financial instruments would generally be offset by an increase in the fair value of our underlying exposures.

Interest Rates

Our Company maintains our percentage of fixed and variable rate debt within defined parameters. We enter into interest rate swap agreements that maintain the fixed-to-variable mix within these parameters. We recognize any differences paid or received on interest rate swap agreements as adjustments to interest expense over the life of each swap.

Our value-at-risk calculation estimates interest rate risk on our derivatives and other financial instruments. The average value at risk represents the simple average of quarterly amounts for the past year. According to our calculations, we estimate with 95 percent confidence that any increase in our average and in our December 31, 1999, net interest expense due to an adverse move in interest rates over a one-week period would not have a material impact on our Consolidated Financial Statements. Our December 31, 1998, estimate also was not material to our Consolidated Financial Statements.

NOTE 9: HEDGING TRANSACTIONS AND DERIVATIVE FINANCIAL INSTRUMENTS

Our Company uses derivative financial instruments primarily to reduce our exposure to adverse fluctuations in interest rates and foreign exchange rates and, to a lesser extent, to reduce our exposure to adverse fluctuations in commodity prices and other market risks. When entered into, these financial instruments are designated as hedges of underlying exposures. Because of the high correlation between the hedging instrument and the underlying exposure being hedged, fluctuations in the value of the instruments are generally offset by changes in the value of the underlying exposures. Virtually all our derivatives are "over-the-counter" instruments. Our Company does not enter into derivative financial instruments for trading purposes.

The estimated fair values of derivatives used to hedge or modify our risks fluctuate over time. These fair value amounts should not be viewed in isolation, but rather in relation to the fair values of the underlying hedging transactions and investments and to the overall reduction in our exposure to adverse fluctuations in interest rates, foreign exchange rates, commodity prices and other market risks.

The notional amounts of the derivative financial instruments do not necessarily represent amounts exchanged by the parties and, therefore, are not a direct measure of our exposure from our use of derivatives. The amounts exchanged are calculated by reference to the notional amounts and by other terms of the derivatives, such as interest rates, exchange rates or other financial indices.

We have established strict counterparty credit guidelines and enter into transactions only with financial institutions of investment grade or better. We monitor counterparty exposures daily and review any downgrade in credit rating immediately. If a downgrade in the credit rating of a counterparty were to occur, we have provisions requiring collateral in the form of U.S. government securities for substantially all of our transactions. To mitigate presettlement risk, minimum credit standards become more stringent as the duration of the derivative financial instrument increases. To minimize the concentration of credit risk, we enter into derivative transactions with a portfolio of financial institutions. As a result, we consider the risk of counterparty default to be minimal.

Interest Rate Management

Our Company maintains a percentage of fixed and variable rate debt within defined parameters. We enter into interest rate swap agreements that maintain the fixed/variable mix within these parameters. These contracts had maturities ranging from one to four years on December 31, 1999. Variable rates are predominantly linked to the London Interbank Offered Rate. Any differences paid or received on interest rate swap agreements are recognized as adjustments to interest expense over the life of each swap, thereby adjusting the effective interest rate on the underlying obligation.

Foreign Currency Management

The purpose of our foreign currency hedging activities is to reduce the risk that our eventual dollar net cash inflows resulting from sales outside the United States will be adversely affected by changes in exchange rates.

We enter into forward exchange contracts and purchase currency options (principally European currencies and Japanese yen) to hedge firm sale commitments denominated in foreign currencies. We also purchase currency options (principally European currencies and Japanese yen) to hedge certain anticipated sales. Premiums paid and realized gains and losses, including those on any terminated contracts, are included in prepaid expenses and other assets. These are recognized in income, along with unrealized gains and losses in the same period the hedging transactions are realized. Approximately $85 million and $43 million of realized losses on settled contracts entered into as hedges of firmly committed transactions that have not yet occurred were deferred on December 31, 1999 and 1998, respectively. Deferred gains/losses from hedging anticipated transactions were not material on December 31, 1999 or 1998. In the unlikely event that the underlying transaction terminates or becomes improbable, the deferred gains or losses on the associated derivative will be recorded in our income statement.

Gains and losses on derivative financial instruments that are designated and effective as hedges of net investments in international operations are included in share-owners' equity as a foreign currency translation adjustment, a component of accumulated other comprehensive income.

The following table presents the aggregate notional principal amounts, carrying values, fair values and maturities of our derivative financial instruments outstanding on December 31, 1999 and 1998 (in millions):

December 31,	Notional Principal Amounts	Carrying Values	Fair Values	Maturity
1999				
Interest rate management				
Swap agreements				
Assets	$ 250	$ 2	$ 6	2000–2003
Liabilities	200	(1)	(8)	2000–2003
Foreign currency management				
Forward contracts				
Assets	1,108	57	71	2000–2001
Liabilities	344	(6)	(3)	2000–2001
Swap agreements				
Assets	102	9	16	2000
Liabilities	412	—	(77)	2000–2002
Purchased options				
Assets	1,770	47	18	2000
Other				
Assets	185	—	2	2000
Liabilities	126	(8)	(8)	2000
	$ 4,497	$ 100	$ 17	

December 31,	Notional Principal Amounts	Carrying Values	Fair Values	Maturity
1998				
Interest rate management				
Swap agreements				
Assets	$ 325	$ 2	$ 19	1999–2003
Liabilities	200	(2)	(13)	2000–2003
Foreign currency management				
Forward contracts				
Assets	809	6	(54)	1999–2000
Liabilities	1,325	(6)	(73)	1999–2000
Swap agreements				
Assets	344	4	6	1999–2000
Liabilities	704	—	(51)	1999–2002
Purchased options				
Assets	232	5	3	1999
Other				
Liabilities	243	(25)	(26)	1999–2000
	$ 4,182	$ (16)	$ (189)	

Maturities of derivative financial instruments held on December 31, 1999, are as follows (in millions):

2000	2001	2002	2003
$ 4,018	$ 268	$ 136	$ 75

Accounting for Derivatives

One of the most controversial issues in the derivatives world is the proper accounting treatment of derivatives transactions. Because of the unusual characteristics of many derivatives and the relative newness of many of these instruments, the accounting profession has not, until recent years, begun to catch up with the derivatives world. For many years derivatives were off-balance-sheet items, meaning that it was difficult, if not impossible, to determine from traditional financial statements what types of derivatives were being used and the effects of those derivative transactions on earnings. Much of the problem stems from the fact that the most widely used and accepted application of derivatives, hedging, leads to considerable complications in accounting. Hedges often generate cash losses and gains while the transactions they are designed to hedge generate only paper gains and losses. If derivative gains and losses are realized and reflected in income statements while gains and losses on the transactions they are designed to hedge are not realized until later, a hedge, which is designed to reduce volatility, will give the appearance through accounting statements of an increase in volatility.

Hedge accounting is a method of accounting for derivatives transactions such that gains and losses on the derivatives are tied to gains and losses on the instruments being hedged.

One solution to the problem is to use **hedge accounting.** Hedge accounting permits the firm to defer the gains and losses on the derivative until later when the hedge is completed. For example, a firm that holds a stock and hedges its future sale with a derivative would not recognize the derivative gains and losses until the security is actually sold. Unfortunately, hedge accounting can lead to abuses that mislead users of financial statements. For example, suppose a firm plans to borrow money at a later date. It enters into a derivative to hedge any increase in interest rates. Suppose it incurs a gain on the derivative resulting from an increase in interest rates. Then suppose it ultimately decides not to borrow the money. It records a profit on the derivative and does not take out the loan. Had it incurred a loss on the derivative, it might well have gone ahead and borrowed, imbedding the derivatives loss in the higher interest rate on the loan. Was this even a hedge? Probably not because there was clearly no firm commitment to borrow. Yet hedge accounting was used.

Swaps, forwards, and futures pose an interesting issue in derivatives accounting. They have a zero value at the start and yet gain and lose value as the underlying moves. As the derivative gains value, it effectively becomes an asset; as it loses value, it effectively becomes a liability. Should that asset/liability be shown on the balance sheet? The practice of good accounting suggests that it should. But how?

In the United States the appropriate methods for accounting are established by the Financial Accounting Standards Board (FASB). A worldwide organization, the International Accounting Standards Committee (IASC) attempts to coordinate and standardize accounting principles across countries. Neither of these bodies has any legal authority. They simply represent efforts on the part of the accounting profession to establish acceptable norms. Auditors' reports must indicate whether established accounting norms have been followed. For publicly traded companies, the securities regulators, such as the Securities and Exchange Commission in the United States, require certain standards and prohibit misleading information in accounting statements. Thus, while accounting standards technically carry no legal weight, they effectively constitute a rule of law.

In 1996 the FASB undertook a project to study and establish standards for accounting for derivatives. This culminated in the release in 1998 of Financial Accounting Standard 133, called **FAS 133,** *Accounting for Derivative Instruments and Hedging Activities.* This controversial document has undergone much scrutiny and criticism but has survived and appears to be the norm to which derivatives accounting will conform. Here we shall look at the important elements of FAS 133, which goes into effect for most firms in June 2000. The International Accounting Standards Committee adopted a similar document, IAS 39, which is somewhat broader in that it applies to all financial assets and liabilities while FAS 133 applies only to derivatives.

FAS 133 basically takes the position that all derivatives transactions will be marked to market, meaning that the gains and losses incurred from derivatives transactions over the accounting period will be determined, regardless of whether the derivative transaction has been terminated, and reported in financial statements. In addition, derivatives will appear on the balance sheet as assets and liabilities. But first, FAS 133 had to define what a derivative is.

> *Under FAS 133 a derivative has one or more underlyings and one or more notional amounts, which combine to determine the settlement or payoff. It must require either no initial outlay or an outlay that is smaller than would be required for other contracts with similar payoffs. In addition it requires a net settlement or physical delivery of the underlying.*

FAS 133 is the policy of the U.S. Financial Accounting Standards Board that specifies appropriate procedures for accounting for derivatives.

FAS 133 permits some exceptions to the rule. For example, purchases of assets on time are not derivatives. The purchase of assets with payment to occur very shortly are not derivatives. Insurance is not a derivative. Options used in executive compensation are not derivatives, at least not with respect to the regulations prescribed by FAS 133; these instruments do, however, have their own accounting requirements. Certain imbedded derivatives may or may not be derivatives. For example, interest-only and principal-only strips are not generally derivatives, but options imbedded in certain floating-rate securities may be considered derivatives and, therefore, may have to be separated and conform to FAS 133.

FAS 133 classifies all derivatives transactions into one of four categories: fair value hedges, cash flow hedges, net investment in foreign currency operations, and speculation.

A fair value hedge is one in which the derivative and the instrument being hedged are both marked to market and gains and losses on both are recorded in current income.

FAIR VALUE HEDGES   A **fair value hedge** is a transaction in which a firm hedges the market value of a position in an asset or a liability. The gain or loss on the derivative is recorded and reflected in current earnings. In addition, the asset or liability is marked to market and its gain or loss is also reflected in current earnings.

For example, a firm holds a security and enters into a derivative transaction to hedge the future sale of the security. At the end of the quarter the firm is preparing its financial statements and the hedge is still in place. Let us say it realizes a loss in value of the security of $100,000. Its derivative, however, incurs a gain of $96,000. It records the following accounting entries:

Debit Derivative (e.g., swap, futures, etc.)	96,000
Credit Unrealized Gain on Derivative	96,000
Debit Unrealized Loss on Security	100,000
Credit Security	100,000

Remember that debits increase and credits decrease assets, and debits decrease and credits increase liabilities and capital. Credits increase and debits decrease income. Thus, in the first entry, an asset account (the derivative) is increased and income (the unrealized gain) is increased. In the second entry, income is decreased (the unrealized loss) and an asset (the security) is decreased. The net effect is that income is decreased by 4,000 and assets decrease by 4,000.

If the hedge is effective, it will have little effect on income and, therefore, on earnings. Otherwise, earnings will fluctuate. Hence, effective and ineffective hedging will be properly reflected in earnings.

To qualify for fair value accounting, firms must maintain proper documentation of every transaction and the hedge must be expected to be effective. The sale of options, however, is ordinarily not eligible for fair value accounting. In addition bonds that are expected to be held to maturity are not eligible for hedge accounting. Certain anticipated transactions, however, can be eligible for hedge accounting, though many of these will fall under the following category.

CASH FLOW HEDGES   In a **cash flow hedge,** the risk of a future cash flow is hedged with a derivative. A classic example is a firm planning to take out a loan. It might sell a Eurodollar futures or buy an FRA to hedge the risk of an increase in interest rates. Cash flow hedging is somewhat more complicated than fair value hedging and must meet a more stringent requirement.

In a cash flow hedge, the firm marks the derivative to market, thereby recognizing the gain or loss in its value. The derivative will then show up on the balance sheet at its current market value. The firm then records that gain or loss in a separate category called Other Comprehensive Income or

OCI. OCI is not an ordinary income account; it is actually a capital account and appears next to equity in the balance sheet. Thus, gains and losses on derivatives go into capital. Then, at the hedge termination date, the underlying transaction, such as the firm taking out a loan, is completed. Then the derivative is removed from the books and the amount recorded to OCI is moved from OCI and adjusts the value of the underlying transaction as well as showing up in earnings. Thus, derivatives gains and losses do not affect income while the hedge is in place but instead show up in a temporary holding account that appears as a part of capital. Ultimately, the transaction the derivative is designed to hedge is undertaken, and the derivatives gain or loss is moved to income as well as to the underlying transaction. In addition, cash flow hedge accounting requires a separation of a hedge's results into "effective" and "ineffective" components.

Let us consider an example of a loan that the firm anticipates. Suppose that six months from now the firm plans to issue a $1,000,000 one-year zero coupon note. It buys an FRA to hedge against rising interest rates. While the hedge is in place interest rates go down and the FRA incurs a loss of $10,000. Eventually the FRA expires with a loss of $12,000 and the note is issued. The firm issues the note at 7 percent for one year, thereby generating an initial cash inflow of $(1 - .07)\$1,000,000 = \$930,000$. With cash flow hedging, there would be an interim transaction of

Debit Other Comprehensive Income	10,000
Credit FRA	10,000

with the FRA showing up on the liability side. When the loan is taken out, the transactions are

Debit Cash	930,000
Credit Notes Payable	930,000
Debit FRA	10,000
Debit Other Comprehensive Income	2,000
Credit Cash	12,000
Debit Notes Payable	12,000
Credit Other Comprehensive Income	12,000

The first entry reflects the fact that a note was issued for $930,000 and cash was received. In the second entry, the FRA is removed from the books as a liability and a further 2,000 loss is recorded in Other Comprehensive Income. Cash of $12,000 is expended to cover the payout on the FRA. In the third entry, Other Comprehensive Income is zeroed out and the note balance is reduced from $930,000 to $918,000. In other words, we have now effectively borrowed $918,000 and will later owe $1 million.

Suppose, however, that this were not a perfect hedge. Assume that at the interim period, the loss was $11,000 but the effective part of the loss was

$10,000. Thus, there is an ineffective part of the hedge that resulted in a loss of $1,000. We would record the following entry:

Debit Current Income	1,000
Debit Other Comprehensive Income	10,000
Credit FRA	11,000

At expiration, let us say the cumulative loss on the FRA is $15,000 and of that amount, $12,000 is effective and $3,000 is ineffective. The first entry above for the $930,000 note is the same. The next two entries become:

Debit FRA	11,000
Credit Other Comprehensive Income	11,000
Debit Current Income	2,000
Debit Other Comprehensive Income	1,000
Debit Notes Payable	12,000
Credit Cash	15,000

The first entry above removes the FRA from liabilities and removes all but $1,000 of the Other Comprehensive Income account. The third entry zeroes out Other Comprehensive Income and reduces Current Income by $2,000. Notes Payable will go from $930,000 to $918,000, reflecting the loss of $12,000 as the effective part of the hedge. The ineffective part is $2,000, which goes into Current Income and combines with the $1,000 previously added to Current Income in the earlier entry to reflect a $3,000 loss for the ineffective part of the hedge.

A cash flow hedge is one in which a future cash flow is hedged. Derivatives are marked to market and gains and losses are recorded to a temporary capital account until the hedge is completed. Hedging gains and losses must be separated into effective and ineffective components.

As noted, cash flow hedging requires a separation of the effective and ineffective parts of hedging. The effective part is deferred and carried in the equity account whereas the ineffective part must be recorded immediately into income. The FASB has not prescribed precisely how the effective and ineffective components are to be separated. Rough rules of thumb have emerged suggesting that an effective hedge is one in which 80 to 125 percent of the gain or loss on the hedged instrument is matched with a gain or loss on the derivative. Nonetheless, the rules are still murky here and cash flow accounting remains somewhat more difficult to use, even though a firm may have no choice in whether it has to use it. In particular, futures, where maturities do not line up perfectly with hedge termination dates, are more likely to be ineffective hedges—at least by FASB rules—and, therefore, may lead to more volatile earnings.

As with fair value hedges, cash flow hedges must be well documented at the start and must be expected to be effective, and firms must specify how they will determine the hedge's effectiveness. Anticipated transactions must be highly likely to occur and the details of the transaction must be spelled out quite specifically. Generally, written options do not qualify.

FOREIGN INVESTMENT HEDGES   Foreign currency hedging had already been treated in Statement of Financial Accounting Standard 52 (SFAS 52), a document released a number of years prior to the release of FAS 133. The primary rules in SFAS 52 were retained. Firms often hedge currency translations of their foreign operations. These hedges are permitted and qualify for hedge accounting if certain conditions are met. Those conditions are similar to those we have previously identified. The hedges must be documented and expected to be effective. Measurement criteria for effectiveness must be clearly specified. Foreign currency hedges not designed to hedge translation can still qualify for fair value or cash flow accounting under the criteria listed above.

SPECULATION   Trades that do not qualify for fair value, cash flow, or foreign currency hedge accounting must be considered speculation. Derivatives are marked to market and gains and losses are recorded in current income with no offsetting adjustments to any other accounts.

SOME PROBLEMS IN THE APPLICATION OF FAS 133   One area in particular in which FAS 133 creates problems is in the use of purchased options to hedge. FAS 133 requires that for options, only the intrinsic value qualifies for hedge accounting. Thus, in a cash flow hedge, changes in the intrinsic value go into the effective portion of the hedge, thereby going into OCI and not affecting income until the underlying transaction is completed. Changes in the time value are considered ineffective and will go directly into income, causing earnings volatility. Problems also exist when options are used in fair value hedges. Since an option moves less than the value of the underlying, income will fluctuate as the underlying moves more than the value of the option. Consequently, FAS 133 may have the effect of discouraging the use of purchased options. This can have a serious impact on such strategies as protective puts and interest rate caps.

As noted, FASB does not prescribe what constitutes effective hedging. Thus, there is some fear that restatements of earnings will be required if later it is determined that the effectiveness test used by a firm is not acceptable.

FAS 133 also requires that some embedded derivatives be stripped out and valued. This can be quite complex.

FAS 133 does not permit hedge accounting for bonds designed to be held to maturity. It reflects the all-too-common and naive view that as long as a bond is to be held to maturity, any losses in value are ultimately recouped. This ruling overlooks the opportunity cost of holding a bond in an environment of higher interest rates. It reflects, not surprisingly, an accounting view of a transaction rather than an economic view.

Under FAS 133 valuation of derivative instruments and the hedged instrument is critical. Although we have placed a great deal of emphasis on valuation in this book, it is not a simple task for a firm to obtain a reliable value for a derivative or for the hedged instrument. Nonetheless, if FAS 133 forces firms to pay attention to market values of derivatives and hedged instruments, it probably serves a good purpose.

FAS 133 does not permit macro hedges. In a macro hedge, a firm takes all of its positions into account and hedges the net exposure. For example, a firm may have exposures to a variety of asset classes. Due to correlations among those asset classes, there may be considerable risk reduction. The firm may then choose to hedge only the remaining risk. Yet, such hedges will now no longer qualify for hedge accounting. Hedges must be transaction specific.

Finally, one of the most popular hedging strategies, the covered call, does not qualify for hedge accounting treatment. Any gains or losses on the call go into current earnings while gains or losses on the security go into OCI. This practice could discourage one of the simplest forms of hedging or make it result in misleading and more volatile accounting earnings.

The U.S. Securities and Exchange Commission requires that publicly traded firms provide qualitative and quantitative disclosures of their derivatives and risk management activities.

DISCLOSURE   Closely related to the issue of accounting for derivatives is the matter of how much information about a firm's use of derivatives is disclosed in annual reports and 10-Ks. In 1997 the U.S. Securities and Exchange Commission ordered that large firms and banks would be required to provide more disclosure of their accounting policies with respect to derivatives; more quantitative and qualitative information about their market risk; and more information about instruments used, positions taken, commitments, and expected transactions. Companies must categorize their derivatives into one of two categories: trading, meaning essentially speculative, and non-trading, meaning essentially hedging.

For their quantitative disclosure, companies must present either (1) tabular information on the market values of their derivatives and relevant contract terms categorized by expiration date, (2) sensitivity analysis of potential losses, or (3) the Value at Risk. For their qualitative disclosure, companies must identify their primary exposures and how they manage those exposures.

The SEC's disclosure requirements have been controversial, requiring that firms reveal information that could be useful to competitors. Moreover, the requirement that firms reveal their financial risks and how they manage them overlooks the fact that firms face a variety of nonfinancial risks, which they are not required to disclose. For example, an airline faces the risk of a crash, resulting in catastrophic human and financial loss. Yet, it is not required to disclose how it manages that risk or what the effect of a crash would be on its VAR. Such rules have the potential for penalizing users who are prudently managing their financial risks.

Avoiding Derivatives Losses

As we have seen throughout this book, derivatives are highly efficient instruments that can be used to manage risk. Nonetheless, part of the price we pay for such instruments is that they are highly leveraged and can be easily misused. Since every derivative generates a gain that is matched by a loss on the other side of the transaction, someone must lose money. In some cases, those losses have been large and surprising to those who incurred the losses. Large losses also tend to make for good headlines, and, consequently, many firms have found themselves embarrassingly portrayed on the front pages of newspapers. Table 16.5 contains a partial list of well-known derivatives losses incurred by organizations since 1988. The losses have ranged from small amounts to almost unbelievably large sums of money. The types of organizations and derivatives used have run the gamut. Fortunately, the incidence of losses, which seemed to peak around 1994, has decreased in recent years. Four of the most celebrated stories of

TABLE 16.5   **Partial List of Organizations Reporting Derivatives Losses**

Time	Organization	Size of Losses	Transactions
1988	Hammersmith and Fulham	£500 million	swaps
March 1991	Allied Lyons	£150 million	currency options
November 1992	Dell Computer	$8 million	currency options and forwards
February 1993	Showa Shell Shekiyu	¥165 billion	currency options and forwards
December 1993	Metallgesellschaft	$1.3 billion	energy futures
January 1994	Codelco	$207 million	copper futures
March 1994	Cargill (Minnetonka Fund)	$100 million	mortgage derivatives
March 1994	Gibson Greetings	$20 million	interest rate swaps
April 1994	Kashima Oil	$1.5 billion	currency derivatives
April 1994	Mead	$12.1 million	interest rate swap
April 1994	Procter & Gamble	$157 million	interest rate and currency swaps
April 1994	Askin Capital Management	$600 million	repurchase agreements and mortgage derivatives
May 1994	Air Products and Chemicals	$113 million	interest rate and currency swaps
May 1994	Sandoz	$78.5 million	misc. derivatives
May 1994	Dell Computer	$34.6 million	options and leveraged swaps
May 1994	Arco Money Market Plus Fund	$22 million	misc. derivatives
June 1994	International Family Entertainment	$2 million	misc. derivatives
June 1994	Paine Webber Bond Mutual Fund	$33 million	mortgage derivatives
June 1994	Investors Equity Life Insurance Co. of Hawaii	$90 million	bond futures
June 1994	Bank of Montreal's Harris Trust and Savings Bank	$51.3 million	mortgage derivatives
July 1994	CS First Boston Investment Management	$40 million	misc. derivatives
July 1994	Glaxo	£115 million	mortgage derivatives
July 1994	Federal Paper	$19 million	currency derivatives
August 1994	Caterpillar Financial	$13.2 million	interest rate caps and swaptions
August 1994	Piper Jaffray Cos.	$700 million	mortgage derivatives

(continued)

TABLE 16.5   *(continued)*

Time	Organization	Size of Losses	Transactions
September 1994	Odessa College	$11 million	mortgage derivatives
September 1994	Shoshone Indian Tribe	$5 million	mortgage derivatives
September 1994	Investors Equity Life	$90 million	futures
September 1994	Sears	$237 million	swaps
October 1994	Portage County, Ohio	$8 million	mortgage derivatives and structured notes
October 1994	Community A Management	$44 million	structured notes
November 1994	Three Farm Credit System Banks	$23 million	structured notes
December 1994	Chemical Bank	$70 million	currency derivatives
December 1994	Orange County, California	$1.6 billion	leveraged repurchase agreements
February 1995	Capital Corporate Federal Credit Union	$126 million	mortgage derivatives
February 1995	Barings PLC	£900 million	stock index futures and options
March 1995	Connecticut Pension Fund	$25 million	mortgage derivatives
March 1995	Escambia County, Florida	$19 million	mortgage derivatives
March 1995	MCN Corporation	$10 million	forwards
March 1995	State of Wisconsin Investment Board	$95 million	currency and interest rate swaps
May 1995	Five clients of Morgan Stanley	$28 million	forwards, options, repurchase agreements
June 1995	Sumitomo Bank	$1.8 billion	copper futures
July 1995	The Common Fund	$137.6 billion	stock index futures
July 1995	Westchester Jewish Center	$630,000	mortgage derivatives
July 1995	First Capital Strategists	$128 million	stock index futures
August 1995	Postipankki	$110 million	mortgage derivatives and structured notes
July 1996	BZW	£11.5 million	currency derivatives
August 1996	Seita	$29.8 million	currency swaps
February 1997	NatWest	£90 million	interest rate options

SOURCES: Information taken from a variety of sources, including various issues of *The Wall Street Journal;* Charles W. Smithson, *Managing Financial Risk: 1995 and 1996 Yearbooks* (Chase Manhattan Bank and CIBC Wood Gundy); *Euromoney,* August 1994; *Futures,* October 1995. A more complete list is provided in Brandon Becker and Jennifer Yoon, "Derivatives Financial Losses," *Journal of Corporate Law* 21 (fall 1995): 215–239.

losses, Metallgesellschaft, Orange County, Barings, and Procter & Gamble are told in the appendix to this chapter.

The experience of these organizations has undoubtedly taught many lessons that have saved other organizations from loss and embarrassment. The industry has made many efforts to establish practices that lead to effective risk management. Two notable efforts in particular are the **G-30 Report** and the **Risk Standards Working Group Report.** The G-30, which stands for Group of 30, is a private international organization of economic and financial experts who study and evaluate various issues facing the international economic community. In 1993 the G-30 issued a report on derivatives practices. The key elements of the G-30 Report are provided in Table 16.6. The report is primarily aimed at the dealer community, but also

TABLE 16.6   **The Group of 30 Recommendations on Derivatives and Risk Management Practices**

GENERAL POLICIES

Recommendation 1: The Role of Senior Management
Dealers and end users should use derivatives in a manner consistent with the overall risk management and capital policies approved by their boards of directors. These policies should be reviewed as business and market circumstances change. Policies governing derivatives use should be clearly defined, including the purposes for which these transactions are to be undertaken. Senior management should approve procedures and controls to implement these policies, and management at all levels should enforce them.

VALUATION AND MARKET-RISK MANAGEMENT

Recommendation 2: Marking to Market
Dealers should mark their derivatives positions to market, on at least a daily basis, for risk management purposes.

Recommendation 3: Market Valuation Methods
Derivatives portfolios of dealers should be valued based on mid-market levels less specific adjustments, or on appropriate bid or offer levels. Mid-market valuation adjustments should allow for expected future costs, such as unearned credit spread, closeout costs, investing and funding costs, and administrative costs.

Recommendation 4: Identifying Revenue Sources
Dealers should measure the components of revenue regularly and in sufficient detail to understand the sources of risk.

Recommendation 5: Measuring Market Risk
Dealers should use a consistent measure to calculate daily the market risk of their derivatives positions and compare it to market risk limits.

- Market risk is best measured as "value at risk" using probability analysis based upon a common confidence interval (e.g., two standard deviations) and time horizon (e.g., one-day exposure).

- Components of market risk that should be considered across the term structure include: absolute price or rate change (delta); convexity (gamma); volatility (vega); time decay (theta); basis or correlation; and discount rate (rho).

Recommendation 6: Stress Simulation
Dealers should periodically perform simulations to determine how their portfolios would perform under stress conditions.

Recommendation 7: Investing and Funding Forecasts
Dealers should periodically forecast the cash investing and funding requirements arising from their derivatives portfolios.

Recommendation 8: Independent Market-Risk Management
Dealers should have a market-risk management function, with clear independence and authority, to ensure that the following responsibilities are carried out:

- The development of risk limit policies and the monitoring of transactions and positions for adherence to these policies. (See Recommendation 5.)

- The design of stress scenarios to measure the impact of market conditions, however improbable, that might cause market gaps, volatility swings, or disruptions of major relationships, or might reduce liquidity in the face of unfavorable market linkages, concentrated market making, or credit exhaustion. (See Recommendation 6.)

- The design of revenue reports quantifying the contribution of various risk components, and of market-risk measures such as value at risk. (See Recommendations 4 and 5.)

- The monitoring of variance between the actual volatility of portfolio value and that predicted by the measure of market risk.

- The review and approval of pricing models and valuation systems used by front- and back-office personnel, and the development of reconciliation procedures if different systems are used.

(continued)

TABLE 16.6 *(continued)*

Recommendation 9: Practices by End Users
As appropriate to the nature, size, and complexity of their derivatives activities, end users should adopt the same valuation and market-risk management practices that are recommended for dealers. Specifically they should consider regularly marketing to market their derivatives transactions for risk-management purposes; periodically forecasting the cash investing and funding requirements arising from their derivatives transactions; and establishing a clearly independent and authoritative function to design and assure adherence to prudent risk limits.

CREDIT RISK MEASUREMENT AND MANAGEMENT

Recommendation 10: measuring Credit Exposure
Dealers and end users should measure credit exposure on derivatives in two ways:

- Current exposure, which is the replacement cost of derivative transactions, that is, their market value, and
- Potential exposure, which is an estimate of the future replacement cost of derivatives transactions. It should be calculated using probability analysis based upon broad confidence intervals (e.g., two standard deviations) over the remaining terms of the transactions.

Recommendation 11: Aggregating Credit Exposures
Credit exposures on derivatives, and all other credit exposures to a counterparty, should be aggregated taking into consideration enforceable netting arrangements. Credit exposures should be calculated regularly and compared to credit limits.

Recommendation 12: Independent Credit Risk Management
Dealers and end users should have a credit risk management function with clear independence and authority, and with analytical capabilities in derivatives, responsible for

- Approving credit exposure measurement demands.
- Setting credit limits and monitoring their use.
- Reviewing credits and concentrations of credit risk.
- Reviewing and monitoring risk-reduction arrangements.

Recommendation 13: Master Agreements
Dealers and end users are encouraged to use one master agreement as widely as possible with each counterparty to document existing and future derivatives transactions, including foreign-exchange forwards and options. Master agreements should provide for payments netting and close-out netting, using a full two-way payments approach.

Recommendation 14: Credit Enhancement
Dealers and end users should assess both the benefits and costs of credit enhancement and risk-reduction arrangements. Where it is proposed that credit downgrades would trigger early termination or collateral requirements, participants should carefully consider their own capacity and that of their counterparties to meet the potentially substantial funding needs that might result.

ENFORCEABILITY

Recommendation 15: promoting Enforceability
Dealers and end users should work together on a continuing basis to identify and recommend solutions for issues of legal enforceability, both within and across jurisdictions, as activities evolve and new types of securities are developed.

SYSTEMS, OPERATIONS, AND CONTROLS

Recommendation 16: Professional Expertise
Dealers and end users must ensure that their derivatives activities are undertaken by professionals in sufficient number and with the appropriate experience, skill levels, and degrees of specialization. These professionals include specialists who transact and manage the risks involved, their supervisors, and those responsible for processing, reporting, controlling, and auditing the activities.

TABLE 16.6   *(continued)*

Recommendation 17: Systems
Dealers and end users must ensure that adequate systems for data capture, processing, settlement, and management reporting are in place so that derivatives transactions are conducted in an orderly and efficient manner in compliance with management policies. Dealers should have risk-management systems that measure the risks incurred in their derivatives activities including market and credit risks. End users should have risk-management systems that measure the risks incurred in their derivatives activities based upon their nature, size, and complexity.

Recommendation 18: Authority
Management of dealers and end users should delegate who is authorized to commit their institutions to derivatives transactions.

ACCOUNTING AND DISCLOSURE

Recommendation 19: Accounting Policies
International harmonization of accounting standards for derivatives is desirable. Pending the adoption of harmonized standards, the following accounting practices are recommended:

- Dealers should account for derivatives transactions by marking them to market, taking changes in value to income each period.
- End users should account for derivatives used to manage risks so as to achieve a consistency of income recognition treatment between those instruments and the risks being managed. Thus, if the risk being managed is accounted for at cost (or, in the case of an anticipatory hedged, not yet recognized), changes in the value of a qualifying risk-management instrument should be deferred until a gain or loss is recognized on the risk being managed. Or, if the risk being managed is marked to market with changes in value being taken to income, a qualifying risk-management instrument should be treated in a comparable fashion.
- End users should account for derivatives not qualifying for risk-management treatment on a mark-to-market basis.
- Amounts due to and from counterparties should only be offset when there is a legal right to set off or when enforceable netting arrangements are in place.
- Where local regulations prevent adoption of these practices, disclosure along these lines is nevertheless recommended.

Recommendation 20: Disclosures
Financial statements of dealers and end users should contain sufficient information about their use of derivatives to provide an understanding of the purposes for which transactions are undertaken, the extent of the transactions, the degree of risk involved, and how the transactions have been accounted for. Pending the adoption of harmonized accounting standards, the following disclosures are recommended:

- Information about management's attitude to financial risk, how instruments are used, and how risks are monitored and controlled.
- Accounting policies.
- Analysis of position at the balance-sheet date.
- Analysis of the credit risk inherent in those positions.
- For dealers only, additional information about the extent of their activities in financial instruments.

RECOMMENDATIONS FOR LEGISLATIORS, REGULATORS, AND SUPERVISORS

Recommendation 21: Recognizing Netting
Regulators and supervisors should recognize the benefits of netting arrangements where and to the full extent that they are enforceable, and encourage their use by reflecting these arrangements in capital adequacy standards. Specifically, they should promptly implement the recognition of the effectiveness of bilateral close-out netting in bank capital regulations.

(continued)

TABLE 16.6   *(continued)*

Recommendation 22: Legal and Regulatory Uncertainties
Legislators, regulators, and supervisors, including central banks, should work in concert with dealers and end users to identify and remove any remaining legal and regulatory uncertainties with respect to:

- The form of documentation required to create legally enforceable agreements (stature of frauds).
- The capacity of parties, such as governmental entities, insurance companies, pension funds, and building societies, to enter into transactions (ultra vires).
- The enforceability of bilateral close-out netting and collateral arrangements in bankruptcy.
- The enforceability of multibranch netting arrangements in bankruptcy.
- The legality/enforceability of derivatives transactions.

Recommendation 23: Tax Treatment
Legislators and tax authorities are encouraged to review and, where appropriate, amend tax laws and regulations that disadvantage the use of derivatives in risk-management strategies. Tax impediments include the inconsistent or uncertain tax treatment of gains and losses on the derivatives, in comparison with the gains and losses that arise from the risks being managed.

Recommendation 24: Accounting Standards
Accounting standards-setting bodies in each country should, as a matter of priority, provide comprehensive guidance on accounting and reporting of transactions in financial instruments, including derivatives, and should work toward harmonization of standards on this subject. Also, the International Accounting Standards Committee should finalize its accounting standard on financial instruments.

SOURCE: The Group of Thirty, *Derivatives: Practices and Principles* (1993).

contains recommendations for end users and even for regulators. The report emphasizes the importance of senior management's involvement in the process and the necessity for having an effective and independent risk management system in place. Note also the importance of such concepts as VAR, delta, gamma, and vega, the need for market *and* credit risk management, and the emphasis on netting.

The Risk Standards Working Group is an informal committee of consultants and practitioners from the institutional investment industry, which largely consists of pension funds. The group's efforts are directed toward improving risk management in the investment management business. The essential recommendations of the Risk Standards report are provided in Table 16.7. The report's emphasis is similar to that of the G-30 Report, but adapted to investment management organizations.

The risk management industry has made substantial progress in improving the practice of risk management. Though much has been learned from mistakes, much has also been learned from research and practice. Today risk management is firmly established as a serious profession that makes a significant contribution to global society.

TABLE 16.7	Risk Standards Working Group on Recommendations on Derivatives and Risk Management Practices for Institutional Investors

I. Management

Risk Standard 1: Acknowledgement of fiduciary responsibility
Fiduciary responsibilities should be defined in writing and acknowledged in writing by the parties responsible.

Risk Standard 2: Approved written policies, definitions, guidelines and investment documentation
The Primary and Manager Fiduciaries should approve formal written policies which reflect their overall risk management objectives. The Primary and Manager Fiduciaries also should approve investment guidelines, management agreements and all other contracts that govern investments. Technical terms should be defined. All policies, definitions, guidelines and investment documentation should be reviewed and updated as appropriate and more often if significant market events or changes in strategy occur.

Risk Standard 3: Independent risk oversight, checks and balances, written procedures and controls
Oversight of compliance with risk policies should be independent of line investment activity and conducted according to up-to-date, written policies and procedures. Front, middle, and back office activities should be separate wherever possible and sufficient checks and balances and appropriate controls should exist. When separation is not possible due to limited staff, alternative checks, balances and controls should be established.

Risk Standard 4: Clearly defined organizational structure and key roles
Organizational structure and reporting lines should be defined clearly and distributed to all parties. Key personnel and their roles in all front, middle and back office areas should be identified. Changes in key personnel should be communicated immediately to all relevant parties.

Risk Standard 5: Consistent application of risk policies
The Primary Fiduciary's risk policies should apply both to internal and external managers and should be consistent across similar asset classes and strategies.

Risk Standard 6: Adequate education, systems and resources, back-up and disaster recovery plans
The Primary and Manager Fiduciaries should ensure that adequate education, systems and resources are available to implement and administer their risk policies. They should also establish and test back-up procedures and disaster recovery plans.

Risk Standard 7: Identification and understanding of key risks
Risks should be analyzed to determine relevancy. This entails understanding strategies and their vulnerabilities, as well as assumptions built into an instrument, system, process, model or strategy. Key risks should be reviewed periodically as well as when significant events occur.

Risk Standard 8: Setting risk limits
Risk limits should be set for the aggregate portfolio and all individual portfolios. These may include limits on asset classes, individual instruments and specific types of risk.

Risk Standard 9: Routine reporting, exception reporting, and escalation procedures
The Primary and Manager Fiduciaries should specify what positions, risks and other information must be reported and to whom. This policy also should define what constitutes required reporting or an exception to guidelines, to whom the exception should be reported, what action must be taken for different levels of violation and what procedures must be followed for ongoing or increased violations.

II. Measurement

Risk Standard 10: Valuation procedures
All readily priced instruments should be valued daily, less-readily priced instruments at least weekly and non-readily priced instruments as often as feasible and whenever a material event occurs. The pricing mechanism and methodologies must be known, understood, follow written policies and be applied consistently by the Primary and Manager Fiduciaries, Managers, custodian and other subcontractors.

(continued)

TABLE 16.7   *(continued)*

Risk Standard 11: Valuation reconciliation, bid/offer adjustments and overrides
Material discrepancies in valuations from different sources should be reconciled following established procedures. A procedure for bid/offer adjustments and overrides to valuations should be established in writing and monitored independently.

Risk Standard 12: Risk measurement and risk/return attribution analysis
The Primary and Manager Fiduciaries should regularly measure relevant risks and quantify the key drivers of risk and return.

Risk Standard 13: Risk-adjusted return measures
Risk-adjusted returns should be measured at the aggregate and individual portfolio level to gain a true measure of relative performance.

Risk Standard 14: Stress testing
Simulation or other stress tests should be performed to ascertain how the aggregate portfolio and individual portfolios would behave under various conditions. These include changes in key risk factors, correlations or other key assumptions and unusual events such as large market moves.

Risk Standard 15: Back testing
Risk and return forecasts and models should be back tested at least quarterly and whenever material events occur to assess their reliability.

Risk Standard 16: Assessing model risk
Dependence on models and assumptions for valuation, risk measurement and risk management should be evaluated and monitored.

III. Oversight

Risk Standard 17: Due diligence, policy compliance and guideline monitoring
The Primary and Manager Fiduciaries should perform frequent, independent reviews of all Managers' risk policies and controls. Where policies and controls fall short of the requirements set forth by the Primary or Manager Fiduciaries, plans for future compliance or corrective action should be documented and communicated. Managers should ensure continuing compliance with their clients' risk policies and guidelines.

Risk Standard 18: Comparison of Manager strategies to compensation and investment activity
The Primary Fiduciary should require each Manager to submit a statement of strategy and ensure that the Manager's activities and compensation are consistent with that strategy. Key risk and return factors should be documented and reviewed at least annually and updated whenever the strategy changes.

Risk Standard 19: Independent review of methodologies, models and systems
All methodologies, models and related systems should be independently reviewed or audited prior to use as well as annually. Significant market moves or changes in market practice should trigger interim reviews.

Risk Standard 20: Review process for new activities
The Primary and Manager Fiduciaries should document the review process for permitting the use of new instruments, strategies or asset classes. Policies for initiating new activities should be consistent with the Primary and Manager Fiduciaries' risk and return goals as well as the Manager's strategy and expertise.

SOURCE: Capital Market Risk Advisors, www.cmra.com.

Summary

In this concluding chapter we have looked at the concept of risk management, meaning to determine the appropriate level of risk, to determine the level of risk a firm currently has, and to take action to ensure that the former is equal to the latter. We examined the risk management industry and noted the differences between how end users and dealers approach risk management.

We looked at some techniques for managing market risk, including delta, gamma, and vega hedging. We also examined the concept of Value at Risk (VAR), which measures the minimum loss expected over a period of time with a given probability. VAR is becoming widely used in the financial world today. We also looked at credit risk, noting how current risk differs from potential risk, and we examined some procedures for reducing credit risk, including the netting of payments owed by parties to each other, and the use of credit derivatives to separate and trade the credit risk. We looked at various other types of risks, including operational risk, model risk, liquidity risk, accounting risk, legal risk, tax risk, regulatory risk, and settlement risk. From a broader perspective, we discussed systemic risk, which is the risk of a meltdown of the entire financial system. We looked at procedures and practices for ensuring that an organizational structure is conducive to effective risk management. We examined the procedures for accounting for derivatives under the new FAS 133. We looked at the recommendations of the Group of 30 and the Risk Standards Working Group on best practices for risk management.

This book has brought you on a tour of the world of derivatives. As you no doubt feel, the subject is a complex one, but you now have the tools to move on to further study of this fascinating subject. When the time comes that you execute your first derivatives trade, it is hoped that you will ask yourself one simple question: Am I practicing risk management?

Key Terms

You should be able to give brief definitions of the following terms.

- risk management/financial risk management
- multilateral netting
- payment netting
- end user
- dealer
- market risk
- Value at Risk (VAR)
- analytical/variance-covariance/ delta normal method
- historical method
- Monte Carlo simulation method
- stress test
- credit/default risk
- current credit risk
- potential credit risk
- enhanced derivatives product company/special purpose vehicles
- netting
- bilateral netting
- cross payment netting
- netting by novation
- credit derivative
- total return swap
- credit swap/credit default swap
- credit spread option
- credit linked security
- credit event
- closeout netting
- operational risk
- model risk

- liquidity risk
- accounting risk
- legal risk
- tax risk
- regulatory risk
- settlement/Herstatt risk
- systemic risk
- front office
- back office
- hedge accounting
- FAS 133
- fair value hedge
- cash flow hedge
- foreign investment/currency hedge
- G-30 Report
- Risk Standards Working Group Report

Further Reading

Risk management in general:

Chew, L. *Managing Derivatives Risk: The Use and Abuse of Leverage.* New York: Wiley, 1996.

Gastineau, G. L., and M. P. Kritzman. *The Dictionary of Financial Risk Management*, 2d ed. New Hope, PA: Frank Fabozzi Associates, 1999.

Smithson, Charles W. *Managing Financial Risk: A Guide to Derivative Products, Financial Engineering, and Value Maximization*, 3d ed. New York: McGraw-Hill, 1998.

The following are good references on credit risk and credit derivatives:

Risk Books. *Credit Derivatives: Applications for Risk Management, Investment and Portfolio Optimisation.* London: Risk Books, 1998.

Risk Books. *Credit Risk: Models and Management.* London: Risk Books, 1999.

Risk Books. *Derivatives Credit Risk: Further Advances in Measurement and Management*, 2d ed. London: Risk Books, 1999.

Saunders, A. *Credit Risk Measurement: New Approaches to Value-at-Risk and Other Paradigms.* New York: Wiley, 1999.

Value at Risk is widely covered in the literature. Two excellent books are:

Dowd, K. *Beyond Value at Risk: The New Science of Risk Management.* Chichester, UK: Wiley, 1998.

Jorion, P. *Value at Risk: A New Benchmark for Controlling Derivatives Risk.* Chicago: Irwin, 1996.

Some books covering accounting, legal, and organization aspects of derivatives are:

Anson, M. J. P. *Accounting and Tax Rules for Derivatives.* New Hope, PA: Frank Fabozzi Associates, 1999.

Johnson, P. M. *Derivatives: A Manager's Guide to the World's Most Powerful Financial Instruments.* New York: McGraw-Hill, 1999.

Klein, R. A., and J. Lederman. *Derivatives Risk and Responsibility*. Chicago: Irwin, 1996.

McLaughlin, R. M. *Over-the-Counter Derivative Products: A Guide to Business and Legal Risk Management and Documentation*. New York: McGraw-Hill, 1999.

Stories of some famous derivatives losses are told in:

Dunbar, N. *Inventing Money: The Story of Long-Term Capital Management and the Legends Behind It*. Chichester, UK: Wiley, 2000.

Fay, S. *The Collapse of Barings*. New York: W. W. Norton, 1997.

Jorion, P., and R. Roper. *Big Bets Gone Bad: Derivatives and Bankruptcy in Orange County*. Orlando: Academic Press, 1995.

Questions and Problems

1. How is the practice of risk management similar to hedging and how is it different?

2. Explain how the function of risk management in an end user differs from risk management in a dealer.

3. Explain the difference between market risk and credit risk. Are techniques for managing market risk appropriate for managing credit risk?

4. Answer the following questions about credit derivatives.

   a. Explain how a total return swap differs from a standard swap and how that difference is designed to capture the credit risk of an underlying bond.

   b. Explain how a credit spread option differs from an ordinary option and how that difference is designed to capture the credit risk of an underlying bond.

   c. Explain how a credit swap differs from an ordinary swap and how that difference is designed to capture the credit risk of a loan.

5. If a portfolio of derivatives is delta hedged by adding a position in Eurodollar futures, what other forms of market risk might remain? How can these risks be eliminated?

6. Interpret the following statements about Value at Risk so that they would be easily understood by a nontechnical corporate executive.

   a. VAR of $1.5 million, one week, probability = .01

   b. VAR of $3.75 million, one year, probability = .05

7. Critique each of the three methods of calculating Value at Risk, giving one advantage and one disadvantage of each.

8. Comment on the current credit risk you have for each of the following positions. Treat them separately, that is, not combined with anything else.

   a. You are short an out-of-the-money interest rate call option.

   b. You entered into a pay fixed–receive floating interest rate swap a year ago. Since that time, interest rates have increased.

   c. You are long an in-the-money currency put option.

   d. You are long a forward contract. During the life of the contract the price of the underlying asset has decreased below the contract price.

9. Explain how closeout netting reduces the credit risk for two firms engaged in several derivatives contracts.

10. How does the legal system impose risk on a derivatives dealer?

11. Explain why it is critical that the back office not be responsible to the front office in a risk-management system.

12. What role should senior management play in a risk-management system?

13. Explain how government can be a source of risk for a firm using derivatives.

14. What is Herstatt risk?

15. Suppose your firm is a derivatives dealer and has recently created a new product. In addition to market and credit risk, what additional risks does it face that are associated more with new products?

16. Explain the difference between fair value hedging and cash flow hedging.

17. What is the most important part of an effective risk-management system?

18. Consider a portfolio consisting of $10 million invested in the S&P 500 and $7.5 million invested in U.S. Treasury bonds. The S&P 500 has an expected return of 14 percent and a standard deviation of 16 percent. The Treasury bonds have an expected return of 9 percent and a standard deviation of 8 percent. The correlation between the S&P 500 and the bonds is .35. All figures are stated on an annual basis.

   a. Find the VAR for one year at a probability of .05. Identify and use the most appropriate method given the information you have.

   b. Using the information you obtained in part a, find the VAR for one day.

19. Calculate the VAR for the following situations:

   a. Use the analytical method and determine the VAR at a probability of .05 for a portfolio in which the standard deviation of annual returns is $2.5 million. Assume an expected return of $0.0.

b. Use the historical method and the following information for the last 120 days of returns to calculate an approximate VAR for a portfolio of $20 million using a probability of .05:

Less than −10%	5
−10% to −5%	18
−5% to 0%	42
0% to 5%	36
5% to 10%	15
Great than 10%	4

20. The following table lists three financial instruments with their deltas, gammas, and vegas for each $1 million notional principal under the assumption of a long position. (Long in a swap or FRA means to pay fixed and receive floating.) Assume that you hold a $12 million notional principal long position in the three-year call option, an $8 million notional principal short position in the three-year swap, and an $11 million notional principal long position in the FRA. Each derivative is based on the 90-day LIBOR.

Instrument	Delta	Gamma	Vega
3-year call option with exercise rate of .12	$40	$1,343	$5.02
3-year swap with fixed rate of .1125	$152	−$678	$0
2-year FRA with fixed rate of. 11	$72	−$390	$0

a. As described above, you have three instruments currently in your portfolio. Determine your current portfolio delta, gamma, and vega. Describe in words the risk properties of your portfolio based on your calculations.

b. Assume that you have to maintain your current position in the call option but are free to increase or decrease your positions in the swap and FRA and you can add a position in a one-year call with delta of $62, gamma of $2,680, and vega of $2.41. Find the combination of notional principals that would make your overall position be delta-, gamma-, and vega-hedged.

21. Answer the following questions about accounting for derivatives:

a. Suppose a firm engages in a derivative transaction that qualifies for fair value hedging. The firm holds a security and hedges it by selling a derivative. During the course of the hedge, the security increases in value by $20,000 while the derivative decreases in value by $22,000. Explain what accounting entries would be done and how the firm's earnings and balance sheet would be affected.

b. Suppose a firm plans to purchase an asset at a future date. The forward price of the asset is $200,000. It hedges that purchase by buying a forward contract at a price of $205,000. During the hedging period, the forward contract incurs a paper loss of $15,000. At the end of the hedge, the forward contract has lost an accumulated value of $20,000 and the asset is $20,000 cheaper. Explain what accounting entries would be done and how the firm's earnings and balance sheet would be affected. What would be different if it were not an effective hedge?

22. (Concept Problem) Suppose you enter into a bet with someone in which you pay $5 up front and are allowed to throw a pair of dice. You receive a payoff equal to the total in dollars of the numbers on the two dice. In other words, if you roll a 1 and a 2, your payoff is $3 and your profit is $3 − $5 = −$2. Determine the probability associated with a Value at Risk of $0.

APPENDIX 16
Some Lessons in Risk Management

Throughout this chapter we have learned about methods for practicing good risk management. Unfortunately, not all firms have followed the best risk management practices. In fact, some of them have hardly practiced risk management at all. During the first few years of the 1990s, an increasing number of firms announced large losses from trading derivatives. Some of the losses were barely large enough to merit an article in *The Wall Street Journal*. In two cases, however, the losses were large enough to bankrupt the organizations. Because learning what not to do is as valuable as learning what to do, we shall take a look at four of the most significant instances where risk management left much to be desired.

Metallgesellschaft: To Hedge or Not to Hedge?

Our proposed risk management program not only protects the pump profit margins with a minimum amount of risk from the spot market, but also offers us an opportunity for extraordinary upside profit with no additional risk.

METALLGESELLSCHAFT'S BUSINESS PLAN
Quoted in Antonio S. Mello and John E. Parsons
"Maturity Structure of a Hedge Matters:
Lessons from the Metallgesellschaft Debacle"
Working Paper, February 1995, Columbia University

The industrial firm Metallgesellschaft A.G. (MG) was the fourteenth largest corporation in Germany in 1993. Founded in 1883, it employed 58,000 people, had 251 subsidiaries worldwide, and was engaged in a variety of businesses primarily related to mining, metals, and energy products. In late 1993 and early 1994, it incurred losses in futures trading totaling about $1.3 billion, which was approximately one-half of its capital at that time. The losses were all the more remarkable for the fact that MG had traded futures successfully for many years. Although the firm was saved by a $1.9 billion bailout by a consortium of banks, the affair has raised concerns on several counts. If an extremely experienced firm can be nearly bankrupted trading derivatives, how can less-experienced firms expect to use them successfully? And, if losses of that size can be generated trading on the highly regulated exchange-listed futures markets, how dangerous can the unregulated over-the-counter markets be? MG's loss was all the more remarkable for the fact that *it was designed to be a hedge.* Or was it?

The troubles were caused by a U.S. subsidiary of MG called MG Refining and Marketing (MGRM). In 1992, MGRM developed a marketing strategy whereby it would offer to U.S. firms long-term fixed-price purchase contracts on gasoline, heating oil, and diesel fuel. MGRM's customers were able to lock in their purchase prices for up to 10 years provided they agreed to buy from MGRM. These transactions were forward contracts at prices $3 to $5 per barrel lower than the spot prices at that time. Since MGRM was committed to delivering the products at expiration, it was short in the forward markets for these various energy products.

To hedge its risk MGRM entered into long futures contracts on the New York Mercantile Exchange. Its futures hedges accounted for about 40 percent of its commitment while over-the-counter derivatives contracts covered about 60 percent. Recognizing the illiquidity of all but the shortest futures contracts, MGRM hedged its position primarily in the shortest-term futures contracts for unleaded gasoline, heating oil, and crude oil. Its over-the-counter contracts were also short-term. MGRM also entered into a contract with a partially owned U.S. firm, Castle Energy, to purchase all of Castle's output at fixed margins for up to 10 years.

By late 1993, MGRM was long futures contracts for 55 million barrels of various energy products and had swaps in place to purchase at least another 100 million barrels. These quantities were almost precisely the amount of its forward commitments to its customers. In other words, MGRM used what we described in Chapter 10 as "a naive hedge ratio" of one-to-one.

As we learned, however, a one-to-one hedge ratio is rarely appropriate. If the hedged instrument moves more or less than the hedging instrument, the position may be underhedged or overhedged. Also since the hedging instruments, futures, had a short maturity, they had to be rolled over as each contract expired. MGRM simply settled up expiring contracts and purchased the next shortest maturity contract. This strategy, called a stack hedge or stack-and-roll hedge, works successfully provided that the markets were in backwardation, meaning, as we covered in Chapter 9, the more distant futures price was lower than the spot or nearby futures price. Energy markets are often in backwardation, a result of the convenience yield, a concept we also previously covered. We emphasize that while energy markets are *often* in backwardation, they can convert to contango without much notice and that is precisely what they did.

In late 1993, energy prices began falling and over the course of that year fell by almost a third. MGRM's long futures positions began incurring losses, resulting in large margin calls. While the firm was theoretically gaining on its fixed supply contracts, those gains would not be realized until the oil was delivered. As we noted, the delivery commitments were spread out up to 10 years in the future. The company's realized losses drained its cash and its paper gains produced no cash to offset. Soon the company was staggering under the weight of these huge losses. The parent company had to make a decision about unwinding its position or continuing to fund the account. It chose to unwind. In retrospect that was the worst thing it could have done. In less than six months energy prices recovered all of their lost ground, meaning that MGRM's now unhedged short forward delivery contracts incurred further losses.

As we noted in the first paragraph of this story, the parent company was bailed out by a consortium of banks, some of which were on its own board of directors. The chairman of MG and the head of MGRM's U.S. oil trading operation were both fired and filed suits for conspiracy and defamation against their former employers. MG ultimately reported a loss of over $1.7 billion for its fiscal year ending September 30, 1994.

It is not clear exactly why MGRM's hedge was so poorly balanced. Some experts suggest that MGRM was speculating and knew exactly what it was doing. Others say that MGRM had an effective hedge in place and could have produced the cash to meet its margin calls without liquidating its futures contracts, which, in hindsight, would have recouped their losses less than a year later. The CFTC, exercising a rarely used and somewhat controversial authority, fined MGRM $2.2 million for failing to exercise adequate internal controls and ordered it to demonstrate in the future that such controls were in place.

Orange County, California: Playing the Odds

I am one of the largest investors in America. I know these things.

ROBERT CITRON
Quoted in Philippe Jorion
Big Bets Gone Bad
(Academic Press, 1996)

Due to my inexperience, I placed a great deal of reliance on the advice of market professionals. . . . I wish I had more training in complex government securities.

ROBERT CITRON
Testimony before Senate Special Committee
on Local Government Investments, January 17, 1995
Quoted in *RISK,* March 1995

Orange County, California, is one of the wealthiest communities in the United States. Home to Disneyland, the California Angels, and the John Wayne airport, it reported a loss of $1.6 billion in its investment account in 1994 and declared the largest municipal bankruptcy in U.S. history. How this could have happened is not at all a mystery. Orange County's treasurer, Robert Citron, was engaged in a clever investment scheme that turned a low-risk essentially money market fund into a turbo-charged investment account.

The 69-year-old Citron, with 24 years' experience as the county treasurer, operated a fund that invested in short-term, fixed-income securities. The fund not only invested Orange County funds but also accepted the funds of almost 200 other municipal governments in California. How it did this is not surprising. The Orange County fund had been earning 300 to 400 basis points above the returns earned on a similar fund operated by the state of California. The Orange County fund's market value was almost $7.5 billion. In June 1994, Citron was reelected county treasurer in spite of warnings by his opponent that the portfolio was excessively leveraged.

By late 1994, a series of sharp increases in interest rates, triggered by the Federal Reserve's efforts to control inflation, brought the value of the fund down by a staggering $2 billion. Orange County was forced to declare bankruptcy. Citron and his chief investment officer were arrested. Citron declared that he had been tricked by his brokerage firm, Merrill Lynch, into making these investments, about which he now stated that he knew little. Orange County went into reorganization, cut services drastically, laid off employees, and filed a $3 billion lawsuit against Merrill Lynch.

It did not take long to determine what had gone wrong. Citron had used leverage to purchase additional government securities through reverse repurchase agreements. Recall from Chapter 9 that we introduced the concept of a repurchase agreement. Let us say that another municipality gives Mr. Citron $100 million to invest. Citron purchases intermediate-term U.S. Treasury notes, which have an average maturity of about 4 years and a duration of about 3.5 years. Citron then executes a reverse repurchase agreement with a securities dealer or bank, pledging the $100 million of securities for a loan of almost $100 million, let us say $90 million. He then uses the $90 million to purchase additional similar securities. This can be done several times with the same money. Ultimately Citron had leveraged the county about threefold, bringing its total invested funds to about $20 billion while its total equity was only about $7 billion. This tripled its duration. Thus, what should have been a fairly low-risk, short- to intermediate-term fund had the risk of a fund of long-term bonds. When bankruptcy was declared and Citron's strategy was revealed, it should have come as no surprise. *The Wall Street Journal* had reported as early as April 1994 that Citron had leveraged the portfolio almost threefold. It was noted that one municipality withdrew about $4 million at that time because it considered the fund too risky. This probably proved to be the best decision of that treasurer's career.

As in any leveraged bond investment, the results are quite good when interest rates are falling. When the 1994 interest rate increases caused the fund to have a series of huge margin calls from their broker, Orange County began dipping into its cash reserves. When it could no longer generate enough cash to meet its margin calls, its lenders began selling the collateral, which amounted to about $10 billion. This sent shock waves into the bond market and prices tumbled.

It should be noted that the word *derivatives* has not been mentioned in conjunction with this Orange County story. Although there were some derivatives in the portfolio, mostly in the form of structured notes, the damage had little to do with derivatives. Citron had simply used U.S. government intermediate-term notes, combined with the leveraging power of repurchase agreements, to destroy almost 20 percent of the fund's value.

To say that Orange County invested unwisely and did not practice risk management is probably an understatement. There was no risk management whatsoever. Citron was supposed to be monitored by the elected county board but little monitoring was done. The board trusted the veteran treasurer and let him do what he wanted.

Orange County offered to repay the municipalities and other agencies whose funds it had invested about three-fourths of their money, plus other securities that would be repayable over a long period of time, but most of the payments were contingent on winning the lawsuit against Merrill Lynch. Almost 2,000 of the 15,000 county employees lost their jobs. The county sold nearly $100 million of its assets and proposed a sales tax increase but the voters overwhelmingly turned it down. The county even tried to sell the John Wayne airport but found that it was not permitted by federal law. Citron pled guilty to six felony counts and was sentenced to a year in jail and fined $100,000 in 1996. Orange County was able to issue new debt, deferred repayment of old debt, and by mid-1996 had emerged from bankruptcy. Eventually it settled its lawsuit with Merrill Lynch.

Barings PLC: How One Man Blew Up a Bank

There is little argument about who was the derivatives technology salesman of 1995. Most people will agree that Nick Leeson did more than anyone to raise the awareness of the need for firm-wide risk management.

CLIVE DAVIDSON
"Profiting from Doom"
Risk, January 1996

Barings PLC was a British investment bank that had been founded in 1763. It had played a major role in British history, financing the Napoleonic Wars, and included Queen Elizabeth II among its many well-heeled clients. One weekend in February 1995 Barings was forced to declare bankruptcy, a result of losses of about $1.2 billion or nearly twice its capital. The losses were attributed to futures trading in its Singapore office by a 28-year-old former clerk named Nick Leeson. Barings was rescued by the Dutch banking concern Internationale Nederlanden Groep (ING), which purchased its assets (approximately $900 million) and assumed most of its liabilities for about $1.61.[1] ING immediately injected about $1 billion in capital. Some of Barings' liabilities, however, were not assumed and those bondholders suffered big losses.

Leeson had joined the bank in July 1989, having previously worked in London for the American bank Morgan Stanley. As a clerk handling the settling of transactions, he proved to be exceptionally well organized and his work in Barings' back office impressed his superiors. In March 1992 he requested and received a transfer to the Singapore office, which was actively involved in futures trading in Tokyo and Osaka, Japan, and at the Singapore International Monetary Exchange (SIMEX). Again Leeson proved to be excellent at organizing the back office. All the while, Leeson was learning the ropes of trading futures. Soon he was executing arbitrage transactions, buying Japanese stock index futures in Singapore and simultaneously selling the same contract in Osaka, capturing differences in the prices of the same contract on the two exchanges.

Transactions of this sort should be low risk. One position will gain and the other will lose a similar amount. The net should be a small profit resulting from slight differences in the prices of the contract on the two exchanges. As Leeson relates the story in his book, *Rogue Trader,* in 1992 he began hiding his losses in a special account. Soon it began appearing that Leeson was generating huge profits. Because Leeson was responsible for the back office and his employees were loyal to him, he was able to keep the losses tucked safely away whenever reports were required or auditors showed up. In 1994, he reported profits of about £28 million but had hidden losses of £180 million. From January 1, 1995, to February 24, Barings' last day, Leeson produced profits of almost £19 million and losses of over £600 million and it was getting increasingly difficult to cover his trail.

Recall from Chapter 7 that we discussed the straddle, a strategy involving long positions in puts and calls with the same exercise price. Leeson was generating more funds by entering into short straddles, a total of almost 20,000 contracts. This meant that Leeson profited as long as the market stayed fairly stable. With high volatility he would lose big. In late January 1995, Leeson held over 3,000 contracts long of the Japanese Nikkei 225 stock index futures at the Osaka exchange. On January 17, an

---

[1]Yes, that is one dollar and 61 cents, which at that time was equivalent to approximately one British pound.

earthquake struck the Japanese city of Kobe and the index fell about 13 percent over the next five weeks. Leeson was generating large losses but increased his bets that the market would turn around. Ultimately Leeson held a $7 billion position that would gain if the market moved up and lose if it moved down. He held about 17,000 contracts in Osaka and over 40,000 in Singapore. He also held huge positions in Japanese government bonds and Euroyen.

The evidence suggests that Barings' executives in London had been warned about Leeson's trading as early as 1992. In 1994, an audit concluded that while Leeson had done nothing wrong, though in fact he had, the potential for wrongdoing was there. It noted that Leeson was running both the front office and back office, though generating large profits with little risk.

Thursday, February 23, was Leeson's last day of work at Barings' Singapore office. He and his wife secretly fled Singapore the next day. They went to several Asian countries before eventually flying to Frankfurt, Germany, where he was arrested by German police a week after fleeing Singapore. Singapore sought extradition while Leeson's British lawyers worked toward having him charged and extradited by England. British authorities were unable to determine that he had violated any of their laws and in October 1995 a German court agreed to turn him over to Singapore. Leeson returned to Singapore and plea bargained a potential 14-year prison sentence down to 6 1/2 years for fraud.

The Barings story shocked the financial world. There were concerns that the SIMEX clearinghouse might fail or use customer funds to cover its losses. The Bank of England, which had rescued Barings once in 1890, considered doing so again, but it quickly became apparent that only investors and not customers would lose money over the Barings failure. While the financial system suffered a shock, it showed no threat of widespread failure, the systemic risk that we previously mentioned. When ING purchased Barings about a week after the failure, the market settled down quickly and no further shocks were felt.

Barings is a classic story in bad risk management. It violates virtually every rule. Leeson was in control of both the back and front offices and, hence, had the ability to hide losses for an extremely long time. Barings' risk management system was nothing more than auditing and regular reports from Leeson showing his positions and performance. The reports were falsified and the auditors' examinations were not sufficient to identify the problem, though they did warn of the potential for fraud. It hardly mattered because they were ignored. The London office was under the impression that this 28-year-old clerk with no college degree was earning large profits arbitraging price differences in two markets. It never questioned how unlikely these profits really were.

Barings was a wake-up call to the rest of the financial world. Risk management became of paramount importance.

Procter & Gamble: Going Up in Suds

I've seen things in the market where I scratch my head and can't imagine why people did it. For example, when P&G lost all that money, I couldn't fathom what anyone at that company was thinking when they looked at that formula of the swap and said, "Yes, that's exactly what I want to put on."

ANONYMOUS
"Confessions of a Structured Note Salesman"
Derivatives Strategy, November 11, 1995

The Procter & Gamble Corporation (P&G) is one of America's best-known companies. It is also a large multinational corporation with extensive foreign operations and significant interest rate and foreign exchange risk. In late October 1993, P&G entered into an exotic swap with its dealer, Banker's Trust (BT). The payment on the swap was determined by a complex formula relating short-term interest rates to long-term interest rates. In early 1994, P&G entered into another exotic swap, this one linked to the exchange rate on the German mark. This transaction was similar to the range floaters that we discussed in Chapter 15. Both parties paid floating rates tied to German interest rates. P&G was betting on deutsche mark swap rates staying between 4.05 percent and 6.10 percent. Both of its positions were essentially bets that U.S. and German interest rates would not increase significantly. If P&G were correct, it would be locking in an attractive below-market borrowing rate of 40 basis points below the commercial paper rate. If it were wrong, P&G would suffer large losses by being forced to borrow at substantially above market rates. The transactions also contained option features that allowed P&G to lock in a cumulative gain or loss.

In April 1994, P&G disclosed that it had taken a $157 million pretax charge as a result of those transactions. Effectively P&G ended up borrowing at 1,412 basis points more than the commercial paper rate. Though the amount lowered its earnings per share only 15 cents, it became a public relations nightmare. P&G's treasurer Norman Mains was reassigned. Later in 1994, P&G filed suit against BT for $130 million under four counts: fraud, negligent misrepresentation, breach of fiduciary duties, and negligence. P&G also pursued charges against BT under the federal RICO (Racketeering Influenced and Corrupt Organizations) Act, a law designed to punish organized crime. The RICO Act had been applied successfully in cases not involving organized crime and it permitted punishment of up to treble damages.

BT argued that P&G ran a sophisticated derivatives operation and was highly experienced in currency and interest rate derivatives. On that point, BT was certainly correct. P&G had many years of successful experience with these types of instruments, some of them being quite leveraged and exotic. So what was P&G's basis for arguing that BT had defrauded it? BT routinely tape recorded all its conversations with its derivatives clients. P&G got a court order to obtain the tapes and found that BT derivatives personnel had made statements to the effect that P&G had no idea it was being taken advantage of. P&G argued that BT was its advisor and that it had, therefore, relied on BT's advice and that it was fraudulent for BT to have led it into these transactions.

In the summer of 1996, BT's newly appointed chairman, though confident of a victory in court, elected to put the matter behind them by settling with P&G. BT ended up paying about $80 million to P&G. BT had also settled a number of other cases out of court. Regulators fined it and forced it to agree to take various actions to change its derivatives sales and operating procedures.

In response, a number of leading derivatives dealers organized an informal working group to develop self-regulatory procedures. Though these procedures are nonbinding, they represent an effort by the industry to develop standards of practice in derivatives sales and trading. Of particular note was the fact that, unless made specific, all transactions are at arm's length, meaning that the dealer is not an advisor to the end user.

People are not apologizing anymore for using derivatives. They've realized that they are not the evil instruments they have been made out to be.

SARAH ORSAY
Derivatives Strategy, April 1997.

LIST OF SYMBOLS

AI, AI_t, AI_T = accrued interest today, at time t, and at time T

b, b_t, b_T = basis today, at time t, and at expiration, T

B, B_T = price of bond or T-bill today, and at maturity, T

β, β_S, β_f, β_p = beta, beta of spot asset, beta of futures, beta of portfolio

β_T = target beta

C = (abbreviated) price of call

$C(S_0,T,X)$ = price of either European or American call on asset with price S_0, expiration T, and exercise price X

$C_e(S_0,T,X)$ = price of European call on asset with price S_0, expiration T, and exercise price X

$C_a(S_0,T,X)$ = price of American call on asset with price S_0, expiration T, and exercise price X

$C(f_0,T,X)$ = price of either European or American call on futures with price f_0, expiration T, and exercise price X

C_{asian} = price of asian call option

$C_e(f_0,T,X)$ = price of European call on futures with price f_0, expiration T, and exercise price X

$C_a(f_0,T,X)$ = price of American call on futures with price f_0, expiration T, and exercise price X

C_u, C_d, C_u^2, C_{ud}, C_d^2 = call price sequence in binomial model

χ = convenience yield

CI_t = coupon interest paid at time t

CP_t = cash payment (principal or interest) on bond at time t

CF = conversion factor on CBOT T-bond contract

$CF(t)$, $CF(T)$ = conversion factor on CBOT T-bond contracts deliverable at times t and T

c = coupon rate

Δ = delta of an option

ΔS, Δf = change in spot price, change in futures price

δ = dividend yield

d = (without subscript) 1.0 + downward return on stock in binomial model

d_1, d_2 = variables in Black-Scholes model

D_j = dividend paid at time j

D_T = compound future value of reinvested dividends

DUR, DUR_S, DUR_f = duration ,duration of spot, implied duration of futures

ϵ = standard normal random variable in Monte Carlo simulation

X, X_1, X_2 = exercise price

$E(x)$ = expected value of the argument x

$e^* =$ measure of hedging effectiveness

$f_0(T), f_t(T), f_T(T) =$ futures price or futures exchange rate today, at time t, and at expiration T

$f^{\ddagger\ddagger}_{o(a)} =$ critical futures price for early exercise of American option on futures

$F(O,T, F(t,T) =$ forward price or forward exchange for contracts written today and at time t, expiring at T

$FV =$ face value of bond

$h, h_u, h_d =$ hedge ratios in binomial model

$i =$ interest rate for storage problem

$J =$ number of observations in sample

$j =$ counter in summation procedure

$K =$ parameter in break forward contract

$k =$ discount rate (required rate) on stock

$\Lambda_i =$ volatility in Ho-Lee model

$LIBOR =$ London Interbank Offer Rate, a Eurodollar rate

$MOS =$ number of months in computing CBOT conversion factor

$MOS^* =$ number of months in computing CBOT conversion factor rounded down to nearest quarter

$\mu_x =$ unsystematic return on stock

$N(d_1), N(d_2) =$ cumulative normal probabilities in Black-Scholes model

$NPV =$ net present value of box spread

$N_C, N_P, N_S, N_f, N_E =$ number of calls, puts, shares of stock, futures, and T-bills held in a position

$n =$ number of time periods in n-period binomial model

$O_{aon} =$ value of asset-or-nothing option

$O_{con} =$ value of cash-or-nothing option

$\Pi =$ profit from strategy

$P =$ (abbreviated) price of put

$P(S_0,T,X) =$ price of either European or American put on asset with price S_0, expiration T, and exercise price X

$P_e(S_0,T,X) =$ price of European put on asset with price S_0, expiration T, and exercise price X

$P_a(S_0,T,X) =$ price of American put on asset with price S_0, expiration T, and exercise price X

$P(f_0,T,X) =$ price of either European or American put on futures with price f_0, expiration T, and exercise price X

$P_e(f_0,T,X) =$ price of European put on futures with price f_0, expiration T, and exercise price X

$P_a(f_0,T,X) =$ price of American put on futures with price f_0, expiration T, and exercise price X

$p =$ binomial probability

$PVBP_S, PVBP_f =$ present value of basis point change for spot, futures

$E(\phi) =$ expected risk premium

$Q =$ number of ways to reach a cell in Ho-Lee model

$r =$ discrete risk-free rate

$r(a,b)$ = interest rate over time interval (a,b)

$\hat{r}$ = implied repo rate

r_h = return on hedged portfolio

r_c = continuously compounded risk-free rate

r_f = percentage change in futures price

r_S = return on stock or spot position

r_{St} = return on stock at time t

r_{Sf} = return on portfolio of stock and futures

r_M = return on market

r_{Mt} = return on market at time t

r^c = continuously compounded return

r_t^C = continuously compounded return at time t

$\bar{r}^c$ = mean continuously compounded return

ρ = foreign risk-free rate

s = storage costs

S_0' = stock price minus present value of dividends

S_{avg} = average stock price during life of option

S_{max} = maximum stock price during life of option

S_{min} = minimum stock price during life of option

S_0, S_t, S_T = stock price (or spot price or spot exchange rate) today, at time t, and at time T

$S_u, S_u^2, S_{ud}, S_d, S_d^2$ = stock price sequence in binomial model

S_T^* = breakeven stock price at expiration

σ = standard deviation or volatility (σ^2 = variance)

σ_{xz} = covariance between x and z

σ_x^2 = variance of x

T, T_1, T_2 = expiration or time to expiration from the current time

t = future point in time or time until a particular future date

θ = cost of carry

u = 1+ upward return on stock in binomial model

$v_0(T), v_t(T)$ = value of futures contract at time 0 and time t expiring at time t

v^f = value of futures contract in hedged portfolio

$V_0(0,T), V_t(0,T)$ = value of forward contract at time 0 and time t, created at time 0 expiring at time T

V_{min} = minimum or insured value of portfolio

V_u, V_d, V_{ud} = sequence of hedge portfolio values of portfolio in binomial model

YRS = number of years in computation of CBOT conversion factor

y, y_s, y_v = bond yield, yield on spot bond, yield on portfolio worth V

y_f = implied yield on futures

VAR = value at risk

LIST OF FORMULAS

Intrinsic Value of American Call

$$C_a(S_0,T,X) \geq \text{Max}(0,S_0, - X)$$

Maximum Spread of European Calls

$$(X_2 - X_1)(1 + r)^{-T} \geq C_e(S_0,T,X_1) - C_e(S_0,T,X_2)$$

Maximum Spread of American Calls

$$(X_2 - X_1) \geq C_a(S_0,T,X_1) - C_a(S_0,T,X_2)$$

Lower Bound of European Call

$$C_e(S_0,T,X) \geq \text{Max}[0, S_0 - X(1 + r)^{-T}]$$

Intrinsic Value of American Put

$$P_a(S_0,T,X) \geq \text{Max}(0,X - S_0)$$

Maximum Spread of European Puts

$$(X_2 - X_1)(1 + r)^{-T} \geq P_e(S_0,T,X_2) - P_e(S_0,T,X_1)$$

Maximum Spread of American Puts

$$(X_2 - X_1) \geq P_a(S_0,T,X_2) - P_a(S_0,T,X_1)$$

Lower Bound of European Put

$$P_e(S_0,T,X) \geq \text{Max}[0,X(1 + r)^{-T} - S_0]$$

Put-Call Parity for American Options

$$C_a(S_0{}',T,X) + X + \sum_{j=1}^{n} D_j (1 + r)^{-t_j} \geq S_0{}' + P_a(S_0{}',T,X) \geq C_a(S_0{}',T,X) + X(1 + r)^{-T}$$

Put-Call Parity for European Options

$$S_0 + P_e(S_0,T,X) = C_e(S_0,T,X) + X(1 + r)^{-T}$$

Stock Prices in Binomial Model

$$S_u = Su$$
$$S_d = Sd$$
$$S_{u^2} = Su^2$$
$$S_{d^2} = Sd^2$$
$$S_{ud} = Sud$$

Call Prices in One-Period Binomial Model

$$C_u = \text{Max}[0, Su - X]$$
$$C_d = \text{Max}[0, Sd - X]$$
$$C = \frac{pC_u + (1 - p)C_d}{1 + r}$$

Call Prices in Two-Period Binomial Model

$$C_{u^2} = \text{Max}[0, Su^2 - X]$$
$$C_{d^2} = \text{Max}[0, Sd^2 - X]$$
$$C_{ud} = \text{Max}[0, Sud - X]$$
$$C_u = \frac{pC_{u^2} + (1 - p)C_{ud}}{1 + r}$$

$$C_d = \frac{pC_{ud} + (1 - p)C_{d^2}}{1 + r}$$

$$C = \frac{pC_u + (1 - p)C_d}{1 + r}$$

Binomial Probabilities

$$u = e^{\sigma\sqrt{T/n}}, d = 1/u$$

, or

$$u = e^{(r - \sigma^2/2)(T/n) + \sigma\sqrt{T/n}}$$

$$d = e^{(r - \sigma^2/2)(T/n) - \sigma\sqrt{T/n}}$$

Risk-free Rate in Binomial Model

$$(1 + r)^{T/n}$$

Value of p in Binomial Model

$$p = \frac{1 + r - d}{u - d}$$

Hedge Ratios in Binomial Model

$$h = \frac{C_u - C_d}{S_u - S_d}$$

$$h_u = \frac{C_{u^2} - C_{ud}}{S_{u^2} - S_{ud}}$$

$$h_d = \frac{C_{ud} - C_{d^2}}{S_{ud} - S_{d^2}}$$

Sequence of Hedge Portfolio Values in Binomial Model

$$V = hS - C$$
$$V_u = hSu - C_u$$
$$V_d = hSd - C_u$$

Black-Scholes Call Option Pricing Model

$$C = S_0N(d_1) - Xe^{-r_cT}N(d_2)$$

$$d_1 = \frac{\ln(S_0/X) + [r_c + \sigma^2/2]T}{\sigma\sqrt{T}}$$

$$d_2 = d_1 - \sigma\sqrt{T}$$

Black Scholes Put Option Pricing Model

$$P = Xe^{-r_cT}[1 - N(d_2)] - S_0[1 - N(d_1)]$$

Call Delta

$$\text{Call Delta} = N(d_1)$$

Call Gamma

$$\text{Call Gamma} = \frac{e^{-d_1^2/2}}{S_0\sigma\sqrt{2\pi T}}$$

Call Rho

$$\text{Call Rho} = TXe^{-r_cT}N(d_2)$$

Call Vega

$$\text{Call Vega} = \frac{S_0\sqrt{T}e^{-d_1^2/2}}{\sqrt{2\pi}}$$

Call Theta

$$\text{Call Theta} = -\frac{S_0 \sigma e^{-d_1^2/2}}{2\sqrt{2\pi T}} - r_c X e^{-r_c T} N(d_2)$$

Put Delta

$$\text{Put Delta} = N(d_1) - 1$$

Put Gamma

$$\text{Put Gamma} = \frac{e^{-d_1^2/2}}{S_0 \sigma \sqrt{2\pi T}}$$

Put Rho

$$\text{Put Rho} = -TX e^{-r_c T}[1 - N(d_2)]$$

Put Vega

$$\text{Put Vega} = \frac{S_0 \sqrt{T} e^{-d_1^2/2}}{\sqrt{2\pi}}$$

Put Theta

$$\text{Put Theta} = \frac{S_0 \sigma e^{-d_1^2/2}}{2\sqrt{2\pi T}} + r_c X e^{-r_1 T}(1 - N(d_2)$$

Present Value of a Series of Discrete Dividends

$$\sum_{j=1}^{T} D_j(1 + r)^{-t_j}$$

Stock Price Minus Present Value of Dividends

$$S_0' = S_0 - D_t e^{-r_c T} \text{ (one dividend)}$$
$$S_0' = S_0 e^{-\delta T} \text{ (continuous dividends)}$$

Sample Estimate of Mean of Continuously Compounded Return

$$\bar{r}^c = \sum_{t=1}^{J} r_t^c / J$$

Sample Estimate of Variance of Continuously Compounded Return

$$\sigma^2 = \frac{\sum_{t=1}^{J} (r_t^c - \bar{r}^c)^2}{(J - 1)} = \frac{\sum_{t=1}^{J} (r_t^c)^2 - \left(\sum_{t=1}^{J} r_t^c\right)^2 / J}{J - 1)}$$

Implied Volatility of At-the-Money Call

$$\sigma \approx \frac{C}{(0.398)S_0 \sqrt{T}}$$

Profit from Call Transaction Held to Expiration

$$\Pi = N_C[\text{Max}(0, S_T - X) - C]$$

Profit from Call Transaction Terminated at T_1

$$\Pi = N_C[C(S_{T_1}, T - T_1, X) - C]$$

Profit from Put Transaction Held to Expiration

$$\Pi = N_p[\text{Max}(0, X - S_T) - P]$$

Profit from Put Transaction Terminated at T_1

$$\Pi = N_p[P(S_{T_1}, T - T_1, X) - P]$$

Profit from Stock Transaction

$$\Pi = N_S(S_T - S_0)$$

Ratio of Calls in Riskless Spread

$$\frac{N_1}{N_2} = -\frac{\Delta_2}{\Delta_1}$$

Conversion of IMM Index to Futures Price per $100

$$f = 100 - (100 - \text{IMM Index})(90/360)$$

Conversion Factors for CBOT T-Bond Contract

$$CF_0 = (c/2)\left(\frac{1 - (1.03)^{-2*\text{YRS}}}{.03}\right) + (1.03)^{(-2*\text{YRS})}$$

$$CF_3 = (CF_0 + c/2)(1.03)^{-.5} - c/4$$

$$CF_6 = (c/2)\left(\frac{1 - (1.03)^{-2*\text{YRS}+1}}{.03}\right) + (1.03)^{(-2*\text{YRS}+1)}$$

$$CF_9 = (CF_6 + c/2)(1.03)^{-.5} - c/4$$

Bond Price Using Term Structure

$$B = \sum_{t=1}^{T} CI_t[1 + r(0,t)]^{-t} + FV[1 + r(0,T)]^{-T}$$

Bond Price Using Yield

$$B = \sum_{t=1}^{T} CP_t(1 + y)^{-t}$$

$$= CI\left[\frac{1 - (1 + y)^{-T}}{y}\right] + FV(1 + y)^{-T}$$

Duration

$$DUR = \frac{\displaystyle\sum_{t=1}^{T} tCP_t(1 + y)^{-t}}{B} = \frac{CI(1 + y)[(1 + y)^T - 1] + Ty(FVy - CI)}{CIy[(1 + y)^T - 1] + FVy^2}$$

Bond Price Percentage Change

$$\frac{\Delta B}{B} \approx -DUR\frac{\Delta y}{(1 + y)}$$

Capital Asset Pricing Model

$$E(r_S) = r + [E(r_M) - r]\beta$$

Beta

$$\beta = \frac{\sigma_{SM}}{\sigma_M^2}$$

Sample Estimate of Covariance between Returns on Stock and Market

$$\sigma_{SM} = \frac{\displaystyle\sum_{t=1}^{J} r_{St}r_{Mt} - \left(\sum_{t=1}^{J} r_{St} \sum_{t=1}^{J} r_{Mt}\right)/J}{J - 1}$$

Sample Estimate of Variance of Return on Market

$$\sigma_M^2 = \frac{\displaystyle\sum_{t=1}^{J} r_{Mt^2} - \left(\sum_{t=1}^{J} r_{Mt}\right)^2/J}{J - 1}$$

Spot Price under Uncertainty and Risk Neutrality

$$S_0 = E(S_T) - s - iS_0$$

Spot Price under Uncertainty and Risk Aversion

$$S_0 = E(S_T) - s - iS_0 - E(\phi)$$

Value of a Forward Contract at Time t Prior to Expiration

$$V_t(0,T) = (F(t,T) - F(0,T))(1 + r)^{-(T-t)}$$

Cost of Carry Futures Pricing Model

$$f_0 = S_0 + \theta$$

Cost of Carry Futures Pricing Model with Convenience Yield

$$f_0 = S_0 + \theta - \chi$$

Stock Index Futures Pricing Model

$$f_0 = S_0 e^{(r_c - \delta)T}$$

Stock Index Futures Pricing Model with Discrete Dividend

$$f_0 = S_0(1 + r)^T - \sum_{j=1}^{T} D_j(1 + r)^{T-\mathfrak{h}}$$

Futures Spread Pricing Model

$$f_0(2) - f_0(1) = \theta_2 - \theta_1$$

Basis Today

$$b_0 = S_0 - f_0$$

Basis at Time t

$$b_t = S_t - f_t$$

Profit from a Short Hedge

$$\Pi = b_t - b_0$$

Variance of Profit from Hedge

$$\sigma_\Pi^2 = \sigma_{\Delta S}^2 + \sigma_{\Delta f}^2 N_f^2 + 2\sigma_{\Delta s \Delta f} N_f$$

Duration of Futures

$$DUR_f \approx -\left(\frac{\Delta f}{f}\right)\left(\frac{1 + y_f}{\Delta y_f}\right)$$

Minimum Variance Hedge Ratio

$$N_f = -\frac{\sigma_{\Delta s \Delta f}}{\sigma_{\Delta f}^2}$$

Price Sensitivity Hedge Ratio

$$N_f = -\left(\frac{DUR_S}{DUR_f}\right)\left(\frac{S}{f}\right)\left(\frac{1 + y_f}{1 + y_s}\right)$$

Stock Index Futures Hedge Ratio

$$N_f = -\beta_S\left(\frac{S}{f}\right)$$

Hedging Effectiveness

$$e^* = \frac{\sigma_{\Delta S}^2 - \sigma_\Pi^2}{\sigma_{\Delta S}^2}$$

Implied Repo on T-Bill or Eurodollar Cash and Carry

$$r = \left(\frac{f_0(t)}{S_0}\right)^{(1/t)} - 1$$

Spot Price for Justifying Exercise of Wild Card Option

$$S_5 < f_3(CF)$$

Implied Repo on T-Bond or T-Note Cash and Carry

$$\hat{r} = \left[\frac{(CF)(f_0(T) + AI_T)}{S_0 + AI_0} \right]^{-(1/T)} - 1$$

Implied Repo Rate on T-Bond or T-Note Spread

$$\hat{r} = \left[\frac{(CF(T)f_0(T)}{CF(t)f_0(t)} \right]^{-1(T-t)} - 1$$

Put-Call-Forward/Futures Parity

$$P_e(S_0, T, X) = C_e(S_0, T, X) + (X - f_0)(1 + r)^{-T}$$

Futures Contracts Required to Achieve Target Duration

$$N_f = \left(\frac{DUR_S - DUR_T}{DUR_f} \right)\left(\frac{S}{f} \right)\left(\frac{1 + y_f}{1 + y_s} \right)$$

Futures Contracts Required to Achieve Target Beta

$$N_f = (\beta_T - \beta_S)\left(\frac{S}{f} \right)$$

Intrinsic Value of American Call Option on Futures

$$C_a(f_0, T, X) \geq Max(0, f_0 - X)$$

Intrinsic Value of American Put Option on Futures

$$P_a(f_0, T, X) \geq Max(0, X - f_0)$$

Lower Bound of European Call Option on Futures

$$C_e(f_0, T, X) \geq Max[0, (f - X)(1 + r)^{-T}]$$

Lower Bound of European Put Option on Futures

$$P_e(f_0, T, X) \geq Max[0, (X - f_0)(1 + r)^{-T}]$$

Put-Call Parity of Options on Futures

$$P_e(f_0, T, X) = C_e(f_0, T, X) + (X - f_0)(1 + r)^{-T}$$

Black Call Option on Futures Pricing Model

$$C = e^{-r_cT}[f_0N(d_1) - XN(d_2)]$$

$$d_1 = \frac{\ln(f_0/X) + (\sigma^2/2)T}{\sigma\sqrt{T}}$$

$$d_2 = d_1 - \sigma\sqrt{T}$$

Black Put Options on Futures Pricing Model

$$P = Xe^{-r_cT}[1 - N(d_2)] - f_0e^{-r_cT}[1 - N(d_1)]$$

Interest Rate Parity

$$F_0 = S_0(1 + r)^T/(1 + \rho)^T$$

Lower Bound of European Foreign Currency Call

$$C_e(S_0, T, X) \geq Max[0, S_0(1 + \rho)^{-T} - X(1 + r)^{-T}]$$

Lower Bound of European Foreign Currency Put

$$P_e(S_0, T, X) \geq Max[0, X(1 + r)^{-T} - S_0(1 + \rho)^{-T}]$$

Put-Call Parity of Foreign Currency Options

$$C_e(S_0, T, X) = P_e(S_0, T, X) + S_0(1 + \rho)^{-T} - X(1 + r)^{-T}$$

Garman-Kohlhagen Foreign Currency Call Option Pricing Model

$$C = S_0 e^{-\rho_c T} N(d_1) - Xe^{-r_c T} N(d_2)$$

$$d_1 = \frac{\ln(S_0 e^{-\rho_c T}/X) + [r_c + (\sigma^2/2)]T}{\sigma\sqrt{T}}$$

$$d_2 = d_1 - \sigma\sqrt{T}$$

Payoff to Holder of Long FRA

$$(\text{Notional principal})(\text{LIBOR} - \text{Agreed upon rate})\left(\frac{\text{Days}}{360}\right)$$

$$\text{Swap Rate} = \frac{1 - \text{final discount factor}}{\text{Sum of discount factors}}$$

Cash Flow to Floating Rate Receiver in Plain Vanilla Swap

$$(\text{Notional principal})(\text{LIBOR} - \text{Swap rate})\left(\frac{\text{Days}}{360}\right)$$

Payoff from Interest Rate Call

$$(\text{Notional principal})\text{Max}(0, \text{LIBOR} - X)\left(\frac{\text{Days}}{360}\right)$$

Payoff from Interest Rate Put

$$(\text{Notional principal})\text{Max}(0, X - \text{LIBOR})\left(\frac{\text{Days}}{360}\right)$$

Number of Shares and Puts to Insure Portfolio

$$N = \frac{V}{S_0 + P}$$

Minimum Value of Insured Portfolio

$$V_{min} = \frac{XV}{S_0 + P}$$

Number of Treasury Bills to Insure Portfolio with Calls and Treasury Bills

$$N_B = \frac{V_{min}}{B_T}$$

Number of Calls to Insure Portfolio with Calls and Treasury Bills

$$N_C = \frac{(V - N_B B)}{C} = \frac{V}{S_0 + P}$$

Number of Futures in Dynamic Hedge with Stock Index Futures

$$N_f = \left[\left(\frac{V_{min}}{X}\right)N(d_1) - \left(\frac{V}{S_0}\right)\right]e^{-r_c T}$$

Number of Treasury Bills in Dynamic Hedge

$$N_B = \frac{V - N_S S_0}{B}$$

Number of Shares of Stock in Dynamic Hedge with Treasury Bills

$$N_S = \left(\frac{V_{min}}{X}\right)N(d_1)$$

Value of Asset-or-Nothing Option

$$O_{aon} = S_0 N(d_1)$$

Value of Cash-or-Nothing Option
$$O_{con} = Xe^{-r_cT}N(d_2)$$
Payoff of Average Price Call
$$Max(0, S_{avg} - X)$$
Payoff of Average Price Put
$$Max(0, X - S_{avg})$$
Payoff of 3-Period Average Strike Call
$$Max(0, S_3 - S_{avg})$$
Payoff of 3-Period Average Strike Put
$$Max(0, S_{avg} - S_3)$$
Payoff of 3-Period Lookback Call
$$Max(0, S_3 - S_{min})$$
Payoff of 3-Period Lookback Put
$$Max(0, S_{max} - S_3)$$
Payoff of 3-Period Fixed-Strike Lookback Call
$$Max(0, S_{max} - X)$$
Payoff of 3-Period Fixed-Strike Lookback Put
$$Max(0, X - S_{min})$$

REFERENCES

This compilation of books, articles, and monographs includes items referenced in this book as well as classic references and other useful articles dealing with topics covered in this book. It is not intended as a comprehensive bibliography of derivatives.

Abken, Peter A. "An Introduction to Portfolio Insurance." *Federal Reserve Bank of Atlanta Economic Review* 72 (November-December 1987), 2–25.

Abken, Peter A. "Interest Rate Caps, Collars, and Floors." *Federal Reserve Bank of Atlanta Economic Review* 74 (November-December 1989): 2–24.

Abken, Peter A. "Beyond Plain Vanilla: A Taxonomy of Swaps." *Federal Reserve Bank of Atlanta Economic Review* 76 (1991): 12–29.

Abken, Peter A. "Valuation of Default-Risky Interest-Rate Swaps." *Advances in Futures and Options Research* 6 (1993): 93–116.

Anderson, Ronald W. "The Regulation of Futures Contract Innovations in the United States." *The Journal of Futures Markets* 3 (1984): 297–332.

Anson, Mark J. P. *Accounting and Tax Rules for Derivatives.* New Hope, Pennsylvania: Frank Fabozzi Associates, 1999.

Arak, Marcelle, Arturo Estrella, Laurie Goodman, and Andrew Silver. "Interest Rate Swaps: An Alternative Explanation." *Financial Management* 17 (1988): 12–18.

Arak, Marcelle, Philip Fischer, Laurie Goodman, and Raj Daryanani. "The Municipal-Treasury Futures Spread." *The Journal of Futures Markets* 7 (1987): 355–371.

Arak, Marcelle, Laurie Goodman, and Susan Ross. "The Cheapest to Deliver Bond on the Treasury Bond Futures Contract." *Advances in Futures and Options Research* 1, part B (1986): 49–74.

Arditti, Fred D. *Derivatives: A Comprehensive Resource for Options, Futures, Interest Rate Swaps, and Mortgage Securities.* Boston: Harvard Business School Press, 1996.

Austin, Michael. "Index Option Overwriting: Strategies and Results." *Derivatives Quarterly* 1 (Summer 1995): 77–84.

Baer, Herbert L., Virginia Grace France, and James T. Moser. "What Does a Clearinghouse Do?" *Derivatives Quarterly* 1 (Spring 1995): 39–46.

Barone-Adesi, Giovanni, and Robert E. Whaley. "Efficient Analytic Approximation of American Option Values." *The Journal of Finance* 42 (June 1987): 301–320.

Baxter, Martin, and Andrew Rennie. *Financial Calculus.* Cambridge, U.K.: Cambridge University Press, 1996.

Beckers, Stan. "Standard Deviations Implied in Option Prices as Predictors of Future Stock Price Variability." *Journal of Banking and Finance* 5 (September 1981): 363–382.

Becketti, Sean. "The Prepayment Risk of Mortgage-Backed Securities." *Federal Reserve Bank of Kansas City Economic Review* 74 (1989): 43–57.

Beder, Tanya Styblo. "Equity Derivatives for Investors." *The Journal of Financial Engineering* 1 (September 1992): 174–195.

Behof, John P. "Reducing Credit Risk in Over-the-Counter Derivatives." *Federal Reserve Bank of Chicago Economic Perspectives* 17 (January-February 1993): 21–31.

Bernardo, Antonio E., and Bradford Cornell. "The Valuation of Complex Derivatives by Investment Firms: Empirical Evidence." *The Journal of Finance* 52 (June 1997): 785–798.

Bernstein, Peter L. *Capital Ideas: The Improbable Origins of Modern Wall Street.* New York: The Free Press, 1992.

Bernstein, Peter L. *Against the Gods: The Remarkable Story of Risk.* New York: Wiley, 1996.

Bessembinder, Hendrik. "An Empirical Analysis of Risk Premia in Futures Markets." *The Journal of Futures Markets* 13 (September 1993): 611–630.

Bhansali, Javesh D. "Managing Interest Rate Risk through Caps." *Derivatives Quarterly* 3 (Spring 1997): 39–45.

Bhattacharya, Mihir. "Transaction Data Tests of Efficiency of the Chicago Board Options Exchange." *Journal of Financial Economics* 12 (1983): 161–185.

Bicksler, James, and Andrew Chen. "An Economic Analysis of Interest Rate Swaps." *The Journal of Finance* 41 (July 1876): 645–656.

Billingsley, Randall S., and Don M. Chance. "Options Market Efficiency and the Box Spread Strategy." *The Financial Review* 20 (November 1985): 287–301.

Black, Fischer. "Fact and Fantasy in the Use of Options." *Financial Analysts Journal* 31 (July-August 1975): 36–41, 61–72.

Black, Fischer. "The Pricing of Commodity Contracts." *Journal of Financial Economics* 3 (January-February 1976): 167–179.

Black, Fischer. "How to Use the Holes in Black-Scholes." *Journal of Applied Corporate Finance* 1 (Winter 1989): 67–73.

Black, Fischer. "How We Came Up with the Option Formula." *Journal of Portfolio Management* 15 (Winter 1989): 4–8.

Black, Fischer, Emanuel Derman, and William Toy. "A One-Factor Model of Interest Rates and Its Application to Treasury Bond Options." *Financial Analysts Journal* 46 (January-February 1990): 33–39.

Black, Fischer, and Myron Scholes. "The Valuation of Option Contracts and a Test of Market Efficiency." *The Journal of Finance* 27 (May 1972): 399–418.

Black, Fischer, and Myron Scholes. "The Pricing of Options and Corporate Liabilities." *Journal of Political Economy* 81 (May-June 1973): 637–659.

Black, Fischer, and Piotr Karasinski. "Bond and Option Pricing When Short Rates Are Lognormal." *Financial Analysts Journal* 47 (July-August 1991): 52–59.

Blomeyer, Edward C., and James C. Boyd. "Empirical Tests of Boundary Conditions for Options on Treasury Bond Futures." *The Journal of Futures Markets* 4 (1988): 185–198.

Blomeyer, Edward C., and Robert C. Klemkosky. "Tests of Market Efficiency of American Call Options." In *Option Pricing,* edited by Menachem Brenner. Lexington, Massachusetts: Heath, 1983.

Bodurtha, James N., and Georges R. Courtadon. "Efficiency Tests of the Foreign Currency Options Market." *The Journal of Finance* 13 (March 1986): 151–162.

Bookstaber, Richard M. *Option Pricing and Investment Strategies.* Chicago: Probus Publishing, 1989.

Breen, Richard. "The Accelerated Binomial Option Pricing Model." *Journal of Financial and Quantitative Analysis* 25 (1991): 153–164.

Brennan, Michael J. "The Pricing of Contingent Claims in Discrete Time Models." *The Journal of Finance* 34 (1979): 53–68.

Brennan, Michael J., and Eduardo S. Schwartz. "The Valuation of American Put Options." *The Journal of Finance* 32 (May 1977): 449–462.

Brenner, Menachem, and Marti G. Subrahmanyam. "A Simple Formula to Compute the Implied Volatility." *Financial Analysts Journal* 45 (September-October 1988): 80–83.

Briys, Eric, Mondher Bellalah, Huu Minh Mai, and Françoise de Varenne. *Options, Futures and Exotic Derivatives: Theory, Application and Practice.* Chichester, U.K.: Wiley, 1998.

Brooks, Robert. *Building Financial Derivatives Applications with C++.* Westport, Connecticut: Quorum Books, 1999.

Brooks, Robert. *Interest Rate Modeling and the Risk Premiums in Interest Rate Swaps.* Charlottesville, Virginia: Association for Investment Management and Research, 1997.

Brooks, Robert, and Miles Livingston. "A Closed-Form Equation for Bond Convexity." *Financial Analysts Journal* 45 (November-December 1989): 78–79.

Brown, Keith C., ed. *Derivative Strategies for Managing Portfolio Risk.* Charlottesville, Virginia: Institute for Chartered Financial Analysts, 1993.

Brown, Keith C., Van W. Harlow, and Donald J. Smith. "The Empirical Analysis of Interest Rate Swap Spreads." *Journal of Fixed Income* 3 (1993): 61–78.

Brown, Keith C., and Donald J. Smith. "Forward Swaps, Swap Options, and the Management of Callable Debt." *Journal of Applied Corporate Finance* 2 (1990): 59–71.

Brown, Keith C., and Donald J. Smith. "Default Risk and Innovations in the Design of Interest Rate Swaps." *Financial Management* 22 (Summer 1993): 94–105.

Brown, Keith C., and Donald J. Smith. *Interest Rate and Currency Swaps: A Tutorial.* Charlottesville, Virginia: The Research Foundation of the Institute of Chartered Financial Analysts, 1995.

Burghardt, Galen, and Morton Lane. "How to Tell If Options Are Cheap." *Journal of Portfolio Management* 16 (Winter 1990): 72–78.

Caks, John, William R. Lane, Robert W. Greenleaf, and Reginald G. Joules. "A Simple Formula for Duration." *The Journal of Financial Research* 8 (Fall 1985): 245–249.

Campbell, Tim S., and William A. Kracaw. *Financial Risk Management: Fixed Income and Foreign Exchange.* New York: Harper Collins, 1993.

Carpenter, Jennifer N. "Current Issues in Accounting for Derivatives." *The Journal of Derivatives* 3 (Spring 1996): 65–71.

Castelino, Mark G. "Minimum-Variance Hedging with Futures Revisited." *Journal of Portfolio Management* 16 (Spring 1990): 74–80.

Celebuski, Matthew J., Joanne M. Hill, and John J. Kilgannon. "Managing Currency Exposures in International Portfolios." *Financial Analysts Journal* 46 (January-February 1990): 16–23.

Chance, Don M. *Managed Futures and Their Role in Investment Portfolios.* Charlottesville, Virginia: Research Foundation of the Institute of Chartered Financial Analysts, 1994.

Chance, Don M. "Translating the Greek: The Real Meaning of Call Option Derivatives." *Financial Analysts Journal* 50 (July-August 1994): 43–49.

Chance, Don M. "A Chronology of Derivatives." *Derivatives Quarterly* 2 (Winter 1995): 53–60.

Chance, Don. M. *Essays in Derivatives.* New Hope, Pennsylvania: Frank Fabozzi Associates, 1998.

Chance, Don M. "Research Trends in Derivatives and Risk Management Since Black-Scholes." *The Journal of Portfolio Management* 25th Anniversary Issue (May 1999): 35–46.

Chance, Don M., and Stephen P. Ferris. "The CBOE Call Option Index: A Historical Record." *The Journal of Portfolio Management* 12 (Fall 1985): 75–83.

Chance, Don M., and Hillary E. Fredericks. "Some Computational Problems in the Pedagogy of the Black-Scholes Model." *The Journal of Financial Education* 24 (Fall 1998): 61–70.

Chance, Don M., and Michael L. Hemler. "The Impact of Delivery Options on Futures Prices: A Survey." *The Journal of Futures Markets* 13 (April 1993): 127–155.

Chang, Carolyn W., and Jack S. K. Chang. "Forward and Futures Prices: Evidence from the Foreign Exchange Markets." *The Journal of Finance* 4 (September 1990): 1333–1336.

Chang, Eric C. "Returns to Speculators and the Theory of Normal Backwardation." *The Journal of Finance* 40 (March 1985): 193–208.

Chang, Eric C., Peter R. Locke, and Steven C. Mann. "The Effect of CME Rule 552 on Dual Traders." *The Journal of Futures Markets* 4 (1994): 493–510.

Chang, Jack S. K., and Latha Shanker. "Hedging Effectiveness of Options and Currency Futures." *The Journal of Futures Markets* 6 (Summer 1986): 289–305.

Chen, Andrew H., Marcia Millon Cornett, and Prafulla G. Nabar. "An Empirical Examination of Interest-Rate Futures Prices." *The Journal of Futures Markets* 13 (October 1993): 781–797.

Chen, K. C., and R. Stephen Sears. "Pricing the SPIN." *Financial Management* 19 (Summer 1990): 36–47.

Chew, Lilian. *Managing Derivatives Risk: The Use and Abuse of Leverage.* New York: Wiley, 1996.

Chicago Board Options Exchange. *Market Statistics 1996.* Chicago: Chicago Board Options Exchange, 1996.

Chiras, Donald P., and Steven Manaster. "The Information Content of Option Prices and a Test of Market Efficiency." *Journal of Financial Economics* 6 (June-September 1978): 213–234.

Chriss, Neil A. *Black-Scholes and Beyond.* Chicago: Irwin Professional, 1997.

Chua, Jess H. "A Closed-Form Formula for Calculating Bond Duration." *Financial Analysts Journal* 40 (May-June 1984): 76–78.

Clarke, Roger G. *Options and Futures: A Tutorial.* Charlottesville, Virginia: The Research Foundation of the Institute of Chartered Financial Analysts, 1992.

Clarke, Roger G., and Robert D. Arnott. "The Cost of Portfolio Insurance: Tradeoffs and Choices." *Financial Analysts Journal* 43 (November-December 1987): 35–47.

Clarke, Roger G., and Mark P. Kritzman. *Currency Management: Concepts and Practices.* Charlottesville, Virginia: The Research Foundation of the Institute of Chartered Financial Analysts, 1996.

Clewlow, Les, and Chris Strickland. *Implementing Derivatives Models.* Chichester, U.K.: Wiley, 1998.

Coleman, Thomas C., and Roger D. Rutz. "Self-Regulation and Government Regulation of Futures and Options Markets." *Journal of Business* 59 (1986): S1–S4.

Commodity Futures Trading Commission. *Annual Report,* various years.

Conine, Thomas E., and Maurry Tamarkin. "A Pedagogic Note on the Derivation of the Comparative Statics of the Option Pricing Model." *Financial Review* 19 (November 1984): 397–400.

Corcoran, Andrea M. "Developing a Risk Management Plan: A System Checklist for Derivatives." *Derivatives Quarterly* 1 (Winter 1994): 10–15.

Cornell, Bradford. "Spot Rates, Forward Rates and Exchange Market Efficiency." *Journal of Financial Economics* 5 (August 1977): 55–65.

Cornell, Bradford, and Mark Reinganum. "Forward and Futures Prices: Evidence from the Foreign Exchange Market." *The Journal of Finance* 36 (December 1981): 1035–1045.

Corrado, Charles J., and Tie Su. "Implied Volatility Skews and Stock Index Skewness and Kurtosis Implied by S&P 500 Index Option Prices." *The Journal of Derivatives* 4 (Summer 1997): 8–19.

Cox, John C., Jonathan E. Ingersoll, Jr., and Stephen A. Ross. "The Relation between Forward Prices and Futures Prices." *Journal of Financial Economics* 9 (December 1981): 321–346.

Cox, John C., and Stephen A. Ross. "The Valuation of Options for Alternative Stochastic Processes." *Journal of Financial Economics* 3 (1976): 145–166.

Cox, John C., Stephen A. Ross, and Mark Rubinstein. "Option Pricing: A Simplified Approach." *Journal of Financial Economics* 7 (September 1979): 229–263.

Cox, John C., and Mark Rubinstein. "A Survey of Alternative Option Pricing Models." In *Option Pricing,* edited by Menachem Brenner. Lexington, Massachusetts: Heath, 1983.

Cox, John C., and Mark Rubinstein. *Options Markets.* Englewood Cliffs, New Jersey: Prentice-Hall, 1985.

Crabbe, Leland E. and Joseph D. Argilagos. "Anatomy of the Structured Note Market." *Journal of Applied Corporate Finance* 7 (1994): 85–98.

Credit Derivatives: Applications for Risk Management, Investment and Portfolio Optimisation. London: Risk Books, 1998.

Credit Risk: Models and Management. London: Risk Books, 1999.

Crouhy, Michel, Dan Galai, and Robert Mark. "Model Risk." *The Journal of Financial Engineering* 7 (September-December 1998): 267–288.

Crowley, Paul. "Why and How Fundamental Managers Should Use Options: Part I." *Derivatives Quarterly* 2 (Spring 1996): 52–66.

Crowley, Paul. "Why and How Fundamental Managers Should Use Options: Part II." *Derivatives Quarterly* 2 (Summer 1996): 40–55.

Daigler, Robert T. *Financial Futures Markets: Concepts, Evidence, and Applications.* New York: Harper Collins, 1993.

Daigler, Robert T. *Financial Futures & Options Markets: Concepts and Strategies.* New York: Harper Collins, 1994.

Dawson, Frederic S. "Risks and Returns in Continuous Option Writing." *The Journal of Portfolio Management* 5 (Winter 1979): 58–63.

Dawson, Paul. "Comparative Pricing of American and European Index Options: An Empirical Analysis." *The Journal of Futures Markets* 14 (May 1994): 363–378.

Derivatives Credit Risk: Further Advances in Measurement and Management, 2nd ed. London: Risk Books, 1999.

Derman, Emanuel, and Iraj Kani. "Riding on a Smile." *Risk* 7 (January 1994): 32–39.

Derman, Emanuel, and Iraj Kani. "The Ins and Outs of Barrier Options: Part I." *Derivatives Quarterly* 3 (Winter 1996): 55–67.

Derman, Emanuel, and Iraj Kani. "The Ins and Outs of Barrier Options: Part II." *Derivatives Quarterly* 3 (Spring 1997): 73–80.

DeRosa, David F. *Currency Derivatives.* New York: Wiley, 1998.

DiMartino, Dawn, Linda Ward, Janet Stevens, and Winn Sargisson. "Procter & Gamble's Derivatives Loss: Isolated Incident or Wake-Up Call?" *Derivatives Quarterly* 2 (Spring 1996): 10–21.

Dowd, Kevin. *Beyond Value at Risk: The New Science of Risk Management.* Chichester, U.K.: Wiley, 1998.

Drennan, Ann S. "Keys to Successful Risk Management: Part 1." *Derivatives Quarterly* 1 (Summer 1995): 54–58.

Drennan, Ann S. "Keys to Successful Risk Management: Part 2." *Derivatives Quarterly* 2 (Winter 1995): 46–51.

Drennan, Ann S. "Keys to Successful Risk Management: Part 3." *Derivatives Quarterly* 2 (Spring 1996): 47–51.

Dubofsky, David A. *Options and Financial Futures: Valuation and Uses*. New York: McGraw-Hill, 1992.

Duffie, Darrell. *Futures Markets*. Englewood Cliffs, New Jersey: Prentice-Hall, 1989.

Duffie, Darrell. "Corporate Risk Management 101: Why Hedge?" *Corporate Risk Management* 3 (May 1991): 22–25.

Duffie, Darrell, and Kenneth J. Singleton. "An Econometric Model of the Term Structure of Interest-Rate Swap Yields." *The Journal of Finance* 52 (1997): 1287–1321.

Dunbar, Nicholas. *Inventing Money: The Story of Long-Term Capital Management and the Legends Behind It.* Chichester, U.K.: Wiley, 2000.

Dupire, Bruno. "Pricing with a Smile." *Risk* 7 (January 1994): 18–20.

Dusak, Katherine. "Futures Trading and Investor Returns: An Investigation of Commodity Risk Premiums." *Journal of Political Economy* 81 (December 1973): 1387–1406.

Eaker, Mark R., and Dwight M. Grant. "Currency Hedging Strategies for International Diversified Equity Portfolios." *Journal of Portfolio Management* 17 (Fall 1990): 30–32.

Eckerdt, Walter L., Jr., and Stephen L. Williams. "The Complete Options Indexes." *Financial Analysts Journal* 40 (July-August 1984): 48–57.

Ederington, Louis H. "The Hedging Performance of the New Futures Market." *The Journal of Finance* 34 (March 1979): 157–170.

Edwards, Franklin R., and Cindy W. Ma. *Futures and Options*. New York: McGraw-Hill, 1992.

Edwards, Franklin R., and Jimmy Liew. "Hedge Funds versus Managed Futures as Asset Classes." *The Journal of Derivatives* 6 (Summer 1999): 45–64.

Einzig, Robert, and Bruce Lange. "Swaps at Transamerica: Applications and Analyses." *Journal of Applied Corporate Finance* 2 (Winter 1990): 48–58.

El-Jahel, Lina, William Perraudin, and Peter Sellin. "Value at Risk for Derivatives." *The Journal of Derivatives* 6 (Summer 1999): 7–26.

Elton, Edwin, Martin Gruber, and Joel Rentzler. "Intra-Day Tests of Efficiency of the Treasury Bill Futures Market." *Review of Economics and Statistics* 66 (1984): 129–137.

Equity Derivatives: Applications in Risk Management and Investment. London: Risk Publications, Ltd., 1997.

Evans, John, and Stephen H. Archer. "Diversification and the Reduction of Dispersion: An Empirical Analysis." *The Journal of Finance* 23 (December 1968): 761–767.

Fabozzi, Frank. *The Handbook of Fixed Income Securities*, 4th ed. Homewood, Illinois: Business One Irwin, 1994.

Fay, Stephen. *The Collapse of Barings*. New York: W. W. Norton, 1997.

Ferguson, Robert. "Some Formulas for Evaluating Two Popular Option Strategies." *Financial Analysts Journal* 49 (September-October 1993): 71–76.

Figlewski, Stephen. "Explaining the Early Discounts on Stock Index Futures: The Case for Disequilibrium." *Financial Analysts Journal* 40 (1984): 43–47, 67.

Figlewski, Stephen. "Hedging Performance and Basis Risk in Stock Index Futures." *The Journal of Finance* 39 (July 1984): 657–669.

Figlewski, Stephen. "Hedging with Stock Index Futures: Theory and Application in a New Market." *The Journal of Futures Markets* 5 (Summer 1985): 183–199.

Figlewski, Stephen. "What Does an Option Pricing Model Tell Us about Option Prices?" *Financial Analysts Journal* 45 (September-October 1989): 12–15.

Figlewski, Stephen. "The Birth of the AAA Derivatives Subsidiary." *The Journal of Derivatives* 1 (Summer 1994): 80–84.

Figlewski, Stephen. "How to Lose Money in Derivatives." *The Journal of Derivatives* 2 (Winter 1994): 75–82.

Figlewski, Stephen, William L. Silber, and Marti G. Subrahmanyam. *Financial Options: From Theory to Practice*. Homewood, Illinois: Business One Irwin, 1990.

Financial Derivatives: New Instruments and Their Uses. Atlanta: Federal Reserve Bank of Atlanta, 1993.

Finnerty, John D. "Financial Engineering in Corporate Finance: An Overview." *Financial Management* 17 (Winter 1988): 14–33.

Finnerty, John D. "The Time Warner Rights Offering: A Case Study in Financial Engineering." *The Journal of Financial Engineering* 1 (June 1992): 38–61.

Francis, Jack Clark, and Avner Wolf. *The Handbook of Interest Rate Risk Management*. Burr Ridge, Illinois: Irwin Professional Publishing, 1994.

Franckle, Charles T. "The Hedging Performance of the New Futures Market: Comment." *The Journal of Finance* 35 (December 1980): 1273–1279.

French, Kenneth. "A Comparison of Futures and Forward Prices." *Journal of Financial Economics* 12 (1983): 311–342.

French, Kenneth. "Detecting Spot Price Forecasts in Futures Prices." *The Journal of Business* 59 (1986): S39–S54.

French, Kenneth. "Pricing Financial Futures Contracts: An Introduction." *The Journal of Applied Corporate Finance* 1 (1989): 59–66.

From Black-Scholes to Black Holes. London: Risk/FINEX, 1992.

Furbush, Dean. "Program Trading and Price Movements: Evidence from the October 1987 Market Crash." *Financial Management* 18 (Autumn 1989): 68–83.

Gadkari, Vilas. "Relative Pricing of Currency Options: A Tutorial." *Advances in Futures and Options Research* 1, part A (1986): 227–245.

Galai, Dan. "Test of Market Efficiency of the Chicago Board Options Exchange." *The Journal of Business* 50 (April 1977): 167–197.

Galai, Dan. "Characterization of Options." *Journal of Banking and Finance* 1 (December 1977): 373–385.

Galai, Dan. "Empirical Tests of Boundary Conditions for CBOE Options." *Journal of Financial Economics* 6 (1978): 187–211.

Galai, Dan. "A Convexity Test for Traded Options." *Quarterly Review of Economics and Business* 19 (Summer 1979): 83–90.

Galai, Dan. "A Survey of Empirical Tests of Option Pricing Models." *Option Pricing*, ed. M. Brenner, pp. 45–80. Lexington, Mass.: D.C. Heath, 1983.

Garcia, C. B., and F. J. Gould. "An Empirical Study of Portfolio Insurance." *Financial Analysts Journal* 43 (July-August 1987): 44–54.

Garman, Mark B., and Steven W. Kohlhagen. "Foreign Currency Option Values." *Journal of International Money and Finance* 2 (1983): 231–237.

Gastineau, Gary L. "An Index of Listed Options Premiums." *Financial Analysts Journal* 33 (May-June 1977): 70–75.

Gastineau, Gary. *The Options Manual*, 3d ed. New York: McGraw-Hill, 1988.

Gastineau, Gary. "An Introduction to Special Purpose Derivatives: Options with a Payout Depending on More Than One Variable." *The Journal of Derivatives* 1 (Fall 1993): 98–104.

Gastineau, Gary L. "An Introduction to Special Purpose Derivatives: Path-Dependent Options." *The Journal of Derivatives* 1 (Winter 1993): 78–86.

Gastineau, Gary L., and Mark P. Kritzman. *Dictionary of Financial Risk Management*, 2nd ed. New Hope, Pennsylvania: Frank Fabozzi Associates, 1999.

Gastineau, Gary L., and Albert Madansky. "Some Comments on the Chicago Board Options Exchange Call Option Index." *Financial Analysts Journal* 40 (July-August 1984): 58–67.

Gay, Gerald D., and Robert W. Kolb. "Immunizing Bond Portfolios with Interest Rate Futures." *Financial Management* 11 (Summer 1982): 81–89.

Gay, Gerald D., Robert W. Kolb, and Raymond Chiang. "Interest Rate Hedging: An Empirical Test of Alternative Strategies." *The Journal of Financial Research* 6 (Fall 1983): 1–13.

Gemmill, Gordon. *Options Pricing: An International Perspective.* London: McGraw-Hill, 1993.

George, Thomas J., and Francis A. Longstaff. "Bid-Ask Spreads and Trading Activity in the S&P 100 Index Options Market." *Journal of Financial and Quantitative Analysis* 28 (September 1993): 381–397.

Geske, Robert. "The Valuation of Compound Options." *Journal of Financial Economics* 7 (March 1979): 63–81.

Geske, Robert. "A Note on an Analytic Formula for Unprotected American Call Options on Stocks with Known Dividends." *Journal of Financial Economics* 7 (December 1979): 375–380.

Geske, Robert, and H. E. Johnson. "The American Put Option Valued Analytically." *The Journal of Finance* 39 (December 1984): 1511–1524.

Gibson, Rajna. *Option Valuation.* New York: McGraw-Hill, 1991.

Gombola, Michael J., Rodney L. Roenfeldt, and Philip L. Cooley. "Spreading Strategies in CBOE Options: Evidence on Market Performance." *The Journal of Financial Research* 1 (Winter 1978): 35–44.

Goodman, Laurie S. "The Use of Interest Rate Swaps in Managing Corporate Liabilities." *Journal of Applied Corporate Finance* 2 (1990): 35–47.

Goodman, Laurie S. "Anatomy of the Secondary Structured Note Market." *Derivatives Quarterly* 2 (1995), 39–43.

Gould, John P., and Dan Galai. "Transactions Costs and the Relationship between Put and Call Prices." *Journal of Financial Economics* 1 (1974): 105–129.

Grabbe, J. Orlin. "The Pricing of Call and Put Options on Foreign Exchange." *Journal of International Money and Finance* 2 (1983): 239–253.

Gramm, Wendy L., and Gerald D. Gay. "Scams, Scoundrels, and Scapegoats: A Taxonomy of CEA Regulation over Derivative Instruments." *The Journal of Derivatives* 1 (Spring 1994): 6–24.

Gray, Roger W. "The Search for a Risk Premium." *Journal of Political Economy* 64 (June 1961): 250–260.

Group of Thirty. *Derivatives: Practices and Principles.* Washington, D.C.: Group of Thirty, 1993.

Grube, R. Corwin, Don B. Panton, and J. Michael Terrell. "Risks and Rewards in Covered Call Positions." *The Journal of Portfolio Management* 5 (Winter 1979): 64–68.

Hart, James F. "The Riskless Option Hedge: An Incomplete Guide." *The Journal of Portfolio Management* 4 (Winter 1978): 58–63.

Hartzmark, Michael L. "Returns to Individual Traders of Futures: Aggregate Results." *Journal of Political Economy* 95 (1987): 1292–1306.

Hartzmark, Michael L. "Luck versus Forecasting Ability: Determinants of Trader Performance in Futures Markets." *Journal of Business* 64 (1991): 49–74.

Haug, Espen Gaarder. *The Complete Guide to Option Pricing Formulas.* New York: McGraw-Hill, 1997.

Heath, David, Robert Jarrow, and Andrew Morton. "Bond Pricing and the Term Structure of Interest Rates." *Econometrica* 60 (January 1992): 77–105.

Heath, David, Robert Jarrow, and Andrew Morton. "Contingent Claim Valuation with a Random Evolution of Interest Rates." *The Review of Futures Markets* 9 (1990): 54–76.

Heath, David, Robert Jarrow, and Andrew Morton. "Bond Pricing and the Term Structure of Interest Rates: A Discrete Time Approximation." *Journal of Financial and Quantitative Analysis* 25 (1990): 419–440.

Hentschel, Ludger, and Clifford W. Smith, Jr. "Controllings Risks in Derivatives Markets." *The Journal of Financial Engineering* 4 (June 1995): 101–125.

Herbst, A. F., D. D. Kare, and S. C. Caples. "Hedging Effectiveness and Minimum Risk Hedge Ratios in the Presence of Autocorrelation: Foreign Currency Futures." *The Journal of Futures Markets* 3 (1989): 185–197.

Hicks, J. R. *Value and Capital,* 2d ed. Oxford: Clarendon Press, 1939.

Hieronymous, Thomas A. *The Economics of Futures Trading.* New York: Commodity Research Bureau, 1977.

Hill, Joanne, and Frank J. Jones. "Equity Trading, Program Trading, Portfolio Insurance, Computer Trading and All That." *Financial Analysts Journal* 44 (July-August 1988): 29–38.

Hill, Joanne, and Thomas Schneeweis. "The Hedging Effectiveness of Foreign Currency Futures." *The Journal of Financial Research* 5 (Spring 1982): 95–104.

Ho, Thomas S. Y., and Sang-Bin Lee. "Term Structure Movements and Pricing Interest Rate Contingent Claims." *The Journal of Finance* 41 (December 1986): 1011–1030.

Houthakker, H. S. "Can Speculators Forecast Prices?" *Review of Economics and Statistics* 39 (1957): 143–151.

Howard, Charles T., and Louis J. D'Antonio. "The Cost of Hedging and the Optimal Hedge Ratio." *The Journal of Futures Markets* 14 (April 1994): 237–258.

Hsia, Chi-Cheng. "On Binomial Option Pricing." *The Journal of Financial Research* 6 (1983), 41–46.

Hsieh, David A., and Merton H. Miller. "Margin Regulation and Stock Market Volatility." *The Journal of Finance* 45 (March 1990): 3–29.

Hull, John. *Introduction to Options and Futures Markets,* 2nd ed. Englewood Cliffs, New Jersey: Prentice-Hall, 1995.

Hull, John. *Options, Futures and Other Derivatives,* 4th ed. Upper Saddle River, New Jersey: Prentice-Hall, 1999.

James, Jessica, and Nick Webber. *Interest Rate Modelling.* Chichester, U.K.: Wiley, 2000.

Jarrow, Robert A. *Modelling Fixed Income Securities and Interest Rate Options.* New York: McGraw-Hill, 1996.

Jarrow, Robert, ed. *Over the Rainbow: Developments in Exotic Options and Complex Swaps.* London: Financial Engineering Ltd., 1995.

Jarrow, Robert, and George Oldfield. "Forward Contracts and Futures Contracts." *Journal of Financial Economics* 9 (1981): 373–382.

Jarrow, Robert, and Andrew Rudd. *Option Pricing.* Homewood, Illinois: Irwin, 1983.

Jarrow, Robert, and Stuart Turnbull. *Derivative Securities.* 2nd ed. Cincinnati: South-Western, 2000.

Johnson, L. L. "The Theory of Hedging and Speculation in Commodity Futures Markets." *Review of Economic Studies* 27 (October 1960): 139–151.

Johnson, Philip McBride. *Derivatives: A Manager's Guide to the World's Most Powerful Financial Instruments.* New York: McGraw-Hill, 1999.

Jones, Frank J. "Spreads: Tails, Turtles, and All That." *The Journal of Futures Markets* 2 (Spring 1981): 63–82.

Jorion, Philippe. *Value at Risk: A New Benchmark for Controlling Derivatives Risk.* Chicago: Irwin Professional, 1996.

Jorion, Philippe, and Sarkis Joseph Khoury. *Financial Risk Management: Domestic and International Dimensions.* Cambridge, Massachusetts: Blackwell, 1996.

Jorion, Philippe, and Robert Roper. *Big Bets Gone Bad: Derivatives and Bankruptcy in Orange County.* Orlando: Academic Press, 1995.

Kairys, Joseph P., Jr., and Nicholas Valerio III. "The Market for Equity Options in the 1870s." *The Journal of Finance* 52 (September 1997): 1707–1723.

Kamara, Avraham. "Issues in Futures Markets: A Survey." *The Journal of Futures Markets* 2 (Fall 1982): 261–294.

Kamara, Avraham. "The Behavior of Futures Prices: A Review of Theory and Evidence." *Financial Analysts Journal* 40 (July-August 1984): 68–75.

Kane, Edward J. "Regulatory Structure in Futures Markets: Jurisdictional Competition Between the SEC, the CFTC and Other Agencies." *The Journal of Futures Markets* 3 (1984): 367–384.

Kat, Harry M. "Portfolio Insurance: A Comparison of Alternative Strategies." *The Journal of Financial Engineering* 2 (December 1993): 415–442.

Kawaller, Ira G. "A Note: Debunking the Myth of the Risk-Free Return." *The Journal of Futures Markets* 7 (1987): 327–331.

Kawaller, Ira G. "Interest Rate Swaps versus Eurodollar Strips." *Financial Analysts Journal* 45 (September-October 1989): 55–61.

Kawaller, Ira G. "Choosing the Best Interest Rate Hedge Ratio." *Financial Analysts Journal* 48 (September-October 1992): 74–77.

Kawaller, Ira G. "Foreign Exchange Hedge Management Tools: A Way to Enhance Performance." *Financial Analysts Journal* 49 (September-October 1993): 79–80.

Kawaller, Ira G. "Comparing Eurodollar Strips to Interest Rate Swaps." *The Journal of Derivatives* 2 (Fall 1994): 67–79.

Kawaller, Ira G. "Understanding Structured Notes." *Derivatives Quarterly* 1 (Spring 1995): 29–32.

Kawaller, Ira G. "Trading and Hedging with Option Calendar Spreads." *Derivatives Quarterly* 1 (Summer 1995): 73–76.

Kawaller, Ira G. "Short-Term Interest Rate Hedging: Hedge Ratios Revisited." *The Journal of Financial Engineering* 3 (September 1996): 267–277.

Kawaller, Ira G. "The TED Spread." *Derivatives Quarterly* 3 (Spring 1997): 46–54.

Kawaller, Ira G. "Tailing Futures Hedges/Tailing Spreads." *The Journal of Derivatives* 5 (Winter 1997): 62–70.

Keynes, John Maynard. *A Treatise on Money.* London: Macmillan, 1930.

Klein, Robert A., and Jess Lederman, eds. *Derivatives Risk and Responsibility.* Chicago: Irwin Professional, 1996.

Klemkosky, Robert C., and Bruce G. Resnick. "Put-Call Parity and Market Efficiency." *The Journal of Finance* 34 (December 1979): 1141–1155.

Klemkosky, Robert C., and Bruce G. Resnick. "An Ex-Ante Analysis of Put-Call Parity." *Journal of Financial Economics* 8 (1980): 363–378.

Kolb, Robert W. *Options: An Introduction.* Miami: Kolb Publishing, 1991.

Kolb, Robert W. *Understanding Futures Markets,* 3rd. ed. Miami: Kolb Publishing, 1991.

Kolb, Robert W. *The Financial Derivatives Reader.* Miami: Kolb Publishing, 1992.

Kolb, Robert W. *Futures, Options and Swaps.* Malden, Massachusetts: Blackwell, 2000.

Kolb, Robert W. *Financial Derivatives,* 2nd ed. Cambridge, Massachusetts: Blackwell, 1996.

Kolb, Robert W., and Raymond Chiang. "Improving Hedging Performance Using Interest Rate Futures." *Financial Management* 10 (Autumn 1981): 72–79.

Kolb, Robert W., Gerald D. Gay, and William C. Hunter. "Liquidity Requirements for Financial Futures Hedges." *Financial Analysts Journal* 41 (May-June 1985): 60–68.

Kritzman, Mark. "What Practitioners Need to Know About Option Replication." *Financial Analysts Journal* 48 (January-February 1992): 21–23.

Kritzman, Mark. "The Minimum-Risk Currency Hedge Ratio and Foreign Asset Exposure." *Financial Analysts Journal* 49 (September-October 1993): 77–78.

Kupiec, Paul. "Stress Testing in a Value at Risk Framework." *The Journal of Derivatives* 6 (Fall 1998): 7–24.

Kuserk, Gregory J., and Peter R. Locke. "Scalper Behavior in Futures Markets: An Empirical Examination." *The Journal of Futures Markets* 13 (June 1993): 409–431.

Kuserk, Gregory J., and Peter R. Locke. "Market Maker Competition on Futures Exchanges." *The Journal of Derivatives* 1 (Summer 1994): 56–66.

Kuserk, Gregory J., and Peter R. Locke. "Market Making with Price Limits." *The Journal of Futures Markets* 16 (September 1996): 677–696.

Labuszewski, John. *Trading Options on Futures.* New York: Wiley, 2000.

Latané, Henry A., and Richard J. Rendleman, Jr. "Standard Deviations of Stock Price Ratios Implied in Option Prices." *The Journal of Finance* 31 (May 1976): 369–382.

Leeson, Nick, and Edward Whitley. *Rogue Trader: How I Brought Down Barings Bank and Shook the Financial World.* Boston: Little, Brown, 1996.

Leuthold, Raymond M., Joan C. Junkus, and Jean E. Cordier. *The Theory and Practice of Futures Markets.* Englewood Cliffs, New Jersey: Prentice-Hall, 1989.

Lewent, Judy C., and A. John Kearney. "Identifying, Measuring, and Hedging Currency Risk at Merck." *Journal of Applied Corporate Finance* 2 (Winter 1990): 19–28.

Lintner, John. "The Valuation of Risk Assets and the Selection of Risky Investments in Stock Portfolios and Capital Budgets." *Review of Economics and Statistics* 47 (February 1965): 13–37.

Litzenberger, Robert H. "Swaps: Plain and Fanciful." *The Journal of Finance* 47 (July 1992): 831–850.

Locke, Peter R., Asani Sarker, and Lifan Wu. "Market Liquidity and Trade Welfare in Multiple Dealer Markets: Evidence from Dual Trading Restrictions." *Journal of Financial and Quantitative Analysis* 34 (March 1999): 57–88.

Longstaff, Francis A. "The Benefits and Costs of Dual Trading." *Journal of Financial Engineering* 2 (1993): 51–54.

Macbeth, James D., and Larry J. Merville. "An Empirical Examination of the Black-Scholes Call Option Pricing Model." *The Journal of Finance* 34 (December 1979): 1173–1186.

Macbeth, James D., and Larry J. Merville. "Tests of the Black-Scholes and Cox Call Option Valuation Models." *The Journal of Finance* 35 (May 1980): 285–300.

Mackay, Robert J. "Removing the Major Tax Impediment to Business Hedging." *The Journal of Financial Engineering* 2 (March 1993): 19–26.

MacKinlay, A. Craig, and Krishna Ramaswamy. "Index-Futures Arbitrage and the Behavior of Stock Index Futures Prices." *The Review of Financial Studies* 1 (1988): 137–158.

Malkiel, Burton G., and Richard E. Quandt. *Strategies and Rational Decisions in the Securities Options Market.* Cambridge, Massachusetts: M.I.T. Press, 1969.

Managing Currency Risk. Charlottesville Association for Investment Mangement and Research, 1987.

Manaster, Steven, and Gary Koehler. "The Calculation of Implied Variances from the Black-Scholes Model: A Note." *The Journal of Finance* 37 (March 1982): 227–230.

Manaster, Stephen, and Steven C. Mann. "Life in the Pits: Competitive Market Making and Inventory Control." *Review of Financial Studies* 9 (Fall 1996): 953–975.

Mann, Steven V. "Calls Are Like Air Conditioners; Puts Are Like Heaters." *Journal of Financial Education* 22 (Spring 1996): 61–64.

Margrabe, William. "The Value of an Option to Exchange One Asset for Another." *The Journal of Finance* 33 (March 1978): 177–186.

Marshall, John F., and Vipul K. Bansal. *Financial Engineering,* 2nd. ed. Miami: Kolb Publishing, 1993.

Marshall, John F., and Kenneth R. Kapner. *The Swaps Market,* 2nd. ed. Miami: Kolb Publishing, 1993.

Mason, Scott, Robert Merton, André Perold, and Peter Tufano. *Cases in Financial Engineering: Applied Studies of Financial Innovation.* Englewood Cliffs, New Jersey: Prentice-Hall, 1995.

McCabe, George M., and Charles T. Franckle. "The Effectiveness of Rolling the Hedge Forward in the Treasury Bill Futures Market." *Financial Management* 12 (Summer 1983): 21–29.

McCabe, George M., and Donald P. Solberg. "Hedging in the Treasury Bill Futures Market When the Hedged Instrument and the Delivered Instrument Are Not Matched." *The Journal of Futures Markets* 9 (December 1989): 529–537.

McIver, Jeffrey. "Tree Power." *Risk* 6 (December 1993): 58–64.

McLaughlin, Robert. *Over-the-Counter Derivative Products.* New York: McGraw-Hill, 1999.

McMillan, Lawrence G. *McMillan on Options.* New York: John Wiley, 1996.

Merton, Robert C. "The Relationship between Put and Call Option Prices: Comment." *The Journal of Finance* 28 (March 1973): 183–184.

Merton, Robert C. "Theory of Rational Option Pricing." *Bell Journal of Economics and Management Science* 4 (Spring 1973): 141–183.

Meulbroek, Lisa. "A Comparison of Forward and Futures Prices of an Interest Rate–Sensitive Financial Asset." *The Journal of Finance* 47 (March 1992): 381–396.

Midanek, Deborah Hicks, and James I. Midanek. "Understanding Mortgage-Backed Securities." *Derivatives Quarterly* 2 (Spring 1996): 39–46.

Miller, Merton H. "Financial Innovation: Achievements and Prospects." *The Journal of Financial Engineering* 1 (June 1992): 1–13.

Miller, Merton H. "Index Arbitrage: Villain or Scapegoat?" *The Journal of Financial Engineering* 1 (December 1992): 319–324.

Modest, David M., and Mahedevan Sundaresan. "The Relationship between Spot and Futures Prices in Stock Index Futures Markets: Some Preliminary Evidence." *The Journal of Futures Markets* 3 (1983): 15–41.

Mossin, Jan. "Equilibrium in a Capital Asset Market." *Econometrica* 34 (October 1966): 768–783.

Mueller, Paul A. "Covered Call Options: An Alternative Investment Strategy." *Financial Management* 10 (Winter 1981): 64–71.

Musiela, Marek, and Marek Rutkowski. *Martingale Methods in Financial Modelling.* Berlin, Germany: Springer-Verlag, 1997.

Nance, Deana R., Clifford W. Smith, Jr., and Charles W. Smithson. "On the Determinants of Corporate Hedging." *The Journal of Finance* 48 (March 1993): 267–284.

Nawalkha, Sanjay, and Donald Chambers. "The Binomial Model and Risk Neutrality: Some Important Details." *The Financial Review* 30 (1995): 605–618.

Neftci, Salih N. *An Introduction to the Mathematics of Financial Derivatives.* San Diego: Academic Press, 1996.

Nelken, Israel. *The Handbook of Exotic Options: Instruments, Analysis and Applications.* Chicago: Irwin Professional, 1996.

Neuberger, Anthony. "Hedging Long-Term Exposures with Multiple Short-Term Futures Contracts." *The Review of Financial Studies* 12 (Fall 1999): 429–459.

Nielsen, Lars Tyge. *Pricing and Hedging of Derivative Securities.* Oxford, U.K.: Oxford University Press, 1999.

O'Brien, Thomas J. "The Mechanics of Portfolio Insurance." *The Journal of Portfolio Management* 14 (Spring 1985): 40–47.

The Options Institute. *Options: Essential Concepts and Trading Strategies.* 2nd ed. New York: McGraw-Hill, 1994.

Over the Rainbow. London: Risk, 1996.

Parkinson, Michael. "Option Pricing: The American Put." *The Journal of Business* 50 (January 1977): 21–36.

Petzel, Todd E. "How Expensive Is It to Insure Your U.S. Equity Portfolio?" *Derivatives Quarterly* 3 (Spring 1997): 81–83.

Phillips, Susan M., and Clifford W. Smith, Jr. "Trading Costs for Listed Options: The Implications for Market Efficiency." *Journal of Financial Economics* 8 (1980): 179–201.

Pirrong, Stephen Craig. "The Self-Regulation of Commodity Exchanges: The Case of Market Manipulation." *Journal of Law and Economics* 38 (April 1995): 141–206.

Pirrong, Stephen Craig. "Market Liquidity and Depth on Computerized and Open Outcry Trading Systems." *The Journal of Futures Markets* 16 (August 1996): 519–543.

Pirrong, Stephen Craig. "Metalgesellschaft: A Prudent Hedger Ruined, or a Wildcatter on NYMEX? *The Journal of Futures Markets* 17 (August 1997): 543–578.

Poitras, Geoffrey. "Turtles, Tails, and Stereos: Arbitrage and the Design of Futures Spread Trading Strategies." *The Journal of Derivatives* 5 (Winter 1997): 71–87.

Pounds, Henry M. "Covered Call Option Writing: Strategies and Results." *The Journal of Portfolio Management* 5 (Winter 1978): 31–42.

Pozen, Robert. "The Purchase of Protective Puts by Financial Institutions." *Financial Analysts Journal* 34 (July-August 1978): 47–60.

Rao, Ramesh K. S. "Modern Option Pricing Models: A Dichotomous Classification." *The Journal of Financial Research* 4 (Spring 1981): 33–44.

Rendleman, Richard J., Jr. "A Reconciliation of Potentially Conflicting Approaches to Hedging with Futures." *Advances in Futures and Options Research* 6 (1993): 81–92.

Rendleman, Richard J., Jr."Option Investing from a Risk-Return Perspective." *The Journal of Portfolio Management* 25th Anniversary Issue (May 1999): 109–121.

Rendleman, Richard J., Jr. "Duration-Based Hedging with Treasury Bond Futures." *The Journal of Fixed Income* 9 (June 1999): 84–91.

Rendlemen, Richard J., Jr. "First Derivatives National Bank: A Case Problem in the Management of Interest Rate Risk." *The Journal of Risk* 1 (1999): 63–85.

Rendleman, Richard J., Jr., and Brit J. Barter. "Two-State Option Pricing." *The Journal of Finance* 34 (December 1979): 1093–1110.

Rendleman, Richard J., Jr., and Christopher Carabini. "The Efficiency of the Treasury Bill Futures Market." *The Journal of Finance* 44 (September 1979): 895–914.

Rendleman, Richard J., Jr., and Richard W. McEnally. "Assessing the Cost of Portfolio Insurance." *Financial Analysts Journal* 43 (May-June 1987): 27–37.

Rentzler, Joel C. "Trading Treasury Bond Spreads against Treasury Bill Futures: A Model and Empirical Tests of the Turtle Trade." *The Journal of Futures Markets* 6 (1986): 41–61.

Resnick, Bruce G. "The Relationship between Futures Prices for U.S. Treasury Bonds." *Review of Research in Futures Markets* 3 (1984): 88–104.

Resnick, Bruce G., and Elizabeth Hennigar. "The Relationship between Futures and Cash Prices for U.S. Treasury Bonds." *Review of Research in Futures Markets* 2 (1983): 282–298.

Ritchken, Peter. *Options: Theory, Strategy, and Applications.* Glenview, Illinois: Scott, Foresman, 1987.

Ritchken, Peter. *Derivative Markets: Theory, Strategy and Applications.* New York: HarperCollins, 1996.

Ritchken, Peter H., and Harvey M. Salkin. "Safety First Selection Techniques for Option Spreads." *The Journal of Portfolio Management* 9 (1981): 61–67.

Ritter, Jay R. "How I Helped Make Fischer Black Wealthier." *Financial Management* 25 (Winter 1996): 104–107.

Roll, Richard. "An Analytic Valuation Formula for Unprotected American Call Options on Stocks with Known Dividends." *Journal of Financial Economics* 5 (November 1977): 251–258.

Roll, Richard, and Stephen A. Ross. "The Arbitrage Pricing Theory Approach to Strategic Portfolio Planning." *Financial Analysts Journal* 40 (May-June 1984): 14–26.

Ronn, Aimee Gerbarg, and Ehud I. Ronn. "The Box Spread Arbitrage Conditions: Theory, Tests, and Investment Strategies." *The Review of Financial Studies* 2 (1989): 91–108.

Rubinstein, Mark. "Nonparametric Tests of Alternative Option Pricing Models Using All Reported Trades and Quotes on the 30 Most Active CBOE Option Classes from August 23, 1976, through August 31, 1978." *The Journal of Finance* 40 (June 1985): 455–480.

Rubinstein, Mark. "Alternative Paths to Portfolio Insurance." *Financial Analysts Journal* 41 (July-August 1985): 42–52.

Rubinstein, Mark. "Derivative Assets Analysis." *The Journal of Economic Perspectives* 1 (Fall 1987): 73–93.

Rubinstein, Mark. "Portfolio Insurance and the Market Crash." *Financial Analysts Journal* 44 (January-February 1988): 38–47.

Rubinstein, Mark. "Implied Binomial Trees." *The Journal of Finance* 49 (July 1994): 771–818.

Rubinstein, Mark. *Derivatives: A PowerPlus Picture Book: Volume 1: Futures, Options and Dynamic Strategies.* Corte Madera, California: Mark Rubinstein, 1999.

Rubinstein, Mark. "The Valuation of Uncertain Income Streams and the Pricing of Options." *Bell Journal of Economics* 7 (1976): 407–425.

Rubinstein, Mark, and Hayne E. Leland. "Replicating Options with Positions in Stock and Cash." *Financial Analysts Journal* 37 (July-August 1981): 63–72.

Rubinstein, Mark, and Eric Reiner. "Breaking Down the Barriers." *Risk* 4 (September 1991): 28–35.

Santoni, G. J., and Tung Liu. "Circuit Breakers and Stock Market Volatility." *The Journal of Futures Markets* 13 (May 1993): 261–277.

Saunders, Anthony. *Credit Risk Measurement: New Approaches to Value-at-Risk and Other Paradigms.* New York: Wiley, 1999.

Schachter, Barry. "Swap Pricing and Swap Mispricing." *Derivatives Quarterly* 2 (Summer 1996): 59–64.

Senchak, Andrew J., and John C. Easterwood. "Cross Hedging CD's with Treasury Bill Futures." *The Journal of Futures Markets* 3 (1983): 429–438.

Shafer, Carl E. "Hedge Ratios and Basis Behavior: An Intuitive Insight?" *The Journal of Futures Markets* 13 (December 1993): 837–847.

Shapiro, Alan C. *Multinational Financial Management,* 6th ed. New York: Wiley, 1999.

Sharpe, William F. "Capital Asset Prices: A Theory of Market Equilibrium under Conditions of Risk." *The Journal of Finance* 19 (September 1964): 425–442.

Shastri, Kuldeep, and Kishore Tandon. "Arbitrage Tests of the Efficiency of the Foreign Currency Options Markets." *Journal of International Money and Finance* 4 (December 1985): 455–468.

Shastri, Kuldeep, and Kishore Tandon. "On the Use of European Models to Price American Options on Foreign Currency." *The Journal of Futures Markets* 6 (Spring 1986): 93–108.

Shastri, Kuldeep, and Kishore Tandon. "Options on Futures Contracts: A Comparison of European and American Pricing Models." *The Journal of Futures Markets* 6 (Winter 1986): 593–618.

Sheikh, Aamir M. "Transaction Data Tests of S&P 100 Call Option Pricing." *Journal of Financial and Quantitative Analysis* 26 (December 1991): 459–475.

Shimko, David C. *Finance in Continuous Time.* Miami: Kolb Publishing, 1992.

Siegel, Daniel R., and Diane F. Siegel. *Futures Markets.* Hinsdale, Illinois: Dryden Press, 1990.

Siems, Thomas F. "Risk Management: Turning Volatility into Profitability." *Derivatives Quarterly* 2 (Spring 1996): 22–31.

Silber, William L. "Marketmaker Behavior in an Auction Market: An Analysis of Scalpers in Futures Markets." *The Journal of Finance* 39 (September 1984): 937–953.

Silber, William L. "Technical Trading: When It Works and When It Doesn't." *The Journal of Derivatives* 1 (Spring 1994): 39–44.

Singleton, J. Clay, and Robin Grieves. "Synthetic Puts and Portfolio Insurance Strategies." *The Journal of Portfolio Management* 10 (Spring 1984): 63–69.

Slivka, Ronald T. "Risk and Return for Option Investment Strategies." *Financial Analysts Journal* 36 (September-October 1980): 67–73.

Slivka, Ronald T. "Call Option Spreading." *The Journal of Portfolio Management* 7 (Spring 1981): 71–76.

Smith, Clifford W., Jr. "Option Pricing: A Review." *Journal of Financial Economics* 3 (January-March 1976): 3–51.

Smith, Clifford W. Jr. "Corporate Risk Management: Theory and Practice." *The Journal of Derivatives* 2 (Summer 1995): 21–30.

Smith, Clifford W., Jr., and Charles W. Smithson. *The Handbook of Financial Engineering: New Financial Product Innovations, Applications, and Analyses.* New York: Harper Business, 1990.

Smith, Clifford W., Jr., Charles W. Smithson, and Lee Macdonald Wakeman. "The Evolving Market for Swaps." *Midland Corporate Financial Journal* 3 (Winter 1986): 20–32.

Smith, Clifford W., Jr., and René M. Stulz. "The Determinants of Firms' Hedging Policies." *Journal of Financial and Quantitative Analysis* 20 (1985): 391–405.

Smith, Donald J. "The Arithmetic of Financial Engineering." *Journal of Applied Corporate Finance* 1 (1989): 49–58.

Smith, Donald. J. "Aggressive Corporate Finance: A Close Look at the Procter & Gamble-Bankers Trust Leveraged Swap." *The Journal of Derivatives* 4 (Summer 1997): 67–79.

Smith, Donald R. "A Simple Method for Pricing Interest Rate Swaptions." *Financial Analyst Journal* 47 (May-June 1991): 72–76.

Smith, Stephen D. "Analyzing Risk and Return for Mortgage-Backed Securities." *Federal Reserve Bank of Atlanta Economic Review* 76 (1991): 2–13.

Smith, Tom, and Robert E. Whaley. "Assessing the Costs of Regulation: The Case of Dual Trading." *Journal of Law and Economics* 37 (1994): 215–246.

Smithson, Charles W. *Managing Financial Risk: A Guide to Derivative Products, Financial Engineering, and Value Maximization,* 3rd ed. New York: McGraw-Hill, 1998.

Sofianos, George. "Index Arbitrage Profitability." *The Journal of Derivatives* 1 (Fall 1993): 6–20.

Solnik, Bruno H. *International Investments,* 4th ed. Reading, Massachusetts: Addison-Wesley, 1999.

Srivastava, Sanjay. "Value-at-Risk Analysis of a Leverage Swap." *The Journal of Risk* 1 (1999): 87–101.

Stapleton, Richard, and Marti Subrahmanyam. "The Valuation of Options When Asset Returns Are Generated by a Binomial Process." *The Journal of Finance* 39 (1984): 1525–1539.

Stein, Jerome L. "The Simultaneous Determination of Spot and Futures Prices." *The American Economic Review* 51 (December 1961): 1012–1025.

Stoll, Hans R. "The Relationship between Put and Call Option Prices." *The Journal of Finance* 31 (May 1969): 319–332.

Stoll, Hans R. "Principles of Inter-Market Regulation." *The Journal of Financial Engineering* 2 (March 1993): 65–71.

Stoll, Hans R. "Lost Barings: A Tale in Three Parts Concluding with a Lesson." *The Journal of Derivatives* 3 (Fall 1995): 109–115.

Stoll, Hans R., and Robert E. Whaley. "Program Trading and Expiration Day Effects." *Financial Analysts Journal* 43 (March-April 1987): 16–28.

Stoll, Hans R., and Robert E. Whaley. "Futures and Options on Stock Indexes: Economic Purpose, Arbitrage, and Market Structure." *The Review of Futures Markets* 7 (1988): 224–229.

Stoll, Hans R., and Robert E. Whaley. *Futures and Options: Theory and Applications.* Cincinnati: South-Western, 1993.

Stone, Charles A., and Anne Zissu. "The Risk of Mortgage Backed Securities and Their Derivatives." *Journal of Applied Corporate Finance* 7 (1994): 99–111.

Strong, Robert A. *Speculative Markets,* 2nd. ed. New York: Harper Collins, 1994.

Stulz, René M. "Options on the Minimum or the Maximum of Two Risky Assets: Analysis and Applications." *Journal of Financial Economics* 10 (July 1982): 161–185.

Sun, Tong-Sheng, Suresh Sundaresan, and Ching Wang. "Interest Rate Swaps: An Empirical Investigation." *Journal of Financial Economics* 34 (1993): 77–99.

Sundaram, Rangarajan K. "Equivalent Martingale Measures and Risk Neutral Pricing: An Expository Note." *The Journal of Derivatives* 5 (Fall 1997): 85–98.

Sundaresan, Suresh. "Futures Prices on Yields, Forward Prices, and Implied Forward Prices from Term Structure." *Journal of Financial and Quantitative Analysis* 26 (September 1991): 409–424.

Sundaresan, Suresh. *Fixed Income Markets and Their Derivatives.* Cincinnati: South-Western, 1997.

Taleb, Nassim. *Dynamic Hedging: Managing Vanilla and Exotic Options.* New York: Wiley, 1997.

Telser, Lester G. "Futures Trading and the Storage of Cotton and Wheat." *Journal of Political Economy* 66 (June 1958): 233–255.

Telser, Lester G. "Why There Are Organized Futures Markets." *Journal of Law and Economics* 24 (1981): 1–22.

Telser, Lester G., and Harlow N. Higinbotham. "Organized Futures Markets: Costs and Benefits." *Journal of Political Economy* 85 (1977): 969–1000.

Thomsett, Michael. *Getting Started in Options.* 3rd ed. New York: Wiley, 1997.

Toevs, Alden L., and David P. Jacob. "Futures and Alternative Hedge Ratio Methodologies." *Journal of Portfolio Management* 12 (Spring 1986): 60–70.

Tosini, Paula A. "Stock Index Futures and Stock Market Activity in October 1987." *Financial Analysts Journal* 44 (January-February 1988): 28–37.

Trennepohl, Gary. "A Comparison of Listed Option Premiums and Black-Scholes Model Prices: 1973–1979." *The Journal of Financial Research* 4 (Spring 1981): 11–20.

Trennepohl, Gary L., and William P. Dukes. "Return and Risk from Listed Option Investments." *The Journal of Financial Research* 2 (Spring 1979): 37–49.

Trippi, Robert R. "A Test of Option Market Efficiency Using a Random-Walk Valuation Model." *Journal of Economics and Business* 29 (Winter 1977): 93–98.

Tucker, Alan L. "Empirical Tests of the Efficiency of the Currency Option Market." *The Journal of Financial Research* 8 (Winter 1985): 275–285.

Tucker, Alan L. *Financial Futures, Options, and Swaps.* St. Paul: West Publishing, 1991.

Turnbull, Stuart M. "Swaps: A Zero Sum Game?" *Financial Management* 16 (Spring 1987): 15–21.

Veit, W. Theodore, and Wallace W. Reiff. "Commercial Banks and Interest Rate Futures: A Hedging Survey." *The Journal of Futures Markets* 3 (1983): 283–293.

Vignola, Anthony, and Charles Dale. "The Efficiency of the Treasury Bill Futures Market: An Analysis of Alternative Specifications." *The Journal of Financial Research* 3 (1980): 169–188.

Wagner, Wayne, and Sheila Lau. "The Effect of Diversification on Risk." *Financial Analysts Journal* 27 (November-December 1971): 48–53.

Wall, Larry D., and John J. Pringle. "Interest Rate Swaps: A Review of the Issues." *Federal Reserve Bank of Atlanta Economic Review* (November-December 1988): 22–40.

Wall, Larry D., and John J. Pringle. "Alternative Explanations of Interest Rate Swaps: A Theoretical and Empirical Analysis." *Financial Management* 18 (1989): 59–73.

Welch, Robert L., and Louis Culumovic. "A Profitable Call Spreading Strategy on the CBOE." *The Journal of Derivatives* 2 (Spring 1995): 24–44.

Whaley, Robert E. "On the Valuation of American Call Options on Stocks with Known Dividends." *Journal of Financial Economics* 9 (June 1981): 207–212.

Whaley, Robert E. "Valuation of American Call Options on Dividend Paying Stocks: Empirical Tests." *Journal of Financial Economics* 19 (March 1982): 29–58.

Whaley, Robert E. "On Valuing American Futures Options." *Financial Analysts Journal* 42 (May-June 1986): 49–59.

Wilmott, Paul. *Derivatives: The Theory and Practice of Financial Engineering.* Chichester, U.K.: Wiley, 1999.

Wilmott, Paul, Sam Howison, and Jeff DeWynne. *The Mathematics of Financial Derivatives.* Cambridge, U.K.: Press Syndicate of the University of Cambridge, 1995.

Yadav, Pradeep K., and Peter F. Pope. "Stock Index Futures Arbitrage: International Evidence." *The Journal of Futures Markets* 9 (December 1990): 573–604.

Yaksick, Rudy. "Swaps, Caps, and Floors: Some Parity and Price Identities." *The Journal of Financial Engineering* 1 (June 1992): 105–115.

Yates, James W., Jr., and Robert W. Kopprasch, Jr. "Writing Covered Call Options: Profits and Risks." *The Journal of Portfolio Management* 6 (Fall 1980): 74–80.

Zivney, Terry L. "The Value of Early Exercise in Option Prices: An Empirical Investigation." *Journal of Financial and Quantitative Analysis* 26 (March 1991): 129–138.

GLOSSARY

Accounting risk The risk associated with improper accounting treatment for a transaction, which may arise when accounting procedures and rulings change or have not yet been established.

Accreting swap A swap in which the notional principal increases through time. *See also* Index amortizing swap.

Accrued interest The amount of interest accumulated on a bond since its last coupon payment date.

Against actuals *See* Exchange for physicals.

All or none order An order to purchase or sell a security or derivative in which the broker is instructed to fill the entire order or not fill any of the order.

All or none, same price order An order to purchase or sell a security or derivative in which the broker is instructed to fill the entire order at the same price or not fill any of the order.

Alternative currency option An option in which the payoff is a function of the performance of two or more currencies. The holder has the right to decide which currency will be compared with the exercise price to determine the payoff.

Alternative option An option involving more than one underlying asset whose payoff is determined by either the better performing (max) of the two assets or the worse performing (min) of the two assets. The rate of return of the better or worse performing of the two assets is compared to the exercise rate.

American option An option that can be exercised on any day during its life.

Amortizing swap *See* Index amortizing swap.

Analytical method A method for estimating the Value-at-Risk in which knowledge of the input values and a pricing model are used with an assumption about the type of probability distribution associated with the risk. Also known as Variance/covariance method and Delta normal method.

Anticipatory hedge A transaction in which a hedger expects to make a transaction in the spot market at a future date and is attempting to protect against a change in the spot price by trading a derivative.

Arbitrage A transaction based on the observation of the same asset or derivative selling at two different prices. The transaction involves buying the asset or derivative at the lower price and selling it at the higher price.

Arbitrage pricing theory A theory of asset pricing in which the expected return is a function of the asset's sensitivity to one or more underlying economic factors.

Arbitrageur An individual who engages in an arbitrage transaction.

Arrears swap A fixed-for-floating rate swap in which the payment is made on the same day that the floating interest rate is determined. *See also* Delayed settlement swap.

Asian option An option in which the final payoff is determined by the average price of the asset during the option's life. *See also* Average price option *and* Average strike option.

Ask price The price at which a market maker offers to sell a security or derivative.

Asset-backed security   A security providing the holder returns based on the payments from a portfolio of underlying securities.

Asset-or-nothing option   An option, which if it expires in-the-money, pays the holder the underlying asset while the holder does not have to pay the exercise price.

Asset pricing theory   The study of the economic processes through which prices and expected returns on securities are formulated.

Assignment   The procedure in which the holder of a short position in an option is instructed to buy or sell the underlying asset or futures from or to the holder of the long position.

Associated person (AP)   An individual affiliated with a firm engaged in any line of futures-related business but excluding individuals who execute trades, manage portfolios or pools, give advice, or perform clerical duties.

At-the-money   An option in which the price of the underlying stock or futures equals the exercise price.

Average price option   An Asian option in which the average price of the asset over the life of the option replaces the price of the asset at expiration in determining the option's payoff.

Average strike option   An Asian option in which the average price of the asset over the life of the option replaces the exercise price at expiration in determining the option's payoff.

Back office   The clerical, record-keeping function in a derivatives/risk management system.

Backwardation   A condition in financial markets in which the forward or futures price is less than the spot price. Also known as an *inverted market*.

Barrier option   An option that either does not begin or terminates early if the underlying asset price hits a certain level called the barrier. If the option does not begin or terminates early, the holder might be paid a rebate. *See also* In-option *and* Out-option.

Basis   The difference between the spot price and the futures or forward price or the difference between a nearby futures or forward price and a deferred futures or forward price.

Basis point   A measure commonly applied to interest rates or yields equal to one 1/100 of 1 percent.

Basis swap   A swap in which both parties make payments at different floating rates.

Basket options   A single option written on a prespecified combination of securities or currencies.

Bear   A person who expects the market to go down. Sometimes referred to as *bearish*.

Bear market   A market in which prices are falling.

Bear spread   An option spread designed to profit in a bear market. Also known as a *bearish spread*.

Beta   A measure of the responsiveness of a security or portfolio to the market as a whole.

Biased expectations   A condition in which investors' expectations of a rate, a security price, or a return systematically differ from the subsequent long-run average rate, price, or return.

Bid price   The price at which a market maker offers to buy a security or derivative.

Bid-ask spread   The difference between the ask price or rate and the bid price or rate.

Bilateral netting   Netting between two parties. *See also* Netting *and* Multilateral netting.

Binary option   *See* Asset-or-nothing option *and* Cash-or-nothing option.

Binomial model   An option pricing model based on the assumption that at any point in time the price of the underlying can change to one of only two possible values.

Binomial option pricing model
See Binomial model.

Black model   A pricing model for an option on a forward or futures contract.

Black-Scholes model   A widely used pricing model for an option on an asset.

Black-Scholes option pricing model   *See* Black-Scholes model.

Block trade   The sale of at least 10,000 shares of stock normally conducted with considerable care so as to minimize the impact on the stock price.

Board broker   *See* Order book official.

Bond option   An option to buy or sell a bond.

Boundary condition   A statement specifying the maximum or minimum price or some other limitation on the price of an option.

Box spread   A risk-free combination of a call money spread and a put money spread.

Breakeven price   The underlying asset price at which a strategy has a zero profit.

Break forward   A forward contract with an upside payoff

like a call, but which has a possible negative value at expiration so as to compensate for the fact that it has no initial value.

Broker   A person who arranges a financial transaction by bringing a buyer and seller together and usually earns a commission.

Bull   A person who expects the market to go up. Sometimes referred to as *bullish*.

Bull market   A market in which prices are rising.

Bull spread   An option spread designed to profit in a bull market. Also known as a *bullish spread*.

Business risk   The risk associated with a particular line of business.

Butterfly spread   An option transaction consisting of one long call at a particular exercise price, another otherwise identical long call at a different exercise price, and two otherwise identical short calls at an exercise price between the other two.

Buy-back   A method of terminating a swap in which a party makes or receives a cash payment to or from the counterparty in the amount of the value of the swap. Also called a *close-out*.

Calendar spread   An option transaction consisting of the purchase of an option with a given expiration and the sale of an otherwise identical option with a different expiration.

Call   An option to buy an asset, currency, or futures. Also refers to the early retirement of a bond.

Call date   The earliest date at which a bond can be called.

Callability   A feature associated with many bonds in which the issuer is permitted to pay off the bond prior to its scheduled maturity date.

Callable bond   A bond that the issuer can retire prior to its maturity date.

Cap   An option transaction in which a party borrowing at a floating rate pays a premium to another party, which reimburses the borrower in the event that the borrower's interest costs exceed a certain level, thus making the effective interest paid on a floating rate loan have a cap or maximum amount. Can also be used in other cases where the underlying is an asset price, commodity price, or exchange rate.

Capital Asset Pricing Model   A model that gives the equilibrium expected return on an asset as a function of the risk-free rate, the expected return on the market, and the asset's beta or systematic risk.

Capital market   The financial market in which long-term securities such as stocks and long-term bonds are traded.

Caplet   One of the component options of a cap.

Carry   The difference between the cash received from holding an asset and the interest forgone or other costs associated with holding it.

Cash and carry   A theoretically riskless transaction consisting of a long position in the spot asset and a short position in the futures contract.

Cash flow hedge   A type of hedge in which a future cash flow from an asset or liability is being hedged and which may qualify for hedge accounting. *See also* Hedge accounting.

Cash market   *See* Spot market.

Cash-or-nothing option   An option, which if it expires in-the-money, pays the holder the exercise price.

Cash settlement   The feature of certain derivatives that allows delivery or exercise to be conducted with an exchange of cash rather than the physical transfer of assets.

Cheapest bond to deliver (CTD)   The bond that if delivered on the Chicago Board of Trade's Treasury bond or note contract provides the largest difference between the invoice price and the cost of the bond.

Chooser option   An option in which the holder decides at a specific time during the option's life whether it will be a put or a call. Sometimes called an *as-you-like-it option*.

Circuit breaker   *See* Trading halt.

Class   All of the options of a particular type (call or put) on a given stock, index, currency, or futures commodity.

Clearing firm   A company that is a member of a futures or options clearinghouse.

Clearinghouse   An institution associated with an options or futures exchange that guarantees the performance of both parties to the contract, collects margins, and maintains records of the parties to all transactions.

Cliquet option   An option that allows an upward resetting of the exercise price as the asset price crosses a series of thresholds.

Closeout netting   Netting in which at the termination of a transaction only the net amount is owed.

CMO   *See* Collateralized mortgage obligation.

CMT rate   Constant Maturity Treasury rate, the rate on a Treasury security of a given maturity. Often used as a floating rate in a Constant maturity swap.

Collar   An option strategy in which a position in an asset is hedged by buying a put with an exercise price typically lower than the current asset price with the cost of the put partially covered by the premium from selling a call at a higher exercise price. For interest rate options designed to protect a loan, the put is a floor and the call is a cap. *See also* Zero cost collar.

Collateral   Any type of cash or security set aside as protection for the lender in a loan. Also, used as a credit enhancement in a derivative transaction.

Collateralized mortgage obligation   A type of mortgage-backed security in which mortgage payments are divided into tranches with different payment characteristics, different priorities, and different risks and are passed through, less a service fee, to holders.

Combination   An option strategy involving positions in a put and a call. Sometimes used to refer to any option strategy involving more than one option.

Commercial paper   A short-term promissory note issued by a large, creditworthy corporation.

Commission   A fee paid by the parties in a transaction to a broker for arranging the transaction.

Commission broker   A trader on the floor of a futures exchange who executes transactions for off-the-floor customers.

Commodity   Any asset, but more frequently used to refer to an agricultural product or sometimes a metal or natural resource.

Commodity fund   *See* Futures fund.

Commodity futures   Any futures contract, but primarily a futures on an agricultural product or sometimes a metal or natural resource.

Commodity Futures Trading Commission   The federal agency that regulates the futures markets.

Commodity option   An option on a commodity, but more often an option on a futures contract.

Commodity pool   A private investment arrangement in which individuals combine their funds and the total amount of funds is used to trade futures contracts, with a cash reserve set aside to meet margin calls.

Commodity pool operator (CPO)   The organizer or manager of a commodity pool.

Commodity swap   A swap in which two parties agree to make payments to each other with at least one party's payments calculated according to the price

of a commodity. The other party's payments can be calculated according to any formula.

Commodity trading advisor (CTA)   An individual who specializes in offering advice regarding the trading of futures contracts.

Comparative statics   An examination of the effects on a model of changes in the variables that influence the model.

Compound option   An option to buy or sell another option.

Constant maturity swap   A swap where one side pays a rate associated with an instrument of constant maturity, which is usually greater than the settlement period of the swap. *See also* CMT rate.

Contango   A condition in financial markets in which the forward or futures price is greater than the spot price.

Contingent premium option   An option in which the premium is paid at expiration and only if the option is in-the-money. *See also* Pay-later option.

Continuous time   A characteristic describing a class of option pricing models in which time moves in extremely small (infinitesimal) units. The Black-Scholes model is a continuous time model. *Contrast with* Discrete time.

Continuously compounded rate   A rate of return in which the asset value grows continuously.

Convenience yield   A premium imbedded in the spot price that provides an extra return for those holding the commodity and is usually observed during shortages of the commodity.

Conversion   An arbitrage transaction consisting of the sale of a call and the purchase of a synthetic call.

Conversion factor   An adjustment factor applied to the settlement price of the Chicago Board of Trade's Treasury bond and note contracts that gives the holder of the short position a choice of several different bonds or notes to deliver.

Convertible bond   A bond in which the holder can convert into a specified number of shares of stock.

Convexity   A mathematical relationship between the change in a bond price and the change in its yield, beyond that explained by its duration. Knowledge and use of convexity is helpful in obtaining effective hedge results.

Cost of carry   The cost involved in holding or storing an asset that consists of storage costs and interest lost on funds tied up. *See also* Cost of Carry model.

Cost of carry model   A model for pricing futures and forward contracts in which the futures or forward price is determined by executing a strategy of buying the asset and selling the futures or forward and which assures that no arbitrage profits will be earned. *See also* Cost of carry.

Coupon   The interest paid on a bond.

Covariance   A measure of the association between two random variables.

Covered call   A combination of a long position in an asset, futures, or currency and a short position in a call on the same.

Credit default swap   *See* Credit swap.

Credit derivative   A derivative contract based on the credit risk of a particular party. *See also* Total return swap, Credit swap, Credit spread option, Credit linked security.

Credit enhancements   Any of several means used to reduce the credit risk on a swap or other derivative transaction.

Credit event   The occurrence of an event related to the credit risk of a party, such as failure to make a scheduled payment, declaration of bankruptcy, repudiation of a liability, or acceleration of payment of another liability.

Credit linked security   A security that pays off less than its face value in the event of a default by a third party on a separate obligation.

Credit risk   The risk that a party to an over-the-counter derivative contract will not pay off as required. Also known as *default risk*.

Credit spread   An option spread in which the amount paid for the purchased option is less than the amount received from the sold option.

Credit spread option   An option in which the underlying is the spread on a credit-risky security over an otherwise comparable Treasury security.

Credit swap   A type of credit derivative in the form of a swap in which one party makes periodic payments to the other and the other party makes payments to the first if a particular credit-related event, such as a default or downgrade, occurs.

Cross product netting   Netting in which payments owed for one transaction are netted against payments owed for another type of transaction. Thus, parties could net one type of derivative against another, as well as against loans.

Cross-rate relationship   The association among the exchange rates of three currencies.

Currency swap   A transaction in which two parties agree to make a series of payments to each other in different currencies.

Currency option   *See* Foreign currency option.

Currency warrants   Options on various foreign currencies underwritten by investment banking firms and trading on the American Stock Exchange.

Current credit risk   The risk that a party to a transaction will be unable to make payments that are currently due.

Daily price limits   The maximum and minimum prices at which a futures contract can trade. These are established by the clearinghouse and are expressed in relation to the previous day's settlement price.

Daily settlement   The process in a futures market in which the daily price changes are paid by the parties incurring losses to the parties making profits. Also known as *marking to market*.

Day order   An order to purchase or sell a security or derivative that is canceled if unfilled by the end of the day.

Day trader   A derivatives trader who closes out all positions by the end of the trading session.

Dealer   A person or firm engaged in the business of buying and selling securities or derivatives for profit. A dealer stands ready to buy or sell at any time.

Debit spread   An option spread in which the amount paid for the purchased option exceeds the amount received from the sold option.

Deductible   A concept in insurance representing the amount by which an insurance payoff is reduced as a result of the insured assuming some of the risk.

Deep in-the-money   An option that is in-the-money by a significant, though unspecific, amount.

Deep out-of-the-money   An option that is out-of-the-money by a significant, though unspecific, amount.

Default risk   *See* Credit risk.

Deferred strike option   An option in which the exercise price is not set until a later time during the option's life but prior to expiration.

Delayed settlement swap   The standard procedure in an interest rate swap in which the floating interest rate is observed at the beginning of the settlement period and the interest is paid at the end. *See also* Arrears swap.

Delivery   The process in which a futures or forward contract can be terminated at expiration through the sale of the asset by the short to the long.

Delivery day   The day on which an asset is delivered to terminate a futures or forward contract.

Delivery option   Any special right or option inherent in a futures contract, held by the holder of the short position and granting flexibility with regard to the item delivered or the timing of delivery. *See also* Timing option, Quality option, End-of-month option, Switching option.

Delta   The ratio of the change in a derivative's price to a given change in the price of the underlying asset or futures.

Delta hedge   A transaction in which an asset or derivative is hedged with another asset or derivative in such a manner that the hedge is adjusted so that the effect of small changes in the underlying is removed and the hedge provides a risk-free return.

Delta neutral   The condition in which an investor's portfolio is delta hedged and, therefore, unaffected by small changes in the value of the underlying.

Delta normal method   *See* Analytical method.

Derivative   A contract between two parties providing for a payoff from one party to the other

determined by the price of an asset, an exchange rate, a commodity price, or an interest rate.

Diagonal spread   An option spread in which the options differ by both time to expiration and exercise price.

Diff swap   A swap in which one party's interest payments are denominated in one currency while the notional principal is stated in another currency.

Diffs   Futures contracts based on the difference between two prices, exchange rates, or interest rates.

Digital option   *See* Asset-or-nothing option *and* Cash-or-nothing option. Same as Binary option.

Discrete time   A characteristic describing a class of option pricing models in which time moves in distinct (finite) units. The binomial model is in discrete time. *Contrast with* Continuous time.

Diversification   An investment strategy in which funds are allocated across numerous different assets.

Dividend protection   A feature associated with the original over-the-counter options market in which the exercise price was adjusted by the amount of any dividend paid on the underlying stock.

Dividend yield   The ratio of the dividend to the stock price.

DOT   An acronym for Designated Order Turnaround, the New York Stock Exchange's system for expediting stock transactions that is used frequently in program trading.

Down-and-in option   An in barrier option in which the premium is paid but the option does not actually begin unless the asset price falls to a specified barrier.

Down-and-out option   An out barrier option in which the premium is paid but the option terminates early if the asset price falls to a specified barrier.

Down-option   A type of barrier option in which the barrier is below the current level of the underlying.

Dual trading   The practice of a floor trader on a derivatives exchange trading for his or her own account as well as for a customer.

Duration   A measure of the size and timing of a bond's cash flows. It also reflects the weighted average maturity of the bond and indicates the sensitivity of the bond's price to a change in its yield.

Dynamic hedge   An investment strategy, often associated with portfolio insurance, in which a stock is hedged by selling futures or buying Treasury bills in such a manner that the position is adjusted frequently and simulates a protective put.

Early exercise   Exercise of an American option before its expiration date.

EDPC   *See* Enhanced derivatives products company.

Efficient market   A market in which the price of an asset reflects its true economic value.

Electronic trading   A system of trading derivatives or securities in which bids and offers are posted to an electronic medium, such as a computer system or the Internet, and which transactions then take place by executing orders through the system. *See also* Open outcry.

Empirical test   A procedure in which data are subjected to various statistical measures to determine if a theory, model, or hypothesis is correct.

End-of-month option   Either the right to defer delivery on the Chicago Board of Trade's Treasury bond futures contract until the final business days of the month during which the contract does not trade or any similar right inherent in a futures contract. Can also refer to exchange-listed options whose expirations are on the last business day of the month.

End user   A firm that enters into derivative transactions with a dealer for the purpose of managing its risk.

Enhanced derivatives products company   A subsidiary established by a bank or swap dealer for the execution of swaps and designed so as to have a higher credit rating than the parent company itself.

Equity basket   A combination of equity securities, otherwise known as a portfolio, but upon which a derivative contract is created.

Equity collar   *See* Collar.

Equity derivative   Any type of derivative contract in which the payoff is based on a stock or stock index.

Equity forward   A forward contract in which the payoff is based on a stock or stock index.

Equity-linked debt   A security that promises a minimum return plus a given percentage of any change in the market above a certain level.

Equity option   An option on a common stock.

Equity swap   A swap in which two parties agree to make payments to each other with at least one party's payments calculated according to the performance of a stock or index.

The other party's payments can be calculated according to any formula.

Euro　The new currency used in Belgium, Germany, France, Spain, Ireland, Italy, Luxembourg, Netherlands, Austria, Portugal, and Finland, which was created as a composite of the currencies of those countries.

Eurodollar　A dollar deposited in a European bank or a European branch of an American bank.

Eurolibor/Euribor　An interest rate paid on deposits of euros. Eurolibor is based on deposits in London while Euribor is based on deposits elsewhere in Europe. *See also* euro.

European Monetary Unit　The single unit of currency planned to replace all currencies of participating countries upon completion of the European unification.

European option　An option that can be exercised only when it expires.

Exchange for physicals　A method of delivery on a futures contract in which the long and short agree to delivery terms different from those specified in the futures contract.

Exchange-listed derivative　An option or futures that trades on an exchange.

Exchange option　An option granting the right to acquire one asset by giving up another asset.

Exchange rate　The rate at which a given amount of one currency converts to another currency.

Ex-dividend date　A day designated four business days prior to the holder-of-record date after which an investor purchasing a stock does not receive the upcoming dividend.

Exercise　The process by which a call option is used to purchase or a put option is used to sell the underlying security, futures, or currency or convert to its cash value.

Exercise limit　The maximum number of option contracts that any one investor can exercise over a specific time period.

Exercise price　The price at which an option permits its owner to buy or sell the underlying security, futures, or currency.

Exercise rate　The fixed rate in an interest rate option, cap, or floor.

Exercise value　*See* Intrinsic value.

Exotic options　A family of options with payoff features different from those of standard European and American options.

Expiration　The date after which a derivative contract no longer exists. Also known as Expiration date.

Extendible bond　A bond in which the holder can choose prior to or at maturity to extend the maturity date.

Face value　The principal amount borrowed on a loan.

FAS 133　A ruling established by the U.S. Financial Accounting Standards Board that specifies the appropriate manner for accounting for derivatives transactions.

Fair value hedge　A type of hedge in which the market value of an asset or liability is being hedged and may qualify for hedge accounting. *See also* Hedge accounting.

Fiduciary call　A form of portfolio insurance in which funds are allocated to calls and Treasury bills such that the transaction is equivalent to a protective put.

Financial asset　An asset representing a claim of one party on another.

Financial engineering　The process of developing, designing, and implementing creative financial contracts, frequently involving derivatives, for the purpose of solving specific risk management problems.

Financial futures   Futures on securities, sometimes including futures on foreign currencies.

Financial risk   The risk associated with changes in such factors as interest rates, stock prices, commodity prices, and exchange rates.

Fixed-for-floating rate swap   An interest rate swap involving the exchange of fixed interest payments for floating interest payments.

FLEX options   Options traded at the Chicago Board Options Exchange that allow the user to specify the strike price, expiration date, and other contract terms in contrast to ordinary CBOE options in which the terms are standardized.

Floating-floating swap   *See* Basis swap.

Floating rate bond   A bond in which the interest payments are adjusted periodically to be consistent with current market interest rates. Also in the form of a loan or note.

Floor   An option transaction in which a party lending at a floating rate pays a premium to another party, which reimburses the lender in the event that the lender's interest revenues are below a certain level, thus making the interest received on a floating rate loan have a floor or

minimum value. It can also be used in other cases where the payoff is tied to an asset price, commodity price, or exchange rate.

Floor broker   A trader on the floor of the options exchange who executes trades for others who are off the floor.

Floorlet   One of the component options of a floor.

Foreign currency futures   A futures contract providing for the purchase of a foreign currency.

Foreign currency option   An option providing for the purchase or sale of a foreign currency.

Foreign investment hedge   A type of hedge related to transactions in foreign currencies and which may qualify for hedge accounting. *See also* Hedge accounting.

Forward commitment   *See* Forward contract.

Forward contract   An agreement between two parties, a buyer and a seller, to buy an asset or currency at a later date at a fixed price.

Forward discount   The relationship between the spot and forward exchange rates of a foreign currency in which the forward rate of a currency is less than the spot rate.

Forward market   A market in which forward contracts are constructed.

Forward premium   The relationship between the spot and forward exchange rates of a foreign currency in which the forward rate of a currency is greater than the spot rate.

Forward rate   The rate agreed upon in a forward contract for a loan or implied by the relationship between short- and long-term interest rates.

Forward rate agreement (FRA)   A transaction, similar to a forward contract, in which one party agrees to make a future interest payment based on an agreed-upon fixed rate of interest and receives a future interest payment based on a floating rate, such as LIBOR.

Forward start option   An option in which the premium is paid today but the option's life does not begin until later.

Forward swap   A forward contract obligating the two parties to enter into a swap at a future date.

FRA   *See* Forward rate agreement.

Free market   A market characterized by a high degree of efficiency and little or no regulatory influence.

Front office   The trading function in a derivatives/risk management system.

Full carry   A condition associated with a futures contract in which the futures price exceeds the spot price by no less than the cost of carry.

Futures commission merchant   A firm in the business of executing futures transactions for the public.

Futures contract   An agreement between two parties, a buyer and a seller, to purchase an asset or currency at a later date at a fixed price and that trades on a futures exchange and is subject to a daily settlement procedure to guarantee to each party that claims against the other party will be paid.

Futures exchange   An organized facility for trading futures, which is governed by a corporate charter with rules and regulations. It may utilize a trading floor or may be an electronic exchange. *See also* Electronic trading.

Futures fund   A mutual fund that specializes in trading futures contracts.

Futures option   An option on a futures contract.

FX swap   A strategy of going long a currency forward contract of one expiration and short a

contract with a different expiration.

Gamma   The rate of change of a derivative's delta with respect to a change in the price of the underlying asset or derivative.

Gamma hedge   A hedged position, usually combined with a delta hedge, in which changes in the delta will be unaffected by large movements in the underlying.

Garman-Kohlhagen model   A model for pricing European foreign currency options.

Generic swap   *See* Fixed-for-floating rate swap.

Geometric Brownian motion   A statistical model based on random movements often used to describe changes in asset prices from which derivative prices can often be obtained.

GLOBEX2   A system of automated trading operated by the Chicago Mercantile Exchange in which bids and offers are entered into a computer and executed electronically.

Good-till-canceled order   An order that is in effect until canceled and is used most often with stop orders and limit orders that may take some time to execute.

Grade   A measure of a commodity's relative quality.

Group of Thirty   An organization of bankers and economists who conduct studies on various issues important to the efficient operation of international financial markets and systems.

Hedge   A transaction in which an investor seeks to protect a position or anticipated position in the spot market by using an opposite position in derivatives.

Hedge accounting   A form of accounting for derivatives transactions in which certain transactions, qualifying as hedges, are accounted for in such a manner that the gains or losses from hedges are, to an extent limited by specified rules, combined with gains and losses from transactions they are designed to hedge, so as to minimize the impact on reported earnings.

Hedge fund   A type of mutual fund in which positions are potentially taken in a broad variety of instruments, often including short positions, and often but not always associated with highly speculative trading.

Hedge portfolio   A portfolio being hedged, often used in the context of a long stock–short call or long stock–long put in which the hedge ratio is adjusted through time to produce a risk-free portfolio.

Hedge ratio   The ratio of derivatives to a spot position (or vice versa) that achieves an objective such as minimizing or eliminating risk.

Hedger   An investor who executes a hedge transaction.

Herstatt risk   *See* Settlement risk.

Historical method   A method for estimating Value-at-Risk that uses historical information on the portfolio's recent performance to estimate its future probability distribution.

Historical volatility   The standard deviation of a security, futures, or currency obtained by estimating it from historical data over a recent time period.

Holder-of-record date   The day on which all current shareholders are entitled to receive the upcoming dividend.

Holding period   The time period over which an investment is held.

Horizontal spread   *See* Calendar spread.

Hybrid   An instrument or contract that possesses some of the characteristics of a derivative.

IMM Index   The method of quoting the price of a Treasury bill or Eurodollar futures contract on the International Monetary Market in which the price is stated in terms of a discount from par of 100.

Immunization   A bond portfolio strategy in which the return is protected against changes in interest rates and is obtained when the duration equals the holding period.

Implied duration   The duration of the bond underlying a futures contract that is implied by using the futures price as though it were the price of the bond.

Implied repo rate   The cost of financing a cash-and-carry transaction that is implied by the relationship between the spot and futures price.

Implied volatility   The standard deviation obtained when the market price of an option equals the price given by a particular option pricing model.

Implied yield   The yield on the bond underlying a futures contract that is implied by using the futures price as though it were the price of the bond.

In-arrears swap   *See* Arrears swap.

Index amortizing swap   A swap in which the notional principal is reduced according to a schedule that may call for an accelerated reduction the lower interest rates fall.

Index arbitrage   The purchase (sale) of a portfolio of stocks representing an index and the sale (purchase) of the

corresponding futures contract. The trade is designed to profit from mispricing in the relationship between the spot and futures prices.

Index option   An option on an index of securities.

Index swap   A swap in which one party's payments are based on an index, such as an equity index. *See also* Equity swap.

Initial margin   The minimum amount of money that must be in an investment account on the day of a transaction. On futures accounts, the initial margin must be met on any day in which the opening balance starts off below the maintenance margin requirement.

In-option   A type of barrier option in which the premium is paid but the option does not actually begin unless the asset price crosses a specified barrier. *See also* Down-and-in option *and* Up-and-in option.

Installment option   An option in which the premium is paid in equal installments. At each payment date, the holder decides whether to continue paying the premium or let the option expire.

Institutional investor   A term used to refer to a firm or organization as an investor as opposed to an individual investor.

Interbank market   An informal organization of banks that execute spot and forward transactions in foreign currency.

Intercommodity spread   A futures transaction involving a long position in a futures on one commodity and a short position in a futures on another commodity.

Interest-only strip   A type of mortgage-backed security in which mortgage interest payments are passed through, less a service fee, to holders. *See also* Principal-only strip.

Interest rate cap   A cap in which the payoff is determined by a floating interest rate.

Interest rate collar   A collar in which the payoff is determined by a floating interest rate.

Interest rate derivative   An option, forward, futures, swap, or other derivative instrument in which the underlying instrument is an interest rate. In some uses, the underlying instrument can be a bond.

Interest rate floor   A floor in which the payoff is determined by a floating interest rate.

Interest rate futures   A futures contract on a fixed-income security.

Interest rate option   An option on an interest rate rather than on a security, commodity, or futures

price. Exercise is determined by whether the interest rate is above or below the strike.

Interest rate parity   The relationship between the spot and forward exchange rates and the interest rates in two countries.

Interest rate swap   A transaction between two parties who agree to make interest payments to each other according to different formulas.

Internal rate of return   The discount rate on an investment that equates the present value of the future cash flows with the price.

International Swaps and Derivatives Association   An organization of derivatives dealers, a major activity of which is the simplification and promotion of standardized low cost derivatives procedures.

In-the-money   A call (put) option in which the price of the asset or futures or the currency exchange rate exceeds (is less than) the exercise price.

Intracommodity spread   A futures transaction consisting of a long position in a futures expiring in one month and a short position in an otherwise identical futures expiring in another month.

Intrinsic value   For a call (put) option, the greater of zero or the

difference between the stock (exercise) price and the exercise (stock) price. Also called *parity value*.

Introducing broker (IB)   A broker who arranges futures transactions for customers but contracts with another firm or individual for the execution of the trade.

Inverse floater   A type of floating rate structured note that pays more interest as interest rates fall and less as interest rates rise.

Inverted market   *See* Backwardation.

IO   *See* Interest-only strip.

ISDA   *See* International Swaps and Derivatives Association.

Johnson-Shad Agreement   The 1982 agreement between CFTC chairman Phillip McBryde Johnson and SEC chairman John Shad that established the lines of regulatory authority over options.

Kappa   *See* Vega.

Knock-in option   *See* In-option.

Knock-out option   *See* Out-option.

Lambda   *See* Vega.

Law of One Price   The principle that two identical assets or portfolios cannot sell for different prices.

LEAPS   Long-term Equity Anticipation Securities. Exchange-listed options on individual stocks and indices with expirations of more than one year.

Legal risk   The risk that the legal system will fail to enforce a contract. Legal risk is primarily faced by dealers and may arise when an end user loses money in a transaction and claims that the dealer mislead it or that the end user had no legal authority to enter into the transaction and the dealer should have informed it of such.

Leverage   The use of debt to magnify investment returns.

Limit down   An occurrence in which the futures price moves down to the lower daily price limit.

Limit move   An occurrence in which a futures price hits the upper or lower daily price limit.

Limit order   A request to purchase or sell a security or derivative that specifies the maximum price to pay or minimum price to accept.

Limit up   An occurrence in which the futures price moves up to the upper daily price limit.

Liquidity   A feature of a market in which transactions can be quickly executed with little impact on prices.

Liquidity risk   The risk associated with a thin market for a transaction, as manifested by few dealers and wide bid-ask spreads.

Listing   The offering of a security, option, or futures for public trading on an exchange.

Local   A trader on the floor of the futures exchange who executes trades for his or her personal account.

Lock-in option   An option which, when the underlying asset reaches a certain level, allows the holder to set the final payout as the current intrinsic value.

Lognormal distribution   A probability distribution of asset returns that is often used to develop option pricing models.

London Interbank Offer Rate (LIBOR)   The interest rate on certain Eurodollar deposits involving London banks.

Long   A position involving the purchase of a security or derivative. It also refers to the party holding the long position.

Long hedge   A hedge involving a short position in the spot market and a long position in the futures market.

Lookback option   An option granting the right to either buy the underlying asset at its lowest price during the option's life or sell the asset at its highest price

during the option's life. Also called a *no-regrets option*.

Lower bound   A value established as the lowest possible price of an option.

Maintenance margin   The minimum amount of money that must be kept in a margin account on any day other than the day of a transaction.

Managed futures   An arrangement in which commodity trading advisors are allocated funds for the purpose of trading futures contracts for a client. Structured as private arrangements, futures funds, and commodity pools.

Margin   Funds kept in a margin account for the purpose of covering losses.

Market efficiency   A concept referring to a market in which prices reflect the true economic values of the underlying assets.

Market maker   A trader in a market who is responsible for buying and selling to the public.

Market-on-close order   An order to purchase or sell securities or derivatives that requests the broker to execute the transaction at a price as close as possible to the closing price.

Market order   A request to purchase or sell a security or derivative in which the broker is instructed to execute the transaction at the current market price.

Market portfolio   The portfolio consisting of all assets in the market.

Market risk   The risk that a firm's value or cash flows will be affected by movements in interest rates, exchange rates, stock prices, or commodity prices.

Market timing   An investment strategy in which the investor attempts to profit by predicting the direction of the market.

Mark-to-market   *See* Daily settlement.

Master swap agreement   A contract form developed by ISDA for simplifying and standardizing swap transactions.

Middle office   A component function of a derivatives/risk management system between the front and back office.

Minimum variance hedge ratio The ratio of futures contracts for a given spot position that minimizes the variance of the profit from the hedge.

Min-max option   An option involving more than one underlying asset whose payoff is determined by either the higher value (max) of the two assets or the lower value (min) of the two assets. The value of the better or worse performing of the two

assets is compared to the exercise price. Also called a *rainbow option.*

Model risk   The risk associated with the use of an incorrect or inappropriate model, or a model containing errors or incorrect inputs.

Modified lookback option   A lookback option in which the payoff is determined by replacing the exercise price by either the high or low price reached by the asset during the option's life.

Money market   The market for short-term securities.

Money spread   An option transaction that involves a long position in one option and a short position in an otherwise identical option with a different exercise price.

Monte Carlo simulation   A procedure for pricing derivatives that involves the generation of random numbers representing prices of the underlying and calculating the derivative value as an average of the possible derivative values obtained from the simulations.

Mortgage-backed security   A security providing the holder returns based on the payments from a portfolio of underlying mortgages.

Mortgage-pass through   A type of mortgage-backed security in which mortgage principal and interest payments are passed

through, less a service fee, to holders of the security.

Mortgage strip   *See* Interest-only strip *and* Principal-only strip.

Multi-asset option   An option whose payoff is based on the performance of more than one underlying asset. *See also* Exchange option *and* Min-max option.

Multilateral netting   Netting between more than two parties, which is essentially equivalent to a clearinghouse.

Multiple listing   The listing of identical options on more than one exchange.

Mutual fund   A company whose shareholders' money is pooled and used to purchase securities.

Naked call   *See* Uncovered call.

National Association of Securities Dealers   An organization of firms that serve as market makers for stocks traded over-the-counter.

National Futures Association An organization of firms engaged in the futures business that serves as the industry's self-regulatory body.

Net interest   The interest opportunity cost of holding any asset less any cash flow in the form of explicit interest or dividends received.

Net present value　The present value of an investment's cash flows minus the initial cost of the investment.

Netting　The practice of aggregating all swaps between two parties and determining the net amount owed from one party to the other.

Netting by novation　Netting in which the net value of a combination of transactions is replaced by a single transaction.

No risk premium hypothesis　A theory of futures markets in which the futures price is determined such that a speculator in futures contracts does not expect to earn a risk premium. In this case the futures prices will be an unbiased predictor of the future spot price.

Normal backwardation　A condition in which the forward or futures price or rate is less than the expected future spot price or rate at expiration.

Normal contango　A condition in which the forward or futures price or rate is greater than the expected future spot price or rate at expiration.

Normal distribution　A probability distribution often described as a bell-shaped curve. Also called a standard normal distribution. *See also* Normal probability.

Normal probability　The probability that a normally distributed random variable will be less than or equal to a given value.

Notice of intention day　The second day in the three-day sequence leading to delivery in which the clearinghouse notifies the holder of the long position that delivery will be made the next business day.

Notional principal　A measure of the size of a swap or derivative, stated in units of a currency, on which the payments are calculated.

Offset　A method of terminating a swap in which a party enters into a new swap with payments occurring on the same dates as the old swap. Both swaps remain in effect. *See also* Offsetting order.

Offsetting order　A derivative transaction that is the exact opposite of a previously established long or short position and cancels the previous outstanding position.

Open interest　The number of futures or options contracts that have been established and not yet been offset or exercised.

Open outcry　A system of trading derivatives or securities in which bids and offers are announced and accepted orally in an open medium such as the trading pit of an exchange.

Operational risk　The risk of a breakdown in the operations of a derivatives program or risk management system.

Option　A contract granting the right to buy or sell an asset, currency, or futures at a fixed price for a specific time period.

Option on futures　An option to buy or sell a futures contract.

Option pricing model　A mathematical equation or procedure that produces the theoretical fair value of an option.

Options Clearing Corporation　The firm that operates as a clearinghouse for the various exchanges that trade options on stocks and indices.

Options exchange　An organized facility for trading options, which is governed by a corporate charter with rules and regulations. It may utilize a trading floor or may be an electronic exchange. *See also* Electronic trading.

Order book official　An employee of the Chicago Board Options Exchange who keeps public limit orders and attempts to fill them at the best available price.

Out-of-the-money　A call (put) in which the price of the asset, currency, or futures is less (greater) than the exercise price.

Out-option A type of barrier option in which the premium is paid but the option terminates early if the asset price crosses a specified barrier. *See also* Down-and-out option *and* Up-and-out option.

Outperformance option An option involving two underlying assets in which the final payout is based on the difference between the values or relative performances of the two assets.

Overnight repo A repurchase agreement with a maturity of one night. *See also* Term repo.

Overpriced A condition in which a security or derivative is trading at more than its value.

Over-the-counter derivative A derivative created in an over-the-counter market and in which there is no active secondary market.

Over-the-counter market A market for securities or derivatives in which the transactions are conducted among dealers, brokers, and the public off of an organized exchange.

Parity *See* Intrinsic value.

Path dependence A characteristic of options in which the payoff of the option is affected by the sequence of prices of the underlying asset as it moves toward expiration. *See also* Path independence.

Path independence A characteristic of options in which the payoff of the option is not affected by the sequence of prices of the underlying asset as it moves toward expiration. *See also* Path dependence.

Payer swaption A swaption in which the party holding the option has the right to enter into a swap and pay the fixed rate.

Pay-later option An option in which the premium is paid at expiration.

Payment netting Netting in which two parties to a transaction settle the amounts simultaneously owed by having one party pay the other the net amount.

Payoff The amount of money received from a transaction at the end of the holding period.

PERCS (Preference Equity Redemption Cumulative Stock) Convertible preferred stock with a maximum payoff, which makes it similar to a covered call.

Perfect hedge A hedge in which the gain on one side of the transaction exactly offsets the loss on the other under all possible outcomes. Rarely exists in the real world.

Performance bond A preferred name for the margin deposit required in futures markets. Makes a distinction between stock market margin, which reflects the borrowing of funds, and futures market margin, which is simply a good-faith deposit.

Pit An octagonally or hexagonally shaped, multi-tiered area on the trading floor of a derivatives exchange within which a group of contracts trades.

Plain vanilla swap *See* Fixed-for-floating rate swap.

Planned amortization class bonds One component tranche of a collateralized mortgage obligation in which an assumed rate of prepayments is embedded into the contract terms. Also called PAC bond.

PO *See* Principal-only strip.

Portfolio insurance An investment strategy employing combinations of securities, Treasury bills, or derivatives that is designed to provide a minimum or floor value of the portfolio at a future date.

Portfolio theory The study of the economic processes through which investors' portfolio decisions are made.

Position day The first day in the three-day sequence leading to delivery in which the holder of the short position notifies the clearinghouse of the intention to make delivery two business days later.

Position limit   The maximum number of options or futures contracts that any one investor can hold.

Position trader   A futures trader who normally holds open positions for a period longer than a day.

Potential credit risk   The risk that a party to a transaction will be unable to make payments due in the future.

Preferred habitat theory   *See* Market segmentation theory.

Prepayment risk   In mortgage- or asset-backed securities, the risk to the holder that the underlying mortgage or other underlying securities will be paid off early due to falling interest rates.

Price sensitivity hedge ratio The number of futures contracts used in a hedge that leaves the value of a portfolio unaffected by a change in an underlying variable, such as an interest rate.

Primary market   The market for securities originally issued and not previously traded among the public.

Principal-only strip   A type of mortgage-backed security in which mortgage principal payments are passed through,

less a service fee, to holders. *See also* Interest-only strip.

Program trading   The trading of large blocks of stock as part of a program of index arbitrage or portfolio insurance.

Protective put   An investment strategy involving the use of a long position in a put and the underlying asset, futures, or currency to provide a minimum selling price for the asset, futures, or currency.

Pure discount bond   A bond, such as a Treasury bill, that pays no coupon but sells for a discount from par value.

Put   An option to sell an asset, currency, or futures.

Put-call-forward/futures parity The relationship among the prices of puts, calls, and futures on a security, commodity, or currency.

Put-call parity   The relationship between the prices of puts, calls, and the underlying security, commodity, or currency.

Quality option   The right to deliver any one from a set of eligible bonds on the Chicago Board of Trade's Treasury Bond futures contract or a similar right inherent in any other futures contract.

Quantity risk   The risk involved in a hedge in which the hedger does not know how many units of

the spot asset he or she will own or sell.

Quanto   A derivative in which a foreign currency price or rate is converted to another currency at a fixed rate.

Quanto swap   *See* Diff swap.

Quasi arbitrage   An arbitrage transaction in which the holder of an asset sells the asset, replaces it with a futures contract, and then reverses the transaction later when the price converges to the cost of carry price.

Range floater   A type of floating rate structured note in which the interest payments can change depending on whether a reference interest rate remains in a particular range.

Range forward   A forward contract with a limited gain and loss. Also known as a *risk reversal* and a *collar*.

Ratio spread   A spread transaction in which the number of contracts is weighted to produce a risk-free position.

Real asset   A tangible asset such as real estate or equipment.

Receiver swaption   A swaption in which the party holding the option has the right to enter into a swap and receive the fixed rate.

Registered option trader   An options trader on the floor of the

American Stock Exchange who trades options for his or her personal account.

Regulatory risk   The risk that regulations or the current regulatory style will change, with adverse consequences for a firm. Regulatory risk may render certain existing or contemplated transactions illegal or hinder the development of new products and solutions.

Repo   *See* Repurchase agreement.

Reportable position   The number of contracts that if held by a futures trader must be law be reported to the regulatory authorities.

Repurchase agreement   A securities transaction in which an investor sells a security and promises to repurchase it a specified number of days later at a higher price reflecting the prevailing interest rate.

Reset option   An option that permits the holder to change the exercise price if the stock price hits a certain level.

Residual tranche   One component tranche of a collateralized mortgage obligation entitling the holder to whatever cash remains after all other tranches have been repaid.

Retractable bond   A bond in which the holder can choose to redeem prior to maturity.

Return   A measure of the increase in wealth from an investment.

Reversal   *See* Offset.

Reverse conversion   An arbitrage transaction consisting of the sale of a put and the purchase of a synthetic put.

Reverse floater   *See* Inverse floater.

Rho   The rate of change of an option's price with respect to the risk-free interest rate.

Risk   In the financial sense, a measure of the variability or uncertainty of a transaction or portfolio.

Risk aversion   The characteristic referring to an investor who dislikes risk and will not assume more risk without an additional return.

Risk-free rate   The return offered by an investment in an asset with no risk.

Risk management   The practice of identifying the risk level a firm desires, identifying the risk level it currently has, and using derivative or other financial instruments to adjust the actual risk level to the desired risk level.

Risk-neutral probability   The probability that would be assigned to an outcome by a person who is risk neutral

(indifferent) to risk. *See also* Risk neutrality.

Risk neutrality   The characteristic referring to an investor who is indifferent toward risk.

Risk preferences   An investor's feelings toward risk.

Risk premium   The additional return risk-averse investors expect for assuming risk.

Risk premium hypothesis   A theory of futures markets in which the futures price is determined such that a speculator in futures contracts expects to earn a risk premium for assuming risk, a result of the transferral of the risk premium from hedgers. In this case the futures price will be a biased predictor of the future spot price.

Risk-return trade-off   The concept in which additional risk must be accepted to increase the expected return.

Risk reversal   *See* Collar.

Risk Standards Working Group An organization of professionals in the investment management industry who develop risk management standards for best practices.

Rolling strip hedge   A strip hedge with a relatively long hedge horizon in which the longer maturity futures are added as nearby futures expire.

Rolling up   A covered call strategy using an out-of-the-money call in which an investor buys back the call when the stock price rises to near the exercise price and sells another out-of-the-money call.

Sale or assignment   A method of terminating a swap in which a party makes or receives a cash payment and passes on its swap payment obligations to another party.

Scalper   A trader on the floor of a derivatives exchange whose trading style involves short holding periods and small profits based on small price changes.

Scratch trade   A trade primarily executed to adjust a dealer's inventory and in which no profit or loss is made.

Seat   A term used to refer to a membership on a derivatives or stock exchange.

Secondary market   The market for assets that were issued previously and are now trading among investors.

Securities and Exchange Commission   The federal agency responsible for regulating the securities and listed options markets.

Securities Investor Protection Corporation   A federal agency that provides investors with insurance against failure of a brokerage firm.

Securitization   The process of creating asset-backed securities.

Series   All of the options of a given class with the same exercise price and expiration.

Settlement price   The official price established by the clearinghouse at the end of each day for use in the daily settlement.

Settlement risk   The risk often faced in international transactions in which a firm exchanges payments with another party and is subject to the risk that its payments may be sent before receipt of the other party's payments, which may not be sent due to bankruptcy, insolvency, or fraud.

Short   A term used to refer to holding a short position or to the party holding the short position.

Short hedge   A hedge transaction involving a long position in the spot market and a short position in the futures market.

Short sale   An investment transaction in which securities are borrowed from a broker and sold to a buyer and, at a later time, repurchased and paid back to the broker.

Short selling   *See* Short sale.

Shout option   An option which, when the underlying asset

reaches a certain level, allows the holder to set the minimum value of the final payout as the current intrinsic value.

Simple return   A rate of return that is not compounded.

SPDV (Special purpose derivatives vehicle)   *See* Enhanced derivatives products company.

Specialist   A trader on the floor of an exchange who is responsible for making a market in certain securities or derivatives.

Speculation   Investments characterized by a high degree of risk and usually short holding periods.

Speculative value   *See* Time value.

Speculator   One who engages in speculative transactions.

Spot market   The market for assets that involves the immediate sale and delivery of the asset.

Spot price   The price of an asset on the spot market.

Spot rate   An interest rate on a loan or bond created in the spot market.

Spread   A derivatives transaction consisting of a long position in one contract and a short position in another, similar contract.

Spreader   A person or institution that engages in a spread transaction.

Stack hedge   A hedge in which the hedge horizon is longer than the expiration of the shortest-lived futures contract but due to lower liquidity of longer maturity futures, extra contracts of shorter maturity futures are used. Sometimes called a *stack*.

Standard deviation   A measure of the dispersion of a random variable around its mean, equal to the square root of the variance.

Stock index   A combination of stock prices designed to measure the performance of the stocks as a whole.

Stock index futures   A futures contract on an underlying stock index.

Stock option   *See* Equity option.

Stop order   An order to purchase or sell securities or derivatives that is not executed until the price reaches a certain level.

Storage   The process in which an asset is held for a certain time period.

Storage cost   The cost of holding an asset, including the physical costs of storage and the interest lost on funds tied up.

Straddle   An option transaction that involves a long position in a put and a call with the same exercise price and expiration.

Strangle   A long put at one exercise price and a long call at a higher exercise price.

Strap   An option transaction that involves a long position in two calls and one put, or two calls for every put, with the same exercise price and expiration.

Stress test   A method of testing a risk management system in which a portfolio's performance under extremely large changes in the underlying is examined.

Strike price   *See* Exercise price.

Strike rate   *See* Exercise rate.

Strike spread   *See* Money spread.

Striking price   *See* Exercise price.

Strip   An option transaction that involves a long position in two puts and one call, or two puts for every call, with the same exercise price and expiration. *See also* Strip hedge.

Strip hedge   A hedge in which a series of futures contracts of successively longer expirations are used to cover a hedge horizon longer than the expiration of the shortest-lived futures contract. Sometimes called a *strip*.

Stripped treasuries   Securities that represent claims on coupons and principal of Treasury bonds. The Treasury bond is purchased and stripped treasuries are sold against the coupons and principal on the Treasury bond.

Structured note   A promissory note, usually with a floating rate, in which the coupon has been enhanced by a derivative to provide for an increased or decreased payment.

Swap   A derivative transaction in which two parties agree to exchange cash flows calculated according to different formulas. *See also* Interest rate swap, Currency swap, Commodity swap, Equity swap.

Swap book   A swap dealer's inventory of swaps.

Swap dealer   A firm that arranges an interest rate or currency swap between two other parties.

Swap option   *See* Swaption.

Swap rate   The fixed rate that a swap dealer will pay or receive on a swap.

Swap spread   The difference between the fixed rate that a swap dealer will pay or receive and the rate on the U.S. Treasury note of equivalent maturity.

Swaption   An option granting the right to enter into a swap. *See* *also* Payer swaption and Receiver swaption.

Switching option   Sometimes defined as the right to switch bonds in a cash-and-carry transaction using Treasury Bond futures although this right is a result of the quality option. *See also* Quality option.

Synthetic call   A combination of a long put and long asset, futures, or currency that replicates the behavior of a call. It may sometimes include a short position in risk-free bonds.

Synthetic futures   A combination of a long call and a short put that replicates the behavior of a long futures contract. It may sometimes include a long or short position in risk-free bonds.

Synthetic put   A combination of a long call and short asset, currency, or futures that replicates the behavior of a put. It may sometimes include a long position in risk-free bonds.

Systematic risk   The risk associated with the market or economy as a whole.

Systemic risk   The risk that failure of one or more financial institutions will trigger more failures, ultimately leading to a breakdown of the financial system.

Tail   The number of additional futures contracts purchased or sold to complete a wild card or quality option delivery.

Tailing the hedge   Adjusting the hedge ratio so that the effects of the interest earned or paid from the daily settlement are taken into account.

Tandem option   An option that actually represents a sequence of options, with a new option automatically beginning as soon as a given option expires.

Target beta   The desired beta of a stock portfolio.

Target duration   The desired duration of a bond portfolio.

Tax risk   The risk that tax laws or the interpretation of tax laws will change, with adverse consequences for a firm.

TED spread   A transaction in which one takes a long position in either a Treasury bill or Treasury bill futures and a short position in a Eurodollar or Eurodollar futures or vice versa. Alternatively, the difference between Treasury bill spot or futures and Eurodollar spot or futures rates.

Term repo   A repurchase agreement with a maturity of more than one day. *See also* Overnight repo.

Term structure of interest rates The relationship between interest rates and maturities of zero coupon bonds.

Term structure of volatility The relationship between the implied volatility of an option and the expiration of the option.

Theoretical fair price   The price of a derivative that permits no arbitrage opportunities. *See also* Theoretical fair value.

Theoretical fair value   The true or appropriate worth of an asset or derivative, which is obtained from a model based on rational investor behavior and the absence of arbitrage opportunities. *See also* Theoretical fair price.

Theta   The rate of change of an option's price with respect to time.

Tick   The minimum permissable price fluctuation.

Time spread   *See* Calendar spread.

Time value   The difference between an option's price and its intrinsic value.

Time value decay   The erosion of an option's time value as expiration approaches.

Timing option   Either the right to defer delivery until any acceptable delivery date on the Chicago Board of Trade's Treasury bond futures contracts or any similar right inherent in a futures contract.

Total return swap A type of credit derivative in the form of a swap in which one party agrees to pay the return on a specific security, usually a bond. The other party usually agrees to pay a fixed or floating interest rate.

Trading halt A rule associated with futures or stock trading in which trading will temporarily cease if prices move by a specified amount during a specified period of time.

Tranche One component of a collateralized mortgage obligation entitling the holder to a specific stream of payments that may differ in characteristics, priority, and risk from another tranche.

Treasury bill A short-term pure-discount bond issued by the U.S. government with original maturities of 91, 182, and 365 days.

Treasury bond A coupon-bearing bond issued by the U.S. government with an original maturity of at least 10 years.

Treasury note A coupon-bearing bond issued by the U.S. government with an original maturity of one to ten years.

Triangular arbitrage The foreign currency arbitrage transaction that forces the cross-rate relationship to hold. *See also* Cross-rate relationship.

Turtle trade An arbitrage spread transaction in which a forward borrowing (or lending) rate is locked in on the Treasury bond or note futures market and a forward lending (or borrowing) rate is locked in on the Treasury bill futures market.

Two-state model *See* Binomial model.

Unbiased A characteristic of a forecast in which the prediction equals the actual outcome on average over a large number of predictions.

Unbiased expectations theory *See* Expectations theory.

Uncovered call An option strategy in which an investor writes a call on a stock not owned.

Underlying The asset or instrument on which a derivative's payoff is based.

Underpriced A condition in which a security or derivative is trading at less than its value.

Unsystematic return The portion of a security's return that is related to factors associated with the individual security and not to the market as a whole.

Unsystematic risk The risk of a security related to factors specific to it and not to the market as a whole.

Up-and-in option An in barrier option in which the premium is paid but the option does not actually begin unless the asset price rises to a specified barrier.

Up-and-out option An out barrier option in which the premium is paid but the option terminates early if the asset price rises to a specified barrier.

Up-option A type of barrier option in which the barrier is above the current level of the underlying.

Upside capture The percentage of the market value of an uninsured portfolio earned by an insured portfolio in a bull market.

Uptick An increase in the price of a security or contract equal to one tick.

Utility A measure of satisfaction usually obtained from money or wealth.

Value A monetary measure of the worth of an investment or contract that reflects its contribution to the investor's wealth.

Value-at-Risk (VAR) A dollar measure of the minimum loss that would be expected over a period of time with a given probability.

Variance A measure of the dispersion of a random variable around its mean, equal to the square of the standard deviation.

Variance/covariance method
See Analytical method.

Variation margin   Money added to or subtracted from a futures account that reflects profits or losses accruing from the daily settlement.

Vega   The rate of change of an option's price with respect to the volatility of the underlying asset or futures.

Vega hedge   A hedged position, usually combined with a delta hedge and a gamma hedge, in which changes in the value of the position are unaffected by changes in the volatility of the underlying.

Vertical spread   *See* Money spread.

Volatility   The characteristic of fluctuations in price. Usually refers to Standard deviation.

Volatility smile/skew   The relationship between the implied volatility of an option and the exercise price, which often takes the shape of a smile or a slightly distorted smile (skew).

Volatility strategy   An option strategy designed to profit from

unusually high or low volatility of the underlying asset.

Warehousing   The practice in which a dealer holds positions in various swaps in an inventory.

Warrant   An option issued by a corporation to buy or sell its stock. Usually has a life of several years when originally issued.

Wash sale   A transaction in which a stock is sold at a loss and an essentially identical stock, or a call option on the stock, is purchased within a 61-day period surrounding the sale. Tax laws prohibit deducting the loss on the sale.

Wild card option   The right to deliver on the Chicago Board of Trade's Treasury bond futures contract after the close of trading in the futures market or a similar right inherent in any other futures contract.

Writer   A person or institution that sells an option.

Yield   The discount rate on a bond that equates the present value of the coupons and principal to the price.

Yield beta   The slope coefficient from a regression of the yield on a spot bond on the yield implied

by the futures contract. Measures the relationship between the spot yield and the yield implied by the futures price.

Yield curve   The relationship between yields on bonds and their maturities.

Yield to maturity   *See* Yield.

Z-bond   One component tranche of a collateralized mortgage obligation in which interest accrues but no principal or interest is paid until higher priority tranches are repaid.

Z statistic   A statistic based on a normal distribution. The probability of observing such a statistic is obtained from the normal distribution. *See also* Normal probability.

Zero cost collar   A collar in which the premiums on the long cap and short floor offset so that there is no premium paid up front.

Zero coupon bond   *See* Pure discount bond.

Zero-plus tick   A situation in a financial market in which a trade takes place at the same price as the last trade but the last time a price changed, it increased.

INDEX